Principles and Practice of
AMERICAN POLITICS

Principles and Practice of
AMERICAN POLITICS

CLASSIC AND CONTEMPORARY READINGS

Fourth Edition

Edited by

Samuel Kernell
University of California, San Diego

Steven S. Smith
Washington University, St. Louis

CQ PRESS

A Division of SAGE
Washington, D.C.

CQ Press
2300 N Street, NW, Suite 800
Washington, DC 20037

Phone: 202-729-1900; toll-free, 1-866-4CQ-PRESS (1-866-427-7737)

Web: www.cqpress.com

Cover design: Silverander Communications
Cover photos: Top left, Klaas Lingbeek-van Kranen; top right, Corbis, Zhang Yan; bottom left, Steve Christensen; bottom right, Smiling Dog Images, LLC
Composition: C&M Digitals (P) Ltd.

♾ The paper used in this publication exceeds the requirements of the American National Standard for Information Sciences—Permanence of Paper for Printed Library Materials, ANSI Z39.48-1992.

Printed and bound in the United States of America

13   12   11   10   09   1   2   3   4   5

Library of Congress Cataloging-in-Publication Data

Principles and practice of American politics : classic and contemporary readings / edited by Samuel Kernell, Steven S. Smith.—4th ed.
    p. cm.
Includes bibliographical references.
    ISBN 978-1-60426-463-0 (pbk. : alk. paper) 1. United States—Politics and government. 2. Political culture—United States. I. Kernell, Samuel II. Smith, Steven S.

JK21.P76 2010
320.973—dc22

                                                                    2009021467

CONTENTS

PREFACE

ASSEMBLING THIS SET of readings for students of American politics has been a pleasure and a challenge. The pleasure has come in discovering so many articles that illuminate American politics. The challenge has come in finding far more than can be contained in a single volume. Consequently, despite its heft, *Principles and Practice* represents a small sampling of the available literature.

Our shared perspective on politics has guided the selection of articles. Political actors pursue goals informed by self-interest. This perspective does not require abandoning all hope that politics can result in public policy that serves the common interests of the public today and for future generations. It says simply that to understand politics we need to understand what different political actors want and how this leads them to engage in various strategies to achieve their goals. For government actors these goals will largely reflect the offices they hold, the constituents they represent, and the constitutional obligations and opportunities that define their roles. Other major actors—the public, the news media, and activists in political parties and interest groups—are similarly motivated by self-interest. They do not occupy government positions, and so their behavior is regulated by a different constellation of opportunities and limitations. Each chapter's readings introduce the interests, rules, and strategic contexts of political action in a major national political forum.

A presidential transition, the election of America's first African-American president, the new White House staff, and the tremendous challenges facing the Congress are among the subjects of the new selections for this edition. Our selections reflect the changing composition of the Supreme Court and the intensification of fights over Court nominations, the debates over the polarization of the American electorate and the place of parties and interest groups in our polity, the ever-evolving state of civil liberties (including the assertion of the right of the press to protect sources), and the role of television in campaigns and governance. Selections that explore media developments and their implications for American democracy round out the many new additions to this new edition.

We have chosen the readings to serve two audiences. Many instructors will employ *Principles and Practice* as a supplement to an introductory American politics textbook. For others, this book may constitute the core reading material for a course. For the former, we selected readings that will animate the institutional processes described in the text. For the latter, we have sought readings that can stand alone and do not assume more than an elementary knowledge of American government and politics.

Some of the selections are classics that all instructors will recognize; others, which may be less familiar, address contemporary political developments or proposals for reform. Each article adds emphasis and depth to textbook coverage and illustrates an important theme; most also introduce an important writer on American politics. We hope all of the articles enrich students' understanding of American politics.

We have taken care to include as much of each original source as possible. We have edited some of the pieces to make them appropriate for classroom use. Ellipses indicate where material has been excised, and brackets enclose editorial interpolations. Other changes are explained in the source note for the reading.

We wish to thank the editorial staff of CQ Press for its expertise, energy, and patience in helping us bring this project to completion. Brenda Carter and Charisse Kiino offered essential encouragement and guidance throughout the effort. Jennifer Campi and Belinda Josey provided superb editorial assistance, and Jason McMann persisted in acquiring permission to reprint the selections. Several anonymous reviewers and the following political scientists provided very helpful comments on our plans for this fourth edition: Suzanne M. Chod, Penn State University; Jack Citrin, University of California–Berkeley; Emily Clough, University of North Texas; Erik Engstrom, University of North Carolina; Timothy R. Johnson, University of Minnesota; Joanna Mosser, Drake University; J. P. Nelson, Florida State University; Paul J. Quirk, University of British Columbia; and Robert R. Robinson, University of Alabama–Birmingham.

Samuel Kernell
Steven S. Smith

ABOUT THE EDITORS

Samuel Kernell is professor of political science at the University of California, San Diego, where he has taught since 1977. He taught previously at the University of Mississippi and the University of Minnesota and served as a senior fellow at the Brookings Institution. Kernell's research interests focus on the presidency, political communication, and American political history. His recent books include *Going Public: New Strategies of Presidential Leadership,* 4th edition (2007); an edited collection of essays, *James Madison: The Theory and Practice of Republican Government;* and *The Logic of American Politics,* 4th edition, coauthored with Gary C. Jacobson. Kernell and Erik J. Engstrom are currently writing *Manufactured Responsiveness,* an analysis of the effects of nineteenth-century state electoral laws on national politics.

Steven S. Smith is professor of political science and director of the Weidenbaum Center at Washington University in St. Louis. He has taught at the University of Minnesota, Northwestern University, and George Washington University and has served as a senior fellow at the Brookings Institution. His research interests include American politics, congressional politics, Russian politics, positive theories of politics, and theories of institutional development. He is author or coauthor of *Party Influence in Congress; Politics or Principle: Filibustering in the United States Senate; Committees in Congress,* 3rd edition; *The American Congress; Call to Order: Floor Politics in the House and Senate; Managing Uncertainty in the House of Representatives;* and *The Politics of Institutional Choice: The Formation of the Russian State Duma.*

ABOUT THE EDITORS

Chapter 1

Designing Institutions

————◆◆————

1-1

from *The Logic of Collective Action*

Mancur Olson Jr.

With the publication of The Logic of Collective Action *in 1965, Mancur Olson introduced the fundamental dilemma of collective action to all who study politics. When members of a group agree to work together to achieve a collective goal, each member as an individual faces powerful disincentives, Olson showed, that can frustrate the efforts of the group as a whole. For example, when each can foresee that his or her relatively small contribution to a collective enterprise will not affect its overall success, many will fail to contribute—a phenomenon known as free riding—and leave to everyone else the burden of supplying the collective good. As a consequence, collective enterprises based on cooperation, and supported by the entire collectivity, nevertheless often fail.*

IT IS OFTEN taken for granted, at least where economic objectives are involved, that groups of individuals with common interests usually attempt to further those common interests. Groups of individuals with common interests are expected to act on behalf of their common interests much as single individuals are often expected to act on behalf of their personal interests. This opinion about

Source: Mancur Olson Jr., *The Logic of Collective Action: Public Goods and the Theory of Groups* (Cambridge: Harvard University Press, 1971), 1–19.

group behavior is frequently found not only in popular discussions but also in scholarly writings. Many economists of diverse methodological and ideological traditions have implicitly or explicitly accepted it. This view has, for example, been important in many theories of labor unions, in Marxian theories of class action, in concepts of "countervailing power," and in various discussions of economic institutions. It has, in addition, occupied a prominent place in political science, at least in the United States, where the study of pressure groups has been dominated by a celebrated "group theory" based on the idea that groups will act when necessary to further their common or group goals. Finally, it has played a significant role in many well-known sociological studies.

The view that groups act to serve their interests presumably is based upon the assumption that the individuals in groups act out of self-interest. If the individuals in a group altruistically disregarded their personal welfare, it would not be very likely that collectively they would seek some selfish common or group objective. Such altruism is, however, considered exceptional, and self-interested behavior is usually thought to be the rule, at least when economic issues are at stake; no one is surprised when individual businessmen seek higher profits, when individual workers seek higher wages, or when individual consumers seek lower prices. The idea that groups tend to act in support of their group interests is supposed to follow logically from this widely accepted premise of rational, self-interested behavior. In other words, if the members of some group have a common interest or objective, and if they would all be better off if that objective were achieved, it has been thought to follow logically that the individuals in that group would, if they were rational and self-interested, act to achieve that objective.

But it is *not* in fact true that the idea that groups will act in their self-interest follows logically from the premise of rational and self-interested behavior. It does *not* follow, because all of the individuals in a group would gain if they achieved their group objective, that they would act to achieve that objective, even if they were all rational and self-interested. Indeed, unless the number of individuals in a group is quite small, or unless there is coercion or some other special device to make individuals act in their common interest, *rational, self-interested individuals will not act to achieve their common or group interests.* In other words, even if all of the individuals in a large group are rational and self-interested, and would gain if, as a group, they acted to achieve their common interest or objective, they will still not voluntarily act to achieve that common or group interest. The notion that groups of individuals will act to achieve their common or group interests, far from being a logical implication of the assumption that the individuals in a group will rationally further their individual interests, is in fact inconsistent with that assumption. . . .

A Theory of Groups and Organizations

The Purpose of Organization

Since most (though by no means all) of the action taken by or on behalf of groups of individuals is taken through organizations, it will be helpful to consider organizations in a general or theoretical way.[1] The logical place to begin any systematic study of organizations is with their purpose. But there are all types and shapes and sizes of organizations, even of economic organizations, and there is then some question whether there is any single purpose that would be characteristic of organizations generally. One purpose that is nonetheless characteristic of most organizations, and surely of practically all organizations with an important economic aspect, is the furtherance of the interests of their members. That would seem obvious, at least from the economist's perspective. To be sure, some organizations may out of ignorance fail to further their members' interests, and others may be enticed into serving only the ends of the leadership.[2] But organizations often perish if they do nothing to further the interests of their members, and this factor must severely limit the number of organizations that fail to serve their members.

The idea that organizations or associations exist to further the interests of their members is hardly novel, nor peculiar to economics; it goes back at least to Aristotle, who wrote, "Men journey together with a view to particular advantage, and by way of providing some particular thing needed for the purposes of life, and similarly the political association seems to have come together originally, and to continue in existence, for the sake of the *general* advantages it brings."[3] More recently Professor Leon Festinger, a social psychologist, pointed out that "the attraction of group membership is not so much in sheer belonging, but rather in attaining something by means of this membership."[4] The late Harold Laski, a political scientist, took it for granted that "associations exist to fulfill purposes which a group of men have in common."[5]

The kinds of organizations that are the focus of this study are *expected* to further the interests of their members.[6] Labor unions are expected to strive for higher wages and better working conditions for their members; farm organizations are expected to strive for favorable legislation for their members; cartels are expected to strive for higher prices for participating firms; the corporation is expected to further the interests of its stockholders;[7] and the state is expected to further the common interests of its citizens (though in this nationalistic age the state often has interests and ambitions apart from those of its citizens).

Notice that the interests that all of these diverse types of organizations are expected to further are for the most part *common* interests: the union members' common interest in higher wages, the farmers' common interest in favorable legislation, the cartel members' common interest in higher prices, the stockholders' common interest in higher dividends and stock prices, the citizens' common interest in good government. It is not an accident that the diverse types of organizations listed are all supposed to work primarily for the *common* interests of their members. Purely personal or individual interests can be advanced, and usually advanced most efficiently, by individual, unorganized action. There is obviously no purpose in having an organization when individual, unorganized action can serve the interests of the individual as well as or better than an organization; there would, for example, be no point in forming an organization simply to play solitaire. But when a number of individuals have a common or collective interest—when they share a single purpose or objective—individual, unorganized action (as we shall soon see) will either not be able to advance that common interest at all, or will not be able to advance that interest adequately. Organizations can therefore perform a function when there are common or group interests, and though organizations often also serve purely personal, individual interests, their characteristic and primary function is to advance the common interests of groups of individuals.

The assumption that organizations typically exist to further the common interests of groups of people is implicit in most of the literature about organizations, and two of the writers already cited make this assumption explicit: Harold Laski emphasized that organizations exist to achieve purposes or interests which "a group of men have in common," and Aristotle apparently had a similar notion in mind when he argued that political associations are created and maintained because of the "general advantages" they bring. . . . As Arthur Bentley, the founder of the "group theory" of modern political science, put it, "there is no group without its interest."[8] The social psychologist Raymond Cattell was equally explicit, and stated that "every group has its interest."[9] This is also the way the word "group" will be used here.

Just as those who belong to an organization or a group can be presumed to have a common interest,[10] so they obviously also have purely individual interests, different from those of the others in the organization or group. All of the members of a labor union, for example, have a common interest in higher wages, but at the same time each worker has a unique interest in his personal income, which depends not only on the rate of wages but also on the length of time that he works.

Public Goods and Large Groups

The combination of individual interests and common interests in an organization suggests an analogy with a competitive market. The firms in a perfectly competitive industry, for example, have a common interest in a higher price for the industry's product. Since a uniform price must prevail in such a market, a firm cannot expect a higher price for itself unless all of the other firms in the industry also have this higher price. But a firm in a competitive market also has an interest in selling as much as it can, until the cost of producing another unit exceeds the price of that unit. In this there is no common interest; each firm's interest is directly opposed to that of every other firm, for the more other firms sell, the lower the price and income for any given firm. In short, while all firms have a common interest in a higher price, they have antagonistic interests where output is concerned. . . .

For these reasons it is now generally understood that if the firms in an industry are maximizing profits, the profits for the industry as a whole will be less than they might otherwise be.[11] And almost everyone would agree that this theoretical conclusion fits the facts for markets characterized by pure competition. The important point is that this is true because, though all the firms have a common interest in a higher price for the industry's product, it is in the interest of each firm that the other firms pay the cost—in terms of the necessary reduction in output—needed to obtain a higher price.

About the only thing that keeps prices from falling in accordance with the process just described in perfectly competitive markets is outside intervention. Government price supports, tariffs, cartel agreements, and the like may keep the firms in a competitive market from acting contrary to their interests. Such aid or intervention is quite common. It is then important to ask how it comes about. How does a competitive industry obtain government assistance in maintaining the price of its product?

Consider a hypothetical, competitive industry, and suppose that most of the producers in that industry desire a tariff, a price-support program, or some other government intervention to increase the price for their product. To obtain any such assistance from the government, the producers in this industry will presumably have to organize a lobbying organization; they will have to become an active pressure group.[12] This lobbying organization may have to conduct a considerable campaign. If significant resistance is encountered, a great amount of money will be required.[13] Public relations experts will be needed to influence the newspapers, and some advertising may be necessary. Professional organizers will probably be needed to organize "spontaneous grass roots" meetings among the distressed producers in the industry, and to get those in the industry to write letters to their congressmen.[14] The campaign for the government assistance will take the time of some of the producers in the industry, as well as their money.

There is a striking parallel between the problem the perfectly competitive industry faces as it strives to obtain government assistance, and the problem it faces in the marketplace when the firms increase output and bring about a fall in price. *Just as it was not rational for a particular producer to restrict his output in order that there might be a higher price for the product of his industry, so it would not be rational for him to sacrifice his time and money to support a lobbying organization to obtain government assistance for the industry. In neither case would it be in the interest of the individual producer to assume any of the costs himself. A lobbying organization, or indeed a labor union or any other organization, working in the interest of a large group of firms or workers in some industry, would get no assistance from the rational, self-interested individuals in that industry.* This would be true even if everyone in the industry were absolutely convinced that the proposed program was in their interest (though in fact some might think otherwise and make the organization's task yet more difficult).

Although the lobbying organization is only one example of the logical analogy between the organization and the market, it is of some practical importance. There are many powerful and well-financed lobbies with mass support in existence now, but these lobbying organizations do not get that support because of their legislative achievements. . . .

Some critics may argue that the rational person will, indeed, support a large organization, like a lobbying organization, that works in his interest, because he knows that if he does not, others will not do so either, and then the organization will fail, and he will be without the benefit that the organization could have provided. This argument shows the need for the analogy with the perfectly competitive market. For it would be quite as reasonable to argue that prices will never fall below the levels a monopoly would have charged in a perfectly competitive market, because if one firm increased its output, other firms would also, and the price would fall; but each firm could foresee this, so it would not start a chain of price-destroying increases in output. In fact, it does not work out this way in a competitive market; nor in a large organization. When the number of firms involved is large, no one will notice the effect on price if one firm increases its output, and so no one will change his plans because of it. Similarly, in a large organization, the loss of one dues payer will not noticeably increase the burden for any other one dues payer, and so a rational person would not believe that if he were to withdraw from an organization he would drive others to do so.

The foregoing argument must at the least have some relevance to economic organizations that are mainly means through which individuals attempt to obtain the same things they obtain through their activities in the market. Labor unions, for example, are organizations through which workers strive to get the same things they get with their individual efforts in the market—higher wages, better working conditions, and the like. It would be strange indeed if the workers did not confront some of the same problems in the union that they meet in the market, since their efforts in both places have some of the same purposes.

However similar the purposes may be, critics may object that attitudes in organizations are not at all like those in markets. In organizations, an emotional or ideological element is often also involved. Does this make the argument offered here practically irrelevant?

A most important type of organization—the national state—will serve to test this objection. Patriotism is probably the strongest non-economic motive for organizational allegiance in modern times. This age is sometimes called the age of nationalism. Many nations draw additional strength and unity from some powerful ideology, such as democracy or communism, as well as from a common religion, language, or cultural inheritance. The state not only has many such powerful sources of support; it also is very important economically. Almost any government is economically beneficial to its citizens, in that the law and order it provides is a prerequisite of all civilized economic activity. But despite the force of patriotism, the appeal of the national ideology, the bond of a common culture, and the indispensability of the system of law and order, no major state in modern history has been able to support itself through voluntary dues or contributions. Philanthropic contributions are not even a significant source of revenue for most countries. Taxes, *compulsory* payments by definition, are needed. Indeed, as the old saying indicates, their necessity is as certain as death itself.

If the state, with all of the emotional resources at its command, cannot finance its most basic and vital activities without resort to compulsion, it would seem that large private organizations might also have difficulty in getting the individuals in the groups whose interests they attempt to advance to make the necessary contributions voluntarily.[15]

The reason the state cannot survive on voluntary dues or payments, but must rely on taxation, is that the most fundamental services a nation-state provides are, in one important respect, like the higher price in a competitive market: they must be available to everyone if they are available to anyone. The basic and most elementary goods or services provided by government, like defense and police protection, and the system of law and order generally, are such that they go to everyone or practically everyone in the nation. It would obviously not be feasible, if indeed it were possible, to deny the protection provided by the military services, the police, and the courts to those who did not voluntarily pay their share of the costs of government, and taxation is accordingly necessary. The common or collective benefits provided by governments are usually called "public goods" by economists, and the concept of public goods is one of the oldest and most important ideas in the study of public finance. A common, collective, or public good is here defined as any good such that, if any person X_i in a group $X_1, \ldots, X_i, \ldots, X_n$ consumes it, it cannot feasibly be withheld from the others in that group.[16] In other words, those who do not purchase or pay for any of the public or collective good cannot be excluded or kept from sharing in the consumption of the good, as they can where noncollective goods are concerned.

Students of public finance have, however, neglected the fact that *the achievement of any common goal or the satisfaction of any common interest means that a public or collective good has been provided for that group.*[17] The very fact that a goal or purpose is *common* to a group means that no one in the group is excluded from the benefit or satisfaction brought about by its achievement. As the opening paragraphs of this chapter indicated, almost all groups and organizations have the purpose of serving the common interests of their members. As R. M. MacIver puts it, "Persons . . . have common interests in the degree to which they participate in a cause . . . which indivisibly embraces them all."[18] It is of the essence of an organization that it provides an inseparable, generalized benefit. It follows that the provision of public or collective goods is the fundamental function of organizations generally. A state is first of all an organization that provides public goods for its members, the citizens; and other types of organizations similarly provide collective goods for their members.

And just as a state cannot support itself by voluntary contributions, or by selling its basic services on the market, neither can other large organizations support themselves without providing some sanction, or some attraction distinct from the public good itself, that will lead individuals to help bear the burdens of maintaining the organization. The individual member of the typical large organization is in a position analogous to that of the firm in a perfectly competitive market, or the taxpayer in the state: his own efforts will not have a noticeable effect on the situation of his organization, and he can enjoy any improvements brought about by others whether or not he has worked in support of his organization.

There is no suggestion here that states or other organizations provide *only* public or collective goods. Governments often provide noncollective goods like electric power, for example, and they usually sell such goods on the market much as private firms would do. Moreover . . . large organizations that are not able to make membership compulsory *must also* provide some noncollective goods in order to give potential members an incentive to join. Still, collective goods are the characteristic organizational goods, for ordinary noncollective goods can always be provided by individual action, and only where common purposes or collective goods are concerned is organization or group action ever indispensable.[19]

NOTES

1. Economists have for the most part neglected to develop theories of organizations, but there are a few works from an economic point of view on the subject. See, for example, three papers by Jacob Marschak, "Elements for a Theory of Teams," *Management Science,* I (January 1955), 127–137, "Towards an Economic Theory of Organization and Information," in *Decision*

Processes, ed. R. M. Thrall, C. H. Combs, and R. L. Davis (New York: John Wiley, 1954), pp. 187–220, and "Efficient and Viable Organization Forms," in *Modern Organization Theory,* ed. Mason Haire (New York: John Wiley, 1959), pp. 307–320; two papers by R. Radner, "Application of Linear Programming to Team Decision Problems," *Management Science,* V (January 1959), 143–150, and "Team Decision Problems," *Annals of Mathematical Statistics,* XXXIII (September 1962), 857–881; C. B. McGuire, "Some Team Models of a Sales Organization," *Management Science,* VII (January 1961), 101–130; Oskar Morgenstern, *Prolegomena to a Theory of Organization* (Santa Monica, Calif.: RAND Research Memorandum 734, 1951); James G. March and Herbert A. Simon, *Organizations* (New York: John Wiley, 1958); Kenneth Boulding, *The Organizational Revolution* (New York: Harper, 1953).

2. Max Weber called attention to the case where an organization continues to exist for some time after it has become meaningless because some official is making a living out of it. See his *Theory of Social and Economic Organization,* trans. Talcott Parsons and A. M. Henderson (New York: Oxford University Press, 1947), p. 318.

3. *Ethics* viii.9.1160a.

4. Leon Festinger, "Group Attraction and Membership," in *Group Dynamics,* ed. Dorwin Cartwright and Alvin Zander (Evanston, Ill.: Row, Peterson, 1953), p. 93.

5. *A Grammar of Politics,* 4th ed. (London: George Allen & Unwin, 1939), p. 67.

6. Philanthropic and religious organizations are not necessarily expected to serve only the interests of their members; such organizations have other purposes that are considered more important, however much their members "need" to belong, or are improved or helped by belonging. But the complexity of such organizations need not be debated at length here, because this study will focus on organizations with a significant economic aspect. The emphasis here will have something in common with what Max Weber called the "associative group"; he called a group associative if "the orientation of social action with it rests on a rationally motivated agreement." Weber contrasted his "associative group" with the "communal group," which was centered on personal affection, erotic relationships, etc., like the family. (See Weber, pp. 136–139, and Grace Coyle, *Social Process in Organized Groups,* New York: Richard Smith, Inc., 1930, pp. 7–9.) The logic of the theory developed here can be extended to cover communal, religious, and philanthropic organizations, but the theory is not particularly useful in studying such groups. See Olson, pp. 61n17, 159–162.

7. That is, its members. This study does not follow the terminological usage of those organization theorists who describe employees as "members" of the organization for which they work. Here it is more convenient to follow the language of everyday usage instead, and to distinguish the members of, say, a union from the employees of that union. Similarly, the members of the union will be considered employees of the corporation for which they work.

8. Arthur Bentley, *The Process of Government* (Evanston, Ill.: Principia Press, 1949), p. 211. David B. Truman takes a similar approach; see his *The Governmental Process* (New York: Alfred A. Knopf, 1958), pp. 33–35. See also Sidney Verba, *Small Groups and Political Behavior* (Princeton, N.J.: Princeton University Press, 1961), pp. 12–13.

9. Raymond Cattell, "Concepts and Methods in the Measurement of Group Syntality," in *Small Groups,* ed. A. Paul Hare, Edgard F. Borgatta, and Robert F. Bales (New York: Alfred A. Knopf, 1955), p. 115.

10. Any organization or group will of course usually be divided into subgroups or factions that are opposed to one another. This fact does not weaken the assumption made here that

organizations exist to serve the common interests of members, for the assumption does not imply that intragroup conflict is neglected. The opposing groups within an organization ordinarily have some interest in common (if not, why would they maintain the organization?), and the members of any subgroup or faction also have a separate common interest of their own. They will indeed often have a common purpose in defeating some other subgroup or faction. The approach used here does not neglect the conflict within groups and organizations, then, because it considers each organization as a unit only to the extent that it does in fact attempt to serve a common interest, and considers the various subgroups as the relevant units with common interests to analyze the factional strife.

11. For a fuller discussion of this question see Mancur Olson, Jr., and David McFarland, "The Restoration of Pure Monopoly and the Concept of the Industry," *Quarterly Journal of Economics*, LXXVI (November 1962), 613–631.

12. Robert Michels contends in his classic study that "democracy is inconceivable without organization," and that "the principle of organization is an absolutely essential condition for the political struggle of the masses." See his *Political Parties*, trans. Eden and Cedar Paul (New York: Dover Publications, 1959), pp. 21–22. See also Robert A. Brady, *Business as a System of Power* (New York: Columbia University Press, 1943), p. 193.

13. Alexander Heard, *The Costs of Democracy* (Chapel Hill: University of North Carolina Press, 1960), especially note 1, pp. 95–96. For example, in 1947 the National Association of Manufacturers spent over $4.6 million, and over a somewhat longer period the American Medical Association spent as much on a campaign against compulsory health insurance.

14. "If the full truth were ever known . . . lobbying, in all its ramifications, would prove to be a billion dollar industry." U.S. Congress, House, Select Committee on Lobbying Activities, *Report*, 81st Cong., 2nd Sess. (1950), as quoted in the *Congressional Quarterly Almanac*, 81st Cong., 2nd Sess., VI, 764–765.

15. Sociologists as well as economists have observed that ideological motives alone are not sufficient to bring forth the continuing effort of large masses of people. Max Weber provides a notable example:

> All economic activity in a market economy is undertaken and carried through by individuals for their own ideal or material interests. This is naturally just as true when economic activity is oriented to the patterns of order of corporate groups. . . .
>
> Even if an economic system were organized on a socialistic basis, there would be no fundamental difference in this respect. . . . The structure of interests and the relevant situation might change; there would be other means of pursuing interests, but this fundamental factor would remain just as relevant as before. It is of course true that economic action which is oriented on purely ideological grounds to the interest of others does exist. But it is even more certain that the mass of men do not act this way, and it is an induction from experience that they cannot do so and never will. . . .
>
> In a market economy the interest in the maximization of income is necessarily the driving force of all economic activity. (Weber, pp. 319–320)

Talcott Parsons and Neil Smelser go even further in postulating that "performance" throughout society is proportional to the "rewards" and "sanctions" involved. See their *Economy and Society* (Glencoe, Ill.: Free Press, 1954), pp. 50–69.

16. This simple definition focuses upon two points that are important in the present context. The first point is that most collective goods can only be defined with respect to some

specific group. One collective good goes to one group of people, another collective good to another group; one may benefit the whole world, another only two specific people. Moreover, some goods are collective goods to those in one group and at the same time private goods to those in another, because some individuals can be kept from consuming them and others can't. Take for example the parade that is a collective good to all those who live in tall buildings overlooking the parade route, but which appears to be a private good to those who can see it only by buying tickets for a seat in the stands along the way. The second point is that once the relevant group has been defined, the definition used here, like Musgrave's, distinguishes collective good in terms of infeasibility of excluding potential consumers of the good. This approach is used because collective goods produced by organizations of all kinds seem to be such that exclusion is normally not feasible. To be sure, for some collective goods it is physically possible to practice exclusion. But, as Head has shown, it is not necessary that exclusion be technically impossible; it is only necessary that it be infeasible or uneconomic. Head has also shown most clearly that nonexcludability is only one of two basic elements in the traditional understanding of public goods. The other, he points out, is "jointness of supply." A good has "jointness" if making it available to one individual means that it can be easily or freely supplied to others as well. The polar case of jointness would be Samuelson's pure public good, which is a good such that additional consumption of it by one individual does not diminish the amount available to others. By the definition used here, jointness is not a necessary attribute of a public good. As later parts of this chapter will show, at least one type of collective good considered here exhibits no jointness whatever, and few if any would have the degree of jointness needed to qualify as pure public goods. Nonetheless, most of the collective goods to be studied here do display a large measure of jointness. On the definition and importance of public goods, see John G. Head, "Public Goods and Public Policy," *Public Finance,* vol. XVII, no. 3 (1962), 197–219; Richard Musgrave, *The Theory of Public Finance* (New York: McGraw-Hill, 1959); Paul A. Samuelson, "The Pure Theory of Public Expenditure," "Diagrammatic Exposition of A Theory of Public Expenditure," and "Aspects of Public Expenditure Theories," in *Review of Economics and Statistics,* XXXVI (November 1954), 387–390, XXXVII (November 1955), 350–356, and XL (November 1958), 332–338. For somewhat different opinions about the usefulness of the concept of public goods, see Julius Margolis, "A Comment on the Pure Theory of Public Expenditure," *Review of Economics and Statistics,* XXXVII (November 1955), 347–349, and Gerhard Colm, "Theory of Public Expenditures," *Annals of the American Academy of Political and Social Science,* CLXXXIII (January 1936), 1–11.

17. There is no necessity that a public good to one group in a society is necessarily in the interest of the society as a whole. Just as a tariff could be a public good to the industry that sought it, so the removal of the tariff could be a public good to those who consumed the industry's product. This is equally true when the public-good concept is applied only to governments; for a military expenditure, or a tariff, or an immigration restriction that is a public good to one country could be a "public bad" to another country, and harmful to world society as a whole.

18. R. M. MacIver in *Encyclopaedia of the Social Sciences,* VII (New York: Macmillan, 1932), 147.

19. It does not, however, follow that organized or coordinated group action is *always* necessary to obtain a collective goal.

The Tragedy of the Commons

Garrett Hardin

In this seminal article, Garrett Hardin identifies another class of collective action problems, the "tragedy of the commons." The concept—a "tragedy" because of the inevitability with which public goods, or the "commons," will be exploited—is generally applied to study cases in which natural resources are being misused. Unlike the problems we have already encountered, which concern the production of public goods, the tragedy of the commons affects their conservation. Because public goods are freely available, members of the community will be tempted to overly consume them—to overfish, to overuse national parks, to pollute public water or air—even as they realize their behavior and that of their neighbors is destroying the goods. Hardin discusses social arrangements that can substitute for the commons, or public ownership of scarce resources, and argues that the tragedy of the commons is becoming a more pressing concern as the population increases. As with the problem of free riding described by Mancur Olson, government authority offers one solution extricating participants from their bind.

AT THE END of a thoughtful article on the future of nuclear war, Wiesner and York concluded that: "Both sides in the arms race are . . . confronted by the dilemma of steadily increasing military power and steadily decreasing national security. *It is our considered professional judgment that this dilemma has no technical solution.* If the great powers continue to look for solutions in the area of science and technology only, the result will be to worsen the situation."[1]

I would like to focus your attention not on the subject of the article (national security in a nuclear world) but on the kind of conclusion they reached, namely that there is no technical solution to the problem. An implicit and almost universal assumption of discussions published in professional and semipopular scientific journals is that the problem under discussion has a technical solution. A technical solution may be defined as one that requires a change only in the techniques of the natural sciences, demanding little or nothing in the way of change in human values or ideas of morality.

Source: Garrett Hardin, "The Tragedy of the Commons," *Science*, December 3, 1968, 1243–1248.

In our day (though not in earlier times) technical solutions are always welcome. . . . [Yet of the] class of human problems which can be called "no technical solution problems" . . . [i]t is easy to show that [it] is not a null class. Recall the game of tick-tack-toe. Consider the problem, "How can I win the game of tick-tack-toe?" It is well known that I cannot, if I assume (in keeping with the conventions of game theory) that my opponent understands the game perfectly. Put another way, there is no "technical solution" to the problem. I can win only by giving a radical meaning to the word "win." I can hit my opponent over the head; or I can drug him; or I can falsify the records. Every way in which I "win" involves, in some sense, an abandonment of the game, as we intuitively understand it. (I can also, of course, openly abandon the game—refuse to play it. This is what most adults do.)

The class of "No technical solution problems" has members. My thesis is that the "population problem," as conventionally conceived, is a member of this class. How it is conventionally conceived needs some comment. It is fair to say that most people who anguish over the population problem are trying to find a way to avoid the evils of overpopulation without relinquishing any of the privileges they now enjoy. They think that farming the seas or developing new strains of wheat will solve the problem—technologically. I try to show here that the solution they seek cannot be found. The population problem cannot be solved in a technical way, any more than can the problem of winning the game of tick-tack-toe.

What Shall We Maximize?

Population, as Malthus said, naturally tends to grow "geometrically," or, as we would now say, exponentially. In a finite world this means that the per capita share of the world's goods must steadily decrease. Is ours a finite world?

A fair defense can be put forward for the view that the world is infinite; or that we do not know that it is not. But, in terms of the practical problems that we must face in the next few generations with the foreseeable technology, it is clear that we will greatly increase human misery if we do not, during the immediate future, assume that the world available to the terrestrial human population is finite. "Space" is no escape.[2]

A finite world can support only a finite population; therefore, population growth must eventually equal zero. . . . When this condition is met, what will be the situation of mankind? Specifically, can [Jeremy] Bentham's goal of "the greatest good for the greatest number" be realized? . . .

The . . . reason [why not] springs directly from biological facts. To live, any organism must have a source of energy (for example, food). This energy is utilized for two purposes: mere maintenance and work. For man, maintenance of life requires about 1600 kilocalories a day ("maintenance calories"). Anything that he does over and above merely staying alive will be defined as work, and is supported by "work calories" which he takes in. Work calories are used not only for what we call work in common speech; they are also required for all forms of enjoyment, from swimming and automobile racing to playing music and writing poetry. If our goal is to maximize population it is obvious what we must do: We must make the work calories per person approach as close to zero as possible. No gourmet meals, no vacations, no sports, no music, no literature, no art. . . . I think that everyone will grant, without argument or proof, that maximizing population does not maximize goods. Bentham's goal is impossible. . . .

The optimum population is, then, less than the maximum. The difficulty of defining the optimum is enormous; so far as I know, no one has seriously tackled this problem. Reaching an acceptable and stable solution will surely require more than one generation of hard analytical work—and much persuasion. . . .

We can make little progress in working toward optimum population size until we explicitly exorcize the spirit of Adam Smith in the field of practical demography. In economic affairs, *The Wealth of Nations* (1776) popularized the "invisible hand," the idea that an individual who "intends only his own gain," is, as it were, "led by an invisible hand to promote . . . the public interest."[3] Adam Smith did not assert that this was invariably true, and perhaps neither did any of his followers. But he contributed to a dominant tendency of thought that has ever since interfered with positive action based on rational analysis, namely, the tendency to assume that decisions reached individually will, in fact, be the best decisions for an entire society. If this assumption is correct it justifies the continuance of our present policy of laissez-faire in reproduction. If it is correct we can assume that men will control their individual fecundity so as to produce the optimum population. If the assumption is not correct, we need to reexamine our individual freedoms to see which ones are defensible.

Tragedy of Freedom in a Commons

The rebuttal to the invisible hand in population control is to be found in a scenario first sketched in a little-known pamphlet in 1833 by a mathematical amateur named William Forster Lloyd (1794–1852).[4] We may well call it "the tragedy of the commons," using the word "tragedy" as the philosopher Whitehead used it: "The essence of dramatic tragedy is not unhappiness. It resides in the solemnity of the remorseless working of things."[5] He then goes on to say, "This inevitableness of destiny can only be illustrated in terms of human life by incidents which in fact involve unhappiness. For it is only by them that the futility of escape can be made evident in the drama."

The tragedy of the commons develops in this way. Picture a pasture open to all. It is to be expected that each herdsman will try to keep as many cattle as possible on the commons. Such an arrangement may work reasonably satisfactorily for centuries because tribal wars, poaching, and disease keep the numbers of both man and beast well below the carrying capacity of the land. Finally, however, comes the day of reckoning, that is, the day when the long-desired goal of social stability becomes a reality. At this point, the inherent logic of the commons remorselessly generates tragedy.

As a rational being, each herdsman seeks to maximize his gain. Explicitly or implicitly, more or less consciously, he asks, "What is the utility *to me* of adding one more animal to my herd?" This utility has one negative and one positive component.

1. The positive component is a function of the increment of one animal. Since the herdsman receives all the proceeds from the sale of the additional animal, the positive utility is nearly +1.

2. The negative component is a function of the additional overgrazing created by one more animal. Since, however, the effects of overgrazing are shared by all the herdsmen, the negative utility for any particular decision-making herdsman is only a fraction of –1.

Adding together the component partial utilities, the rational herdsman concludes that the only sensible course for him to pursue is to add another animal to his herd. And another. . . . But this is the conclusion reached by each and every rational herdsman sharing a commons. Therein is the tragedy. Each man is locked into a system that compels him to increase his herd without limit—in a world that is limited. Ruin is the destination toward which all men rush, each pursuing his own best interest in a society that believes in the freedom of the commons. Freedom in a commons brings ruin to all.

Some would say that this is a platitude. Would that it were! In a sense, it was learned thousands of years ago, but natural selection favors the forces of psychological denial.[6] The individual benefits as an individual from his ability to deny the truth even though society as a whole, of which he is a part, suffers. Education can counteract the natural tendency to do the wrong thing, but the inexorable succession of generations requires that the basis for this knowledge be constantly refreshed.

A simple incident that occurred a few years ago in Leominster, Massachusetts, shows how perishable the knowledge is. During the Christmas shopping season the parking meters downtown were covered with plastic bags that bore tags reading: "Do not open until after Christmas. Free parking courtesy of the mayor and city council." In other words, facing the prospect of an increased demand for already scarce space, the city fathers reinstituted the system of the commons. (Cynically, we suspect that they gained more votes than they lost by this retrogressive act.)

In an approximate way, the logic of the commons has been understood for a long time, perhaps since the discovery of agriculture or the invention of private property in real estate. But it is understood mostly only in special cases which are not sufficiently generalized. Even at this late date, cattlemen leasing national land on the western ranges demonstrate no more than an ambivalent understanding, in constantly pressuring federal authorities to increase the head count to the point where overgrazing produces erosion and weed-dominance. Likewise, the oceans of the world continue to suffer from the survival of the philosophy of the commons. Maritime nations still respond automatically to the shibboleth of the "freedom of the seas." Professing to believe in the "inexhaustible resources of the oceans," they bring species after species of fish and whales closer to extinction.[7]

The National Parks present another instance of the working out of the tragedy of the commons. At present, they are open to all, without limit. The parks themselves are limited in extent—there is only one Yosemite Valley—whereas population seems to grow without limit. The values that visitors seek in the parks are steadily eroded. Plainly, we must soon cease to treat the parks as commons or they will be of no value to anyone.

What shall we do? We have several options. We might sell them off as private property. We might keep them as public property, but allocate the right to enter them. The allocation might be on the basis of wealth, by the use of an auction system. It might be on the basis of merit, as defined by some agreed-upon standards. It might be by lottery. Or it might be on a first-come, first-served basis, administered to long queues. These, I think, are all the reasonable possibilities. They are all objectionable. But we must choose—or acquiesce in the destruction of the commons that we call our National Parks.

Pollution

In a reverse way, the tragedy of the commons reappears in problems of pollution. Here it is not a question of taking something out of the commons, but of putting something in—sewage, or chemical, radioactive, and heat wastes into water; noxious and dangerous fumes into the air; and distracting and unpleasant advertising signs into the line of sight. The calculations of utility are much the same as before. The rational man finds that his share of the cost of the wastes he discharges into the commons is less than the cost of purifying his wastes before releasing them. Since this is true for everyone, we are locked into a system of "fouling our own nest," so long as we behave only as independent, rational, free-enterprisers.

The tragedy of the commons as a food basket is averted by private property, or something formally like it. But the air and waters surrounding us cannot readily be fenced, and so the tragedy of the commons as a cesspool must be prevented by different means, by coercive laws or taxing devices that make it cheaper for the polluter to treat his pollutants than to discharge them untreated. We have not progressed as far with the solution of this problem as we have with the first. Indeed, our particular concept of private property, which deters us from exhausting the positive resources of the earth, favors pollution. The owner of a factory on the bank of a stream—whose property extends to the middle of the stream—often has difficulty seeing why it is not his natural right to muddy the waters flowing past his door. The law, always behind the times, requires elaborate stitching and fitting to adapt it to this newly perceived aspect of the commons.

The pollution problem is a consequence of population. It did not much matter how a lonely American frontiersman disposed of his waste. "Flowing water purifies itself every 10 miles," my grandfather used to say, and the myth was near enough to the truth when he was a boy, for there were not too many people. But as population became denser, the natural chemical and biological recycling processes became overloaded, calling for a redefinition of property rights.

How to Legislate Temperance?

Analysis of the pollution problem as a function of population density uncovers a not generally recognized principle of morality, namely: *the morality of an act is a function of the state of the system at the time it is performed.*[8] Using the commons as a cesspool does not harm the general public under frontier conditions, because there is no public; the same behavior in a metropolis is unbearable. A hundred and fifty years ago a plainsman could kill an American bison, cut out only the tongue for his dinner, and discard the rest of the animal. He was not in any important sense being wasteful. Today, with only a few thousand bison left, we would be appalled at such behavior.

In passing, it is worth noting that the morality of an act cannot be determined from a photograph. One does not know whether a man killing an elephant or setting fire to the grassland is harming others until one knows the total system in which his act appears. "One picture is worth a thousand words," said an ancient

Chinese; but it may take 10,000 words to validate it. It is as tempting to ecologists as it is to reformers in general to try to persuade others by way of the photographic shortcut. But the essence of an argument cannot be photographed: it must be presented rationally—in words.

That morality is system-sensitive escaped the attention of most codifiers of ethics in the past. "Thou shalt not . . ." is the form of traditional ethical directives which make no allowance for particular circumstances. The laws of our society follow the pattern of ancient ethics, and therefore are poorly suited to governing a complex, crowded, changeable world. Our epicyclic solution is to augment statutory law with administrative law. Since it is practically impossible to spell out all the conditions under which it is safe to burn trash in the back yard or to run an automobile without smog-control, by law we delegate the details to bureaus. The result is administrative law, which is rightly feared for an ancient reason—*Quis custodiet ipsos custodes?*—"Who shall watch the watchers themselves?" John Adams said that we must have "a government of laws and not men." Bureau administrators, trying to evaluate the morality of acts in the total system, are singularly liable to corruption, producing a government by men, not laws.

Prohibition is easy to legislate (though not necessarily to enforce); but how do we legislate temperance? Experience indicates that it can be accomplished best through the mediation of administrative law. We limit possibilities unnecessarily if we suppose that the sentiment of *Quis custodiet* denies us the use of administrative law. We should rather retain the phrase as a perpetual reminder of fearful dangers we cannot avoid. The great challenge facing us now is to invent the corrective feedbacks that are needed to keep custodians honest. We must find ways to legitimate the needed authority of both the custodians and the corrective feedbacks.

Freedom to Breed Is Intolerable

The tragedy of the commons is involved in population problems in another way. In a world governed solely by the principle of "dog eat dog"—if indeed there ever was such a world—how many children a family had would not be a matter of public concern. Parents who bred too exuberantly would leave fewer descendants, not more, because they would be unable to care adequately for their children. David Lack and others have found that such a negative feedback demonstrably controls the fecundity of birds.[9] But men are not birds, and have not acted like them for millenniums, at least.

If each human family were dependent only on its own resources; *if* the children of improvident parents starved to death; *if,* thus, overbreeding brought its own "punishment" to the germ line—*then* there would be no public interest in controlling the breeding of families. But our society is deeply committed to the welfare state,[10] and hence is confronted with another aspect of the tragedy of the commons.

In a welfare state, how shall we deal with the family, the religion, the race, or the class (or indeed any distinguishable and cohesive group) that adopts over-breeding as a policy to secure its own aggrandizement?[11] To couple the concept of freedom to breed with the belief that everyone born has an equal right to the commons is to lock the world into a tragic course of action.

Unfortunately this is just the course of action that is being pursued by the United Nations. In late 1967, some 30 nations agreed to the following: "The Universal Declaration of Human Rights describes the family as the natural and fundamental unit of society. It follows that any choice and decision with regard to the size of the family must irrevocably rest with the family itself, and cannot be made by anyone else."[12] It is painful to have to deny categorically the validity of this right; denying it, one feels as uncomfortable as a resident of Salem, Massachusetts, who denied the reality of witches in the 17th century. At the present time, in liberal quarters, something like a taboo acts to inhibit criticism of the United Nations. There is a feeling that the United Nations is "our last and best hope," that we shouldn't find fault with it; we shouldn't play into the hands of the archconservatives. However, let us not forget what Robert Louis Stevenson said: "The truth that is suppressed by friends is the readiest weapon of the enemy." If we love the truth we must openly deny the validity of the Universal Declaration of Human Rights, even though it is promoted by the United Nations. We should also join with Kingsley Davis in attempting to get Planned Parenthood–World Population to see the error of its ways in embracing the same tragic ideal.[13] . . .

. . . The argument has here been stated in the context of the population problem, but it applies equally well to any instance in which society appeals to an individual exploiting a commons to restrain himself for the general good—by means of his conscience. To make such an appeal is to set up a selective system that works toward the elimination of conscience from the race.

Pathogenic Effects of Conscience

It is a mistake to think that we can control the breeding of mankind in the long run by an appeal to conscience. . . . If we ask a man who is exploiting a commons to desist "in the name of conscience," what are we saying to him? What does he hear?—not only at the moment but also in the wee small hours of the night when, half asleep, he remembers not merely the words we used but also the nonverbal communication cues we gave him unawares? Sooner or later, consciously or subconsciously, he senses that he has received two communications, and that they are contradictory: (i) (intended communication) "If you don't do as we ask, we will openly condemn you for not acting like a responsible citizen"; (ii) (the unintended communication) "If you *do* behave as we ask, we will secretly condemn you for a simpleton who can be shamed into standing aside while the rest of us exploit the commons." . . .

To conjure up a conscience in others is tempting to anyone who wishes to extend his control beyond the legal limits. Leaders at the highest level succumb to this temptation. Has any President during the past generation failed to call on labor unions to moderate voluntarily their demands for higher wages, or to steel companies to honor voluntary guidelines on prices? I can recall none. The rhetoric used on such occasions is designed to produce feelings of guilt in noncooperators.

For centuries it was assumed without proof that guilt was a valuable, perhaps even an indispensable, ingredient of the civilized life. Now, in this post-Freudian world, we doubt it.

Paul Goodman speaks from the modern point of view when he says: "No good has ever come from feeling guilty, neither intelligence, policy, nor compassion. The guilty do not pay attention to the object but only to themselves, and not even to their own interests, which might make sense, but to their anxieties." [14]

One does not have to be a professional psychiatrist to see the consequences of anxiety. We in the Western world are just emerging from a dreadful two-centuries-long Dark Ages of Eros that was sustained partly by prohibition laws, but perhaps more effectively by the anxiety-generating mechanisms of education. Alex Comfort has told the story well in *The Anxiety Makers;* it is not a pretty one. [15]

Since proof is difficult, we may even concede that the results of anxiety may sometimes, from certain points of view, be desirable. The larger question we should ask is whether, as a matter of policy, we should ever encourage the use of a technique the tendency (if not the intention) of which is psychologically pathogenic. We hear much talk these days of responsible parenthood; the coupled words are incorporated into the titles of some organizations devoted to birth control. Some people have proposed massive propaganda campaigns to instill responsibility into the nation's (or the world's) breeders. But what is the meaning of the word responsibility in this context? Is it not merely a synonym for the word conscience? When we use the word responsibility in the absence of substantial sanctions are we not trying to browbeat a free man in a commons into acting against his own interest? Responsibility is a verbal counterfeit for a substantial *quid pro quo.* It is an attempt to get something for nothing.

If the word responsibility is to be used at all, I suggest that it be in the sense Charles Frankel uses it.[16] "Responsibility," says this philosopher, "is the product of definite social arrangements." Notice that Frankel calls for social arrangements—not propaganda.

Mutual Coercion, Mutually Agreed Upon

The social arrangements that produce responsibility are arrangements that create coercion, of some sort. Consider bank-robbing. The man who takes money from a bank acts as if the bank were a commons. How do we prevent such action? Certainly not by trying to control his behavior solely by a verbal appeal to his sense of responsibility. Rather than rely on propaganda we follow Frankel's lead and insist that a bank is not a commons; we seek the definite social arrangements that will keep it from becoming a commons. That we thereby infringe on the freedom of would-be robbers we neither deny nor regret.

The morality of bank-robbing is particularly easy to understand because we accept complete prohibition of this activity. We are willing to say "Thou shalt not rob banks," without providing for exceptions. But temperance also can be created by coercion. Taxing is a good coercive device. To keep downtown shoppers temperate in their use of parking space we introduce parking meters for short periods, and traffic fines for longer ones. We need not actually forbid a citizen to park as long as he wants to; we need merely make it increasingly expensive for him to do so. Not prohibition, but carefully biased options are what we offer him. A Madison Avenue man might call this persuasion; I prefer the greater candor of the word coercion.

Coercion is a dirty word to most liberals now, but it need not forever be so. As with the four-letter words, its dirtiness can be cleansed away by exposure to the light, by saying it over and over without apology or embarrassment. To many, the word coercion implies arbitrary decisions of distant and irresponsible bureaucrats; but this is not a necessary part of its meaning. The only kind of coercion I recommend is mutual coercion, mutually agreed upon by the majority of the people affected.

To say that we mutually agree to coercion is not to say that we are required to enjoy it, or even to pretend we enjoy it. Who enjoys taxes? We all grumble about them. But we accept compulsory taxes because we recognize that voluntary taxes would favor the conscienceless. We institute and (grumblingly) support taxes and other coercive devices to escape the horror of the commons.

An alternative to the commons need not be perfectly just to be preferable. With real estate and other material goods, the alternative we have chosen is the institution of private property coupled with legal inheritance. Is this system perfectly just? As a genetically trained biologist I deny that it is. It seems to me that, if there are to be differences in individual inheritance, legal possession should be perfectly correlated with biological inheritance—that those who are biologically more fit to be the custodians of property and power should legally inherit more. But genetic recombination continually makes a mockery of the doctrine of "like father, like son" implicit in our laws of legal inheritance. An idiot can inherit millions, and a trust fund can keep his estate intact. We must admit that our legal system of private property plus inheritance is unjust—but we put up with it because we are not convinced, at the moment, that anyone has invented a better system. The alternative of the commons is too horrifying to contemplate. Injustice is preferable to total ruin.

It is one of the peculiarities of the warfare between reform and the status quo that it is thoughtlessly governed by a double standard. Whenever a reform measure is proposed it is often defeated when its opponents triumphantly discover a flaw in it. As Kingsley Davis has pointed out,[17] worshippers of the status quo sometimes imply that no reform is possible without unanimous agreement, an implication contrary to historical fact. As nearly as I can make out, automatic rejection of proposed reforms is based on one of two unconscious assumptions: (i) that the status quo is perfect; or (ii) that the choice we face is between reform and no action; if the proposed reform is imperfect, we presumably should take no action at all, while we wait for a perfect proposal.

But we can never do nothing. That which we have done for thousands of years is also action. It also produces evils. Once we are aware that the status quo is action, we can then compare its discoverable advantages and disadvantages with the predicted advantages and disadvantages of the proposed reform, discounting as best we can for our lack of experience. On the basis of such a comparison, we can make a rational decision which will not involve the unworkable assumption that only perfect systems are tolerable.

Recognition of Necessity

Perhaps the simplest summary of this analysis of man's population problems is this: the commons, if justifiable at all, is justifiable only under conditions of low-population density. As the human population has increased, the commons has had to be abandoned in one aspect after another.

First we abandoned the commons in food gathering, enclosing farm land and restricting pastures and hunting and fishing areas. These restrictions are still not complete throughout the world.

Somewhat later we saw that the commons as a place for waste disposal would also have to be abandoned. Restrictions on the disposal of domestic sewage are widely accepted in the Western world; we are still struggling to close the commons to pollution by automobiles, factories, insecticide sprayers, fertilizing operations, and atomic energy installations.

In a still more embryonic state is our recognition of the evils of the commons in matters of pleasure. There is almost no restriction on the propagation of sound waves in the public medium. The shopping public is assaulted with mindless music, without its consent. Our government is paying out billions of dollars to create supersonic transport which will disturb 50,000 people for every one person who is whisked from coast to coast 3 hours faster. Advertisers muddy the airwaves of radio and television and pollute the view of travelers. We are a long way from outlawing the commons in matters of pleasure. Is this because our Puritan inheritance makes us view pleasure as something of a sin, and pain (that is, the pollution of advertising) as the sign of virtue?

Every new enclosure of the commons involves the infringement of somebody's personal liberty. Infringements made in the distant past are accepted because no contemporary complains of a loss. It is the newly proposed infringements that we vigorously oppose; cries of "rights" and "freedom" fill the air. But what does "freedom" mean? When men mutually agreed to pass laws against robbing, mankind became more free, not less so. Individuals locked into the logic of the commons are free only to bring on universal ruin; once they see the necessity of mutual coercion, they become free to pursue other goals. I believe it was Hegel who said, "Freedom is the recognition of necessity."

The most important aspect of necessity that we must now recognize, is the necessity of abandoning the commons in breeding. No technical solution can rescue us from the misery of overpopulation. Freedom to breed will bring ruin to all. At the moment, to avoid hard decisions many of us are tempted to propagandize for conscience and responsible parenthood. The temptation must be resisted, because an appeal to independently acting consciences selects for the disappearance of all conscience in the long run, and an increase in anxiety in the short.

The only way we can preserve and nurture other and more precious freedoms is by relinquishing the freedom to breed, and that very soon. "Freedom is the recognition of necessity"—and it is the role of education to reveal to all the necessity of abandoning the freedom to breed. Only so, can we put an end to this aspect of the tragedy of the commons.

NOTES

1. J. B. Wiesner and H. F. York, *Sci. Amer.* 211 (No. 4), 27 (1964).

2. G. Hardin, *J. Hered.* 50, 68 (1959); S. von Hoernor, *Science* 137, 18 (1962).

3. A. Smith, *The Wealth of Nations* (Modern Library, New York, 1937), p. 423.

4. W. F. Lloyd, *Two Lectures on the Checks to Population* (Oxford Univ. Press, Oxford, England, 1833), reprinted (in part) in *Population, Evolution, and Birth Control,* G. Hardin, Ed. (Freeman, San Francisco, 1964), p. 37.

5. A. N. Whitehead, *Science and the Modern World* (Mentor, New York, 1948), p. 17.

6. G. Hardin, Ed. *Population, Evolution and Birth Control* (Freeman, San Francisco, 1964), p. 56.

7. S. McVay, *Sci. Amer.* 216 (No. 8), 13 (1966).

8. J. Fletcher, *Situation Ethics* (Westminster, Philadelphia, 1966).

9. D. Lack, *The Natural Regulation of Animal Numbers* (Clarendon Press, Oxford, 1954).

10. H. Girvetz, *From Wealth to Welfare* (Stanford Univ. Press, Stanford, Calif., 1950).

11. G. Hardin, *Perspec. Biol. Med.* 6, 366 (1963).

12. U. Thant, *Int. Planned Parenthood News,* No. 168 (February 1968), p. 3.

13. K. Davis, *Science* 158, 730 (1967).

14. P. Goodman, *New York Rev. Books* 10(8), 22 (23 May 1968).

15. A. Comfort, *The Anxiety Makers* (Nelson, London, 1967).

16. C. Frankel, *The Case for Modern Man* (Harper, New York, 1955), p. 203.

17. J. D. Roslansky, *Genetics and the Future of Man* (Appleton-Century-Crofts, New York, 1966), p. 177.

1-3

The Prosperous Community

SOCIAL CAPITAL AND PUBLIC LIFE

Robert D. Putnam

The solutions to all of the problems presented in this chapter require partici-
pants to cooperate—to pay their taxes, to refrain from overfishing, to fix their
polluting vehicles, and the like—even as each participant recognizes that he
or she would be rewarded by failing to cooperate. This situation not only
endangers a community's ability to achieve its collective goals but also engenders
mutual suspicion and hostility among community members. In the article that
follows, Robert Putnam argues persuasively that successful cooperation breeds
success in the future. If we trust our neighbors to follow through on their
commitments, then we are more likely to do the same.

> Your corn is ripe today; mine will be so tomorrow. 'Tis profitable for us
> both, that I should labour with you today, and that you should aid me
> tomorrow. I have no kindness for you, and know you have as little for
> me. I will not, therefore, take any pains upon your account; and should
> I labour with you upon my own account, in expectation of a return,
> I know I should be disappointed, and that I should in vain depend upon
> your gratitude. Here then I leave you to labour alone; You treat me in the
> same manner. The seasons change; and both of us lose our harvests for
> want of mutual confidence and security.
>
> —DAVID HUME

THE PREDICAMENT of the farmers in Hume's parable is all too familiar in communities and nations around the world:

- Parents in communities everywhere want better educational opportunities
  for their children, but collaborative efforts to improve public schools falter.
- Residents of American ghettos share an interest in safer streets, but
  collective action to control crime fails.
- Poor farmers in the Third World need more effective irrigation and
  marketing schemes, but cooperation to these ends proves fragile.

Source: Robert D. Putnam, "The Prosperous Community: Social Capital and Public Life," *The American Prospect*, March 21, 1993.

- Global warming threatens livelihoods from Manhattan to Mauritius, but joint action to forestall this shared risk founders.

Failure to cooperate for mutual benefit does not necessarily signal ignorance or irrationality or even malevolence, as philosophers since Hobbes have underscored. Hume's farmers were not dumb, or crazy, or evil; they were trapped. Social scientists have lately analyzed this fundamental predicament in a variety of guises: the tragedy of the commons; the logic of collective action; public goods; the prisoners' dilemma. In all these situations, as in Hume's rustic anecdote, everyone would be better off if everyone could cooperate. In the absence of coordination and credible mutual commitment, however, everyone defects, ruefully but rationally, confirming one another's melancholy expectations.

How can such dilemmas of collective action be overcome, short of creating some Hobbesian Leviathan? Social scientists in several disciplines have recently suggested a novel diagnosis of this problem, a diagnosis resting on the concept of *social capital*. By analogy with notions of physical capital and human capital—tools and training that enhance individual productivity—"social capital" refers to features of social organization, such as networks, norms, and trust, that facilitate coordination and cooperation for mutual benefit. Social capital enhances the benefits of investment in physical and human capital.

Working together is easier in a community blessed with a substantial stock of social capital. This insight turns out to have powerful practical implications for many issues on the American national agenda—for how we might overcome the poverty and violence of South Central Los Angeles, or revitalize industry in the Rust Belt, or nurture the fledgling democracies of the former Soviet empire and the erstwhile Third World. . . .

How does social capital undergird good government and economic progress? First, networks of civic engagement foster sturdy norms of generalized reciprocity: I'll do this for you now, in the expectation that down the road you or someone else will return the favor. "Social capital is akin to what Tom Wolfe called the 'favor bank' in his novel *The Bonfire of the Vanities*," notes economist Robert Frank. A society that relies on generalized reciprocity is more efficient than a distrustful society, for the same reason that money is more efficient than barter. Trust lubricates social life.

Networks of civic engagement also facilitate coordination and communication and amplify information about the trustworthiness of other individuals. Students of prisoners' dilemmas and related games report that cooperation is most easily sustained through repeat play. When economic and political dealing is embedded in dense networks of social interaction, incentives for opportunism and malfeasance are reduced. This is why the diamond trade, with its extreme possibilities for fraud, is concentrated within close-knit ethnic enclaves. Dense social ties facilitate gossip and other valuable ways of cultivating reputation—an essential foundation for trust in a complex society.

Finally, networks of civic engagement embody past success at collaboration, which can serve as a cultural template for future collaboration. The civic traditions of north-central Italy provide a historical repertoire of forms of cooperation that, having proved their worth in the past, are available to citizens for addressing new problems of collective action.

Sociologist James Coleman concludes, "Like other forms of capital, social capital is productive, making possible the achievement of certain ends that would not be attainable in its absence. . . . In a farming community . . . where one farmer got his hay baled by another and where farm tools are extensively borrowed and lent, the social capital allows each farmer to get his work done with less physical capital in the form of tools and equipment." Social capital, in short, enables Hume's farmers to surmount their dilemma of collective action.

Stocks of social capital, such as trust, norms, and networks, tend to be self-reinforcing and cumulative. Successful collaboration in one endeavor builds connections and trust—social assets that facilitate future collaboration in other, unrelated tasks. As with conventional capital, those who have social capital tend to accumulate more—them as has, gets. Social capital is what the social philosopher Albert O. Hirschman calls a "moral resource," that is, a resource whose supply increases rather than decreases through use and which (unlike physical capital) becomes depleted if *not* used.

Unlike conventional capital, social capital is a "public good," that is, it is not the private property of those who benefit from it. Like other public goods, from clean air to safe streets, social capital tends to be underprovided by private agents. This means that social capital must often be a by-product of other social activities. Social capital typically consists in ties, norms, and trust transferable from one social setting to another. . . .

Social Capital and Economic Development

Social capital is coming to be seen as a vital ingredient in economic development around the world. Scores of studies of rural development have shown that a vigorous network of indigenous grassroots associations can be as essential to growth as physical investment, appropriate technology, or (that nostrum of neoclassical economists) "getting prices right." Political scientist Elinor Ostrom has explored why some cooperative efforts to manage common pool resources, like grazing grounds and water supplies, succeed, while others fail. Existing stocks of social capital are an important part of the story. Conversely, government interventions that neglect or undermine this social infrastructure can go seriously awry.

Studies of the rapidly growing economies of East Asia almost always emphasize the importance of dense social networks, so that these economies are sometimes said to represent a new brand of "network capitalism." These networks, often based on the extended family or on close-knit ethnic communities like the overseas Chinese, foster trust, lower transaction costs, and speed information and innovation. Social capital can be transmuted, so to speak, into financial capital: In novelist Amy Tan's *Joy Luck Club,* a group of mah-jong–playing friends evolves into a joint investment association. China's extraordinary economic growth over the last decade has depended less on formal institutions than on *guanxi* (personal connections) to underpin contracts and to channel savings and investment. . . .

Bill Clinton's proposals for job-training schemes and industrial extension agencies invite attention to social capital. The objective should not be merely an assembly-line injection of booster shots of technical expertise and work-related skills into individual firms and workers. Rather, such programs could provide a matchless opportunity to create productive new linkages among community groups, schools, employers, and workers, without creating costly new bureaucracies. Why not experiment with modest subsidies for training programs that bring together firms, educational institutions, and community associations in innovative local partnerships? The latent effects of such programs on social capital accumulation could prove even more powerful than the direct effects on technical productivity.

Conversely, when considering the effects of economic reconversion on communities, we must weigh the risks of destroying social capital. Precisely because social capital is a public good, the costs of closing factories and destroying communities go beyond the personal trauma borne by individuals. Worse yet, some government programs themselves, such as urban renewal and public housing projects, have heedlessly ravaged existing social networks. The fact that these collective costs are not well measured by our current accounting schemes does not mean that they are not real. Shred enough of the social fabric and we all pay.

Social Capital and America's Ills

Fifty-one deaths and 1 billion dollars in property damage in Los Angeles . . . put urban decay back on the American agenda. Yet if the ills are clear, the prescription is not. Even those most sympathetic to the plight of America's ghettos are not persuaded that simply reviving the social programs dismantled in the last decade or so will solve the problems. The erosion of social capital is an essential and under-appreciated part of the diagnosis.

Although most poor Americans do not reside in the inner city, there is something qualitatively different about the social and economic isolation experienced by the chronically poor blacks and Latinos who do. Joblessness, inadequate education, and poor health clearly truncate the opportunities of ghetto residents. Yet so do profound deficiencies in social capital.

Part of the problem facing blacks and Latinos in the inner city is that they lack "connections" in the most literal sense. Job-seekers in the ghetto have little access, for example, to conventional job referral networks. Labor economists Anne Case and Lawrence Katz have shown that, regardless of race, inner-city youth living in neighborhoods blessed with high levels of civic engagement are more likely to finish school, have a job, and avoid drugs and crime, controlling for the individual characteristics of the youth. That is, of two identical youths, the one unfortunate enough to live in a neighborhood whose social capital has eroded is more likely to end up hooked, booked, or dead. Several researchers seem to have found similar neighborhood effects on the incidence of teen pregnancy, among both blacks and whites, again controlling for personal characteristics. Where you live and whom you know—the social capital you can draw on—helps to define who you are and thus to determine your fate.

Racial and class inequalities in access to social capital, if properly measured, may be as great as inequalities in financial and human capital, and no less portentous. Economist Glenn Loury has used the term "social capital" to capture the fundamental fact that racial segregation, coupled with socially inherited differences in community networks and norms, means that individually targeted "equal opportunity" policies may not eliminate racial inequality, even in the long run. Research suggests that the life chances of today's generation depend not only on their parents' social resources, but also on the social resources of their parents' ethnic group. Even workplace integration and upward mobility by successful members of minority groups cannot overcome these persistent effects of inequalities in social capital. William Julius Wilson has described in tragic detail how the exodus of middle-class and working-class families from the ghetto has eroded the social capital available to those left behind. The settlement houses that nurtured sewing clubs and civic activism a century ago, embodying community as much as charity, are now mostly derelict.

It would be a dreadful mistake, of course, to overlook the repositories of social capital within America's minority communities. . . . Historically, the black church has been the most bounteous treasure-house of social capital for African Americans. The church provided the organizational infrastructure for political mobilization in the civil rights movement. Recent work on American political participation by political scientist Sidney Verba and his colleagues shows that the church is a uniquely powerful resource for political engagement among blacks—an arena in which to learn about public affairs and hone political skills and make connections.

In tackling the ills of America's cities, investments in physical capital, financial capital, human capital, and social capital are complementary, not competing alternatives. Investments in jobs and education, for example, will be more effective if they are coupled with reinvigoration of community associations.

Some churches provide job banks and serve as informal credit bureaus, for example, using their reputational capital to vouch for members who may be ex-convicts, former drug addicts, or high school dropouts. In such cases the church does not merely provide referral networks. More fundamentally, wary employers and financial institutions bank on the church's ability to identify parishioners whose formal credentials understate their reliability. At the same time, because these parishioners value their standing in the church, and because the church has put its own reputation on the line, they have an additional incentive to perform. Like conventional capital for conventional borrowers, social capital serves as a kind of collateral for men and women who are excluded from ordinary credit or labor markets. In effect, the participants pledge their social connections, leveraging social capital to improve the efficiency with which markets operate.

The importance of social capital for America's domestic agenda is not limited to minority communities. Take public education, for instance. The success of private schools is attributable, according to James Coleman's massive research, not so much to what happens in the classroom nor to the endowments of individual students, but rather to the greater engagement of parents and community members in private school activities. Educational reformers like child psychologist James Comer seek to improve schooling not merely by "treating" individual children but by deliberately involving parents and others in the educational process. Educational policymakers need to move beyond debates about curriculum and governance to consider the effects of social capital. Indeed, most commonly discussed proposals for "choice" are deeply flawed by their profoundly individualist conception of education. If states and localities are to experiment with voucher systems for education or child care, why not encourage vouchers to be spent in ways that strengthen community organization, not weaken it? Once we recognize the importance of social capital, we ought to be able to design programs that creatively combine individual choice with collective engagement.

Many people today are concerned about revitalizing American democracy. Although discussion of political reform in the United States focuses nowadays on such procedural issues as term limits and campaign financing, some of the ills that afflict the American polity reflect deeper, largely unnoticed social changes.

"Some people say that you usually can trust people. Others say that you must be wary in relations with people. Which is your view?" Responses to this question, posed repeatedly in national surveys for several decades, suggest that social trust in the United States has declined for more than a quarter century. By contrast, American politics benefited from plentiful stocks of social capital in earlier times. Recent historical work on the Progressive Era, for example, has uncovered evidence of the powerful role played by nominally non-political associations (such as women's literary societies) precisely because they provided a dense social network. Is our current predicament the result of a long-term erosion of social capital, such as community engagement and social trust?

Economist Juliet Schorr's discovery of "the unexpected decline of leisure" in America suggests that our generation is less engaged with one another outside the marketplace and thus less prepared to cooperate for shared goals. Mobile, two-career (or one-parent) families often must use the market for child care and other services formerly provided through family and neighborhood networks. Even if market-based services, considered individually, are of high quality, this deeper social trend is eroding social capital. There are more empty seats at the PTA and in church pews these days. While celebrating the productive, liberating effects of fuller equality in the workplace, we must replace the social capital that this movement has depleted.

Our political parties, once intimately coupled to the capillaries of community life, have become evanescent confections of pollsters and media consultants and independent political entrepreneurs—the very antithesis of social capital. We have too easily accepted a conception of democracy in which public policy is not the outcome of a collective deliberation about the public interest, but rather a residue of campaign strategy. The social capital approach, focusing on the indirect effects of civic norms and networks, is a much-needed corrective to an exclusive emphasis on the formal institutions of government as an explanation for our collective discontents. If we are to make our political system more responsive, especially to those who lack connections at the top, we must nourish grass-roots organization.

Classic liberal social policy is designed to enhance the opportunities of *individuals,* but if social capital is important, this emphasis is partially misplaced. Instead we must focus on community development, allowing space for religious organizations and choral societies and Little Leagues that may seem to have little to do with politics or economics. Government policies, whatever their intended effects, should be vetted for their indirect effects on social capital. If, as some suspect, social capital is fostered more by home ownership than by public or private tenancy, then we should design housing policy accordingly. Similarly, as Theda Skocpol has suggested, the direct benefits of national service programs might be dwarfed by the indirect benefits that could flow from the creation of social networks that cross class and racial lines. In any comprehensive strategy for improving the plight of America's communities, rebuilding social capital is as important as investing in human and physical capital. . . .

Wise policy can encourage social capital formation, and social capital itself enhances the effectiveness of government action. From agricultural extension services in the last century to tax exemptions for community organizations in this one,

American government has often promoted investments in social capital, and it must renew that effort now. A new administration that is, at long last, more willing to use public power and the public purse for public purpose should not overlook the importance of social connectedness as a vital backdrop for effective policy.

Students of social capital have only begun to address some of the most important questions that this approach to public affairs suggests. What are the actual trends in different forms of civic engagement? Why do communities differ in their stocks of social capital? What *kinds* of civic engagement seem most likely to foster economic growth or community effectiveness? Must specific types of social capital be matched to different public problems? Most important of all, how is social capital created and destroyed? What strategies for building (or rebuilding) social capital are most promising? How can we balance the twin strategies of exploiting existing social capital and creating it afresh? The suggestions scattered throughout this essay are intended to challenge others to even more practical methods of encouraging new social capital formation and leveraging what we have already.

We also need to ask about the negative effects of social capital, for like human and physical capital, social capital can be put to bad purposes. Liberals have often sought to destroy some forms of social capital (from medieval guilds to neighborhood schools) in the name of individual opportunity. We have not always reckoned with the indirect social costs of our policies, but we were often right to be worried about the power of private associations. Social inequalities may be embedded in social capital. Norms and networks that serve some groups may obstruct others, particularly if the norms are discriminatory or the networks socially segregated. Recognizing the importance of social capital in sustaining community life does not exempt us from the need to worry about how that community is defined—who is inside and thus benefits from social capital, and who is outside and does not. Some forms of social capital can impair individual liberties, as critics of communitarianism warn. Many of the Founders' fears about the "mischiefs of faction" apply to social capital. Before toting up the balance sheet for social capital in its various forms, we need to weigh costs as well as benefits. This challenge still awaits.

Progress on the urgent issues facing our country and our world requires ideas that bridge outdated ideological divides. Both liberals and conservatives agree on the importance of social empowerment, as E. J. Dionne recently noted ("The Quest for Community (Again)," *TAP,* Summer 1992). The social capital approach provides a deeper conceptual underpinning for this nominal convergence. Real progress requires not facile verbal agreement, but hard thought and ideas with high fiber content. The social capital approach promises to uncover new ways of combining private social infrastructure with public policies that work, and, in turn, of using wise public policies to revitalize America's stocks of social capital.

Chapter 2

The Constitutional Framework

2-1

The Founding Fathers: A Reform Caucus in Action

John P. Roche Jr.

Textbook consideration of the Constitution's Framers reverentially casts them as political philosophers conveying to future generations timeless laws of proper civic relations. Students of the era delve into arguments of The Federalist and other source materials to detect the intellectual roots of the Framers in the political theories of Locke, Montesquieu, Hume, and even Machiavelli. In this essay Roche reminds us that we should not forget that these were politicians charged with proposing a reform that had to win the endorsement of at least nine states before it became more than the collective ruminations of thirty-nine delegates. The Framers were certainly conversant with the leading political thought of their era—so conversant, indeed, that they exhibited great versatility in invoking these theorists in behalf of whatever scheme they were endorsing. Roche makes a persuasive case that the Constitution reflects the at times brilliant but always pragmatic choices of Framers ever mindful of the preferences of their constituents. Consequently, the Constitution was, in Roche's assessment, a "patch-work sewn together under the pressure of both time and events."

Source: John P. Roche, "The Founding Fathers: A Reform Caucus in Action," *American Political Science Review 55,* no. 4 (December 1961): 799–816. Some notes appearing in the original have been deleted.

OVER THE LAST CENTURY and a half, the work of the Constitutional Convention and the motives of the Founding Fathers have . . . undergone miraculous metamorphoses: at one time acclaimed as liberals and bold social engineers, today they appear in the guise of sound Burkean conservatives. . . . The implicit assumption is that if James Madison were among us, he would be President of the Ford Foundation, while Alexander Hamilton would chair the Committee for Economic Development.

The "Fathers" have thus been admitted to our best circles; the revolutionary ferocity which confiscated all Tory property in reach and populated New Brunswick with outlaws has been converted by . . . American historians into a benign dedication to "consensus" and "prescriptive rights." The Daughters of the American Revolution have . . . at last found ancestors worthy of their descendants. It is not my purpose here to argue that the "Fathers" were, in fact, radical revolutionaries; that proposition has been brilliantly demonstrated by Robert R. Palmer in his *Age of the Democratic Revolution.* My concern is with the further position that not only were they revolutionaries, but also they were democrats. Indeed, . . . they were first and foremost superb democratic politicians. I suspect that in a contemporary setting, James Madison would be Speaker of the House of Representatives and Hamilton would be the *eminence grise* dominating . . . the Executive Office of the President. They were, with their colleagues, *political men* . . . and as recent research into the nature of American polities in the 1780s confirms,[1] they were committed (perhaps willy-nilly) to working within the democratic framework, within a universe of public approval. Charles Beard *and* the filiopietists to the contrary notwithstanding, the Philadelphia Convention was not a College of Cardinals or a council of Platonic guardians working within a manipulative, predemocratic framework; it was a *nationalist* reform caucus which had to operate with great delicacy and skill in a political cosmos full of enemies to achieve the one definitive goal-popular approbation.

Perhaps the time has come, to borrow Walton Hamilton's fine phrase, to raise the Framers from immortality to mortality, to give them credit for their magnificent demonstration of the art of democratic politics. The point must be reemphasized; they *made* history and did it within the limits of consensus. There was nothing inevitable about the future in 1787. . . . What they did was to hammer out a pragmatic compromise which would both bolster the "National interest" and be acceptable to the people. What inspiration they got came from their collective experience as professional politicians in a democratic society. As John Dickinson put it to his fellow delegates on August 13, "Experience must be our guide. Reason may mislead us."

In this context, let us examine the problems they confronted and the solutions they evolved. The Convention has been described picturesquely as a counter-revolutionary junta and the Constitution as a *coup d'etat*,[2] but this has been accomplished by withdrawing the whole history of the movement for constitutional reform from its true context. No doubt the goals of the constitutional elite were "subversive" to the existing political order, but it is overlooked that their subversion could only have succeeded if the people of the United States endorsed it by regularized procedures. Indubitably they were "plotting" to establish a much stronger central government than existed under the Articles, but only in the sense in which one could argue equally well that John F. Kennedy was, from 1956 to 1960, "plotting" to become President. In short, on the fundamental *procedural* level, the Constitutionalists had to work according to the prevailing rules of the game. . . .

I

When the Constitutionalists went forth to subvert the Confederation, they utilized the mechanisms of political legitimacy. And the roadblocks which confronted them were formidable. At the same time, they were endowed with certain potent political assets. The history of the United States from 1786 to 1790 was largely one of a masterful employment of political expertise by the Constitutionalists as against bumbling, erratic behavior by the opponents of reform. Effectively, the Constitutionalists had to induce the states, by democratic techniques of coercion, to emasculate themselves. To be specific, if New York had refused to join the new Union, the project was doomed; yet before New York was safely in, the reluctant state legislature had *sua s'ponte* to take the following steps: (1) agree to send delegates to the Philadelphia Convention; (2) provide maintenance for these delegates (these were distinct stages: New Hampshire was early in naming delegates, but did not provide for their maintenance until July); (3) set up the special *ad hoc* convention to decide on ratification; and (4) concede to the decision of the *ad hoc* convention that New York should participate. New York admittedly was a tricky state, with a strong interest in a *status quo* which permitted her to exploit New Jersey and Connecticut, but the same legal hurdles existed in every state. And at the risk of becoming boring, it must be reiterated that the *only* weapon in the Constitutionalist arsenal was an effective mobilization of public opinion.

The group which undertook this struggle was an interesting amalgam of a few dedicated nationalists with the self-interested spokesmen of various parochial bailiwicks. The Georgians, for example, wanted a strong central authority to provide military protection for their huge, underpopulated state against the Creek

Confederacy; Jerseymen and Connecticuters wanted to escape from economic bondage to New York; the Virginians hoped to establish a system which would give that great state its rightful place in the councils of the republic. The dominant figures in the politics of these states therefore cooperated in the call for the Convention. . . . There was, of course, a large element of personality in the affair: there is reason to suspect that Patrick Henry's opposition to the Convention and the Constitution was founded on his conviction that Jefferson was behind both, and a close study of local politics elsewhere would surely reveal that others supported the Constitution for the simple (and politically quite sufficient) reason that the "wrong" people were against it.

To say this is not to suggest that the Constitution rested on a foundation of impure or base motives. It is rather to argue that in politics there are no immaculate conceptions, and that in the drive for a stronger general government, motives of all sorts played a part. Few men in the history of mankind have espoused a view of the "common good" or "public interest" that militated against their private status; even Plato with all his reverence for disembodied reason managed to put philosophers on top of the pile. Thus it is not surprising that a number of diversified private interests joined to push the nationalist public interest; what would have been surprising was the absence of such a pragmatic united front. And the fact remains that, however motivated, these men did demonstrate a willingness to compromise their parochial interests in behalf of an ideal which took shape before their eyes and under their ministrations.

. . . [W]hat distinguished the leaders of the Constitutionalist caucus from their enemies was a "Continental" approach to political, economic and military issues. To the extent that they shared an institutional base of operations, it was the Continental Congress (thirty-nine of the delegates to the Federal Convention had served in Congress), and this was hardly a locale which inspired respect for the state governments. . . . [M]embership in the Congress under the Articles of Confederation worked to establish a continental frame of reference, that a Congressman from Pennsylvania and one from South Carolina would share a universe of discourse which provided them with a conceptual common denominator *vis-à-vis* their respective state legislatures. This was particularly true with respect to external affairs: the average state legislator was probably about as concerned with foreign policy then as he is today, but Congressmen were constantly forced to take the broad view of American prestige, were compelled to listen to the reports of Secretary John Jay and to the dispatches and pleas from their frustrated envoys in Britain, France and Spain. From considerations such as these, a "Continental" ideology developed which seems to have demanded a revision of our domestic institutions primarily on the ground that only by invigorating our general government could we assume our rightful place in the international arena. Indeed, an argument with great force-particularly since Washington was its incarnation-urged that our very survival in the Hobbesian jungle of world politics depended upon a reordering and strengthening of our national sovereignty.[3]

. . . [T]he great achievement of the Constitutionalists was their ultimate success in convincing the elected representatives of a majority of the white male population that change was imperative. A small group of political leaders with a Continental vision and essentially a consciousness of the United States' *international* impotence provided the matrix of the movement. To their standard other leaders rallied with their own parallel ambitions. Their great assets were (1) the presence in their caucus of the one authentic American "father figure," George Washington, whose prestige was enormous;[4] (2) the energy and talent of their leadership (in which one must include the towering intellectuals of the time, John Adams and Thomas Jefferson, despite their absence abroad), and their communications "network," which was far superior to anything on the opposition side;[5] (3) the preemptive skill which made "their" issue The Issue and kept the locally oriented opposition permanently on the defensive; and (4) the subjective consideration that these men were spokesmen of a new and compelling credo: *American* nationalism, that ill-defined but nonetheless potent sense of collective purpose that emerged from the American Revolution.

Despite great institutional handicaps, the Constitutionalists managed in the mid-1780s to mount an offensive which gained momentum as years went by. Their greatest problem was lethargy, and paradoxically, the number of barriers in their path may have proved an advantage in the long run. Beginning with the initial battle to get the Constitutional Convention called and delegates appointed, they could never relax, never let up the pressure. In practical terms, this meant that the local "organizations" created by the Constitutionalists were perpetually in movement building up their cadres for the next fight. (The word organization has to be used with great caution: a political organization in the United States—as in contemporary England—generally consisted of a magnate and his following, or a coalition of magnates. This did not necessarily mean that it was "undemocratic" or "aristocratic," in the Aristotelian sense of the word: while a few magnates such as the Livingstons could draft their followings, most exercised their leadership without coercion on the basis of popular endorsement. The absence of organized opposition did not imply the impossibility of competition any more than low public participation in elections necessarily indicated an undemocratic suffrage.)

The Constitutionalists got the jump on the "opposition" . . . at the outset with the demand for a Convention. Their opponents were caught in an old political trap: they were not being asked to approve any specific program of reform, but only to endorse a meeting to discuss and recommend needed reforms. If they took a hard line at the first stage, they were put in the position of glorifying the *status quo* and of denying the need for *any* changes. Moreover, the Constitutionalists could go to the people with a persuasive argument for "fair play"—"How can you condemn reform before you know precisely what is involved?" Since the state legislatures obviously would have the final say on any proposals that might emerge from the Convention, the Constitutionalists were merely reasonable men asking for a chance. Besides, since they did not make any concrete proposals at that stage, they were in a position to capitalize on every sort of generalized discontent with the Confederation.

Perhaps because of their poor intelligence system, perhaps because of overconfidence generated by the failure of all previous efforts to alter the Articles,[6] the opposition awoke too late to the dangers that confronted them in 1787. Not only did the Constitutionalists manage to get every state but Rhode Island . . . to appoint delegates to Philadelphia, but when the results were in, it appeared that they dominated the delegations. Given the apathy of the opposition, this was a natural phenomenon: in an ideologically nonpolarized political atmosphere those who get appointed to a special committee are likely to be the men who supported the movement for its creation. Even George Clinton, who seems to have been the first opposition leader to awake to the possibility of trouble, could not prevent the New York legislature from appointing Alexander Hamilton— though he did have the foresight to send two of his henchmen to dominate the delegation. Incidentally, much has been made of the fact that the delegates to Philadelphia were not elected by the people; some have adduced this fact as evidence of the "undemocratic" character of the gathering. But put in the context of the time, this argument is wholly specious: the central government under the Articles was considered a creature of the component states and in all the states but Rhode Island, Connecticut and New Hampshire, members of the national Congress were chosen by the state legislatures. This was not a consequence of elitism or fear of the mob; it was a logical extension of states'-rights doctrine to guarantee that the national institution did not end-run the state legislatures and make direct contact with the people.[7]

II

With delegations safely named, the focus shifted to Philadelphia. While waiting for a quorum to assemble, James Madison got busy and drafted the so-called Randolph or Virginia Plan with the aid of the Virginia delegation. This was a political master-stroke. Its consequence was that once business got underway, the framework of discussion was established on Madison's terms. There was no interminable argument over agenda; instead the delegates took the Virginia Resolutions—"just for purposes of discussion"—as their point of departure. And along with Madison's proposals, many of which were buried in the course of the summer, went his major premise: a new start on a Constitution rather than piece-meal amendment. This was not necessarily revolutionary—a little exegesis could demonstrate that a new Constitution might be formulated as "amendments" to the Articles of Confederation—but Madison's proposal that this "lump sum" amendment go into effect after approval by nine states (the Articles required unanimous state approval for any amendment) was thoroughly subversive.[8]

Standard treatments of the Convention divide the delegates into "nationalists" and "states'-righters" with various improvised shadings ("moderate national-ists," etc.), but these are *a posteriori* categories which obfuscate more than they clarify. What is striking to one who analyzes the Convention as a case-study in democratic politics is the lack of clear-cut ideological divisions in the Convention. Indeed, I submit that the evidence—Madison's *Notes,* the corre-spondence of the delegates, and debates on ratification—indicates that this was a remarkably homogeneous body on the ideological level. Yates and Lansing, Clinton's two chaperones for Hamilton, left in disgust on July 10. (Is there any-thing more tedious than sitting through endless disputes on matters one deems fundamentally misconceived? It takes an iron will to spend a hot summer as an ideological *agent provocateur.*) Luther Martin, Maryland's bibulous narcissist, left on September 4 in a huff when he discovered that others did not share his self-esteem; others went home for personal reasons. But the hard core of delegates accepted a grinding regimen throughout the attrition of a Philadelphia summer precisely because they shared the Constitutionalist goal.

Basic differences of opinion emerged, of course, but these were not ideologi-cal; they were *structural.* If the so-called "states'-rights" group had not accepted the fundamental purposes of the Convention, they could simply have pulled out and by doing so have aborted the whole enterprise. Instead of bolting, they returned day after day to argue and to compromise. An interesting symbol of this basic homogeneity was the initial agreement on secrecy: these professional politicians did not want to become prisoners of publicity; they wanted to retain that freedom of maneuver which is only possible when men are not forced to take public stands in the preliminary stages of negotiation.[9] There was no legal means of binding the tongues of the delegates: at any stage in the game a dele-gate with basic principled objections to the emerging project could have taken the stump (as Luther Martin did after his exit) and denounced the convention to the skies. Yet Madison did not even inform Thomas Jefferson in Paris of the course of the deliberations[10] and available correspondence indicates that the del-egates generally observed the injunction. Secrecy is certainly uncharacteristic of any assembly marked by strong ideological polarization. This was noted at the time: the *New York Daily Advertiser,* August 14, 1787, commented that the " . . . profound secrecy hitherto observed by the Convention [we consider] a happy omen, as it demonstrates that the spirit of party on any great and essential point cannot have arisen to any height." [11]

Commentators on the Constitution who have read *The Federalist* in lieu of reading the actual debates have credited the Fathers with the invention of a sublime concept called "Federalism." Unfortunately *The Federalist* is probative evidence for only one proposition: that Hamilton and Madison were inspired propagandists with a genius for retrospective symmetry. Federalism, as the theory is generally defined, was an improvisation which was later promoted into a political theory. Experts on "federalism" should take to heart the advice of David Hume, who warned in his *Of the Rise and Progress of the Arts and Sciences* that " . . . there is no subject in which we must proceed with more caution than in [history], lest we assign causes which never existed and reduce what is merely contingent to stable and universal principles." In any event, the final balance in the Constitution between the states and the nation must have come as a great disappointment to Madison, while Hamilton's unitary views are too well known to need elucidation.

It is indeed astonishing how those who have glibly designated James Madison the "father" of Federalism have overlooked the solid body of fact which indicates that he shared Hamilton's quest for a unitary central government. To be specific, they have avoided examining the clear import of the Madison-Virginia Plan,[12] and have disregarded Madison's dogged inch-by-inch retreat from the bastions of centralization. The Virginia Plan envisioned a unitary national government effectively freed from and dominant over the states. The lower house of the national legislature was to be elected directly by the people of the states with membership proportional to population. The upper house was to be selected by the lower and the two chambers would elect the executive and choose the judges: The national government would be thus cut completely loose from the states.[13]

The structure of the general government was freed from state control in a truly radical fashion, but the scope of the authority of the national sovereign as Madison initially formulated it was breathtaking. . . . The national legislature was to be empowered to disallow the acts of state legislatures, and the central government was vested, in addition to the powers of the nation under the Articles of Confederation, with plenary authority wherever ". . . the separate States are incompetent or in which the harmony of the United States may be interrupted by the exercise of individual legislation." [14] Finally, just to lock the door against state intrusion, the national Congress was to be given the power to use military force on recalcitrant states.[15] This was Madison's "model" of an ideal national government, though it later received little publicity in *The Federalist*.

The interesting thing was the reaction of the Convention to this militant program for a strong autonomous central government. Some delegates were startled, some obviously leery of so comprehensive a project of reform,[16] but nobody set off any fireworks and nobody walked out. Moreover, in the two weeks that followed, the Virginia Plan received substantial endorsement *en principe*; the initial temper of the gathering can be deduced from the approval "without debate or dissent," on May 31, of the Sixth Resolution which granted Congress the authority to disallow state legislation ". . . contravening *in its opinion* the Articles of Union." Indeed, an amendment was included to bar states from contravening national treaties.[17]

The Virginia Plan may therefore be considered, in ideological terms, as the delegates' Utopia, but as the discussions continued and became more specific, many of those present began to have second thoughts. After all, they were not residents of Utopia or guardians in Plato's Republic who could simply impose a philosophical ideal on subordinate strata of the population. They were practical politicians in a democratic society, and no matter what their private dreams might be, they had to take home an acceptable package and defend it—and their own political futures—against predictable attack. On June 14 the breaking point between dream and reality took place. Apparently realizing that under the Virginia Plan, Massachusetts, Virginia and Pennsylvania could virtually dominate the national government—and probably appreciating that to sell this program to "the folks back home" would be impossible—the delegates from the small states dug in their heels and demanded time for a consideration of alternatives. One gets a graphic sense of the inner politics from John Dickinson's reproach to Madison: "You see the consequences of pushing things too far. Some of the members from the small States wish for two branches in the General Legislature and are friends to a good National Government; but we would sooner submit to a foreign power than . . . be deprived of an equality of suffrage in both branches of the Legislature, and thereby be thrown under the domination of the large States." [18] . . .

III

According to the standard script, at this point the "states'-rights" group intervened in force behind the New Jersey Plan, which has been characteristically portrayed as a reversion to the *status quo* under the Articles of Confederation with but minor modifications. A careful examination of the evidence indicates that only in a marginal sense is this an accurate description. It is true that the New Jersey Plan put the states back into the institutional picture, but one could argue that to do so was a recognition of political reality rather than an affirmation of states'-rights.

A serious case can be made that the advocates of the New Jersey Plan, far from being ideological addicts of states'-rights, intended to substitute for the Virginia Plan a system which would both retain strong national power and have a chance of adoption in the states. The leading spokesman for the project asserted quite clearly that his views were based more on counsels of expediency than on principle; said Paterson on June 16: "I came here not to speak my own sentiments, but the sentiments of those who sent me. Our object is not such a Government as may be best in itself, but such a one as our Constituents have authorized us to prepare, and as they will approve." . . . With a shrewd eye, Paterson queried:

> Will the Operation and Force of the [central] Govt. depend upon the mode of Representn.—No—it will depend upon the Quantum of Power lodged in the leg. ex. and judy. Departments—Give [the existing] Congress the same Powers that you intend to give the two Branches, [under the Virginia Plan] and I apprehend they will act with as much Propriety and more Energy . . .[19]

In other words, the advocates of the New Jersey Plan concentrated their fire on what they held to be the *political liabilities* of the Virginia Plan—which were matters of institutional structure—rather than on the proposed scope of national authority. Indeed, the Supremacy Clause of the Constitution first saw the light of day in Paterson's Sixth Resolution; the New Jersey Plan contemplated the use of military force to secure compliance with national law; and finally Paterson made clear his view that under either the Virginia or the New Jersey systems, the general government would ". . . act on individuals and not on states." [20] From the states'-rights viewpoint, this was heresy: the fundament of that doctrine was the proposition that any central government had as its constituents the states, not the people, and could only reach the people through the agency of the state government.

Paterson then reopened the agenda of the Convention, but he did so within a distinctly nationalist framework. Paterson's position was one of favoring a strong central government in principle, but opposing one which in fact *put the big states in the saddle*. (The Virginia Plan, for all its abstract merits, did very well by Virginia.) As evidence for this speculation, there is a curious and intriguing proposal among Paterson's preliminary drafts of the New Jersey Plan:

> Whereas it is necessary in Order to form the People of the U. S. of America in to a Nation, that the States should be consolidated, by which means all the Citizens thereof will become equally intitled to and will equally participate in the same Privileges and Rights . . . it is therefore resolved, that all the Lands contained within the Limits of each state individually, and of the U. S. generally be considered as constituting one Body or Mass, and be divided into thirteen or more integral parts.

> Resolved, That such Divisions or integral Parts shall be styled Districts.[21]

This makes it sound as though Paterson was prepared to accept a strong unified central government along the lines of the Virginia Plan if the existing states were eliminated. He may have gotten the idea from his New Jersey colleague Judge David Brearley, who on June 9 had commented that the only remedy to the dilemma over representation was " . . . that a map of the U. S. be spread out, that all the existing boundaries be erased, and that a new partition of the whole be made into 13 equal parts." [22] According to Yates, Brearley added at this point " . . . then a government on the present [Virginia Plan] system will be just." [23]

This proposition was never pushed—it was patently unrealistic—but one can appreciate its purpose: it would have separated the men from the boys in the large-state delegations. How attached would the Virginians have been to their reform principles if Virginia were to disappear as a component geographical unit (the largest) for representational purposes? Up to this point, the Virginians had been in the happy position of supporting high ideals with that inner confidence born of knowledge that the "public interest" they endorsed would nourish their private interest. Worse, they had shown little willingness to compromise. Now the delegates from the small states announced that they were unprepared to be offered up as sacrificial victims to a "national interest" which reflected Virginia's parochial ambition. Caustic Charles Pinckney was not far off when he remarked sardonically that " . . . the whole [conflict] comes to this": "Give N. Jersey an equal vote, and she will dismiss her scruples, and concur in the Natil. system." [24] What he rather unfairly did not add was that the Jersey delegates were not free agents who could adhere to their private convictions; they had to take back, sponsor and risk their reputations on the reforms approved by the Convention—and in New Jersey, not in Virginia.

Paterson spoke on Saturday, and one can surmise that over the weekend there was a good deal of consultation, argument, and caucusing among the delegates. One member at least prepared a full length address: on Monday Alexander Hamilton, previously mute, rose and delivered a six-hour oration. [25] It was a remarkably apolitical speech; the gist of his position was that *both* the Virginia and New Jersey Plans were inadequately centralist, and he detailed a reform program which was reminiscent of the Protectorate under the Cromwellian *Instrument of Government* of 1653. It has been suggested that Hamilton did this in the best political tradition to emphasize the moderate character of the Virginia Plan,[26] to give the cautious delegates something *really* to worry about; but this interpretation seems somehow too clever. Particularly since the sentiments Hamilton expressed happened to be completely consistent with those he privately—and sometimes publicly—expressed throughout his life. He wanted, to take a striking phrase from a letter to George Washington, a "strong well mounted government";[27] in essence, the Hamilton Plan contemplated an elected life monarch, virtually free of public control, on the Hobbesian ground that only in this fashion could strength and stability be achieved. The other alternatives, he argued, would put policy-making at the mercy of the passions of the mob; only if the sovereign was beyond the reach of selfish influence would it be possible to have government in the interests of the whole community.[28]

From all accounts, this was a masterful and compelling speech, but (aside from furnishing John Lansing and Luther Martin with ammunition for later use against the Constitution) it made little impact. Hamilton was simply transmitting on a different wavelength from the rest of the delegates; the latter adjourned after his great effort, admired his rhetoric, and then returned to business.[29] It was rather as if they had taken a day off to attend the opera. Hamilton, never a particularly patient man or much of a negotiator, stayed for another ten days and then left, in considerable disgust, for New York.[30] Although he came back to Philadelphia sporadically and attended the last two weeks of the Convention, Hamilton played no part in the laborious task of hammering out the Constitution. . . .

IV

On Tuesday morning, June 19, the vacation was over. James Madison led off with a long, carefully reasoned speech analyzing the New Jersey Plan which, while intellectually vigorous in its criticisms, was quite conciliatory in mood. "The great difficulty," he observed, "lies in the affair of Representation; and if this could be adjusted, all others would be surmountable." [31] (As events were to demonstrate, this diagnosis was correct.) When he finished, a vote was taken on whether to continue with the Virginia Plan as the nucleus for a new constitution: seven states voted "Yes"; New York, New Jersey, and Delaware voted "No"; and Maryland, whose position often depended on which delegates happened to be on the floor, divided. Paterson, it seems, lost decisively; yet in a fundamental sense he and his allies had achieved their purpose: from that day onward, it could never be forgotten that the state governments loomed ominously in the background and that no verbal incantations could exorcise their power. Moreover, nobody bolted the convention: Paterson and his colleagues took their defeat in stride and set to work to modify the Virginia Plan, particularly with respect to its provisions on representation in the national legislature. Indeed, they won an immediate rhetorical bonus; when Oliver Ellsworth of Connecticut rose to move that the word "national" be expunged from the Third Virginia Resolution ("Resolved that a *national* Government ought to be established consisting of a *supreme* Legislative, Executive and Judiciary" [32]), Randolph agreed and the motion passed unanimously.[33] The process of compromise had begun.

For the next two weeks, the delegates circled around the problem of legislative representation. The Connecticut delegation appears to have evolved a possible compromise quite early in the debates, but the Virginians and particularly Madison (unaware that he would later be acclaimed as the prophet of "federalism") fought obdurately against providing for equal representation of states in the second chamber. There was a good deal of acrimony and at one point Benjamin Franklin—of all people—proposed the institution of a daily prayer; practical politicians in the gathering, however, were meditating more on the merits of a good committee than on the utility of Divine intervention. On July 2, the ice began to break when through a number of fortuitous events[34]—and one that seems deliberate[35]—the majority against equality of representation was converted into a dead tie. The Convention had reached the stage where it was "ripe" for a solution (presumably all the therapeutic speeches had been made), and the South Carolinians proposed a committee. Madison and James Wilson wanted none of it, but with only Pennsylvania dissenting, the body voted to establish a working party on the problem of representation.

The members of this committee, one from each state, were elected by the delegates—and a very interesting committee it was. Despite the fact that the Virginia Plan had held majority support up to that date, neither Madison nor Randolph was selected (Mason was the Virginian) and Baldwin of Georgia, whose shift in position had resulted in the tie, was chosen. From the composition, it was clear that this was not to be a "fighting" committee: the emphasis in membership was on what might be described as "second-level political entrepreneurs." On the basis of the discussions up to that time, only Luther Martin of Maryland could be described as a "bitter-ender." Admittedly, some divination enters into this sort of analysis, but one does get a sense of the mood of the delegates from these choices—including the interesting selection of Benjamin Franklin, despite his age and intellectual wobbliness, over the brilliant and incisive Wilson or the sharp, polemical Gouverneur Morris, to represent Pennsylvania. His passion for conciliation was more valuable at this juncture than Wilson's logical genius, or Morris' acerbic wit.

There is a common rumor that the Framers divided their time between philosophical discussions of government and reading the classics in political theory. Perhaps this is as good a time as any to note that their concerns were highly practical, that they spent little time canvassing abstractions. A number of them had some acquaintance with the history of political theory (probably gained from reading John Adams' monumental compilation *A Defense of the Constitutions of Government,*[36] the first volume of which appeared in 1786), and it was a poor rhetorician indeed who could not cite Locke, Montesquieu, or Harrington *in support* of a desired goal. Yet up to this point in the deliberations, no one had expounded a defense of states'-rights or the "separation of powers" on anything resembling a theoretical basis. It should be reiterated that the Madison model had no room either for the states or for the "separation of powers": effectively *all* governmental power was vested in the national legislature. The merits of Montesquieu did not turn up until *The Federalist;* and although a perverse argument could be made that Madison's ideal was truly in the tradition of John Locke's *Second Treatise of Government,*[37] the Locke whom the American rebels treated as an honorary president was a pluralistic defender of vested rights,[38] not of parliamentary supremacy.

It would be tedious to continue a blow-by-blow analysis of the work of the delegates; the critical fight was over representation of the states and once the Connecticut Compromise was adopted on July 17, the Convention was over the hump. Madison, James Wilson, and Gouverneur Morris of New York (who was there representing Pennsylvania!) fought the compromise all the way in a last-ditch effort to get a unitary state with parliamentary supremacy. But their allies deserted them and they demonstrated after their defeat the essentially opportunist character of their objections—using "opportunist" here in a non-pejorative sense, to indicate a willingness to swallow their objections and get on with the business. Moreover, once the compromise had carried (by five states to four, with one state divided), its advocates threw themselves vigorously into the job of strengthening the general government's substantive powers—as might have been predicted, indeed, from Paterson's early statements. It nourishes an increased respect for Madison's devotion to the art of politics, to realize that this dogged fighter could sit down six months later and prepare essays for *The Federalist* in contradiction to his basic convictions about the true course the Convention should have taken.

V

Two tricky issues will serve to illustrate the later process of accommodation. The first was the institutional position of the Executive. Madison argued for an executive chosen by the National Legislature and on May 29 this had been adopted with a provision that after his seven-year term was concluded, the chief magistrate should not be eligible for reelection. In late July this was reopened and for a week the matter was argued from several different points of view. A good deal of desultory speech-making ensued, but the gist of the problem was the opposition from two sources to election by the legislature. One group felt that the states should have a hand in the process; another small but influential circle urged direct election by the people. There were a number of proposals: election by the people, election by state governors, by electors chosen by state legislatures, by the National Legislature (James Wilson, perhaps ironically, proposed at one point that an Electoral College be chosen by lot from the National Legislature!), and there was some resemblance to three-dimensional chess in the dispute because of the presence of two other variables, length of tenure and reeligibility. Finally, after opening, reopening, and re-reopening the debate, the thorny problem was consigned to a committee for resolution.

The Brearley Committee on Postponed Matters was a superb aggregation of talent and its compromise on the Executive was a masterpiece of political improvisation. (The Electoral College, its creation, however, had little in its favor as an *institution*—as the delegates well appreciated.) The point of departure for all discussion about the presidency in the Convention was that in immediate terms, the problem was non-existent; in other words, everybody present knew that under any system devised, George Washington would be President. Thus they were dealing in the future tense and to a body of working politicians the merits of the Brearley proposal were obvious: everybody got a piece of cake. (Or to put it more academically, each viewpoint could leave the Convention and argue to its constituents that it had *really* won the day.) First, the state legislatures had the right to determine the mode of selection of the electors; second, the small states received a bonus in the Electoral College in the form of a guaranteed minimum of three votes while the big states got acceptance of the principle of proportional power; third, if the state legislatures agreed (as six did in the first presidential election), the people could be involved directly in the choice of electors; and finally, if no candidate received a majority in the College, the right of decision passed to the National Legislature with each state exercising equal strength. (In the Brearley recommendation, the election went to the Senate, but a motion from the floor substituted the House; this was accepted on the ground that the Senate already had enough authority over the executive in its treaty and appointment powers.)

This compromise was almost too good to be true, and the Framers snapped it up with little debate or controversy. No one seemed to think well of the College as an *institution;* indeed, what evidence there is suggests that there was an assumption that once Washington had finished his tenure as President, the electors would cease to produce majorities and the chief executive would usually be chosen in the House. George Mason observed casually that the selection would be made in the House nineteen times in twenty and no one seriously disputed this point. The vital aspect of the Electoral College was that it got the Convention over the hurdle and protected everybody's interests. The future was left to cope with the problem of what to do with this Rube Goldberg mechanism.

In short, the Framers did not in their wisdom endow the United States with a College of Cardinals—the Electoral College was neither an exercise in applied Platonism nor an experiment in indirect government based on elitist distrust of the masses. It was merely a jerry-rigged improvisation which has subsequently been endowed with a high theoretical content. When an elector from Oklahoma in 1960 refused to cast his vote for Nixon (naming Byrd and Goldwater instead) on the ground that the Founding Fathers intended him to exercise his great independent wisdom, he was indulging in historical fantasy. If one were to indulge in counter-fantasy, he would be tempted to suggest that the Fathers would be startled to find the College still in operation—and perhaps even dismayed at their descendants' lack of judgment or inventiveness.[39]

The second issue on which some substantial practical bargaining took place was slavery. The morality of slavery was, by design, not at issue;[40] but in its other concrete aspects, slavery colored the arguments over taxation, commerce, and representation. The "Three-Fifths Compromise," that three-fifths of the slaves would be counted both for representation and for purposes of direct taxation (which was drawn from the past—it was a formula of Madison's utilized by Congress in 1783 to establish the basis of state contributions to the Confederation treasury) had allayed some Northern fears about Southern overrepresentation (no one then foresaw the trivial role that direct taxation would play in later federal financial policy), but doubts still remained. The Southerners, on the other hand, were afraid that Congressional control over commerce would lead to the exclusion of slaves or to their excessive taxation as imports. Moreover, the Southerners were disturbed over "navigation acts," *i.e.,* tariffs, or special legislation providing, for example, that exports be carried only in American ships; as a section depending upon exports, they wanted protection from the potential voracity of their commercial brethren of the Eastern states. To achieve this end, Mason and others urged that the Constitution include a proviso that navigation and commercial laws should require a two-thirds vote in Congress.

These problems came to a head in late August and, as usual, were handed to a committee in the hope that, in Gouverneur Morris' words, " . . . these things may form a bargain among the Northern and Southern states." [41] The Committee reported its measures of reconciliation on August 25, and on August 29 the package was wrapped up and delivered. What occurred can best be described in George Mason's dour version (he anticipated Calhoun in his conviction that permitting navigation acts to pass by majority vote would put the South in economic bondage to the North—it was mainly on this ground that he refused to sign the Constitution):

> The Constitution as agreed to till a fortnight before the Convention rose was such a one as he would have set his hand and heart to. . . . [Until that time] The 3 New England States were constantly with us in all questions . . . so that it was these three States with the 5 Southern ones against Pennsylvania, Jersey and Delaware. With respect to the importation of

slaves, [decision-making] was left to Congress. This disturbed the two Southernmost States who knew that Congress would immediately suppress the importation of slaves. Those two States therefore struck up a bargain with the three New England States. If they would join to admit slaves for some years, the two Southern-most States would join in changing the clause which required the 2/3 of the Legislature in any vote [on navigation acts]. It was done.[42]

On the floor of the Convention there was a virtual love-feast on this happy occasion. Charles Pinckney of South Carolina attempted to overturn the committee's decision, when the compromise was reported to the Convention, by insisting that the South needed protection from the imperialism of the Northern states. But his Southern colleagues were not prepared to rock the boat and General C. C. Pinckney arose to spread oil on the suddenly ruffled waters; he admitted that:

> It was in the true interest of the S[outhern] States to have no regulation of commerce; but considering the loss brought on the commerce of the Eastern States by the Revolution, their liberal conduct towards the views of South Carolina [on the regulation of the slave trade] and the interests the weak Southn. States had in being united with the strong Eastern states, he thought it proper that no fetters should be imposed on the power of making commercial regulations; *and that his constituents, though prejudiced against the Eastern States, would be reconciled to this liberality.* He had himself prejudices agst the Eastern States before he came here, but would acknowledge that he had found them as liberal and candid as any men whatever. (Italics added)[43]

Pierce Butler took the same tack, essentially arguing that he was not too happy about the possible consequences, but that a deal was a deal.[44] . . .

VI

Drawing on their vast collective political experience, utilizing every weapon in the politician's arsenal, looking constantly over their shoulders at their constituents, the delegates put together a Constitution. It was a makeshift affair; some sticky issues (for example, the qualification of voters) they ducked entirely; others they mastered with that ancient instrument of political sagacity, studied ambiguity (for example, citizenship), and some they just overlooked. In this last category, I suspect, fell the matter of the power of the federal courts to determine the constitutionality of acts of Congress. When the judicial article was formulated (Article III of the Constitution), deliberations were still in the stage where the legislature was endowed with broad power under the Randolph formulation, authority which by its own terms was scarcely amenable to judicial review. In essence, courts could hardly determine when " . . . the separate States are incompetent or . . . the harmony of the United States may be interrupted"; the National Legislature, as critics pointed out, was free to define its own jurisdiction. Later the definition of legislative authority was changed into the form we know, a series of stipulated powers, *but the delegates never seriously reexamined the jurisdiction of the judiciary under this new limited formulation.*[45] All arguments on the intention of the Framers in this matter are thus deductive and a *posteriori*, though some obviously make more sense than others.

The Framers were busy and distinguished men, anxious to get back to their families, their positions, and their constituents, not members of the French Academy devoting a lifetime to a dictionary. They were trying to do an important job, and do it in such a fashion that their handiwork would be acceptable to very diverse constituencies. No one was rhapsodic about the final document, but it was a beginning, a move in the right direction, and one they had reason to believe the people would endorse. In addition, since they had modified the impossible amendment provisions of the Articles (the requirement of unanimity which could always be frustrated by "Rogues Island") to one demanding approval by only three-quarters of the states, they seemed confident that gaps in the fabric which experience would reveal could be rewoven without undue difficulty. . . .

Madison, despite his reservations about the Constitution, was the campaign manager in ratification. His first task was to get the Congress in New York to light its own funeral pyre by approving the "amendments" to the Articles and sending them on to the state legislatures. Above all, momentum had to be maintained. The anti-Constitutionalists, now thoroughly alarmed and no novices in politics, realized that their best tactic was attrition rather than direct opposition. Thus they settled on a position expressing qualified approval but calling for a second Convention to remedy various defects (the one with the most demagogic appeal was the lack of a Bill of Rights). Madison knew that to accede to this demand would be equivalent to losing the battle, nor would he agree to conditional approval (despite wavering even by Hamilton). This was an all-or-nothing proposition: national salvation or national impotence with no intermediate positions possible. Unable to get congressional approval, he settled for second best: a unanimous resolution of Congress transmitting the Constitution to the states for whatever action they saw fit to take. The opponents then moved from New York and the Congress, where they had attempted to attach amendments and conditions, to the states for the final battle.

At first the campaign for ratification went beautifully: within eight months after the delegates set their names to the document, eight states had ratified.

Only in Massachusetts had the result been close (187-168). Theoretically, a ratification by one more state convention would set the new government in motion, but in fact until Virginia and New York acceded to the new Union, the latter was a fiction. New Hampshire was the next to ratify; Rhode Island was involved in its characteristic political convulsions (the Legislature there sent the Constitution out to the towns for decision by popular vote and it got lost among a series of local issues); North Carolina's convention did not meet until July and then postponed a final decision. This is hardly the place for an extensive analysis of the conventions of New York and Virginia. Suffice it to say that the Constitutionalists clearly outmaneuvered their opponents, forced them into impossible political positions, and won both states narrowly. The Virginia Convention could serve as a classic study in effective floor management: Patrick Henry had to be contained, and a reading of the debates discloses a standard two-stage technique. Henry would give a four- or five-hour speech denouncing some section of the Constitution on every conceivable ground (the federal district, he averred at one point, would become a haven for convicts escaping from state authority!);[46] when Henry subsided, "Mr. Lee of Westmoreland" would rise and literally poleaxe him with sardonic invective (when Henry complained about the militia power, "Lighthorse Harry" really punched below the belt: observing that while the former Governor had been sitting in Richmond during the Revolution, *he* had been out in the trenches with the troops and thus felt better qualified to discuss military affairs).[47] Then the gentlemanly Constitutionalists (Madison, Pendleton and Marshall) would pick up the matters at issue and examine them in the light of reason.

Indeed, modern Americans who tend to think of James Madison as a rather desiccated character should spend some time with this transcript. Probably Madison put on his most spectacular demonstration of nimble rhetoric in what might be called "The Battle of the Absent Authorities." Patrick Henry in the course of one of his harangues alleged that Jefferson was known to be opposed to Virginia's approving the Constitution. This was clever: Henry hated Jefferson, but was prepared to use any weapon that came to hand. Madison's riposte was superb: First, he said that with all due respect to the great reputation of Jefferson, he was not in the country and therefore could not formulate an adequate judgment; second, no one should utilize the reputation of an outsider—the Virginia Convention was there to think for itself; third, if there were to be recourse to outsiders, the opinions of George Washington should certainly be taken into consideration; and finally, he knew from privileged personal communications from Jefferson that in fact the latter *strongly favored* the Constitution.[48] To devise an assault route into this rhetorical fortress was literally impossible.

VII

The fight was over; all that remained now was to establish the new frame of government in the spirit of its framers. And who were better qualified for this task than the Framers themselves? Thus victory for the Constitution meant simultaneous victory for the Constitutionalists; the anti-Constitutionalists either capitulated or vanished into limbo—soon Patrick Henry would be offered a seat on the Supreme Court[49] and Luther Martin would be known as the Federalist "bull-dog." [50] And irony of ironies, Alexander Hamilton and James Madison would shortly accumulate a reputation as the formulators of what is often alleged to be our political theory, the concept of "federalism." . . .

Thus we can ask what the Framers meant when they gave Congress the power to regulate interstate and foreign commerce, and we emerge, reluctantly perhaps, with the reply that . . . they may not have known what they meant, that there may not have been any semantic consensus. The Convention was not a seminar in analytic philosophy or linguistic analysis. Commerce was *commerce*—and if different interpretations of the word arose, later generations could worry about the problem of definition. The delegates were in a hurry to get a new government established; when definitional arguments arose, they characteristically took refuge in ambiguity. If different men voted for the same proposition for varying reasons, that was politics (and still is); if later generations were unsettled by this lack of precision, that would be their problem.

There was a good deal of definitional pluralism with respect to the problems the delegates did discuss, but when we move to the question of extrapolated intentions, we enter the realm of spiritualism. When men in our time, for instance, launch into elaborate talmudic exegesis to demonstrate that federal aid to parochial schools is (or is not) in accord with the intentions of the men who established the Republic and endorsed the Bill of Rights, they are engaging in historical Extra-Sensory Perception. (If one were to join this E. S. P. contingent for a minute, he might suggest that the hard-boiled politicians who wrote the Constitution and Bill of Rights would chuckle scornfully at such an invocation of authority: obviously a politician would chart his course on the intentions of the living, not of the dead, and count the number of Catholics in his constituency.)

The Constitution, then, was not an apotheosis of "constitutionalism," a triumph of architectonic genius; it was a patch-work sewn together under the pressure of both time and events by a group of extremely talented democratic politicians. They refused to attempt the establishment of a strong, centralized sovereignty on the principle of legislative supremacy for the excellent reason that the people would not accept it. They risked their political fortunes by opposing the established doctrines of state sovereignty because they were convinced that the existing system was leading to national impotence and probably foreign domination. For two years, they worked to get a convention established. For over three months, in what must have seemed to the faithful participants an endless process of give-and-take, they reasoned, cajoled, threatened, and bargained amongst themselves. The result was a Constitution which the people, in fact, by democratic processes, did accept, and a new and far better national government was established.

Beginning with the inspired propaganda of Hamilton, Madison and Jay, the ideological build-up got under way. *The Federalist* had little impact on the ratification of the Constitution, except perhaps in New York, but this volume had enormous influence on the image of the Constitution in the minds of future generations, particularly on historians and political scientists who have an innate fondness for theoretical symmetry. Yet, while the shades of Locke and Montesquieu *may* have been hovering in the background, and the delegates *may* have been unconscious instruments of a transcendent *telos,* the careful observer of the day-to-day work of the Convention finds no over-arching principles. The "separation of powers" to him seems to be a by-product of suspicion, and "federalism" he views as a *pis aller,* as the farthest point the delegates felt they could go in the destruction of state power without themselves inviting repudiation.

To conclude, the Constitution was neither a victory for abstract theory nor a great practical success. Well over half a million men had to die on the battlefields of the Civil War before certain constitutional principles could be defined—a baleful consideration which is somehow overlooked in our customary tributes to the farsighted genius of the Framers and to the supposed American talent for "constitutionalism." The Constitution was, however, a vivid demonstration of effective democratic political action, and of the forging of a national elite which literally persuaded its countrymen to hoist themselves by their own boot straps. American pro-consuls would be wise not to translate the Constitution into Japanese, or Swahili, or treat it as a work of semi-Divine origin; but when students of comparative politics examine the process of nation-building in countries newly freed from colonial rule, they may find the American experience instructive as a classic example of the potentialities of a democratic elite.

NOTES

1. The view that the right to vote in the states was severely circumscribed by property qualifications has been thoroughly discredited in recent years. See Chilton Williamson,

American Suffrage from Property to Democracy, 1760–1860 (Princeton, 1960). The contemporary position is that John Dickinson actually knew what he was talking about when he argued that there would be little opposition to vesting the right of suffrage in freeholders since "The great mass of our Citizens is composed at this time of freeholders, and will be pleased with it." Max Farrand, *Records of the Federal Convention*, Vol. 2, p. 202 (New Haven, 1911). (Henceforth cited as *Farrand*.)

2. The classic statement of the *coup d'etat* theory is, of course, Charles A. Beard, *An Economic Interpretation of the Constitution of the United States* (New York, 1913). . . .

3. "[T]he situation of the general government, if it can be called a government, is shaken to its foundation, and liable to be overturned by every blast. In a word, it is at an end; and, unless a remedy is soon applied, anarchy and confusion will inevitably ensue." Washington to Jefferson, May 30, 1787, *Farrand*, III, 31. See also Irving Brant, *James Madison, The Nationalist* (New York, 1948), ch. 25.

4. The story of James Madison's cultivation of Washington is told by Brant, *op. cit.*, pp. 394–97.

5. The "message center" being the Congress; nineteen members of Congress were simultaneously delegates to the Convention. One gets a sense of this coordination of effort from Broadus Mitchell, *Alexander Hamilton, Youth to Maturity* (New York, 1957), ch. 22.

6. The Annapolis Convention, called for the previous year, turned into a shambles: only five states sent commissioners, only three states were legally represented, and the instructions to delegates named varied quite widely from state to state. Clinton and others of his persuasion may have thought this disaster would put an end to the drive for reform. See Mitchell, *op. cit.*, pp. 362–67; Brant, *op. cit.*, pp. 375–87.

7. The terms "radical" and "conservative" have been bandied about a good deal in connection with the Constitution. This usage is nonsense if it is employed to distinguish between two economic "classes"—*e.g.*, radical debtors versus conservative creditors, radical farmers versus conservative capitalists, etc.—because there was no polarization along this line of division; the same types of people turned up on both sides. And many were hard to place in these terms: does one treat Robert Morris as a debtor or a creditor? or James Wilson? See Robert E. Brown, *Charles Beard and the Constitution* (Princeton, 1956), passim. The one line of division that holds up is between those deeply attached to states'-rights and those who felt that the Confederation was bankrupt. Thus, curiously, some of the most narrow-minded, parochial spokesmen of the time have earned the designation "radical" while those most willing to experiment and alter the *status quo* have been dubbed "conservative"! See Cecelia Kenyon, "Men of Little Faith," *William and Mary Quarterly*, Vol. 12, p. 3 (1955).

8. Yet, there was little objection to this crucial modification from any quarter—there almost seems to have been a gentlemen's agreement that Rhode Island's *liberum veto* had to be destroyed.

9. See Mason's letter to his son, May 27, 1787, in which he endorsed secrecy as "a proper precaution to prevent mistakes and misrepresentation until the business shall have been completed, when the whole may have a very different complexion from that in which the several crude and indigested parts might in their first shape appear if submitted to the public eye." *Farrand*, III, 28.

10. See Madison to Jefferson, June 6, 1787, *Farrand*, III, 35.

11. Cited in Charles Warren, *The Making of the Constitution* (Boston, 1928), p. 138.

12. "I hold it for a fundamental point, that an individual independence of the states is utterly irreconcilable with the idea of an aggregate sovereignty," Madison to Randolph, cited in Brant, *op. cit.*, p. 416.

13. The Randolph Plan was presented on May 29, see *Farrand*, I, 18–23; the state legislatures retained only the power to *nominate* candidates for the upper chamber. Madison's view of the appropriate position of the states emerged even more strikingly in Yates' record of his speech on June 29: "Some contend that states are sovereign when in fact they are only political societies. There is a gradation of power in all societies, from the lowest corporation to the highest sovereign. The states never possessed the essential rights of sovereignty. . . . The states, at present, are only great corporations, having the power of making by-laws, and these are effectual only if they are not contradictory to the general confederation. The states ought to be placed under the control of the general government—at least as much so as they formerly were under the king and British parliament." *Farrand*, I, 471. Forty-six years later, after Yates' "Notes" had been published, Madison tried to explain this statement away as a misinterpretation: he did not flatly deny the authenticity of Yates' record, but attempted a defense that was half justification and half evasion. Madison to W. C. Rives, Oct. 21, 1833. *Farrand*, III, 521–24.

14. Resolution 6.

15. *Ibid.*

16. See the discussions on May 30 and 31. "Mr. Charles Pinkney wished to know of Mr. Randolph whether he meant to abolish the State Governts. Altogether . . . Mr. Butler said he had not made up his mind on the subject and was open to the light which discussion might throw on it . . . Genl. Pinkney expressed a doubt . . . Mr. Gerry seemed to entertain the same doubt." *Farrand*, I, 33–34. There were no denunciations—though it should perhaps be added that Luther Martin had not yet arrived.

17. *Farrand*, I, 54. (Italics added.)

18. *Ibid.*, p. 242. Delaware's delegates had been instructed by their general assembly to maintain in any new system the voting equality of the states. *Farrand*, III, 574.

19. *Ibid.*, pp. 275–76.

20. "But it is said that this national government is to act on individuals and not on states; and cannot a federal government be so framed as to operate in the same way? It surely may." *Ibid.*, pp. 182–83; also *ibid.* at p. 276.

21. *Farrand*, III, 613.

22. *Farrand*, I, 177.

23. *Ibid.*, p. 182.

24. *Ibid.*, p. 255.

25. J. C. Hamilton, cited *ibid.*, p. 293.

26. See, *e.g.*, Mitchell, *op. cit.*, p. 381.

27. Hamilton to Washington, July 3, 1787, *Farrand*, III, 53.

28. A reconstruction of the Hamilton Plan is found in *Farrand*, III, 617–30.

29. Said William Samuel Johnson on June 21: "A gentleman from New-York, with boldness and decision, proposed a system totally different from both [Virginia and New Jersey]; and though he has been praised by every body, he has been supported by none." *Farrand*, I, 363.

30. See his letter to Washington cited *supra* note 43.

31. *Farrand*, I, 321.

32. This formulation was voted into the Randolph Plan on May 30, 1787, by a vote of six states to none, with one divided. *Farrand*, I, 30.

33. *Farrand*, I, 335–36. In agreeing, Randolph stipulated his disagreement with Ellsworth's rationale, but said he did not object to merely changing an "expression." Those who subject the Constitution to minute semantic analysis might do well to keep this instance in mind; if Randolph could so concede the deletion of "national," one may wonder if any word changes can be given much weight.

34. According to Luther Martin, he was alone on the floor and cast Maryland's vote for equality of representation. Shortly thereafter, Jenifer came on the floor and "Mr. King, from Massachusetts, valuing himself on Mr. Jenifer to divide the State of Maryland on this question . . . requested of the President that the question might be put again; however, the motion was too extraordinary in its nature to meet with success." Cited from "The Genuine Information, . . ." *Farrand*, III, 188.

35. Namely Baldwin's vote *for* equality of representation which divided Georgia—with Few absent and Pierce in New York fighting a duel, Houston voted against equality and Baldwin shifted to tie the state. Baldwin was originally from Connecticut and attended and tutored at Yale, facts which have led to much speculation about the pressures the Connecticut delegation may have brought on him to save the day (Georgia was the last state to vote) and open the way to compromise. To employ a good Russian phrase, it was certainly not an accident that Baldwin voted the way he did. See *Warren*, p. 262.

36. For various contemporary comments, see *Warren*, pp. 814–18. On Adams' technique, see Zoltan Haraszti, "The Composition of Adams' *Defense*," in *John Adams and the Prophets of Progress* (Cambridge, 1952), ch. 9. In this connection it is interesting to check the Convention discussions for references to the authority of Locke, Montesquieu and Harrington, the theorists who have been assigned various degrees of paternal responsibility. There are no explicit references to James Harrington; one to John Locke (Luther Martin cited him on the state of nature, *Farrand*, I, 437); and seven to Montesquieu, only one of which related to the "separation of powers" (Madison in an odd speech, which he explained in a footnote was given to help a friend rather than advance his own views, cited Montesquieu on the separation of the executive and legislative branches, *Farrand*, II, 34). This, of course, does not prove that Locke and Co. were without influence; it shifts the burden of proof, however, to those who assert ideological causality. See Benjamin F. Wright, "The Origins of the Separation of Powers in America," *Economica*, Vol. 13 (1933), p. 184.

37. I share Willmoore Kendall's interpretation of Locke as a supporter of parliamentary supremacy and majoritarianism; see Kendall, *John Locke and the Doctrine of Majority Rule* (Urbana, 1941). Kendall's general position has recently received strong support in the definitive edition and commentary of Peter Laslett, *Locke's Two Treatises of Government* (Cambridge, 1960).

38. The American Locke is best delineated in Carl Becker, *The Declaration of Independence* (New York, 1948).

39. See John P. Roche, "The Electoral College: A Note on American Political Mythology," *Dissent* (Spring, 1961), pp. 197–99. The relevant debates took place July 19–26, 1787, *Farrand*, II, 50–128, and September 5–6, 1787, *ibid.*, pp. 505–31.

40. See the discussion on August 22, 1787, *Farrand*, II, 366–75; King seems to have expressed the sense of the Convention when he said, "the subject should be considered in a political light only." *Ibid.* at 373.

41. *Farrand,* II, 374. Randolph echoed his sentiment in different words.

42. Mason to Jefferson, cited in *Warren,* p. 584.

43. August 29, 1787, *Farrand,* II, 449–50.

44. *Ibid.,* p. 451. The plainest statement of the matter was put by the three North Carolina delegates (Blount, Spaight and Williamson) in their report to Governor Caswell, September 18, 1787. After noting that "no exertions have been wanting on our part to guard and promote the particular interest of North Carolina," they went on to explain the basis of the negotiations in cold-blooded fashion: "While we were taking so much care to guard ourselves against being over reached and to form rules of Taxation that might operate in our favour, it is not to be supposed that our Northern Brethren were Inattentive to their particular Interest. A navigation Act or the power to regulate Commerce in the Hands of the National Government . . . is what the Southern States have given in Exchange for the advantages we Mentioned." They concluded by explaining that while the Constitution did deal with other matters besides taxes—"there are other Considerations of great Magnitude involved in the system"—they would not take up valuable time with boring details! *Farrand,* III, 83–84.

45. The Committee on Detail altered the general grant of legislative power envisioned by the Virginia Plan into a series of specific grants; these were examined closely between August 16 and August 23. One day only was devoted to the Judicial Article, August 27, and since no one raised the question of judicial review of *Federal* statutes, no light was cast on the matter. A number of random comments on the power of the judiciary were scattered throughout the discussions, but there was another variable which deprives them of much probative value: the proposed Council of Revision which would have joined the Executive with the judges in *legislative* review. Madison and Wilson, for example, favored this technique—which had nothing in common with what we think of as judicial review except that judges were involved in the task.

46. See *Elliot's Debates on the Federal Constitution* (Washington, 1836), Vol. 3, pp. 436–38.

47. This should be quoted to give the full flavor: "Without vanity, I may say I have had different experience of [militia] service from that of [Henry]. It was my fortune to be a soldier of my country. . . . I saw what the honorable gentleman did not see—our men fighting. . . ." *Ibid.,* p. 178,

48. *Ibid.,* p. 329.

49. Washington offered him the Chief Justiceship in 1796, but he declined; Charles Warren, *The Supreme Court in United States History* (Boston, 1947), Vol. 1, p. 139.

50. He was a zealous prosecutor of seditions in the period 1798–1800; with Justice Samuel Chase, like himself an alleged "radical" at the time of the Constitutional Convention, Martin hunted down Jeffersonian heretics. See James M. Smith, *Freedom's Fetters* (Ithaca, 1956), pp. 342–43.

2-2

Anti-Federalist No. 3

Brutus
November 15, 1787

After the Constitutional Convention, most of the delegates returned home to promote ratification by their states. Some, however, had opposed the final plan for the new government. They, along with allies who had boycotted the Convention, began lobbying their state legislatures to reject ratification. The two sides battled each other in the nation's newspapers. We celebrate the winners as the Framers, as contemporaries frequently called them.

Weeks after the Convention, Alexander Hamilton, James Madison, and John Jay launched a series of pro-ratification newspaper articles under the pen name Publius; collectively, they called themselves "Federalists," in order to allay misgivings about the creation of the new, more resourceful national government. After ratification, their eighty-five essays were published in book form as The Federalist, and subsequently as The Federalist Papers. (Thomas Jefferson immediately added it to the required reading list of all University of Virginia undergraduates.)

Their opponents, known as the "Anti-Federalists," were also capable political thinkers. While history has tended to denigrate them as "men of little faith," it is difficult to find fault with much of their reasoning. In the essay below—one of sixteen penned by Brutus (likely New York delegate Robert Yates)—the author highlights some serious issues with the new Constitution and its plan of "nominal" representation. How can the presence of a distant, national government advance democracy (popular control) over that presently provided by the smaller states' own assemblies? Why should a small, unelected, malapportioned Senate be permitted to veto any proposal arising in the more democratic institution, the House of Representatives? Both are serious problems which Madison grapples with in his famous "rebuttals" in the next readings.

TO THE CITIZENS of the State of New-York.In the investigation of the constitution, under your consideration, great care should be taken, that you do not form your opinions respecting it, from unimportant provisions, or fallacious appearances.

On a careful examination, you will find, that many of its parts, of little moment, are well formed; in these it has a specious resemblance of a free government—but this is not sufficient to justify the adoption of it—the gilded pill, is often found to contain the most deadly poison.

You are not however to expect, a perfect form of government, any more than to meet with perfection in man: your views therefore, ought to be directed to the main pillars upon which a free government is to rest. . . . Under these impressions, it has been my object to turn your attention to the principal defects in this system. . . . I shall now [in this third essay] proceed . . . to examine its parts more minutely, and show that the powers are not properly deposited, for the security of public liberty.

The first important object that presents itself in the organization of this government, is the legislature. This is to be composed of two branches; the first to be called the general assembly [the House of Representatives], and is to be chosen by the people of the respective states, in proportion to the number of their inhabitants, and is to consist of sixty five members, with powers in the legislature to increase the number, not to exceed one for every thirty thousand inhabitants. The second branch is to be called the senate, and is to consist of twenty-six members, two of which are to be chosen by the legislatures of each of the states.

In the former of these there is an appearance of justice, in the appointment of its members—but if the clause, which provides for this branch, be stripped of its ambiguity, it will be found that there is really no equality of representation, even in this house.

The words are "representatives and direct taxes, shall be apportioned among the several states, which may be included in this union, according to their respective numbers, which shall be determined by adding to the whole number of free persons, including those bound to service for a term of years, and excluding Indians not taxed, three fifths of all other persons."—What a strange and unnecessary accumulation of words are here used to conceal from the public eye what might have been expressed in the following concise manner. Representatives are to be proportioned among the states respectively, according to the number of freemen and slaves inhabiting them, counting five slaves for three free men.

"In a free state." says the celebrated Montesquieu, "every man. who is supposed to be a free agent, ought to be concerned in his own government. Therefore the legislature should reside in the whole body of the people, or their representatives." But it has never been alleged that those who are not free agents, can, upon any rational principle, have any thing to do in government, either by themselves or others. If they have no share in government, why is the number of members in the assembly, to be increased on their account? Is it because in some of the states, a considerable part of the property of the inhabitants consists in a number of their fellow men, who are held in bondage, in defiance of every idea of benevolence, justice, and religion, and contrary to all the principles of liberty, which have been publicly avowed in the late glorious revolution? If this be a just ground for representation, the horses in some of the states, and the oxen in others, ought to be represented—for a great share of property in some of them consists in these animals; and they have as much control over their own actions, as these poor unhappy creatures, who are intended to be described in the above recited clause, by the words, "all other persons." By this mode of apportionment, the representatives of the different parts of the union will be extremely unequal. . . .

There appears at the first view a manifest inconsistency in the apportionment of representatives in the senate, upon the plan of a consolidated government. On every principle of equity, and propriety, representation in a government should be in exact proportion to the numbers, or the aids afforded by the persons represented. How unreasonable and unjust then is it that Delaware should have a representation in the senate, equal to Massachusetts, or Virginia, the latter of which contains ten times her numbers . . . ? This article of the constitution will appear the more objectionable, if it is considered, that the powers vested in this branch of the legislature are very extensive, and greatly surpass those lodged in the assembly [House of Representatives], not only for general purposes, but in many instances, for the internal police of the states. The Other branch of the legislature, in which, if in either, a faint spark of democracy is to be found, should have been properly organized and established—but upon examination you will find, that this branch does not possess the qualities of a just representation, and that there is no kind of security, imperfect as it is for its remaining in the hands of the people. . . .

The very term, representative, implies, that the person or body chosen for this purpose, should resemble those who appoint them. A representation of the people of America, if it be a true one, must be like the people. It ought to be so constituted, that a person, who is a stranger to the country, might be able to form a just idea of their character, by knowing that of their representatives. . . . Society instituted government to promote the happiness of the whole, and this is the great end always in view in the delegation of powers. It must then have been intended, that those who are placed instead of the people, should possess their sentiments and feelings, and be governed by their interests, or, in other words, should bear the strongest resemblance of those in whose room they are substituted. It is obvious, that for an assembly to be a true likeness of the people of any country, they must be considerably numerous. One man or a few men cannot possibly represent the feelings, opinions, and characters of a great multitude. In this respect, the new constitution is radically defective. The house of assembly, which is intended as a representation of the people of America, will not, nor cannot, in the nature of things, be a proper one. Sixty-five men cannot be found in the United States, who hold the sentiments, possess the feelings, or are acquainted with the wants and interests of this vast country. This extensive continent is made up of a number of different classes of people; and to have a proper representation of them each class ought to have an opportunity of choosing their best informed men for the purpose; but this cannot possibly be the case in so small a number. The state of New York, on the present apportionment, will send six members to the assembly: I will venture to affirm, that number cannot be found in the state, who will bear a just resemblance to the several classes of people who compose it. In this assembly, the farmer, merchant, mechanic and other various orders of people, ought to be represented according to their respective weight and numbers; and the representatives ought to be intimately acquainted with the wants, understand the interests of the several orders in the society, and feel a proper sense and becoming zeal to promote their prosperity.

I cannot conceive that any six men in this state can be found properly qualified in these respects to discharge such important duties: but supposing it possible to find them, is there the least degree of probability that the choice of the people will fall upon such men? According to the common course of human affairs, the natural aristocracy of the country will be elected. Wealth always creates influence, and this is generally much increased by large family connections: this class in society will for ever have a great number of dependents; besides, they will always favor each other—it is their interest to combine—they will therefore constantly unite their efforts to procure men of their own rank to be elected—they will concentrate all their force in every part of the state into one point, and by acting together, will most generally carry their election. It is probable, that but few of the merchants, and those most opulent and ambitious, will have a representation from their body. Few of them are characters sufficiently conspicuous to attract the notice of the electors of the state in so limited a representation. The great body of the yeomen of the country cannot expect any of their order in this assembly. The station will be too elevated for them to aspire to. The distance between the people and their representatives will be so very great that there is no probability that a farmer, however respectable, will be chosen. The mechanics of every branch, must expect to be excluded from a seat in this Body. It will and must be esteemed a station too high and exalted to be filled by any but the first men in the state, in point of fortune; so that in reality there will be no part of the people represented, but the rich, even in that branch of the legislature, which is called the democratic. The well born, and highest orders in life, as they term themselves, will be ignorant of the sentiments of the middling class of citizens, strangers to their ability, wants, and difficulties, and void of sympathy, and fellow feeling. This branch of the legislature will not only be an imperfect representation, but there will be no security in so small a body, against bribery, and corruption. It will consist at first, of sixty-five, and can never exceed one for every thirty thousand inhabitants; a majority of these, that is, thirty-three, are a quorum, and a majority of which, or seventeen, may pass any law—so that twenty-five men, will have the power to give away all the property of the citizens of these states. What security therefore can there be for the people, where their liberties and property are at the disposal of so few men? It will literally be a government in the hands of the few to oppress and plunder the many. . . . The rulers of this country must be composed of very different materials . . . if the majority of the legislature are not, before many years, entirely at the devotion of the executive. . . .

The more I reflect on this subject, the more firmly am I persuaded, that the representation is merely nominal—a mere burlesque; and that no security is provided against corruption and undue influence. No free people on earth, who have elected persons to legislate for them, ever reposed that confidence in so small a number. The British house of commons consists of five hundred and fifty-eight members; the number of inhabitants in Great Britain is computed at eight millions. This gives one member for a little more than fourteen thousand, which exceeds double the proportion this country can ever have: and yet we require a larger representation in proportion to our numbers, than Great-Britain, because this country is much more extensive, and differs more in its productions, interests, manners, and habits. The democratic branch of the legislatures of the several states in the union consists, I believe at present, of near two thousand; and this number was not thought too large for the security of liberty by the framers of our state constitutions: some of the states may have erred in this respect, but the difference between two thousand, and sixty-five, is so very great, that it will bear no comparison.

Other objections offer themselves against this part of the constitution. I shall reserve them for a future paper, when I shall show, defective as this representation is, no security is provided that even this shadow of the right will remain with the people.

2-3

Federalist No. 10

James Madison
November 22, 1787

When one reads this tightly reasoned, highly conceptual essay, it is easy to forget that it was published in a New York newspaper with the purpose of persuading that state's ratification convention to endorse the Constitution. Although after ratification this essay went unnoticed for more than a century, today it stands atop virtually every scholar's ranking of The Federalist essays. Written in November 1787, it was James Madison's first contribution to the ratification debate. In responding to Brutus's claim that only small democracies are viable, Madison develops a persuasive rationale for a large, diverse republic—one that he had employed several times in debates at the Convention and that his pro-ratification allies had popularized. The modern reader can appreciate how it resonates with the nation's diversity of interests in the twenty-first century. And everyone, then and now, can admire the solid logic employed by this intelligent man, who begins with a few unobjectionable assumptions and derives from them the counterintuitive conclusion that the surest way to avoid the tyranny of faction is to design a political system in which factions are numerous and none can dominate. This essay repays careful reading.

AMONG THE NUMEROUS advantages promised by a well-constructed Union, none deserves to be more accurately developed than its tendency to break and control the violence of faction. The friend of popular governments never finds himself so much alarmed for their character and fate, as when he contemplates their propensity to this dangerous vice. He will not fail, therefore, to set a due value on any plan which, without violating the principles to which he is attached, provides a proper cure for it. The instability, injustice, and confusion introduced into the public councils, have, in truth, been the mortal diseases under which popular governments have everywhere perished; as they continue to be the favorite and fruitful topics from which the adversaries to liberty derive their most specious declamations. The valuable improvements made by the American constitutions on the popular models, both ancient and modern, cannot certainly be too much admired; but it would be an unwarrantable partiality, to contend that they have as effectually obviated the danger on this side, as was wished and expected. Complaints are everywhere heard from our most considerate and virtuous citizens, equally the friends of public and private faith, and of public and personal liberty, that our governments are too unstable, that the public good is disregarded in the conflicts of rival parties, and that measures are too often decided, not according to the rules of justice and the rights of the minor party, but by the superior force of an interested and over-bearing majority. However anxiously we may wish that these complaints had no foundation, the evidence, of known facts will not permit us to deny that they are in some degree true. It will be found, indeed, on a candid review of our situation, that some of the distresses under which we labor have been erroneously charged on the operation of our governments; but it will be found, at the same time, that other causes will not alone account for many of our heaviest misfortunes; and, par-ticularly, for that prevailing and increasing distrust of public engagements, and alarm for private rights, which are echoed from one end of the continent to the other. These must be chiefly, if not wholly, effects of the unsteadiness and injustice with which a factious spirit has tainted our public administrations.

By a faction, I understand a number of citizens, whether amounting to a majority or a minority of the whole, who are united and actuated by some com-mon impulse of passion, or of interest, adversed to the rights of other citizens, or to the permanent and aggregate interests of the community.

There are two methods of curing the mischiefs of faction: the one, by remov-ing its causes; the other, by controlling its effects. There are again two methods of removing the causes of faction: the one, by destroying the liberty which is essential to its existence; the other, by giving to every citizen the same opinions, the same passions, and the same interests.

It could never be more truly said than of the first remedy, that it was worse than the disease. Liberty is to faction what air is to fire, an aliment without which it instantly expires. But it could not be less folly to abolish liberty, which is essential to political life, because it nourishes faction, than it would be to wish the annihilation of air, which is essential to animal life, because it imparts to fire its destructive agency.

The second expedient is as impracticable as the first would be unwise. As long as the reason of man continues fallible, and he is at liberty to exercise it, different opinions will be formed. As long as the connection subsists between his reason and his self-love, his opinions and his passions will have a reciprocal influence on each other; and the former will be objects to which the latter will attach them-selves. The diversity in the faculties of men, from which the rights of property originate, is not less an insuperable obstacle to a uniformity of interests. The pro-tection of these faculties is the first object of government. From the protection of different and unequal faculties of acquiring property, the possession of differ-ent degrees and kinds of property immediately results; and from the influence of these on the sentiments and views of the respective proprietors, ensues a division of the society into different interests and parties.

The latent causes of faction are thus sown in the nature of man; and we see them everywhere brought into different degrees of activity, according to the different circumstances of civil society. A zeal for different opinions concerning religion, concerning government, and many other points, as well of speculation as of practice; an attachment to different leaders ambitiously contending for pre-eminence and power; or to persons of other descriptions whose fortunes have been interesting to the human passions, have, in turn, divided mankind into parties, inflamed them with mutual animosity, and rendered them much more disposed to vex and oppress each other than to co-operate for their common good. So strong is this propensity of mankind to fall into mutual animosities, that where no substantial occasion presents itself, the most frivolous and fanciful distinctions have been sufficient to kindle their unfriendly passions and excite their most violent conflicts. But the most common and durable source of factions has been the various and unequal distribution of property. Those who hold and those who are without property have ever formed distinct interests in society. Those who are creditors, and those who are debtors, fall under a like discrimination. A landed interest, a manufacturing interest, a mercantile interest, a moneyed interest, with many lesser interests, grow up of necessity in civilized nations, and divide them into different classes, actuated by different sentiments and views. The regulation of these various and interfering interests forms the principal task of modern legislation, and involves the spirit of party and faction in the necessary and ordinary operations of the government.

No man is allowed to be a judge in his own cause, because his interest would certainly bias his judgment, and, not improbably, corrupt his integrity. With equal, nay with greater reason, a body of men are unfit to be both judges and parties at the same time; yet what are many of the most important acts of legislation, but so many judicial determinations, not indeed concerning the rights of single persons, but concerning the rights of large bodies of citizens? And what are the different classes of legislators but advocates and parties to the causes which they determine? Is a law proposed concerning private debts? It is a question to which the creditors are parties on one side and the debtors on the other. Justice ought to hold the balance between them. Yet the parties are, and must be, themselves the judges; and the most numerous party, or, in other words, the most powerful faction must be expected to prevail. Shall domestic manufactures be encouraged, and in what degree, by restrictions on foreign manufactures? are questions which would be differently decided by the landed and the manufacturing classes, and probably by neither with a sole regard to justice and the public good. The apportionment of taxes on the various descriptions of property is an act which seems to require the most exact impartiality; yet there is, perhaps, no legislative act in which greater opportunity and temptation are given to a predominant party to trample on the rules of justice. Every shilling with which they overburden the inferior number, is a shilling saved to their own pockets.

It is in vain to say that enlightened statesmen will be able to adjust these clashing interests, and render them all subservient to the public good. Enlightened statesmen will not always be at the helm. Nor, in many cases, can such an adjustment be made at all without taking into view indirect and remote considerations, which will rarely prevail over the immediate interest which one party may find in disregarding the rights of another or the good of the whole. The inference to which we are brought is, that the causes of faction cannot be removed, and that relief is only to be sought in the means of controlling its effects.

If a faction consists of less than a majority, relief is supplied by the republican principle, which enables the majority to defeat its sinister views by regular vote. It may clog the administration, it may convulse the society; but it will be unable to execute and mask its violence under the forms of the Constitution. When a majority is included in a faction, the form of popular government, on the other hand, enables it to sacrifice to its ruling passion or interest both the public good and the rights of other citizens. To secure the public good and private rights against the danger of such a faction, and at the same time to preserve the spirit and the form of popular government, is then the great object to which our inquiries are directed. Let me add that it is the great desideratum by which this form of government can be rescued from the opprobrium under which it has so long labored, and be recommended to the esteem and adoption of mankind.

By what means is this object attainable? Evidently by one of two only. Either the existence of the same passion or interest in a majority at the same time must be prevented, or the majority, having such coexistent passion or interest, must be rendered, by their number and local situation, unable to concert and carry into effect schemes of oppression. If the impulse and the opportunity be suffered to coincide, we well know that neither moral nor religious motives can be relied on as an adequate control. They are not found to be such on the injustice and violence of individuals, and lose their efficacy in proportion to the number combined together, that is, in proportion as their efficacy becomes needful.

From this view of the subject it may be concluded that a pure democracy, by which I mean a society consisting of a small number of citizens, who assemble and administer the government in person, can admit of no cure for the mischiefs of faction. A common passion or interest will, in almost every case, be felt by a majority of the whole; a communication and concert result from the form of government itself; and there is nothing to check the inducements to sacrifice the weaker party or an obnoxious individual. Hence it is that such democracies have ever been spectacles of turbulence and contention; have ever been found incompatible with personal security or the rights of property; and have in general been as short in their lives as they have been violent in their deaths. Theoretic politicians, who have patronized this species of government, have erroneously supposed that by reducing mankind to a perfect equality in their political rights, they would, at the same time, be perfectly equalized and assimilated in their possessions, their opinions, and their passions.

A republic, by which I mean a government in which the scheme of representation takes place, opens a different prospect, and promises the cure for which we are seeking. Let us examine the points in which it varies from pure democracy, and we shall comprehend both the nature of the cure and the efficacy which it must derive from the Union.

The two great points of difference between a democracy and a republic are: first, the delegation of the government, in the latter, to a small number of citizens elected by the rest; secondly, the greater number of citizens, and greater sphere of country, over which the latter may be extended. The effect of the first difference is, on the one hand, to refine and enlarge the public views, by passing them through the medium of a chosen body of citizens, whose wisdom may best discern the true interest of their country, and whose patriotism and love of justice will be least likely to sacrifice it to temporary or partial considerations. Under such a regulation, it may well happen that the public voice, pronounced by the representatives of the people, will be more consonant to the public good than if pronounced by the people themselves, convened for the purpose. On the other hand, the effect may be inverted. Men of factious tempers, of local prejudices, or of sinister designs, may, by intrigue, by corruption, or by other means, first obtain the suffrages, and then betray the interests, of the people. The question resulting is, whether small or extensive republics are more favorable to the election of proper guardians of the public weal; and it is clearly decided in favor of the latter by two obvious considerations.

In the first place, it is to be remarked that, however small the republic may be, the representatives must be raised to a certain number, in order to guard against the cabals of a few; and that, however large it may be, they must be limited to a certain number, in order to guard against the confusion of a multitude. Hence, the number of representatives in the two cases not being in proportion to that of the two constituents, and being proportionally greater in the small republic, it follows that, if the proportion of fit characters be not less in the large than in the small republic, the former will present a greater option, and consequently a greater probability of a fit choice.

In the next place, as each representative will be chosen by a greater number of citizens in the large than in the small republic, it will be more difficult for unworthy candidates to practice with success the vicious arts by which elections are too often carried; and the suffrages of the people being more free, will be more likely to centre in men who possess the most attractive merit and the most diffusive and established characters.

It must be confessed that in this, as in most other cases, there is a mean, on both sides of which inconveniences will be found to lie. By enlarging too much the number of electors, you render the representatives too little acquainted with all their local circumstances and lesser interests; as by reducing it too much, you render him unduly attached to these, and too little fit to comprehend and pursue great and national objects. The federal Constitution forms a happy combination in this respect; the great and aggregate interests being referred to the national, the local and particular to the State legislatures.

The other point of difference is, the greater number of citizens and extent of territory which may be brought within the compass of republican than of democratic government; and it is this circumstance principally which renders factious combinations less to be dreaded in the former than in the latter. The smaller the society, the fewer probably will be the distinct parties and interests composing it; the fewer the distinct parties and interests, the more frequently will a majority be found of the same party; and the smaller the number of individuals composing a majority, and the smaller the compass within which they are placed, the more easily will they concert and execute their plans of oppression. Extend the sphere, and you take in a greater variety of parties and interests; you make it less probable that a majority of the whole will have a common motive to invade the rights of other citizens; or if such a common motive exists, it will be more difficult for all who feel it to discover their own strength, and to act in unison with each other. Besides other impediments, it may be remarked that, where there is a consciousness of unjust or dishonorable purposes, communication is always checked by distrust in proportion to the number whose concurrence is necessary.

Hence, it clearly appears, that the same advantage which a republic has over a democracy, in controlling the effects of faction, is enjoyed by a large over a small republic,—is enjoyed by the Union over the States composing it. Does the advantage consist in the substitution of representatives whose enlightened views and virtuous sentiments render them superior to local prejudices and schemes of injustice? It will not be denied that the representation of the Union will be most likely to possess these requisite endowments. Does it consist in the greater security afforded by a greater variety of parties, against the event of any one party being able to outnumber and oppress the rest? In an equal degree does the increased variety of parties comprised within the Union, increase this security. Does it, in fine, consist in the greater obstacles opposed to the concert and accomplishment of the secret wishes of an unjust and interested majority? Here, again, the extent of the Union gives it the most palpable advantage.

The influence of factious leaders may kindle a flame within their particular States, but will be unable to spread a general conflagration through the other States. A religious sect may degenerate into a political faction in a part of the Confederacy; but the variety of sects dispersed over the entire face of it must secure the national councils against any danger from that source. A rage for paper money, for an abolition of debts, for an equal division of property, or for any other improper or wicked project, will be less apt to pervade the whole body of the Union than a particular member of it; in the same proportion as such a malady is more likely to taint a particular county or district, than an entire State.

In the extent and proper structure of the Union, therefore, we behold a republican remedy for the diseases most incident to republican government. And according to the degree of pleasure and pride we feel in being republicans, ought to be our zeal in cherishing the spirit and supporting the character of Federalists.

2-4

Federalist No. 51

James Madison
February 8, 1788

Where Federalist No. 10 finds solution to tyranny in the way society is organized, No. 51 turns its attention to the Constitution. In a representative democracy citizens must delegate authority to their representatives. But what is to prevent these ambitious politicians from feathering their own nests or usurping power altogether at their constituencies' expense? The solution, according to James Madison, is to be found in "pitting ambition against ambition," just as the solution in No. 10 lay in pitting interest against interest. In this essay, Madison explains how the Constitution's system of checks and balances will accomplish this goal. Note that he does not try to refute Brutus directly by defending the design of the Senate, which would have been a tough argument. Rather he assumes a different premise—namely, the popularly elected House of Representatives will push the envelope of its authority. He then avers that the Senate and the executive may find the House irresistible, requiring some future Convention to strengthen these institutions to buttress separation of powers.

To what expedient, then, shall we finally resort, for maintaining in practice the necessary partition of power among the several departments, as laid down in the Constitution? The only answer that can be given is, that as all these exterior provisions are found to be inadequate, the defect must be supplied, by so contriving the interior structure of the government as that its several constituent parts may, by their mutual relations, be the means of keeping each other in their proper places. Without presuming to undertake a full development of this important idea, I will hazard a few general observations, which may perhaps place it in a clearer light, and enable us to form a more correct judgment of the principles and structure of the government planned by the convention.

In order to lay a due foundation for that separate and distinct exercise of the different powers of government, which to a certain extent is admitted on all hands to be essential to the preservation of liberty, it is evident that each department should have a will of its own; and consequently should be so constituted that the members of each should have as little agency as possible in the appointment of the members of the others. Were this principle rigorously adhered to, it would require that all the appointments for the supreme executive, legislative, and judiciary magistracies should be drawn from the same fountain of authority, the people, through channels having no communication whatever with one another. Perhaps such a plan of constructing the several departments would be less difficult in practice than it may in contemplation appear. Some difficulties, however, and some additional expense would attend the execution of it. Some deviations, therefore, from the principle must be admitted. In the constitution of the judiciary department in particular, it might be inexpedient to insist rigorously on the principle: first, because peculiar qualifications being essential in the members, the primary consideration ought to be to select that mode of choice which best secures these qualifications; secondly, because the permanent tenure by which the appointments are held in that department, must soon destroy all sense of dependence on the authority conferring them.

It is equally evident, that the members of each department should be as little dependent as possible on those of the others, for the emoluments annexed to their offices. Were the executive magistrate, or the judges, not independent of the legislature in this particular, their independence in every other would be merely nominal.

But the great security against a gradual concentration of the several powers in the same department, consists in giving to those who administer each department the necessary constitutional means and personal motives to resist encroachments of the others. The provision for defense must in this, as in all other cases, be made commensurate to the danger of attack. Ambition must be made to counteract ambition. The interest of the man must be connected with the constitutional rights of the place. It may be a reflection on human nature, that such devices should be necessary to control the abuses of government. But what is government itself, but the greatest of all reflections on human nature? If men were angels, no government would be necessary. If angels were to govern men, neither external nor internal controls on government would be necessary. In framing a government which is to be administered by men over men, the great difficulty lies in this: you must first enable the government to control the governed; and in the next place oblige it to control itself. A dependence on the people is, no doubt, the primary control on the government; but experience has taught mankind the necessity of auxiliary precautions.

This policy of supplying, by opposite and rival interests, the defect of better motives, might be traced through the whole system of human affairs, private as well as public. We see it particularly displayed in all the subordinate distributions of power, where the constant aim is to divide and arrange the several offices in such a manner as that each may be a check on the other; that the private interest of every individual may be a sentinel over the public rights. These inventions of prudence cannot be less requisite in the distribution of the supreme powers of the State.

But it is not possible to give to each department an equal power of self-defense. In republican government, the legislative authority necessarily predominates. The remedy for this inconveniency is to divide the legislature into different branches; and to render them, by different modes of election and different principles of action, as little connected with each other as the nature of their common functions and their common dependence on the society will admit. It may even be necessary to guard against dangerous encroachments by still further precautions. As the weight of the legislative authority requires that it should be thus divided, the weakness of the executive may require, on the other hand, that it should be fortified. An absolute negative on the legislature appears, at first view, to be the natural defense with which the executive magistrate should be armed. But perhaps it would be neither altogether safe nor alone sufficient. On ordinary occasions it might not be exerted with the requisite firmness, and on extraordinary occasions it might be perfidiously abused. May not this defect of an absolute negative be supplied by some qualified connection between this weaker department and the weaker branch of the stronger department, by which the latter may be led to support the constitutional rights of the former, without being too much detached from the rights of its own department? . . .

Chapter 3

Federalism

—————※◦※—————

3-1

Federalism as an Ideal Political Order and an Objective for Constitutional Reform

James M. Buchanan

In this essay Nobel laureate economist James M. Buchanan makes a case for federalism. Buchanan, a market-oriented economist, arrives at a solution to the threat of concentrated power nearly opposite to that proposed by Madison. Whereas Madison thought that the nation would be safe from such a threat if power were reposed in an inherently factious and weak national majority, Buchanan prefers a more decentralized approach. He would give states greater authority and let market mechanisms regulate them—as in the residence decisions of a mobile citizenry, the subject of the excerpt below.

MY AIM HERE is to discuss federalism, as a central element in an inclusive political order, in two, quite different, but ultimately related, conceptual perspectives. First, I examine federalism as an ideal type, as a stylized component of a constitutional structure of governance that might be put in place ab initio, as emergent from agreement among citizens of a particular community before that community, as such, has experienced its own history. Second, the discussion shifts dramatically toward reality, and the critical importance of defining the historically

Source: James Buchanan, "Federalism as an Ideal Political Order and an Objective for Constitutional Reform," *Publius: The Journal of Federalism* 25 (spring 1995): 19–27.

determined status quo is recognized as a necessary first step toward reform that may be guided by some appreciation of the federalist ideal.

Ideal Theory

Federalism as an Analogue to the Market

An elementary understanding and appreciation of political federalism is facilitated by a comparable understanding and appreciation of the political function of an economy organized on market principles. Quite apart from its ability to produce and distribute a highly valued bundle of "goods," relative to alternative regimes, a market economy serves a critically important political role. To the extent that allocative and distributive choices can be relegated to the workings of markets, the necessity for any politicization of such choices is eliminated.

But why should the politicization of choices be of normative concern? Under the standard assumptions that dominated analysis before the public choice revolution, politics is modeled as the activity of a benevolently despotic and monolithic authority that seeks always and everywhere to promote "the public interest," which is presumed to exist independently of revealed evaluations and which is amenable to discovery or revelation. If this romantic image of politics is discarded and replaced by the empirical reality of politics, any increase in the relative size of the politicized sector of an economy must carry with it an increase in the potential for exploitation.[1] The well-being of citizens becomes vulnerable to the activities of politics, as described in the behavior of other citizens as members of majoritarian coalitions, as elected politicians, and as appointed bureaucrats.

This argument must be supplemented by an understanding of why and how the market, as the alternative to political process, does not also expose the citizen-participant to comparable exploitation. The categorical difference between market and political interaction lies in the continuing presence of an effective exit option in market relationships and in its absence in politics. To the extent that the individual participant in market exchange has available effective alternatives that may be chosen at relatively low cost, any exchange is necessarily voluntary. In its stylized form, the market involves no coercion, no extraction of value from any participant without consent. In dramatic contrast, politics is inherently coercive, independently of the effective decision rules that may be operative.

The potential for the exercise of individual liberty is directly related to the relative size of the market sector in an economy. A market organization does not, however, emerge spontaneously from some imagined state of nature. A market economy must, in one sense, be "laid on" through the design, construction, and implementation of a political-legal framework (i.e., an inclusive constitution) that protects property and enforces voluntary contracts. As Adam Smith emphasized, the market works well only if these parameters, these "laws and institutions," are in place.[2]

Enforceable constitutional restrictions may constrain the domain of politics to some extent, but these restrictions may not offer sufficient protection against the exploitation of citizens through the agencies of governance. That is to say, even if the market economy is allowed to carry out its allocational-distributional role over a significant relative share of the political economy, the remaining domain of actions open to politicization may leave the citizen, both in person and property, vulnerable to the expropriation of value that necessarily accompanies political coercion.

How might the potential for exploitation be reduced or minimized? How might the political sector, in itself, be constitutionally designed so as to offer the citizen more protection?

The principle of federalism emerges directly from the market analogy. . . . Under a federalized political structure, persons, singly and/or in groups, would be guaranteed the liberties of trade, investment, and migration across the inclusive area of the economy. Analogously to the market, persons retain an exit option; at relatively low cost, at least some persons can shift among the separate political jurisdictions. Again analogously to the market, the separate . . . state governments would be forced to compete, one with another, in their offers of publicly provided services. The federalized structure, through the forces of interstate competition, effectively limits the power of the separate political units to extract surplus value from the citizenry.

Principles of Competitive Federalism

The operating principles of a genuinely competitive federalism can be summarized readily.[3] As noted, the central or federal government would be constitutionally restricted in its domain of action, severely so. Within its assigned sphere, however, the central government would be strong, sufficiently so to allow it to enforce economic freedom or openness over the whole of the territory. The separate states would be prevented, by federal authority, from placing barriers on the free flow of resources and goods across their borders.

The constitutional limits on the domain of the central or federal government would not be self-enforcing, and competition could not be made operative in a manner precisely comparable to that which might restrict economic exploitation by the separate states. If the federal (central) government, for any reason, should move beyond its constitutionally dictated mandate of authority, what protection might be granted—to citizens individually or to the separate states—against the extension of federal power?

The exit option is again suggested, although this option necessarily takes on a different form. The separate states, individually or in groups, must be constitutionally empowered to secede from the federalized political structure, that is, to form new units of political authority outside of and beyond the reach of the existing federal government. Secession, or the threat thereof, represents the only means through which the ultimate powers of the central government might be held in check. Absent the secession prospect, the federal government may, by overstepping its constitutionally assigned limits, extract surplus value from the citizenry almost at will, because there would exist no effective means of escape.[4]

With an operative secession threat on the part of the separate states, the federal or central government could be held roughly to its assigned constitutional limits, while the separate states could be left to compete among themselves in their capacities to meet the demands of citizens for collectively provided services. . . .

We should predict, of course, that the separate states of a federal system would be compelled by the forces of competition to offer tolerably "efficient" mixes of publicly provided goods and services, and, to the extent that citizens in the different states exhibit roughly similar preferences, the actual budgetary mixes would not be predicted to diverge significantly, one from the other. However, the point to be emphasized here (and which seems to have been missed in so much of the discussion about the potential European federalism) is that any such standardization or regularization as might occur, would itself be an emergent property of competitive federalism rather than a property that might be imposed either by constitutional mandate or by central government authority.

The Path Dependency of Constitutional Reform

From Here to There: A Schemata

The essential principle for meaningful discourse about constitutional-institutional reform (or, indeed, about any change) is the recognition that reform involves movement from some "here" toward some "there." The evaluative comparison of alternative sets of rules and alternative regimes of political order, as discussed above in the first section, aims exclusively at defining the "there," the idealized objective toward which any change must be turned. But the direction for effective reform also requires a definition of the "here." Any reform, constitutional or otherwise, commences from some "here and now," some status quo that is the existential reality. History matters, and the historical experience of a political community is beyond any prospect of change; the constitutional-institutional record can neither be ignored nor rewritten. The question for reform is, then: "How do we get there from here?"

These prefatory remarks are necessary before any consideration of federalism in discussion of practical reform. The abstracted ideal—a strong but severely limited central authority with the capacity and the will to enforce free trade over the inclusive territory, along with several separate "states," each one of which stands in a competitive relationship with all other such units—of this ideal federal order may be well-defined and agreed upon as an objective for change. However, until and unless the "here," the starting point, is identified, not even the direction of change can be known.

A simple illustration may be helpful. Suppose that you and I agree that we want to be in Washington, D.C. But, suppose that you are in New York and I am in Atlanta. We must proceed in different directions if we expect to get to the shared or common objective.

Constitutional reform aimed toward an effective competitive federalism may reduce or expand the authority of the central government relative to that of the separate state governments. . . . If the status quo is described as a centralized and unitary political authority, reform must embody devolution, a shift of genuine political power from the center to the separate states. On the other hand, if the status quo is described by a set of autonomous political units that may perhaps be geographically contiguous but which act potentially in independence one from another, reform must involve a centralization of authority, a shift of genuine power to the central government from the separate states.

Figure 1 offers an illustrative schemata. Consider a well-defined territory that may be organized politically at any point along the abstracted unidimensional spectrum that measures the extent to which political authority is centralized. At the extreme left of this spectrum, the territory is divided among several fully autonomous political units, each one of which possesses total "sovereignty," and among which any interaction, either by individuals or by political units, must be subjected to specific contractual negotiation and agreement. At the extreme right of this spectrum, the whole of the territory is organized as an inclusive political community, with this authority centralized in a single governmental unit. Individuals and groups may interact, but any such interaction must take place within the uniform limits laid down by the monolithic authority.

An effective federal structure may be located somewhere near the middle of the spectrum, between the regime of fully autonomous localized units on the one hand and the regime of fully centralized authority on the other. This simple illustration makes it easy to see that constitutional reform that is aimed toward the competitive federal structure must be characterized by some increase in centralization, if the starting point is on the left, and by some decrease in centralization, if the starting point is on the right.

Figure 1. A Constitutuional Reform Schemata

Fully autonomous   Competitive   Centralized
separate states   federalism   unitary polity

The illustration prompts efforts to locate differing regimes at differing places in their own separate histories on the unidimensional scalar. In 1787, James Madison, who had observed the several former British colonies that had won their independence and organized themselves as a confederation, located the status quo somewhere to the left of the middle of the spectrum, and he sought to secure an effective federalism by establishing a stronger central authority, to which some additional powers should be granted. Reform involved a reduction in the political autonomy of the separate units. In the early post–World War II decades, the leaders of Europe, who had observed the terrible nationalistic wars, located their status quo analogously to Madison. They sought reform in the direction of a federalized structure—reform that necessarily involved some establishment of central authority, with some granting of power independently of that historically claimed by the separate nation-states.

By comparison and contrast, consider the United States in 1995, the history of which is surely described as an overshooting of Madison's dreams for the ideal political order. Over the course of two centuries, and especially after the demise of any secession option, as resultant from the great Civil War of the 1860s, the U.S. political order came to be increasingly centralized. The status quo in 1995 lies clearly to the right of the spectrum, and any reform toward a federalist ideal must involve some devolution of central government authority and some increase in the effective independent power of the several states. . . .

Constitutional reform in many countries, as well as the United States, would presumably involve devolution of authority from the central government to the separate states.

Constitutional Strategy and the Federalist Ideal

The simple construction of Figure 1 is also helpful in suggesting that it may be difficult to achieve the ideal constitutional structure described as competitive federalism. Whether motivated by direct economic interest, by some failure to understand basic economic and political theory, or by fundamental conservative instincts, specific political coalitions will emerge to oppose any shift from the status quo toward a federal structure, no matter what the starting point. If, for example, the status quo is described by a regime of fully autonomous units (the nation-states of Europe after World War II), political groups within each of these units will object to any sacrifice of national sovereignty that might be required by a shift toward federalism. . . .

Similar comments may be made about the debates mounted from the opposing direction. If a unitary centralized authority describes the status quo ante, its supporters may attempt to and may succeed in conveying the potential for damage through constitutional collapse into a regime of autonomous units, vulnerable to economic and political warfare. The middle way offered by devolution to a competitive federalism may, in this case, find few adherents.[5] . . .

As the construction in Figure 1 also suggests, however, the fact that the federalist structure is, indeed, "in the middle," at least in the highly stylized sense discussed here, may carry prospects for evolutionary emergence in the conflicts between centralizing and decentralizing pressures. Contrary to the poetic pessimism of William Butler Yeats, the "centre" may hold, if once attained, not because of any intensity of conviction, but rather due to the location of the balance of forces.[6]

Federalism and Increasing Economic Interdependence

In the preceding discussion, I have presumed that the economic benefits of a large economic nexus, defined both in territory and membership, extend at least to and beyond the limits of the political community that may be constitutionally organized anywhere along the spectrum in Figure 1, from a regime of fully autonomous political units to one of centralized political authority. Recall that Adam Smith emphasized that economic prosperity and growth find their origins in the division (specialization) of labor and that this division, in turn, depends on the extent of the market. Smith placed no limits on the scope for applying this principle. But we know that the economic world of 1995 is dramatically different from that of 1775. Technological development has facilitated a continuing transformation of local to regional to national to international interactions among economic units. Consistently with Smith's insights, economic growth has been more rapid where and when political intrusions have not emerged to prevent entrepreneurs from seizing the advantages offered by the developing technology.

Before the technological revolution in information processing and communication, however, a revolution that has occurred in this half-century, politically motivated efforts to "improve" on the workings of market processes seemed almost a part of institutional reality. In this setting, it seemed to remain of critical economic importance to restrict the intrusiveness of politics, quite apart from the complementary effects on individual liberties. Political federalism, to the extent that its central features were at all descriptive of constitutional history, did serve to facilitate economic growth.

The modern technological revolution in information processing and communications may have transformed, at least to some degree, the setting within which politically motivated obstructions may impact on market forces. This technology may, in itself, have made it more difficult for politicians and governments, at any and all levels, to check or to limit the ubiquitous pressures of economic interdependence.[7] When values can be transferred worldwide at the speed of light and when events everywhere are instantly visible on CNN, there are elements of competitive federalism in play, almost regardless of the particular constitutional regimes in existence.

Finally, the relationship between federalism, as an organizing principle for political structure, and the freedom of trade across political boundaries must be noted. An inclusive political territory, say, the United States or Western Europe, necessarily places limits on its own ability to interfere politically with its own internal market structure to the extent that this structure is, itself, opened up to the free workings of international trade, including the movement of capital. On the other hand, to the extent that the internal market is protected against the forces of international competition, other means, including federalism, become more essential to preserve liberty and to guarantee economic growth.

Conclusion

The United States offers an illustrative example. The United States prospered mightily in the nineteenth century, despite the wall of protectionism that sheltered its internal markets. It did so because political authority, generally, was held in check by a constitutional structure that did contain basic elements of competitive federalism. By comparison, the United States, in this last decade of the twentieth century, is more open to international market forces, but its own constitutional structure has come to be transformed into one approaching a centralized unitary authority.

Devolution toward a competitive federal structure becomes less necessary to the extent that markets are open to external opportunities. However, until and unless effective constitutional guarantees against political measures to choke off external trading relationships are put in place, the more permanent constitutional reform aimed at restoring political authority to the separate states offers a firmer basis for future economic growth along with individual liberty. . . .

NOTES

1. James M. Buchanan, "Politics without Romance: A Sketch of Positive Public Choice Theory and Its Normative Implications," Inaugural Lecture, Institute for Advanced Studies, Vienna, Austria, *IHS Journal, Zeitschrift des Instituts für Höhere Studien* 3 (1979): B1–B11.

2. Adam Smith, *The Wealth of Nations* (1776; Modern Library ed.; New York: Random House, 1937).

3. See Geoffrey Brennan and James M. Buchanan, *The Power to Tax: Analytical Foundations of a Fiscal Constitution* (New York: Cambridge University Press, 1980), pp. 168–186, for more comprehensive treatment.

4. For formal analysis of secession, see James M. Buchanan and Roger Faith, "Secession and the Limits of Taxation: Towards a Theory of Internal Exit," *American Economic Review* 5 (December 1987): 1023–1031; for a more general discussion, see Allen Buchanan, *Secession: The Morality of Political Divorce from Fort Sumter to Lithuania and Quebec* (Boulder, Colo.: Westview, 1991).

5. The theory of agenda-setting in public choice offers analogies. If the agenda can be manipulated in such fashion that the alternatives for choice effectively "bracket" the ideally preferred position, voters are confronted with the selection of one or the other of the extreme alternatives, both of which may be dominated by the preferred option. See Thomas Romer and Howard Rosenthal, "Political Resource Allocation, Controlled Agendas, and the Status Quo," *Public Choice* 33 (Winter 1978): 27–43.

6. William Butler Yeats, "The Second Coming," *The Collected Works of W. B. Yeats,* vol. 1, *The Poems,* Ed. Richard J. Finneran (New York: Macmillan, 1989), p. 187.

7. Richard McKenzie and Dwight Lee, *Quicksilver Capital: How the Rapid Movement of Wealth Has Changed the World* (New York: Free Press, 1991).

Federalism: Battles on the Front Lines of Public Policy

Donald F. Kettl

The phrase "separation of powers" refers to the division of authority across the institutions of the national government; "federalism" refers to the vertical division of authority and responsibility between Washington and the states. The Constitution keeps state authority separate and distinct, but its Framers did not build walls separating these governments into exclusive domains of policy. Instead American federalism, like separation of powers, is a system of shared powers. During the twentieth century, power and responsibility have undoubtedly shifted to the national (or, as it is commonly called, "federal") government. Yet the states remain key participants, meaning that successful programs involve continuous coordination across these levels of government. Mostly the arrangement works reasonably well. But as Hurricane Katrina taught us in 2005, America's federalism is anything but a finely tuned machine. In the following essay, Donald Kettl, one of the nation's authorities on the subject, finds the difficult lessons this disaster taught the public and policymakers.

IN THE EYES of many sad observers, Hurricane Katrina's assault on the Gulf Coast over Labor Day weekend 2005 was not only a stunning reminder of just how far the nation still must go to resolve deep racial and class divisions in American society. It also marked a collapse—both political and administrative—of American federalism. Thousands of New Orleans residents found themselves marooned at the tattered Superdome. CNN got its cameras there, but neither the city, the state, nor the federal government could seem to get food, water, or medicine to the trapped residents. The military and an armada of buses finally arrived to take the trapped refugees to safety, but not before people died in the chaos.

Standing in front of the St. Louis Cathedral in New Orleans just days after the Superdome evacuation, President Bush applauded the work of government officials. Nevertheless, he admitted, "the system, at every level of government, was not well coordinated and was overwhelmed in the first few

Source: This piece is an original essay commissioned for this volume. Some of the material in this reading first appeared in the author's "Potomac Chronicle" column, which is featured every other month in *Governing* magazine, a publication for state and local governments.

days." He stunned state and local officials with what came next. "It is now clear," he said, "that a challenge on this scale requires greater federal authority and a broader role for the armed forces—the institution of our government most capable of massive logistical operations on a moment's notice."[1] The glaring headlines and searing pictures had painted a portrait of the failure of federalism. The initial chaos quickly gave way to finger-pointing, with federal officials saying they were awaiting clear requests, submitted in the proper form, from state and local officials. Louisiana Governor Kathleen Blanco, in her first phone call to the president, asked for "all federal firepower." She continued, "I meant everything. Just send it. Give me planes, give me boats. . . ."[2]

New Orleans Mayor Ray Nagin sent out his own plea: "I need everything." He criticized federal officials and said, "They're thinking small, man. And this is a major, major, major deal. And I can't emphasize it enough, man. This is crazy." When top federal officials told them help was on the way, Nagin countered, "They're not here." Frustrated, he added, "Now get off your asses and do something, and let's fix the biggest goddamn crisis in the history of this country."[3] But help was painfully slow in coming.

Challenging Federalism

Mayor Nagin was stuck for four days in the battered Hyatt Hotel, with no air conditioning in the sweltering, late summer heat. The mayor and his staff found their temporary headquarters in shambles. Not only had the storm isolated them, but it spun off a tornado that ripped away part of the hotel. For the first two days, Nagin had no communication with the outside world except through press releases to CNN reporters. One of his technology aides then remembered that he had established an Internet phone account. The mayor's technology aides eventually found a working Internet connection in one of the hotel's conference rooms and managed to get eight lines hooked up just in time to get a call from President Bush in *Air Force One*. Conditions were brutal. When a gang tried to break into the hotel and steal their small supply of food, the mayor and his small party had to evacuate from the fourth to the 27th floor. The phones they were using worked only if the caller leaned over the balcony into the indoor atrium. "This was when the last parts of the government were about to come undone," explained Greg Meffert, New Orleans's chief technology officer. "It felt like the Alamo—we were surrounded and had only short bursts of communication."[4]

It was little wonder that the president considered a larger role for the military in disaster response. Katrina literally and figuratively swamped the ability of state and local governments to respond. But although the nation's governors saw an important federal role, they rejected the idea of federal control. A month after the storm hit, *USA Today* published a survey of the governors. A total of thirty-eight governors had responded. Only two supported the president's plan. Mississippi Governor Haley Barbour, a Republican who had once headed the party, whose state took a direct hit from Katrina, said the states might need some federal help. "But we don't need them coming and running things," said the governor's spokesman. Michigan Governor Jennifer Granholm, a Democrat, was blunter. "Whether a governor is a Republican or Democrat, I would expect the response would be, 'Hell no,'" she said.[5]

Lurking behind the terrible difficulty in marshaling an effective response to Katrina's devastation was a more subtle political battle over how to manage the inevitable political fallout. Shortly after the storm overwhelmed news coverage on television sets around the nation, the Pew Research Center for the People and the Press surveyed Americans about how they viewed government's response to the storm. The survey revealed an enormous gulf with enormous implications for federalism: When asked whether President Bush had done all he could, 53 percent of Republicans agreed. However, 85 percent of Democrats and 71 percent of independents believed he could have done more. When asked about the response of state and local governments, there was little partisan difference in the answers. Among Republicans, 54 percent rated the response of state and local governments as only "fair" or "poor." For Democrats the figure was 51 percent, and for independents, 52 percent.[6]

There were big partisan divisions in Americans' assessment of the federal government's response to the disaster. Top Republicans quickly calculated that conversations about what went wrong at the federal level—whether the Federal Emergency Management Agency (FEMA) could or should have acted differently, for example—could only go in the wrong direction, from President Bush's point of view. So they resisted calls for a national commission to examine the government's response and instead relied on the polls to point to a different interpretation: that state and local governments should have responded better and had failed their citizens. In part, that explains President Bush's suggestion about a stronger military role in responding to disasters. His underlying argument was that when the crisis occurred, state and local governments could not rise to the challenge. Only the federal government—at least, the federal military—could respond effectively. Coming from a former governor, the argument might have seemed strange. But for a president facing devastating performance by his own emergency response agency and equally devastating findings in public opinion polls, it made sense to deflect blame to state and local governments and to rely on the military's response to deflect criticism of his actions.

Wilma's Test

Soon after Katrina's floodwaters subsided, another enormous storm, Hurricane Wilma, flared up in the Gulf of Mexico. This time the storm struck at southern Florida. Although the devastation was not nearly as brutal as that from Katrina's blow at New Orleans and southern Mississippi, Wilma left hundreds of thousands of residents without food, water, or electric power for days.

The storm got much less attention from the news media, but government officials and administrators put planning and response under a microscope. Before Wilma hit, Florida Governor Jeb Bush firmly told members of Congress, "I can say with certainty that federalizing emergency response to catastrophic events would be a disaster as bad as Hurricane Katrina." In fact, he concluded, "If you federalize, all the innovation, creativity, and knowledge at the local level would subside." [7] If the storm did its worst, the state's Division of Emergency Management promised, residents would have ice, food, and water within twenty-four hours. The storm hit hard, but it stopped short of Category 5. Six million residents found themselves without ice, food, water, or electricity. Long lines snaked around the few operating gasoline pumps. A three-star army general called state officials to say he wanted to fly in and take command. According to later reports, Governor Bush told federal Department of Homeland Security officials that the federal takeover effort was "insulting" to him personally.

Florida officials launched a clever countercoup. Craig Fugate, Florida's emergency manager, seized the Department of Homeland Security's National Incident Management System. In principle, every incident must have a single commander, to prevent battles over who is in charge of what. "I'd now like to introduce the incident commander," Fugate told federal officials during a videoconference. To the stunned surprise of the feds from the Department of Homeland Security, he pulled in Governor Bush. Under the federal government's own rules, federal officials were required to support the incident commander, and Fugate's maneuver had outflanked them. One of Fugate's first acts was to seize control of 300 satellite phones that the federal department had sent to Florida for the use of its officials and give them to local emergency workers instead. FEMA sent in a large team of workers, but its employees ended up working under the overall authority of state officials.

Governor Bush said the state was responsible for the problems that developed, but everyone had basic supplies within seventy-two hours. And if state officials did not meet their twenty-four-hour response target, they nevertheless retained control of the operation—and overall command of the federal response. When big storms hit, Fugate—a rabid University of Florida fan—puts on a weather-beaten, orange Gators cap. When the crisis ebbs, he switches to a clean blue one. Within days of Wilma's assault on southern Florida, Fugate was wearing his blue Gators cap again.

Federalism's Arenas

In the storms, federalism played itself out in a host of complex ways. In part the issue was a political one: With so many different players at all levels involved in the difficult process, finger-pointing and blame-shifting became inevitable. In part it was fiscal: Given the enormity of the damage, who ought to pay for—and control decisions about—rebuilding the region? And in part it was administrative: Why did the federal, state, and local governments find it so difficult to provide a coordinated, effective response?

And as with everything else in federalism, complicated issues became entangled with each other. In mid-2005, America's governors had pushed hard for fundamental changes in the Medicaid program, the nation's most important program for providing medical and nursing home care for the poor, including the poor elderly. From 1998 to 2003, Medicaid spending increased 62 percent, compared with a 36 percent increase for Medicare, the federal program that pays doctor and hospital bills for seniors. Experts estimated that over the next fifteen years Medicaid's cost would grow 145 percent, an annual growth rate of 8.2 percent for the states.[8] For most governors, Medicaid was the fastest-growing item in the budget, and they looked for help in funding a program that, after all, was mostly federal. "Governors believe that Medicaid reform must be driven by good public policy and not by the federal budget process," the National Governors Association concluded in a 2005 report.[9]

The secretary of the federal Department of Health and Human Services, Michael Leavitt, created a special commission to study Medicaid and strategies for putting it on a sounder financial footing. The commission proposed giving states more flexibility in managing the program, including new options for reducing the cost of prescription drugs. It also argued for making it harder for individuals to transfer their assets to others so as to qualify sooner for Medicaid benefits (which have strict limits on recipients' income, savings, and other assets). The commission, however, did not solve the biggest problems: dealing with the rising cost of long-term care, especially in nursing homes, and as the commission put it, "expanding the number of people covered with quality care while recognizing budget constraints." [10]

The governors hoped that their work, coupled with the special commission's, would build momentum for fundamental reform. The two projects, they thought, could come together in President Bush's budget address early in 2006 and set the stage for sweeping changes. But the rising costs of the war in Iraq, coupled with the enormous, uncounted costs of federal assistance for the Gulf Coast, torpedoed that plan. Thus, in addition to the administrative, financial, and political implications of the hurricanes, the states had to reckon with significant collateral damage: The storms blew away what governors hoped would be their best chance for Medicaid reform. No one in Washington had the resources or the energy for a major assault on such a difficult set of questions, so the states concluded they might well end up having to attack the problems piecemeal and on their own.

Federalism behaved, at once, exactly as the Founders designed it—and precisely as some of them feared it would stumble in crisis. However, the Founders never intended this American invention of "federalism" to be a bold, sweeping innovation. They were supremely practical men (women were not invited to Philadelphia to help frame the new nation) with a supremely practical problem. Northern states did not trust southern states. Farmers did not trust merchants. Most of all, larger states did not trust smaller states and vice versa. The fledgling nation's army had won independence from Great Britain, but the notables gathered in Philadelphia in 1787 needed to find some glue to hold the new country together. If they had failed, the individual states would have been too small to endure—and would surely have proved easy pickings for European nations eager to expand.

It is not surprising, therefore, that the nation's Founders relied on a supremely pragmatic strategy for solving the practical problem of how to balance power among the states. They made the national[11] government supreme, but they also created the Tenth Amendment to the Constitution to remind everyone that the states retained any power not explicitly given to the national government. Except for forbidding the states from interfering with commerce between them, the Constitution allowed the states to govern themselves.

The system of federalism that the Founders created had few rules and fewer fixed boundaries. As federalism has developed over the centuries, however, two important facts about the system have become clear. First, federalism's very strength comes from its enormous flexibility—its ability to adapt to new problems and political cross-pressures. Second, it creates alternative venues for political action. Interests that fight and lose at the state level have been able to find clever ways of taking their battles to the national government. Losers at the national level have been able to refight their wars in the states.

Throughout American history, we have frequently looked on federalism as a rather sterile scheme for determining who is in charge of what in our governmental system. But that misses most of what makes federalism important and exciting. It makes far more sense to view federalism as an ever-evolving, flexible system for creating arenas for political action. Americans have long celebrated their basic document of government as a "living Constitution." No part of it has lived more—indeed, changed more—than that involving the relationship between the national and the state governments and the relationships among the states. This can be seen clearly in the rich variations on the three themes that Katrina highlighted: political, fiscal, and administrative federalism.

Political Federalism

In the 1990s some South Carolina business owners launched the *Tropic Sea* as a casino boat for "cruises to nowhere." However, the enterprise soon became a cruise to a very important somewhere by raising the question, Just how far can—and should—federal power intrude on the prerogatives of the states?

This balance-of-power question is as old as the American republic and in fact predates the Constitution. When the colonies declared their independence from King George III, they formed a loose confederation. It proved barely strong enough to win the war and not nearly strong enough to help govern the new nation. Problems with the country's Articles of Confederation led to the nation's leaders to gather in Philadelphia to draft a new constitution. At the core of their debate was the question of how much power to give the national government and how much to reserve to the states. The Founders followed a time-honored tradition in resolving such tough issues—they sidestepped it. The Constitution is silent on the question, and the Tenth Amendment simply reinforces the obvious: The national government has only the powers that the Constitution gives it. By leaving the details vague, the authors of the Constitution avoided a wrenching political battle. They also ensured that generations of Americans after them would refight the same battles—most often with legal stratagems in the nation's courts, but sometimes, as in the Civil War, with blood.

A Cruise to Somewhere?

The *Tropic Sea* sailed into an ongoing struggle in South Carolina politics. Although developers loved gambling ships such as the *Tropic Sea,* which lured tourists to the state, several legislators and local officials did not, and they had been actively campaigning against the ships. As a result, when the *Tropic Sea* asked permission to dock at Charleston's State Ports Authority (SPA) Pier, the SPA said no. The boat ended up at anchor in the harbor while its owners sought help from the Federal Maritime Commission (FMC). The FMC sided with the boat owners but was overturned by a federal appeals court. The case eventually ended up in the U.S. Supreme Court.

South Carolina argued that, as a state government, it wasn't subject to the FMC's jurisdiction, and in a bitter five-to-four decision at the end of its 2002 term, the Supreme Court agreed. Writing for the majority, Justice Clarence Thomas looked past the usual foundation of political struggles over state power, the Tenth Amendment, and instead built his argument on the little-noticed Eleventh Amendment, ratified in 1798, which specifies that the judicial power of the United State[s] does not extend to the states. This amendment supported the notion of "dual federalism"—separate spheres of federal and state action. In the decades after its ratification, however, the dual federalism argument gradually eroded, especially after 1868, under the weight of the "equal protection" clause of the Fourteenth Amendment. That amendment asserts that all citizens have the right to equal treatment under the law. In establishing a national standard, the Fourteenth Amendment gave the courts power to enforce national policy over state objections. That pushed away the dual federalism concept and helped shift the balance of power to the national government. After William Rehnquist became chief justice in 1986, however, dual federalism resurfaced and surged ahead again.

In ruling for South Carolina, Justice Thomas admitted that there was little textual evidence to support his position. Rather, he said, dual federalism was "embedded in our constitutional structure." The concept helped uphold the "dignity" of the states as dual sovereigns. That, he said, was the core of the decision.[12]

Asserting the dignity of the states is a new constitutional standard. The Eleventh Amendment explicitly applies to federal courts, not federal administrators, such as employees of the FMC. Conservatives, of course, had long criticized liberals for making law from the bench. In this case, however, it was the conservatives on the Court who crafted a new principle, which they used to push back the scope of the national government's power.

Federalism Means War

The Supreme Court under Rehnquist gradually chipped away at national power and aggressively worked to strengthen the role of the states. The major federalism decisions have all been by votes of five to four, built on the conservative bloc of Rehnquist, Thomas, Anthony Kennedy, Sandra Day O'Connor, and Antonin Scalia. The disputes, on the Court as well as off, have become increasingly intense. As *New York Times* reporter Linda Greenhouse put it, "These days, federalism means war." [13]

The battles became so sharp that candidates' views on federalism were critical in the battles over new appointments to the Supreme Court, especially those of Chief Justice John Roberts and Justice Samuel Alito. Given the ages of several other justices, more appointment battles are certain—and so are questions about the Court's role in reframing federalism. Will the Court remain on its dual federalism course? Staying that course raises two very difficult questions.

First, just how far is the Court prepared to go in pursuing dual federalism? In the past it has ruled that workers cannot sue states for discrimination under federal age and disability standards. It has also protected states from suits by people who claimed unfair competition from state activities in the marketplace, such as photocopying by state universities. Bit by bit the Court has extended state power at the expense of the national government's jurisdiction.

At some point, however, the pursuit of state "dignity" will collide with national standards for equal protection. At some point, state protection against national labor standards will crash into national protection of civil rights and civil liberties. That point might come in debates over family leave or prescription drugs, over voting rights or transportation of nuclear waste. But a collision is certain. From the Fourteenth Amendment, there is a long tradition of asserting national power over the states. From the Rehnquist court, there is a new legal argument for reasserting state power.

Neither argument is an absolute. In some issues (such as civil rights) there is a strong case for national preeminence. In other issues (such as the states' own systems of law) there is a strong case for state preeminence. Still other issues, however (such as gambling boats), rest squarely in the middle. The nation then has to determine how best to balance competing policy goals and constitutional principles. Sometimes those battles are fought out in the legislative and executive branches, but most often they are contested in the courts.

Since the dawn of Roosevelt's New Deal in the 1930s, national power has grown at the expense of the states. Now, with an uncommon purpose, the conservatives on the Supreme Court are pushing that line back. The Roberts Court can continue the campaign to reassert the power of the states, but clearly at some point it will have to hold national interests paramount. What is less clear is where and how the Court will draw that line.

The second question that the Court's pro-dual federalism course raises is even tougher: How far can the Court advance state-centered federalism without running headlong into the new campaign for homeland security, which demands a strong national role? It is one thing for the Court to pursue the principles of state sovereignty and dignity. But beefing up homeland security inevitably means strengthening federal power. There is a vital national interest in ensuring that state and local governments protect critical infrastructure, such as water systems and harbors. The nation needs not only a strong intelligence apparatus but also a powerful emergency response system.

Federalism and the Living Constitution

It may be that relatively few Americans care about whether a gambling boat can dock at a South Carolina port. But the basic issue—where to draw the line between national and state power, and who ought to draw it—is an issue that all Americans care about, even if they spend little time thinking about it in those terms. It has been the stuff of bloody battles and endless debate. As political scientist Howard Gillman told the *New York Times,* federalism has become "the biggest and deepest disagreement about the nature of our constitutional system." [14] The equal protection and homeland security issues will only intensify that disagreement as we wade deeper into the real meaning of the states' "dignity."

These issues are scarcely ones that the Founders could have anticipated when they wrote the Constitution and the Bill of Rights. Few present-day Americans, after all, had heard the phrase "homeland security" before September 11, 2001. The genius of the Founders was that they recognized the importance of federalism, that they put broad boundaries around it but did not try to resolve it for all time, and that they created a mechanism for Americans in subsequent generations to adjust the balance, subtly and continually.

It was no easy matter to recognize the key questions out of thousands that engaged the members of the Constitutional Convention in Philadelphia. It was even tougher to resolve the questions just sufficiently to win the Constitution's adoption, without pushing so hard as to deepen the divisions. And it was quite remarkable to do so in a way that has allowed us to reshape the balance in our time.

Fiscal Federalism

These grand debates are what most Americans think of when they think of "federalism." They are the stuff of high school civics classes and the enduring classics of American history. For national, state, and local policymakers, however, the soft underbelly of federalism is much more often the question of who pays for what.

That has not always been the case. But in the 1950s, as the nation—and the national government—became much more ambitious about domestic policy, fiscal federalism became increasingly important. During that period, citizens and national policymakers wanted the country to undertake new, large-scale projects, such as building a national network of highways and tearing down decaying slums. State and local governments could not, or would not, move ahead on such matters. Often they simply did not have the funds to do so; sometimes local political forces opposed the policies. Even without those impediments, state and local governments almost always lacked the ability to coordinate the creation of such complex systems as effective high-speed highways with other jurisdictions. (Who would want to drive on a modern, four-lane road only to hit a two-lane gravel path at the state line?) Therefore citizens and national policymakers pressed to empower the national government to undertake the projects.

National Goals through Intergovernmental Grants

The national government tackled the problem of getting local and state governments to do what it wanted done by offering them grants. If local governments lacked the resources to tear down dilapidated housing, the national government could create an "urban renewal" program and provide the money, thus avoiding the constitutional problem that would have come with national coercion. The national government did not *make* local governments accept the money or tear down the slums. But few local officials could resist a national program that helped them do what they, too—or at least many of their constituents—wanted done.

The same was true at the state level. In the 1950s Americans were buying cars in record numbers, but they found the roads increasingly clogged. Long-distance driving often proved a special chore because road systems did not connect well and the quality of the roads fell far below the performance ability of the cars driving on them. During the Eisenhower administration the national government decided to tackle that problem by creating a new program—the interstate highway system—and inducing states to join it by funding 90 percent of the construction costs. With motorists demanding better roads, the offer was too good to refuse. Since this was occurring amid the hottest moments of the cold war, President Dwight D. Eisenhower reinforced the idea of a national interest by arguing that the system served both transportation and defense goals—it would allow troops to move quickly to wherever they might be needed. (Wags have since joked that the system could best serve the national defense by luring Russian tanks onto the [Beltway around Washington, D.C.,] and challenging them to cope with the traffic and find the right exit.)[15]

The strategy continued to be used through the 1960s. When Lyndon B. Johnson announced his War on Poverty, he decided to fight it primarily through national grants to state and local governments. He created the Model Cities program, which provided aid to local communities trying to uproot poverty and rebuild urban neighborhoods, and established other programs to provide better housing for poor Americans. He founded Medicaid, which provided grants to state governments so that they, in turn, could provide health care to the poor. More grants followed, to support job training, criminal justice, public health, and a host of other national goals.

It was a clever strategy in a number of ways. For one, it sidestepped constitutional limitations on national interference in state and local issues: The national government did not force state and local governments to join the programs; it simply made them financially irresistible. No state or local officials wanted to have to explain to constituents why they left cheap money on the table, especially when their neighbors were benefiting from the programs.

This approach sidestepped another tough constitutional problem as well: the national government's dealing directly with local governments. Through long-standing constitutional interpretation and practice, local governments are considered creatures of the states, not the national government. The states created the national government, so constitutionally the national government must deal with the states. Hence the states alone have the power to control what local governments can—and cannot—do. Before Johnson's program, local governments struggled with increasing problems of poverty, substandard housing, and other human needs. They often found themselves without power or enough money to attack the problems. Few state governments themselves had adequate resources to address these serious issues, and in many states, political forces prevented the creation of new programs that might have helped.

Many analysts concluded that the only solution was to create a direct link between the national and local governments—a link that bypassed the states. But given both constitutional limits and political conflicts, how could such a link be established? Federal grants to local governments proved the answer. Across the nation, state governments gave permission for local governments to receive the money. If the national government agreed to take on the problems and keep state officials out of the process, the programs seemed an attractive proposition to state and local officials alike.

From the 1950s through the 1970s, these intergovernmental aid programs became increasingly popular and important. They not only grew in size but also became ever more vital elements of state and local government financing. In 1938 federal aid had amounted to just 8.7 percent of state and local revenue. It surged to 22 percent—more than one out of every five dollars raised by state and local governments—in 1978, at the high-water mark of federal aid.

As the national government used its funds to support state and local governments and to induce them to do things they might not have done otherwise, federal aid became not only an increasingly important part of the policy system but also something on which those governments became ever more dependent. When the national government began tightening its fiscal belt in the late 1970s, state and local governments felt the effects keenly. In 1980, federal aid was 40 percent of all spending by state and local governments from their own sources. By 2002 it had dropped to 29 percent.[16] Few federal programs were abolished, however. Rather, the national government simply cut back support—leaving state and local governments to deal with ongoing commitments and, in many cases, powerful supporters who fought hard to keep the programs alive. In the federal highway program, federal support mostly provided aid for construction, not maintenance. As highways aged, state governments found themselves with huge bills for repairing crumbling bridges and old roadbeds.

When recession hit in 2002, state and local governments looked expectantly to Washington for some hope—and help.

No News Was Bad News

The nation's governors, in particular, were hoping for good news when President George W. Bush began 2003 by announcing his plans for a $670 billion tax cut. They hoped the speech would contain at least some help for their ailing budgets. Except for a modest proposal on unemployment insurance, however, they found themselves left out in the January cold.

With their budgets in the biggest crisis since World War II, governors had been lobbying hard for national help. They hoped for a short-term resuscitation of revenue sharing, the federal government's program of distributing broad grants to state and local governments to use as they wished. The program ended in 1982, but they wanted to bring it back. Failing that, they pressed for at least some tinkering with the formula for reimbursing Medicaid spending, the fastest-growing program in many state budgets and one, as noted earlier, that was originally launched through the incentive of national grants. Changes in the Medicaid formulas, the governors hoped, would ease their budget worries.

Ignoring most of the states' pleas, Bush instead advanced a bold stroke to restructure the national tax system. The administration did suggest some changes to Medicaid, but the changes proposed would have reduced aid (or increased costs) for the poor, and they immediately incited opposition from groups struggling to protect the program. The states were left on their own with a $90 billion budget shortfall that threatened to soak up all of the short-term economic stimulus Bush was proposing, and more. The net effect promised to be an economic wash surrounded by political conflict.

Who is at fault here? The feds, for failing to extend a helping hand when the states needed it most? Or the states, for digging themselves into the hole and whining when Bush refused to help them out? As with most questions of fault, the answer is, both.

If Bush truly had been interested in jump-starting the economy, pumping money through the states would quickly have done just that. But the president was concerned more with long-term revision of the tax code than with short-term economic stimulus, especially through the states. As for the states, their fault lies in having hitched their spending to the booming economy of the 1990s. They forgot "Stein's Law," derived by the late Herbert Stein, once chairman of the president's Council of Economic Advisers: "Things that can't go on forever—won't."[17] When the boom collapsed, the states found themselves hooked on spending increases they could not support.

Exploding Health Care Costs

In the 1990s national aid to state and local governments had actually resumed its upward course (see Figure 1), but not because the national government had decided to resume its generosity to state and local governments. Rather, the reason was that national aid for payments to individuals—mostly through Medicaid—suddenly accelerated, as the benefits became more generous and health care costs began to grow rapidly. Grants for all other purposes had leveled off or shrunk, but national aid for health care had swung quickly upward, as had state governments' own spending for their matching share of the costs. In 1960 federal grants for payments to individuals amounted to 31 percent of all grants. By 2009, budget experts estimate, the figure will swell to 71 percent (see Figure 2). There will little federal aid for anything but payments to individuals, most of which will be Medicaid.

As the new century began, health care costs, particularly under Medicaid, exploded at precisely the same moment that state revenues collapsed. Spending for doctor visits, hospital care, and especially prescription drugs swelled at the highest rate in a decade, growing to 30 percent of state spending, and it could not have come at a worse time for state governments. It has swamped the states' efforts to control the rest of their budgets and aggravated their financial hemorrhage. The monster in the states' budgetary basement has become health care: treating the uninsured, providing long-term care for the elderly, and buying

Figure 1. Federal Aid to State and Local Governments

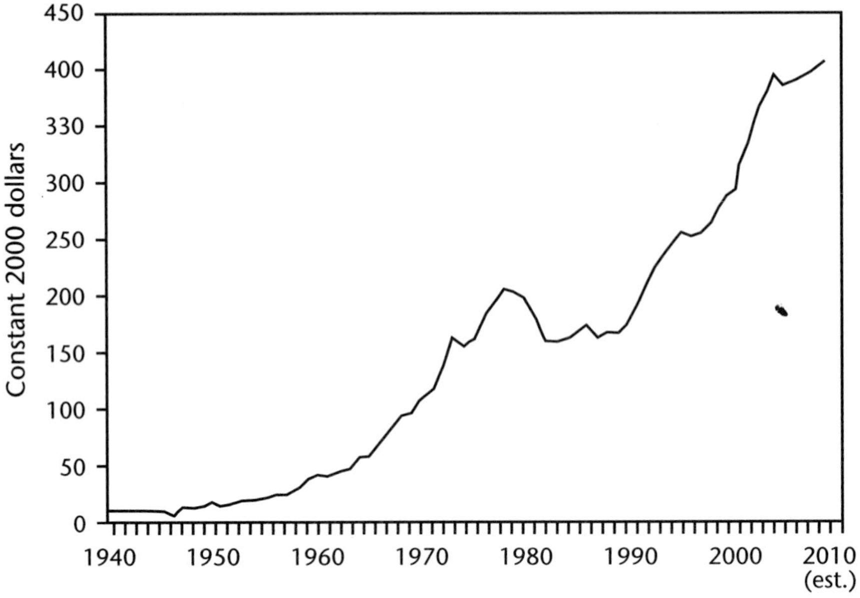

Source: U.S. Office of Management and Budget, *Budget of the United States Government, Fiscal Year 2005: Historical Tables* (Table 12.1), www.gpoaccess.gov/usbudget/fy05/hist.html (accessed January 21, 2006). Figures for fiscal years 2004–2009 are estimates.

prescription drugs. With the baby boomers reaching retirement age, the budgetary problem promises to get worse.

State spending pegged to unsustainable revenue growth and the sudden increase in health care costs threaten a continuing, profound crisis for state policymakers. Aggravating it is the projection by most economists that economic growth will not proceed fast enough to bail out the states any time soon. It's little wonder that in some states Democrats were quietly rooting for Republican governors to make the hard budgetary decisions, and vice versa. If the states are the laboratories of democracy, the lurching of budgetary Frankensteins could litter broken test tubes across the floor. This is a long way from the salad days of national-state relations in the 1960s and early 1970s. The feds then saw state and local problems as their own. Democrats and Republicans joined together to provide national funds to leverage state and local action. The partnership might have been paternalistic, but it shaped policy for decades. When budget cuts hit in the late 1970s and early 1980s, national-state ties became increasingly frayed. They unraveled further with the Bush administration's 2002 loosening of air pollution regulations, which complicated the job many states faced in meeting

Figure 2. Grants for Payments to Individuals as a Share of All Grants

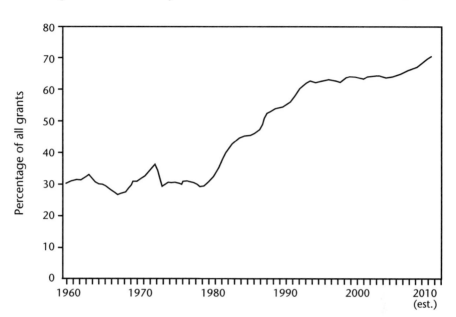

Source: U.S. Office of Management and Budget, *Budget of the United States Government, Fiscal Year 2005: Historical Tables* (Table 12.1), http://www.gpoaccess.gov/usbudget/fy05/hist.html (accessed January 21, 2006). Figures for fiscal years 2004–2009 are estimates.

pollution standards, and frayed some more with the administration's capital gains tax plan.

The states can—indeed, they have to—deal with some of these problems by putting their spending back into balance with a realistic view of their revenues. They need to update their revenue systems. But they cannot solve their fundamental fiscal problems without a new partnership between the states and the feds. And that will be hard to realize as long as the two groups move in such different orbits that the fundamental problems they share never come together.

Administrative Federalism

A close corollary of the rise of fiscal federalism has been the growing importance of state and local governments as administrative agents of national programs. As close observers of Washington politics know, the national government has increased its spending without increasing (in fact, while decreasing) the number of bureaucrats. The reason it has been able to do so? The national government has leveraged the activity of state and local governments as agents to do much of its work. As is the case in fiscal federalism, the states usually have discretion about whether to enlist as national agents, but the construction of programs typically leaves them little choice. Consider, for example, the case of environmental policy. Under national environmental laws, state governments have substantial responsibility for issuing permits and monitoring emissions.

The Environmental Protection Agency (EPA) relies heavily on state governments for much of the frontline work. In the process, however, some states have used that role to set their own policies, which often have been far broader than those of the EPA. In a peculiar, up-from-the-bottom style of federalism, that has meant that some states have, in practice, set policy for the entire nation.

Policymaking for the Nation—in Sacramento

Top officials in the capital have been increasingly consumed by a war about the air, and there is a good chance that a decade from now the EPA administrator will not be setting much environmental policy. Recent agency administrators, both Republican and Democratic, have been pinned down in a fierce guerrilla battle between some congressional members who are trying to lighten the burden of environmental regulations and others who are trying to toughen pollution standards and reduce global warming. The administrator's job increasingly has been to chart the EPA's course through the political crossfire. As the melee has raged in Washington, the policy initiative has shifted to the states and to foreign governments.

It is little wonder that California has been so aggressive in campaigning to reduce air pollution. Pollution problems in the Los Angeles basin are legendary. Medical research has shown that kids growing up in the area suffer a 10 percent to 15 percent decrease in lung function and suffer more from asthma and respiratory infections than their counterparts elsewhere in the country. Autopsies of 152 young people who died suddenly from crime or health problems revealed that all of them had inflamed airways and 27 percent had severe lung damage.

The state has set tougher standards than federal regulations required, and in the past twenty-five years the results have been remarkable. The number of health advisories for high levels of ozone shrank from 166 in 1976 to just fifteen in 2001.

In July 2002 California took another tough step. The legislature passed a bill requiring that all cars sold in California after 2009 meet tough standards for greenhouse gases, the carbon-based emissions scientists believe promote global warming. In signing the bill, Governor Gray Davis chided the national government for "failing to ratify the Kyoto treaty on global warming." They "missed their opportunity to do the right thing," Davis said. "So it is left to California, the nation's most populous state and the world's fifth largest economy, to take the lead." California was proud to "join the long-standing and successful effort of European nations against global warming." [18]

With its legislation, California rendered moot President Bush's March 2001 decision to withdraw the United States from the Kyoto treaty, at least with respect to carbon dioxide pollution from cars. Carmakers had waged a fierce battle against the California bill, but in the end they could not beat the forces of environmentalists and citizens worried about public health. They found themselves trooping off to Sacramento to haggle over the details of the new regulations.

No automaker can afford to ignore California and its huge market, as was clear after the state's earlier decision to mandate cleaner gas and catalytic converters. When California mandated catalytic converters to scrub auto exhaust, it soon became impossible to buy cars in Wisconsin or Texas that did not contain the device as well. As California goes, at least in air pollution, so goes the nation.

For California regulators, the aggressive antipollution campaign has not been a one-way street. The new California law requires regulators to reduce not only smog but also greenhouse gases, such as carbon dioxide. New-generation diesel engines are more fuel efficient than many gasoline-powered engines. That means less fuel and fewer carbon dioxide emissions. And that, in turn, has brought California regulators into close negotiations with automakers about encouraging production of diesel-powered cars.

For those who have long seen diesels as blue-smoke-belching behemoths, the idea that diesel power might be a pollution-reducing strategy may seem preposterous. It may seem even more unlikely that government would be encouraging a shift to diesel engines or that government regulators would be in conversations with automakers hammering out deals to do so. Above all, it may seem incredible that the government taking the action would be a state government. But that is exactly what is happening in California.

All this, in turn, has led to budding ties between state regulators and the European Union (EU). European nations have been working as hard and as long on global warming as anyone. The EU's aggressive efforts to reduce greenhouse gases have stimulated new diesel technologies. So California regulators find themselves steering in the same direction as their counterparts abroad. Put together, this means that American policy for auto emissions is subtly shifting course, driven by activities at the state and international levels.

State governments have long prided themselves on being the nation's policy laboratories, and healthy competition among them might produce new breakthroughs. But there is also a profound risk that the nation could find its policy strategies increasingly evolving through accidental bits and bumps, without a national debate about what is truly in the national interest. The trend is already briskly under way. General Electric chief executive Jeffrey Immelt has said that 99 percent of all new regulations the company faces are, over time, coming not from the national government but from the European Union.[19] The states are vigorously developing new pollution standards. Meanwhile, as Washington policymakers focus on the interest group battles that constantly consume them, they risk fighting more and more about less and less.

Conclusion

If James Madison today rode his horse to Washington, down the interstate from his Virginia estate at Montpelier, would he recognize the system of federalism he helped to craft? He would undoubtedly be stunned at the very idea of using federalism to work out problems of ship-based gambling, health care for the poor, or global warming. However, on a few moments' reflection—and perhaps after a bit of conversation to get up to speed on the stunning policy predicaments of the twenty-first century—he would see in these puzzles echoes of the issues he and his colleagues dealt with at the end of the eighteenth century. He would surely recognize the tough battles that raged in the days after the fierce hurricanes of 2005. They were little different in tone from the ones he and his colleagues waged in Philadelphia.

The glue holding together America's special—and peculiar—democratic system comes from a unique blending of federal, state, and local responsibilities. Early Americans faced a fundamental, dramatic choice: to assign those responsibilities clearly to different levels of government and then write rules for governments to coordinate their inevitable differences, or to allow governments to share responsibilities and then to negotiate their differences through a political process. The latter is the cornerstone of American federalism.

Thus federalism is a much-revered constitutional principle, rooted deeply in the American tradition, which draws its life from political bargaining. It is tempting to read the Constitution, think of the stirring rhetoric of the Founders, and celebrate federalism as a set of rules. In reality, federalism is a set of political action arenas. It is far less an institution than a living organism, one that breathes, grows, shrinks, and changes in response to the forces pressing upon it.

Federalism has helped Americans survive the pressures that led to the Civil War, and it has often made possible programs and policies that might not otherwise have existed. It would be hard, for example, to imagine the national government itself taking on the job of building the massive interstate highway system. Only through federalism did this crucial system come into being, as federalism introduced the possibility of a political, fiscal, and administrative partnership that made possible a program no one government alone could have produced. By the same means, federalism has transformed American cities (for better or worse) through urban renewal, launched a war on poverty, helped clean the environment, and produced a health care program for the nation's poor.

Of course, this partnership has not always been a happy or peaceful one. Governors are never convinced that the national government provides enough money, and national policymakers constantly find it difficult to corral fifty different states—and tens of thousands of local governments—into a coherent policy system. When Hurricane Katrina devastated the Gulf Coast, federalism created a series of roadblocks that vastly complicated the job of getting critical relief to suffering citizens. New Orleans's mayor blamed Louisiana's governor. The governor called on the federal government to send everything it had, but the feds said that the governor had not requested the information in the right way. When the process of rebuilding began, New Orleans residents complained that the feds were slow in providing everything from new maps of the flood plain to trailers for displaced residents. Louisiana residents complained that citizens in Mississippi, the state next door, received more money per capita.

In the storm's wake, study after study pointed to failures of leadership and coordination. It is no exaggeration to conclude that the struggle to coordinate the intergovernmental system cost some people their lives. When quick, coordinated governmental response is needed, federalism has sometimes proved slow and disjointed. It is a system far better equipped to broaden participation in the political process than to produce efficient government.

Of course, if we had wanted that kind of government, we would long ago have sided with Alexander Hamilton in his effort to bring energy to the executive and to strengthen presidential power. Other Founders rejected his argument, and the resulting political system has proved remarkably resilient. The system's flexibility has not only made it possible to work out accommodations for the tough issues but also created arenas in which Americans with many different points of view can continue to contest the future of the nation's public policy. But the new challenges of homeland security and Katrina-like disasters raise tough questions about how to ensure that the quest for responsiveness does not prove administratively chaotic.

NOTES

1. George W. Bush, "Address to the Nation," September 15, 2005, www.whitehouse.gov/news/releases/2005/09/2005915-8.html (accessed January 19, 2006).

2. CNN, *American Morning,* September 2, 2005, http://transcripts.cnn.com/TRANSCRIPTS/0509/02/ltm.03.html (accessed January 19, 2006).

3. CNN.com, "Transcript of Radio Interview with Mayor Nagin," September 2, 2005, www.cnn.com/2005/US/09/02/nagin.transcript/ (accessed January 19, 2006).

4. Christopher Rhoads and Peter Grant, "City Officials Struggled to Keep Order with Crisis," *Wall Street Journal*, September 9, 2005, A1.

5. Bill Nichols and Richard Benedetto, "Govs to Bush: Relief Our Job," *USA Today*, October 2, 2005, www.usatoday.com/news/washington/2005-10-02-gov-survey_x.htm (accessed January 19, 2006).

6. Pew Research Center for the People and the Press, "Two-in-Three Critical of Bush's Relief Efforts," September 8, 2005, http://people-press.org/reports/display.php3? ReportID=255 (accessed January 20, 2006).

7. The facts and quotations in this discussion come from Robert Block and Amy Schatz, "Local and Federal Authorities Battle to Control Disaster Relief," *Wall Street Journal*, December 8, 2005, A1.

8. Bipartisan Commission on Medicaid Reform, "The Medicaid Commission," September 1, 2005, 8.

9. National Governors Association, "Medicaid Reform: A Preliminary Report," June 15, 2005, 1, www.nga.org/Files/pdf/0506medicaid.pdf (accessed January 21, 2006).

10. Ibid., 14.

11. Throughout this chapter, I will use *national* to refer to what most people call the *federal* government. To use *federal* in discussing *federalism* often causes endless confusion, so I am resorting to the less-common usage to maintain clarity. Readers who find that in itself confusing can simply substitute *federal* for *national* wherever it appears.

12. *Federal Maritime Commission v. South Carolina Ports Authority*, No. 01-46. See Linda Greenhouse, "Justices Expand States' Immunity in Federalism Case," *New York Times*, May 29, 2002, sec. A.

13. Linda Greenhouse, "The Nation: 5-to-4, Now and Forever; At the Court, Dissent over States' Rights Is Now War," *New York Times*, June 9, 2002, sec. 4.

14. Ibid.

15. For a map of the system, see www.fhwa.dot.gov/hep10/nhs.

16. U.S. Census Bureau, *Statistical Abstract of the United States, 2006* (Washington, D.C.: Government Printing Office), Table 421.

17. Herbert Stein, interview with the author.

18. Gray Davis, "California Takes on Air Pollution," *Washington Post*, July 22, 2002, sec. A.

19. Brandon Mitchener, "Increasingly, Rules of Global Economy Are Set in Brussels," *Wall Street Journal*, April 23, 2002, sec. A.

3-3

A Separate Peace

Jonathan Rauch

The previous essay presents American federalism the way it is typically portrayed—as an amalgam of state and federal responsibilities whose separate administration challenges effective coordination. Disaster policy, for example, has gravitated from the states to the federal government. Secondary education has witnessed an expanded federal role, but primary responsibility remains with the states. Both areas, however, exhibit serious friction between these levels of government. Jonathan Rauch considers in this essay another commonly expressed virtue of federalism: the states' capacity to act independently allows many different policy approaches to be tested simultaneously. Successes tend to be copied by other states and frequently serve as models for national policy. Rauch finds an additional virtue in independent state action: it moderates easily inflamed cultural issues. In the case of abortion, the issue became highly contentious after the Supreme Court proclaimed the right to an abortion to be a national privacy right. But with gay marriage, the national government has stayed clear. As states pass their own laws, mostly banning gay marriage, the issue has remained defused.

MITT ROMNEY, the former governor of Massachusetts and a 2008 Republican presidential candidate, is a thoughtful politician, for a politician. So it was not surprising to find him recently debating one of the country's core conundrums. It was a little surprising, though, to find him debating himself.

Romney believes abortion is wrong, but he thinks the decision on whether to allow it should be left to the states. In February, *National Journal* asked him if he favored a constitutional amendment banning abortion. No, he replied:

What I've indicated is that I am pro-life and that my hope is that the Supreme Court will give to the states . . . their own ability to make their own decisions with regard to their own abortion law. . . . My view is not to impose a single federal rule on the entire nation, a one-size fits all approach, but instead allow states to make their own decisions in this regard.

Romney also believes gay marriage is wrong, but he thinks the decision on whether to allow it should *not* be left to the states. Last year, he poured scorn on Senator John McCain, who (like Romney) opposes gay marriage, but who (unlike

Source: Jonathan Rauch, "A Separate Peace," *The Atlantic Monthly,* April 2007.

Romney) opposes a U.S. constitutional amendment banning it. "Look," Romney said, "if somebody says they're in favor of gay marriage, I respect that view. If someone says—like I do—that I oppose same-sex marriage, I respect that view. But those who try and pretend to have it both ways, I find it to be disingenuous."

Taking the two quotations side by side, one could be excused for supposing Romney was trying to have it both ways. However, in fairness to him, now is not the first time Republicans have argued with themselves over moral federalism— or, what may be a better term, moral pluralism: leaving states free to go their separate ways when a national moral consensus is lacking.

In 1973, when the Supreme Court (in *Roe v. Wade*) declared abortion to be a constitutional right, conservatives were outraged. But what to do? Republicans were divided. Abortion opponents wanted the practice banned by a constitutional amendment, and supporters of Ronald Reagan soon took up the cause. Reagan, of course, was preparing a conservative primary challenge to the politically vulnerable and ideologically moderate Republican president, Gerald Ford—and Ford was in a bind, because his wife, Betty, had already endorsed Roe ("a great, great decision").

Ford's response was also to call for a constitutional amendment—but one that would return authority over abortion to the states, not impose a federal ban. In the end, Ford won the presidential nomination but lost the struggle within his party: The 1976 Republican platform called for "enactment of a constitutional amendment to restore protection of the right to life for unborn children."

The more things change, the more they stay the same: In this decade, Vice President Cheney—a Ford administration alumnus, as it happens—has called for the gay-marriage issue to be left to the states. But his party's cultural right has insisted on a national ban: not one gay marriage on U.S. soil! When President [George W.] Bush sided with the right, he effectively cast the deciding vote, and moral pluralism lost.

WHO was right, Cheney or Bush? Ford or Reagan? Romney or Romney? A priori, the answer isn't obvious, but the country has recently run, in effect, a laboratory experiment. On abortion, it went with a uniform national rule. On gay marriage, it has gone the other way.

Abortion started in the state legislatures, where it was sometimes contentious but hardly the stuff of a nationwide culture war. Neither party's national political platform had an abortion plank until 1976. In the late 1960s and early 1970s, some liberal-minded states began easing restrictive abortion laws. When the Supreme Court nationalized the issue, in 1973, it short-circuited a debate that was only just getting started.

By doing that, it moved abortion out of the realm of normal politics, which cuts deals and develops consensus, and into the realm of protest politics, which rejects compromise and fosters radicalism. Outraged abortion opponents mobilized;

alarmed abortion-rights advocates countermobilized; the political parties migrated to extreme positions and entrenched themselves there; the Supreme Court became a punching bag; and abortion became an indigestible mass in the pit of the country's political stomach.

Gay marriage started out looking similarly intractable and inflammable. As with abortion, a few liberal states began breaking with tradition, thereby initiating a broader moral debate; and, as with abortion, purists on both extremes denounced the middle as unsustainable or intolerable, saying that gay marriage (like abortion) must be illegal (or legal) everywhere in order to be effectively illegal (or legal) anywhere. The purists got help when two important actors preemptively rejected compromise. The Massachusetts Supreme Judicial Court ordered same-sex marriage in 2003, and then refused even to consider civil unions. That decision provoked President Bush's equally provocative endorsement of a constitutional ban on gay marriage. The battle lines appeared to have been drawn for a national culture war, waged by extremes of left and right over the heads of a marginalized center.

But the political system, and the public, refused to be hustled. Congress rejected a federal constitutional ban. The federal courts stayed out of the argument (and Bush's appointment of two conservative Supreme Court justices who look favorably on states' rights probably ensures that the Court will keep its distance). With the federal government standing aside, the states got busy. All but a handful passed bans on gay marriage. Several adopted civil unions instead of gay marriage. One, Massachusetts, is tussling over efforts to revoke gay marriage.

The result is a diversity of practice that mirrors the diversity of opinion. And gay marriage, not incidentally, is moving out of the realm of protest politics and into the realm of normal politics; in the 2006 elections, the issue was distinctly less inflammatory than two years earlier. It is also moving out of the courts. According to Carrie Evans, the state legislative director of the Human Rights Campaign (a gay-rights organization), most gay-marriage litigation has already passed through the judicial pipeline; only four states have cases under way, and few other plausible venues remain. "It's all going to shift to the state legislatures," she says. "The state and national groups will have to go there."

Barring the unexpected, then, same-sex marriage began in the courts and will wind up in the state legislatures and on state ballots: the abortion tape runs backward. The issue will remain controversial, producing its share of flare-ups and fireworks; but it will become more tractable over time, as the country works its way toward a consensus. As a political issue, gay marriage will be around for years, but as a catalyst for culture war, it has already peaked.

Although I bow to no one in my support for gay marriage—society needs more marriages, not fewer, and gay couples need the protections and obligations of marriage, and gay individuals need the hope and promise of marriage—the last few years have provided a potent demonstration of the power of moral pluralism to act as a political shock absorber. Even moral absolutists—people who believe gay marriage is a basic human right or, for that matter, people who believe abortion is murder—should grudgingly support pluralism, because it makes the world safe for their moral activism by keeping the cultural peace. Someone should tell Mitt Romney. Maybe Mitt Romney could tell him.

Chapter 4

Civil Rights

4-1

Immigration and the Future of Identity Politics in the United States

Taeku Lee

Considering the same demographic trends pondered in the last essay, Taeku Lee asks how race and ethnicity will influence American society and politics a decade from now. Answering this question is not a simple matter of projecting population trends. Lee argues that the answer lies in how Americans define themselves and their place in relation to others in our multiracial, multicultural society. Race, ethnicity, class, and a more subjective quality that Lee calls "nation" combine in several ways to create alternative vignettes of the future.

MUCH HAS BEEN made of the dramatic influx of immigration to the United States since the mid-1960s. According to federal statistics, immigrants and their children make up nearly one in four American residents. More than 34 million foreign-born persons and almost 32 million second generation immigrants lived in the United States in 2002 (U.S. Census Bureau 2002). The so-called Fourth Wave of immigration has swept in a sea change in the racial and ethnic composition of the United States. Up until the first decade of the twentieth century, about 90 percent of new migrants to the United States set sail from European shores. By the 1990s the proportion had dwindled to about 15 percent, and more

Source: Adapted from the article originally appearing in *Perspectives on Politics*, 2003, Volume 3, Issue 3, pp. 557–561.

than 80 percent of new migrants came from Asia and the Americas (U.S. Immigration and Naturalization Service 2002).

Much too has been made of the changes in how the U.S. government classifies and counts by race and ethnicity. In 1977 the Office of Management and Budget (OMB) issued its Directive No. 15, requiring all federal agencies to collect data for at least five groups—American Indians and Alaska Natives, Asians and Pacific Islanders, non-Hispanic blacks, non-Hispanic whites, and Hispanics. OMB then revised the directive in 1997 to include the instruction to "mark one or more" responses, thus allowing people to identify themselves with multiple races or ethnicities (Perlmann and Waters 2002). As a result of the changes, the U.S. government today formally recognizes sixty-three distinct "races" and 126 unique ethno-racial combinations.

The face of America is changing before us and, with it, the names and categories we use to identify ourselves. These changes have emboldened some scholars to conjure Panglossian reveries of a multiracial city on the hill, while others portend the rise of Manichean "race wars," "culture wars," and the end of our national identity as we know it. Several pointed questions prefigure these debates, however. Will Asians increasingly be "honorary whites"? Will Latinos increasingly be racialized, assimilated, or fragmented? Will African Americans remain relatively unified, or will they find themselves increasingly divided by class, political ideology, or something else? What effect will the multiracial population of America have on these trends? Lastly, what can the work of social science tell us about the likely configuration of race and ethnic politics over a finite future, say, ten years hence?[1]

Demography as Destiny

A fine line separates forecasting from fortune-telling in a domain as complex and dynamic as racial and ethnic politics, but some predictions seem obvious. Foremost among them is that current demographic trends will persist. In the coming decade we can expect the foreign-born population—and the proportion of Asians and Latinos in the United States—to continue to rise (Bean and Stevens 2003). Sometime in this century, we are told, whites (as conventionally defined) will no longer be a majority of the voting-age population. Based on the last two Censuses, moreover, the migration of Asians and Latinos to the United States is likely to spread well beyond gateway cities like New York, Los Angeles, and Miami into more geographically dispersed locales (Frey 2002). Thus in ten years fewer Americans will be able to claim no direct encounter with an Asian or Latino person.

A second prediction is that the population of Americans who identify themselves with more than one race and ethnic group is likely to increase by 2015. This is likely for several reasons, first among them being our greater familiarity with the option of identifying ourselves as multiracial. Another reason is the continuing increase in the number of interracial marriages, with Asian Americans in particular being likelier to marry outside the group than African Americans or, to a lesser extent, Latinos (Bean and Stevens 2003). Third, the best evidence suggests that only a small fraction of the Americans who might have identified with more than one race did so in 2000 (Goldstein and Morning 2000). That conclusion is buttressed by the fact that modest changes in how we ask people to self-identify ethno-racially can produce dramatic increases in the estimated population of multiracial Americans.[2] Finally, the trend of growing social acceptance of interracial families and political legitimacy of multiracial identity will likely continue, amplifying each of the other factors leading to greater multiracial identification (Schuman et al. 1997).

These predictions about demographic change, however, do not translate neatly into predictions about the likely effect on race relations and politics. We commonly think of politics as a game of numbers. Perhaps, then, their increasing numbers will fuel a high-octane Latino and Asian political power in America. Such expectations have thus far been dashed. Asian Americans and Latinos are less likely to be citizens, less likely to register to vote, and less likely to engage in all realms of politics (voting or otherwise) than their white and African American counterparts (Ramakrishnan 2005). Moreover, the politics of these new Americans is characterized by the relative absence of party mobilization, the salience of dual citizenship and transnational political ties, the persistence of language barriers, little discretionary time, the instability and uncertainty of social and political group identities, and other impediments to full incorporation and greater participation (DeSipio 1996, Jones-Correa 1998, Wong 2005).

In civic and economic realms it is similarly far from clear whether the influx of new ethnic Americans will herald the formation of harmonious, multiracial, multiethnic coalitions or portend the activation of invidious interethnic conflicts and competition. That diversity is a boon is a widely held belief. It enriches our social and cultural lives and enhances the kind of creative, adaptive, collective decision making that U.S. businesses need to compete and prevail in a globalized economy. Some evidence does tell us that—under conditions of equal status, mutual interdependence, common goals, and strong leadership—the fact of diversity tempers deep-rooted prejudices and fosters interracial harmony and tolerance (Allport 1954). Yet other studies tell us that a changing demography—especially under conditions of economic scarcity and competition—preconditions race riots, hate crimes, heightened intolerance and distrust, and the general outbreak of incivility and ill-will between fellow Americans (Blalock 1967, Bobo and Hutchings 1996, Green, Strolovich, and Wong 1998).

The prospect of a growing multiracial population in America too yields no clear story about the future. Some scholars see the growing recognition of our multiple racial lineages and envisage a radical transformation of how we conceive of families (DaCosta 2003). Some see the mounting tendency of groups to lobby and contest how our government categorizes and counts its population and contemplate the possibility of a groundswell of politics organized around multiracial identity (Williams 2006). Some see the rise in immigration and interracial marriages and fret about the emergence of a *mestizo* nation and a *mestizaje* politics (Huntington 2004). Many envision the abandonment of existing ethnoracial categories altogether but differ about what follows: Some think such categories would be replaced with a renewed interest in ancestry (Glazer 2002); others, with a renewed interest in pigmentation (Hochschild 2005). Yet others suggest that although the categories we use may vanish, "race" as an organizing principle in American life will remain intact (Hollinger 2003).

Beyond Black-White

What then can we say beyond merely that growth and complexity will continue? We might, alternatively, presume that the past is prologue and work as though past trends and current realities will morph mechanically into future projections. This approach typically leads to the conclusion that our current racial order will be recapitulated, putting whites on top, blacks at the bottom, and Asians and Latinos somewhere in between. Pressed further, we might also extrapolate that Asians will grow indistinct from ethnic whites and that Latinos and African Americans will continue to share the common lot of economic hardship, social segregation, and political marginalization. Moreover, we might expect Asians and Latinos to continue to become immersed in, and integrated into, the fabric of American society through processes of assimilation and incorporation that are segmented and uneven across the multiple contexts of immigrant life (Portes and Zhou 1993, Bean and Stevens 2003).

Such predictions, however, are often as indiscriminate and incomplete as they are unsurprising. For one thing, we often miss crucial diversity within groups when we focus reflexively on differences between groups. Historically, for instance, immigrants of European descent, such as Irish, Italian, and Jewish Americans, were not always categorized as "white," nor were the attendant privileges of "whiteness" easily obtained (Roediger 1991). Today the material conditions facing Southeast Asians are discernibly worse than those facing other Asians; the economic and political power of Florida's Cuban American community is substantial compared with that of other Latinos; and the persecution facing

Muslims, Arabs, and South Asians since the terrorist attacks of September 11, 2001, is more acute than that facing other immigrants in America. Even within the supposedly homogeneous African American community, there is considerable (and, by some accounts, growing) ideological diversity, economic division, and conflict across gender, sexual orientation, and immigrant identities (Dawson 2001, Wilson 1978, Cohen 1999, Rogers 2006).

More important, especially given the speed and scope of the changes that are occurring, it is far from obvious that the best way to understand a dynamic phenomenon like race and immigration in the United States is by using static tools and theories wrought from the past. Viewing race through a black-white lens or immigration through an assimilation-racialization lens is only helpful if it fits with our current circumstances. It is far from clear, for instance, why current U.S. Census classification treats distinct populations that share a common Asian national origin—Chinese, Filipino, Japanese, and so on—as separate "races" (but not ethnicities), while it treats populations of distinct Latin American national origins as a single "ethnicity" (but not race). More on this in a moment.

I propose that we think about our future prospects quite differently. The approach I have in mind starts by digging deeper into existing black-white and assimilation-racialization frameworks and identifying the root dimensions that Americans use to define themselves. I suggest that when most Americans ask themselves the question, Who am I? their answer reflects one or a combination of four durable, overlapping dimensions of "identity"—race, ethnicity, class, and nation (Smith 2003, Lie 2004). These dimensions also serve as the basis for organizing, perpetuating, and contesting much of the existing powers and privileges of contemporary American society. It is crucial, as many scholars have noted, to understanding race as separate from, and not reducible to, ethnicity, class, and nation (e.g., Omi and Winant 1994). But it is equally crucial to note that these dimensions are not independent of one another. Rather, they overlap and reinforce each other and are sure to continue to do so in the foreseeable future.

So in asking the question, What will race and immigration look like ten years from now? I propose that we consider how these root dimensions currently stack up and how they may be rearranged in the future. Specifically, let us consider three vignettes in which race pairs with class, ethnicity, and nation, respectively. For each, I give a rendition of how Asian Americans, African Americans, Latinos, and whites are currently situated relative to one another and then briefly speculate on how the relation might change in the next decade or so. The first two vignettes enlist current, standard definitions of "race" and "ethnicity," and in the third I consider race in its more subjective and ideologically nuanced sense. To preview, the purpose of this exercise is to demonstrate that how we currently think of whites, blacks, Asians, and Latinos vis-à-vis one another depends on which root dimensions we employ. How the four primary ethno-racial groups might relate to one another in the future will likely depend on whether and how the root dimensions are rearranged and become most salient to a person's identity.

Vignette 1: Race and Class

The first vignette depicts the standard black-white paradigm on which contemporary debates over racial progress and racial attitudes are typically founded. Here race and class trump all other potentially defining features of a person's identity. The emergence of a black middle class, some say, implies the declining significance of race (Wilson 1978). The political failures of race-based affirmative action policies, others say, necessitate a move to class-based education and employment policies (Wilson 1987). We are all too familiar with such arguments, where race and class are spoken of as two sides of the same coin.

In the diagram in Figure 1, race and class, taken together, situate whites and blacks at the antipodes with respect to each other.[3] Both dimensions inform the everyday experiences of African Americans, whereas white Americans typically ignore race as an integral aspect of their lives. Racial considerations are more easily rendered invisible to white Americans, it is argued, because of the prevailing belief among many whites in individualism and meritocracy. That is, they tend to believe that opportunities to succeed are equal between blacks and whites and that whites are better off than blacks simply because they work with greater spirit and industry to avail themselves of those opportunities. That core division between blacks and whites has been such a durable and defining characteristic of America's racial order that it is unlikely to change over the next ten years.

What about Asians and Latinos? If we hew narrowly to the current government definitions of Asian or Pacific Islander "races" and Latino "ethnicity," Asians and Latinos, too, are situated opposite one another in the two-dimensional space depicted in Figure 1. That Asians and Latinos enter the twenty-first century facing quite different socioeconomic conditions would appear uncontroversial. The material circumstances of Asian Americans are comparable to those of whites and quite unlike those of Latinos (especially Mexicans), who continue to function in the U.S. economy as its principal source of low-wage labor (Massey, Durand, and Malone 2002). In 2004 the per capita incomes of non-Hispanic whites and Asian Americans were $27,414 and $26,217, respectively. For African Americans and Latinos the comparable figures were $16,035 and $14,106 (DeNavas-Walt, Proctor, and Lee 2005). It is important to note that the different national origin groups among Asians and Latinos are not equally well off. For instance, whereas the poverty rate for Asian Americans in

Figure 1. Mapping Class Identity onto Racial Identity

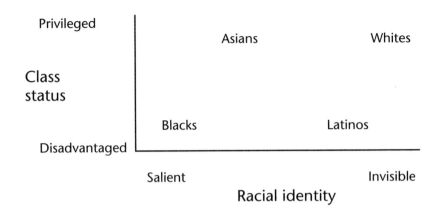

1999 was 12.6 percent (very close to the national average of 12.4 percent), the proportion of Asians living below the poverty line ranged from 6.3 percent for Filipinos, to 29.3 percent for Cambodians, and 37.8 percent for Hmongs (Reeves and Bennett 2004).

Racially, Asians are given a high salience, and Latinos a low salience in part because government agencies such as the Census Bureau consider Asian Americans a "racial" group and Latinos an "ethnic" group. In addition, the relatively greater salience of race for Asians is suggested by the fact that Asian Americans are about as likely to report being discriminated against on account of race as Latinos—a rather striking result given that Asian Americans enjoy substantially greater material advantages than Latino Americans (Lee 2000). Many will likely balk at such a claim. From the standpoint of Asians as a "race," some have noted that the differences in class mobility among national origin groups likely work against the development of a durable pan-ethnic solidarity. For Latinos, second generation immigrants are much likelier to view their experiences in a racial light than are their first generation counterparts (Portes and Rumbaut 2001), so this representation of Asians and Latinos as in opposite situations may not hold for long. In 1990 and 2000, more than 40 percent of Americans who identified themselves as Latino on the Census Bureau's "ethnicity" identifier also identified racially as "Other race"; conversely, 97 percent of those who identified as "Other race" were Americans who also identified as Latino (Lopez 2005). It is hard to interpret these outcomes as anything other than an explicit rejection of the deracialization of Latino identity. They may say more about the ironies of the present-day ethno-racial classification system than about any real differences in how ordinary Americans apply existing ethnic/racial labels to themselves.

Vignette 2: Race and Ethnicity

The second vignette goes deeper into the shaky foundations of the present-day classification system. How does race, as currently defined by government agencies and social science research, join together with ethnicity? The diagram in Figure 2 proposes that we consider ethnicity as relatively invisible for blacks and whites. Doing that for African Americans will surprise few readers, as racial definitions continue to dominate the viability of ethnic options for Americans of African descent.[4] The laundering of ethnic claims for white Americans, however, may evoke protest from readers who would point to the seas of green that flood Boston, Chicago, and other cities every Saint Patrick's Day or the many "Little Italy's" that continue to thrive across the American urban landscape. Yet as sociologists have shown, while ethnic claims are perhaps more readily accessible for whites than for blacks, the era of European national ancestry as a defining identity for white Americans is largely in its twilight, coming to light only episodically in symbolic celebrations like Saint Patrick's Day parades, Oktoberfests, and tulip festivals (Alba 1990, Waters 1990). By contrast, there is significant evidence that for Asians and Latinos ethnicity is a substantive, instrumental identity. Beyond ritual celebrations of Cinco de Mayo, Lunar New Year, Diwali, and the like, ethnic ties and ethnic discrimination are instrumental in defining where Latinos and Asians live, the civic and religious associations they belong to, and even, at times, whether and when they are politically mobilized (Espiritu 1992, Jones-Correa 1998, Bobo et al. 2000).

If this way of thinking about how race and ethnicity come together holds up, one outcome is that whites and Asians stand opposite each another. This result contrasts starkly against the prevailing views that whites and Asians are more alike than different and that whites and Asians growing ever-closer over time.

One might object that I have managed to situate whites and Asians opposite one another by using an ethno-racial classification scheme that simply fails to capture the complexity of our times. One might also object that the classification scheme that the Office of Management and Budget and the Census Bureau currently use has no scientific basis and is the result of political compromises. Note, for instance, that in other contexts, such as current Equal Employment Opportunity Commission affirmative action guidelines, Latinos, Asians, and Native Americans are rather seamlessly included in the same administrative class as African Americans (Skrentny 2002). More generally, other scholars have noted the ubiquity of a "one-hate rule," in which whites are singled out as distinct from nonwhites and in which all kinds of white racism are treated as equivalent regardless of the group against which it is directed (Hollinger 2005).

Figure 2. Mapping Ethnic Identity onto Racial Identity

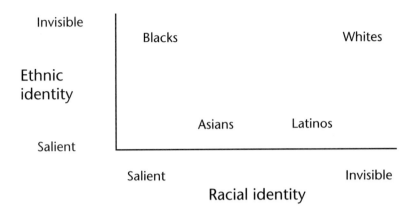

These are valid contentions. They point to the absurdity of current governmental definitions of race and ethnicity. Bureaucratic illogics are often a generative force for change, and one likely future is that the way race and ethnicity are currently defined will change. Government actors (professors, too) are not simply "consumers" of predetermined racial/ethnic names and labels (Omi and Winant 1994, Smith 2003). They are producers as well. So, too, increasingly, are the diverse and proliferating citizen groups that seek recognition, representation, and the right to be named. In fact, most of the recent changes to governmental definitions of race and ethnicity—the separation of Latino "ethnicity" from non-Latino "races," the fragmentation of nationally specific Asian and Pacific Islander "races," the creation of a hybrid multiracial identity—have been the result of such interest group mobilization. Thus the future is likely to bring new ethno-racial classification systems, most likely ones that try to bring emerging groups such as Asians and Latinos more in line with a black-white racial hierarchy.

Vignette 3: Race and Nation

What should not be lost in the rush to change the way we classify people to better fit preconceived notions of "race" is the fact that the experiences of Asians and Latinos are in crucial respects distinct from those of both whites and African Americans. The palpable divide separating Asians and Latinos from whites and African Americans is illuminated by considering how we think of our national identity—who belongs and who does not.

The third and final vignette thus considers race alongside nation. In considering race and nation together, I now take race beyond incongruous governmental definitions and the way most Americans today think of Asians and Latinos racially, with Asians grouped closer to whites and Latinos grouped closer to African Americans. That ordering of groups is consistent with contemporary stories of Asian Americans as a "model minority" acclaimed for their penchant for industry, zeal to succeed, and the socioeconomic results to show for it (Tuan 1999). It is also consistent with pervasive views of Latinos, who are subjected to many of the same slurs and stereotypes cast at African Americans and similarly severe socioeconomic disadvantages (Bobo et al. 2000).

What then groups Asians together with Latinos and apart from both whites and African Americans? As Figure 3 illustrates, the differentiation occurs on the axis of national belonging. As newcomers to America, both Asians and Latinos are commonly viewed as outsiders whose cultures are unassimilable and whose loyalties are suspect. Evidence for this includes the stubborn belief that most Latinos are undocumented "aliens" and the fear that the continued influx of Mexicans into the United States will lead to balkanization and the demise of the nation's core Anglo-Protestant culture (Huntington 2004). With respect to Asian Americans, the evidence includes a long history in which the loyalties of U.S. citizens of Asian descent have been presumed to be to their Asian home countries and not to the United States—a history that ranges from the forced internment of Japanese Americans during World War II, to contemporary cases like the alleged foreign influence peddling of Asian American donors in the 1996 presidential election and alleged espionage by Dr. Wen Ho Lee, a Taiwanese American nuclear scientist working at Los Alamos (see, e.g., Kim 1999). Especially in post–9/11 America, there is a bright line of national belonging that separates immigrant-based ethnic groups such as Asians, Latinos, and Arabs from whites and African Americans.

This vignette reveals a third possible ordering. As Figure 3 shows, whites and Latinos are now at the antipodes of the main diagonal axis, with blacks and Asians opposite each other on the "off-diagonal" axis. Thus one upshot of the three vignettes is that any group—blacks, Latinos, or Asians—might be situated opposite to whites, depending on how "race" is defined and which overlapping identity classes are paired with it. A second upshot is that the pairings of race with class, ethnicity, and nationhood are not equally likely to be durable over the next decade. Class and race are likely to continue to go hand in hand, as a group's socioeconomic attainments are likely to match their status in America's racial hierarchy in the foreseeable future. That racial hierarchy, however, is an uncomfortable fit with the current government system of classifying people into racial and ethnic categories. Moreover, if the post–9/11 drumbeat for patriotism and

Figure 3. Mapping National Ideology onto Racial Ideology

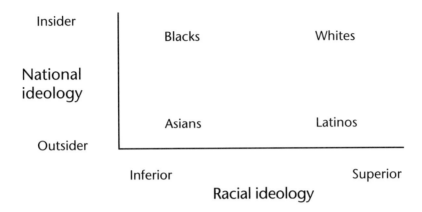

national identity continues with greater force and urgency, the relative status of whites, blacks, Asians, and Latinos in the American landscape may shift yet again away from strictly race-based hierarchies and toward a more ethnocentric view of national belonging.

Two Steps Back

At this point, the vignettes sputter and clang like a jalopy, implying conclusions without the benefit of testable premises. That said, however, in the spirit of taking risks rather than hedging bets, I close by being even more specific about [what] can be predicted for the next decade or so. First, as suggested earlier, we are not likely to grin and bear the current ethno-racial classification system for long. In particular, the current convention—most evident in the Census—that only ethnicity distinguishes Hispanics from non-Hispanics, while assorted Asian-national-origin groups are defined as separate "races," is untenable and likely to change in the near future.

Such a prospect is often taken to imply a gradual decline of the primacy of race in American life. In my view, such a prediction is either naïvely optimistic or willfully blind. The ubiquity of race/ethnicity, class, and nationhood is likely to continue into the near future. This is especially so given the social and political environment in which we currently live—one characterized by Republican control of all branches of the federal government, with nativist vigilantes policing the United States–Mexico border, sustained efforts to unmake the racial progress of the 1960s and remake the "wall of separation" dividing religion and politics, public embrace of ethno-religious criminal profiling, and other spectacles of nostalgia and jingoism. The names and labels used to describe and categorize individuals in America may change, but the use of social and political constructions that divide a people into us and them, insider and outsider, citizen and alien, or deserving and undeserving, and so on, will continue.

What does this mean, really? It means that the adaptation and inclusion of immigrants into American life, if they are Afro-Caribbean, Arab, Asian, or Latino, will remain a clash of fates—success with scorn, hope with despair. Immigrants who come matched to skills in demand in the U.S. economy will continue to enjoy the material fruits of their labor, but never without the thorns of social ostracism and ethno-national chauvinism. Similarly, it means that a select few blacks will continue to move onward and upward in America, but never without sobering reminders that—in a society that presently privileges the principle of color-blindness as a goal over the unfulfilled reality of color-blindness in the antidiscriminatory practices of our institutions—the success of the few will only come at the expense of the abject failure of the many. With or without affirmative action, deep-rooted formal and informal practices will leave African Americans conspicuously underrepresented in most privileged and powerful walks of American life into the future.

Finally, the prospects for communities of color seizing their own destinies by engaging in multiracial politics are dim. To be fair, there have been intermittent glimmers of hope, as in the elections of Harold Washington as mayor of Chicago in 1983, Gary Locke as governor of Washington in 1996, and Antonio Villaraigosa as mayor of Los Angeles in 2005. But our current milieu is one in which the political labors that bear fruit are seemingly the labors of working "within the system," as seen in the appointments of Colin Powell, Condoleezza Rice, Alberto Gonzalez, Elaine Chao, Norman Mineta, Carlos Gutierrez, and others by the current administration.[5] These gestures of the Republican Party to reach out to blacks, Asians, and Latinos may be purely symbolic, or they may be genuine, but over the short duration of a decade their greatest effect (especially for Asians and Latinos) is likely to be the increased dispersion of votes across party lines. Barring some restoration of the left, the Democratic Party's historic hold on the partisan loyalties (if not actual votes) of communities of color will likely continue to attenuate. We have already seen this in the higher proportion of Latino and Asian American Republican voters in the 2004 presidential election. Good or bad, this dispersion of votes is quite likely to further weaken the ability of blacks, Asians, and Latinos to demand and achieve substantive policy representation. Here again, ours is an era that favors the few haves over the many have-nots.

This view into the future is decidedly bleak. To adapt Donald Rumsfeld's poetics to present circumstances, it is created from "known knowns" and "known unknowns." But there are "unknown unknowns" that too may adjudicate between the soothsayer and sophist in this essay. Ultimately, time (and perhaps our will to make a difference) will tell that tale.

NOTES

1. Given the economy of space in these essays, I do not discuss the racial positioning of Native Americans. This is a regrettable omission not just because a corner of the "ethno-racial pentagon" is abandoned, but more so because it has been a transformative space, with the dramatic political and demographic "resurgence of the native" in the last several decades (but see, e.g., Nagel 1997).

2. A 2003 survey of Californians, for example, found that more than one in four respondents identified multiracially when asked to self-identify using "identity points," a substantially greater proportion than the one in twenty Californians who identified multiracially under the "Mark one or more" format of the 2000 Census (Lee 2006).

3. These figures are used purely for illustrative purposes and are not intended imply the specific placement of any group—e.g., that race is equally salient for Asians as for blacks.

4. Important exceptions here are the salience of ethnic claims of African or Afro-Caribbean immigrants and cultural strands of underlying Afro-centrism and the Black Muslim movement in America.

5. Colin Powell was U.S. secretary of state from 2001 to 2004; Condoleeza Rice was national security adviser from 2001 to 2004 and has been secretary of state since 2005; Alberto Gonzalez was White House counsel from 2001 to 2004 and has been attorney general since 2005; Elaine Chao has been secretary of labor since 2001; Norman Mineta has been secretary of transportation since 2001; Carlos Gutierrez has been secretary of commerce since 2005.

REFERENCES

Alba, Richard D. 1990. *Ethnic Identity: The Transformation of White America.* New Haven: Yale University Press.

Allport, Gordon. 1954. *The Nature of Prejudice.* Cambridge, Mass.: Addison-Wesley.

Bean, Frank D., and Gillian Stevens. 2003. *America's Newcomers and the Dynamics of Diversity.* New York: Russell Sage.

Blalock, Hubert. 1967. *Toward a Theory of Minority-Group Relations.* New York: Wiley.

Bobo, Lawrence, and Vincent Hutchings. 1996. "Perceptions of Racial Group Competition." *American Sociological Review* 61(6): 951–972.

Bobo, Lawrence, Melvin Oliver, James Johnson Jr., and Abel Valenzuela Jr., eds. 2000. *Prismatic Metropolis: Inequality in Los Angeles.* New York: Russell Sage.

Cohen, Cathy. 1999. *Boundaries of Blackness: AIDS and the Breakdown of Black Politics.* Chicago: University of Chicago Press.

DaCosta, Kimberly McClain. 2003. "Multiracial Identity: From Personal Problem to Public Issue." In *New Faces in a Changing America,* ed. Loretta Winters and Herman DeBose. Thousand Oaks, Calif.: Sage.

Dawson, Michael C. 2001. *Black Visions.* Chicago: University of Chicago Press.

DeNavas-Walt, Carmen, Bernadette D. Proctor, and Cheryl Hill Lee. 2005. *Income, Poverty, and Health Insurance Coverage in the United States: 2004.* U.S. Census Bureau, Current Population Reports, 60-229. Washington, D.C.: U.S. Government Printing Office.

DeSipio, Louis. 1996. *Counting on the Latino Vote: Latinos as a New Electorate.* Charlottesville: University of Virginia Press.

Espiritu, Yen Le. 1992. *Asian American Panethnicity.* Philadelphia: Temple University Press.

Frey, William H. 2002. *Census 2000 Reveals New Native-Born and Foreign-Born Shifts across U.S.* PSC Research Report 02-520. Ann Arbor, Mich.: Population Studies Center, Institution for Social Research.

Glazer, Nathan. 2002. "Do We Need the Census Race Question?" *Public Interest,* Fall, 21–31.

Goldstein, Joshua, and Ann Morning. 2000. "The Multiple-Race Population of the United States: Issues and Estimates." *Proceedings of the National Academy of Sciences* 97 (11): 6230–6235.

Green, Donald Philip, Dara Strolovich, and Janelle Wong. 1998. "Defended Neighborhoods, Integration, and Racially Motivated Crime." *American Journal of Sociology* 104 (2): 372–403.

Hochschild, Jennifer. 2005. "Looking Ahead: Racial Trends in the United States." *Daedalus,* Winter, 70–81.

Hollinger, David. 2003. "Amalgamation and Hypodescent: The Question of Ethnoracial Mixture in the History of the United States." *American Historical Review* 108 (5): 1363–1390.

———. 2005. "The One Drop Rule and the One Hate Rule." *Daedalus,* Winter, 18–28.

Huntington, Samuel P. 2004. *Who Are We? The Challenges to America's National Identity.* New York: Simon and Schuster.

Jones-Correa, Michael. 1998. *Between Two Nations: The Political Predicament of Latinos in New York City.* Ithaca, N.Y.: Cornell University Press.

Kim, Claire Jean. 1999. *Bitter Fruit: The Politics of Black-Korean Conflict in New York City.* New Haven: Yale University Press.

Lee, Taeku. 2000. "Racial Attitudes and the Color Line(s) at the Close of the Twentieth Century." In *The State of Asian Pacific Americans: Transforming Race Relations,* ed. Paul Ong. Los Angeles: LEAP/UCLA Asian Pacific American Public Policy Institute.

———. 2006. "Between Social Theory and Social Science Practice: Towards a New Approach to the Survey Measurement of Race." In *Identity as a Variable: A Guide to Conceptualization and Measurement of Identity,* ed. Rawi Abdelal, Yoshiko Herrera, Alastair Iain Johnston, and Rose McDermott. New York: Cambridge University Press.

Lie, John. 2004. *Modern Peoplehood.* Cambridge, Mass.: Harvard University Press.

Lopez, Ian Haney. 2005. "Race on the 2010 Census: Hispanics and the Shrinking White Majority." *Daedalus,* Winter, 42–52.

Massey, Douglas S., Jorge Durand, and Nolan J. Malone. 2002. *Beyond Smoke and Mirrors: Mexican Immigration in an Era of Economic Integration.* New York: Russell Sage.

Nagel, Joane. 1997. *American Indian Ethnic Renewal: Red Power and the Resurgence of Identity and Culture.* New York: Oxford University Press.

Omi, Michael, and Howard Winant. 1994. Rev. ed. *Racial Formation in the United States.* New York: Routledge.

Perlmann, J., and Mary J. Waters, eds. 2002. *The New Race Question: How the Census Counts Multi-racial Individuals.* New York: Russell Sage.

Portes, Alejandro, and Min Zhou. 1993. "The New Second Generation: Segmented Assimilation and its Variants." *Annals of the American Academy of Political and Social Science* 530:74–97.

Portes, Alejandro, and Rubén G. Rumbaut. 2001. *Legacies: The Story of the Immigrant Second Generation*. Berkeley: University of California Press.

Ramakrishnan, Karthick. 2005. *Democracy in Immigrant America*. Palo Alto, Calif.: Stanford University Press.

Reeves, Terrance, and Claudette Bennett. 2004. *We the People: Asians in the United States*. U.S. Census Bureau, Census 2000 Special Reports, CENSR-17. Washington, D.C.: U.S. Government Printing Office.

Roediger, David. 1991. *Wages of Whiteness: Race and the Making of the American Working Class*. London: Verso.

Rogers, Reuel. 2006. *Afro-Caribbean Immigrants and the Politics of Incorporation: Ethnicity, Exception, and Exit*. New York: Cambridge University Press.

Schuman, Howard, Charlotte Steeh, Lawrence Bobo, and Maria Krysan. 1997. *Racial Attitudes in America*, rev. ed. Cambridge, Mass.: Harvard University Press.

Skrentny, John D. 2002. *The Minority Rights Revolution*. Cambridge, Mass.: Harvard University Press.

Smith, Rogers. 2003. *Stories of Peoplehood: The Politics and Morals of Political Membership*. New York: Cambridge University Press.

Tuan, Mia. 1999. *Forever Foreigners or Honorary Whites?* New Brunswick, N.J.: Rutgers University Press.

U.S. Census Bureau. 2002. *Current Population Survey: Monthly Demographic File*. March. Washington, D.C.: U.S. Census Bureau.

U.S. Immigration and Naturalization Service. 2002. *2000 INS Statistical Yearbook*. Washington, D.C.: Government Printing Office.

Waters, Mary C. 1990. *Ethnic Options: Choosing Identities in America*. Berkeley: University of California Press.

Williams, Kim. 2006. *Race Counts: American Multiracialism and Civil Rights Policies*. Ann Arbor, Mich.: University of Michigan Press.

Wilson, William Julius. 1978. *The Declining Significance of Race: Blacks and Changing American Institutions*. Chicago: University of Chicago Press.

———. 1987. *The Truly Disadvantaged: The Inner City, the Underclass, and Public Policy*. Chicago: University of Chicago Press.

Wong, Janelle. 2005. *Democracy's Promise: Immigrants and American Civic Institutions*. Ann Arbor, Mich.: University of Michigan Press.

4-2

American Diversity and the 2000 Census

Nathan Glazer

Since the earliest days of the republic, race has proved a difficult issue for each generation of politicians to resolve. While the problem began with slavery, it did not, of course, end with the institution's eradication during the Civil War. Throughout the nineteenth and twentieth centuries, the core issues of "white over black" never receded far from the surface of America's politics. As the country has entered the twenty-first century there have been signs of change in the racial picture, change that has been occurring for some time but has suddenly become manifest. For one, Hispanics have now eclipsed African Americans as the nation's largest racial minority. In this essay, Nathan Glazer ponders a couple of fundamental, yet easily overlooked, issues of race for this next century. They concern how the government defines race and, more importantly, how in our increasingly multiracial and at the same time assimilated society we define ourselves.

THE 2000 CENSUS, on which the Census Bureau started issuing reports in March and April of 2001, reflected, in its structure and its results, the two enduring themes of American racial and ethnic diversity, present since the origins of American society in the English colonies of the Atlantic coast: first, the continued presence of what appears to be an almost permanent lower caste composed of the black race; and second, the ongoing process of immigration of races and peoples from all quarters of the globe, who seem, within a few generations, to merge into a common American people.

To make two such large generalizations is admittedly a bold move. Undoubtedly, as further data from the census is released, we will have evidence of the continuing progress of American blacks in education, occupational diversity, and income. We will have grounds for arguing that the effects of integration into a common people can be seen, at long last, among American blacks. And when it comes to the new waves of immigration of the past few decades, some will question whether the process of assimilation and incorporation, which has swallowed up so many groups and races and religions into a common American people, will continue to work its effects on the new groups now gathered together under the

Source: Nathan Glazer, "American Diversity and the 2000 Census," *Public Interest* 144 (summer 2001): 3–18.

terms "Hispanic" and "Asian." Yet I believe it can be argued that this large distinction in the processes of assimilation and integration that has persisted during the three- or four-century history of American diversity—the distinction between blacks and others—still shows itself, and still poses some of the most difficult questions for American society.

The First Census

The distinction makes itself evident in the very history and structure of the census, and in the character of the data that it first presents to the public today. In the first census of 1790, required for purposes of apportionment [seats in the House of Representatives] by the U.S. Constitution adopted in 1787, the separation between blacks and whites was already made. Indeed, that separation was itself foreshadowed by the Constitution, which, in a famous compromise, decreed that "Representatives . . . shall be apportioned among the several states . . . according to their respective numbers, which shall be determined by adding to the whole number of free persons . . . three-fifths of all other persons." Those "other persons" were slaves. The "three-fifths" was a compromise between excluding all slaves for purposes of apportionment (which would have reduced the weight of the Southern slave states in the union) or counting them simply as persons (which would have given the slave states too great weight).

The census could have fulfilled the requirements of the Constitution by counting only slaves. But what was to be done with free blacks? There were, even then, free blacks, but their civil status was sharply below that of whites. It was apparently decided that they could not be simply numbered among the "free persons" referred to in the Constitution but had to be clearly distinguished from whites. So the first census went beyond the Constitution: It counted "free white males and females" as one category, "slaves" as another, but then added a category of "all other free persons." The count of "other persons"—slaves—and "all other free persons"—free blacks—produced the total number of blacks. Thus from the beginning, white could be differentiated from black. That has remained the most enduring distinction in the U.S. census.

In that first census, following the apportionment provision of the Constitution, "Indians not taxed" were also excluded. Over time, this simple scheme has been extended to cover other races and ethnic groups as they entered the new nation through immigration, to a degree which is possibly unique among national censuses, and which we will explore below. But the census begins crucially with the distinction between white and black. As Clara Rodriguez writes in her book *Changing Race:*

Between the drafting of the Constitution of 1787 and the taking of the first census in 1790, the term white became an explicit part of [the free population]. . . . Theoretically, those in political charge could have chosen another definition for the [free population]. . . . They could have chosen "free English-speaking males over sixteen" or "free males of Christian descent" or "of European descent." But they chose color. Having named the central category "white" gave a centrality and power to color that has continued throughout the history of the census.

But of course this reflected the centrality of the black-white distinction in American society and the American mind. Rodriguez goes on to note that on occasion in the pre-Civil War censuses "aliens and foreigners not naturalized," separately numbered, are combined in one table with native whites and citizens in a table of "total white." "In the 1850 census, the category 'free whites' is changed to simply 'whites,' which suggests by this time it was evident that all the people in this category were free."

The Color Line

Color—race—has since been elaborated to a remarkable degree in the U.S. census. The most striking aspect of the American census of 2000—as of the few before—is that the short form, which goes to all American households, consists mostly of questions on race and "Hispanicity." Two large questions ask for the respondent's race, and whether the respondent is of "Spanish/Hispanic" origin, and both go into considerable detail in trying to determine just what race, and just what kind of "Hispanic," the respondent is. The race question lists many possibilities to choose from, including, to begin with, "white" and "black," and going on to "Indian (Amer.)," with an additional request to list the name of the tribe, "Eskimo," or "Aleut." And then under the general heading "Asian or Pacific Islander (API)," it lists as separate choices Chinese, Filipino, Hawaiian, Korean, Vietnamese, Japanese, Asian Indian, Samoan, Guamanian, "Other API," and finally "Other race (print name)." In the 2000 census, it was possible for the first time for the respondent to check more than one race. This change was made after an extended discussion in the 1990s about how to account for those with parents of different races, who wanted to check off both, or perhaps more than two.

The question on whether one is Spanish/Hispanic also goes on to list a range of possibilities: "Mexican, Mexican-Am. [for "American"], or Chicano" (to account for the fact that Mexican Americans choose different terms to describe themselves), "Puerto Rican," "Cuban," and "other Spanish/Hispanic," with again the request to write in one group. In the 1990 census, a host of examples—"Argentinean,

Colombian, Dominican, Nicaraguan, Salvadoran, Spaniard, and so on," was offered.

The observant and conscientious citizen may note that many other matters of interest to the census and the polity—whether one is of foreign birth or not, a citizen or not, and one's education, occupation, income, housing status, etc.—are all relegated to the long form, which goes to a large sample of citizens. And he may also ask why the census pays such great and meticulous attention to race and ethnicity (or rather one kind of ethnicity, that of Spanish-Hispanic background).

Many answers, going back to the first census of 1790, and before that, to the Constitution that prescribed a regular decennial census, and before that, to the first arrival of black slaves in the English colonies in the early seventeenth century, are available to explain why the first statistics the census makes available today, along with the raw number of the population in each state and locality, are those describing race and ethnicity. But there is also an immediate and proximate answer of much more recent currency: Congress requires that ethnic and racial statistics be available within a year of the census for the purpose of redrawing the boundaries of congressional districts, and the other electoral districts for state legislative assemblies, and for city and county elected officials.

Ethnic and racial statistics have become so significant for redistricting because of the Civil Rights Act of 1964, the Voting Rights Acts of 1965, and the latter's amendments of 1970, 1975, and 1982. . . . The right enshrined in the Voting Rights statute, to the free exercise of the vote, has been extended through litigation and administrative and judicial rule-making to cover rights to the drawing of congressional and other district boundaries in such a way as to protect or enhance the ability of minority groups, blacks in particular, but others too, to elect representatives of their own group. If blacks are to be protected from discrimination . . . then detailed statistics of how a race is distributed are necessary.

That is why the first statistics that come out of the census are those that make it possible to redraw district lines immediately on the basis of the new census, and for various groups to challenge the new district lines if they are aggrieved. . . . For those with the responsibility of drawing up the new districts—the state legislatures primarily—the central concern is generally the maximization of the number of representatives of the party in power in the state legislature. A second concern is to maintain for the incumbents of the favored party district boundaries that secure their return. But overlaying these historic political reasons for drawing district lines, which courts accept in some measure as legitimate, is a new imperative, the protection of minority groups.

The Four "Official" Minorities

"Portrait of a Nation" is the title of a major story on the first results of the census in the *New York Times,* and it is accompanied by elaborate colored maps. The colors provide information on the distribution of the minority population—blacks, Hispanics, Asians, American Indians.

To explain how these have become the American minorities—to the exclusion of many other possible minorities—and why their numbers and distribution are in every newspaper report considered the most important information to look for in the census, would require a precis of American history. It is hardly necessary to explain why blacks are the first of the minority groups. They have been a significant presence in the United States and its predecessor colonies from the beginning. Our greatest national trauma—the Civil War—was directly occasioned by the problem of black slavery, and the most significant amendments to the Constitution became part of that quasi-sacred document in order to deal with the consequences of black slavery.

American Indians were there even before the beginning but were considered outside the society and polity unless they individually entered into non-Indian-American society, as many have, through intermarriage and assimilation. Their status has changed over time, from outside the polity as semi-sovereign foreign nations, to subjects almost without rights, to a population confined on reservations, to one that now increasingly becomes part of the society. Indeed, today, to be able to claim an American-Indian heritage is a plus for one's social status. This is too complex a history to be reviewed here. There is good reason to maintain a separate count of Indians, though there are great complexities in doing so.

"Hispanics," too, were there from before the beginning, if we take into account the Spaniards and Creoles moving up from Mexico who had already established colonial settlements in northern Mexico—what is now the Southwest of the United States—before the first English colonists had established permanent settlements on the Atlantic coast. Of course, they were not "Hispanics" then. Two hundred and fifty years later, this mixed population became part of the United States as a result of the annexation of the northern part of Mexico after the Mexican-American war. But it contained then a small population of Mexicans and Indians, and interestingly enough, despite the sense of racial difference felt by the Anglo-Americans, and despite the prejudice against Mexicans, they were not differentiated in the census as a separate group until 1930. Until then, one presumes, they were "white." In that year, Clara Rodriguez notes, a census publication, responding to the increase in immigration from Mexico as a result of the revolutionary wars and troubles of the 1920s, reported that "persons of Mexican birth or parentage who were not definitely reported as white or Indian were designated

Mexican" and included in "other races." In 1940, this policy was changed, and Mexicans became white again. By 1950, added to the growing number of Mexicans in the Southwest, as a result of immigration in the previous decades, was a large number of Puerto Ricans in New York City, migrants from the island of Puerto Rico, which had been annexed after the Spanish-American war of 1898. In that census year, the two were combined in the census—along with smaller numbers of other groups—into a "Spanish-surnamed" group.

In the wake of Castro's victory in Cuba, a third large group of Latin Americans emigrated to the United States. Whether or not one could make a single meaningful category out of Mexicans, Puerto Ricans, and Cubans, separated as they are by culture, history, and to some extent by racial characteristics, they were so combined, with a host of other Spanish-speaking groups, into a "Hispanic" category in the census of 1970. The creation of the category was a response to political pressure from Mexican Americans. It now includes large numbers of Nicaraguans, Guatemalans, Salvadorans, Dominicans, Colombians, Ecuadorians, and others fleeing the political and economic troubles of their homelands.

Racial and ethnic groups are conventionally described today as "constructed," but it is worth noting that this "construction" is not simply the result of white determinations—it is also the result of group insistence, at least to some degree. As Peter Skerry tells us in his book *Counting on the Census:*

> The finalized questionnaires for the 1970 census were already at the printers when a Mexican American member of the U.S. Interagency Committee on Mexican American affairs demanded that a specific Hispanic-origin question be included. . . . Over the opposition of Census Bureau officials, who argued against inclusion of an untested question so late in the process, [President] Nixon ordered the secretary of commerce and the census director to add the question.

And so "Hispanics" were born. The pressure to maintain the category, with all its subdistinctions, persists. The distinguished demographer Stanley Lieberson has written about a well-intentioned intervention at a conference preparatory to the 1990 census:

> I naively suggested that there was no reason to have an Hispanic question separate from the ethnic ancestry question [an ancestry question has been part of the long form since 1980] since the former . . . could be classified as a subpart of the latter. Several participants from prominent Hispanic organizations were furious at such a proposal. They were furious, by the way, not at me (just a naive academic), rather it was in the form of a warning to census personnel of the consequences that would follow were this proposal to be taken seriously.

The last of the four minorities distinguished in the census is the "Asian," a creation—or construction—that has as complex a history as that of the Hispanic. Chinese and Japanese individuals were undoubtedly present in the United States before they were first listed as "races" in 1870—by then there was a substantial population of Chinese in California, and they were already the subject of racist legislation. In 1930, "Filipino," "Hindu" [sic], and "Korean" were added as separate races, and it became the pattern to add a new "race" for each Asian immigrant group as it became numerous. Eventually, we have the complex category of "Asian and Pacific Islander" (API), with all its listed subgroups.

As in the case of the Mexicans, the initial discrimination that made each of these a separate group was undoubtedly racist and reflected a sense of white superiority. The Asian groups were all subjected to discriminatory legislation. One could be naturalized as a citizen only if one were "white" (or, after the Civil War, black). All sorts of restrictions, from land ownership to the pursuit of certain professions or occupations, were imposed on them by various states because they were noncitizens. But Asian immigrants were denied because of race the right of becoming citizens. These groups were indeed nonwhite, but their separate classification was more than a matter of keeping neat statistics. An identity was being selected for a group felt to be inferior. This identity may well have been the one the members of the group would have chosen, but it was not they who decided they should be numbered aside from the dominant whites. . . .

A Melting Pot?

These then are the four "official" minorities, though no law names these and only these as minorities. But what has happened then to all those others once considered "minorities," ethnic groups that were in the first quarter of the twentieth century in the eye of public attention because of the recency of their immigration, their lower social and economic status, and the concern that they could not be assimilated? Immigration was largely cut off by law in the 1920s because of these concerns. The United States has been a country of immigration since its origins, and by some measures the immigration of the first two decades of the twentieth century was much greater than the immigration of the last three decades, which has swelled the numbers of the new minorities. Had one picked up a book on American minorities and race relations in the 1950s, Jews might have been presented as the typical minority: Much of the social theory and social psychology on minority status was formulated with the position of Jews in mind. Jews were a major element in the mass immigration that preceded the present one, from the 1880s to the 1920s. Other major components of this immigration were Italians,

Poles, Hungarians, Czechs, Slovaks, Slovenes, Croats, Serbs, Greeks, Armenians, Lebanese, Syrians, and many other peoples of Eastern and Southern Europe and the Near East. Are they no longer included in the story of American minorities?

One can go further back and ask, what has happened to the Irish, the Germans, the Swedes, Norwegians, and Danes, and the host of immigrants who came earlier and were also once sharply distinguished as separate groups, different from the founding group, the English? Does not the story of American diversity include all these too? How has the palette become restricted to the four minorities that play so large a role in the current census?

The simple answer is that integration and assimilation reduce over time the differences that distinguish one group from another, or from the original settler group, what Tocqueville called the "Anglo-Americans." We have no good term for this group. WASP ("White Anglo-Saxon Protestant") has been used in recent decades, ironically or derisively, for the founding element and their descendants. But aside from the necessity to distinguish such a group historically, no term is currently really necessary: Immigrants merge in two or three generations into a common American people, and ethnic distinctions become less and less meaningful. Ethnicity becomes symbolic, a matter of choice, to be noted on the basis of name or some other signifier on occasion, of little matter for most of one's life.

At one time, the census distinguished the foreign-born by place of birth, and the foreign-born parents of the native-born by place of birth, permitting us to track ethnic groups (somewhat uncertainly, owing to the lack of fit between ethnicity and national boundaries) for two generations. The rest of the population was classed as natives of native parentage, not further distinguishable, at least in the census, on the basis of their ethnicity. In 1980, the question on birthplace of parents was dropped, to the distress of sociologists and students of ethnicity. A new question on "ancestry" was added, which, in theory, would permit us to connect people to ethnic groups in the third generation and beyond. But the amount of mixture among groups, through marriage, is today such that the answers to the ancestry question, if one is not an immigrant or the child of an immigrant with a clear sense of ancestry, are not helpful in distinguishing an ethnic group much beyond the second generation. The answers then become so variable, so dependent on cues from the census itself—such as the examples the census form gives to the respondent regarding what is intended by the term "ancestry," which is by no means clear to many people—as to be hardly meaningful. It is a question that permits some 40 million Americans, seven times the population of Ireland, to declare that they are of "Irish" ancestry.

There are indeed differences of some significance based on ethnicity among the native white population, and sometimes these become evident—when home countries are involved in conflict, for example—or even paramount. This is particularly evident for Jews, who are marked not only as a religion (but the census rigorously refrains from asking any question or accepting any response on religion) but also by ethnicity (but to the census, Jews are not an ethnic group but a religion). The exceptional history that resulted in the killing of most of the Jews of Europe, and the creation of a regularly imperiled State of Israel, ties Jews to their past and to their co-religionists abroad much more than other ethnic groups. They are not to be found in any census count—they are not a "race" and not even, for the census, an "ancestry," even though that answer would make sense for most Jews.

Sociologists and political scientists can plumb for differences among the native white population, and they will find not insignificant differences in income, occupation, political orientation, and so on. Jews, for example, are exceptional among "whites" for their regular overwhelming support for Democrats. Indeed, the differences among native whites, ethnically distinguished, may be greater than those among the official minority groups or between any of them and the native white population. Yet from the point of view of public opinion and official notice, these differences are not significant. The ethnic groups of the great immigrations of the nineteenth and early twentieth century have sunk below the horizon of official attention. They have merged into the "white" population, become integrated and assimilated, and only emerge as a special interest on occasion, stimulated by a conflict or crisis involving the home country.

"Whiteness Theory"

Recently, this somewhat benign view of American history, one in which immigrant groups steadily assimilate to, and become part of, the common American people, has been challenged by historians who argue that this was a strictly limited process, available only to whites, and, further, that many of those who were eventually included as full Americans had to overcome a presumption that they were not "really" white. In other words, race is crucial, both at its beginning and, by implication, throughout American history, for full inclusion. To take one powerful and clear statement of this position:

> The saga of European immigration has long been held up as proof of the openness of American society, the benign and absorptive powers of American capitalism, and the robust health of American democracy. "Ethnic inclusion," "ethnic mobility," and "ethnic assimilation" on the European model set the standard upon which "America," as an ideal, is presumed to work; they provide the normative experience against which others are measured. But this pretty story suddenly fades once one recognizes how crucial Europeans' racial status as "free white persons" was

to their gaining entrance in the first place; how profoundly dependent their racial inclusion was upon the racial exclusion of others; how racially accented the native resistance was even to their inclusion for something over half a century. [Matthew Frye Jacobsen, in *Whiteness of a Different Color.*] The implication of this point of view is that the present minorities as commonly understood exist not only because of the recency of their immigration but primarily because of color: They are not white. Their ability to become full and equal participants in American society is thereby limited because of America's racist character.

But I believe these "whiteness theorists" are wrong. The racist character of the past is clear, and a degree of racism in the present is also evident, despite radical changes in public opinion and major changes in law and legal enforcement. But there has been a striking and irreversible change between the 1920s—when immigration from Eastern and Southern Europe was sharply reduced and immigration from Asia was banned entirely—and the postwar decades and, in particular, the period since the 1960s. Public institutions and significant private institutions today may only take account of race for the purpose of benefiting minorities.

The whiteness theorists may have a story to tell about the past, but it is one that has limited bearing on the present. The new immigrant groups are for the most part distinguished by race or quasi-racial characteristics from the population of European white origin. Yet it seems likely they progress pretty much at the same rate, affected by the same factors—their education and skills, their occupations, the areas of the country in which they settle, and the like—as the European immigrants of the past.

They merge into the common population at the same rate too. We will soon have analyses of marriages between persons of different race and ethnicity, to the extent the census makes possible, but we already know that the number and percentage of intermarriages between persons from the minorities and the majority has grown greatly in recent decades. One analysis of the 1990 census, reported by David T. Canon in his *Race, Redistricting and Representation,* shows that "for married people between the ages of twenty-five and thirty-four, 70 percent of Asian women and 39 percent of Hispanic women have white [*sic*] husbands." But only 2 percent of black women in the same age group were married to white men. The theme of black difference contrasted with the intermixture and merger of other groups is clearly sounded in these and other statistics.

The End of "Race"?

The first studies conducted by independent analysts of the 2000 census statistics brought up sharply the degree to which blacks are still distinguished from other minorities or subgroups in the United States by residential segregation. "Analysis of Census Finds Segregation Along With Diversity," reads one headline. "Segregation" in this analysis is measured by the diversity of census tracts, as experienced by the "average" person of a given group or race. The average white person lives in a tract that is 80 percent white, down from 85 percent in 1990; the average black person lives in a tract that is 51 percent black, down from 56 percent in 1990; the average Hispanic is less "segregated" by this measure—his tract is 45 percent Hispanic, and increased from 43 percent in 1990. But one may explain this degree of segregation and its rise since 1990 by the huge increase, based on immigration, much of it illegal, of the Hispanic population. The average Asian lives in a tract that is not particularly Asian—18 percent, as against 15 percent in 1990. This rise reflects to some degree the 50 percent increase of the Asian population, mostly through immigration, in the decade.

Local reporting focused on the relative proportions of the minority groups in each community, and also on the degree of segregation. Integration proceeds, but slowly. There are black census tracts in Boston with almost no whites and white tracts with almost no blacks. We calculate these figures every census, as if watching a fever report. The overall picture is that the segregation of blacks is great, the segregation of Hispanic groups, despite the recency of their immigration and their foreign tongue, is rather less, and little segregation is noted among Asians.

The big news of the census was that "Hispanics" had for the first time surpassed blacks in number, but that was only the case if one excluded from the black population those individuals who had chosen the race "black" along with another race. Hispanics rose to 35.3 million, a 61 percent increase in 10 years; blacks rose by about 16 percent to 34.7 million, or 36.4 million if one added those who chose more than one race. Blacks are 12.3 percent of the population, about the same percentage they have maintained for the past century. The increase in Hispanics was much greater than expected: It was generally agreed that one reason for this increase was a larger number of illegal immigrants than had been previously calculated, 9 million according to one demographer instead of 7, perhaps as much as 11 million according to another demographer.

Making the comparison between the two largest minorities was complicated by the fact that respondents could choose more than one race for the first time, and 7 million did so. Analysis of these mixed-race choices, even reporting on them, is not easy. A reporter writes: "Five percent of blacks, 6 percent of Hispanics, 14 percent of Asians and 2.5 percent of whites identified themselves as multi-racial." But why are these multi-race choosers labeled "black" or "Asian"? Is the "one drop" rule once used by the southern states operating here? If someone chooses "American Indian" and another race, do we include that person in the count of American Indians? If we do, that would increase the number of

American Indians by more than 50 percent. The Office of Management and Budget oversees the race and ethnic statistics compiled by federal agencies, and it has determined that for their purposes (affirmative-action monitoring and the like) all multi-race choosers who chose white and a minority race are to be counted as being part of the minority, a decision that has pleased minority advocates. But does it reflect how these individuals see themselves?

The mixed-race choices complicate the issue of choosing a base on which to measure the progress of, or possible discrimination against, minorities, an important step in affirmative action programs. That is the reason some minority leaders opposed allowing the mixed-race option. If the base becomes smaller, the degree of discrimination that one may claim in noting how many members of the group have attained this or that position is reduced.

Now that the option exists, it is clear many are eager to choose two or even more races. Among blacks there seems to be less willingness to choose two races than among Asians and American Indians—perhaps because it may be seen as something like race betrayal. But it is noteworthy that younger persons more often choose two races than older ones. If one creates a combined black group by putting together blacks with those who choose black as one of the races they tick off, 2.3 percent of this combined group 50 years of age or older turn out to be multi-race choosers, but 8.1 percent of those 17 and younger choose more than one race. But those who choose the option of black-white are still quite few—fewer in number than those who choose white-other ("other" in the racial category means Hispanic), or white-Asian, or white-American Indian.

When the statistics of intermarriage are analyzed, one can be sure there will be a considerable rise in white-black marriages since 1990, even if the percentage of such intermarriages is considerably less than white-Asian or Hispanic-non-Hispanic marriages. Blacks are still more segregated, more separated, in residence than other minority groups. They are more sharply defined in their consciousness as separate: History has made them so. But even among blacks, one sees the process of assimilation and integration, as measured by choice of race and by intermarriage, at work. By the census of 2010 or 2020, these processes will be further advanced. Indeed, one may perhaps look forward to a time when our complex system of racial and ethnic counting is made so confusing by the number of possible choices, singular and multiple, that the whole scheme is abandoned. Many Americans hope so.

Chapter 5

Civil Liberties

5-1

From *Republic.com 2.0*

Cass R. Sunstein

It is difficult to think of more universal and absolute language concerning free speech than the First Amendment's provision: "Congress shall make no law . . . abridging the freedom of speech." Yet, jurists have long noted that it cannot be absolute. Justice Oliver Wendell Holmes famously observed that the amendment does not allow a person to yell "Fire!" in a crowded theater. In this essay, Cass Sunstein cites numerous circumstances—many involving new communications technologies—that appear equally problematic. Where and how should the line be drawn between speech that is protected and speech that is not? He presents and assesses two competing principles of free speech. One is a kind of libertarian, "consumerist" principle that individuals and organizations invoke to protect whatever speech they want to say or sponsor. The alternative, favored by Sunstein, is the democratic principle that holds some speech to be more sacrosanct than other speech. In this scheme, the most protected speech is that which affects democratic control of government; government is allowed to regulate other forms of speech, such as statements that are patently harmful.

WERE THOSE RESPONSIBLE for the ILOVEYOU virus protected by the free-speech principle? It would be silly to say that they are. But if this form of speech may be regulated, what are the limits on government's power?

Source: Cass R. Sunstein, from "Freedom of Speech," in *Republic.com 2.0*, by Cass R. Sunstein (Princeton, N.J.: Princeton University Press, 2007), 165–189.

Consider a case involving not email but a website—a case that may, in some ways, turn out to be emblematic of the future. The site in question had a dramatic name: "The Nuremberg Files." It began, "A coalition of concerned citizens throughout the USA is cooperating in collecting dossiers on abortionists in anticipation that one day we may be able to hold them on trial for crimes against humanity." The site contained a long list of "Alleged Abortionists and Their Accomplices," with the explicit goal of recording "the name of every person working in the baby slaughter business in the United States of America." The list included the names, home addresses, and license-plate numbers of many doctors who performed abortions, and also included the names of their spouses and children.

So far, perhaps, so good. But three of these doctors had been killed. Whenever a doctor was killed, the website showed a line drawn through his name. The site also included a set of "wanted posters," Old West—style, with photographs of doctors with the word "Wanted" under each one. A group of doctors brought suit, contending the practices of which this site was a part amounted in practice to "a hit list" with death threats and intimidation. The jury awarded them over $100 million in damages; the verdict was upheld on appeal, though the dollar award was reduced substantially (it remained in the millions of dollars).

Should the free-speech principle have protected the Nuremberg Files? Maybe it should have. But if you think so, would you allow a website to post names and addresses of doctors who performed abortions, with explicit instructions about how and where to kill them? Would you allow a website to post bomb-making instructions? To post such instructions alongside advice about how and where to use the bombs? To show terrorists exactly where and how to strike? As we have seen, there is nothing fanciful about these questions. Dozens of sites now contain instructions about how to make bombs—though to my knowledge, none of them tells people how and where to use them. If you have no problem with bomb-making instructions on websites, you might consider some other questions. Does your understanding of free speech allow people to work together at a site called pricefixing.com, through which competitors can agree to set prices and engage in other anticompetitive practices? (I made that one up.) Does your understanding of free speech allow people to make unauthorized copies of movies, music, and books, and to give or sell those copies to dozens, thousands, or millions of others? (I didn't make that one up.)

My basic argument here is that the free-speech principle, properly understood, is not an absolute and that it allows government to undertake a wide range of restrictions on what people want to say on the Internet. However the hardest questions should be resolved, the government can regulate computer viruses, criminal conspiracy, and explicit incitement to engage in criminal acts, at least if the incitement is likely to be effective. In my view, it would also be acceptable for government to require broadcasters to provide educational programming for children on television, as in fact it now does; to mandate free air time for candidates for public office; and to regulate contributions to and expenditures on political campaigns, at least within certain boundaries.

This is not the place for a full discussion of constitutional doctrines relating to freedom of expression. But in the process of showing the democratic roots of the system of free expression, I attempt to provide an outline of the basic constitutional principles.[1]

Emerging Wisdom? Televisions as Toasters

An emerging view is that the First Amendment to the Constitution requires government to respect consumer sovereignty. Indeed, the First Amendment is often treated as if it incorporates the economic ideal—as if it is based on the view that consumer choice is what the system of communications is all about. Although it is foreign to the original conception of the free-speech principle, this view can be found in many places in current law.

For one thing, it helps to explain the constitutional protection given to commercial advertising. This protection is exceedingly recent. Until 1976,[2] the consensus within the Supreme Court and the legal culture in general was that the First Amendment did not protect commercial speech at all. Since that time, commercial speech has come to be treated more and more like ordinary speech, to the point where Justice Thomas has even doubted whether the law should distinguish at all between commercial and political speech.[3] To date, Justice Thomas has not prevailed on this count. But the Court's commercial-speech decisions often strike down restrictions on advertising, and for that reason, those decisions are best seen as a way of connecting the idea of consumer sovereignty with the First Amendment itself.

Belonging in the same category is the frequent constitutional hostility to campaign-finance regulation. The Supreme Court has held that financial expenditures on behalf of political candidates are generally protected by the free-speech principle—and in what seems to me an act of considerable hubris, the Court has also held that it is illegitimate for government to try to promote political equality by imposing ceilings on permissible expenditures.[4] The inequality that comes from divergences in wealth is not, [i]n the Court's view, a proper subject for democratic control. According to the Court, campaign-finance restrictions cannot be justified by reference to equality at all. It is for this reason that candidate *expenditures* from candidates' personal funds may not be regulated. It is also for this reason that restrictions on campaign *contributions* from one person to a candidate can be regulated only as a way of preventing the reality or appearance of corruption.

The constitutional debate over campaign-finance regulation remains complex and unresolved, and the members of the Supreme Court are badly divided.[5] Some of the justices would further reduce the government's existing authority to regulate campaign contributions, on the theory that such contributions lie at the heart of what the free-speech principle protects. Here too an idea of consumer sovereignty seems to be at work. In many of the debates over campaign expenditures and contributions, the political process itself is being treated as a kind of market in which citizens are seen as consumers, expressing their will not only through votes and statements but also through money. I do not mean to suggest that the government should be able to impose whatever restrictions it wishes. I mean only to notice, and to question, the idea that the political domain should be seen as a market and the influential claim that government is entirely disabled from responding to the translation of economic inequality into political equality.

Even more relevant for present purposes is the widespread suggestion, with some support in current constitutional law, that the free-speech principle forbids government from interfering with the communications market by, for example, attempting to draw people's attention to serious issues or regulating the content of what appears on television networks.[6] To be sure, everyone agrees that the government is permitted to create and protect property rights, even if this means that speech will be regulated as a result. We have seen that the government may give property rights to websites and broadcasters; there is no constitutional problem with that. Everyone also agrees that the government is permitted to control monopolistic behavior and thus to enforce antitrust law, which is designed to ensure genuinely free markets in communications. Structural regulation, not involving direct control of speech but intended to make sure that the market works well, is usually unobjectionable. Hence government can create copyright law and, at least within limits, forbid unauthorized copying. (There is, however, an extremely important and active debate about how to reconcile copyright law and the free-speech principle.)[7] But if government attempts to require television broadcasters to cover public issues, or to provide free air time for candidates, or to ensure a certain level of high-quality programming for children, many people will claim that the First Amendment is being violated.

What lies beneath the surface of these debates?

Two Free-Speech Principles

We might distinguish here between the free-speech principle as it operates in courts and the free-speech principle as it operates in public debate. As far as courts are concerned, there is as yet no clear answer to many of the constitutional questions that would be raised by government efforts to make the speech market work better. For example, we do not really know, as a matter of constitutional law, whether government can require educational and public-affairs programming on television. The Court allowed such regulation when three or four television stations dominated the scene, but it has left open the question of whether such regulation would be legitimate today.[8] As a matter of prediction, the most that can be said is that there is a reasonable chance that the Court would permit government to adopt modest initiatives, so long as it was promoting goals associated with deliberative democracy.

Indeed the Court has been very cautious, and self[-]consciously so, about laying down firm rules governing the role of the free-speech principle on new technologies. The Court is aware that things are changing rapidly and that there is much that it does not know. Because issues of fact and value are in a state of flux, it has tended to offer narrow, case-specific rulings that offer little guidance, and constraint, for the future.[9]

But the free-speech principle has an independent life outside of the courtroom. It is often invoked, sometimes strategically though sometimes as a matter of principle, in such a way as to discourage government initiatives that might make the communications market serve democratic goals. Outside of the law, and inside the offices of lobbyists, newspapers, radio stations, and recording studios, as well as even in ordinary households, the First Amendment has a large *cultural* presence. This is no less important than its technical role in courts. Here the identification of the free-speech principle with consumer sovereignty is becoming all the tighter. Worst of all, the emerging cultural understanding severs the link between the First Amendment and democratic self-rule.

Recall here Bill Gates's words: "It's already getting a little unwieldy. When you turn on DirectTV and you step through every channel—well, there's three minutes of your life. When you walk into your living room six years from now, you'll be able to just say what you're interested in, and have the screen help you pick out a video that you care about. It's not going to be 'Let's look at channels 4, 5, and 7.'" Taken to its logical extreme, the emerging wisdom would identify the First Amendment with the dream of unlimited consumer sovereignty with respect to speech. It would see the First Amendment in precisely Gates's terms. It would transform the First Amendment into a constitutional guarantee of consumer sovereignty in the domain of communications.

I have had some experience with the conception of the First Amendment as an embodiment of consumer sovereignty, and it may be useful to offer a brief account of that experience. From 1997 to 1998, I served on the President's Advisory Committee on the Public Interest Obligations of Digital Television Broadcasters. Our task was to consider whether and how television broadcasters should be required to promote public-interest goals—through, for example, closed captioning for the hearing-impaired, emergency warnings, educational programming for children, and free air time for candidates. About half of the committee's members were broadcasters, and most of them were entirely happy to challenge proposed government regulation as intrusive and indefensible. One of the two co-chairs was the redoubtable Leslie Moonves, president of CBS. Moonves is an obviously intelligent, public-spirited man but also the furthest thing from a shrinking violet, and he is, to say the least, attuned to the economic interests of the television networks. Because of its composition, this group was not about to recommend anything dramatic. On the contrary, it was bound to be highly respectful of the prerogatives of television broadcasters. In any case the Advisory Committee was just that—an advisory committee—and we had power only to write a report, and no authority to impose any duties on anyone at all.

Nonetheless, the committee was subject to a sustained, intense, high-profile, and evidently well-funded lobbying effort by economic interests, generally associated with the broadcasting industry, seeking to invoke the First Amendment to suggest that any and all public-interest obligations should and would be found unconstitutional. An elegantly dressed and high-priced Washington lawyer testified before us for an endless hour, making quite outlandish claims about the meaning of the First Amendment. A long stream of legal documents was generated and sent to all of us, most of them arguing that (for example) a requirement of free air time for candidates would offend the Constitution. At our meetings, the most obvious (omni) presence was Jack Goodman, the lawyer for the National Association of Broadcasters (NAB), the lobbying and litigating arm of the broadcast industry, which wields the First Amendment as a kind of protectionist weapon against almost everything that government tries to do. To say that Goodman and the NAB would invoke the free-speech principle at the drop of a hat, or the faintest step of a Federal Communications Commission official in the distance, is only a slight exaggeration.

Of course all this was an entirely legitimate exercise of free speech. But when the President's Advisory Committee on the Public Interest Obligations of Digital Television Broadcasters already consists, in large part, of broadcasters, and when that very committee is besieged with tendentious and implausible interpretations of the First Amendment, something does seem amiss. There is a more general point. The National Association of Broadcasters and others with similar economic interests typically use the First Amendment in precisely the same way that the National Rifle Association uses the Second Amendment. We should think of the two camps as jurisprudential twins. The National Association of Broadcasters is prepared to make self-serving and outlandish claims about the First Amendment before the public and before courts, and to pay lawyers and publicists a lot of money to help establish those claims. (Perhaps they will ultimately succeed.) The National Rifle Association does the same thing with the Second Amendment. In both cases, those whose social and economic interests are at stake are prepared to use the Constitution, however implausibly invoked, in order to give a veneer of principle and respectability to arguments that would otherwise seem hopelessly partisan and self-interested.

Indeed our advisory committee heard a great deal about the First Amendment, and about marginally relevant Supreme Court decisions, and about footnotes in lower-court opinions, but exceedingly little, in fact close to nothing, about the pragmatic and empirical issues on which many of our inquiries should have turned. If educational programming for children is required on CBS, NBC, and ABC, how many children will end up watching? What would they watch, or do, instead? Would educational programming help them? When educational programming is required, how much do the networks lose in dollars, and who pays the tab—advertisers, consumers, network employees, or someone else? What would be the real-world effects, on citizens and fund-raising alike, of free air time for candidates? Would such a requirement produce more substantial attention to serious issues? Would it reduce current pressures to raise money? What are the consequences of violence on television for both children and adults? Does television violence actually increase violence in the real world? Does it make children anxious in a way that creates genuine psychological harm? How, exactly, are the hard-of-hearing affected when captions are absent?

We can go further still. In the early part of the twentieth century, the due process clause of the Fourteenth Amendment was used to forbid government from regulating the labor market through, for example, minimum-wage and maximum-hour legislation.[10] The Court thought that the Constitution allowed workers and employers to set wages and hours as they "choose," without regulatory constraints. This is one of the most notorious periods in the entire history of the Supreme Court. Judicial use of the Fourteenth Amendment for these purposes is now almost universally agreed to have been a grotesque abuse of power. Nearly everyone now sees that the underlying questions were democratic ones, not ones for the judiciary. The Court should not have forbidden democratic experimentation that would, plausibly at least, have done considerable good.

In fact a central animating idea, in these now-discredited decisions, was that of consumer sovereignty—ensuring that government would not "interfere" with the terms produced by workers, employers, and consumers. (The word "interfere" has to be in quotation marks because the government was there already; the law of property, contract, and torts helps account for how much workers receive, how long they work, and how much consumers pay.) But in the early part of the twenty-first century, the First Amendment is serving a similar purpose in popular debate and sometimes in courts as well. All too often, it is being invoked on behalf of consumer sovereignty in a way that prevents the democratic process from resolving complex questions that turn on issues of fact and value that are ill-suited to judicial resolution.

To say this is not to say that the First Amendment should play no role at all. On the contrary, it imposes serious limits on what might be done. But some imaginable initiatives, responding to the problems I have discussed thus far, are fully consistent with the free-speech guarantee. Indeed, they would promote its highest aspirations.

Free Speech Is Not an Absolute

We can identify some flaws in the emerging view of the First Amendment by investigating the idea that the free-speech guarantee is "an absolute" in the specific sense that government may not regulate speech at all. This view plays a large role in public debate, and in some ways it is a salutary myth. Certainly the idea that the First Amendment is an absolute helps to discourage government from doing things that it ought not to do. At the same time it gives greater rhetorical power to critics of illegitimate government censorship. But a myth, even if in some ways salutary, remains a myth; and any publicly influential myth is likely to create many problems.

There should be no ambiguity on the point: free speech is not an absolute. We have seen that the government is allowed to regulate speech by imposing neutral rules of property law, telling would-be speakers that they may not have access to certain speech outlets. But this is only the beginning. Government is permitted to regulate computer viruses; unlicensed medical advice; attempted bribery; perjury; criminal conspiracies ("let's fix prices!"); threats to assassinate the president; blackmail ("I'll tell everyone the truth about your private life unless you give me $100"); criminal solicitation ("might you help me rob this bank?"); child pornography; violations of the copyright law; false advertising; purely verbal fraud ("this stock is worth $100,000"); and much more. Many of these forms of speech will not be especially harmful. A fruitless and doomed attempt to solicit someone to commit a crime, for example, is still criminal solicitation; a pitifully executed attempt at fraud is still fraud; sending a computer virus that doesn't actually work is still against the law.

Perhaps you disagree with the view, settled as a matter of current American law (and so settled in most other nations as well), that *all* of these forms of speech are unprotected by the free-speech principle. There is certainly a good argument that some current uses of the copyright law impose unnecessary and unjustifiable restrictions on free speech—and that these restrictions are especially troublesome in the era of the Internet.[11] But you are not a free-speech absolutist unless you believe that *each* of these forms of speech should be protected by that principle. And if this is your belief, you are a most unusual person (and you will have a lot of explaining to do).

This is not the place for a full account of the reach of the First Amendment of the American Constitution.[12] But it is plain that some distinctions must be made among different kinds of speech. It is important, for example, to distinguish between speech that can be shown to be quite harmful and speech that is relatively harmless. As a general rule, the government should not be able to regulate the latter. We might also distinguish between speech that bears on democratic self-government and speech that does not; certainly an especially severe burden should be placed on any government efforts to regulate political speech. Less simply, we might want to distinguish among the *kinds of lines* that government is drawing in terms of the likelihood that government is acting on the basis of illegitimate reasons (a point to which I will return).

These ideas could be combined in various ways, and indeed the fabric of modern free-speech law in America reflects one such combination. Despite the increasing prominence of the idea that the free-speech principle requires unrestricted choices by individual consumers, the Court continues to say that political speech receives the highest protection and that government may regulate (for example) commercial advertising, obscenity, and libel of ordinary people without meeting the especially stringent burden of justification required for political speech. But for present purposes, all that is necessary is to say that no one really believes that the free-speech principle, or the First Amendment, is an absolute. We should be very thankful for that.

The First Amendment and Democratic Deliberation

The fundamental concern of this book is to see how unlimited consumer options might compromise the preconditions of a system of freedom of expression, which include unchosen exposures and shared experiences. To understand the nature of this concern, we will make most progress if we insist that the free-speech principle should be read in light of the commitment to democratic deliberation. In other words, a central point of the free-speech principle is to carry out that commitment.

There are profound differences between those who emphasize consumer sovereignty and those who stress the democratic roots of the free-speech principle. For the latter, government efforts to regulate commercial advertising need not be objectionable. Certainly false and misleading commercial advertising is more readily subject to government control than false and misleading political speech. For those who believe that the free-speech principle has democratic foundations and is not fundamentally about consumer sovereignty, government regulation of television, radio, and the Internet is not always objectionable, at least so long as it is reasonably taken as an effort to promote democratic goals.

Suppose, for example, that government proposes to require television broadcasters (as indeed it now does) to provide three hours per week of educational programming for children. Or suppose that government decides to require television broadcasters to provide a certain amount of free air time for candidates for public office, or a certain amount of time on coverage of elections. For those who believe in consumer sovereignty, these requirements are quite troublesome, indeed they seem like a core violation of the free-speech guarantee. For those who associate the free-speech principle with democratic goals, these requirements are fully consistent with its highest aspirations. Indeed in many democracies—including, for example, Germany and Italy—it is well understood that the mass media can be regulated in the interest of improving democratic self-government.[13]

There is nothing novel or iconoclastic in the democratic conception of free speech. On the contrary, this conception lay at the heart of the original understanding of freedom of speech in America. In attacking the Alien and Sedition Acts, for example, James Madison claimed that they were inconsistent with the free-speech principle, which he linked explicitly to the American transformation of the concept of political sovereignty. In England, Madison noted, sovereignty was vested in the King. But "in the United States, the case is altogether different. The People, not the Government, possess the absolute sovereignty." It was on this foundation that any "Sedition Act" must be judged illegitimate. "[T]he right of electing the members of the Government constitutes . . . the essence of a free and responsible government," and "the value and efficacy of this right depends on the knowledge of the comparative merits and demerits of the candidates for the public trust."[14] It was for this reason that the power represented by a Sedition Act ought, "more than any other, to produce universal alarm; because it is levelled against that right of freely examining public characters and measures, and of free communication among the people thereon, which has ever been justly deemed the only effectual guardian of every other right."

In this way Madison saw "free communication among the people" not as an exercise in consumer sovereignty, in which speech was treated as a kind of commodity, but instead as a central part of self-government, the "only effectual guardian of every other right." Here Madison's conception of free speech was a close cousin of that of Justice Louis Brandeis, who . . . saw public discussion as a "political duty" and believed that the greatest menace to liberty would be "an inert people." A central part of the American constitutional tradition, then, places a high premium on speech that is critical to democratic processes, and centers the First Amendment on the goal of self-government. If history is our guide, it follows that government efforts to promote a well-functioning system of free expression, as through extensions of the public-forum idea, may well be acceptable. It also follows that government faces special burdens when it attempts to regulate political speech, burdens that are somewhat more severe than those it faces when it attempts to regulate other forms of speech.

American history is not the only basis for seeing the First Amendment in light of the commitment to democratic deliberation. The argument can be justified by basic principle as well.[15]

Consider the question whether the free-speech principle should be taken to forbid efforts to make communications markets work better from the democratic point of view. Return to our standard examples: educational programming for children, free air time for candidates for public office, closed-captioning for the hearing-impaired. (I am putting the Internet to one side for now because it raises distinctive questions.) Perhaps some of these proposals would do little or no good, or even harm; but from what standpoint should they be judged inconsistent with the free-speech guarantee?

If we believe that the Constitution gives all owners of speech outlets an unbridgeable right to decide what appears on "their" outlets, the answer is clear: government could require none of these things. But why should we believe that? If government is not favoring any point of view, and if it is really improving the operation of democratic processes, it is hard to find a legitimate basis for complaint. Indeed, the Supreme Court has expressly held that the owner of shopping centers—areas where a great deal of speech occurs—may be required to keep their property open for expressive activity.[16] Shopping centers are not television broadcasters; but if a democratic government is attempting to build on the idea of a public forum so as to increase the likelihood of exposure to and debate about diverse views, is there really a reasonable objection from the standpoint of free speech itself?

In a similar vein, it makes sense to say that speech that is political in character, in the sense that it relates to democratic self-government, cannot be regulated without an especially strong showing of government justification—and that commercial advertising, obscenity, and other speech that is not political in that sense can be regulated on the basis of a somewhat weaker government justification. I will not attempt here to offer a full defense of this idea, which of course raises some hard line-drawing problems. But in light of the importance of the question to imaginable government regulation of new technologies, there are three points that deserve brief mention.

First, an insistence that government's burden is greatest when it is regulating political speech emerges from a sensible understanding of government's own incentives. It is here that government is most likely to be acting on the basis of illegitimate considerations, such as self-protection, or giving assistance to powerful private groups. Government is least trustworthy when it is attempting to control speech that might harm its own interests; and when speech is political, government's own interests are almost certainly at stake. This is not to deny that government is often untrustworthy when it is regulating commercial speech, art, or other speech that does not relate to democratic self-government. But we have the strongest reasons to distrust government regulation when political issues are involved.

Second, an emphasis on democratic deliberation protects speech not only when regulation is most likely to be biased, but also when regulation is most likely to be harmful. If government regulates child pornography on the Internet or requires educational programming for children on television, it remains possible to invoke the normal democratic channels to protest these forms of regulation as ineffectual, intrusive, or worse. But when government forbids criticism of an ongoing war effort, the normal channels are foreclosed, in an important sense, by the very regulation at issue. Controls on public debate are uniquely damaging because they impair the process of deliberation that is a precondition for political legitimacy.

Third, an emphasis on democratic deliberation is likely to fit, far better than any alternative, with the most reasonable views about particular free-speech problems. However much we disagree about the most difficult speech problems, we are likely to believe that at a minimum, the free-speech principle protects political expression unless government has exceedingly strong grounds for regulating it. On the other hand, forms of speech such as perjury, attempted bribery, threats, unlicensed medical advice, and criminal solicitation are not likely to seem to be at the heart of the free-speech guarantee.

An understanding of this kind certainly does not answer all constitutional questions. It does not provide a clear test for distinguishing between political and non-political speech, a predictably vexing question.[17] (To those who believe that the absence of a clear test is decisive against the distinction itself, the best response is that any alternative test will lead to line-drawing problems of its own. Because everyone agrees that some forms of speech are regulable, line drawing is literally inevitable. If you're skeptical, try to think of a test that eliminates problems of this kind.) It does not say whether and when government may regulate art or literature, sexually explicit speech, or libelous speech. In all cases, government is required to have a strong justification for regulating speech, political or not. But the approach I am defending does help to orient inquiry. When government is regulating false or fraudulent commercial advertising, libel of private persons, or child pornography, it is likely to be on firm ground. When government is attempting to control criminal conspiracy or speech that contains direct threats of violence aimed at particular people, it need not meet the stringent standards required for regulation of political dissent. What I have suggested here, without fully defending the point, is that a conception of the First Amendment that is rooted in democratic deliberation is an exceedingly good place to start.

Forms of Neutrality

None of this means that the government is permitted to regulate the emerging communications market however it wishes. To know whether to object to what government is doing, it is important to know what *kind* of line it is drawing.[18] There are three possibilities here.

- The government might be regulating speech in a way that is *neutral with respect to the content of the speech at issue*. This is the least objectionable way of regulating speech. For example, government is permitted to say that people may not use loudspeakers on the public streets after midnight or that speakers cannot have access to the front lawn immediately in front of the White House. A regulation of this kind imposes no controls on speech of any particular content. An Internet example: if government says that no one may use the website of CNN unless CNN gives permission, it is acting in a way that is entirely neutral with respect to speech content. So too with restrictions on sending computer viruses. The government bans the ILOVEYOU virus, but it also bans the IHATEYOU virus and the IAMINDIFFERENTTOYOU virus. What is against the law is sending viruses; their content is irrelevant.

- The government might regulate speech in a way that depends on the content of what is said, but without discriminating against any particular point of view. Suppose, for example, that government bans commercial speech on the subways but allows all other forms of speech on the subways. In the technical language of First Amendment law, this form of regulation is "content-based" but "viewpoint-neutral." Consider the old fairness doctrine, which required broadcasters to cover public issues and to allow speech by those with opposing views. Here the content of speech is highly relevant to what government is requiring, but no specific point of view is benefited or punished. The same can be said for the damages award against the Nuremburg Trials website; the content of the speech definitely mattered, but no particular point of view was being punished. The same award would be given against a website that treated pro-life people in the same way that the Nuremburg Trials treated doctors. In the same category would be a regulation saying that in certain areas, sexually explicit speech must be made inaccessible to children. In these cases, no lines are being drawn directly on the basis of point of view.

- The government might regulate a point of view that it fears or dislikes. This form of regulation is often called "viewpoint discrimination." Government might say, for example, that no one may criticize a decision to go to war, or that no one may claim that one racial group is inferior to another, or that no one may advocate violent overthrow of government. Here the government is singling out a point of view that it wants to ban, perhaps because it believes that the particular point of view is especially dangerous.

It makes sense to say that these three kinds of regulations should be treated differently, on the Internet as elsewhere. Viewpoint discrimination is the most objectionable. Content-neutral regulation is the least objectionable. If officials are regulating speech because of the point of view that it contains, their action is almost certainly unconstitutional. Government should not be allowed to censor arguments and positions merely because it fears or disapproves of them. If officials are banning a disfavored viewpoint, they ought to be required to show, at the very least, that the viewpoint really creates serious risks that cannot be adequately combated with more speech. Officials ought also be required to explain, in altogether convincing terms, why they are punishing one point of view and not its opposite.

A content-neutral regulation is at the opposite extreme, and such regulations are often legitimate. If the government has acted in a content-neutral way, courts usually do not and should not intervene, at least if the basic channels of communications remain open, and if government has a solid reason for the regulation. Of course a gratuitous or purposeless regulation must be struck down even if it is content-neutral. Suppose that government says that the public streets—or for that matter the Internet—may be used for expressive activity, but only between 8 p.m. and 8:30 p.m. If so, the neutrality of the regulation is no defense. But content-neutral regulations are frequently easy to justify; their very neutrality, and hence breadth, ensures that there is a good reason for them. The government is unlikely to ban expressive activity from 8:30 p.m. until 7:59 a.m. because so many people would resist the ban. The more likely regulation prohibits noisy demonstrations when people are trying to sleep, and there is nothing wrong with such prohibitions.

Now consider the intermediate case. When government is regulating in a way that is based on content but neutral with respect to point of view, there are two issues. The first is whether the particular line being drawn suggests lurking viewpoint discrimination—a hidden but detectable desire to ban a certain point of view. When it does, the law should probably be struck down. If government says that the most recent war, or abortion, may not be discussed on television, it is, as a technical matter, discriminating against a whole topic, not against any particular point of view; but there is pretty good reason to suspect government's motivations. A ban on discussion of the most recent war is probably an effort to protect the government from criticism.

The second and perhaps more fundamental issue is whether government is able to invoke strong, content-neutral grounds for engaging in this form of regulation. A ban on televised discussion of the most recent war should be struck down for this reason. The ban seems to have no real point, aside from forbidding certain points of view from being expressed. But the government has a stronger argument if, for example, it is requiring broadcasters to offer three hours of educational programming for children. In that case, it is trying to ensure that television serves children, an entirely legitimate interest.

Of course some cases may test the line between discrimination on the basis of content and discrimination on the basis of viewpoint. If government is regulating sexually explicit speech when that speech offends contemporary community standards, is it regulating on the basis of viewpoint or merely content? This is not an easy question, and many people have argued over the right answer. But an understanding of the three categories discussed here should be sufficient to make sense out of the bulk of imaginable free-speech challenges—and should provide some help in approaching the rest of them as well.

Penalties and Subsidies

Of course government can do a range of things to improve the system of free speech. Here it is important to make a further distinction, between "subsidies" on the one hand and "penalties" on the other. Government is likely to have a great deal of trouble when it is imposing penalties on speech. Such penalties are the model of what a system of free expression avoids. Government will have more room to maneuver if it is giving out selective subsidies. Public officials are not required to give money out to all speakers, and if they are giving money to some people but not to others, they may well be on firm ground. But the distinction between the penalties and subsidies is not always obvious.

The most conspicuous penalties are criminal and civil punishments. If government makes it a crime to libel people over the Internet or imposes civil fines on television broadcasters who do not provide free air time for candidates for office, it is punishing speech. The analysis of these penalties should depend on the considerations discussed thus far—whether political speech is involved, what kind of line the government is drawing, and so forth.

Somewhat trickier, but belonging in the same category, are cases in which government is *withdrawing a benefit to which people would otherwise be entitled* when the reason for the withdrawal is the government's view about the appropriate content of speech. Suppose, for example, that government gives an annual cash subsidy to all speakers of a certain kind—say, those networks that agree to provide educational programming for children. But suppose that government withdraws the subsidy from those networks that provide speech of which the government disapproves. Imagine, for example, that the government withdraws the subsidy from networks whose news shows are critical of the president. For the most part, these sorts of penalties should be analyzed in exactly the same way as criminal or civil punishment. When benefits are being withdrawn, just as when ordinary punishment is being imposed, government is depriving people of goods to which they would otherwise be entitled, and we probably have excellent reason to distrust its motives. If government responds to dissenters by taking away benefits that they would otherwise receive, it is violating the free-speech principle.

But a quite different issue is posed when government gives out selective subsidies to speakers. It often does this by, for example, funding some museums and artists but not others, and generally through the National Endowment for the Arts and the Public Broadcasting System. Imagine a situation in which government is willing to fund educational programming for children and pays a station to air that programming on Saturday morning—without also funding situation comedies or game shows. Or imagine that government funds a series of historical exhibits on the Civil War without also funding exhibits on the Vietnam War, or on World War II, or on the history of sex equality in America. What is most important here can be stated very simply: *under current law in the United States (and generally elsewhere), government is permitted to subsidize speech however it wishes.*[19]

Government often is a speaker, and as such, it is permitted to say whatever it likes. No one thinks that there is a problem if officials endorse one view and reject another. And if government seeks to use taxpayer funds to subsidize certain projects and enterprises, there is usually no basis for constitutional complaint. The only exception to this principle is that if government is allocating funds to private speakers in a way that discriminates on the basis of viewpoint, there might be a First Amendment problem.[20] The precise nature of this exception remains unclear. But it would certainly be possible to challenge, on constitutional grounds, a decision by government to fund the Republican Party website without also funding the Democratic Party website.

Of course this kind of discrimination goes far beyond anything that I shall be suggesting here. What is important, then, is that government has a great deal of room to maneuver insofar as it is not penalizing speech but instead subsidizing it.

A Restrained, Prudent First Amendment

This chapter has dealt with a range of free-speech issues, some of them briskly, and it is important not to lose the forest for the trees. My basic claims have been that the First Amendment in large part embodies a democratic ideal, that it should not be identified with the notion of consumer sovereignty, and that it is not an absolute. The core requirement of the free-speech principle is that with respect to politics, government must remain neutral among points of view. Content regulation is disfavored; viewpoint discrimination is almost always out of bounds. A key task is to ensure compliance with these requirements in the contemporary environment.

NOTES

1. For more detailed treatments, see Cass R. Sunstein, *Democracy and the Problem of Free Speech* (New York: Free Press, 1993); Alexander Meiklejohn, *Free Speech and its Relation to Self-Government* (New York: Harper, 1948); and C. Edwin Baker, *Human Liberty and Freedom of Speech* (New York: Oxford University Press, 1995).

2. *Virginia State Bd. of Pharmacy v. Virginia Citizens Consumer Council,* 425 U.S. 748 (1976).

3. 44 *Liquormart, Inc. v. Rhode Island,* 517 U.S. 484 (1996).

4. See *Buckley v. Valeo,* 424 U.S. 1 (1979).

5. See, e.g., *Randall v. Sorrell,* 126 S. Ct. 2479 (2006); *McConnell v. FEC,* 540 U.S. 93 (2003).

6. See, e.g., Thomas Krattenmaker and L. A. Powe, "Converging First Amendment Principles for Converging Communications Media," *Yale LJ* 104 (1995): 1719, 1725.

7. For discussion, see Lessig, *Free Culture,* Benkler, *Wealth of Networks.*

8. The old case, allowing government action, is *Red Lion Broadcasting v. FCC,* 395 U.S. 367 (1969).

9. See, e.g., *Denver Area Educational Telecommunications Consortium, Inc. v. FCC,* 518 U.S. 727 (1996). The Court's caution is defended in Cass R. Sunstein, *One Case at a Time* (Cambridge, Mass.: Harvard University Press, 1999).

10. See *Lochner v. New York,* 198 U.S. 45 (1905).

11. See Lessig, *Free Culture*; Benkler, *Wealth of Networks.*

12. For an effort in this direction, see Sunstein, *Democracy and the Problem of Free Speech.*

13. See ibid., 77–81, for an overview.

14. James Madison, "Report on the Virginia Resolution, January 1800," in *Writings of James Madison* vol. 6, ed. Gaillard Hunt (New York: Putnam, 1906), 385–401.

15. I draw here on Sunstein, *Democracy and the Problem of Free Speech,* 132–36.

16. *Pruneyard Shopping Center v. Robins,* 447 U.S. 74 (1980).

17. I attempt to answer it in Sunstein, *Democracy and the Problem of Free Speech,* 121–65.

18. The best discussion is Geoffrey Stone, "Content Regulation and the First Amendment," *Wm. & Mary L. Rev.* 25 (1983): 189.

19. See *Rumsfeld v. Forum for Academic and Institutional Rights,* 126 S. Ct. 1297 (2006).

20. The murkiness of current law is illustrated by the Court's decisions in ibid., in which the Court unanimously upheld the Solomon Amendment, withdrawing federal funding from educational institutions that refused to provide equal access to the United States military; and in *National Endowment for the Arts v. Finley,* 524 U.S. 569 (1998), in which a sharply divided Court upheld a statute directing the NEA, when making funding decisions, to consider "general standards of decency and respect for the diverse beliefs and values of the American public." In the NEA case, the Court suggested that it would have ruled differently if the statute had discriminated on the basis of viewpoint.

5-2

Miranda v. Arizona

Supreme Court of the United States

In their efforts to protect rights guaranteed by the Constitution, courts sometimes establish rules of behavior for government officials. In 1966 the Supreme Court considered a number of instances in which police officers or prosecutors failed to give arrested individuals notice of their rights at the out-set of the interrogations. The Court held that prosecutors could not use state-ments stemming from custodial interrogation unless they demonstrated the use of procedural safeguards "effective to secure the privilege against self-incrimination" as provided by the Fifth Amendment. To ensure that Fifth Amendment rights were protected, the Court outlined the specific warnings interrogators must give to suspects, including notice of the right to remain silent and the right to have counsel present during questioning.

MIRANDA v. ARIZONA

384 U.S. 436 (1966)

CERTIORARI TO THE SUPREME COURT OF ARIZONA.

Decided June 13, 1966.

MR. CHIEF JUSTICE WARREN delivered the opinion of the Court.

The cases before us raise questions which go to the roots of our concepts of American criminal jurisprudence: the restraints society must observe consistent with the Federal Constitution in prosecuting individuals for crime. More specifi-cally, we deal with the admissibility of statements obtained from an individual who is subjected to custodial police interrogation and the necessity for proce-dures which assure that the individual is accorded his privilege under the Fifth Amendment to the Constitution not to be compelled to incriminate himself. . . .

We dealt with certain phases of this problem recently in *Escobedo v. Illinois* . . . (1964). There, as in the four cases before us, law enforcement officials took the defendant into custody and interrogated him in a police station for the purpose of obtaining a confession. The police did not effectively advise him of his right to remain silent or of his right to consult with his attorney. Rather, they confronted him with an alleged accomplice who accused him of having perpetrated a murder. When the defendant denied the accusation and said "I didn't shoot Manuel, you did it," they handcuffed him and took him to an interrogation room. There, while handcuffed and standing, he was questioned for four hours until he confessed. During this interrogation, the police denied his request to speak to his attorney, and they prevented his retained attorney, who had come to the police station, from consulting with him. At his trial, the State, over his objection, introduced the confession against him. We held that the statements thus made were constitutionally inadmissible.

This case has been the subject of judicial interpretation and spirited legal debate since it was decided two years ago. Both state and federal courts, in assessing its implications, have arrived at varying conclusions. A wealth of scholarly material has been written tracing its ramifications and underpinnings. Police and prosecutor have speculated on its range and desirability. We granted certiorari in these cases . . . in order further to explore some facets of the problems, thus exposed, of applying the privilege against self-incrimination to in-custody interrogation, and to give concrete constitutional guidelines for law enforcement agencies and courts to follow.

We start here, as we did in Escobedo, with the premise that our holding is not an innovation in our jurisprudence, but is an application of principles long recognized and applied in other settings. We have undertaken a thorough re-examination of the Escobedo decision and the principles it announced, and we reaffirm it. That case was but an explication of basic rights that are enshrined in our Constitution—that "No person . . . shall be compelled in any criminal case to be a witness against himself," and that "the accused shall . . . have the Assistance of Counsel"—rights which were put in jeopardy in that case through official overbearing. These precious rights were fixed in our Constitution only after centuries of persecution and struggle. And in the words of Chief Justice Marshall, they were secured "for ages to come, and . . . designed to approach immortality as nearly as human institutions can approach it," *Cohens v. Virginia*, 6 Wheat. 264, 387 (1821).

Over 70 years ago, our predecessors on this Court eloquently stated:

> The maxim *nemo tenetur seipsum accusare* had its origin in a protest against the inquisitorial and manifestly unjust methods of interrogating accused persons, which [have] long obtained in the continental system, and, until the expulsion of the Stuarts from the British throne in 1688, and the erection of additional barriers for the protection of the people against the exercise of arbitrary power, [were] not uncommon even in England. While the admissions or confessions of the prisoner, when voluntarily and freely made, have always ranked high in the scale of incriminating evidence, if an accused

person be asked to explain his apparent connection with a crime under investigation, the ease with which the questions put to him may assume an inquisitorial character, the temptation to press the witness unduly, to browbeat him if he be timid or reluctant, to push him into a corner, and to entrap him into fatal contradictions, which is so painfully evident in many of the earlier state trials, notably in those of Sir Nicholas Throckmorton, and Udal, the Puritan minister, made the system so odious as to give rise to a demand for its total abolition. The change in the English criminal procedure in that particular seems to be founded upon no statute and no judicial opinion, but upon a general and silent acquiescence of the courts in a popular demand. But, however adopted, it has become firmly embedded in English, as well as in American jurisprudence. So deeply did the iniquities of the ancient system impress themselves upon the minds of the American colonists that the States, with one accord, made a denial of the right to question an accused person a part of their fundamental law, so that a maxim, which in England was a mere rule of evidence, became clothed in this country with the impregnability of a constitutional enactment. *Brown v. Walker*, 161 U.S. 591, 596–597 (1896).

In stating the obligation of the judiciary to apply these constitutional rights, this Court declared in *Weems v. United States* . . . (1910):

. . . our contemplation cannot be only of what has been but of what may be. Under any other rule a constitution would indeed be as easy of application as it would be deficient in efficacy and power. Its general principles would have little value and be converted by precedent into impotent and lifeless formulas. Rights declared in words might be lost in reality. And this has been recognized. The meaning and vitality of the Constitution have developed against narrow and restrictive construction.

This was the spirit in which we delineated, in meaningful language, the manner in which the constitutional rights of the individual could be enforced against overzealous police practices. . . .

Our holding will be spelled out with some specificity in the pages which follow but briefly stated it is this: the prosecution may not use statements, whether exculpatory or inculpatory, stemming from custodial interrogation of the defendant unless it demonstrates the use of procedural safeguards effective to secure the privilege against self-incrimination. By custodial interrogation, we mean questioning initiated by law enforcement officers after a person has been taken into custody or otherwise deprived of his freedom of action in any significant way. As for the procedural safeguards to be employed, unless other fully effective means are devised to inform accused persons of their right of silence and to assure a continuous opportunity to exercise it, the following measures are required. Prior to any questioning, the person must be warned that he has a right to remain silent, that any statement he does make may be used as evidence against him, and that he has a right to the presence of an attorney, either retained or appointed. The defendant may waive effectuation of these rights, provided the waiver is made voluntarily, knowingly and intelligently. If, however, he indicates in any manner and at any stage of the process that he wishes to consult with an attorney before speaking there can be no questioning. Likewise, if the individual is alone and indicates in any manner that he does not wish to be interrogated, the police may not question him. The mere fact that he may have answered some questions or volunteered some statements on his own does not deprive him of the right to refrain from answering any further inquiries until he has consulted with an attorney and thereafter consents to be questioned. . . .

The constitutional issue we decide in each of these cases is the admissibility of statements obtained from a defendant questioned while in custody or otherwise deprived of his freedom of action in any significant way. In each, the defendant was questioned by police officers, detectives, or a prosecuting attorney in a room in which he was cut off from the outside world. In none of these cases was the defendant given a full and effective warning of his rights at the outset of the interrogation process. In all the cases, the questioning elicited oral admissions, and in three of them, signed statements as well which were admitted at their trials. They all thus share salient features—incommunicado interrogation of individuals in a police-dominated atmosphere, resulting in self-incriminating statements without full warnings of constitutional rights.

An understanding of the nature and setting of this in-custody interrogation is essential to our decisions today. The difficulty in depicting what transpires at such interrogations stems from the fact that in this country they have largely taken place incommunicado. From extensive factual studies undertaken in the early 1930's, including the famous Wickersham Report to Congress by a Presidential Commission, it is clear that police violence and the "third degree" flourished at that time. In a series of cases decided by this Court long after these studies, the police resorted to physical brutality—beating, hanging, whipping— and to sustained and protracted questioning incommunicado in order to extort confessions. The Commission on Civil Rights in 1961 found much evidence to indicate that "some policemen still resort to physical force to obtain confessions," 1961 Comm'n on Civil Rights Rep., Justice, pt. 5, 17. The use of physical brutality and violence is not, unfortunately, relegated to the past or to any part of the country. Only recently in Kings County, New York, the police brutally beat, kicked and placed lighted cigarette butts on the back of a potential witness under interrogation for the purpose of securing a statement incriminating a third party. . . .

The examples given above are undoubtedly the exception now, but they are sufficiently widespread to be the object of concern. Unless a proper limitation upon custodial interrogation is achieved—such as these decisions will advance—there can be no assurance that practices of this nature will be eradicated in the foreseeable future. . . .

Again we stress that the modern practice of in-custody interrogation is psychologically rather than physically oriented. As we have stated before, "Since *Chambers v. Florida,* 309 U.S. 227, this Court has recognized that coercion can be mental as well as physical, and that the blood of the accused is not the only hallmark of an unconstitutional inquisition." *Blackburn v. Alabama,* 361 U.S. 199, 206 (1960). Interrogation still takes place in privacy. Privacy results in secrecy and this in turn results in a gap in our knowledge as to what in fact goes on in the interrogation rooms. A valuable source of information about present police practices, however, may be found in various police manuals and texts which document procedures employed with success in the past, and which recommend various other effective tactics. These texts are used by law enforcement agencies themselves as guides. . . .

. . . the setting prescribed by the manuals and observed in practice becomes clear. In essence, it is this: To be alone with the subject is essential to prevent distraction and to deprive him of any outside support. The aura of confidence in his guilt undermines his will to resist. He merely confirms the preconceived story the police seek to have him describe. Patience and persistence, at times relentless questioning, are employed. To obtain a confession, the interrogator must "patiently maneuver himself or his quarry into a position from which the desired objective may be attained." When normal procedures fail to produce the needed result, the police may resort to deceptive stratagems such as giving false legal advice. It is important to keep the subject off balance, for example, by trading on his insecurity about himself or his surroundings. The police then persuade, trick, or cajole him out of exercising his constitutional rights. . . .

In the cases before us today, given this background, we concern ourselves primarily with this interrogation atmosphere and the evils it can bring. In No. 759, *Miranda v. Arizona,* the police arrested the defendant and took him to a special interrogation room where they secured a confession. In No. 760, *Vignera v. New York,* the defendant made oral admissions to the police after interrogation in the afternoon, and then signed an inculpatory statement upon being questioned by an assistant district attorney later the same evening. In No. 761, *Westover v. United States,* the defendant was handed over to the Federal Bureau of Investigation by local authorities after they had detained and interrogated him for a lengthy period, both at night and the following morning. After some two hours of questioning, the federal officers had obtained signed statements from the defendant. Lastly, in No. 584, *California v. Stewart,* the local police held the defendant five days in the station and interrogated him on nine separate occasions before they secured his inculpatory statement. . . .

It is obvious that such an interrogation environment is created for no purpose other than to subjugate the individual to the will of his examiner. This atmosphere carries its own badge of intimidation. To be sure, this is not physical intimidation, but it is equally destructive of human dignity. The current practice of incommunicado interrogation is at odds with one of our Nation's most cherished principles—that the individual may not be compelled to incriminate himself. Unless adequate protective devices are employed to dispel the compulsion inherent in custodial surroundings, no statement obtained from the defendant can truly be the product of his free choice. . . .

. . . unless we are shown other procedures which are at least as effective in apprising accused persons of their right of silence and in assuring a continuous opportunity to exercise it, the following safeguards must be observed.

At the outset, if a person in custody is to be subjected to interrogation, he must first be informed in clear and unequivocal terms that he has the right to remain silent. For those unaware of the privilege, the warning is needed simply to make them aware of it—the threshold requirement for an intelligent decision as to its exercise. More important, such a warning is an absolute prerequisite in overcoming the inherent pressures of the interrogation atmosphere. It is not just the subnormal or woefully ignorant who succumb to an interrogator's imprecations, whether implied or expressly stated, that the interrogation will continue until a confession is obtained or that silence in the face of accusation is itself damning and will bode ill when presented to a jury. Further, the warning will show the individual that his interrogators are prepared to recognize his privilege should he choose to exercise it.

The Fifth Amendment privilege is so fundamental to our system of constitutional rule and the expedient of giving an adequate warning as to the availability of the privilege so simple, we will not pause to inquire in individual cases whether the defendant was aware of his rights without a warning being given. Assessments of the knowledge the defendant possessed, based on information as to his age, education, intelligence, or prior contact with authorities, can never be more than speculation; a warning is a clearcut fact. More important, whatever the background of the person interrogated, a warning at the time of the interrogation is indispensable to overcome its pressures and to insure that the individual knows he is free to exercise the privilege at that point in time.

The warning of the right to remain silent must be accompanied by the explanation that anything said can and will be used against the individual in court. This warning is needed in order to make him aware not only of the privilege, but also of the consequences of forgoing it. It is only through an awareness of these consequences that there can be any assurance of real understanding and intelligent exercise of the privilege. Moreover, this warning may serve to make the individual more acutely aware that he is faced with a phase of the adversary system—that he is not in the presence of persons acting solely in his interest.

The circumstances surrounding in-custody interrogation can operate very quickly to overbear the will of one merely made aware of his privilege by his interrogators. Therefore, the right to have counsel present at the interrogation is indispensable to the protection of the Fifth Amendment privilege under the system we delineate today. Our aim is to assure that the individual's right to choose between silence and speech remains unfettered throughout the interrogation process. . . .

The presence of counsel at the interrogation may serve several significant subsidiary functions as well. If the accused decides to talk to his interrogators, the assistance of counsel can mitigate the dangers of untrustworthiness. With a lawyer present the likelihood that the police will practice coercion is reduced, and if coercion is nevertheless exercised the lawyer can testify to it in court. The presence of a lawyer can also help to guarantee that the accused gives a fully accurate statement to the police and that the statement is rightly reported by the prosecution at trial. . . .

An individual need not make a pre-interrogation request for a lawyer. While such request affirmatively secures his right to have one, his failure to ask for a lawyer does not constitute a waiver. No effective waiver of the right to counsel during interrogation can be recognized unless specifically made after the warnings we here delineate have been given. The accused who does not know his rights and therefore does not make a request may be the person who most needs counsel. . . .

If an individual indicates that he wishes the assistance of counsel before any interrogation occurs, the authorities cannot rationally ignore or deny his request on the basis that the individual does not have or cannot afford a retained attorney. The financial ability of the individual has no relationship to the scope of the rights involved here. The privilege against self-incrimination secured by the Constitution applies to all individuals. The need for counsel in order to protect the privilege exists for the indigent as well as the affluent. In fact, were we to limit these constitutional rights to those who can retain an attorney, our decisions today would be of little significance. . . .

In order fully to apprise a person interrogated of the extent of his rights under this system then, it is necessary to warn him not only that he has the right to consult with an attorney, but also that if he is indigent a lawyer will be appointed to represent him. Without this additional warning, the admonition of the right to consult with counsel would often be understood as meaning only that he can consult with a lawyer if he has one or has the funds to obtain one. . . .

Once warnings have been given, the subsequent procedure is clear. If the individual indicates in any manner, at any time prior to or during questioning, that he wishes to remain silent, the interrogation must cease. At this point he has shown that he intends to exercise his Fifth Amendment privilege; any statement taken after the person invokes his privilege cannot be other than the product of compulsion, subtle or otherwise. Without the right to cut off questioning, the setting of in-custody interrogation operates on the individual to overcome free choice in producing a statement after the privilege has been once invoked. If the individual states that he wants an attorney, the interrogation must cease until an attorney is present. At that time, the individual must have an opportunity to confer with the attorney and to have him present during any subsequent questioning. If the individual cannot obtain an attorney and he indicates that he wants one before speaking to police, they must respect his decision to remain silent. . . .

If the interrogation continues without the presence of an attorney and a statement is taken, a heavy burden rests on the government to demonstrate that the defendant knowingly and intelligently waived his privilege against self-incrimination and his right to retained or appointed counsel. *Escobedo v. Illinois,* 378 U.S. 478, 490, n. 14. . . .

An express statement that the individual is willing to make a statement and does not want an attorney followed closely by a statement could constitute a waiver. But a valid waiver will not be presumed simply from the silence of the accused after warnings are given or simply from the fact that a confession was in fact eventually obtained. . . .

The principles announced today deal with the protection which must be given to the privilege against self-incrimination when the individual is first subjected to police interrogation while in custody at the station or otherwise deprived of his freedom of action in any significant way. It is at this point that our adversary system of criminal proceedings commences, distinguishing itself at the outset from the inquisitorial system recognized in some countries. Under the system of warnings we delineate today or under any other system which may be devised and found effective, the safeguards to be erected about the privilege must come into play at this point. . . .

To summarize, we hold that when an individual is taken into custody or otherwise deprived of his freedom by the authorities in any significant way and is subjected to questioning, the privilege against self-incrimination is jeopardized. Procedural safeguards must be employed to protect the privilege, and unless other fully effective means are adopted to notify the person of his right of silence and to assure that the exercise of the right will be scrupulously honored, the following measures are required. He must be warned prior to any questioning that he has the right to remain silent, that anything he says can be used against him in a court of law, that he has the right to the presence of an attorney, and that if he cannot afford an attorney one will be appointed for him prior to any questioning if he so desires. Opportunity to exercise these rights must be afforded to him throughout the interrogation. After such warnings have been given, and such opportunity afforded him, the individual may knowingly and intelligently waive these rights and agree to answer questions or make a statement. But unless and until such warnings and waiver are demonstrated by the prosecution at trial, no evidence obtained as a result of interrogation can be used against him. . . .

5-3

Roe v. Wade

Supreme Court of the United States

To what extent can rights perceived by the people, but not explicitly protected by the Constitution, be recognized as constitutional principles by the courts? Judges often disagree on where the lines should be drawn. This question arose in Roe v. Wade, *the Supreme Court's 1973 decision on abortion. The specific issue was, does the Constitution embrace a woman's right to terminate her pregnancy by abortion? A 5–4 majority on the Supreme Court held that a woman's right to an abortion fell within the right to privacy protected by the Fourteenth Amendment. The decision gave a woman autonomy over the pregnancy during the first trimester and defined different levels of state interest for the second and third trimesters. The Court's ruling affected the laws of forty-six states. Justice Harry Blackmun, arguing for the majority, insisted that the Court had recognized such a right in a long series of cases and that it was appropriate to extend the right to a woman's decision to terminate a pregnancy. In a dissenting opinion, Justice William Rehnquist, who later became chief justice, argued that because abortion was not considered an implicit right at the time the Fourteenth Amendment, states must be allowed to regulate it.*

ROE ET AL. v. WADE, DISTRICT ATTORNEY OF DALLAS COUNTY

410 U.S. 113

APPEAL FROM THE UNITED STATES DISTRICT COURT FOR THE NORTHERN DISTRICT OF TEXAS.

Decided January 22, 1973.

MR. JUSTICE BLACKMUN delivered the opinion of the Court.

This Texas federal appeal and its Georgia companion, Doe v. Bolton, post, . . . present constitutional challenges to state criminal abortion legislation. The Texas statutes under attack here are typical of those that have been in effect in many States for approximately a century. . . .

We forthwith acknowledge our awareness of the sensitive and emotional nature of the abortion controversy, of the vigorous opposing views, even among physicians, and of the deep and seemingly absolute convictions that the subject inspires. One's philosophy, one's experiences, one's exposure to the raw edges of human existence, one's religious training, one's attitudes toward life and family and their values, and the moral standards one establishes and seeks to observe, are all likely to influence and to color one's thinking and conclusions about abortion. . . .

Our task, of course, is to resolve the issue by constitutional measurement, free of emotion and of predilection. We seek earnestly to do this, and, because we do, we have inquired into, and in this opinion place some emphasis upon, medical and medical-legal history and what that history reveals about man's attitudes toward the abortion procedure over the centuries. We bear in mind, too, Mr. Justice Holmes' admonition in his now-vindicated dissent in *Lochner v. New York,* 198 U. S. 45, 76 (1905):

> [The Constitution] is made for people of fundamentally differing views, and the accident of our finding certain opinions natural and familiar or novel and even shocking ought not to conclude our judgment upon the question whether statutes embodying them conflict with the Constitution of the United States.

. . . Jane Roe [a pseudonym used to protect the identity of the woman], a single woman who was residing in Dallas County, Texas, instituted this federal action in March 1970 against the District Attorney of the county. She sought a declaratory judgment that the Texas criminal abortion statutes were unconstitutional on their face, and an injunction restraining the defendant from enforcing the statutes.

Roe alleged that she was unmarried and pregnant; that she wished to terminate her pregnancy by an abortion "performed by a competent, licensed physician, under safe clinical conditions"; that she was unable to get a "legal" abortion in Texas because her life did not appear to be threatened by the continuation of her pregnancy; and that she could not afford to travel to another jurisdiction in order to secure a legal abortion under safe conditions. She claimed that the Texas statutes were unconstitutionally vague and that they abridged her right of personal privacy, protected by the First, Fourth, Fifth, Ninth, and Fourteenth Amendments. By an amendment to her complaint Roe purported to sue "on behalf of herself and all other women" similarly situated. . . .

The principal thrust of appellant's attack on the Texas statutes is that they improperly invade a right, said to be possessed by the pregnant woman, to choose to terminate her pregnancy. Appellant would discover this right in the concept of personal "liberty" embodied in the Fourteenth Amendment's Due Process Clause; or in personal, marital, familial, and sexual privacy said to be protected by the Bill of Rights or its penumbras, . . . or among those rights reserved to the people by the Ninth Amendment. . . .

It perhaps is not generally appreciated that the restrictive criminal abortion laws in effect in a majority of States today are of relatively recent vintage. Those laws, generally proscribing abortion or its attempt at any time during pregnancy except when necessary to preserve the pregnant woman's life, are not of ancient or even of common-law origin. Instead, they derive from statutory changes effected, for the most part, in the latter half of the 19th century. . . .

It is thus apparent that at common law, at the time of the adoption of our Constitution, and throughout the major portion of the 19th century, abortion was viewed with less disfavor than under most American statutes currently in effect. Phrasing it another way, a woman enjoyed a substantially broader right to terminate a pregnancy than she does in most States today. At least with respect to the early stage of pregnancy, and very possibly without such a limitation, the opportunity to make this choice was present in this country well into the 19th century. Even later, the law continued for some time to treat less punitively an abortion procured in early pregnancy. . . .

The Constitution does not explicitly mention any right of privacy. In a line of decisions, however, going back perhaps as far as *Union Pacific R. Co. v. Botsford* . . . (1891), the Court has recognized that a right of personal privacy, or a guarantee of certain areas or zones of privacy, does exist under the Constitution. In varying contexts, the Court or individual Justices have, indeed, found at least the roots of that right in the First Amendment . . . ; in the Fourth and Fifth Amendments . . . ; in the penumbras of the Bill of Rights . . . ; in the Ninth Amendment . . . ; or in the concept of liberty guaranteed by the first section of the Fourteenth Amendment. . . . These decisions make it clear that only personal rights that can be deemed "fundamental" or "implicit in the concept of ordered liberty," . . . are included in this guarantee of personal privacy. They also make it clear that the right has some extension to activities relating to marriage . . . ; procreation . . . ; contraception . . . ; family relationships . . . ; and child rearing and education. . . .

This right of privacy, whether it be founded in the Fourteenth Amendment's concept of personal liberty and restrictions upon state action, as we feel it is, or, as the District Court determined, in the Ninth Amendment's reservation of rights to the people, is broad enough to encompass a woman's decision whether or not to terminate her pregnancy. The detriment that the State would impose upon the pregnant woman by denying this choice altogether is apparent. Specific and direct harm medically diagnosable even in early pregnancy may be involved.

Maternity, or additional offspring, may force upon the woman a distressful life and future. Psychological harm may be imminent. Mental and physical health may be taxed by child care. There is also the distress, for all concerned, associated with the unwanted child, and there is the problem of bringing a child into a family already unable, psychologically and otherwise, to care for it. In other cases, as in this one, the additional difficulties and continuing stigma of unwed motherhood may be involved. All these are factors the woman and her responsible physician necessarily will consider in consultation.

On the basis of elements such as these, appellant and some *amici* argue that the woman's right is absolute and that she is entitled to terminate her pregnancy at whatever time, in whatever way, and for whatever reason she alone chooses. With this we do not agree. Appellant's arguments that Texas either has no valid interest at all in regulating the abortion decision, or no interest strong enough to support any limitation upon the woman's sole determination, are unpersuasive. The Court's decisions recognizing a right of privacy also acknowledge that some state regulation in areas protected by that right is appropriate. As noted above, a State may properly assert important interests in safeguarding health, in maintaining medical standards, and in protecting potential life. At some point in pregnancy, these respective interests become sufficiently compelling to sustain regulation of the factors that govern the abortion decision. The privacy right involved, therefore, cannot be said to be absolute. . . .

We, therefore, conclude that the right of personal privacy includes the abortion decision, but that this right is not unqualified and must be considered against important state interests in regulation. . . .

Where certain "fundamental rights" are involved, the Court has held that regulation limiting these rights may be justified only by a "compelling state interest," . . . and that legislative enactments must be narrowly drawn to express only the legitimate state interests at stake. . . .

In the recent abortion cases . . . courts have recognized these principles. Those striking down state laws have generally scrutinized the State's interests in protecting health and potential life, and have concluded that neither interest justified broad limitations on the reasons for which a physician and his pregnant patient might decide that she should have an abortion in the early stages of pregnancy. Courts sustaining state laws have held that the State's determinations to protect health or prenatal life are dominant and constitutionally justifiable. . . .

The District Court held that the appellee [the district attorney, defending the Texas law] failed to meet his burden of demonstrating that the Texas statute's infringement upon Roe's rights was necessary to support a compelling state interest, and that, although the appellee presented "several compelling justifications for state presence in the area of abortions," the statutes outstripped these justifications and swept "far beyond any areas of compelling state interest." 314 F. Supp., at 1222–1223. Appellant and appellee both contest that holding. Appellant, as has been indicated, claims an absolute right that bars any state imposition of criminal penalties in the area. Appellee argues that the State's determination to recognize and protect prenatal life from and after conception constitutes a compelling state interest. As noted above, we do not agree fully with either formulation.

A. The appellee and certain *amici* argue that the fetus is a "person" within the language and meaning of the Fourteenth Amendment. In support of this, they outline at length and in detail the well-known facts of fetal development. If this suggestion of personhood is established, the appellant's case, of course, collapses, for the fetus' right to life would then be guaranteed specifically by the Amendment. The appellant conceded as much on reargument. On the other hand, the appellee conceded on reargument that no case could be cited that holds that a fetus is a person within the meaning of the Fourteenth Amendment.

The Constitution does not define "person" in so many words. Section 1 of the Fourteenth Amendment contains three references to "person." The first, in defining "citizens," speaks of "persons born or naturalized in the United States." The word also appears both in the Due Process Clause and in the Equal Protection Clause. "Person" is used in other places in the Constitution: in the listing of qualifications for Representatives and Senators, Art. I, § 2, cl. 2, and § 3, cl. 3; in the Apportionment Clause, Art. I, § 2, cl. 3; in the Migration and Importation provision, Art. I, § 9, cl. 1; in the Emolument Clause, Art. I, § 9, cl. 8; in the Electors provisions, Art. II, § 1, cl. 2, and the superseded cl. 3; in the provision outlining qualifications for the office of President, Art. II, § 1, cl. 5; in the Extradition provisions, Art. IV, § 2, cl. 2, and the superseded Fugitive Slave Clause 3; and in the Fifth, Twelfth, and Twenty-second Amendments, as well as in §§ 2 and 3 of the Fourteenth Amendment. But in nearly all these instances, the use of the word is such that it has application only postnatally. None indicates, with any assurance, that it has any possible pre-natal application.

All this, together with our observation, *supra,* that throughout the major portion of the 19th century prevailing legal abortion practices were far freer than they are today, persuades us that the word "person," as used in the Fourteenth Amendment, does not include the unborn. This is in accord with the results reached in those few cases where the issue has been squarely presented. . . . Indeed, our decision in *United States v. Vuitch,* 402 U. S. 62 (1971), inferentially is to the same effect, for we there would not have indulged in statutory interpretation favorable to abortion in specified circumstances if the necessary consequence was the termination of life entitled to Fourteenth Amendment protection.

This conclusion, however, does not of itself fully answer the contentions raised by Texas, and we pass on to other considerations.

B. The pregnant woman cannot be isolated in her privacy. She carries an embryo and, later, a fetus, if one accepts the medical definitions of the developing young in the human uterus. See Dorland's *Illustrated Medical Dictionary* 478–479, 547 (24th ed. 1965). The situation therefore is inherently different from marital intimacy, or bedroom possession of obscene material, or marriage, or procreation, or education, with which *Eisenstadt* and *Griswold*, *Stanley*, *Loving*, *Skinner*, and *Pierce* and *Meyer* were respectively concerned. As we have intimated above, it is reasonable and appropriate for a State to decide that at some point in time another interest, that of health of the mother or that of potential human life, becomes significantly involved. The woman's privacy is no longer sole and any right of privacy she possesses must be measured accordingly.

Texas urges that, apart from the Fourteenth Amendment, life begins at conception and is present throughout pregnancy, and that, therefore, the State has a compelling interest in protecting that life from and after conception. We need not resolve the difficult question of when life begins. When those trained in the respective disciplines of medicine, philosophy, and theology are unable to arrive at any consensus, the judiciary, at this point in the development of man's knowledge, is not in a position to speculate as to the answer.

It should be sufficient to note briefly the wide divergence of thinking on this most sensitive and difficult question. There has always been strong support for the view that life does not begin until live birth. This was the belief of the Stoics. It appears to be the predominant, though not the unanimous, attitude of the Jewish faith. It may be taken to represent also the position of a large segment of the Protestant community, insofar as that can be ascertained; organized groups that have taken a formal position on the abortion issue have generally regarded abortion as a matter for the conscience of the individual and her family. As we have noted, the common law found greater significance in quickening. Physicians and their scientific colleagues have regarded that event with less interest and have tended to focus either upon conception, upon live birth, or upon the interim point at which the fetus becomes "viable," that is, potentially able to live outside the mother's womb, albeit with artificial aid. Viability is usually placed at about seven months (28 weeks) but may occur earlier, even at 24 weeks. The Aristotelian theory of "mediate animation," that held sway throughout the Middle Ages and the Renaissance in Europe, continued to be official Roman Catholic dogma until the 19th century, despite opposition to this "ensoulment" theory from those in the Church who would recognize the existence of life from the moment of conception. The latter is now, of course, the official belief of the

Catholic Church. As one brief *amicus* discloses, this is a view strongly held by many non-Catholics as well, and by many physicians. Substantial problems for precise definition of this view are posed, however, by new embryological data that purport to indicate that conception is a "process" over time, rather than an event, and by new medical techniques such as menstrual extraction, the "morning-after" pill, implantation of embryos, artificial insemination, and even artificial wombs. . . .

In view of all this, we do not agree that, by adopting one theory of life, Texas may override the rights of the pregnant woman that are at stake. We repeat, however, that the State does have an important and legitimate interest in preserving and protecting the health of the pregnant woman, whether she be a resident of the State or a nonresident who seeks medical consultation and treatment there, and that it has still *another* important and legitimate interest in protecting the potentiality of human life. These interests are separate and distinct. Each grows in substantiality as the woman approaches term and, at a point during pregnancy, each becomes "compelling." . . .

The judgment of the District Court as to intervenor Hallford is reversed, and Dr. Hallford's complaint in intervention is dismissed. In all other respects, the judgment of the District Court is affirmed. Costs are allowed to the appellee.

It is so ordered.

MR. JUSTICE REHNQUIST, dissenting.

The Court's opinion brings to the decision of this troubling question both extensive historical fact and a wealth of legal scholarship. While the opinion thus commands my respect, I find myself nonetheless in fundamental disagreement with those parts of it that invalidate the Texas statute in question, and therefore dissent. . . .

. . . I have difficulty in concluding, as the Court does, that the right of "privacy" is involved in this case. Texas, by the statute here challenged, bars the performance of a medical abortion by a licensed physician on a plaintiff such as Roe. A transaction resulting in an operation such as this is not "private" in the ordinary usage of that word. Nor is the "privacy" that the Court finds here even a distant relative of the freedom from searches and seizures protected by the Fourth Amendment to the Constitution, which the Court has referred to as embodying a right to privacy. *Katz v. United States,* 389 U. S. 347 (1967).

If the Court means by the term "privacy" no more than that the claim of a person to be free from unwanted state regulation of consensual transactions may be a form of "liberty" protected by the Fourteenth Amendment, there is no doubt that similar claims have been upheld in our earlier decisions on the basis of that liberty. I agree with the statement of MR. JUSTICE STEWART in his concurring opinion that the "liberty," against deprivation of which without due process the Fourteenth Amendment protects, embraces more than the rights found in the Bill of Rights. But that liberty is not guaranteed absolutely against deprivation, only against deprivation without due process of law. The test traditionally applied in the area of social and economic legislation is whether or not a law such as that challenged has a rational relation to a valid state objective. . . . The Due Process Clause of the Fourteenth Amendment undoubtedly does place a limit, albeit a broad one, on legislative power to enact laws such as this. If the Texas statute were to prohibit an abortion even where the mother's life is in jeopardy, I have little doubt that such a statute would lack a rational relation to a valid state objective under the test stated in *Williamson, supra.* But the Court's sweeping invalidation of any restrictions on abortion during the first trimester is impossible to justify under that standard, and the conscious weighing of competing factors that the Court's opinion apparently substitutes for the established test is far more appropriate to a legislative judgment than to a judicial one.

The Court eschews the history of the Fourteenth Amendment in its reliance on the "compelling state interest" test. . . . But the Court adds a new wrinkle to this test by transposing it from the legal considerations associated with the Equal Protection Clause of the Fourteenth Amendment to this case arising under the Due Process Clause of the Fourteenth Amendment. Unless I misapprehend the consequences of this transplanting of the "compelling state interest test," the Court's opinion will accomplish the seemingly impossible feat of leaving this area of the law more confused than it found it.

While the Court's opinion quotes from the dissent of Mr. Justice Holmes in *Lochner v. New York* . . . (1905), the result it reaches is more closely attuned to the majority opinion of Mr. Justice Peckham in that case. As in *Lochner* and similar cases applying substantive due process standards to economic and social welfare legislation, the adoption of the compelling state interest standard will inevitably require this Court to examine the legislative policies and pass on the wisdom of these policies in the very process of deciding whether a particular state interest put forward may or may not be "compelling." The decision here to break pregnancy into three distinct terms and to outline the permissible restrictions the State may impose in each one, for example, partakes more of judicial legislation than it does of a determination of the intent of the drafters of the Fourteenth Amendment.

The fact that a majority of the States reflecting, after all, the majority sentiment in those States, have had restrictions on abortions for at least a century is a strong indication, it seems to me, that the asserted right to an abortion is not "so rooted in the traditions and conscience of our people as to be ranked as fundamental,"

Snyder v. Massachusetts . . . (1934). Even today, when society's views on abortion are changing, the very existence of the debate is evidence that the "right" to an abortion is not so universally accepted as the appellant would have us believe.

To reach its result the Court necessarily has had to find within the scope of the Fourteenth Amendment a right that was apparently completely unknown to the drafters of the Amendment. As early as 1821, the first state law dealing directly with abortion was enacted by the Connecticut Legislature. . . . By the time of the adoption of the Fourteenth Amendment in 1868, there were at least 36 laws enacted by state or territorial legislatures limiting abortion. While many States have amended or updated their laws, 21 of the laws on the books in 1868 remain in effect today. Indeed, the Texas statute struck down today was, as the majority notes, first enacted in 1857 and "has remained substantially unchanged to the present time." . . .

There apparently was no question concerning the validity of this provision or of any of the other state statutes when the Fourteenth Amendment was adopted. The only conclusion possible from this history is that the drafters did not intend to have the Fourteenth Amendment withdraw from the States the power to legislate with respect to this matter. . . .

For all of the foregoing reasons, I respectfully dissent.

The Real World of Constitutional Rights

THE SUPREME COURT AND THE IMPLEMENTATION
OF THE ABORTION DECISIONS

Gerald N. Rosenberg

When one considers how exposed the Constitution's "religious establish-ment" clause is to continuous revision, it is not surprising to find other, less established rights deeply enmeshed in politics as well. The next essay exam-ines the right to an abortion, a controversial aspect of civil liberties policy that has been defended as an application of the "right to privacy."

The Supreme Court began asserting the right to privacy in earnest with Griswold v. Connecticut in 1965, when it ruled that a married couple's decision to use birth control lay beyond the purview of the government. The 1973 Roe v. Wade decision establishing a woman's right to an abortion—the best known and most controversial privacy right—has further established privacy as a class of rights implicit in the Bill of Rights. But, as Gerald Rosenberg explains, Roe v. Wade *left many aspects of abortion rights unre-solved, and a lively public debate on the subject continues today.*

IN *ROE V. WADE* and *Doe v. Bolton* (1973) the Supreme Court held unconstitutional Texas and Georgia laws prohibiting abortions except for "the purpose of saving the life of the mother" (Texas) and where "pregnancy would endanger the life of the pregnant mother or would seriously and permanently injure her health" (Georgia). The Court asserted that women had a fundamental right of privacy to decide whether or not to bear a child. Dividing pregnancy roughly into three trimesters, the Court held that in the first trimester the choice of abortion was a woman's alone, in consultation with a physician. During the second trimester, states could regulate abortion for the preservation and protection of women's health, and in approximately the third trimester, after fetal viability, could ban abortions outright, except where necessary to preserve a woman's life or health.

Source: Gerald N. Rosenberg, "The Real World of Constitutional Rights: The Supreme Court and the Implementation of the Abortion Decisions," in *Contemplating Courts,* ed. Lee Epstein (Washington, D.C.: CQ Press, 1995), 390–419. Some notes and bibliographic references appearing in the original have been deleted.

Although responding specifically to the laws of Texas and Georgia, the broad scope of the Court's constitutional interpretation invalidated the abortion laws of almost every state and the District of Columbia.[1] According to one critic, *Roe* and *Doe* "may stand as the most radical decisions ever issued by the Supreme Court" (Noonan 1973, 261).

Roe and *Doe* are generally considered leading examples of judicial action in support of relatively powerless groups unable to win legislative victories. In these cases, women were that politically disadvantaged group; indeed, it has been claimed, "No victory for women's rights since enactment of the 19th Amendment has been greater than the one achieved" in *Roe* and *Doe* ("A Woman's Right" 1973, A4). But women are not the only disadvantaged interests who have attempted to use litigation to achieve policy ends. Starting with the famous cases brought by civil rights groups, and spreading to issues raised by environmental groups, consumer groups, and others, reformers have over the past decades looked to the courts as important producers of political and social change. Yet, during the same period, students of judicial politics have learned that court opinions are not always implemented with the speed and directness that rule by law assumes. This is particularly the case with decisions that touch on controversial, emotional issues or deeply held beliefs, such as abortion.

This chapter contains an exploration of the effect of the Court's abortion decisions, both *Roe* and *Doe,* and the key decisions based on them. How did the public, politicians, medical professionals, and interest groups react to them? Were the decisions implemented? Did they bring safe and legal abortions to all American women? To some American women? If the answer turns out to be only some, then I want to know why. What are the factors that have led a constitutional right to be unevenly available? More generally, are there conditions under which Court decisions on behalf of relatively powerless groups are more or less likely to be implemented.[2]

The analysis presented here shows that the effect and implementation of the Court's abortion decisions have been neither straightforward nor simple. Political response has varied and access to legal and safe abortion has increased, but in an uneven and nonuniform way. These findings are best explained by two related factors. First, at the time of the initial decisions there was widespread support for legal abortion from several sets of actors, including relevant political and professional elites on both the national and local level, the public at large, and activists. Second, the Court's decisions, by allowing clinics to perform abortions, made it possible for women to obtain abortions in some places where hospitals refused to provide them. Implementation by private clinics, however, has led to uneven availability of abortion services and has encouraged local political opposition.

The Abortion Cases

Roe and *Doe* were the Court's first major abortion decisions, but they were not its last.[3] In response to these decisions, many states rewrote their abortion laws, ostensibly to conform with the Court's constitutional mandate but actually with the goal of restricting the newly created right. Cases quickly arose, and continue to arise, challenging state laws as inconsistent with the Court's ruling, if not openly and clearly hostile to it. In general, the Court's response has been to preserve the core holding of *Roe* and *Doe* that a woman has a virtually unfettered constitutional right to an abortion before fetal viability, but to defer to legislation in areas not explicitly dealt with in those decisions. These cases require brief mention.

Areas of Litigation

Since *Roe* and *Doe,* the Court has heard three kinds of cases on abortion. One type involves state and federal funding for abortion. Here, the Court has consistently upheld the right of government not to fund abortion services and to prohibit the provision of abortions in public hospitals, unless the abortion is medically necessary. In perhaps the most important case, *Harris v. McRae* (1980), the Court upheld the most restrictive version of the so-called Hyde Amendment, which barred the use of federal funds for even medically necessary abortions, including those involving pregnancies due to rape or incest.

A second area that has provoked a great deal of litigation is the degree of participation in the abortion decision constitutionally allowed to the spouse of a pregnant married woman or the parents of a pregnant single minor. The Court has consistently struck down laws requiring spousal involvement but has upheld laws requiring parental notification or consent, as long as there is a "judicial bypass" option allowing minors to bypass their parents and obtain permission from a court.

A third area generating litigation involves the procedural requirements that states can impose for abortions. Most of these cases have arisen from state attempts to make abortion as difficult as possible to obtain. Regulations include requiring all post–first trimester abortions to be performed in hospitals; the informed, written consent of a woman before an abortion can be performed; a twenty-four-hour waiting period before an abortion can be performed; a pathology report for each abortion and the presence of a second physician at abortions occurring after potential viability; the preservation by physicians of the life of viable fetuses; and restrictions on the disposal of fetal remains. The Court's most recent pronouncement on these issues, *Planned Parenthood of Southeastern Pennsylvania v. Casey* (1992), found informed consent, a twenty-four-hour waiting period, and certain reporting requirements constitutional.

Trends in Court Treatment of Abortion Cases

Since the late 1980s, as *Casey* suggests, the Court has upheld more restrictions on the abortion right. In *Webster v. Reproductive Health Services* (1989), the Court upheld a 1986 restrictive Missouri law, and in 1991, in *Rust v. Sullivan,* it upheld government regulations prohibiting family-planning organizations that receive federal funds from counseling patients about abortion or providing abortion referrals. Most important, in *Casey* the Court abandoned the trimester framework of *Roe.* Although the justices did not agree on the proper constitutional standard for assessing state restrictions on abortion, Justices Sandra Day O'Connor, Anthony M. Kennedy, and David H. Souter adopted an "undue burden" standard. Under this standard, states may regulate abortion but may not place an undue burden on women seeking an abortion of a nonviable fetus.

Many commentators expected *Casey* to generate an avalanche of litigation centering directly on the abortion rights. Given the ambiguity of the undue burden standard, they expected expanded state activity to limit abortion. These expectations may yet be fulfilled, but, interestingly, Court cases since *Casey* have not specifically focused on the abortion right per se. Rather, in recent litigation the Court has been asked to resolve questions concerning access to abortion; namely, what steps can courts take to prevent antiabortion advocates from interfering with public access to family-planning and abortion clinics. The reason these kinds of questions arose is not difficult to discern; the 1990s has seen the rise of militant tactics—ranging from boisterous protests to harassment of clinic workers and even to the murder of physicians performing abortions—by certain segments of the antiabortion movement.

These "access" cases have generated mixed Court rulings. In *Bray v. Alexandria Women's Health Clinic* (1993), the Court rejected an attempt by pro-choice groups to use the 1871 Ku Klux Klan Act as a way to bring federal courts into this area. But, in *Madsen v. Women's Health Center* (1994), the Court upheld parts of a Florida trial court injunction permanently enjoining antiabortion protesters from blocking access to an abortion clinic and from physically harassing persons leaving or entering it. With the enactment by Congress of the Freedom of Access to Clinic Entrances Act in 1994, and the immediate filing of a legal challenge, it is likely that the Court will have another opportunity to address this issue.

Implementing Constitutional Rights

How have the public, politicians, medical professionals, and interest groups reacted to the Court decisions since *Roe* and *Doe*? How has access to legal and safe abortion changed in the wake of these decisions? In other words, when the Supreme Court announces a new constitutional right, what happens?

Figure 1. Legal Abortions, 1966–1992

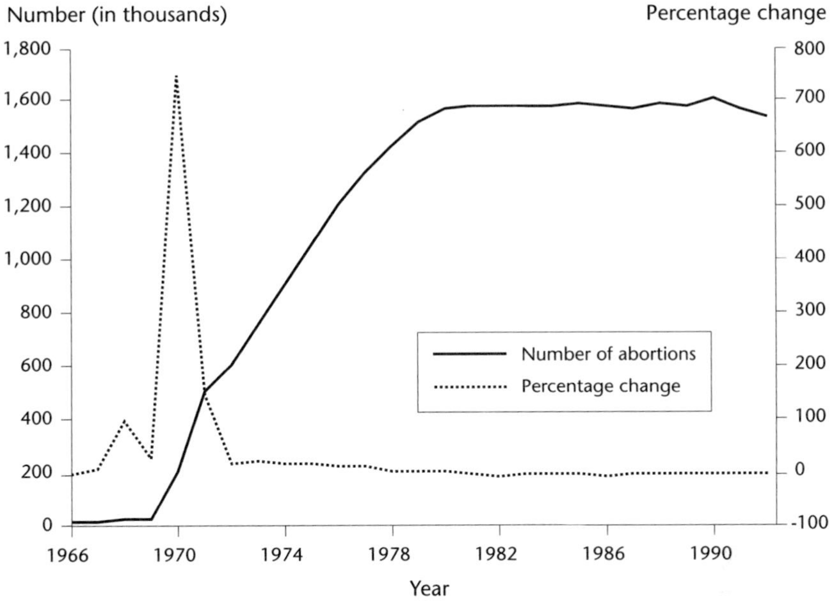

Number (in thousands)   Percentage change

Year

Sources: Estimates by the Alan Guttmacher Institute and the Centers for Disease Control and Prevention in Henshaw and Van Vort 1994, 100–106, 112; Lader 1973, 209; U.S. Congress 1974, 1976; Weinstock et al. 1975, 23. When sources differed, I have relied on data from the Alan Guttmacher Institute since its estimates are based on surveys of all known abortion providers and are generally more complete. Data points for 1983, 1986, and 1990 are estimates based on interpolations made by the Alan Guttmacher Institute.

Legal Abortions: The Numbers

An obvious way to consider this question, at least in the abortion realm, is to look at the number of legal abortions performed before and after the 1973 decisions. For, if the Court has had an important effect on society in this area, we might expect to find dramatic increases in the number of legal abortions obtained after 1973. Collecting statistics on legal abortion, however, is not an easy task. Record keeping is not as precise and complete as one would hope. Two organizations, the public Centers for Disease Control and Prevention in Atlanta and the private Alan Guttmacher Institute in New York, are the most thorough and reliable collectors of the information. The data they have collected on the number of legal abortions performed between 1966 and 1992 and the yearly percentage change are shown in Figure 1.

Interestingly, these data present a mixed picture of the effect of the abortion decisions. On the one hand, they suggest that after *Roe* the number of legal abortions increased at a strong pace throughout the 1970s (the solid line in Figure 1).

On the other hand, they reveal that the changes after 1973 were part of a trend that started in 1970, three years before the Court acted. Strikingly, the largest increase in the number of legal abortions occurs between 1970 and 1971, two years before *Roe*! In raw numerical terms, the increase between 1972 and 1973 is 157,800, a full 134,500 fewer than the pre-*Roe* increase in 1970–1971. It is possible, of course, that the effect of *Roe* was not felt in 1973. Even though the decision was handed down in January, perhaps the 1973–1974 comparison gives a more accurate picture. If this is the case, the increase, 154,000, is still substantially smaller than the change during 1970–1971. And while the number of legal abortions continued to increase in the years immediately after 1974, that rate eventually stabilized and by the 1990s had actually declined. The dotted line in Figure 1 (representing the percentage change in the number of legal abortions performed from one year to the next) shows, too, that the largest increases in the number of legal abortions occurred in the years prior to *Roe*. . . .

The data presented above show that the largest numerical increases in legal abortions occurred in the years prior to initial Supreme Court action. . . . There was no steep or unusual increase in the number of legal abortions following *Roe*. To be sure, it is possible that without constitutional protection for abortion no more states would have liberalized or repealed their laws and those that had done so might have overturned their previous efforts. And the fact that the number of legal abortions continued to increase after 1973 suggests that the Court was effective in easing access to safe and legal abortion. But those increases, while large, were smaller than those of previous years. Hence, the growth in the number of legal abortions can be only partially attributed to the Court; it might even be the case that the increases would have continued without the Court's 1973 decisions.

What Happened?

Particularly interesting about the data presented above is that they suggest that *Roe* itself failed to generate major changes in the number of legal abortions. This finding is compatible with political science literature, in which it is argued that Supreme Court decisions, particularly ones dealing with emotional and controversial issues, are not automatically and completely implemented. It also appears to fit nicely with an argument I have made elsewhere (Rosenberg 1991), which suggests that several factors must be present for new constitutional rights to be implemented. These include widespread support from political and professional elites on both the national and local level, from the public at large, and from activists and a willingness on the part of those called on to implement the decision to act accordingly. This is true, as Alexander Hamilton pointed out two centuries ago, because courts lack the power of "either the sword or the purse." To a greater extent than other government institutions, courts are dependent on both elite and popular support for their decisions to be implemented.

To fill out my argument in greater detail, I examine both pre- and post-1973 actions as they relate to the implementation of the abortion right. In so doing, I reach two important conclusions. First, by the time the Court reached its decisions in 1973, little political opposition to abortion existed on the federal level, relevant professional elites and social activists gave it widespread support, it was practiced on a large scale (see Figure 1), and public support for it was growing. These positions placed abortion reform in the American mainstream. Second, in the years after 1973, opposition to abortion strengthened and grew.

Pre-*Roe* Support

In the decade or so prior to *Roe,* there was a sea change in the public position of abortion in American life. At the start of the 1960s, abortion was not a political issue. Abortions, illegal as they were, were performed clandestinely, and women who underwent the procedure did not talk about it.[4] By 1972, however, abortion had become a public and political issue. While little legislative or administrative action was taken on the federal level, a social movement, organized in the mid- and late 1960s, to reform and repeal prohibitions on abortion met with some success at the state level, and public opinion swung dramatically from opposition to abortion in most cases to substantial support.

Elites and Social Activists

Although abortions have always been performed, public discussion did not surface until the 1950s. In 1962 the American Law Institute (ALI) published its Model Penal Code on abortion, permitting abortion if continuing the pregnancy would adversely affect the physical or mental health of the woman, if there was risk of birth defects, or if the pregnancy resulted from rape or incest. Publicity about birth defects caused by Thalidomide, a drug prescribed in the 1960s to cure infertility, and a German measles epidemic in the years 1962–1965 kept the issue prominent. By November 1965 the American Medical Association Board of Trustees approved a report urging adoption of the ALI law.

In 1966, reform activists began making numerous radio and television appearances.[5] By then there were several pro-choice groups, including the Society for Humane Abortion in California; the Association for the Study of

Abortion in New York, a prestigious board of doctors and lawyers; and the Illinois Committee for Medical Control of Abortion, which advocated repeal of all abortion laws. Abortion referral services were also started. Previously, pro-choice activists had made private referrals to competent doctors in the United States and Mexico, who performed illegal but safe abortions. But by the late 1960s, abortion referral groups operated publicly. In New York City, in 1967, twenty-two clergy announced the formation of their group, gaining front-page coverage in the *New York Times* (Fiske 1967). The Chicago referral service took out a full page ad in the *Sun-Times* announcing its services. In Los Angeles, the referral service was serving more than a thousand women per month. By the late 1960s pro-choice organizations, including abortion-referral services, were operating in many major U.S. cities. And by 1971, the clergy referral service operated publicly in eighteen states with a staff of about 700 clergy and lay people (Hole and Levine 1971, 299).

In order to tap this emerging support, the National Association for the Repeal of Abortion Laws (NARAL) was founded.[6] Protesting in the streets, lecturing, and organizing "days of anger" began to have an effect. Women who had under-gone illegal abortions wrote and spoke openly about them. Seventy-five leading national groups endorsed the repeal of all abortion laws between 1967 and the end of 1972, including twenty-eight religious and twenty-one medical groups. Among the religious groups, support ranged from the American Jewish Congress to the American Baptist Convention. Medical groups included the American Public Health Association, the American Psychiatric Association, the American Medical Association, the National Council of Obstetrics-Gynecology, and the American College of Obstetricians and Gynecologists. Among other groups, support included the American Bar Association and a host of liberal organizations. Even the YWCA supported repeal (U.S. Congress 1976, 4:53–91).

The Federal Government

In the late 1960s, while the abortion law reform battle was being fought in the states, the federal arena was quiet. For example, although states with less restrictive laws received Medicaid funds that paid for some abortions, for "six years after 1967, not a single bill was introduced, much less considered, in Congress to curtail the use of federal funds for abortion" (Rosoff 1975, 13). The pace momentarily quickened in 1968 when the Presidential Advisory Council on the Status of Women, appointed by President Lyndon Johnson, recommended the repeal of all abortion laws (Lader 1973, 81–82).

Still, abortion was not a major issue in the 1968 presidential campaign. Despite his personal beliefs, the newly elected president, Richard M. Nixon, did not take active steps to limit abortion, and the U.S. government did not enter *Roe* nor, after the decision, did it give support to congressional efforts to limit abortion.[7] Although it is true that in 1973 and 1974 President Nixon was occupied with other matters, his administration essentially avoided the abortion issue.

In Congress there was virtually no abortion activity prior to 1973. In April 1970, Sen. Bob Packwood (R-Ore.) introduced a National Abortion Act designed to "guarantee and protect" the "fundamental constitutional right" of a woman "to control her own fertility" (U.S. Congress 1970a). He also introduced a bill to liberalize the District of Columbia's abortion law (U.S. Congress 1970b). Otherwise, Congress remained essentially inactive on the abortion issue.

The States

It is not at all surprising that the president and Congress did not involve themselves in the abortion reform movement of the 1960s. Laws banning abortion were state laws, so most of the early abortion law reform activity was directed at state governments. In the early and middle parts of the decade there was some legislative discussion in California, New Hampshire, and New York. By 1967, reform bills were introduced in twenty-eight states, including California, Colorado, Delaware, Florida, Georgia, Maryland, Oklahoma, New Jersey, New York, North Carolina, and Pennsylvania (Rubin 1982). The first successful liberalization drive was in Colorado, which adopted a reform bill, modeled on the ALI's Model Penal Code. Interestingly, another early reform state was California, where Gov. Ronald Reagan, despite intense opposition, signed a reform bill.

These victories further propelled the reform movement, and in 1968, abortion legislation was pending in some thirty states. During 1968–1969 seven states— Arkansas, Delaware, Georgia, Kansas, Maryland, New Mexico, and Oregon— enacted reform laws based on or similar to the ALI model (Lader 1973, 84). In 1970, four states went even further. In chronological order, Hawaii, New York, Alaska, and Washington essentially repealed prohibitions on abortions in the first two trimesters.

To sum up, in the five or so years prior to the Supreme Court's decisions, reform and repeal bills had been debated in most states, and seventeen plus the District of Columbia acted to liberalize their laws (Craig and O'Brien 1993, 75). State action had removed some obstacles to abortion, and safe and legal abortions were thus available in scattered states. And, as indicated in Figure 1, in 1972, nearly 600,000 legal abortions were performed. Activity was widespread, vocal, and effective.

Public Opinion

Another important element in the effectiveness of the Court is the amount of support from the population at large. By the eve of the Court's decision in 1973, public opinion had dramatically shifted from opposition to abortion in most cases to substantial, if not majority, support. Indeed, in the decades that have followed, opinion on abortion has remained remarkably stable.[8]

Looking at the 1960s as a whole, Blake (1971, 543, 544) found that opinions on discretionary abortion were "changing rapidly over time" and polls were recording "rapidly growing support." For example, relying on data from Gallup polls, Blake (1977b, 49) found that support for elective abortion increased approximately two and one-half times from 1968 to 1972. One set of Gallup polls recorded a fifteen-point drop in the percentage of respondents disapproving of abortions for financial reasons in the eight months between October 1969 and June 1970 (Blake 1977a, 58). . . . In 1971, a national poll taken for the Commission on Population Growth and the American Future found 50 percent of its respondents agreeing with the statement that the abortion "decision should be left up to persons involved and their doctor" (Rosenthal 1971, 22). Thus, in the words of one study, "[b]y the time the Supreme Court made its ruling, there was strong public support behind the legalization of abortion" (Ebaugh and Haney 1980, 493).

Much of the reason for the growth in support for the repeal of the laws on abortion, both from the public and from organizations, may have come from changes in opinion by the professional elite. Polls throughout the late 1960s reported that important subgroups of the American population were increasingly supportive of abortion law reform and repeal. Several nonscientific polls of doctors, for example, suggested a great deal of support for abortion reform. A scientific poll of nearly thirteen thousand respondents in nursing, medical, and social work schools in the autumn and winter of 1971 showed strong support for repeal. The poll found split opinions among nursing students and faculty but found that 69 percent of medical students, 71 percent of medical faculty, 76 percent of social work students, and 75 percent of social work faculty supported "freely accessible abortion" (Rosen et al. 1974, 165). And a poll by the American Council of Education of 180,000 college freshmen in 1970 found that 83 percent favored the legalization of abortion (Currivan 1970). It is clear that in the late 1960s and early 1970s, the public was becoming increasingly supportive of legal abortion.

Post-*Roe* Activity

The relative quiet of the early 1960s has yet to return to the abortion arena. Rather than settling the issue, the Court's decisions added even more controversy. On the federal level, legislative and administrative action dealing with abortion has swung back and forth, from more or less benign neglect prior to 1973 to open antipathy to modest support. State action has followed a different course. Legislative efforts in the 1960s and early 1970s to reform and repeal abortion laws gave way to efforts to limit access to abortions. Public opinion remained stable until the *Webster* decision, after which there was a noticeable shift toward the prochoice position. Finally, the antiabortion movement grew both more vocal and more violent.

The Federal Government: The President

On the presidential level, little changed in the years immediately after *Roe*. Nixon, as noted, took no action, and Gerald R. Ford, during his short term, said little about abortion until the presidential campaign in 1976, when he took a middle-of-the-road, antiabortion position, supporting local option, the law before *Roe*, and opposing federal funding of abortion (Craig and O'Brien 1993, 160–161). His Justice Department, however, did not enter the case of *Planned Parenthood of Central Missouri v. Danforth*, in which numerous state restrictions on the provision of abortion were challenged, and the Ford administration took no major steps to help the antiabortion forces.[9]

The Carter administration, unlike its Republican predecessors, did act to limit access to abortion. As a presidential candidate Carter opposed federal spending for abortion, and as president, during a press conference in June 1977, he stated his support for the Supreme Court's decisions allowing states to refuse Medicaid funding for abortions (Rubin 1982, 107). The Carter administration also sent its solicitor general into the Supreme Court to defend the Hyde Amendment.

Ronald Reagan was publicly committed to ending legal abortion. Opposition to *Roe* was said to be a litmus test for federal judicial appointments, and Reagan repeatedly used his formidable rhetorical skills in support of antiabortion activists. Under his presidency, antiabortion laws enacted included prohibiting fetal tissue research by federal scientists, banning most abortions at military hospitals, and denying funding to organizations that counseled or provided abortion services abroad. His administration submitted amicus curiae cases in all the Court's abortion cases, and in two (*Thornburgh v. American College of Obstetricians and Gynecologists,* 1986, and *Webster*) urged that *Roe* be overturned. Yet, despite the rhetoric and the symbolism, these actions had little effect on the abortion rate. As Craig and O'Brien (1993, 190) put it, "in spite of almost eight years of antiabortion rhetoric, Reagan had accomplished little in curbing abortion."

The administration of George Bush was as, if not more, hostile to the constitutional right to abortion as its predecessor. It filed antiabortion briefs in several abortion cases and urged that *Roe* be overturned. During Bush's presidency, the Food and Drug Administration placed RU-486, a French abortion drug, on the list of unapproved drugs, making it ineligible to be imported for personal use. And, in the administration's most celebrated antiabortion action, the secretary of the Health and Human Services Department, Louis W. Sullivan, issued regulations prohibiting family-planning organizations that received federal funds from counseling patients about abortion or providing referrals (the "gag rule" upheld in *Rust*).

President Bill Clinton brought a sea change to the abortion issue. As the first pro-choice president since *Roe*, he acted quickly to reverse decisions of his predecessors. In particular, on the third day of his administration, and the twentieth anniversary of *Roe*, Clinton issued five abortion-related memos.

1. He rescinded the ban on abortion counseling at federally financed clinics (negating *Rust*).
2. He rescinded restrictions on federal financing of fetal tissue research.
3. He eased U.S. policy on abortions in military hospitals.
4. He reversed Reagan policy on aid to international family planning programs involved in abortion-related activities.
5. He called for review of the ban on RU-486, the French abortion pill (Toner 1993).

In addition, in late May 1994, he signed the Freedom of Access to Clinic Entrances Act, giving federal protection to facilities and personnel providing abortion services. And, in early August 1994, the U.S. Justice Department sent U.S. marshals to help guard abortion clinics in at least twelve communities around the country (Thomas 1994). Furthermore, his two Supreme Court appointees as of 1994, Ruth Bader Ginsburg and Stephen Breyer, are apparently both pro-choice.

The Federal Government: Congress

In contrast to the executive branch, Congress engaged in a great deal of antiabortion activity after 1973, although almost none of it was successful, and some supportive activity actually occurred in the late 1980s and early 1990s. By means of legislation designed to overturn *Roe*, riders to various spending bills, and constitutional amendments, many members of Congress made their opposition to abortion clear. Perhaps the most important congressional action was the passage of the Hyde Amendment, which restricted federal funding of abortion: First passed in 1976, and then in subsequent years, the amendment prohibited the use of federal funds for abortion except in extremely limited circumstances. Although the wording varied in some years, the least limited version allowed funding only to save the life of the woman, when rape or incest had occurred, or when some long-lasting health damage, certified by two physicians, would result from the pregnancy. The amendment has been effective and the number of federally funded abortions fell from 294,600 in 1977 to 267 in 1992 (Daley and Gold 1994, 250).

Despite the amount of congressional activity, the Hyde Amendment was the only serious piece of antiabortion legislation enacted.[10] And, in 1994, Congress actually enacted legislation granting federal protection to abortion clinics. Thus, Congress was hostile in words but cautious in action with abortion. While not supporting the Court and the right to abortion, congressional action did not bar legal abortion.[11]

The States

Prior to 1973 the states had been the main arena for the abortion battle, and Court action did not do much to change that. In the wake of the Court decisions, all but a few states had to rewrite their abortion laws to conform to the Court's constitutional mandate. Their reactions, like those on the federal level, varied enormously. Some states acted to bring their laws into conformity with the Court's ruling, while others reenacted their former restrictive laws or enacted regulations designed to impede access to abortion. Since abortion is a state matter, the potential for state action affecting the availability of legal abortion was high.

At the outset, a national survey reported that state governments "moved with extreme caution in implementing the Supreme Court's ruling" (Brody 1973, A1). By the end of 1973, Blake (1977b, 46) reports, 260 abortion-related bills had been introduced in state legislatures and 39 enacted. In 1974, 189 bills were introduced and 19 enacted. In total, in the two years immediately following the Court decisions, 62 laws relating to abortion were enacted by 32 states. And state activity continued, with more abortion laws enacted in 1977 than in any year since 1973 (Rubin 1982, 126, 136).

Many of these laws were hostile to abortion. "Perhaps the major share," Blake (1977b, 61 n. 2) believes, was "obstructive and unconstitutional." They included spousal and parental consent requirements, tedious written-consent forms describing the "horrors" of abortion, funding limitations, waiting periods, hospitalization requirements, elaborate statistical reporting requirements, and burdensome medical procedures. Other action undertaken by states was simple and directly to the point. North Dakota and Rhode Island, for example, responded to the Court's decisions by enacting laws allowing abortion only to preserve the life of the woman (Weinstock et al. 1975, 28; "Rhode Island" 1973). Virginia rejected a bill bringing its statutes into conformity with the Court's order (Brody 1973, 46). Arkansas enforced a state law allowing abortion only if the pregnancy threatened the life or health of the woman ("Abortions Legal for Year" 1973, A14). In Louisiana, the attorney general threatened to take away the license of any physician performing an abortion, and the state medical society declared that any physician who performed an abortion, except to save the woman's life, violated the ethical principles of medicine (Weinstock et al. 1975, 28). The Louisiana State Board of Medical Examiners also pledged to prevent physicians from performing abortions (Brody 1973). In Pennsylvania, the state medical society announced that it did "not condone abortion on demand" and retained its strict standards (King 1973, 35). And in Saint Louis, the city attorney threatened to arrest any physician who performed an abortion (King 1973). Given this kind of activity, it can be concluded that in many states the Court's intent was "widely and purposively frustrated" (Blake 1977b, 60–61).

Variation in state response to the constitutional right to an abortion continues to this day. Although legal abortions are performed in all states, the availability of abortion services varies enormously. As noted, a variety of restrictions on abortion have been enacted across the country. In the wake of the Court's decision in *Webster* (1989), which upheld a restrictive Missouri law, a new round of state restrictions on abortion was generally expected. Indeed, within two years of the decision nine states and Guam enacted restrictions. Nevertheless, four states enacted legislation protecting a woman's right to abortion (Craig and O'Brien 1993, 280). The Pennsylvania enactments were challenged in *Casey* (1992), in which the "undue burden" standard was announced. The lack of clarity in this standard virtually ensures that restrictions will continue to be enacted.

Public Opinion

As shown in Figure 2, public opinion changed little from the early 1970s (pre-*Roe*) until the *Webster* decision in 1989, after which a small but important growth in pro-choice support occurred. Although differently worded questions produce different results, it is clear that the American public remains strongly supportive of abortion when the woman's health is endangered by continuing the pregnancy, when there is a strong chance of a serious fetal defect, and when the pregnancy is the result of rape or incest. The public is more divided when abortion is sought for economic reasons, by single unmarried women unwilling to marry, and by married women who do not want more children. "The overall picture

Figure 2. Public Opinion and Abortion, Selected Years, 1975–1992

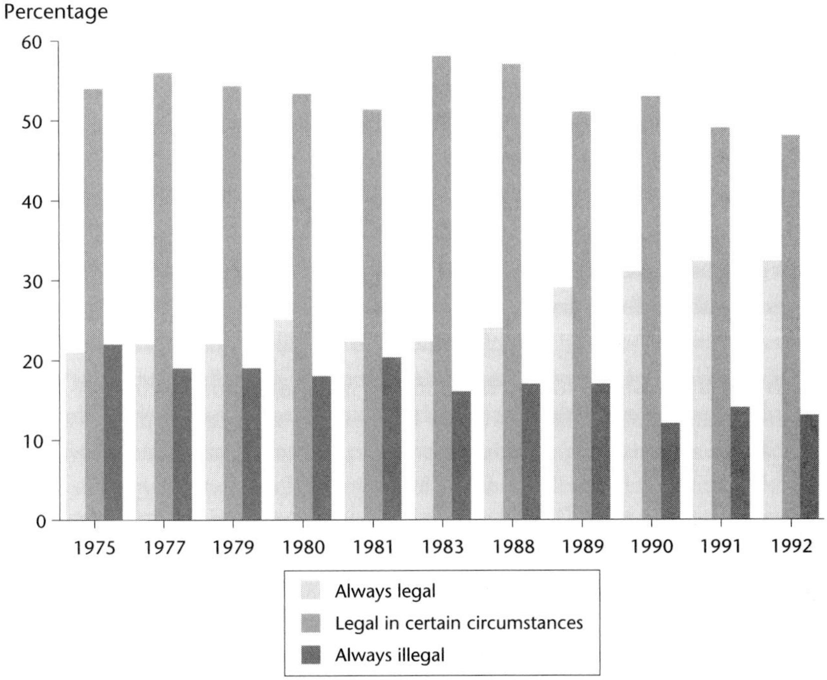

Percentage

Source: Newport and McAneny 1992, 51–52.
Note: "No opinion" omitted.

that emerges is that a majority supports leaving abortion legal and available to women unfortunate enough to need it, though many in the majority remain concerned about the moral implications" (Craig and O'Brien 1993, 269). . . .

Anti-Abortion Activity

Organized opposition to abortion increased dramatically in the years following the Court's initial decisions. National groups such as the American Life Lobby, Americans United for Life, the National Right to Life Committee, the Pro-Life Action League, and Operation Rescue and numerous local groups have adopted some of the tactics of the reformers. They have marched, lobbied, and protested, urging that abortion be made illegal in most or all circumstances. In addition, in the 1980s, groups like Operation Rescue began to adopt more violent tactics. And, since 1982, the U.S. Bureau of Alcohol, Tobacco and Firearms has reported

Table 1. Abortion Clinics Reporting Harassment,
1985 and 1988 (in percentage)

Activity	1985	1988
Picketing	80	81
Picketing with physical contact or blocking	47	46
Demonstrations resulting in arrests	—	38
Bomb threats	48	36
Vandalism	28	34
Picketing homes of staff members	16	17

Note: Dash = question not asked.
Source: Surveys of all abortion providers taken by the Alan Guttmacher Institute in Henshaw (1991, 246–252, 263).

146 incidents of bombing, arson, or attempts against clinics and related sites in thirty states, causing more than $12 million in damages (Thomas 1994). The high level of harassment of abortion clinics is shown in Table 1.

The level of harassment appears to have increased over time. In just 1992 and 1993 the U.S. Bureau of Alcohol, Tobacco and Firearms recorded thirty-six incidents, which resulted in an estimated $3.8 million in damages (Thomas 1994). The National Abortion Federation, representing roughly half of the nation's clinics, noted that incidents of reported vandalism at its clinics more than doubled from 1991 to 1992 (Barringer 1993). From May 1992 to August 1993 the U.S. Bureau of Alcohol, Tobacco and Firearms reported that 123 family-planning clinics were bombed or burned (Baum 1993). In 1992 more than forty clinics were attacked with butyric acid (a chemical injected through key holes, under doors, or into ventilation shafts) forcing clinic closures and requiring costly repairs (Anderson and Binstein 1993, C27). One of the aims of this violence appears to be to raise the cost of operating abortion clinics to such an extent as to force their closure. In 1992 and 1993, for example, arson destroyed clinics in Missoula and Helena, Montana, and in Boise, Idaho. The clinics have either been unable to reopen or have had great difficulty in doing so because of the difficulty of finding owners willing to rent to them and obtaining insurance coverage. In 1990, in the wake of such violence, one major insurer, Traveler's Insurance Company, decided not to insure any abortion-related concerns (Baum 1993).

Another tactic aimed at shutting down abortion clinics is to conduct large, sustained protests. During the summer of 1991, for example, Operation Rescue staged forty-six days of protest in Wichita, Kansas, resulting in the arrest of approximately 2,700 people. During the summer of 1993, Operation Rescue launched a seven-city campaign with similar aims. In addition, there have been individual acts of violence against abortion providers. Dr. David Gunn was murdered in March 1993 outside an abortion clinic in Pensacola, Florida; Dr. George Tiller was shot in August 1993 in Wichita, Kansas; and Dr. John Britton and his escort, James Barrett, a retired air force lieutenant colonel, were murdered in late July 1994, also in Pensacola. Commenting on the murders of Dr. Britton and James Barrett, Don Treshman, director of the antiabortion group Rescue America, issued an ominous warning: "Up to now, the killings have been on one side, with 30 million dead babies and hundreds of dead and maimed mothers. On the other side, there are two dead doctors. Maybe the balance is going to shift" (quoted in Lewin 1994, A7).[12] In sum, as Forrest and Henshaw (1987, 13) concluded, "antiabortion harassment in the United States is widespread and frequent."

Two important facts can be gleaned from the foregoing discussion. First, at the time of the 1973 abortion decisions, large segments of the political and professional elite were either indifferent to or supported abortion reform. Second, after the decisions, many political leaders vociferously opposed abortion. Congress enacted antiabortion legislation as did some of the states. In addition, activist opposition was growing. How this opposition affected the implementation of the decisions is the focus of the next section.

The Effect of Opposition on the Implementation of Abortion Rights

On the eve of the abortion decisions, there was widespread support from critical professional elites, growing public support, successful reform in many states, and indifference from most national politicians. Is this sufficient for the implementation of constitutional rights?

Constitutional rights are not self-implementing. That is, to make a right a reality, the behavior of individuals and the policies of the institutions in which they work must change. Because abortion is a medical procedure, and because safe abortion requires trained personnel, the implementation of abortion rights depends on the medical profession to provide abortion services. When done properly, first-term and most second-term abortions can be performed on an outpatient basis, and there is less risk of death in the procedure than there is in childbirth or in such routine operations as tonsillectomies. Thus, no medical or technical reasons stand in the way of the provision of abortion services. Following Supreme Court action, however, the medical profession moved with "extreme caution" in making abortion available (Brody 1973, 1). Coupled with the hostility of some state legislatures, barriers to legal abortion remained.

Table 2. Hospitals Providing Abortions, Selected Years,
1973–1992 (percentage)

Year	Private, short-term non-Catholic, general	Public
1973	24	—
1974	27	17
1975	30	—
1976	31	20
1977	31	21
1978	29	—
1979	28	—
1980	27	17
1982	26	16
1985	23	17
1988	21	15
1992	18	13

Note: Dash = unavailable.
Sources: Forrest, Sullivan, and Tietze 1978, table 5; Henshaw 1986, 253; Henshaw et al.
1982, table 7; Henshaw, Forrest, and Van Vort 1987, 68; Henshaw and Van Vort1990, 102–108,
142; Henshaw and Van Vort 1994, 100–106, 122; Rubin 1982, 154; Sullivan, Tietze, and Dryfoos, 1977, figure 10; Weinstock et al. 1975, 32.

These barriers have proved to be strong. Perhaps the strongest barrier has been
opposition from hospitals. In Table 2, I track the response of hospitals to the
Court's decisions. The results are staggering. Despite the relative ease and safety
of the abortion procedure, and the unambiguous holding of the Court, both public and private hospitals throughout America have refused to perform abortions.
The vast majority of public and private hospitals have never performed an abortion! In
1973 and the first quarter of 1974, for example, slightly more than three-quarters
of public and private non-Catholic general care short-term hospitals did not
perform a single abortion (Weinstock et al. 1975, 31). As illustrated in the table,
the passage of time has not improved the situation. By 1976, three years after the
decision, at least 70 percent of hospitals provided no abortion services. By 1992
the situation had further deteriorated: only 18 percent of private non-Catholic
general care short-term hospitals and only 13 percent of public hospitals provided
abortions. As Stanley Henshaw (1986, 253, emphasis added) concluded, reviewing the data in 1986, "most hospitals have *never* performed abortions."

These figures mask the fact that even the limited availability of hospital abortions detailed here varies widely across states. In 1973, for example, only 4 percent of all abortions were performed in the eight states that make up the East

South Central and West South Central census divisions (Weinstock et al. 1975, 25).[13] Two states, on the other hand, New York and California (which are home to about 20 percent of all U.S. women), accounted for 37 percent of all abortions in 1974 (Alan Guttmacher Institute 1976). In eleven states, "not a single public hospital reported performance of a single abortion for any purpose whatsoever in all of 1973" (Weinstock et al. 1975, 31). By 1976, three years after Court action, no hospitals, public or private, in Louisiana, North Dakota, and South Dakota performed abortions. The Dakotas alone had thirty public and sixty-two private hospitals. In five other states, which had a total of eighty-two public hospitals, not one performed an abortion. In thirteen additional states, less than 10 percent of each state's public hospitals reported performing any abortions (Forrest, Sullivan, and Tietze 1979, 46). Only in the states of California, Hawaii, New York, and North Carolina and in the District of Columbia did more than half the public hospitals perform any abortions during 1974–1975 (Alan Guttmacher Institute 1976, 30). By 1992, the situation was little better, with five states (California, New York, Texas, Florida, and Illinois) accounting for 49 percent of all legal abortions (Henshaw and Van Vort 1994, 102).

This refusal of hospitals to perform abortions means that women seeking them, particularly from rural areas, have to travel, often a great distance, to exercise their constitutional rights. In 1973, for example, 150,000 women traveled out of their state of residence to obtain abortions. By 1982 the numbers had dropped, but more than 100,000 women were still forced to travel to another state for abortion services. ...

Even when women can obtain abortions within their states of residence, they may still have to travel a great distance to do so. In 1974, the year after *Roe,* the Guttmacher Institute found that between 300,000 and 400,000 women left their home communities to obtain abortions (Alan Guttmacher Institute 1976). In 1980, across the United States, more than one-quarter (27 percent) of all women who had abortions had them outside of their home counties (Henshaw and O'Reilly 1983, 5). And in 1988, fifteen years after *Roe,* an estimated 430,000 (27 percent) women who had abortions in nonhospital settings traveled more than fifty miles from their home to reach their abortion provider. This includes over 140,000 women who traveled more than 100 miles to obtain a legal abortion (Henshaw 1991, 248).[14]

The general problem that faces women who seek to exercise their constitutional right to abortion is the paucity of abortion providers. From the legalization of abortion in 1973 to the present, at least 77 percent of all U.S. counties have been without abortion providers. And the problem is not merely rural. In 1980, seven years after Court action, there were still fifty-nine metropolitan areas in which no facilities could be identified that provided abortions (Henshaw et al. 1982, 5). The most recent data suggest that the problem is worsening. In 1992, 84 percent of all U.S. counties, home to 30 percent of all women of reproductive age, had no abortion providers. Ninety-one of the country's 320 metropolitan (28 percent) areas have no identified abortion provider, and an additional 14 (4 percent) have providers who perform fewer than fifty abortions per year. . . .

Even when abortion service is available, providers have tended to ignore the time periods set out in the Court's opinions. In 1988, fifteen years after the decisions, only 43 percent of all providers perform abortions after the first trimester. More than half (55 percent) of the hospitals that perform abortions have refused to perform second-trimester procedures, a time in pregnancy at which hospital services may be medically necessary. Only at abortion clinics have a majority of providers been willing to perform abortions after the first trimester. Indeed, in 1988 a startling 22 percent of all providers refused to perform abortions past the tenth week of pregnancy, several weeks within the first trimester, during which, according to the Court, a woman's constitutional right is virtually all-encompassing (Henshaw 1991, 251).

Finally, although abortion is "the most common surgical procedure that women undergo" (Darney et al. 1987, 161) and is reportedly the most common surgical procedure performed in the United States, an *increasing* percentage of residency programs in obstetrics and gynecology do not provide training for it. A survey taken in 1985 of all such residency programs found that 28 percent of them offered no training at all, a nearly fourfold increase since 1976. According to the results of the survey, approximately one-half of the programs made training available as an option, while only 23 percent included it routinely (Darney et al. 1987, 160). By 1992 the percentage of programs requiring abortion training had dropped nearly to half, to 12 percent (Baum 1993). In a study done in 1992 of 216 of 271 residency programs, it was found that almost half (47 percent) of graduating residents had never performed a first-trimester abortion, and only 7 percent had ever performed one in the second trimester (Cooper 1993). At least part of the reason for the increasing lack of training is harassment by antiabortion activists. "Antiabortion groups say these numbers prove that harassment of doctors, and in turn, medical schools which train residents in abortion procedures, is an effective tactic," Cooper reported. "'You humiliate the school. . . . We hope that in 10 years, there'll be none' that train residents how to perform abortions" (Randall Terry, founder of Operation Rescue, quoted in Cooper 1993, B3). . . .

It is clear that hospital administrators, both public and private, refused to change their abortion policies in reaction to the Court decisions. In the years since the Court's decisions, abortion services have remained centered in metropolitan areas and in those states that reformed their abortion laws and regulations prior to the Court's decisions. In 1976 the Alan Guttmacher Institute (1976, 13) concluded that "[t]he response of hospitals to the legalization of abortion continues to be so limited . . . as to be tantamount to no response." Jaffe, Lindheim, and Lee (1981, 15) concluded that "the delivery pattern for abortion services that has emerged since 1973 is distorted beyond precedent." Reviewing the data in the mid-1980s, Henshaw, Forrest, and Blaine (1984, 122) summed up the situation this way: "There is abundant evidence that many women still find it difficult or impossible to obtain abortion services because of the distance of their home to the nearest provider, the cost, a lack of information on where to go, and limitations on the circumstances under which a provider will make abortions available." Most recently, Henshaw (1991, 253) concluded that "an American woman seeking abortion services will find it increasingly difficult to find a provider who will serve her in an accessible location and at an affordable cost."

Implementing Constitutional Rights: The Market

The foregoing discussion presents a seeming dilemma. There has been hostility to abortion from some politicians, most hospital administrators, many doctors, and parts of the public. On the whole, in response to the Court, hospitals did not change their policies to permit abortions. Yet, as demonstrated in Figure 1, the number of legal abortions performed in the United States continued to grow. How is it, for example, that congressional and state hostility seemed effectively to prevent progress in civil rights in the 1950s and early 1960s but did not prevent abortion in the 1970s? The answer to this question not only removes the dilemma but also illustrates why the Court's abortion decisions were effective in making legal abortion more easily available. The answer, in a word, is *clinics.*

The Court's decisions prohibited the states from interfering with a woman's right to choose an abortion, at least in the first trimester. They did not uphold hospitalization requirements, and later cases explicitly rejected hospitalization requirements for second-trimester abortions.[15] Room was left for abortion reformers, population control groups, women's groups, and individual physicians to set up clinics to perform abortions. The refusal of many hospitals, then, to perform abortions could be countered by the creation of clinics willing to do the job. And that's exactly what happened.

In the wake of the Court's decisions the number of abortion providers sharply increased. In the first year after the decisions, the number of providers grew by nearly 25 percent. Over the first three years the percentage increase was almost 58 percent. The number of providers reached a peak in 1982 and has declined more than 18 percent since then. These raw data, however, do not indicate who these providers were.

. . . [T]he number of abortion providers increased because of the increase in the number of clinics. To fill the void that hospitals had left, clinics opened in large numbers. Between 1973 and 1974, for example, the number of nonhospital abortion providers grew 61 percent. Overall, between 1973 and 1976 the number of nonhospital providers grew 152 percent, nearly five times the rate of growth of hospital providers. In metropolitan areas . . . the growth rate was 140 percent between 1973 and 1976, five times the rate for hospital providers; in nonmetropolitan areas it was a staggering 304 percent, also about five times the growth rate for nonmetropolitan hospitals.

The growth in the number of abortion clinics was matched by the increase in the number of abortions performed by them. By 1974, nonhospital clinics were performing approximately 51 percent of all abortions, and nearly an additional 3 percent were being performed in physicians' offices. Between 1973 and 1974, the number of abortions performed in hospitals rose 5 percent, while the number performed in clinics rose 39 percent. By 1976, clinics accounted for 62 percent of all reported abortions, despite the fact that they were only 17 percent of all providers (Forrest, Sullivan, and Tietze 1979). From 1973 to 1976, the years immediately following Court action, the number of abortions performed in hospitals increased by only 8 percent, whereas the number performed in clinics and physicians' offices increased by a whopping 113 percent (Forrest et al. 1979).[16] The percentages continued to rise, and by 1992, 93 percent of all abortions were performed in nonhospital settings. Clinics satisfied the need that hospitals, despite the Court's actions, refused to meet.

In permitting abortions to be performed in clinics as well as hospitals, the Court's decisions granted a way around the intransigence of hospitals. The decisions allowed individuals committed to safe and legal abortion to make use of the market and create their own structures to meet the demand. They also provided a financial incentive for services to be provided. At least some clinics were formed solely as money-making ventures. As the legal activist Janice Goodman put it, "Some doctors are going to see a very substantial amount of money to be made on this" (quoted in Goodman, Schoenbrod, and Stearns 1973, 31). Nancy Stearns, who filed a pro-choice amicus brief in Roe, agreed: "[In the abortion cases] the people that are necessary to effect the decision are doctors, most of whom are not opposed, probably don't give a damn, and in fact have a whole lot to gain . . . because of the amount of money they can make" (quoted in Goodman et al. 1973, 29). Even the glacial growth of hospital abortion providers in the early and mid-1970s may be due, in part, to financial considerations. In a study of thirty-six general hospitals in Harris County (Houston), Texas, the need for increased income was found to be an important determinant of whether hospitals performed abortions. Hospitals with low occupancy rates, and therefore low income, the study reported, "saw changing abortion policy as a way to fill beds and raise income" (Kemp, Carp, and Brady 1978, 27).

Although the law of the land was that the choice of an abortion was not to be denied a woman in the first trimester, and regulated only to the extent necessary to preserve a woman's health in the second trimester, American hospitals, on the whole, do not honor the law. By allowing the market to meet the need, however, the Court's decisions resulted in at least a continuation of some availability of safe and legal abortion. Although no one can be sure what might have happened if clinics had not been allowed, if the sole burden for implementing the decisions had been on hospitals, hospital practice suggests that resistance would have been strong. After all, the Court did find abortion constitutionally protected, and most hospitals simply refused to accept that decision.

The implementation of constitutional rights, then, may depend a great deal on the beliefs of those necessary to implement them. The data suggest that without clinics the Court's decisions, constitutional rights notwithstanding, would have been frustrated.

Court Decisions and Political Action

It is generally believed that winning a major Supreme Court case is an invaluable political resource. The victorious side can use the decision to dramatize the issue, encourage political mobilization, and ignite a political movement. In an older view, however, this connection is dubious. Writing at the beginning of the twentieth century, Thayer (1901) suggested that reliance on litigation weakens political organizing. Because there have been more than twenty years of litigation in regard to abortion, the issue provides a good test of these competing views.

The evidence suggests that *Roe* and *Doe* may have seriously weakened the political effectiveness of the winners—pro-choice forces—and inspired the losers. After the 1973 decisions, many pro-choice activists simply assumed they had won and stopped their activity. According to J. Hugh Anwyl, then the executive director of Planned Parenthood of Los Angeles, pro-choice activists went "on a long siesta" after the abortion decisions (quoted in Johnston 1977, 1). Alfred F. Moran, an executive vice president at Planned Parenthood of New York, put it this way: "Most of us really believed that was the end of the controversy. The Supreme Court had spoken, and while some disagreement would remain, the issue had been tried, tested and laid to rest" (Brozan 1983, A17). These views were joined by a NARAL activist, Janet Beals: "Everyone assumed that when the Supreme Court made its decision in 1973 that we'd got what we wanted and the battle was over. The movement afterwards lost steam" (quoted in Phillips 1980, 3). By 1977 a survey of pro-choice and antiabortion activity in thirteen states nationwide revealed that abortion rights advocates had failed to match the activity of their opponents (Johnston 1977).[17] The political organization and momentum that had changed laws nationwide dissipated in reaction to Court victory. This may help explain why abortion services remain so unevenly available.

Reliance on Court action seems to have harmed the pro-choice movement in a second way. The most restrictive version of the Hyde Amendment, banning federal funding of abortions even where abortion is necessary to save the life of the woman, was passed with the help of a parliamentary maneuver by pro-choice legislators. Their strategy, as reported the following day on the front pages of the *New York Times* and the *Washington Post,* was to pass such a conservative bill that the Court would have no choice but to overturn it (Russell 1977; Tolchin 1977). This reliance on the Court was totally unfounded. With hindsight, Karen Mulhauser, a former director of NARAL, suggested that "had we made more gains through the legislative and referendum processes, and taken a little longer at it, the public would have moved with us" (quoted in Williams 1979, 12). By winning a Court case "without the organization needed to cope with a powerful opposition" (Rubin 1982, 169), pro-choice forces vastly overestimated the power and influence of the Court.

By the time of *Webster* (1989), however, pro-choice forces seemed to have learned from their mistakes, while right-to-life activists miscalculated. In early August 1989, just after *Webster,* a spokesperson for the National Right to Life Committee proclaimed: "[F]or the first time since 1973, we are clearly in a position of strength" (Shribman 1989, A8). Pro-choice forces, however, went on the offensive by generating a massive political response. Commenting on *Webster,* Nancy Broff, NARAL's legislative and political director, noted, "It finally gave us the smoking gun we needed to mobilize people" (quoted in Kornhauser 1989, 11). Membership and financial support grew rapidly. "In the year after *Webster,* membership in the National Abortion Rights Action League jumped from 150,000 to 400,000; in the National Organization for Women [NOW], from 170,000 to 250,000" (Craig and O'Brien 1993, 296). Furthermore, NARAL "nearly tripled" its income in 1989, and NOW "nearly doubled" its income, as did the Planned Parenthood Federation of America (Shribman 1989, A8). In May 1989 alone, NARAL raised $1 million (Kornhauser 1989).

This newfound energy was turned toward political action. In gubernatorial elections in Virginia and New Jersey in the fall of 1989, pro-choice forces played an important role in electing the pro-choice candidates L. Douglas Wilder and James J. Florio over antiabortion opponents. Antiabortion legislation was defeated in Florida, where Gov. Bob Martinez, an opponent of abortion, called a special session of the legislature to enact it. Congress passed legislation that allowed the District of Columbia to use its own tax revenues to pay for abortions and that essentially repealed the so-called gag rule, but President Bush vetoed both bills, and the House of Representatives failed to override the vetoes. As Paige Cunningham, of the antiabortion group Americans United for Life, put it: "The pro-life movement has been organized and active for twenty years, and some of us are tired. The pro-choice movement is fresh so they're operating with a much greater energy reserve. They've really rallied in light of *Webster*" (quoted in Berke 1989, 1).

This new understanding was also seen in *Casey*. Although pro-choice forces had seen antiabortion restrictions upheld in *Webster* and *Rust,* and the sure antiabortion vote of Justice Clarence Thomas had replaced the pro-choice vote of Justice Thurgood Marshall on the Supreme Court in the interim, pro-choice forces appealed the lower-court decision to the Supreme Court. As the *New York Times* reported, this was "a calculated move to intensify the political debate on abortion before the 1992 election" (Berke 1989, 1). Further increasing the stakes, they asked the Court either to reaffirm women's fundamental right to abortion or to overturn *Roe.* Berke (1991, B8) declared that "[t]he action marked an adjustment in strategy by the abortion rights groups, who seem now to be looking to the Court as a political foil rather than a source of redress."

All this suggests that Thayer may have the stronger case. That is, Court decisions do seem to have a mobilizing potential, but for the losers![18] Both winners and losers appear to assume that Court decisions announcing or upholding constitutional rights will be implemented, but they behave in different ways. Winners celebrate and relax, whereas losers redouble their efforts. Note, too, that in the wake of *Webster,* public opinion moved in a pro-choice direction, counter to the tenor of the opinion. Court decisions do matter, but in complicated ways.

Conclusion

"It does no good to have the [abortion] procedure be legal if women can't get it," stated Gwenyth Mapes, the executive director of the Missoula (Montana) Blue Mountain Clinic destroyed by arson in March 1993 (quoted in Baum 1993, A1).

Courts do not exist in a vacuum. Supreme Court decisions, even those finding constitutional rights, are not implemented automatically or in any straightforward or simple way. They are merely one part of the broader political picture. At best, they can contribute to the process of change. In and of themselves, they accomplish little.

The implementation of the Court's abortion decisions, partial though it has been, owes its success to the fact that the decisions have been made in a time when the role of women in American life is changing dramatically. Out of the social turmoil of the 1960s grew a women's movement that continues to press politically, socially, and culturally for ending restrictions on women's opportunities. Access to safe and legal abortion is part of this movement. In 1973 the Supreme Court lent its support by finding a constitutional right to abortion. And in the years since, it has maintained its support for that core constitutional right. Yet, I have argued that far more important in making safe and legal abortion available are the beliefs of politicians, relevant professionals, and the public. When these groups are supportive of abortion choice, that choice is available. Where they have opposed abortion, they have fought against the Court's decisions, successfully minimizing access to abortion. Lack of support from hospital administrators and some politicians and intense opposition from a small group of politicians and activists have limited the availability of abortion services. On the whole, in states that were supportive of abortion choice before Court action, access remains good. In the states that had the most restrictive abortion laws before *Roe,* abortion services are available but remain difficult to obtain. As Gwenyth Mapes put it, "It does no good to have the [abortion] procedure be legal if women can't get it."

This analysis suggests that in general, constitutional rights have a greater likelihood of being implemented when they reflect the preexisting beliefs of politicians, relevant professionals, and the public. When at least some of these groups are opposed, locally or nationally, implementation is less likely. The assumption that the implementation of Court decisions and constitutional rights is unproblematic both reifies and removes courts from the political, social, cultural, and economic systems in which they operate. Courts are political institutions, and their role must be understood accordingly. Examining their decisions without making the political world central to that examination may make for fine reading in constitutional-law textbooks, but it tells the reader very little about the lives people lead.

NOTES

1. Alaska, Hawaii, New York, and Washington had previously liberalized their laws. The constitutional requirements set forth in *Roe* and *Doe* were basically, although not completely, met by these state laws.

2. For a fuller examination, see Rosenberg 1991.

3. In 1971, before *Roe* and *Doe,* the Court heard an abortion case (*United States v. Vuitch*) from Washington, D.C. The decision, however, did not settle the constitutional issues involved in the abortion controversy.

4. Estimates of the number of legal abortions performed each year prior to *Roe* vary enormously, ranging from 50,000 to nearly 2 million. See Rosenberg 1991, 353–355.

5. The following discussion, except where noted, is based on Lader 1973.

6. After the 1973 decisions, NARAL kept its acronym but changed its name to the National Abortion Rights Action League.

7. Nixon's "own personal views" were that "unrestricted abortion policies, or abortion on demand" could not be squared with his "personal belief in the sanctity of human life" (quoted in Lader 1973, 176–177).

8. Franklin and Kosaki (1989, 762) argue that in the wake of *Roe* opinions hardened. That is, those who were pro-choice before the decision became even more so after; the same held true for those opposed to abortion. Court action did not change opinions; abortion opponents did not become abortion supporters (and vice versa). See Epstein and Kobylka 1992, 203.

9. Ford did veto the 1977 appropriations bill containing the Hyde Amendment. He stated that he did so for budgetary reasons (the bill was $4 billion over his budget request) and reasserted his support for "restrictions on the use of federal funds for abortion" (quoted in Craig and O'Brien 1993, 161).

10. The Congressional Research Service reports that Congress enacted thirty restrictive abortion statutes during 1973–1982 (Davidson 1983).

11. The growth in violent attacks on abortion clinics, and illegal, harassing demonstrations in front of them, may demonstrate a growing awareness of this point by the foes of abortion.

12. Treshman is not the only antiabortion activist to express such views. Goodstein (1994, A1) writes that "there is a sizable faction among the antiabortion movement's activists . . . who have applauded Hill [the convicted killer of Dr. Britton and Mr. Barrett] as a righteous defender of babies."

13. The East South Central states are Kentucky, Tennessee, Alabama, and Mississippi. The West South Central states are Arkansas, Louisiana, Oklahoma, and Texas. Together, these eight states contained 16 percent of the U.S. population in 1973.

14. It is possible, of course, that some women had personal reasons for not obtaining an abortion in their home town. Still, that seems an unlikely explanation as to why 100,000 women each year would leave their home states to obtain abortions.

15. *Akron v. Akron Center for Reproductive Health* (1983); *Planned Parenthood v. Ashcroft* (1983). The vast majority of abortions in the United States are performed in the first trimester. As early as 1976, the figure was 90 percent. See Forrest et al. 1979, 32.

16. The percentage for clinics is not artificially high because there were only a small number of clinic abortions in the years preceding Court action. In 1973, clinics performed more than 330,000 abortions, or about 45 percent of all abortions (see Alan Guttmacher Institute 1976, 27).

17. Others in agreement with this analysis include Tatalovich and Daynes (1981, 101, 164), participants in a symposium at the Brookings Institution (in Steiner 1983), and Jackson and Vinovskis (1983, 73), who found that after the decisions "state-level pro-choice grounds disbanded, victory seemingly achieved."

18. This also appears to have been the case in 1954 with the Court's school desegregation decision, *Brown v. Board of Education*. After that decision, the Ku Klux Klan was reinvigorated

and the White Citizen's Councils were formed, with the aim of preserving racial segregation through violence and intimidation.

REFERENCES

"Abortions Legal for Year, Performed for Thousands." 1973. *New York Times,* December 31, Sec. A.

Alan Guttmacher Institute. 1976. *Abortion 1974–1975: Need and Services in the United States, Each State and Metropolitan Area.* New York: Planned Parenthood Federation of America.

Anderson, Jack, and Michael Binstein. 1993. "Violent Shift in Abortion Battle." *Washington Post,* March 18, Sec. C.

Barringer, Felicity. 1993. "Abortion Clinics Said to Be in Peril." *New York Times,* March 6, Sec. A.

Baum, Dan. 1993. "Violence Is Driving Away Rural Abortion Clinics." *Chicago Tribune,* August 21, Sec. A.

Berke, Richard L. 1989. "The Abortion Rights Movement Has Its Day." *New York Times,* October 15, Sec. 4.

_____.1991. "Groups Backing Abortion Rights Ask Court to Act." *New York Times,* November 8, Sec. A.

Blake, Judith. 1971. "Abortion and Public Opinion: The 1960–1970 Decade." *Science,* February 12.

_____.1977a. "The Abortion Decisions: Judicial Review and Public Opinion." In *Abortion: New Directions for Policy Studies,* edited by Edward Manier, William Liu, and David Solomon. Notre Dame, Ind.: University of Notre Dame Press.

_____.1977b. "The Supreme Court's Abortion Decisions and Public Opinion in the United States." *Population and Development Review* 3:45–62.

Brody, Jane E. 1973. "States and Doctors Wary on Eased Abortion Ruling." *New York Times,* February 16, Sec. A.

Brozan, Nadine. 1983. "Abortion Ruling: 10 Years of Bitter Conflict." *New York Times,* January 15, Sec. A.

Cooper, Helene. 1993. "Medical Schools, Students Shun Abortion Study." *Wall Street Journal,* Midwest edition, March 12, Sec. B.

Craig, Barbara Hinkson, and David M. O'Brien. 1993. *Abortion and American Politics.* Chatham, N.J.: Chatham House.

Currivan, Gene. 1970. "Poll Finds Shift to Left among College Freshmen." *New York Times,* December 20, Sec. 1.

Daley, Daniel, and Rachel Benson Gold. 1994. "Public Funding for Contraceptive, Sterilization, and Abortion Services, Fiscal Year 1992." *Family Planning Perspectives* 25:244–251.

Darney, Philip D., Uta Landy, Sara MacPherson, and Richard L. Sweet. 1987. "Abortion Training in U.S. Obstetrics and Gynecology Residency Programs." *Family Planning Perspectives* 19:158–162.

Davidson, Roger H. 1983. "Procedures and Politics in Congress." In *The Abortion Dispute and the American System,* edited by Gilbert Y. Steiner. Washington, D.C.: Brookings Institution.

Ebaugh, Helen Rose Fuchs, and C. Allen Haney. 1980. "Shifts in Abortion Attitudes: 1972–1978." *Journal of Marriage and the Family* 42:491–499.

Epstein, Lee, and Joseph F. Kobylka. 1992. *The Supreme Court and Legal Change.* Chapel Hill: University of North Carolina Press.

Fiske, Edward B. 1967. "Clergymen Offer Abortion Advice." *New York Times,* May 22, Sec. A.

Forrest, Jacqueline Darroch, and Stanley K. Henshaw. 1987. "The Harassment of U.S. Abortion Providers." *Family Planning Perspectives* 19:9–13.

Forrest, Jacqueline Darroch, Ellen Sullivan, and Christopher Tietze. 1978. "Abortion in the United States, 1976–1977." *Family Planning Perspectives* 10:271–279.

———. 1979. *Abortion 1976–1977: Need and Services in the United States, Each State and Metropolitan Area.* New York: Alan Guttmacher Institute.

Franklin, Charles H., and Liane C. Kosaki. 1989. "Republican Schoolmaster: The U.S. Supreme Court, Public Opinion, and Abortion." *American Political Science Review* 83:751–771.

Goodman, Janice, Rhonda Copelon Schoenbrod, and Nancy Stearns. 1973. "Doe and Roe." *Women's Rights Law Reporter* 1:20–38.

Goodstein, Laurie. 1994. "Life and Death Choices: Antiabortion Faction Tries to Justify Homicide." *Washington Post,* August 13, Sec. A.

Henshaw, Stanley K. 1986. "Induced Abortion: A Worldwide Perspective." *Family Planning Perspectives* 18:250–254.

———. 1991. "The Accessibility of Abortion Services in the United States." *Family Planning Perspectives* 23:246–252, 263.

Henshaw, Stanley K., and Kevin O'Reilly. 1983. "Characteristics of Abortion Patients in the United States, 1979 and 1980." *Family Planning Perspectives* 15:5.

Henshaw, Stanley K., and Jennifer Van Vort. 1990. "Abortion Services in the United States, 1987 and 1988." *Family Planning Perspectives* 22:102–108, 142.

———. 1994. "Abortion Services in the United States, 1991 and 1992." *Family Planning Perspectives* 26:100–106, 122.

Henshaw, Stanley K., Jacqueline Darroch Forrest, and Ellen Blaine. 1984. "Abortion Services in the United States, 1981 and 1982." *Family Planning Perspectives* 16:119–127.

Henshaw, Stanley K., Jacqueline Darroch Forrest, and Jennifer Van Vort. 1987. "Abortion Services in the United States, 1984 and 1985." *Family Planning Perspectives* 19:63–70.

Henshaw, Stanley K., Jacqueline Darroch Forrest, Ellen Sullivan, and Christopher Tietze. 1982. "Abortion Services in the United States, 1979 and 1980." *Family Planning Perspectives* 14:5–15.

Henshaw, Stanley K., Lisa M. Koonin, and Jack C. Smith. 1991. "Characteristics of U.S. Women Having Abortions, 1987." *Family Planning Perspectives* 23:75–81.

Hole, Judith, and Ellen Levine. 1971. *Rebirth of Feminism.* New York: Quadrangle.

Jackson, John E., and Maris A. Vinovskis. 1983. "Public Opinion, Elections, and the 'Single-Issue' Issue." In *The Abortion Dispute and the American System,* edited by Gilbert Y. Steiner. Washington, D.C.: Brookings Institution.

Jaffe, Frederick S., Barbara L. Lindheim, and Phillip R. Lee. 1981. *Abortion Politics.* New York: McGraw-Hill.

Johnston, Laurie. 1977. "Abortion Foes Gain Support as They Intensify Campaign." *New York Times,* October 23, Sec. 1.

Kemp, Kathleen A., Robert A. Carp, and David W. Brady. 1978. "The Supreme Court and Social Change: The Case of Abortion." *Western Political Quarterly* 31:19–31.

King, Wayne. 1973. "Despite Court Ruling, Problems Persist in Gaining Abortions." *New York Times,* May 20, Sec. 1.

Kornhauser, Anne. 1989. "Abortion Case Has Been Boon to Both Sides." *Legal Times,* July 3.

Lader, Lawrence. 1973. *Abortion II: Making the Revolution.* Boston: Beacon Press.

Lewin, Tamar. 1994. "A Cause Worth Killing For? Debate Splits Abortion Foes." *New York Times,* July 30, Sec. A.

Newport, Frank, and Leslie McAneny. 1992. "Whose Court Is It Anyhow? O'Connor, Kennedy, Souter Position Reflects Abortion Views of Most Americans." *Gallup Poll Monthly* 322 (July): 51–53.

Noonan, John T., Jr. 1973. "Raw Judicial Power." *National Review,* March 2.

Phillips, Richard. 1980. "The Shooting War over 'Choice' or 'Life' Is Beginning Again." *Chicago Tribune,* April 20, Sec. 12.

"Rhode Island Abortion Law Is Declared Unconstitutional." 1973. *New York Times,* May 17, Sec. A.

Rosen, R. A. Hudson, H. W. Werley Jr., J. W. Ager, and F. P. Shea. 1974. "Health Professionals' Attitudes toward Abortion." *Public Opinion Quarterly* 38:159–173.

Rosenberg, Gerald N. 1991. *The Hollow Hope: Can Courts Bring About Social Change?* Chicago: University of Chicago Press.

Rosenthal, Jack. 1971. "Survey Finds 50% Back Liberalization of Abortion Policy." *New York Times,* October 28, Sec. A.

Rosoff, Jeannie I. 1975. "Is Support for Abortion Political Suicide?" *Family Planning Perspectives* 7:13–22.

Rubin, Eva R. 1982. *Abortion, Politics, and the Courts.* Westport, Conn.: Greenwood Press.

Russell, Mary. 1977. "House Bars Use of U.S. Funds in Abortion Cases." *Washington Post,* June 18, Sec. A.

Shribman, David. 1989. "Abortion-Issue Foes, Preaching to the Converted in No Uncertain Terms, Step Up Funding Pleas." *Wall Street Journal,* December 26, Sec. A.

Steiner, Gilbert Y., ed. 1983. *The Abortion Dispute and the American System.* Washington, D.C.: Brookings Institution.

Sullivan, Ellen, Christopher Tietze, and Joy G. Dryfoos. 1977. "Legal Abortion in the United States, 1975–1976." *Family Planning Perspectives* 9:116.

Tatalovich, Raymond, and Byron W. Daynes. 1981. *The Politics of Abortion.* New York: Praeger.

Thayer, James Bradley. 1901. *John Marshall.* Boston: Houghton, Mifflin.

Thomas, Pierre. 1994. "U.S. Marshals Dispatched to Guard Abortion Clinics." *Washington Post,* August 2, Sec. A.

Tolchin, Martin. 1977. "House Bars Medicaid Abortions and Funds for Enforcing Quotas." *New York Times,* June 18, Sec. A.

Toner, Robin. 1993. "Clinton Orders Reversal of Abortion Restrictions Left by Reagan and Bush." *New York Times,* January 23, Sec. A.

United States. Congress. Senate. 1970a. *Congressional Record.* Daily ed. 91st Cong., 2d sess. April 23, S3746.

_____. 1970b. *Congressional Record.* Daily ed. 91st Cong., 2d sess. February 24, S3501.

_____. 1974. Committee on the Judiciary. *Hearings before the Subcommittee on Constitutional Amendments.* Vol. 2. 93d Cong., 2d sess.

_____. 1976. Committee on the Judiciary. *Hearings before the Subcommittee on Constitutional Amendments.* Vol. 4. 94d Cong., 1st sess.

Weinstock, Edward, Christopher Tietze, Frederick S. Jaffe, and Joy G. Dryfoos. 1975. "Legal Abortions in the United States since the 1973 Supreme Court Decisions." *Family Planning Perspectives* 7:23–31.

Williams, Roger M. 1979. "The Power of Fetal Politics." *Saturday Review,* June 9.

"A Woman's Right." 1973. *Evening Star* (Washington, D.C.), January 27, Sec. A.

The Puzzling Case of the Abortion Attitudes of the Millennial Generation

Clyde Wilcox and Patrick Carr

When the Supreme Court ruled in Roe v. Wade *(1972) that a woman enjoyed a privacy right to terminate a pregnancy, it ignited a debate that crystallized women's movements into feminist and antifeminist camps. Commonly, even contentious Supreme Court rulings tend to become accepted and recede from controversy. Not abortion, as Jonathan Rauch observed in an earlier essay (3-3). Although abortion has become commonplace throughout much of the nation, recent public opinion surveys find it losing support among young Americans, even those who register liberal views on other political issues. This essay examines the generation gap on abortion and suggests some possible explanations.*

OVER THE LAST THIRTY-FIVE YEARS, groups on both sides of the abortion issue have spent an enormous amount of money and effort on mobilizing public opinion. They have conducted surveys and focus groups to better understand how the public thinks about abortion and how to frame the debate. They have designed videos, direct-mail packages, and television, radio, and Internet ads to try to influence opinion. They also have organized marches and demonstrations and trained activists in how best to discuss abortion in debates and in personal conversations (Staggenborg 1991; Maxwell 2002; Shields 2007).

And yet for thirty-five years aggregate support for abortion has remained unchanged. Gallup polls from 1977 through 2008 reveal only small differences over time in the percentages of Americans who would allow abortion under all circumstances, under some circumstances, or under no circumstances.[1] Although individuals sometimes change their minds on abortion, in the aggregate the public has been remarkably consistent, apparently resistant to the efforts and arguments of groups and activists on both sides of the issue (Cook, Jelen, and Wilcox 1992).

Surveys have shown that the public is ambivalent about abortion: many are morally troubled by abortion, but they also are troubled by government limits on women's moral choices. Although the activists on both sides of the issue have staked out consistent and uncompromising positions on abortion, many

Source: Clyde Wilcox and Patrick Carr, "The Puzzling Case of the Abortion Attitudes of the Millennial Generation," in *Understanding Public Opinion*, by Barbara Norrander and Clyde Wilcox (Washington, D.C.: CQ Press, 2009), 123–130, 138–142. Some notes appearing in the original have been deleted.

Americans support abortion under some circumstances but not under others. They weigh why a woman wants an abortion, her circumstances, and how far along she is in the pregnancy (Cook, Jelen, and Wilcox 1992; Tribe 1992). Many seek to balance two compelling values—the moral autonomy of women and an emergent fetal life with claims that become more compelling in the last months of pregnancy.

This ambivalence has played out in a variety of ways in state legislatures and referenda. The public has generally supported restrictions on abortions, including parental notification, informed consent, and waiting periods, but majorities have consistently opposed overturning *Roe v. Wade,* the 1973 Supreme Court decision that established a constitutional right to abortion, or imposing serious restrictions on abortion rights. In 2008 voters in two states rejected referenda that would have severely limited women's choice of abortion. The outcomes of these battles have been predictable, because public support for and ambivalence about abortion has remained unchanged for thirty-five years.

But the long-term stability in abortion attitudes may be about to change. During the 1970s, 1980s, and 1990s, two different processes balanced each other. On the one hand, Americans of all generations were becoming less pro-choice. On the other, the attitudes of the youngest Americans who entered the electorate were consistently more liberal than those of the oldest Americans who were leaving it. Thus generational replacement offset trends toward more conservative attitudes among all generations.

Today, however, the youngest Americans entering the electorate are less pro-choice than the oldest generation they are replacing. Indeed, the cohort often referred to as the Millennial Generation or Generation Y is less pro-choice than any age group so far in the twenty-first century and less pro-choice than any other young cohort since the Supreme Court overturned abortion restrictions in 1973. If this trend continues, generational replacement will no longer offset trends toward more conservative attitudes—it will instead reinforce them. The stability of aggregate abortion attitudes will then end, and support for legal abortion in the aggregate will decline.

Since 1972, the General Social Survey (GSS) has asked Americans whether it should be possible for a woman to obtain a legal abortion—legal under each of six separate circumstances:

- If the woman's own health is seriously endangered by the pregnancy
- If there is a strong chance of a serious defect in the baby
- If the woman became pregnant as the result of rape

Figure 1. Abortion Attitudes by Age Group over Time

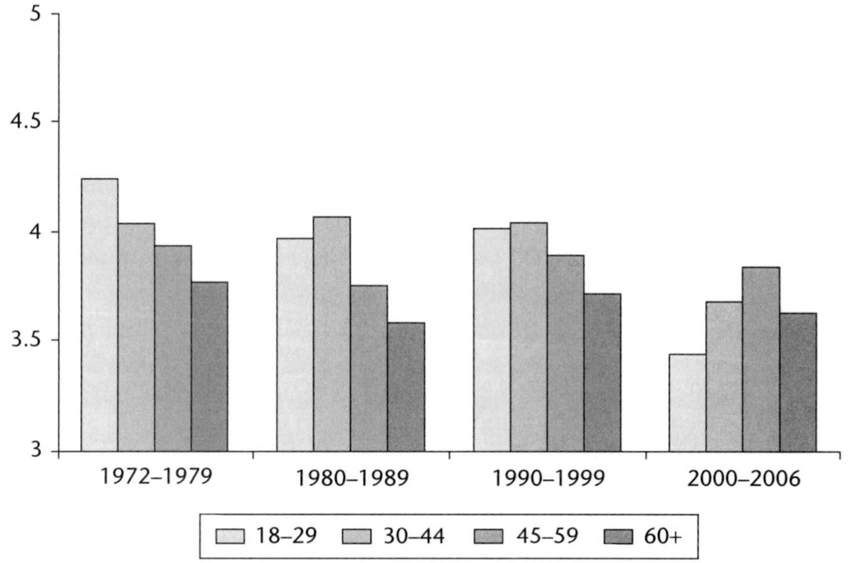

Source: General Social Survey, 1972–2006.
Note: In the scale partially shown, 1 indicates opposition to legal abortion for all six circumstances under which it might be performed (see text) and 6 indicates support for allowing legal abortion for each circumstance.

- If the family has a very low income and cannot afford any more children

- If the woman is not married and does not want to marry the man

- If the woman is married and does not want any more children.

To measure abortion attitudes, we have summed all "yes" answers to create a scale in which 0 indicates opposition to legal abortion for all six circumstances and 6 indicates support for allowing legal abortion for each circumstance.[3] Higher scores therefore represent greater support for abortion rights.

Figure 1 shows the abortion attitudes of four age groups over four decades. In the 1970s, the youngest cohort was the most pro-choice, and it was the second most pro-choice cohort in the 1980s and 1990s. Meanwhile, throughout these decades the oldest Americans were the least pro-choice. The impact of generational replacement is clear by simply comparing the height of the bars for the youngest and oldest citizens.

By weighting the data from the 1990s to reflect the generational distribution in the 1970s, we are able to estimate the impact of generational replacement more precisely (not shown). This procedure discounts any Americans who reached adulthood after 1979, and it increases the number of those who were born early in the twentieth century. This calculation reveals that, in the 1990s, respondents averaged 3.95 on the six-point abortion scale, but without generational replacement the

Table 1. Abortion Attitudes of Youngest Cohort with Comparisons,
2000–2006 (percent)

	Age cohort			
	18–29	30–44	45–59	60+
Woman's health	86%	89%**	89%***	89%***
Rape	78	79	79	79
Fetal defect	71	76***	78***	78***
Poverty	39	43**	46***	40
Single woman	35	40***	46***	39***
Wants no more kids	37	44***	47***	39
None of these	9	9	8	8
All of these	29	34	39	30
Number of cases	1,033	1,709	1,459	1,328

Source: General Social Survey, 2000–2006.
Note: Statistical tests are made relative to eighteen- to twenty-nine-year-olds.
** p ≤ .05
*** p ≤ .01

figure would have been 3.81. We can then look at the mean, or average, score on this scale for the total sample or any subgroup.

However, in the first decade of the twenty-first century younger citizens are markedly less pro-choice than the oldest cohort—indeed, they are more conservative than any other age group. The Millennial Generation is also markedly less pro-choice than any young cohort in any previous decade. Clearly, something is distinctive about the abortion attitudes of the Millennial Generation of Americans.

The absolute magnitude of the differences between age groups is substantively small. The difference between young adults in the period 2000–2006 and young adults in the 1990s is about half of a point on the abortion scale. But because of the large number of cases in the GSS, we are statistically confident that the Millennial Generation is less pro-choice than the other age cohorts. The differences are worth exploring, both because there is no theoretical reason to expect them and because they are politically important.

It is possible that the youngest cohort is especially distinctive on one or two of the questions in the six-item battery, but not all questions. Table 1 shows the responses to each question from 2000 to 2006, and also shows the percentage who opposed and supported abortion for all six circumstances.

The data reveal that younger Americans are slightly less pro-choice than any other cohort on every question, but that the differences are small for the health of the mother and not significant for rape. The oldest cohort mirrors the youngest in its lower support for abortion for reasons of poverty or when a married woman simply wants no more children. But younger Americans are distinctive in their lower support for abortion in cases of fetal defect and for single women who do not wish to marry. The gap between the Millennial Generation and those who are ages forty-five to fifty-nine is 10–11 percent for single women and for married couples who want no more children, and 7 percent for poverty and fetal defect.

Although the Millennial Generation is less likely to support abortion for each specific circumstance, it is not more likely to oppose abortion under all circumstances. The bottom of the table shows that although the youngest citizens are less likely than other groups to support abortion for all six circumstances, they are no more likely to oppose it for all circumstances. Instead, they are more likely to support abortion under some but not all circumstances—and fewer circumstances than older cohorts.

Distinctive on Abortion, or on Something Else?

It may be that the Millennial Generation is not distinctive primarily in its abortion attitudes, but rather on other characteristics that influence these attitudes. Studies have consistently reported that demographic characteristics, religious affiliations and behaviors, and social and political attitudes are strong predictors of abortion attitudes. Perhaps the Millennial cohort is more religious, more Republican, or more generally conservative than older cohorts, which, in turn influences its abortion attitudes.

In fact, the Millennial Generation differs from the older cohorts in its demographic characteristics, religious affiliations, and social and political attitudes—but each of these differences predicts that the youngest Americans will be more *liberal* on abortion than older cohorts, not more conservative. Compared with older cohorts, members of the Millennial Generation have higher levels of education, are more likely to live in urban areas, are more likely to be single and to not be parents, and are more likely to be in the labor force. Each of these factors has been associated with more pro-choice attitudes in at least some previous studies.

More important, the Millennials are more secular than older cohorts, not more religious. According to past studies, abortion attitudes are strongly associated with religious affiliations, practices, and beliefs. The Catholic Church and most evangelical denominations have adopted antiabortion positions, and committed members of these churches have been less pro-choice than other Americans. Those who attend church regularly are consistently less supportive of abortion, as are those who believe the Bible to be the literal word of God.

Table 2. Generational Differences in Religion and Other Attitudes, 2000–2006

	Age cohort			
	18–29	30–44	45–59	60+
Committed evangelical	13%	16%***	19%***	18%***
Committed Catholic	6	7**	8**	12***
Secular	23	17***	14***	8***
Attend church seldom	47	42***	41***	35***
Attend church weekly/more	17	23***	26***	35***
Bible is literally true	31	34**	30	38***
Republican	30	35***	34***	36***
Conservative	29	34***	34***	37***
Sex always wrong				
Extramarital	83	80*	77**	82
Premarital	19	26***	25***	38***
Teens 14–16	59	71***	74***	81***
Same-sex couples	46	55***	54***	70***
Gender equality families	75	68***	64***	41***
Gender equality politics	79	78	81	68***
Working mothers are able parents	63	59**	49***	37***
Euthanasia	71	70	69	62***
Right to end life if incurable disease	61	61	64	42***
Ideal family, 3–4 children	46	36***	34***	44
Number of cases	1,033	1,709	1,459	1,328

Source: General Social Survey, 2000–2006.
Note: Statistical tests are made relative to eighteen- to twenty-nine-year-olds.
* p ≤ .10.
** p ≤ .05.
*** p ≤ .01.

Table 2 shows that younger respondents are less likely than older cohorts to be committed evangelicals or committed Catholics, and they are more likely to be secular than older cohorts. They are more likely to attend church seldom (a few times a year or less), and are less likely than older cohorts to attend weekly or more. And they are somewhat less likely to believe that the Bible is literally true. Thus the religious characteristics of the Millennial cohort predict that it should be more pro-choice than older Americans.

Abortion attitudes are also increasingly associated with partisanship and ideology. In the 1970s, Republicans and Democrats had similar attitudes on abortion, but by the 1990s Republicans were far more conservative. Over time, Republican candidates increasingly took antiabortion positions, and Democrats adopted pro-choice ones (Abramowitz 1995). Some voters were persuaded by party leaders and changed their attitudes on abortion, while others who felt strongly about abortion changed their party identification (Layman and Carsey 2002).

The data in Table 2 show that young people are less likely to identify as Republicans than older cohorts, although they also are less likely to be Democrats and more likely to identify as independents. Ideologically, they are less likely to call themselves conservatives and more likely to identify themselves as liberals. But neither of these attitudes helps us understand the distinctive abortion attitudes of this cohort.

Abortion attitudes also are associated with other, more specific social and political attitudes. For many people, abortion is tied up in larger questions of sexual morality. Those with traditional sexual values—who oppose sex outside of marriage, for example—sometimes argue that abortion removes the connection between sexuality and fertility (Luker 1984). But Table 2 shows that the Millennial Generation has more permissive sexual values than other generations. It is far less likely than older cohorts to believe that premarital sex, sex among younger teens, and sexual activity among gays and lesbians are always wrong. The sole exception is attitudes toward extramarital affairs.[4] On other measures not shown in Table 2, the youngest cohort is the most liberal on distributing birth control information to young people without a parent's permission and on the availability of pornography. They are also more likely to report having seen an X-rated movie recently. Again, none of these attitudes predicts conservative opinions on abortion.

Abortion attitudes are also tied up in larger questions about gender equality. Feminists argue that women's equality is ensured only if they can control their fertility, because unwanted pregnancies can interfere with education and career advancement. Those who favor traditional gender roles frequently focus on women's roles as mothers (Luker 1984). Table 2 reveals that the Millennial Generation is no less supportive of overall gender equality than other cohorts, and is actually the most egalitarian in attitudes toward family roles. Once again, these attitudes predict that the Millennials should be slightly more pro-choice than older groups.

Opponents of abortion generally frame their arguments around the sanctity of life. Many of these groups take strong stands against stem cell research and against physician-assisted suicide. The Millennial Generation is more likely to support physician-assisted suicide, and also to believe that people should have the right to end their lives if they have an incurable disease (Table 2).

Finally, attitudes toward abortion are related to a desire for larger families. Those who think the ideal family has several children are likely to think of an unexpected pregnancy as an opportunity and not a constraint. The data suggest that the Millennial Generation is more likely than other cohorts to think that three or more children are the ideal family size. This finding is especially true of young women, nearly half of whom think a family of three or more children is ideal.

Table 2, then, does little to explain the distinctive conservatism of the Millennial Generation on abortion. On only one question—ideal family size—are the attitudes of the Millennial Generation consistent with a profile that predicts more conservative abortion attitudes. Every other religious characteristic or attitude predicts that the Millennials will be the most pro-choice cohort. This prediction is best seen by comparing the youngest and oldest cohorts—the two least pro-choice cohorts in (2000–2006) in Figure 1.

But the reasons for the conservatism of the oldest cohort are evident in Table 2. Members of this cohort are more religious. Compared with the Millennial Generation, for example, they are twice as likely to be a committed Catholic and one-third as likely to be secular. They are also more conservative in general ideology, far more conservative on sexual morality, far less supportive of gender equality, and more opposed to policies that make it easier to terminate life. The oldest generation is conservative on abortion *because* of these other characteristics, and the youngest generation is conservative *in spite* of them.

In fact, the oldest generation is more pro-choice than its characteristics would predict, and the youngest cohort is far less pro-choice. To demonstrate, we estimated a series of regression equations [not shown], testing the distinctiveness of the Millennial Generation and those age sixty and older against middle-aged respondents. . . . The oldest cohort is more pro-choice than others who share its demographic and religious characteristics. . . .

In general, the data indicate that abortion attitudes among the Millennial Generation are shaped by the same forces that affect the attitudes of older respondents. For both groups, those who are better educated are more pro-choice, and those who attend church most frequently are the least pro-choice. Also for both groups, those who are ideologically conservative are less supportive of legal abortion than liberals, and those who have conservative attitudes on issues relating to the inviolability of life are less pro-choice as well, as are those who think large families are ideal. Thus, although the Millennials attend church less often and are more liberal on sexual morality questions than older Americans, among this younger cohort those who attend church the most often and who are the most conservative on sexual morality issues are more conservative than others in their age group. . . .

Why Is the Millennial Generation Less Pro-Choice?

The Millennial Generation has come of age during a period of less support for legal abortion. During this time, the public debate has focused largely on popular restrictions on abortion, such as a ban on partial-birth abortion, informed consent laws, and a continuing push for parental notification and consent. There has been little media coverage of the possibility that abortion rights might disappear if *Roe* were overturned, and state referenda designed to limit abortion rights have gone down to defeat in recent years. Thus the dominant frame for abortion since 1998 has included an assumption that basic abortion rights are guaranteed, and focused therefore on which restrictions should be imposed. This distinctive frame is probably sufficient to explain the declining support for abortion among older generations during the 1997–2006 period.

Because it has come of age during a period of declining support for abortion, the Millennial Generation might be expected to enter the electorate with lower levels of support for legal abortion. Indeed, the youngest cohorts are especially shaped by the dominant frame of issues as they reach adulthood, so we would expect them to enter the electorate less supportive of abortion rights. But is this likely to persist over a lifetime? Will the Millennials remain a distinctive generation, such as the sixties and post–*Roe* generations, or will they change their attitudes as the parental notification cohort did . . .?

Whether members of the Millennial Generation will continue to hold less pro-choice views throughout their lifetimes may hinge on whether they are currently responding only to the partial-birth abortion frame, or whether other factors are shaping their abortion opinions. Three other factors might be shaping the abortion attitudes of this cohort. First, popular culture framings of pregnancy, childbirth, and abortion have shaped the opinions of the youngest cohort. A series of television shows and movies have depicted single, pregnant young women who choose to have their babies and whose stories end happily. Most recently, the movie *Juno* portrayed a pregnant high school girl who briefly considered an abortion, but ultimately decided to place the baby with an adoptive family.[5] This outcome is consistent with the Millennial Generation's preference of a larger ideal family size, suggesting a stronger pro-natal attitude.

Second, as ultrasound technology has improved, more mothers are including these images in their collection of baby pictures. The antiabortion movement's placards featuring photos of bloody aborted fetuses were ineffective primarily because they were so gruesome that people seldom looked at them. By contrast, an ultrasound image of "Jason" in a book of baby pictures is something over which viewers linger. In *Juno*, the heroine chooses not to have an abortion in part because a classmate tells her that the fetus has fingernails. For Millennials, the act of viewing pictures of developing fetuses and associating them with children may lead them to place a somewhat higher value on fetal life.

Although we have no survey data to confirm that viewing ultrasound images influences attitudes, opponents of abortion forces clearly believe they do exert such an influence. Many states have endured political struggles about requiring ultrasounds for all abortion patients, and Oklahoma now requires patients to listen to a description of what they are seeing on the ultrasound image. In 2008 four states required ultrasound images before an abortion was performed. But scattered media surveys in recent years do indicate that the Millennial Generation is not more likely to believe that life begins at conception. Like many other Americans, the Millennials attempt to balance the value of fetal life with that of women's autonomy, and in that balancing they appear to assign slightly higher value to fetal life than do other cohorts.

Third, unlike middle-aged cohorts, the Millennials do not associate equality for women with attitudes toward abortion, perhaps because they do not believe that having an unexpected child poses difficulty for women. This attitude may reflect media portrayals. For example, when the television character Murphy Brown had a baby in 1991, her perennial housepainter served as nanny and Murphy's professional life was unimpeded. When the character Rachel had a child in 2002 on the TV show *Friends*, she was able to continue down a demanding career track, with time to socialize with her friends. And even though Juno, the teenage heroine of the 2007 movie by the same name, suffered from the normal inconveniences of pregnancy and some nasty looks, her life nevertheless appeared to be largely on course by the movie's end.

It is difficult to predict the future of abortion attitudes among this and coming generations, for the owl of Minerva flies at dusk. But at least two possible scenarios could have very different consequences for the politics of abortion.

Scenario 1: The Millennials Are Like the Parental Notification Generation

. . . The generation that came of age while the nation debated parental notification laws in the 1980s was distinctively less pro-choice when young, but when abortion rights were later threatened by state restrictions on abortion, it increased markedly its support for legal abortion over the 1989–1996 period. In response to the political debate over restrictions on abortion, members of this cohort tended to be more conservative when they were young, but the new frame of a threat to abortion rights affected their attitudes. Over time, then, this generation became less distinctive in its abortion attitudes. The Millennial Generation may be shaped by media factors beyond the political debate over partial-birth abortion, but over time it may come to see that unexpected pregnancies can affect lives to an extent not portrayed in television shows and movies. If the Supreme Court were to allow further restrictions on abortion, the Millennials might become markedly more liberal, as did the parental notification cohort.

In 2008 support for this prospect was found in the voting of the Millennial Generation on ballot initiatives to limit abortion. In California, Proposition 4 would have amended the state constitution to require parental notification on abortion, although the measure allowed many exceptions. The Millennial Generation voted against this relatively mild abortion measure by nearly two to one and was the most solidly opposed of any cohort. The measure passed among voters ages thirty to forty-four and those sixty-five and over. South Dakota Initiative 11 would have banned abortions, except to protect the health and life of the mother and in cases of rape or incest in which the pregnancy was less than twenty weeks. All age groups opposed this more severe restriction, but once again opposition was strongest among those under thirty. In Michigan, a somewhat related ballot measure to allow stem cell research passed, with young voters providing the largest margin.

This scenario is made more plausible by the fact that the abortion attitudes of this cohort are not anchored securely in religious worldviews or other social attitudes. As noted earlier, Barack Obama's election to the presidency in November 2008 makes it less likely that the Supreme Court will overturn *Roe v. Wade*, but the current majority may allow further restrictions. The Millennials might then consider the possible loss of abortion rights, which would lead to greater support for abortion.

Scenario 2: A Juno Generation?

Because the values of the Millennials are shaped by more than simply the political debate on abortion, they may remain less pro-choice than older generations throughout their lives. A generation with somewhat higher pro-natal views and a tendency to place a higher value on fetal life may retain its distinctiveness over its life cycle. There is evidence that these values have influenced life decisions, because recent studies find that the abortion rate has declined primarily among the youngest cohorts.

On some of the questions in the GSS abortion battery, the Millennials may be distinctive because of life experiences that will always shape their attitudes. A generation that grew up with divorce and single mothers may well find that being single is an insufficient rationale to justify abortion. And a generation that grew up in a world in which mentally and physically challenged children attend school and benefit from special attention and technology may be less convinced that these are justifications for abortion. In one *Newsweek* survey in 2006, the youngest cohort was especially distinctive in rejecting the rationale that abortion should be allowed for cases in which the baby would be mentally handicapped. Attitudes toward other rationales for abortion may be more transitory. A generation that came of age during a record-setting economic expansion might find poverty to be a less-than-compelling rationale for abortion, but it might reassess that viewpoint in economic hard times.

If the Millennials remain distinctive, the next question is how large will the cohort be? The forces that have likely shaped the abortion attitudes of the youngest cohort have not changed, so that young people reaching adulthood late in this decade and into the next may also be more conservative on abortion. Over the next few years, the Millennials are replacing an older cohort that is only slightly more conservative on abortion, but within a decade they might be replacing the sixties generation, which has consistently been one of the most liberal. At that point, generational replacement would push aggregate opinion in a conservative direction.

This process could have a substantial impact on the politics of abortion. As Millennial Generation voters replace baby boomers, average support for abortion might decline to the point at which a majority favor limiting abortion to only the physically traumatic circumstances of danger to the health of the mother, rape, incest, or severe fetal defect. Some surveys have shown that the Millennial Generation remains supportive of abortion if the physical health of the woman is in danger, but is less supportive if her mental health is endangered. It is possible that the generation that comes after the Millennials will be even less pro-choice.

If the Millennials retain their distinctively low support for abortion throughout the life cycle and if their generation is large or the one after it is also conservative, then aggregate support for abortion will rapidly decline. This situation could change the dynamics of abortion attitudes in many states and lead to more limits on abortion rights.

NOTES

1. See www.gallup.com/poll/1576/Abortion.aspx.

2. "Informed consent" laws on abortion are like those for other medical procedures—they require that a doctor tell a patient about various considerations. But legislators in some states have written specific statements for doctors, some of which are incorrect.

3. Those who did not respond to more than two of the six questions were excluded from the analysis, but those who indicated that they were unsure of their position on one or two items received a score of 0.5 for these questions.

4. These questions on sexual activity probably evoke different images for the youngest and older cohorts. Because the Millennial Generation is less likely than older cohorts to be married, many will reference their parents when considering this question, but will consider questions on premarital sex and teen sex in terms of their own generation. By contrast, older Americans will consider extramarital sex questions in relation to their own generation, but premarital sex and teen sex will prompt them to think of their children.

5. *Juno* is only the most recent in a series of depictions of pregnant women who choose to have a baby.

REFERENCES

Abramowitz, Alan I. 1995. "It's Abortion, Stupid: Policy Voting in the 1992 Presidential Election." *Journal of Politics* 57: 176–186.

Cook, Elizabeth Adell, Ted G. Jelen, and Clyde Wilcox. 1992. *Between Two Absolutes: Public Opinion and the Politics of Abortion*. Boulder, Colo.: Westview Press.

Layman, Geoffrey C., and Thomas M. Carsey. 2002a. "Party Polarization and 'Conflict Extension' in the American Electorate." *American Journal of Political Science* 46: 786–802.

Luker, Kristin. 1984. *Abortion and the Politics of Motherhood*. Berkeley: University of California Press.

Maxwell, Carol J. C. 2002. *Pro-life Activists in America: Meaning, Motivation, and Direct Action*. New York: Cambridge University Press.

Shields, Jon A. 2007. "Between Passion and Deliberation: The Christian Right and Democratic Ideals." *Political Science Quarterly* 12: 89–113.

Staggenborg, Suzanne. 1991. *The Pro-choice Movement: Organization and Activism in the Abortion Conflict*. New York: Oxford University Press.

Tribe, Laurence H. 1992. *Abortion: The Clash of Absolutes*. New York: Norton.

Chapter 6

Congress

6-1

Congress, The Troubled Institution

Steven S. Smith

Political scientist Steven Smith outlines major trends in congressional politics—the polarization of Congress, the abuse of congressional procedures by the parties, the flow of power from Congress to the president, and the public's low esteem for Congress. Smith shows how these developments are interrelated and concludes that, while some reforms would improve Congress, addressing the underlying polarization will require a more basic change in American politics.

CONGRESS IS CURRENTLY A troubled institution. It usually is. At the moment, Congress appears handcuffed by deep partisan polarization, seems to thwart the will of the people when it fails to act on important problems, looks weak in comparison with the president and other executive officials, and is held in low esteem by most Americans. Presidents of both parties complain about its slowness, the media highlights "earmarks," "pork," and other characterizations of what some consider wasteful spending, and scandals involving members of Congress surface on a seemingly regular basis. Even legislators who retire from Congress carp about the institution to which they so frequently sought reelection.

It also is true that Congress is the most powerful national legislature in the world. It is formally independent of the chief executive, its jurisdiction is very

Source: This piece is an original essay commissioned for this volume.

broad, it sets its own agenda, and its members are elected independently of the executive. The executive and judicial branches cannot spend money without Congress's approval, the president needs the approval of the Senate to appoint senior executive officials and judges and to implement treaties, and Congress has wide-ranging powers to investigate the executive branch.

Nevertheless, in everyday politics Congress is at a severe disadvantage in its relationship with the president and the courts. Unlike the executive branch, Congress is not led by a single leader, like the president, who can deliberate in private and articulate a single policy for his branch. Instead, every member has an equal vote and the two houses must negotiate their differences on legislation. Unlike any federal court, Congress is large and unwieldy, it is bicameral, its deliberations are quite visible, and its floor proceedings are televised. Congress does not speak with one voice, cannot move quickly most of the time, and is quite permeable to outside influence.

Congress's political weaknesses have been exposed in recent years. Partisanship, deadlock on key issues, readiness to defer to the president in a crisis, and public despair with its performance have plagued Congress. This article outlines and evaluates these weaknesses.

A Polarized Congress

The partisan tone of legislators may be the most conspicuous feature of polarized congressional politics over the past twenty-five years. There is more to polarization than the derisive tone of the legislators' rhetoric. The deep and wide differences existing between the parties and are evident in legislators' floor voting behavior. Figure 1, shows the distribution of the members of the House and Senate on a liberal-to-conservative scale, based on a statistical analysis of all roll-call votes. The distribution covers two Congresses, the 92nd (1971–1972) and the 110th (2007–2008).

In the early 1970s, Democrats were far more liberal than Republicans on average and Republicans were more cohesive than the Democrats, but neither house was very polarized by party. In the House, the voting patterns of nearly half of the membership fell between the most liberal Republican and most conservative Democrat. In the Senate, this middle group comprised over a third of the Senate membership. These large blocs of legislators in the middle of the policy spectrum dictated outcomes.

The pattern has been different since the late 1980s. In the Senate of 2007–2008, only Democrat Ben Nelson of Nebraska and Republicans Arlen Specter of Pennsylvania and Susan Collins and Olympia Snowe of Maine occupy the middle space between the otherwise cohesive parties. By voting behavior, not just rhetoric, the parties are sharply polarized.

Figure 1. Liberal-Conservative Scores in Selected Congresses,
Democrats in Gray, Republicans in White

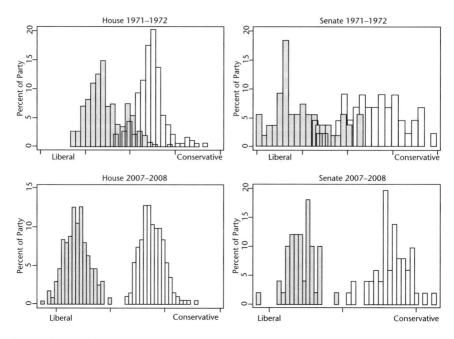

Source: http://voteview.com

The polarization of congressional parties and politics is the product of multiple forces in American politics. The social upheaval of the 1960s and early 1970s generated the civil rights movement, the feminist movement, the anti-Vietnam War movement, the youth culture, and other social and cultural developments, which in turn spawned a reaction that attracted the support of conservatives of both parties, particularly in rural America and the South. *Roe v. Wade,* the 1973 Supreme Court decision on abortion, seemed to catalyze Christian conservatives, formerly a dormant group in American politics, to mobilize for the Republicans. Republican candidates and strategists recognized an opportunity to join economic and social conservatives in a larger coalition that could upset the long-standing Democratic majorities, consisting of an uneasy alliance between northern liberals and white southern conservatives.

The realignment of political values and party preferences that started in the late 1960s began to alter the composition of Congress in the 1970s. In many places in the South, Republican legislators replaced conservative Democrats, thus making the congressional Democrats more uniformly liberal and reinforcing the conservative forces among congressional Republicans. In the Northeast, Midwest, and West Coast, many moderate Republicans lost to more liberal Democrats, which reinforced the liberal leanings among congressional Democrats and the conservative trend among Republicans. In the 1980s, the Republicans began to elect conservative leaders from the South, and the Democrats lost the mix of southern leaders who were important to the party in the mid-twentieth century.

As the composition of the party elites changed, the electorate began to sort itself so that political attitudes on economic and social issues were more strongly aligned with party preferences. In nearly every part of the country, the electorate supporting the Democrats became more liberal and the electorate supporting the Republicans became more conservative. As a result, political pressures from home became more uniform among the legislators of each party.

The successive elections of the 1970s, 1980s, and 1990s brought in legislators who were even more polarized by party. The strategies of party leaders, first among Republicans and then the Democrats, enhanced this polarization. In the late 1980s and early 1990s, Republicans in the House, led by Georgia's Newt Gingrich, sought disciplined voting within the party to force Democratic leaders to draw support from conservative Democrats to win floor votes. Conservative Democrats, in turn, had more difficulty gaining reelection in their conservative districts and states.

These developments were mutually reinforcing. As each party became more cohesive, its leadership became more assertive and placed more pressure on misfits within the party. As national party leaders, local party activists, and the electorate sorted themselves by party, primary election winners became more polarized and the electorate was more frequently given a choice on the extremes, between quite liberal Democrats and quite conservative Republicans. Only liberal legislators had a chance to be elected a leader among congressional Democrats; only conservative legislators had a chance to be elected a leader among congressional Republicans. As the parties became more polarized, their leaders became more partisan.

Contrary to popular belief, redrawing district lines to stack House districts with the partisans of one party does not explain this degree of polarization. The Senate, for which state lines are never changed, suffers from the same party polarization as the House, which is subject to redistricting. Instead, the sorting of the electorate and legislators into parties with distinctive political attitudes accounts for the durable pattern of the past two decades.

Legislative Pathologies in Congress

The consequences of partisan polarization in Congress are quite different in the two houses. Polarization in the House has yielded a streamlined, centralized process that can speed legislation to passage, but this process often excludes the minority party in ways that intensify minority frustration and partisan passions. In contrast, polarized parties and super-majority rule in the Senate cause delay and inaction, an outcome that encourages both parties to engage in a blame game out of frustration. Because both houses must approve legislation, Senate obstructionism can kill many bills.

Features of a Polarized House

The House majority party is able to control the floor agenda and pass legislation as long as it is reasonably cohesive. Cohesion is the product of several features of the modern House:

- The Speaker, as leader of the majority party, serves as the presiding officer and can freely recognize members to make motions on the floor, such as calling up bills for consideration.

- The Committee on Rules, which has been under the control of the Speaker since the early 1970s, can report resolutions that, if adopted by a House majority, can bring bills and conference reports to the floor and limit debate and amendments. A cohesive majority party can get these resolutions, called "special rules," adopted.

- The Speaker appoints conference committees and can structure their membership to suit his party's needs.

Polarized parties mean that a cohesive majority party can readily gain House approval of special rules, limit minority opportunities to offer proposals, pass legislation, and control conference committee negotiations with the Senate. These features of a polarized House speed legislative action.

Unfortunately for the House minority party, partisan polarization also tends to produce a process so dominated by majority party members that minority party members are often excluded from meaningful participation. Both Democratic and Republican majority parties have moved decisions on the most important policies from standing committees, where the minority is represented proportionately in most cases, to the leadership and informal work groups of the majority party, where the minority is not represented at all. Both Democratic and Republican majority parties have so restricted floor amendments on major bills that the minority party often does not have a meaningful opportunity to propose alternatives and attract some support from majority party members for them.

Features of a Polarized Senate

1. The majority party's leader, the Majority Leader, does not preside and instead attempts to influence the Senate by making motions from the floor.

2. Most motions can be filibustered—that is, subjected to unending debate—and so the minority can attempt to obstruct action on bills it dislikes.

3. To overcome a filibuster or threatened filibuster of most bills, a three-fifths majority of all elected senators (60 when 99 or all 100 seats are filled) is required to invoke cloture (close debate) and get a vote to pass a bill.

4. The ability of the minority to filibuster proposals to change these rules means that the majority party cannot put in place rules similar to those that so advantage a House majority party. A two-thirds majority of senators voting (67 when 100 senators are voting) is required to invoke cloture on legislation that changes the rules.

Polarized parties mean that a sizable minority party—one with 41 or more members—can block majority party legislation on the floor. This feature of a polarized Senate can delay or even kill legislation.

For the Senate majority party, partisan polarization tends to produce public expectations that the majority party can pass its legislation but gives the minority party the parliamentary tools to prevent that from happening. And the minority party has been exploiting those parliamentary tools with greater frequency. Figure 2 shows the number of filibusters and cloture votes in Congresses since the mid-twentieth century. Counting filibusters is not easy (distinguishing between talk and obstructionism is often difficult and even threatened filibusters can be effective in killing a bill), but the count reflects real experience. Plainly, the record of increased filibustering since the late 1980s is very different than the previous decades.

Partisan polarization contributes to filibustering in powerful ways. A minority party leader finds it much easier to employ obstructionist tactics when no one from his party objects. Moreover, obstructionism is more likely to succeed in blocking majority party legislation, forcing compromise, or killing legislation, when the minority party is united and can prevent cloture. In response, the majority party leader attempts cloture more frequently, often several times on the same bill. The majority party members complain about minority obstructionism and minority party members complain that the majority is too quick to attempt to shut off debate and minority amendments.

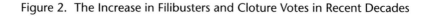

Figure 2. The Increase in Filibusters and Cloture Votes in Recent Decades

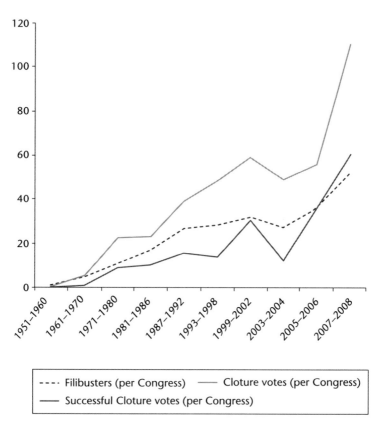

Source: Barbara Sinclair, "The New World of U.S. Senators," in Lawrence C. Dodd and Bruce I. Oppenheimer, eds., *Congress Reconsidered*, 9th ed. (Washington, D.C.: CQ Press, 2009), p. 7.

Do filibusters matter? In the polarized Congress of the last two decades, fili-busters have made the Senate the primary burial ground of legislation. Political scientist Barbara Sinclair has demonstrated that in Congresses since the early 1990s 33 of 80 major bills that died at some stage had passed the House but died in the Senate; only 3 died in the House after passing the Senate (others passed neither house or were vetoed). In contrast, in the 1970s and 1980s, only 12 of 42 major bills that died at some stage had passed the House but died in the Senate; 8 died in the House after passing the Senate.

The problems associated with the filibuster continue to intensify. In March 2009 Senate Republicans—all 41 of them—signed a letter to President Barack Obama to encourage the president to renominate President Bush's nominees for the federal courts. They warned, "Regretfully, if we are not consulted on, and approve of, a nominee from our states, the Republican Conference will be unable to support moving forward on that nominee. And we will act to preserve this principle and the rights of our colleagues if it is not." That is, before President Obama offered a single nomination to the federal courts, the Republican minority demanded that the president defer to them under threat of blocking his nominees by filibuster.

In the polarized Congress, conference committees have fallen into disuse. Because conference committees approve compromise legislation with the majority support of conferees from each house, the like-minded majority party conferees do not need the support of minority party members and can largely ignore them. As a result, majority party members consult with each other without any minority legislators or staff present and appear to announce outcomes. In recent Congresses, the majority party went so far as to circumvent conference committees altogether by having majority party and committee leaders of the two houses negotiate compromises without appointing conference committees and then having the agreements incorporated as amendments between the houses. Even the formality of minority party participation is avoided.

These patterns have intensified and even personalized partisan conflict. Legislators who value a meaningful voice in policymaking are either frustrated at being excluded (the House minority party) or for having a majority that is less than the super majority required to pass legislation (the Senate majority party). Tolerance of the other party has become very thin. Distrust of the other side is so widespread that opportunities for real cross-party deliberation are ignored.

Largely because of the unique features of the Senate, and often with the contribution of divided party control of the House, Senate, and presidency, polarized parties create a strong bias against passing legislation. As Sinclair shows, more major legislation has been killed after the parties became so polarized in the late 1980s than in the previous two decades. A polarized Senate gets hung up on filibusters, while a House, Senate, and presidency controlled by different and polarized parties cannot agree on legislation.

A Weakened Congress

Over the past decade the power of Congress has been challenged on several fronts. A series of crises—terrorism, the war in Iraq, and the economic crisis has led the president to seek and receive broad powers with almost no detailed direction from Congress in the legislation. The president also has asserted broad powers without any congressional participation by acting through executive orders or other means. President George W. Bush and his top advisers claimed a general theory of presidential power known as the theory of the unitary executive that the president can control the actions of all executive branch agencies, even when the law gives authority directly to department and agency officials.

To follow is a brief description of the major ways in which Congress has yielded power to the president in recent years. Congress, under the basic constitutional framework, must delegate some power to the executive branch to implement policies Congress deems desirable. Unless the president has constitutional power of his own, Congress can detail how the delegated power is to be used. If Congress fails to provide the detail, or at least to limit the delegation to a short period or to carefully control spending for the purpose, the president is granted power that Congress could reserve for itself.

Incentives to delegate broad power to the president are greatest in emergencies. In an emergency a president can argue that the national interest requires that the chief executive quickly be given authority act with the flexibility required to meet unknown contingencies. Legislators can hope that Congress's control over spending and oversight activities will keep the executive in check, but, in practice, the president's advantage in public relations, control over information, and partisan considerations may limit Congress's ability to check the use of power once it is delegated to the president. In a Congress highly polarized by party, the tendency to grant unfettered power to the executive is exceptionally great when the same party controls both houses of Congress and the White House.

During the six years from 2001 to 2006 of Republican majorities in Congress and a Republican president, the fight against terrorism and the wars in Iraq and Afghanistan led Congress to grant sweeping powers to President George W. Bush. By historical standards, Congress held very few hearings on the broad sweep of issues during the period—prewar intelligence, the conduct of the war in Iraq, the National Security Agency's surveillance program, the treatment of detainees, and reform of the intelligence apparatus. The use of federal dollars and the constitutionality of executive actions were frequently questioned by legislators and the media but seldom in congressional hearings or investigations. Once the Department of Homeland Security was created in 2003 out of 22 agencies, Congress did not seriously scrutinize the functioning of the new department until one of its units, the Federal Emergency Management Agency, mismanaged the response to Hurricane Katrina in 2005. In the intensely partisan atmosphere of Washington, serious oversight of a Republican administration by a Republican Congress would only give the Democratic opposition opportunities to score points. Partisan convenience, rather than a commitment to check the use of power, seemed to drive the congressional oversight agenda.

In the meantime, President Bush took existing trends in presidential assertions of unilateral power to a greater extreme. The administration broadened its interpretation of executive privilege to deny information to Congress. President Bush used executive orders more broadly to direct executive agencies, sometimes in contravention of statutes. President Bush used signing statements liberally when signing legislation into law to assert that he would not implement features of the law that he considered unconstitutional infringements on his power.

More generally, President Bush and key figures in his administration subscribed to the theory of a unitary executive. The theory holds that the president has line authority over all parts of the executive branch. Bush administration officials used the logic of the argument to justify presidential signing statements and other intrusions into statutory governance of executive agencies. To be sure, there is a compelling argument that the commander-in-chief role assigned to the president by the Constitution gives the president strong authority over the use of the armed forces. But, it is reasonable to argue and even seems historically accurate to say, Congress is free to direct or constrain other executive agencies by law.

Democrats, once again in the majority after the 2006 mid-term elections, objected to Bush's view of his powers but were unable to do much about it before the end of Bush's second term. The Democrats stepped up oversight activities, forced dozens of administration officials to testify, and attempted to impose a timetable for withdrawal from Iraq, but the president proved to have a strategic advantage in most of the confrontations with Congress. Once his policy was in place, he could rely on Senate Republicans to obstruct votes on unfriendly legislation and, if need be, veto legislation to block it. And President Bush could delay or assert executive privilege when hostile congressional committees attempted to investigate executive actions—and the approaching end of his second term meant that he did not have to delay for long. President Obama, of course, dealing with a friendly Congress, ordered executive agencies to ignore President Bush's signing statements unless they first consulted the Department of Justice.

National emergencies can motivate even an opposition Congress to grant sweeping authority to a president, as the Democrats did in 2008 in response to the economic crisis. With Wall Street investment banks about to the collapse in late 2008, the Bush administration requested and received a $700 billion authorization for the Troubled Asset Relief Program (TARP) to "restore liquidity and stability to the financial system," primarily by purchasing soured assets, mainly mortgage-backed securities, and thus stabilizing the banking system. The fear, widely shared by economists and administration officials, was that the national economy would suffer badly if major financial institutions failed. While some conservative Republicans opposed the bill, most Republicans and nearly all Democrats supported the legislation. To the surprise of many members of Congress, the administration used most of the first half of the TARP funds to buy ownership stakes in banks and insurance companies to shore up their balance sheets. The second half, which Congress could have denied by passing a resolution of disapproval, was not fully dedicated at the time of this writing.

Many members of Congress were nervous about a broad delegation of power to the Treasury and so imposed multiple mechanisms overlapping oversight and reporting responsibilities. A Congressional Oversight Panel, soon chaired by a Harvard professor, was created to review the work of Treasury and report to Congress every thirty days. The comptroller general of the General Accountability Office, an arm of Congress, was required to monitor the program and report every sixty days. Treasury itself was required to file reports with Congress, a special inspector general was created, and a board comprised of executive officials was established to oversee implementation of the bill and report to Congress quarterly.

The oversight was likely to be taken seriously, but the delegation of power nevertheless represented one of the vaguest delegations of power for the authorization of such a large sum of money. Moreover, the administration moved so quickly in dedicating the funds that congressional oversight would long post-date irreversible executive action. Later reports indicated that the executive branch had a difficult time accounting for the way the banks used federal funds.

The Unpopular Congress

The popularity of Congress ebbs and flows with the public's confidence in government. When the president's ratings and trust in government improved after the tragic events of September 11, 2001, Congress's approval ratings improved, too (Figure 3). Nevertheless, Congress's performance ratings are almost always below those of the president and the Supreme Court—when President George W. Bush earned approval ratings in the 20s, Congress managed to fall into the teens.

The legislative process is easy to dislike—it often generates political posturing and grandstanding, it necessarily involves bargaining, and it often leaves broken promises in its trail. Members of Congress often appear self-serving as they pursue their political careers and represent interests and reflect values

Figure 3. Percent Approving Congressional Performance, 1993-2008

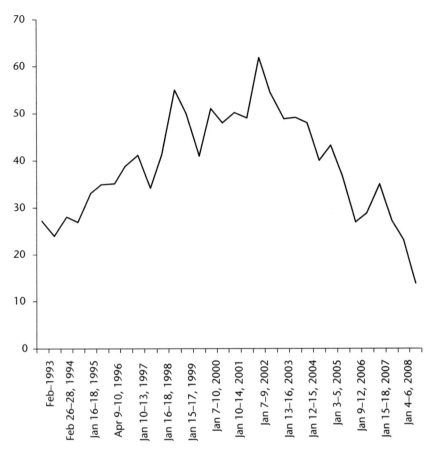

Source: Gallup Poll.

that are controversial. And many Americans find the intense partisanship that Congress has exhibited in the last two decades to be quite distasteful . The public relations efforts of the congressional parties probably make matters worse by emphasizing partisan and derisive messages. In contrast, the Supreme Court is cloaked in ritual and is seldom seen or heard by the general public. The president is represented by a single, large, and professional public relations machine.

Some of Congress's low standing is the fault of a few of its members. Scandals, even when they involve a single member, add to the public's frustration with Congress and have contributed to the institution's poor ratings in opinion polls. In fact, Congress seems to be a never-ending source of comic relief, like the joke about the legislator who kept referring to the presiding officer as "Your Honor."

HIGHLIGHTS OF RECENT CONGRESSIONAL ETHICS SCANDALS

- 1989: House Speaker James Wright (D-Texas) resigned after Republicans charged him with ethics violations for receiving extraordinarily large royalties on a book.
- 1989: Questions about the propriety of campaign contributions were raised in the "Keating Five" affair, which concerned the relationship between five senators and a prominent savings-and-loan owner seeking to block an investigation of his financial dealings.
- 1991: Sen. David Durenburger (R-Minn.) was condemned in a unanimously approved Senate resolution for signing a book deal and for seeking reimbursement for expenses for staying in a condo that he owned.
- 1992: The disclosure that many House members had repeatedly overdrawn their accounts at the House disbursement office led people to believe that members enjoyed special privileges.
- 1995: A long investigation of sexual harassment charges against Senator Robert Packwood (R-Oregon) led to his forced resignation from office.
- 1995: Rep. Dan Rostenkowski (D-Ill.), former chairman of the House Ways and Means Committee, was found guilty of illegally receiving cash for personal use from the House post office. He later served a prison term.
- 1995: Rep. Enid Waldholtze (R-Utah) retired after her husband was charged with felonies in conjunction with raising funds for her campaign.
- 1997: Speaker Newt Gingrich (R-Georgia) agreed to pay $300,000 in fines based on charges that he used nonprofit organizations for political purposes and misled the House Committee on Standards of Official Conduct.
- 1998: Rep. Jay Kim (R-Cal.) pleaded guilty to charges involving over $250,000 in illegal campaign contributions.
- 2002: Rep. James A. Traficant Jr. (D-Ohio) was convicted of receiving bribes in exchange for helping businesses get government contracts and of engaging in a pattern of racketeering since taking office in 1985.
- 2004: House Majority Leader Tom Delay (R-Texas) was issued letters of admonition by the House ethics committee for improperly promising to endorse the son of Rep. Nick Smith (R-Mich.) in exchange for Smith's vote on a bill and for attending a fundraising event with lobbyists for a company that was lobbying him on pending legislation.

Box continued

- 2005: Rep. Duke Cunningham (R-Calif.) resigned and pleaded guilty to taking more than $2.4 million in bribes and related tax evasion and fraud, the largest financial sum involving an individual member.
- 2006: Rep. Tom Delay (R-Texas) resigned after being indicted in Texas for laundering money through a national party committee in his effort to redistrict Texas congressional districts.
- 2006: Rep. William Jefferson (D-La.) won reelection to the House but was denied a Ways and Means committee assignment after FBI agents video-taped him appearing to solicit a bribe and later found $90,000 of the marked cash in his freezer—making this "the cold cash scandal." Jefferson was defeated for reelection in 2008. The prosecution continues at this writing.
- 2006: Rep. Mark Foley (R-Fla.) resigned after it was disclosed that he sent sexually explicit e-mail messages to underage House pages.
- 2006: Rep. Bob Ney (R-Ohio) pleaded guilty to making false statements and conspiracy in relation to receiving thousands of dollars in gifts from lobbyist Jack Abramoff. A Ney aide also pleaded guilty for receiving gifts. Separately, Abramoff pleaded guilty to charges of conspiracy, fraud, and tax evasion.
- 2008: Sen. Ted Stevens (R-Alaska) was convicted of seven counts of failing to disclose gifts related to the renovation of his Alaska home on his Senate financial disclosure forms. At this writing, Stevens is pursuing additional legal avenues, but he was defeated for reelection in November 2008. His conviction was set aside in 2009 because of prosecutorial improprieties.
- 2008: Rep. Tim Mahoney (D-Fla) confessed that he had had an extra-marital affair with a staff member. Shortly after news reports indicated that Mahoney attempted to buy the staff member's silence, his wife filed for divorce and he was defeated for reelection.

There is no doubt that a large majority of today's members behave ethically. There is also no doubt that the ethical standards applied by the public, the media, and Congress itself are higher today than at any other time. Yet, there is no denying that the seemingly regular flow of scandals harms Congress's standing with the American people.

Incumbents and candidates for Congress contribute to the generally low esteem of their colleagues in another way. Many of them, maybe most, complain about the institution to which they work so hard to get and stay elected. Denigrating the institution is an old technique in American campaigns that has become even more conspicuous in recent decades. Indeed, many recent arrivals on Capitol Hill promised to end "business as usual" in Washington and to push through reforms to "fix" Congress—to end partisanship, reform the system of congressional perks and earmarks, to stop the influence of special interests, and so on. Yet while Congress languishes with mediocre approval ratings, individual members of Congress continue to do quite well. Typically, Gallup polls find that about 70 percent of the public approves of the way its own member of Congress handles the job. Most incumbents, typically more than 90 percent, successfully gain reelection when they seek it. Running *for* Congress by running *against* Congress seems to work quite well.

Congressional campaigns have become personal and often very ugly. In the polarized environment of the recent past, candidates win their parties' primaries to get on the general election ballot by demonstrating their commitment to party principles. In the general election campaign, the candidates demonize their opponents. The winning candidates emerging from these campaigns have acquired a partisan style that they carry with them into Congress, reinforcing the partisan polarization.

Directions for Reform

Partisanship, mean and ugly campaigns, congressional gridlock, and the low esteem of Congress feed on each other. They have produced a dysfunctional Congress that alienates the public, discourages qualified people from running for seats in the House and Senate, and far too often fails to act on serious problems. Presidents fill the voids created by a handcuffed Congress when they can, weakening congressional participation in important policy arenas and undermining the representational basis for policymaking.

What can be done? First, it is important to keep in mind that the partisan polarization that is behind much of Congress's problems is not readily remedied by Congress. We have a right to expect more civil and tolerant behavior by legislators and their leaders, but we cannot expect legislators to move far from the policy positions that got them elected. Thus, in the short run, the burden is on American voters to elect more moderate candidates who, as legislators, will demand less partisan behavior from their leaders and insist on the compromises necessary to address the policy challenges facing the country. I am not hopeful.

Nevertheless, legislators should take steps to improve their institution. In both houses, policymaking and interpersonal relations would be improved with fewer three- and four-day work weeks and more five-day work weeks, which would create less conflict between floor and committee sessions and perhaps keep legislators in Washington for more weekends. It's not easy for legislators to keep their partisanship in check when they spend little time with each other except to rush from place to place and cast votes. Moreover, we cannot expect Congress to engage in creative legislative activity and meaningful oversight on the part-time schedule that Congress has maintained in recent decades. Unfortunately, legislators are not likely to happily give up time in their districts and states to make this possible.

In the House, the majority party must work much harder to protect the minority party's ability to participate in policymaking in a meaningful way. The standing committees should be used whenever possible as forums for the exchange of ideas. Other rulemaking reforms include observing layover rules guaranteeing the passage of time before action is taken and preserving amendment opportunities in committees and on the floor. The majority party cannot be expected to tolerate a minority that repeatedly fails to propose serious amendments and uses nearly all of its opportunities to participate to score political points. So again, legislators would have to set aside their real differences to reduce partisanship and find a way to compromise across a wide partisan divide. In the present polarized atmosphere, this is perhaps not too realistic.

In the Senate, no reform could be more important than filibuster reform. The practice is long-standing, but is justified by neither the Constitution nor early Senate rules. It developed quite accidentally when the Senate failed to include the motion of the previous question, used in the House to limit debate, in a codification of its rules. The practice of filibustering has come to be a regular means of obstructionism for the minority, effectively raising the threshold for passing legislation from 51 to 60 for nearly all legislation of more than modest importance. The Senate minority party is not likely to endorse filibuster reform anytime soon.

6-2

The Transition to Democratic Leadership in a Polarized House

Kathryn Pearson and Eric Schickler

Political scientists Kathryn Pearson and Eric Schickler observe that the polariza-tion of parties in the House of Representatives has yielded a decision-making process that often excludes the minority party from meaningful participation. This process, they argue, has survived changes in party control, is becoming insti-tutionalized, and will likely survive for years to come in the House.

ON THE OPENING DAY of the 110th Congress in January 2007, newly elected Speaker of the House Nancy Pelosi, D-Calif., announced, "I accept this gavel in the spirit of partnership, not partisanship, and look forward to working with you, Mr. Boehner, and the Republicans in the Congress for the good of the American people."[1] At the close of the 110th Congress, however, it was clear that the change in majority party control had not reduced the high level of partisan conflict that has characterized recent Congresses. After gaining the majority in the 2006 elec-tions, Democratic leaders attempted to pass a largely partisan legislative agenda over the opposition of President George W. Bush, and in doing so they were will-ing to exclude the minority party from the legislative process when necessary.

Many congressional observers bemoan the current state of Congress. High on their list of complaints is its intense partisanship; the House is sharply divided into competing camps that appear unwilling to work with one another. Debate on major issues is typically full of partisan acrimony, and majority party leaders often use heavy-handed tactics to shut out the minority. Democrats complained bitterly about similar behavior by Republican leaders when the GOP controlled Congress from 1995 to 2006. When Republicans enjoyed unified control of the national government, they often cut House Democrats out of the bargaining process. Democrats charged that this produced policies out of step with a nation essentially divided evenly between the parties; Republicans, however, believed it imperative to adopt an ambitious program to persuade voters to grant them a longer hold on power.

Source: Kathryn Pearson and Eric Schickler, "The Transition to Democratic Leadership in a Polarized House," in *Congress Reconsidered*, 9th ed., ed. Lawrence C. Dodd and Bruce I. Oppenheimer (Washington, D.C.: CQ Press, 2009), 165–168, 170–187. Some notes appearing in the original have been deleted.

Unified Republican control of the government ended after the 109th Congress. After twelve years in the minority, Democrats picked up thirty House seats and six Senate seats in the 2006 elections to gain control of both chambers. National tides clearly favored Democratic candidates; no Democratic incumbent lost, and nineteen new Democrats won in House districts that had voted for President Bush in 2004.

The Democratic election victory promoted Pelosi, the minority leader in the preceding Congress, to prominence as the first female Speaker of the House and the first Democratic Speaker since 1994. Presiding over a relatively cohesive caucus appreciative of its newfound majority status, Pelosi wields considerable power. She also faced significant challenges in the 110th Congress, some unique to her speakership and others shared by her predecessors. When Democrats took over in January 2007, the United States was nearly four years into an increasingly unpopular war in Iraq. In the context of divided government, the Democratic leaders in the House of Representatives and the Senate were responsible for the Democratic majority's legislative response to the war. And the public wanted change: Republicans' loss of control of Congress occurred in large part because of public dissatisfaction with President Bush's handling of Iraq.[2] The Democrats' margin was narrow, and Pelosi needed to balance competing demands: pursuing change to satisfy the liberal Democratic base in Congress and in the electorate, while at the same time ensuring the reelection of her more moderate members, including several new and vulnerable members from swing districts. This task was complicated by most Republicans' calculation that sticking with the president on the war was still their best strategy.

In this essay we assess party leadership in the House of Representatives. After providing an overview of the Democratic leadership and its challenges and strategies in the 110th Congress, we consider its continuities with past Republican- and Democratic-controlled Congresses. We also discuss the Republicans' response to Democratic majority control. We conclude by discussing the highly partisan order that is becoming institutionalized in the House.

The Return to Democratic Majority Control

House Democratic leaders promoted their "first one hundred hours agenda" during the 2006 campaign, providing a blueprint of their legislative plans. Unlike the Republicans' 1994 legislative campaign manifesto, the "Contract with America," the hundred-hours agenda was an informal list of legislative ideas that evolved throughout the campaign. Pelosi began to refer to the plan in July and promoted it during the campaign season, although it never really resonated with voters.[3] Both the Contract with America and the hundred-hours agenda were products of the leadership, but the majority of House GOP candidates in 1994 actually signed the Contract with America, whereas individual House candidates did not formally sign onto the hundred-hours agenda.

When they gained majority control, Democratic leaders rushed to pass the hundred-hours agenda's six items, which included legislation to tax the oil industry, enact the 9/11 Commission's recommendations, raise the federal minimum wage, provide discounts for Medicare prescription drugs, cut student loan costs, and expand embryonic stem cell research. All of the legislation passed with overwhelming support among Democrats and some support from Republicans as well, allowing Democratic leaders to claim an early victory—even if it was short-lived.

Although the vote margins reflected Democratic consensus on the legislative items, the leadership drove both the agenda and the process. The six bills came to the House floor under closed rules and without any committee action. This strategy allowed Democratic leaders to pass them quickly (with several hours to spare, even) and tout their accountability and fulfillment of campaign promises. The hundred-hours agenda also sent a strong signal about party leaders' agenda-setting power and their willingness to shut both the minority and committee chairs out of important policy decisions. Party leaders determined the agenda and bypassed the "normal" legislative process. By bringing the legislation to the floor without giving committees the opportunity to hold hearings or markups on any of the six items, party leaders all but excluded committee chairmen from the process. Minority members protested vehemently that the bills came to the House floor under closed rules that did not allow any amendments. The scene reflected a rapid role reversal, as the formerly ascendant Republicans went from defending closed rules to attacking majority tyranny, and the newly empowered Democrats abandoned their calls for minority rights in favor of the need to act with dispatch.

In addition to passing the party's legislative priorities, party leaders moved quickly on reform measures. Democratic rules changes included two designed to promote fiscal discipline and accountability: earmark reform and pay-as-you-go budgeting. The earmark reform added transparency to the process by requiring that conference reports include a list of earmarks and their sponsors. The pay-as-you-go budget rule stipulated that any new spending measure or tax cut be offset by equal spending cuts. Both reforms proved only moderately effective and were difficult to carry out in that they created several openings for Republicans to use procedural stratagems to stall Democratic proposals.

Only some of the Democratic agenda items that passed the House became law, given the combination of presidential opposition and a closely divided Senate. . . . The House initially passed a bill to promote energy efficiency during the first hundred hours; it pushed through a second, more expansive bill in August 2007. The

Senate watered the measure down, but the final version nonetheless contained many items on the Democrats' agenda to promote fuel economy and energy efficiency. This victory was overshadowed, however, by partisan conflict over oil drilling at the close of the 2008 session. The minimum wage increase, also passed during the first hundred hours, was enacted after it was attached as an amendment to a supplemental appropriations bill. Democrats could also declare victory on a farm bill enacted over the president's veto. Ethics reform, another Democratic priority, was stalled by partisan conflict for much of the 110th Congress. But in March 2008, with prodding from Speaker Pelosi and with support from thirty-three Republicans, the Democrats' efforts culminated in narrow passage of legislation to create an outside Office of Congressional Ethics.

On other domestic policy priorities, such as children's health insurance (SCHIP) and stem cell research, the Democrats achieved only symbolic victories, as the measures passed the House but were not ultimately enacted into law because of presidential vetoes. . . .

Institutional Reforms and Powerful Speakers

The Speaker's power has grown over the last several decades. Pelosi has benefited in particular from the expansion of the Speaker's power that occurred during the Gingrich and Hastert years. When Pelosi was first elected to the House of Representatives in 1987, she witnessed Speaker Jim Wright presiding over the 100th Congress (1987–1988)—a Congress characterized by heated conflict between Democratic Party leaders and President Ronald Reagan over policy. Speaker Wright used his prerogatives more aggressively than his predecessors had, but the institutional and political roots supporting leaders' potential use of party discipline had been planted in the preceding decades.

In the late 1960s and early 1970s, political changes and institutional reforms began to shift the focus of power in the House from committee chairmen to party leaders. An influx of Republicans in the South led to a decrease in the proportion of conservatives in the Democratic Caucus and an increase in its ideological homogeneity.[4] Reforms from 1969 to 1975 endowed party leaders with tools not possessed by a leader since Speaker Joe Cannon, R-Ill., in 1910. Following Cannon's downfall, the Democrats' Ways and Means Committee delegation had doubled as the Committee on Committees, determining members' committee assignments and committee transfers. In 1974 Democrats created the leadership-controlled Steering and Policy Committee and gave it the power to make committee assignments. The Speaker controlled the staff for the Steering and Policy Committee, further enhancing his power. In January 1973 Democratic rules were reformed to require an automatic secret ballot on committee chairs at the start of each Congress.

The reforms gave the Speaker increased control over the legislative agenda. In December 1974 the Speaker alone was granted the authority to select the chairman and Democratic members of the House Rules Committee, making the committee an arm of the leadership. In addition, the Speaker was given the power to refer legislation to more than one committee, to set time limits on committee consideration, and to expedite consideration of legislation in committee and on the House Floor. Wright pushed these prerogatives to the limit during his stormy tenure as Speaker (1987–1988), but his successor, Tom Foley, D-Wash., proved more reluctant to exert power. Foley's tenure was characterized by legislative failures in the domestic policy arena and disunity among the Democratic Caucus, particularly during the two years of unified Democratic control of government (1993–1994). The 1994 election debacle owed at least in part to Democrats' failure to act effectively as a team during Clinton's first two years in office.

Republicans gained fifty-two seats in the 1994 elections, giving them a majority in the House of Representatives for the first time in forty years. During their subsequent twelve years in the majority, Republicans centralized power in the hands of party leaders to an even greater extent than had their Democratic predecessors. Perhaps most important, Speaker Newt Gingrich, R-Ga., seized a more active role in determining committee assignments and in selecting committee chairs. In the past, committee chairmanships had been largely governed by the seniority system, in which the majority party member with the longest tenure on a committee would be its chair, subject to a vote of the Democratic Caucus. This system had limited the Democrats' ability to control committee politics, which often were dominated by cooperative relationships between senior members of both parties. But Gingrich bypassed the seniority system in appointing more junior, conservative loyalists to chair three key committees, including the Appropriations Committee, which handles the spending bills that Congress considers. The appointments made clear that this would be an activist, assertive leadership. When committees drafted legislation that did not satisfy party leaders, Gingrich circumvented them by appointing special party task forces to shape legislation for the floor. The Republicans adopted new rules setting a six-year term limit for committee and subcommittee chairs, further eroding committee leaders' power.

When Dennis Hastert, R-Ill., replaced Gingrich as Speaker following the 1998 elections, many observers expected a shift to "regular order" and a degree of comity. Although Hastert largely remained out of the public spotlight, many of the centralizing moves that Gingrich—along with his Democratic predecessors, particularly Jim Wright—had made were extended under his leadership. Despite their narrow majorities from 1995 to 2006, Republican leaders relied on their own members' votes to pass their legislative program instead of trying to attract support from centrist Democrats. Indeed, Speaker Hastert made it clear that he was not interested in passing legislation that required Democrats' support when he announced that nothing would come to the House floor for a vote unless a majority of Republicans approved of it—a practice that has since been dubbed the "Hastert rule." Democrats seeking to cooperate with Republicans in the policy-making process were rebuffed.

To the surprise of some rank-and-file Democrats, Democratic leaders kept in place many of the Republicans' centralizing reforms. Most significantly, they retained the six-year term limits for committee chairs. Although it is possible—indeed likely, according to an aide to Speaker Pelosi[5]—that Democrats will undo this rule before the clock runs out, the decision to retain it at all indicates that the balance of power has shifted toward party leaders and away from committee chairmen, compared to the last time Democrats were in control. The Democrats also kept in place the Republican restriction that a member may only chair one committee or subcommittee, although they made three exceptions for representatives David Obey, D-Wis., Zoe Lofgren, D-Calif., and Ed Markey, D-Mass.[6]

The Democrats made some substantive and symbolic committee changes in line with their core constituencies and political goals. Their oversight goals were manifest in the creation of four new subcommittees for oversight, and what had been the House Government Reform Committee in the 109th Congress became the House Oversight and Government Reform Committee in the 110th Congress. And "Labor," "Natural," and "Wildlife" were all reincorporated into the committee names from which the Republicans had deleted them.

On the other hand, the seniority system—which had eroded under Republican control—remains largely intact. In the 110th Congress, all standing committees were chaired by their most senior Democrat. When the Steering Committee's recommendations came before the Democratic Caucus, Michael Michaud, D-Maine, challenged Bob Filner, D-Calif., for chair of the Veterans Affairs Committee, but he was defeated by a two-to-one margin.[7] The Speaker has sole discretion in appointing the chair of the House Permanent Select Committee on Intelligence. Pelosi bypassed the most senior Democrat on the committee, Jane Harman, Calif., and the second-most-senior, Alcee Hastings, Fla. Instead of deferring to Harman's seniority, Pelosi appointed the less experienced—but more partisan—Silvestre Reyes, D-Texas, a move that angered some Harman supporters, particularly Blue Dog Democrats.[8]

When Republicans took control of Congress in 1995 after forty years in the minority, none of the new committee chairs had ever headed a committee before. In 2007, by contrast, four committee chairs had been chairs during the 103rd Congress (two of the same committees, two of other committees), and they likely assumed they would pick up where they had left off twelve years ago. Another ten new committee chairs had chaired subcommittees the last time Democrats controlled Congress.[9] Despite this institutional memory, Speaker Pelosi made it clear that she, not the committee chairs, control the legislative agenda.

Indeed, although Pelosi has been careful to include committee chairs in policy discussions, she has asserted her authority to a greater extent than past Democratic Speakers. Two experienced committee chairmen posed potential challenges to her leadership. Energy and Commerce Committee chair John Dingell, D-Mich., threatened to be a major barrier to Democrats' plans to forward legislation to combat global warming. The longest-serving House member and an experienced committee chair, Dingell was more concerned about the auto industry in his Michigan district than the Democrats' environmental agenda. Pelosi responded by creating a new Select Committee on Energy Independence and Global Warming. Dingell responded: "These kind of committees are as useful and relevant as feathers on a fish."[10] Pelosi gave in to Dingell's demand to put in writing that the new task force would not infringe on his power to write legislation. However, when Dingell brought his legislation to the Democratic Caucus, Pelosi wielded control over the agenda, declaring that Dingell's bill was harmful to the environment—and thus the Democrats' agenda—and that it would not be considered.[11] A second potential trouble spot came from liberal Judiciary Committee chair John Conyers, who in the past had expressed support for impeaching President Bush. Before Congress convened, Pelosi instructed Conyers that the committee should not pursue impeachment, and Conyers complied.

The House Committee on Rules has been considered an arm of the leadership since the reforms of the 1970s, but leadership control has tightened considerably in recent Congresses. The extent to which the leadership controls the committee, at the expense of rank-and-file influence, was starkly obvious during the committee assignment process for the 110th Congress. Pelosi had a difficult time filling the five open seats on the committee, which had typically been considered a plum assignment. Democrats' experiences on the committee had been difficult under GOP control. According to a top Pelosi aide, no one requested the vacant seats.[12] To fill the nine majority slots, Pelosi added four first-term Democrats (doubling the total number of newcomers assigned there in the past twenty-five years) and, most significantly, allowed members of the committee to serve also on another committee. With the increase in leadership-dictated closed rules, which bar any amendments, Rules Committee members have less influence in the legislative process. Dropping the committee's "exclusive" designation indicates that leadership control over the Rules Committee is so strong that membership is no longer considered particularly valuable.

Majority Leadership Team

The Democratic leadership team partly reflected the demographic and ideological diversity of the caucus membership. For several decades political scientists argued that party leaders were "middle men" whose policy views situated them somewhere in the center of their party.[13] In most Congresses over the past two decades, however, party leaders have tended to come from the parties' more ideological wings. They have also demonstrated a strong commitment to building electoral majorities by fund raising. With the exception of Speaker Tom Foley, who led House Democrats from 1989 to 1994, the last several Speakers have aggressively pursued a partisan agenda at the expense of minority participation and have been viewed almost entirely as party leaders rather than leaders of the House as a whole.

Pelosi epitomizes these recent trends: She is a liberal Democrat, an extraordinary fund-raiser, and is pursuing a partisan agenda. She was first elected to the House in a special election in 1987. Although it was her first bid for office, Pelosi had partisan and political roots. Her father, Thomas D'Alessandro, served in the House from 1939 to 1947 and was mayor of Baltimore for twelve years after that. Pelosi chaired the California Democratic Party from 1981 to 1983, chaired the national party's Compliance Review Commission on delegate rules in 1984, and was the Democratic Senatorial Campaign Committee's finance chairman from 1985 to 1987. Pelosi's district, California's eighth, encompasses three-quarters of San Francisco and is among the most Democratic districts in the country, delivering 85 percent of its votes to John Kerry in 2004. Pelosi's liberal constituents reelect her by big margins every cycle: in 2006 she received 80 percent of the vote. From the start Pelosi has been an active legislator on behalf of her district. She has championed human rights in China; increased funding to research, prevent, and treat AIDS; and the establishment of a private-public trust fund to restore the Presidio.[14] Pelosi's policy pursuits on behalf of her district have made it easy for her opponents to label her a "San Francisco liberal."

Pelosi's committee assignments have facilitated the development of her policy expertise and leadership. From 1991 to 2003 she served on the Appropriations Committee, and from 1997 to 2001 she was the ranking minority member on its Foreign Operations Subcommittee. She was also a member of the Select House Intelligence Committee from 1993 to 2003, and the ranking minority member from 2001 to 2003. Pelosi was particularly active as a committee leader in the wake of the September 11 attacks.

Pelosi won her first leadership post—minority whip—in October 2001, in a competitive race against political rival Steny Hoyer, D-Md. Pelosi had been a loyal partisan throughout her career. Her party support score, as measured annually by

Congressional Quarterly, never dipped below 96 percent. But it was her fund-raising loyalty to the party—raising and distributing money for Democratic congressional candidates nationwide—that proved critical. In 2000 Pelosi raised more than $3 million for Democratic candidates.[15] Hoyer's AmeriPAC, on the other hand, only raised $680,000 that year.[16] Pelosi defeated Hoyer among House Democrats 118–95.[17] In her next race in 2002 Pelosi defeated Harold Ford Jr., D-Tenn., 177–29, to become minority leader.

While some worried that Pelosi's liberalism would hinder her leadership, Pelosi established a reputation as a pragmatic leader who enforced party discipline. After becoming minority leader in 2002, she quit the Progressive Caucus (composed of liberals) and reached out to moderate and conservative Democrats, although some members complained that her liberal colleagues remained her closest advisers.[18] When they were in the minority, Democrats voted together more often under Pelosi's leadership than they had in fifty years, according to *Congressional Quarterly.* Pelosi was aided by demographic shifts. Democratic members had become increasingly like-minded. By the time Pelosi became the Democratic leader, the share of southern Democrats had shrunk considerably, and the Democratic Caucus was more homogeneous than it ever had been or has been since. Pelosi showed a willingness that her predecessors had not to demand and enforce party discipline.[19] Given Pelosi's pragmatism—and Democrats' electoral victories under her leadership while they were the minority—Pelosi faced no opposition from her colleagues in her bid to become the fifty-second Speaker in 2007.

The Democratic leadership generally works as a team. The top leaders in the 110th Congress included Pelosi; her second in command, Majority Leader Hoyer; majority whip James Clyburn, S.C.; Democratic Caucus chair Rahm Emanuel, Ill., and chairman of the Democratic Congressional Campaign Committee (DCCC) Christopher Van Hollen, Md. In 2007 each of these Democratic leaders voted with the party more often than the average Democratic member did (92 percent of the time was the average unity score for all Democrats). Party leaders actively campaign for their colleagues, frequently attending their fund-raisers and raising money to distribute. With the exception of Clyburn, all of the Democrats' top leaders formed leadership political action committees (PACs) and contributed generously to federal candidates during the 2006 cycle. Hoyer's PAC contributed $916,000, followed by Emanuel's $723,000, Pelosi's $663,500, and Van Hollen's $111,500.[20]

Hoyer is more ideologically moderate than Pelosi, and the Democrats' two top leaders brought with them to the new majority a long-running rivalry rooted in differences that are mainly personal but partly ideological. Pelosi strongly supported John Murtha's, D-Pa., challenge to Hoyer for the post of majority leader and lobbied members aggressively to support him. After

Hoyer's decisive victory, however, it seems that he and Pelosi generally worked together effectively. Moderate Democrats typically turned to Hoyer rather than Pelosi. Between the two, Democrats across the ideological spectrum felt represented in the leadership. Hoyer was also better situated, and more inclined, to work with Republicans than Pelosi. When the Democrats needed to negotiate with Republicans to end an impasse over the disclosure of earmarks in the appropriations process, it was Hoyer, not Pelosi, who worked out the deal.[21]

Democratic whip James Clyburn advanced from Democratic Caucus chair to become the highest-ranking African American party leader in the 110th Congress and the second African American to serve as Democratic whip. Elected to the House in 1992, Clyburn brought considerable experience to the post of whip. He had led the Congressional Black Caucus, been Democratic Caucus vice chairman, and had chaired the Democratic Caucus since 2005. Clyburn expanded the whip's role and influence, working with the senior chief deputy whip, John Lewis, D-Ga. Clyburn also worked with committee chairs and groups within the Democratic Caucus to ascertain members' views early in the legislative process.[22] Clyburn was quoted early in the session: "Members get very nervous in being asked to vote for something where they were not intimately involved. The committee chairmen will reap the benefits of whatever product we [in the whip operation] have, to make sure that concerns are addressed."[23]

After his widely recognized success as chair of the DCCC during the 2006 election cycle, Rahm Emanuel was elected chairman of the Democratic Caucus, the fourth-highest-ranking leadership post. Emanuel was widely considered a rising star. He was first elected to the House in 2002 after serving as a policy adviser to President Bill Clinton. Under Emanuel's leadership, the DCCC raised $64 million to spend on House races in the 2006 cycle—an increase of nearly 75 percent over the previous cycle.[24] As caucus chair, Emanuel played a critical role in policy making and as a party strategist. Emanuel considered challenging Clyburn for whip, but to avoid a contested election and the consternation of the Congressional Black Caucus, he instead ran unopposed for caucus chair.[25]

Christopher Van Hollen chaired the DCCC, a position appointed by party leaders, and at the same time he gained a seat on the powerful Ways and Means Committee. These moves were considered rewards for his efforts leading up to the successful 2006 elections.[26] During the 2006 cycle, Van Hollen led the DCCC's ten-member candidate recruitment team and with Debbie Wasserman Schultz, D-Fla., co-chaired the "Red to Blue" drive to funnel extra resources to Democratic challengers within striking distance of defeating GOP incumbents.

The Democratic Steering Committee, chaired by Pelosi, grew to fifty-two members in the 110th Congress (from thirty-five in the 103rd Congress). Many of its new members had strong allegiance to Pelosi, including its two co-chairs,

Rosa DeLauro, Conn., and George Miller, Calif.[27] Pelosi is known to have a tight circle of Democratic allies in which personal loyalty is strong and reciprocal. Frequently cited Pelosi confidants include Miller, Anna G. Eshoo, Calif., Zoe Lofgren, Calif., Edward J. Markey, DeLauro, and John P. Murtha. Her loyalty to these friends and others initially worried some of her colleagues on the outside, particularly when she strongly supported Murtha's leadership bid over Hoyer.[28]

Nonetheless, most Democrats seem to think that Pelosi recovered quickly from the Murtha misstep, and she has generally received good marks from her Democratic colleagues and congressional observers for her ability to unify the party and pass Democratic priorities in the House. Pelosi makes extensive efforts to reach out to all the Democratic members, holding frequent sessions with committee chairs, new members, and other lawmakers.[29] Indeed, party unity among Democrats reached a record high during the first session of the 110th Congress. According to CQ Weekly the average Democrat voted with his or her party 92 percent of the time in votes in which the majority of one party voted against the majority of the other. The gap between northern and southern Democrats was small; the groups averaged 93 percent and 90 percent respectively. Republicans' average party unity dipped to 85 percent.

The number of party unity votes, in which one or both parties voted unanimously against the other, has skyrocketed since the late 1990s.[30] As Figure 1 shows, since 2003 unanimity among members of both parties has been strikingly high. Democratic unity reached an all-time high in 2003 and 2004; Democrats voted unanimously on 27 percent of all roll call votes in which the two parties opposed each other in both years. Republicans' high-water mark occurred in 2001, when they voted unanimously on 32 percent of the party unity votes. But both parties continued to vote as unified blocs at a high rate in the 110th Congress. In 2007 Democrats voted unanimously on 170 party unity votes, and Republicans did so on 177 (constituting 23 percent and 24 percent of party unity votes, respectively). In the 1970s and 1980s, the number of unanimous votes achieved by either party typically ranged between ten and twenty and rarely exceeded 10 percent of all party unity votes. The number of unanimous votes increased dramatically for Republicans in the 1990s, whereas Democrats began to achieve perfect unity with greater frequency only in 2002. Although unanimous votes partly reflect the increased ideological divergence between the two parties, they also reflect and reinforce the sense that the House now comprises two unified teams who view themselves as engaged in an intense, no-holds-barred battle.

The Democrats' high level of unity is particularly striking given that scholars and Democratic House members alike frequently assert that the Democratic membership is more diverse than the Republican, and that the Democrats' ideological diversity poses challenges to their leaders. Without question, the Democratic Caucus is

Figure 1. Unanimous Party Votes, 1955–2007

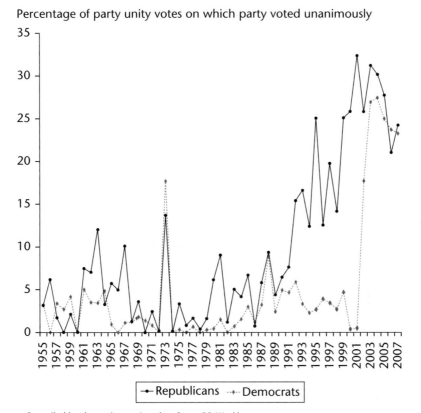

Percentage of party unity votes on which party voted unanimously

Source: Compiled by the authors using data from *CQ Weekly*.

more diverse in race, ethnicity, and gender than the Republican Conference, and more diverse than it has been in the past. In the 110th Congress, there were 40 African Americans, 20 Latinos, 4 Asian Americans, and 50 women among the Democrats. Among Republicans there were 3 Latinos, 1 American Indian, and 21 women. Democratic leaders are explicitly responsive to gender, ethnic, and racial balance when distributing power among their members.

From an ideological perspective, however, Democratic diversity is actually less than in the past because there are fewer conservative, southern Democrats. This is illustrated in Figures 2 and 3, which present the distribution of Democrats' and Republicans' ideology ratings in the 103rd and 110th Congresses, respectively. Notice that Democrats were more dispersed across the ideological spectrum than the Republicans in the 103rd Congress, with a fair number of moderate and conservative members. By contrast, Democratic members were much more tightly concentrated in the 110th Congress, with the vast majority close to the party's

Figure 2.   Density of Member Ideology (First Dimension DW-NOMINATE
Scores), 103rd Congress (1993–1994)

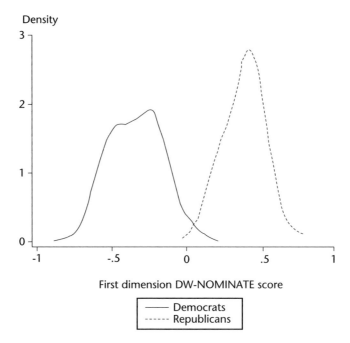

First dimension DW-NOMINATE score

——— Democrats
------ Republicans

Source: Compiled by the authors using data from http://voteview.com/dwnomin.htm.

ideological median. So while Democratic leaders have had notable success in keeping members in line and in structuring the agenda to exclude attractive minority party alternatives, increasing ideological homogeneity facilitates their efforts.

Even if Democratic diversity is overstated, Democratic concern about some of their vulnerable members as the 2008 elections approached was not. Nineteen of the new members came from districts that President Bush won in 2004. Although not giving these members many centrist options to vote for, Democratic leaders have been more frank about the need to protect vulnerable freshmen—dubbed "majority makers"—than leaders were in the past. They helped vulnerable members, freshmen in particular, both inside the institution and with campaign fundraising. For example, five freshman Democrats served as subcommittee chairs, and not coincidentally they were among the Democrats facing the toughest reelection races.[31] Democratic leaders gave vulnerable first-term representative Nancy Boyda, D-Kan., an early legislative victory by bringing to the floor her bill to revoke the pensions of members of Congress who are convicted of crimes. Debbie Wasserman

Figure 3.   Density of Member Ideology (First Dimension DW-NOMINATE Scores), 110th Congress (2007–2008)

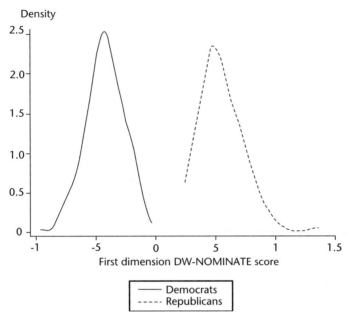

Source: Compiled by the authors using data from http://voteview.com/dwnomin.htm.

Schultz headed the "Frontline" program to help vulnerable new members with fund raising. Interestingly, although the new Democrats from "Bush districts" were a bit less loyal than Democrats from more liberal districts, they have compiled party-voting records that are high compared with the levels typically reached by Democrats in the 1960s. The average unity score for the Bush district freshmen in 2007 was 87 percent, compared with 97 percent for the other freshmen and 96 percent for all Democrats. By contrast, the average southern Democrat in the 92nd Congress (1971–1972) voted with his or her party only 46 percent of the time, the lowest point of the era leading up to the reforms of the 1970s.[32]

Democratic defections on procedural votes, most notably motions to recommit, are a glaring exception to the high level of Democratic cohesion and a surprise to longtime congressional observers. According to a senior Pelosi aide, "there is nothing that has produced more turmoil inside our Caucus than those things [motions to recommit]."[33] Given that most controversial bills in the contemporary era come up under restrictive rules, a motion to recommit provides one of the few opportunities for minority members to offer legislative alternatives. A member opposed to a bill can offer a motion to recommit immediately before a vote on final passage, followed by only five minutes of debate on each side. During Republican-controlled Congresses, Republican members viewed motions to recommit as largely procedural rather than substantive measures. When they were the majority party, Republican leaders kept their members from supporting motions to recommit, and Republicans lost on only eleven of them during the twelve years they were in the majority, none in the 109th Congress.[34]

From the start of the 110th Congress it became clear that the Republicans had found a crack in the Democrats' procedural armor with motions to recommit. Indeed, Republicans indicated that they use the motions to "put vulnerable Democrats on the spot and force them to make a choice between the interests of their constituents back home or supporting their leadership on something that could be used against them in the fall."[35] In 2007 alone, Republicans won on twenty-one motions to recommit, including some high-profile embarrassments.[36] For example, Republicans won a victory on the Democrats' lobbyist bundling disclosure bill when they passed a motion to recommit to include disclosure requirements for leadership PACs. Democrats were forced to pull a District of Columbia voting rights bill because of a threat from a motion to recommit to include an anti–gun control provision. Many of the defections were by Democratic freshmen who represent moderate districts and did not witness past discipline on these votes, but it is nonetheless surprising that some in the party leadership have been willing to allow members to break ranks on these votes. Now that some members have come to see motions to recommit as substantive rather than procedural measures, it will be hard for the leadership to recast them as simply procedural, party-line votes. But many rank-and-file Democrats are upset. In May 2008, Maxine Waters sent a "Dear Colleague" letter to fellow Democrats expressing concern that the leadership's willingness to allow some Democrats to vote for GOP motions to recommit will "only serve to fracture the Democratic Caucus." Waters wrote, "I cannot help wondering if our Caucus will be torn apart by frequent support for Republican motions to recommit."[37]

The Republican Response

Republican leaders have faced challenges of their own adjusting to life in the minority with a heavy-handed majority. Just as Democratic leaders did in previous Congresses, Republican leaders have responded by criticizing the majority party on procedural and substantive grounds at every turn. In many respects GOP leaders' vocal criticism of Democratic legislation on the House floor and in press conferences and their willingness to obstruct legislative business mirror the tactics of the Gingrich-led "bomb-throwers" during the 1980s and early 1990s. The critical difference is that this is now an explicit leadership strategy, whereas Gingrich's group generally worked outside of the leadership.

The Republican leadership went through significant change in the year leading up to the 110th Congress. Majority whip Tom DeLay, R-Texas, resigned amid ethics scandals, forcing several new leadership elections in February 2006. Although those elections did not affect Hastert's position as Speaker, Republicans elected a new majority leader, John Boehner of Ohio. Following Republicans' loss of majority control in the 2006 elections, Hastert announced that he would not run for his party's leadership, and he retired from office altogether midway through the 110th Congress.[38] In addition to Boehner the Republicans elected Roy Blunt, Mo., as minority whip; Adam Putnam, Fla., as conference chair; and Tom Cole, Okla., as National Republican Congressional Committee (NRCC) chair.

In the 110th Congress this leadership team reflected Republicans' conservative policy positions. With the defeat of long-serving moderate Republicans such as Nancy Johnson, Conn., Sue Kelly, N.Y., and James Leach, Iowa, in the 2006 elections, fewer Republican moderates remained in the House, and they were not represented in the top ranks of the leadership. Unlike previous Congresses, the leadership was all male. Tom Cole is a Native American. As was the case among Democratic leaders, the Republican leaders voted with their party more often than the average Republican member. They all formed leadership PACs that made ample contributions to federal candidates in the 2006 cycle: Boehner contributed $1,033,831; Blunt contributed $985,921; Cole contributed $531,611; and Putnam contributed $125,475.

Boehner was the highest-ranking and most visible Republican leader. He was often seen fiercely criticizing House Democrats or expressing support for President Bush in his handling of the Iraq war. Elected in 1990, Boehner quickly adopted then–minority whip Newt Gingrich's confrontational style in attacking the Democratic majority and the management of Congress.[39] When Republicans took the majority in 1995, Boehner was elected Republican Conference chairman. After the 1998 elections, however, he was defeated for reelection to the leadership. Boehner turned his energy to legislating, chairing the Education and the Workforce Committee from 2001 to 2006 and rehabilitating his image in the process. At the same time, Boehner increased his fund-raising efforts for the party. DeLay's resignation provided an opportunity for Boehner to return to the leadership, and he challenged majority whip Roy Blunt for DeLay's position. Boehner defeated Blunt 122–109 in early 2006 and became the second-highest-ranking Republican. In the 110th Congress, Boehner was challenged by Mike Pence, Ind., the Republican Study chairman, but Pence only garnered twenty-seven votes.

Roy Blunt has been the Republican whip since 2003. He is another conservative voice in the leadership, although conservatives are not always happy with his leadership style. Blunt was a close ally of DeLay, who appointed him chief deputy whip in the 106th Congress. Blunt's style is more conciliatory than DeLay's, and that can be an advantage when he works with members but a disadvantage when it comes to extracting votes. When Boehner and Blunt competed for majority leader in 2006, Blunt did not give up his position as whip. Although this frustrated some colleagues, it turned out to be a smart move. At the start of the 110th Congress, Blunt ran for whip again, defeating John Shadegg, R-Ariz., 137–57. In the minority, GOP defections were more frequent, but Blunt had some notable successes in keeping most of his members in line, particularly on votes concerning the war in Iraq.

Republican Conference chair Adam Putnam was the youngest member of the leadership, and he was widely viewed as a rising star. In his leadership bid Putnam defeated Jack Kingston, Ga., 100–91, on the third ballot. Nine months earlier he had been elected chair of the Policy Committee. Putnam was elected to the House in 2000. Speaker Hastert appointed him to the Rules Committee when a vacancy occurred in 2004, and Putnam raised his profile by taking the lead in many debates over special rules. Putnam was a consistently conservative voice, responsible for helping to craft policy. Even with little chance to set the policy agenda in the minority, Putnam takes ideas seriously and provides policy research for other Republicans.[40] Like his colleagues in the leadership, he strongly blasted Democrats in the press.

Although Tom Cole only arrived in Congress in 2003, he already had years of political experience, including a stint as the executive director of the NRCC. That experience, combined with his prolific fund-raising in the 2006 cycle, helped him defeat Republicans Pete Sessions, Texas, and Phil English, Pa., in the race to chair the NRCC at the start of the 110th Congress. Cole early made it clear that every Republican member is expected to raise significant amounts of money for the party. While establishing such fundraising quotas is not new, the large amounts and explicit instructions are. According to *CQ Weekly,* every House Republican was given a table detailing expectations by date and by status. In 2007 Republican leaders were expected to contribute $375,000 to the party; committee ranking members between $205,000 and $255,000; subcommittee ranking members between $155,000 and $205,000; rank-and-file members between $110,000 and $130,000; and freshmen $60,000.[41]

Chairing the NRCC was a particularly important—and difficult—job in the 110th Congress because of the political challenges House Republicans faced going into the 2008 elections. During the 110th Congress, Democrats gained three additional House seats in special elections to replace departing Republican members.

At the same time, Republican retirements outnumbered Democrats' by a sizable margin. Management problems also hindered the NRCC. Its former treasurer, Christopher Ward, was accused of submitting fake committee audits and funneling hundreds of thousands of dollars from the NRCC to his personal accounts over five years.[42] In March 2008 Cole revealed that the NRCC debt from 2006 amounted to between $18 million and $19 million.[43] Given these challenges, Boehner added an extra leadership team of Republican members to help the NRCC.

Republican leaders emphasize the importance of presenting a unified opposition to Democrats' major legislative priorities. By providing Democrats with little or no support for their proposals, Republican leaders hope to force conflicted Democrats to cast votes that are tough to defend in their districts, or better yet, cause Democratic leaders to suffer the embarrassment of losing on the House floor or pulling a bill from consideration. Although they still lost on most votes, the Republican whip team managed to embarrass the Democrats in some cases. Most notably they used motions to recommit to challenge Democrats' agenda control. When determining what issues to highlight in their motions to recommit, the Republicans shrewdly selected issues that would appeal to Democrats representing moderate districts, such as immigration and gun control.

Republicans also undermined Democrats' efforts to claim credit for earmark reform and ethics reform. Most members of Congress, regardless of party, seek out earmarks. Under GOP control they had become an embarrassment, and Democrats capitalized on this by passing earmark reform when they took control. However, when Appropriations Committee chair David Obey wanted to wait until after the conference committee stage to reveal the list of earmarks, Republicans seized the opportunity to criticize the Democrats for backtracking on reform.

Republicans turned to procedural moves to highlight their anger by disrupting business on the House floor. In the first session of the 110th Congress alone, Republicans called for votes on motions to adjourn twenty-three times.[44] In July 2007, when the electronic voting machines malfunctioned, Republicans accused Democrats of foul play in narrowly defeating a Republican amendment to an agriculture appropriations bill that would have barred benefits to illegal immigrants. The dispute led to an investigation.[45] In May 2008, Republicans used procedural tactics to highlight their anger over Democrats' handling of a supplemental appropriations bill to fund the war in Iraq. They stalled the process for two days with moves such as requesting recorded votes on the journal, offering motions to adjourn, and objecting to suspending the rules because a quorum was not present. Republicans were upset with Democratic leaders' plan to bring the bill directly to the floor, bypassing committee consideration, because that route prevented them from offering a motion to recommit.[46] While Congress was out of session during the August 2008 recess, Republican members nonetheless spoke on the House floor daily to criticize Democrats' handling of energy policy, most notably Democratic leaders' refusal to allow a vote on off-shore drilling. In the end, pressure from moderate Democrats compelled leaders to allow a vote on an offshore drilling compromise.

In the minority, the Republicans' centralization of party leadership is less significant and less obvious than it was when they were in the majority, but it persists nonetheless. Republican leaders have continued to make party loyalty a requirement when selecting ranking minority members on committees. Five members who were not the most senior became ranking members on their committees in the 110th Congress.

The most consequential Republican strategic decision was to stick with President Bush on the war and related issues, notwithstanding Bush's low approval ratings and the perception that Bush's policies had cost the GOP their majority, at least in part. From the Republican standpoint, cooperating with Bush on the war made sense inasmuch as most party members represented districts that continued to support the president, and the resulting impasse left Democrats unable to point to the enactment of one of their most important agenda items. Democrats cast Republicans as obstructionists, but Republicans countered that Democrats left them out of the legislative process.

The 110th Congress in Historical Context

Is the centralized leadership of both parties in the 110th Congress an aberration? Or does it instead reflect a return to prior historical precedent? In many ways the contemporary House resembles the House in the era of so-called czar rule, when powerful Republican Speakers Thomas Reed (1889–1891, 1895–1899) and Joseph Cannon (1903–1911) dominated. Speakers Reed and Cannon used control of committee assignments and of the Rules Committee to shape legislation. The few dissenters from the GOP program were marginalized in the early twentieth century, just as moderates today face intense pressure to toe the party line. Cannon's leadership was dramatically weakened in 1910 when a coalition of insurgent Republicans and Democrats voted to remove the Speaker from the Rules Committee and to expand the committee and make it subject to election by the House. Following the 1910 revolt, committee leaders gradually gained the security provided by the seniority system, and party leaders largely became brokers among contending ideological and committee-based factions.

In the decades that followed, even the most prominent Speaker, Democrat Sam Rayburn of Texas (1940–1961), lacked the influence over his caucus that Reed and Cannon once wielded over theirs. Instead Rayburn was constantly pleading with chairs to report bills favored by most Democrats and generally lacked the power to bypass the powerful, often conservative committee leaders. It was not until the 1970s, when liberals gained an overwhelming majority in the Democratic Caucus, that party leadership began to revive.

In the last edition of *Congress Reconsidered,* we speculated about the prospect that the Republican system of strong party government would become institutionalized. The extent to which Democrats have thus far followed Republican practices suggests that a durable shift has indeed occurred. The sources of Joe Cannon's downfall in 1910–1911 provide a framework for evaluating the prospects for Democratic leaders, Pelosi in particular, to sustain centralized party government or to lose power because of a resentful caucus and House chamber, as Speaker Cannon did.

Two major forces combined to foster the success of the revolt against Cannon. First, starting in 1905 a progressive faction gained strength within the GOP, as President Theodore Roosevelt began to give voice to demands for major policy change. Although progressive Republicans only numbered approximately two dozen or so members by 1910—arguably fewer than the number of Democratic moderates today—Roosevelt's public support combined with the popularity of Progressivism in their home districts made them far more confrontational and aggressive than present-day moderates. Ideological divisions within the GOP became more pronounced than is currently the case.

The most likely faction to become disillusioned among Democrats is the moderate-to-conservative Blue Dogs, who numbered forty-nine by the end of the 110th Congress. Thus far the Blue Dogs have not pursued an agenda independent of the party but have worked within party channels to achieve their goals. Indeed, they tout their influence in the reinstatement of pay-as-you-go budgeting rules and in the budget resolutions passed by Democrats in the 110th Congress. The average Blue Dog had a party loyalty score of 88 in 2007, suggesting that most of these members are not far from the Democratic mainstream on most issues. The Blue Dogs, however, have positioned themselves to make demands on Democratic leaders with a new internal rule that binds all of their members to the group's position if two-thirds of the members support the position. In 2008 they became more vocal in their insistence on several policy provisions, including offsets on supplemental appropriations, a compromise on the executive branch's electronic surveillance power (FISA), and allowing offshore drilling, forcing the Democratic leadership to accommodate their positions at critical points in the process. It is plausible that the Blue Dogs' increasing boldness will engender further intraparty troubles if a future Democratic administration makes major liberal policy initiatives possible.

A second force exacerbating dissatisfaction with Cannon was the perception that his tight personal control deprived individual members of opportunities to exert influence. A major difference today is that Pelosi's leadership of the Democratic Caucus is more collegial than was Cannon's: Where Cannon worked with a small circle of personal intimates in attempting to run the House, Pelosi's team is far more extensive, drawing on several deputy whips to reach out to members based on regional and even ideological interests and investing more members in the process. In the current organization, Democrats who demonstrate party loyalty through their voting record and fund-raising efforts have considerable opportunities to advance within the power structure of the House. Party leaders also contribute generously to members' campaigns, particularly the campaigns of those who need help. Parties also recognize, to some extent, individual legislative leadership. As long as the member supports the party position, leaders are happy to cede leadership on particular issues to knowledgeable members on the House floor, particularly committee chairs who might otherwise resent strong party leadership and electorally vulnerable members who need a record of legislative accomplishments. Again, this mitigates the resistance to vigorous party leadership without sacrificing the Democrats' ability to close off opportunities for Republicans to undermine the party's priorities. On a cautionary note, however, Pelosi has emphasized personal ties and personal loyalty more than Hastert did, and that has already generated some resentment among those Democrats who lack such ties to the Speaker.

An additional factor that will influence the prospects for institutionalizing the highly partisan contemporary system is unified party control of Congress and the White House. Traditionally, strong congressional parties have been identified with movements to defend congressional power against executive branch encroachments. But when the GOP controlled both the lower chamber and the White House from 2001 to 2006, strong House leadership coincided with close working relations with the White House to attain common legislative goals. Indeed, the cooperative relationship between Republican leaders and the Bush administration contrasted sharply with the unruly interactions between the Clinton White House and Democratic leaders in 1993–1994. Should Democrats recapture the White House in 2008 while holding onto their majorities in Congress, a key question will be whether the party is able to emulate Republicans' close working relationship across the branches. In the meantime, divided government in 2007 and 2008 brought more aggressive executive oversight on the part of congressional committees and efforts to defend congressional power from executive encroachment.

Still, on the whole the conditions that produced the Cannon revolt do not appear likely to recur anytime soon. The prospects for institutionalizing the highly partisan system under Democratic control are reinforced by turnover patterns. A mere 142 members serving in the 110th Congress had served in the House prior to Gingrich's election as Speaker in 1995. Therefore, less than one-third of these members had direct experience with an era prior to the intense partisan warfare of recent years. The era in which the Speaker and the minority leader played golf and poker together precedes the tenure of all but the most senior members. Beyond the policy differences between the parties, partisan acrimony and the uncertainty of party control going into every election reinforce the "teamlike" mentality of the parties on Capitol Hill. In such an environment the bitter partisanship and strong party leadership characteristic of today's Congress are likely to persist for the foreseeable future.

NOTES

Thanks to Michael Brady, Aaron King, Frank Orlando, and Brittany Perry, of the Political Institutions and Public Choice Program at Duke University, for research assistance in the preparation of this chapter.

1. *Congressional Record*, 110th Cong., 1st sess., 2007, H4.

2. Gary Jacobson, "The War, the President, and the 2006 Midterm Congressional Elections," paper presented at the annual meeting of the Midwest Political Science Association, Chicago, 2007.

3. "Manifesto for the 'First 100 Hours,'" *CQ Weekly Online*, November 20, 2006, 3104.

4. David W. Rohde, *Parties and Leaders in the Postreform House* (Chicago: University of Chicago Press, 1991).

5.George Kundanis, interview by author, May 29, 2008.

6. Rebecca Kimitch, "CQ Guide to the Committees: Democrats Opt to Spread the Power," *CQ Weekly Online*, April 16, 2007, 1080–1083.

7. Ibid.

8. Chris Strohm, "Homeland Security—Harman Finally Lands Intel Post on Homeland Panel," *CongressDaily*, January 18, 2007.

9. Kimitch, "CQ Guide to the Committees."

10. Darren Goode and Christian Bourge, "Environment—Pelosi Creating Global Warming Panel; Dingell Shrugs," *CongressDailyPM*, January 17, 2007.

11. Jonathan Weisman, "Edging away from Inner Circle, Pelosi Asserts Authority," *Washington Post*, July 9, 2007, A01.

12. Kundanis, interview.

13. See, e.g., David Truman, *The Congressional Party* (New York: Wiley, 1959).

14. Michael Barone and Richard E. Cohen, "Nancy Pelosi," *The Almanac of American Politics 2008*, Web edition (Washington, D.C.: National Journal Group, 2008).

15. Karen Foerstel, "Pelosi: A Tireless Fundraiser Sees Herself as a 'Fresh' Face," *CQ Weekly Online*, October 6, 2001, 2324–2325.

16. Data from www.opensecrets.org.

17. Karen Foerstel, "Pelosi's Vote-Counting Prowess Earns Her the House Democrats' No. 2 Spot," *CQ Weekly Online,* October 13, 2001, 2397–2398.

18. Jill Barshay, "Woman of the House Brings a Sense of Power," *CQ Weekly Online,* November 13, 2006, 2970–2973.

19. Alan K. Ota and Susan Ferrechio, "Experience Counts in the House," *CQ Weekly Online,* November 20, 2006, 3128–3131.

20. Obtained from www.opensecrets.org.

21. Susan David and Steven T. Dennis, "Pelosi, Hoyer Mend Fences—Gradually," *Roll Call,* July 17, 2007.

22. "Clyburn, James E.," in *CQ's Politics in America 2008: The 110th Congress,* ed. Jackie Koszczuk and Martha Angle (Washington, D.C.: Congressional Quarterly, 2008).

23. Richard E. Cohen, "Congress—A Different Kind of Whip," *National Journal,* January 20, 2007.

24. "Emanuel, Rahm," in *CQ's Politics in America 2008: The 110th Congress.*

25. Ibid.

26. "Van Hollen, Christopher," in *CQ's Politics in America 2008: The 110th Congress.*

27. Kimitch, "CQ Guide to the Committees."

28. Weisman, "Edging away from Inner Circle."

29. Ibid.

30. "Party Unity Background," *CQ Weekly Online,* January 14, 2008, 147.

31. They include Christopher Carney, Pa., Homeland Security; Heath Shuler, N.C., and Jason Altmire, Pa., Small Business; John Hall, N.Y., and Harry E. Mitchell, Ariz., Veterans Affairs.

32. Rohde, *Parties and Leaders,* 55.

33. Kundanis, interview.

34. Betsy Palmer, Congressional Research Service, Library of Congress, "The Motion to Recommit in the House: The Minority's Motion," February 2, 2007. CRS report RL33860.

35. Lauren W. Whittington and Steven T. Dennis, "Waters Issues Warning to House Leadership," *Roll Call,* May 8, 2008.

36. Data for 110th Congress compiled by Don Wolfensberger from the THOMAS Web site of the Library of Congress, http://thomas.loc.gov.

37. Whittington and Dennis, "Waters Issues Warning."

38. Adding insult to injury, his seat was filled by a Democrat, Bill Foster, in a special election.

39. "Boehner, John," in *CQ's Politics in America 2008: The 110th Congress.*

40. "Putnam, Adam," in *CQ's Politics in America 2008: The 110th Congress.*

41. Shawn Zeller and Michael Teitelbaum, "GOP Fundraising on Quota System," *CQ Weekly Online,* January 15, 2007, 154.

42. Lauren W. Whittington, "Cole: NRCC Debt Neared $19 Million," *Roll Call,* March 17, 2008.

43. Ibid.

44. Katherine Rizzo, "House GOP Perfects Parliamentary Ploys," *CQ Today Online News,* May 1, 2008.

45. Alexander Bolton, "Pelosi, Boehner Fight over Scope of 'Stolen Vote' Probe," *The Hill,* September 8, 2007.

46. Jennifer Bendery, "House Republicans Mount Procedural Protest over War Spending Bill," *Roll Call,* May 6, 2008.

Congressional Committees in a Continuing Partisan Era

John H. Aldrich and David W. Rohde

In the essay below, John Aldrich and David Rohde describe the theory of conditional party government. This theory posits that a cohesive party, one in which the party members agree on most issues, will empower its leadership to play a central role in policymaking. With cohesive majority parties over the last three decades, majority party leaders have directed the actions of standing committees and assumed a direct role in designing legislation.

THE TWO PRINCIPAL organizing structures of Congress are the political parties and the committee system. During the history of the institution, the relative influence of the two has shifted back and forth. From 1890 to 1910, the majority party dominated the House of Representatives, with the Speaker empowered to appoint committees and their chairs and to control the legislative agenda. After the revolt against Speaker Joe Cannon in 1910, power shifted to committees, whose leaders were selected based on seniority. From the 1920s through the 1970s party influence was relatively weak, and that period became known as the era of committee government. Then, beginning with the reform period in the 1970s, institutional changes were adopted that strengthened parties and weakened the sway of committees and their chairs. Moreover, the extent and intensity of partisan conflict in Congress increased. Of course, even in strong party eras Congress members did not abandon the committee system. Speaker Cannon's powers, for example, were exercised in large part through the committee system. This shifting balance of power therefore reflects the degree of autonomy of the committees and their chairs from their legislative party organizations, as well as any additional, independent powers granted the party.

In this chapter we discuss the transformation of the party-committee balance from the 1970s to the present, focusing mainly on the House but also considering the Senate. We begin by considering the Democratic Party reforms of the 1970s that launched the transformation and how the Democrats applied the party leadership's new powers. Then we consider further developments after the Republicans won control of both houses in the 1994 elections. We also discuss

Source: John H. Aldrich and David W. Rohde, "The Congressional Committees in a Continuing Partisan Era," in *Congress Reconsidered*, 9th ed., ed. Lawrence C. Dodd and Bruce I. Oppenheimer (Washington, D.C.: CQ Press, 2009), 217–229, 232–240. Some notes appearing in the original have been deleted.

additional institutional changes that the GOP made and the ways in which the Republican Party leadership interacted with the committee system to achieve its legislative goals. The return of the Democratic majority after the 2006 elections gives us a single but important session to examine the party-committee balance under new party (and committee) leadership. We will also briefly discuss Senate committees and then offer some conclusions.

The Committee System and the Era of Committee Government

The most important thing to recognize about the House and Senate committee systems is that they are designed institutions. That is, they are created by the membership to serve the interests of the chamber and its members. Committees, through division of labor, permit the chamber to stretch its capabilities by having only a subset of members consider each issue and piece of legislation in detail. Furthermore, committees encourage the development of expertise through members' specialization in the issue areas covered by their committees' jurisdictions.[1] In addition to these benefits to the chamber, committees also provide benefits to individual members. Richard Fenno has argued that members of Congress pursue one or more of three goals: reelection, power within the chamber, and good public policy.[2] The achievement of each of these goals is potentially influenced by committee membership. Members can use committee service to identify themselves with issues that are important to constituents and to secure benefits for their districts, thus enhancing their chances for reelection.[3] Committee and subcommittee chairmanships also provide members with positions of power in the chamber. And committee members are in the best position to influence public policy within their committees' jurisdictions.[4]

Congress used committees to conduct business from the beginning of the institution, although it took most of a century for the system to develop into the form we know today.[5] Standing committees (that is, permanent committees with recognized substantive jurisdictions) were widely used by the 1820s. They included members from both the majority and minority parties, and as the committees developed expertise their parent chambers began to defer to their judgments on legislative policy. Throughout the 1800s, the influence of the majority party leadership over committees grew. Speakers had the right to appoint committee members and chairs, and they chaired the Rules Committee, which set the terms of debate for bills on the House floor. The Speaker lost these powers in the revolt against Speaker Cannon in 1910. After that the Speaker could no longer appoint committees, and each party developed its own procedures for that purpose.

Seniority in committee service became the almost inviolable basis for choosing committee chairs. Moreover, the Rules Committee was autonomous and the Speaker barred from serving on it.

As a result of these developments, committees became largely independent from party influence. Because committee chairs were chosen and maintained in power by seniority, they had no particular incentive to be responsive to the wishes of their party or its leaders in producing legislation. The chairs shaped their committees' agendas, appointed subcommittees (and usually chose their chairs), and decided when hearings would be held and how bills would be handled. These developments might have been less consequential if the committee leaders were ideologically representative of their party, but that was not the case. From 1930 on, the Democrats were usually in the majority, and because southern Democrats were more likely to accumulate seniority than their northern counterparts, they were disproportionately represented among committee leaders. Conservative southerners often allied with Republicans to block or alter Democratic legislation, a situation that greatly frustrated northerners. Although that pattern had begun in the 1930s, their frustration became particularly pronounced in the 1950s and 1960s.

Party Reform: Gateway to the Partisan Era

Initial attempts at reform of committee government included a successful effort in 1961 to expand the Rules Committee to reduce the influence of southern conservatives on the panel. Then in 1970 Congress passed the Legislative Reorganization Act. It contained a number of important features, such as the requirement that committees make public roll call votes, and it generally required committees to permit the public to attend their meetings. The act also made it much easier to obtain recorded votes on amendments on the House floor and set the stage for electronic voting, which markedly sped up floor voting. These changes started to shift the locus of legislative decision making from the committees to the floor. The reorganization act, however, took no action to revise the seniority system or to reduce the powers of committee chairs.[6] The conservative coalition was able to block any such actions that would have undermined their institutional position.

However, the makeup of the House (and Senate) membership was changing. The Voting Rights Act of 1965 had enfranchised black voters in the South, and their strong tilt to the Democratic Party was liberalizing the party's voter base there. Reinforcing that effect was the gradual departure from the party of conservative voters who no longer saw the Democrats as standing for their interests. As a consequence of these developments, new southern Democrats were becoming more like their northern colleagues, and the Democratic membership in Congress was becoming less divided and more homogeneous.[7] This set the stage for efforts to strengthen the majority party leadership relative to the committee system. Since the revolt against Cannon, the diverse memberships of the congressional parties had been reluctant to enhance party power because their very diversity meant that there would be great uncertainty about the ends for which that power would be used. That is, members could not be sure what policies leaders would seek, and so individual members feared that powerful leaders would seek policies far different from their own preferred outcome. If, on the other hand, the preferences of party members were to become more similar, members would not have to be as concerned that leaders with preferences different from theirs would be chosen, and it would be safer to grant leaders stronger powers.

This relationship is the essence of the theoretical perspective that we have labeled *conditional party government,* or CPG for short.[8] If the legislators in a party have very heterogeneous policy preferences, they will not be likely to grant strong powers to their leadership. As policy preferences become more homogeneous, members will be progressively more likely to empower their party leaders because they will have less reason to fear the use of those powers. This tendency will be further reinforced as the positions of the two parties become more different because the consequences to each party's members of the other party's winning the competition to control policy will become more and more negative.

By the early 1970s, liberal Democrats were a clear majority of the House Democratic caucus, but not of the entire House membership. Because they could not muster a majority on the floor for the kinds of reforms they favored, the liberals targeted the rules of the Democratic caucus instead. Only Democrats could vote on these efforts, which combined strategies dealing both with committees and with the party and its leadership. First they sought to undermine the independence and power of committee leaders, so that the remaining conservatives would be less able to impede passage of their desired legislation. This strategy followed two tracks. First, the liberals wanted to end the automatic nature of the seniority system. To this end the caucus adopted rules providing for a secret ballot vote on all committee chairs at the beginning of every Congress. If the prospective chair (usually still the most senior Democrat on the committee) was voted down, there would be a competitive election of the chair in the caucus. This change was shown to have real consequences in 1975 when three southern Democrats were removed from committee chairmanships and replaced by more loyal northerners. Chairs were put on notice that they could not buck their party's policy wishes with impunity.

The second track of the strategy involved adopting rules that restricted the powers of those chosen as chairs. The principal vehicle was a set of rules known as the Subcommittee Bill of Rights, which required that committee members bid for the chairs of subcommittees in order of seniority, ending the ability of full committee chairs simply to appoint those positions. Subcommittees had to receive specific jurisdictions, and committee legislation had to be referred to subcommittees accordingly. In addition, subcommittee chairs would control their own budgets and staffs, rather than the chair of the full committee doing so.

The other strategy of the reformers was to give more powers to the party leadership. The Speaker received the right to appoint the chair and the Democratic members of the Rules Committee. That meant that the leadership could again control the flow of legislation and strategically shape the terms of floor consideration. In addition, the power to assign Democrats to other committees was vested in a new Steering and Policy Committee, most of whose members were party leaders or appointed by the Speaker. The reformers wanted the leadership to have more influence over the allocation of prized assignments, to make members more responsive to the leaders. Finally, the Speaker was given the authority to refer bills to more than one committee and to set deadlines for reporting, further reducing the ability of committees to act as roadblocks.

Partisanship Takes Hold: 1983–1994

The reforms were adopted by the mid-1970s and some of their consequences were quickly apparent, but divisions remained in the Democratic caucus, preventing the full effects of the changes from being visible. Indeed, many observers complained that the reforms had merely made Congress less efficient by further decentralizing power to subcommittees. This viewpoint was reinforced by Ronald Reagan's success in 1981 at splitting off southern Democrats to support his budget and tax proposals. The recession of 1982, however, helped bring fifty-seven Democrats to the House, including many moderate-to-liberal southerners. Consequently the conservative coalition was no longer a majority of the House. The newcomers made up over one-fifth of the Democratic caucus, and they provided support for stronger use of the leadership's powers to advance the party agenda and to compete with the priorities of the Reagan administration.

As we noted earlier, one reform strategy sought to induce committee chairs to refrain from blocking party bills and to support the Democratic Party's legislative program. After the removal of the three southern chairs in 1975, committee chairs recognized that their continued hold on their positions depended to a degree on their party support, and their behavior changed accordingly.

Research shows that members who occupied, or were close in seniority to, committee chairs dramatically increased their levels of party support between 1971 and 1982.[9] For example, in 1973–1974 the party unity score of Rep. Jamie Whitten, D-Miss., was thirty-eight points below the party average and eighteen points below the average for southern Democrats. Anticipating a liberal challenge when the chairmanship of the Appropriations Committee (where he ranked second) became vacant, Whitten began to change his behavior. By 1988, Whitten's party unity score was not only higher than the average southern Democrat's, it was two points higher than the average Democrat's.[10] Moreover, the Democratic caucus continued to use the mechanism for voting on chair candidates to pressure or remove committee leaders whose performance was deemed unsatisfactory.

The other reform strategy was to strengthen the party leadership, and it had a substantial impact on the relationship between the leadership and committees. As Barbara Sinclair has said, "Party and committee leaders must work together . . . since both are agents of and ultimately responsible to the Democratic Caucus."[11] In the changed environment, most committee leaders came to think of themselves as part of a team with the majority leadership. Committee chairs realized that they could not act independently of party priorities in drafting legislation. In turn, they expected party leaders to provide adequate staff support and assistance in moving bills to passage on the floor.[12]

One of the most important tools available to the party leadership was control of the Rules Committee. During the 1980s, the Democrats increasingly used the resolutions (called "special rules") that set the terms for floor consideration of legislation to structure the agenda to the advantage of the party.[13] For example, special rules could bar amendments completely, giving members a take-it-or-leave-it choice between the bill the leadership favored and nothing. Or the rule could permit just those amendments that the leadership wanted to consider, barring others that the Republican minority wanted but that would cause policy or electoral difficulties for some Democrats. Moreover, if the reporting committee had not adequately taken the majority party's wishes into account, special rules could be used to alter the bill as reported to bring the policy closer to the preference of the majority. This was done multiple times on defense authorization bills reported from the Armed Services Committee.

Not surprisingly, the majority party's use of its powers provoked anger and frustration among Republicans. One response from the GOP was to change its party rules to mimic those of the Democrats, so as to make its own leadership more able to compete. For example, the Republicans gave the minority leader the right to make Republican appointments to the Rules Committee and created a new committee assignment system in which the leadership had more voting power. The party leader was also empowered to designate "leadership issues," and on those bills all members of the party leadership were obliged to support the positions of the Republican Conference.

The Republicans also adopted progressively more confrontational tactics to protest their treatment and to undermine the Democratic majority. Some complaints came from GOP leaders and mainline conservatives, but most active were members of a group of populist conservatives known as the Conservative Opportunity Society (COS), led by Newt Gingrich of Georgia, then a backbencher. Gingrich and COS believed that the Republicans would be a perpetual minority unless they stopped going along with the Democrats as a means of attempting to have some influence on legislation. Instead, they argued that the GOP had to draw contrasts with the Democrats and let the public make a choice. The COS organized protests against the Democrats' management of the chamber and fought against the use of special rules to control the agenda and limit Republican influence. These efforts culminated in late 1988, when Gingrich filed a formal complaint with the House Ethics Committee against Speaker Jim Wright, D-Texas. The ensuing investigation led to Wright's resignation from the House.

Republican Rule and Its Consequences: 1994–2000

Republican confrontations with the Democratic majority continued into the 1990s, especially after President Bill Clinton was elected in 1992, restoring unified government. The GOP was able to take advantage of the political context in 1994, successfully exploiting negative public feelings about government performance, the condition of the nation, and Clinton personally.[14] The Republicans won majority control of both houses of Congress for the first time since the election of 1952. The new majority in the House chose Newt Gingrich as their Speaker, and the party set out to transform the operation of the chamber to set the stage for major changes in government policy.

Republican Procedural Changes

Gingrich's transforming efforts commenced almost immediately.[15] Little more than a week after election day he made clear his intent to depart from the seniority system in selecting committee chairs to a greater extent than the Democrats ever did, announcing that he had chosen Bob Livingston, La., as the new chair of the Appropriations Committee. Livingston ranked fifth in committee seniority but was considered more ideologically dependable and more effective than the more senior committee members. A few days later, Gingrich again bypassed seniority to select more dependable chairs for Judiciary and Commerce. Gingrich was asserting the right to name the new chairs before the newly elected majority had yet arrived in Washington, and the Republican Conference members tacitly ratified his decisions by their acquiescence.

The powers of committees and their chairs were also changed significantly. Three committees were abolished outright, and most remaining committees were limited to five subcommittees. These actions eliminated twenty-five sub-committees and 12 percent of full committee slots. As one COS member said, "Our system will prevent members from getting locked into the status quo."[16]

The Republican leadership gave its chairs the right to appoint subcommittee chairs and control over committee staff. This reflected Gingrich's view that chairs should control their committees, but he also believed that the party should control the chairs. He required committee chairs to consult with him before choosing subcommittee heads, and he pressured one chair to name two freshman representatives to head subcommittees. Gingrich also required each member of the Appropriations Committee to sign a "letter of fidelity," pledging to cut the budget as much as the Speaker wanted. To further weaken the capacities of committee leaders to build an independent power base, the Republicans adopted a six-year term limit for all committee and subcommittee chairmen.

Gingrich also announced a new Republican committee assignment process, and it was adopted by the Republican Conference in December. It gave the Speaker control over a much larger fraction of votes on the Committee on Committees. Republican House members also confirmed their leader's right to appoint the members and chair of the Rules Committee. Overall, under the new GOP majority, committees had less independent power and the party leadership had more.

It is worth noting one thing that the GOP did not do. It didn't adopt a wholesale realignment of committee jurisdictions, as some reformers had wanted. The existing pattern of jurisdictions had too many implications for the reelection, policy, and power goals of members, and most of them were unwilling to accept the risks involved in major change.[17] When the GOP took over the majority, Gingrich authorized Rep. David Dreier of California (vice chair of a joint committee on congressional reform in the previous Congress) to draft four plans of varying comprehensiveness for revamping the committee system. After it became apparent that there would be significant resistance from the chairs and members of affected committees, Gingrich opted for a version of the least-extensive plan. Thus we see that although Republican members were willing to support strengthening their leadership's influence over committees, they were not willing to sacrifice their other interests that were served by the committee system.

Party Leaders and Committees

The rules changes that the new Republican majority adopted thus set the stage for greater influence by party leaders over the activities and legislative products of committees. Because of limited space we can only present a few examples, mostly drawn from the 104th Congress (1995–1997), which we can then compare with the first session under the Democratic majority in the 110th.

Influencing Bill Creation in Committees. Majority leadership involvement in the crafting of bills in committee did not originate with the 104th Congress. As Sinclair shows,[18] such activity had become more frequent as committee autonomy decreased in the postreform era. It was, however, still infrequent in the Democrat-controlled Congresses, as most leader activity involved stages of the process after initial drafting. The 104th marked a major increase in this role for majority leadership.

The most extensive instance of leadership influence on bill creation was the drafting and revision of the legislation designed to implement the Contract with America.[19] Although there was substantial initial consultation on general matters during the crafting of the contract, the top GOP leaders determined which issues would be included and many of the particulars. For example, it was Gingrich who decided that school prayer would not be included. Committee consideration of these predrafted bills was largely pro forma, a necessary consequence of the leadership's pledge to pass them in the Congress's first hundred days.

The contract was of central importance, but the leadership's involvement in committees' initial consideration of bills was not limited to that legislation. Another example involves the major reform of agriculture subsidy policy that became known as the Freedom to Farm Act. In September 1995, the GOP leadership sent a letter to the Agriculture Committee chair, Pat Roberts of Kansas. They wrote, "We give the committee leave" to write major budget-cutting farm legislation. They indicated that they hoped the committee would support Roberts's bill, but if not "we will feel compelled" to bring the bill to the floor allowing unlimited amendments, or to replace the committee's bill with true reforms.[20] Moreover, during the consideration of the bill in committee, John Boehner of Ohio (a member, who was also GOP Conference chair) went so far as to say, "If this committee can't do it [make $13 billion in cuts called for in the budget plan], the future of this committee is seriously in doubt."[21] Rarely in congressional history has the majority leadership sought to dictate to and threaten a committee in so direct a fashion.

Bypassing Committees and Postcommittee Adjustments. In some instances, the Republican leadership simply bypassed committees altogether to achieve its policy and political goals. Gingrich had personally picked the chair of the Judiciary Committee, the independent-minded Henry Hyde of Illinois. Hyde was suitably responsive to the leadership and the Republican Conference during the speedy processing of a large number of bills from the Contract with America. However, the bill to repeal the 1994 ban on assault weapons, which Hyde opposed, went to the floor without committee consideration. When asked why Judiciary was not given the opportunity to consider the bill, the chairman said: "We have a reputation of being deliberative."[22]

Another device for bypassing committees was the use of leader-appointed party task forces.[23] Often, but not always, task forces had the assent of committees (or at least of their leaders), and they usually contained some members of the appropriate committees. A key difference, however, was that they contained only Republicans, and at times they were used to secure a different policy outcome than the committee of jurisdiction preferred. For example, in 1995 the Government Reform and Oversight Committee approved a bill to abolish the Commerce Department that was insufficiently radical to satisfy many of the GOP freshmen. The dissenters expressed their displeasure, and in response the leadership chose a different, more radical bill to accomplish the goal. The source of the bill was a GOP task force set up by Gingrich and chaired by a freshman. The bill had no hearings and no committee markup.[24]

The leadership could also use its control over the Rules Committee to make adjustments in the content of legislation after the committees had made their decisions. Barbara Sinclair's research shows that under the Republicans this kind of action was most frequent in the "revolutionary" 104th Congress, occurring on nearly half the major bills. But postcommittee adjustments continued to occur in later Congresses, for example, on more than one-third of the major bills in the 105th Congress.[25] One instance was the 1997 budget resolution, when Gingrich supervised adjustments to placate dissident Republicans and the White House. Another occurred in 1999, when moderate Republicans threatened to oppose the GOP tax bill because it was not sufficiently concerned with deficit reduction. Speaker Hastert brokered a change that made the tax rate cut dependent on a declining national debt.[26]

Special Rules and Control of the Floor. As we noted earlier, leaders of the majority can use their powers to support and defend the decisions of committees or to undermine them if the committees have not produced a result the party wanted. One way is through their general control of the floor agenda.

We saw that when they were in the minority, GOP members frequently attacked the Democrats for writing rules that barred them from offering amendments. As the majority in the 104th, however, they demonstrated that they were quite prepared to do the same thing. In one instance, on the recissions bill (legislation to make cuts in previously appropriated funds) taken up in March 1995, the Rules Committee wrote a rule that had the effect of blocking cutting defense spending to increase social spending. The rule prompted strong objections from a number of GOP moderates.[27]

In another example, a group of conservative Democrats wanted to offer a substitute amendment for the Republican Medicare reform plan, but the Rules Committee barred their amendment. Gene Taylor, D-Miss., said, "I am furious. . . . The Republicans came to power promising change, open rules." He charged, "They are no more fair than the Democrats."[28]

Not Everything Is Partisan

To this point we have focused our attention on the increased partisanship in Congress and on the strengthening of the influence of the party structure relative to committees. In this section we want to emphasize that one should not overinterpret these patterns. Specifically, it is important to recognize that much of Congress's business does not involve party conflict, as the data displayed in Table 1 demonstrate.[29] The table shows data from three Congresses on the proportion of bills over which there was some conflict, either in committee or on the floor. The standard for conflict was very minimal: Was there even one roll call on the bill on which there was a minority larger than 10 percent? Despite this low threshold, however, only about one-third of the bills saw any conflict at all.

Why was there so seldom conflict on legislation, if Congress has become ever more partisan over the period covered by these data? The reason is that the agenda that Congress deals with is multifaceted and diverse, and only a portion of it deals with the types of issues that provoke interparty disagreement. The parties care intensely about bills that relate to divisions among their members, their activists, and their electoral coalitions—things such as tax policy, the scope of government, regulation of business, and social issues such as abortion and gay rights. Most legislation, however, does not tap into these divisive subjects. Much legislation involves renewal of, or funding for, existing programs with wide support in the country or Congress, or proposals for new policies with many perceived benefits. This type of bill provides all members the chance to (in David Mayhew's words) "claim credit" or "take positions" and thereby enhance their chances for reelection.[30] Because

Table 1. Conflict on Legislation in the 96th, 100th, and 104th Congresses

	96th Congress (1979–1980)	100th Congress (1987–1988)	104th Congress (1995–1996)
Prestige committees	51.3% (150)	65.7% (67)	76.3% (93)
Policy committees	40.7% (317)	28.7% (394)	34.3% (376)
Constituency committees	20.8% (438)	17.8% (499)	23.8% (315)
All committees	32.8% (905)	25.6% (960)	35.1% (784)

Note: Given above are the percentages of bills considered by those committees that exhibited some conflict, either in committee or on the floor (the number of bills in each category is in parentheses). See endnote 29.

members do not run directly against one another, there is not a zero-sum relationship among them, and all members can potentially benefit from the adoption of legislation.

This relationship is readily apparent in Table 1 when we consider different types of committees.[31] The prestige committees—those most important to the party leadership—deal with more conflictual legislation in every Congress and also exhibit a systematic increase in conflict over time. The policy committees, which process most of Congress's substantive legislation, reveal an intermediate level of conflict and no systematic increase. Finally, the constituency committees—those most involved with providing electoral benefits to members—show the least amount of conflict on legislation.

Not only does the propensity for partisan disagreement vary across types of committees and from bill to bill, but it also varies within a single piece of legislation. Consider the Freedom to Farm Act that we mentioned earlier, which in 1996 sought to reform federal farm policy. Table 2 shows the results of two roll calls on that bill.[32] The first vote involved an effort to cut the peanut price support program, a typical "distributive" policy issue that had offered electorally important benefits to some members from agricultural districts. In this instance, within both the Democratic and Republican Parties, the members from the agriculture committees responded quite differently from other members, being much less inclined to support the abolition of peanut supports. Differences between the parties are small, and differences within them are large.

The second vote was on the Democrats' substitute proposal, which sought to keep farm policy closer to the status quo. Here the interparty differences are great. Only one Republican supported the Democrats' proposal, but 86 percent of the Democrats did. Moreover, the voting of committee members is virtually the same as that of members not on the

Table 2. Votes on the 1996 Freedom to Farm Act

	Phase out peanut supports	*Democratic substitute*
Republicans		
Agriculture committees	8.8% (34)	0.0% (34)
Others	61.3% (199)	0.5% (200)
All members	53.6% (233)	0.4% (234)
Democrats		
Agriculture committees	20.0% (25)	100.0% (23)
Others	48.5% (163)	84.8% (164)
All members	44.6% (188)	86.6% (187)
All members		
Agriculture committees	13.6% (59)	40.4% (57)
Others	55.5% (362)	38.5% (364)
All members	49.6% (421)	38.7% (421)

Note: Given above are the percentages of members voting "aye" on the two votes (the number of members is in parentheses). "Agriculture committees" means representatives who are on either the Committee on Agriculture or on the Appropriations Subcommittee on Agriculture and Rural Development. "Others" includes all other members.

committees. Thus some issues can provoke partisan responses while others do not, even within a single bill.

Senate Contrasts

Committees are less central to the work of the Senate than of the House because of a number of institutional differences between the two chambers. First, the Senate must deal with essentially the same legislative jurisdiction with less than one-fourth the number of members. Senators are therefore spread more thinly and are less specialized. For example, in 2001 senators served on an average of 3.3 standing committees and 8.9 subcommittees; the corresponding numbers for representatives were 1.9 and 3.9. On the other hand, only about half of House members are the chair or ranking minority member of a committee or subcommittee, whereas most senators are, giving them an institutional power base on which to focus.[33]

The Senate's rules and traditions also vest more power in individuals and small groups than those of the House. The most familiar manifestation of this is the ability of a minority to block passage of legislation through filibuster, but there are many other aspects of the institution that reinforce individual power to delay or block Senate action. The House is a "majoritarian" institution, in which the majority can work its will with even one more vote than the minority, but in the Senate the majority must usually pay attention to at least some minority views to achieve any results.

Another major difference is the role of the House Rules Committee that we discussed earlier. Through special rules, the majority party can decide which amendments, if any, may be considered on the floor. Moreover, regular House rules require that amendments be germane. In the Senate, neither of these conditions holds. Usually the only way to limit amendments is if senators *unanimously* consent to do so, and amendments need not be germane. Thus the Senate floor plays a much larger role in shaping the content of legislative outcomes than does the House floor, and it is much easier for senators who do not serve on the committee with jurisdiction to have an impact.

As a result of these differences, both Senate committees and Senate parties have been institutionally weaker than their House counterparts, and individual senators have been more consequential. Furthermore, because the majority party leadership usually has had to deal with some members of the minority, partisan conflict in the Senate has tended to be less frequent and less vitriolic. Nevertheless, over the last couple of decades party conflict has intensified in the Senate as well.[34] We have already considered some of the similarities and differences between the House and Senate over appropriations. As another example, in 1995 the new GOP majority adopted some rules to enhance party influence in the Senate. As in the House, six-year term limits were imposed on committee chairs. Chairs were to be chosen by successive, secret ballot votes, first among Republican committee members, then in the whole GOP Conference. Moreover, on some aspects of the Senate's business partisan conflict was as vigorous as any seen in the House. The prime example was confirmation of judicial nominations, in which only the Senate has a role. Democrats used the power of the filibuster to block nominations by President George W. Bush that they regarded as unacceptable, while frustrated Republicans railed against their actions. . . .

The House under Speakers Hastert and Pelosi

We developed the theory of conditional party government to explain the ebb and flow of party influence in Congress over time. We have argued that as the policy preferences of party members become more homogeneous, and as the ideological centers of gravity of the two parties become more divergent, rank-and-file members will be progressively more willing to delegate strong powers to their leaders to advance the party's program and to benefit it electorally. In this chapter we described how the relationship between the party organizations in Congress and the committee systems changed, arguing that the changes were in accord with the expectations of CPG, especially after the Republican takeover in 1994. Although most observers found the arguments and evidence persuasive with respect to the Gingrich Congresses, some also raised the reasonable question of whether CPG would continue to account for congressional organization and policy making.[35] In this concluding section, we address that issue by discussing developments in Congress in the last decade, during the speakerships of Dennis Hastert and Nancy Pelosi.

CPG theory has a number of key features that we have to account for to demonstrate continued applicability: (1) Have intraparty homogeneity and interparty divergence remained high? (2) If so, has the majority party in particular continued to delegate strong powers to its leadership? and (3) Has the majority leadership continued to exercise its powers to facilitate achievement of the party's legislative and electoral goals?

With regard to the first question, the data are unequivocal. All research on the subject shows that the polarization of the parties continues.[36] The median positions of the parties on roll call measures have even been a bit farther apart during the last ten years than they were in the 104th Congress. Moreover, the proportion of Congress that takes positions in the middle of the ideological spectrum is smaller than ever. This evidence indicates that the underlying "condition" for CPG is still well satisfied. We will now consider the other two features of the argument separately for the periods of Gingrich's two successors, as each provides a separate opportunity to test the predictions of CPG against data based on new members, leaders, and circumstances.

Hastert's Speakership

The selection of Dennis Hastert, R-Ill., as Speaker provided a strong challenge for CPG theory because on taking office he promised that regular procedures would be restored. However, with regard to the willingness of members to delegate power to party leaders, none of the significant authority granted to the Republican House leadership was rescinded. To the contrary, Hastert sought and was granted additional power. For example, in late 2002 Hastert asked the GOP conference to give him and the party even more influence over the Appropriations Committee by requiring that the chairs of its subcommittees be approved by the party Steering Committee.[37] In addition the Speaker arranged to give the Steering Committee the right to approve full committee chairs. In 2001 and 2003, under Hastert's leadership, the committee bypassed a number of more senior and more moderate members to pick more junior and more conservative candidates for chairmanships. For example, Chris Shays of Connecticut, who had joined with Democrats against his party leaders in the successful fight for campaign finance reform legislation, was passed over for chair of the Government Reform Committee (where he was most senior) in favor of Tom Davis of Virginia, who had served on the committee only half as long. And in 2005, in perhaps the strongest use of leadership power against a committee chairman in a century, Chris Smith of New Jersey was removed from the top spot on Veterans Affairs because of his persistent efforts to increase spending on veterans programs. The leadership had warned Smith to be more compliant with their priorities or risk punishment.[38] When he continued, the threats were fulfilled.

Moreover, regarding the continued exercise of leadership powers, Hastert and his colleagues showed that they were more than willing to manipulate the legislative process for majority party advantage. For example, Hastert and then–Senate majority leader Bill Frist, R-Tenn., presented a compromise that they had negotiated on the Medicare bill in late 2003, and Hastert pressured Ways and Means Committee chair Bill Thomas of California to accept it against his will.[39] Around the same time, majority leader Tom DeLay of Texas gave the Armed Services Committee chair an ultimatum to pass the defense authorization bill within two days, or else the leadership would strip out a popular provision and send it to the floor alone.[40]

Thus the Republican leadership continued to pressure and influence committees' actions. They also continued to use the tools at their disposal to structure the floor agenda and actions taken after bills are passed. Despite Hastert's promise to restore the use of regular procedures, the GOP continued to use restrictive special rules to block the Democrats from offering many of their preferred amendments. David Dreier, R-Calif., noted as chair of the Rules Committee that he used to complain about Democrats' use of special rules but that he learned "pretty quickly" that the majority party needed to use that device. "'I had not known what it took to govern,' he acknowledged. Now 'our number one priority is to move our agenda.'"[41] Indeed, Don Wolfensberger, former head of the Republican staff on the Rules Committee, concluded, "By the 107th Congress (2001–2003) . . . the Republicans had far exceeded the Democrats' worst excesses in restricting floor amendments."[42]

The GOP leadership in both chambers at times restricted minority members from participation in the deliberations of conference committees. (These are temporary panels set up to resolve differences in legislation after bills have been passed by both houses.) For example, in 2003 only two moderate Democratic senators and no House Democrats were permitted to participate in the conference on the Medicare bill, and on the energy bill no Democrats at all were permitted in conference meetings. In using all of these techniques, the Republicans denied that they were being unfair to the Democrats. They contended that they were just doing what was necessary to enact their legislative agenda. As Speaker Hastert said in an interview in late 2003, "While a Speaker should strive to be fair, he is also judged by how he gets the job done. The job of the Speaker is to rule fairly, but ultimately to carry out the will of the majority."[43]

Pelosi's Speakership

The transition to Democratic rule after the elections of 2006 offered another opportunity to assess the predictions of CPG theory, especially the expectation that while polarization continued, the House Democrats could be expected to delegate strong powers to their leadership. The rules package for the 110th Congress that Speaker Nancy Pelosi, Calif., and her allies drafted and submitted confirmed the accuracy of that expectation. The package included all the main leadership powers that the Democrats exercised the last time they were the majority, plus some new ones from the era of Republican control. The most striking of these was Pelosi's decision to retain the six-year term limit for committee chairs. Moreover, she did not even inform senior Democrats of this decision until shortly before the vote on the new rules. Many of them objected (including John Dingell, the incoming chair of the Energy and Commerce Committee, who said, "I think it's dumb"), but all party members including Dingell voted for the provisions.

CPG theory would also lead us to expect the vigorous exercise of leadership powers on behalf of the party's program in the new Congress, with the support of the vast majority of Democratic representatives. This expectation is also borne out. Pelosi selected six bills—all high priorities for the party—to be considered in the first one hundred hours of legislative business. These bills bypassed committee consideration and were put together without GOP input. All were considered under closed or restrictive rules, so that Republicans were blocked from offering amendments. The Democrats successfully completed consideration of all six well before the hundred-hour deadline.

Of course the Democratic Party is not so homogeneous that it lacks any recalcitrant members. John Dingell was one, and his committee had jurisdiction over one of the Democrats' priority issues for the new Congress: the energy bill. Seeking to return processes to the regular order of the past, Dingell proceeded to construct a bill according to his own lights, and his committee's draft included two significant provisions that were at odds with leadership priorities: They were an attempt to preempt states from regulating greenhouse gases from automobiles and a provision to override a recent Supreme Court decision confirming the authority of the Environmental Protection Agency to act to combat global warming.[44]

Pelosi called Dingell and some other members of the Energy Committee to a meeting in her office with the leadership. There she demanded that Dingell remove the two provisions from the draft bill. After some negotiations, Dingell agreed to comply.[45] Rep. Henry Waxman, D-Calif., chairman of the Energy Committee's

Oversight Subcommittee, who attended the meeting, later said, "I have never seen a speaker take such an active and forceful role on policy. . . . [Former Speakers] Tip O'Neill or Tom Foley would not have told John Dingell or Dan Rostenkowski [a former Ways and Means chair] not to report out a bill, or what kind of bill to report out of committee. . . . [Dingell] was shocked by her action."[46] Pelosi also succeeded in other conflicts with Dingell, including the creation of a select committee on global warming and pushing through a floor amendment to the energy bill on renewable energy standards, over the chairman's objections.[47]

Despite these conflicts, it should be clear from our earlier discussion that CPG theory does not anticipate that the general relationship between the leadership and the committee chairs would necessarily be confrontational. Just as the Speaker is the top agent of the party caucus, chairs are agents too in the current era, of both the party and the leadership. Party leaders would prefer that they be faithful agents who can be trusted to pursue shared goals on their own. Leaders must also, however, be able to monitor activity and constrain chairs if they stray. That occurred in the 2007 interactions over energy policy. As majority leader Steny Hoyer, D-Md., put it, "There is a necessity for a unity of voice and purpose in the Democratic Party . . . and the only way you're going to do that was to have a central management to create consensus, not simply individual discrete committee agendas."[48] But as Barney Frank, D-Mass., chairman of the Financial Services Committee, said, "This is not a zero-sum game. . . . It's a mutually supportive relationship."[49]

Pelosi also repeatedly demonstrated her willingness to employ control of the floor agenda through special rules to give preference to party priorities. As was the case with the six bills with which the Democrats opened the Congress, special rules that restricted or prohibited amendments were applied to the overwhelming majority of bills that came to the floor during 2007. These rules were drafted at the direction of the Democratic leadership, and partisan conflict over procedural arrangements reached unprecedented levels. In the 100th Congress, when there were substantial efforts at procedural manipulation under the direction of Speaker Wright, 90 percent of the Democrats opposed 90 percent of the Republicans on only 18 percent of the floor votes on special rules. In the 104th Congress, the first with Newt Gingrich as Speaker, that proportion increased to 58 percent. In the first session of the 110th Congress, however, fully 99 percent of the special rules votes saw this degree of party conflict![50]

Another development in this Congress regarding the Rules Committee is a remarkable and telling indicator of how much the relationship between parties and committees has changed since the prereform era. Before 1974, when the Speaker regained the right to appoint the majority members and the chair of the Rules Committee, the committee was an independent center of power, and many members desired appointment to it so that they could exercise influence within the House. Virtually all appointees to Rules had to serve a number of terms in office before they could secure a place. Moreover, the committee was deemed so important and desirable that it was designated an "exclusive" committee—a member of it could serve on no other standing committee. In 2007, however, when the Democrats had to appoint five new members because they had regained majority status, four of the five were freshmen. The exclusive designation was removed, and Rules Committee members were given additional committee assignments as well. Having lost its independent power, Rules was no longer as important or desirable a post. It was merely an extension of the majority party leadership.

Control over special rules is not the only procedural advantage the majority leadership can bring to bear on behalf of their party. For example, in April 2008 President Bush sought approval for a trade agreement that his administration had negotiated with Colombia. He expected that a vote would take place within sixty legislative days because of the stipulation in congressional rules known as "fast-track," giving such measures priority.[51] Bush knew that there was opposition to the agreement among some Democrats, but he judged that the short time frame and the oncoming election would exert pressure on Congress to comply with his wishes. Democrats, on the other hand, had been trying to persuade the administration to take some additional action to help economically distressed Americans before they addressed the trade deal. Speaker Pelosi responded to the Bush stratagem by bringing to the House floor a rules change that stripped fast-track procedures from this trade agreement. The change, which puts off a vote until the Speaker decides the time is right, secured the support of all but ten Democrats.

Moreover, the new Republican minority has sought to use its limited capabilities to encourage solidarity among its members and to compete with the majority. For example, Rep. Walter Jones, R-N.C., a generally conservative member who nonetheless had become a vigorous opponent of the war in Iraq, was passed over twice during the 110th Congress for the top minority position on a subcommittee of the Armed Services Committee because of his deviation from party orthodoxy.[52] Also, Jeff Flake, R-Ariz., another conservative who frequently disagreed with his party leaders in the previous Congress about their support for too much spending, was removed from his place on the Judiciary Committee. The minority leader, John Boehner, R-Ohio, later informed him that the action was taken because of Flake's verbal attacks on party leaders.[53]

Thus all indications are that the theoretical account offered by CPG is as applicable in 2008 as it was in 1995. Partisan policy disagreement is at least as strong and partisan conflict just as intense. Indeed, these conditions continue to be reinforced by the close division of the two chambers. In every election since 1994, members of both parties have believed that they had a good chance to win majority control. That perception makes every decision on policy and legislative strategy potentially a high-stakes choice, giving the majority party strong incentive to use its institutional powers to the maximum. Therefore, as long as the legislative parties remain ideologically homogeneous and the ideological divergence between the two parties remains great, and as long as the partisan division of the chambers is close, we expect conditional party government theory to continue to provide a good explanation for congressional organization and activity.

NOTES

1. This interest in developing and sharing expertise is the central focus in the "informational" theory of legislative organization presented by Keith Krehbiel in *Information and Legislative Organization* (Chicago: University of Chicago Press, 1991).

2. Richard F. Fenno Jr., *Congressmen in Committees* (Boston: Little Brown, 1973), chap. 1.

3. Indeed, David Mayhew contended that the institutional structure of the Congress was principally designed to foster members' reelection. See David R. Mayhew, *Congress: The Electoral Connection* (New Haven: Yale University Press, 1974). Also see E. Scott Adler, *Why Congressional Reforms Fail: Reelection and the House Committee System* (Chicago: University of Chicago Press, 2002).

4. See Richard C. Hall, *Participation in Congress* (New Haven: Yale University Press, 1996); and C. Lawrence Evans, *Leadership in Committee* (Ann Arbor: University of Michigan Press, 2001).

5. For more information on the history of the committee system, see Joseph Cooper, *The Origins of the Standing Committees and the Development of the Modern House* (Houston: Rice University Studies, 1970); and Christopher J. Deering and Steven S. Smith, *Committees in Congress,* 3rd ed. (Washington, D.C.: CQ Press, 1997).

6. For a detailed analysis of the growth of amending activity on the floors of both chambers see Steven S. Smith, *Call to Order: Floor Politics in the House and Senate* (Washington, D.C.: Brookings Institution Press, 1989).

7. For more details, see David W. Rohde, *Parties and Leaders in the Postreform House* (Chicago: University of Chicago Press, 1991), chap. 3.

8. See Rohde, *Parties and Leaders,* chap. 2; and John H. Aldrich, *Why Parties? The Origin and Transformation of Political Parties in America* (Chicago: University of Chicago Press, 1995), chaps. 6 and 7. An alternative (but compatible) theory of partisan organization of Congress is offered by Gary W. Cox and Mathew D. McCubbins, *Legislative Leviathan* (Berkeley: University of California Press, 1993).

9. Sara Brandes Crook and John R. Hibbing, "Congressional Reform and Party Discipline: The Effects of Changes in the Seniority System on Party Loyalty in the House of Representatives," *British Journal of Political Science* 15 (1985): 207–226. See also Fiona M. Wright, "The Caucus Reelection Requirement and the Transformation of Committee Chairs," *Legislative Studies Quarterly* 25 (2000): 469–480.

10. See Rohde, *Parties and Leaders,* 75–76.

11. Barbara Sinclair, *Legislators, Leaders, and Lawmaking: The U.S. House of Representatives in the Postreform Era* (Baltimore: Johns Hopkins University Press, 1995), 164.

12. For more details on this transformed relationship see Sinclair, *Legislators, Leaders, and Lawmaking,* chap. 9; and Rohde, *Parties and Leaders,* chap. 4.

13. Much has been written about the new role of the Rules Committee. See, for example, Bruce I. Oppenheimer, "The Rules Committee: New Arm of Leadership in a Decentralized

House," in *Congress Reconsidered,* ed. Lawrence C. Dodd and Bruce I. Oppenheimer (New York: Praeger, 1977), 96–116; Stanley Bach and Steven S. Smith, *Managing Uncertainty in the House of Representatives* (Washington, D.C.: Brookings Institution Press, 1988); Sinclair, *Legislators, Leaders, and Lawmaking,* chap. 8; and Rohde, *Parties and Leaders,* 98–118.

14. See Gary C. Jacobson, *The Politics of Congressional Elections,* 5th ed. (New York: Longman, 2001), 178–185.

15. The discussion in this section is drawn from John H. Aldrich and David W. Rohde, "The Transition to Republican Rule in the House: Implications for Theories of Congressional Politics," *Political Science Quarterly* 112 (1997–1998): 541–567; and C. Lawrence Evans and Walter J. Oleszek, *Congress under Fire: Reform Politics and the Republican Majority* (Boston: Houghton Mifflin, 1997).

16. Quoted in Guy Gugliotta, "In New House, Barons Yield to the Boss," *Washington Post,* December 1, 1994, 1.

17. See Adler, *Why Congressional Reforms Fail.*

18. Sinclair, *Legislators, Leaders, and Lawmaking,* 163–197.

19. For more detail on the contract and Congress's actions on it, see James G. Gimpel, *Fulfilling the Contract: The First 100 Days* (Boston: Allyn and Bacon, 1996).

20. *Washington Post,* October 8, 1995, A5.

21. *Roll Call,* October 2, 1995, 20.

22. *Washington Post,* March 26, 1996, A9.

23. Task forces had been used before the GOP majority took over. See Sinclair, *Legislators, Leaders, and Lawmaking.* For more recent details on task force use, see Barbara Sinclair, *Unorthodox Lawmaking: New Legislative Processes in the U.S. Congress,* 2nd ed. (Washington, D.C.: CQ Press, 2000).

24. See *CQ Weekly,* September 23, 1995, 2886; *Roll Call,* October 12, 1995, 3. For more systematic analysis of bypassing committees, see Charles J. Finocchiaro, "Setting the Stage: Party and Procedure in the Pre-Floor Agenda Setting of the U.S. House," PhD diss., Michigan State University, 2003; and Sinclair, *Unorthodox Lawmaking.*

25. Sinclair, *Unorthodox Lawmaking,* 94.

26. Ibid., 211 and 20, respectively.

27. *Roll Call,* March 20, 1995, 18.

28. *Congressional Quarterly Weekly Report,* October 21, 1995, 3207.

29. The data are adapted from Tables 1–4 in Jamie L. Carson, Charles J. Finocchiaro, and David W. Rohde, "Consensus and Conflict in House Decision Making: A Bill-Level Examination of Committee and Floor Behavior," paper delivered at the annual meeting of the Midwest Political Science Association, Chicago, April 2001. The data include all public bills and joint resolutions referred to a committee and either reported by the committee or debated on the floor.

30. See Mayhew, *Congress: The Electoral Connection,* 52–73.

31. The classification was developed by Deering and Smith, *Committees in Congress,* 3rd ed., chap. 3. The prestige committees are Appropriations and Ways and Means; the policy committees are Banking, Commerce, Education, Foreign Affairs, Government Operations, and Judiciary; the constituency committees are Agriculture, Armed Services, Interior, Merchant Marine, Science, Transportation, and Veterans Affairs. (Committee names change over time. These are the names for the 96th Congress.) The committees that the authors term "unrequested" are omitted, as are Rules and Budget because they consider few bills. Note that bills referred to more than one committee are counted for each committee to which they were referred.

32. These data are taken from Mark S. Hurwitz, Roger J. Moiles, and David W. Rohde, "Distributive and Partisan Issues in Agriculture Policy in the 104th House," *American Political Science Review* 95 (2001): 915.

33. The dominant role of Senate subcommittee chairs is discussed in C. Lawrence Evans, *Leadership in Committee: A Comparative Analysis of Leadership Behavior in the U.S. Senate* (Ann Arbor: University of Michigan Press, 2001).

34. For discussions of various ways in which parties can be consequential in the Senate, see *Why Not Parties? Party Effects in the United States Senate,* ed. Nathan W. Monroe, Jason M. Roberts, and David W. Rohde (Chicago: University of Chicago Press, 2008).

35. See, for example, Lawrence C. Dodd and Bruce I. Oppenheimer, "Congress and the Emerging Order: Conditional Party Government or Constructive Partisanship?" in *Congress Reconsidered,* 6th ed., ed. Lawrence C. Dodd and Bruce I. Oppenheimer (Washington, D.C.: CQ Press, 1997), 390–413.

36. See, for example, Richard Fleisher and Jon R. Bond, "The Shrinking Middle in the U.S. Congress," *British Journal of Political Science* 34 (July 2004): 429–451; and Sean Theriault, "The Case of the Vanishing Moderates: Party Polarization in the Modern Congress," manuscript, University of Texas, 2004.

37. Remember that the Steering Committee is weighted toward leadership influence. See *Roll Call,* November 18, 2002, 1.

38. *CQ Weekly,* July 26, 2003, 1910.

39. *Washington Post,* November 30, 2003, A8.

40. *CQ Weekly,* November 8, 2003, 2785.

41. Jim VandeHei, "Using the Rules Committee to Block Democrats," *Washington Post,* June 16, 2003, A21.

42. Don Wolfensberger, "The Motion to Recommit in the House: The Creation, Evisceration, and Restoration of a Minority Right," paper prepared for the Conference on the History of Congress, Stanford University, December 5–6, 2003, 31.

43. *Roll Call,* November 17, 2003, 4.

44. See Richard E. Cohen, "Power Surge," *National Journal,* July 21, 2007, 23.

45. *The Hill,* June 19, 2007, 3.

46. Quoted in Cohen, "Power Surge," 22.

47. *The Hill,* February 6, 2007, 1. Pelosi did, however, agree to Dingell's request that the select committee would not have any legislative jurisdiction.

48. Quoted in *Washington Post,* July 9, 2007, A4.

49. Quoted in *Roll Call,* November 5, 2007, 22.

50. The data on the 100th and 104th Congresses come from the PIPC House roll call database ("Roll Call Voting Data for the United States House of Representatives, 1953–2004," compiled by the Political Institutions and Public Choice Program, Michigan State University). The data are available from Michael Crespin's Web site, http://crespin.myweb.uga.edu. The data on the 110th Congress were compiled for this essay.

51. Fast-track legislation had expired in July 2007, but since the Colombia agreement was negotiated before expiration, the rules continued to apply to it.

52. See *The Hill,* October 16, 2007, 3.

53. See Robert D. Novak, "Bad Behavior?" January 13, 2007, at http://townhall.com.

Chapter 7

The Presidency

7-1

from *Presidential Power*

Richard E. Neustadt

In his classic treatise Presidential Power, *Richard E. Neustadt presents a problem that confronts every occupant of the White House: His authority does not match the expectations for his performance. We expect our presidents to be leaders, Neustadt tells us, but the office guarantees no more than that they will be clerks. In the following excerpt, Neustadt explains that the key to presidential success lies in persuasion and shows how the ability to persuade depends on bargaining.*

THE LIMITS ON COMMAND suggest the structure of our government. The Constitutional Convention of 1787 is supposed to have created a government of "separated powers." It did nothing of the sort. Rather, it created a government of separated institutions *sharing* powers.[1] "I am part of the legislative process," Eisenhower often said in 1959 as a reminder of his veto.[2] Congress, the dispenser of authority and funds, is no less part of the administrative process. Federalism adds another set of separated institutions. The Bill of Rights adds others. Many public purposes can only be achieved by voluntary acts of private institutions; the press, for one, in Douglass Cater's phrase, is a "fourth branch of government."[3]

Source: Richard Neustadt, *Presidential Power and the Modern Presidents: The Politics of Leadership from Roosevelt to Reagan* (1960; New York: Simon & Schuster, 1990), 29–49.

And with the coming of alliances abroad, the separate institutions of a London, or a Bonn, share in the making of American public policy.

What the Constitution separates our political parties do not combine. The parties are themselves composed of separated organizations sharing public authority. The authority consists of nominating powers. Our national parties are confederations of state and local party institutions, with a headquarters that represents the White House, more or less, if the party has a President in office. These confederacies manage presidential nominations. All other public offices depend upon electorates confined within the states.[4] All other nominations are controlled within the states. The President and congressmen who bear one party's label are divided by dependence upon different sets of voters. The differences are sharpest at the stage of nomination. The White House has too small a share in nominating congressmen, and Congress has too little weight in nominating presidents for party to erase their constitutional separation. Party links are stronger than is frequently supposed, but nominating processes assure the separation.[5]

The separateness of institutions and the sharing of authority prescribe the terms on which a President persuades. When one man shares authority with another, but does not gain or lose his job upon the other's whim, his willingness to act upon the urging of the other turns on whether he conceives the action right for him. The essence of a President's persuasive task is to convince such men that what the White House wants of them is what they ought to do for their sake and on their authority. (Sex matters not at all; for *man* read *woman*.)

Persuasive power, thus defined, amounts to more than charm or reasoned argument. These have their uses for a President, but these are not the whole of his resources. For the individuals he would induce to do what he wants done on their own responsibility will need or fear some acts by him on his responsibility. If they share his authority, he has some share in theirs. Presidential "powers" may be inconclusive when a President commands, but always remain relevant as he persuades. The status and authority inherent in his office reinforce his logic and his charm.

Status adds something to persuasiveness; authority adds still more. When Truman urged wage changes on his secretary of commerce [Charles Sawyer] while the latter was administering the [recently seized] steel mills, he and Secretary Sawyer were not just two men reasoning with one another. Had they been so, Sawyer probably would never have agreed to act. Truman's status gave him special claims to Sawyer's loyalty or at least attention. In Walter Bagehot's charming phrase, "no man can *argue* on his knees." Although there is no kneeling in this country, few men—and exceedingly few cabinet officers—are immune to the impulse to say "yes" to the President of the United States. It grows harder to say "no" when they are seated in his Oval Office at the White

House, or in his study on the second floor, where almost tangibly he partakes of the aura of his physical surroundings. In Sawyer's case, moreover, the President possessed formal authority to intervene in many matters of concern to the secretary of commerce. These matters ranged from jurisdictional disputes among the defense agencies to legislation pending before Congress and, ultimately, to the tenure of the secretary, himself. There is nothing in the record to suggest that Truman voiced specific threats when they negotiated over wage increases. But given his formal powers and their relevance to Sawyer's other interests, it is safe to assume that Truman's very advocacy of wage action conveyed an implicit threat.

A President's authority and status give him great advantages in dealing with the men he would persuade. Each "power" is a vantage point for him in the degree that other men have use for his authority. From the veto to appointments, from publicity to budgeting, and so down a long list, the White House now controls the most encompassing array of vantage points in the American political system. With hardly an exception, those who share in governing this country are aware that at some time, in some degree, the doing of *their* jobs, the furthering of *their* ambitions, may depend upon the President of the United States. Their need for presidential action, or their fear of it, is bound to be recurrent if not actually continuous. Their need or fear is his advantage.

A President's advantages are greater than mere listing of his "powers" might suggest. Those with whom he deals must deal with him until the last day of his term. Because they have continuing relationships with him, his future, while it lasts, supports his present influence. Even though there is no need or fear of him today, what he could do tomorrow may supply today's advantage. Continuing relationships may convert any "power," any aspect of his status, into vantage points in almost any case. When he induces other people to do what he wants done, a President can trade on their dependence now and later.

The President's advantages are checked by the advantages of others. Continuing relationships will pull in both directions. These are relationships of mutual dependence. A President depends upon the persons whom he would persuade; he has to reckon with his need or fear of them. They too will possess status or authority, or both, else they would be of little use to him. Their vantage points confront his own; their power tempers his.

Persuasion is a two-way street. Sawyer, it will be recalled, did not respond at once to Truman's plan for wage increases at the steel mills. On the contrary, the secretary hesitated and delayed and only acquiesced when he was satisfied that publicly he would not bear the onus of decision. Sawyer had some points of vantage all his own from which to resist presidential pressure. If he had to reckon with coercive implications in the President's "situations of strength," so had Truman to be mindful of the implications underlying Sawyer's place as a department head, as steel administrator, and as a cabinet spokesman for business. Loyalty is reciprocal. Having taken on a dirty job in the steel crisis, Sawyer had strong claims to loyal support. Besides, he had authority to do some things that the White House could ill afford. . . . [H]e might have resigned in a huff (the removal power also works two ways). Or . . . he might have declined to sign necessary orders. Or he might have let it be known publicly that he deplored what he was told to do and protested its doing. By following any of these courses Sawyer almost surely would have strengthened the position of management, weakened the position of the White House, and embittered the union. But the whole purpose of a wage increase was to enhance White House persuasiveness in urging settlement upon union and companies alike. Although Sawyer's status and authority did not give him the power to prevent an increase outright, they gave him capability to undermine its purpose. If his authority over wage rates had been vested by a statute, not by revocable presidential order, his power of prevention might have been complete. So Harold Ickes [Sr.] demonstrated in the famous case of helium sales to Germany before the Second World War.[6]

The power to persuade is the power to bargain. Status and authority yield bargaining advantages. But in a government of "separated institutions sharing power," they yield them to all sides. With the array of vantage points at his disposal, a President may be far more persuasive than his logic or his charm could make him. But outcomes are not guaranteed by his advantages. There remain the counter pressures those whom he would influence can bring to bear on him from vantage points at their disposal. Command has limited utility; persuasion becomes give-and-take. It is well that the White House holds the vantage points it does. In such a business any President may need them all—and more.

THIS VIEW OF POWER as akin to bargaining is one we commonly accept in the sphere of congressional relations. Every textbook states and every legislative session demonstrates that save in times like the extraordinary Hundred Days of 1933—times virtually ruled out by definition at mid-century—a President will often be unable to obtain congressional action on his terms or even to halt action he opposes. The reverse is equally accepted: Congress often is frustrated by the President. Their formal powers are so intertwined that neither will accomplish very much, for very long, without the acquiescence of the other. By the same token, though, what one demands the other can resist. The stage is set for that great game, much like collective bargaining, in which each seeks to profit from the other's needs and fears. It is a game played catch-as-catch-can, case by case. And everybody knows the game, observers and participants alike.

The concept of real power as a give-and-take is equally familiar when applied to presidential influence outside the formal structure of the federal government. . . . When he deals with [governors, union officials, company executives and even citizens or workers] a President draws bargaining advantage from his status or authority. By virtue of their public places or their private rights they have some capability to reply in kind.

In spheres of party politics the same thing follows, necessarily, from the confederal nature of our party organizations. Even in the case of national nominations a President's advantages are checked by those of others. In 1944 it is by no means clear that Roosevelt got his first choice as his running mate. In 1948 Truman, then the President, faced serious revolts against his nomination. In 1952 his intervention from the White House helped assure the choice of Adlai Stevenson, but it is far from clear that Truman could have done as much for any other candidate acceptable to him.[7] In 1956 when Eisenhower was President, the record leaves obscure just who backed Harold Stassen's efforts to block Richard Nixon from renomination as vice president. But evidently everything did not go quite as Eisenhower wanted, whatever his intentions may have been.[8] The outcomes in these instances bear all the marks of limits on command and of power checked by power that characterize congressional relations. Both in and out of politics these checks and limits seem to be quite widely understood.

Influence becomes still more a matter of give-and-take when Presidents attempt to deal with allied governments. A classic illustration is the long unhappy wrangle over Suez policy in 1956. In dealing with the British and the French before their military intervention, Eisenhower had his share of bargaining advantages but no effective power of command. His allies had their share of counterpressures, and they finally tried the most extreme of all: action despite him. His pressure then was instrumental in reversing them. But had the British government been on safe ground at home, Eisenhower's wishes might have made as little difference after intervention as before. Behind the decorum of diplomacy—which was not very decorous in the Suez affair—relationships among allies are not unlike relationships among state delegations at a national convention. Power is persuasion, and persuasion becomes bargaining. The concept is familiar to everyone who watches foreign policy.

In only one sphere is the concept unfamiliar: the sphere of executive relations. Perhaps because of civics textbooks and teaching in our schools, Americans instinctively resist the view that power in this sphere resembles power in all others. Even Washington reporters, White House aides, and congressmen are not immune to the illusion that administrative agencies comprise a single structure, "the" executive branch, where presidential word is law, or ought to be. Yet . . . when a President seeks something from executive officials his persuasiveness is subject to the same sorts of limitations as in the case of congressmen, or governors, or national committeemen, or private citizens, or foreign governments. There are no generic differences, no differences in kind and only sometimes in degree. The incidents preceding the dismissal of [General Douglas] MacArthur and the incidents surrounding seizure of the steel mills make it plain that here as elsewhere influence derives from bargaining advantages; power is a give-and-take.

Like our governmental structure as a whole, the executive establishment consists of separated institutions sharing powers. The President heads one of these; cabinet officers, agency administrators, and military commanders head others. Below the departmental level, virtually independent bureau chiefs head many more. Under mid-century conditions, federal operations spill across dividing lines on organization charts; almost every policy entangles many agencies; almost every program calls for interagency collaboration. Everything somehow involves the President. But operating agencies owe their existence least of all to one another—and only in some part to him. Each has a separate statutory base; each has its statutes to administer; each deals with a different set of subcommittees at the Capitol. Each has its own peculiar set of clients, friends, and enemies outside the formal government. Each has a different set of specialized careerists inside its own bailiwick. Our Constitution gives the President the "take-care" clause and the appointive power. Our statutes give him central budgeting and a degree of personnel control. All agency administrators are responsible to him. But they also are responsible to Congress, to their clients, to their staffs, and to themselves. In short, they have five masters. Only after all of those do they owe any loyalty to each other.

"The members of the cabinet," Charles G. Dawes used to remark, "are a president's natural enemies." Dawes had been Harding's budget director, Coolidge's vice president, and Hoover's ambassador to London; he also had been General Pershing's chief assistant for supply in World War I. The words are highly colored, but Dawes knew whereof he spoke. The men who have to serve so many masters cannot help but be somewhat the "enemy" of any one of them. By the same token, any master wanting service is in some degree the "enemy" of such a servant. A President is likely to want loyal support but not to relish trouble on his doorstep. Yet the more his cabinet members cleave to him, the more they may need help from him in fending off the wrath of rival masters. Help, though, is synonymous with trouble. Many a cabinet officer, with loyalty ill rewarded by his lights and help withheld, has come to view the White House as innately hostile to department heads. Dawes's dictum can be turned around.

A senior presidential aide remarked to me in Eisenhower's time: "If some of these cabinet members would just take time out to stop and ask themselves, 'What would I want if I were President?' they wouldn't give him all the trouble he's been having." But even if they asked themselves the question, such officials often could not act upon the answer. Their personal attachment to the President is all too often overwhelmed by duty to their other masters.

Executive officials are not equally advantaged in their dealings with a President. Nor are the same officials equally advantaged all the time. Not every officeholder can resist like a MacArthur or Sawyer. . . . The vantage points conferred upon officials by their own authority and status vary enormously. The variance is heightened by particulars of time and circumstance. In mid-October 1950, Truman, at a press conference, remarked of the man he had considered firing in August and would fire the next April for intolerable insubordination:

> Let me tell you something that will be good for your souls. It's a pity that you . . . can't understand the ideas of two intellectually honest men when they meet. General MacArthur . . . is a member of the Government of the United States. He is loyal to that Government. He is loyal to the President. He is loyal to the President in his foreign policy. . . . There is no disagreement between General MacArthur and myself.[9]

MacArthur's status in and out of government was never higher than when Truman spoke those words. The words, once spoken, added to the general's credibility thereafter when he sought to use the press in his campaign against the President. And what had happened between August and October? Near victory had happened, together with that premature conference on postwar plans, the meeting at Wake Island.

If the bargaining advantages of a MacArthur fluctuate with changing circumstances, this is bound to be so with subordinates who have at their disposal fewer powers, lesser status, to fall back on. And when officials have no powers in their own right, or depend upon the President for status, their counterpressure may be limited indeed. White House aides, who fit both categories, are among the most responsive men of all, and for good reason. As a director of the budget once remarked to me, "Thank God I'm here and not across the street. If the President doesn't call me, I've got plenty I can do right here and plenty coming up to me, by rights, to justify my calling him. But those poor fellows over there, if the boss doesn't call them, doesn't ask them to do something, what *can* they do but sit?" Authority and status so conditional are frail reliances in resisting a President's own wants. Within the White House precincts, lifted eyebrows may suffice to set an aide in motion; command, coercion, even charm aside. But even in the White House a President does not monopolize effective power. Even there persuasion is akin to bargaining. A former Roosevelt aide once wrote of cabinet officers:

Half of a President's suggestions, which theoretically carry the weight of orders, can be safely forgotten by a Cabinet member. And if the President asks about a suggestion a second time, he can be told that it is being investigated. If he asks a third time, a wise Cabinet officer will give him at least part of what he suggests. But only occasionally, except about the most important matters, do Presidents ever get around to asking three times.[10]

The rule applies to staff as well as to the cabinet, and certainly has been applied *by* staff in Truman's time and Eisenhower's.

Some aides will have more vantage points than a selective memory. Sherman Adams, for example, as the assistant to the President under Eisenhower, scarcely deserved the appellation "White House aide" in the meaning of the term before his time or as applied to other members of the Eisenhower entourage. Although Adams was by no means "chief of staff" in any sense so sweeping—or so simple—as press commentaries often took for granted, he apparently became no more dependent on the President than Eisenhower on him. "I need him," said the President when Adams turned out to have been remarkably imprudent in the Goldfine case, and delegated to him, at least nominally, the decision on his own departure.[11] This instance is extreme, but the tendency it illustrates is common enough. Any aide who demonstrates to others that he has the President's consistent confidence and a consistent part in presidential business will acquire so much business on his own account that he becomes in some sense independent of his chief. Nothing in the Constitution keeps a well-placed aide from converting status into power of his own, usable in some degree even against the President—an outcome not unknown in Truman's regime or, by all accounts, in Eisenhower's.

The more an officeholder's status and his powers stem from sources independent of the President, the stronger will be his potential pressure on the President. Department heads in general have more bargaining power than do most members of the White House staff; but bureau chiefs may have still more, and specialists at upper levels of established career services may have almost unlimited reserves of the enormous power which consists of sitting still. As Franklin Roosevelt once remarked:

> The Treasury is so large and far-flung and ingrained in its practices that I find it almost impossible to get the action and results I want—even with Henry [Morgenthau] there. But the Treasury is not to be compared with the State Department. You should go through the experience of trying to get any changes in the thinking, policy, and action of the career diplomats and then you'd know what a real problem was. But the Treasury and the State Department put together are nothing compared with the Na-a-vy. The admirals are really something to cope with—and I should know. To change anything in the Na-a-vy is like punching a feather bed. You punch it with your right

and you punch it with your left until you are finally exhausted, and then you find the damn bed just as it was before you started punching.[12]

In the right circumstances, of course, a President can have his way with any of these people. . . . [But] as between a President and his "subordinates," no less than others on whom he depends, real power is reciprocal and varies markedly with organization, subject matter, personality and situation. The mere fact that persuasion is directed at executive officials signifies no necessary easing of his way. Any new congressman of the Administration's party, especially if narrowly elected, may turn out more amenable (though less useful) to the President than any seasoned bureau chief "downtown." *The probabilities of power do not derive from the literary theory of the Constitution.*

THERE IS a widely held belief in the United States that were it not for folly or for knavery, a reasonable President would need no power other than the logic of his argument. No less a personage than Eisenhower has subscribed to that belief in many a campaign speech and press-conference remark. But faulty reasoning and bad intentions do not cause all quarrels with Presidents. The best of reasoning and of intent cannot compose them all. For in the first place, what the President wants will rarely seem a trifle to the people he wants it from. And in the second place, they will be bound to judge it by the standard of their own responsibilities, not his. However logical his argument according to his lights, their judgment may not bring them to his view.

Those who share in governing this country frequently appear to act as though they were in business for themselves. So, in a real though not entire sense, they are and have to be. When Truman and MacArthur fell to quarreling, for example, the stakes were no less than the substance of American foreign policy, the risks of greater war or military stalemate, the prerogatives of Presidents and field commanders, the pride of a proconsul and his place in history. Intertwined, inevitably, were other stakes as well: political stakes for men and factions of both parties; power stakes for interest groups with which they were or wished to be affiliated. And every stake was raised by the apparent discontent in the American public mood. There is no reason to suppose that in such circumstances men of large but differing responsibilities will see all things through the same glasses. On the contrary, it is to be expected that their views of what ought to be done and what they then should do will vary with the differing perspectives their particular responsibilities evoke. Since their duties are not vested in a "team" or a "collegium" but in themselves, as individuals, one must expect that they will see things for themselves. Moreover, when they are responsible to many masters and when an event or policy turns loyalty against loyalty—a day-by-day occurrence in the nature of the case—one must assume that those who have the duties to perform will choose the terms of reconciliation. This is the essence of their personal responsibility. When their own duties pull in opposite directions, who else but they can choose what they will do?

When Truman dismissed MacArthur, the latter lost three posts: the American command in the Far East, the Allied command for the occupation of Japan, and the United Nations command in Korea. He also lost his status as the senior officer on active duty in the United States armed forces. So long as he held those positions and that status, though, he had a duty to his troops, to his profession, to himself (the last is hard for any man to disentangle from the rest). As a public figure and a focus for men's hopes he had a duty to constituents at home, and in Korea and Japan. He owed a duty also to those other constituents, the UN governments contributing to his field forces. As a patriot he had a duty to his country. As an accountable official and an expert guide he stood at the call of Congress. As a military officer he had, besides, a duty to the President, his constitutional commander. Some of these duties may have manifested themselves in terms more tangible or more direct than others. But it would be nonsense to argue that the last negated all the rest, however much it might be claimed to override them. And it makes no more sense to think that anybody but MacArthur was effectively empowered to decide how he himself would reconcile the competing demands his duties made upon him.

. . . Reasonable men, it is so often said, *ought* to be able to agree on the requirements of given situations. But when the outlook varies with the placement of each man, and the response required in his place is for each to decide, their reasoning may lead to disagreement quite as well—and quite as reasonably. Vanity, or vice, may weaken reason, to be sure, but it is idle to assign these as the cause of . . . MacArthur's defiance. Secretary Sawyer's hesitations, cited earlier, are in the same category. One need not denigrate such men to explain their conduct. For the responsibilities they felt, the "facts" they saw, simply were not the same as those of their superiors; yet they, not the superiors, had to decide what they would do.

Outside the executive branch the situation is the same, except that loyalty to the President may often matter *less*. There is no need to spell out the comparison with governors of Arkansas, steel company executives, trade union leaders, and the like. And when one comes to congressmen who can do nothing for themselves (or their constituents) save as they are elected, term by term, in districts and through party structures differing from those on which a President depends, the case is very clear. An able Eisenhower aide with long congressional experience remarked to me in 1958: "The people on the Hill don't do what they might *like* to do, they do what they think they *have* to do in their own interest as *they* see it." This states the case precisely.

The essence of a President's persuasive task, with congressmen and everybody else, is to induce them to believe that what he wants of them is what their own appraisal of their own responsibilities requires them to do in their interest, not his. Because men may differ in their views on public policy, because differences in outlook stem from differences in duty—duty to one's office, one's constituents, oneself—that task is bound to be more like collective bargaining than like a reasoned argument among philosopher kings. Overtly or implicitly, hard bargaining has characterized all illustrations offered up to now. This is the reason why: Persuasion deals in the coin of self-interest with men who have some freedom to reject what they find counterfeit.

A President draws influence from bargaining advantages. But does he always need them? . . . [S]uppose most players of the governmental game see policy objectives much alike, then can he not rely on logic (or on charm) to get him what he wants? The answer is that even then most outcomes turn on bargaining. The reason for this answer is a simple one: Most who share in governing have interests of their own beyond the realm of policy objectives. The sponsorship of policy, the form it takes, the conduct of it, and the credit for it separate their interest from the President's despite agreement on the end in view. In political government the means can matter quite as much as ends; they often matter more. And there are always differences of interest in the means.

Let me introduce a case externally the opposite of my previous examples: the European Recovery Program of 1948, the so-called Marshall Plan. This is perhaps the greatest exercise in policy agreement since the Cold War began. When the then secretary of state, George Catlett Marshall, spoke at the Harvard commencement in June 1947, he launched one of the most creative, most imaginative ventures in the history of American foreign relations. What makes this policy most notable for present purposes, however, is that it became effective upon action by the Eightieth Congress, at the behest of Harry Truman, in the election year 1948.[13]

Eight months before Marshall spoke at Harvard, the Democrats had lost control of both houses of Congress for the first time in fourteen years. Truman, whom the secretary represented, had just finished his second troubled year as President-by-succession. Truman was regarded with so little warmth in his own party that in 1946 he had been urged not to participate in the congressional campaign. At the opening of Congress in January 1947, Senator Robert A. Taft, "Mr. Republican," had somewhat the attitude of a President-elect. This was a vision widely shared in Washington, with Truman relegated thereby to the role of caretaker-on-term. Moreover, within just two weeks of Marshall's commencement address, Truman was to veto two prized accomplishments of Taft's congressional majority: the Taft-Hartley Act and tax reduction.[14] Yet scarcely ten months later the Marshall Plan was under way on terms to satisfy its sponsors, its authorization completed, its first-year funds in sight, its administering agency in being: all managed by as thorough a display of executive-congressional cooperation as any we have seen since the Second World War. For any President at any time this would have been a great accomplishment. In years before mid-century it would have been enough to make the future reputation of his term. And for a Truman, at this time, enactment of the Marshall Plan appears almost miraculous.

How was the miracle accomplished? How did a President so situated bring it off? In answer, the first thing to note is that he did not do it by himself. Truman had help of a sort no less extraordinary than the outcome. Although each stands for something more complex, the names of Marshall, Vandenberg, Patterson, Bevin, Stalin tell the story of that help.

In 1947, two years after V-J Day, General Marshall was something more than secretary of state. He was a man venerated by the President as "the greatest living American," literally an embodiment of Truman's ideals. He was honored at the Pentagon as an architect of victory. He was thoroughly respected by the secretary of the Navy, James V. Forrestal, who that year became the first secretary of defense. On Capitol Hill, Marshall had an enormous fund of respect stemming from his war record as Army chief of staff, and in the country generally no officer had come out of the war with a higher reputation for judgment, intellect, and probity. Besides, as secretary of state, he had behind him the first generation of matured foreign service officers produced by the reforms of the 1920s, and mingled with them, in the departmental service, were some of the ablest of the men drawn by the war from private life to Washington. In terms both of staff talent and staff use, Marshall's years began a State Department "golden age" that lasted until the era of McCarthy. Moreover, as his undersecretary, Marshall had, successively, Dean Acheson and Robert Lovett, men who commanded the respect of the professionals and the regard of congressmen. (Acheson had been brilliantly successful at congressional relations as assistant secretary in the war and postwar years.) Finally, as a special undersecretary Marshall had Will Clayton, a man highly regarded, for good reason, at both ends of Pennsylvania Avenue.

Taken together, these are exceptional resources for a secretary of state. In the circumstances, they were quite as necessary as they obviously are relevant. The Marshall Plan was launched by a lame-duck Administration "scheduled" to leave office in eighteen months. Marshall's program faced a congressional leadership traditionally isolationist and currently intent upon economy. European aid was viewed with envy by a Pentagon distressed and virtually disarmed through budget cuts, and by domestic agencies intent on enlarged welfare programs. It was not viewed with liking by a Treasury intent on budget surpluses. The plan had need of every asset that could be extracted from the personal position of its nominal author and from the skills of his assistants.

Without the equally remarkable position of the senior senator from Michigan, Arthur H. Vandenberg, it is hard to see how Marshall's assets could have been enough. Vandenberg was chairman of the Senate Foreign Relations Committee. Actually, he was much more than that. Twenty years a senator, he was the senior member of his party in the chamber. Assiduously cultivated by FDR and Truman, he was a chief Republican proponent of bipartisanship in foreign policy and consciously conceived himself its living symbol to his party, to the country, and abroad. Moreover, by informal but entirely operative agreement with his colleague Taft, Vandenberg held the acknowledged lead among Senate Republicans in the whole field of international affairs. This acknowledgment meant more in 1947 than it might have meant at any other time. With confidence in the advent of a Republican administration two years hence, most of the gentlemen were in a mood to be responsive and responsible. The war was over, Roosevelt dead, Truman a caretaker, theirs the trust. That the senator from Michigan saw matters in this light his diaries make clear.[15] And this was not the outlook from the Senate side alone; the attitudes of House Republicans associated with the Herter Committee and its tours abroad suggest the same mood of responsibility. Vandenberg was not the only source of help on Capitol Hill. But relatively speaking his position there was as exceptional as Marshall's was downtown.

Help of another sort was furnished by a group of dedicated private citizens who organized one of the most effective instruments for public information seen since the Second World War: the Committee for the Marshall Plan, headed by the eminent Republicans whom FDR in 1940 had brought to the Department of War: Henry L. Stimson as honorary chairman and Robert P. Patterson as active spokesman. The remarkable array of bankers, lawyers, trade unionists, and editors, who had drawn together in defense of "internationalism" before Pearl Harbor and had joined their talents in the war itself, combined again to spark the work of this committee. Their efforts generated a great deal of vocal public support to buttress Marshall's arguments, and Vandenberg's, in Congress.

But before public support could be rallied, there had to be a purpose tangible enough, concrete enough, to provide a rallying ground. At Harvard, Marshall had voiced an idea in general terms. That this was turned into a hard program susceptible of presentation and support is due, in major part, to Ernest Bevin, the British foreign secretary. He well deserves the credit he has sometimes been assigned as, in effect, coauthor of the Marshall Plan. For Bevin seized on

Marshall's Harvard speech and organized a European response with prompt-ness and concreteness beyond the State Department's expectations. What had been virtually a trial balloon to test reactions on both sides of the Atlantic was hailed in London as an invitation to the Europeans to send Washington a bill of particulars. This they promptly organized to do, and the American Administration then organized in turn for its reception without further argu-ment internally about the pros and cons of issuing the "invitation" in the first place. But for Bevin there might have been trouble from the secretary of the treasury and others besides.[16]

If Bevin's help was useful at that early stage, Stalin's was vital from first to last. In a mood of self-deprecation Truman once remarked that without Moscow's "crazy" moves "we would never have had our foreign policy . . . we never could have got a thing from Congress." [17] George Kennan, among others, had deplored the anti-Soviet overtone of the case made for the Marshall Plan in Congress and the country, but there is no doubt that this clinched the argument for many segments of American opinion. There also is no doubt that Moscow made the crucial contributions to the case.

By 1947 events, far more than governmental prescience or open action, had given a variety of publics an impression of inimical Soviet intentions (and of Europe's weakness) and a growing urge to "do something about it." Three months before Marshall spoke at Harvard, Greek-Turkish aid and promulgation of the Truman Doctrine had seemed rather to crystallize than to create a public mood and a congressional response. The Marshall planners, be it said, were poorly placed to capitalize on that mood, nor had the secretary wished to do so. Their object, indeed, was to cut across it, striking at the cause of European weak-ness rather than at Soviet aggressiveness, per se. A strong economy in Western Europe called, ideally, for restorative measures of continental scope. American assistance proffered in an anti-Soviet context would have been contradictory in theory and unacceptable in fact to several of the governments that Washington was anxious to assist. As Marshall, himself, saw it, the logic of his purpose for-bade him to play his strongest congressional card. The Russians then proceeded to play it for him. When the Europeans met in Paris, Molotov walked out. After the Czechs had shown continued interest in American aid, a Communist coup overthrew their government while Soviet forces stood along their borders within easy reach of Prague. Molotov transformed the Marshall Plan's initial presentation; Czechoslovakia assured its final passage, which followed by a month the takeover in Prague.

Such was the help accorded Truman in obtaining action on the Marshall Plan. Considering his politically straitened circumstances he scarcely could have done with less. Conceivably some part of Moscow's contribution might have been dispensable, but not Marshall's or Vandenberg's or Bevin's or Patterson's or that of the great many other men whose work is represented by their names in my account. Their aid was not extended to the President for his own sake. He was not favored in this fashion just because they liked him personally or were spellbound by his intellect or charm. They might have been as helpful had all held him in disdain, which some of them certainly did. The Londoners who seized the ball, Vandenberg and Taft and the congressional majority, Marshall and his planners, the officials of other agencies who actively supported them or "went along," the host of influential private citizens who rallied to the cause—all these played the parts they did because they thought they had to, in their interest, given their responsibilities, not Truman's. Yet they hardly would have found it in their interest to collaborate with one another or with him had he not furnished them precisely what they needed from the White House. Truman could not do without their help, but he could not have had it without unremitting effort on his part.

The crucial thing to note about this case is that despite compatibility of views on public policy, Truman got no help he did not pay for (except Stalin's). Bevin scarcely could have seized on Marshall's words had Marshall not been plainly backed by Truman. Marshall's interest would not have comported with the exploitation of his prestige by a president who undercut him openly or subtly or even inadvertently at any point. Vandenberg, presumably, could not have backed proposals by a White House that begrudged him deference and access gratifying to his fellow partisans (and satisfying to himself). Prominent Republicans in private life would not have found it easy to promote a cause identified with Truman's claims on 1948—and neither would the prominent New Dealers then engaged in searching for a substitute.

Truman paid the price required for their services. So far as the record shows, the White House did not falter once in firm support for Marshall and the Marshall Plan. Truman backed his secretary's gamble on an invitation to all Europe. He made the plan his own in a well-timed address to the Canadians. He lost no opportunity to widen the involvements of his own official family in the cause. Averell Harriman, the secretary of commerce; Julius Krug, the secretary of the interior; Edwin Nourse, the Economic Council chairman; James Webb, the director of the budget—all were made responsible for studies and reports contributing directly to the legislative presentation. Thus these men were committed in advance. Besides, the President continually emphasized to everyone in reach that he did not have doubts, did not desire complications and would foreclose all he could. Reportedly his emphasis was felt at the Treasury, with good effect. And Truman was at special pains to smooth the way for Vandenberg. The senator insisted on "no politics" from the Administration side; there was none. He thought a survey of American resources and capacity essential; he got it in the

Krug and Harriman reports. Vandenberg expected advance consultation; he received it, step by step, in frequent meetings with the President and weekly conferences with Marshall. He asked for an effective liaison between Congress and agencies concerned; Lovett and others gave him what he wanted. When the senator decided on the need to change financing and administrative features of the legislation, Truman disregarded Budget Bureau grumbling and acquiesced with grace. When, finally, Vandenberg desired a Republican to head the new administering agency, his candidate, Paul Hoffman, was appointed despite the President's own preference for another. In all these ways Truman employed the sparse advantages his "powers" and his status then accorded him to gain the sort of help he had to have.

Truman helped himself in still another way. Traditionally and practically, no one was placed as well as he to call public attention to the task of Congress (and its Republican leadership). Throughout the fall and winter of 1947 and on into the spring of 1948, he made repeated use of presidential "powers" to remind the country that congressional action was required. Messages, speeches, and an extra session were employed to make the point. Here, too, he drew advantage from his place. However, in his circumstances, Truman's public advocacy might have hurt, not helped, had his words seemed directed toward the forthcoming election. Truman gained advantage for his program only as his own endorsement of it stayed on the right side of that fine line between the "caretaker" in office and the would-be candidate. In public statements dealing with the Marshall Plan he seems to have risked blurring this distinction only once, when he called Congress into session in November 1947 asking both for interim aid to Europe and for peacetime price controls. The second request linked the then inflation with the current Congress (and with Taft), becoming a first step toward one of Truman's major themes in 1948. By calling for both measures at the extra session he could have been accused—and was—of mixing home-front politics with foreign aid. In the event no harm was done the European program (or his politics). But in advance a number of his own advisers feared that such a double call would jeopardize the Marshall Plan. Their fears are testimony to the narrowness of his advantage in employing his own "powers" for its benefit.[18]

It is symptomatic of Truman's situation that bipartisan accommodation by the White House then was thought to mean congressional consultation and conciliation on a scale unmatched in Eisenhower's time. Yet Eisenhower did about as well with opposition congresses as Truman did, in terms of requests granted for defense and foreign aid. It may be said that Truman asked for more extraordinary measures. But it also may be said that Eisenhower never lacked for the prestige his predecessor had to borrow. It often was remarked, in Truman's time, that he seemed a split personality, so sharply did his conduct differentiate domestic politics from national security. But personality aside, how else could he, in his first term, gain ground for an evolving foreign policy? The plain fact is that Truman had to play bipartisanship as he did or lose the game.

HAD TRUMAN LACKED the personal advantages his "powers" and his status gave him, or if he had been maladroit in using them, there probably would not have been a massive European aid program in 1948. Something of the sort, perhaps quite different in its emphasis, would almost certainly have come to pass before the end of 1949. Some American response to European weakness and to Soviet expansion was as certain as such things can be. But in 1948 temptations to await a Taft plan or a Dewey plan might well have caused at least a year's postponement of response had the outgoing Administration bungled its congressional or public or allied or executive relations. Quite aside from the specific virtues of their plan, Truman and his helpers gained that year, at least, in timing the American response. As European time was measured then, this was a precious gain. The President's own share in this accomplishment was vital. He made his contribution by exploiting his advantages. Truman, in effect, lent Marshall and the rest the perquisites and status of his office. In return they lent him their prestige and their own influence. The transfer multiplied his influence despite his limited authority in form and lack of strength politically. Without the wherewithal to make this bargain, Truman could not have contributed to European aid.

Bargaining advantages convey no guarantees. Influence remains a two-way street. In the fortunate instance of the Marshall Plan, what Truman needed was actually in the hands of men who were prepared to "trade" with him. He personally could deliver what they wanted in return. Marshall, Vandenberg, Harriman, et al., possessed the prestige, energy, associations, staffs essential to the legislative effort. Truman himself had a sufficient hold on presidential messages and speeches, on budget policy, on high-level appointments, and on his own time and temper to carry through all aspects of his necessary part. But it takes two to make a bargain. It takes those who have prestige to lend it on whatever terms. Suppose that Marshall had declined the secretaryship of state in January 1947; Truman might not have found a substitute so well equipped to furnish what he needed in the months ahead. Or suppose that Vandenberg had fallen victim to a cancer two years before he actually did; Senator Wiley of Wisconsin would not have seemed to Taft a man with whom the world need be divided. Or suppose that the secretary of the treasury had been possessed of stature, force, and charm commensurate with that of his successor in Eisenhower's time, the redoubtable George M. Humphrey. And what if Truman then had seemed to the Republicans what he turned out to be in 1948, a formidable candidate for President? It is unlikely that a single one of these "supposes" would have changed the final outcome; two or three, however, might have altered it entirely. Truman was not guaranteed more power than his "powers" just because he had continuing relationships with cabinet secretaries and with senior senators. Here, as everywhere, the outcome was conditional on who they were and what he was and how each viewed events, and on their actual performance in response.

Granting that persuasion has no guarantee attached, how can a President reduce the risks of failing to persuade? How can he maximize his prospects for effectiveness by minimizing chances that his power will elude him? The Marshall Plan suggests an answer: He guards his power prospects in the course of making choices. Marshall himself, and Forrestal and Harriman, and others of the sort held office on the President's appointment. Vandenberg had vast symbolic value partly because FDR and Truman had done everything they could, since 1944, to build him up. The Treasury Department and the Budget Bureau—which together might have jeopardized the plans these others made—were headed by officials whose prestige depended wholly on their jobs. What Truman needed from those "givers" he received, in part, because of his past choice of men and measures. What they received in turn were actions taken or withheld by him, himself. The things they needed from him mostly involved his own conduct where his current choices ruled. The President's own actions in the past had cleared the way for current bargaining. His actions in the present were his trading stock. Behind each action lay a personal choice, and these together comprised his control over the give-and-take that gained him what he wanted. In the degree that Truman, personally, affected the advantages he drew from his relationships with other men in government, his power was protected by his choices.

By "choice" I mean no more than what is commonly referred to as "decision": a President's own act of doing or not doing. Decision is so often indecisive, and indecision is so frequently conclusive, that *choice* becomes the preferable term. "Choice" has its share of undesired connotations. In common usage it implies a black-and-white alternative. Presidential choices are rarely of that character. It also may imply that the alternatives are set before the choice maker by someone else. A President is often left to figure out his options for himself. . . .

If Presidents could count upon past choices to enhance their current influence, as Truman's choice of men had done for him, persuasion would pose fewer difficulties than it does. But Presidents can count on no such thing. Depending on the circumstances, prior choices can be as embarrassing as they were helpful in the instance of the Marshall Plan. . . . Truman's hold upon MacArthur was weakened by his deference toward him in the past.

Assuming that past choices have protected influence, not harmed it, present choices still may be inadequate. If Presidents could count on their own conduct to provide them enough bargaining advantages, as Truman's conduct did where Vandenberg and Marshall were concerned, effective bargaining might be much easier to manage than it often is. In the steel crisis, for instance, Truman's own persuasiveness with companies and union, both, was burdened by the conduct of an independent wage board and of government attorneys in the courts, to say nothing of Wilson, Arnall, Sawyer, and the like. Yet in practice, if not theory, many of *their* crucial choices never were the President's to make. Decisions that are legally in others' hands, or delegated past recall, have an unhappy way of proving just the trading stock most needed when the White House wants to trade. One reason why Truman was consistently more influential in the instance of the Marshall Plan than in the steel case or the MacArthur case is that the Marshall Plan directly involved Congress. In congressional relations there are some things that no one but the President can do. His chance to choose is higher when a message must be sent, or a nomination submitted, or a bill signed into law, than when the sphere of action is confined to the executive, where all decisive tasks may have been delegated past recall.

But adequate or not, a President's choices are the only means in his own hands of guarding his own prospects for effective influence. He can draw power from continuing relationships in the degree that he can capitalize upon the needs of others for the Presidency's status and authority. He helps himself to do so, though, by nothing save ability to recognize the preconditions and the chance advantages and to proceed accordingly in the course of the choice making that comes his way. To ask how he can guard prospective influence is thus to raise a further question: What helps him guard his power stakes in his own acts of choice?

NOTES

1. The reader will want to keep in mind the distinction between two senses in which the word *power* is employed. When I have used the word (or its plural) to refer to formal constitutional, statutory, or customary authority, it is either qualified by the adjective "formal" or placed in quotation marks as "power(s)." Where I have used it in the sense of effective influence on the conduct of others, it appears without quotation marks (and always in the singular). Where clarity and convenience permit, *authority* is substituted for "power" in the first sense and *influence* for power in the second.

2. See, for example, his press conference of July 22, 1959, as reported in the *New York Times,* July 23, 1959.

3. See Douglass Cater, *The Fourth Branch of Government* (Boston: Houghton Mifflin, 1959).

4. With the exception of the vice presidency, of course.

5. See David B. Truman's illuminating study of party relationships in the Eighty-first Congress, *The Congressional Party* (New York: Wiley, 1959), especially chaps. 4, 6, 8.

6. As secretary of the interior in 1939, Harold Ickes refused to approve the sale of helium to Germany despite the insistence of the State Department and the urging of President Roosevelt. Without the secretary's approval, such sales were forbidden by statute. See *The Secret Diaries of Harold L. Ickes* (New York: Simon & Schuster, 1954), vol. 2, especially pp. 391–93, 396–99.

In this instance the statutory authority ran to the secretary as a matter of his discretion. A President is unlikely to fire cabinet officers for the conscientious exercise of such authority. If the President did so, their successors might well be embarrassed both publicly and at the Capitol were they to reverse decisions previously taken. As for a President's authority to set aside discretionary determinations of this sort, it rests, if it exists at all, on shaky legal ground not likely to be trod save in the gravest of situations.

7. Truman's *Memoirs* indicate that having tried and failed to make Stevenson an avowed candidate in the spring of 1952, the President decided to support the candidacy of Vice President Barkley. But Barkley withdrew early in the convention for lack of key northern support. Though Truman is silent on the matter, Barkley's active candidacy nearly was revived during the balloting, but the forces then aligning to revive it were led by opponents of Truman's Fair Deal, principally Southerners. As a practical matter, the President could not have lent his weight to their endeavors and could back no one but Stevenson to counter them. The latter's strength could not be shifted, then, to Harriman or Kefauver. Instead the other Northerners had to be withdrawn. Truman helped withdraw them. But he had no other option. See Harry S Truman, *Memoirs, vol. 2, Years of Trial and Hope* (Garden City, N.Y.: Doubleday, Time Inc., 1956), pp. 495–96.

8. The reference is to Stassen's public statement of July 23, 1956, calling for Nixon's replacement on the Republican ticket by Governor Herter of Massachusetts, the later secretary of state. Stassen's statement was issued after a conference with the President. Eisenhower's public statements on the vice-presidential nomination, both before and after Stassen's call, permit of alternative inferences: either that the President would have preferred another candidate, provided this could be arranged without a showing of White House dictation, or that he wanted Nixon on condition that the latter could show popular appeal. In the event, neither result was achieved. Eisenhower's own remarks lent strength to rapid party moves that smothered Stassen's effort. Nixon's nomination thus was guaranteed too quickly to appear the consequence of popular demand. For the public record on this matter see reported statements by Eisenhower, Nixon, Stassen, Herter, and Leonard Hall (the National Republican Chairman) in the *New York Times* for March 1, 8, 15, 16; April 27; July 15, 16, 25–31; August 3, 4, 17, 23, 1956. See also the account from private sources by Earl Mazo in *Richard Nixon: A Personal and Political Portrait* (New York: Harper, 1959), pp. 158–87

9. Stenographic transcript of presidential press conference, October 19, 1950, on file in the Truman Library at Independence, Missouri.

10. Jonathan Daniels, *Frontier on the Potomac* (New York: Macmillan, 1946), pp. 31–32.

11. Transcript of presidential press conference, June 18, 1958, in *Public Papers of the Presidents Dwight D. Eisenhower, 1958* (Washington, D.C.: National Archives, 1959), p. 479. In the summer of 1958, a congressional investigation into the affairs of a New England textile manufacturer, Bernard Goldfine, revealed that Sherman Adams had accepted various gifts and favors from him (the most notoriety attached to a vicuna coat). Adams also had made inquiries about the status of a Federal Communications Commission proceeding in which Goldfine was

involved. In September 1958 Adams was allowed to resign. The episode was highly publicized and much discussed in that year's congressional campaigns.

12. As reported in Marriner S. Eccles (*Beckoning Frontiers,* New York: Knopf, 1951), p. 336.

13. In drawing together these observations on the Marshall Plan, I have relied on the record of personal participation by Joseph M. Jones, *The Fifteen Weeks* (New York: Viking, 1955), especially pp. 89–256; on the recent study by Harry Bayard Price, *The Marshall Plan and Its Meaning* (Ithaca: Cornell University Press, 1955), especially pp. 1–86; on the Truman *Memoirs,* vol. 2, chaps. 7–9; on Arthur H. Vandenberg Jr., ed., *The Private Papers of Senator Vandenberg* (Boston: Houghton Mifflin, 1952), especially pp. 373 ff.; and on notes of my own made at the time. This is an instance of policy development not covered, to my knowledge, by any of the university programs engaged in the production of case studies.

14. Secretary Marshall's speech, formally suggesting what became known as the Marshall Plan, was made at Harvard on June 5, 1947. On June 20 the President vetoed the Taft-Hartley Act; his veto was overridden three days later. On June 16 he vetoed the first of two tax reduction bills (HR 1) passed at the first session of the Eightieth Congress; the second of these (HR 3950), a replacement for the other, he also disapproved on July 18. In both instances his veto was narrowly sustained.

15. *Private Papers of Senator Vandenberg,* pp. 378–79, 446.

16. The initial reluctance of the Secretary of the Treasury, John Snyder, to support large-scale spending overseas became a matter of public knowledge on June 25, 1947. At a press conference on that day he interpreted Marshall's Harvard speech as a call on Europeans to help themselves, by themselves. At another press conference the same day, Marshall for his own part had indicated that the United States would consider helping programs on which Europeans agreed. The next day Truman held a press conference and was asked the inevitable question. He replied, "General Marshall and I are in complete agreement." When pressed further, Truman remarked sharply, "The secretary of the treasury and the secretary of state and the President are in complete agreement." Thus the President cut Snyder off, but had programming gathered less momentum overseas, no doubt he would have been heard from again as time passed and opportunity offered.

The foregoing quotations are from the stenographic transcript of the presidential press conference June 26, 1947, on file in the Truman Library at Independence, Missouri.

17. A remark made in December 1955, three years after he left office, but not unrepresentative of views he expressed, on occasion, while he was President.

18. This might also be taken as testimony to the political timidity of officials in the State Department and the Budget Bureau where that fear seems to have been strongest. However, conversations at the time with White House aides incline me to believe that there, too, interjection of the price issue was thought a gamble and a risk. For further comment see my "Congress and the Fair Deal: A Legislative Balance Sheet," *Public Policy,* vol. 5 (Cambridge: Harvard University Press, 1954), pp. 362–64.

7-2

The Gatekeeper: Rahm Emanuel on the Job

Ryan Lizza

During his first month in office, President Barack Obama unveiled the most ambitious legislative agenda proposed by a president since Lyndon Johnson's Great Society in 1965. Not only did President Obama include unprecedented spending to stimulate the economy out of recession, but he also proposed comprehensive health care reform, major cuts in seemingly untouchable programs, such as agriculture support, and a shift of the tax burden to upper income brackets. Even with healthy Democratic majorities in both houses of Congress, success would clearly require extensive compromise among moderate Democrats and Republicans. Just how much of his program Congress would enact was anyone's guess. As most of the consequential action during his first term would occur in Congress, the president selected savvy Democratic politician Rahm Emanuel to run the White House as his chief of staff. Typically, presidents have selected their chiefs to manage the operation of the White House staff, comprised of some 500 aides, and to serve as a gatekeeper to those who would seek to influence him. By picking Emanuel, however, President Obama appeared poised to place his White House on a mobilization footing to push his program through Congress.

RAHM EMANUEL'S office, which is no more than a three-second walk from the Oval Office, is as neat as a Marine barracks. On his desk, the files and documents, including leatherbound folders from the National Security Council, are precisely arranged, each one parallel with the desk's edge. During a visit hours before Congress passed President Barack Obama's stimulus package, on Friday, February 13th, I absently jostled one of Emanuel's heavy wooden letter trays a few degrees off kilter. He glared at me disapprovingly. Next to his computer monitor is a smaller screen that looks like a handheld G.P.S. device and tells Emanuel where the President and senior White House officials are at all times. Over all, the office suggests the workspace of someone who, in a more psychologized realm than the West Wing of the White House and with a less exacting job than that of the President's chief of staff, might be cited for "control issues."

Source: Ryan Lizza, "The Gatekeeper: Rahm Emanuel on the Job," *The New Yorker*, March 2, 2009.

Because the atmosphere of crisis is now so thick at the White House, any moment of triumph has a fleeting half-life, but the impending passage of the seven-hundred-and-eighty-seven-billion-dollar stimulus bill provided, at least for an afternoon, a sense of satisfaction. As Emanuel spoke about the complications of the legislation, he was quick to credit colleagues for shepherding the bill to victory—Peter Orszag, the budget director; Phil Schiliro, the legislative-affairs director; Jason Furman, the deputy director of the National Economic Council— but, in fact, nearly everyone in official Washington acknowledges that, besides Obama himself, Emanuel had done the most to coax and bully the bill out of Congress and onto the President's desk for signing.

That afternoon, Emanuel and his team were already concentrating on the next major project: the President's budget, which will be released on February 26th. Emanuel had just come from a budget meeting in the Roosevelt Room with the President's senior staff. (The President was downstairs in the Situation Room; coincidentally or not, hours later U.S. Predators attacked a Pakistani Taliban compound in South Waziristan.) After the budget meeting broke up, staffers hurried through the West Wing reception area: Carol Browner, who is in charge of energy policy; Larry Summers, Obama's top economic adviser; Gene Sperling, an adviser to the Treasury Secretary; Orszag; Furman. Like Emanuel, all had worked in the Clinton Administration, all are strong-willed, and all know how to navigate the White House bureaucracy to advance their views. Emanuel personally recruited several of them, and it is now his job to manage their competing egos. . . .

Unlike recent chiefs of staff from the Bush and Clinton eras, who tended to be relatively quiet inside players, Emanuel is a former congressional leader, a Democratic Party power, and one of the more colorful Beltway celebrities. He is a political John McEnroe, known for both his mercurial temperament and his tactical brilliance. In the same conversation, he can be wonkish and thoughtful, blunt and profane. (When Emanuel was a teen-ager, he lost half of his right middle finger, after cutting it on a meat slicer—an accident, Obama once joked, that "rendered him practically mute.") And, like McEnroe, Emanuel seems to employ his volcanic moments for effect, intimidating opponents and referees alike but never quite losing himself in the midst of battle. "I've seen Rahm scream at a candidate for office one moment and then quickly send him a cheese-cake," Chris Van Hollen, a Democratic representative from Maryland, and a friend of Emanuel's, told me.

Emanuel has long since learned to balance his outsized personality, which has made him a subject of intrigue in Washington, with a compulsion for order, which makes him an effective manager. As a child, he attended a Jewish day school in Chicago, where students received written evaluations, instead of A's and B's. "My first-grade teacher," he told me, "said two things that were very interesting: 'Rahm likes to clean up after cleanup time is over.' " He pointed to his desk. "I am fastidious about it. In fact, this is messy today." The second point was about Emanuel's "personality being larger than life." In the first grade.

By any measure, what Obama's White House has achieved in passing the stimulus bill is historic. The last President to preside over a legislative victory of this magnitude so early in his Administration was Franklin Roosevelt, who on the sixth day of his Presidency persuaded Congress to enact a wholesale restructuring of the banking system. (That, too, is likely in the offing for the Obama team.) Yet praise for Obama was surprisingly grudging. Some liberal Democrats said that Emanuel and his team had made too many concessions to House Republicans, all of whom voted against the legislation. Meanwhile, conservatives complained that Obama had broken his pledge of bipartisan cooperation. Both arguments infuriated Emanuel, who spent hours on the Hill during the negotiations, arranged private meetings with Obama in the Oval Office for the Republican senators Susan Collins, Olympia Snowe, and Arlen Specter, whose votes were critical to the bill's passage, and personally haggled over the smallest spending details during a crucial evening of bargaining that lasted until the early morning.

"They have never worked the legislative process," Emanuel said of critics like the *Times* columnist Paul Krugman, who argued that Obama's concessions to Senate Republicans—in particular, the tax cuts, which will do little to stimulate the economy—produced a package that wasn't large enough to respond to the magnitude of the recession. "How many bills has he passed?"

Emanuel has heard such complaints before. As a senior aide in the Clinton White House, he successfully fought a Republican Congress to pass the State Children's Health Insurance Program (S-CHIP), which now provides health care for seven million kids. "I worked children's health care," he said. "President Clinton had pediatric care, eye, and dental, inside Medicaid. The Republicans had pediatric care, no eye and dental, outside of Medicaid. The deal Chris Jennings, Bruce Reed, and Rahm Emanuel cut for President Clinton was eye, dental, and pediatric, but the Republican way—outside of Medicaid. At that time, I was eviscerated by the left." He slammed his fist on the desk, his voice rising. "I had sold out! Today, who are the greatest defenders of kids' health care? The very people that opposed it when it passed," Emanuel said. "Back then, you'd have thought I was a whore! How could we do this outside of Medicaid? They warned that it had to be in Medicaid—not that they gave a rat's ass that the kid had eye or dental care. But, for getting it outside of Medicaid, we got kids' eye and dental care. O.K.? That was the swap. Now, my view is that Krugman as an economist is not wrong. But in the art of the possible, of the deal, he is wrong. He couldn't get his legislation."

The stimulus bill was essentially held hostage to the whims of Collins, Snowe, and Specter, but if Al Franken, the apparent winner of the disputed Minnesota Senate race, had been seated in Washington, and if Ted Kennedy, who is battling brain cancer, had been regularly available to vote, the White House would have needed only one Republican to pass the measure. "No disrespect to Paul Krugman," Emanuel went on, "but has he figured out how to seat the Minnesota senator?" (Franken's victory is the subject of an ongoing court challenge by his opponent, Norm Coleman, which the national Republican Party has been happy to help finance.) "Write a fucking column on how to seat the son of a bitch. I would be fascinated with that column. O.K.?" Emanuel stood up theatrically and gestured toward his seat with open palms. "Anytime they want, they can have it," he said of those who are critical of his legislative strategies. "I give them my chair."

His task has been made no easier by Obama's desire for bipartisanship, which Emanuel argues the press has misunderstood. "The public wants bipartisanship," he said. "We just have to try. We don't have to succeed." Still, he insisted, they have been succeeding. All Obama's other major accomplishments to date—winning approval for three hundred and fifty billion dollars in additional funding for the Troubled Asset Relief Program (TARP), passing the Lilly Ledbetter Fair Pay Act, expanding S-CHIP [medical coverage for children in poor families], signing an executive order to shutter the detention camp at Guantánamo Bay and a memorandum to increase the fuel efficiency of cars—were supported by at least some Republicans. The G.O.P., Emanuel said, decided that opposing the stimulus "was definitional, and I will make an argument to you, both on political and economic grounds: they will lose. I don't think the onus is on us. We tried. The story is they failed.". . .

The office of chief of staff was created by Dwight Eisenhower, who redesigned the working structure of the White House along the hierarchal staff system he had learned as supreme commander of Allied forces in the Second World War. His chief of staff—though he didn't officially use the title, because Eisenhower worried that "politicians think it sounds too military"—was Sherman Adams, who accrued enormous influence, power, and enemies. Neither John F. Kennedy nor Lyndon Johnson had a chief of staff, and largely managed the White House themselves. Richard Nixon returned to Eisenhower's system and delegated vast managerial authority to H. R. Haldeman, the Watergate conspirator whose iron-fisted management of the White House abetted Nixon's own self-destructive behavior in office. In reaction, both Gerald Ford and Jimmy Carter tried to operate without chiefs of staff, but both men reversed course when the flat management structure of their respective White Houses produced staff disarray. Since Carter, every President has acknowledged the need for a strong chief of staff.

Over the years, some clear patterns about what kind of person succeeds in the job have emerged. James Pfiffner, a professor at George Mason University who has written extensively on the history of the office, cites four chiefs of staff as notable failures: Adams, Haldeman, Donald Regan, who was Ronald Reagan's second chief of staff, and John Sununu, George H. W. Bush's first chief of staff. "All of them got power-hungry, they alienated members of Congress, they alienated members of their own Administration, they had reputations for a lack of common civility, and they had hostile relations with the press. And each one of them resigned in disgrace and hurt their Presidents," Pfiffner said. "Being able to be firm and tough without being obnoxious and overbearing is crucial."

Emanuel's début as chief of staff featured him on the Hill making deals with lawmakers—politely and with due deference, by all accounts—but a chief of staff's primary job is to serve as the gatekeeper to the President, controlling the flow of information and people into the Oval Office. Constrict that flow too much and you deprive the President of opposing points of view; increase it too much and you drown him in extraneous detail and force him to arbitrate disputes better settled at a lower level. Emanuel saw both extremes in the Clinton White House. Clinton's first chief of staff, Thomas (Mack) McLarty, a childhood friend from Arkansas, was known as Mack the Nice, and under his leadership the White House was chaotic. Leon Panetta, who is now Obama's C.I.A. director and, like Emanuel, was a congressman, took over from McLarty. Arguably, he overcompensated for McLarty's laxness, limiting access to the President so drastically that Clinton surreptitiously sought counsel outside the channels that Panetta controlled. "The President set up a parallel White House, led by Dick Morris, while Leon was chief of staff," a former senior Clinton White House official told me. "If you clamp down too tight the principal says, 'You're not letting me have access to the people and the information I really want, so I'm just going to go build some other structure.'"

Obama's managerial instincts tend toward a looser operation, with lots of staff and outside input. The fact that he will keep a BlackBerry to stay in touch with friends outside the West Wing fishbowl is one sign of this. (Emanuel grimaced when I mentioned his boss's devotion to the device.) But early in his Senate career Obama also learned the perils of not having one strong manager in charge. When he arrived in Washington, in 2005, he told one of his senior aides, "My vision of this is having six smart people sitting around the table batting ideas around." A month and a half later, tensions erupted between Obama's Chicago staff and his Washington staff, making it difficult for them to agree on his schedule. Obama was frustrated that no single person was able to make decisions. The aide reminded him, "Don't you remember: 'six smart people sitting around the table'?" Obama replied, "Oh, that was six weeks ago. I'm not on that now."

Emanuel's task will be further complicated by what is a fairly top-heavy White House. David Axelrod, Obama's longtime political strategist, Valerie Jarrett, a close friend and counsellor, and Pete Rouse, Obama's Senate chief of staff, are "senior advisers," a title that in the White House denotes a special place at the top of the hierarchy. Part of Emanuel's job will be to stitch Obama's old campaign hands together with powerful new figures on the policy side, such as Summers— "a dominating personality," according to a senior White House official—and James L. Jones, a retired four-star general and Obama's national-security adviser. In addition, Obama has created four new policy czars at the White House—for health care, energy, Native American affairs, and urban affairs—making the West Wing a more crowded place. Meanwhile, Vice President Joseph Biden has been promised a high-level role in decision-making. Joshua Bolten, George W. Bush's last chief of staff, told me that Emanuel has "the challenge of fitting a lot of large personalities and brains and portfolios into a relatively small space."

Perhaps Emanuel's greatest challenge, however, will be making the adjustment from being a prominent elected official to being a staffer. Bolten, who hosted Emanuel and eleven former chiefs of staff for breakfast at the White House in December, said, "One of the interesting bits of advice that emerged from the breakfast was that you probably shouldn't be a political principal yourself. You need to put aside your own personality and profile and adopt one that serves your boss. I'm not saying you necessarily have to have a low profile, but it can't really be your own independent profile. It's got to be the profile your boss wants reflected, and it has to be a profile that does not compete with the rest of the Cabinet." Emanuel said that he has thought about that advice. "There's no doubt" that this is an issue, he told me. "There are pluses to who I was and what I was and there are perils to who I was and what I was, and you've got to be conscious of them."

David Axelrod is one of Emanuel's best friends. . . . The two men met in 1982, when Emanuel was a spokesman for a Naderite group called the Illinois Public Action Council and Axelrod was a reporter for the Chicago *Tribune*. Emanuel's organization had just helped elect Lane Evans as the first Democratic representative from western Illinois in many years, and Emanuel was eager to get Axelrod to write about it. "He was just relentless," Axelrod told me recently. "Rahm chased me down to the recovery room after my second child was born. He says, 'What is it, a boy or a girl?' I said, 'It's a boy.' He said, 'Mazel tov,' and then a little pause. Then he says, 'When do you think you'll be back at. . . .'"

Emanuel has succeeded in almost every professional endeavor he has undertaken. In Chicago, in 1989 and 1991, he raised money for the successful mayoral campaigns of Richard M. Daley, and this caught the attention of Bill Clinton's campaign, which hired him. Emanuel then raised a record amount of money for Clinton, which kept his Presidential campaign from collapsing during the darkest days of the primaries, when he was fighting allegations of adultery and draft-dodging. In the Clinton White House, after a brief setback—he was demoted after clashing with Hillary Clinton—Emanuel rose to become a top adviser to Bill Clinton, securing for himself the small but coveted office next to the President's private study. . . . When Emanuel left the Clinton Administration, in 1998, he moved back to Chicago, took a job as an investment banker, and in less than three years earned nearly twenty million dollars. In 2002, he won a congressional seat in the city on his first attempt. Three years later, he took over the D.C.C.C., and, more than anyone else, was responsible for restoring Democrats to power the following year. (Not a single Democratic incumbent lost in the general election.) By the time Obama came calling for a chief of staff, Emanuel was the Democratic Caucus chair, making him fourth in the House leadership, and on a path to becoming Speaker.

Obama settled on Emanuel as early as last August. "It was months before the election when Barack said to me, 'You know, Rahm would make a great chief of staff,' " Axelrod said. "He spent six years in the White House, knows this place inside and out, spent four or five years in Congress, and became a leader in a short period of time. He really understands the legislative process, he's a friend who the President has known for a long time from Chicago, and whose loyalty is beyond question, and who thinks like a Chicagoan."

Emanuel did not want the job. A few months before Election Day, Obama sent him an e-mail, with a warning: "Heads up, I'm coming for you." Emanuel was a key negotiator in moving the TARP legislation through Congress, in October. After the bill cleared Congress, Obama, who supported it, sent Emanuel another e-mail. "I told you we made a great team," he said. Emanuel wrote back, "I look forward to being your floor leader in the House." . . .

Over lunch two days before the Inauguration, Emanuel explained to me his decision to give up his congressional seat and return to the White House. We were in a brasserie in the lobby of a Washington hotel, and Emanuel, dressed in a black sweater over a white button-down, was frequently interrupted by people who wanted to wish him well or have their picture taken with him. "The main hesitation was family, because there's no way you will convince me this is good for my family," Emanuel, who has three children, ages eleven, ten, and eight, said. "No matter what every White House says—'We're going to be great, family-friendly'—well, the only family we're going to be good for is the First Family. Everybody else is, like, really a distant second, O.K.?"

Then there was the issue of his congressional ambition. In 2005, when Obama first arrived in Washington, he and Emanuel had dinner and discussed their futures. "He knew what I wanted to do, I knew what he wanted to do," Emanuel told me. "He was going to be President one day, and I was going to run for Speaker. It was not that he was deciding on 2008 but his course was one day he was going to run for President." For Emanuel, being chief of staff meant abandoning his goal.

"I was putting together the pieces of my puzzle for Speaker," he said. "I'd been to the White House—that was a dream, but I'd been there. Now I was on to another dream and professional goal and career. And so I had to give that up." He added, "I had my own personal desire of being the first Jewish Speaker. That's why I took on the D.C.C.C. job, that's why I ran for Caucus chair, that's why I stayed involved."

Emanuel grew up in a political family. His Israeli-born father, Benjamin, was a member of the Irgun, a militant Zionist group from which the modern Likud Party eventually emerged. His mother, Marsha, was a civil-rights activist who was arrested several times. "We were attacked because we were white Jews with African-Americans," Ezekiel said. When Martin Luther King, Jr., marched in Chicago in 1966, and was pelted with eggs, Marsha and her children marched along with him. Ezekiel told me that he knew Rahm would take the job of chief of staff because of Marsha's father, Herman Smulivitz, a boxer and a union organizer. It was Herman who instilled in Rahm a commitment to service, and Rahm was particularly close to him.

When I asked Rahm about his grandfather, his eyes welled up with tears. "I'm a little too tired, a little too stressed," he said. "It's too emotional about Gramp." He poured himself a glass of water and took a sip. Earlier, he had explained his decision in pragmatic terms: "If you got into public life to affect policy, and to affect the direction of the country, where could you do that on the most immediate basis? Everybody knows: chief of staff." . . .

Obama's decision to hire Emanuel says two things about his Presidency. First, like his decision to make Biden, an expert in foreign policy, his running mate, it shows that he is honest enough about what he doesn't know to try to fill in the gaps in his own experience. There are people working for Obama who know as much as Emanuel does about the legislative process, and others who know as much as he does about running the White House, but there isn't anybody who knows as much about both. Obama's choice also says a great deal about the ethos of his White House. He recently characterized his team as a group of "mechanics," which suggests an emphasis not on ideology but on details and problem-solving. In the Clinton White House, Emanuel's specialty was helping to pass legislation that required centrist coalitions, like NAFTA, a crime bill, and welfare reform. "He's a partisan in the sense that he's a strong Democrat, but he's not an ideological Democrat," Stanley Greenberg said. "He's not ideologically liberal. He comes out of Chicago politics, which is more transactional."

During the Senate negotiations, Obama agreed to pare back his tax cut for workers, from five hundred dollars to four hundred dollars. It was Emanuel's job to sell the decision to House Democrats. "Nancy was opposed to it," he told me, referring to Nancy Pelosi, the Speaker of the House, who asked him why he would put the President's tax cut on the table. "I said, 'Because at the end of the day the President believes we have to get this done.' " Emanuel thinks that the stimulus bill speaks for itself: "It is the most progressive tax bill in the history of the United States, bar none, by a quotient of two."

Emanuel laughed as he recounted the final sticking point in the negotiations. It was not, as many people have thought, an argument between the five centrist senators—Ben Nelson, Joe Lieberman, Collins, Snowe, and Specter—and the House but a debate among the centrists themselves. The dispute was over a formula for how Medicaid funds in the bill would be allocated to the states. In the House version of the legislation, fifty per cent of the funds would go to all states and fifty per cent would go to states with high unemployment. In the Senate, where rural interests are more dominant, the formula was 80–20. A deal had been reached between the two chambers to split the difference and make the formula 65–35. "Everybody signed except for Ben Nelson," Emanuel said. "He wants 72–28, or seventy-two and a half, and he says, 'I'm not signing this deal.' Specter says, 'Well, I am not agreeing with you.'" Without Nelson, Collins wasn't likely to vote for the deal, either.

"Collins and Snowe are kind of like, at this point, looking at their shoes," Emanuel went on, "because Specter says, 'Well, why make it seventy-two? What do you mean? We all have it at sixty-five, in the middle.'" Emanuel politely declared that the formula would stay at 65–35. He then asked Nelson to step out of the room with him. After a brief conversation in the hallway, they returned, and Nelson agreed to the stimulus package.

Emanuel stood up and removed his tie as he finished the story, making it clear that he was ready to leave for the airport. He seemed more cheerful, knowing that he was that much closer to seeing his family. I asked him what he promised Nelson to persuade him to drop his objections. Emanuel just smiled. "Everything is going to be O.K.," he said, in a mock-soothing voice. "America is going to be a great place."

7-3

from *Going Public*

Samuel Kernell

Richard Neustadt, writing in 1960, judged that the president's ability to lead depended on skill at the bargaining table in cutting deals with other politicians. In the following essay Samuel Kernell examines how the leadership strategy of modern presidents has evolved. He finds that, rather than limiting their leadership to quiet diplomacy with fellow Washingtonians, modern presidents often "go public," a set of activities borrowed from presidential election campaigns and directed toward persuading other politicians to adopt their policy preferences. Some examples of going public are a televised press conference, a special prime-time address to the nation, traveling outside Washington to deliver a speech to a business or professional convention, and a visit to a day care center with network cameras trailing behind.

Introduction: Going Public in Theory and Practice

WHEN PRESIDENT GEORGE H. W. BUSH delivered his State of the Union address to the joint assembly of the mostly Democratic Congress on January 28, 1992, he assumed what was becoming a familiar stance:

> I pride myself that I am a prudent man, and I believe that patience is a virtue. But I understand that politics is for some a game. . . . I submit my plan tomorrow. And I am asking you to pass it by March 20. And I ask the American people to let you know they want this action by March 20.
>
> From the day after that, if it must be: The battle is joined.
>
> And you know when principle is at stake, I relish a good fair fight.

Once upon a time, these might have been fighting words, but by the 1990s presidents had so routinely come to appeal for public support in their dealings with Congress that Bush's rhetoric scarcely caused a stir among his Washington

Source: Samuel Kernell, *Going Public: New Strategies of Presidential Leadership*, 3d ed. (Washington, D.C.: CQ Press, 1997), 1–12, 17–26, 34–38, 57–64; and Samuel Kernell, *Going Public: New Strategies of Presidential Leadership*, 4th ed. (Washington, D.C.: CQ Press, 2006), 40–57. Some notes appearing in the original have been deleted.

audience. Presidential appeals for public support had, in fact, become common-place. Two years later Bill Clinton would use the same forum to launch a six-month public relations campaign to persuade Congress to expand coverage of federal health care beyond Medicare to include everyone not covered by employer insurance. What raised eyebrows was not the announcement or even the scope of the plan. Rather it was the bravado—some would say hubris—with which Clinton warned the assembled legislators that if they failed to give him a fully comprehensive program "I will take this pen and veto it." Two days after his 2004 reelection George W. Bush held a press conference in which he outlined an ambitious policy agenda headed by overhaul of the Social Security system. He matter-of-factly told reporters, "I earned capital in the campaign, political capital, and now I intend to spend it. It is my style."[1] Six weeks later he unveiled in his State of the Union address his partial privatization scheme for Social Security and announced a "sixty cities in sixty days" campaign to push it through Congress.

I call the approach to presidential leadership that has come into vogue at the White House "going public." It is a strategy whereby a president promotes himself and his policies in Washington by appealing directly to the American public for support. Forcing compliance from fellow Washingtonians by going over their heads to enlist constituents' pressure is a tactic that was known but seldom attempted during the first half of the century. Theodore Roosevelt probably first enunciated the strategic principle of going public when he described the presidency as the "bully pulpit." Moreover, he occasionally put theory into practice with public appeals for his Progressive Party reforms. During the next thirty years, other presidents also periodically summoned public support to help them in their dealings with Congress. Perhaps the most famous such instance is Woodrow Wilson's ill-fated whistle-stop tour of the country on behalf of his League of Nations treaty. Equally noteworthy, historically, is Franklin D. Roosevelt's series of radio "fireside chats," which were designed less to subdue congressional opposition than to remind politicians of his continuing national mandate for the New Deal.

These historical instances are significant in large part because they are rare. Unlike Richard Nixon, who thought it important "to spread the White House around" by traveling and speaking extensively,[2] these earlier presidents were largely confined to Washington and obliged to address the country through the nation's newspapers. The concept and legitimizing precedents of going public may have been established during these years, but the emergence of presidents who *routinely* did so to promote their policies outside Washington awaited the development of modern systems of transportation and mass communications. Going public should be appreciated as a strategic adaptation to the information age.

The regularity with which recent presidents have sought public backing for their Washington dealings has altered the way politicians both inside and outside the White House regard the office. The following chapters present numerous instances of presidents preoccupied with public relations, as if these activities chiefly determined their success. Cases are recounted of other Washington politicians intently monitoring the president's popularity ratings and his addresses on television, as if his performance in these realms governed their own behavior. We shall also examine various testimonials of central institutional figures, including several Speakers of the House of Representatives, citing the president's prestige and rhetoric as they explain Congress's actions. If the public ruminations of politicians are to be believed, the president's effectiveness in rallying public support has become a primary consideration for those who do business with him.

Presidential Theory

Going public has become routine. This was not always the case. After World War I Congress refused to support President Wilson's League of Nations, a peace treaty the president himself had helped negotiate. In this instance Congress determined to amend the treaty and a president equally determined to finalize the agreement the other countries had ratified left him with little choice but to go public to try to marshal public opinion to force the Senate's agreement. Today our information-age presidents opt to go public regardless of the political climate in Washington.

There is another reason to systematically study this leadership strategy. Compared with many other aspects of the modern presidency, scholarship has only recently directed its attention toward this feature of the president's repertoire. Although going public had not become a keystone of presidential leadership in the 1950s and 1960s, when much of the influential scholarship on the subject was written, sufficient precedents were available for scholars to consider its potential for presidential leadership in the future.

Probably the main reason traditional presidential scholarship shortchanged going public is its fundamental incompatibility with bargaining. Presidential power is the "power to bargain," Richard E. Neustadt taught a generation of students of the presidency.[3] When Neustadt published his definitive study of presidential leadership in 1960, the "bargaining president" had already become a centerpiece of pluralist theories of American politics. Nearly a decade earlier, Robert A. Dahl and Charles E. Lindblom had described the politician in America generically as "the human embodiment of a bargaining society." They made a special point to include the president in writing that despite his possessing "more hierarchical controls than any other single figure in the government . . . like everyone else . . . the President must bargain constantly."[4] Since Neustadt's landmark treatise, other major works on the presidency have reinforced and elaborated this theme.[5]

Going public violates bargaining in several ways. First, it rarely includes the kinds of exchanges necessary, in pluralist theory, for the American political system to function properly. At times, going public will be merely superfluous—fluff compared with the substance of traditional political exchange. Practiced in a dedicated way, however, it may displace bargaining.

Second, going public fails to extend benefits for compliance, but freely imposes costs for noncompliance. In appealing to the public to "tell your senators and representatives by phone, wire, and Mailgram that the future hangs in balance," the president seeks the aid of a third party—the public—to force other politicians to accept his preferences.[6] If targeted representatives are lucky, the president's success may cost them no more than an opportunity at the bargaining table to shape policy or to extract compensation. If unlucky, they may find themselves both capitulating to the president's wishes and suffering the reproach of constituents for having resisted him in the first place. By imposing costs and failing to offer benefits, going public is more akin to force than to bargaining. Nelson W. Polsby makes this point when he says that members of Congress may "find themselves ill disposed toward a president who prefers to deal indirectly with them [by going public] through what they may interpret as coercion rather than face-to-face in the spirit of mutual accommodation."[7] This senator may echo the sentiments, if not the actions, of those on Capitol Hill who find themselves repeatedly pressured by the president's public appeals: "A lot of Democrats, even if they like the President's proposal, will vote against him because of his radio address on Saturday."[8]

Third, going public entails public posturing. To the extent that it fixes the president's bargaining position, posturing makes subsequent compromise with other politicians more difficult. Because negotiators must be prepared to yield some of their clients' preferences to make a deal, bargaining proverbially proceeds best behind closed doors. Consider the difficulty Ronald Reagan's widely publicized challenge "My tax proposal is a line drawn in dirt" posed for subsequent budget negotiations in Washington.[9] Similarly, during his nationally televised State of the Union address in 1994, President Bill Clinton sought to repair his reputation as someone too willing to compromise away his principles by declaring to the assembled joint session of Congress, "If you send me [health care] legislation that does not guarantee every American private health insurance that can never be taken away, you will force me to take this pen, veto the legislation, and we'll come right back here and start all over again."[10] Not only did these declarations threaten to cut away any middle ground on which a compromise might be constructed, they probably stiffened the resolve of the president's adversaries, some of whom would later be needed to pass the administration's legislative program.

Finally, and possibly most injurious to bargaining, going public undermines the legitimacy of other politicians. It usurps their prerogatives of office, denies their role as representatives, and questions their claim to reflect the interests of their constituents. For a traditional bargaining stance with the president to be restored, these politicians would first have to reestablish parity, probably at a cost of conflict with the White House.[11]

Given these fundamental incompatibilities, one may further speculate that by spoiling the bargaining environment, going public renders the president's future influence ever more dependent upon his ability to generate popular support for himself and his policies. The degree to which a president draws upon public opinion determines the kind of leader he will be.

Presidential Practice

Bargaining and going public have never been particularly compatible styles of leadership. In the early twentieth century, when technology limited presidents' capacity to engage in public relations, they did so sparingly. On rare occasions, presidents might enlist public support as their contribution to bargains with politicians for whom their position was potentially risky. But generally, these two leadership strategies coexisted in a quiet tension. In modern times, though, going public is likely to take the form of an election campaign. George W. Bush's "sixty cities in sixty days" Social Security reform tour in 2005 is a recent example to which we shall later return. When presidents adopt intensive public relations as their leadership strategy they render bargaining increasingly difficult. The decision to go public at one juncture may preclude and undermine the opportunity to bargain at another, and vice versa. All this means that the decision to bargain or to go public must be carefully weighed.

The two case studies below reveal that modern presidents and their advisers carefully attend to this strategic issue. We compare instances of presidential success and failure in order to understand the potential gains and losses embedded in presidents' choices.

Ronald Reagan Enlists Public Opinion as a Lever

No president has enlisted public strategies to better advantage than did Ronald Reagan. Throughout his tenure, he exhibited a full appreciation of bargaining and going public as the modern office's principal strategic alternatives. The following examples from a six-month survey of White House news coverage show how entrenched this bifurcated view of presidential strategy has become. The survey begins in late November 1984, when some members of the administration were pondering how the president might exploit his landslide victory and others were preparing a new round of budget cuts and a tax reform bill for the next Congress.

November 29, 1984. Washington Post columnist Lou Cannon reported the following prediction from a White House official: "We're going to have confrontation on spending and consultation on tax reform." The aide explained, "We have somebody to negotiate with us on tax reform, but may not on budget cuts."[12] By "confrontation" he was referring to the president's success in appealing to the public on national television, that is, in going public. By "consultation" he meant bargaining.

January 25, 1985. The above prediction proved accurate two months later, when another staffer offered as pristine an evocation of going public as one is likely to find: "We have to look at it, in many ways, like a campaign. He [Reagan] wants to take his case to the people. You have a constituency of 535 legislators as opposed to 100 million voters. But the goal is the same—to get the majority of voters to support your position."[13]

February 10, 1985. In a nationally broadcast radio address, President Reagan extended an olive branch, inviting members of Congress to "work with us in the spirit of cooperation and compromise" on the budget. This public statement probably did little to allay the frequently voiced suspicion of House Democratic leaders that such overtures were mainly intended for public consumption. One Reagan aide insisted, however, that the president simply sought to reassure legislators that "he would not 'go over their heads' and campaign across the country for his budget without trying first to reach a compromise."[14] In this statement the aide implicitly concedes the harm public pressure can create for bargaining but seeks to incorporate it advantageously into the strategic thinking of the politicians with whom the administration must deal by not forswearing its use.

March 9, 1985. After some public sparring, the administration eventually settled down to intensive budget negotiations with the Republican-led Senate Finance Committee. Failing to do as well as he would like, however, Reagan sent a message to his party's senators through repeated unattributed statements to the press that, if necessary, he would "go to the people to carry our message forward." * Again, public appeals, though held in reserve, were threatened.

March 11, 1985. In an interview with a *New York Times* correspondent, a senior Reagan aide sized up his president: "He's liberated, he wants to get into a fight, he feels strongly and wants to push his program through himself. . . . Reagan never quite believed his popularity before the election, never believed the polls. Now he has it, and he's going to push . . . ahead with our agenda."[15]

May 16, 1985. To avoid entangling tax reform with budget deliberations in Congress, Reagan, at the request of Republican leaders, delayed unveiling his tax reform proposal until late May. A couple of weeks before Reagan's national television address on the subject, White House aides began priming the press with leaks on the proposal's content and promises that the president would follow it with a public relations blitz. In the words of one White House official, the plan was to force Congress to make a "binary choice between tax reform or no tax reform."[16] The administration rejected bargaining, as predicted nearly six months earlier by a White House aide, apparently for two strategic reasons. First, Reagan feared that in a quietly negotiated process, the tax reform package would unravel under the concerted pressure of the special interests. Second, by taking the high-profile approach of "standing up for the people against the special interests," in the words of one adviser, tax reform might do for Republicans what Social Security did for Democrats—make them the majority party.[17]

During these six months, when bargaining held out promise—as it had during negotiations with the Senate Finance Committee—public appeals were held in reserve. The White House occasionally, however, threatened an appeal in trying to gain more favorable consideration. On other occasions, when opponents of the president's policies appeared capable of extracting major concessions—House Democrats on the budget and interest groups on tax reform, for example—the White House disengaged from negotiations and tried through public relations to force Congress to accept the president's policies. Although by 1985 news items such as the preceding excerpts seemed unexceptional as daily news, they are a recent phenomenon. One does not routinely find such stories in White House reporting twenty years earlier when, for example, John Kennedy's legislative agenda was stalled in Congress.

---

*Jonathan Fuerbringer, "Reagan Critical of Budget View of Senate Panel," *New York Times*, March 9, 1985. Senate Majority Leader Bob Dole told reporters that if the president liked the Senate's final budget package he would campaign for it "very vigorously ... going to television, whatever he needs to reduce federal spending." Karen Tumulty, "Reagan May Get Draft of Budget Accord Today," *Los Angeles Times*, April 4, 1985, 1.

President Clinton Snares Himself by Bargaining

Shortly after assuming office, Bill Clinton received some bad news. The Bush administration had underestimated the size of the next year's deficit by $50 billion. The president's campaign promises of new domestic programs and a middle-class tax cut would have to be put on hold in favor of fulfilling his third, now urgent pledge to trim $500 billion from the deficit over the next five years. On February 17, 1993, President Clinton appeared before a joint session of Congress and a national television audience to unveil his deficit reduction package. The president's deficit-cutting options were constrained by two considerations: he wanted to include minimal stimulus spending to honor his campaign promise, and he faced a Congress controlled by fellow Democrats who were committed to many of the programs under the budget ax. Even with proposed cuts in defense spending, the only way the budget could accommodate these constraints was through a tax increase. The package raised taxes on the highest-income groups and introduced a broad energy consumption tax. During the following weeks, the president and his congressional liaison team quietly lobbied Congress. He would not again issue a public appeal until the eve of the final vote in August.

The president soon learned that Republicans in both chambers had united in opposition to the administration proposal. Led by Newt Gingrich in the House of Representatives and Bob Dole in the Senate, Republicans retreated to the side-lines and assumed the role of Greek chorus, ominously chanting "tax and spend liberals." This meant that the administration needed virtually every Democratic vote to win. Democratic members appreciated this, and many began exploiting the rising value of their votes to extract concessions that would make the legislation more favorable to their constituents.

By June the president's bargaining efforts had won him a watered-down bill that even he had difficulty being enthusiastic about. Meanwhile, the Republicans' public relations campaign had met with success: the American public had come to regard President Clinton as a "tax and spend liberal." Whereas shortly after the February speech, the *Los Angeles Times* had found half of its polling respondents willing to describe the president's initiative as "bold and innovative" and only 35 percent of them willing to describe it as "tax and spend," by June these numbers had reversed. Now, 53 percent labeled it "tax and spend" and only 28 percent still regarded it as "bold and innovative."[18] Given this turnaround in the public's assessment of the initiative, it was not surprising that the public also downgraded its evaluation of the initiative's sponsor. During the previous five months, President Clinton's approval rating had plunged from 58 to 41 percent.

This was the situation when several of Clinton's senior campaign consultants sounded the alarm in a memo: in only six months the president had virtually exhausted his capacity for leadership. If he did not turn back the current tide of public opinion, he would be weakened beyond repair. In response, the president assembled his senior advisers to evaluate current strategy. This set the stage for a confrontation between those advisers who represented the president in bargaining with other Washingtonians and those staffers who manned the White House public relations machinery. The argument that erupted between these advisers should disabuse anyone of the notion that bargaining and cultivating public support are separate, self-contained spheres of action that do not encroach on one another.[19]

The president's chief pollster, Stanley Greenberg, opened the discussion by stating his and his fellow consultants' position: "We do not exaggerate when we say that our current course, advanced by our economic team and Congressional leaders, threatens to sink your popularity further and weaken your presidency. . . . The immediate problem," he explained, "is that thanks to the Republican effort no one views your economic package as anything other than a tax scheme. You must exercise a 'bold zero option,' which is consultant talk for 'rid your policy of any taxes that affect the middle class.' " (In fact, the only tax still in the bill was a 4.3-cent-per-gallon gasoline tax that would raise a modest $20 billion.) Greenberg then unveiled polling data that found broad public support for such a move. He closed by warning everyone in the room, "We have a very short period of time. And if we don't communicate something serious and focused in the period, we're going to be left with what our detractors used to characterize our plan. . . . Don't assume we can fix it in August." This concluded the case for going public. And in order to use this strategy, Clinton had to change course on taxes.

According to those present, the economic and congressional advisers had listened to this argument "with a slow burn." Finally, the president's chief lobbyist, Howard Paster, blurted out, "This isn't an election! The Senate breaks its ass to get a 4.3-cent-a-gallon tax passed, and we can't just abandon it." Besides, they needed the $20 billion provided by the tax to offset other concessions that would be necessary to get the bill passed. "I need all the chips that are available," Paster pleaded. "Don't bargain them away here. Let me have maximum latitude."

From here, the discussion deteriorated into name calling and blame assigning that stopped only when Clinton started screaming at everyone—"a purple fit" is how one participant described it. In the end the president decided that he had to stay the course but that he would begin traveling around the country to explain to the public that his economic package was the "best" that could be enacted. In mid-August, after a concerted public relations campaign that concluded with a nationally televised address, the legislation barely passed. (In the Senate, Vice President Al Gore cast the tie-breaking vote.) The new administration's first legislative initiative had drained its resources both in Congress and across the nation. From here, the Clinton administration limped toward even more difficult initiatives represented by the North American Free Trade Agreement (NAFTA) and health care reform.

Clearly, as both case studies show, going public appears to foster political relations that are quite at odds with those traditionally cultivated through bargaining. One may begin to examine this phenomenon by asking, what is it about modern politics that would inspire presidents to go public in the first place?

How Washington and Presidents Have Changed

The incompatibility of bargaining and going public presents some pressing theoretical questions. Why should presidents come to favor a strategy of leadership that appears so incompatible with the principles of pluralist theory? Why, if other Washington elites legitimately and correctly represent the interests of their clients and constituents, would anything be gained by going over their heads? The answers to these questions are complex, reflecting changes in the capital and in presidents. In this chapter we consider the changes within Washington, the locale of presidential activity. . . .

Some would account for the rise of going public by resorting to the imperative of technology. Certainly, advances in transportation and communications have been indispensable to this process, but they have not been sufficient in themselves to alter political relations in such a contradictory way. . . .

There are more fundamental reasons for the discrepancy between theory and current practice. Politics in Washington may no longer be as tractable to bargaining as it once was. Presidents prefer to go public because the strategy offers a better prospect of success than it did in the past. Perhaps the most consequential development in the modern era is the regularity of divided party control of government. Every president since Jimmy Carter has at some time had to deal with a Congress in which the opposition party controlled one or both chambers. On such occasions, each side frequently finds political advantage in frustrating the other and playing a blame game. Posturing in preparation for the next election takes precedence over bargaining and passing new policy.

Moreover, beginning in the 1970s close observers of American politics detected a pervasive decoupling of traditional allegiances. The most prominent of these trends saw voters abandoning their political party affiliations. From the 1960s to the 1980s the proportion of survey respondents who classified themselves as Independent (or some other noncommittal category) grew from 24 to 41 percent; twenty-five years later, despite a resurgent partisanship among both voters and politicians on a number of dimensions, this basic, defining fact has not changed. Entering the 2006 midterm election period, most surveys show Independent to be the single most popular choice when respondents are asked their party identification.[20] And voters continue to split their ballots, if not quite at the record rates of the 1980s, still to a degree unknown in the 1950s and 1960s.* Consequently, political relations among politicians in Washington remain loose and individualistic. In part ballot split-ting reflects the dramatic growth of incumbency advantage, especially in House elections, during the 1980s. From 1976 until 1992 at least 90 percent of these incumbents who sought reelection won both their primary and general elections. Some years the figure reached a 98 percent success rate. If this suc-cess better insulated these politicians from party and institutional leaders, it served paradoxically to make many of them more sensitive to public opinion from their constituencies. After all, they were winning, in their view, by dint of heroic effort to respond to their constituents.[21]

As politicians in Washington became more sensitive (and perhaps responsive) to public pressure, presidents learned that mobilizing these pressures worked. For exposition I classify the earlier era up to the 1970s as "institutionalized pluralism" and the latter era as "individualized plural-ism." Since the 1994 midterm congressional elections, when an ideologi-cally infused resurgent Republican Party surprisingly took over control of the House of Representatives and the Senate for the first time in a genera-tion, politics in Washington has in one important respect shifted away from those relations described by individualized pluralism. Specifically, a series of vigorous Republican Party leaders in Congress have restored a level of discipline and policy coherence unseen since the 1960s. Nonetheless, given the recentness and limited scope of this development and continuing, unabated expectations of presidential leadership via public relations, I have retained this bifurcated classification of the modern evo-lution of Washington politics from predominantly private elite transac-tions to the mobilization of interested publics. We will consider how recently strengthened partisanship in Congress may temper presidents' incentives to go public. . . .

---

*During the 1990s, the American National Election Surveys found 30 percent of respondent voters reporting that they had split their ballot between the presidential and House candidates. This compares to 18 percent in 2004 and the 1960s and 14 percent during the 1950s. The author wishes to thank Martin B. Wattenberg for supplying these figures in a personal communication, March 10, 2006.

The President's Place in Institutionalized Pluralism

Constructing coalitions across the broad institutional landscape of Congress, the bureaucracy, interest groups, courts, and state governments requires a politician who possesses a panoramic view and commands the resources necessary to engage the disparate, parochial interests of Washington's political elites. Only the president enjoys such vantage and resources. Traditional presidential scholarship leaves little doubt as to how they should be employed. Nowhere has Dahl and Lindblom's framework of the bargaining society been more forcefully employed than in Richard E. Neustadt's classic *Presidential Power*, published in 1960. Neustadt observes:

> Status and authority yield bargaining advantages. But in a government of "separated institutions sharing powers," they yield them to all sides. With the array of vantage points at his disposal, a President may be far more persuasive than his logic or his charm could make him. But outcomes are not guaranteed by his advantages. There remain the counter pressures those whom he would influence can bring to bear on him from vantage points at their disposal. Command has limited utility; persuasion becomes give-and-take. . . .

> The President's advantages are checked by the advantages of others. Continuing relationships will pull in both directions. These are relationships of mutual dependence. A President depends upon the men he would persuade; he has to reckon with his need or fear of them. They too will possess status, or authority, or both, else they would be of little use to him. Their vantage points confront his own; their power tempers his.*

Bargaining is thus the essence of presidential leadership, and pluralist theory explicitly rejects unilateral forms of influence as usually insufficient and ultimately costly. The ideal president is one who seizes the center of the Washington bazaar and actively barters with fellow politicians to build winning coalitions. He must do so, according to this theory, or he will forfeit any claim to leadership. . . .

The Calculus of Those Who Deal with the President

Those Washingtonians who conduct business with the president observe his behavior carefully. Their judgment about his leadership guides them in their dealings with

---

* Richard E. Neustadt, *Presidential Power*, 28–29. Copyright 1980. Reprinted by permission of John Wiley and Sons, Inc. Compare with Dahl and Lindblom's earlier observation: "The President possesses more hierarchical controls than any other single figure in the government; indeed, he is often described somewhat romantically and certainly ambiguously as the most powerful democratic executive in the world. Yet like everyone else in the American policy process, the President must bargain constantly—with Congressional leaders, individual Congressmen, his department heads, bureau chiefs, and leaders of nongovernmental organizations" (Dahl and Lindblom, *Politics, Economics, and Welfare*, 333).

him. Traditionally, the professional president watchers have asked themselves the following questions: What are his priorities? How much does he care whether he wins or loses on a particular issue? How will he weigh his options? Is he capable of winning?

Each person will answer these questions about the president's will and skill somewhat differently, of course, depending upon his or her institutional vantage. The chief lobbyist for the United Auto Workers, a network White House correspondent, and the mayor of New York City may size up the president differently depending upon what they need from him. Nonetheless, they arrive at their judgments about the president in similar ways. Each observes the same behavior, inspects the same personal qualities, evaluates the views of the same recognized opinion leaders—columnists and commentators, among others—and tests his or her own tentative opinions with those of fellow community members. Local opinion leaders promote a general agreement among Washingtonians in their assessments of the president. Their agreement is his reputation.[22]

A president with a strong reputation does better in his dealings largely because others expect fewer concessions from him. Accordingly, he finds them more compliant; an orderly marketplace prevails. Saddled with a weak reputation, conversely, a president must work harder. Because others expect him to be less effective, they press him harder in expectation of greater gain. Comity at the bargaining table may give way to contention as other politicians form unreasonable expectations of gain. Through such expectations, the president's reputation regulates community relations in ways that either facilitate or impede his success. In a world of institutionalized pluralism, bargaining presidents seldom actively traded upon their prestige, leaving it to influence Washington political elites only through their anticipation of the electorate's behavior. As a consequence, prestige remained largely irrelevant to other politicians' assessments of the president.* Once presidents began going public and interjecting prestige directly into their relations with fellow politicians, and once these politicians found their resistance to this pressure diminished because of their own altered circumstances, the president's ability to marshal public opinion soon became an important ingredient of his reputation. New questions were added to traditional ones: Does the president feel strongly enough about an issue to go public? Will he follow through on his threats to do so? Does his standing in the country run so deep that it will likely be converted into mail to members of Congress, or is it so shallow that it will expire as he attempts to use it?

In today's Washington, the answers to these questions contribute to the president's reputation. Consequently, his prestige and reputation have lost much of

---

* Neustadt observed that President Truman's television appeal for tighter price controls in 1951 had little visible effect on how Washington politicians viewed the issue. This is the only mention of a president going public in the original eight chapters of the book. Neustadt, *Presidential Power*, 45.

their separateness. The community's estimates of Carter and Reagan rose and fell with the polls. Through reputation, prestige has begun to play a larger role in regulating the president's day-to-day transactions with other community members. Grappling with the unclear causes of Carter's failure in Washington, Neustadt arrived at the same conclusion:

> A President's capacity to draw and stir a television audience seems every bit as inter-esting to current Washingtonians as his ability to wield his formal powers. This interest is his opportunity. While national party organizations fall away, while con-gressional party discipline relaxes, while interest groups proliferate and issue net-works rise, a President who wishes to compete for leadership in framing policy and shaping coalitions has to make the most he can out of his popular connection. Anticipating home reactions, Washingtonians . . . are vulnerable to any breeze from home that presidential words and sights can stir. If he is deemed effective on the tube they will anticipate. That is the essence of professional reputation.[23]

The record supports Neustadt's speculation. In late 1978 and early 1979, with his monthly approval rating dropping to less than 50 percent, President Carter complained that it was difficult to gain Congress's attention for his legislative proposals. As one congressional liaison official stated, "When you go up to the Hill and the latest polls show Carter isn't doing well, then there isn't much rea-son for a member to go along with him."[24] A member of Congress concurred: "The relationship between the President and Congress is partly the result of how well the President is doing politically. Congress is better behaved when he does well. . . . Right now, it's almost as if Congress is paying no attention to him."[25]

The President's Calculus

The limited goods and services available for barter to the bargaining president would be quickly exhausted in a leaderless setting where every coalition partner must be dealt with individually. When politicians are more subject to environ-mental forces, however, other avenues of presidential influence open up. No politician within Washington is better positioned than the president to go outside the community and draw popular support. With members more sensitive to influences beyond Washington, the president's hand in mobilizing public opinion has been strengthened. For the new Congress—indeed, for the new Washington generally—going public may at times be the most effective course available.

Under these circumstances, the president's prestige becomes his political cap-ital. It is something to be spent when the coffers are full, to be conserved when they are low, and to be replenished when they are empty. Early in 1997, when asked by campaign-weary news reporters why President Clinton maintained such a heavy travel schedule after his election victory, press secretary Michael D.

McCurry lectured them on modern political science: "Campaigns are about framing a choice for the American people. . . .When you are responsible for governing you have to use the same tools of public persuasion to advance your program, to build public support for the direction you are attempting to lead."[26]

If public relations are to be productive the message must be tailored to a correctly targeted audience. For this, presidents require accurate, precisely measured readings of public opinion. Modern presidents must be attentive to the polls, but they need not crave the affection of the public. Their relationship with it may be purely instrumental. However gratifying public approval may be, popular support is a resource the expenditure of which must be coolly calculated. As another Clinton aide explained, "Clinton has come to believe that if he keeps his approval ratings up and sells his message as he did during the campaign, there will be greater acceptability for his program. . . . The idea is that you have to sell it as if in a campaign."[27]

Bargaining presidents require the sage advice of politicians familiar with the bargaining game; presidents who go public need pollsters. Compare the relish with which President Nixon reportedly approached the polls with the disdain Truman expressed. "Nixon had all kinds of polls all the time," recalled one of his consultants. "He sometimes had a couple of pollsters doing the same kind of survey at the same time. He really studied them. He wanted to find the thing that would give him an advantage."[28] The confidant went on to observe that the president wanted poll data "on just about anything and everything" throughout his administration.

Indicative of current fashion, presidents from Carter through Bush have all had in-house pollsters taking continuous—weekly, even daily—readings of public opinion.[29] When George H. W. Bush reportedly spent $216,000 of Republican National Committee (RNC) money on in-house polling in one year, many Washington politicians probably viewed it as an excessive indulgence, reflecting the RNC's largesse more than any practical need for data. But this figure soon looked modest after Clinton spent nearly ten times that amount in 1993, when he averaged three or four polls and an equal number of focus groups each month.[30]

Pollsters vigilantly monitor the pulse of opinion to warn of slippage and to identify opportunities for gain. Before recommending a policy course, they assess its costs in public support. Sometimes, as was the case with Clinton's pollsters, they go so far as to ask the public whether the president should bargain with congressional leaders or challenge them by mobilizing public opinion. These advisers' regular and frequently unsolicited denials that they affected policy belie their self-effacement.

To see how the strategic prescriptions of going public differ from those of bargaining, consider the hypothetical case of a president requiring additional votes if he is to prevail in Congress. If a large number of votes is needed, the most obvious and direct course is to go on prime-time television to solicit the public's active support. Employed at the right moment by a popular president, the effect may be dramatic. This tactic, however, has considerable costs and risks. A real debit of lost public support may occur when a president takes a forthright position. There is also the possibility that the public will not respond, which damages the president's future credibility. Given this, a president understandably finds the *threat* to go public frequently more attractive than the *act*. To the degree that such a threat is credible, the anticipated responses of some representatives and senators may suffice to achieve victory.

A more focused application of influence via public relations becomes available as an election nears. Fence-sitting representatives and senators may be plied with promises of reelection support. This may be done privately and selectively, or it may be tendered openly to all who may vote on the president's program. Presidential support can be much more substantial than endorsement. Presidents at least as far back as 1938, when Franklin Roosevelt failed to purge anti–New Deal Democrats in the midterm elections, have at times actively sought to improve their own fortunes in the next Congress by influencing the current election. During the 1970 midterm congressional election campaigns, President Nixon raced around the country "in a white heat," trying desperately to secure a Republican Congress that would not convene for another generation.[31] In the 1999–2000 election cycle outgoing President Clinton pushed the modern president's efforts to serve his party's candidates to what would seem to be an individual's physical limits. By one count he participated in 295 congressional fund-raising events garnering more than $160 million for his party's candidates. Were it not for the tragic events of 9/11 and the subsequent invasion of Afghanistan, President Bush might have matched his predecessor. After getting off to a slow start in the next election cycle, the president made up ground rapidly. By the 2002 election he had attended seventy-four fund-raisers, an impressive number except when compared to Clinton, but he garnered significantly more money for Republican congressional candidates than had his Democratic counterpart. . . .

The variety of methods for generating publicity notwithstanding, going public offers fewer and simpler stratagems than does its pluralist alternative. At the heart of the latter lies bargaining, which must involve choice: choice among alternative coalitions, choice of specific partners, and choice of the goods and services to be bartered. Above all, it requires empathy, the ability of one politician to discern what his or her counterpart minimally needs in return for cooperation. The number, variety, and subtlety of choices place great demands upon strategic calculation, so much so that pluralist leadership must be understood as an art. In Neustadt's schema, the president's success ultimately reduces to intuition an ability to sense "right choices."[32]

Going public also requires choice, and it leaves ample room for the play of talent. If anyone doubts it, consider the obviously staged town meetings that

President Bush's advance team assembled during his [2005] "sixty cities in sixty days" promotion of Social Security reform. Public relations is a less obscure matter than bargaining with fellow politicians, every one of them a professional bent on extracting as much from the president while surrendering as little as possible. Going public promises a more straightforward presidency than its pluralist counterpart—its options fewer, its strategy simpler, and consequently, its practitioner's actions both more predictable and easily observed.

NOTES

1. Dan Froomkin, "Bush Agenda: Bold but Blurry," *Washington Post*, November 5, 2004.

2. Robert B. Semple Jr., "Nixon Eludes Newsmen on Coast Trip," *New York Times*, August 3, 1970, 16.

3. Richard E. Neustadt, *Presidential Power* (New York: John Wiley and Sons, 1980).

4. Robert A. Dahl and Charles E. Lindblom, *Politics, Economics, and Welfare* (New York: Harper and Row, 1953), 333.

5. Among them are Aaron Wildavsky, *The Politics of the Budgetary Process* (Boston: Little, Brown, 1964); Graham T. Allison, *The Essence of Decision: Explaining the Cuban Missile Crisis* (New York: HarperCollins, 1987); Hugh Heclo, *The Government of Strangers* (Washington, D.C.: Brookings Institution, 1977); and Nelson W. Polsby, *Consequences of Party Reform* (New York: Oxford University Press, 1983).

6. From Ronald Reagan's address to the nation on his 1986 budget. Jack Nelson, "Reagan Calls for Public Support of Deficit Cuts," *Los Angeles Times*, April 25, 1985, 1.

7. Nelson W. Polsby, "Interest Groups and the Presidency: Trends in Political Intermediation in America," in *American Politics and Public Policy*, ed. Walter Dean Burnham and Martha Wagner Weinbey (Cambridge: MIT Press, 1978), 52.

8. Hedrick Smith, "Bitterness on Capitol Hill," *New York Times*, April 24, 1985, 14.

9. Ed Magnuson, "A Line Drawn in Dirt," *Time*, February 22, 1982, 12–13.

10. William J. Clinton, *Public Papers of the Presidents of the United States: William J. Clinton, 1994*, vol. 1 (Washington, D.C.: Government Printing Office, 1995), 126–135.

11. See David S. Broder, "Diary of a Mad Majority Leader," *Washington Post*, December 13, 1981, C1, C5; David S. Broder, "Rostenkowski Knows It's His Turn," *Washington Post National Weekly Edition*, June 10, 1985, 13.

12. Lou Cannon, "Big Spending-Cut Bill Studied," *Washington Post*, November 29, 1984, A8.

13. Bernard Weinraub, "Reagan Sets Tour of Nation to Seek Economic Victory," *New York Times*, January 25, 1985, 43.

14. Bernard Weinraub, "Reagan Calls for 'Spirit of Cooperation' on Budget and Taxes," *New York Times*, February 10, 1985, 32. On Democratic suspicions of Reagan's motives see Hedrick Smith, "O'Neill Reflects Democratic Strategy on Budget Cuts and Tax Revisions," *New York Times*, December 6, 1984, B20; and Margaret Shapiro, "O'Neill's New Honeymoon with Reagan," *Washington Post National Weekly Edition*, February 11, 1985, 12.

15. Bernard Weinraub, "In His 2nd Term, He Is Reagan the Liberated," *New York Times*, March 11, 1985, 10.

16. David E. Rosenbaum, "Reagan Approves Primary Elements of Tax Overhaul," *New York Times*, May 16, 1985, 1.

17. Robert W. Merry and David Shribman, "G.O.P. Hopes Tax Bill Will Help It Become Majority Party Again," *Wall Street Journal*, May 23, 1985. See also Rosenbaum, "Reagan Approves Primary Elements of Tax Overhaul," 14. Instances such as those reported here continued into summer. See, for example, Jonathan Fuerbringer, "Key Issues Impede Compromise on Cutting Deficit," *New York Times*, June 23, 1985, 22.

18. These figures are reported in Richard E. Cohen, *Changing Course in Washington* (New York: Macmillan, 1994), 180.

19. The account of this meeting comes from Bob Woodward, *The Agenda* (New York: Simon and Schuster, 1994).

20. An excellent source for monitoring these trends is www.pollingreport.com.

21. Gary C. Jacobson, *The Politics of Congressional Elections*, 5th ed. (New York: Longman, 2001), 21–34.

22. This discussion of reputation follows closely that of Neustadt in *Presidential Power*, chap. 4.

23. Neustadt, *Presidential Power*, 238.

24. Cited in Gary C. Jacobson, *The Politics of Congressional Elections*, 4th ed. (New York: Longman, 1997), 193–194.

25. Statement by Rep. Richard B. Cheney cited in Charles O. Jones, "Congress and the Presidency," in *The New Congress*, eds. Thomas E. Mann and Norman J. Ornstein (Washington, D.C.: American Enterprise Institute, 1981), 241.

26. Alison Mitchell, "Clinton Seems to Keep Running Though the Race Is Run and Won," *New York Times*, February 12, 1997, A1, A12.

27. Ibid., A12.

28. Cited in George C. Edwards III, *The Public Presidency* (New York: St. Martin's Press, 1983), 14.

29. B. Drummond Ayres Jr., "G.O.P. Keeps Tabs on Nation's Mood," *New York Times*, November 16, 1981, 20.

30. These figures are cited in George C. Edwards III, "Frustration and Folly: Bill Clinton and the Public Presidency," in *The Clinton Presidency: First Appraisals*, eds. Colin Campbell and Bert A. Rockman (Chatham, N.J.: Chatham House, 1996), 234.

31. Rowland Evans and Robert Novak, *Nixon in the White House: The Frustration of Power*, (New York: Random House, 1971).

32. Neustadt, *Presidential Power*, especially chap. 8.

7-4

How Cable Ended the Golden Age of Presidential Television: From 1969 to 2006

Matthew A. Baum and Samuel Kernell

Numerous technological advances in communications and transportation during the twentieth century steadily expanded opportunities for presidents to go public. None was more important than television. From the late 1950s on, virtually every home had at least one television set. President John Kennedy grasped the opportunity television afforded presidents when he conducted the first live televised press conference in 1961. From then until the rise of cable television, presidents pretty much enjoyed the prerogative to enter America's homes whenever they "asked" the networks for airtime. More recently, however, technology has turned against presidents' easy access to the public. In this article Matthew Baum and Samuel Kernell trace the growth of cable and satellite subscription services and show that this trend is closely associated with the sharply declining audiences for presidents' national television addresses.

"THE PRESIDENT IS not irrelevant here." Bill Clinton's response to a reporter's pointed question during a nationally televised, prime-time news conference on April 18, 1995, came across as little more than a desperate denial of the truth. Having seized firm control of Congress in the previous fall's midterm elections and now marching in step toward enacting their legislative program, the "Contract with America," congressional Republicans had given the nation ample reason to suspect that perhaps this Democratic president had indeed become irrelevant.

Many Americans had apparently already answered the question for themselves. Nielsen Media Research reported that only 6.5 percent of households with televisions watched the president assert his relevance. In March 1969, in contrast, when President Richard Nixon conducted one of his routine prime-time press conferences, all three networks broadcast it, and according to Nielsen, 59 percent of America's television households tuned in.[1] Figure 1 shows more systematic evidence of this trend. The average audience ratings depicted in the figure, based on 158 televised, prime-time addresses and news conferences, show a steady downward trend, beginning with the Reagan presidency.[2]

Source: This essay summarizes, partially excerpts, and updates research originally reported in Baum and Kernell, "Has Cable Ended the Golden Age of Presidential Television?" *American Political Science Review* 55 (March 1999): 99–114.

Figure 1. Average Percentage of Households with Televisions Watching
Prime-Time Presidential TV Appearances, 1969–2006

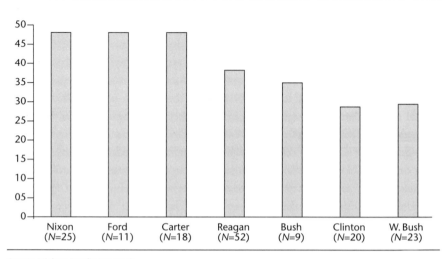

Source: Nielsen Media Research
Note: "Rating" is a commonly reported variable that Nielsen Media Research defines as the percentage of households owning televisions that are tuned in to an average minute of a given program.

Presidents appear to be losing their television audience at precisely the time when they most need it. Increasingly they have staked their leadership in Washington on their ability to attract the public's support for themselves and their policies (Kernell 1997). Whether measured by public appearances, number of speeches, or days of travel, each recent president has in some way matched or eclipsed his predecessors' efforts to communicate directly with the American people. Substantial research has also demonstrated "going public" to be a viable leadership strategy. Through speeches, popular presidents can influence public preferences on policy (Mondak 1993; Page, Shapiro, and Dempsey 1987) and elevate the salience of some national issues over others (Bartels 1993; Cohen 1995). As Bill Clinton conclusively demonstrated with his 1998 State of the Union address, a president's public appeals can also boost his standing in the polls (Brace and Hinckley 1993; Simon and Ostrom 1989; Ragsdale 1984).[3] More than ever, presidents act on Neustadt's (1960) early insight that good things happen to popular presidents. Given these benefits, it comes as no surprise to find that about a third of the White House staff is engaged in some aspect of public relations to promote the president and his policies with the American public.

If modern presidents lose their prime-time audience, they will have surrendered a political asset that will be difficult to replace by other means. The alternative of speaking to the American public through the news media is being closed off by increasingly unobliging journalistic practices. Presidents complain, with some justification, that the news media prefer to report unfavorable news about them (Groeling and Kernell 1998; Patterson 1996, Baum and Groeling 2004). More importantly, however, network television news no longer allows presidents to speak for themselves. The average presidential sound bite on the network evening news has shrunk from forty seconds in 1968 to less than seven seconds in 1996 (Center for Media and Public Affairs 1996; Hallin 1994). With reporters and anchors on camera more, and presidents less, how reporters and their editors decide to frame a story can greatly influence how the audience will consume it (Miller and Krosnik 1996). The finding that news coverage of a president's policy preferences generally fails to influence public opinion is therefore unsurprising (Page, Shapiro, and Dempsey 1987; Edwards 2003). Modern news practices offer presidents a poor substitute for direct appeals on television.

Why are modern presidents losing their television audience? This is the central question we seek to answer in this study. Past research has largely ignored audience ratings, and so the scholarly literature offers few answers. We investigate the question in two distinct ways: In the next section we examine survey responses to questions measuring individuals' consumption of presidential messages. The statistical relationships reported below offer suggestive evidence of the underlying opinion dynamics that account for the trend in Figure 1. The cumulative evidence indicates that cable (and, more recently, satellite) technology has allowed the public to become strategically discriminating in its viewing decisions. So, too, our evidence suggests, have presidents and network executives, as they appraise this increasingly fickle audience in deciding, respectively, whether to deliver and broadcast a prime-time press conference or address to the nation.

The Utility of Watching the President

Twenty-five years ago, CBS, NBC and ABC enjoyed an oligopoly. As one network executive reminisced, "When viewers turned on the TV set, they had five choices, and the networks were three of them . . . [They] collectively accounted for about 90% of the television audience" (Lowry 1997). Between 1969 and 2005, the number of households subscribing to cable rose sharply from 6 percent to 83 percent.[4] Moreover, in 1983 cable subscribers received, on average, less than fifteen channels; today the average exceeds one hundred (*IT Facts*; Webster and Lichty 1991). As Figure 2 shows, both trends in cable subscriptions and programming choices have taken a heavy toll on the audience shares of the major networks.[5]

To appreciate how cable and other potential factors might erode the president's audience, we begin by stating the viewing decision using the standard utility model, *PB - C*. The "expected benefit" of consuming a president's message

Figure 2. Network Audience Share and Households
with Cable, 1969–2006

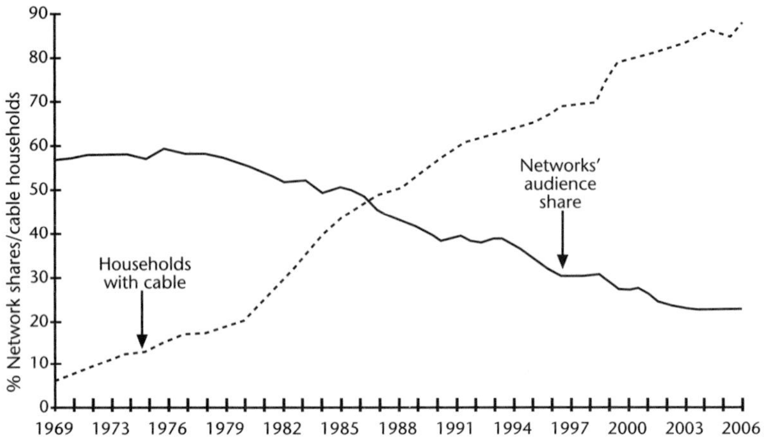

Sources: (1) Cable households data - *Statistical Abstract of the United States* (Washington, D.C.: U.S. Government Printing Office, various years); (2) Networks' audience shares supplied by A.C, Nielsen.
Note: "% Network shares" refers to the combined prime-time Nielsen ratings of the three major broadcast networks (each rating point is equivalent to 1% of U.S. households); "Cable households" refers to the percentage of U.S. households subscribing to cable.

is made up of two terms: *B*, representing the potential benefit or value to the viewer of information that the president might provide, discounted by *P*, which is the probability that the president will actually offer credible information on a subject. When the viewing decision is stated in these terms, we can see that citizens who think politicians are crooks and liars will expect to derive little benefit from watching the president, regardless of what he has to say.

Against this expected benefit the viewer must weigh various costs, or *C*, and here is where cable programming enters the equation. Aside from the direct effort, or "transaction cost," of tuning in to the president's address, the viewer considers the "opportunity costs" entailed in watching the president rather than watching some other program or undertaking some other pleasurable activity. Back in the days when the several broadcast networks dominated the airwaves, they could manipulate viewers' opportunity costs by agreeing to suspend commercial programming and jointly broadcast the president's address. (They even used the same cameras.) This practice left voters with few programming alternatives. That, in turn, served the networks' purposes, in preventing serious audience erosion when commercial programming resumed, and the president's goal, by guaranteeing the largest possible audience.

The success of this practice depended, of course, on viewers' staying tuned throughout the president's appearance. Networks had little cause to worry. One study (Foote 1988) found sixteen of President Gerald Ford's nineteen television appearances commanding market shares as high as, or higher than, the regularly scheduled commercial programming the president's appearance had preempted. That even President Ford's notably uncharismatic appearances did not prompt viewers to turn off their televisions (or tune over to public or local independent programming) offers compelling evidence that during the pre-cable era, watching the president imposed minimal opportunity costs. Even those viewers who might have anticipated negligible benefit from watching President Ford nonetheless did so. Viewers behaved as if media critics were right in calling them "captives" of network television. Throughout our discussion we will enlist this term to characterize the predicament of this once-dominant class of broadcast viewers. As it concerns presidential television, a viewer's "captive" status results from the combination of limited channels, an unwillingness to turn off the television, and the networks' joint suspension of commercial programming during a presidential appearance.

Cable gives viewers choices, and for this reason, it makes watching the president costly. As the number of alternative programs increases, so too does the likelihood that one of them will prove more attractive than the president's message, prompting the viewer to change channels.[6] So, cable subscribers will be less likely to watch a presidential appearance than will those viewers who remain captive to the broadcast signal.

Although it is substantively important, this prediction is intuitive and does not need to be depicted formally to be appreciated. There is, however, a second, less-obvious hypothesis embedded in the utility calculus of watching the president, particularly when one of the prominent possible states is that of captive viewer. In Figure 3 we graph the probability of watching the president as a function of these cost-benefit comparisons. Because captive viewers will experience negligible opportunity costs in watching the president, they will tend to do so even when they anticipate minimal benefit. Cable subscribers, on the other hand, are free to move along Figure 3's curve, and so their assessment of benefit will heavily influence their viewing decision. The qualitative difference between captive, antenna-tethered viewers and cable viewers in the choice to watch the president should show up statistically in an interaction between cable access and those variables that reflect the attractiveness of a presidential appearance. Below we test this utility hypothesis in two ways: on individuals' self-reported viewing habits and on aggregate trends of audience shares. Although they similarly confirm the model, each level of analysis offers distinct insights into the president's declining audience.

Figure 3. The Probability of Viewing the President
as a Function of Expected Utility

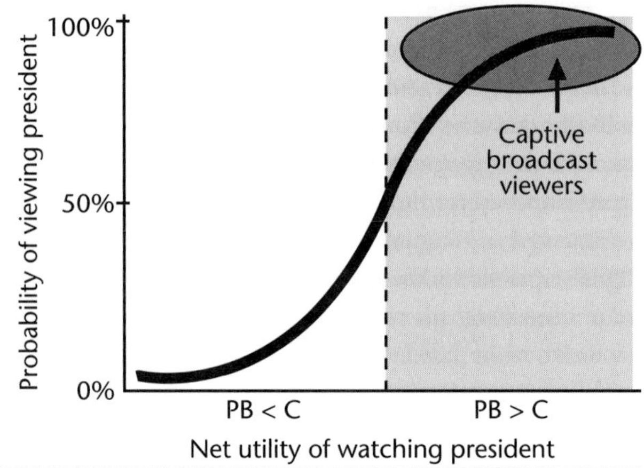

Watching the 1996 Presidential Debates

For the vast majority of the American people television has emerged over the past few decades as the primary source of information about politics. For some it represents their sole means of becoming informed about the issues of the day. Newspaper readership, conversely, has declined steadily since the 1960s and in a way that suggests a massive substitution of television for newspapers as a source for civic information (Briller 1990; Lichty and Gomery 1992; Moisy 1997; Stanley and Niemi 1998).[7]

Reflecting the rise of alternative information technologies, recent American National Election Study (NES) surveys, which are the chief source of scholarly research on voting behavior in national elections, have queried respondents about their preferred sources of information about politics. The 1996 NES survey asked respondents if they subscribed to cable or satellite television service, giving us an opportunity to examine systematically its effect on political communication. The survey also asked respondents whether they watched the first and second presidential debates between President Bill Clinton and his Republican opponent, Bob Dole. Although debates represent a different kind of presidential appearance, we have little reason to suspect that they differ materially from the addresses to the nation and press conferences tallied in Figure 1. In recent years the American public has shown just as great an inclination to abandon presidential debates as other forms of televised presidential communication. More people typically watch the debates, but Nielsen (2006) reports erosion in the share of television viewers who tune in to them from more than half of those watching television to roughly a third in recent elections.[8]

We have hypothesized that respondents with cable will approach their viewing choices differently, since they enjoy numerous programming options unavailable to the broadcast audience and hence are more likely to engage in a cost-benefit calculation with respect to watching the president. In an extensive analysis of the covariates of debate watching reported elsewhere (Baum and Kernell 1999), we found a much stronger propensity to watch the debates among those cable subscribers who are highly informed about politics than among their poorly informed counterparts. Among broadcast viewers, this difference did not emerge.[9] The relationships displayed in Figure 4 closely follow the utility logic of viewing decisions depicted in Figure 3.[10] Among cable subscribers, reported debate watching is strongly related to the respondent's level of political information. The differences between these low- and high-information respondents are eighteen and twenty-seven percentage points ($p < .05$) for the first and second debates, respectively, and highly informed cable subscribers actually eclipsed their captive counterparts in tuning in to these events. Additionally, the differences between cable subscribers and nonsubscribers are greatest among the least-well-informed respondents. Poorly informed cable subscribers dropped out of the debate audience in droves, presumably because they changed channels in favor of entertainment programming.

Also as predicted, noncable respondents confirm their captive status by reporting watching the debates at about the same rate regardless of how politically informed they are. In neither debate did the percentage point differences of -.12 and -.07 between low- and high-information nonsubscribers reach the .05 significance level. Nonetheless, the fact that subscribers and nonsubscribers trend in opposite directions across levels of political awareness presents an intriguing possibility: Why would the least politically informed broadcast viewers be the most likely to watch the presidential debates? Perhaps the answer lies in their greater overall exposure to television programming. If these poorly informed captive viewers watch more television, then more of them than their better informed counterparts might well have been tuned in when the networks (including Fox) preempted evening commercial programming to present the debates.

Unfortunately, the NES survey does not ask about overall viewing habits, and so we cannot directly control for the effects of overall exposure to television programming on these relationships. Yet suggestive circumstantial evidence is available in the 1996 General Social Survey (GSS), which did include respondents' viewing habits and found the amount of time logged in front of the television to be inversely associated with education (Davis 1996).[11] Political information is highly correlated with education in the NES survey ($r = .49$). Hence, more of our low-information respondents in Figure 4 might have watched the debates simply because more of them were watching TV when the debates aired.

Assigning the GSS respondents' television-viewing levels for the different educational categories to our low- and high-political-information, noncable NES respondents allows us to estimate these groups' different levels of exposure to television. By this estimate, our low-information respondents averaged almost an hour more of daily television viewing than high-information respondents— 3.4 compared to 2.6 hours per day. Perhaps, then, the inverse relationship of political information and debate watching for noncable respondents is not so paradoxical. Tuning in to the debates might impose comparatively low opportunity costs for the captive viewers who, despite their typically poorer understanding of politics, are nonetheless drawn to it merely by virtue of their relatively heavy diet of television.

If, as these relationships suggest, the changing media marketplace frees uninterested viewers to abandon political programming, the effects should manifest over time in a steady decline of the president's audience ratings, as cable and satellite services offer more programming alternatives to more citizens.

The President's Audience Ratings

As suggestive as the survey differences between cable and broadcast viewers may be, we need information over time to confirm that they are at the root of recent presidents' audience losses. The presidents' average audience ratings in Figure 1 are based on the 158 prime-time presidential addresses and press conferences for which we have Nielsen ratings data. These ratings reflect the percentage of households with television that are viewing the appearance.

Our key treatment variable is cable's share of the household audience. We could measure this in various ways, including, obviously, the percentage of households subscribing to cable, as shown in Figure 2. Instead, however, we have adopted a closely correlated indicator, Network Share, or the average share of the audience watching one of the three broadcast networks during prime time. This measure performs slightly better, we suspect because it takes into account not only the fast-growing share of homes wired to cable or sporting a satellite dish but also the increasing number of viewing options available to subscribers. We also test a number of other situational variables that might contribute to the utility of viewing the president. Others have found the public's receptivity to the president's messages closely associated with its assessment of

Figure 4. Probability of Watching the 1996 Presidential Debates:
Cable Subscribers versus Nonsubscribers

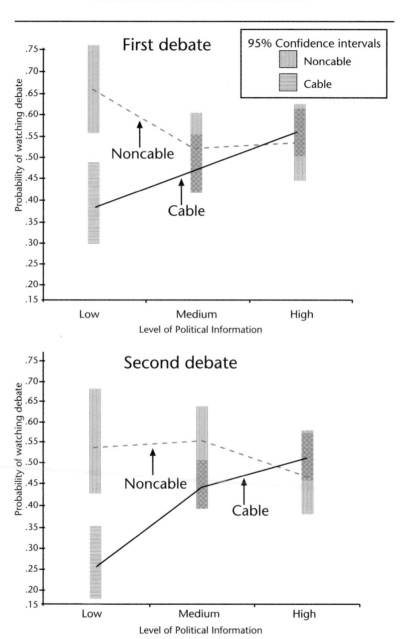

Source: Baum and Kernell (1999): Probabilities represent percentages derived from transformed logit coefficients.

his job performance (Page, Shapiro, and Dempsey 1987; Zaller 1997). Hence we have added "Approve," the Gallup poll's familiar share of the public approving the president's job performance at the time of the television appearance. We take into account the effect of the economy on the public's receptivity to presidential appearances.[12] The variable "Bad Economy" is based on the percentage of respondents who answered "bad" when asked to forecast the next year's business conditions in the University of Michigan's monthly Survey of Consumer Sentiment.

This group of variables may reflect the viewer's assessment of the value or benefit of watching the president's address. On the cost side of the ledger, we have identified several variables that might influence these time-series relationships. During the Clinton administration, the networks began rotating coverage of some presidential appearances. Of the twenty Clinton prime-time addresses and press conferences for which we have audience data, only fourteen were broadcast by all three major networks. President George W. Bush has fared somewhat better, perhaps reflecting the crisis content of many of his addresses during his first term. During the first five years of his presidency only seven of his twenty-three appearances failed to receive full network coverage. Selective network broadcasts are a modern development that rarely occurred in past administrations. We suspect the change reflects the growing costliness to the networks of interrupting their commercial programming and finding large shares of their audience subsequently changing to a cable channel and not returning to the networks for the remainder of the prime-time evening. When a network opts out of covering a presidential event, it adds a major programming alternative to the menus of *both* broadcast and cable viewers. This sharply increases the opportunity costs associated with watching the president and should, according to our model, reduce his audience share commensurately. In a preliminary analysis we found the largest audience losses occurring when only one network carried an event, such as President Clinton's ill-starred press conference, with which we opened our discussion. Accordingly we shall represent these instances with a dummy variable, "One Network."

Media research (Webster and Lichty 1991, 154–157) identifies two other variables—represented in our analysis by "Summer" and "9 p.m."—relating to costs that systematically limit the size of the prime-time audience. For television producers, July and August are indeed "the dog days of summer." Longer days and vacations conspire to reduce the numbers of people watching television, and hence reruns become the staple. Similarly, whatever the season or day of the week, the 9:00 p.m.-to-10:00 p.m. time slot normally finds a television turned on in more households than at any other time of the day. If a president runs afoul of

Table 1. The Presidents' Audience Rating as a Function
of Network Share, Political Setting, and Schedule

Independent Variable	Equation 1 Full Series (N = 158)		Equation 2 Nixon–Carter (N = 54)		Equation 3 Reagan–W. Bush (N = 104)	
	Coef.	Std. Error	Coef.	Std. Error	Coef.	Std. Error
Network share	.51***	.05	-.57	1.25	.34***	.07
Approve	.00	.00	.19*	.10	.00	.00
Bad economy	.08	.04	.11	.08	.12*	.05
Crisis	.06**	.02	.06	.03	.06**	.02
Summer	-.06***	.02	-.11**	.03	-.05**	.02
9:00 p.m.	.05***	.01	.06***	.02	.03*	.01
One network	-.08**	.03			-.10***	.03
Constant	.02	.04	.63	.73	.05	.04
Adjusted R^2	.05		.27		.43	

*$p < .05$, **$p < .01$, ***$p < .001$

Source: Baum and Kernell (1999), updated through 2006 by authors. The above equations report OLS regression estimates of the full and partial time series of presidents' national audience ratings.

these preferred viewing times and seasons, fewer viewers will be watching TV when he appears.

In the first equation of Table 1 (whose results appear in the first two columns) we have regressed the 158 presidential audience ratings summarized in Figure 1 on these benefit and costs variables. For the most part, the relationships closely follow our expectations and parallel the survey results. The presence of viewing options is, again, a powerful predictor of the president's audience share. Presidential approval displays the correct sign and is significant; concern with the economy significantly increases the audience. International crises attract audiences; apparently, crises give viewers a special reason to learn what the president has to say. Two days after the attack of 9/11, a record 88 percent of America's households tuned in to see how President Bush planned to respond. The several schedule variables reflecting time of address, season, and number of networks showing the president are all significantly related to watching the president. The same structural features of the market mediate the president's audience rating as do so for commercial programming.[13] The one variable that fails to produce a statistically significant relationship for the full 1969 to 2006 series is the president's approval rating; more on this below.

Earlier we argued that variations in an address's expected benefit will have less effect on the viewing choices of those who remain dependent on the broadcast signal, for the simple reason that they have nowhere else to go. The ideal way of testing this hypothesis on marginal changes in the president's audience shares over time entails analyzing the relationships separately for cable and broadcast viewers. Unfortunately, Nielsen Media Research does not provide such partially disaggregated data for scholarly research. There is, however, another, indirect approach available. Note that Figure 2 shows neither cable penetration of households nor network audience shares changing greatly until the early 1980s. During the Nixon-to-Carter era, for example, the big three networks' share of the market declined only about one percentage point (from 56 percent to 55 percent), compared to a thirty-four percentage point decline (from 55 percent to 21 percent) for the 1981–2006 period. Consequently, presidents' audience ratings (see Figure 1) were both higher and more stable during the Nixon, Ford, and Carter presidencies than for more recent presidents. By estimating the equations separately for these two time periods, we obtain series with distinct mixes of cable and broadcast audiences. According to our model, stronger time-series relationships should occur for the second period, when far more members of the television audience possessed many more viewing options and consequently a meaningful choice whenever the president appeared on the screen.

This is precisely what we find in the second and third equations of Table 1. Only the scheduling variables are statistically significant for both the first and second periods. This is perfectly consistent with our model, since these variables capture *whether* people are watching television, rather than their particular choice of programming. Moreover, "Network Share" is appropriately weak and insignificant during the early period, reflecting cable's limited penetration into American households. By comparison, the president's audience ratings during the Reagan-to-G. W. Bush era tracked all of the independent variables except, again, presidential approval ("Approve"). At first glance, this null finding is surprising. Elsewhere, however, we offer evidence suggesting that because it is important, other actors incorporate the president's public prestige into their strategic decisions of whether ("One Network") and when ("9:00 p.m.") to broadcast the event (Baum and Kernell, 1999).

Conclusion

The textbook assessment that "television has brought about . . . the greater ease with which American presidents can communicate directly with the American people" (Erikson and Tedin 1995, 235) increasingly represents the reality of a bygone "golden age" of presidential television. In the 1960s and 1970s, when more homes in America had televisions than had indoor plumbing and virtually all viewers (including early cable subscribers) depended on the networks for their programming, presidents possessed an enviable tool of persuasion. President Kennedy introduced the live, prime-time press conference in 1961 so that he could, as he explained to a reporter at the inaugural session, "speak directly to the American people." Over the next several decades, direct appeals to the captive American audience became commonplace. In 1970 President Nixon delivered nine prime-time addresses to the nation. He and other presidents did not hesitate to take to the airwaves to exhort the public to write, call, and send mailgrams to their members of Congress in support of their policies. The urge to go public with a prime-time address was tempered only by the consideration that the president might wear out his welcome (Kernell 1997, 107).

What broadcast technology gave the president, cable technology appears to be taking away. In recent years, as the number of television households receiving cable has swelled, along with the programming alternatives it offers, the number of viewers who reach for their remote at the first sight of the president has grown steadily. That in turn has prompted the broadcast networks to reassess their willingness to surrender prime-time slots to the president. Rotating coverage is increasingly favored, and some presidential coverage requests have been rejected outright. Gone are the days when a president could "appear simultaneously on all national radio and television networks at prime, large-audience evening hours, virtually whenever and however the president wishes" (Minow et al. 1973).

The recent origin of this phenomenon necessarily renders speculative any assessment of its implications. We can reasonably conclude, nonetheless, that presidents' diminished access to the national television audience will present future presidents with a serious strategic dilemma: How will they promote their policies to a citizenry that depends almost entirely on television for its news and information yet is increasingly unwilling to allow the president into their homes?

NOTES

1. Over the years, A. C. Nielsen Company has established itself as the authoritative source and arbiter of television viewing habits. Two of Nielsen's better known audience rating indexes gauge audience size as a percentage of households using television (HUT) and as a percentage of households owning televisions, which it calls "Average Audience Household" (AAH). The former is best suited for assessing a program's performance in a given time slot and consequently is favored by network producers. The latter better measures a program's overall audience penetration and allows program comparisons across time slots. AAH is the Nielsen rating for an average minute of programming. For our study, we use AAH, which represents the percentage of those U.S. households possessing television that tuned into the president's address during an average minute of that program.

2. At least one of the four major networks (including Fox) broadcast each of these addresses and press conferences. Only since 1993 has a presidential address or press conference received less than full coverage.

3. Shortly after the Monica Lewinsky sex scandal broke into the news, President Clinton's political standing became so unstable that several newspaper and network surveys launched daily tracking surveys to monitor the president's pulse in public opinion. But then the president delivered a well-received State of the Union address, his polling numbers shot up to their highest levels ever, and the polling subsided. The results of the CBS/*New York Times* Survey are typical (Berke 1998).

4. The 2005 figure include satellite subscriptions. Henceforth we shall drop references to these subscriptions, which are functionally equivalent to cable and have been added to subsequent figures as "cable" subscribers.

5. Recently even the broadcast market has started to expand and offer viewers more choices. A fourth broadcast network, Fox, started up in 1991, and in 1994 UPN and WB entered the market.

6. During President Clinton's much-anticipated 1998 State of the Union speech, during the first days of the Lewinsky scandal, the fledgling WB network enjoyed its highest-rated program ever, when almost eight million viewers tuned in to a new series (Snow 1998).

7. Over the past decade, the Internet has begun to emerge as an important alternative to television as a source of political information. However, survey evidence (e.g., Pew Center 2002, 2004) suggests that for a vast majority Americans, television remains the overwhelmingly predominant source of news about politics.

8. Fifty-one percent of NES respondents claimed to have watched the first debate when it was broadcast on all four network channels, PBS, and CNN on October 6, 1996, and 47 percent reported watching the second debate ten days later. The Nielsen ratings, comparable to those in Figure 1, record much more modest audiences of 32 percent and 26 percent of households with television, respectively, for the two debates.

9. This variable represents the NES interviewer's estimate of the respondent's level of political information. Despite problems of reliability that would appear inherent in such a subjective measure, Zaller (1992) found that this variable, measured in the preelection interview, performs as well as or better than any other NES-based indicator of political awareness, including education, political participation, media exposure, interest in politics, and various informational indices he constructed (which we replicated).

10. Following a simulation procedure for generating significance levels developed by King, Tomz, and Wittenberg (2000), we have also plotted the 95 percent confidence intervals for each expected probability.

11. The 1996 General Social Survey asked respondents how many hours per day they watched television. Responses were coded 0 through 24 hours per day. Separating respondents by education level, those with less than a ninth grade education averaged fully two more hours per day of television viewing than their college educated counterparts—4.2 versus 2.2 hours per day.

12. We also tested the effects of various presidential scandals during this era. These events drive down a president's approval rating, which apparently accounts for their failure to yield significant statistical relationships in the multivariate analysis.

13. Although the scheduling of presidential addresses is constrained by events (e.g., a sudden international crisis) or obligations (e.g., the State of the Union address), they are

not randomly distributed with respect to time and season. Instead, the address schedule represents a negotiated agreement between network executives and White House advisers and consequently may be partly endogenous to the equation.

REFERENCES

Bartels, Larry M. 1993. "Messages Received: The Political Impact of Media Exposure." *American Political Science Review* 87 (June): 267–285.

Baum, Matthew A., and Tim Groeling. 2004. "Crossing the Water's Edge: Elite Rhetoric, Media Coverage and the Rally-Round-the-Flag Phenomenon, 1979–2003." Paper presented to the annual meeting of the American Political Science Association, Chicago, Ill., Sept.

Baum, Matthew A., and Samuel Kernell. 1999. "Has Cable Ended the Golden Age of Presidential Television?" *American Political Science Review* 93 (March): 99–114.

Berke, Richard L. 1998. "A Wild Ride, with No End Now in Sight." *New York Times,* January 30, A14.

Brace, Paul, and Barbara Hinckley. 1993. "Presidential Activities from Truman through Reagan: Timing and Impact." *Journal of Politics* 55 (May): 382–398.

Briller, Bert R. 1990. "Zooming in Closer on the News Audience." *Television Quarterly* 25 (Winter): 107–116.

Center for Media and Public Affairs (CMPA). 1996. "Markle Presidential Election Watch: Report Card." www.cmpa.com/politics/Elections/ewarchiv.htm.

Cohen, Jeffrey, E. 1995. "Presidential Rhetoric and the Public Agenda." *American Journal of Political Science* 39 (February): 7–107.

Davis, James Allen. 1996. "General Social Surveys, 1972–1999." [computer file]: Principal investigator, James A. Davis; director and co-principal investigator, Tom W. Smith. Chicago: National Opinion Research Center [producer]; Storrs, [Conn.]: Roper Public Opinion Research Center [distributor, 1996]. NORC edition.

Edwards, George C. 2003. *On Deaf Ears.* New Haven: Yale University Press.

Erikson, Robert S., and Kent L. Tedin. 1995. *American Public Opinion: Its Origins, Content, and Impact.* 5th edition. Boston: Allyn and Bacon.

Foote, Joe S. 1988. "Ratings Decline of Presidential Television." *Journal of Broadcasting and Electronic Media* 32 (Spring): 225–230.

Groeling, Tim, and Samuel Kernell. 1998. "Is Network News Coverage of the President Biased?" *Journal of Politics* 60 (November): 1064–1086.

Hallin, Daniel C. 1994. *We Keep America on Top of the World: Television Journalism and the Public Sphere.* London and New York: TJ Press (Padstow) Ltd.

IT Facts. 2004. www.itfacts.biz/index.php?id=P1654 (original source: A. C. Nielsen).

Kernell, Samuel. 1997. *Going Public.* 3rd edition. Washington, D.C.: CQ Press.

King, Gary, Michael Tomz, and Jason Wittenberg. 2000. "Making the Most of Statistical Analyses: Improving Interpretation and Presentation." *American Journal of Political Science* 44 (April): 347–361.

Lichty, Lawrence W., and Douglas Gomery. 1992. "More Is Less." In *The Future of News: Television, Newspapers, Wire Services, News Magazines.* Washington, D.C.: Woodrow Wilson Center Press.

Lowry, Brian. 1997. "Cable Stations Gather Strength." *Los Angeles Times,* September 2, F1.

Media Monitor. 1991. Newsletter of the Center for Media and Public Affairs, Washington, D.C. Spring, 4.

Miller, Joanne, and Jon Krosnick. 1996. "News Media Impact on the Ingredients of Presidential Evaluations: A Program of Research on the Priming Hypothesis." In *Presidential Persuasion and Attitudinal Change,* ed. Diana C. Mutz and Paul M. Sniderman. Ann Arbor: University of Michigan Press.

Minow, Newton N., John Bartlow Martin, and Lee M. Mitchell. 1973. *Presidential Television.* New York: Basic Books.

Moisy, Claude. 1997. "Myths of the Global Information Village." *Foreign Policy* 107 (Summer): 78–87.

Mondak, Jeffrey J. 1993. "Source Cues and Policy Approval: The Cognitive Dynamics of Public Support for the Reagan Agenda." *American Journal of Political Science* 37 (February): 186–212.

Neustadt, Richard E. 1960. *Presidential Power and the Modern Presidents.* New York: John Wiley.

Nielsen Media Research. 2006. *Nielsen Tunes in to Politics.* New York: Nielsen Media Research.

Page, Benjamin, Robert Shapiro, and G. Dempsey. 1987. "What Moves Public Opinion." *American Political Science Review* 81 (September): 815–831.

Patterson, Thomas. 1996. "Bad News, Period." *PS: Political Science and Politics* 29 (March): 17–20.

Pew Research Center for the People and the Press. 2002. *Biennial Media Consumption Survey.* Princeton Survey Research Associates (April).

———. 2004. *Biennial Media Consumption Survey.* Princeton Survey Research Associates (April).

Ragsdale, Lyn. 1984. "The Politics of Presidential Speechmaking, 1949–1980." *American Political Science Review* 78 (December): 971–984.

Rosenstone, Steven J., Donald R. Kinder, Warren E. Miller, and the National Election Studies. 1997. *American National Election Study, 1996: Pre- and Post-Election Survey* [Computer file]. 2nd release. Ann Arbor, Mich.: University of Michigan, Center for Political Studies [producer], 1997. Ann Arbor, Mich.: Inter-university Consortium for Political and Social Research [distributor], 1997.

Simon, Dennis M., and Charles W. Ostrom Jr. 1989. "The Impact of Televised Speeches and Foreign Travel on Presidential Approval." *Public Opinion Quarterly* 53 (Spring): 58–82.

Snow, Shauna. 1998. "Morning Report: Arts and Entertainment Reports from the Times, National and International News Services and the Nation's Press." *Los Angeles Times,* January 22, F50.

Stanley, Harold W., and Richard G. Niemi. 1998. *Vital Statistics on American Politics, 1997–1998.* Washington D.C.: CQ Press.

Webster, James G., and Lawrence W. Lichty. 1991. *Ratings Analysis: Theory and Practice.* New Jersey and London: Lawrence Erlbaum Associates.

Zaller, John, R. 1992. *The Nature and Origins of Mass Opinion.* New York: Cambridge University Press.

———. 1997. "A Model of Communication Effects at the Outbreak of the Gulf War." In *Do the Media Govern? Politicians, Voters, and Reporters in America.* Ed. Shanto Iyengar and Richard Reeves. Thousand Oaks, Calif.: Sage. 296–311

Chapter 8

The Bureaucracy

8-1

The Politics of Bureaucratic Structure

Terry M. Moe

Legislators, presidents, and other political players care about the content and implementation of policy. They also care about the way executive agencies are structured: Where in the executive branch are new agencies placed? What kind of bureaucrat will be motivated to aggressively pursue, or to resist the pursuit of, certain policy goals? Who should report to whom? What rules should govern bureaucrats' behavior? In the following essay, Terry M. Moe observes that these questions are anticipated and answered by politicians as they set policy. They are the subjects of "structural" politics. The federal bureaucracy is not structured on the basis of a theory of public administration, Moe argues, but should instead be viewed as the product of politics.

AMERICAN PUBLIC BUREAUCRACY is not designed to be effective. The bureaucracy arises out of politics, and its design reflects the interests, strategies, and compromises of those who exercise political power.

This politicized notion of bureaucracy has never appealed to most academics or reformers. They accept it—indeed, they adamantly argue its truth—and the social science of public bureaucracy is a decidedly political body of work as a result. Yet, for the most part, those who study and practice public administration have a thinly

Source: John E. Chubb and Paul E. Peterson, eds., *Can the Government Govern?* (Washington, D.C.: Brookings Institution Press, 1989), 267–285. Some notes appearing in the original have been deleted.

veiled disdain for politics, and they want it kept out of bureaucracy as much as possible. They want presidents to stop politicizing the departments and bureaus. They want Congress to stop its incessant meddling in bureaucratic affairs. They want all politicians to respect bureaucratic autonomy, expertise, and professionalism.[1]

The bureaucracy's defenders are not apologists. Problems of capture, inertia, parochialism, fragmentation, and imperialism are familiar grounds for criticism. And there is lots of criticism. But once the subversive influence of politics is mentally factored out, these bureaucratic problems are understood to have bureaucratic solutions—new mandates, new rules and procedures, new personnel systems, better training and management, better people. These are the quintessential reforms that politicians are urged to adopt to bring about effective bureaucracy. The goal at all times is the greater good: "In designing any political structure, whether it be the Congress, the executive branch, or the judiciary, it is important to build arrangements that weigh the scale in favor of those advocating the national interest."[2]

The hitch is that those in positions of power are not necessarily motivated by the national interest. They have their own interests to pursue in politics—the interests of southwest Pennsylvania or cotton farmers or the maritime industry—and they exercise their power in ways conducive to those interests. Moreover, choices about bureaucratic structure are not matters that can be separated off from all this, to be guided by technical criteria of efficiency and effectiveness. Structural choices have important consequences for the content and direction of policy, and political actors know it. When they make choices about structure, they are implicitly making choices about policy. And precisely because this is so, issues of structure are inevitably caught up in the larger political struggle. Any notion that political actors might confine their attention to policymaking and turn organizational design over to neutral criteria or efficiency experts denies the realities of politics.

This essay is an effort to understand bureaucracy by understanding its foundation in political choice and self-interest. The central question boils down to this: what sorts of structures do the various political actors—interest groups, presidents, members of Congress, bureaucrats—find conducive to their own interests, and what kind of bureaucracy is therefore likely to emerge from their efforts to exercise political power? In other words, why do they build the bureaucracy they do? . . .

A Perspective on Structural Politics

Most citizens do not get terribly excited about the arcane details of public administration. When they choose among candidates in elections, they pay attention to such things as party or image or stands on policy. If pressed, the candidates would probably have views or even voting records on structural issues—for example, whether the Occupational Safety and Health Administration should be required to carry out cost-benefit analysis before proposing a formal rule or whether the Consumer Product Safety Commission should be moved into the Commerce Department—but this is hardly the stuff that political campaigns are made of. People just do not know or care much about these sorts of things.

Organized interest groups are another matter. They are active, informed participants in their specialized issue areas, and they know that their policy goals are crucially dependent on precisely those fine details of administrative structure that cause voters' eyes to glaze over. Structure is valuable to them, and they have every incentive to mobilize their political resources to get what they want. As a result, they are normally the only source of political pressure when structural issues are at stake. Structural politics is interest group politics.

Interest Groups: The Technical Problem of Structural Choice

Most accounts of structural politics pay attention to interest groups, but their analytical focus is on the politicians who exercise public authority and make the final choices. This tends to be misleading. It is well known that politicians, even legislators from safe districts, are extraordinarily concerned about their electoral popularity and, for that reason, are highly responsive to their constituencies. To the extent this holds true, their positions on issues are not really their own, but are induced by the positions of others. If one seeks to understand why structural choices turn out as they do, then, it does not make much sense to start with politicians. The more fundamental questions have to do with how interest groups decide what kinds of structures they want politicians to provide. This is the place to start.

In approaching these questions about interest groups, it is useful to begin with an extreme case. Suppose that, in a given issue area, there is a single dominant group (or coalition) with a reasonably complex problem—pollution, poverty, job safety, health—it seeks to address through governmental action, and that the group is so powerful that politicians will enact virtually any proposal the group offers, subject to reasonable budget constraints. In effect, the group is able to exercise public authority on its own by writing legislation that is binding on everyone and enforceable in the courts.

The dominant group is an instructive case because, as it makes choices about structure, it faces no political problems. It need not worry about losing its grip on public authority or about the influence of its political opponents—considerations which would otherwise weigh heavily in its calculations. Without the usual uncertainties and constraints of politics, the group has the luxury of concerning itself entirely with the technical requirements of effective organization. Its job is to identify those structural arrangements that best realize its policy goals.

It is perhaps natural to think that, since a dominant group can have anything it wants, it would proceed by figuring out what types of behaviors are called for by what types of people under what types of conditions and by writing legislation spelling all this out in the minutest detail. If an administrative agency were necessary to perform services, process applications, or inspect business operations, the jobs of bureaucrats could be specified with such precision that they would have little choice but to do the group's bidding.

For simple policy goals—requiring, say, little more than transfer payments—these strategies would be attractive. But they are quite unsuited to policy problems of any complexity. The reason is that, although the group has the political power to impose its will on everyone, it almost surely lacks the knowledge to do it well. It does not know what to tell people to do.

In part, this is an expertise problem. Society as a whole simply has not developed sufficient knowledge to determine the causes of or solutions for most social problems; and the group typically knows much less than society does, even when it hires experts of its own. These knowledge problems are compounded by uncertainty about the future. The world is subject to unpredictable changes over time, and some will call on specific policy adjustments if the group's interests are to be pursued effectively. The group could attempt to specify all future contingencies in the current legislation and, through continuous monitoring and intervention, update it over time. But the knowledge requirements of a halfway decent job would prove enormously costly, cumbersome, and time-consuming.

A group with the political power to tell everyone what to do, then, will typically not find it worthwhile to try. A more attractive option is to write legislation in general terms, put experts on the public payroll, and grant them the authority to "fill in the details" and make whatever adjustments are necessary over time. This compensates nicely for the group's formidable knowledge problems, allowing it to pursue its own interests without knowing exactly how to implement its policies and without having to grapple with future contingencies. The experts do what the group is unable to do for itself. And because they are public officials on the public payroll, the arrangement economizes greatly on the group's resources and time.

It does, however, raise a new worry: there is no guarantee the experts will always act in the group's best interests. Experts have their own interests—in career, in autonomy—that may conflict with those of the group. And, due largely to experts' specialized knowledge and the often intangible nature of their outputs, the group cannot know exactly what its expert agents are doing or why.

These are problems of conflict of interest and asymmetric information, and they are unavoidable. Because of them, control will be imperfect.

When the group's political power is assured, as we assume it is here, these control problems are at the heart of structural choice. The most direct approach is for the group to impose a set of rules to constrain bureaucratic behavior. Among other things, these rules might specify the criteria and procedures bureaucrats are to use in making decisions; shape incentives by specifying how bureaucrats are to be evaluated, rewarded, and sanctioned; require them to collect and report certain kinds of information on their internal operations, and set up oversight procedures by which their activities can be monitored. These are basic components of bureaucratic structure.

But some slippage will remain. The group's knowledge problems, combined with the experts' will and capacity to resist (at least at the margins), make perfect control impossible. Fortunately, though, the group can do more than impose a set of rules on its agents. It also has the power to choose who its agents will be—and wise use of this power could make the extensive use of rules unnecessary.

The key here is reputation. Most individuals in the expert market come with reputations that speak to their job-relevant traits: expertise, intelligence, honesty, loyalty, policy preferences, ideology. "Good" reputations provide reliable information. The reason is that individuals value good reputations, they invest in them—by behaving honestly, for instance, even when they could realize short-term gains through cheating—and, having built up reputations, they have strong incentives to maintain them through consistent behavior. To the group, therefore, reputation is of enormous value because it allows predictability in an uncertain world. And predictability facilitates control.

To see more concretely how this works, consider an important reputational syndrome: professionalism. If individuals are known to be accountants or securities lawyers or highway engineers, the group will immediately know a great deal about their "type." They will be experts in certain issues. They will have specialized educations and occupational experiences. They will analyze issues, collect data, and propose solutions in characteristic ways. They will hew to the norms of their professional communities. Particularly when professionalism is combined with reputational information of a more personal nature, the behavior of these experts will be highly predictable.

The link between predictability and control would seem especially troublesome in this case, since professionals are widely known to demand autonomy in their work. And, as far as restrictive rules and hierarchical directives are concerned, their demand for autonomy does indeed pose problems. But the group is forced to grant experts discretion anyway, owing to its knowledge problems. What professionalism does—via reputation—is allow the group to anticipate how expert discretion will be exercised under various conditions; it can then plan accordingly as it designs a structure that takes best advantage of their expertise. In the extreme, one might think of professionals as automatons, programmed to behave in specific ways. Knowing how they are programmed, the group can select those with the desired programs, place them in a structure designed to accommodate them, and turn them loose to exercise free choice. The professionals would see themselves as independent decision makers. The group would see them as under control. And both would be right.

The purpose of this illustration is not to emphasize professionalism per se, but to clarify a general point about the technical requirements of organizational design. A politically powerful group, acting under uncertainty and concerned with solving a complex policy problem, is normally best off if it resists using its power to tell bureaucrats exactly what to do. It can use its power more productively by selecting the right types of bureaucrats and designing a structure that affords them reasonable autonomy. Through the judicious allocation of bureaucratic roles and responsibilities, incentive systems, and structural checks on bureaucratic choice, a select set of bureaucrats can be unleashed to follow their expert judgment, free from detailed formal instructions.

Interest Groups: The Political Problem of Structural Choice

Political dominance is an extreme case for purposes of illustration. In the real world of democratic politics, interest groups cannot lay claim to unchallenged legal authority. Because this is so, they face two fundamental problems that a dominant group does not. The first I will call political uncertainty, the second political compromise. Both have enormous consequences for the strategic design of public bureaucracy—consequences that entail substantial departures from effective organization.

Political uncertainty is inherent in democratic government. No one has a perpetual hold on public authority nor, therefore, a perpetual right to control public agencies. An interest group may be powerful enough to exercise public authority today, but tomorrow its power may ebb, and its right to exercise public authority may then be usurped by its political opponents. Should this occur, they would become the new "owners" of whatever the group had created, and they could use their authority to destroy—quite legitimately—everything the group had worked so hard to achieve.

A group that is currently advantaged, then, must anticipate all this. Precisely because its own authority is not guaranteed, it cannot afford to focus entirely on technical issues of effective organization. It must also design its creations so that they have the capacity to pursue its policy goals in a world in which its enemies may achieve the right to govern. The group's task in the current period, then, is to build agencies that are difficult for its opponents to gain control over later. Given the way authority is allocated and exercised in a democracy, this will often mean building agencies that are insulated from public authority in general—and thus insulated from formal control by the group itself.

There are various structural means by which the group can try to protect and nurture its bureaucratic agents. They include the following:

- It can write detailed legislation that imposes rigid constraints on the agency's mandate and decision procedures. While these constraints will tend to be flawed, cumbersome, and costly, they serve to remove important types of decisions from future political control. The reason they are so attractive is rooted in the American separation-of-powers system, which sets up obstacles that make formal legislation extremely difficult to achieve—and, if achieved, extremely difficult to overturn. Should the group's opponents gain in political power, there is a good chance they would still not be able to pass corrective legislation of their own.

- It can place even greater emphasis on professionalism than is technically justified, since professionals will generally act to protect their own autonomy and resist political interference. For similar reasons, the group can be a strong supporter of the career civil service and other personnel systems that insulate bureaucratic jobs, promotion, and pay from political intervention. And it can try to minimize the power and number of political appointees, since these too are routes by which opponents may exercise influence.

- It can oppose formal provisions that enhance political oversight and involvement. The legislative veto, for example, is bad because it gives opponents a direct mechanism for reversing agency decisions. Sunset provisions, which require reauthorization of the agency after some period of time, are also dangerous because they give opponents opportunities to overturn the group's legislative achievements.

- It can see that the agency is given a safe location in the scheme of government. Most obviously, it might try to place the agency in a friendly executive department, where it can be sheltered by the group's allies. Or it may favor formal independence, which provides special protection from presidential removal and managerial powers.

- It can favor judicialization of agency decision making as a way of insulating policy choices from outside interference. It can also favor making various types of agency actions—or inactions—appealable to the courts. It must take care to design these procedures and checks, however, so that they disproportionately favor the group over its opponents.

The driving force of political uncertainty, then, causes the winning group to favor structural designs it would never favor on technical grounds alone:

designs that place detailed formal restrictions on bureaucratic discretion, impose complex procedures for agency decision making, minimize opportunities for oversight, and otherwise insulate the agency from politics. The group has to protect itself and its agency from the dangers of democracy, and it does so by imposing structures that appear strange and incongruous indeed when judged by almost any reasonable standards of what an effective organization ought to look like.

But this is only part of the story. The departure from technical rationality is still greater because of a second basic feature of American democratic politics: legislative victory of any consequence almost always requires compromise. This means that opposing groups will have a direct say in how the agency and its mandate are constructed. One form that this can take, of course, is the classic compromise over policy that is written about endlessly in textbooks and newspapers. But there is no real disjunction between policy and structure, and many of the opponents' interests will also be pursued through demands for structural concessions. What sorts of arrangements should they tend to favor?

- Opponents want structures that work against effective performance. They fear strong, coherent, centralized organization. They like fragmented authority, decentralization, federalism, checks and balances, and other structural means of promoting weakness, confusion, and delay.

- They want structures that allow politicians to get at the agency. They do not want to see the agency placed within a friendly department, nor do they favor formal independence. They are enthusiastic supporters of legislative veto and reauthorization provisions. They favor onerous requirements for the collection and reporting of information, the monitoring of agency operations, and the review of agency decisions—thus laying the basis for active, interventionist oversight by politicians.

- They want appointment and personnel arrangements that allow for political direction of the agency. They also want more active and influential roles for political appointees and less extensive reliance on professionalism and the civil service.

- They favor agency decision making procedures that allow them to participate, to present evidence and arguments, to appeal adverse agency decisions, to delay, and, in general, to protect their own interests and inhibit effective agency action through formal, legally sanctioned rules. This means that they will tend to push for cumbersome, heavily judicialized decision processes, and that they will favor an active, easily triggered role for the courts in reviewing agency decisions.

- They want agency decisions to be accompanied by, and partially justified in terms of, "objective" assessments of their consequences: environmental impact statements, inflation impact statements, cost-benefit analysis. These are costly, time-consuming, and disruptive. Even better, their methods and conclusions can be challenged in the courts, providing new opportunities for delaying or quashing agency decisions.

Political compromise ushers the fox into the chicken coop. Opposing groups are dedicated to crippling the bureaucracy and gaining control over its decisions, and they will pressure for fragmented authority, labyrinthine procedures, mechanisms of political intervention, and other structures that subvert the bureaucracy's performance and open it up to attack. In the politics of structural choice, the inevitability of compromise means that agencies will be burdened with structures fully intended to cause their failure.

In short, democratic government gives rise to two major forces that cause the structure of public bureaucracy to depart from technical rationality. First, those currently in a position to exercise public authority will often face uncertainty about their own grip on political power in the years ahead, and this will prompt them to favor structures that insulate their achievements from politics. Second, opponents will also tend to have a say in structural design, and, to the degree they do, they will impose structures that subvert effective performance and politicize agency decisions.

Legislators and Structural Choice

If politicians were nothing more than conduits for political pressures, structural choice could be understood without paying much attention to them. But politicians, especially presidents, do sometimes have preferences about the structure of government that are not simple reflections of what the groups want. And when this is so, they can use their control of public authority to make their preferences felt in structural outcomes.

The conduit notion is not so wide of the mark for legislators, owing to their almost paranoid concern for reelection. In structural politics, well informed interest groups make demands, observe legislators' responses, and accurately assign credit and blame as decisions are made and consequences realized. Legislators therefore have strong incentives to do what groups want—and, even in the absence of explicit demands, to take entrepreneurial action in actively representing group interests. They cannot satisfy groups with empty position taking. Nor can they costlessly "shift the responsibility" by delegating tough decisions to the bureaucracy. Interest groups, unlike voters, are not easily fooled.

This does not mean that legislators always do what groups demand of them. Autonomous behavior can arise even among legislators who are motivated by

nothing other than reelection. This happens because politicians, like groups, recognize that their current choices are not just means of responding to current
pressures, but are also means of imposing structure on their political lives. This
will sometimes lead them to make unpopular choices today in order to reap
political rewards later on.

It is not quite right, moreover, to suggest that legislators have no interest of
their own in controlling the bureaucracy. The more control legislators are able
to exercise, the more groups will depend on them to get what they want; and
this, in itself, makes control electorally attractive. But the attractiveness of control is diluted by other factors. First, the winning group—the more powerful
side—will pressure to have its victories removed from political influence.
Second, the capacity for control can be a curse for legislators in later conflict,
since both sides will descend on them repeatedly. Third, oversight for purposes
of serious policy control is time-consuming, costly, and difficult to do well; legislators typically have much more productive ways to spend their scarce
resources.

The result is that legislators tend not to invest in general policy control.
Instead, they value "particularized" control: they want to be able to intervene
quickly, inexpensively, and in ad hoc ways to protect or advance the interests of
particular clients in particular matters. This sort of control can be managed by an
individual legislator without collective action; it has direct payoffs; it will generally be carried out behind the scenes; and it does not involve or provoke conflict.
It generates political benefits without political costs. Moreover, it fits in quite
nicely with a bureaucratic structure designed for conflict avoidance: an agency
that is highly autonomous in the realm of policy yet highly constrained by complex procedural requirements will offer all sorts of opportunities for particularistic interventions.

The more general point is that legislators, by and large, can be expected either
to respond to group demands in structural politics or to take entrepreneurial
action in trying to please them. They will not be given to flights of autonomous
action or statesmanship.

Presidents and Structural Choice

Presidents are motivated differently. Governance is the driving force behind the
modern presidency. All presidents, regardless of party, are expected to govern
effectively and are held responsible for taking action on virtually the full range of
problems facing society. To be judged successful in the eyes of history—arguably
the single most important motivator for presidents—they must appear to be
strong leaders. They need to achieve their policy initiatives, their initiatives must

be regarded as socially valuable, and the structures for attaining them must appear to work.

This raises two basic problems for interest groups. The first is that presidents are not very susceptible to the appeals of special interests. They want to make groups happy, to be sure, and sometimes responding to group demands will contribute nicely to governance. But this is often not so. In general, presidents have incentives to think in grander terms about what is best for society as a whole, or at least broad chunks of it, and they have their own agendas that may depart substantially from what even their more prominent group supporters might want. Even when they are simply responding to group pressures—which is more likely, of course, during their first term—the size and heterogeneity of their support coalitions tend to promote moderation, compromise, opposition to capture, and concern for social efficiency.

The second problem is that presidents want to control the bureaucracy. While legislators eagerly delegate their powers to administrative agencies, presidents are driven to take charge. They do not care about all agencies equally, of course. Some agencies are especially important because their programs are priority items on the presidential agenda. Others are important because they deal with sensitive issues that can become political bombshells if something goes wrong. But most all agencies impinge in one way or another on larger presidential responsibilities—for the budget, for the economy, for national defense—and presidents must have the capacity to direct and constrain agency behavior in basic respects if these larger responsibilities are to be handled successfully. They may often choose not to use their capacity for administrative control; they may even let favored groups use it when it suits their purposes. But the capacity must be there when they need it.

Presidents therefore have a unique role to play in the politics of structural choice. They are the only participants who are directly concerned with how the bureaucracy as a whole should be organized. And they are the only ones who actually want to run it through hands-on management and control. Their ideal is a rational, coherent, centrally directed bureaucracy that strongly resembles popular textbook notions of what an effective bureaucracy, public or private, ought to look like.

In general, presidents favor placing agencies within executive departments and subordinating them to hierarchical authority. They want to see important oversight, budget, and policy coordination functions given to department superiors—and, above them, to the Office of Management and Budget and other presidential management agencies—so that the bureaucracy can be brought under unified direction. While they value professionalism and civil service for their contributions to expertise, continuity, and impartiality, they want authority in the hands of their own political appointees—and they want to choose appointees whose types appear most conducive to presidential leadership.

This is just what the winning group and its legislative allies do not want. They want to protect their agencies and policy achievements by insulating them from politics, and presidents threaten to ruin everything by trying to control these agencies from above. The opposing groups are delighted with this, but they cannot always take comfort in the presidential approach to bureaucracy either. For presidents will tend to resist complex procedural protections, excessive judicial review, legislative veto provisions, and many other means by which the losers try to protect themselves and cripple bureaucratic performance. Presidents want agencies to have discretion, flexibility, and the capacity to take direction. They do not want agencies to be hamstrung by rules and regulations—unless, of course, they are presidential rules and regulations designed to enhance presidential control.

Legislators, Presidents, and Interest Groups

Obviously, presidents and legislators have very different orientations to the politics of structural choice. Interest groups can be expected to anticipate these differences from the outset and devise their own strategies accordingly.

Generally speaking, groups on both sides will find Congress a comfortable place in which to do business. Legislators are not bound by any overarching notion of what the bureaucracy as a whole ought to look like. They are not intrinsically motivated by effectiveness or efficiency or coordination or management or any other design criteria that might limit the kind of bureaucracy they are willing to create. They do not even want to retain political control for themselves.

The key thing about Congress is that it is open and responsive to what the groups want. It willingly builds, piece by piece—however grotesque the pieces, however inconsistent with one another—the kind of bureaucracy interest groups incrementally demand in their structural battles over time. This "congressional bureaucracy" is not supposed to function as a coherent whole, nor even to constitute one. Only the pieces are important. That is the way groups want it.

Presidents, of course, do not want it that way. Interest groups may find them attractive allies on occasion, especially when their interests and the presidential agenda coincide. But, in general, presidents are a fearsome presence on the political scene. Their broad support coalitions, their grand perspective on public policy, and their fundamental concern for a coherent, centrally controlled bureaucracy combine to make them maverick players in the game of structural politics. They want a "presidential bureaucracy" that is fundamentally at odds with the congressional bureaucracy everyone else is busily trying to create.

To the winning group, presidents are a major source of political uncertainty over and above the risks associated with the future power of the group's opponents. This gives it even greater incentives to pressure for structures that are insulated from politics—and, when possible, disproportionately insulated from presidential politics. Because of the seriousness of the presidency's threat, the winning group will place special emphasis on limiting the powers and numbers of political appointees, locating effective authority in the agency and its career personnel, and opposing new hierarchical powers—of review, coordination, veto—for units in the Executive Office or even the departments.

The losing side is much more pragmatic. Presidents offer important opportunities for expanding the scope of conflict, imposing new procedural constraints on agency action, and appealing unfavorable decisions. Especially if presidents are not entirely sympathetic to the agency and its mission, the losing side may actively support all the trappings of presidential bureaucracy—but only, of course, for the particular case at hand. Thus, while presidents may oppose group efforts to cripple the agency through congressional bureaucracy, groups may be able to achieve much the same end through presidential bureaucracy. The risk, however, is that the next president could turn out to be an avid supporter of the agency, in which case presidential bureaucracy might be targeted to quite different ends indeed. If there is a choice, sinking formal restrictions into legislative concrete offers a much more secure and permanent fix.

Bureaucracy

Bureaucratic structure emerges as a jerry-built fusion of congressional and presidential forms, their relative roles and particular features determined by the powers, priorities, and strategies of the various designers. The result is that each agency cannot help but begin life as a unique structural reflection of its own politics.

Once an agency is created, the political world becomes a different place. Agency bureaucrats are now political actors in their own right. They have career and institutional interests that may not be entirely congruent with their formal missions, and they have powerful resources—expertise and delegated authority—that might be employed toward these selfish ends. They are new players whose interests and resources alter the political game.

It is useful to think in terms of two basic types of bureaucratic players: political appointees and careerists. Careerists are the pure bureaucrats. As they carry out their jobs, they will be concerned with the technical requirements of effective organization, but they will also face the same problem that all other political actors face: political uncertainty. Changes in group power, committee composition, and presidential administration represent serious threats to things that bureaucrats hold dear. Their mandates could be restricted, their budgets cut, their discretion curtailed, their reputations blemished. Like groups and politicians, bureaucrats cannot afford to concern themselves solely with technical matters. They must take action to reduce their political uncertainty.

One attractive strategy is to nurture mutually beneficial relationships with groups and politicians whose political support the agency needs. If these are to provide real security, they must be more than isolated quid pro quos; they must be part of an ongoing stream of exchanges that give all participants expectations of future gain and thus incentives to resist short-term opportunities to profit at one another's expense. This is most easily done with the agency's initial supporters. Over time, however, the agency will be driven to broaden its support base, and it may move away from some of its creators—as regulatory agencies sometimes have, for example, in currying favor with the business interests they are supposed to be regulating. All agencies will have a tendency to move away from presidents, who, as temporary players, are inherently unsuited to participation in stable, long-term relationships.

Political appointees are also unattractive allies. They are not long-term participants, and no one will treat them as though they are. They have no concrete basis for participating in the exchange relationships of benefit to careerists. Indeed, they may not want to, for they have incentives to pay special attention to White House policy, and they will try to forge alliances that further those ends. Their focus is on short-term presidential victories, and relationships that stabilize politics for the agency may get in the way and have to be challenged.

As this begins to suggest, the strategy of building supportive relationships is inherently limited. In the end, much of the environment remains out of control. This prompts careerists to rely on a second, complementary strategy of uncertainty avoidance: insulation. If they cannot control the environment, they can try to shut themselves off from it in various ways. They can promote further professionalization and more extensive reliance on civil service. They can formalize and judicialize their decision procedures. They can base decisions on technical expertise, operational experience, and precedent, thus making them "objective" and agency-centered. They can try to monopolize the information necessary for effective political oversight. These insulating strategies are designed, moreover, not simply to shield the agency from its political environment, but also to shield it from the very appointees who are formally in charge.

All of this raises an obvious question: why can't groups and politicians anticipate the agency's alliance and insulationist strategies and design a structure ex ante that adjusts for them? The answer, of course, is that they can. Presidents may push for stronger hierarchical controls and greater formal power for appointees than they otherwise would. Group opponents may place even greater emphasis on opening the agency up to political oversight. And so on. The agency's design, therefore, should from the beginning incorporate everyone's anticipations about its incentives to form alliances and promote its own autonomy.

Thus, however active the agency is in forming alliances, insulating itself from politics, and otherwise shaping political outcomes, it would be a mistake to regard the agency as a truly independent force. It is literally manufactured by the other players as a vehicle for advancing and protecting their own interests, and their structural designs are premised on anticipations about the roles the agency and its bureaucrats will play in future politics. The whole point of structural choice is to anticipate, program, and engineer bureaucratic behavior. Although groups and politicians cannot do this perfectly, the agency is fundamentally a product of their designs, and so is the way it plays the political game. That is why, in our attempt to understand the structure and politics of bureaucracy, we turn to bureaucrats last rather than first.

Structural Choice as a Perpetual Process

The game of structural politics never ends. An agency is created and given a mandate, but, in principle at least, all of the choices that have been made in the formative round of decision making can be reversed or modified later.

As the politics of structural choice unfolds over time, three basic forces supply its dynamics. First, group opponents will constantly be on the lookout for opportunities to impose structures of their own that will inhibit the agency's performance and open it up to external control. Second, the winning group must constantly be ready to defend its agency from attack—but it may also have attacks of its own to launch. The prime reason is poor performance: because the agency is burdened from the beginning with a structure unsuited to the lofty goals it is supposed to achieve, the supporting group is likely to be dissatisfied and to push for more productive structural arrangements. Third, the president will try to ensure that agency behavior is consistent with broader presidential priorities, and he will take action to impose his own structures on top of those already put in place by Congress. He may also act to impose structures on purely political grounds in response to the interests of either the winning or opposing group.

All of this is going on all the time, generating pressures for structural change that find expression in both the legislative and executive processes. These are potentially of great importance for bureaucracy and policy, and all the relevant participants are intensely aware of it. However, the choices about structure that are made in the first period, when the agency is designed and empowered with a mandate, are normally far more enduring and consequential than those that will be made later. They constitute an institutional base that is protected by all the impediments to new legislation inherent in separation of powers, as well as by the political clout of the agency's supporters. Most of the pushing and hauling in subsequent years is likely to produce only incremental change. This, obviously, is very much on everyone's minds in the first period.

NOTES

1. Harold Seidman and Robert Gilmour, *Politics, Position, and Power: From the Positive to the Regulatory State,* 4th ed. (Oxford University Press, 1986); and Frederick C. Mosher, *Democracy and the Public Service,* 2d ed. (Oxford University Press, 1982).

2. Seidman and Gilmour, *Politics, Position, and Power,* p. 330.

8-2

Bush and the Bureaucracy: A Crusade for Control

Paul Singer

Every president seeks to influence policy by controlling the decisions of executive agencies and their personnel. Presidents accomplish this by means such as increasing the authority of presidential appointees and establishing procedures that govern the regulatory activities of agencies. In this essay, reporter Paul Singer reports on the efforts of the George W. Bush administration (2001–2009) and considers the views of its critics.

TWO WEEKS BEFORE George W. Bush's 2001 inauguration, the Heritage Foundation issued a paper offering the new president advice on "taking charge of federal personnel."

The authors—two former officials at the Office of Personnel Management and a former congressional staffer who is now at OPM—laid out an ambitious agenda to overhaul civil service rules and "reassert managerial control of government." The paper emphasized the importance of appointing strong leaders to key government positions and holding bureaucrats "personally accountable for achievement of the president's election-endorsed and value-defined program."

Reminded of this paper recently, co-author Robert Moffit, who has moved on to other issues at Heritage, dusted off a copy and called a reporter back with a hint of rejoicing in his voice. "They apparently are really doing this stuff," he said.

To Moffit and other proponents of strong management, the Bush White House has indeed initiated a dramatic transformation of the federal bureaucracy, trying to create a leaner, more results-oriented government that can better account for taxpayer dollars. Reshaping the agenda of government to match the president's priorities is the purpose of democratic elections, Moffit said.

But critics charge that the White House is embarking on a crusade to replace expert judgment in federal agencies with political calculation, to marginalize or eliminate longtime civil servants, to change laws without going through Congress,

Source: Paul Singer, "Bush and the Bureaucracy: A Crusade for Control," *National Journal,* March 25, 2005.

to silence dissenting views within the government, and to centralize decision-making in the White House.

"A president cannot wave a wand and wipe prior policy, as implemented by duly enacted statutes, off the books," said Rena Steinzor, a founder and board member of the Center for Progressive Regulation, a think tank of liberal academics. "We have made a judgment as a nation, for decades, that an independent bureaucracy is very important." The Bush administration, she said, is "politicizing and terrorizing the bureaucracy, and turning it 180 degrees."

Critics point to a long list of manifestations of greater White House control. Among them:

> Reorganizations in various federal agencies, such as major staff cuts anticipated at NASA, that eliminate career civil service staff, or replace managers with political appointees;
>
> New management systems to grade federal agencies on the results they achieve, with the White House in charge of defining "success";
>
> Increased White House oversight of regulations issued by the Environmental Protection Agency, the Department of Labor, and other departments and agencies;
>
> The president's proposal to replace the civil service employment system with new, government-wide "pay-for-performance" rules that make it easier for managers to promote, reward, or fire employees;
>
> "Competitive sourcing" requirements that force thousands of federal workers to compete against private contractors to keep their jobs;
>
> A series of steps that may weaken traditional watchdogs and the office that protects whistle-blowers;
>
> New restrictions on the public release of government information, including a huge jump in the number of documents labeled "classified";
>
> A growing cadre of government employees who are going public with charges that their recommendations were ignored, their reports edited, or their conclusions reversed by their political-appointee managers, at the behest of the White House.

Many presidents have tried to reshape the federal bureaucracy to their liking. President Nixon had his "Management by Objective" program that attempted to rein in anti-poverty programs; President Clinton had his "Reinventing Government" initiative that aimed to improve government services and streamline rules. But under Bush, White House control of the federal agencies is "more coordinated and centralized than it has ever been," said New York University professor of public service Paul Light, who is also a senior fellow at the Brookings Institution. "It is a sea change from what it was under the Clinton administration."

Clay Johnson, who as deputy director for management at the Office of Management and Budget is the point man for Bush's "management agenda," denied any "Republican conspiracy" to control the bureaucracy or silence civil servants. "It's about things working better; it's not about controlling," Johnson said. "The thing that we can impose more of than anything else is clarity—clarity of purpose. We want to have a real clear definition of what success is," he said.

"The overall goal of all that we are doing," Johnson added, "is, we want to get to the point in three or four years where we can say to the American taxpayer that every program is getting better every year."

The federal bureaucracy is a notoriously unwieldy beast. It includes about 1.9 million civilian employees, many of whom have agendas that differ from the president's. Each administration, Republican or Democratic, struggles with its relationship with an army of workers who were on the job before the new political team arrived, and who expect to be there after the team leaves.

"You have this bizarre cycle, where the leader comes into the room and says, 'We are going to march north,' and the bureaucracy all applaud," said former House Speaker Newt Gingrich, R-Ga. "Then the leader leaves the room, and the bureaucracy says, 'Yeah, well, this "march north" thing is terrific, but this year, to be practical, we have to keep marching south. But what we'll do is, we'll hire a consultant to study marching north, so that next year we can begin to think about whether or not we can do it.'"

The White House is proud of its management initiatives and Bush's reputation as "the M.B.A. president." The administration regularly issues press releases to announce progress on the President's Management Agenda—a list of priorities that includes competitive sourcing and development of "e-government." And Bush's fiscal 2006 budget includes cuts based on performance assessments for hundreds of individual federal programs. But critics fear that the management agenda, combined with an array of other administration initiatives, has established a framework that makes it easier for political appointees to overrule, marginalize, or even fire career employees who question the president's agenda.

For example, the Environmental Protection Agency issued a rule earlier this month to regulate emissions of mercury from power plants. In unveiling the rule, the EPA asserted that it represents the most stringent controls on mercury ever issued. According to the agency, the requirements are cost-effective, will achieve significant health benefits, and will create an economic incentive for companies to continually improve their environmental performance.

But the rule is driven by the Bush administration's novel—some say, illegal—interpretation of the Clean Air Act that allows the EPA to avoid imposing mandatory emissions controls on each facility. Environmentalists, and some EPA staff, contend that the mercury rule is far weaker than one the Clinton administration proposed, and that political appointees at the agency ignored the scientific and legal judgment of career staff to push the rule through the regulatory process.

The battle over the mercury rule has been bitter and public. Many other efforts to tighten central control are buried deep within the bowels of the bureaucracy.

Structures

The Natural Resources Conservation Service is not generally a political hotbed. A division of the Agriculture Department, the NRCS—working through "conservationist" offices in each state—is responsible for helping farmers implement soil and water conservation measures, such as restoring wetlands, building dams, and designing systems to prevent animal waste from running off into waterways.

In a major reorganization over the past two years, NRCS chief Bruce Knight eliminated the service's six regional offices, which were headed by career managers and oversaw the state offices. He replaced the six regional managers with three political appointees in Washington and shuffled 200 career staffers from the regional offices into other offices throughout the agency.

Knight said the reorganization is "really just a strong business case." It created a "flatter, leaner structure" that relies much more heavily on the expertise of the state conservationists and makes better use of employees, he said. "I had about 200 highly valuable [employees] scattered around the country, and I needed to put them at the mission of the agency."

But in so doing, Knight has also raised concerns about the independence of the technical staffers who oversee conservation measures across the country.

Under the new structure, career NRCS scientists might worry that their technical decisions about where to spend money and how to implement programs will be overruled for political purposes, said Rich Duesterhaus, a former NRCS staffer and now director of government affairs for the National Association of Conservation Districts.

"They clearly now have a direct line from the politically appointed chief, through these three politically appointed regional assistant chiefs, to the line officers who supervise and carry out these programs," Duesterhaus said. And why should political control over a soil and water conservation agency matter? Because the 2002 farm bill doubled the NRCS's budget for assistance to farmers, from about $1.5 billion in 2001 to $2.8 billion in 2006, with a total increase of $18 billion slated through 2012.

"In the old days, the money wasn't big enough to matter," Duesterhaus said, but the influx of cash in 2002 has made the NRCS "a contender in terms of spoils, and where those spoils go becomes an issue." With direct political oversight of the state conservationists, Duesterhaus said, "it becomes a little easier to say, 'Well, we need Ohio, so make sure we put a little extra money in Ohio.'"

Earlier this month, Charles Adams, one of the six career regional conservationists who were unseated in the reorganization, filed a discrimination complaint against Knight and other agency officials, arguing that the reorganization derailed his 37-year career in favor of three political appointees with far less expertise. "I allege that . . . a calculated, arbitrary, and capricious decision was made to preclude me from the line and leadership of this agency," Adams wrote in his complaint to the Agriculture Department's Office of Civil Rights.

Knight rejects any suggestion that he has politicized the work of a technical agency. "The real power is in the state conservationist, the career individual in the state who manages the budget and the people," he said. "Most people will agree that we are more scientifically and technologically based now" than before the reorganization. The agency has about 12,500 staff members and only a dozen political appointees, Knight said.

But employees in other federal agencies have also asserted that reorganization plans have bumped career managers from senior positions, or diluted their authority.

The Centers for Disease Control and Prevention is instituting a major overhaul that will create a new layer of "coordinating centers"—including a strategic center responsible for developing long-term goals for the agency—between CDC Director Julie Gerberding and the health and science centers that formerly reported directly to her. Gerberding said, "I don't think our goal is to have control over the organization—our goal is to have an impact on health."

But some career staffers say they are being pushed aside and losing the ability to manage their programs. *The Washington Post* earlier this month reported a memo from a top CDC official warning that CDC employees are suffering a "crisis of confidence" and that they feel "cowed into silence." CDC aides—who are unwilling to have their names published for fear of reprisals—say they are losing the ability to make independent professional judgments on topics ranging from sexual abstinence, to drug use, to influenza. Gerberding replied, "I think that is a very inaccurate assessment of what is going on at CDC."

Nevertheless, throughout the federal government, complaints can be heard from disgruntled civil servants who feel they are being elbowed aside by the political leadership—though it is hard to assess whether the invariably anonymous sources have been targeted for elimination or are simply frightened of the change.

Some of the administration's efforts have attracted congressional scrutiny. On March 16, the House Science panel's Space and Aeronautics Subcommittee held a hearing on the administration's plan to slash funding for aeronautics research at NASA and to eliminate 2,000 jobs in order to focus the agency on the president's "Vision for Space Exploration," which includes the goal of manned missions to Mars.

But the administration is not backing down. In fact, it wants more authority to carry out these reorganizations. The White House has said it is drafting legislative proposals to create a "sunset" process requiring federal programs to rejustify their existence every 10 years and to set up "reform" commissions giving the president authority to initiate major restructuring of programs. House Government Reform Committee Chairman Tom Davis, R-Va., said in an interview this month that he believes that Congress should restore the president's unilateral authority to reorganize executive branch agencies—authority that presidents held from the late 1930s until 1984, and that Nixon used when he created the Environmental Protection Agency in 1970.

Procedures

Beyond its tinkering with organizational structures, the White House is pursuing a sweeping overhaul of personnel rules that is aimed at giving managers across the federal government more flexibility to promote, punish, or fire hundreds of thousands of civil servants. While a proposed transformation of the pay systems at the Defense and Homeland Security departments has spurred vigorous debate—fueled by the administration's announcement in January that it wants to extend these systems to the rest of the federal government—less fanfare attended last year's rollout of a new pay-for-performance plan for the roughly 6,000 veteran federal government managers who constitute the Senior Executive Service.

Together, the two new approaches give political appointees in federal agencies greater authority to reward or discipline senior career managers, and give managers the same authority over the civil servants below them. The White House calls this a "modern" personnel system, where everyone is judged on results. Critics call it a process for weeding out recalcitrant civil servants or political opponents.

The new pay-for-performance plan for the Senior Executive Service eliminates annual raises for top career managers and replaces them with a system of merit ratings. Some career executives fear that the system will allow the White House to simply push aside managers who are unenthusiastic about the president's agenda.

"We all know that performance is in the eyes of the beholder, no matter what you say about wanting to have many numerical indicators and so forth," said Carol Bonosaro, president of the Senior Executives Association, which represents members of the SES. "The concern is that if you know that your boss has the total authority to not give you a pay raise, are you going to be more inclined to skirt an ethics requirement for them? Are you going to be more inclined to do what is perhaps not really right?"

And the layers of performance ratings based on the president's goals serve to reinforce the agenda throughout the bureaucracy, Bonosaro said. "You kick the general, and the general comes back and kicks the soldiers, and it goes down the line."

In another move, which could affect thousands of civil servants, Bush has made "competitive sourcing" one of his primary management goals for federal agencies, requiring government workers to compete for their jobs against private contractors.

In January, OMB reported that government employees had won about 90 percent of the 30,000 jobs awarded in 2003 and 2004, with decisions still to be made on about 15,000 jobs offered for competition in those years. But in February, the Federal Aviation Administration announced that Lockheed Martin had won the government's largest-ever job competition, covering about 2,300 flight-service jobs. FAA workers slated to be displaced under the contract filed an appeal this month, complaining that the agency's bidding process was flawed.

"Everything they do is sending the signal [to employees] that they can be replaced easily by contractors, if the work they do isn't done by whatever standards the president is going to put out in his new measurement system," said Colleen Kelley, president of the National Treasury Employees Union.

"It's all about putting more power in the hands of the appointees and making it easier to downgrade, get rid of, use the rules as a weapon against employees who are not in lockstep with you," said Mark Roth, general counsel of the American Federation of Government Employees.

OMB's Johnson denies any intent to enforce political orthodoxy on the civil service. "Rewarding people for their political views is against the law. It's like incest: verboten. Not allowed. Doesn't happen," Johnson said.

"You are being encouraged, and evaluated, and mentored, and managed, and held accountable for doing things that the administration considers to be important," he said. "That does not mean vote Republican versus Democrat; that doesn't mean be pro-life or pro-choice, or be for strict-constructionist judges, or be against strict-constructionist judges," Johnson contended.

"We are controlling what the definition of success is, but shame on us if that's a bad idea. I think it's a really good idea," Johnson said. "It is a mind-set and an approach, and it is a focus on results that [the president] is imposing. It's not 'I want everyone to be like me and have the same political beliefs as me.'"

Checks and Balances

But what if "incest" does happen? Where would a civil servant go to report "verboten" behavior?

Critics of the administration charge that the White House is tampering with the independent structures that protect against waste, fraud, abuse, and political retribution—the federal inspectors general and the Office of General Counsel. The White House vehemently denies the charge.

Rep. Henry Waxman, D-Calif., the top Democrat on the House Government Reform Committee, issued a report last October—and updated it in January—declaring that the Bush administration was appointing inspectors general with political connections to the White House much more frequently than the Clinton administration did. Working with a very small sample—11 IGs appointed by Bush, 32 appointed by Clinton—Waxman's report concludes that 64 percent of the Bush appointees had political experience on their resumes, and only 18 percent had audit experience. For the Clinton appointees, the ratios were reversed: 22 percent had political backgrounds, 66 percent had audit experience.

Gaston Gianni, who until his retirement in December was the Clinton-appointed inspector general at the Federal Deposit Insurance Corporation and vice chairman of the President's Council on Integrity and Efficiency—an IG professional group—said, "I've read the Waxman report. Factually, it's correct. The conclusions, I don't think flow from the facts."

Gianni said it is true that the Bush administration is favoring political background rather than investigative experience in appointing IGs, but he said there is no evidence that the people Bush has appointed have any less independence or zeal for their work.

Nevertheless, Gianni said, the practice worries him. "The environment is such, as we go forward, that the perception will be that, rather than 'small-p' political appointees, they are going to become 'capital-P' Political appointees. Even though nothing else has changed, that is what the perception will be."

Steinzor and NYU's Light agree that the White House has generally sent the message to inspectors that an excess of independence may be bad for their careers.

Last July, Johnson and Gianni signed a memo to inspectors general and agency heads, spelling out the "working relationship principles" for both positions and emphasizing the need for mutual respect, objectivity, and communication between an IG and his or her agency head. Johnson serves as the chairman of the president's council on integrity, and the memo was his idea. Some critics read it as a warning to IGs not to be too aggressive, but Johnson denies any such message.

"The IGs should not be, by definition, adversarial agents," Johnson said. "They are there to prevent waste, fraud, and abuse. The heads of agency are there to prevent waste, fraud, and abuse. The IGs, by definition, are for positive change. . . . Where you get into disagreements is when somebody tries to constantly play 'gotcha,' or where the IG gets a little too enamored of their independent status and tries to do things in a negative fashion, tries to uproot things, or identify things that will hurt the agency," he said. "The IG is there to help the agency."

Johnson said that he had recommended the "relationship principles" to the professional group, but that IGs and agency officials drafted the principles.

Light said there is nothing untoward about principles extolling the virtues of communication and common decency, but he argued that the memo—together with the pattern noted in the Waxman report and some high-profile firings of IGs early in the Bush administration—sets a tone that may have a chilling effect on inspectors.

Johnson dismisses this concern. "I don't think there is any information that suggests that the IGs are less critical than they have been. I don't think there is anything that says they are finding less waste, fraud, and abuse, that they are being less effective IGs as a result of this 'Republican conspiracy.'"

The Office of Special Counsel is a bigger concern for administration critics. Established as an independent agency charged with protecting whistle-blowers and civil servants who are mistreated for political or other reasons unconnected with their performance, the office is in a bitter feud with several of its employees who argue that they are being punished for resisting attempts by Bush's appointee to dismantle the operation.

Among other things, current and former employees charge that Special Counsel Scott Bloch has summarily dismissed hundreds of whistle-blower complaints, instigated a reorganization of the office that will significantly increase political control of investigations, and forced senior staff members critical of his work to choose between relocating to regional offices or being fired. Several anonymous employees, joined by four public-interest groups, filed formal charges against Bloch on March 3, and at least half a dozen staff members have resigned or been fired for refusing to relocate.

Bloch characterizes the complaints against his office as the work of a few disgruntled employees, reinforced by groups that are on a mission to embarrass the White House. Together, these critics are "going out and making reckless allegations that have no truth. They don't like the success Bush officials are having in dealing with the bureaucracy," Bloch said. "They don't want a Bush appointee like myself to get credit" for reducing a large backlog of old cases that were languishing when Bloch took office in 2004. "We have doubled our enforcement over prior years in all areas," Bloch said. His critics "hurl accusations at the office and basically say insulting things about their fellow employees, and they are false."

Levers of Government

An Interior Department official who has worked in the federal government for 30 years denied that the White House is trying to marginalize the civil service, arguing that what people are seeing is simply better executive management from the White House.

"This administration runs a more effective management of the government than did the previous administration, which was a lot more loosey-goosey," this person said, requesting anonymity to speak freely about his bosses. "They bring more of a business mind-set, but I don't think that's a particularly bad thing. They are more organized, and they are smart about it."

The sharper management focus extends into the minutiae of government, giving the White House oversight and control of the executive branch at several levels. In some cases, the Bush administration is creating new approaches, but in most cases, officials are simply using authorities created under prior administrations and applying them more aggressively.

For example, Clinton issued a regulatory-review executive order in 1993, charging OMB's Office of Information and Regulatory Affairs with ensuring that regulations "are consistent with applicable law [and] the president's priorities." The order emphasized use of the best available science and the most cost-effective approach to regulations.

The Bush administration has built on this executive order, setting new requirements for reviewing the costs and benefits of regulatory proposals, establishing a higher threshold for reaching scientific certainty in regulatory decisions, and creating new opportunities for outside experts to challenge the government's conclusions about the dangers that a rule is designed to mitigate.

A regulatory agency career official who demanded anonymity said that OIRA, under the Bush administration, is "much more active" in the regulatory process. "They get involved much earlier in the process on large rules," the official said. "They are reviewing drafts of preambles as they are being written for some rules, or sections of rules."

The executive order gives OMB 90 days to review agency rules, but OIRA Administrator John Graham said in an e-mail response to a reporter's query: "During an important rule-making, OIRA may work informally with agencies at the early stages of the rule-making. This early OIRA participation is designed to make sure that our benefit-cost perspective receives a fair hearing, before key decisions are made and final documents are drafted."

Graham added, "A key benefit of early OIRA involvement is that the pace of rule-making is accelerated by building consensus early in the process and avoiding contentious delays beyond the 90-day review period." He said that the majority of

OMB staffers are career civil servants with significant expertise in their issue areas and that, contrary to the assumptions of many critics, OMB involvement does not always result in an outcome that is more favorable to industry. For example, he said, OMB initiated a Food and Drug Administration rule-making to require that producers add the trans-fat content of foods to nutritional labels.

Sally Katzen, who held both John Graham's job and Clay Johnson's job during her years in the Clinton administration, said, "There is nothing wrong with more-centralized review, guidance, and oversight. It is, after all, a president—singular—who is the head of the executive branch." But, she cautioned, "the problems we face are often highly technical or otherwise highly complicated, and those who serve in the White House or OMB do not have all the answers. And they certainly don't have the manpower, the expertise, or the intimate familiarity with the underlying detail. They cannot—and, in my mind, should not—replace the agency expertise, the agency knowledge, and the agency experience."

While OIRA serves as the central regulatory-review office for the White House, OMB has also positioned itself as the central performance-accountability office, with the establishment of the "President's Management Agenda" and the Program Assessment Rating Tool, or PART, under which the White House grades every agency and program on the basis of its management activities and real-world results. After several years of conducting the assessments without imposing any real consequences for failure, the administration, in the first budget proposal of Bush's second term, used the results assessments to justify eliminating or significantly reducing funding for about 150 federal programs.

John Kamensky, who was deputy director of the National Performance Review (the "reinventing government" initiative) in the Clinton administration, said that Bush's White House is, in many ways, simply expanding on efforts begun in the previous administration.

"We had proposed, in the Clinton administration, tying performance to budget, but there wasn't enough performance information to do that. The Bush administration has that information, finally, so it's sort of a natural progression," Kamensky said.

But critics worry that the review process gives the administration the opportunity to establish its own measures of success for programs, without taking into account the requirements established by Congress.

For example, OMB's review declared the Housing and Urban Development Department's Community Development Block Grant program "ineffective," charging that its mission is unclear, it has few measures of success, and it "does not effectively target funds to the most-needy communities."

But a study by a National Academy of Public Administration panel in February disputed OMB's assessment. The program's "statutory mission or purpose seems clear," the panel said. As a block grant, CDBG is able to fund a broad range of community-development functions, and "if the CDBG program lacks clarity, it is likely because the statute intended it so," according to the report. The breadth of the program's activities makes it difficult to provide specific measures of success, the panel concluded, and the White House suggestion that funding be geographically targeted "seems to contradict the statute's intent."

Donald Plusquellic, mayor of Akron, Ohio, and president of the U.S. Conference of Mayors, defends the CDBG program. "I can evaluate anything as a failure if I get to set up the standards," he said.

Johnson acknowledges that CDBG fails the test in part because the administration is applying a new definition of success. "We believe the goal of housing programs is not just to build houses, but the economic development that comes with them. So those are the results we want to focus on," Johnson said. "You can say we are imposing our political views on people, or our favored views of the housing world or the CDBG world on people. Well, guilty as charged. It's important to focus on outcomes, not outputs."

The president has proposed to eliminate the $4 billion block-grant program and shift its functions into a new community and economic development initiative in the Commerce Department. The Senate voted 66–32 last week for a budget amendment designed to block the administration plan.

NYU's Light says the administration has instituted a host of other procedures that centralize power in the White House, ranging from a vetting process for political appointees that allows little independent decision-making for Cabinet officials, to regular conference calls between the White House and the agency chiefs of staff that help to "focus [the staffers'] attention up Pennsylvania Avenue to the White House, and away from down in your department."

But is that a bad thing? The Heritage Foundation's Moffit doesn't think so. "Why would that be anything other than 100 percent American?" Moffit asks. "I elected a president, and I expect the president to run the executive branch of the government. And there is an issue about whether he is? That's absurd."

The role of the civil service is "to make the car run," Moffit said. "And if they have been driving the car east for the past 25 years of their professional life, but the president says, 'Fine, I know you've been going east, but now we're going to go west; you're going to do a 180-degree turn and go in exactly the opposite direction,' their job is to make sure the car goes exactly in the opposite direction. Nobody elected them to do anything else."

Roth of the American Federation of Government Employees disagrees. "You do not entirely change your entire focus every time a president is elected, because it is not the job of the president to pass the laws. It is the job of the president to execute the laws," Roth said. "These laws are on the books, these programs are in regulations." An administration "can't just say, 'We don't like it, so don't do it.'"

8-3

from *The Politics of Presidential Appointments*

David E. Lewis

In this essay, political scientist David Lewis outlines the remarkable history of presidential efforts to control the federal bureaucracy through personnel appointments. Presidents have replaced merit-based positions with presidential appointments, created new layers of political appointees over civil servants, added staff aides to top offices, laid off civil servants, and reorganized departments to accommodate more presidential appointees. As a result, the merit-based civil service today comprises a smaller portion of the federal workforce than it did in the mid-twentieth century.

FEW PEOPLE have heard of Schedule C appointments to the federal service. If queried most would connect a discussion of "Schedule C" to Internal Revenue Service tax forms, but in 1953 the creation of the Schedule C by President Eisenhower was a watershed event in the history of federal personnel management. Eisenhower created this new category of appointments after his inauguration not only in response to pressure from Republican partisans to create more jobs for party members, but also to help rein in the sprawling New Deal bureaucracy created and staffed by presidents Roosevelt and Truman for the previous twenty years. The creation of this new category of federal personnel gave the administration the authority to add over one thousand new appointees to the executive branch and immediately gain substantial influence in important public-policy areas like conservation and the environment.

Prior to Eisenhower's order, important bureaucratic jobs—like director and assistant director of the U.S. Fish and Wildlife Service, director of the National Park Service, and chief and deputy chief of the Soil Conservation Service—had to be filled by career employees who had worked their way up through the agency

Source: David E. Lewis, *The Politics of Presidential Appointments: Political Control and Bureaucratic Performance,* by David E. Lewis, (Princeton, N.J.: Princeton University Press: 2008), 11–25, 27–37, 39–43, 49–50. Notes appearing in the original have been deleted.

according to nonpolitical criteria. After Eisenhower's order, these jobs could and were filled by political appointees reviewed by the Republican National Committee and named by the White House. Future presidential administrations expanded the number of jobs included in Schedule C, both managerial positions and other confidential positions like staff, counsel, and special assistant positions.

It is hard to understand the details or importance of President Eisenhower's order without an understanding of the history and details of the civil service system in the United States. Very important and practical choices about the number and location of appointees occur in the context of a unique history and sometimes complex set of civil service laws and rules.

This chapter . . . begins with a brief history of the federal personnel system. It then describes the contours of the modern personnel system, including an explanation of the different types of appointed positions and how they get created. The chapter then describes the presidential personnel operation and how it responds to pressures to fill existing positions and satisfy demands for patronage. The next section describes the most common politicization techniques and the tools Congress has used to rein them in. The chapter concludes with a case study of the reorganization of the Civil Service Commission to illustrate the different politicization techniques and demonstrate how politicization is used to change public policy.

A Brief History of the Federal Personnel System

One of the unique features of the Constitution is that it makes virtually no mention of the bureaucracy; its few limited references to departments or officers give virtually no detail apart from the fact that principal officers are to be nominated by the president and confirmed by the Senate. Congress is empowered to determine the means of appointing inferior officers, and the president is granted the ability to request information from principal officers in writing. Apart from these few details the Constitution is silent about the design, function, and administration of the bureaucratic state.

The Constitution's silence leaves responsibility for the creation, nurturing, and maintenance of the continuing government to elected officials, who are divided by different constituencies, institutional responsibilities, and political temperaments. It is the decisions of these persons in the context of a shifting electoral, partisan, and historical landscape that shapes the nature and history of the modern personnel system.

The Personnel System before Merit

The personnel system that presided from 1789 to 1829 was selected and populated by and with persons from the same social class, who were defined by enfranchisement, property, common upbringing, and shared values. They were drawn from what Leonard White calls "a broad class of gentlemen." The selection of federal personnel was dictated in large part by "fitness for public office," but fitness for office was itself defined by standing, wealth, or public reputation rather than relevant experience, expertise, or demonstrated competence.

Long tenure and expectations of continued service were the norm, reinforced by the long dominance of one party in power from 1800 to 1829, the absence of a national party system, and, apparently, the personal conviction of early presidents that persons should not be removed from office because of their political beliefs. Presidents did fill vacancies and newly created offices in the expanding federal government with their partisans, but outright removals of Federalists by Republicans were rare. Regular rotation only occurred at the level of department heads.

The increasingly permanent and class-based federal service did have its detractors. There was a growing sentiment, particularly with expanded franchise, that more positive action needed to be taken to democratize the public service itself. Of particular concern to many were instances where sons inherited the jobs of their fathers, accentuating fears that federal jobs were becoming a type of property or privilege. In 1820 Congress enacted the Tenure of Office Act, requiring the explicit reappointment of all federal officials every four years as a way of contravening the establishment of a professional class.

The old system was not overturned fully until the presidency of Andrew Jackson. Upon assuming office in 1829 Jackson said, "The duties of all public officers are, or at least admit of being made, so plain and simple that men of intelligence may readily qualify themselves for their performance; I can not but believe that more is lost by the long continuance of men in office than is generally to be gained by their experience." Jackson believed that public office was not reserved for a particular class or incumbents in government. Rather, it should be opened to the broader public. The political benefits of such an action were not lost on Jackson.

While his actions to democratize the federal service only led to the turnover of 10 percent of the federal workforce, his actions set in motion a full-fledged patronage system in the United States. Undergirded by the development of national parties hungry for federal office as a way of securing funds and votes, the regular rotation of a large percentage of federal offices became the norm. The national parties, loose confederations of state and local parties, gave out offices and expected activity for the party and political assessments in return. Office holders would return 1 to 6 percent of their salaries to the party. . . .

The vast majority of federal jobs were located outside of Washington, D.C. They were an important political resource and were viewed proprietarily by congressmen who sought to distribute patronage to local and state machines that brought them to power. Presidents were expected to consult with the senators and, to a lesser extent, representatives in the states where appointments were made. The power of this norm was reinforced by the practice of senatorial courtesy whereby the Senate would refuse to confirm a nomination if an objection was raised by the senator from the state where the appointment was being made. While some strong presidents, such as Jackson or Polk, resisted this norm in principle, all usually followed it in practice.

The deleterious consequences of the spoils system for bureaucratic performance were somewhat mitigated by several factors. First, Andrew Jackson was partly right that many federal jobs did not require a tremendous amount of expertise or special training. . . . Most of the work in the civil service was still clerical and very little authority or discretion was delegated to subcabinet officials. In addition, many of the persons turned out of office with electoral turnover would return once their party returned to power.

Second, jobs requiring more expertise were sometimes filled by persons who did not turn over with each administration. Certain auditors, comptrollers, clerks, and personnel in the scientific offices stayed from administration to administration to conduct the business of government. . . . Indeed, some employees of long tenure moved up to key positions because of their expertise. Their competence and expertise in public work outweighed party patronage considerations in their selection.

This dual personnel system persisted during a period when the size and activities of government were limited. As the federal government grew in size and complexity, however, the weaknesses of the spoils system became increasingly apparent. The quality of the federal service suffered. Rotation in office did lead to the dismissal of many qualified federal officials, such as those who kept the accounts and records, made it difficult to sustain reforms, and prevented the development of consistent, purposeful management practices. Rotation-induced instability prevented functional specialization and the development of managerial and policy-specific expertise. These factors, coupled with low pay, decreased the prestige of federal jobs and their reliability as long-term careers. Day-to-day performance was also hindered by the low quality of patronage appointees who were only competent in their jobs by happy accident or the limited requirements of their occupations. Many appointees spent a portion of their time in other jobs, in work for the party, or in leisure.

. . . . The challenges of the Civil War, economic and territorial expansion, periodic monetary crises, massive immigration, and technological change meant the federal government would need to take on new responsibilities and expand to fit its new roles; and public pressure for greater federal government involvement meant the administration of government would have to change. It would have to specialize, organize, and stabilize in order to provide the expertise and services demanded by agricultural interests, businesses, pensioners, consumers, and voters of all types through their elected officials. Congress and the president faced increasing pressure to build a professional bureaucracy by enacting civil service reforms.

The Creation and Extension of Merit

A number of different groups were involved in the nascent push for civil service reform. Included among these groups were urban merchants, bankers, and brokers, often motivated by their own frustrating experience with corrupt and inefficient postal offices and customs houses. A larger class of professionals including lawyers, academics, journalists, and clergy were also supportive of reform, partly as a moral crusade against the corruptions of the spoils system but also as a means of confronting a political system not responsive enough to their interests. Agency officials were also supportive of reform as a means of improving the performance of offices they were supposed to manage.

Efforts to alter the system usually engendered hostility from the parties and their sympathizers in Congress. As public pressure to change the personnel system mounted, however, the national parties acquiesced reluctantly, fearful of giving up the patronage they held or hoped to gain in the next election. They became more supportive when they needed to cultivate reform-oriented voters. They were also more supportive when they were out of power or expected to lose power since civil service would limit the opposition party's control over spoils. . . .

The first serious government-wide attempt at reform came in the 1870s during the Grant Administration. The reform was motivated more by a desire to heal divisions in the Republican Party than that for substantive reform. Republicans had experienced significant losses in the 1870 elections and a split emerged among reformers within the party and Grant-aligned machine elements, particularly in the Senate. To appease reformers, Grant requested a law authorizing the president to issue regulations governing the admission of persons to the civil service, to hire employees to assess the fitness of persons for the civil service, and to establish regulations governing the conduct of civil servants appointed under the new regulations. In response, the Republican majority delegated to the president sweeping authority to create a civil service system with the hope of bridging the rift before the 1872 elections.

When the commission recommended its first set of rules in 1872, Republicans in Congress said little. After the 1872 elections, however, their tone changed. When the first civil service examinations came on-line in the Treasury Department in 1873, members of Congress were openly hostile. They responded by refusing appropriations for the commission in 1874. Since Grant's primary interest in the commission was to hold together the different factions in the party, he did little to defend it. When Congress refused to appropriate funds again in 1875, Grant revoked the commission's rules and closed its offices.

Rutherford B. Hayes pledged to support civil service reform during his candidacy in 1876. When he assumed office in 1877 he requested appropriations from Congress to reactivate the Grant Civil Service Commission. Congress turned down his request, but Hayes took a number of other actions to further the cause of civil service. He appointed noted civil service reformer Carl Schurz as Secretary of the Interior, where Schurz installed a vigorous merit system. Hayes also instituted competitive examinations in the New York City customhouse and post office after a public investigation of the customhouse and a bitter feud with Senator Conkling from New York over patronage.

Hayes's actions coincided with the formation of a number of civil service reform associations. These organizations appeared earliest in the northeast where Hayes's controversy over appointments to the New York customhouse drew the most attention. By 1881 the number of groups had grown substantially and societies existed from San Francisco to New York.

The assassination of Hayes's successor, James Garfield, by a disappointed office seeker in the summer of 1881 galvanized popular support for a more concrete and permanent merit system. One month after Garfield's assassination, the local civil service reform associations that started during the Hayes administration coalesced into the National Civil Service Reform League. In December 1881, Democratic Senator George Pendleton introduced reform legislation drafted by the league. The bill was reported from committee in May 1882 but had little support in the Republican Congress. The league, however, pressured for the legislation with a poster campaign and the publication of lists of opponents to civil service reform. With Garfield's assassination reformers had their crystallizing event and leading journals and newspapers aided their efforts.

Enthusiasm for reform increased after the elections in the fall of 1882. Republicans fared poorly and reform was clearly an issue. President Chester Arthur expressed his support for the legislation, and debate on the Pendleton bill began as soon as Congress convened on December 12, 1882. Debate lasted through December 27 and on January 16, 1883, President Arthur signed the Pendleton Act into law. The law created—for the first time in the United States—a merit-based federal civil service.

The law provided for the creation of a three-person bipartisan Civil Service Commission (CSC) that would administer exams and promulgate rules under the act. Under the provisions of the Pendleton Act only 10.5 percent of all federal workers were included in the merit system, and these were primarily employees in large post offices or customs houses. Some employees from the departmental service in

Washington, D.C.[,] were also included. At this time being under the merit system meant only that persons had to do well on competitive examinations to be appointed. There were no effective protections against adverse job actions or firing after appointment. Job tenure was only protected by the requirement that new persons appointed to the job had to have done well on the same competitive examination. Formal job tenure and protection from partisan dismissal were not established until the late 1890s. Rigorous prohibition on political activity by civil servants was not enacted until Congress passed the Hatch Act in 1939.

The Pendleton Act delegated to the president authority to add the remaining unclassified federal jobs into the merit system with the exception of positions requiring Senate confirmation and common laborers. Presidents added significantly to the civil service through presidential action; 65 percent of the growth in civil service coverage between 1884 and 1903 was through executive order. Once positions were added, it was difficult for Congress to remove them since they would presumably have to do so over the president's veto. They were unlikely to override a president's veto given that one party was sure to prefer to have these positions under civil service at any given time. . . .

Presidents, with a few exceptions, resisted pressures to remove positions once they had been included in the merit system. Presidents were bolstered by the interests that had pushed for the enactment of civil service reform in the first place. Notably, civil service reform leagues continued to push for the preservation and expansion of the federal merit system while also pressuring states and localities to adopt reforms of their own. Efforts to roll back merit system gains were met with howls of protest . . . .

Nascent government unions also pushed for the expansion of the merit system. The passage of the Pendleton Act provided an environment in which federal employees could organize more easily since the act weakened the ties of federal employees to political patrons. Workers in several occupations, such as mail carriers and postal clerks, organized in the late 1880s and early 1890s. Postal unions were particularly effective at lobbying for pay increases and tenure protections. . . .

These unions were instrumental in the passage of the Lloyd-Lafollette Act in 1912 that formally allowed the unionization of government workers (provided they joined unions that would not strike). The act also prohibited dismissal for reasons other than efficiency, and gave employees the right to be notified of possible firing in writing and respond.

The Lloyd-Lafollette [A]ct spurred a period of more aggressive unionization and the National Federation of Federal Employees organized in 1917 under the auspices of the American Federation of Labor (AFL). This was followed by the American Federation of Government Employees (AFGE) in 1932 and the United Federal Workers of America (under the Congress of Industrial Organizations

[CIO]) in 1937. These unions, along with the occupation-specific unions like the postal unions, were instrumental in securing higher salaries and benefits for federal workers. They helped secure the enactment of the Civil Service Retirement Act of 1920 and the Classification Acts of 1923 and 1949. The former provided retirement and survivor benefits as well as improved tenure protections for civil service workers. The latter two acts created a job classification and pay system on the principle of equal pay for equal work and outlined detailed grievance procedures that strengthened worker protections against adverse personnel actions. . . .

The merit system continued to expand as all nineteenth-century and most twentieth-century presidents through Franklin Delano Roosevelt used executive orders to include new classes of employees in the merit system. Presidents frequently blanketed positions into the civil service just prior to leaving office. It was not unusual for Congress to allow new agencies to be created outside the merit system originally, only to add them into the system later. For example, many agencies created to mobilize for war or to combat the Great Depression were originally created outside the merit system. In some cases, the creation of new agencies and new programs provided patronage opportunities that excited either the president or Congress. In fact, in the 1930s Congress on occasion specifically prohibited the president from placing agencies in the merit system. Once these agencies were populated according to the dictates of the politicians in power, they moved to blanket them into the civil service system. This protected their partisans from removal and ensured a degree of long-term loyalty to the programmatic mission of the agencies or to the patrons themselves.

The percentage of federal jobs in the traditional merit system has varied substantially over time (figure 1). By 1897, the advent of the McKinley presidency, close to 50 percent of the federal civilian workforce was under the merit system, and by 1932 close to 80 percent of federal workers held merit positions, a proportion that dipped during the New Deal but reached its peak of almost 88 percent in 1951. This figure underestimates the actual extension of the merit system because many employees not covered by the traditional merit system were employed under other agency-specific personnel systems, like the Tennessee Valley Authority (TVA) or the Foreign Service, which included merit-like provisions. In addition, many of the excluded employees were employed overseas and were unlikely to be consequential for patronage.

While the percentage of jobs included in the merit system peaked at midcentury, it is now decreasing as the federal government shifts its strategy away from a one-size-fits-all personnel system to an agency-specific model. This trend has accelerated at the start of the twenty-first century, since Congress enacted legislation providing both the Department of Homeland Security and the Department of Defense with authority to create their own personnel systems. If

Figure 1. Percentage of Federal Civilian Jobs in the Traditional
Merit System, 1883–2004

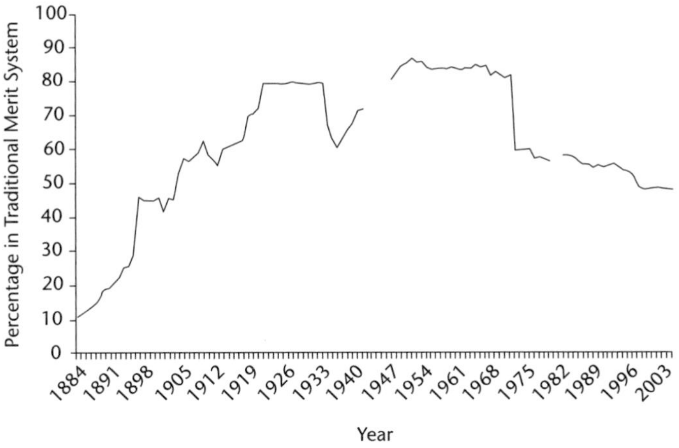

these new systems are implemented effectively, the number of federal employees under the traditional merit system will dip below 30 percent of the federal
civilian workforce.

The Modern Personnel System

Today the federal government employs 2.5 million civilians in full-time positions (and 1.4 million uniformed military personnel). Each civilian job is defined
by a pay category and an appointment authority. To ensure equal pay for equal
work, an elaborate pay system, including three primary classification schemes
for blue-collar, white-collar, and top-level management positions, has been
developed. The Federal Wage System (FWS) covers trade, craft, skilled, and
unskilled laborers. The General Schedule (GS) defines the pay rates for administrative, technical, and professional jobs, while the Senior Level and Scientific
and Professional (SL/ST) system does the same for high-level, but nonmanage-
rial, positions. Top-level management and professional jobs are covered under
the Senior Executive Service (SES) pay schedule or the Executive Schedule
(EX). The EX, with a few exceptions, is reserved for positions requiring presidential nomination and Senate confirmation. In each pay system there is a series
of numerical pay categories that in the GS system are called *grades*. There are
currently fifteen grades in the GS system. These pay categories define a pay
range for jobs with equivalent levels of responsibility, qualifications, or experience. Each pay category allows for some flexibility in differentiating between

employees who hold similar positions but have different levels of experience or backgrounds. In the GS system these are called *steps*. . . .

Of the 2.5 million full-time civilian employees, about 1.32 million are included in the traditional merit system. At the heart of the civil service system is a series of rules and regulations governing how people can obtain federal jobs and what their rights are with regard to promotion, removal, and other personnel actions. Merit system principles demand that persons be hired, promoted, and fired only on the basis of merit rather than on other factors, such as party membership, gender, or race. Persons initially establish their merit through competitive examination or, in some cases, appropriate background qualifications. Once a person's qualifications have been established, a determination is made about his or her eligibility for both position and pay grade. Persons employed under the merit system have a series of rights formerly defined in the *Federal Personnel Manual,* most notably rights to notification and appeal in cases of adverse personnel actions such as demotion or removal. These rights are now defined in the *Code of Federal Regulations* and various Office of Personnel Management (OPM) handbooks.

Excepted Positions

As suggested above, more than half of all federal jobs are now "excepted" from the traditional merit system described above (figure 2). The excepted service is a residual category, catching all jobs that are not subject to the appointment provisions of Title 5 of the United States Code. There are four categories of excepted jobs: positions requiring presidential nomination and Senate confirmation (PAS); jobs filled by persons in the SES; positions in what are known as Schedules A, B, and C; and positions in agency-specific personnel systems.

The most visible positions outside the traditional merit system are those that require presidential nomination and Senate confirmation. These positions are at the top of the federal personnel hierarchy. The United States Constitution (Article II, sec. 2, cl. 2) requires that all "ambassadors, other public ministers and consuls, judges of the Supreme Court, and all other officers of the United States" be appointed in this manner. The manner of appointing "inferior" officers is up to Congress (and the president) as the result of legislative determinations. Where one draws the line between "principal" and "inferior" officers, however, is unclear. In 2004 there were 1,137 PAS positions in the executive branch, about 945 of which were policymaking positions. The remainder is comprised of appointments to minor advisory or committee-supervisory roles often requiring only part-time employment, paid on a per diem basis. Of the 945 positions, about 186 were U.S. attorneys or U.S. marshals and 154 were ambassadors, leaving 550–600 key executive PAS positions in the cabinet departments and major independent

Figure 2. Federal Civilian Personnel System Appointment Authorities

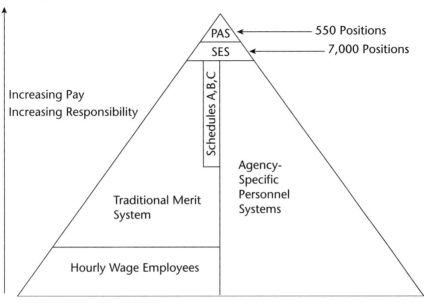

Note: Excludes job-specific excepted positions. PAS excludes part-time, advisory, U.S. Attorneys. U.S. Marshals, and ambassadorial positions. The "excepted service" includes PAS, SES, Schedules A, B, C, and personnel in agency-specific personnel systems.

agencies. The average cabinet department dealing with domestic affairs has fifteen to thirty PAS positions, including a secretary, a deputy secretary, a handful of under- and assistant secretaries, an inspector general, and a chief financial officer.

Between PAS positions and the competitive civil service in the federal hierarchy is a space filled by a mixture of career employees from the Senior Executive Service (SES) and political appointees who will be designated noncareer members of this service. The SES was created by the Civil Service Reform Act of 1978 and is comprised of a cadre of approximately 7,000 senior management officials. The OPM, based on its own assessment and the requests of agencies, allocates a certain number of SES positions to each department or agency, and the administration chooses which of the jobs in the agency will be SES jobs. Presidents or their subordinates can choose either an existing member of the SES (a career civil servant who applied to be a part of the SES) or a political appointee from outside who will fill an SES job. By law political appointees cannot exceed 10 percent of the entire SES or 25 percent of the allocated SES positions in a specific agency. In 2004 there were 6,811 persons in the SES, 674 of whom were appointees. Some examples of appointed SES positions include Chief of Staff at the U.S Agency for International Development, Director of Intergovernmental Affairs for the Department of Defense, Deputy Assistant Secretary for Special Education and

Rehabilitative Services, and Deputy General Counsel in the Department of Health and Human Services.

A key motivation in creating the SES was to give presidents more flexibility in controlling policy and programmatic positions pivotal for implementing the administration's program. One way in which it did this was to provide more appointees at this level; another was to increase the ease with which presidents could reassign career senior management officials. Under the law the president can reassign a career SES executive to any other position, provided the president and the new agency head have been in office for at least 120 days and the executive has been given 15 days notice (60 if the reassignment includes a geographical change).

Since the creation of the merit system it has been clear that there are some positions for which it is not feasible to hold exams, even in agencies where the merit system is otherwise entirely appropriate. There are three classes of such positions, designated as Schedules A, B, and C. There are no examinations at all for Schedule A positions, which historically have included lawyers, military chaplains, or positions in isolated localities. Schedule B positions have examinations attached to them but they establish a threshold level of acceptability and do not utilize comparisons among applicants. This schedule has included positions in new agencies or programs for which there are no established directions or guidelines, federal work-study positions, and positions set aside for those with certain types of disabilities.

The third schedule, Schedule C, is reserved for positions of a confidential or policy-determining nature. As the start of the chapter suggested, the schedule was created by President Eisenhower in 1953. Schedule C originally included both management positions below the PAS level and the assorted staff assigned to appointees (confidential assistants, drivers, and so forth). As such, the pay range for Schedule C appointees varied dramatically according to position. Top-level management positions in Schedule C were eventually converted to NEA positions in 1966 and SES positions in 1978. Lower-paying Schedule C positions remain (GS 15 and below). In 2004 there were 1,596 persons appointed to Schedule C positions in the federal government.

These constitute an important subtype of political appointment and, while technically selected by agency officials, presidents since Reagan have exercised substantial control over them. . . . Typical Schedule C posts include special or confidential assistants to PAS appointees, directors of communications, press, or outreach offices, and officials in legislative liaison offices. Some current examples include the White House liaison in the Department of Interior, the confidential assistant to the Assistant Secretary of Education for Vocational and Adult Education, and the Director of Media Affairs in the Department of Labor.

Table 1. Examples of Agencies with Broad Exceptions from the
Traditional Merit Personnel System

Department of Defense
Department of Homeland Security
Federal Aviation Agency
United States Postal Service
Postal Rates Commission
Central Intelligence Agency
National Security Agency
Tennessee Valley Authority
Federal Bureau of Investigation
General Accounting Office
Panama Canal Commission
Board of Governors, Federal Reserve System
Peace Corps
Railroad Retirement Board
Overseas Private Investment Corporation
Nuclear Regulatory Commission
Federal Election Commission

Source. U.S. General Accounting Office 1997a; U.S. Senate 2000.

The last, and by far the largest, set of positions are excepted because they are located in agencies that have authority to govern their own personnel systems (table 1). They can be low- or high-paying jobs of varying levels of responsibility and character. Calling them "excepted" is something of a misnomer, however, since the rights of employees in these personnel systems are usually very similar to those in the Title 5 civil service system. There has been a dramatic increase in the number of "excepted" jobs because recent congressional decisions give certain agencies authority to create their own personnel systems outside the merit system defined by Title 5. The most significant actions in this regard have been the reorganization in 1970 of the postal service into a government corporation, with its own personnel system (800,000 employees); the creation of the Department of Homeland Security in 2002, with authority to create its own personnel system (170,000 civilian employees); and Congress's decision in 2003 to grant the Department of Defense authority to create its own personnel system (660,000 civilian employees). Agencies, bolstered by outside critiques of the federal personnel system, have long clamored for more control over their own personnel systems, claiming that they need more flexibility in hiring, promoting, and firing in order to improve performance. Flexible personnel systems allow them to respond more quickly to changes in the job market, agency personnel needs, and new programmatic responsibilities. Increased flexibility, however, can also lead to fewer protections against abuses in hiring, firing, and promotion, as well as inequities in pay, bene-fits, and treatment for comparable work.

In sum, politicization, when it does occur, is, at the top levels, defined both by pay and by appointment authority. It involves an increase in the number of PAS, SES, Schedule C, and similarly excepted agency-specific appointees.

The Modern Presidential Personnel Process

Given these different types of appointments, it is worth reviewing how presi-dents and their staffs go about filling PAS positions and determining where to place SES and Schedule C appointees. Both policy and patronage concerns shape modern personnel politics. On the policy side, presidents are confronted with a need to fill hundreds of executive-level PAS positions across the government requiring specific skills, experience, and expertise. These jobs range from the Secretary of Defense to the Assistant Secretary of Labor for Occupational Safety and Health to the Under Secretary of Commerce for Intellectual Property. The success of the administration in controlling the bureaucracy depends upon their success in filling these slots. . . .

There is almost uniform concern articulated voluntarily by persons involved in presidential personnel about how important it is to find loyal people with the right skills and background to fill these jobs. . . . Personnel is policy and White House officials recognize that in order to get control of policy, you need people who are loyal to the president and qualified for the job to which they have been appointed. In practice, evaluations of competence can be colored by ideology and the immediate need to fill literally thousands of jobs. Reagan aide Lyn Nofziger, for example, stated, "As far as I'm concerned, anyone who supported Reagan is competent." That said, and importantly, most senior personnel offi-cials define their job as finding the most competent people for senior adminis-tration posts.

Starting with President Nixon, many presidents have employed profes-sional recruiters to help identify qualified persons for top executive posts. The most important personnel task at the start of each administration is that of identifying candidates to fill these positions. Each administration has pro-duced lists of positions to be filled first. These include positions important for public safety but also usually positions that need to be filled early to advance the president's policy agenda. Transition advice to President Kennedy focused on the "pressure points" in government. In the Reagan administration the transition focused first on the "Key 87" positions, which included executive posts necessary for implementation of Reagan's economic program. These priority positions naturally receive the most attention throughout the president's term whenever vacancies occur. In some cases, the existing number of positions is sufficient to gain control and advance the president's agenda; in others, it is not.

On the patronage side, presidents and their personnel operations are besieged by office seekers who have a connection to the campaign, to the party, interest groups, or patrons in Congress important to the administration. Recent administrations have received tens of thousands of resumes, and even more recommendations and communications dealing with specific candidates or jobs. . . . Overall, the Clinton administration received over 100,000 resumes. . . .

Dealing with requests for jobs involves evaluating the skills and backgrounds of priority job seekers and locating appropriate or defensible jobs in levels of pay and responsibility. In many cases, priority placements are young, inexperienced, or primarily qualified through political work. This makes them unqualified for top executive posts. The less background experience, the harder it is to find them jobs. Such applicants are usually given staff, liaison, advance, and public affairs jobs for which they are best qualified given their campaign experience. In other cases, people connected to the candidates either through personal relationships or contributions are too senior to take such jobs but are either not qualified for or not interested in top executive posts. Personnel officials often recommend these persons for ambassadorships, positions on commissions, or advisory posts. . . .

In practice, presidents and their subordinates in presidential personnel (PPO) determine the number and location of political appointees by starting with where their predecessor had appointees and then making incremental adjustments. Each administration learns what jobs were filled by appointees in the last administration through a variety of sources, including transition reports produced by teams sent to the different agencies in the executive branch prior to the inauguration, contacts with the previous administration, and government publications. Subsequent adjustments to the number and location of appointees are made based upon concerns about policy and the need to satisfy concerns for patronage.

The distinction drawn between policy and patronage activities in presidential personnel is not to suggest that policy-driven personnel practices have no patronage component or that efforts to reward campaign supporters cannot influence policy. On the contrary, patronage concerns invariably influence appointments, and appointees of all types can influence policy outputs. Rather, the point is that one process revolves primarily around filling *positions* and the other process revolves primarily around placing *persons.* These two fundamentally different goals are managed differently and have different effects on the number and penetration of political appointments in the bureaucracy.

Common Politicization Techniques

One factor that can influence the number and penetration of appointees in specific cases is the extent to which presidents and their appointees confront career personnel in management positions that do not share their ideology or priorities. Conflict between the president and agencies can emerge for a number of reasons. Sometimes the disagreement stems from what agencies do. Some agencies are designed with a specific policy goal in mind. For example, the Office of Economic Opportunity was the hallmark of Lyndon Johnson's Great Society. It was anathema to Richard Nixon, and he set about politicizing (and dismantling) it in the early 1970s.

In other cases the political biases of a particular agency have less to do with the mission of the agency embedded in law or executive decree than with issues of personnel. Career managers can be unresponsive because they are known to be partisans from the other party. For example, surveys of top executives from the Nixon and Ford administrations showed that many top managers, particularly executives in social service agencies, were unsympathetic to the policy goals of the Nixon administration. More recent surveys confirm that top careerists in defense agencies are more likely to be Republican and conservative, whereas top careerists in social welfare agencies are likely to be Democrats and liberal.

Career managers also often feel bound by legal, moral, or professional norms to certain courses of action and these courses of action may be at variance with the president's agenda. Agencies act to implement policy directives spelled out in statutes, executive decrees, or informal directions from Congress. They are legally bound to implement the laws enacted, and the amount of discretion administrators possess to alter policy is not always clear. Differences of opinion arise about both managers' power and their responsibilities given this power. This is starkly illustrated in cases where career employees are asked to implement administrative policies they believe to be of questionable legality. For instance, career employees make administrative changes in the level and type of civil rights enforcement that might or might not include affirmative action as a remedy. Directions from political appointees can also bump up against professional norms. The ranger in the Forest Service, the statistician in the Bureau of Labor Statistics, and the

Figure 3. Hypothetical Agency Problem

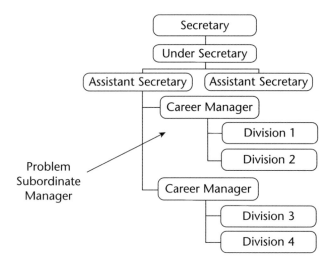

lawyer in the Justice Department has a point beyond which they cannot go and still maintain their professional integrity. . . .

A number of different techniques for politicizing agencies address the perceived lack of responsiveness from career officials. These techniques are often used concurrently with other strategies for gaining control of the bureaucracy, such as budgeting, public statements, and administrative actions. To help visualize what this problem looks like, consider figure 3, an organizational chart from a hypothetical department in which the top three levels are filled by presidential appointments with Senate confirmation. Below this is a level of career managers who direct the operating programs and bureaus. Assume that one of these career managers is unresponsive or problematic to the administration in power for one of the reasons listed above.

Replacement

The first and most obvious solution to this dilemma is to remove the resistant career manager and replace this person with an appointee or more acceptable career person. If the position is a general SES position the president can replace the career SES manager with an appointee after a period of time, provided doing so will not put the agency over the statutory limit for the number of appointees in the SES or agency.

The president can also try to change the appointment authority of the position in question (figure 4). For example, a presidential administration could change a GS 15 career management position to a Schedule C position or a general SES position. Changes in appointment authority can sometimes be performed internally, as in the case of deciding which jobs are SES jobs. In other cases changes are performed with a request to the Office of Personnel Management (or earlier, the CSC). Most experienced personnel officers know how to use the appropriate terms of art to ensure their applications are approved. The OPM director and many of her subordinates serve at the pleasure of the president, easing the way for the White House to get its way. . . .

There are . . . three techniques well known in bureaucratic lore for getting unwanted employees to leave their current jobs. The first and most obvious strategy for convincing a careerist to leave is the *frontal assault*. Political appointees meet privately with the career manager in question and tell the manager that her services are no longer needed. Career managers are offered help finding another job, a going-away party, and even a departmental award. The career manager is informed that if she refuses to leave, her employment record and references will suffer.

The career manager can also be *transferred* within the agency to a position she is unlikely to accept. The transfer offer is usually accompanied by a raise and perhaps a promotion to a newly created position. In such cases, appointees know ahead of time the types of jobs the career employee is likely or unlikely to accept. For example, the career manager known to have strong ties to the East Coast may be offered a job in Dallas or St. Louis. Appointees inform the career employee that if she does not want the new job, she can resign without prejudice from the agency and stay on in their current position for a limited amount of time until she finds another position.

With a change in administration, careerists identified with the past administration's policies worry about being transferred to "turkey farms"—jobs with few responsibilities, limited staff, and no access to policymaking. . . . As noted above, by law SES careerists cannot be removed without consent for 120 days by the new administration, but many waive these rights if the new administration requests it. If career employees do not waive this right, the new administration can transfer them after 120 days, provided they have been given appropriate written notice.

A related strategy is the *new-activity* technique. Political appointees hatch plans for a new agency initiative, and the career employee in question is selected for the job ostensibly on the basis of his past performance and unique qualifications. The career manager is even promoted and given an increase in pay. The new initiative appears to be meaningful, but the real purpose behind it is to move the career manager out of his current position. . . .

Figure 4. Replacement

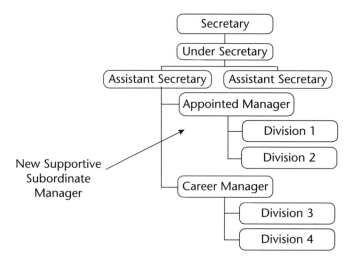

Layering

Political appointees' difficulty in getting what they want through attempting to remove career employees and reclassifying their jobs often leads them to adopt other strategies. One of the most prominent is *layering,* the practice of adding politically appointed managers on top of career managers as a means of enhancing political control. . . . These new appointees can more carefully monitor the career managers and assume some of their policy-determining responsibilities through their influence in budget preparation, personnel decisions, and other administrative responsibilities. . . .

Add Appointed Ministerial Staff

A similar strategy is to *add appointed ministerial staff.* For instance, the Senate-confirmed assistant secretary adds two special assistants. Titled positions like assistant secretaries often acquire title-riding appointees like chiefs of staff, special assistants, counsels, and public affairs personnel to help them perform their job. The strategy of adding ministerial staff is different from layering in that the appointees added have little formal authority. While they have little formal authority, such appointees can acquire substantial informal authority as experts, gatekeepers, and public spokespeople.

Ministerial staff of this type usually comprises Schedule C appointees. Schedule C positions are created specifically for persons attached to the incoming appointees. Schedule C appointees gain power from being the primary advisors to higher-level appointees and from speaking with the implied authority of the appointee. In other contexts ministerial staff is given special projects, review budgets and legal documents, and help in personnel and administrative decisions. Schedule C positions can be training grounds for other appointed positions. Persons working for higher-level appointees often gain valuable experience and exposure and move from these positions into managerial positions with more formal responsibility.

Reorganization

A fourth common politicization technique is *reorganization*. Reorganization has been used strategically by managers to diminish the influence of problematic career managers and enhance political control. . . . The nominal purpose of the reorganization can be to align organizational structure to better meet the bureau's stated goals or to increase efficiency but have the real or dual purpose of getting better control of the bureau. In large, modern agencies with complicated organizational structures, reorganizations can be subtle and effective means of getting political appointees in charge of important administrative responsibilities. In reorganizations, positions are created and disbanded, upgraded and downgraded, and these decisions are informed by the political needs of administration officials.

For example, in the 1980s enforcement activities within the Environmental Protection Agency (EPA) were reorganized at least three times. In 1981 the Office of Enforcement was disbanded and the legal staff was parsed out to various other offices within the agency. EPA director Anne Burford assembled a new Office of Legal and Enforcement Counsel not long after, but key positions remained vacant into 1982. In 1983 a distinct Office of Enforcement Counsel was created under an assistant administrator. The effect of Burford's reorganizations, however, was to diminish the influence of inherited personnel partly through a decline in morale and high turnover among attorneys who had served in the old Office of Enforcement.

Reorganization can also be used to create parallel bureaucratic structures or processes to circumvent existing structures. This form of politicization takes two common forms. In the first, a new manager who is sympathetic to the goals of the administration is added to the management structure with staff and resources. . . . In this case, however, it is not the problematic career manager who is given this post; rather, it is the trusted, sympathetic manager with closer ties to the administration. This manager duplicates or explicitly assumes tasks performed by the division headed by the less-responsive career manager. The administration then cuts the disfavored manager out of decision making and downgrades the manager's division. . . .

Reductions-in-Force (RIF)

The final prominent technique for politicizing is the *reduction-in-force (RIF)*. While RIFs are a normal part of organizational life in both the private and public sectors, they can also be used strategically to transform an unresponsive agency. Through RIFs federal officials cut employment as a way of getting control of the bureau. According to a general rule of "save grade, save pay," those career employees with the least experience lose their jobs first during RIFs, but those who stay with more seniority are bumped down in position and often assume tasks that are new or are different from what they were doing before. They often have to do more work for the same amount of pay, and the new tasks they assume are frequently jobs not performed by people in their pay scale. These ripple effects increase attrition beyond that caused by the initial RIF. For example, reducing the employment of Division 1 and Division 2 will lead to attrition in both divisions. The career manager in charge of these divisions and her subordinates will have to do more work with fewer employees and manage through declining morale for an administration with whom they likely disagree ideologically.

The Reagan administration's treatment of the Council on Environmental Quality (CEQ) is a good example of this approach. In 1982 the CEQ's staff had been reduced from forty-nine, under President Carter, to fifteen. The administration fired all of the immediate council staff, some of whom had served since the Nixon and Ford administrations. Appointees from the campaign staff replaced those removed.

Informal Aids to Politicization

There are also a number of ways to augment politicization efforts informally. One common technique for politicizing administration is to leave career positions vacant for significant periods of time and have appointees take over these responsibilities in an acting role. For example, during the second George W. Bush administration, when Sandra Bates, a career manager within the General Services Administration (GSA), decided to leave her position as Commissioner of the Federal Technology Service (FTS), Barbara Shelton was selected to fill that job in an acting role until a replacement was found. Although career managers generally assume acting roles when appointees leave, Shelton was an appointee. She was the politically appointed regional administrator of the GSA's Mid-Atlantic region. No immediate plans were announced to select a permanent replacement in the agency. GSA was pursuing an internal reorganization wherein the FTS would be merged with the Federal Supply Service.

With lax oversight and informal norms, different presidential administrations have also been successful in influencing personnel choices inside the *civil service* without changing the appointment authority of the jobs themselves. Technically, personnel chosen for positions under the merit system are to be chosen outside the influence of politics. In reality, both Congress and the president can strongly influence the hiring of careerists at higher levels in the permanent federal service. The most formal and blatant attempt to do this was the Eisenhower administration's "Willis Directive." Charles Willis, an assistant to Eisenhower chief-of-staff Sherman Adams, wrote and circulated an elaborate personnel plan for the new administration. The plan invited officials from the Republican National Committee (RNC), Republican congressmen, or other prominent state Republicans to recommend personnel for jobs both *inside* and outside the civil service. All jobs at GS 14 and above were called "controlled" positions. Federal agencies were to announce vacancies on forms supplied by the RNC and make regular reports to the RNC on how vacancies were filled. Both the spirit and contents of the plan violated Civil Service Rule 4, which state[s] that career positions are to be filled "without regard to political or religious affiliation." . . .

In total, the numbers and percentages of appointees vary from administration to administration because of replacement, layering, reorganization, and RIFs. These politicization techniques can be augmented by less formal techniques, such as strategic vacancies, political influence in the hiring of careerists, and bending of the rules in administrative determinations and rulings.

Congressional Responses

Of course, politicization choices happen with an eye toward Congress since the legislative branch has both the means of learning about politicization and a variety of ways to respond. . . .Civil servants in the affected agencies complain to the press or friendly members of Congress. As one personnel official explained to me, "the *Washington Post* is their inspector general." Others confirmed that the possibility that their actions might appear on the front page of the *Washington Post* constrained personnel actions. Personnel officials also suggested that members of Congress were attentive to appointee head-counts, and the existence of congressional reports including such counts confirms their claim.

Personnel officials recognize that their missteps can lead to problems for the president and adjust their behavior accordingly. At minimum, an influential member of

Congress can informally communicate his displeasure with the agency or the White House. Members can also publicize the president's action, creating an embarrassing situation for the White House. For example, in 1987 several Democratic members of Congress accused the Reagan administration of "packing" the top ranks of government with appointees to the detriment of the federal service. Backed by a GAO report tracking appointments, these members denounced an increase in appointees to the SES, particularly in the agencies that manage the government such as the OPM (personnel), the GSA (facilities), and the OMB (finances). During the Clinton administration, Republicans publicly complained about the politicization of the Commerce Department, and they requested that the GAO investigate the burrowing of Democratic appointees and staff into civil service positions. In the second George W. Bush administration, the Democratic minority used charges of cronyism coupled with data on appointee increases to score political points.

More concretely, Congress can refuse presidential requests to create new Senate-confirmed positions or use their appropriations power to limit these and other types of appointed positions. For example, efforts to elevate the EPA to a cabinet department in the George H. W. Bush administration were derailed partly due to Congress's refusal to accede to the president's requests for additional appointees. Congress has also enacted limits on the number of positions that could be paid at appointee-level salaries as a means of limiting the number of appointees. They occasionally include specific language in appropriations bills mandating that none of the appropriations be used to pay the salaries of more than a set number of appointees. For example, the Department of Transportation and Related Agencies Appropriations Act, enacted in the late 1980s, includes the following language, "None of the funds in this Act shall be available for salaries and expenses of more than [insert number] political and Presidential appointees in the Department of Transportation." The number of appointees allowed has varied in other bills from a low of 88 to a high of 138.

These instances are rare but this should not be taken as evidence that presidents can act with a free hand. On the contrary, White House officials anticipate the likely response of Congress and adjust their behavior accordingly. They are less likely to politicize if they expect Congress to overturn their action or impose serious political costs on the president. . . .

Conclusion

To understand politicization decisions from administration to administration one has to understand the context of both the history of the merit system and the details defining the different strategies and techniques employed. The professional merit-based civil service system was a late arrival in the United States. The United States federal government operated for almost one hundred years without a formal professional civil service, yet the importance of ensuring both loyalty and competence in the federal service was already evident. During the height of the spoils system, a dual personnel system existed with a continuing body of professionals working side by side with patronage appointees. The dual system presaged numerous attempts to institute merit systems in the period leading up to the formal creation of the merit system.

The 1883 reforms embodied in the Pendleton Act were focused on the task of eliminating spoils. Reformers sought to end assessments, political activity by public employees, and patronage hiring and firing through the expansion of merit protection and the merit system. The U.S. personnel system's narrow focus on spoils had a lasting effect on public personnel management. The United States was slow to focus on positive human resource management activities like recruitment, training, morale, and benefits. Instead, the personnel system was defined by rules designed to protect workers from the evil of spoils. Part of Congress's recent motivation for allowing individual agencies to develop personnel systems outside the traditional merit-based civil service system is to allow them to escape the cumbersome and antiquated federal personnel system. Isolated exceptions to Title 5 have now become a landslide, with less than one-half of all federal personnel under the traditional merit system. The Merit Systems Protection Board, the appellate body that hears employee complaints, is cutting its budget and closing regional offices.

While the federal personnel system continues to change dramatically, the politicization calculus remains much the same. Political actors are making decisions about the numbers of Senate-confirmed, noncareer SES, and Schedule C appointees in an effort to make the bureaucracy responsive to them and satisfy demands for patronage. In the same way they feared turning over competent, long-tenured professionals in the Jacksonian era, so, too, they fear politicizing too much now. . . .

Chapter 9

The Judiciary

9-1

from *A Matter of Interpretation: Federal Courts and the Law*

Antonin Scalia

Supreme Court judges and indeed—as we learn in the essay by Carp, Manning, and Stidham, later in this section—judges at every level of the federal judiciary decide cases in close accord with the political views of those who appointed them. Years of Democratic control of the White House and Congress created the activist federal judiciary of the 1960s and 1970s that advanced federal protections of civil rights and civil liberties. With the resurgence of the Republican Party in national politics, the federal judiciary has gradually, with turnover in members, become more conservative. Some observers note these trends and conclude that judges are little more than partisan politicians disguised in robes. Unsurprisingly, judges do not view themselves this way. Instead, they account for their sometimes sharply differing opinions on criteria that do not fit neatly on the familiar partisan or ideological dimensions that are used to classify elected officeholders. In the next two essays, two current Supreme Court justices—one conservative and appointed by a Republican president, the other a moderate, appointed by a Democrat—explain how they approach decisions, decisions on which they frequently disagree. As you

Source: Antonin Scalia, "Common-Law Courts in a Civil-Law System: The Role of United States Federal Courts in Interpreting the Constitution and Laws," from *A Matter of Interpretation: Federal Courts and the Law,* (Princeton University Press: 1997), 3–47. Some notes appearing in the original have been deleted.

read and weigh these alternative views, note that both judges begin with the same assumption—that as the unelected branch the judiciary should, when possible, defer to the decisions of democratically elected officeholders.

In the following essay, excerpted from his highly regarded series of lectures to Princeton law students, Justice Antonin Scalia explains how he approaches decisions. Some call this style "literalist" or "originalist," in that Scalia weighs decisions against a close reading of the texts of laws and the Constitution. He reminds us that in a constitutional democracy judges are not charged with deciding what fair and just policy should be. This responsibility belongs with elected officials, who better reflect their citizenry's views on such matters. Nor should judges try to read the minds of those who make the law. A judge's role begins and ends with applying the law (including the Constitution) to the particular circumstances of a legal disagreement. Scalia's critics have complained that the application of law is frequently not so simple. Laws conflict or fail to consider the many contingencies that reach the Supreme Court.

THE FOLLOWING ESSAY attempts to explain the current neglected state of the science of construing legal texts, and offers a few suggestions for improvement. It is addressed not just to lawyers but to all thoughtful Americans who share our national obsession with the law.

The Common Law

The first year of law school makes an enormous impact upon the mind. Many students remark upon the phenomenon. They experience a sort of intellectual rebirth, the acquisition of a whole new mode of perceiving and thinking. Thereafter, even if they do not yet know much law, they do—as the expression goes—"think like a lawyer."

The overwhelming majority of the courses taught in that first year, and surely the ones that have the most profound effect, teach the substance, and the methodology, of the common law—torts, for example; contracts; property; criminal law. American lawyers cut their teeth upon the common law. To understand what an effect that must have, you must appreciate that the common law is not really common law, except insofar as judges can be regarded as common. That is to say, it is not "customary law," or a reflection of the people's practices, but is rather law developed by the judges. Perhaps in the very infancy of Anglo-Saxon law it could have been thought that the courts were mere expositors of generally accepted social practices; and certainly, even in the full maturity of the common law, a well-established commercial or social practice could form the basis for a court's decision. But from an early time—as early as the Year Books, which record English judicial decisions from the end of the thirteenth century to the beginning of the sixteenth—any equivalence between custom and common law had ceased to exist, except in the sense that the doctrine of *stare decisis* rendered prior judicial decisions "custom." The issues coming before the courts involved, more and more, refined questions to which customary practice provided no answer.

Oliver Wendell Holmes's influential book *The Common Law*[1]—which is still suggested reading for entering law students—talks a little bit about Germanic and early English custom. . . . This is the image of the law—the common law—to which an aspiring American lawyer is first exposed, even if he has not read Holmes over the previous summer as he was supposed to. He learns the law, not by reading statutes that promulgate it or treatises that summarize it, but rather by studying the judicial opinions that invented it. This is the famous case-law method, pioneered by Harvard Law School in the last century, and brought to movies and TV by the redoubtable Professor Kingsfield of *Love Story* and *The Paper Chase*. The student is directed to read a series of cases, set forth in a text called a "casebook," designed to show how the law developed. . . . Famous old cases are famous, you see, not because they came out right, but because the rule of law they announced was the intelligent one. Common-law courts performed two functions: One was to apply the law to the facts. All adjudicators—French judges, arbitrators, even baseball umpires and football referees—do that. But the second function, and the more important one, was to *make* the law.

If you were sitting in on Professor Kingsfield's class when *Hadley* v. *Baxendale* was the assigned reading, you would find that the class discussion would not end with the mere description and dissection of the opinion. [This case, a familiar example of 19th century English common law, involves liability in failing to perform a contracted obligation.-Ed.] Various "hypotheticals" would be proposed by the crusty (yet, under it all, good-hearted) old professor, testing the validity and the sufficiency of the "foreseeability" rule. What if, for example, you are a blacksmith, and a young knight rides up on a horse that has thrown a shoe. He tells you he is returning to his ancestral estate, Blackacre, which he must reach that very evening to claim his inheritance, or else it will go to his wicked, no-good cousin, the sheriff of Nottingham. You contract to put on a new shoe, for the going rate of three farthings. The shoe is defective, or is badly shod, the horse goes lame, and the knight reaches Blackacre too late. Are you really liable for the full amount of his inheritance? Is it reasonable to impose that degree of liability for three farthings? Would not the parties have set a different price if liability of that amount had been contemplated? Ought there not to be, in other words, some limiting principle to damages beyond mere foreseeability? Indeed, might not that principle—call it presumed assumption of risk—explain why *Hadley* v. *Baxendale* reached the right result after all, though not for the precise reason it assigned?

What intellectual fun all of this is! It explains why first-year law school is so exhilarating: because it consists of playing common-law judge, which in turn consists of playing king—devising, out of the brilliance of one's own mind, those laws that ought to govern mankind. How exciting! And no wonder so many law students, having drunk at this intoxicating well, aspire for the rest of their lives to be judges!

Besides the ability to think about, and devise, the "best" legal rule, there is another skill imparted in the first year of law school that is essential to the making of a good common-law judge. It is the technique of what is called "distinguishing" cases. That is a necessary skill, because an absolute prerequisite to common-law lawmaking is the doctrine of *stare decisis*—that is, the principle that a decision made in one case will be followed in the next. Quite obviously, without such a principle common-law courts would not be making any "law"; they would just be resolving the particular dispute before them. It is the requirement that future courts adhere to the principle underlying a judicial decision which causes that decision to be a legal rule. (There is no such requirement in the civil-law system, where it is the text of the law rather than any prior judicial interpretation of that text which is authoritative. Prior judicial opinions are consulted for their persuasive effect, much as academic commentary would be; but they are not *binding*.)

Within such a precedent-bound common-law system, it is critical for the lawyer, or the judge, to establish whether the case at hand falls within a principle that has already been decided. Hence the technique—or the art, or the game—of "distinguishing" earlier cases. It is an art or a game, rather than a science, because what constitutes the "holding" of an earlier case is not well defined and can be adjusted to suit the occasion. . . .

It should be apparent that by reason of the doctrine of *stare decisis*, as limited by the principle I have just described, the common law grew in a peculiar fashion—rather like a Scrabble board. No rule of decision previously announced could be *erased*, but qualifications could be *added* to it. The first case lays on the board: "No liability for breach of contractual duty without privity"; the next player adds "unless injured party is member of household." And the game continues.

As I have described, this system of making law by judicial opinion, and making law by distinguishing earlier cases, is what every American law student, every newborn American lawyer, first sees when he opens his eyes. And the impression remains for life. His image of the great judge—the Holmes, the Cardozo—is the man (or woman) who has the intelligence to discern the best rule of law for the case at hand and then the skill to perform the broken-field run-ning through earlier cases that leaves him free to impose that rule: distinguish-ing one prior case on the left, straight-arming another one on the right, high-stepping away from another precedent about to tackle him from the rear, until (bravo!) he reaches the goal—good law. That image of the great judge remains with the former law student when he himself becomes a judge, and thus the common-law tradition is passed on.

Democratic Legislation

All of this would be an unqualified good, were it not for a trend in government that has developed in recent centuries, called democracy. In most countries, judges are no longer agents of the king, for there are no kings. . . . [O]nce we have taken this realistic view of what common-law courts do, the uncomfortable relationship of common-law lawmaking to democracy (if not to the technical doctrine of the sepa-ration of powers) becomes apparent. Indeed, that was evident to many even before legal realism carried the day. It was one of the principal motivations behind the law-codification movement of the nineteenth century. . . .

The nineteenth-century codification movement . . . was generally opposed by the bar, and hence did not achieve substantial success, except in one field: civil procedure, the law governing the trial of civil cases.[2] (I have always found it curi-ous, by the way, that the only field in which lawyers and judges were willing to abandon judicial lawmaking was a field important to nobody except litigants, lawyers, and judges. Civil procedure used to be the *only* statutory course taught in first-year law school.) Today, generally speaking, the old private-law fields—contracts, torts, property, trusts and estates, family law—remain firmly within the control of state common-law courts.[3] Indeed, it is probably true that in these fields judicial lawmaking can be more freewheeling than ever, since the doctrine of *stare decisis* has appreciably eroded. Prior decisions that even the cleverest mind cannot distinguish can nowadays simply be overruled.

My point in all of this is not that the common law should be scraped away as a barnacle on the hull of democracy. I am content to leave the common law, and the process of developing the common law, where it is. It has proven to be a good method of developing the law in many fields—and perhaps the very best method. An argument can be made that development of the bulk of private law by judges (a natural aristocracy, as Madison accurately portrayed them)[4] is a desirable limitation upon popular democracy. . . .

But though I have no quarrel with the common law and its process, I do ques-tion whether the *attitude* of the common-law judge—the mind-set that asks,

"What is the most desirable resolution of this case, and how can any impediments to the achievement of that result be evaded?"—is appropriate for most of the work that I do, and much of the work that state judges do. We live in an age of legislation, and most new law is statutory law. . . . Every issue of law resolved by a federal judge involves interpretation of text—the text of a regulation, or of a statute, or of the Constitution. Let me put the Constitution to one side for the time being, since many believe that that document is in effect a charter for judges to develop an evolving common law of freedom of speech, of privacy rights, and the like. I think that is wrong—indeed, as I shall discuss below, I think it frustrates the whole purpose of a written constitution. But we need not pause to debate that point now, since a very small proportion of judges' work is constitutional interpretation in any event. (Even in the Supreme Court, I would estimate that well less than a fifth of the issues we confront are constitutional issues—and probably less than a twentieth if you exclude criminal-law cases.) By far the greatest part of what I and all federal judges do is to interpret the meaning of federal statutes and federal agency regulations. Thus the subject of statutory interpretation deserves study and attention in its own right, as the principal business of judges and (hence) lawyers. It will not do to treat the enterprise as simply an inconvenient modern add-on to the judge's primary role of common-law lawmaker. Indeed, attacking the enterprise with the Mr. Fix-it mentality of the common-law judge is a sure recipe for incompetence and usurpation.

The Science of Statutory Interpretation

The state of the science of statutory interpretation in American law is accurately described by a prominent treatise on the legal process as follows:

> Do not expect anybody's theory of statutory interpretation, whether it is your own or somebody else's, to be an accurate statement of what courts actually do with statutes. The hard truth of the matter is that American courts have no intelligible, generally accepted, and consistently applied theory of statutory interpretation.[5]

Surely this is a sad commentary: We American judges have no intelligible theory of what we do most.

Even sadder, however, is the fact that the American bar and American legal education, by and large, are unconcerned with the fact that we have no intelligible theory. Whereas legal scholarship has been at pains to rationalize the common law—to devise the *best* rules governing contracts, torts, and so forth—it has

intention was. I only want to know what the words mean." [9] And I agree with Holmes's other remark, quoted approvingly by Justice Jackson: "We do not inquire what the legislature meant; we ask only what the statute means." [10]

Textualism

The philosophy of interpretation I have described above is known as textualism. In some sophisticated circles, it is considered simpleminded—"wooden," "unimaginative," "pedestrian." It is none of that. To be a textualist in good standing, one need not be too dull to perceive the broader social purposes that a statute is designed, or could be designed, to serve; or too hidebound to realize that new times require new laws. One need only hold the belief that judges have no authority to pursue those broader purposes or write those new laws.

Textualism should not be confused with so-called strict constructionism, a degraded form of textualism that brings the whole philosophy into disrepute. I am not a strict constructionist, and no one ought to be—though better that, I suppose, than a nontextualist. A text should not be construed strictly, and it should not be construed leniently; it should be construed reasonably, to contain all that it fairly means. The difference between textualism and strict constructionism can be seen in a case my Court decided four terms ago.[11] The statute at issue provided for an increased jail term if, "during and in relation to . . . [a] drug trafficking crime," the defendant "uses . . . a firearm." The defendant in this case had sought to purchase a quantity of cocaine; and what he had offered to give in exchange for the cocaine was an unloaded firearm, which he showed to the drug-seller. The Court held, I regret to say, that the defendant was subject to the increased penalty, because he had "used a firearm during and in relation to a drug trafficking crime." The vote was not even close (6–3). I dissented. Now I cannot say whether my colleagues in the majority voted the way they did because they are strict-construction textualists, or because they are not textualists at all. But a proper textualist, which is to say my kind of textualist, would surely have voted to acquit. The phrase "uses a gun" fairly connoted use of a gun for what guns are normally used for, that is, as a weapon. As I put the point in my dissent, when you ask someone, "Do you use a cane?" you are not inquiring whether he has hung his grandfather's antique cane as a decoration in the hallway.

But while the good textualist is not a literalist, neither is he a nihilist. Words do have a limited range of meaning, and no interpretation that goes beyond that range is permissible. My favorite example of a departure from text—and certainly the departure that has enabled judges to do more freewheeling law-making than any other—pertains to the Due Process Clause found in the Fifth and Fourteenth Amendments of the United States Constitution, which says that no person shall "be deprived of life, liberty, or property without due process of law." It has been interpreted to prevent the government from taking away certain liberties *beyond* those, such as freedom of speech and of religion, that are specifically named in the Constitution. (The first Supreme Court case to use the Due Process Clause in this fashion was, by the way, *Dred Scott*[12]-not a desirable parentage.) Well, it may or may not be a good thing to guarantee additional liberties, but the Due Process Clause quite obviously does not bear that interpretation. By its inescapable terms, it guarantees only process. Property can be taken by the state; liberty can be taken; even life can be taken; but not without the *process* that our traditions require—notably, a validly enacted law and a fair trial. To say otherwise is to abandon textualism, and to render democratically adopted texts mere springboards for judicial lawmaking.

Of all the criticisms leveled against textualism, the most mindless is that it is "formalistic." The answer to that is, *of course it's formalistic!* The rule of law is *about* form. If, for example, a citizen performs an act—let us say the sale of certain technology to a foreign country—which is prohibited by a widely publicized bill proposed by the administration and passed by both houses of Congress, *but not yet signed by the President*, that sale is lawful. It is of no consequence that everyone knows both houses of Congress and the President wish to prevent that sale. Before the wish becomes a binding law, it must be embodied in a bill that passes both houses and is signed by the President. Is that not formalism? A murderer has been caught with blood on his hands, bending over the body of his victim; a neighbor with a video camera has filmed the crime; and the murderer has confessed in writing and on videotape. We nonetheless insist that before the state can punish this miscreant, it must conduct a full-dress criminal trial that results in a verdict of guilty. Is that not formalism? Long live formalism. It is what makes a government a government of laws and not of men. . . .

Legislative History

Let me turn now . . . to an interpretive device whose widespread use is relatively new: legislative history, by which I mean the statements made in the floor debates, committee reports, and even committee testimony, leading up to the enactment of the legislation. My view that the objective indication of the words, rather than the intent of the legislature, is what constitutes the law leads me, of course, to the conclusion that legislative history should not be used as an authoritative indication of a statute's meaning. This was the traditional English, and the traditional American, practice. Chief Justice Taney wrote:

> In expounding this law, the judgment of the court cannot, in any degree, be influenced by the construction placed upon it by individual

members of Congress in the debate which took place on its passage, nor by the motives or reasons assigned by them for supporting or opposing amendments that were offered. The law as it passed is the will of the majority of both houses, *and the only mode in which that will is spoken is in the act itself*; and we must gather their intention from the language there used, comparing it, when any ambiguity exists, with the laws upon the same subject, and looking, if necessary, to the public history of the times in which it was passed.[13]

That uncompromising view generally prevailed in this country until the present century. The movement to change it gained momentum in the late 1920s and 1930s, driven, believe it or not, by frustration with common-law judges' use of "legislative intent" and phonied-up canons to impose their own views—in those days views opposed to progressive social legislation. I quoted earlier an article by Dean Landis inveighing against such judicial usurpation. The solution he proposed was not the banishment of legislative intent as an interpretive criterion, but rather the use of legislative history to place that intent beyond manipulation.[14]

Extensive use of legislative history in this country dates only from about the 1940s. . . . In the past few decades, however, we have developed a legal culture in which lawyers routinely—and I do mean routinely—make no distinction between words in the text of a statute and words in its legislative history. My Court is frequently told, in briefs and in oral argument, that "Congress said thus-and-so"—when in fact what is being quoted is not the law promulgated by Congress, nor even any text endorsed by a single house of Congress, but rather the statement of a single committee of a single house, set forth in a committee report. Resort to legislative history has become so common that lawyerly wags have popularized a humorous quip inverting the oft-recited (and oft-ignored) rule as to when its use is appropriate: "One should consult the text of the statute," the joke goes, "only when the legislative history is ambiguous." Alas, that is no longer funny. Reality has overtaken parody. A few terms ago, I read a brief that *began* the legal argument with a discussion of legislative history and then continued (I am quoting it verbatim): "Unfortunately, the legislative debates are not helpful. Thus, we turn to the other guidepost in this difficult area, statutory language." [15]

As I have said, I object to the use of legislative history on principle, since I reject intent of the legislature as the proper criterion of the law. What is most exasperating about the use of legislative history, however, is that it does not even make sense for those who *accept* legislative intent as the criterion. It is much more likely to produce a false or contrived legislative intent than a genuine one. . . .

Ironically, but quite understandably, the more courts have relied upon legislative history, the less worthy of reliance it has become. In earlier days, it was at least genuine and not contrived—a real part of the legislation's *history*, in the sense that it was part of the *development* of the bill, part of the attempt to inform and persuade those who voted. Nowadays, however, when it is universally known and expected that judges will resort to floor debates and (especially) committee reports as authoritative expressions of "legislative intent," affecting the courts rather than informing the Congress has become the primary purpose of the exercise. It is less that the courts refer to legislative history because it exists than that legislative history exists because the courts refer to it. One of the routine tasks of the Washington lawyer-lobbyist is to draft language that sympathetic legislators can recite in a prewritten "floor debate"—or, even better, insert into a committee report. . . .

I think that Dean Landis, and those who joined him in the prescription of legislative history as a cure for what he called "willful judges," would be aghast at the results a half century later. On balance, it has facilitated rather than deterred decisions that are based upon the courts' policy preferences, rather than neutral principles of law. Since there are no rules as to how much weight an element of legislative history is entitled to, it can usually be either relied upon or dismissed with equal plausibility. If the willful judge does not like the committee report, he will not follow it; he will call the statute not ambiguous enough, the committee report too ambiguous, or the legislative history (this is a favorite phrase) "as a whole, inconclusive." . . .

Interpreting Constitutional Texts

Without pretending to have exhausted the vast topic of textual interpretation, I wish to address a final subject: the distinctive problem of constitutional interpretation. The problem is distinctive, not because special principles of interpretation apply, but because the usual principles are being applied to an unusual text. Chief Justice Marshall put the point as well as it can be put in *McCulloch* v. *Maryland*:

> A constitution, to contain an accurate detail of all the subdivisions of which its great powers will admit, and of all the means by which they may be carried into execution, would partake of the prolixity of a legal code, and could scarcely be embraced by the human mind. It would probably never be understood by the public. Its nature, therefore, requires, that only its great outlines should be marked, its important objects designated, and the minor ingredients which compose those objects be deduced from the nature of the objects themselves.[16]

In textual interpretation, context is everything, and the context of the Constitution tells us not to expect nit-picking detail, and to give words and phrases an expansive rather than narrow interpretation—though not an interpretation that the language will not bear.

Take, for example, the provision of the First Amendment that forbids abridgment of "the freedom of speech, or of the press." That phrase does not list the full range of communicative expression. Handwritten letters, for example, are neither speech nor press. Yet surely there is no doubt they cannot be censored. In this constitutional context, speech and press, the two most common forms of communication, stand as a sort of synecdoche for the whole. That is not strict construction, but it is reasonable construction.

It is curious that most of those who insist that the drafter's intent gives meaning to a statute reject the drafter's intent as the criterion for interpretation of the Constitution. I reject it for both. . . . [T]he Great Divide with regard to constitutional interpretation is not that between Framers' intent and objective meaning, but rather that between *original* meaning (whether derived from Framers' intent or not) and *current* meaning. The ascendant school of constitutional interpretation affirms the existence of what is called The Living Constitution, a body of law that (unlike normal statutes) grows and changes from age to age, in order to meet the needs of a changing society. And it is the judges who determine those needs and "find" that changing law. Seems familiar, doesn't it? Yes, it is the common law returned, but infinitely more powerful than what the old common law ever pretended to be, for now it trumps even the statutes of democratic legislatures. . . .

If you go into a constitutional law class, or study a constitutional law casebook, or read a brief filed in a constitutional law case, you will rarely find the discussion addressed to the text of the constitutional provision that is at issue, or to the question of what was the originally understood or even the originally intended meaning of that text. The starting point of the analysis will be Supreme Court cases, and the new issue will presumptively be decided according to the logic that those cases expressed, with no regard for how far that logic, thus extended, has distanced us from the original text and understanding. Worse still, however, it is known and understood that if that logic fails to produce what in the view of the current Supreme Court is the *desirable* result for the case at hand, then, like good common-law judges, the Court will distinguish its precedents, or narrow them, or if all else fails overrule them, in order that the Constitution might mean what it *ought* to mean. Should there be—to take one of the less controversial examples—a constitutional right to die? If so, there is.[17] Should there be a constitutional right to reclaim a biological child put out for adoption by the other parent? Again, if so, there is.[18] If it is good, it is so. Never mind the text that we are supposedly construing; we will smuggle these new rights in, if all else fails, under the Due Process Clause (which, as I have described, is textually incapable of containing them). Moreover, what the Constitution meant yesterday it does not necessarily mean today. As our opinions say in the context of our Eighth Amendment jurisprudence (the Cruel and Unusual Punishments Clause), its meaning changes to reflect "the evolving standards of decency that mark the progress of a maturing society." [19]

This is preeminently a common-law way of making law, and not the way of construing a democratically adopted text. . . . Proposals for "dynamic statutory construction," such as those of Judge Calabresi . . . are concededly avant-garde. The Constitution, however, even though a democratically adopted text, we formally treat like the common law. What, it is fair to ask, is the justification for doing so?

One would suppose that the rule that a text does not change would apply *a fortiori* to a constitution. If courts felt too much bound by the democratic process to tinker with statutes, when their tinkering could be adjusted by the legislature, how much more should they feel bound not to tinker with a constitution, when their tinkering is virtually irreparable. It certainly cannot be said that a constitution naturally suggests changeability; to the contrary, its whole purpose is to prevent change—to embed certain rights in such a manner that future generations cannot readily take them away. A society that adopts a bill of rights is skeptical that "evolving standards of decency" always "mark progress," and that societies always "mature," as opposed to rot. Neither the text of such a document nor the intent of its framers (whichever you choose) can possibly lead to the conclusion that its only effect is to take the power of changing rights away from the legislature and give it to the courts.

Flexibility and Liberality of the Living Constitution

The argument most frequently made in favor of the Living Constitution is a pragmatic one: Such an evolutionary approach is necessary in order to provide the "flexibility" that a changing society requires; the Constitution would have snapped if it had not been permitted to bend and grow. This might be a persuasive argument if most of the "growing" that the proponents of this approach have brought upon us in the past, and are determined to bring upon us in the future, were the *elimination* of restrictions upon democratic government. But just the opposite is true. Historically, and particularly in the past thirty-five years, the "evolving" Constitution has imposed a vast array of new constraints—new inflexibilities—upon administrative, judicial, and legislative action. To mention only a few things that formerly could be done or not done, as the society desired, but now cannot be done:

- admitting in a state criminal trial evidence of guilt that was obtained by an unlawful search;[20]
- permitting invocation of God at public-school graduations;[21]
- electing one of the two houses of a state legislature the way the United States Senate is elected, i.e., on a basis that does not give all voters numerically equal representation;[22]
- terminating welfare payments as soon as evidence of fraud is received, subject to restoration after hearing if the evidence is satisfactorily refuted;[23]
- imposing property requirements as a condition of voting;[24]
- prohibiting anonymous campaign literature;[25]
- prohibiting pornography.[26]

And the future agenda of constitutional evolutionists is mostly more of the same—the creation of *new* restrictions upon democratic government, rather than the elimination of old ones. *Less* flexibility in government, not *more*. As things now stand, the state and federal governments may either apply capital punishment or abolish it, permit suicide or forbid it—all as the changing times and the changing sentiments of society may demand. But when capital punishment is held to violate the Eighth Amendment, and suicide is held to be protected by the Fourteenth Amendment, all flexibility with regard to those matters will be gone. No, the reality of the matter is that, generally speaking, devotees of The Living Constitution do not seek to facilitate social change but to prevent it.

There are, I must admit, a few exceptions to that—a few instances in which, historically, greater flexibility has been the result of the process. But those exceptions serve only to refute another argument of the proponents of an evolving Constitution, that evolution will always be in the direction of greater personal liberty. (They consider that a great advantage, for reasons that I do not entirely understand. All government represents a balance between individual freedom and social order, and it is not true that every alteration of that balance in the direction of greater individual freedom is necessarily good.) But in any case, the record of history refutes the proposition that the evolving Constitution will invariably enlarge individual rights. The most obvious refutation is the modern Court's limitation of the constitutional protections afforded to property. The provision prohibiting impairment of the obligation of contracts, for example, has been gutted.[27] I am sure that We the People agree with that development; we value property rights less than the Founders did. So also, we value the right to bear arms less than did the Founders (who thought the right of self-defense to be absolutely fundamental), and there will be few tears shed if and when the Second Amendment is held to guarantee nothing more than the state National Guard.

But this just shows that the Founders were right when they feared that some (in their view misguided) future generation might wish to abandon liberties that they considered essential, and so sought to protect those liberties in a Bill of Rights. We may *like* the abridgment of property rights and *like* the elimination of the right to bear arms; but let us not pretend that these are not *reductions* of *rights*.

Or if property rights are too cold to arouse enthusiasm, and the right to bear arms too dangerous, let me give another example: Several terms ago a case came before the Supreme Court involving a prosecution for sexual abuse of a young child. The trial court found that the child would be too frightened to testify in the presence of the (presumed) abuser, and so, pursuant to state law, she was permitted to testify with only the prosecutor and defense counsel present, with the defendant, the judge, and the jury watching over closed-circuit television. A reasonable enough procedure, and it was held to be constitutional by my Court.[28] I dissented, because the Sixth Amendment provides that "[i]n *all* criminal prosecutions the accused shall enjoy the right . . . to be confronted with the witnesses against him" (emphasis added). There is no doubt what confrontation meant—or indeed means today. It means face-to-face, not watching from another room. And there is no doubt what one of the major purposes of that provision was: to induce *precisely* that pressure upon the witness which the little girl found it difficult to endure. It is difficult to accuse someone to his face, particularly when you are lying. Now no extrinsic factors have changed since that provision was adopted in 1791. Sexual abuse existed then, as it does now; little children were more easily upset than adults, then as now; a means of placing the defendant out of sight of the witness existed then as now (a screen could easily have been erected that would enable the defendant to see the witness, but not the witness the defendant). But the Sixth Amendment nonetheless gave *all* criminal defendants the right to *confront* the witnesses against them, because that was thought to be an important protection. The only significant things that *have* changed, I think, are the society's sensitivity to so-called psychic trauma (which is what we are told the child witness in such a situation suffers) and the society's assessment of where the proper balance ought to be struck between the two extremes of a procedure that assures convicting 100 percent of all child abusers, and a procedure that assures acquitting 100 percent of those falsely accused of child abuse. I have no doubt that the society is, as a whole, happy and pleased with what my Court decided. But we should not pretend that the decision did not *eliminate* a liberty that previously existed. . . .

It seems to me that that is where we are heading, or perhaps even where we have arrived. Seventy-five years ago, we believed firmly enough in a rock-solid, unchanging Constitution that we felt it necessary to adopt the Nineteenth Amendment to give women the vote. The battle was not fought in the courts, and few thought that it could be, despite the constitutional guarantee of Equal

Protection of the Laws; that provision did not, when it was adopted, and hence did not in 1920, guarantee equal access to the ballot but permitted distinctions on the basis not only of age but of property and of sex. Who can doubt that if the issue had been deferred until today, the Constitution would be (formally) unamended, and the courts would be the chosen instrumentality of change? The American people have been converted to belief in The Living Constitution, a "morphing" document that means, from age to age, what it ought to mean. And with that conversion has inevitably come the new phenomenon of selecting and confirming federal judges, at all levels, on the basis of their views regarding a whole series of proposals for constitutional evolution. If the courts are free to write the Constitution anew, they will, by God, write it the way the majority wants; the appointment and confirmation process will see to that. This, of course, is the end of the Bill of Rights, whose meaning will be committed to the very body it was meant to protect against: the majority. By trying to make the Constitution do everything that needs doing from age to age, we shall have caused it to do nothing at all.

NOTES

I am grateful for technical and research assistance by Matthew P. Previn, and for substantive suggestions by Eugene Scalia.

1. Oliver Wendell Holmes, Jr., *The Common Law* (1881).

2. The country's first major code of civil procedure, known as the Field Code (after David Dudley Field, who played a major role in its enactment), was passed in New York in 1848. By the end of the nineteenth century, similar codes had been adopted in many states. *See* Lawrence M. Friedman, *A History of American Law* 340–47 (1973).

3. The principal exception to this statement consists of so-called Uniform Laws, statutes enacted in virtually identical form by all or a large majority of state legislatures, in an effort to achieve nationwide uniformity with respect to certain aspects of some common-law fields. *See, e.g.*, Uniform Commercial Code, 1 U.L.A. 5 (1989); Uniform Marriage and Divorce Act 9A U.L.A. 156 (1987); Uniform Consumer Credit Code, 7A U.L.A. 17 (1985).

4. "The [members of the judiciary department], by the mode of their appointment, as well as by the nature and permanency of it, are too far removed from the people to share much in their prepossessions." *The Federalist* No. 49, at 341 (Jacob E. Cooke ed., 1961).

5. Henry M. Hart, Jr. & Albert M. Sacks, *The Legal Process* 1169 (William N. Eskridge, Jr. & Philip P. Frickey eds., 1994).

6. *See* 1 William Blackstone, *Commentaries on the Laws of England* 59–62, 91 (photo reprint 1979) (1765).

7. Joel Prentiss Bishop, *Commentaries on the Written Laws and Their Interpretation* 57–58 (Boston: Little, Brown, & Co. 1882) (emphasis added) (citation omitted).

8. James M. Landis, *A Note on "Statutory Interpretation,"* 43 Harv. L. Rev. 886, 891 (1930).

9. Felix Frankfurter, *Some Reflections on the Reading of Statutes*, 47 Colum. L. Rev. 527, 538 (1947).

10. Oliver Wendell Holmes, *Collected Legal Papers* 207 (1920), *quoted in* Schwegmann Bros. v. Calvert Distillers Corp., 341 U.S. 384, 397 (1951) (Jackson, J., concurring).

11. Smith v. United States, 508 U.S. 223 (1993).

12. Dred Scott v. Sandford, 60 U.S. (19 How.) 393, 450 (1857).

13. Aldridge v. Williams, 44 U.S. (3 How.) 9, 24 (1845) (emphasis added).

14. *See* Landis, *supra* note 17, at 891–92.

15. Brief for Petitioner at 21, Jett v. Dallas Indep. Sch. Dist., 491 U.S. 701 (1989), *quoted in* Green v. Bock Laundry Machine Co., 490 U.S. 504, 530 (1989) (Scalia, J., concurring).

16. McCulloch v. Maryland, 17 U.S. (4 Wheat.) 316, 407 (1819).

17. *See* Cruzan v. Director, Mo. Dep't of Health, 497 U.S. 261, 279 (1990).

18. *See In re* Kirchner, 649 N.E.2d 324, 333 (Ill.), *cert. denied*, 115 S. Ct. 2599 (1995).

19. Rhodes v. Chapman, 452 U.S. 337, 346 (1981), quoting from Trop v. Dulles, 356 U.S. 86, 101 (1958) (plurality opinion).

20. *See* Mapp v. Ohio, 367 U.S. 643 (1961).

21. *See* Lee v. Weisman, 505 U.S. 577 (1992).

22. *See* Reynolds v. Sims, 377 U.S. 533 (1964).

23. *See* Goldberg v. Kelly, 397 U.S. 254 (1970).

24. *See* Kramer v. Union Free Sch. Dist., 395 U.S. 621 (1969).

25. *See* McIntyre v. Ohio Elections Comm'n, 115 S. Ct. 1511 (1995).

26. Under current doctrine, pornography may be banned only if it is "obscene," *see* Miller v. California, 413 U.S. 15 (1973), a judicially crafted term of art that does not embrace material that excites "normal, healthy sexual desires," Brocket v. Spokane Arcades, Inc., 472 U.S. 491, 498 (1985).

27. *See* Home Building & Loan Ass'n v. Blaisdell, 290 U.S. 398 (1934).

28. *See* Maryland v. Craig, 497 U.S. 836 (1990).

9-2

from *Active Liberty*

Stephen Breyer

Justice Stephen Breyer's book Active Liberty, *from which this essay is excerpted, has been widely viewed as an activist judge's response to Justice Scalia's paean to judicial restraint. Yet Breyer does not envision a broadly activist role for judges in shaping social policy. For one thing, he agrees fundamentally with Scalia that unelected, life-tenured judges should subordinate their personal views on policy to those who are elected to make these decisions. Reflecting this, Breyer's decisions show his reluctance to overrule acts of Congress and executive decisions. For Breyer, the primacy of democracy requires that judges play a special role as guardians of citizens' rights and opportunities to influence government. On a variety of issues, this hierarchy of values leads Breyer to decide cases in ways that Scalia believes overstep judges' mandate. Breyer accepts broad regulation of campaign finance as advancing the performance of democracy, whereas Scalia argues that such laws affront First Amendment protections of free speech.*

THE THEME AS I here consider it falls within an interpretive tradition. . . . That tradition sees texts as driven by *purposes*. The judge should try to find and "honestly . . . say what was the underlying purpose expressed" in a statute. The judge should read constitutional language "as the revelation of the great purposes which were intended to be achieved by the Constitution" itself, a "framework for" and a "continuing instrument of government." The judge should recognize that the Constitution will apply to "new subject matter . . . with which the framers were not familiar." Thus, the judge, whether applying statute or Constitution, should "reconstruct the past solution imaginatively in its setting and project the purposes which inspired it upon the concrete occasions which arise for their decision." Since law is connected to life, judges, in applying a text in light of its purpose, should look to *consequences*, including "contemporary conditions, social, industrial, and political, of the community to be affected." And since "the purpose of construction is the ascertainment of meaning, nothing that is logically relevant should be excluded." [1]

Source: Stephen Breyer, from *Active Liberty: Interpreting Our Democratic Constitution,* (Alfred A. Knopf: 2005), 17–34, 85–101. Some notes appearing in the original have been deleted.

That tradition does not expect highly general instructions themselves to determine the outcome of difficult concrete cases where language is open-ended and precisely defined purpose is difficult to ascertain. Certain constitutional language, for example, reflects "fundamental aspirations and . . . 'moods,' embodied in provisions like the due process and equal protection clauses, which were designed not to be precise and positive directions for rules of action." A judge, when interpreting such open-ended provisions, must avoid being "willful, in the sense of enforcing individual views." A judge cannot "enforce whatever he thinks best." "In the exercise of" the "high power" of judicial review, says Justice Louis Brandeis, "we must be ever on our guard, lest we erect our prejudices into legal principles," At the same time, a judge must avoid being "wooden, in uncritically resting on formulas, in assuming the familiar to be the necessary, in not realizing that any problem can be solved if only one principle is involved but that unfortunately all controversies of importance involve if not a conflict at least an interplay of principles." [2]

How, then, is the judge to act between the bounds of the "willful" and the "wooden"? The tradition answers with an *attitude*, an attitude that hesitates to rely upon any single theory or grand view of law, of interpretation, or of the Constitution. It champions the need to search for purposes; it calls for restraint, asking judges to "speak . . . humbly as the voice of the law." And it finds in the democratic nature of our system more than simply a justification for judicial restraint. Holmes reminds the judge as a general matter to allow "[c]onsiderable latitude . . . for differences of view." . . .

[O]ne can reasonably view the Constitution as focusing upon active liberty, both as important in itself and as a partial means to help secure individual (modern) freedom. The Framers included elements designed to "control and mitigate" the ill effects of more direct forms of democratic government, but in doing so, the Framers "did not see themselves as repudiating either the Revolution or popular government." Rather, they were "saving both from their excesses." The act of ratifying the Constitution, by means of special state elections with broad voter eligibility rules, signaled the democratic character of the document itself.[3]

As history has made clear, the original Constitution was insufficient. It did not include a majority of the nation within its "democratic community." It took a civil war and eighty years of racial segregation before the slaves and their descendants could begin to think of the Constitution as theirs. Nor did women receive the right to vote until 1920. The "people" had to amend the Constitution, not only to extend its democratic base but also to expand and more fully to secure basic individual (negative) liberty.

But the original document sowed the democratic seed. Madison described something fundamental about American government, then and now, when he said the Constitution is a "charter . . . of power . . . granted by liberty," not (as in Europe) a "charter of liberty . . . granted by power." [4] . . .

In sum, our constitutional history has been a quest for workable government, workable democratic government, workable democratic government protective of individual personal liberty. Our central commitment has been to "government of the people, by the people, for the people." And the applications following illustrate how this constitutional understanding helps interpret the Constitution—in a way that helps to resolve problems related to *modern* government. . . .

Statutory Interpretation

The [first] example concerns statutory interpretation. It contrasts a literal text-based approach with an approach that places more emphasis on statutory purpose and congressional intent. It illustrates why judges should pay primary attention to a statute's purpose in difficult cases of interpretation in which language is not clear. It shows how overemphasis on text can lead courts astray, divorcing law from life-indeed, creating law that harms those whom Congress meant to help. And it explains why a purposive approach is more consistent with the framework for a "delegated democracy" that the Constitution creates.[5]

The interpretive problem arises when statutory language does not clearly answer the question of what the statute means or how it applies. Why does a statute contain such language? Perhaps Congress used inappropriate language. Perhaps it failed to use its own drafting expertise or failed to have committee hearings, writing legislation on the floor instead. Perhaps it chose politically symbolic language or ambiguous language over more precise language—possibilities that modern, highly partisan, interest-group-based politics (responding to overly simplified media accounts) make realistic. Perhaps no one in Congress thought about how the statute would apply in certain circumstances. Perhaps it is impossible to use language that foresees how a statute should apply in all relevant circumstances.

The founding generation of Americans understood these or similar possibilities. They realized that judges, though mere "fallible men," would have to exercise judgment and discretion in applying newly codified law. But they expected that judges, when doing so, would remain faithful to the legislators' will. The problem of statutory interpretation is how to meet that expectation.

Most judges start in the same way. They look first to the statute's language, its structure, and its history in an effort to determine the statute's purpose. They then use that purpose (along with the language, structure, and history) to determine the proper interpretation. Thus far, there is agreement. But when the problem is truly difficult, these factors without more may simply limit the universe of possible answers without clearly identifying a final choice. What then?

At this point judges tend to divide in their approach. Some look primarily to text, i.e., to language and text-related circumstances, for further enlightenment. They may try to tease further meaning from the language and structure of the statute itself. They may look to language-based canons of interpretation in the search for an "objective" key to the statute's proper interpretation, say a canon like *noscitur a sociis*, which tells a judge to interpret a word so that it has the same kind of meaning as its neighbors. Textualism, it has been argued, searches for "meaning . . . in structure." It means "preferring the language and structure of the law whenever possible over its legislative history and imputed values." It asks judges to avoid invocation of vague or broad statutory purposes and instead to consider such purposes at "lower levels of generality." It hopes thereby to reduce the risk that judges will interpret statutes subjectively, substituting their own ideas of what is good for those of Congress.[6]

Other judges look primarily to the statute's purposes for enlightenment. They avoid the use of interpretive canons. They allow context to determine the level of generality at which they will describe a statute's purpose—in the way that context tells us not to answer the lost driver's request for directions, "Where am I?" with the words "In a car." They speak in terms of congressional "intent," while understanding that legal conventions govern the use of that term to describe, not the intent of any, or every, individual legislator, but the intent of the group—in the way that linguistic conventions allow us to speak of the intentions of an army or a team, even when they differ from those of any, or every, soldier or member. And they examine legislative history, often closely, in the hope that the history will help them better understand the context, the enacting legislators' objectives, and ultimately the statute's purposes. At the heart of a purpose-based approach stands the "reasonable member of Congress"—a legal fiction that applies, for example, even when Congress did not in fact consider a particular problem. The judge will ask how this person (real or fictional), aware of the statute's language, structure, and general objectives (actually or hypothetically), *would have wanted* a court to interpret the statute in light of present circumstances in the particular case.

[A] recent case illustrate[s] the difference between the two approaches. In [it] the majority followed a more textual approach; the dissent, a more purposive approach. . . . The federal habeas corpus statute is ambiguous in respect to the time limits that apply when a state prisoner seeks access to federal habeas corpus. It says that a state prisoner (ordinarily) must file a federal petition within one year after his state court conviction becomes final. But the statute tolls that one-year period during the time that "a properly filed application for State post-conviction *or other collateral review*" is pending. Do the words "other collateral review" include an earlier application for a federal habeas corpus petition? Should the one-year period be tolled, for example, when a state prisoner mistakenly files a habeas petition in federal court before he exhausts all his state collateral remedies?"

It is unlikely that anyone in Congress thought about this question, for it is highly technical. Yet it is important. More than half of all federal habeas corpus petitions fall into the relevant category—i.e., state prisoners file them prematurely before the prisoner has tried to take advantage of available state remedies. In those cases, the federal court often dismisses the petition and the state prisoner must return to state court to exhaust available state remedies before he can once again file his federal habeas petition in federal court. If the one-year statute of limitations is not tolled while the first federal habeas petition was pending, that state prisoner will likely find that the one year has run—and his federal petition is time-barred—before he can return to federal court.[7]

A literal reading of the statute suggests that this is just what Congress had in mind. It suggests that the one-year time limit is tolled only during the time that *state* collateral review (or similar) proceedings are in process. And that reading is supported by various linguistic canons of construction.[8]

Nonetheless, the language does not foreclose an alternative interpretation— an interpretation under which such petitions would fall within the scope of the phrase "other collateral review." The word "State" could be read to modify the phrase "post-conviction . . . review," permitting "*other* collateral review" to refer to federal proceedings. The phrase "properly filed" could be interpreted to refer to purely formal filing requirements rather than calling into play more important remedial questions such as the presence or absence of "exhaustion." A purposive approach favors this latter linguistic interpretation.[9]

Why? [Consider] our hypothetical legislator, the reasonable member of Congress. Which interpretation would that member favor (if he had thought of the problem, which he likely had not)? Consider the consequences of the more literal interpretation. That interpretation would close the doors of federal habeas courts to many or most state prisoners who mistakenly filed a federal habeas petition too soon, but not to all such prisoners. Whether the one-year window was still open would depend in large part on how long the federal court considering the premature federal petition took to dismiss it. In cases in which the court ruled quickly, the short time the federal petition was (wrongly) present in the federal court might not matter. But if a premature federal petition languishes on the federal court's docket while the one year runs, the petitioner would likely lose his one meaningful chance to seek federal habeas relief. By way of contrast, state court delay in considering a prisoner petition in state court would not matter. Whenever *state* proceedings are at issue, the statute tolls the one-year limitations period.

Now ask *why* our reasonable legislator would want to bring about these consequences. He might believe that state prisoners have too often abused the federal writ by filing too many petitions. But the distinction that a literal interpretation would make between those allowed to file and those not allowed to file—a distinction that in essence rests upon federal court processing delay—is a *random* distinction, bearing no logical relation to any abuse-related purpose. Would our reasonable legislator, even if concerned about abuse of the writ, choose to deny access to the Great Writ on a *random* basis? Given our traditions, including those the Constitution grants through its habeas corpus guarantees, the answer to this question is likely no. Would those using a more literal text-based approach answer this question differently? I do not think so. But my real objection to the text-based approach is that it would prevent them from posing the question at all.[10]

[This] example suggest[s] the danger that lurks where judges rely too heavily upon just text and textual aids when interpreting a statute. . . . [W]hen difficult statutory questions are at issue, courts do better to focus foremost upon statutory purpose, ruling out neither legislative history nor any other form of help in order to locate the role that Congress intended the statutory words in question to play.

For one thing, near-exclusive reliance upon canons and other linguistic interpretive aids in close cases can undermine the Constitution's democratic objective. Legislation in a delegated democracy is meant to embody the people's will, either directly (insofar as legislators see themselves as translating how their constituents feel about each proposed law) or indirectly (insofar as legislators see themselves as exercising delegated authority to vote in accordance with what they see as the public interest). Either way, an interpretation of a statute that tends to implement the legislator's will helps to implement the public's will and is therefore consistent with the Constitution's democratic purpose. For similar reasons an interpretation that undercuts the statute's objectives tends to undercut that constitutional objective. . . .

Use of a "reasonable legislator" fiction also facilitates legislative accountability. Ordinary citizens think in terms of general purposes. They readily understand their elected legislators' thinking similarly. It is not impossible to ask an ordinary citizen to determine whether a particular law is consistent with a general purpose the ordinary citizen might support. It is not impossible to ask an ordinary citizen to determine what general purpose a legislator sought to achieve in enacting a particular statute. And it is not impossible for the ordinary citizen to judge the legislator accordingly. But it *is* impossible to ask an ordinary citizen (or an ordinary legislator) to understand the operation of linguistic canons of interpretation. And it *is* impossible to ask an ordinary citizen to draw any relevant electoral conclusion from consequences that might flow when courts reach a purpose-thwarting interpretation of the statute based upon their near-exclusive use of interpretive canons. Were a segment of the public unhappy about application of the Arbitration Act to ordinary employment contracts, whom should it blame?

For another thing, that approach means that laws will work better for the people they are presently meant to affect. Law is tied to life, and a failure to understand how a statute is so tied can undermine the very human activity that the law seeks to benefit. The more literal text-based, canon-based interpretation of the Foreign Sovereign Immunities jurisdictional statute, for example, means that foreign nations, those using tiered corporate ownership, will find their access to federal courts cut off, undermining the statute's basic jurisdictional objectives. The textual approach to the habeas corpus statute randomly closes courthouse doors in a way that runs contrary to our commitment to basic individual liberty. And it does so because it tends to stop judges from asking a relevant purpose-based question: Why would Congress have wanted a statute that produces those consequences?[11]

In sum, a "reasonable legislator" approach is a workable method of implementing the Constitution's democratic objective. It permits ready translation of the general desire of the public for certain ends, through the legislator's efforts to embody those ends in legislation, into a set of statutory words that will carry out those general objectives. I have argued that the Framers created the Constitution's complex governmental mechanism in order better to translate public will, determined through collective deliberation, into sound public policy. The courts constitute part of that mechanism. And judicial use of the "will of the reasonable legislator"—even if at times it is a fiction—helps statutes match their means to their overall public policy objectives, a match that helps translate the popular will into sound policy. An overly literal reading of a text can too often stand in the way.

Constitutional Interpretation: Speech

The [next] example focuses on the First Amendment and how it . . . show[s] the importance of reading the First Amendment not in isolation but as seeking to maintain a system of free expression designed to further a basic constitutional purpose: creating and maintaining democratic decision-making institutions.

The example begins where courts normally begin in First Amendment cases. They try to classify the speech at issue, distinguishing among different speech-related activities for the purpose of applying a strict, moderately strict, or totally relaxed presumption of unconstitutionality. Is the speech "political speech," calling for a strong pro-speech presumption, "commercial speech," calling for a mid-range presumption, or simply a form of economic regulation presumed constitutional?

Should courts begin in this way? Some argue that making these kinds of categorical distinctions is a misplaced enterprise. The Constitution's language makes no such distinction. It simply protects "the freedom of speech" from government restriction. "Speech is speech and that is the end of the matter." But to limit distinctions to the point at which First Amendment law embodies the slogan "speech is speech" cannot work. And the fact that the First Amendment seeks to protect active liberty as well as modern liberty helps to explain why.[12]

The democratic government that the Constitution creates now regulates a host of activities that inevitably take place through the medium of speech. Today's workers manipulate information, not wood or metal. And the modern information-based workplace, no less than its more materially based predecessors, requires the application of community standards seeking to assure, for example, the absence of anti-competitive restraints; the accuracy of information; the absence of discrimination; the protection of health, safety, the environment, the consumer; and so forth.

Laws that embody these standards obviously affect speech. Warranty laws require private firms to include on labels statements of a specified content. Securities laws and consumer protection laws insist upon the disclosure of information that businesses might prefer to keep private. Health laws forbid tobacco advertising, say, to children. Anti-discrimination laws insist that employers prevent employees from making certain kinds of statements. Communications laws require cable broadcasters to provide network access. Campaign finance laws restrict citizen contributions to candidates.

To treat all these instances alike, to scrutinize them all as if they all represented a similar kind of legislative effort to restrain a citizen's "modern liberty" to speak, would lump together too many different kinds of activities under the aegis of a single standard, thereby creating a dilemma. On the one hand, if strong First Amendment standards were to apply across the board, they would prevent a democratically elected government from creating necessary regulation. The strong free speech guarantees needed to protect the structural democratic governing process, if applied without distinction to all governmental efforts to control speech, would unreasonably limit the public's substantive economic (or social) regulatory choices. The limits on substantive choice would likely exceed what any liberty-protecting framework for democratic government could require, depriving the people of the democratically necessary room to make decisions, including the leeway to make regulatory mistakes. . . . Most scholars, including "speech is speech" advocates, consequently see a need for distinctions. The question is, Which ones? Applied where?

At this point, reference to the Constitution's more general objectives helps. First, active liberty is particularly at risk when law restricts speech directly related to the shaping of public opinion, for example, speech that takes place in areas related to politics and policy-making by elected officials. That special risk justifies especially strong pro-speech judicial presumptions. It also justifies careful review whenever the speech in question seeks to shape public opinion, particularly if that opinion in turn will affect the political process and the kind of society in which we live.

Second, whenever ordinary commercial or economic regulation is at issue, this special risk normally is absent. Moreover, strong pro-speech presumptions risk imposing what is, from the perspective of active liberty, too severe a restriction upon the legislature—a restriction that would dramatically limit the size of the legislative arena that the Constitution opens for public deliberation and action. The presence of this second risk warns against use of special, strong pro-speech judicial presumptions or special regulation-skeptical judicial review.

The upshot is that reference to constitutional purposes in general and active liberty in particular helps to justify the category of review that the Court applies to a given type of law. But those same considerations argue, among other things, against category boundaries that are too rigid or fixed and against too mechanical an application of those categories. Rather, reference to active liberty will help courts define and apply the categories case by case.

Consider campaign finance reform. The campaign finance problem arises out of the explosion of campaign costs, particularly those related to television advertising, together with the vast disparity in ability to make a campaign contribution. In the year 2000, for example, election expenditures amounted to $1.4 billion, and the two presidential candidates spent about $310 million. In 2002, an off-year without a presidential contest, campaign expenditures still amounted to more than $1 billion. A typical House election cost $900,000, with an open seat costing $1.2 million; a typical Senate seat cost about $4.8 million, with an open contested seat costing about $7.1 million.[13] . . .

A small number of individuals and groups underwrite a very large share of these costs. In 2000, about half the money the parties spent, roughly $500 million, was soft money, i.e., money not subject to regulation under the then current campaign finance laws. Two-thirds of that money—almost $300 million—came from just 800 donors, each contributing a minimum of $120,000. Of these donors, 435 were corporations or unions (whose *direct* contributions the law forbids). The rest, 365, were individual citizens. At the same time, 99 percent of the 200 million or so citizens eligible to vote gave less than $200. Ninety-six percent gave nothing at all.[14]

The upshot is a concern, reflected in campaign finance laws, that the few who give in large amounts may have special access to, and therefore influence over, their elected representatives or, at least, create the appearance of undue influence. (One study found, for example, that 55 percent of Americans believe that large contributions have a "great deal" of impact on how decisions are made in Washington; fewer than 1 percent believed they had no impact.) These contributions (particularly if applied to television) may eliminate the need for, and in that sense crowd out, smaller individual contributions. In either case, the public may lose confidence in the political system and become less willing to participate in the political process. That, in important part, is why legislatures have tried to regulate the size of campaign contributions.[15]

Our Court in 1976 considered the constitutionality of the congressional legislation that initially regulated campaign contributions, and in 2003 we considered more recent legislation that tried to close what Congress considered a loophole— the ability to make contributions in the form of unregulated soft money. The basic constitutional question does not concern the desirability or wisdom of the legislation but whether, how, and the extent to which the First Amendment permits the legislature to impose limits on the amounts that individuals or organizations or parties can contribute to a campaign. Here it is possible to sketch an approach to decision-making that draws upon the Constitution's democratic objective.[16]

It is difficult to find an easy answer to this basic constitutional question in language, in history, or in tradition. The First Amendment's language says that Congress shall not abridge "the freedom of speech." But it does not define "the freedom of speech" in any detail. The nation's Founders did not speak directly about campaign contributions. . .

Neither can we find the answer through the use of purely conceptual arguments. Some claim, for example, that "money is speech." Others say, "money is not speech." But neither contention helps. Money is not speech, it is money. But the expenditure of money enables speech, and that expenditure is often necessary to communicate a message, particularly in a political context. A law that forbade the expenditure of money to communicate could effectively suppress the message.

Nor does it resolve the problem simply to point out that campaign contribution limits inhibit the political "speech opportunities" of those who wish to contribute more. Indeed, that is so. But the question is whether, in context, such a limitation is prohibited as an abridgment of "the freedom of speech." To announce that the harm imposed by a contribution limit is under no circumstances justified is simply to state an ultimate constitutional conclusion; it is not to explain the underlying reasons.[17]

Once we remove our blinders, however, paying increased attention to the Constitution's general democratic objective, it becomes easier to reach a solution. To understand the First Amendment as seeking in significant part to protect active liberty, "participatory self-government," is to understand it as protecting more than the individual's modern freedom. It is to understand the amendment as seeking to facilitate a conversation among ordinary citizens that will encourage their informed participation in the electoral process. It is to suggest a constitutional purpose that goes beyond protecting the individual from government restriction of information about matters that the Constitution commits to individual, not collective, decision-making. It is to understand the First Amendment as seeking primarily to encourage the exchange of information and ideas necessary for citizens themselves to shape that "public opinion which is the final source of government in a democratic state." In these ways the Amendment helps to maintain a form of government open to participation (in Constant's words) by "all the citizens, without exception." [18]

To focus upon the First Amendment's relation to the Constitution's democratic objective is helpful because the campaign laws seek to further a similar objective. They seek to democratize the influence that money can bring to bear upon the electoral process, thereby building public confidence in that process, broadening the base of a candidate's meaningful financial support, and encouraging greater public participation. Ultimately, they seek thereby to maintain the integrity of the political process—a process that itself translates political speech into governmental action. Insofar as they achieve these objectives, those laws, despite the limits they impose, will help to further the kind of open public political discussion that the First Amendment seeks to sustain, both as an end and as a means of achieving a workable democracy.

To emphasize the First Amendment's protection of active liberty is not to find the campaign finance laws automatically constitutional. Rather, it is to recognize that basic democratic objectives, including some of a kind that the First Amendment seeks to further, lie on both sides of the constitutional equation. Seen in terms of modern liberty, they include protection of the citizen's speech from government interference; seen in terms of active liberty, they include promotion of a democratic conversation. That, I believe, is why our Court has refused to apply a strong First Amendment presumption that would almost automatically find the laws unconstitutional. Rather the Court has consistently rejected "strict scrutiny" as the proper test, instead examining a campaign finance law "close[ly]" while applying what it calls "heightened scrutiny. In doing so, the Court has emphasized the power of large campaign contributions to "erod[e] public confidence in the electoral process." It has noted that contribution limits are "aimed at protecting the integrity of the process"; pointed out that in doing so they "tangibly benefit public participation in political debate"; and concluded that that is why "there is no place for the strong presumption against constitutionality, of the sort often thought to accompany the words 'strict scrutiny.' " In this statement it recognizes the possibility that, just as a restraint of trade is sometimes lawful because it furthers, rather than restricts, competition, so a restriction on speech, even when political speech is at issue, will sometimes prove reasonable, hence lawful. Consequently the Court has tried to look realistically both at a campaign finance law's *negative* impact upon those primarily wealthier citizens who wish to engage in more electoral communication and its *positive* impact upon the public's confidence in, and ability to communicate through, the electoral process. And it has applied a constitutional test that I would describe as one of proportionality. Does the statute strike a reasonable balance between electoral speech-restricting and speech-enhancing consequences? Or does it instead impose restrictions on speech that are disproportionate when measured against their electoral and speech-related benefits, taking into account the kind, the importance, and the extent of those benefits, as well as the need for the restriction in order to secure them?[19]

In trying to answer these questions, courts need not totally abandon what I have referred to as judicial modesty. Courts can defer to the legislature's own judgment insofar as that judgment concerns matters (particularly empirical matters) about which the legislature is comparatively expert, such as the extent of the campaign finance problem, a matter that directly concerns the realities of political life. But courts should not defer when they evaluate the risk that reform legislation will defeat the participatory self-government objective itself. That risk is present, for example, when laws set contribution limits so low that they elevate the reputation-related or media-related advantages of incumbency to the point of insulating incumbent officeholders from effective challenge.[20]

A focus upon the Constitution's democratic objective does not offer easy answers to the difficult questions that campaign finance laws pose. But it does clarify the First Amendment's role in promoting active liberty and suggests an approach for addressing those and other vexing questions. In turn, such a focus can help the Court arrive at answers faithful to the Constitution, its language, and its parts, read together as a consistent whole. Modesty suggests when, and how, courts should defer to the legislature in doing so. . . .

My argument is that, in applying First Amendment presumptions, we must distinguish among areas, contexts, and forms of speech. Reference . . . back to at least one general purpose, active liberty, helps both to generate proper distinctions and also properly to apply the distinctions generated. The active liberty reference helps us to preserve speech that is essential to our democratic form of government, while simultaneously permitting the law to deal effectively with such modern regulatory problems as campaign finance. . . .

NOTES

1. Hand, *supra* note I, at 109; *United States v. Classic,* 313 U.S. 299, 316 (1941) (Stone, J.); Hand, *id.*, at 157; Aharon Barak, *A Judge on Judging: The Role of a Supreme Court in a Democracy,* 116 Harv. L. Rev. 16, 28 (2002) ("The law regulates relationships between people. It prescribes patterns of behavior. It reflects the values of society. The role of the judge is to understand the purpose of law in society and to help the law achieve its purpose."); Goldman, *supra* note I, at 115; Felix Frankfurter, *Some Reflections on the Reading of Statutes,* 47 Colum. L. Rev. 527, 541 (1947).

2. Felix Frankfurter, *The Supreme Court in the Mirror of Justices,* in *Of Law and Life & Other Things That Matter* 94 (Philip B. Kurland ed., 1965); *id.* at 95; Hand, *supra* note I, at 109; *New State Ice Co. v. Liebmann,* 285 U.S. 262, 311 (1932) (Brandeis, J., dissenting); Frankfurter, *supra* note 3, at 95.

3. *Id.* at 517.

4. Bailyn, *supra* note I, at 55 (quoting James Madison).

5. Aharon Barak, *A Judge on Judging: The Role of a Supreme Court in a Democracy,* 116 Harv. L. Rev. 28-29 (2002).

6. See, e.g., Antonin Scalia, *Common-Law Courts in a Civil-Law System: The Role of United States Federal Courts in Interpreting the Constitution and Laws,* in *A Matter of Interpretation: Federal Courts and the Law* 26–27 (Amy Gutmann ed., 1997); see William N. Eskridge Jr., Philip P. Frickey, & Elizabeth Garrett, *Cases and Materials on Legislation-Statutes and the Creation of Public Policy* 822 (3d ed. 2001); Frank H. Easterbrook, *Text, History, and Structure in Statutory Interpretation,* 17 Harv. J. L. & Pub. Pol'y 61, 64 (1994).

7. *Duncan,* 533 U.S. 167 at 185 (Breyer, J. dissenting) (citing U.S. Dept. of Justice, Office of Justice Programs, Bureau of Justice Statistics, *Federal Habeas Corpus Review: Challenging State Court Criminal Convictions* 17 [1995]).

8. See *id.* at 172–75.

9. *Id.* at 190–93 (Breyer, J., dissenting).

10. *Id.* at 190 (Breyer, J., dissenting).

11. Barak, *supra* note I, at 28–29.

12. See, e.g., Alex Kozinski & Stuart Banner, *Who's Afraid of Commercial Speech?* 76 Va. L. Rev. 627, 631 (1990); Martin H. Redish, *The First Amendment in the Marketplace: Commercial Speech and the Values of Free Expression,* 39 Geo. Wash. L. Rev. 429, 452–48 (1971); cf. 44 *Liquormart, Inc. v. Rhode Island,* 517 U.S. 484, 522 (1996) (Thomas, J., concurring in part and concurring in the judgment); U.S. Const. art. I.

13. Ctr. for Responsive Politics, *Election Overview, 2000 Cycle: Stats at a Glance,* at http://www.opensecrets.org/overview/index.asp?Cycle=2000 accessed Mar. 8, 2002 (aggregating totals using Federal Election Commission data); Ctr. for Responsive Politics, *Election Overview,* at http://www.opensecrets.org/overview/stats.asp accessed Nov. 21, 2003 (based on FEC data).

14. Taken from the record developed in *McConnell v. Federal Election Comm'n*, No. 02-1674 et al., Joint Appendix 1558. In the 2002 midterm election, less than one-tenth of one percent of the population gave 83 percent of all (hard and soft) itemized campaign contributions. Ctr. for Responsive Politics, see *supra* note 2.

15. Taken from the record developed in *McConnell*, No. 02-1674 et al., Joint Appendix 1564.

16. *Buckley v. Valeo*, 424 U.S. I (1976); *McConnell v. FEC*, 540 U.S. 93 (2003).

17. U.S. Const. amend. I.

18. *Masses Publishing Co. v. Patten*, 244 F.535, 540 (S.D.N.Y. 1917 [(Hand, J.)]; Benjamin Constant, *The Liberty of the Ancients Compared with That of the Moderns* (1819), in *Political Writings*, at 327 (Biancamaria Fontana trans. & ed., 1988).

19. *McConnell*, 540 U.S. at 136, 231; see also *Nixon v. Shrink Mo. Gov't PAC*, 528 U.S. 377, 399–402 (2000) (Breyer, J., concurring); *id.* at 136 (internal quotation marks omitted); *id.* at 137 (internal quotation marks omitted); see *Board of Trade of Chicago v. United States*, 246 U.S. 231 (1918); see *McConnell*, 540 U.S. at 134–42.

20. *McConnell*, 540 U.S. at 137.

9-3

Federalist No. 78

Alexander Hamilton
May 28, 1788

Of the several branches laid out in the Constitution, the judiciary is the least democratic—that is, the least responsive to the expressed preferences of the citizenry. Indeed, it is hard to imagine an institution designed to be less responsive to the public than the Supreme Court, whose unelected judges enjoy lifetime appointments. During the Constitution's ratification, this fact exposed the judiciary to all sorts of wild speculation from opponents about the dire consequences the judiciary would have for the new republic. In one of the most famous passages of The Federalist, *Alexander Hamilton seeks to calm fears by declaring the judiciary to be "the least dangerous branch." Unlike the president, the Court does not control a military force, and unlike Congress, it cannot confiscate citizens' property through taxation. At the same time, Hamilton does not shrink from assigning the judiciary a critical role in safeguarding the Constitution against congressional and presidential encroachments he sees as bound to occur from time to time. By assigning it this role, he assumed that the Supreme Court has the authority of "judicial review" even though there was no provision for it in the Constitution.*

WE PROCEED now to an examination of the judiciary department of the proposed government. In unfolding the defects of the existing Confederation, the utility and necessity of a federal judicature have been clearly pointed out. It is the less necessary to recapitulate the considerations there urged, as the propriety of the institution in the abstract is not disputed; the only questions which have been raised being relative to the manner of constituting it, and to its extent. To these points, therefore, our observations shall be confined.

The manner of constituting it seems to embrace these several objects: 1st. The mode of appointing the judges. 2d. The tenure by which they are to hold their places. 3d. The partition of the judiciary authority between different courts, and their relations to each other.

First.

As to the mode of appointing the judges; this is the same with that of appointing the officers of the Union in general, and has been so fully discussed . . . that nothing can be said here which would not be useless repetition.

Second.

As to the tenure by which the judges are to hold their places; this chiefly concerns their duration in office; the provisions for their support; the precautions for their responsibility.

According to the plan of the convention, all judges who may be appointed by the United States are to hold their offices during good behavior. . . . The standard of good behavior for the continuance in office of the judicial magistracy, is certainly one of the most valuable of the modern improvements in the practice of government. In a monarchy it is an excellent barrier to the despotism of the prince; in a republic it is a no less excellent barrier to the encroachments and oppressions of the representative body. And it is the best expedient which can be devised in any government, to secure a steady, upright, and impartial administration of the laws.

Whoever attentively considers the different departments of power must perceive, that, in a government in which they are separated from each other, the judiciary, from the nature of its functions, will always be the least dangerous to the political rights of the Constitution; because it will be least in a capacity to annoy or injure them. The Executive not only dispenses the honors, but holds the sword of the community. The legislature not only commands the purse, but prescribes the rules by which the duties and rights of every citizen are to be regulated. The judiciary, on the contrary, has no influence over either the sword or the purse; no direction either of the strength or of the wealth of the society; and can take no active resolution whatever. It may truly be said to have neither FORCE nor WILL, but merely judgment; and must ultimately depend upon the aid of the executive arm even for the efficacy of its judgments.

This simple view of the matter suggests several important consequences. It proves incontestably, that the judiciary is beyond comparison the weakest of the three departments of power[1]; that it can never attack with success either of the other two; and that all possible care is requisite to enable it to defend itself against their attacks. It equally proves, that though individual oppression may now and then proceed from the courts of justice, the general liberty of the people can never be endangered from that quarter; I mean so long as the judiciary remains truly distinct from both the legislature and the Executive. For I agree, that "there is no liberty, if the power of judging be not separated from the legislative and executive powers."[2] And it proves, in the last place, that as liberty can have nothing to fear from the judiciary alone, but would have every thing to fear from its union with either of the other departments; that as all the effects of such a union must ensue from a dependence of the former on the latter, notwithstanding a nominal and apparent separation; that as, from the natural feebleness of the judiciary, it is in continual jeopardy of being overpowered, awed, or influenced by its co-ordinate branches; and that as nothing can contribute so much to its firmness and independence as permanency in office, this quality may therefore be justly regarded as an indispensable ingredient in its constitution, and, in a great measure, as the citadel of the public justice and the public security.

The complete independence of the courts of justice is peculiarly essential in a limited Constitution. By a limited Constitution, I understand one which contains certain specified exceptions to the legislative authority; such, for instance, as that it shall pass no bills of attainder, no ex post facto laws, and the like. Limitations of this kind can be preserved in practice no other way than through the medium of courts of justice, whose duty it must be to declare all acts contrary to the manifest tenor of the Constitution void. Without this, all the reservations of particular rights or privileges would amount to nothing.

Some perplexity respecting the rights of the courts to pronounce legislative acts void, because contrary to the Constitution, has arisen from an imagination that the doctrine would imply a superiority of the judiciary to the legislative power. It is urged that the authority which can declare the acts of another void, must necessarily be superior to the one whose acts may be declared void. As this doctrine is of great importance in all the American constitutions, a brief discussion of the ground on which it rests cannot be unacceptable.

There is no position which depends on clearer principles, than that every act of a delegated authority, contrary to the tenor of the commission under which it is exercised, is void. No legislative act, therefore, contrary to the Constitution, can be valid. To deny this, would be to affirm, that the deputy is greater than his principal; that the servant is above his master; that the representatives of the people are superior to the people themselves; that men acting by virtue of powers, may do not only what their powers do not authorize, but what they forbid.

If it be said that the legislative body are themselves the constitutional judges of their own powers, and that the construction they put upon them is conclusive upon the other departments, it may be answered, that this cannot be the natural presumption, where it is not to be collected from any particular provisions in the Constitution. It is not otherwise to be supposed, that the Constitution could intend to enable the representatives of the people to substitute their will to that of their constituents. It is far more rational to suppose, that the courts were designed to be an intermediate body between the people and the legislature, in order, among other things, to keep the latter within the limits assigned to their authority. The interpretation of the laws is the proper and peculiar province of the courts. A constitution is, in fact, and must be regarded by the judges, as a fundamental law. It therefore belongs to them to ascertain its meaning, as well as the meaning of any particular act proceeding from the legislative body. If there should happen to be an irreconcilable variance between the two, that which has the superior obligation and validity ought, of course, to be preferred; or, in other words, the Constitution ought to be preferred to the statute, the intention of the people to the intention of their agents.

Nor does this conclusion by any means suppose a superiority of the judicial to the legislative power. It only supposes that the power of the people is superior to both; and that where the will of the legislature, declared in its statutes, stands in opposition to that of the people, declared in the Constitution, the judges ought to be governed by the latter rather than the former. They ought to regulate their decisions by the fundamental laws, rather than by those which are not fundamental.

This exercise of judicial discretion, in determining between two contradictory laws, is exemplified in a familiar instance. It not uncommonly happens, that there are two statutes existing at one time, clashing in whole or in part with each other, and neither of them containing any repealing clause or expression. In such a case, it is the province of the courts to liquidate and fix their meaning and operation. So far as they can, by any fair construction, be reconciled to each other, reason and law conspire to dictate that this should be done; where this is impracticable, it becomes a matter of necessity to give effect to one, in exclusion of the other. The rule which has obtained in the courts for determining their relative validity is, that the last in order of time shall be preferred to the first. But this is a mere rule of construction, not derived from any positive law, but from the nature and reason of the thing. It is a rule not enjoined upon the courts by legislative provision, but adopted by themselves, as consonant to truth and propriety, for the direction of their conduct as interpreters of the law. They thought it reasonable, that between the interfering acts of an EQUAL authority, that which was the last indication of its will should have the preference.

But in regard to the interfering acts of a superior and subordinate authority, of an original and derivative power, the nature and reason of the thing indicate the converse of that rule as proper to be followed. They teach us that the prior act of a superior ought to be preferred to the subsequent act of an inferior and subordinate authority; and that accordingly, whenever a particular statute contravenes the Constitution, it will be the duty of the judicial tribunals to adhere to the latter and disregard the former.

It can be of no weight to say that the courts, on the pretense of a repugnancy, may substitute their own pleasure to the constitutional intentions of the legislature. This might as well happen in the case of two contradictory statutes; or it might as well happen in every adjudication upon any single statute. The courts must declare the sense of the law; and if they should be disposed to exercise WILL instead of JUDGMENT, the consequence would equally be the substitution of their pleasure to that of the legislative body. The observation, if it prove any thing, would prove that there ought to be no judges distinct from that body.

If, then, the courts of justice are to be considered as the bulwarks of a limited Constitution against legislative encroachments, this consideration will afford a strong argument for the permanent tenure of judicial offices, since nothing will contribute so much as this to that independent spirit in the judges which must be essential to the faithful performance of so arduous a duty.

This independence of the judges is equally requisite to guard the Constitution and the rights of individuals from the effects of those ill humors, which the arts of designing men, or the influence of particular conjunctures, sometimes disseminate among the people themselves, and which, though they speedily give place to better information, and more deliberate reflection, have a tendency, in the meantime, to occasion dangerous innovations in the government, and serious oppressions of the minor party in the community. . . . Until the people have, by some solemn and authoritative act, annulled or changed the established form, it is binding upon themselves collectively, as well as individually; and no presumption, or even knowledge, of their sentiments, can warrant their representatives in a departure from it, prior to such an act. But it is easy to see, that it would require an uncommon portion of fortitude in the judges to do their duty as faithful guardians of the Constitution, where legislative invasions of it had been instigated by the major voice of the community.

But it is not with a view to infractions of the Constitution only, that the independence of the judges may be an essential safeguard against the effects of occasional ill humors in the society. These sometimes extend no farther than to the injury of the private rights of particular classes of citizens, by unjust and partial laws. Here also the firmness of the judicial magistracy is of vast importance in mitigating the severity and confining the operation of such laws. It not only serves to moderate the immediate mischiefs of those which may have been passed, but it operates as a check upon the legislative body in passing them; who, perceiving that obstacles to the success of iniquitous intention are to be expected from the scruples of the courts, are in a manner compelled, by the very motives of the injustice they meditate, to qualify their attempts. . . .

That inflexible and uniform adherence to the rights of the Constitution, and of individuals, which we perceive to be indispensable in the courts of justice, can certainly not be expected from judges who hold their offices by a temporary commission. Periodical appointments, however regulated, or by whomsoever made, would, in some way or other, be fatal to their necessary independence. If the power of making them was committed either to the Executive or legislature, there would be danger of an improper complaisance to the branch which possessed it; if to both, there would be an unwillingness to hazard the displeasure of either; if to the people, or to persons chosen by them for the special purpose, there would be too great a disposition to consult popularity, to justify a reliance that nothing would be consulted but the Constitution and the laws.

There is yet a further and a weightier reason for the permanency of the judicial offices, which is deducible from the nature of the qualifications they require. It has been frequently remarked, with great propriety, that a voluminous code of laws is one of the inconveniences necessarily connected with the advantages of a free government. To avoid an arbitrary discretion in the courts, it is indispensable that they should be bound down by strict rules and precedents, which serve to define and point out their duty in every particular case that comes before them; and it will readily be conceived from the variety of controversies which grow out of the folly and wickedness of mankind, that the records of those precedents must unavoidably swell to a very considerable bulk, and must demand long and laborious study to acquire a competent knowledge of them. Hence it is, that there can be but few men in the society who will have sufficient skill in the laws to qualify them for the stations of judges. And making the proper deductions for the ordinary depravity of human nature, the number must be still smaller of those who unite the requisite integrity with the requisite knowledge. . . .

NOTES

1. The celebrated Montesquieu, speaking of them, says: "Of the three powers above mentioned, the judiciary is next to nothing." "Spirit of Laws." vol. i., page 186. [See Charles de Secondat, Baron de Montesquieu, *The Spirit of Laws,* trans. Thomas Nugent, rev. J. V. Pritchard (London: G. Bell & Sons Ltd., 1914)].

2. Idem, page 181.

9-4

Congress and the Politics of Judicial Appointments

Sarah A. Binder and Forrest Maltzman

In distributing power across the separate branches of government, the Constitution's Framers followed the blueprint of "checks and balances" wherever possible. Clearly, requiring Senate confirmation ("advice and consent") of presidential nominations to the Supreme Court and secondary federal courts was intended to put in place justices who enjoyed broad support. Whenever opposing political parties controlled the executive and the legislature, judicial appointments have been susceptible to conflict, in part because, unlike budgets, a single appointment is difficult to compromise. Historically, presidential nomination and judicial confirmation decisions were generally transacted in a bipartisan fashion. Quiet diplomacy in identifying acceptable nominees and informal rules of "senatorial courtesy" guided the delicate business of recruiting federal judges. Over the past several decades, however, Supreme Court appointments have emerged as among the most contentious issues to confront politicians in Washington. In this essay, Sarah Binder and Forrest Maltzman test various possible explanations for this development. In the course of their investigation they account for the numerous ways in which national politics has changed in recent years.

HALF A DOZEN computers and network servers seized, a renowned counterespionage and antiterrorism forensic expert hired, Secret Service investigators brought in, and scores of Senate staff interviewed by the Senate's sergeant-at-arms. Murder in the Capitol? Terrorist plot? No, it was just another skirmish in the battle over confirming federal judges. This time, in fall 2003, Republican staff pilfered computer files from Democrats, revealing the Democrats' collusion with organized interests to block controversial judicial nominees. Although Republicans cried foul, the stolen memos confirmed what seasoned observers of the Senate had come to expect: Selecting and confirming federal judges has become a no-holds-barred game among senators, presidents, and organized interests, each seeking to influence the ideological tenor of the federal bench.

Source: Sarah A. Binder and Forrest Maltzman, "Congress and the Politics of Judicial Appointments," in *Congress Reconsidered*, by Lawrence C. Dodd and Bruce I. Oppenheimer (CQ Press: 2005), 13:1–13:21. Some notes appearing in the original have been deleted.

In this chapter we explore the politics of judicial selection, focusing on partisan, institutional, and temporal forces that shape the fate of presidential appointments to the lower federal courts. Assessing patterns over the past fifty years, we depict broad trends in the process of judicial selection and pinpoint recent developments that have fueled conflict over the makeup of the federal bench. Although today's tactics in the battles over federal judges—from stolen memos to successful filibusters—are new, the underlying struggle to shape the federal bench is not. Both cooperation and competition are recurring themes in the politics of judicial selection, a politics strongly shaped not only by recent partisan pique but by enduring constitutional and institutional forces as well.

The Evolving Role of the Senate in Judicial Selection

Article II, Section 2 of the Constitution stipulates that presidential appointments must be made with the "Advice and Consent" of the Senate. Although Alexander Hamilton claimed in *Federalist No. 76* that the Senate's role would be limited, this means that the president and the Senate share the appointment power.[1] The Senate's constitutionally prescribed role clearly grants senators opportunities to influence the fate of presidential appointees and thus the chance to shape the makeup of the federal bench.

The geographic design of the federal courts strongly shapes the nature of Senate involvement in selecting federal judges. Because federal trial and appellate-level courts are territorially defined, each federal judgeship is associated with a home state, and new judges are typically drawn from that state. As a result, senators attempt to influence the president's choice of appointees to federal courts in their states. There is considerable variation across the states in how senators handle their role in the selection process. In some states, the more senior senator recommends candidates for White House consideration; in most states, only senators or other elected officials from the president's party participate—a practice stemming from the treatment of judgeships as party patronage starting in the nineteenth century.[2] And in just a few states today—including California and Wisconsin—bipartisan selection commissions generate judicial candidates for White House review. However designed, the selection process affords senators the opportunity to influence the selection of judicial nominees from their states.[3] Presidents are not obliged to heed senators' views in selecting nominees. Although the Constitution prescribes Senate "advice" as well as "consent," nothing in the Constitution requires the president to respect the views of interested senators from the state. In practice, however, judicial nominees must pass muster with the entire chamber, and thus presidents have an incentive to anticipate objections from home state and other interested senators in making appointments. In the past, federal judgeships rarely elicited the interest of senators outside the nominee's home state, and so the views of the home state senators from the president's party were typically sufficient to determine whether or not nominees would be confirmed. Other senators would defer to the views of the home state senator from the president's party, thus establishing the norm of *senatorial courtesy*.[4] Moreover, the Senate Judiciary Committee in the early twentieth century established the "blue slip" to solicit the views of home state senators—regardless of whether they were of the president's party—once nominees were referred to the committee.[5] By institutionalizing home state senators' role in the confirmation process, senators also gained some leverage over the president at the nomination stage. Threats to block a nominee during confirmation could theoretically be used to encourage the president to consider senators' views before making an appointment.

By the early twentieth century, the modern process for judicial selection had been shaped. Because in the past judicial selection has rarely elicited national attention, and because Senate nominations have only occasionally triggered open conflict, the received wisdom emphasizes the cooperative relationship between presidents and senators in shaping the federal bench. Senate observers have often said that the president merely defers to the views of the home state senators from his party when selecting judges for the nation's trial courts, the U.S. District Courts. Senators themselves fuel such perceptions of the process. As Sen. Phil Gramm, R-Texas, once boasted, "I'm given the power to make the appointment. . . . The people elected me to do that."[6] Presidents are said to be less likely to defer to senators over the selection of appellate judges for the U.S. Circuit Courts of Appeals. Nevertheless, even here the process frequently reflects cooperation between home state senators and the White House.

Despite the conventional wisdom that cooperation is the rule, trends in the nomination and confirmation process suggest otherwise. Figure 1 shows the increasing length of time it takes a president to make a nomination for a vacant seat on the bench.[7] The amount of time it takes for the president to make a nomination surely reflects in large part the degree of disagreement over who should serve on the bench. The recent and marked increase in how long it takes to select nominees confirms recent charges that the process of advice and consent is newly politicized.

An examination of the confirmation process shows a similar pattern. The Senate took, on average, just one month to confirm judicial nominees during President Ronald Reagan's first term. By the end of President Bill Clinton's second term, the wait had increased on average fivefold for district court

Figure 1. Length of Nomination Process for Judicial Nominees:
Mean Number of Days, by Congress, between
Vacancy and Nomination, 1947–1998

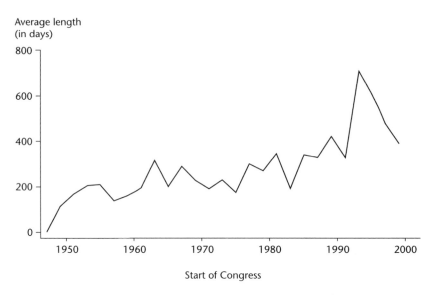

Source: Data compiled from Final Legislative and Executive Calendars, Senate Judiciary Committee, 80th–105th Congresses.

nominees and sevenfold for appellate court nominees. At least a fourth of Clinton's judicial nominees in the 106th Congress (1999–2000) waited more than six months to be confirmed, including U.S. District Court Judge Richard Paez, who had waited nearly four years to be confirmed to the U.S. Court of Appeals for the Ninth Circuit. Confirmation delay continued to increase under President George W. Bush, reaching a record for appellate court nominees in the 107th Congress (2001–2002).

Still, delays weathered by recent presidents in securing confirmation of their nominees reflect more than Clinton's polarized relations with a Republican Senate or Bush's polarized relations with a Democratic Senate. Delays in the confirmation process were considerable in the mid-1980s, when Reagan saw Democratic Senates take, on average, nearly four months to confirm his judicial nominees. Even during a rare episode of unified Democratic control during 1993 and 1994, the Senate took an average of three months to confirm the majority party's nominees.

It would be a mistake to conclude that recent confirmation delays are entirely an aberration from the Senate's traditional mode of advice and consent. During Eisenhower's last term, for example, the Democratic Senate averaged four months to confirm the president's judicial nominees. Parallel to the foot-dragging that has occurred in recent years, it sometimes took the Democratic Senate led by Lyndon Johnson longer than seven months to conclude action on nominees slated by Eisenhower for vacancies on the federal bench. Although confirmation delay may be especially pronounced in recent years, disagreement between the president and Senate over federal judges has historical precedent.

The roots of today's impasse over federal judges are also visible in confirmation rates for judicial nominees. In Figure 2, a sharp decline in the rate of confirmation for district and appellate court appointees is quite striking. A perfect 100 percent of appellate court nominees were confirmed in the 1950s, but less than 40 percent were confirmed in the 107th Congress (2001–2002). Although confirmation rates for trial court nominees are quite variable, the fates of these lower court nominees roughly parallel the experience of appellate court nominees before the Senate. Overall, the data support the notion that the Senate confirmation process has markedly changed over the past ten years. Oddly enough, although the White House now spends longer than ever vetting potential federal judges, the chance of confirmation is at a fifty-year low. Still, it is important to remember that polarization of the process is not entirely new. Troubled waters for judicial nominees were pronounced as early as the early 1970s, no doubt reflecting partisan and ideological disagreements between President Richard Nixon and a Democratic Senate.

The Politics of Advice and Consent

How do we account for the Senate's uneven performance in confirming federal judges? Why were nominees of the past decade particularly likely to be denied a seat on the federal bench, and why does it take so long for the Senate to render its decision? Five forces are at the root of the difficulties presidents face in securing confirmation of judicial nominees. First and foremost are ideological forces: the array of policy views across the three branches affects the probability of confirmation. Second, partisan forces matter: political contests between the president and the opposing Senate party help account for the Senate's treatment of judicial nominees. Third, institutional rules and practices in the Senate shape the likelihood of confirmation. Fourth, presidential capital and resources may matter. And finally, temporal forces shape the Senate's treatment of potential judges: the congressional calendar, electoral cycles, and historical changes in the importance of the federal bench combine to affect the fate of the president's nominees. We explore each of the forces in turn.

Figure 2. Confirmation Rates for Judicial Nominees, 1947–2002

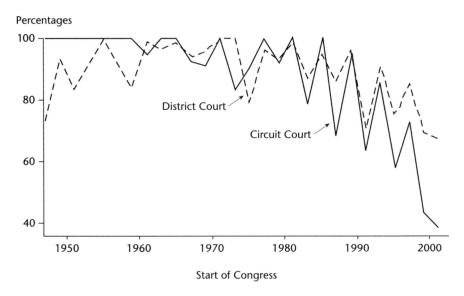

Percentages

District Court

Circuit Court

Start of Congress

Sources: Data compiled from Final Legislative and Executive Calendars, Senate Judiciary Committee, 80th–105th Congresses. Data for 106th and 107th Congresses compiled from United States Senate Committee on the Judiciary Web site, http://judiciary.senate.gov.

Partisan and Ideological Forces

Partisan and ideological forces are of course inextricably linked in the contemporary Congress as the two legislative parties have diverged ideologically in recent decades. Not surprisingly then, pundits assessing the Senate's treatment of Clinton's nominees have typically pointed to poisoned relations between conservative Republicans and Clinton. It was often suggested that personal, partisan, and ideological antagonisms between Clinton and far-right conservatives led Republican senators to delay even the most highly qualified nominees. Democrats' obstruction of several of Bush's nominees in the 108th Congress (2003–2004) was similarly attributed to partisan pique, as liberal Democrats criticized Bush's tendency to nominate extremely conservative (and presumably Republican) judges.

Partisan politics may affect the process of advice and consent more broadly in the guise of divided party government. Because judges have lifetime tenure and the capacity to make lasting decisions on the shape of public law, senators have good cause to scrutinize the views of all potential federal judges. Because presidents overwhelmingly seek to appoint judges of the president's party, Senate scrutiny of judicial nominees should be particularly intense when different parties control the White House and the Senate. It is not a surprise, then, that nominees considered during a period of divided control take significantly longer to be confirmed than those nominated during unified control. Judicial nominees are also less likely to be confirmed during divided government: Over the past fifty-five years, the Senate has confirmed an average of 94 percent of district and appellate court nominees considered during periods of unified control but roughly only 80 percent of nominees during divided government.

Partisan control of the branches is particularly likely to affect the course of nominations when presidents seek to fill vacancies on appellate courts whose judges are evenly balanced between the two parties. [As the ideological distance increases between the president and the opposing party (regardless of whether it is the majority in the Senate), the probability of swift confirmation goes down. . . . Efforts by majority party Republicans on the Senate Judiciary Committee during Clinton's second term to delay hearings on his nominees are a prime example of how ideological disagreement between the parties can lead to long delays in the confirmation process.] Because most appellate court cases are heard by randomly generated three-judge panels, nominations to courts that are evenly divided are likely to have a more significant impact on the law's development, compared with appointments to courts that lean decidedly in one ideological direction. Senate majorities are especially reluctant to confirm nominees to such courts when the appointment would tip the court balance in the favor of a president from the opposing party. One of the hardest hit courts is the Sixth Circuit Court of Appeals, straddling populous Midwest states such as Michigan and Ohio. In recent years, a quarter of the bench has been vacant, including one seat declared a judicial emergency after sitting empty for five years. Moreover, the Sixth Circuit has been precariously balanced between the parties, with the bench roughly half-filled by judges appointed by Democrats. The Senate slowdown on appointments to that circuit during the Clinton administration was likely motivated by its strategic importance, since confirming Clinton's nominees would have eliminated the opportunity for a future Republican president to move a balanced court into the conservative camp. Similarly, once Bush took office, the two Michigan senators (both Democrats) went to great lengths to prevent the Senate from taking action on Bush's conservative nominees for that court. In short, partisan dynamics—fueled in part by ideological conflict—strongly shape the Senate's conduct of advice and consent, making it difficult for presidents to stack the federal courts as they would prefer.

Institutional Forces

Partisan and ideological forces do not, of course, operate in a vacuum. The process of advice and consent is equally shaped by an array of Senate rules that distribute power in a unique way across the institution. Thus, to explain the fate of the president's judicial nominees, we need to know something about not only the partisan and ideological context, but also the institutional arena in which senators dispense their advice and consent. Senators are wise to the ways in which Senate rules and practices may be exploited in the confirmation process. Understanding how senators motivated by policy and political interests exploit pivotal rules and practices is essential for explaining the outcomes of advice and consent.

A prime institutional step for any nominee is securing approval from the Senate Judiciary Committee. Two significant hurdles await judicial nominees in that committee. First, by tradition, senators from the home state of each judicial nominee cast the first judgment on him or her. As suggested above, the veto power of home state senators is institutionalized in Judiciary panel procedures. Both of the state's senators are asked their views about judicial nominees from their home state pending before the committee. Senators can return the "blue slip," demarking their support of or objection to the nominee, or they can refuse to return the blue slip altogether—an action signaling opposition. One negative blue slip from a home state senator traditionally was sufficient to block further action on a nominee. As the process has become more polarized in recent years, committee chairs have been tempted to ignore objections from minority party senators. At a minimum, blue slips today weigh heavily in the committee chair's assessment concerning whether, when, and how to proceed on a nominee, but senators' objections do not necessarily prevent the committee from proceeding.

Historically, large ideological differences between the president and the home state senator have led to longer confirmation proceedings than normal for appellate court nominees, suggesting the power of home state senators to affect panel proceedings. Conversely, the strong support of one's home state senator is essential in navigating the committee successfully. Given the often fractured attention of the Senate and the willingness of senators to heed the preferences of the home state senator, having a strong advocate in the Senate with an interest in seeing the nomination proceed is critical in smoothing the way for nominees.

Second, the experience of judicial nominees in committee drives home the importance of Senate rules that grant considerable procedural powers to committee chairs. Because of the generally low salience of most judicial nominations, the Senate largely defers to the Judiciary Committee's judgment on whether and when to proceed with a nomination. Discretion over the fate of each nominee is held by the committee chair, who holds the power to convene hearings and to schedule a committee vote to report a nomination to the chamber. Not surprisingly, then, ideological differences between the panel chair and the president show a discernible effect on the course of judicial nominations. The greater the ideological differences between the president and the chair of the Judiciary panel, the longer it takes for the committee to act.

Once approved by committee, a nomination has a second broad institutional hurdle to clear: making it onto the Senate's crowded agenda. By rule and precedent, both majority and minority party coalitions can delay nominations after they clear committee. Because the presiding officer of the chamber gives the majority leader priority in being recognized to speak on the Senate floor, the majority leader has the upper hand in setting the chamber's agenda. This is especially so given his control of the executive session agenda, the arena in which nominations are called up for confirmation. When the president's party controls the Senate, this means that nominations are usually confirmed more quickly; under divided control, nominations can be kept off the floor by the majority leader. Such procedural advantages clearly enhance the importance of support from the majority leader in shaping the fate of presidential appointees.

The majority leader's discretion over the executive session agenda is not wielded without challenge, however: nominations can be filibustered. The chance that a nomination might be filibustered usually motivates the majority leader to seek unanimous consent of the full chamber before bringing a nomination before the Senate. Such consultation between the two parties means that nominations are unlikely to clear the Senate without the endorsement of the minority party.

The de facto requirement of minority party assent suggests that the party opposing the president retains significant power to affect the fate of nominees, even when the opposing party does not control the Senate. As policy differences increase between the president and the opposing party, that party is more likely to exercise its power to delay nominees. Given the high degree of polarization between the two parties today, it is not surprising that judicial nominations have become such a flash point for the parties. As we discuss below, when Democrats lost control of the Senate after the 2002 elections, they turned to a new tactic to block objectionable nominees: the filibuster. Although in the past Senate majorities have periodically had to fight to close debate on judicial nominees via cloture, successful filibusters are without modern precedent for nominees to lower courts. Such extreme tactics clearly result from the increased polarization between the two parties and the rising salience of the federal courts across the interest group community. Much of the variation in the fates of judicial nominees before the Senate is thus seemingly driven by ideologically motivated players and parties in both the executive and legislative branches who exploit the rules of the game in an effort to shape the makeup of the federal bench.

Presidential Forces

Presidents are not powerless in trying to shape the outcome of advice and consent. Although the president lacks a formal means of pushing nominations through to confirmation, presidents have a few tools that may affect the fates of their appointees. . . . The president's ability to encourage confirmation may . . . be shaped by his popularity with the public. Presidents who are highly regarded tend to store up political capital that can be used to increase the chances of confirmation for judicial nominees. All told, presidents have some influence over the speed of advice and consent, but their influence likely is exercised only at the margins of the legislative arena.

Temporal Forces

Finally, it is important to consider how secular or cyclical elements of the political calendar may shape the fate of judicial nominees. It is often suggested, for example, that extreme delays encountered by judicial nominees in recent years may be a natural consequence of an approaching presidential election. For example, with control of both the Senate and the White House up for grabs in November 2000, it was expected that Republican senators would approach their duties of advice and consent with extreme caution. Rather than confirming an outgoing Democratic president's last judicial nominees, pragmatic politics would dictate, Republicans should save these lifetime appointments for a president of their own party. Not surprisingly, in the run-up to the 2000 election, forty judicial nominees remained in limbo. Most of them had not even received a hearing before the Senate Judiciary panel.

There is certainly some truth to the idea that an approaching presidential election affects the politics of advice and consent. Over the past fifty years, Senate treatment of judicial nominations submitted or pending during a presidential election year has been significantly different than its treatment of other judicial nominations. First, the Senate has historically taken longer to confirm nominees pending before a presidential election than those submitted earlier in a president's term. Second, and more notably, presidential-election-year nominees are significantly less likely to be confirmed. For all judicial nominations submitted between 1947 and 2002, appointments pending in the Senate before a presidential election were 25 percent less likely to be confirmed than ones submitted earlier in a president's term.

All the same, presidents can also benefit from the political calendar. Strategically timing referral of a nomination is essential, as nominations made earlier in a president's term tend to move more swiftly. Nominations also move more swiftly when the Senate's confirmation load is lighter. The fewer nominees pending, the quicker a nominee will sail to confirmation.

Finally, and perhaps most important, the broad belief that the confirmation process has become more protracted over time is confirmed by the evidence in Figures 1 and 2, which shows the increasing amount of time it takes for presidents to select nominees and the declining rate of confirmation for both levels of the federal bench. As we explore below, such a secular increase in the length of the advice and consent process may result from the rising importance of the federal courts as policymaking players. Interest groups and politicians frequently and increasingly have used the federal courts as a means of resolving political disputes.[8] The result, we suspect, has been increased concern among political actors about the makeup of the federal bench and thus a heightened salience of the confirmation process beyond the affected court and state. . . .

The New Wars of Judicial Selection

Partisan conflict over advice and consent came to a head in March 2004 when the Senate Democratic Caucus vowed to block all executive and judicial nominations.[9] At issue were the president's decision to grant recess appointments to two of the judicial nominees filibustered by the Democrats and the White House's refusal to nominate Democratic choices for several bipartisan commissions. Such actions, Minority Leader Tom Daschle, D-S.D., charged on the Senate floor, "not only poison the nomination process, but they strike at the heart of the principle of checks and balances that is one of the pillars of the American democracy."[10] Democrats said they would lift the blockade after a couple of dozen Democrats had been appointed to bipartisan boards and commissions and after Bush had guaranteed that he would not make any more recess appointments.

Although that particular blockade was lifted two months later, the broader breakdown of the nomination process in 2004 suggests that the politics of judicial selection have changed markedly in recent years: the character of the process seems qualitatively different today than in the past. To be sure, not every nominee experiences intense opposition, as Democrats acquiesced to over a hundred of Bush's judicial appointees. But why has the process become so intensely polarized in recent years? The changing face of Senate obstruction in the battles over judges bears a deeper look.

Perhaps most striking about the new war over advice and consent is its visibility beyond the halls of the Senate. The rising salience of federal judgeships is visible on several fronts. First, intense interest in the selection of federal judges is no longer limited to the home state senators. Second, negative blue slips from home state senators no longer guarantee that a nomination will be killed, as recent Judiciary panel chairs have been hesitant to accord such influence to objections from the minority party. Third, recorded floor votes are now the norm for confirmation of appellate court judges, as nominations are of increased importance to groups outside the institution. And fourth, nominations now draw the attention of strategists within both political parties—as evidenced by the president's focus on judicial nominations in stumping for Republican Senate candidates in the 2002 midterm elections.

How do we account for the rising salience of federal judgeships to actors in and out of the Senate? It is tempting to claim that the activities of organized interests after the 1987 Supreme Court confirmation battle over Robert Bork are responsible. But interest groups have kept a close eye on judicial selection for quite some time. Both liberal and conservative groups were involved periodically from the late 1960s into the 1980s. And in 1984, liberal groups under the umbrella of the Alliance for Justice commenced systematic monitoring of judicial appointments, as had the conservative Judicial Reform Project of the Free Congress Foundation earlier in the decade. Although interest group tactics may have fanned the fires over judicial selection in recent years, the introduction of new blocking tactics in the Senate developed long after groups had become active in the process.[11] Outside groups may encourage senators to take more aggressive stands against judicial nominees, but by and large Senate opposition reflects senators' concerns about the policy impact of judges on the federal bench.

Rather than attribute the state of judicial selection to the lobbying of outside groups, we believe that the politics of judicial selection have been indelibly shaped by two concurrent trends. First, the two political parties are more ideologically opposed today than they have been for the past few decades. . . . Ideological differences between the parties encourage senators to exploit the rules of the game to their party's advantage.

Second, it is important to remember that if the courts were of little importance to the two parties, then polarized relations would matter little to senators and presidents in conducting advice and consent. However, the federal courts today are intricately involved in the interpretation and enforcement of federal law, particularly as the Supreme Court has limited its docket in recent years. . . . Intense ideological disagreement, coupled with the rising importance of a closely balanced federal bench, has brought combatants in the wars of advice and consent to new tactics and new crises, as the two parties struggle to shape the future of the federal courts. . . .

There are few signs that the wars of advice and consent will abate anytime soon. Reflecting on the Democrats' filibusters, Lindsay Graham, R-S.C., observed that "if you don't think down the road it will be answered in kind by the Republican Party, I think you are very naïve."[12] The new tactics, Graham warned, would become the norm. "Payback," Graham aptly summed up, "is hell." So long as ideological divisions lead senators to disagree over the makeup of the federal bench, and so long as the courts remain central in the interpretation of public law, battles over judicial selection are unlikely to go away. More likely, they will intensify—especially when the next vacancy on the Supreme Court occurs. Unless the president selects someone with moderate ideological stripes, past battles over confirming federal judges will pale in comparison. The stakes of who sits on the federal bench are simply too high for combatants in the battles of advice and consent to view the contest from the sidelines. Policy motivations and institutional opportunities will continue to shape the ideological character of the federal bench.

NOTES

1. For a discussion of the Framers' intentions regarding "advice and consent," see John Ferling, "The Senate and Federal Judges: The Intent of the Founding Fathers," *Capitol Studies* 2 (winter 1974): 57–70.

2. On the emergence of federal judgeships as patronage, see Kermit Hall, *The Politics of Justice* (Lincoln: University of Nebraska Press, 1979).

3. The influence of home state senators in the selection of nominees is probed in Sarah A. Binder and Forrest Maltzman, "The Limits of Senatorial Courtesy," *Legislative Studies Quarterly* 24 (February 2004): 5–22; and Donald Songer, Thomas Hansford, and Tajuana Massie, "The Timing of Presidential Nominations to the Lower Federal Courts," *Political Research Quarterly* (March 2004): 145–154.

4. The logic of senatorial courtesy is explored in Tonja Jacobi, "The Senatorial Courtesy Game: Explaining the Norm of Informal Vetoes in 'Advice and Consent' Nominations," *Legislative Studies Quarterly* (forthcoming).

5. See Sarah A. Binder, "Origins of the Senate 'Blue Slip': The Creation of Senate Norms" (paper presented at the annual meeting of the Midwest Political Science Association, Chicago, April 2004).

6. As cited in Robert A. Carp and Ronald Stidham, *Judicial Process in America*, 2nd ed. (Washington, D.C.: CQ Press, 1993), 232.

7. The data include all nominees for the federal District Courts and Circuit Courts of Appeal eventually confirmed by the Senate.

8. See Robert Kagan, *Adversarial Legalism* (Cambridge: Harvard University Press, 2001); Thomas F. Burke, *Lawyers, Lawsuits, and Legal Rights: The Battle over Litigation in American Society* (Berkeley: University of California Press, 2004); and Gordon Silverstein, *How Law Kills Politics* (New York: Norton, forthcoming).

9. See Paul Kane, "Nominations Put on Ice," *Roll Call,* March 29, 2004.

10. Sen. Tom Daschle, "Politicization of the Nomination Process," *Congressional Record,* March 26, 2004, S3200.

11. Recent tactics of two leading interest groups are detailed in Bob Davis and Robert S. Greenberger, "Two Old Foes Plot Tactics in Battle over Judgeships," *Wall Street Journal,* March 2, 2004.

12. As cited in Jennifer A. Dlouhy, "Judicial War far From Over," *CQ Weekly,* November 15, 2003, 2824.

The Voting Behavior of George W. Bush's Judges: How Sharp a Turn to the Right?

Robert A. Carp, Kenneth L. Manning, and Ronald Stidham

In recent years politics in Washington has become as intensely partisan and polarized ideologically as at any time in the past half-century. Partisanship periodically flares up in its most virulent form during divided government when the Senate deliberates confirmation of the president's judicial nominees. Democratic President Clinton complained continually that the Republican Senate was not giving his nominees a fair shake. Similarly, President Bush has blasted Democratic obstructionism. In this essay, the authors contribute a very important fact to our understanding of these political imbroglios: President Bush's appointments to the federal district courts appear in their decisions to be among the most ideologically homogeneous—in this instance, conservative—of any president's appointees.

WHAT IS THE ideological direction of the judges whom President George W. Bush has appointed during his first five years in office? Until now most of the information about this question has been anecdotal in nature or has come from quantitative studies with relatively small numbers.[1] Critics of the president, often liberal Democrats, have suggested that Bush's judicial appointees are ultraconservatives who are hostile to the interests of racial minorities, women, the environment, personal privacy, and so on. As vice president of the liberal People for the American Way, Elliot Mincberg sees Bush's judgeships

as a way that the White House can continue to appeal to and mobilize the far right base which sometimes may be disappointed with the president on taxes or on spending or on other kinds of issues. There are many disparate parts of the far right base. There's the more libertarian right, there's the religious right, there's others. All of them seem to be unified on the notion of, "We want judges and justices like Scalia and Thomas," which, of course, has been the President's slogan and mantra.[2]

Source: This piece is an original essay commissioned for this volume.

President Bush and his supporters clearly have a very different view of the men and women he is selecting for federal judicial posts. Former assistant attorney general Viet Dinh conceded that the administration was eschewing candidates who might appear to be "judicial activists," but he asserted,

> We are extremely clear in following the President's mandate that we should not, and do not employ any [political-ideological] litmus test on any one particular issue, because in doing so we would be guilty of politicizing the judiciary[,] and that is as detrimental as if we were unable to identify men and women who would follow the law rather than legislate from the bench.[3]

In this chapter we seek to shed some light on whether or not President Bush is making ideologically based appointments and whether his judicial cohort is deciding cases in the manner anticipated by most court observers. We have organized the chapter around two basic questions: What might we expect of the Bush administration's potential to have an ideological impact on the federal courts? and What do the empirical data tell us so far about the way that the Bush cohort has been deciding cases during the five years of his presidency?

Judicial scholars have identified four general factors that determine whether chief executives can obtain a judiciary that is sympathetic to their political values and attitudes: the degree of the president's commitment to making ideologically based appointments; the number of vacancies to be filled; the level of the chief executive's political clout; and the ideological climate that the new judicial appointees enter.[4]

Presidential Support for Ideologically Based Appointments

One key aspect of the success of chief executives in appointing a federal judiciary that mirrors their own political beliefs is the depth of their commitment to doing so. Some presidents may be content merely to fill the federal bench with party loyalists and pay little attention to their nominees' specific ideologies. Some may consider ideological factors when appointing Supreme Court justices but may not regard them as important for trial and appellate judges. Other presidents may discount ideologically grounded appointments because they themselves tend to be nonideological. Still others may place factors such as past political loyalty ahead of ideology in selecting judges.

For example, Harry Truman had strong political views, but when selecting judges he placed loyalty to himself ahead of the candidate's overall political orientation. On the other hand, Ronald Reagan and Lyndon Johnson are examples of presidents who had strong ideological beliefs on many issues and took great pains to select judges who shared those beliefs.

What do we know about whether President George W. Bush is committed to making ideologically based judicial appointments? The evidence suggests that the president is indeed using ideology as a basis for his nominations. Recall, for example that just prior to the election of 2000 George W. Bush publicly expressed admiration for Justice Antonin Scalia, who is one of the most conservative members of the Supreme Court.[5] Justice Scalia usually interprets the Constitution as restraining congressional power to regulate commerce and seeks to limit the expansion of many Bill of Rights freedoms (generally conservative positions).

In May 2001, after making his first batch of judicial nominations, President Bush made it clear that his judges will adhere to his conservative judicial philosophy: "Every judge I appoint will be a person who clearly understands the role of a judge is to interpret the law, not to legislate from the bench," he said.[6] And early in 2003, Bush's then assistant attorney general said in an interview, "We want to ensure that the president's mandate to us that the men and women who are nominated by him to be on the bench have his vision of the proper role of the judiciary. That is, a judiciary that will follow the law, not make the law. . . ." [7]

Surely there is no doubt that judicial appointments have commanded a key and central portion of President Bush's domestic agenda. As associate White House counsel Dabney Friedrich noted, "It is one of the president's most important domestic priorities. He has given a great deal of attention to judgeships over the past four years, and he will continue to do so." [8] Furthermore one Republican Senate aide observed that Bush's judicial policy agenda has been taken up by the Republican Senate leadership. The aide said that "it has been discussed at the vast majority of leadership meetings which are every week. It has come up at the vast majority of Policy Committee meetings over in the Capitol. And every week we are in session we go to lunch with all the Republican senators and it always comes up. It is always an issue, a constant issue." [9]

Still, as always, actions speak louder than words. So rather than quote the president and his spokesmen about what kind of judges they say they want to appoint, it is probably best to look at the backgrounds and records of the men and women they have already selected. In his thorough study of the lower court judges President Bush appointed during his first term in office, Sheldon Goldman and his fellow researchers found a group of individuals who are highly competent and comparatively diverse in their backgrounds. Still, the picture is of a cohort with highly conservative credentials and backgrounds, many of whom were selected from and vetted by the conservative Federalist Society.[10] As for the president's most visible judicial candidates, his nominees to the U.S. Supreme Court, their conservative backgrounds and values are incontrovertible. Not counting Harriet Miers, who withdrew from the nomination process early in the game, both John Roberts and Samuel Alito have long and well-established voting records that strongly recommended them to their conservative supporters.[11]

In sum, the evidence is very compelling that President Bush does possess a strong desire to make ideologically based nominations to the federal judiciary and that he is prepared to spend considerable political capital to secure their confirmation.

The Number of Vacancies to be Filled

A second element affecting the capacity of chief executives to establish a policy link between themselves and the judiciary is the number of appointments available to them. The more judges a president can select, the greater his potential to put his stamp on the judicial branch. For example, George Washington's influence on the Supreme Court was significant because he was able to nominate ten individuals to the High Court. Jimmy Carter's was nil because no vacancies occurred during his term as president.

The number of appointment opportunities depends on several factors: how many judicial vacancies are inherited from the previous administration (Clinton, for example, was left with a whopping one hundred district and trial court vacancies—14 percent of the total—by his predecessor, George H. W. Bush), how many judges and justices die or resign during the president's term, how long the president serves, and whether Congress passes legislation that significantly increases the number of judgeships.

Historically, the last factor seems to have been the most important in influencing the number of judgeships available, and politics in its most basic form permeates that process. A study of proposals in thirteen Congresses to create new judgeships tested the following two hypotheses: (1) "Proposals to add new federal judges are more likely to pass if the same party controls the Presidency and Congress than if different parties are in power," and (2) "Proposals to add new federal judges are more likely to pass during the first two years of the president's term than during the second two years." The study author concluded that his "data support both hypotheses—proposals to add new judges are about five times more likely to pass if the same party controls the presidency and Congress than if different parties control, and about four times more likely to pass during the first two years of the president's term than during the second two years." He then noted that these findings serve "to remind us that not only is judicial selection a political process, but so is the creation of judicial posts." [12]

When George W. Bush assumed the presidency he inherited 82 vacancies, quite a sizable number by historical standards. The reason was largely the bitter partisan politics that had prevailed during the Clinton administration, which caused many of Clinton's judicial nominees to go without Senate confirmation. A second factor in the equation is that judges are dying or retiring from the bench at about the same rate during the Bush administration as during previous ones. By the end of 2005 President Bush had appointed 182 individuals to the federal district courts, or just over 27 percent of the total. (At the same time there were an additional 37 vacancies on the district courts and 14 nominations pending.) By January 1, 2006, the president had made 41 appointments to the courts of appeals, about 23 percent of the total. (There were also 14 vacancies and 5 pending nominations.) If the present trend continues, by the end of his two terms President Bush will have appointed about 40 percent of the total lower federal judiciary—a very substantial impact, although not an unprecedented one for a two-term president.

What about the possibility of Congress passing a new omnibus judges bill that would give the president the opportunity to pack the judiciary with men and women who share his values? Such an enactment greatly enhanced Presidents Kennedy and Carter's ideological impacts on the judiciary. Unfortunately for President Bush, he had had no such luck. It is true that in 2001 the Judicial Conference of the United States recommended to Congress that it create fifty-four new district and appellate judgeships. It also called for "permanent authorization" of seven previously established, temporary district judgeships. However, the politically divided Congress did not oblige. Congress refused to create any new appellate judgeships, established only eight new district court judgeships, and granted permanent authorization to only four temporary positions.[13] More recently, however, the president's prospects in this realm have started to look up. There is currently a bill pending in Congress, which experts believe has some real chance of success, that would create 9 permanent and 3 temporary circuit judgeships and 44 permanent and 12 temporary district judgeships. This measure also has the backing of the U.S. Judicial Conference.[14] If these legislative proposals are enacted into law, President Bush would appoint an additional 5 percent of the lower court judges in the United States.

So what is one to conclude about this second predictor of whether President Bush will potentially have a substantial impact on the ideological direction of the federal judiciary—the number of vacancies he can fill? The data suggest that in terms of pure numbers the president is having about an average set of opportunities to make an ideological impact on the federal bench. That means that after his second term almost half of the federal judges will likely bear the Bush stamp—a factor of no little consequence.

The President's Political Clout

Presidential skill in overcoming political obstacles is also a factor. The U.S. Senate can be a stumbling block. If the Senate is controlled by the president's party, the White House will find it much easier to secure confirmations. Sometimes, when the opposition is in power in the Senate, presidents are forced into political horse-trading to get their nominees approved. For example, in summer 1999 President Clinton was obliged to make a deal with the conservative chairman of the Senate Judiciary Committee, Orrin Hatch. To obtain smooth sailing for at least ten of Clinton's judicial nominations that were blocked in the Senate, the president agreed to nominate a Utah Republican, Ted Stewart, who was vigorously opposed by liberals and environmental groups.

The Senate Judiciary Committee can be another roadblock. Some presidents have been more adept than others at easing their candidates through the jagged rocks of the Judiciary Committee rapids. Both Presidents Kennedy and Johnson, for example, had to deal with the formidable James Eastland of Mississippi, then committee chairman, but only Johnson seems to have had the political adroitness to get most of his liberal nominees approved. Kennedy lacked that skill. Clinton, despite his considerable political acumen, was never able to parlay those skills into much clout with the conservative and often hostile Senate Judiciary Committee.

Finally, the president's personal popularity is another element in the political power formula. Chief executives who are well liked by the public and who command respect among opinion makers in the news media, the rank-and-file of their political party, and the leaders of the nation's major interest groups are much more likely to prevail over any forces that seek to thwart their judicial nominations.

How would we assess President Bush's capacity to make an ideological impact on the federal judiciary in light of this "political clout" variable? Immediately after the 2000 election, the Senate was evenly divided between the two political parties, but with Vice President Cheney available to break any tie vote, the Republicans were in control of the chamber. In principle, that should have enhanced President Bush's ability to obtain confirmation of judicial nominees of like-minded values. But soon after the election a series of events occurred that greatly clouded the scenario. First, the Democrats regained control of the Senate when Vermont senator Jim Jeffords unexpectedly left the Republican Party caucus. All legislative action came to a halt for several weeks as the struggle to reorganize the Senate became the major focus of attention. Equally important, after Jeffords's defection control of the Judiciary Committee went to the Democrats. The new committee chair, Sen. Patrick Leahy, was in no frame of mind to become a rubber stamp for President Bush's judicial nominees. Then came the terrorist attacks on September 11, 2001, and public and legislative attention became riveted on antiterrorism legislation and national security.

At the end of President Bush's first two years in office, his scorecard showed mixed results. On the downside, two of his nominees, Priscilla Owen and Charles Pickering, received negative votes from the Judiciary Committee, and the committee returned the names of twenty-eight other district and appellate court candidates to the president without taking any action. But the news was by no means all bad for the president. None of his judicial nominations was defeated on the floor of the Senate, and ninety-nine individuals, presumably all staunch conservatives, obtained approval by the Judiciary Committee and the full Senate.

Next, two series of events produced countervailing effects on the president's political clout in the Senate. On the positive side for President Bush, the Republicans regained control of the Senate, and thus control of the Judiciary Committee, in the midterm elections of 2002. The GOP retained control (and the president's reelection bid was successful) in 2004.

On the other hand, during the final year of his first term Senate Democrats were successful in blocking a number of the president's appellate court nominations by use of the filibuster. The Republicans, with a bare majority in the Senate, did not have the votes to cut off debate. President Bush retaliated by using recess appointments on two occasions, infuriating Democrats. In May 2004 a deal of sorts was cut between the White House and the Senate. Under it the president agreed to make no more recess appointments during the remainder of his first term, which ended January 20, 2005. "In return, Democrats, who had been holding up action on all of Bush's judicial choices since March to protest the recess appointments, agreed to allow votes on 25 mostly noncontroversial nominations to district and appeals posts over the next several weeks." [15] Then in spring 2005 there formed in the Senate what was dubbed the "Gang of Fourteen," a bipartisan group of moderates who (temporarily at least) ended the filibuster fight over the aforementioned appellate court nominations. They brought about an agreement that permitted some of the president's most controversial judges to take their seats on the appellate courts and denied Republicans the opportunity to exercise the so-called nuclear option of altering Senate rules to bar filibusters on judicial nominations. According to the agreement, the pivotal Gang of Fourteen would support a filibuster only in "extraordinary circumstances," a term left for the senators to define in their own way.

A second negative for the president was that after the elections of 2004 the chairmanship of the Senate Judiciary Committee went from the highly conservative Republican Orrin Hatch to middle-of-the-road Republican Arlen Specter of Pennsylvania. Coming from a state that voted for John Kerry in 2004, and with a sustained record as a moderate rather than a staunch conservative, Specter made it clear that as committee chair he did not intend to be a rubber stamp for the Bush administration. For example, immediately after President's Bush's reelection Specter said, "When you talk about judges who would change the right of a woman to choose, who'd overturn *Roe versus Wade,* I think that is unlikely. . . . . And I have said that bluntly during the course of the campaign, that *Roe versus Wade* was inviolate." That led the founder of the nonprofit Christian organization Focus on the Family, James Dobson, to comment that Senator Specter "is a big-time problem." [16] President Bush may well have similar thoughts about the chairman of the Judiciary Committee.

Yet a third negative for President Bush has been his declining popularity in the public opinion polls ever since his narrow reelection. The enduring war in Iraq has become more and more of a drag on the president's public support, and a variety of other factors have cost Bush support in the polls, as well (e.g., the apparent inaction and impotence of the government in the face of Hurricane Katrina, rising gasoline prices, charges of corruption and improprieties against various Republican members of Congress and the executive branch, and so on). By early 2006 some 54 percent of the American public disapproved of the way the president was handling his job.[17] Moderate members of the Senate and the Judiciary Committee are not oblivious to these polls; they can see that there might be little or no political cost to them from opposing the president's judicial nominees.

Perhaps the real test of the president's political clout in this area is his record in appointing members of the U.S. Supreme Court. When President Bush nominated the conservative but competent John Roberts to be chief justice of the United States, opposition was minimal and the president prevailed. Likewise, when the president nominated the equally conservative but somewhat more controversial Samuel Alito to the high Court, he prevailed. In the interim, however, when President Bush nominated White House counsel Harriet Miers to the Court, the result was quite different. Charged with being a mere political crony of the president and inexperienced in judicial matters, Miers wilted under a barrage of criticism from both liberals and conservatives. Not only did the president not possess the clout to push her nomination through, but Miers withdrew from the nomination process before she could even be considered by the Senate Judiciary Committee.

What, then, are we to conclude about this third determinant of whether a president will be successful in making ideologically based appointments—his political clout? Despite some notable setbacks, President Bush has enjoyed considerable success in securing the confirmation of most of his conservative judicial nominees. The only times when he has run into serious trouble have been when his nominees promised to be so extreme that they roused the opposition

of Senate moderates (e.g., the Gang of Fourteen) or when they lacked the traditional measure of judicial competence.

The Judicial Climate the New Judges Enter

A final matter affects the capacity of chief executives to secure a federal judiciary that reflects their own political values: the philosophical orientations of
the currently sitting district and appellate court judges, with whom the new
appointees would interact. Because federal judges serve lifetime appointments during good behavior, presidents must accept the composition and
value structure of the judiciary as it exists when they take office. If the existing judiciary already reflects the president's political and legal orientations,
the impact of the new judicial appointees will be immediate and substantial.
However, if the new chief executive faces a trial and appellate judiciary
whose values are radically different from his own, the impact of that president's subsequent judicial appointments will be weaker and slower to materialize. New judges must respect the controlling legal precedents and the
constitutional interpretations that prevail in the judiciary at the time they
enter it, or they risk being overturned by a higher court. That reality may
limit the capacity of a new set of judges to go their own way—at least in the
short run.

President Reagan's impact on the judicial branch continues to be substantial.
By the end of his second term he had appointed an unprecedented 368 federal
judges, 50 percent of those on the bench. When he entered the White House, the
Supreme Court was already teetering to the right because of Richard Nixon's
and Gerald R. Ford's conservative appointments. Although Jimmy Carter's liberal appointees were still serving on trial and appellate benches, Reagan found a
good many conservative Nixon and Ford judges on the bench when he took
office. Thus he had a major role in shaping the entire federal judiciary in his own
conservative image for some time to come. The George H. W. Bush judges had
a much easier time making their impact felt because they entered a judicial realm
wherein well over half of the judges already professed conservative Republican
values.

President Clinton's impact on the judiciary was slower to manifest itself
because his judicial nominees entered an arena in which more than 75 percent
of the trial and appellate court judgeships were held by the appointees of GOP
presidents with very conservative orientations. When George W. Bush entered
the White House, 51 percent of the federal judges had been appointed by
Democratic presidents.

How does this affect President Bush's potential to leave his ideological mark on the composition of the judiciary? When the president first took office, the partisan backgrounds of the judges were balanced with almost mathematical precision: 51 percent of those on the lower federal bench had been appointed by Republican presidents; 49 percent by Democrats. In such a situation, even a slight change in numbers can give one party a controlling edge in the judicial decision-making process and, perhaps more important, in the composition of the policymaking appeals court panels. Evidence that this is so was already compelling at the beginning of President Bush's sixth year in office. First of all, as we entered 2006, Republican control of the lower courts was roughly at the two-thirds level, and of course, seven of the nine members of the U.S. Supreme Court are Republican appointees.[18] Second, turning to the appellate courts, which make important policy decisions and which, at least in principle, oversee the decision making of the trial court judges, by January 2006, of the twelve U.S. circuits (including the District of Columbia Circuit but excluding what is known as the Federal Circuit), the appointees of Republican presidents now have a majority in ten. The Second Circuit is almost evenly split, and only in the Ninth Circuit do appointees of Democratic presidents make up a majority.[19]

In sum, the overall evidence suggests that President Bush should be able to continue to move the federal judiciary in a more conservative direction. He has indicated a clear desire to appoint more conservative jurists, and his Supreme Court appointments are vivid evidence of his commitment. He is filling an average number of new vacancies, although his declining popularity and the looming prospect of Republican losses in the 2006 elections may be clouds on the horizon. Finally, given the narrow balance of the judiciary between Republicans and Democrats at the beginning of his term, President Bush continues to be in a critical position to tilt the ideological balanced in a decidedly conservative direction.

Sources and Definitions

Before we examine the data we have collected, we need to say a word about the data's source, and offer working definitions of the terms "conservative" and "liberal." The data on trial court decisions were taken from a database consisting of more than 75,000 opinions, by almost 1,800 judges, published in the *Federal Supplement* from 1933 through fall 2005. Included in this overall data set were 795 decisions handed down by judges appointed by President George W. Bush.[20] Only those cases that fit easily into one of twenty-eight case types and that contained a clear, underlying liberal-conservative dimension were used. This included cases such as state and federal habeas corpus pleas, labor-management disputes, questions involving the right to privacy, and environmental protection cases. Excluded were cases involving patents, admiralty disputes, and land condemnation hearings. The number of cases not selected was about the same as the number included.

In the realm of civil rights and civil liberties, "liberal" judges would generally take a broadening position; that is, they would seek in their rulings to extend those freedoms. "Conservative" jurists, by contrast, would prefer to limit such rights. For example, in a case in which a government agency wanted to prevent a controversial person from speaking in a public park or at a state university, a liberal judge would be more inclined than a conservative to uphold the right of the would-be speech giver. Or, in a case concerning affirmative action in public higher education, a liberal judge would be more likely to take the side favoring special admissions for minority petitioners.

In the area of government regulation of the economy, liberal judges would probably uphold legislation that benefited working people or the economic underdog. Thus, if the secretary of labor sought an injunction against an employer for paying less than the minimum wage, a liberal judge would be more disposed to endorse the labor secretary's arguments, whereas a conservative judge would tend to side with business, especially big business.

Another broad category of cases often studied by judicial scholars is criminal justice. Liberal judges are, in general, more sympathetic to the motions made by criminal defendants. For instance, in a case in which the accused claimed to have been coerced by the government to make an illegal confession, liberal judges would be more likely than their conservative counterparts to agree that the government had acted improperly.

What the Data Reveal

In Figure 1 we compare the total "liberalism" scores of the judicial cohorts appointed by eight of the most recent chief executives, three Democrats and five Republicans.[21] The data indicate that only 33 percent of the decisions of the George W. Bush jurists have been decided in a liberal direction. This not only makes the Bush team the most conservative among those of the eight most recent presidents, but indeed it is the most conservative number that we have for all American presidents going back to Woodrow Wilson![22] The numbers are certainly more conservative than the scores of Presidents Johnson, Carter, and Clinton are liberal; their appointees' scores were respectively 52 percent, 52 percent, and 45 percent liberal. Bush appointees' decisions are also more right of center than those of his GOP predecessors Nixon, Ford, Reagan, and Bush Sr.,

Figure 1. Decisions Scored as Liberal by Judges Appointed
by the Eight Most Recent Presidents

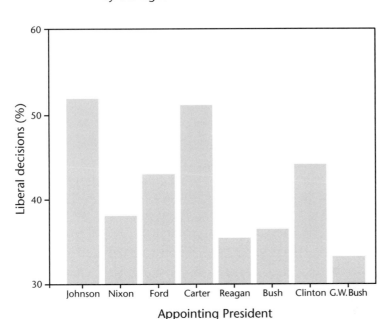

which were respectively 38 percent, 43 percent, 36 percent, and 37 percent.[23] The differences between George W. Bush's judicial cohort and those of his three Republican predecessors are large enough that they are not likely to result from mere chance.

Let us turn up our examining microscope a notch and compare the voting patterns of Bush jurists with the patterns of other modern presidents' appointees on the three composite variables civil rights and liberties, criminal justice, and labor and economic regulation. The first column in Table 1 focuses on civil rights and liberties; that is, it examines judges' voting behavior on issues such as abortion, freedom of speech, the right to privacy, charges of racial minority discrimination, and so on. It is here that we find some of the best evidence for some meaningful ideological screening by President's Bush judicial appointment staff. Only 27 percent of the decisions of Bush cohort judges fell on the liberal side of issues pertaining to Bill of Rights and civil rights matters, giving the president the lowest score of any modern chief executive. Not only are Bush's trial judges more conservative than the next-most-conservative cohort—Ronald Reagan's appointees—but the odds ratio score of .79 indicates that Bush judges are approximately 20 percent less likely than Reagan judges to hand down a liberal opinion

Table 1. Percentages of Liberal Decisions in Three Case Types by Judges Appointed by the Eight Most Recent Presidents

Appointing president	Civil liberties and rights	Criminal justice	Economic labor regulation	All cases
Johnson	57.9	36.6	62.9	51.9
Nixon	37.8	27.0	48.5	38.0
Ford	39.7	34.5	52.4	43.0
Carter	50.9	38.0	60.9	51.2
Reagan	32.0	25.3	48.6	35.5
Bush	32.1	29.0	49.8	36.5
Clinton	41.2	38.8	54.2	44.0
G.W. Bush	27.2	29.8	47.3	33.3

in this issue area.[24] Such differences are statistically significant, meaning that they are very unlikely to have occurred by mere chance. Thus G. W. Bush judges are significantly more conservative in civil rights and liberties cases than judges selected by any other president.

This should come as little surprise, since the major controversies surrounding President Bush's judicial nominees have focused on their stances on issues such as affirmative action, gay rights, abortion, establishment of religion, and the right to privacy (all of which are included in our civil rights and liberties composite variable). Furthermore, the president's electoral base has clearly centered on these same issues, and there is considerable evidence to suggest that he has sought to please and strengthen that base through his judicial appointments.

The number of decisions we have in our database for the G. W. Bush judges is not large enough for us to examine all twenty-eight variables that go into our overall composite. However, the variable with the largest number of cases, Fourteenth Amendment and civil rights cases, contains some 170 decisions. Because of its comparatively large size and because it highlights a realm where the Bush jurists are singularly conservative, we will examine it here. In Table 2 we show the voting patterns of the Bush cohort compared with those of our seven other recent chief executives.

In the table we see that Bush appointees have decided only 19 percent of civil liberties cases in a liberal direction. Set against the background of the president's vigorous defense of the PATRIOT Act, indefinite detentions of "enemy combatants" in the war on terrorism, and unauthorized domestic surveillance of

Table 2. Percentages of Liberal Decisions in Fourteenth Amendment Cases by Judges Appointed by the Eight Most Recent Presidents

Appointing president	% Liberal decisions (N)	% Conservative decisions (N)
Johnson	53.9 (709)	46.1 (607)
Nixon	32.7 (585)	67.3 (1,204)
Ford	34.8 (144)	65.2 (270)
Carter	41.2 (868)	58.8 (1,241)
Reagan	26.8 (656)	73.2 (1,788)
Bush	27.5 (264)	72.5 (697)
Clinton	34.5 (404)	65.5 (766)
G.W. Bush	19.4 (33)	80.6 (137)

American citizens, it is perhaps not surprising that the G. W. Bush judges have taken a more minimalist approach to the expansion and protection of individual liberties. That low number of 19 percent contrasts markedly with the liberal numbers of Presidents Johnson, Carter, and Clinton, which were respectively 54 percent, 41 percent, and 35 percent. But even compared with the numbers of Bush's GOP predecessors, Nixon, Ford, Reagan, and Bush Sr. (33 percent, 35 percent, 27 percent, and 28 percent, respectively) the G. W. Bush team is singularly right of center in this policymaking realm.

The battles over the nominations of John Roberts, Harriet Miers, and Samuel Alito to the Supreme Court focused primarily on the issues of abortion, right to life, gay rights, and so on—all components of our variable "Right to privacy." Unfortunately, the number of cases for this variable is too small for us justify in the production of a formal table. Still, the results we have are tantalizing and merit a brief reference: So far only 17 percent of the decisions that Bush judges have rendered in the realm of abortion, right to life, gay rights, and so on have been in a liberal direction. That compares with figures of 29 percent for Reagan's judges and 49 percent for the Bush Sr. cohort. As one might expect, Clinton's team is the most liberal in this key policy realm, with a liberalism score of 54 percent. Again, these conclusions are somewhat tentative until the numbers increase, but if additional data validate them, the G. W. Bush cohort is a clear and vivid reflection of the president's own values in this area.

Few observers, friend or foe, have commented on Bush's nominations in terms of their possible effect on judicial issues pertaining to labor-management disputes, the power of the bureaucracy, or major curtailments of the rights of routine criminal defendants. In previous presidential campaigns, Republican candidates have called for an end to "big government," for curtailment of the power of labor unions, for reversal of the key criminal justice decisions of the Warren Court, or for an end to deficit spending. But those issues carried little weight, if any, in the Bush campaign of 2004, which focused much more on issues of who could be better trusted to fight terrorism and which candidate was the better embodiment of moral values (often code words for issues pertaining to abortion, gay rights, and right to life issues). Thus one would not expect Bush's judicial candidates to be vetted for their stances on labor and economic questions or on (nonterrorist) criminal justice matters. One would therefore predict that G. W. Bush's judicial cohort in those two areas would be more moderate, and the data do not disappoint.

The second, "Criminal justice" column in Table 1 shows judges' voting on issues such as habeas corpus pleas, motions made before and during a criminal trial, and forfeiture of property in criminal cases. In this realm, the voting record of the Bush team is 30 percent liberal. It is certainly more conservative than the records of the cohorts appointed by Democratic presidents Johnson, Carter, and Clinton, which were respectively 37 percent, 38 percent, and 39 percent. But it is right in line with the scores of Reagan and Bush Sr., which were 25 percent and 29 percent. Again we would note that whereas President George W. Bush has been critical of the federal courts on issues such as abortion and the right to life, he has said little or nothing about routine issues of criminal justice. Thus, while G. W. Bush's jurists are distinctly conservative in this realm, they are well within the charts.

Table 1's third column shows judges' voting patterns in the realm of labor and economic regulation, in which a typical case might be that of a labor union versus a company, a worker alleging a violation of the Fair Labor Standards Act, or a petitioner challenging the right of a government regulator to circumscribe his activity. On this composite variable, 47 percent of the decisions of the Bush appointees have been on the liberal side. This puts his cohort several points to the right of center compared with those of Nixon, Reagan, and Bush Sr., which were respectively 49 percent, 49 percent, and 50 percent. The group is distinctly more conservative when contrasted with the liberal scores of the Johnson, Carter, and Clinton jurists—63 percent, 61 percent, and 54 percent. What are we to make of these findings?

First, there should be little surprise that the Bush cohort is not as dramatically conservative in the realm of labor and economic regulation as on civil rights and liberties. In his campaigns for the presidency, George W. Bush made no serious calls for cutting back the power of organized labor or for curtailing the power of federal government regulators. During his presidency there have been no major initiatives against organized labor; furthermore, the size of the federal government and the size of its deficits have soared. Thus there would be little reason to predict that the Bush administration has been screening its judicial nominees for particularly conservative values on labor and economic issues.

Second, what is notable about the labor and economic regulation scores of all appointees in the past quarter-century is how similar they are. This is part of a larger political-judicial phenomenon that we have discussed elsewhere: Since the end of the New Deal, and particularly since the 1950s, the major political battles between the presidential candidates, in Congress, and within the Supreme Court have been over Bill of Rights and Fourteenth Amendment issues, not over matters of labor and economic regulation.[25]

Moreover, in recent decades Congress has legislated, often with precision, in the areas of economic regulation and labor relations and thus has restricted the discretion of judges in these fields. In sum, the serious political and judicial battles of recent decades have not been fought in the labor and economic arenas, and relatively clear guidelines provided by Congress and the courts have reduced whatever wiggle room there might have been for Republicans to be inordinately conservative or Democrats to be correspondingly liberal. The moderate scores of Bush judges are a manifestation of this overall phenomenon.

Traditional versus Nontraditional Judges

One final subject of interest is the decision-making patterns of Bush's traditional (that is, white male) appointees compared with those of his nontraditional appointees (women and minorities). Such comparisons are increasingly meaningful because President Bush has appointed the largest number of women and minorities to the federal bench of any Republican president (of the Democrats, Clinton appointed the most).[26] Conventional wisdom often suggests that women and minorities might be somewhat more liberal in their voting patterns than their white male counterparts (although the evidence tends to be inconclusive).[27] The reason is that historically women and minorities have been subjected to racial and gender discrimination by law, as well as in the workplace in terms of equal pay for equal work and promotion to managerial positions.

Table 3. Percentages of Liberal Decisions by Traditional and Nontraditional
Judges Appointed by George W. Bush[a]

	% Liberal decisions (N)	% Conservative decisions (N)
Traditional	32.1	67.9
	(159)	(337)
Nontraditional	35.5	64.5
	(106)	(193)

Notes: Odds ratio (a) = .859; chi square = .968 (p = .182).
[a] "Nontraditional" judges are women and/or members of an ethnic minority group.
"Traditional" jurists are white males.

Table 3 provides some modest evidence for that conventional wisdom:
Overall, 32 percent of the decisions of Bush's traditional judges have been in a
liberal direction, whereas 36 percent of the rulings handed down by his female
and minority jurists have been liberal. We are cautious in our conclusions here
because the differences are substantively not very great, nor are they at levels of
statistical significance that would allow us to have great confidence in the findings. We must await the accumulation of a larger number of decisions in our
database before we can offer any final conclusions about this phenomenon.

Conclusion

We have explored the ideological impact that President George W. Bush has had
so far on the decision-making patterns of the trial court judiciary. To perform
this task, we sought to determine the degree to which Bush and his appointment
team have possessed a strong commitment to make ideologically based appointments, the number of vacancies to be filled, the extent of the president's political
clout, and the ideological climate that his judicial cohort is entering.

Our estimation is that President Bush is having a substantial impact on the ideological orientation of the federal judiciary, particularly in the realm of civil
rights and liberties, since it is Bill of Rights and equality issues that have defined
much of the president's domestic political and judicial agenda, and that is an area
where judges still have maximum room for honest differences (as opposed to the
more settled area of labor and economic regulation). The quantitative data from
our investigation lend support to that estimation.

First, in their overall voting patterns President Bush's judges are not only the
most conservative of the eight most recent administrations examined here, but

indeed they are the most conservative for all presidential cohorts going back to Woodrow Wilson. The overall scores of the Bush judges are perhaps not "off the charts" in their level of conservatism, but they are sharply right of center. That is most evident in the realm of civil rights and liberties, where the Bush team is a full five percentage points more conservative than even the trial judges appointed by Presidents Reagan and Bush Sr. Our tentative look at the cases in the areas that make up the right to privacy variable suggests that the Bush cohort is highly reflective of the president's own social conservatism in this realm also. Finally, President Bush's nontraditional judges seem to be deciding cases in a somewhat more liberal manner than the white males who have been selected for judicial service.

NOTES

1. For example, see Robert A. Carp, Kenneth L. Manning, and Ronald Stidham, "The Decision-Making Behavior of George W. Bush's Judicial Appointees," *Judicature* 88, no. 1 (2004): 20–28.

2. Elliot Mincberg, quoted in Sheldon Goldman, Elliot Slotnick, Gerard Gryski, and Sara Schiavoni, "W. Bush's Judiciary: The First Term Record," *Judicature* 88, no. 6 (2005): 245–246.

3. Carp, Manning, and Stidham, "The Decision-Making Behavior," 20.

4. For a summary of this literature, see Robert A. Carp, Ronald Stidham, and Kenneth Manning, *Judicial Process in America*, 6th ed., chap. 7 (Washington, D.C.: CQ Press, 2004).

5. Stuart Taylor Jr., "The Supreme Question," *Newsweek*, July 10, 2000, 20.

6. Bennett Roth, "Bush Submits 11 names for Federal Bench," *Houston Chronicle*, May 10, 2001, A1.

7. Goldman et al., "W. Bush's Judiciary," 284.

8. Ibid., 245.

9. Ibid., 245–246.

10. Ibid., 244–275.

11. For example, see Evan Thomas and Stuart Taylor Jr., "Judging Roberts," *Newsweek*, August 1, 2005, 22–33; and Patty Reinert, "Battle Begins over Alito Record," *Houston Chronicle*, November 2, 2005, A1.

12. Jon R. Bond, "The Politics of Court Structure: The Addition of New Federal Judges," *Law and Policy Quarterly* 2 (1980): 182, 183, and 187.

13. Act of November 2, 2002; 116 Stat. 1786.

14. "Judiciary Gets Funding Increase, but Cuts May Still Come," *The Third Branch* 37 (2005): 4 and 6.

15. Helen Dewar, "President, Senate Reach Pact on Judicial Nominations," *Washington Post*, May 19, 2004, A21.

16. Retrieved from www.cnn.com/2004/ALLPOLITICS/11/07/specter.judiciary, November 9, 2004.

17. *Rasmussen Reports*, January 10, 2006, http://rasmussenreports.com/.

18. It should be remembered that not all of President Bush's judicial appointments are net gains for the Republicans, since many of the judges who are currently stepping aside are GOP jurists appointed by Ronald Reagan and Bush Sr. The really key gains will come when the Clinton judges begin to retire en masse in the coming years. In such situations a Democrat will be replaced by a Republican, which will be a sort of two-for-one gain obviously not possible when a Reagan or Bush Sr. Republican is replaced by another GOP jurist.

19. The Ninth Circuit comprises Washington, Oregon, California, Alaska, Hawaii, Montana, Idaho, Nevada, and Arizona.

20. These rulings were handed down in three key issue areas: civil liberties and rights, $n = 394$; criminal justice, $n = 181$; and labor and economic regulation, $n = 220$. Though we coded only district court rulings, prior research suggests that the behavior of jurists at this level is comparable to that of judges appointed by the same president to the courts of appeals. See Ronald Stidham, Robert A. Carp, and Donald R. Songer, "The Voting Behavior of President Clinton's Judicial Appointees," *Judicature* 80 (1996): 16–20; and Robert A. Carp, Donald Songer, C. K. Rowland, and Lisa Richey-Tracy, "The Voting Behavior of Judges Appointed by President Bush," *Judicature* 76 (1993): 298–302.

21. The reader will note that we have made few references to President Gerald Ford in our generalizations about the voting behavior of recent Republican presidential cohorts. The reason is that President Ford was something of an outlier and an exception to the rule that the judges appointed by GOP chief executives are generally more conservative than those selected by Democratic presidents. (Ford's overall liberalism score of 44 percent makes him the most liberal of recent Republican presidents, although still more conservative than recent Democratic chief executives.) First, Ford was much less of a political ideologue than his predecessor in the White House, Richard Nixon, or his Republican successors, Reagan, Bush Sr., and George W. Bush. Also, because Ford's circuitous route to the presidency did not enhance his political effectiveness with the Senate, he would not have had the clout to force highly conservative Republican nominees through a liberal, Democratic Senate, even if he had wished to.

22. See Figure 7-1 in Carp, Stidham, and Manning, *Judicial Process in America*, 158.

23. It might be argued that the relationship between the appointing president and the voting patterns of his appointees would be comparatively weak for district judges because of the phenomenon of "senatorial courtesy," which in principle acts to restrict the president's appointing power. On the other hand, one might argue that the appointment effects would be greater for circuit court appointments, for which senatorial courtesy does not apply. In fact, however, studies over the years have demonstrated that presidential effects at the district court level have been quite robust. For example, see Carp, Stidham, and Manning, *Judicial Process in America*, 157–168 and 289–294.

24. For a brief explanation of the meaning of the odds ratio score, see Carp, Stidham, and Manning, *Judicial Process in America*, 292.

25. Ibid., 314–317.

26. Goldman et al., "W. Bush's Judiciary."

27. See Robert A. Carp, Kenneth L. Manning, and Ronald Stidham, "President Clinton's District Judges: 'Extreme Liberals' or Just Plain Moderates," *Judicature* 84 (2001): 284–288; and Carp, Stidham, and Manning, *Judicial Process in America*, 106–107.

Chapter 10

Public Opinion

10-1

Analyzing and Interpreting Polls

Herbert Asher

Public opinion polls have gained a prominent place in modern American politics. Polls themselves often are newsworthy, particularly during campaigns and times of political crisis. Unfortunately, as Herbert Asher shows in the following essay, polls are open to misinterpretation and misuse. The wording of questions, the construction of a sample, the choice of items to analyze and report, the use of surveys to measure trends, and the examination of subsets of respondents all pose problems of interpretation. Every consumer of polling information must understand these issues to properly use the information polls provide.

INTERPRETING A POLL is more an art than a science, even though statistical analysis of poll data is central to the enterprise. An investigator examining poll results has tremendous leeway in deciding which items to analyze, which sample subsets or breakdowns to present, and how to interpret the statistical results. Take as an example a poll with three items that measure attitudes toward arms control negotiations. The investigator may construct an index from these three items. . . . Or the investigator may emphasize the results from one question, perhaps because of space and time constraints and the desire to keep matters simple, or because

Source: Herbert Asher, *Polling and the Public: What Every Citizen Should Know,* 4th ed. (Washington, D.C.: CQ Press, 1998), 141–169.

those particular results best support the analyst's own policy preferences. The investigator may examine results from the entire sample and ignore subgroups whose responses deviate from the overall pattern. Again time and space limitations or the investigator's own preferences may influence these choices. Finally, two investigators may interpret identical poll results in sharply different ways depending on the perspectives and values they bring to their data analysis; the glass may indeed be half full or half empty.

As the preceding example suggests, the analysis and interpretation of data entail a high degree of subjectivity and judgment. Subjectivity in this context does not mean deliberate bias or distortion, but simply professional judgments about the importance and relevance of information. Certainly, news organizations' interpretations of their polls are generally done in the least subjective and unbiased fashion. But biases can slip in—sometimes unintentionally, sometimes deliberately—when, for example, an organization has sponsored a poll to promote a particular position. Because this final phase of polling is likely to have the most direct influence on public opinion, this chapter includes several case studies to illustrate the judgmental aspects of analyzing and interpreting poll results.

Choosing Items to Analyze

Many public opinion surveys deal with multifaceted, complex issues. For example, a researcher querying Americans about their attitudes toward tax reform might find initially that they overwhelmingly favor a fairer tax system. But if respondents are asked about specific aspects of tax reform, their answers may reflect high levels of confusion, indifference, or opposition. And depending upon which items the researcher chooses to emphasize, the report might convey support, indifference, or opposition toward tax reform. American foreign policy in the Middle East is another highly complex subject that can elicit divergent reactions from Americans depending on which aspects of the policy they are questioned about.

Some surveys go into great depth on a topic through multiple items constructed to measure its various facets. The problem for an investigator in this case becomes one of deciding which results to report. Moreover, even though an extensive analysis is conducted, the media might publicize only an abbreviated version of it. In such a case the consumer of the poll results is at the mercy of the media to portray accurately the overall study. Groups or organizations that sponsor polls to demonstrate support for a particular position or policy option often disseminate results in a selective fashion which enables them to put the organization and its policies in a favorable light.

In contrast with in-depth surveys on a topic, *omnibus surveys* are superficial in their treatment of particular topics because of the need to cover many subjects in the same survey. Here the problem for an investigator becomes one of ensuring that the few questions employed to study a specific topic really do justice to the substance and complexity of that topic. It is left to the consumer of both kinds of polls to judge whether they receive the central information on a topic or whether other items might legitimately yield different substantive results.

The issue of prayer in public schools is a good example of how public opinion polling on a topic can be incomplete and potentially misleading. Typically, pollsters ask Americans whether they support a constitutional amendment that would permit voluntary prayer in public schools, and more than three-fourths of Americans respond that they would favor such an amendment. This question misses the mark. Voluntary prayer by individuals is in no way prohibited; the real issue is whether there will be *organized* voluntary prayer. But many pollsters do not include items that tap this aspect of the voluntary prayer issue. Will there be a common prayer? If so, who will compose it? Will someone lead the class in prayer? If so, who? Under what circumstances and when will the prayer be uttered? What about students who do not wish to participate or who prefer a different prayer?

The difficulty with both the in-depth poll and the omnibus survey is that the full set of items used to study a particular topic is usually not reported and thus the consumer cannot make informed judgments about whether the conclusions of the survey are valid. Recognizing this, individuals should take a skeptical view of claims by a corporate executive or an elected officeholder or even a friend that the polls demonstrate public support for or opposition to a particular position. The first question to ask is: What is the evidence cited to support the claim? From there one might examine the question wording, the response alternatives, the screening for nonattitudes, and the treatment of "don't know" responses. Then one might attempt the more difficult task of assessing whether the questions used to study the topic at hand were really optimal. Might other questions have been used? What aspects of the topic were not addressed? Finally, one might ponder whether different interpretations could be imposed on the data and whether alternative explanations could account for the reported patterns.

In evaluating poll results, there is always the temptation to seize upon those that support one's position and ignore those that do not. The problem is that one or two items cannot capture the full complexity of most issues. For example, a *Newsweek* poll conducted by the Gallup Organization in July 1986 asked a number of questions about sex laws and lifestyles. The poll included the following three items (Alpern 1986, 38):

Do you approve or disapprove of the Supreme Court decision upholding a state law against certain sexual practices engaged in privately by consenting adult homosexuals? [This question was asked of the 73 percent who knew about the Supreme Court decision.]

Disapprove	47%
Approve	41%

In general, do you think that states should have the right to prohibit particular sexual practices conducted in private between consenting adult homosexuals?

No	57%
Yes	34%

Do you think homosexuality has become an accepted alternative lifestyle or not?

Yes	32%
No	61%
Don't know	7%

Note that the first two items tap citizens' attitudes toward the legal treatment of homosexuals, while the third addresses citizens' views of homosexuality as a lifestyle. Although differently focused, all three questions deal with aspects of gay life. It would not be surprising to see gay rights advocates cite the results of the first two questions as indicating support for their position. Opponents of gay rights would emphasize the results of the third question.

An Eyewitness News/*Daily News* poll of New York City residents conducted in February 1986 further illustrates how the selective use and analysis of survey questions can generate very different impressions of popular opinion on an issue. This poll asked a number of gay rights questions:

On another matter, would you say that New York City needs a gay rights law or not?

Yes, need gay rights law	39%
No, do not need gay rights law	54%
Don't know/no opinion	8%

On another matter, do you think it should be against the law for landlords or private employers to deny housing or a job to someone because that person is homosexual or do you think landlords and employers should be allowed to do that if they want to?

Yes, should be against law	49%
No, should not be against law	47%
Volunteered responses	
Should be law only for landlord	1%
Should be law only for employers	8%
Don't know/no opinion	3%

Although a definite majority of the respondents oppose a gay rights law in response to the first question, a plurality also believe that it should be illegal for landlords and employers to deny housing and jobs to persons because they are homosexual. Here the two questions both address the legal status of homosexuals, and it is clear which question gay rights activists and gay rights opponents would cite in support of their respective policy positions. It is not clear, however, which question is the better measure of public opinion. The first question is unsatisfactory because one does not know how respondents interpreted the scope of a gay rights law. Did they think it referred only to housing and job discrimination, or did they think it would go substantially beyond that? The second question is inadequate if it is viewed as equivalent to a gay rights law. Lumping housing and jobs together constitutes another flaw since citizens might have divergent views on these two aspects of gay rights.

Additional examples of the importance of item selection are based on polls of Americans' attitudes about the Iraqi invasion of Kuwait in 1990. Early in the Persian Gulf crisis, various survey organizations asked Americans, using different questions, how they felt about taking military action against Iraq. Not surprisingly, the organizations obtained different results.

Do you favor or oppose direct U.S. military action against Iraq at this time? (Gallup, August 3–4, 1990)

Favor	23%
Oppose	68%
Don't know/refused	9%

Do you agree or disagree that the U.S. should take all actions necessary, including the use of military force, to make sure that Iraq withdraws its forces from Kuwait? (ABC News/*Washington Post*, August 8, 1990)

Agree	66%
Disagree	33%
Don't know	1%

Would you approve or disapprove of using U.S. troops to force the Iraqis to leave Kuwait? (Gallup, August 9–12, 1990, taken from *Public Perspective*, September/October 1990, 13)

Approve	64%
Disapprove	36%

(I'm going to mention some things that may or may not happen in the Middle East and for each one, please tell me whether the U.S. should or should not take military action in connection with it). . . . If Iraq refuses to withdraw from Kuwait? (NBC News/*Wall Street Journal*, August 18–19, 1990, taken from *Public Perspective*, September/October 1990, 13)

No military action	51%
Military action	49%

Note that the responses to these questions indicate varying levels of support for military action even though most of the questions were asked within two weeks of each other. The first question shows the most opposition to military action. This is easily explained: the question concerns military action *at this time,* an alternative that many Americans may have seen as premature until other means had been tried. The other three questions all indicate majority support for military action, although that support ranges from a bare majority to about two-thirds of all Americans. It is clear which question proponents and opponents of military action would cite to support their arguments.

Throughout the Persian Gulf crisis, public opinion was highly supportive of President Bush's policies; only in the period between October and December 1990 did support for the president's handling of the situation drop below 60 percent. For example, a November 1990 CBS News/*New York Times* poll showed the following patterns of response:

Do you approve or disapprove of the way George Bush is handling Iraq's invasion of Kuwait?

Approve	50%
Disapprove	41%
Don't know/NA	8%

Likewise, an ABC News/*Washington Post* poll in mid-November reported:

Do you approve or disapprove of the way George Bush is handling the situation caused by Iraq's invasion of Kuwait?

Approve	59%
Disapprove	36%
Don't know/NA	5%

Some opponents of the military buildup tried to use these and similar polls to demonstrate that support for the president's policies was decreasing, since earlier polls had indicated support levels in the 60–70 percent range. Fortunately, the *Washington Post* poll cited above asked respondents who disapproved of Bush's policy whether the president was moving too slowly or too quickly. It turned out that 44 percent of the disapprovers said "too slowly" and 37 percent "too quickly." Thus, a plurality of the disapprovers preferred more rapid action against Iraq—a result that provided little support for those critics of the president's policies who were arguing against a military solution.

Shortly before the outbreak of the war, the *Washington Post* conducted a survey of American attitudes about going to war with Iraq. To assess the effects of question wording, the *Post* split its sample in half and used two different versions of the same question followed by the identical follow-up question to each item.

Version 1

As you may know, the U.N. Security Council has authorized the use of force against Iraq if it doesn't withdraw from Kuwait by January 15. If Iraq does not withdraw from Kuwait, should the United States go to war against Iraq to force it out of Kuwait at some point after January 15 or not?

Go to war sometime after January 15	62%
No, do not go to war	32%

How long after January 15 should the United States wait for Iraq to withdraw from Kuwait before going to war to force it out?

Do not favor war at any point	32%
Immediately	18%
Less than one month	28%
1–3 months	8%
4 months or longer	2%

Version 2

The United Nations has passed a resolution authorizing the use of military force against Iraq if they do not withdraw their troops from Kuwait by January 15. If Iraq does not withdraw from Kuwait by then, do you think the United States should start military actions against Iraq, or should the United States wait longer to see if the trade embargo and economic sanctions work?

U.S. should start military actions	49%
U.S. should wait longer to see if sanctions work	47%

How long after January 15 should the United States wait for Iraq to withdraw from Kuwait before going to war to force it out?

U.S. should start military actions	49%

For those who would wait:

Less than a month	15%
1–3 months	17%
4 months or longer	9%

Morin (1991) points out how very different portraits of the American public can be painted by examining the two versions with and without the follow-up question. For example, version 1 shows 62 percent of Americans supporting war against Iraq, while version 2 shows only 49 percent. These different results stem from inclusion of the embargo and sanctions option in the second version. Thus it appears that version 2 gives a less militaristic depiction of the American public. Responses to the follow-up question, however, provide a different picture of the public. For example, the first version shows that 54 percent of Americans (18 + 28 + 8) favor going to war within three months. But the second version shows that 81 percent of Americans (49 + 15 + 17) favor war within three months. The point, of course, is that the availability of different items on a survey can generate differing descriptions of the public's preferences.

The importance of item selection is illustrated in a final example on the Gulf War from an April 3, 1991, ABC News/*Washington Post* poll conducted just after the conflict. It included the following three questions:

> Do you approve or disapprove of the way that George Bush is handling the situation involving Iraqi rebels who are trying to overthrow Saddam Hussein?
>
> | | |
> |---|---|
> | Approve | 69% |
> | Disapprove | 24% |
> | Don't know | 7% |
>
> Please tell me if you agree or disagree with this statement: The United States should not have ended the war with Iraqi President Saddam Hussein still in power.
>
> | | |
> |---|---|
> | Agree | 55% |
> | Disagree | 40% |
> | Don't know | 5% |
>
> Do you think the United States should try to help rebels overthrow Hussein or not?
>
> | | |
> |---|---|
> | Yes | 45% |
> | No | 51% |
> | Don't know | 4% |

Note that the responses to the first item indicate overwhelming approval for the president. But if one analyzed the second question in isolation, one might conclude that a majority of Americans did not support the president and indeed wanted to restart the war against Saddam Hussein. But the third item shows that a majority of Americans oppose helping the rebels. The lesson of this and the previous examples is clear. Constructing an interpretation around any single survey item can generate a very inaccurate description of public opinion. Unfortunately, advocates of particular positions have many opportunities to use survey results selectively and misleadingly to advance their cause.

The health care debate in 1993 and 1994 also provides examples of how the selection of items for analysis can influence one's view of American public opinion. *Washington Post* polls asked Americans whether they thought the Clinton health plan was better or worse than the present system (Morin 1994). In one version of the question, the sample was given the response options "better" or "worse," while in the other version respondents could choose among "better," "worse," or "don't know enough about the plan to say." The following responses were obtained:

Version 1		Version 2	
better	52%	better	21%
worse	34%	worse	27%
don't know (volunteered)	14%	don't know enough	52%

Clearly, very different portrayals of American public opinion are presented by the two versions of the question. The first version suggests that a majority of Americans believed that the Clinton plan was better than the status quo, while the second version suggests that a plurality of citizens with opinions on the issue felt that the Clinton plan was worse. It is obvious which version of the question supporters and opponents of the Clinton health plan would be more likely to cite.

Another example from the health care reform area deals with Americans' feelings about the seriousness of the health care problem. Certainly, the more seriously the problem was viewed, the greater the impetus for changing the health care system. Different polling organizations asked a variety of questions designed to tap the importance of the health care issue (questions taken from the September/October 1994 issue of *Public Perspective, 23, 26*):

> Louis Harris and Associates (April 1994): Which of the following statements comes closest to expressing your overall view of the health care system in this country? . . . There are some good things in our health care system, but fundamental changes are needed to make it better. . . . Our health care system has so much wrong with it that we need to completely rebuild it. . . . On the whole, the health care system works pretty well and only minor changes are necessary to make it work.

Fundamental changes needed	54%
Completely rebuild it	31%
Only minor changes needed	14%

> NBC/*Wall Street Journal* (March 1994): Which of the following comes closest to your belief about the American health care system—the system is in crisis; the system has major problems, but is not in crisis; the system has problems, but they are not major; or the system has no problems?

Crisis	22%
Major problems	50%
Minor problems	26%

> Gallup (June 1994): Which of these statements do you agree with more: The country has health care problems, but no health care crisis, or, the country has a health care crisis?

Crisis	55%
Problems but no crisis	41%
Don't know	4%

> Gallup (June 1994): Which of these statements do you agree with more: The country has a health care crisis, or the country has health care problems, but no health care crisis?

Crisis	35%
Problems but no crisis	61%
Don't know	4%

Certainly if one were trying to make the case that health care reform was an absolute priority, one would cite the first version of the Gallup question in which 55 percent of the respondents labeled health care a crisis. But if one wanted to move more slowly and incrementally on the health care issue, one would likely cite the NBC News/ *Wall Street Journal* poll in which only 22 percent of Americans said there was a crisis. Health care reform is the kind of controversial public policy issue that invites political leaders to seize upon those poll results to advance their positions. In such situations, citizens should be sensitive to how politicians are selectively using the polls.

Schneider (1996) has provided an excellent example of how examination of a single trial heat question may give a misleading impression of the electoral strength of presidential candidates. A better sense of the candidates' true electoral strength is achieved by adding to the analysis information about the incumbent's job approval rating. For example, in a trial heat question in May 1980 incumbent president Jimmy Carter led challenger Ronald Reagan by 40 to 32 percent, yet at the time Carter's job rating was quite negative: 38 percent approval and 51 percent disapproval. Thus Carter's lead in the trial heat item was much more fragile than it appeared; indeed, Reagan went on to win the election. Four years later, in May of 1984, President Reagan led challenger Walter Mondale by 10 percentage points in the trial heat question. But Reagan's job rating was very positive: 54 percent approval compared with 38 percent disapproval. Thus Reagan's 10-point lead looked quite solid in view of his strong job ratings, and he won overwhelmingly in November. Finally, in April 1992, incumbent president George Bush led challenger Bill Clinton by 50 to 34 percent in the trial heat question, a huge margin. But Bush's overall job rating was negative—42 percent approval versus 48 percent disapproval. Bush's lead over Clinton, then, was not as strong as it appeared, and Clinton ultimately won the election.

By collecting information on multiple aspects of a topic, pollsters are better able to understand citizens' attitudes (Morin and Berry 1996). One of the anomalies of 1996 was the substantial number of Americans who were worried about the health of the economy at a time when by most objective indicators the economy was performing very well. Part of the answer to this puzzle was Americans' ignorance and misinformation about the country's economic health. For example, even though unemployment was substantially lower in 1996 than in 1991, 33 percent of Americans said it was higher in 1996 and 28 percent said the same. The average estimate of the unemployment rate was 20.6 percent when in reality it was just over 5 percent. Americans' perceptions of inflation and the deficit were similar; in both cases Americans thought that the reality was much worse than it actually was. It is no wonder that many Americans expressed economic insecurity during good economic times; they were not aware of how strongly the economy was performing.

The final example in this section focuses on how the media selects what we learn about a poll even when the complete poll and analyses are available to the citizenry. The example concerns a book entitled *Sex in America: A Definitive Survey* by Robert T. Michael et al., published in 1994, along with a more specialized and comprehensive volume, *The Social Organization of Sexuality: Sexual Practices in the United States* by Edward O. Laumann et al. Both books are based on an extensive questionnaire administered by the National Opinion Research Center to 3,432 scientifically selected respondents. . . .

Because of the importance of the subject matter and because sex sells, media coverage of the survey was widespread. How various media reported the story indicates how much leeway the media have and how influential they are in determining what citizens learn about a given topic. For example, the *New York Times* ran a front-page story on October 7, 1994, entitled "Sex in America: Faithfulness in Marriage Thrives After All." Less prominent stories appeared in subsequent issues, including one on October 18, 1994, inaccurately entitled "Gay Survey Raises a New Question."

Two of the three major news magazines featured the sex survey on the covers of their October 17, 1994, issues. The *Time* cover simply read "Sex in America: Surprising News from the Most Important Survey since the Kinsey Report." The *U.S. News & World Report* cover was more risqué, showing a partially clad man and woman in bed; it read "Sex in America: A Massive New Survey, the Most Authoritative Ever, Reveals What We Do Behind the Bedroom Door." In contrast, *Newsweek* simply ran a two-page story with the lead "Not Frenzied, But Fulfilled. Sex: Relax. If you do it—with your mate—around twice a week, according to a major new study, you basically wrote the book of love."

Other magazines and newspapers also reported on the survey in ways geared to their readership. The November issue of *Glamour* featured the survey on its cover with the teaser "Who's doing it? And how? MAJOR U.S. SEX SURVEY." The story that followed was written by the authors of the book. While the cover of the November 15, 1994, *Advocate* read "What That Sex Survey Really Means," the story focused largely on what the survey had to say about the number of gays and lesbians in the population. The lead stated "10%: Reality or Myth? There's little authoritative information about gays and lesbians in the landmark study *Sex in America*—but what there is will cause big trouble." Finally, the *Chronicle of Higher Education,* a weekly newspaper geared to college and university personnel, in its October 17, 1994, issue headlined its story "The Sex Lives of Americans. Survey that had been target of conservative attacks produces few startling results."

Both books about the survey contain a vast amount of information and a large number of results and findings. But most of the media reported on such topics as marital fidelity, how often Americans have sex, how many sex partners people have, how often people experience orgasm, what percentages of the population are gay and lesbian, how long sex takes, and the time elapsed between a couple's first meeting and their first sexual involvement. Many of the reports also presented results for married vs. singles, men vs. women, and other analytical groupings. While most of the media coverage cited above was accurate in reporting the actual survey results, it also was selective in focusing on the more titillating parts of the survey, an unsurprising outcome given the need to satisfy their readerships.

Examining Trends with Polling Data

Researchers often use polling data to describe and analyze trends. To isolate trend data, a researcher must ensure that items relating to the topic under investigation are included in multiple surveys conducted at different points in time. Ideally, the items should be identically worded. But even when they are, serious problems of comparability can make trend analysis difficult. Identically worded items may not mean the same thing or provide the same stimulus to respondents over time because social and political changes in society have altered the meaning of the questions. For example, consider this question:

> Some say that the civil rights people have been trying to push too fast. Others feel they haven't pushed fast enough. How about you? Do you think that civil rights leaders are trying to push too fast, are going too slowly, or are they moving at about the right speed?

The responses to this item can be greatly influenced by the goals and agenda of the civil rights leadership at the time of the survey. A finding that more Americans think that the civil rights leaders are moving too fast or too slowly may reflect not a change in attitude from past views about civil rights activism but a change in the civil rights agenda itself. In this case, follow-up questions designed to measure specific components of the civil rights agenda are needed to help define the trend.

There are other difficulties in achieving comparability over time. For example, even if the wording of an item were to remain the same, its placement within the questionnaire could change, which in turn could alter the meaning of a question. Likewise, the definition of the sampling frame and the procedures used to achieve completed interviews could change. In short, comparability entails much more than simply wording questions identically. Unfortunately, consumers of poll results seldom receive the information that enables them to judge whether items are truly comparable over time.

Two studies demonstrate the advantages and disadvantages of using identical items over time. Abramson, Silver, and Anderson (1990) complained that the biennial National Election Studies (NES) conducted by the Survey Research Center at the University of Michigan, Ann Arbor, were losing their longitudinal comparability as new questions were added to the surveys and old ones removed. Baumgartner and Walker (1988), in contrast, complained that the use of the same standard question over time to assess the level of group membership in the United States had systematically underestimated the extent of such activity. They argued that new measures of group membership should be employed, which, of course, would make comparisons between past and present surveys more problematic. Although both the old and the new measures can be included in a survey, this becomes very costly if the survey must cover many other topics.

Two other studies show how variations in question wording can make the assessment of attitude change over time difficult. Borrelli and colleagues (1987) found that polls measuring Americans' political party loyalties in 1980 and in 1984 varied widely in their results. They attributed the different results in these polls to three factors: whether the poll sampled voters only; whether the poll emphasized "today" or the present in inquiring about citizens' partisanship; and whether the poll was conducted close to election day, which would tend to give the advantage to the party ahead in the presidential contest. The implications of this research for assessing change in party identification over time are evident—that is, to conclude that genuine partisan change occurred in either of the two polls, other possible sources of observed differences, such as modifications in the wording of questions, must be ruled out. In a study of support for aid to the Nicaraguan contras between 1983 and 1986, Lockerbie and Borrelli (1990) argue that much of the observed change in American public opinion was not genuine. Instead, it was attributable to changes in the wording of the questions used to measure support for the contras. Again, the point is that one must be able to eliminate other potential explanations for observed change before one can conclude that observed change is genuine change.

Smith's (1993) critique of three major national studies of anti-Semitism conducted in 1964, 1981, and 1992 is an informative case study of how longitudinal comparisons may be undermined by methodological differences across surveys. The 1981 and 1992 studies were ostensibly designed to build upon the 1964 effort, thereby facilitating an analysis of trends in anti-Semitism. But, as Smith notes, longitudinal comparisons among the three studies were problematic because of differences in sample definition and interview mode, changes in question order and question wording, and insufficient information to evaluate the quality of the sample and the design execution. In examining an eleven-item anti-Semitism scale, he did find six items highly comparable over time that indicated a decline in anti-Semitic attitudes.

Despite the problems of sorting out true opinion change from change attributable to methodological factors, there are times when public opinion changes markedly and suddenly in response to a dramatic occurrence and the observed change is indeed genuine. Two examples from CBS News/*New York Times* polls in 1991 about the Persian Gulf war illustrate dramatic and extensive attitude change. The first example concerns military action against Iraq. Just before the January 15 deadline imposed by the UN for the withdrawal of Iraq from Kuwait, a poll found that 47 percent of Americans favored beginning military action against Iraq if it did not withdraw; 46 percent were opposed. Two days after the deadline and after the beginning of the allied air campaign against Iraq, a poll found 79 percent of Americans saying the United States had done the right thing in beginning military action against Iraq. The second example focuses on people's attitudes toward a ground war in the Middle East. Before the allied ground offensive began, only 11 percent of Americans said the United States should begin fighting the ground war soon; 79 percent said bombing from the air should continue. But after the ground war began, the numbers shifted dramatically: 75 percent of Americans said the United States was right to begin the ground war, and only 19 percent said the nation should have waited longer. Clearly, the Persian Gulf crisis was a case in which American public opinion moved dramatically in the direction of supporting the president at each new stage.

Examining Subsets of Respondents

Although it is natural to want to know the results from an entire sample, often the most interesting information in a poll comes from examining the response patterns of subsets of respondents defined according to certain theoretically or substantively relevant characteristics. For example, a January 1986 CBS News/*New York Times* poll showed President Reagan enjoying unprecedented popularity for a six-year incumbent: 65 percent approved of the president's performance, and only 24 percent disapproved. But these overall figures mask some analytically interesting variations. For example, among blacks only 37 percent approved of the president's performance; 49 percent disapproved. The sexes also differed in their views of the president, with men expressing a 72 percent approval rate compared with 58 percent for women. (As expected among categories of party loyalists, 89 percent of the Republicans, 66 percent of the independents, and only 47 percent of the Democrats approved of the president's performance.) Why did blacks and whites—and men and women—differ in their views of the president?

There is no necessary reason for public opinion on an issue to be uniform across subgroups. Indeed, on many issues there are reasons to expect just the opposite. That is why a fuller understanding of American public opinion is gained by taking a closer look at the views of relevant subgroups of the sample. In doing so, however, one should note that dividing the sample into subsets increases the sampling error and lowers the reliability of the sample estimates. For example, a sample of 1,600 Americans might be queried about their attitudes on abortion. After the overall pattern is observed, the researcher might wish to break down the sample by religion—yielding 1,150 Protestant, 400 Catholic, and 50 Jewish respondents—to determine whether religious affiliation is associated with specific attitudes toward abortion. The analyst might observe that Catholics on the whole are the most opposed to abortion. To find out which Catholics are most likely to oppose abortion, she might further divide the 400 Catholics into young and old Catholics or regular church attenders and nonregular attenders, or into four categories of young Catholic churchgoers, old Catholic churchgoers, young Catholic nonattenders, and old Catholic nonattenders. The more breakdowns done at the same time, the quicker the sample size in any particular category plummets, perhaps leaving insufficient cases in some categories to make solid conclusions.

Innumerable examples can be cited to demonstrate the advantages of delving more deeply into poll data on subsets of respondents. An ABC News/*Washington Post* poll conducted in February 1986 showed major differences in the attitudes of men and women toward pornography; an examination of only the total sample would have missed these important divergences. For example, in response to the question "Do you think laws against pornography in this country are too strict, not strict enough, or just about right?" 10 percent of the men said the laws were too strict, 41 percent said not strict enough, and 47 percent said about right. Among women, only 2 percent said the laws were too strict, a sizable 72 percent said they were not strict enough, and 23 percent thought they were about right (Sussman 1986b, 37).

A CBS News/*New York Times* poll of Americans conducted in April 1986 found widespread approval of the American bombing of Libya; 77 percent of the sample approved of the action, and only 14 percent disapproved. Despite the overall approval, differences among various subgroups are noteworthy. For example, 83 percent of the men approved of the bombing compared with 71 percent of the women. Of the white respondents, 80 percent approved in contrast to only 53 percent of the blacks (Clymer 1986). Even though all of these demographically defined groups gave at least majority support to the bombing, the differences in levels of support are both statistically and substantively significant.

Polls showed dramatic differences by race in the O. J. Simpson case, with blacks more convinced of Simpson's innocence and more likely to believe that he could not get a fair trial. For example, a field poll of Californians (*U.S. News & World Report,* August 1, 1994) showed that only 35 percent of blacks believed that Simpson could get a fair trial compared with 55 percent of whites. Also, 62 percent of whites thought Simpson was "very likely or somewhat likely" to be guilty of murder compared with only 38 percent for blacks. Comparable results were found in a national *Time*/CNN poll (*Time,* August 1, 1994): 66 percent of whites thought Simpson got a fair preliminary hearing compared with only 31 percent of black respondents, while 77 percent of the white respondents thought the case against Simpson was "very strong" or "fairly strong" compared with 45 percent for blacks. A *Newsweek* poll (August 1, 1994) revealed that 60 percent of blacks believed that Simpson was set up (20 percent attributing the setup to the police); only 23 percent of whites believed in a setup conspiracy. When asked whether Simpson had been treated better or worse than the average white murder suspect, whites said better by an overwhelming 52 to 5 percent margin, while blacks said worse by a 30 to 19 percent margin. These reactions to the Simpson case startled many Americans who could not understand how their compatriots of another race could see the situation so differently.

School busing to achieve racial integration has consistently been opposed by substantial majorities in national public opinion polls. A Harris poll commissioned by *Newsweek* in 1978 found that 85 percent of whites opposed busing (Williams 1979, 48). An ABC News/*Washington Post* poll conducted in February 1986 showed 60 percent of whites against busing (Sussman 1986a). The difference between the two polls might reflect genuine attitude change about busing in that eight-year period, or it might be a function of different question wording or different placement within the questionnaire. Whatever the reason, additional analysis of both these polls shows that whites are not monolithic in their opposition to busing. For example, the 1978 poll showed that 56 percent of white parents whose children had been bused viewed the experience as "very satisfactory." The 1986 poll revealed sharp differences in busing attitudes among younger and older whites. Among whites age thirty and under, 47 percent supported busing and 50 percent opposed it, while among whites over age thirty, 32 percent supported busing and 65 percent opposed it. Moreover, among younger whites whose families had experienced busing firsthand, 54 percent approved of busing and 46 percent opposed it. (Of course, staunch opponents of busing may have moved to escape busing, thereby guaranteeing that the remaining population would be relatively more supportive of busing.)

Another example of the usefulness of examining poll results within age categories is provided by an ABC News/*Washington Post* poll conducted in May 1985 on citizens' views of how the federal budget deficit might be cut. One item read, "Do you think the government should give people a smaller Social Security cost-of-living increase than they are now scheduled to get as a way of reducing the budget deficit, or not?" Among the overall sample, 19 percent favored granting a smaller cost-of-living increase and 78 percent opposed. To test the widespread view that young workers lack confidence in the Social Security system and doubt they will ever get out of the system what they paid in, Sussman (1985c) investigated how different age groups responded to the preceding question. Basically, he found that all age groups strongly opposed a reduction in cost-of-living increases. Unlike the busing issue, this question showed no difference among age groups—an important substantive finding, particularly in light of the expectation that there would be divergent views among the old and young. Too often people mistakenly dismiss null (no difference) results as uninteresting and unexciting; a finding of no difference can be just as substantively significant as a finding of a major difference.

An example where age does make a difference in people's opinions is the topic of physician-assisted suicide. A *Washington Post* poll conducted in 1996 asked a national sample of Americans, "Should it be legal or illegal for a doctor to help a terminally ill patient commit suicide?" (Rosenbaum 1997). The attitudes of older citizens and younger citizens were markedly different on this question—the older the age group, the greater the opposition to doctor-assisted suicide. For example, 52 percent of respondents between ages eighteen and twenty-nine thought doctor-assisted suicide should be legal; 41 percent said it should be illegal. But for citizens over age seventy, the comparable figures were 35 and 58 percent. Even more striking were some of the racial and income differences on this question. Whites thought physician involvement in suicide should be legal by a 55 to 35 percent margin; blacks opposed it 70 to 20 percent. At the lowest income levels, doctor-assisted suicide was opposed by a 54 to 37 percent margin; at the highest income level it was supported by a 58 to 30 percent margin.

In many instances the categories used for creating subgroups are already established or self-evident. For example, if one is interested in gender or racial differences, the categories of male and female or white and black are straightforward candidates for investigation. Other breakdowns require more thought. For example, what divisions might one use to examine the effects of age? Should they be young, middle-aged, and old? If so, what actual ages correspond to these categories? Is middle age thirty-five to sixty-five, forty to sixty, or what? Or should more than three categories of age be defined? In samples selected to study the effects of religion, the typical breakdown is Protestant, Catholic, and Jewish. But this simple threefold division might overlook some interesting variations; that is, some Protestants are evangelical, some are fundamentalist, and others are considered mainline denominations. Moreover, since most blacks are Protestants, comparisons of Catholics and Protestants that do not also control for race may be misleading.

Establishing categories is much more subjective and judgmental in other situations. For example, religious categories can be defined relatively easily by denominational affiliation, as mentioned earlier, but classifying respondents as evangelicals or fundamentalists is more complicated. Those who actually belong to denominations normally characterized as evangelical or fundamentalist could be so categorized. Or an investigator might identify some evangelical or fundamentalist beliefs, construct some polling questions around them, and then classify respondents according to their responses to the questions. Obviously, this would require some common core of agreement about the definition of an evangelical or fundamentalist. Wilcox (1984, 6) argues:

> Fundamentalists and evangelicals have a very similar set of religious beliefs, including the literal interpretation of the Bible, the need for a religious conversion known as being "born-again," and the need to convert sinners to the faith. The evangelicals, however, are less anti-intellectual and more involved in the secular world, while the fundamentalists criticize the evangelicals for failing to keep themselves "pure from the world."

Creating subsets by ideology is another common approach to analyzing public opinion. The most-often-used categories of ideology are liberal, moderate, and conservative, and the typical way of obtaining this information is to ask respondents a question in the following form: "Generally speaking, do you think of yourself as a liberal, moderate, or conservative?" However, one can raise many objections to this procedure, including whether people really assign common meanings to these terms. Indeed, the levels of ideological sophistication and awareness have been an ongoing topic of research in political science.

Journalist Kevin Phillips (1981) has cited the work of political scientists Stuart A. Lilie and William S. Maddox, who argue that the traditional liberal-moderate-conservative breakdown is inadequate for analytical purposes. Instead, they propose a fourfold classification of liberal, conservative, populist, and libertarian, based on two underlying dimensions: whether one supports or opposes governmental intervention in the economy and whether one supports or opposes expansion of individual behavioral liberties and sexual equality. They define liberals as those who support both governmental intervention in the economy and expansion of personal liberties, conservatives as those who oppose both, libertarians as citizens who favor expanding personal liberties but oppose governmental intervention in the economy, and populists as persons who favor governmental economic intervention but oppose the expansion of personal liberties. According to one poll, populists made up 24 percent of the electorate, conservatives 18 percent, liberals 16 percent, and libertarians 13 percent, with the rest of the electorate not readily classifiable or unfamiliar with ideological terminology.

This more elaborate breakdown of ideology may help us to better understand public opinion, but the traditional categories still dominate political discourse. Thus, when one encounters citizens who oppose government programs that affect the marketplace but support pro-choice court decisions on abortion, proposed gay rights statutes, and the Equal Rights Amendment, one feels uncomfortable calling them liberals or conservatives since they appear to be conservative on economic issues and liberal on lifestyle issues. One might feel more confident in classifying them as libertarians.

Additional examples of how an examination of subsets of respondents can provide useful insights into the public's attitudes are provided by two CBS News/*New York Times* surveys conducted in 1991, one dealing with the Persian Gulf crisis and the other with attitudes toward police. Although the rapid and successful conclusion of the ground war against Iraq resulted in widespread approval of the enterprise, before the land assault began there were differences of opinion among Americans about a ground war. For example, in the February 12–13 CBS News/*New York Times* poll, Americans were asked: "Suppose several thousand American troops would lose their lives in a ground war against Iraq. Do you think a ground war against Iraq would be worth the cost or not?" By examining the percentage saying it would be worth the cost, one finds the following results for different groups of Americans:

All respondents	45%	Independents	46%
Men	56%	Republicans	54%
Women	35%	Eighteen to twenty-nine year-olds	50%
Whites	47%	Thirty to forty-four year-olds	44%
Blacks	30%	Forty-five to sixty-four year-olds	51%
Democrats	36%	Sixty-five years and older	26%

Note that the youngest age group, the one most likely to suffer the casualties, is among the most supportive of a ground war. Note also the sizable differences between men and women, whites and blacks, and Democrats and Republicans.

Substantial racial differences in opinion also were expressed in an April 1–3, 1991, CBS News/*New York Times* poll on attitudes toward local police. Overall, 55 percent of the sample said they had substantial confidence in the local police, and 44 percent said little confidence. But among whites the comparable percentages were 59 percent and 39 percent, while for blacks only 30 percent had substantial confidence and fully 70 percent expressed little confidence in the police. Even on issues in which the direction of white and black opinion was the same, there were still substantial racial differences in the responses. For example, 69 percent of whites said that the police in their own community treat blacks and whites the same, and only 16 percent said the police were tougher on blacks than on whites. Although a plurality—45 percent—of blacks agreed that the police treat blacks and whites equally, fully 42 percent of black respondents felt that the police were tougher on blacks. Certainly if one were conducting a study to ascertain citizens' attitudes about police performance, it would be foolish not to examine the opinions of relevant subgroups.

Another example of the importance of examining subsets of respondents is provided by a January 1985 ABC News/*Washington Post* poll that queried Americans about their attitudes on a variety of issues and presented results not only for the entire sample but also for subsets of respondents defined by their attentiveness to public affairs (Sussman 1985b). Attentiveness to public affairs was measured by whether the respondents were aware of four news events: the subway shooting in New York City of four alleged assailants by their intended victim; the switch in jobs by two key Reagan administration officials, Donald Regan and James Baker; the Treasury Department's proposal to simplify the tax system; and protests against South African apartheid held in the United States. Respondents then were divided into four levels of awareness, with 27 percent in the highest category, 26 percent in the next highest, 25 percent in the next category, and 22 percent falling in the lowest. The next step in the analysis was to compare the policy preferences of the highest and lowest awareness subsets.

There were some marked differences between these two groups. For example, on the issue of support for the president's military buildup, 59 percent of the lowest awareness respondents opposed any major cuts in military spending to lessen the budget deficit. In contrast, 57 percent of the highest awareness group said that military spending should be limited to help with the budget deficit. On the issue of tax rates, a majority of both groups agreed with the president that taxes were too high, but there was a difference in the size of the majority. Among the lowest awareness respondents, 72 percent said taxes were too high and 24 percent said they were not, while among the highest awareness respondents, 52 percent said taxes were too high and 45 percent said they were not (Sussman 1985b).

Opinions about the future of Social Security and Medicare also are affected by citizens' knowledge about the two programs (Pianin and Brossard 1997). In one poll, the more people knew about Social Security and Medicare, the more likely they were to believe that these programs were in crisis and that major governmental action was needed. For example, among highly knowledgeable respondents, 88 percent believed that Social Security either was in crisis or had major problems; only 70 percent of respondents with little knowledge agreed. Likewise, 89 percent of the highly knowledgeable respondents believed Social Security would go bankrupt if Congress did nothing compared to only 61 percent for the less-informed respondents.

All these findings raise some interesting normative issues about public opinion polls. . . . [T]he methodology of public opinion polls is very democratic. All citizens have a nearly equal chance to be selected in a sample and have their views counted; all respondents are weighted equally (or nearly so) in the typical data analysis. Yet except at the polls all citizens do not have equal influence in shaping public policy. The distribution of political resources, whether financial or informational, is not uniform across the population. Polls themselves become a means to influence public policy, as various decision makers cite poll results to legitimize their policies. But should the views of all poll respondents be counted equally? An elitist critic would argue that the most informed segments of the population should be given the greatest weight. Therefore, in the preceding example of defense spending, more attention should be given to the views of the highest awareness subset (assuming the validity of the levels of awareness), which was more supportive of reducing military spending. An egalitarian argument would assert that all respondents should be counted equally. . . .

Interpreting Poll Results

An August 1986 Gallup poll on education showed that 67 percent of Americans would allow their children to attend class with a child suffering from AIDS, while 24 percent would not. What reaction might there be to this finding? Some people might be shocked and depressed to discover that almost one-fourth of Americans could be so mean-spirited toward AIDS victims when the scientific evidence shows that AIDS is not a disease transmitted by casual contact. Others might be reassured and relieved that two-thirds of Americans are sufficiently enlightened or tolerant to allow their children to attend school with children who have AIDS. Some people might feel dismay: How could 67 percent of Americans foolishly allow their children to go to school with a child who has AIDS when there is no absolute guarantee that AIDS cannot be transmitted casually?

Consider this example from a 1983 poll by the National Opinion Research Center (NORC): "If your party nominated a black for President, would you vote for him if he were qualified for the job?" Eighty-five percent of the white respondents said yes. How might this response be interpreted? One might feel positive about how much racial attitudes have changed in the United States. A different perspective would decry the fact that in this supposedly tolerant and enlightened era, 15 percent of white survey respondents could not bring themselves to say they would vote for a qualified black candidate.

In neither example can we assign a single correct meaning to the data. Instead, the interpretation one chooses will be a function of individual values and beliefs, and purposes in analyzing the survey. This is demonstrated in an analysis of two national surveys on gun control, one sponsored by the National Rifle Association (NRA) and conducted by Decision/Making/Information, Inc., and the other sponsored by the Center for the Study and Prevention of Handgun Violence and conducted by Cambridge Reports, Inc. (pollster Patrick Caddell's firm). Although the statistical results from both surveys were comparable, the two reports arrived at substantially different conclusions. The NRA's analysis concluded:

> Majorities of American voters believe that we do *not* need more laws governing the possession and use of firearms and that more firearms laws would *not* result in a decrease in the crime rate. (Wright 1981, 25)

In contrast, the center's report stated:

> It is clear that the vast majority of the public (both those who live with handguns and those who do not) want handgun licensing and registration. . . . The American public wants some form of handgun control legislation. (Wright 1981, 25)

Wright carefully analyzed the evidence cited in support of each conclusion and found that

> the major difference between the two reports is not in the findings, but in what is said about or concluded about the findings: what aspects of the evidence are emphasized or de-emphasized, what interpretation is given to a finding, and what implications are drawn from the findings about the need, or lack thereof, for stricter weapons controls. (Wright 1981, 38)

In essence, it was the interpretation of the data that generated the difference in the recommendations.

Two polls on tax reform provide another example of how poll data can be selectively interpreted and reported (Sussman 1985a). The first poll, sponsored by the insurance industry, was conducted by pollster Burns Roper. Its main conclusion, reported in a press conference announcing the poll results, was that 77 percent of the American public "said that workers should not be taxed on employee benefits" and that only 15 percent supported such a tax, a conclusion very reassuring to the insurance industry. However, Roper included other items in the poll that the insurance industry chose not to emphasize. As Sussman points out, the 77 percent opposed to the taxing of fringe benefits were then asked, "Would you still oppose counting the value of employee benefits as taxable income for employees if the additional tax revenues went directly to the reduction of federal budget deficits and not into new spending?" Twenty-six percent were no longer opposed to taxing fringe benefits under this condition, bringing the overall opposition down to 51 percent of the sample.

A second follow-up question asked, "Would you still oppose counting the value of employee benefits as taxable income for employees if the additional tax revenues permitted an overall reduction of tax rates for individuals?" (a feature that was part of the Treasury Department's initial tax proposals). Now only 33 percent of the sample was opposed to taxing fringes, 50 percent supported it, and 17 percent were undecided. Thus, depending upon which results one used, one could show a majority of citizens supportive of or opposed to taxing fringe benefits.

The other poll that Sussman analyzed also tapped people's reactions to the Treasury Department's tax proposal. A number of questions in the survey demonstrated public hostility to the Treasury proposal. One item read:

> The Treasury Department has proposed changing the tax system. Three tax brackets would be created, but most current deductions from income would be eliminated. Non-federal income taxes and property taxes would not be deductible, and many deductions would be limited. Do you favor or oppose this proposal? (Sussman 1985a)

Not surprisingly, 57 percent opposed the Treasury plan, and only 27 percent supported it. But as Sussman points out, the question is highly selective and leading since it focuses on changes in the tax system that hurt the taxpayer. For example, nowhere does it inform the respondent that a key part of the Treasury plan was to reduce existing tax rates so that 80 percent of Americans would be paying either the same amount or less in taxes than they were paying before. Clearly, this survey was designed to obtain a set of results compatible with the sponsor's policy objectives.

Morin (1995) describes a situation in which polling data were misinterpreted and misreported in the *Washington Post* because of faulty communication between a *Post* reporter and a local polling firm that was conducting an omnibus survey in the Washington, D.C., area. Interested in how worried federal employees were about their jobs given the budgetary battles between the Clinton White House and the Republican Congress in 1995, the reporter commissioned the polling firm to include the following questions in its survey: "Do you think your agency or company will probably be affected by federal budget cutbacks? Do you think your own job will be affected?" The poll discovered that 40 percent of the federal workers interviewed believed their own jobs might be affected. Unfortunately, when the polling outfit prepared a report for its client, the reporter, the report concluded that these federal workers felt their jobs were jeopardized. And then the reporter's story stated, "Four out of every 10 federal employees fear losing their jobs because of budget reductions." As Morin points out, this conclusion does not follow from the polling questions asked. The belief that one's job will likely be affected is not equivalent to the fear of losing one's job. Instead, the effects might be lower salary increases, decreased job mobility, increased job responsibilities, and the like. A correction quickly appeared in the *Post* clarifying what the polling data actually had said. One lesson of this example is the responsibility that pollsters have to clients to communicate carefully and accurately what poll results mean. Another lesson is that one should not try to read too much into the responses to any single survey item. In this case, if the reporter wanted to know exactly how federal workers thought their jobs would be affected, a specific question eliciting this information should have been included in the survey.

Weighting the Sample

Samples are selected to be representative of the population from which they are drawn. Sometimes adjustments must be made to a sample before analyzing and reporting results. These adjustments may be made for substantive reasons or because of biases in the characteristics of the selected sample. An example of adjustments made for substantive reasons is pollsters' attempts to determine who the likely voters will be and to base their election predictions not on the entire sample but on a subset of likely voters.

To correct for biases, weights can be used so that the sample's demographic characteristics more accurately reflect the population's overall properties. Because sampling and interviewing involve statistics and probability theory as well as logistical problems of contacting respondents, the sample may contain too few blacks, or too few men, or too few people in the youngest age category. Assuming that one knows the true population proportions for sex, race, and age, one can adjust the sample by the use of weights to bring its numbers into line with the overall population values. For example, if females constitute 60 percent of the sample but 50 percent of the overall population, one might weight each female respondent by five-sixths, thereby reducing the percentage of females in the sample to 50 percent (five-sixths times 60 percent).

A 1986 *Columbus Dispatch* preelection poll on the gubernatorial preferences of Ohioans illustrates the consequences of weighting. In August 1986 the *Dispatch* sent a mail questionnaire to a sample of Ohioans selected from the statewide list of registered voters. The poll showed that incumbent Democratic governor Richard Celeste was leading former GOP governor James Rhodes, 48 percent to 43 percent, with Independent candidate and former Democratic mayor of Cleveland Dennis Kucinich receiving 9 percent; an undecided alternative was not provided to respondents (Curtin 1986a). Fortunately, the *Dispatch* report of its poll included the sample size for each category (unlike the practice of the national media). One table presented to the reader showed the following relationship between political party affiliation and gubernatorial vote preference (Curtin 1986b):

Gubernatorial preference	Democrat	Republican	Independent
Celeste	82%	14%	33%
Rhodes	9	81	50
Kucinich	9	5	17
Total %	100	100	100
(N)	(253)	(245)	(138)

Given the thrust of the news story that Celeste was ahead, 48 to 43 percent, the numbers in the table were surprising because Rhodes was running almost as well among Republicans as Celeste was among Democrats, and Rhodes had a substantial lead among Independents. Because the N's were provided, one could calculate the actual number of Celeste, Rhodes, and Kucinich votes in the sample as follows:

Celeste votes $= .82(253) + .14(245) + .33(138) = 287$

Rhodes votes $= .09(253) + .81(245) + .50(138) = 291$

Kucinich votes $= .09(253) + .05(245) + .17(138) = 58$

The percentages calculated from these totals show Rhodes slightly *ahead,* 46 to 45 percent, rather than trailing. At first I thought there was a mistake in the poll or in the party affiliation and gubernatorial vote preference. In rereading the news story, however, I learned that the sample had been weighted. The reporter wrote, "Results were adjusted, or weighted, slightly to compensate for demographic differences between poll respondents and the Ohio electorate as a whole" (Curtin 1986b). The reporter did inform the reader that the data were weighted, but nowhere did he say that the adjustment affected who was ahead in the poll.

The adjustment probably was statistically valid since the poll respondents did not seem to include sufficient numbers of women and blacks, two groups that were more supportive of the Democratic gubernatorial candidate. However, nowhere in the news story was any specific information provided on how the weighting was done. This example illustrates that weighting can be consequential, and it is probably typical in terms of the scant information provided to citizens about weighting procedures.

When Polls Conflict: A Concluding Example

A variety of factors can influence poll results and their subsequent interpretation. Useful vehicles for a review of these factors are the polls that led up to the 1980, 1984, 1988, 1992, and 1996 presidential elections—polls that were often highly inconsistent. For example, in the 1984 election, polls conducted at comparable times yielded highly dissimilar results. A Harris poll had Reagan leading Mondale by 9 percentage points, an ABC News / *Washington Post* poll had Reagan ahead by 12 points, a CBS News / *New York Times* survey had Reagan leading by 13 points, a *Los Angeles Times* poll gave Reagan a 17-point lead, and an NBC News poll had the president ahead by 25 points (Oreskes 1984). In September 1988 seven different polls on presidential preference were released within a three-day period with results ranging from Bush ahead by 8 points to a Dukakis lead of 6 points (Morin 1988). In 1992 ten national polls conducted in the latter part of August showed Clinton with leads over Bush ranging from 5 to 19 percentage points (Elving 1992). And in 1996, the final preelection polls showed Clinton leading Dole by margins ranging from 7 to 18 percentage points. How can polls on an ostensibly straightforward topic such as presidential vote preference differ so widely? Many reasons can be cited, some obvious and others more subtle in their effects.

Among the more subtle reasons are the method of interviewing and the number of callbacks that a pollster uses to contact respondents who initially were unavailable. According to Lewis and Schneider (1982, 43), Patrick Caddell and George Gallup in their 1980 polls found that President Reagan received less support from respondents interviewed personally than from those queried over the telephone. Their speculation about this finding was that weak Democrats who were going to desert Carter found it easier to admit this in a telephone interview than in a face-to-face situation.

With respect to callbacks, Dolnick (1984) reports that one reason a Harris poll was closer than others in predicting Reagan's sizable victory in 1980 was that it made repeated callbacks, which at each stage "turned up increasing numbers of well-paid, well-educated Republican-leaning voters." A similar situation occurred in 1984. Traugott (1987) found that persistence in callbacks resulted in a more Republican sample, speculating that Republicans were less likely to have been at home or available initially.

Some of the more obvious factors that help account for differences among compared polls are question wording and question placement. Some survey items mention the presidential and vice-presidential candidates, while others mention only the presidential challengers. Some pollsters ask follow-up questions of undecided voters to ascertain whether they lean toward one candidate or another; others do not. Question order can influence responses.

Normally, incumbents and better known candidates do better when the question on vote intention is asked at the beginning of the survey rather than later. If vote intention is measured after a series of issue and problem questions have been asked, respondents may have been reminded of shortcomings in the incumbent's record and may therefore be less willing to express support for the incumbent.

Comparable polls also can differ in how the sample is selected and how it is treated for analytical purposes. Some polls sample registered voters; others query adult Americans. There are differences as well in the methods used to identify likely voters. As Lipset (1980) points out, the greater the number of respondents who are screened out of the sample because they do not seem to be likely voters, the more probable it is that the remaining respondents will be relatively more Republican in their vote preferences. Some samples are weighted to guarantee demographic representativeness; others are not.

It is also possible that discrepancies among polls are not due to any of the above factors, but may simply reflect statistical fluctuations. For example, if one poll with a 4 percent sampling error shows Clinton ahead of Dole, 52 to 43 percent, this result is statistically congruent with other polls that might have a very narrow Clinton lead of 48 to 47 percent or other polls that show a landslide Clinton lead of 56 to 39 percent.

Voss et al. (1995) summarized and compared many of the methodological differences among polls conducted by eight polling organizations for the 1988 and 1992 presidential elections. Even though all eight organizations were studying the same phenomenon, there were enough differences in their approaches that polls conducted at the same time using identical questions might still get somewhat different results for reasons beyond sampling error. One feature Voss et al. examined was the sampling method—how each organization generated a list of telephone numbers from which to sample. Once the sample was selected, polling organizations conducting telephone interviews still had to make choices about how to handle "busy signals, refusals, and calls answered by electronic devices, how to decide which household members are eligible to be interviewed, and how to select the respondent from among those eligible" (Voss et al. 1995). The investigators also examined the various weighting schemes used by each survey operation to ensure a representative sample. Much of this methodological information is not readily available to the consumer of public opinion polls, and if it were many consumers would be overwhelmed by the volume of methodological detail. Yet these factors can make a difference. For example, the eight polling organizations analyzed by Voss et al. treated refusals quite differently. Some of the outfits did not call back after receiving a refusal from a potential respondent; other organizations did make callbacks. One organization generally tried to call back but with a different interviewer, but then gave up if a second refusal was obtained.

Just as different methodological features can affect election polls, they also can influence other surveys. One prominent example dealt with the widely divergent estimates of rape obtained from two different national surveys. Much of this discrepancy stemmed from the methodological differences between the two surveys (Lynch 1996). Because the poll consumer is unaware of many of the design features of a survey, he or she must assume the survey design was appropriate for the topic at hand. Then the consumer can ask whether the information collected by the survey was analyzed and interpreted correctly.

REFERENCES

Abramson, Paul R., Brian Silver, and Barbara Anderson. 1990. "The Decline of Overtime Comparability in the National Election Studies." *Public Opinion Quarterly* 54 (summer): 177–190.

Alpern, David M. 1986. "A *Newsweek* Poll: Sex Laws." *Newsweek,* 14 July, 38.

Baumgartner, Frank R., and Jack L. Walker. 1988. "Survey Research and Membership in Voluntary Associations." *American Journal of Political Science* 32 (November): 908–928.

Borrelli, Stephen, Brad Lockerbie, and Richard G. Niemi. 1987. "Why the Democrat-Republican Partisan Gap Varies from Poll to Poll." *Public Opinion Quarterly* 51 (spring): 115–119.

Clymer, Adam. 1986. "A Poll Finds 77% in U.S. Approve Raid on Libya." *New York Times,* 17 April, A-23.

Curtin, Michael. 1986a. "Celeste Leading Rhodes 48% to 43%, with Kucinich Trailing." *Columbus Dispatch,* 10 August, 1-A.

———. 1986b. "Here Is How Poll Was Taken." *Columbus Dispatch,* 10 August, 8-E.

Dolnick, Edward. 1984. "Pollsters Are Asking: What's Wrong." *Columbus Dispatch,* 19 August, C-1.

Elving, Ronald D. 1992. "Polls Confound and Confuse in This Topsy-Turvy Year." *Congressional Quarterly Weekly Report,* 12 September, 2725–2727.

Laumann, Edward O., et al. 1994. *The Social Organization of Sexuality.* Chicago: University of Chicago Press.

Lewis, I. A., and William Schneider. 1982. "Is the Public Lying to the Pollsters?" *Public Opinion* 5 (April/May): 42–47.

Lipset, Seymour Martin. 1980. "Different Polls, Different Results in 1980 Politics." *Public Opinion* 3 (August/September): 19–20, 60.

Lockerbie, Brad, and Stephen A. Borrelli. 1990. "Question Wording and Public Support for Contra Aid, 1983–1986." *Public Opinion Quarterly* 54 (summer): 195–208.

Lynch, James P. 1996. "Clarifying Divergent Estimates of Rape from Two National Surveys." *Public Opinion Quarterly* 60 (winter): 558–619.

Michael, Robert T., John H. Gagnon, Edward O. Laumann, and Gina Kolata. 1994. *Sex in America: A Definitive Survey.* Boston: Little, Brown.

Morin, Richard. 1988. "Behind the Numbers: Confessions of a Pollster." *Washington Post,* 16 October, C-1, C-4.

_____ . 1991. "2 Ways of Reading the Public's Lips on Gulf Policy." *Washington Post,* 14 January, A-9.

_____ . 1994. "Don't Know Much About Health Care Reform." *Washington Post* National Weekly Edition, 14–20 March, 37.

_____ . 1995. "Reading between the Numbers." *Washington Post* National Weekly Edition, 4–10 September, 30.

Morin, Richard, and John M. Berry. 1996. "Economic Anxieties." *Washington Post* National Weekly Edition, 4–10 November, 6–7.

Oreskes, Michael. 1984. "Pollsters Offer Reasons for Disparity in Results." *New York Times,* 20 October, A-8.

Phillips, Kevin P. 1981. "Polls Are Too Broad in Analysis Divisions." *Columbus Dispatch,* 8 September, B-3.

Pianin, Eric, and Mario Brossard. 1997. "Hands Off Social Security and Medicare." *Washington Post* National Weekly Edition, 7 April, 35.

Rosenbaum, David E. 1997. "Americans Want a Right to Die. Or So They Think." *New York Times,* 8 June, E3.

Schneider, William. 1996. "How to Read a Trial Heat Poll." Transcript, CNN "Inside Politics Extra," 12 May (see AllPolitics Web site).

Smith, Tom W. 1993. "Actual Trends or Measurement Artifacts? A Review of Three Studies of Anti-Semitism." *Public Opinion Quarterly* 57 (fall): 380–393.

Sussman, Barry. 1985a. "To Understand These Polls, You Have to Read the Fine Print." *Washington Post* National Weekly Edition, 4 March, 37.

_____ . 1985b. "Reagan's Support on Issues Relies Heavily on the Uninformed." *Washington Post* National Weekly Edition, 1 April, 37.

_____ . 1985c. "Social Security and the Young." *Washington Post* National Weekly Edition, 27 May, 37.

_____ . 1986a. "It's Wrong to Assume that School Busing Is Wildly Unpopular." *Washington Post* National Weekly Edition, 10 March, 37.

_____ . 1986b. "With Pornography, It All Depends on Who's Doing the Looking." *Washington Post* National Weekly Edition, 24 March, 37.

Traugott, Michael W. 1987. "The Importance of Persistence in Respondent Selection for Preelection Surveys." *Public Opinion Quarterly* 51 (spring): 48–57.

Voss, D. Stephen, Andrew Gelman, and Gary King. 1995. "Preelection Survey Methodology: Details from Eight Polling Organizations, 1988 and 1992." *Public Opinion Quarterly* 59 (spring): 98–132.

Wilcox, William Clyde. 1984. "The New Christian Right and the White Fundamentalists: An Analysis of a Potential Political Movement." Ph.D. diss., Ohio State University.

Williams, Dennis A. 1979. "A New Racial Poll." *Newsweek,* 26 February, 48, 53.

Wright, James D. 1981. "Public Opinion and Gun Control: A Comparison of Results from Two Recent National Surveys." *Annals of the American Academy of Political and Social Science* 455 (May): 24–39.

10-2

Dynamic Representation

James A. Stimson, Michael B. MacKuen, and Robert S. Erikson

The relationship between public opinion and government action is complex. In the United States, with single-member congressional districts, we often consider relationship at the "micro" level—that is, whether individual elected officials are following the wishes of their home constituencies. But the overall relationship between public preferences and government behavior, the "macro" level, is more difficult to assess. In the following essay, James Stimson, Michael MacKuen, and Robert Erikson provide a look at this relationship with the help of a creative invention. These scholars use a statistical technique to build an aggregate measure of public opinion from dozens of polls. The technique allows them to measure change in the liberalism of views expressed in the polls over several decades. Then, using similarly aggregated measures of the behavior of Congress, the president, and the Supreme Court, they evaluate the relationship between the liberalism of public opinion and the behavior of the institutions. Government as a whole proves responsive to public opinion, and Congress and the presidency prove more responsive to public opinion than the Supreme Court.

WHAT DOES IT mean that a government represents public feelings? Responsiveness must be a central part of any satisfactory answer. Representative governments respond to—meaning act as a consequence of—changes in public sentiment. To "act as a consequence of" changes in public sentiment implies a sequence, inherently structured in time. We may say that if, by knowing about earlier changes in public sentiment, we can improve the prediction of public policy over what we could have done from knowing only the history of public policy itself, then opinion causes policy, and this is dynamic representation. . . .

The *dynamic* character of representation has a second aspect. Most political decisions are about change or the prevention of change. Governments decide to change health care systems, to reduce environmental regulations, to develop new weapons systems, or to increase subsidies for long staple cotton growers. Or not. Thus, political decisions have a directional force to them, and their incremental

Source: James A. Stimson, Michael B. MacKuen, and Robert S. Erikson, "Dynamic Representation," *American Political Science Review* 89 (September 1995): 543–564. Notes appearing in the original have been deleted.

character is inherently dynamic. Further, most public opinion judgments concern change as well. The public expresses preferences for "more" or "less" governmental action across different spheres: "faster school integration," "cuts in welfare spending," "getting tougher on crime," and so on. The main difference is that public sentiment is generally more vague, diffuse, than the more concrete government action.

This understanding suggests something akin to the familiar "thermostat" analogy. The public makes judgments about current public policy—most easily that government's actions need to be enhanced or trimmed back. These judgments will change as policy changes, as real-world conditions change, or as "politically colored" perceptions of policy and conditions change. And as the simple model indicates, politicians and government officials sense these changes in public judgment and act accordingly. Thus, when public policy drifts away from the public's demands for policy, the representation system acts as a control mechanism to keep policy on course.

The question now is how. If public opinion governs, how does it find its way into the aggregation of acts that come to be called public policy.

The Mechanisms of Dynamic Representation

Start with a politician facing a policy choice. With both preferences over policy options and a continuing need to protect the electoral career from unwanted termination, the elected official will typically need to balance personal preference against electoral expediency. We presume that politicians have personal preferences for and against particular policies and also that they value reelection. Then for each choice, we can define (1) a personal ideal point in the space of policy options and (2) an *expediency point* (that position most likely to optimize future reelection changes). The expediency point might be the median voter of the relevant constituency or some similar construct. We are not concerned here about particular rules. All that matters is that the politician have a *perception* of the most expedient position.

. . . Politicians create an appropriate margin of safety: those who highly value policy formulation or who feel safe at home choose policy over security; those who face competitive challenge in the next election lean toward "expediency" and security. . . .

. . . [E]lectoral turnover stems from events that overwhelm the margin of safety that the politicians select. Campaign finance, personal scandals, challenger tactics, the framing of electoral choice—all affect outcomes. The victims come both from those who take electoral risk by pursuing policy and also from those who ignore personal preference and concentrate solely on reelection: what matters is the force of electoral events relative to the politician's expectations. . . .

To breathe life into this system, let us put it into motion to see its aggregate and dynamic implications. Assume that public opinion—global attitudes toward the role of government in society—moves over time. Immediately we can expect greater turnover as the force of public opinion augments the normal electoral shocks to upset incumbent politicians' standard calculus. Now, the changes in personnel will prove systematic: rightward shifts in public opinion will replace Democrats with Republicans, and leftward shifts Republicans with Democrats. . . .

Rational Anticipation, Turnover, and Policy Consequence

Turnover from elections works most transparently with politicians who are neither well informed (until hit on the head by the club of election results) nor strategic. But that does not look at all like the politicians we observe. The oft-painted picture of members of Congress, for example, as people who read five or six daily newspapers, work 18-hour days, and leave no stone unturned in anticipating the electoral problems that might arise from policy choices does not suggest either limited information or naïveté.

We explicitly postulate the reverse of the dumb and naïve politician: (1) elected politicians are rational actors; (2) they are well informed about movements in public opinion; and (3) they agree with one another about the nature of those movements. This was well said by John Kingdon: "People in and around government sense a national mood. They are comfortable discussing its content, and believe they know when the mood shifts. The idea goes by different names. . . . But common to all . . . is the notion that a rather large number of people out in the country are thinking along certain common lines, that this national mood changes from one time to another in discernible ways, and that these changes in mood or climate have important impacts on policy agendas and policy outcomes" (1984, 153). . . .

Elected politicians, we believe, sense the mood of the moment, assess its trend, and anticipate its consequence for future elections. Changes in opinion, correctly perceived, will lead politicians to revise their beliefs about future election opportunities and hazards. Revised beliefs imply also revised expedient positions. Such strategic adjustment will have two effects: (1) it will dampen turnover, the conventional path of electoral influence; and (2) it will drive policy through rational anticipation.

When politicians perceive public opinion change, they adapt their behavior to please their constituency and, accordingly, enhance their chances of reelection. Public opinion will still work through elections, however. When they are surprised by the suddenness or the magnitude of opinion change or when they are unable credibly to alter their policies, politicians, despite their best efforts, will occasionally face defeat at the polls. Rather more fitfully than was the case with dumb politicians, public preferences will operate on electoral institutions by changing the personnel and thus the aggregated preferences of elected officials.

But that is not the only public opinion effect. Changing policy from shifting perceptions of what is electorally expedient we will refer to as *rational anticipation*. In a world of savvy politicians, rational anticipation produces dynamic representation without need for actual electoral defeats.

Politicians modify their behavior at the margin. Liberals and conservatives do not change their stripes, but they do engage in strategic behavior either to minimize risk from movements adverse to their positions or to maximize electoral payoff from movements supportive of their positions. For example, in a conservative era, such as the early 1980s, conservative Democrats found it easier to break with their party and did it more often, while liberal Republicans found it more difficult and dangerous and did it less often. The result of such conditions can be substantial shifts in winning and losing coalitions without any change of personnel.

Moreover, such direct anticipation of the electoral future does not exhaust the possibilities. For other actors also anticipate the effects of future elections on the current behavior of elected officials. Those who advance policy proposals— bureaucrats, lobbyists, judges, and citizens—are concerned with what can be done successfully, be it administrative act, judicial decision, or legislative proposal. And other politicians—those who pursue a leadership role or advocate particular policies—may choose to push ahead of the curve, to multiply the effects of even marginal shifts in opinion by anticipating others' anticipated reactions.

The impact of rational anticipation is thus a net shift in policy outputs from the aggregation of all these smallish strategic decisions, which (responding to the same signal) tend to move all in the same direction. It should be observable as the direct response of policy to opinion change, when election turnover effects are controlled.

A Design for Assessing Representation

This two-part setup permits three possible empirical outcomes: (1) two-stage representation may occur through the mechanism of electoral turnover, where candidate success depends upon the public opinion of the moment, which is then reflected in policy behavior; (2) movements in policy acts may reflect opinion

Figure 1. The Pathways to Dynamic Representation

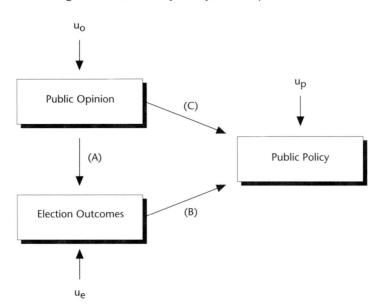

without changes in elite personnel, the rational anticipation scheme; and (3) no representation might occur if both schemes fail. The alternatives are laid out in Figure 1. There we can see three testable linkages. The first, A, is the first stage of the electoral sequence. The question to be answered is, Does public opinion affect election outcomes? The second stage, B, is not much in doubt. Its question is no cliff-hanger: Is there a difference in policy behavior between liberals and conservatives? The third linkage, C, is rational anticipation. Its question is, Does public policy move with public opinion independently of the effects of (past) elections? . . .

. . . The scheme of Figure 1 takes account of reality by positing other sets of causes of all phenomena as disturbances. The first, u_o, is the exogenous factors that account for changes in opinion. Not a focus of attention here (but see Durr 1993), they are such plausible forces as national optimism or pessimism arising from economic performance and reactions to past policies as experienced in daily life.

Elections are influenced by factors such as incumbent party performance, incumbency, macropartisanship, and so forth. Those factors appear as u_e on Figure 1. And finally, u_p captures sets of causes of public policy other than representation—such things as the events and problems to which policy is response or solution. Some of these "disturbances" are amenable to modeling, and will be. Some are irreducible, and must remain unobserved. . . .

Measurement

The raw materials of dynamic representation are familiar stuff: public opinion, elections, and public policy together form the focus of a major proportion of our scholarly activity. But familiar as these concepts are, longitudinal measures of them are (excepting elections) ad hoc at best and more often nonexistent. It is easy to think of movements of public opinion over time and public policy over time. It is not easy to quantify them. The situation—familiar concepts but novel measures—requires more than the usual cursory attention to measurement concerns. We begin with public opinion.

The Measures: Public Opinion and Elections

To tap public opinion over time we have [to] measure domestic policy mood (Stimson 1991). Mood is the major dimension underlying expressed preferences over policy alternatives in the survey research record. It is properly interpreted as left versus right—more specifically, as global preferences for a larger, more active federal government as opposed to a smaller, more passive one across the sphere of all domestic policy controversies. Thus our public opinion measure represents the public's sense of whether the political "temperature" is too hot or too cold, whether government is too active or not active enough. The policy status quo is the baseline, either explicit or implicit, in most survey questions. What the questions (and the mood measure) tap then is relative preference—the preferred direction of policy change.

Displayed in Figure 2, the *policy mood* series portrays an American public opinion that moves slowly back and forth from left (up on the scale) to right (down) over time and is roughly in accord with popular depictions of the eras of modern American politics. It reaches a liberal high point in the early 1960s, meanders mainly in the liberal end of its range through the middle 1970s, moves quite dramatically toward conservatism approaching 1980, and then begins a gradual return to liberalism over the 1980s. Note as well that the neutral point (50% liberal, 50% conservative) means something: points above 50 mean that the public wants more conservative policy. Thus, while the public's conservatism peaked in 1980, the public continued to demand more conservative policy (though by smaller margins) until 1984. (Thus we may think of our mood measure as a signal to politicians about the intensity and the direction of political pressure. It represents a demand for change.) . . .

The Measures: Policy Change

What is policy liberalism, and how can we measure it? What we observe is decisions such as congressional votes—not quite "policy." Our view is that each involves

Figure 2. Public Opinion over Time: Domestic Policy Mood, 1956–1993

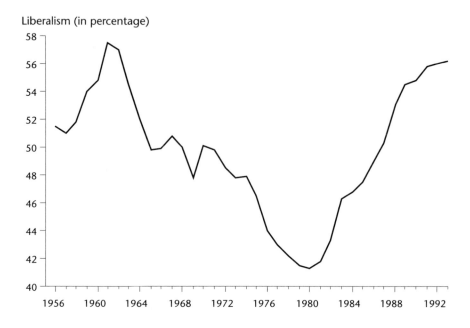

Liberalism (in percentage)

policy *change* at the margin. The issue as it is typically confronted is, Should we move current government policy in more liberal (expansive) directions or in more conservative ones? What we observe is who votes how. We see, for example, a particular vote in which the liberal forces triumph over conservative opponents. We take such a vote to mean that in fact the (unobserved) content of the vote moves policy in a liberal direction—or resists movement in the conservative direction.

This is a direct analogy to public opinion as we measure it. We ask the public whether government should "do more" or "spend more" toward some particular purpose. We take the response, "do more," "do less," "do about the same" to indicate the preferred direction of policy *change.* In both cases direction of change from the status quo is the issue.

Measuring this net liberalism or conservatism of global policy output seems easy enough in concept. We talk about some Congresses being more or less liberal than others as if we knew what that meant. But if we ask how we know, where those intuitions come from, the answer is likely to be nonspecific. The intuitions probably arise from fuzzy processing of multiple indicators of, for example, congressional action. And if none of them by itself is probably "the" defensible measure, our intuitions are probably correct in netting out the sum of many of them, all moving in the same direction. That, at least, is our strategy here. We will exploit several indicators of annual congressional policy output, each by itself dubious. But when they run in tandem with one another, the set will seem much more secure than its members.

Congressional Rating Scales. Rating scales are a starting point. Intended to tap the policy behaviors of individual House members and Senators, scales produced by groups such as Americans for Democratic Action (ADA) and Americans for Constitutional Action (ACA), later American Conservative Union (ACU), are now available for most of the period in question. Neither of these is intended to be a longitudinal measure of congressional action; and from a priori consideration of the properties such a measure would want, this is not how we would derive one. But if scales move similarly across chambers and scales from different organizations move in common over time, then we begin to believe that whatever it is they are measuring is probably global liberalism or conservatism of roll-call voting. Thus, as a measure of *net group rating*, we take the yearly average of the House's (or Senate's) ADA score and (100 minus) the ACA/ACU score.

Congressional Roll-Call Outcomes. The strength of the rating scales is their cross-sectional validity: they discriminate liberals from moderates from conservatives in any given year. Their weakness is longitudinal validity: we are less confident that they discriminate liberal from moderate from conservative Congresses. For greater face validity, we turn to the roll calls themselves as measures of policymaking. A quite direct measure is the answer to the questions, On ideological votes, who wins? and By how much do they win? Provided that we can isolate a set of roll calls that polarize votes along the left-versus-right main dimension of American domestic politics, measuring the degree of, say, liberalism is as easy as counting the votes. If we know which position on the vote is liberal and which conservative, then all that remains is to observe who won and by how much (and then aggregate that roll-call information to the session).

We exploit the cross-sectional strength of the rating scales (specifically, ADA) to classify roll calls. For each of the 25,492 roll-call votes in both houses for 1956–90, we classify the vote as left-right polarized or not (and then in which direction). The criterion for the classification as polarized is that the vote must show a greater association with member ADA scores than a hypothetical party-line vote for the particular members of each Congress. The intuition of this criterion is that we know we are observing a left-right cleavage when defection from party lines is itself along left-right lines—conservative Democrats voting with Republicans, liberal Republicans voting with Democrats. Although the party vote itself might be ideological, we cannot know that it is. One measure of the net liberalism of the session (for each house separately) is then simply the median size of the liberal coalition (on votes where the liberal and conservative sides are defined). A second approach to the same raw data is to focus on winning and losing, rather than coalition size. In this set of measures we simply count the percentage of liberal wins. We are observing quite directly then who wins, who loses, and by how much.

The Dramatic Acts of Congress: Key Votes. Scales of roll-call votes tell us about the overall tenor of public policy. Probably an excellent basis for inference about the net direction of policy movement, they do not distinguish between minor matters and those of enormous public consequence and visibility. Getting a good measure of "importance" presents a formidable challenge, requiring great numbers of subtle judgments about content and context. It is nonetheless desirable to have some indication of whether legislative activity produces something of import. A particular subset of legislation, the *Congressional Quarterly* "key votes" for each session of Congress, does attempt to distinguish the crucial from the trivial. The virtues of this set of votes are that it reflects the wisdom of expert observers of Congress at the time about what was important, and the measures are readily coded into liberal or conservative actions (and some that are neither).

We quantify the key votes as a combination of who wins and by how much. Accordingly, we average (1) the percentage of liberal wins and (2) the size of the liberal winning coalition. Crude, the measures nonetheless tap the issue in question, the direction of highly visible outcomes. The resulting time series are noisy (as would be expected from the small numbers of votes for each year), evincing a good deal of year-to-year fluctuation that seems meaningless. But they also show a picture of episodes of major policy change occurring exactly when expected for the Great Society (liberalism, peaking in 1965) and the Reagan Revolution (conservatism, peaking in 1981) periods respectively.

To get a sense of how legislative policy has moved over the years, look at Figure 3. [Figure 3a] presents our four measures for the House of Representatives. (To keep the eye on systematic movement, we have smoothed the graphs by taking a centered three-year moving average for each series. Note that we smooth only in this graph: we use the measured data for the statistical analysis.) It is clear that each indicator (wins, coalition size, ADA–ACA ratings, and key votes) contains both a common component and an idiosyncratic component. The lines move together, with a bit of zig and zag around the main flow. The panel for the Senate (Figure 3b) carries a similar message. Peaks of liberalism came during the early 1960s and the late 1980s, with conservatism at its height around 1980. While thus similar in outline, the patterns are not quite identical.

Presidential Policy Liberalism. The beginning point of dealing with the presidency is noting the near impossibility of direct measures of presidential liberalism from what presidents say and do. While we have an intuition about various acts and speeches, any attempt to quantify that intuition, to extract acts from the context of actions, quickly becomes hopelessly subjective. The alternative is to

Figure 3. Indicators of Public Policy Change in Four Parts of American Government (Three-Year Moving Averages)

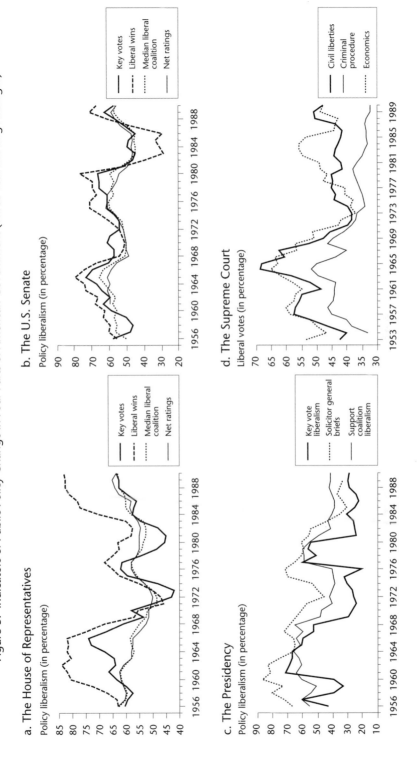

a. The House of Representatives

Policy liberalism (in percentage)

Key votes
Liberal wins
Median liberal coalition
Net ratings

b. The U.S. Senate

Policy liberalism (in percentage)

Key votes
Liberal wins
Median liberal coalition
Net ratings

c. The Presidency

Policy liberalism (in percentage)

Key vote liberalism
Solicitor general briefs
Support coalition liberalism

d. The Supreme Court

Liberal votes (in percentage)

Civil liberties
Criminal procedure
Economics

look instead at presidents through their quantifiable records of interacting with the legislature and judiciary.

We know how often particular members of Congress support and oppose the president. And we can measure the liberalism of individual members in several ways. The most convenient of these is ADA scores, which are present for the entire period, as other comparable indicators are not. And we know that ADA ratings are very highly correlated with other ratings when available—positively or negatively—so that they can serve as a useful instrument of the underlying concept.

How then to combine these different pieces of information? A first approach is to ask the question, How liberal are the regular supporters of the president each year?, and then adopt that standard as a reflection of what the president wanted from Congress. That, however, is confounded by shared partisanship between president and member. We expect members of the president's party to be more likely to be regular supporters—independent of ideological agreement with the president's program. To deal with shared party ties as a confounding factor in presidential support, we opt instead to focus on presidential support within party. The strategy is first to divide each party into support and opposition groups based upon whether member presidential support is above or below the average for the party. The mean ADA rating of each party's "support" group is then an estimate of the president's ideological position. The opposition groups similarly measure the reverse. The measurement question then may be reduced to how such separate estimates are to be combined. For a summary measure of presidential position we perform a principal components analysis of the eight indicators (*support* vs. *oppose,* by party, by house). That analysis shows decisively that each of the eight taps a single underlying dimension. Such a dimension is estimated with a factor score and rescaled . . . to approximate the ADA scales from which it was derived.

For a second legislative presidential position measure we simply take the recorded presidential position for the key votes and compute the percentage of presidential stands each year that are liberal, where again the votes are classified by polarization with individual ADA ratings.

Presidential Interaction with the Court. With less regularity and on a quite different set of issues, presidents make their policy views known to the U.S. Supreme Court. The mechanism for doing so formally is the amicus curiae brief filed by the presidency's designated agent to the courts, the solicitor general. On over 700 occasions in the 1953–89 terms, the solicitor general went on record with the Court, arguing that the holdings of particular judicial decisions ought to be affirmed or reversed. About 90% of these briefs take positions on cases that are themselves classifiably liberal or conservative.

We employ the solicitor general briefs data as leverage to measure presumed presidential position on judicial issues. Using the direction coding from the Spaeth Supreme Court data base for the case and our knowledge of whether the solicitor general argued to affirm or reverse, we code each of the briefs as to direction—liberal, conservative, or nonideological. It is then an easy matter to produce aggregated annual scales as percentage liberal of the ideological positions taken.

A quick comparison of the presidential series with the legislative series (in Figure 3) suggests less coherence in the presidential measures. Much of the discord comes from the *Solicitor General* series (which we retain, nevertheless, for its substantive value). Note also that the presidential series is typically more conservative than the two congressional series, as we might reasonably expect from the historical party control of the two institutions.

Supreme Court Liberalism. For data we have the Supreme Court data base for the period 1953–90. From that, we can content-classify the majority position in individual cases as liberal, conservative, or neither; and from that, the lifetime liberalism or conservatism of individual justices is readily derived. Then we return to the individual cases and scale the majority and dissenting votes by the justices who cast them. This allows a content-free second classification of the majority position as liberal, conservative, or not ideological. From this we build annual measures of the major-case content categories. We have chosen four such categories—*civil rights and liberties, criminal procedure, economics,* and *other*—the number a compromise between separating matters which might in principle produce different alignments and grouping broadly enough to have sufficient cases in each for reliable annual measures.

For each measure we construct a time series consisting of the percentage of all votes cast by the justices on the liberal side of the issue, whichever that is, for the year. This focus on justice decisions, rather than aggregate outcomes of the Court, appears to produce a more moderate measure over time than the alternative. . . .

We examine the first three domains in Figure 3. There we see that the issue domains move pretty much in tandem. All domains show the famous liberalism of the Warren Court in the mid-1960s and the conservative reaction of the Burger Court. Most show a modest rebound of liberalism in the early 1980s, which then reverses from the influence of new Reagan justices.

The pattern of more substantive notice is that the *"criminal procedure"* cases produce no liberal rebound in the 1980s. This is an interesting exception, for public attitudes toward crime and criminals are themselves an exception to the growing liberalism of the 1980s (Stimson 1991). This is a case where the conservative message ("The solution is more punitive law enforcement") is still dominant. . . .

A Summary Analysis of Governmental Responsiveness

For a summation of dynamic representation we slice across the institutional structure of American politics, returning to the familiar questions, Does public opinion influence public policy? and By what process? Our combining the policy output of the four institutions is, of course, a fiction: a single national public policy is not the average of independent branches. We "average" across different branches to provide a rough answer to a rough question. Here we select two indicators from each of the four prior analyses (president, House, Senate, and Supreme Court) and then estimate representation as it works on the American national government as a whole. . . .

We get a better sense of the historical dynamic by examining Figure 4. Plotted here are measures of public opinion, public policy and predicted policy. The first (in the light, solid line) is public opinion, with its liberal peaks during the early 1960s and late 1980s and its conservative peak around 1980. The dark, solid line represents policy, a simple average of our eight policy indicators. Without much work, it is clear that the two series are basically similar: policy reflects the timing and range of public opinion change.

Yet the two paths are not identical. Policy turned much more conservative during the late 1960s and early 1970s than the public demanded. Then, contrary to the continuing turn to the right, policy temporarily shifted leftward under Carter's leadership. Now look at the small dots that show predicted policy. . . . The exceptionally good fit is apparent. More important, the model is now able to account for the otherwise surprising conservatism just before 1972 and the liberalism of the late 1970s by including the Vietnam War and the composition variables. Thus, while the main part of policy moves in accord with public preferences, significant deviations can and do occur. Those deviations seem explicable but not by public preferences. Public opinion is powerful but not all-powerful.

Figure 4 takes us back to where we started, public policy preferences, and forward to the end of the story, the policy liberalism of American government, 1956–90. The point is that the two are a lot alike. . . .

Some Reflections on American Politics

The past four decades of United States history show that politicians translate changes in public opinion into policy change. Further, the evidence suggests that this translation varies by institution, both in the mechanisms that produce the link and in the nature of the dynamics.

Most important, dynamic representation finds strong support. Our work indicates that when the public asks for a more activist or a more conservative government,

Figure 4. Global Public Opinion and Global Public Policy:
Predicted and Actual Policy

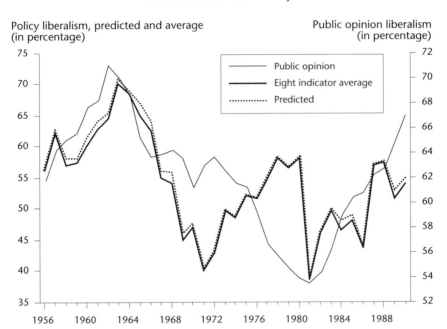

Policy liberalism, predicted and average
(in percentage)

Public opinion liberalism
(in percentage)

politicians oblige. The early peak of public opinion liberalism during the early 1960s produced liberal policy; the turn away from activism and the steady move toward conservatism was similarly reflected in national policy; and the recent 1980s upsurge of public demand for action was also effective (with the exception of the Court). To be sure, other things matter too. We have modeled a late 1960s shift rightward in policy (beyond that driven by public opinion) as a function of the Vietnam War's dominance over domestic political agendas. In addition, we modeled the shift leftward during the years of the Carter presidency (a shift contrary to the prevailing movement in public opinion) as a coincidence of compositional factors.

   While we are confident that the basic result holds, we know that we do not yet fully understand movement in public policy. Nevertheless, the main story is that large-scale shifts in public opinion yield corresponding large-scale shifts in government action.

   The link between opinion and policy is undoubtedly more complicated. While concentrating on policy response to opinion, we have seen little evidence of opinion reaction to policy. Elementary analyses generate contradictory inferences: the matter is subtle, the timing probably complex. We do know enough to assert that opinion reaction cannot explain the structural associations we uncover. We do not know enough to characterize the fuller relationship. This, of course, is a compelling subject for hard work.

Beyond the basic result, we can say that American national institutions vary in the mechanisms that produce responsiveness. It is the Senate, not the House of Representatives, that most clearly mimics the eighteenth-century clockwork meant to produce electoral accountability. When comparing the effectiveness of turnover and rational anticipation, we find that for the Senate (and also for the presidency), the most important channel for governmental representation is electoral replacement. Equally responsive, however, is the House of Representatives. Its members employ rational anticipation to produce a similarly effective public policy response, without the overt evidence of personnel change. The Supreme Court appears to reflect public opinion far more than constitutionally expected; but, in comparison, it is the institution that responds least.

Finally, the dynamics prove interesting. Each of the electoral institutions translates immediately public opinion into public policy. That is to say, when electoral politicians sense a shift in public preferences, they act directly and effectively to shift the direction of public policy. We find no evidence of delay or hesitation. The Court, not surprisingly, moves at a more deliberate speed. But equally important, rational anticipation is based not only on the long-term trends in public opinion but also on year-to-year shifts. That is to say, politicians constantly and immediately process public opinion changes in order to stay ahead of the political curve. Understanding politics well, the constitutional framers were correct in expecting short-term politics to be a fundamental part of dynamic representation.

The United States government, as it has evolved over the years, produces a complex response to public demands. The original constitutional design mixed different political calculations into different institutions so that no personal ambition, no political faction, no single political interest, or no transient passion could dominate. We now see the founders' expectations about complexity manifest in contemporary policymaking. Constitutional mechanisms harness politicians' strategies to the public's demands. In the end, the government combines both short- and long-term considerations through both rational anticipation and compositional change to produce a strong and resilient link between public and policy. . . .

REFERENCES

Durr, Robert H. 1993. "What Moves Policy Sentiment?" *American Political Science Review* 87:158–70.

Kingdon, John W. 1984. *Agendas, Alternatives, and Public Policies.* Boston: Little, Brown.

Stimson, James A. 1991. *Public Opinion in America: Moods, Cycles, and Swings.* Boulder: Westview.

10-3

America's Ignorant Voters

Michael Schudson

The meagerness of the average American's political knowledge has dismayed observers for decades. But Michael Schudson asks whether the informed citizen— meaning one who knows basic facts about government and politics—is truly the foundation of effective democracy. Reviewing the evidence, Schudson argues, contrary to conventional wisdom, that the problem is not growing worse. Moreover, voters may not recall many facts but still be able to vote in a way that reflects reasonable evaluations of candidates and parties.

EVERY WEEK, the *Tonight Show's* Jay Leno takes to the streets of Los Angeles to quiz innocent passersby with some simple questions: On what bay is San Francisco located? Who was president of the United States during World War II? The audience roars as Leno's hapless victims fumble for answers. Was it Lincoln? Carter?

No pollster, let alone a college or high school history teacher, would be surprised by the poor showing of Leno's sample citizens. In a national assessment test in the late 1980s, only a third of American 17-year-olds could correctly locate the Civil War in the period 1850–1900; more than a quarter placed it in the 18th century. Two-thirds knew that Abraham Lincoln wrote the Emancipation Proclamation, which seems a respectable showing, but what about the 14 percent who said that Lincoln wrote the Bill of Rights, the 10 percent who checked the Missouri Compromise, and the nine percent who awarded Lincoln royalties for *Uncle Tom's Cabin?*

Asking questions about contemporary affairs doesn't yield any more encouraging results. In a 1996 national public opinion poll, only 10 percent of American adults could identify William Rehnquist as the chief justice of the Supreme Court. In the same survey, conducted at the height of Newt Gingrich's celebrity as Speaker of the House, only 59 percent could identify the job he held. Americans sometimes demonstrate deeper knowledge about a major issue before the nation, such as the Vietnam War, but most could not describe the thrust of the Clinton health care plan or tell whether the Reagan administration supported the Sandinistas or the contras during the conflict in Nicaragua (and only a third could place that country in Central America).

Source: Michael Schudson, "America's Ignorant Voters," *Wilson Quarterly,* Spring 2000, Vol. 24, Issue 2.

It can be misleading to make direct comparisons with other countries, but the general level of political awareness in leading liberal democracies overseas does seem to be much higher. While 58 percent of the Germans surveyed, 32 percent of the French, and 22 percent of the British were able to identify Boutros Boutros-Ghali as secretary general of the United Nations in 1994, only 13 percent of Americans could do so. Nearly all Germans polled could name Boris Yeltsin as Russia's leader, as could 63 percent of the British, 61 percent of the French, but only 50 percent of the Americans.

How can the United States claim to be [a] model democracy if its citizens know so little about political life? That question has aroused political reformers and preoccupied many political scientists since the early 20th century. It can't be answered without some historical perspective.

Today's mantra that the "informed citizen" is the foundation of effective democracy was not a central part of the nation's founding vision. It is largely the creation of late-19th-century Mugwump and Progressive reformers, who recoiled from the spectacle of powerful political parties using government as a job bank for their friends and a cornucopia of contracts for their relatives. (In those days before the National Endowment for the Arts, Nathaniel Hawthorne, Herman Melville, and Walt Whitman all subsidized their writing by holding down federal patronage appointments.) Voter turnout in the late 19th century was extraordinarily high by today's standards, routinely over 70 percent in presidential elections, and there is no doubt that parades, free whiskey, free-floating money, patronage jobs, and the pleasures of fraternity all played a big part in the political enthusiasm of ordinary Americans.

The reformers saw this kind of politics as a betrayal of democratic ideals. A democratic public, they believed, must reason together. That ideal was threatened by mindless enthusiasm, the wily maneuvers of political machines, and the vulnerability of the new immigrant masses in the nation's big cities, woefully ignorant of Anglo-Saxon traditions, to manipulation by party hacks. E. L. Godkin, founding editor of the Nation and a leading reformer, argued that "there is no corner of our system in which the hastily made and ignorant foreign voter may not be found eating away the political structure, like a white ant, with a group of natives standing over him and encouraging him."

This was in 1893, by which point a whole set of reforms had been put in place. Civil service reform reduced patronage. Ballot reform irrevocably altered the act of voting itself. For most of the 19th century, parties distributed at the polls their own "tickets," listing only their own candidates for office. A voter simply took a ticket from a party worker and deposited it in the ballot box, without needing to read it or mark it in any way. Voting was thus a public act of party affiliation. Beginning in 1888, however, and spreading across the country by 1896, this system was replaced with government-printed ballots that listed all the candidates from each eligible party. The voter marked the ballot in secret, as we do today, in an act that affirmed voting as an individual choice rather than a social act of party loyalty. Political parades and other public spectacles increasingly gave way to pamphlets in what reformers dubbed "educational" political campaigns. Leading newspapers, once little more than organs of the political parties, began to declare their independence and to portray themselves as nonpartisan commercial institutions of public enlightenment and public-minded criticism. Public secondary education began to spread.

These and other reforms enshrined the informed citizen as the foundation of democracy, but at a tremendous cost: Voter turnout plummeted. In the presidential election of 1920, it dropped to 49 percent, its lowest point in the 20th century—until it was matched in 1996. Ever since, political scientists and others have been plumbing the mystery created by the new model of an informed citizenry: How can so many, knowing so little, and voting in such small numbers, build a democracy that appears to be (relatively) successful?

There are several responses to that question. The first is that a certain amount of political ignorance is an inevitable byproduct of America's unique political environment. One reason Americans have so much difficulty grasping the political facts of life is that their political system is the world's most complex. Ask the next political science Ph.D. you meet to explain what government agencies at what level—federal, state, county, or city—take responsibility for the homeless. Or whom he or she voted for in the last election for municipal judge. The answers might make Jay Leno's victims seem less ridiculous. No European country has as many elections, as many elected offices, as complex a maze of overlapping governmental jurisdictions, as the American system. It is simply harder to "read" U.S. politics than the politics of most nations.

The hurdle of political comprehension is raised a notch higher by the ideological inconsistencies of American political parties. In Britain, a voter can confidently cast a vote without knowing a great deal about the particular candidates on the ballot. The Labor candidate generally can be counted on to follow the Labor line, the Conservative to follow the Tory line. An American voter casting a ballot for a Democrat or Republican has no such assurance. Citizens in other countries need only dog paddle to be in the political swim; in the United States they need the skills of a scuba diver.

If the complexity of U.S. political institutions helps explain American ignorance of domestic politics, geopolitical factors help explain American backwardness in foreign affairs. There is a kind of ecology of political ignorance at work. The United States is far from Europe and borders only two other countries. With a vast domestic market, most of its producers have relatively few dealings with customers in other countries, globalization notwithstanding. Americans, lacking the parliamentary form of government that prevails in most other democracies, are also likely to find much of what they read or hear about the wider world politically opaque. And the simple fact of America's political and cultural superpower status naturally limits citizens' political awareness. Just as employees gossip more about the boss than the boss gossips about them, so Italians and Brazilians know more about the United States than Americans know about their countries.

Consider a thought experiment. Imagine what would happen if you transported those relatively well-informed Germans or Britons to the United States with their cultural heritage, schools, and news media intact. If you checked on them again about a generation later, after long exposure to the distinctive American political environment—its geographic isolation, superpower status, complex political system, and weak parties—would they have the political knowledge levels of Europeans or Americans? Most likely, I think, they would have developed typically American levels of political ignorance.

Lending support to this notion of an ecology of political knowledge is the stability of American political ignorance over time. Since the 1940s, when social scientists began measuring it, political ignorance has remained virtually unchanged. It is hard to gauge the extent of political knowledge before that time, but there is little to suggest that there is some lost golden age in U.S. history. The storied 1858 debates between Senator Stephen Douglas and Abraham Lincoln, for example, though undoubtedly a high point in the nation's public discourse, were also an anomaly. Public debates were rare in 19th-century political campaigns, and campaign rhetoric was generally overblown and aggressively partisan.

Modern measurements of Americans' historical and political knowledge go back at least to 1943, when the *New York Times* surveyed college freshmen and found "a striking ignorance of even the most elementary aspects of United States history." Reviewing nearly a half-century of data (1945–89) in *What Americans Know about Politics and Why It Matters* (1996), political scientists Michael Delli Carpini and Scott Keeter conclude that, on balance, there has been a slight gain in Americans' political knowledge, but one so modest that it makes more sense to speak of a remarkable stability. In 1945, for example, 43 percent of a national sample could name neither of their U.S. senators; in 1989, the figure was essentially unchanged at 45 percent. In 1952, 67 percent could name the vice president; in 1989, 74 percent could do so. In 1945, 92 percent of Gallup poll respondents knew that the term of the president is four years, compared with 96 percent in 1989. Whatever the explanations for dwindling voter turnout since 1960 may be, rising ignorance is not one of them.

As Delli Carpini and Keeter suggest, there are two ways to view their findings. The optimist's view is that political ignorance has grown no worse despite the spread of television and video games, the decline of political parties, and a variety of other negative developments. The pessimist asks why so little has improved despite the vast increase in formal education during those years. But the main conclusion remains: no notable change over as long a period as data are available.

Low as American levels of political knowledge may be, a generally tolerable, sometimes admirable, political democracy survives. How? One explanation is provided by a school of political science that goes under the banner of "political heuristics." Public opinion polls and paper-and-pencil tests of political knowledge, argue researchers such as Arthur Lupia, Samuel Popkin, Paul Sniderman, and Philip Tetlock, presume that citizens require more knowledge than they actually need in order to cast votes that accurately reflect their preferences. People can and do get by with relatively little political information. What Popkin calls "low-information rationality" is sufficient for citizens to vote intelligently.

This works in two ways. First, people can use cognitive cues, or "heuristics." Instead of learning each of a candidate's issue positions, the voter may simply rely on the candidate's party affiliation as a cue. This works better in Europe than in America, but it still works reasonably well. Endorsements are another useful shortcut. A thumbs-up for a candidate from the Christian Coalition or Ralph Nader or the National Association for the Advancement of Colored People or the American Association of Retired Persons frequently provides enough information to enable one to cast a reasonable vote.

Second, as political scientist Milton Lodge points out, people often process information on the fly, without retaining details in memory. If you watch a debate on TV—and 46 million did watch the first presidential debate between President Bill Clinton and Robert Dole in 1996—you may learn enough about the candidates' ideas and personal styles to come to a judgment about each one. A month later, on election day, you may not be able to answer a pollster's detailed questions about where they stood on the issues, but you will remember which one you liked best—and that is enough information to let you vote intelligently.

The realism of the political heuristics school is an indispensable corrective to unwarranted bashing of the general public. Americans are not the political dolts they sometimes seem to be. Still, the political heuristics approach has a potentially fatal flaw: It subtly substitutes voting for citizenship. Cognitive shortcuts have their place, but what if a citizen wants to persuade someone else to vote for his or her chosen candidate? What may be sufficient in the voting booth is

inadequate in the wider world of the democratic process: discussion, deliberation, and persuasion. It is possible to vote and still be disenfranchised.

Yet another response to the riddle of voter ignorance takes its cue from the
Founders and other 18th-century political thinkers who emphasized the importance of a morally virtuous citizenry. Effective democracy, in this view, depends
more on the "democratic character" of citizens than on their aptitude for quiz
show knowledge of political facts. Character, in this sense, is demonstrated all
the time in everyday life, not in the voting booth every two years. From Amitai
Etzioni, William Galston, and Michael Sandel on the liberal side of the political
spectrum to William J. Bennett and James Q. Wilson on the conservative side,
these writers emphasize the importance of what Alexis de Tocqueville called
"habits of the heart." These theorists, along with politicians of every stripe, point
to the importance of civil society as a foundation of democracy. They emphasize
instilling moral virtue through families and civic participation through churches
and other voluntary associations; they stress the necessity for civility and democratic behavior in daily life. They would not deny that it is important for citizens
to be informed, but neither would they put information at the center of their
vision of what makes democracy tick.

Brown University's Nancy Rosenblum, for example, lists two essential traits
of democratic character. "Easy spontaneity" is the disposition to treat others
identically, without deference, and with an easy grace. This capacity to act as if
many social differences are of no account in public settings is one of the things
that make[s] democracy happen on the streets. This is the disposition that foreign
visitors have regularly labeled "American" for 200 years, at least since 1818,
when the British reformer and journalist William Cobbett remarked upon Americans' "universal civility." Tocqueville observed in 1840 that strangers in America who meet "find neither danger nor advantage in telling each other freely
what they think. Meeting by chance, they neither seek nor avoid each other.
Their manner is therefore natural, frank, and open."

Rosenblum's second trait is "speaking up," which she describes as "a willingness to respond at least minimally to ordinary injustice." This does not involve
anything so impressive as organizing a demonstration, but something more like
objecting when an adult cuts ahead of a kid in a line at a movie theater, or politely
rebuking a coworker who slurs a racial or religious group. It is hard to define
"speaking up" precisely, but we all recognize it, without necessarily giving it the
honor it deserves as an element of self-government.

We need not necessarily accept Rosenblum's chosen pair of moral virtues.
Indeed a Japanese or Swedish democrat might object that they look suspiciously
like distinctively American traits rather than distinctively democratic ones.
They almost evoke Huckleberry Finn. But turning our attention to democratic

character reminds us that being well informed is just one of the requirements of democratic citizenship.

The Founding Fathers were certainly more concerned about instilling moral virtues than disseminating information about candidates and issues. Although they valued civic engagement more than their contemporaries in Europe did, and cared enough about promoting the wide circulation of ideas to establish a post office and adopt the First Amendment, they were ambivalent about, even suspicious of, a politically savvy populace. They did not urge voters to "know the issues"; at most they hoped that voters would choose wise and prudent legislators to consider issues on their behalf. On the one hand, they agreed that "the diffusion of knowledge is productive of virtue, and the best security for our civil rights," as a North Carolina congressman put it in 1792. On the other hand, as George Washington cautioned, "however necessary it may be to keep a watchful eye over public servants and public measures, yet there ought to be limits to it, for suspicions unfounded and jealousies too lively are irritating to honest feelings, and oftentimes are productive of more evil than good."

If men were angels, well and good—but they were not, and few of the Founders were as extravagant as Benjamin Rush in his rather scary vision of an education that would "convert men into republican machines." In theory, many shared Rush's emphasis on education; in practice, the states made little provision for public schooling in the early years of the Republic. Where schools did develop, they were defended more as tutors of obedience and organs of national unity than as means to create a watchful citizenry. The Founders placed trust less in education than in a political system designed to insulate decision making in the legislatures from the direct influence of the emotional, fractious, and too easily swayed electorate.

All of these arguments—about America's political environment, the value of political heuristics, and civil society—do not add up to a prescription for resignation or complacency about civic education. Nothing I have said suggests that the League of Women Voters should shut its doors or that newspaper editors should stop putting politics on page one. People may be able to vote intelligently with very little information—even well educated people do exactly that on most of the ballot issues they face—but democratic citizenship means more than voting. It means discussing and debating the questions before the political community—and sometimes raising new questions. Without a framework of information in which to place them, it is hard to understand even the simple slogans and catchwords of the day. People with scant political knowledge, as research by political scientists Samuel Popkin and Michael Dimock suggests, have more difficulty than others in perceiving differences between candidates and parties. Ignorance also tends to breed more ignorance; it inhibits people from venturing into situations that make them feel uncomfortable or inadequate, from the voting booth to the community forum to the town hall.

What is to be done? First, it is important to put the problem in perspective. American political ignorance is not growing worse. There is even an "up" side to Americans' relative indifference to political and historical facts: their characteristic openness to experiment, their pragmatic willingness to judge ideas and practices by their results rather than their pedigree.

Second, it pays to examine more closely the ways in which people do get measurably more knowledgeable. One of the greatest changes Delli Carpini and Keeter found in their study, for example, was in the percentage of Americans who could identify the first 10 amendments to the Constitution as the Bill of Rights. In 1954, the year the U.S. Supreme Court declared school segregation unconstitutional in *Brown v. Board of Education,* only 31 percent of Americans could do so. In 1989, the number had moved up to 46 percent.

Why the change? I think the answer is clear: The civil rights movement, along with the rights-oriented Warren Court, helped bring rights to the forefront of the American political agenda and thus to public consciousness. Because they dominated the political agenda, rights became a familiar topic in the press and on TV dramas, sitcoms, and talk shows, also finding their way into school curricula and textbooks. Political change, this experience shows, can influence public knowledge.

This is not to say that only a social revolution can bring about such an improvement. A lot of revolutions are small, one person at a time, one classroom at a time. But it does mean that there is no magic bullet. Indeed, imparting political knowledge has only become more difficult as the dimensions of what is considered political have expanded into what were once nonpolitical domains (such as gender relations and tobacco use), as one historical narrative has become many, each of them contentious, and as the relatively simple framework of world politics (the Cold War) has disappeared.

In this world, the ability to name the three branches of government or describe the New Deal does not make a citizen, but it is at least a token of membership in a society dedicated to the ideal of self-government. Civic education is an imperative we must pursue with the full recognition that a high level of ignorance is likely to prevail—even if that fact does not flatter our faith in rationalism, our pleasure in moralizing, or our confidence in reform.

10-4

from *Culture War? The Myth of a Polarized America*

Morris P. Fiorina

Many observers of politics have asserted that Americans are increasingly polarized, particularly over cultural or social issues. That polarization, it is claimed, has intensified partisanship in the electorate and in Washington. In the following essay, Morris Fiorina challenges the assumption that Americans have become more deeply divided on cultural issues. He argues, rather, that political elites, particularly candidates for office, have become more polarized along party and ideological lines, thus changing the choices available to the voters. That, in turn, has produced a sorting of the electorate and the deceptive appearance of polarization in the mass public.

[Many observers of American politics in recent years refer] to "the 50:50 nation." During the late 1990s and early 2000s this phrase began to appear in popular discussions of American politics, as did a similar phrase, "the 49 percent nation." Such phraseology referred to the closely divided national elections of the late 1990s, when the winning party's popular vote share repeatedly came in right around 49 percent of the total vote:

• 1996 Clinton Vote	49.2%
• 1996 Republican House Vote	48.9
• 1998 Republican House Vote	48.9
• 2000 Gore Vote	48.4
• 2000 Republican House Vote	48.3
• 2002 Republican House Vote	50.9

If we consider only the two-party vote, the parties are almost exactly evenly matched nationally—50:50—or at least they were until the 2002 House elections, when the Republicans broke through that ceiling and got to 52.9 percent. Clearly, recent national elections have been exceedingly close. No presidential candidate has won a majority of the popular vote since 1988, the past three elections constituting the longest such streak since the so-called "era of indecision," when no presidential candidate won a majority of the popular vote in the four elections from 1880 to 1892.

Source: Morris P. Fiorina, *Culture War? The Myth of a Polarized America* (Upper Saddle River, N.J.: Pearson Education, Inc., 2005), 11–26.

Figure 1. Two Very Different Close Election Scenarios

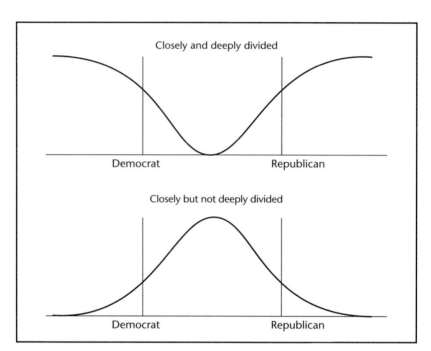

The question is what to make of these recent close elections? For most commentators, the answer is obvious: the American electorate is polarized. In the previously quoted words of the *Economist*, the close recent U.S. elections "*. . . reflect deep demographic divisions. . . . The 50-50 nation appears to be made up of two big, separate voting blocks, with only a small number of swing voters in the middle.*" The top panel of Figure 1 depicts this claim graphically. The electorate is highly polarized: a large number of "progressives" on the left support the Democrats, a large number of "orthodox" on the right support the Republicans, and very few people occupy the middle ground. With a polarized electorate like this, elections will be very close, half the voters will cheer, and half the voters will seethe, as *USA Today* asserts.

But the U-shaped distribution in the top panel of the figure is not the only electoral configuration that will produce close elections. Most obviously, con-sider the bell-shaped distribution in the bottom panel of Figure 1, which is the inverse of the U-shaped distribution in the top. In the lower figure most people hold moderate or centrist positions and relatively few are extreme partisans. But if the Democratic and Republican parties position themselves equidistant from the center on opposite sides, then the bottom configuration too produces close elections. In both examples the electorate is *closely* divided, but only in the top panel of the figure would we say that the voters are *deeply* divided. In the top panel it would be accurate to say that voters are polarized, but in the bottom panel we would more accurately call most voters ambivalent or indifferent.

When an election results in a near 50:50 outcome, the standard interpretation seems to be that the electorate is polarized as in the top panel of Figure 1. Why should that be the default interpretation? When an individual voter reports that he or she is on the fence (50:50) about whom to vote for, everyone understands that there are a number of plausible interpretations; the individual likes both candidates equally, dislikes both candidates equally, or really doesn't give a damn. No one suggests that the individual is polarized. But the aggregate and individual situations are analogous. In each case a continuous variable (percent of the vote/probability of voting for a given candidate) is compressed into a dichotomous variable (Republican or Democratic victory/Republican or Democratic vote), with enormous loss of information. To illustrate, consider the map on the inside back cover of this book, which differs from the red and blue map on the front cover in that a state is colored red or blue only if it was won by a margin of 55:45 or greater, a standard political science definition of marginality. Now a great deal of the map is gray, reflecting the fact that many states are marginal and not securely in the camp of one party or the other. In language analogous to that used to describe individual voters, we might call such states "ambivalent" or "uncertain."

In sum, close elections may reflect equal numbers of voters who hate one candidate and love the other, voters who like both, voters who do not care much at all about either candidate, or various combinations of these conditions. Without taking a detailed look at voter attitudes, we cannot determine whether close elections reflect a polarized electorate that is deeply divided, or an ambivalent electorate that is closely divided between the choices it is offered. So, let us take a closer look at the public opinion that underlies the knife-edge elections of the past few years. Is it as divided as election outcomes seem to suggest?

Is the Country Polarized?

You've got 80% to 90% of the country that look at each other like they are on separate planets. (Bush reelection strategist, Matthew Dowd).

Is America polarized? Strictly speaking the question should be "has America become *more* polarized?" for that is the claim. But if the country is not polarized to begin with, the question of whether it has become more polarized is moot. Barely two months before the supposed "values chasm separating the blue

Table 1. Red Versus Blue States: Political Inclinations

	Blue	Red
Vote intention: Bush	34%	44%
Democratic self-ID	36	32
Republican self-ID	25	31
Liberal self-ID	22	18
Conservative self-ID	33	41
Moderate self-ID	45	41

states from the red ones" emerged in the 2000 election, the Pew Research Center for the People & the Press conducted an extensive national survey that included a wide sampling of issues, a number of those which figure prominently in discussions of the culture war. We have divided the Pew survey respondents into those who resided in states that two months later were to be categorized as blue states and states that two months later were to be categorized as red states. The question is whether there is any indication in these data that the election results would leave one half the country "seething" and one half "cheering," as *USA Today* reports.

Table 1 indicates that the residents of blue and red states certainly intended to vote differently: the percentage expressing an intention to vote for George Bush was ten points higher in the red states. Reminiscent of our discussion of dichotomous choices, however, the partisan and ideological predispositions underlying these voting differences were less distinct. The difference between the proportions of red and blue state respondents who consider themselves Democrats is not statistically significant, and the difference in the proportions who consider themselves Republicans is barely so—in both red and blue states self-identified independents are the largest group. Similarly, about a fifth of the respondents in both red and blue states consider themselves liberals (the four point difference is not statistically significant), and while there are more conservatives in the red states, there are more conservatives than liberals even in the blue states. In both the red and blue states the largest group of people classified themselves as moderates. In sum, while the aggregate voting patterns of red and blue states would turn out to be quite distinct in November, the underlying patterns of political identification were much less so.

Table 2 reports similar results for the group evaluations reported by residents of red and blue states. Unsurprisingly, red state residents regard the Republican Party more favorably than the Democrats, but 55 percent of them regard the Democratic Party favorably. Conversely, blue state residents regard the Democratic Party

Table 2. Red Versus Blue States: Group Evaluations
(Percent very/mostly favorable toward . . .)

	Blue	Red
Republican Party	50%	58%
Democratic Party	64	55
Evangelical Christians	60	63
Jews	79	77
Catholics	77	79
Muslims	56	47
Atheists	37	27

more favorably than the Republicans, but 50 percent report favorable evaluations of the Republican Party. Evangelical Christians are evaluated equally positively by solid majorities in both red and blue states, as are Jews and Catholics. Muslims fare less well overall and red state residents regard them lower still, but one wonders how much experience many people have with actual Muslims—especially in many of the red states—as opposed to the abstract concept of a Muslim. Finally, in a standard finding, neither red nor blue state residents like atheists: Americans do not care very much what or how people believe, but they are generally negative toward people who don't believe in anything.

Across a range of other matters, blue and red state residents differ little, if at all. Figures in Table 3 indicate that similar proportions regard the government as *almost always* wasteful and inefficient—relative to the red states, the blue states clearly are not wellsprings of support for big government. Only small minorities in either category regard discrimination as the main reason that African Americans can't get ahead—the blue states are not hotbeds of racial liberalism. Immigrants receive a warmer reception among blue state residents, but multiculturalism remains a minority position even in the blue states. Blue state residents are less likely to endorse unqualified patriotism.

On the other hand, red state residents are just as likely as blue state residents to believe that large companies have too much power and to think that corporations make too much profit—the red states are not the running dogs of corporate America. Amusingly, majorities in both red and blue states agree that Al Gore is more of a liberal than he lets on, and that George Bush is more of a conservative than he lets on—they were not fooled by all the talk about "progressives" and "compassionate conservatives." And finally—and counter to suggestions of numerous Democrats after the election—majorities in both red

Table 3. Red Versus Blue States: Beliefs and Perceptions:
(Percent strongly supporting statement)

Gov't almost always wasteful and inefficient	39%	44%
Discrimination main reason blacks cannot get ahead	25	21
Immigrants strengthen our country	44	32
Fight for country right or wrong	35	43
Too much power concentrated in large companies	64	62
Corporations make too much profit	44	43
Al Gore is more liberal than he lets on	55	59
George Bush is more conservative than he lets on	59	57
Wish Clinton could run again (strongly disagree)	51	61

and blue states *strongly* disagree with the proposition that they wish Bill Clinton could run again. Clinton was more favorably regarded in the blue states, but Clinton fatigue by no means was limited to the red states.

When it comes to issue sentiments, Table 4 shows that in many cases the small differences we have seen so far become even smaller. Contrary to Republican dogma, red state citizens are equally as unenthusiastic about using the surplus (har!) to cut taxes as blue state citizens. Nearly equal numbers of blue and red state residents think the surplus should be used to pay off the national debt, increase domestic spending, and bolster Social Security and Medicare. Contrary to Democratic dogma, blue state citizens are equally as enthusiastic as red state citizens about abolishing the inheritance tax, giving government grants to religious organizations, adopting school vouchers, and partially privatizing Social Security. Overwhelming majorities in both red and blue states favor providing prescription drugs through Medicare, and solid majorities endorse protecting the environment, whatever it takes. Neither red nor blue state residents attach high priority to increasing defense spending. Looking at this series of issue items, one wonders why anyone would bother separating respondents into red and blue categories—the differences are insignificant.

But, we have not considered the specific issues that define the culture war. Table 5 brings us to the heart of the matter—questions of religion, morality, and sexuality. The proportion of Protestants is significantly higher in the red states, of course, as is the proportion of respondents who report having a "born again" experience. There is a real difference here between the heartland and the coasts. But the significance of this difference fades when we dig deeper. Only a minority of red state respondents reports being very involved in church activities— only marginally more than those blue state respondents who report heavy

Table 4. Red Versus Blue States: Issue Sentiments

	Blue	Red
Should use the surplus to cut taxes	14%	14%
. . . pay off the national debt	21	23
. . . increase domestic spending	28	24
. . . bolster SS and Medicare	35	38
Favor abolition of inheritance tax	70	72
. . . gov't grants to religious organizations	67	66
. . . school vouchers for low and middle income parents	54	50
. . . partial privatization of SS	69	71
. . . Medicare coverage of prescription drugs	91	92
. . . increasing defense sepnding	30	37
Do whatever it takes to protect the environment	70	64

involvement. A higher proportion of red state respondents report that religion is very important in their lives, but a healthy 62 percent majority of blue state respondents feel similarly. Very similar proportions think churches should stay out of politics, and the minority of red state residents who approve of the clergy talking politics from the pulpit is slightly smaller than the minority in the blue states. Book-burners are only slightly more common in the red states. Finally, there is a clear difference in one of the major issues of the culture war, homosexuality, but probably less of a difference than many would have expected. The level of support for societal acceptance of homosexuality is ten percentage points higher in the blue states (twelve points if we add those who waffle to those who fully accept homosexuality). The difference is statistically significant, but it hardly conjures up an image of two coalitions of deeply opposed states engaged in a culture war. Opinion is almost as divided within the red and the blue states as it is between them. Significantly, this ten- to twelve-point difference on the issue of homosexual acceptance is about as large a difference as we found between red and blue state respondents in the survey. Readers can judge for themselves whether differences of this magnitude justify the military metaphors usually used to describe them.

A legitimate objection to the preceding comparisons is that they include all citizens rather than just voters. Only about half of the age-eligible electorate goes to the polls in contemporary presidential elections, and far fewer vote in lower-level elections. It is well known that partisanship and ideology are strong correlates of who votes: more intense partisans and more extreme ideologues

Table 5. Red Versus Blue States: Religion and Morals

	Blue	Red
Protestant	50%	69%
"Born again" or Evangelical Christian	28	45
Very involved in church activities	21	29
Religion is very important in my life	62	74
Churches should keep out of politics	46	43
Ever right for clergy to discuss candidates or issues from the pulpit? (yes)	35	33
Ban dangerous books from school libraries (yes)	37	42
Homosexuality should be accepted by society		
Agree strongly	41	31
Agree not strongly	16	14

are more likely to vote. Thus, it is possible that the *voters* in red states differ more from the *voters* in blue states than the residents do. To consider this possibility we turn to the 2000 National Election Study which—after the election—asks individuals whether and how they voted. In 2000, the NES reported a vote distribution reasonably close to the actual national division: 50.6 percent of the respondents reported voting for Gore, 45.5 percent for Bush, and the remainder for minor candidates.

Tables 6 and 7 report differences among reported voters in the NES that are only marginally larger than those reported among all respondents in the Pew Survey. Again, the largest difference is for the vote itself. To reiterate, even if an individual feels 55:45 between the two candidates, she has to vote one way or the other. The reported vote for Bush is 54 percent in the red states versus 37 percent in the blue states—a seventeen-point gap, which is larger than the ten-point gap in vote *intention* in the earlier Pew Survey. Self-identified Democrats were significantly more common among blue state voters and self-identified Republicans significantly more common among red state voters, but in neither case does the difference reach double digits; independents and minor party affiliates were a third of the actual electorate in both categories. Self-identified liberals are more common in the blue states, but self-identified conservatives were at least as numerous as liberals in blue states. Again, moderates or centrists were the majority in both categories. An overwhelming majority of blue state voters approved of Bill Clinton's general job performance as well as his foreign policy job performance and his economic job performance, but so did a heavy, if smaller, majority of red state voters. Only minorities of both blue state and red state

Table 6. Red Versus Blue States: Political Inclinations

	Blue	Red
Bush vote	37%	54%
Democratic self-ID*	40	32
Republican self-ID	25	34
Liberal self-ID	20	11
Conservative self-ID	24	31
Clinton job approval**	71	57
Clinton foreign policy job approval	70	63
Clinton economic job approval	81	74
Democrats better able to handle economy	35	27
Republicans better able to handle economy	24	29
Prefer unified control	24	24

* Party identifiers include strong and weak identifiers, not independent leaners.
  Liberal identifiers are scale postions 1–2, conservative identifiers 6–7.
**Unless otherwise noted approval figures in the table combine "strongly approve"
  and "approve."

voters thought that one party could better handle the economy. Finally, rather than blue state residents favoring Democratic control of the Presidency and Congress and red state residents favoring Republican control, nearly identical majorities of both prefer divided control.

Table 7 indicates that issue preferences in the two categories of states are surprisingly similar in many instances. Four in ten voters in both red and blue states agree that immigration should decrease, and seven in ten believe that English should be the official language of the United States (the proportion is actually slightly higher in the blue states). Four in ten voters in both categories put environmental considerations above employment considerations, a surprising similarity in light of the image of red states as hotbeds of clear-cutters and blue states as strongholds of tree-huggers. Narrow majorities of voters in both categories support school vouchers, and large majorities support the death penalty. In neither blue nor red states are people wildly in favor of government intervention to ensure fair treatment of African Americans in employment, and virtually identical (small) proportions support racial preferences in hiring.

Again, when we turn to the specific issues that define the culture war, larger differences emerge, but there also are numerous surprises. A solid majority of blue state voters support stricter gun control laws, but so does a narrow majority of red state voters. Support for women's equality is overwhelming and identical among

Table 7. Red Versus Blue States: Issue Preferences

	Blue	Red
Immigration should decrease*	41%	43%
Make English official language	70	66
Environment over jobs	43	42
Favor school vouchers	51	54
Favor death penalty	70	77
Government should ensure fair treatment of blacks in employment	57	51
Blacks should get preferences in hiring	13	14
Stricter gun control	64	52
Equal women's role**	83	82
Attend church regularly	50	65
Moral climate: much worse	26	30
somewhat worse	25	25
Tolerate others' moral views	62	62
Abortion—always legal	48	37
Allow homosexual adoption	52	40
No gay job discrimination	73	62
Favor gays in military (strongly)	60	44

* Unless otherwise noted, the figures in the table combine "strongly" or "completely agree" responses with "mostly" or "somewhat agree" responses.
**Scale positions 1–2

voters in both categories of states. Although regular church attenders are significantly more common in the red states, similar proportions in both red and blue states believe the moral climate of the country has deteriorated since 1992, and identical proportions believe that others' moral views should be tolerated. Support for unrestricted abortion is eleven points higher among blue state voters, but such unqualified support falls short of a majority, and more than a third of red state voters offer similarly unqualified support. The 2000 NES is particularly rich in items tapping people's views about matters related to sexual orientation. Here we find differences between blue and red state voters that are statistically significant, though smaller in magnitude than regular consumers of the news might have expected. A narrow majority of blue state voters would allow homosexuals to adopt children, but so would four in ten red state voters. Solid majorities of voters in both categories support laws that would ban employment discrimination against gays. Sixty percent of blue state voters fully support gays in the military, contrasted with 44 percent of red state voters. This 16 percent difference is the single largest disparity we found between the issue preferences of red and blue state voters. Perhaps Bill Clinton picked the one issue in the realm of sexual orientation that was most likely to create controversy. But the evidence supports the alternative hypothesis that Clinton's executive order polarized the electorate: according to Gallup data, popular support for gays in the military rose through the 1980s and had reached 60 percent in 1989 before plummeting in the wake of Clinton's executive order.

All in all, the comparison of blue and red state residents who claim to have voted in 2000 seems consistent with the picture reflecting comparisons of all residents of blue and red states. There are numerous similarities between red and blue state voters, some differences, and a few notable differences, but little that calls to mind the portrait of a culture war between the states.

Chapter 11

Voting, Campaigns, and Elections

11-1

from *The Reasoning Voter*

Samuel L. Popkin

*Voters confront difficult choices with incomplete and usually biased informa-
tion. Many voters are not strongly motivated to learn more. Even if they want
to learn more, the information they need is often not available in a convenient
form. In the following essay, Samuel L. Popkin argues that this predicament
does not necessarily lead voters to make irrational decisions. Voters instead
rely on low-cost shortcuts to obtain information and make decisions. Popkin's
analysis can help us to better understand the role of campaigns in voters'
decision-making processes as well as other features of American politics.*

IN RECENT DECADES, journalists and reformers have complained with increasing
force about the lack of content in voting and the consequent opportunities for
manipulating the electorate. And yet over the same period academic studies of
voting have begun to expose more and more about the substance of voting decisions and the limits to manipulation of voters. The more we learn about what
voters know, the more we see how campaigns matter in a democracy. And the
more we see, the clearer it becomes that we must change both our critiques of
campaigns and our suggestions for reforming them.

Source: Samuel L. Popkin, *The Reasoning Voter: Communication and Persuasion in Presidential Campaigns,* 2d
ed. (Chicago: University of Chicago Press, 1994), 212–219. Notes appearing in the original have been
deleted.

In this [essay] I summarize my findings about how voters reason and show how some modest changes which follow from my theory could ameliorate some defects of the campaign process.

I have argued . . . that the term *low-information rationality,* or "gut" rationality, best describes the kind of practical reasoning about government and politics in which people actually engage. . . . [L]ow-information reasoning is by no means devoid of substantive content, and is instead a process that economically incorporates learning and information from past experiences, daily life, the media, and political campaigns. . . .

Gut rationality draws on the information shortcuts and rules of thumb that voters use to obtain and evaluate information and to choose among candidates. These information shortcuts and rules of thumb must be considered when evaluating an electorate and considering changes in the electoral system.

How Voters Reason

It is easy to demonstrate that Americans have limited knowledge of basic textbook facts about their government and the political debates of the day. But evaluating citizens only in terms of such factual knowledge is a misleading way to assess their competence as voters.

Because voters use shortcuts to obtain and evaluate information, they are able to store far more data about politics than measurements of their textbook knowledge would suggest. Shortcuts for obtaining information at low cost are numerous. People learn about specific government programs as a by-product of ordinary activities, such as planning for retirement, managing a business, or choosing a college. They obtain economic information from their activities as consumers, from their workplace, and from their friends. They also obtain all sorts of information from the media. Thus they do not need to know which party controls Congress, or the names of their senators, in order to know something about the state of the economy or proposed cuts in Social Security or the controversies over abortion. And they do not need to know where Nicaragua is, or how to describe the Politburo, in order to get information about changes in international tensions which they can relate to proposals for cutting the defense budget.

When direct information is hard to obtain, people will find a proxy for it. They will use a candidate's past political positions to estimate his or her future positions. When they are uncertain about those past positions, they will accept as a proxy information about the candidate's personal demographic characteristics and the groups with which he or she has associated. And since voters find it difficult to gather information about the past competence of politicians who have performed outside their district or state, they will accept campaign competence as a proxy for competence in elected office—as an indication of the political skills needed to handle the issues and problems confronting the government.

Voters use evaluations of personal character as a substitute for information about past demonstrations of political character. They are concerned about personal character and integrity because they generally cannot infer the candidate's true commitments from his past votes, most of which are based on a hard-to-decipher mixture of compromises between ideal positions and practical realities. Evaluating any sort of information for its relevance to politics is a reasoning process, not a reflex projection directly from pocketbook or personal problems to votes. But in making such evaluations, voters use the shortcut of relying on the opinions of others whom they trust and with whom they discuss the news. These opinions can serve as fire alarms that alert them to news deserving more than their minimal attention. As media communities have developed, voters have the additional shortcut of validating their opinions by comparing them with the opinions of political leaders whose positions and reputations people grow to know over time.

People will use simplifying assumptions to evaluate complex information. A common simplifying assumption is that a politician had significant control over an observable result, such as a loss of jobs in the auto industry. This saves people the trouble of finding out which specific actions really caused the result. Another example of a simplifying assumption is the notion that "My enemy's enemy is my friend."

People use party identification as running tallies of past information and shortcuts to storing and encoding their past experiences with political parties. They are able to encode information about social groups prominent in the party, the priorities of the party, and the performance of the party and its president in various policy areas. This generalized information about parties provides "default values" from which voters can assess candidates about whom they have no other information. In keeping generalized tallies by issue area, they avoid the need to know the specifics of every legislative bill.

As a shortcut in assessing a candidate's future performance, without collecting more data, people assemble what data they have about the candidate into a causal narrative or story. Because a story needs a main character, they can create one from their knowledge of people who have traits or characteristics like those of the candidate. This allows them to go beyond the incomplete information they have about a candidate, and to hold together and remember more information than they otherwise could. Because these stories are causal narratives, they allow voters to think about government in causal terms and to evaluate what it will do. Narratives thus help people incorporate their reasoning about government into their projections about candidates; their assumptions "confer political significance on some facts and withhold it from others." They offer people a way to connect personal and political information, to project that information into the future, and to make a complete picture from limited information.

Finally, people use shortcuts when choosing between candidates. When faced with an array of candidates in which some are known well and some are known poorly, and all are known in different and incomparable ways, voters will seek a clear and accessible criterion for comparing them. This usually means looking for the sharpest differences between the candidates which can be related to government performance. Incorporating these differences into narratives allows them to compare the candidates without spending the calculation time and the energy needed to make independent evaluations of each candidate.

Working Attitudes

People do not and cannot use all the information they have at one time. What they use will depend in part on the point of view or frame with which they view the world; attitudes and information are brought to bear if they fit the frame. Of the attitudes and bits of information available, people tend to use those they consider important or those they have used recently. As the changes in voter attitudes entailed by the emergence of new candidates in primaries suggest, attitudes and information will also be brought to the foreground when they fit with what is *expected* in a situation. Our realizations, the thoughts that come clearly to mind, depend in part on what others say about their own thoughts and perceptions.

Thus, as options change, expectations change. If a Democrat were asked in early 1984 what he or she thought of Walter Mondale as a presidential candidate, and the reply was "He'll be all right," that response could be interpreted as coming from a nonthinking voter who was passively following a media report about the thinking of others. But the same response could also be interpreted as an indication of a complex ability to come to grips with the available choices, with issue concerns that cannot be satisfied simultaneously, and with the compromises considered necessary to reach consensus with other people. Similarly, if the same voter were asked a few weeks later what he or she thought about Gary Hart and the reply was "He's just what we need," the response could be interpreted to mean that this voter was simply following the media-reported bandwagon. On the other hand, it could be interpreted to mean that reported changes in public expectations had brought other attitudes and concerns forward in the voter's mind. As this example suggests, the information voters use depends on the reasoning they do, and the reasoning they do depends in part on their expectations. It also indicates that the way in which the content of a voter's response is interpreted depends on a theory about how voters use information and make choices. And I am convinced that any such theory must account for the "working attitudes" of voters—the combinations of feeling, thought, and information they bring to bear when they make their choices at the polls.

Why Campaigns Matter

Changes in government, in society, and in the role of the mass media in politics have made campaigns more important today than they were fifty years ago, when modern studies of them began. Campaign communications make connections between politics and benefits that are of concern to the voter; they offer cognitive focal points, symbolic "smoking guns," and thus make voters more aware of the costs of misperception. Campaigns attempt to achieve a common focus, to make one question and one cleavage paramount in voters' minds. They try to develop a message for a general audience, a call that will reach beyond the "disinterested interest" of the highly attentive, on one hand, and the narrow interests of issue publics, on the other. Each campaign attempts to organize the many cleavages within the electorate by setting the political agenda in the way most favorable to its own candidates. . . .

The spread of education has both broadened and segmented the electorate. Educated voters pay more attention to national and international issues and they are now connected in many more electronic communities—groups of people who have important identifications maintained through media rather than direct, personal contact. There are also today more government programs—Medicare, Social Security, welfare, and farm supports are obvious examples—that have a direct impact on certain groups, which become issue publics. Other issue publics include coalitions organized around policies toward specific countries, such as Israel or Cuba; various conservation and environmental groups; and groups concerned with social issues, such as abortion and gun control. Furthermore, there are now a great many more communications channels with which these people can keep in touch with those outside their immediate neighborhoods or communities. Such extended groups are not new, and modern communications technology is not necessary to mobilize them, as the abolitionist and temperance movements remind us; but the channels to mobilize such groups are more available today, and I believe that the groups they have nurtured are more numerous. When the national political conventions were first telecast in 1952, all three networks showed the same picture at the same time because there was only one national microwave relay; today, with the proliferation of cable systems and satellite relays, television and VCRs can now show over a hundred channels. Furthermore, as channels and options have proliferated, and as commuting time has increased and two-career families become more common, the proportion of people watching mainstream networks and network news is also dropping.

Over the past fifty years, as surveys have become increasingly available to study public opinion, there have been many gains in knowledge about voting and elections. There have also been losses, as national surveys have replaced the detailed community orientation of the original Columbia studies. We know much more about individuals and much less about extended networks, and we have not adequately examined the implications for society and campaigning of the transitions from face-to-face to electronic communities.

Both primaries and the growth of media communication have increased the amount of exposure people get to individual candidates, particularly the quantity of personal information they get about the candidates. This increases the importance of campaigns because it gives voters more opportunities to abandon views based on party default values in favor of views based on candidate information, and also more opportunities to shift from views based on a candidate's record to views based on his or her campaign image. Moreover, as primaries have expanded, parties have had to deal with the additional task of closing ranks after the campaign has pitted factions within the party against each other. Primaries have also changed the meaning of political party conventions. Conventions no longer deliberate and choose candidates; instead, they present the electorate with important cues about the social composition of the candidate's coalition and about the candidate's political history and relations with the rest of the party. The more primaries divide parties, the more cues are needed to reunite parties and remind supporters of losing candidates about their differences with the other party.

The Implications of Shortcuts

Recognizing the role of low-information rationality in voting behavior has important implications for how we measure and study attitudes, how we evaluate the effects of education, and how we evaluate electoral reforms. To begin with, we must acknowledge that the ambivalence, inconsistency, and changes in preference that can be observed among voters are not the result of limited information. They exist because as human beings we can never use all of what we know at any one time. We can be as ambivalent when we have a lot of information and concern as when we have little information and limited concern. Nor do inconsistency, ambivalence, and change result from a lack of education (especially civic education) or a lack of political interest. Ambivalence is simply an immutable fact of life. Economists and psychologists have had to deal with the inconsistencies people demonstrate in cognitive experiments on framing and choice: preference reversals and attitude changes can no longer be attributed to a lack of information, a lack of concern, a lack of attention, low stakes, or the existence of "non-attitudes."

The use of information shortcuts is likewise an inescapable fact of life, and will occur no matter how educated we are, how much information we have, and how much thinking we do. Professionals weighing résumés and past accomplishments against personal interviews, or choosing from an array of diverse objects, have the same problems and use the same shortcuts as voters choosing presidents. What we have called Gresham's law of information—that new and personal information, being easier to use, tends to drive old and impersonal political information out of circulation—applies not only to the inattentive and the uneducated but to all of us. We must therefore stop considering shortcuts pejoratively, as the last refuge of citizens who are uneducated, lacking in the political experience and expertise of their "betters," or cynically content to be freeloaders in our democracy.

Drunkard's Searches and information shortcuts provide an invaluable part of our knowledge and must therefore be considered along with textbook knowledge in evaluating any decision-making process. As Abraham Kaplan has noted, the Drunkard's Search—metaphorically, looking for the lost keys under the nearest streetlight—seems bothersome because of the assumption that we should begin any search rationally, in the most likely places rather than in those that are the best lit and nearest to hand. He adds, "But the joke may be on us. It may be sensible to look first in an unlikely place just *because* 'it's lighter there.' . . . The optimal pattern of search does not simply mirror the pattern of probability density of what we seek. We accept the hypothesis that a thing sought is in a certain place because we remember having seen it there, or because it is usually in places of that kind, or for like reasons. But . . . we look in a certain place for additional reasons: we happen to be in the place already, others are looking elsewhere." At least when people look under the streetlight, they will almost certainly find their keys if they are there; if they look by the car, in the dark, they are far less likely to find them even if they are there.

. . . [W]e should keep in mind the main features about how voters obtain information and reason about their political choices. The Drunkard's Search is an aid to calculation as well as an information shortcut. By telling us where to look, it also tells us how to choose, how to use easily obtained information in making comparisons and choices. As long as this is how we search and choose, people will neither have nor desire all the information about their government that theorists and reformers want them to have.

The faith that increased education would lead to higher levels of textbook knowledge about government, and that this knowledge in turn would enable the electorate to measure up to its role in democratic theory, was misplaced. Education doesn't change *how* we think. Education broadens the voter, because educated voters pay attention to more problems and are more sensitive to connections between their lives and national and international events. However, educated voters still *sample* the news, and they still rely on shortcuts and calculation aids in assessing information, assembling scenarios, and making their choices. Further, an educated, broadened electorate is a more diffuse electorate, an electorate segmented by the very abundance of its concerns. Such an electorate will be harder to form into coalitions. The more divided an electorate, the more time and communication it takes to assemble people around a single cleavage.

Since all citizens sample the news and use shortcuts, they must be judged in part by the quality of the "fire alarms" to which they respond. They must be judged in part by *who* they know and respond to, not simply by *what* they know. Furthermore, this use of fire alarms has an important implication. Since people can only respond to the fire alarms they hear, it matters how the fire alarms to which they are exposed are chosen. If it matters whether the responses to a policy or crisis are mediated electronically by Jesse Jackson and Jesse Helms, or by Bill Bradley and Robert Dole, then attention must be given to how the mediators are chosen by the networks.

11-2

Party Polarization in National Politics:
The Electoral Connection

Gary C. Jacobson

A popular notion among political scientists and other observers is that national politicians have become more polarized and partisan because the electorate has become more polarized. The behavior of elected officials merely reflects the differences in the parties' electoral bases. The map of the nation's congressional districts appears to confirm this supposition. It shows that Democrats win in urban areas while Republicans win in suburban and rural areas, suggesting that a cultural divide in the American electorate has produced partisan polarization among elected members of Congress. In this essay, Gary C. Jacobson describes the polarization of the electorate and Congress but observes that the partisan polarization of Congress seems to have emerged before the polarization of the electorate. He argues that leaders in Congress contributed to the polarization of public opinion.

IN DECEMBER 1998 the House of Representatives voted to impeach President Bill Clinton. The vote was radically partisan: all but four Republicans voted for at least one of the four articles of impeachment, and only five Democrats voted for any of them. Grant every member's claim of a conscience vote, and it becomes all the more remarkable that 98 percent of Republican consciences dictated a vote to impeach the president, while 98 percent of Democratic consciences dictated the opposite. The Senate's verdict after the impeachment trial was only slightly less partisan. Every Democrat voted for acquittal, and 91 percent of the Republicans voted for conviction on at least one article.

Research on congressional roll call voting, notably by several authors represented in this volume, makes it clear that party line voting on the impeachment issue was not an aberration, but the culmination of a trend nearly two decades old. The proportion of partisan roll call votes and party loyalty on these votes have been increasing in both houses of Congress since the 1970s, reflecting growing ideological polarization of the congressional parties. To appreciate how dramatically the parties have diverged since the 1970s, look at Figure 1, which

Source: Jon R. Bond and Richard Fleisher, eds., *Polarized Politics: Congress and the President in a Partisan Era* (Washington, D.C.: CQ Press, 2000), 9–30. Notes and bibliographical references appearing in the original have been deleted.

Figure 1. Ideological Positions on Roll-Call Votes

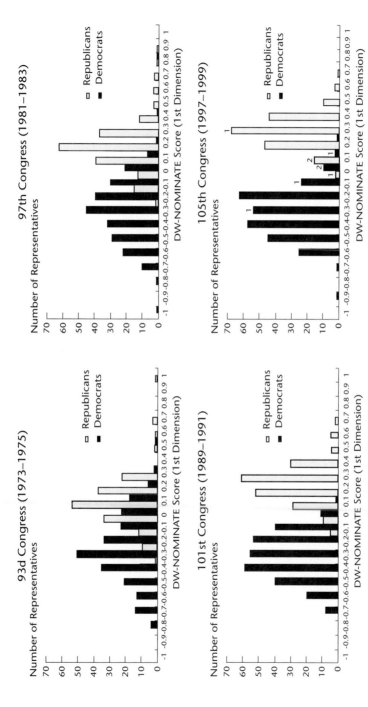

Source: Compiled by the author from Poole and Rosenthal DW-NOMINATE Scores (http://voteview.gsia.cmu.edu.dwnl.htm).

Note: The entries are frequency distributions of Republican and Democratic members of Congress on a liberal-conservative dimension based on non-unanimous roll call votes in which 1 represents the most conservative position and −1 represents the most liberal. Each bar indicates the number of representatives falling into the specified range. For example, in the 105th Congress, sixty-two Republicans had scores between .03 and .04 on the scale.

Figure 2. Difference in Median and Mean DW-NOMINATE Scores of Republicans and Democrats, 83d through 105th Congresses

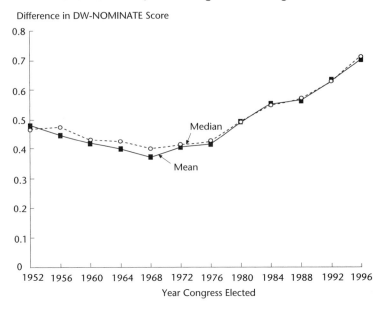

Note: The entries are the difference between the mean and the median positions on the DW-NOMINATE scale of House Republicans and Democrats in the specified Congress. The larger the difference, the farther apart the two parties are ideologically.

displays the distribution of House members' scores on a common measure of political ideology in selected Congresses spanning the past three decades. These scores, known as dw-nominate scores, are calculated from all non-unanimous roll call votes cast from the 80th Congress through the 105th Congress. Each member's pattern of roll call votes locates him or her on a liberal-conservative dimension ranging from –1.0 (most liberal) to 1.0 (most conservative), allowing us to compare the distribution of positions along the dimension taken by Democrats and Republicans in different Congresses.

In the 93d Congress, the ideological locations of House Democrats and Republicans overlapped across the middle half of the scale, and the gap between the two parties' modal locations was comparatively small. In the 97th Congress, the overlap was a bit less extensive but still sizable. By the 101st Congress, the parties had become noticeably more polarized. The 105th Congress, which voted on Clinton's impeachment, was the most sharply polarized of all, with not a single Republican falling below zero on the scale, and only four Democrats scoring above zero.

Trends in partisan polarization in the House over a some what longer period are summarized in Figure 2, which displays the difference in median and mean dw-nominate scores of House Republicans and Democrats in the Congress immediately following each presidential election from 1952 through 1996. Note particularly how dramatically the gap between the parties' average ideological locations grew in the 1990s; in the 105th Congress, the parties' medians and means were more than 0.7 points apart on this 2-point scale. According to Keith Poole and Howard Rosenthal, the first dw-nominate dimension captures, in addition to liberal-conservative ideology, the primary cleavage that distinguishes the two parties, and hence the scores also serve as measures of party loyalty. From this perspective, party unity on the House impeachment vote was simply a manifestation of a broader pattern of partisan polarization highlighted by the nearly complete disappearance of conservative Democrats and liberal Republicans (although a few moderates remain in both parties). The numbers above the columns in the last panel of Figure 1 show how many members bolted their party on impeachment. Note that all but two of the nine who defected on impeachment belong to the small set of members who still have dw-nominate scores adjacent to or overlapping those of members of the opposing party.

The Republicans persisted in their attempts to impeach and remove Clinton even though every one of the myriad national polls taken from the eruption of the Monica Lewinsky scandal in January 1998 through the end of the trial in February 1999 found the public opposed to impeachment and conviction, typically by margins of about two to one. Yet the public, like Congress, was from start to finish sharply polarized on the issue. In poll after poll, a solid majority of self-identified Republicans favored Clinton's impeachment and removal, while more than 80 percent of self-identified Democrats remained opposed. In the end, 68 percent of Republicans wanted the Senate to convict and remove Clinton, while only 30 percent favored acquittal; among Democrats, 89 percent favored acquittal, while only 10 percent preferred conviction. Members of Congress may have voted their consciences, but their consciences were wonderfully in tune with the preferences of their core supporters. Congressional Republicans acted against the manifest preferences of a majority of Americans on a highly salient issue, and they may yet pay for it in the 2000 election by losing the House and—much less likely—the Senate. But they voted the way the majority of Republican voters wanted them to.

Partisan voting on impeachment thus reflected, albeit in an exaggerated and skewed fashion, sharply divided electoral constituencies. It also reflected the power of majority party leaders in the contemporary House to enforce discipline, notably on the adoption of a rule governing the impeachment bill that did not permit consideration of a censure resolution. Moderate Republicans were left with no alternative short of impeachment. These two forces—the emergence of distinct and increasingly homogenous electoral coalitions in both parties and, in consequence, the greater willingness of members to submit to party discipline—are the chief explanations that have been offered for the broader rise in party unity and ideological divergence since the 1970s. Respect for the power of the electoral connection usually concedes causal priority to electoral change. Yet voters can respond only to the options presented by the parties' candidates. If legislative parties become more dissimilar and unified as their respective electoral coalitions become more dissimilar and homogenous, it is also true that the choices offered by more polarized, unified parties encourage polarized electoral responses.

My goal in this chapter is to review the electoral changes that both underlie and reflect the more unified and divergent congressional parties of the 1990s. The story contains few surprises, but fresh observations from the most recent elections point uniformly to a near-term future that is, if anything, substantially more conducive to partisan coherence and division, intensifying conflicts not only within the legislature, but especially—under divided government—between the president and Congress.

Most of the analysis is presented graphically, for this is the most efficient way to summarize and appreciate the various interrelated trends. I begin with some observations on changes in partisanship and voting behavior since the 1970s. Next, I show how the electoral coalitions of House Democrats and Republicans have consequently diverged. The circle is completed by an examination of how patterns of roll call voting have become increasingly predictable from electoral decisions, fulfilling one major condition for responsible party government. An ironic effect of these changes may have been to make divided government even more popular, for the parties in government have polarized much more sharply than have party identifiers in the electorate.

The Growth of Partisan Coherence in the Electorate

The consensus explanation for the rise in party cohesion in Congress since the 1970s is party realignment in the South. The short version is that the civil rights revolution, particularly the Voting Rights Act of 1965, brought southern blacks into the electorate as Democrats, while moving conservative whites to abandon their ancestral allegiance to the Democratic Party in favor of the ideologically more compatible Republicans. The movement of jobs and people to the South also contributed to larger numbers of Republican voters, who gradually replaced conservative Democrats with conservative Republicans in southern House and Senate seats. The constituencies that elected the remaining Democrats became more like Democratic constituencies elsewhere, so the roll call voting of southern Democrats became more like the roll call voting of Democrats from other regions. The southern realignment left both congressional parties with more

Figure 3. The Rise of the Republican South, 1952–1998

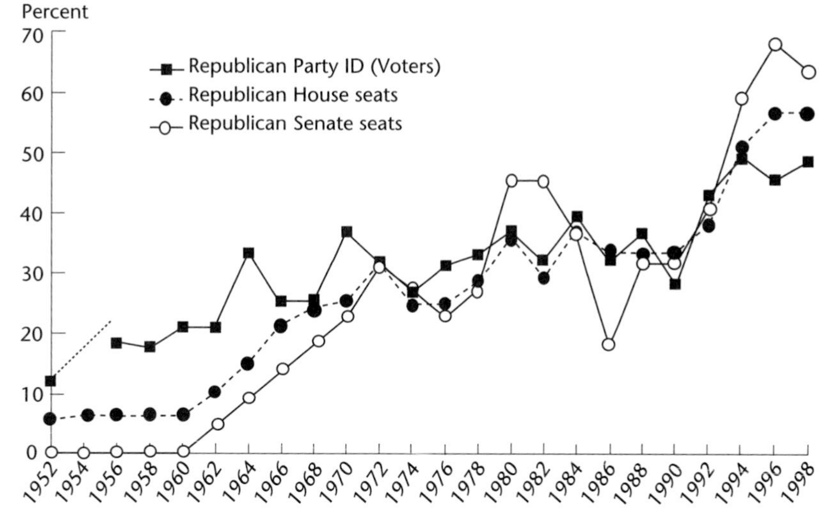

Source: National Election Studies.

politically homogeneous electoral coalitions, reducing internal disagreements and making stronger party leadership tolerable.

This analysis is certainly correct as far as it goes. The realignment of southern political loyalties and electoral habits has been thoroughly documented. Figure 3 summarizes the principal trends. As the proportion of Republicans among major party identifiers has risen, so has the share of southern House and Senate seats won by Republican candidates. Starting from almost nothing in the 1950s, Republicans now enjoy parity with the Democrats among voters and hold solid majorities of southern House and Senate seats.

Realignment in the South contributed to the increasing ideological homogeneity of the parties, but it is by no means the whole story. Other forces have also necessarily been at work, for links between ideology and party identification have grown stronger outside the South as well. Since 1972 the National Election Studies (NES) have asked respondents to place themselves on a 7-point ideological scale ranging from extremely liberal to extremely conservative. On average, nearly 80 percent of respondents who say they voted in House elections are able to locate their position on the scale. As Figure 4 shows, tau-b correlations between the voters' positions on the liberal-conservative scale and the NES's 7-point party identification scale have grown noticeably stronger since 1972 outside the South as well as within. Like other measurements of correlation, the tau-b statistic takes values from –1 (a perfect negative relationship) through 0 (no relationship) to 1 (a perfect positive relationship). In the analysis presented here

Figure 4. Correlation between Party Identification and Ideology of
House Voters, 1972–1998

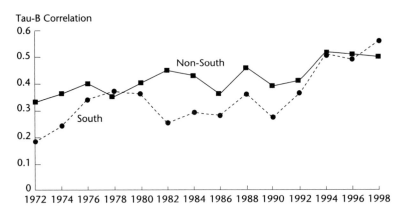

Figure 5. Correlation between Party Identification and Issue Positions,
House Voters, 1972–1998

and in Figure 5, the higher the tau-b correlation, the stronger the positive relationship between party identification and the other variable of interest. The
increase was steeper for southern voters, and by 1994 they had become indistinguishable on this score from voters elsewhere.

A similar pattern of growing partisan coherence within the electorate is evident in
correlations between voters' party identification and positions on several of the

NES's issue scales displayed in Figure 5. On every issue—ranging from the government's economic role, to race, to women's role in society, to abortion policy—the overall trend is upward, with tau-b correlations reaching their highest levels on four of the five scales in 1998. Notice that although economic issue positions are normally most strongly related to partisanship—reflecting the venerable New Deal cleavage—the steepest increases have occurred on social issues. For example, in 1980 opinions on abortion were unrelated to party identification; now we observe a substantial correlation. In 1980 only 30 percent of voters who opposed abortion under all circumstances identified themselves as Republicans; by 1998, 71 percent did so.

More generally, in 1972 the voter's positions on the various scales—ideology, jobs, aid to blacks, and women's role—predicted party identification (Republican, independent, or Democrat) with only 62 percent accuracy; in 1998 the same four variables predicted party identification with 74 percent accuracy. Clearly, citizens now sort themselves into the appropriate party (given their ideological leanings and positions on issues) a good deal more consistently than they did in the 1970s, with the largest increases in consistency occurring in the 1990s. Not surprisingly, partisan evaluations of presidential candidates, presidents, and the parties themselves have become more divergent as well.

The Revival of Electoral Consistency

Both the southern realignment and growing ideological coherence of electoral coalitions have contributed to greater consistency in voting behavior. Among individual voters, party loyalty has risen and ticket splitting has diminished since the 1970s. Figures 6 and 7 display the pertinent data. Party loyalty in congressional elections declined from the 1950s through the 1970s but has subsequently rebounded, recovering about two-thirds of the decline. Party loyalty in presidential elections is trickier to measure, because some years have featured prominent independent or third party candidacies (specifically 1968, 1980, 1992, and 1996), while the rest have not. But even with Ross Perot drawing votes from both parties in 1996, 84 percent of partisans voted for their party's presidential candidate, a higher proportion than in any election from 1952 through 1980. If we consider as defectors only those who voted for the other *major* party's candidate, the rate of defection in both 1992 and 1996 was only 10 percent, the lowest of any election in the NES time series (1988 had the next lowest rate).

The trend in ticket splitting—voting for candidates of different parties on the same ballot—appears, not accidentally, as the inverse of the trend in party loyalty. Ticket splitting was relatively infrequent in the 1950s, grew more common through the 1970s, and since has declined to the levels last seen in the

Figure 6. Party Loyalty in Congressional Elections, 1952–1998

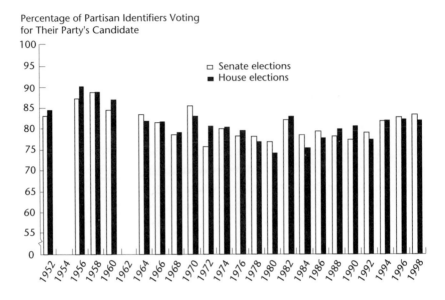

Figure 7. Ticket Splitting, 1952–1998

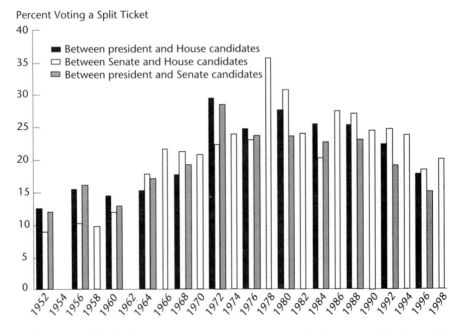

early 1960s. The declines since the 1970s in partisan defections and ticket split-ting are probably even greater than these NES data indicate, because both phe-nomena have been artificially inflated since 1978 by changes in the wording

Figure 8. Correlations Between District-Level House and Presidential Voting, 1952–1996

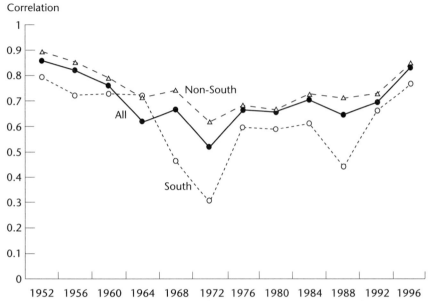

and administration of the vote question that produce an overreport of votes for House incumbents.

An important consequence of greater party loyalty and decreased ticket split-ting is that aggregate electoral results have become more consistent across offices. For example, the simple correlation between a party's district-level House and presidential vote shares has risen sharply from its low point in 1972, as Figure 8 indicates. Both the decrease between 1952 and 1972 and the increase since 1972 are steepest for southern districts, but the same U-shaped trend occurs in districts outside the South as well. By 1996 the association between House and presiden-tial voting had rebounded to a level last seen in the 1950s (.77 in the South, .85 elsewhere, and .83 overall). Similarly, a district's presidential vote predicted which party's candidate would win the House seat with greater accuracy in the 1990s than at any time since the 1950s. The trend toward electoral disintegration across offices I documented a decade ago has clearly gone into reverse since then.

Diverging Electoral Constituencies

The growth in partisan coherence, consistency, and loyalty among voters has made the two parties' respective electoral constituencies—that is, the voters

Figure 9. Difference in Mean Ideological Self-Placement of House Activist and Electoral Constituencies, 1972–1998

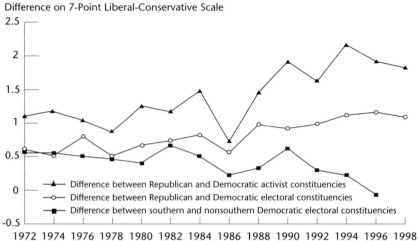

Difference on 7-Point Liberal-Conservative Scale

Legend:
— ▲ — Difference between Republican and Democratic activist constituencies
— ○ — Difference between Republican and Democratic electoral constituencies
— ■ — Difference between southern and nonsouthern Democratic electoral constituencies

who supported the party's winning candidates—politically more homogeneous and more dissimilar. It has also given the president and congressional majorities more divergent electoral constituencies when the branches are divided between the parties.

To begin with an elementary but telling example, according to NES surveys, 48 percent of the respondents who voted for members of the Democratic House majority in 1972 also voted for Richard Nixon; 36 percent of the voters supporting the Democratic House winners voted for Ronald Reagan in 1984; but only 27 percent of the voters supporting members of the Republican House majority voted for Clinton in 1996. The comparatively small proportion of shared electoral constituents was surely one source of Clinton's difficulties with the Republican congressional majority in a divided government.

More generally, the respective parties' electoral constituencies have diverged ideologically since the 1970s, with the parties' most active supporters moving the farthest apart. I measure differences in the ideological makeup of electoral constituencies by subtracting the mean ideological self-placement of NES respondents who voted for one set of winning candidates from the mean for respondents who voted for another set of winning candidates. Ideological divisions among activist constituents are gauged by repeating the analysis for respondents who reported engaging in at least two political acts in addition to voting during the campaign. Figure 9 displays the changes in the ideological distinctiveness of the electoral constituencies of House Republicans and Democrats and of southern and nonsouthern Democrats since 1972.

Figure 10. Difference in Mean Ideological Self-Placement of Senate Activist and Electoral Constituencies, 1976–1998

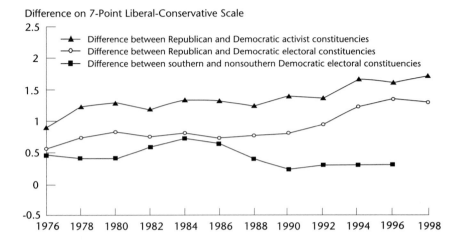

In the 1970s the ideological differences between the two parties' electoral constituencies were modest and no wider than the gap between southern and nonsouthern Democrats' electoral constituencies. By the 1990s the difference between the parties' electoral constituencies had more than doubled, to about 1.2 points on the 7-point scale, and the Democrats' regional divergence had entirely disappeared. Realignment in the South again explains only part of this change, for the gap between Republican and Democratic constituencies also grew (from 0.7 to 1.1 points) outside the South. Note also that the mean ideological difference between the parties' most active electoral constituents widened even more, nearly doubling to about two points on the scale.

Figure 10 presents the equivalent data for Senate electoral constituencies, except that entries are calculated from the three surveys up to and including the year indicated on the chart, so that data from voters electing the entire Senate membership are used to calculate in each observation. The same pattern of ideological polarization between the parties' respective electoral and activist constituencies appears, although somewhat muted, reflecting the greater heterogeneity of the Senate's larger electorates.

The ideological gap between the president's electoral constituency and the congressional majority's electoral constituency under conditions of divided government also has doubled. In 1972 Nixon voters were on average only 0.7 points more conservative than voters for the House Democrats elected that year. In 1996 the House Republicans' electoral constituency was 1.4 points more conservative than Bill Clinton's electoral constituency. The gap between the most active segment of each electoral constituency widened even more, from 1.3 points in 1972 to 2.2 points in 1996. An equivalent analysis of self-placement on issue positions tells the same story; on every issue dimension examined in Figure 5, the congressional parties' respective electoral coalitions are farther apart in the 1990s than they were at the beginning of the time series.

A discussion of changes in electoral coalitions would not be complete without confirming how profoundly the southern realignment has affected the demographic composition of the remaining Democratic coalition. Although it is not news, it is still worth highlighting just how dependent successful southern Democratic candidates are on African American voters. Figure 11 presents the pertinent data. For representatives, the entry is simply the proportion of all votes for the winning Democrat that were cast by black voters in each election year. For senators, it is the African American proportion of all votes for winning southern Democrats in the trio of elections culminating in the year listed. Therefore, the Senate entries indicate the proportion of African Americans in the electoral constituencies of all southern senators in the Congress following the specified election. Blacks were once a negligible part of the electoral constituencies of southern Democrats in Congress. Now they supply more than one-third of their votes. Add to this the fact that southern whites who continue to identify themselves as Democrats now share the socioeconomic profile of white Democrats elsewhere, and the nearly complete disappearance of conservative southern Democrats in Congress is no mystery at all.

Chicken or Egg?

Evidence from examination of the electorate, then, is fully consistent with the standard argument that partisan polarization in Congress reflects electoral changes that have left the parties with more homogeneous and more dissimilar electoral coalitions. When the focus of analysis is Congress, electoral change seems to be the independent variable: changes in roll call voting reflect changes in electoral coalitions. When the focus is on elections, however, it becomes apparent that causality works at least as strongly in the opposite direction: voters sort themselves out politically by responding to the alternatives represented by the two parties.

Realignment in the South *followed* the national Democratic Party's decision to champion civil rights for African Americans and the Republican Party's choice of Sen. Barry Goldwater, who voted against the Civil Rights Act of 1964, as its standard-bearer that year. Partisan divisions on the abortion issue surfaced first in Congress, then in the electorate. Electorates diverged ideologically after the

Figure 11. Share of Votes for Southern Democratic Representatives and Senators
Provided by African American Voters, 1956–1996

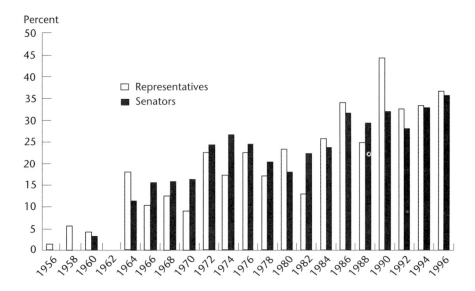

parties had diverged ideologically; the divisions in Congress and among activists
during and after the Reagan years left the two parties with more distinctive
images, making it easier for voters to recognize their appropriate ideological
home. Conservatives moved into the Republican ranks, while liberals remained
Democrats. Notice that most of the trends among voters identified in the figures
show their largest movement in the 1990s, *after* the firming up of congressional
party lines in the 1980s.

This is not to say, however, that members of Congress simply follow their
own ideological fancies, leaving voters no choice but to line up accordingly. As
vote-seeking politicians, they naturally anticipate voters' potential responses and
so are constrained by them. The Republican "southern strategy" emerged
because Republican presidential candidates sensed an opportunity to win con-
verts among conservative white southerners. Ambitious Republicans adopted
conservative positions on social issues to attract voters alienated by the Democrats' tolerance of nontraditional life styles but indifferent at best to Republican
economic policies. Democrats emphasized "choice" on abortion because they
recognized its appeal to well-educated, affluent voters who might otherwise
think of themselves as Republicans. In the budget wars of the past two decades,
Democrats have vigorously defended middle class entitlements such as Social
Security and Medicare, while Republicans have championed tax cuts because
each position has a large popular constituency. In adopting positions, then,

Figure 12. Variance in Roll Call Ideology Explained by District Presidential Vote and Party, 1952–1996

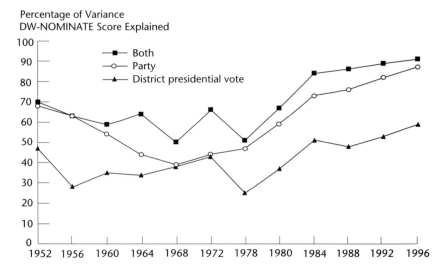

politicians are guided by the opportunities and constraints presented by configurations of public opinion on political issues. Party polarization in Congress depended on the expectation that voters would reward, or at least not punish, voting with one's party's majority.

In reality, therefore, the relationship between mass and elite partisan consistency is inherently interactive. Between the 1970s and the 1990s, changes in electoral and congressional politics reinforced one another, encouraging greater partisan consistency and cohesion in both. One important result is that the linkage between citizens' decisions on election day and the actions of the winners once they assume office has become much tighter. Indeed, election results predict congressional roll call voting on issues that fall along the primary liberal-conservative dimension accurately enough to meet one of the fundamental conditions for responsible party government. This is evident when we regress dw-nominate scores on two variables, party and the district-level presidential vote, and observe how much of the variance they explain. The presidential vote stands here as a serviceable if somewhat imprecise measure of district ideology: the higher the Republican share of the vote in any given election, the more conservative the district. The results are summarized in Figure 12, which tracks the proportion of variance in first-dimension dw-nominate scores explained by party and presidential vote, individually and in combination, in the Congresses immediately following each presidential election since 1952.

As we would expect from the information in Figures 1 and 2, the capacity of party to account for roll call voting on the liberal-conservative dimension declined from the 1950s to the 1970s but since then has risen steeply. The predictive accuracy of the district-level presidential vote remained lower than that of party through most of the period, reaching a low point in 1976 (a consequence of Jimmy Carter's initial appeal to conservative southerners), but then rising to its highest levels in the time series during the 1990s. The *relative* contribution of district ideology to explaining House members' positions on the liberal-conservative dimension tends to be greatest in the 1960s and 1970s, when party's contribution is lowest. Between 1976 and 1996, both variables become increasingly accurate predictors of congressional voting, to the point where by the 105th Congress, party and presidential vote account for a remarkable 91.5 percent of the variance in representatives' dw-nominate scores.

The voting patterns of House members, then, are increasingly predictable from elementary electoral variables: the party of the winner and the district's ideology as reflected in its presidential leanings (with these two variables themselves correlated in 1996 at the highest level since the 1950s). With this development, voters have a much clearer idea of how their collective choices in national elections will translate into congressional action on national issues. Because party labels are so much more predictive of congressional behavior, voters have good reason to use them more consistently to guide voting decisions.

The same circumstances that make the party label such an informative cue also deepen the dilemma faced by moderate voters, however. And, despite the growing divergence between the parties' respective electoral coalitions, most Americans still cluster in the middle of the ideological spectrum. In surveys from the 1990s, about 60 percent of House voters place themselves in one of the middle three positions on the 7-point liberal-conservative scale, down only modestly from about 68 percent in the 1970s. Polarization in Congress has outstripped polarization in the electorate, so the proportion of citizens placing themselves between the two parties has not diminished. Therefore, although the 1998 NES survey found party line voting to be near its highest level in thirty years, it also found that

- only 45 percent of voters preferred the continuation of the two-party system to elections without party labels (29 percent) or new parties to challenge the Republicans and Democrats (26 percent);
- 84 percent thought that the phrase "too involved in partisan politics" described Congress quite well (40 percent) or extremely well (44 percent);
- 56 percent preferred control of the presidency and Congress to be split between the parties, 24 percent preferred one party to control both institutions, and the rest did not care.

With elite polarization outstripping mass polarization, the advent of a central component of responsible party government—unified parties with distinct policy positions—may have had the paradoxical effect of strengthening support for divided government. The more divergent the parties' modal ideological positions, the more reason the remaining centrist voters have to welcome the moderating effect of divided government. But under divided government, the more divergent the parties, the more rancorous the conflict between the president and Congress, and rancorous political conflict is welcomed by almost no one.

The Clinton impeachment put the bitterest of partisan conflicts on full display, and the public did not find it a pretty sight. After the Senate acquitted Clinton, members of Congress, particularly on the Republican side, began looking for ways to soften the image of rabid partisanship that the impeachment had imparted. The trends examined here suggest that any success they achieve is destined to be temporary. Party divisions in Congress have increasingly sturdy electoral roots, particularly among activists, as well as strong institutional reinforcement from the congressional parties. Both parties' holds on their respective branches is tenuous, guaranteeing intense electoral competition across the board in 2000. The party that achieves the upper hand has an excellent chance of winning control of the whole federal government; if the Republicans can win the presidency, they are almost certain to capture undivided national power for the first time in nearly half a century. With so much at stake, no partisan political advantage is likely to be left unexploited. The only constraint on undiluted partisanship is the fear of losing ground by *looking* too partisan; if impeachment politics is any indication, it is not much of a constraint. All signs point to a new partisan era in national politics that is likely to continue for the foreseeable future.

11-3

from *Air Wars*

Darrell M. West

Complaints about negative advertising, voter manipulation, and ever-mounting costs are voiced in all national, and most statewide, election campaigns. Many voters describe campaign advertising as misleading and as not providing adequate information about the candidates. In this essay, Darrell West reviews the criticisms of modern campaigns and describes the strategies and mechanics of television advertising in political campaigns.

IT WAS A HISTORIC ELECTION. After defeating Sen. Hillary Clinton for the Democratic nomination and triumphing over Republican nominee John McCain, Sen. Barack Obama made history by becoming America's first African American president. Noting that the country was mired in a financial meltdown and engulfed in controversial wars in Iraq and Afghanistan, Obama broadcast advertisements explaining that he represented "Change We Can Believe In." His commercials linked McCain to unpopular GOP President George W. Bush with the slogan "More of the Same." Employing McCain's own words from the nominating process, Obama put forth that the Arizona senator supported Bush 90 percent of the time on legislative votes.

For his part, McCain ran a scorched earth strategy that characterized Obama as a vacuous celebrity similar to Paris Hilton and Britney Spears, then as someone who palled around with domestic terrorists, and finally as a tax-and-spend liberal whose philosophy bordered on socialism. One ad hammered Obama with the attack of "Higher Taxes. More Spending. Not Ready." In the end, though, people's fears about the national economy led Obama to a 52 percent to 46 percent margin win over his Republican rival.

As illustrated throughout the campaign, advertisements are a major component of political races. In recent presidential campaigns, campaign spots accounted for the largest item in total fall expenditures.[1] Commercials are used to shape citizens' impressions and affect news coverage.[2] As such, they represent a major strategic tool for campaigners. However, not all spots produce the same

Source: Darrell M. West, "Overview of Ads," from *Air Wars: Television Advertising in Election Campaigns, 1952–2008,* 5th ed. (Washington, D.C.: CQ Press: 2010), 1–24.

results. Some ads work; others do not. To determine which spots are effective, analysts must look at production techniques, ad buys (the frequency and location of ad broadcasting), opposition responses, news coverage, and citizens' predispositions. Through detailed studies of ad campaigns since the 1950s, this book shows how to assess ad messages, media coverage of ads, and ad impact on voters.

The History of Ads

From the earliest days of the Republic, communications devices have been essential to political campaigns. In 1828, handbills distributed by Andrew Jackson's supporters portrayed John Quincy Adams as "driving off with a horsewhip a crippled old soldier who dared to speak to him, to ask an alms." A circular distributed by Adams's forces, meanwhile, attacked Jackson for "ordering other executions, massacring Indians, stabbing a Samuel Jackson in the back, murdering one soldier who disobeyed his commands, and hanging three Indians."[3]

The method, though perhaps not the tone, of communicating with the electorate has changed dramatically since 1828. Handbills have virtually disappeared. Radio became the most popular vehicle in the 1920s and 1930s. After World War II, television emerged as the advertising medium of choice for political candidates. And now, in the twenty-first century, the media marketplace has fragmented into a bewildering variety of communication channels from cable television and talk radio to late-night entertainment shows and the World Wide Web. A new Internet-based lexicon has appeared that distinguishes banner ads (large boxes that span the top of a Web site), interstitial ads (spots that flash while a Web site is being loaded), pop-up ads (spots that appear after a Web site is loaded), transactional ads (spots that allow viewers to make a purchase or request information), and rich media ads (spots that have audio, video, or motion embedded within them).[4] Somehow, in this multifaceted situation, candidates must figure out how to reach voters who will decide key election contests.

The 1952 presidential campaign was the first one to feature television ads. In that year, each party ran television and print ads evoking World War II memories. Republicans, in an effort to support Gen. Dwight Eisenhower and break two decades of Democratic control, reminded voters in a *New York Times* ad that "one party rule made slaves out of the German people until Hitler was conquered by Ike." Not to be outdone, Democratic ads informed voters that "General Hindenburg, the professional soldier and national hero, [was] also ignorant of domestic and political affairs. . . . The net result was his appointment of Adolf Hitler as Chancellor."[5]

In the 1960s, television spots highlighted differences in candidates' personal traits. The 1964 presidential campaign with Lyndon Johnson and Barry Goldwater was one of the most negative races since the advent of television. Johnson's campaign characterized Goldwater as an extremist not to be trusted with America's future. One five-minute ad, "Confession of a Republican," proclaimed, "This man scares me. . . . So many men with strange ideas are working for Goldwater."[6] Johnson's "Daisy" ad made a similar point in a more graphic manner. Along with speeches and news coverage, the visual image of a mushroom cloud rising behind a little girl picking daisies in a meadow helped raise doubts about Goldwater's fitness for office in the nuclear age, even though a firestorm of protest forced the ad off the air after only one showing.

Ads in the 1970s and 1980s took advantage of public fear about the economy. When the United States started to experience the twin ills of inflation and unemployment, a phenomenon that led experts to coin a new word, *stagflation,* campaign commercials emphasized economic themes. In 1980, Republican challenger Ronald Reagan effectively used ads to criticize economic performance under President Jimmy Carter. When the economy came roaring back in 1984, Reagan's serene "Morning in America" ad communicated the simple message that prosperity abounded and the United States was at peace.

The 1988 presidential contest was the zenith of attack politics in the post–World War II period. This campaign illustrated the powerful ability of ads to alter impressions of a candidate who was not well known nationally. Early in the summer of 1988, Massachusetts governor Michael Dukakis held a 17-percentage-point lead over his Republican rival, then vice president George H.W. Bush. Women preferred Dukakis over Bush by a large margin, and the governor was doing well among blacks, elderly citizens, and Democrats who previously had supported Reagan.

Meanwhile, Republicans were test marketing new advertising material. Over Memorial Day weekend in Paramus, New Jersey, Bush aides Jim Baker, Lee Atwater, Roger Ailes, Robert Teeter, and Nicholas Brady stood behind a one-way mirror observing a small group of so-called Reagan Democrats. Information concerning Willie Horton, a convicted black man who—while on furlough from a Massachusetts prison—brutally raped a white woman, was being presented, and the audience was quite disturbed. Atwater later boasted to party operatives, "By the time this election is over, Willie Horton will be a household name."[7] Bush went on to beat Dukakis 53 percent to 46 percent.

The 1992 campaign represented the dangers of becoming overly reliant on attack ads and the power of thirty-minute "infomercials" by Reform Party candidate Ross Perot. Throughout the race, Bush used ads to attack Democratic nominee Bill Clinton's character and his record as governor of Arkansas. But unlike in his 1988 race, Bush did not prevail. The poor economy, the backlash that developed against Bush's advertising attacks, and Clinton's quick responses to criticisms led to Clinton beating Bush 43 percent to 38 percent. Perot finished in third place with 19 percent, the best showing for a third-party candidate since Theodore Roosevelt in 1912.

In 1996, President Clinton coasted to reelection through the help of ads broadcast more than a year before the election. With the advice of political strategist Dick Morris, Clinton defied the conventional wisdom arguing against early advertising. He ran ads both on television and over the Internet that positioned him as the bulwark against GOP extremism. Linking Republican nominee Bob Dole to unpopular House Speaker Newt Gingrich, Clinton portrayed the Republican Party as insensitive to women, children, and minorities and not to be trusted with important issues such as Social Security, Medicare, and education.

In 2000, Al Gore and George W. Bush ran in the closest presidential election in decades. Featuring cautious advertising that played to undecided voters, each candidate, along with outside groups, ran commercials that challenged the integrity and experience of the other. Bush emphasized education reform, whereas Gore focused on health care and Social Security. One Bush ad, popularly known as "RATS," featured the first use of a subliminal message in presidential campaign history when the word RATS was superimposed over a few frames criticizing Gore's prescription drug plan.[8] The election even saw a remake of the infamous 1964 "Daisy" ad ("Daisy II"), when a group of Texans paid for an ad with an image of a girl plucking petals off a daisy while an announcer complained that because of Clinton–Gore deals with "communist Red China" in return for campaign contributions, Democrats had compromised the country's security and made the nation vulnerable to Chinese missile attacks.

In 2004, Bush used images of firefighters carrying victims away from the World Trade Center to explain how he was a "tested" individual who could provide steady leadership in turbulent times. At the same time, he characterized his opponent, Democrat John Kerry, as an unprincipled and untrustworthy "flip-flopper." The campaign produced a commercial showing Senator Kerry windsurfing while a narrator intoned, "In which direction would John Kerry lead? Kerry voted for the Iraq War, opposed it, supported it, and now opposes it again. . . . John Kerry: Whichever way the wind blows."[9] Kerry, meanwhile, attacked Bush's economic record and complained about Bush's foreign policy. One advertisement said "only Herbert Hoover had a worse record on jobs." Another spot showed a picture of Saudi Crown Prince Abdullah and suggested that "the Saudi royal family gets special favors, while our gas prices skyrocket."[10]

The 2008 presidential campaign represented one of the most wide-open races in decades. There was no incumbent or heir-apparent on the ballot of either major party. The result was that eight Democrats and nine Republicans sought their party's nomination. This included a woman (Hillary Clinton), an African American (Barack Obama), a Hispanic (Bill Richardson), a Mormon (Mitt Romney), and a former prisoner of war (John McCain). Between the primaries and the general election, the airwaves were saturated with political commercials. In the fall, McCain attacked Obama in terms of policy vision, lack of foreign policy experience, and personal associations. Obama, meanwhile, said McCain represented "Bush's Third Term" and that his GOP rival was not the party maverick he claimed to be.

Throughout these elections, commercials were a valuable lens on the inner workings of each campaign. Candidates revealed crucial aspects of their vision, leadership style, and substantive positions. As stated by Elizabeth Kolbert, then a news reporter for the *New York Times*, "Every advertising dollar spent represents a clue to a campaign's deepest hopes and a potential revelation about its priorities."[11]

Principles of Advertising

Strategists use the principles of stereotyping, association, demonization, and code words to influence the electorate. A *stereotype* refers to a common portrait or an oversimplified judgment that people hold toward groups or sets of individuals. For example, Republicans are often portrayed as strong on defense, but not very compassionate toward poor people. Democrats are viewed as caring and compassionate toward the downtrodden, but overly eager to raise taxes. Because television ads are brief, generally no more than thirty seconds, campaigners evoke stereotypes knowing they appeal to voters' prejudices and commonly held views.

However, ads cannot create perceptions that do not already exist in people's minds. There must be a kernel of truth in the stereotype for these types of appeals to be effective. If people do not already think that college professors are absent-minded, nurses are caring, or car salespeople are sleazy, it is hard for election ads to play to these kinds of sentiments.

Association is based on linking a candidate or cause to some other idea or person. Politicians love to connect themselves to widely esteemed popular objects while tying their opponents to things that are unpopular, controversial, or divisive. Flags, patriotism, and prominent celebrities are examples of objects with which candidates surround themselves. In contrast, opponents are pictured with unpopular causes or organizations or cast in a light that bonds them to unfavorable objects such as higher taxes, funding cuts for social programs, and ties to fringe groups or corporate "big money."[12]

During the Cold War, it was popular to portray leftist-leaning candidates as communist sympathizers having allegiance to foreign powers. When Kerry received the Democratic nomination, opponents sought to tie him to controversial Vietnam War protester, actress Jane Fonda. The Swift Boat Veterans for Truth ran an ad entitled "Friends" that asserted, "even before Jane Fonda went to Hanoi to meet with the enemy and mock America, John Kerry secretly met with enemy leaders in Paris. . . . Jane Fonda apologized for her activities, but John Kerry refuses to."[13]

In the campaign for the 2008 Democratic presidential nomination, Hillary Clinton used association techniques to tie Obama to controversial African American minister Jeremiah Wright, Obama's hometown minister at Trinity United Church of Christ in Chicago. Using videos of Wright complaining that America was "the No. 1 killer in the world" and that the U.S. government had "started the AIDS virus," she suggested that Obama was outside the political meanstream because he associated with such a controversial speaker.[14]

The 2008 general election saw a similar tactic on the part of McCain. The GOP nominee attempted to link Obama to former 1960s radical William Ayers. Noting that Ayers had admitted to participating in a police station bombing in 1970 and that Obama had held a benefit coffee at Ayers's home in 1995 during his first run for public office, McCain said that this personal link between the men proved that Obama was too extreme for America and not to be trusted.

However, after endorsements by Warren Buffett and Colin Powell, Obama ran spots touting support by these prominent Americans and used these associations to make the point that he represented a safe choice for America. Combined with his own calm demeanor and steady voice, Obama defused what could have come to be seen as negative associations with controversial figures.

To gain credibility, politicians like to associate themselves with such popular people as public figures, sports heroes, astronauts, or Hollywood celebrities. These individuals come from outside the political world and often have a great deal of mainstream influence and respect. By associating with them and winning their endorsements, politicians attempt to piggyback onto the high credibility these individuals have among voters in general.[15]

Demonization is the process of turning an opponent into an evil being or satanic figure Wartime enemies are condemned as murderers, terrorists, or barbarians. Political opponents are portrayed as extremists out of touch with the mainstream or guilty of immoral behavior. Adversaries are identified with policy actions that are widely condemned or seen as socially destructive.

For example, an entry in an anti-Bush ad contest sponsored by the MoveOn.org Voter Fund intermingled pictures of Adolf Hitler and George W. Bush making speeches. In a clear effort to demonize the sitting president, the spot concluded with the tagline, "What were war crimes in 1945 is foreign policy in 2003."[16]

Meanwhile, commercials sponsored by the Progress for America Voter Fund, a conservative political action committee, attacked Kerry by showing pictures of Osama bin Laden and September 11 hijacker Mohamed Atta. The unmistakable message in these spots was that Kerry was not to be trusted with defending America's security.[17]

As with the other principles, demonizing the opposition is a tactic that must be used carefully. There must be some believability in the specific appeal for an ad to have credibility. One cannot simply make charges that are unsubstantiated or so far out of bounds as to exceed voters' ability to internalize them. Demonization must bear some resemblance to the facts for this tactic to influence citizens.

Code words are shorthand communication devices that play on common stereotypes and connotations associated with particular kinds of language. Even in the limited space of thirty seconds, campaigns can use short messages to communicate broader messages to the public. Many people feel that thirty seconds is too brief a period to convey much in the way of substantive themes, but during election campaigns, single words or expressions can take on enormous importance.

For example, in the 1960s and 1970s, Republicans used the phrase "law and order" to play to voter conceptions that Democrats were permissive on crime, race, and morality, whereas Republicans could be counted on to protect the social order. Democrats were paired with images and voice-overs of urban riots and social protests to convey complex political messages.

Democrats, meanwhile, have used a similar tactic in regard to the code word of *right wing*. Following the surprise GOP takeover of the House and Senate in 1994 and Newt Gingrich's ascension to the Speakership, Democrats played to voter stereotypes about Republicans being uncaring and insensitive. Using examples of extreme rhetoric and policy proposals that sought to slow the rate of increase in spending on various federal programs, Democrats associated GOP candidates with unsympathetic and extremist images. Throughout the country in 2000, House Democrats used the phrase *right-wing extremists* to refer to their Republican counterparts.[18]

Code words are powerful communication devices because they allow voters to associate a particular message with a specific code word. One of the most frequently used code words has been *liberal* by Republicans. In 1988, George Bush Sr. called Democratic candidate Dukakis a liberal thirty-one times in his speeches. The message got through to voters. Whereas 31 percent in May 1988 believed Dukakis was liberal, the figure rose to 46 percent by September 1988.

In 1992, Bush's use of the term *liberal* rose to sixty-two times. Similar to 1988, the word took on a number of negative meanings, such as being fiscally irresponsible, soft on crime, and dangerously out of touch with the American public. This approach allowed Bush to condemn Clinton with the single word liberal without having to voice more detailed descriptions of his opponent's position.[19]

By 1996, the country's airwaves were filled with ads using the L-word. Dole ran ads condemning Clinton as a tax-and-spend liberal and as someone whose failed policies were liberal. In one speech in September 1996, Dole used the word fourteen times. Republican congressional candidates used the same appeal all across the country. Ads financed by the Republican National Committee criticized Democratic House and Senate candidates as "liberals," "ultra-liberals," "super-liberals," "unbelievably liberal," "embarrassingly liberal," "foolishly liberal," and "taxingly liberal." Because of the country's changed political climate after the abortive Republican Revolution to downsize government, though, the use of the word liberal as an epithet did not resonate with voters. As one voter in a focus group put it, the term liberal meant helping people. Others felt that "liberal is having an open mind."

This view was supported in a 1996 CBS News/New York Times survey asking people what they thought of when they heard someone described as liberal or conservative, respectively. The most common responses for liberal were open minded (14 percent), free spending (8 percent), high degree of government involvement (7 percent), helps people (5 percent), and pro-handouts (5 percent). The most common responses for conservative were fiscally responsible (17 percent), closed minded (10 percent), careful (8 percent), against change (7 percent), and low degree of government involvement (6 percent).[20]

In the 2004 campaign, however, use of the *liberal* epithet returned to the campaign trail. President George W. Bush criticized Kerry for advocating a return to "massive new government agencies" with power over health care. Through an ad showing a map of a complex federal bureaucracy, Bush charged that Kerry's health care program would cause "rationing" and that "Washington bureaucrats, not your doctor, [would] make final decisions on your health."[21] In addition, the Republican National Committee sent a mass mailing to voters in Arkansas and West Virginia accusing "liberals" of seeking to ban the Bible in order to promote policies on gay marriage.[22]

With conservative disgust over the decision of the French government not to support the war in Iraq, the 2004 election introduced the code word *French* to political discourse. Not only did some lawmakers seek to rename French fries "freedom fries," Bush's Commerce secretary, Don Evans, accused Kerry of looking "French" because he spoke the language, was cosmopolitan, and had French relatives.[23] The National Rifle Association also associated Kerry with France by using a mailing with a French poodle wearing a Kerry campaign sweater and having a bow in its hair to condemn the Democrat's record.[24]

As explained by Françoise Meltzer, a humanities professor at the University of Chicago, in the 2004 electoral context, "French really means un-American." It was a striking contrast to earlier periods, when France was viewed favorably in the United States because it had aided the thirteen colonies during the American Revolution and given America the gift of the Statue of Liberty.[25]

The 2008 presidential election was a code word bonanza. Democrats argued that McCain was an "out of touch" politician who didn't even use a computer or e-mail. Meanwhile, Republicans complained that Obama was a liberal or even a socialist, and that he associated with domestic terrorists. Obama sought to disarm these attacks by joking at the end of the campaign that some people thought he was a secret communist because he'd "shared [his] toys in kindergarten."[26]

How Ads Are Put Together

Production techniques for commercials have improved dramatically since the 1950s. Early ads were rudimentary by contemporary standards. Political spots often took the form of footage from press conferences or testimonials from prominent citizens. Many were of the "talking head" variety in which the candidate (or his or her supporter) looked straight into the camera and spoke for thirty or sixty seconds without any editing.

Contemporary ads, in contrast, are visually enticing. Technological advances in television and on the Internet allow ad producers to use colorful images and sophisticated editing techniques to make spots more compelling. Images can be spliced together, and animated images visually transpose one person into another in a split second using a technique called "morphing." As we see in the next sections, catchy visuals, music, and color capture viewer attention and convey particular political messages in a variety of ways.

Visual Images

The visual aspect of advertising is the most important part of commercials. According to the old adage, a picture is worth a thousand words. Contemporary ads use graphic imagery to grab the public's attention and convey messages. Whereas traditional research focused on the spoken content of ads to determine ways of conveying messages, modern analysts study both audio and visual aspects of advertising.

Candidates often attempt to undermine political opponents by associating them with unfavorable visuals. A 1990 campaign ad by Sen. Bennett Johnston, D-La., against his opponent, state representative David Duke, showed pictures of

Duke addressing a Ku Klux Klan rally in the presence of a burning cross to make his point that Duke was an extremist who should not be elected to a seat in the U.S. Senate.

A similar phenomenon happened in 1996. Taking advantage of House Speaker Newt Gingrich's unpopularity, Democrats across the United States broadcast ads showing pictures of Gingrich side by side with Bob Dole and House and Senate Republican candidates. The message was clear: A vote for the Republican Dole was a vote for Gingrich.

In 2000, George W. Bush positioned himself as a "compassionate conservative" and frequently appeared at election rallies with retired general Colin Powell, a popular African American leader who later became Bush's secretary of state. Bush surrounded himself in photo opportunities and ads with women, minorities, and children to convey the idea he was a different kind of Republican than Gingrich. For his part, Gore relied on pictures of himself with his wife, Mary Elizabeth (Tipper) Gore, to communicate the idea that he was a candidate with firm values and a strong marriage. It was a way to distinguish himself from the personal scandals of the Clinton era.

In 2004, terrorism was mentioned in 13 percent of all the ads run after Labor Day.[27] Some advertisements mentioned Osama bin Laden by name or showed pictures of him. One Republican Senate candidate in Wisconsin even invoked the visual image of a burning World Trade Center on September 11, 2001, to charge that "Russ Feingold voted against the Patriot Act and the Department of Homeland Security."[28]

However, by 2008, public fear over domestic terrorism had faded. In his campaign for the Republican presidential nomination, former New York City mayor Rudy Giuliani attempted to play to citizen concerns by broadcasting ads reminding people of 9/11. But unlike 2004, when these fears helped Bush win reelection, visual images of past terrorist attacks did not resonate with voters; the electorate was much more worried about the economy.

Indeed, the powerful imagery in the fall general election centered on the economy. With the startling meltdown of major financial institutions in the weeks leading up to the November election, voters saw major companies failing or merging and an extraordinary amount of taxpayer dollars infused into banks and insurance companies. Images of unemployed workers, people losing health benefits, and senior citizens forced to scrimp on needed prescription drugs were commonplace. Through these and other devices, Obama effectively tied McCain to Bush and negative perceptions about the Republican Party's economic policies.

The visual aspect of campaign advertising is important because it is the one that has the most impact on viewers. The reason is simple—people remember visuals longer than they do spoken words. Images also have the advantage of creating an emotional response much more powerful than that which results from hearing the spoken word.

CBS news reporter Lesley Stahl tells the story of a hard-hitting evening news piece broadcast on Reagan's presidency in 1984. The story claimed that Reagan had done certain things, such as cut the budget for the elderly, that were contrary to what he said he had done. Accompanying the story was a series of pleasant visual images of Reagan "basking in a sea of flag-waving supporters, beaming beneath red-white-and-blue balloons floating skyward, sharing concerns with farmers in a field." After the story aired, Stahl was surprised by a favorable telephone call from a top Reagan assistant. Asked why he liked the story, given her harsh words, the Reagan adviser explained she had given the White House four and a half minutes of positive pictures of President Reagan: "They don't hear what you are saying if the pictures are saying something different."[29]

Visual Text

Visual text is a print message appearing onscreen, generally in big, bold letters. Printed messages grab viewers' attention and tell them to pay attention to an ad. As an example, Ross Perot's 1992 ads used visual text scrolling up the screen to persuade the American public to vote for him. Spots for Clinton in 1996 used big, splashy text onscreen to make the political point that Republicans wanted to "CUT MEDICARE." Dole sought to characterize Clinton as "LIBERAL" and "UNTRUSTWORTHY." In 2000, Democratic ads often noted that Texas ranked "50TH" in family health care, and Republican ads complained that Gore was guilty of "EXAGGERATIONS." Republican ads against Obama in 2008 superimposed text such as "INEXPERIENCED" or "NOT READY" to argue that the Democrat lacked the necessary credentials for the chief executive position. Obama countered by saying that McCain was "More of the Same." Advertisers have found that memory of a message is greatly enhanced by combining visual text with spoken words and descriptive images.

Music and Sounds

Music sets the tone for an ad. Just as party hosts use upbeat music to accompany festivities or an educational institution plays "Pomp and Circumstance" to set the scene for a graduation ceremony, campaign ads use music to convey the mood of a particular commercial.

Uplifting ads use cheery music to make people feel good about a candidate. For example, the 1984 campaign featured an independently produced ad called "I'm Proud To Be an American" that used music from country singer Lee Greenwood's song by that same name. The music played over scenes of Reagan, the American flag, and cheerful scenes of happy Americans. It conveyed the message that things were good in America and people should vote for Reagan.

Conversely, somber or ominous music in an ad seeks subliminally to undermine support for the opponent. In George H.W. Bush's "Revolving Door" ad in 1988, dark and threatening music accompanied scenes of prisoners walking through a revolving door while an announcer attacked Dukakis's record on crime. The sounds of drums, the footsteps of guards on metal stairs, and threatening voices were integral to the ad's message that voters should reject Dukakis in the November election because he was soft on crime.

Color

Color communicates vivid messages in ads. Media consultants use bright colors to associate their candidates with a positive image and grayish or black and white to associate opponents with a negative image. In 2000, for example, the NAACP-sponsored spot about the dragging death of James Byrd was broadcast in black and white to make the point that something dramatically different and calamitous had taken place and viewers should pay close attention.

The 1992 Bush campaign developed an ad called "Arkansas Record" that featured a vulture looking out over a dark and barren landscape to make its point that Clinton had poorly governed Arkansas. That year, Bush also used a low-quality, grayish photographic negative of Clinton from an April 20, 1992, *Time* magazine cover to exhort voters to defeat the Arkansas governor in November. The cover with the photographic negative of Clinton was entitled, "Why Voters Don't Trust Clinton." Bush's ad juxtaposed a nice color image of himself to reinforce the message that voters should not vote for Clinton.

A 1996 Dole commercial took a color videotape clip in which Clinton said if he had it to do over again, he would inhale marijuana, and rebroadcast the image in black and white to make Clinton look sinister. The opposite technique (going from black and white to color) was used by Gore in his 2000 ad called "Veteran." It opened with a black and white photo of a youthful Gore in Vietnam, then shifted to color frames of Gore with Tipper.

Editing

Editing determines the sequencing and pacing of an ad. The *sequencing* of ad images refers to how images in one scene are related to following scenes. For example, the 1984 Reagan ad "Morning in America" showed images of Reagan interspersed with scenes of Americans at work and a country at peace. The sequencing linked the president with the popular themes of peace and prosperity. These images were accompanied by music that enhanced the emotional impact of the ad.

An Obama attack ad in 2008 showed a shifty-eyed McCain grimacing, raising his eyebrows, and smiling awkwardly to suggest he was not the right man for the presidency. At a time of domestic crisis, according to the spot, the United States needed someone better equipped to handle economic and foreign policy issues.

The *pacing* of an ad refers to whether the images flow smoothly or abruptly from scene to scene. Abrupt cuts from image to image create a jarring effect that tells viewers something bad is appearing before them. Such cuts are commonly used to convey negative feelings in attack ads.

Voice-Overs

Through an off-screen announcer, a voice-over provides a road map that knits together visual scenes. A campaign ad is composed of different pictures that convey particular points. The announcer guides viewers through these scenes to clearly communicate the message of the ad.

Typically, attack ads use male announcers to deliver blistering criticisms, but Dole made history in 1996 by using a female announcer to condemn Clinton's "failed liberal drug policies." The use of a woman for the voice-over was designed to soften any potential backlash from going on the attack and to appeal to women concerned about drug use and moral permissiveness in American society.

However, in 2000, both George W. Bush and Gore reverted to the historical pattern and relied more frequently on male announcers for the audio components of their ads. One exception was a Bush ad called "Compare," which used a female announcer to criticize Gore's prescription drug plan. Female narrators are used for health care ads because market research reveals that women make the preponderance of health care decisions in U.S. households. Another exception took place in 2004 during a Bush ad known as "Wolves." This spot used the image of a pack of wolves to argue that the United States was surrounded by dangerous enemies. It used a female announcer to take the edge off what was a hard-hitting attack on the opposition.

How Ads Are Financed

The financing of campaign ads has changed dramatically in recent decades. In the post-Watergate reforms of the 1970s, candidates generally paid for the bulk of their advertisements out of so-called hard money contributions. These were gifts given directly to candidate organizations for voter persuasion. Campaigners would use these funds to produce and broadcast ads that were put out on the airwaves under a candidate's direct sponsorship. Both the Republican and Democrat nominees broadcast ads designed to frame the contest and set the agenda of political dialogue.

Over time, though, a series of loopholes appeared that transformed campaign ad financing. Interest groups and party organizations began to exploit a loophole that allowed unlimited amounts of money (so-called soft money gifts) to be spent on voter education and get-out-the-vote efforts. Originally created by the 1976 *Buckley v. Valeo* Supreme Court case on the post-Watergate reforms, this loophole was designed to strengthen political parties and outside groups and allow them to mobilize and educate supporters. Donors could give whatever money they desired without being limited to the $1,000 per individual and $5,000 per organization rules for hard money contributions.

This loophole reached its zenith in the 1990s when President Bill Clinton used large amounts of soft money contributions to the Democratic National Committee (DNC) to run ads extolling his virtues and lambasting those of the Republican opposition. Rather than using the money for get-out-the-vote or party-building activities, the DNC ran commercials that were virtually indistinguishable from hard money–financed candidate spots. Republicans did the same thing through the Republican National Committee to criticize Clinton and campaign against Democratic House and Senate candidates.[30]

The ensuing controversy over these funding practices (and a post-election investigation into Clinton's campaign spending) eventually led to enactment of the 2002 Bipartisan Campaign Reform Act (BCRA) sponsored by John McCain and Democrat Russell Feingold. Among its key principles were the outlawing of soft money gifts at the national party level (although state party organizations still could accept these contributions), an increase in individual contributions to $2,000 per candidate per election cycle, and a requirement that candidates personally appear in ads saying they paid for their commercials and took responsibility for their contents.

Groups still could run issue ads that talked about specific policies. For example, they could say that Republicans were harming poor people or that Democrats loved to raise taxes. But ads broadcast by these organizations in the sixty days before a general election could not engage in electoral advocacy. Groups could not criticize the policy stances of a specific federal candidate without registering as a political action committee and being subject to disclosure requirements.

The result of this legislation is a hodgepodge of rules concerning ad financing. Candidates can use hard money gifts to run advertisements, as can national party organizations. State party groups can rely on soft money contributions for political advertisements. Interest groups can spend unlimited amounts of money on issue ads without any disclosure of spending or contributors, except in the last sixty days before a general election. At that point in the campaign, they can run ads criticizing federal candidates, but they have to disclose who paid for the spots.

Unaffected by the 2002 reform legislation are radio ads, direct mail, phone calls, and Internet advertisements. Officials had focused on television ads because they form the bulk of political communications and are the technology that critics most worry about in terms of misleading voters. By restraining the most worrisome television maladies, the hope is that this reform will improve the content and tone of civic discourse. However, as discussed later in this volume, there is little evidence from 2004 or 2008 that the new rules made candidate appeals any more civil.

The 2004 and 2008 elections saw the rise of ad financing through Internet contributions. Howard Dean in 2004 and Obama in 2008 democratized fund-raising by using Web sites to raise large amounts of money from many small donors. With the Democratic base upset at President George W. Bush and alarmed at the Iraq War, these anti-war candidates raised huge amounts of money. Obama's total contributions exceeded $600 million, an all-time record for an American presidential candidate. This allowed him to fund a wide variety of television commercials, radio spots, Internet advertisements, a thirty-minute infomercial the week before the election, and get-out-the-vote efforts on Election Day.

The Impact of Ads on Voters

Ads are fascinating not only because of the manner in which they are put together but also because of their ability to influence voters. People are not equally susceptible to the media, and political observers have long tried to find out how media power actually operates.[31]

Consultants judge the effectiveness of ads by the ultimate results—who wins. This type of test, however, is never possible to complete until after the election. It leads invariably to the immutable law of advertising: Winners have great ads and losers do not.

As an alternative, journalists evaluate ads by asking voters to indicate whether commercials influenced them. When asked directly whether television commercials helped them decide how to vote, most voters say they did not. For example, the results of a Media Studies Center survey placed ads at the bottom of the heap in terms of possible information sources. Whereas 45 percent of voters felt they learned a lot from debates, 32 percent cited newspaper stories, and 30 percent pointed to television news stories, just 5 percent believed they learned a lot from political ads. When asked directly about ads in a CBS News/*New York*

Times survey, only 11 percent reported that any presidential candidate's ads had helped them decide how to vote.[32]

But this is not a meaningful way of looking at advertising. Such responses undoubtedly reflect an unwillingness to admit that external agents have any effect on individual voting behavior. Many people firmly believe that they make up their minds independently of the campaign. Much in the same way teenagers do not like to concede parental influence, few voters are willing to admit they are influenced by television.

In studying campaign ads, one needs to emphasize the overall context in which people make decisions. The same ad can have very different consequences depending on the manner in which an opponent responds, the way a journalist reports the ad, the number of times the spot is broadcast, or the predispositions of the viewer.

A vivid example is found in Kathleen Hall Jamieson's study of the 1988 presidential campaign.[33] The effectiveness of Bush's "Revolving Door" ad on Dukakis's crime record was enhanced by the majority culture's fears about black men raping white women and by earlier news stories that had sensationalized Horton's crime spree. Bush did not have to mention Horton in his ad for viewers to make the connection between Dukakis and heinous crimes.

This idea is central to understanding campaign advertisements. Commercials cannot be explored in isolation from candidate behavior and the general flow of media information. An analysis of thirty-second spots requires a keen awareness of the structure of electoral competition, strategic candidate behavior, media coverage, and public opinion. A variety of long- and short-term factors go into voter decision-making. In terms of long-term forces, things such as party loyalties, ideological predispositions, the rules of the game, and socioeconomic status linked to education, income, sex, race, and region affect how people interpret ads and judge candidates. Meanwhile, there are a variety of short-term factors during a campaign that affect people. These include how the media cover ads, what reporters say about the candidates, candidate strategies, and debate performance.

Generally, the better known candidates are, the less ads are able to sway voter impressions. In a situation in which voters have firm feelings about campaigners based on long-term forces such as party and ideology, it is difficult for any of the short-term forces to make a difference. However, if the candidate is not well known or there is volatility in the political climate, news, ads, and debates can make a substantial difference in the election outcome.

The Structure of Electoral Competition

The structure of the electoral process defines the general opportunities available to candidates. The most important development at the presidential level has been the dramatic change in how convention delegates are selected. Once controlled by party leaders in small-scale caucus settings thought to be immune from media influence, nominations have become open and lengthy affairs significantly shaped by the mass media. The percentage of delegates to national nominating conventions selected through primaries increased significantly after 1968. From the 1920s to the 1960s, about 40 percent of delegates were selected in primaries, with the remainder chosen in caucus settings dominated by party leaders. However, after rule changes set in motion by the Democratic Party's McGovern-Fraser Commission following the 1968 election, about 70 percent of convention delegates in each party now are chosen directly by voters in presidential primaries.

Nominating reforms have required candidates to appeal directly to voters for support and in the eyes of many observers have altered the character of the electoral system.[34] No longer are candidates dependent on negotiations with a handful of party leaders. Instead, they must demonstrate public appeal and run campaigns that win media attention. Campaigns have become longer and have come to depend increasingly on television as a means of attracting public support.[35]

Some campaigns get far more attention than others. Citizens are more interested in and knowledgeable about presidential general election campaigns than nominating contests. Although variation exists among individual contests depending on the candidates involved, nomination races typically generate less citizen interest and less media coverage. Of course, the 2008 Democratic nominating contest sparked unusual interest because of the clash of superstar candidates Obama and Clinton.

These differences in the visibility of the candidates and the extent of media coverage are important for the study of television advertisements. Because less visible races feature candidates who are not well known, ad effects on citizens' opinions of the candidates often are significant. Past research has demonstrated that television's impact is strongest when viewers have weakly formulated views.[36] It is easier to run ads against a candidate who is not well known because there is no preexisting attitudinal profile to shield that individual against critical claims.

In addition, candidate behavior is conditioned by the rules of the game. Presidential elections in the United States are determined by the state-based Electoral College. Candidates seek to assemble a majority of Electoral College votes by winning targeted states. This electoral structure has enormous implications for advertising strategies. Most candidates do not run a fifty-state campaign. Instead, because many states tend to vote consistently over time, they focus on the fifteen to twenty states that swing back and forth between the two major parties.

Daron Shaw has undertaken an innovative study of Electoral College strategies and found that candidates apportion their time and advertising dollars in systematic ways. According to his study, strategies center on five categories: base

Republican, marginal Republican, battleground state, marginal Democratic, and base Democratic.[37] Factors such as electoral history, size of the state's electoral vote, and current competitiveness dictate how campaigners allocate their resources. These decisions tend to be stable across presidential elections. This demonstrates the way in which electoral rules affect candidate strategies.

Advertising and Strategic Politicians

Early research downplayed the power of ads to mold the public images of candidates. The pioneering study in this area was Thomas Patterson and Robert McClure's innovative effort, *The Unseeing Eye*.[38] Looking at both content and effects, they sought to dispel the concerns of the public and journalists regarding political commercials. Using a model of psychological reasoning based on voters' knowledge about candidates, these researchers examined whether television ads enabled voters to learn more about the policy views or about the personal qualities of campaigners. They found that voters learned more about the issues from ads than from the news, because the ads addressed issues whereas the news was dominated by coverage of the "horse race"—who is ahead at a given time. Popular concerns about the strategic dangers of ads affecting how viewers thought of candidates were minimized as uninformed hand-wringing.

The study's results fit with the general view among election experts of the 1960s and 1970s that political strategies were not very decisive in determining election results. Researchers in the era following the 1960 publication of Campbell et al.'s classic work on voting behavior, *The American Voter*, proclaimed such long-term forces as party identification as the most important. Few scholars disputed this interpretation, even as many argued that short-term factors related to media coverage, candidates' advertisements, and campaign spending simply were not crucial to vote choice. For example, Harold Mendelsohn and Irving Crespi claimed in 1970 that the "injection of high doses of political information during the frenetic periods of national campaigns does very little to alter the deeply rooted, tightly held political attitudes of most voters."[39] Even the later emergence of models based on pocketbook considerations did little to change this interpretation. Paid ads were thought to have limited capacity to shape citizens' impressions of economic performance.

Recent decades, though, have begun to see changes in previous viewpoints. Candidates have started to use commercials more aggressively, reporters have devoted more attention to paid advertising, and ad techniques have grown more sophisticated. It now is thought that voters' assessments can change based on short-term information and that candidates have the power to sway undecided voters who wait until the closing weeks of the campaign to make up their minds.

Evidence from elections across the United States suggests that ads are successful in helping candidates develop impressions of themselves.[40]

This is particularly true when campaigners are unknown or in multicandidate nominating contests. The more strategic options that are available with the larger number of candidates involved, the more potential there is for the campaign to affect citizen judgments. One study of the New Hampshire primary by Lynn Vavreck, Constantine Spiliotes, and Linda Fowler, for example, found that a variety of campaign activities affected voters' recognition of and favorability toward specific candidates.[41]

Furthermore, candidates no longer hold a monopoly on advertising. Political parties, interest groups, and even private individuals run commercials around election time. In fact, there are discernible differences in the percentage of attack ads run by different sources. The most negative messages involve issue ads run by interest groups. Fifty-six percent of those ads were attack oriented in recent elections, compared with 20 percent of candidate-sponsored advertisements.[42]

Because paid ads are so important in contemporary campaigns, candidates take the development of advertising strategies quite seriously. Commercials often are pretested through focus groups or public opinion surveys.[43] Themes as well as styles of presentation are tried out before likely voters. What messages are most appealing? When and how often should particular ads be aired? Who should be targeted? How should ads best convey information?

The number of times an ad is broadcast is one of the most important strategic decisions made during the campaign. Professional ad buyers specialize in picking time slots and television shows advantageous for particular candidates. Whereas a candidate interested in appealing to senior citizens may air ads repeatedly during television shows catering to the elderly, youth-oriented politicians may run spots on Fox Network or MTV, and minority candidates may advertise on Black Entertainment Television. Obama, for example, advertised extensively on minority stations, whereas McCain broadcast ads on television shows with large older audiences, such as *NCIS*.

The content and timing of ads are crucial for candidates because of their link to overall success. Campaigns have become a blitz of competing ads, quick responses, and counter-responses. Ads have become serial in nature, with each ad building thematically on previous spots. Election campaigns feature strategic interactions as important as the individual ads themselves.

In the fast-changing dynamics of election campaigns, decisions to advance or delay particular messages can be quite important. Quick-response strategies require candidates to respond immediately when negative ads appear or political conditions are favorable. Candidates often play off each other's ads in an effort to gain the advantage with voters.

Advertising and the News Media

One of the developments of the contemporary period has been coverage of political advertising by reporters. Network news executive William Small described this as the most important news trend of recent years: "Commercials are now expected as part of news stories."[44] Many news outlets have even launched "ad watch" features. These segments, aired during the news and discussed in newspaper articles, present the ad, along with commentary on its accuracy and effectiveness. The most effective ads are those whose basic messages are reinforced by the news media.

Scholars traditionally distinguished the free from the paid media. Free media meant reports from newspapers, magazines, radio, and television that were not billed to candidates. The paid media encompassed commercials purchased by the candidate on behalf of the campaign effort. The two avenues of communications were thought to be independent in terms of effects on viewers because of the way viewers saw them.

But the increase in news coverage of advertising has blurred or even eliminated this earlier division between free and paid media. People who separate the effects of these communications channels need to recognize how intertwined the free and paid media have become. It is now quite common for network news programs to rebroadcast entertaining, provocative, or controversial ads. Even entertainment shows are filled with references to contemporary politics. Journalists and entertainers have begun to evaluate the effects of campaign commercials, and it has become clear that the free media provide significant audiences for television ads.

Ads broadcast for free during the news or discussed in major newspapers have several advantages over those aired purely as commercials. One strength is that viewers traditionally have trusted the news media—at least in comparison with paid ads—for fairness and objectivity. William McGuire has shown that the credibility of the source is one determinant of whether the message is believed.[45] The high credibility of the media gives ads aired during the news an important advantage over those seen as plain ads. Roger Ailes explained it this way: "You get a 30 or 40 percent bump out of [an ad] by getting it on the news. You get more viewers, you get credibility, you get it in a framework."[46]

The 2004 presidential election introduced a new category of advertisements—*phantom,* or *vapor, ads.* These are commercials produced and distributed to journalists but barely broadcast. Journalists complained that Kerry released half a dozen spots on topics such as health care, taxes, and the Iraq War that were never aired to the general public. This made the ads "video news releases purporting to be substantial paid advertising," according to reporters.[47]

In 2008, McCain and Obama did the same thing. One vapor ad by McCain attracted considerable media attention. Although it aired infrequently, it accused Obama of supporting comprehensive sex education for kindergarten children because of a law he had cosponsored while in the Illinois Senate. The ad was misleading because the intent of the legislation was to protect young kids from sexual predators, not to indoctrinate them with sexual content.

Commercials in the news guarantee campaigners a large audience and free air time. Opinion polls have documented that nearly two-thirds of Americans cite television as their primary source of news. This is particularly true for what is referred to as the "inadvertent audience"—those who are least interested in politics and among the most volatile in their opinions.[48]

But there can be disadvantages to having an ad aired during a newscast. When an ad is described as unfair to the opposition, media coverage undermines the sponsor's message. The advantages of airing an ad during the news can also be lost if reporters challenge the ad's factual accuracy.

During recent elections, though, journalists have tried in vain to keep up with the onslaught of negative and misleading appeals.[49] Both candidates in 2004 pushed the envelope of factual inaccuracy. For example, Kerry accused the Bush White House of having a secret plan to reintroduce a military draft and of wanting to privatize Social Security. Bush, meanwhile, complained that Kerry's health care program would create new federal bureaucracies and that Kerry thought terrorism was a nuisance like prostitution and gambling. In 2008, McCain broadcast a number of misleading ads, such as the sex education spot described above, and commercials saying Obama would raise taxes on middle-class families. This led to considerable media criticism alleging that these claims were misleading at best or downright inaccurate.[50]

Reporters write stories criticizing the candidates for misleading and inaccurate claims, but the sheer volume of ad expenditures and campaign trail rhetoric overwhelms press oversight.[51] Journalists simply cannot compete with the hundreds of times ads are broadcast by the candidates. Campaigners are very adroit at communicating directly with the public and ignoring critical press stories about their advertisements.

Changes in Public Opinion

Public opinion and voting behavior have undergone significant changes that are relevant to advertising. Voters are less trusting of government officials today than they were in the past. Whereas 23 percent of voters in 1958 agreed that you cannot trust the government to do what is right most of the time, 84 percent were untrusting at the turn of the twenty-first century. A significant bloc of voters does not identify with either one of the major parties.[52] These citizens are often the kind of voters who swing back and forth between the parties.

The independence of American voters and the volatility in American politics unleashed by corporate downsizing and the end of the Cold War have uprooted some parts of citizen attitudes. People's impressions of short-term political events can be fluid, and the issues or leadership qualities seen as most important at any given time can change.[53]

Each of these developments has altered the tenor of electoral campaigns and led to extensive efforts to appeal to undecided voters. Writing in the 1830s, Alexis de Tocqueville worried that the great masses would make "hasty judgments" based on the "charlatans of every sort [who] so well understand the secret of pleasing them."[54] The prominence today of an open electoral system filled with mistrusting voters and fast-paced ads has done nothing to alleviate this concern.

Conclusion

In short, there are many different things that affect the use, interpretation, and impact of campaign ads. No single perspective can explain why an ad works well at a particular time but may backfire in a different context. One must look at the political environment, the nature of public opinion, how reporters cover the ads, the way in which ads are edited and financed, and the strategies of stereotyping, association, demonization, and code words used by campaigners.

NOTES

1. Ira Chinoy, "In Presidential Race, TV Ads Were Biggest '96 Cost by Far," *Washington Post,* March 31, 1997, A19.

2. Michael Franz, Paul Freedman, Kenneth Goldstein, and Travis Ridout, *Campaign Advertising and American Democracy* (Philadelphia: Temple University Press, 2007).

3. Kathleen Jamieson, *Packaging the Presidency,* 2nd ed. (New York: Oxford University Press, 1992), 6–7.

4. "Ads for a Web Generation," *New York Times,* August 24, 1998, D7.

5. Jamieson, *Packaging the Presidency,* 50.

6. Quoted in Jamieson, *Packaging the Presidency,* 195. For a description of Johnson's strategy, see Edwin Diamond and Stephen Bates, *The Spot* (Cambridge: MIT Press, 1984), 127–140.

7. "How Bush Won," *Newsweek,* November 21, 1988, 117. Also see Paul Taylor and David Broder, "Early Volley of Bush Ads Exceeded Expectations," *Washington Post,* October 28, 1988.

8. Richard Berke, "Democrats See, and Smell, Rats in G.O.P. Ad," *New York Times,* September 12, 2000, A1.

9. Howard Kurtz, "Presidential Attack Ads Move from Land to Water—and Back," *Washington Post,* September 23, 2004, A9.

10. Jim Rutenberg, "Kerry Ads Draw on Saudis for New Attack on Bushes," *New York Times,* October 5, 2004, A16.

11. Elizabeth Kolbert, "Secrecy over TV Ads, or, the Peculiar Logic of Political Combat," *New York Times,* September 17, 1992, A21.

12. Emmett Buell and Lee Sigelman, *Attack Politics: Negativity in Presidential Campaigns since 1960* (Lawrence: University Press of Kansas, 2008).

13. Paul Farhi, "Ad Says Kerry 'Secretly' Met with Enemy; but He Told Congress of It," *Washington Post,* September 22, 2004, A8.

14. Ken Dilanian, "Defenders Say Wright Has Love, Righteous Anger for USA," *USA Today,* March 19, 2008.

15. Darrell M. West and John Orman, *Celebrity Politics* (Upper Saddle River, N.J.: Prentice Hall, 2003).

16. "Anti-Bush Ad Contest Includes Hitler Images," *Washington Post,* January 6, 2004, A4.

17. Howard Kurtz, "Ads Aiming Straight for the Heart," *Washington Post,* October 27, 2004, A1.

18. Darrell M. West, *Patrick Kennedy: The Rise to Power* (Upper Saddle River, N.J.: Prentice Hall, 2000).

19. Harry Berkowitz, "Campaigns Aim at Economy," *Newsday,* September 28, 1996, A13.

20. Marjorie Connelly, "A 'Conservative' Is (Fill in the Blank)," *New York Times,* November 3, 1996, E5.

21. Howard Kurtz, "Bush's Health Care Ads Not Entirely Accurate," *Washington Post,* October 13, 2004, A8.

22. David Kirkpatrick, "Republicans Admit Mailing Campaign Literature Saying Liberals Will Ban the Bible," *New York Times,* September 24, 2004, A20.

23. Paul Begala, "A Good Dirty Fight," *New York Times,* November 4, 2004, A25.

24. Glen Justice, "In Final Days, Attacks Are in the Mail and below the Radar," *New York Times,* October 31, 2004, A30.

25. Sandra Maler, "'French' Becomes Campaign Slur," *Seattle Times,* October 27, 2004, A5.

26. "Today on the Presidential Campaign Trail," *Washington Post,* October 30, 2008.

27. Wisconsin Advertising Project, "Presidential TV Advertising Battle Narrows to Just Ten Battleground States," October 12, 2004, press release.

28. Graeme Zielinski, "Michels Makes Case with Images from 9–11," *Milwaukee Journal Sentinel,* October 19, 2004, A1.

29. Martin Schram, *The Great American Video Game* (New York: William Morrow, 1987), 25–26. For a reassessment of the differential impact of radio and television viewers on the 1960 debates, see David Vancil and Sue Pendell, "The Myth of Viewer-Listener Disagreement in the First Kennedy-Nixon Debate," *Central States Speech Journal* 38 (Spring 1987): 16–27.

30. Kathleen Hall Jamieson, *Everything You Think You Know about Politics . . . and Why You're Wrong* (New York: Basic Books, 2000).

31. Daniel Stevens, "Separate and Unequal Effects: Information, Political Sophistication and Negative Advertising in American Elections," *Political Research Quarterly* 58, no. 3 (September 2005): 413–425; and Ted Brader, "Striking a Responsive Chord: How Political Ads Motivate and Persuade Voters by Appealing to Emotions," *American Journal of Political Science* 49, no. 2 (April 2005): 388–405.

32. The Media Studies Center poll is reported in *Providence Journal,* "Hype Swells as First Presidential Debate Approaches," September 29, 1996, A7. The CBS News/*New York Times* numbers come from Richard Berke, "Should Dole Risk Tough Image? Poll Says He Already Has One," *New York Times,* October 16, 1996, A1.

33. Kathleen Hall Jamieson, "Context and the Creation of Meaning in the Advertising of the 1988 Presidential Campaign," *American Behavioral Scientist* 32 (1989): 415–424. Also see Marion Just et al., *Cross Talk: Citizens, Candidates, and the Media in a Presidential Campaign* (Chicago: University of Chicago Press, 1996).

34. James Ceaser, *Presidential Selection* (Princeton: Princeton University Press, 1979).

35. Karen DeWitt, "Tsongas Pitches Economic Austerity Mixed with Patriotism," *New York Times,* January 1, 1992, A10.

36. Ken Goldstein and Paul Freedman, "New Evidence for New Arguments: Money and Advertising in the 1996 Senate Elections," *Journal of Politics* 62 (2000): 1087–1108.

37. Daron Shaw, "The Methods behind the Madness: Presidential Electoral College Strategies, 1988–1996," *Journal of Politics* 61 (1999): 893–913. Also see his "The Effect of TV Ads and Candidate Appearances on Statewide Presidential Votes, 1988–96,"*American Political Science Review* 93 (1999): 345–361.

38. Thomas Patterson and Robert McClure, *The Unseeing Eye* (New York: Putnam's, 1976). Also see Martin Wattenberg, *The Rise of Candidate-Centered Politics* (Cambridge: Harvard University Press, 1991); and Richard M. Perloff, *Political Communication: Press, Politics, and Policy in America* (Mahway, N.J.: Erlbaum, 1998).

39. The Harold Mendelsohn and Irving Crespi quote comes from their book, *Polls, Television, and the New Politics* (Scranton, Penn.: Chandler, 1970), 248.

40. Craig Leonard Brians and Martin Wattenberg, "Campaign Issue Knowledge and Salience: Comparing Reception from TV Commercials, TV News, and Newspapers," *American Journal of Political Science* 40 (February 1996): 172–193; and Xinshu Zhao and Steven Chaffee, "Campaign Advertisements versus Television News as Sources of Political Issue Information," *Public Opinion Quarterly* 59 (Spring 1995): 41–65.

41. Lynn Vavreck, Constantine Spiliotes, and Linda Fowler, "The Effects of Retail Politics in the New Hampshire Primary," *American Journal of Political Science* 46 (2002): 595–610.

42. Alliance for Better Campaigns, "Spot Comparison," *The Political Standard* 3 (June 2000): 1. See also Jonathan Krasno and Daniel Seltz, "Buying Time: Television Advertising in the 1998 Congressional Elections," Brennan Center for Justice, undated.

43. Elizabeth Kolbert, "Test-Marketing a President: How Focus Groups Pervade Campaign Politics," *New York Times Magazine,* August 30, 1992, 18–21, 60, 68, 72.

44. Quoted in John Foley, Dennis Britton, and Eugene Everett Jr., eds., *Nominating a President: The Process and the Press* (New York: Praeger, 1980), 79.

45. William McGuire, "Persuasion, Resistance, and Attitude Change," in *Handbook of Communication,* ed. Ithiel de Sola Pool (Chicago: Rand McNally, 1973), 216–252; and "The Nature of Attitudes and Attitude Change," in *Handbook of Social Psychology,* 2nd ed., vol. 3, ed. Gardner Lindzey and Elliot Aronson (Reading, Mass.: Addison-Wesley, 1969), 136–314.

46. Quote taken from David Runkel, ed., *Campaign for President: The Managers Look at '88* (Dover, Mass.: Auburn House, 1989), 142.

47. Howard Kurtz, "Some Kerry Spots Never Make the Air," *Washington Post,* October 20, 2004, A6.

48. Michael Robinson, "Public Affairs Television and the Growth of Political Malaise," *American Political Science Review* 70 (1976): 409–432.

49. David Peterson and Paul Djupe, "When Primary Campaigns Go Negative," *Political Research Quarterly* 58, no. 1 (March 2005): 45–54.

50. Larry Rohter, "Ad on Sex Education Distorts Obama Policy," *New York Times,* September 11, 2008, A22.

51. Howard Kurtz, "Ads Push the Factual Envelope," *Washington Post,* October 20, 2004, A1.

52. Seymour Martin Lipset and William Schneider, *The Confidence Gap* (New York: Free Press, 1983), 17; Paul Abramson, John Aldrich, and David Rohde, *Change and Continuity in the 1996 Elections* (Washington, D.C.: CQ Press, 1997); James Campbell, *The Presidential Pulse of Congressional Elections,* 2nd ed. (Lexington: University Press of Kentucky, 1997); and Bruce Keith, *The Myth of the Independent Voter* (Berkeley: University of California Press, 1992).

53. Thomas Holbrook and Scott McClurg, "The Mobilization of Core Supporters: Campaigns, Turnout, and Electoral Composition in United States Presidential Elections," *American Journal of Political Science* 49, no. 4 (October 2005): 689–703.

54. Alexis de Tocqueville, *Democracy in America,* trans. George Lawrence (Garden City, N.J.: Doubleday, 1969), 198.

11-4

The Triumph of Diversity: Barack Obama, Race, and the 2008 Presidential Election

Alan I. Abramowitz

Political scientist Alan Abramowitz examines survey data to evaluate the role of attitudes about race in voting for the U.S. president in 2008. He finds that a significant minority of whites, Hispanics, and Asian Americans expressed reservations about black political influence in general and a black president in particular. These attitudes are correlated with the vote of members of these groups. However, the American electorate has been transformed over the past several decades as a result of the increase in nonwhite voters and that worked to the advantage of Barack Obama. These trends are going to continue for the foreseeable future.

THE 2008 ELECTION WAS ONE of the most remarkable in American history. On November 4, 2008, Barack Obama, the son of a white mother from Kansas and a black father from Kenya, was elected to the nation's highest office. On his way to becoming the country's first African-American president, the first-term senator from Illinois had to overcome not just racial prejudice but persistent rumors that he was a Muslim and concerns about his lack of national experience. Before that, to win his party's nomination Obama had to overcome the enormous financial and organizational resources of the early favorite for the Democratic nomination, New York senator and former First Lady Hillary Clinton, herself a pathbreaking candidate. But Obama did overcome all of these obstacles, and in so doing, made history. In addition to being the first African-American president, the forty-seven-year-old Obama was the first non-southern Democrat to win the White House since John F. Kennedy.

The 2008 presidential election sparked the interest of the American people like no other in the past forty years from the first caucuses and primaries in January all the way until Election Day. Nearly 132 million Americans cast ballots in the presidential election, an increase of more than 8 million over the 2004 total of 123 million. The estimated turnout of 62 percent of eligible voters was one of the highest since World War II and the highest since the vote was extended to eighteen- to twenty-year-olds in 1972. African-American turnout shattered all previous records. And Americans not only voted in record numbers in 2008, they also

Source: This piece is an original essay commissioned for this volume.

volunteered, displayed yard signs and bumper stickers, attended campaign rallies, and donated money to the parties and candidates in record numbers.

It was a campaign full of twists and turns from Barack Obama's surprise victory in the Iowa caucuses to John McCain's selection of little- known Alaska governor Sarah Palin as his running-mate and a major financial and economic crisis that forced both campaigns to react on the fly to a proposed $700-billion federal bailout of some of the nation's largest banks. Through all of these twists and turns, however, the 2008 election was shaped not only by the unpopularity of George Bush and the deteriorating state of the U.S. economy but also by longer-term trends affecting American society and the American electorate, especially the growth of racial and ethnic diversity. In that sense, results of the 2008 presidential election may have been historic not only for the election of the first African-American president but also for signaling the beginning of a new era in American politics.

The Election Results

At precisely 11:00 p.m. Eastern Standard Time on November 4, just as the polls closed in California, Oregon, and Washington, all of the major television networks and news services declared Barack Obama to be the winner of the 2008 presidential election. After more than a year of campaigning it took only a few hours of vote counting to determine that Obama would have the 270 electoral votes that he needed to become the 44th president of the United States. In fact, he would eventually receive 365 electoral votes, the largest total since Bill Clinton's election in 1996.

Obama's margin of more than 9.5 million votes was the largest for any presidential candidate since Ronald Reagan in 1984. More than 69 million Americans cast their ballots for the Democratic ticket of Barack Obama and Delaware Senator Joe Biden, while over 59 million voted for the Republican ticket of John McCain and Alaska Governor Sarah Palin and almost 2 million voted for minor party candidates. The Democratic ticket won approximately 53 percent of the vote to approximately 46 percent for the Republican ticket and just over one percent for minor party candidates. By the standards of post-war presidential elections it was a decisive win but not a landslide. The total number of votes cast for the Obama-Biden ticket was a record, however. Obama was the first Democratic presidential candidate since Jimmy Carter to win a majority of the popular vote, and his 53 percent share of the popular vote was the largest for any presidential candidate since George H. W. Bush in 1988 and the largest for any Democratic candidate since Lyndon Johnson in 1964.

Democrats scored major gains in the congressional elections as well, picking up eight seats in the Senate and twenty-one seats in the House of Representatives. It marked the second consecutive election in which Democrats made significant gains in the House and Senate. In the 2006 midterm elections they had picked up six Senate seats and thirty House seats. When the new Congress convened in January of 2009, Democrats would hold fifty-eight or fifty-nine seats (with the results of the Minnesota election still undecided) in the Senate and 257 seats in the House, both the largest Democratic totals since the 1994 midterm election.

A glance at the 2008 electoral map demonstrates the breadth of the Democratic sweep across the nation. The Obama-Biden ticket carried twenty-eight states and the District of Columbia, including all nineteen states won by John Kerry in 2004 and nine states won by George W. Bush in that election. The nine Bush states that switched to Obama were Florida, Ohio, Virginia, North Carolina, Indiana, Iowa, New Mexico, Colorado, and Nevada. Obama and Biden carried seven of the eight most populous states: California, New York, Florida, Illinois, Pennsylvania, Ohio, and Michigan. Among the most populous states, only President Bush's home state of Texas voted for John McCain.

While Barack Obama's margin in the national popular vote would not be considered a landslide, the Democratic ticket did carry many individual states by landslide or near-landslide margins, including several of the most populous states. For example, Obama carried California by twenty-four points, New York by twenty-seven points, Illinois by twenty-five points, Michigan by sixteen points, and New Jersey by sixteen points. Of the twenty-eight states carried by the Democratic ticket, the margin was greater than ten points in twenty-two states and less than five points in only four states. Despite the decisive Democratic victory, however, many states that voted for the Republican ticket also did so by landslide or near-landslide margins. Of the twenty-two states carried by John McCain, the margin was greater than ten points in fifteen states and less than five points in only two states. And while the nation as a whole was moving in a Democratic direction between 2004 and 2008, Republicans managed to increase their margin of victory in four states: Oklahoma, Arkansas, Louisiana, and Tennessee.

A similar pattern was evident in the election results at the county level. According to an analysis by the *New York Times*, between 2004 and 2008 the Democratic share of the vote increased in 2,437 of the nation's 3,141 counties; at the same time, however, the Republican share of the vote increased in 678 counties. The Democratic share of the vote increased by more than ten points in 1,173 counties; however, the Republican share of the vote increased by more than ten points in 225 counties. Counties with the largest increases in the Democratic share of the vote were generally found in large metropolitan areas with relatively high levels of education and large concentrations of Hispanic and African-American voters.

Counties with the largest increases in the Republican share of the vote were generally found in small towns and rural areas with relatively low levels of education, small minority populations, and high concentrations of Southern Baptists. Many of these Republican-tilting counties were located in Southern states and states that border the South.

A Nation Divided by Region, Age, and Race

The overall picture that emerges from an examination of the 2008 electoral map is one of a country that had moved decisively in a Democratic direction since 2004 but that remained deeply divided. Across all fifty states and the District of Columbia, the average margin of victory for the winning presidential candidate increased from 15.8 points in 2004 to 17.6 points in 2008 while the median increased from 12.1 points to 15.1 points. There were more landslide and near-landslide states and fewer closely contested states. The number of states in which the winning candidate's margin of victory was greater than ten points increased from thirty to thirty-five, while the number in which the winning candidate's margin of victory was less than five points decreased from eleven to six. Of the seven most populous states, only Florida and Ohio were decided by less than five points while New York, California, and Illinois were decided by more than twenty points.

There was wide divergence in support for the presidential candidates across states and regions of the country. Although Barack Obama made inroads into the Republican Party's southern base by carrying Virginia, North Carolina, and Florida, John McCain carried the other eight states of the old Confederacy along with the border states of Kentucky, West Virginia, and Oklahoma, winning most of them by double-digit margins. McCain won 54 percent of the vote in the South while Obama won 57 percent of the vote in the rest of the country.

The high degree of geographical polarization in 2008 is consistent with the pattern evident in other recent presidential elections, including the 2004 election, but it represents a dramatic change from the voting patterns of the 1960s and 1970s. In the closely contested 1960 and 1976 elections, for example, there were far more closely contested states and far fewer landslide states than in recent presidential elections. And in both of those elections every one of the most populous states was closely contested, including California, New York, Illinois, and Texas. The divisions between red states and blue states are far deeper today than they were thirty or forty years ago and the 2008 election did nothing to change that reality.

Further evidence of shifting voting patterns can be seen by comparing support for the Democratic presidential candidates in 2004 and 2008 among various demographic groups. According to the national exit polls, Barack Obama did

Table 1. Democratic Presidential Vote by Age and Race, 2004–2008

Group	2004	2008	Change
18-29	54%	66%	+ 12%
30-44	46%	52%	+ 6%
45-64	48%	50%	+ 2%
65 +	46%	45%	- 1%
White	41%	43%	+ 2%
African-American	88%	95%	+ 7%
Hispanic	53%	67%	+ 14%
Other Race	55%	64%	+ 9%

Source: 2004 and 2008 National Exit Polls

substantially better than the Democrats' 2004 nominee, John Kerry, among most groups of voters including men and women, college graduates and non-graduates, and lower- and upper-income voters. However, the data in Table 1 show that the size of Democratic gains between 2004 and 2008 varied considerably based on two characteristics—age and race. Obama's gains were much greater among younger voters than among older voters. Obama carried voters under the age of thirty by a margin of thirty-four points versus only nine points for Kerry. However, he did slightly worse than Kerry among voters over the age of sixty-five, losing that group by eight points versus six points for Kerry. As a result, the generation gap in candidate preference was much greater in 2008 than in 2004.

Obama also made much larger gains among African-American and Hispanic voters than among white voters. In addition to increasing African-American turnout, Obama also won the African-American vote by a much larger margin than John Kerry—ninety-one points versus seventy-seven points. However, the most dramatic improvement in Democratic performance between 2004 and 2008 occurred among Hispanic voters. According to the exit poll data, Obama won the Hispanic vote by thirty-six points versus Kerry's margin of only ten points. In contrast, the improvement in Democratic performance among white voters was much smaller. Obama lost the white vote by a margin of twelve points versus seventeen points for John Kerry.

No Democratic presidential candidate since Lyndon Johnson has won a majority of the white vote, so the fact that Barack Obama lost the white vote was hardly surprising. Obama's twelve-point deficit among white voters was identical to that of Al Gore in 2000. However, the fact that white voters favored the Republican presidential candidate by a double-digit margin in 2008 despite the poor condition of the economy and the extraordinary unpopularity of the incumbent Republican president suggests that racial prejudice played a role in limiting the level of white support for the Democratic candidate.

Further evidence of the effects of race can be seen in state exit poll results. White support for Barack Obama varied dramatically across regions and states, ranging from a low of around 10 percent in the Deep South to close to 60 percent in parts of the Northeast and West. In many states outside the South, Obama did substantially better than John Kerry among white voters. Between 2004 and 2008 the Democratic share of the white vote increased by five points in California and Washington, seven points in Michigan and Wisconsin, eight points in Colorado, and nine points in Oregon. In many southern and border south states, however, Obama did no better or worse than Kerry among white voters. Between 2004 and 2008 the Democratic share of the white vote fell by four points in Mississippi, six points in Arkansas, nine points in Alabama, and ten points in Louisiana.

Based on these results, it appears very likely that racial prejudice was a factor in limiting support for Barack Obama, especially among white voters in the Deep South and in some of the states bordering the South. But this was not enough to hand the election to John McCain because Obama's losses among these groups of white voters were offset by gains among white voters in other parts of the country, especially among younger whites for whom the opportunity to help elect the country's first African-American president may have enhanced Obama's appeal, and by increased turnout and support among nonwhite voters including Hispanics.

Racial Attitudes and the Election

From the moment that he announced his candidacy in early 2007, Barack Obama's quest for the presidency was dogged by questions about whether white Americans, and perhaps Hispanics and Asian Americans as well, would vote for a black man for president. Many media commentators, and not a few academic experts, were skeptical. Racist attitudes, according to these observers, were deeply ingrained in Americans' psyches and a black presidential candidate, even one as gifted and charismatic as Barack Obama, was bound to pay a heavy "racial cost" as a result.

In the end, as we have seen, Barack Obama was able to overcome any lingering effects of racial prejudice and win a decisive victory. Still, the fact that Obama won only 44 percent of the white vote despite the dire condition of the U.S. economy and the extraordinary unpopularity of the outgoing Republican president, and did particularly poorly among older whites and those in the deep South, suggests that the "racial cost" hypothesis cannot be dismissed as out of hand.

Fortunately the 2008 American National Election Study (NES) included a large number of questions designed to tap respondents' racial attitudes. For the purpose of measuring the impact of racial attitudes on the vote, I chose three questions that focused specifically on the political significance of race. One question asked whether blacks in the United States have too little, too much, or about the right amount of political influence; one asked whether the respondent would feel uncomfortable about having a black person as president; and one asked whether the respondent would feel pleased about having a black person as president. These three questions were combined to form a political racism scale.

The results indicate that, despite the progress that the United States has made in recent decades in overcoming the legacy of slavery and segregation, a significant minority of whites, Hispanics and Asian Americans expressed reservations about black political influence in general and a black president in particular. Twelve percent of whites and 10 percent of Hispanics and Asian Americans felt that blacks had "too much influence" in American government; 15 percent of whites and 15 percent of Hispanics and Asian Americans acknowledged that they were "not pleased at all" by the prospect of an African-American president; and 20 percent of whites and 18 percent of Hispanics and Asian Americans admitted that the idea of a black president made them at least slightly uncomfortable. Thirty-six percent of whites, including 48 percent of those with only a high school education, expressed a negative opinion on at least one of these three items, as did 32 percent of Hispanics and Asian Americans. In contrast, only 19 percent of white college graduates expressed any negative opinions.

The important question, of course, is did these attitudes affect the way Americans voted in 2008? Based on the results displayed in Table 2, the answer to this question appears to be a qualified "yes." At least among white voters there was a fairly strong relationship between the political racism scale and the presidential vote. Only 26 percent of whites who scored high on the political racism scale voted for Obama compared with 49 percent of those who scored in the middle range on the scale and 69 percent of those who scored low on the scale. For Hispanics and other nonwhites, the relationship was not as strong. Even among Hispanics and other nonwhites who fell at the high end of the political racism scale, the large majority voted for Obama.

To conduct a more definitive test of the impact of political racism on the white American vote, this study needed to control for other factors that are known to influence candidate choice, especially party identification, political ideology, and evaluations of the incumbent president's job performance. I hypothesized that the impact of racial attitudes would not be the same for all types of white voters, however. Race would appear to be a classic example of what political scientist James Stimson has characterized as an "easy issue." That is because, compared with other characteristics, a candidate's racial identity is a simple fact that can be readily observed and understood by voters of all levels of political sophistication. I have hypothethized that racial attitudes would to have a stronger influence on

Table 2. Percentage Voting for Obama by Political Racism among Whites,
Blacks, Hispanics, and Other Nonwhites

Political Racism	Whites	Blacks	Hispanics	Other Nonwhites
Low	69	100	86	93
Moderate	49	100	78	78
High	26	92	62	68

Source: 2008 National Election Study

Table 3. Results of Logistic Regression Analyses of Vote Choice among Whites

Independent Variable	All Whites B (S.E.)	High School B (S.E.)	College Grads B (S.E.)
Party Id	1.38 (.18)	1.97 (.42)	1.14 (.32)
Party Lean	1.33 (.24)	3.12 (.77)	.87 (.39)
Ideology	.63 (.12)	.61 (.26)	.66 (.22)
Bush Job	.68 (.11)	.53 (.23)	1.07 (.23)
Pol Racism	.42 (.06)	.69 (.14)	.24 (.13)
Correctly Predicted	89.9%	94.2%	92.1%

Source: 2008 National Election Study

vote choice among relatively unsophisticated voters than among relatively sophisticated voters. To test this hypothesis, I performed separate logistic regression analyses of candidate choice among two groups of white voters in 2008—those with only a high school education and those with a college degree.

The results, displayed in Table 3, show that racial attitudes had a substantial impact on candidate choice among white voters in general. Whites who scored high on the political racism scale were significantly less likely to vote for Barack Obama than whites who scored low on the scale, regardless of their party identification, ideology, or evaluation of President Bush. However, the impact of political racism on vote choice was almost three times stronger among high-school-educated whites than among college graduates. Party identification, like race, is a very simple cue, and also had a stronger influence on vote choice among the high-school educated than among college graduates. In contrast, evaluations of President Bush's job performance had a much stronger influence on vote choice among white college graduates than among those with only a high school education.

These results suggest that racial attitudes had different effects on different types of white voters in 2008. It appears that better educated and presumably more politically sophisticated whites viewed the election primarily as a referendum on the performance of President Bush. Racial attitudes had little influence on their decisions. Moreover, white college graduates were less likely to hold negative opinions about the role of blacks in the political process than whites with less schooling.

Whites with only a high school education were more likely to hold negative opinions about the role of blacks in the political process than those with a college education. And the fact that President Bush was not on the ballot may have limited the ability of these less educated and presumably less politically sophisticated voters to see a connection between his performance and the choice between John McCain and Barack Obama. As a result, the race of the Democratic nominee appears to have been a more salient voting cue for high-school-educated whites than for college-educated whites.

These results suggest that the impact of racist attitudes on the presidential vote in 2008 was concentrated among one segment of the white electorate—those with a high school education or less. However, the damage to Barack Obama's candidacy was limited because whites with a high school education or less make up a declining share of the electorate in the United States. This group made up 25 percent of the overall electorate in 2008, down from 74 percent during the 1950s. In contrast, white college graduates made up 29 percent of the overall electorate in 2008, up from 10 percent during the 1950s. Rising education levels in the American electorate were therefore an important factor in Barack Obama's victory.

The Triumph of Diversity

Barack Obama's victory in the 2008 presidential election can best be understood as a product of three distinct sets of factors: changes in the demographic composition and political attitudes of the American electorate, some of which had been developing for decades and some of which were more recent in origin; short-term forces at work in 2008, including the unpopularity of President Bush and the dire condition of the U.S. economy; and the campaigns conducted by the Democratic and Republican candidates. Economic conditions and the actions of the presidential and vice-presidential candidates received extensive coverage in the media during the campaign, but far less attention was paid to shifts in the demographic composition and political attitudes of the electorate. However, Obama's election would not have been possible without these changes. Moreover, these changes are likely to affect elections for many years to come.

Without question, the most important change in the composition of the American electorate has been a steady increase in the proportion of nonwhite voters. This trend has been evident for at least fifty years but it has accelerated in

Figure 1. Nonwhite Share of U.S. Electorate, 1992–2008

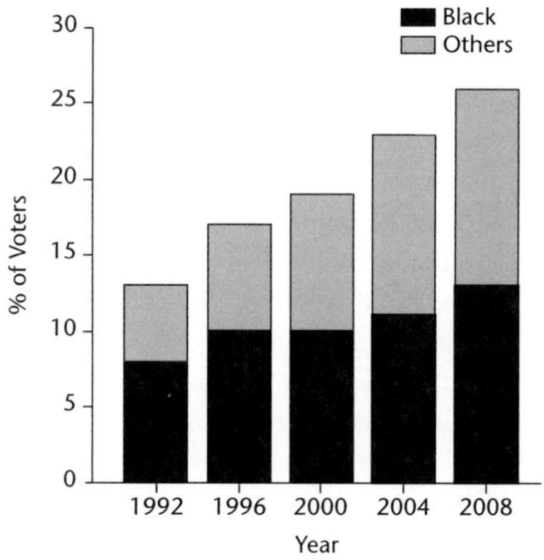

Source: National Exit Polls

the last two decades. It is a result of increased immigration from Asia, Africa, and Latin America, higher birth rates among minority groups, and increased registration and turnout among African-Americans, Hispanics, and other nonwhite citizens. Moreover, this shift is almost certain to continue for the foreseeable future based on Census Bureau projections of the racial and ethnic makeup of the American population between now and 2050.

Figure 1 displays data from national exit polls on the changing racial composition of the U.S. electorate between 1992 and 2008. In the sixteen years between 1976 and 1992, the nonwhite share of the U.S. electorate increased only slightly—going from 11 percent to 13 percent. However, in the sixteen years between 1992 and 2008 the nonwhite share of the electorate doubled, going from 13 percent to 26 percent. Helped by an aggressive Democratic registration and get-out-the-vote campaign in African-American and Hispanic communities, the nonwhite share of the electorate increased from 23 percent in 2004 to 26 percent in 2008 with African-Americans going from 11 percent to 13 percent, and Hispanics going from 8 percent to 9 percent.

Since the 1970s the composition of the nonwhite electorate has itself been changing, with Hispanics (who are included here in the nonwhite population although they can be of any race) and Asian Americans comprising a growing share of nonwhite voters. Both of these groups continue to be underrepresented in the electorate relative to their numbers in the voting-age population due to high rates of noncitizenship and relatively low registration and turnout rates. However, both groups are growing rapidly. Hispanics are now the largest minority group in the U.S. population and their share of the electorate has been rising steadily, reaching 8 percent in 2004 and 9 percent in 2008.

The growth of the nonwhite electorate, beginning with African-Americans in the 1960s and 1970s and continuing with Hispanics and Asian Americans since the 1980s, has had profound consequences for the party system and the electoral process in the United States. African-American and Hispanic voters now comprise a large proportion of the electoral base of the Democratic Party. Thus, according to the 2008 national exit poll, African-Americans made up 24 percent of Obama voters while Hispanics and other nonwhites made up 16 percent of Obama voters. In contrast, despite the rapid growth in the proportion of nonwhite voters over the past two decades, the Republican Party's electoral base has changed very little and remains overwhelmingly white. According to the 2008 national exit poll, African-Americans made up less than one percent of McCain voters while Hispanics and other nonwhites made up only 9 percent of McCain voters.

The expansion of the African-American electorate made Barack Obama's nomination possible, as they provided him with a large proportion of his support in many of the Democratic primaries, especially in the South. The growth of the nonwhite electorate as a whole made Barack Obama's election possible, as African-American and other nonwhite voters provided him with a large enough margin to offset a substantial deficit among white voters. Table 4 displays the trend in the Democratic margin or deficit by race in presidential elections since 1992. Based on the national exit poll results, we can estimate that white voters gave John McCain a plurality of close to 12 million votes in 2008. This was somewhat smaller than George Bush's plurality among white voters in 2004 but more than a million votes larger than Bush's plurality among white voters in 2000. Yet Barack Obama won the national popular vote by more than 9.5 million votes while Al Gore only won the national popular vote by about half a million votes in 2000. The difference between 2000 and 2008 was that Obama's margin among nonwhites was more than 21 million votes while Gore's margin among nonwhites was a little less than 11 million votes.

The nonwhite share of the U.S. electorate is certain to continue growing well into the twenty-first century. This can be seen by examining exit poll data on the racial composition of the 2008 electorate as well as Census Bureau data on the racial composition of the U.S. population by age. According to the 2008 national exit poll, non-Hispanic whites made up 81 percent of voters over the age of forty-five but only 66 percent of voters under the age of forty-five; African-Americans made up 15 percent of voters under the age of forty-five compared with only 9 percent of those forty-five and older while Hispanics and other nonwhites made up 19 percent of voters under the age of forty-five compared with only 10 percent of those forty-five and older.

Table 4. Democratic Plurality in Millions of Votes by Race, 1992–2008

Year	Whites	Nonwhites	Total
1992	−1.8	+7.6	+5.8
1996	−1.6	+9.8	+8.2
2000	−10.3	+10.8	+0.5
2004	−14.9	+11.9	−3.0
2008	−11.6	+21.1	+9.5

Source: National Exit Polls

Table 5. Racial Composition of U.S. Population by Age

Age Group	White	Black	Hispanic	Other
65-plus	80.7%	8.4%	6.6%	4.3%
14-17	59.9%	16.3%	18.0%	5.8%
5-13	57.5%	15.3%	20.6%	6.6%
Under 5	54.1%	15.5%	23.7%	6.7%

Source: U.S. Census Bureau, July 2007

The Census Bureau data displayed in Table 5 show that there is a dramatic difference between the racial composition of the oldest and youngest age groups in the U.S. population. Non-Hispanic whites make up almost 81 percent of Americans over the age of sixty-five but less than 60 percent of those under the age of eighteen. In contrast, African-Americans make up more than15 percent of the population under the age of eighteen compared with only 8 percent of the population over the age of sixty-five and Hispanics make up more than 20 percent of the population under the age of eighteen and almost 24 percent of the population under the age of five, compared with less than 7 percent of the population over the age of sixty-five. While the nonwhite share of the electorate will probably continue to lag behind the nonwhite share of the population due to lower citizenship and turnout rates, these data indicate that we can expect the nonwhite share of the U.S. electorate to continue to grow for many years.

A second trend of more recent origin also made a significant contribution to Barack Obama's victory in 2008—generational realignment. Americans under the age of thirty are now substantially more likely to identify with the Democratic Party, vote for Democratic candidates, and express liberal views on a wide range of issues than their elders. This trend was already evident in 2004 when voters under the age of thirty were the only age group to support John Kerry over George Bush, favoring the Democratic challenger by a margin of nine points. Two years later, in the 2006 midterm elections, eighteen to twenty-nine-year-olds supported Democratic House and Senate candidates over Republicans by better than a twenty point margin. Although younger voters were not solely responsible for the Democrats' victory, they made a significant contribution to their gains in the House and Senate.

In 2008, voters under the age of thirty made an even more substantial contribution to Barack Obama's victory, turning out in large numbers (eighteen to twenty-nine-year-olds comprised 18 percent of the electorate versus 17 percent in 2004) and supporting Obama by a better than two to one margin over John McCain. Obama's 34-point margin among eighteen–twenty-nine-year-old voters was the largest ever recorded in a national exit poll for any presidential candidate in any age group. The youth vote was a major factor in Barack Obama's decisive victory: voters under the age of thirty provided Obama with a plurality of almost 8 million votes, which was more than 80 percent of his overall popular vote margin.

Strong support for Democratic candidates by voters under the age of thirty is explained in part by this age cohort's inclusion of a much larger proportion of African-Americans, Hispanics, and other nonwhites than older cohorts. However, race and ethnicity do not completely explain the current generation gap in voting behavior. There is also a generation gap among white and Hispanic voters: in 2008 white and Hispanic voters under the age of thirty were substantially more likely to support Barack Obama than white and Hispanic voters over the age of thirty. According to the 2008 national exit poll, 54 percent of whites under the age of thirty voted for Obama compared with only 41 percent of whites over the age of thirty; similarly, 76 percent of Hispanics under the age of thirty voted for Obama compared with only 63 percent of Hispanics over the age of thirty.

Part of the reason for the current generation gap in voting behavior is that whites and nonwhites under the age of thirty hold more liberal views on a variety of issues than older whites and nonwhites. This can be seen very clearly in the evidence from the 2008 NES data displayed in Table 6. According to these data, both whites and nonwhites under the age of thirty were more likely to describe themselves as liberal, endorse gay marriage, and support a government-sponsored universal health care plan than whites and nonwhites over the age of thirty. These results suggest that disproportionate support for the Democratic Party by eighteen to twenty-nine-year-old voters in 2008 was not simply a result of Barack Obama's personal appeal to younger Americans but was based on real differences in political outlook between today's younger generation and their elders—differences that cross racial lines. The difference on the issue of gay marriage is particularly striking and suggests that the Republican Party's embrace of social conservatism and the religious right has greatly reduced its appeal to younger voters of all races.

Table 6. Liberalism of Voters by Age and Race in 2008

Issue	Whites		Nonwhites	
	18–29	*30+*	*18–29*	*30+*
Liberal Id	40	24	49	36
Gay Marriage	60	31	66	34
Health Care	55	41	80	60

Source: 2008 National Election Study

Toward the Future: American Politics in an Age of Diversity

In the aftermath of the 2008 election the Democratic Party finds itself in its strongest position in government since the early 1990s. Democrats now control the White House and both chambers of Congress and their majorities in the Senate and House of Representatives are the largest for either party since the 1994 midterm election. President Obama and the Democratic leadership of the House and Senate will be presiding over a nation facing immense challenges at home and overseas, including a failing domestic economy, a global financial crisis, and two wars with no end in sight. And with their expanded majorities in Congress, the Democrats will have to deal with greater regional and ideological diversity in their ranks. Many of the Democrats elected to the House and Senate in 2006 and 2008 are moderates who represent districts and states with a history, until recently, of supporting Republican presidential candidates. Keeping their expanded majorities united behind President Obama's legislative program will be a difficult assignment for House Speaker Nancy Pelosi and Senate Majority Leader Harry Reid. And in the Senate, lacking sixty votes to cut off debate, Democrats will still face the threat of Republican filibusters unless they can win over a few of the handful of remaining Republican moderates.

The Republican Party today faces the opposite problem from the Democrats. With their numbers greatly reduced by the results of the 2006 and 2008 elections, Republicans in Congress are left with a shrunken and overwhelmingly conservative party. The large majority of those who remain represent safe Republican districts and states, many in the South. There are almost no moderate Republicans left in either chamber, and the Republican party has been decimated in the Northeast, where it now holds only a handful of House seats and only three of twenty-two Senate seats.

The GOP's electoral base has also been shrinking. Its voters are disproportionately white, socially conservative, middle-aged or older, and located in small towns and rural areas. In a country that is becoming increasingly urban, non-white, and socially tolerant, that is not a good position for a political party to be in. The party's weakness among younger Americans, who not only voted for Barack Obama over John McCain by a two to one margin but who also increasingly identify with the Democratic Party, should be especially concerning to Republican strategists since research shows that once young adults form an attachment to a political party they frequently maintain that attachment for many years. In order to revive their fortunes, Republicans will need to find a way to reach beyond their current base to appeal to nonwhites, young people, and an increasingly educated and socially moderate electorate.

It is too soon to say whether the results of the 2008 election marked a decisive turning point in the fortunes of the Democratic and Republican parties. History demonstrates that winning a decisive election victory is no guarantee of future success for a political party. In 1964 the Democratic Party won an even bigger victory in the presidential and congressional elections—a victory that allowed President Lyndon Johnson to push an ambitious legislative program through Congress, including civil rights legislation, federal aid to education, the war on poverty, and Medicare. Stories in the media about the demise of the Republican Party were rampant. But two years later, with the country deeply divided over the Vietnam War, racial unrest, and a growing youth culture, Democrats suffered major setbacks in the midterm elections, and in 1968 Richard Nixon defeated Hubert Humphrey to reclaim the White House for the Republicans.

Whether the Democrats will be able to consolidate the gains that they have made since 2006 is very much an open question. The answer to that question will depend largely on how they govern over the next two to four years and how the American people view the results that the Democrats produce. However, based on the evidence presented in this paper it is already clear that the American electorate has been transformed over the past several decades as a result of demographic trends and that these trends are going to continue for the foreseeable future. Barack Obama's election was, to a large extent, a result of those trends. The growing size of the nonwhite electorate in the United States along with the increasing liberalism and Democratic identification of younger Americans of all races mean that a successful Obama presidency could put the Democratic Party in a position to dominate American politics for many years to come. If so, 2008 may be remembered not only for the election of the first African-American president but also as a turning point in the ongoing transformation of the American electorate.

Chapter 12

Political Parties

12-1

from *Why Parties?*

John H. Aldrich

American political parties were created by politicians and committed citizens who sought to win elections and control legislatures, executives, and even the courts. The parties exist at local, state, and national levels—wherever elections are held for coveted offices. The system of political parties that has evolved over time is fragmented and multilayered. In the following essay, John H. Aldrich describes the nature of the political problems that parties solve for candidates and voters. As much as we may dislike partisanship, modern democracies could not, Aldrich explains, function without it.

Is the Contemporary Political Party Strong or in Decline?

The Case for the Importance of Political Parties

THE PATH TO OFFICE for nearly every major politician begins today, as it has for over 150 years, with the party. Many candidates emerge initially from the ranks of party activists, all serious candidates seek their party's nomination, and they become serious candidates in the general election only because they have won

Source: John H. Aldrich, *Why Parties? The Origin and Transformation of Political Parties in America* (Chicago: University of Chicago Press, 1995), 14–27. Notes appearing in the original have been deleted.

their party's endorsement. Today most partisan nominations are decided in primary elections—that is, based on votes cast by self-designated partisans in the mass electorate. Successful nominees count on the continued support of these partisans in the general election, and for good reason. At least since surveys have provided firm evidence, all presidential nominees have won the support of no less than a majority of their party in the electorate, no matter how over-whelming their defeat may have been.

This is an age of so-called partisan dealignment in the electorate. Even so, a substantial majority today consider themselves partisans. The lowest percentage of self-professed (i.e., "strong" and "weak") partisans yet recorded in National Election Studies (NES) surveys was 61 percent in 1974, and another 22 percent expressed partisan leanings that year. Evidence from panel surveys demonstrates that partisan-ship has remained as stable and enduring for most adults after dealignment as it did before it, and it is often the single strongest predictor of candidate choice in the public.

If parties have declined recently, the decline has not occurred in their formal organizations. Party organizations are if anything stronger, better financed, and more professional at all levels now. Although its importance to candidates may be less than in the past, the party provides more support—more money, work-ers, and resources of all kinds—than any other organization for all but a very few candidates for national and state offices.

Once elected, officeholders remain partisans. Congress is organized by parties. Party-line votes elect its leadership, determine what its committees will be, assign members to them, and select their chairs. Party caucuses remain a staple of congressional life, and they and other forms of party organizations in Con-gress have become stronger in recent years. Party voting in committee and on the floor of both houses, though far less common in the United States than in many democracies, nonetheless remains the first and most important standard for understanding congressional voting behavior, and it too has grown stronger, in this case much stronger, in recent years.

Relationships among the elected branches of government are also heavily par-tisan. Conference committees to resolve discrepancies between House and Sen-ate versions of legislation reflect partisan as well as interchamber rivalries. The president is the party's leader, and his agenda is introduced, fought for, and sup-ported on the floor by his congressional party. His agenda becomes his party's congressional agenda, and much of it finds its way into law.

The Case for Weak and Weakening Parties

As impressive as the scenario above may be, not all agree that parties lie at the heart of American politics, at least not anymore. The literature on parties over the past two decades is replete with accounts of the decline of the political party. Even the choice of titles clearly reflects the arguments. David Broder perhaps began this stream of literature with *The Party's Over* (1972). Since then, political scientists have written extensively on this theme: for example, Crotty's *American Political Parties in Decline* (1984), Kirkpatrick's *Dismantling the Parties* (1978), Polsby's *Consequences of Party Reform* (1983) . . . , Ranney's thoughtful *Curing the Mischiefs of Faction* (1975), and Wattenberg's *The Decline of American Political Parties* (1990).

Those who see larger ills in the contemporary political scene often attribute them to the failure of parties to be stronger and more effective. In "The Decline of Collective Responsibility" (1980), Fiorina argued that such responsibility was possible only through the agency of the political party. Jacobson concluded his study of congressional elections (1992) by arguing that contemporary elections induce "responsiveness" of individual incumbents to their districts but do so "without [inducing] responsibility" in incumbents for what Congress does. As a result, the electorate can find no one to hold accountable for congressional failings. He too looked to a revitalized party for redress. These themes reflect the responsible party thesis, if not in being a call for such parties, at least in using that as the standard for measuring how short the contemporary party falls.

The literature on the presidency is not immune to this concern for decaying parties. Kernell's account of the strategy of "going public" (1986)—that is, generating power by marshaling public opinion—is that it became more common as the older strategy of striking bargains with a small set of congressional (and partisan) power brokers grew increasingly futile. The earlier use of the president's power to persuade (Neustadt 1960, 1990) failed as power centers became more diverse and fragmented and brokers could no longer deliver. Lowi argued this case even more strongly in *The Personal President* (1985). America, he claimed, has come to invest too much power in the office of the president, with the result that the promise of the presidency and the promises of individual presidents go unfulfilled. Why? Because the rest of government has become too unwieldy, complicated, and fragmented for the president to use that power effectively. His solution? Revitalize political parties.

Divided partisan control over government, once an occasional aberration, has become the ordinary course of affairs. Many of the same themes in this literature are those sounded above—fragmented, decentralized power, lack of coordination and control over what the government does, and absence of collective responsibility. Strong political parties are, among other things, those that can deliver the vote for most or all of their candidates. Thus another symptom of weakened parties is regularized divided government, in the states as well as in the nation.

If divided government is due to weakened parties, that condition must be due in turn to weakened partisan loyalties in the electorate. Here the evidence is clear. The proportions and strength of party attachments in the electorate declined in the mid-1960s. There was a resurgence in affiliation twenty years later, but to a lower level than before 1966. The behavioral consequences of these changes are if anything even clearer. Defection from party lines and split-ticket voting are far more common for all major offices at national, state, and local levels today than before the mid-1960s. Elections are more candidate centered and less party centered, and those who come to office have played a greater role in shaping their own more highly personalized electoral coalitions. Incumbents, less dependent on the party for winning office, are less disposed to vote the party line in Congress or to follow the wishes of their party's president. Power becomes decentralized toward the individual incumbent and, as Jacobson argues, individual incumbents respond to their constituents. If that means defecting from the party, so be it.

Is the Debate Genuine?

Some believe that parties have actually grown stronger over the past few decades. This position has been put most starkly by Schlesinger: "It should be clear by now that the grab bag of assumptions, inferences, and half-truths that have fed the decline-of-parties thesis is simply wrong" (1985, p. 1152). Rather, he maintains, "Thanks to increasing levels of competition between the parties, then, American political parties are stronger than before" (p. 1168). More common is the claim that parties were weakened in the 1960s but have been revitalized since then. Rohde pointed out that "in the last decade, however, the decline of partisanship in the House has been reversed. Party voting, which had been as low as 27 percent in 1972, peaked at 64 percent in 1987" (1989, p. 1). Changes in party voting in the Senate have been only slightly less dramatic, and Rohde has also demonstrated that party institutions in the House strengthened substantially in the same period (1991). If, as Rohde says, parties in the government are stronger, and if . . . others are correct that party organizations are stronger, a thesis of decline with resurgence must be taken seriously. The electorate's partisan affiliations may be a lagging rather than a leading indicator, and even they have rebounded slightly.

A Theory of Political Parties

As diverse as are the conclusions reached by these and other astute observers, all agree that the political party is—or should be—central to the American political system. Parties are—or should be—integral parts of all political life, from structuring the reasoning and choice of the electorate, through all facets of campaigns and seemingly all facets of the government, to the very possibility of effective governance in a democracy.

How is it that such astute observers of American politics and parties, writing at virtually the same time and looking at much the same evidence, come to such diametrically opposed conclusions about the strength of parties? Eldersveld . . . wrote that "political parties are complex institutions and processes, and as such they are difficult to understand and evaluate" (1982, p. 407). As proof, he went on to consider the decline of parties thesis. At one point he wrote, "The decline in our parties, therefore, is difficult to demonstrate, empirically or in terms of historical perspective" (p. 417). And yet he then turned to signs of party decline and concluded his book with the statement: "Despite their defects they continue today to be the major instruments for democratic government in this nation. With necessary reforms we can make them even more central to the governmental process and to the lives of American citizens. Eighty years ago, Lord James Bryce, after studying our party system, said, 'In America the great moving forces are the parties. The government counts for less than in Europe, the parties count for more. . . .' If our citizens and their leaders wish it, American parties will still be the 'great moving forces' of our system" (1982, pp. 432–33).

The "Fundamental Equation" of the New Institutionalism Applied to Parties

That parties are complex does not mean they are incomprehensible. Indeed complexity is, if not an intentional outcome, at least an anticipated result of those who shape the political parties. Moreover, they are so deeply woven into the fabric of American politics that they cannot be understood apart from either their own historical context and dynamics or those of the political system as a whole. Parties, that is, can be understood only in relation to the polity, to the government and its institutions, and to the historical context of the times.

The study of political parties, second, is necessarily a study of a major pair of political *institutions*. Indeed, the institutions that define the political party are unique, and as it happens they are unique in ways that make an institutional account especially useful. Their establishment and nature are fundamentally extralegal; they are nongovernmental political institutions. Instead of statute, their basis lies in the actions of ambitious politicians that created and maintain them. They are, in the parlance of the new institutionalism, *endogenous institutions*—in fact, the most highly endogenous institutions of any substantial and sustained political importance in American history.

By endogenous, I mean it was the actions of political actors that created political parties in the first place, and it is the actions of political actors that have shaped and altered them over time. And political actors have chosen to alter their parties dramatically at several times in our history, reformed them often, and tinkered with them constantly. Of all major political bodies in the United States, the political party is the most variable in its rules, regulations, and procedures—that is to say, in its formal organization—and in its informal methods and traditions. It is often the same set of actors who write the party's rules and then choose the party's outcomes, sometimes at nearly the same time and by the same method. Thus, for example, one night national party conventions debate, consider any proposed amendments, and then adopt their rules by a majority vote of credentialed delegates. The next night these same delegates debate, consider any proposed amendments, and then adopt their platform by majority vote, and they choose their presidential nominee by majority vote the following night.

Who, then, are these critical political actors? Many see the party-in-the-electorate as comprising major actors. To be sure, mobilizing the electorate to capture office is a central task of the political party. But America is a republican democracy. All power flows directly or indirectly from the great body of the people, to paraphrase Madison's definition. The public elects its political leaders, but it is that leadership that legislates, executes, and adjudicates policy. The parties are defined in relation to this republican democracy. Thus it is political leaders, those Schlesinger (1975) has called "office-seekers"—*those who seek and those who hold elective office*—who are the central actors in the party.

Ambitious office seekers and holders are thus the first and most important actors in the political party. A second set of important figures in party politics comprises those who hold, or have access to, critical resources that office seekers need to realize their ambitions. It is expensive to build and maintain the party and campaign organizations necessary to compete effectively in the electoral arena. Thomas Ferguson, for example, has made an extended argument for the "primary and constitutive role large investors play in American politics" (1983, p. 3). Much of his research emphasizes this primary and constitutive role in party politics in particular, such as in partisan realignments. The study of the role of money in congressional elections has also focused in part on concentrations of such sources of funding, such as from political action committees which political parties are coming to take advantage of. Elections are also fought over the flow of information to the public. The electoral arm of political parties in the eighteenth century was made up of "committees of correspondence," which were primarily lines of communication among political elites and between them and potential voters, and one of the first signs of organizing of the Jeffersonian Republican party was the hiring of a newspaper editor. The press was first a partisan press, and editors and publishers from Thomas Ritchie to Horace Greeley long were critical players in party politics. Today those with specialized knowledge relevant to communication, such as pollsters, media and advertising experts, and computerized fund-raising specialists, enjoy influence in party, campaign, and even government councils that greatly exceeds their mere technical expertise.

In more theoretical terms, this second set of party actors include those Schlesinger (1975) has called "benefit seekers," those for whom realization of their goals depends on the party's success in capturing office. Party activists shade from those powerful figures with concentrations of, or access to, money and information described above to the legions of volunteer campaign activists who ring doorbells and stuff envelopes and are, individually and collectively, critical to the first level of the party—its office seekers. All are critical because they command the resources, whether money, expertise, and information or merely time and labor, that office seekers need to realize their ambitions. As a result, activists' motivations shape and constrain the behavior of office seekers, as their own roles are, in turn, shaped and constrained by the office seekers. The changed incentives of party activists have played a significant role in the fundamentally altered nature of the contemporary party, but the impact of benefit seekers will be seen scattered throughout this account.

Voters, however, are neither office seekers nor benefit seekers and thus are not a part of the political party at all, even if they identify strongly with a party and consistently support its candidates. Voters are indeed critical, but they are critical as the targets of party activities. Parties "produce" candidates, platforms, and policies. Voters "consume" by exchanging their votes for the party's product (see Popkin et al. 1976). Some voters, of course, become partisans by becoming activists, whether as occasional volunteers, as sustained contributors, or even as candidates. But until they do so, they may be faithful consumers, "brand name" loyalists as it were, but they are still only the targets of partisans' efforts to sell their wares in the political marketplace.

Why, then, do politicians create and recreate the party, exploit its features, or ignore its dictates? The simple answer is that it has been in their interests to do so. That is, this is a *rational choice* account of the party, an account that presumes that rational, elective office seekers and holders use the party to achieve their ends.

I do not assume that politicians are invariably self-interested in a narrow sense. This is not a theory in which elective office seekers simply maximize their chances of election or reelection, at least not for its own sake. They may well have fundamental values and principles, and they may have preferences over policies as means to those ends. They also care about office, both for its own sake and for the opportunities to achieve other ends that election and reelection make possible. . . . Just as winning elections is a means to other ends for politicians (whether career or policy ends), so too is the political party a means to these other ends.

Why, then, do politicians turn to create or reform, to use or abuse, partisan institutions? The answer is that parties are designed as attempts to solve problems that current institutional arrangements do not solve and that politicians have come to believe they cannot solve. These problems fall into three general and recurring categories.

The Problem of Ambition and Elective Office Seeking

Elective office seekers, as that label says, want to win election to office. Parties regulate access to those offices. If elective office is indeed valuable, there will be more aspirants than offices, and the political party and the two-party system are means of regulating that competition and channeling those ambitions. Major party nomination is necessary for election, and partisan institutions have been developed—and have been reformed and re-reformed—for regulating competition. Intra-institutional leadership positions are also highly valued and therefore potentially competitive. There is, for example, a fairly well institutionalized path to the office of Speaker of the House. It is, however, a Democratic party institution. Elective politicians, of course, ordinarily desire election more than once. They are typically careerists who want a long and productive career in politics. Schlesinger's ambition theory (1966) . . . is precisely about this general problem. Underlying this theory, though typically not fully developed, is a problem. The problem is that if office is desirable, there will be more, usually many more, aspirants than there are offices to go around. When stated in rigorous form, it can be proved that in fact there is no permanent solution to this problem. And it is a problem that can adversely affect the fortunes of a party. In 1912 the Republican vote was split between William Howard Taft and Theodore Roosevelt. This split enabled Woodrow Wilson to win with 42 percent of the popular vote. Not only was Wilson the only break in Republican hegemony of the White House in this period, but in that year Democrats increased their House majority by sixty-five additional seats and captured majority control of the Senate. Thus failure to regulate intraparty competition cost Republicans dearly.

For elective office seekers, regulating conflict over who holds those offices is clearly of major concern. It is ever present. And it is not just a problem of access to government offices but is also a problem internal to each party as soon as the party becomes an important gateway to office.

The Problem of Making Decisions for the Party and for the Polity

Once in office, partisans determine outcomes for the polity. They propose alternatives, shape the agenda, pass (or reject) legislation, and implement what they enact. The policy formation and execution process, that is, is highly partisan. The parties-in-government are more than mere coalitions of like-minded individuals, however; they are enduring institutions. Very few incumbents change their partisan affiliations. Most retain their partisanship throughout their career, even though they often disagree (i.e., are not uniformly like-minded) with some of their partisan peers. When the rare incumbent does change parties, it is invariably to join the party more consonant with that switcher's policy interests. This implies that there are differences between the two parties at some fundamental and enduring level on policy positions, values, and beliefs. Thus, parties are institutions designed to promote the achievement of collective choices—choices on which the parties differ and choices reached by majority rule. As with access to office and ambition theory, there is a well-developed theory for this problem: *social choice theory.* Underlying this theory is the well-known problem that no method of choice can solve the elective officeholders' problem of combining the interests, concerns, or values of a polity that remains faithful to democratic values, as shown by the consequences flowing from Arrow's theorem (Arrow 1951). Thus, in a republican democracy politicians may turn to partisan institutions to solve the problem of collective choice. In the language of politics, parties may help achieve the goal of attaining policy majorities in the first place, as well as the often more difficult goal of maintaining such majorities.

The Problem of Collective Action

The third problem is the most pervasive and thus the furthest-ranging in substantive content. The clearest example, however, is also the most important. To win office, candidates need more than a party's nomination. Election requires persuading members of the public to support that candidacy and mobilizing as many of those supporters as possible. This is a problem of collective action. How do candidates get supporters to vote for them—at least in greater numbers than vote for the opposition—as well as get them to provide the cadre of workers and contribute the resources needed to win election? The political party has long been the solution.

As important as wooing and mobilizing supporters are, collective action problems arise in a wide range of circumstances facing elective office seekers. Party action invariably requires the concerted action of many partisans to achieve collectively desirable outcomes. Jimmy Carter was the only president in the 1970s and 1980s to enjoy unified party control of government. Democrats in Congress, it might well be argued, shared an interest in achieving policy outcomes. And yet Carter was all too often unable to get them to act in their shared collective interests. In 1980 not only he but the Democratic congressional parties paid a heavy price for failed cooperation. The theory here, of course, is the *theory of public goods* and its consequence, the *theory of collective action*.

The Elective Office Seekers' and Holders' Interests Are to Win

Why should this crucial set of actors, the elective office seekers and officeholders, care about these three classes of problems? The short answer is that these concerns become practical problems to politicians when they adversely affect their chances of winning. Put differently, politicians turn to their political party—that is, use its powers, resources, and institutional forms—when they believe doing so increases their prospects for winning desired outcomes, and they turn from it if it does not.

Ambition theory is about winning per se. The breakdown of orderly access to office risks unfettered and unregulated competition. The inability of a party to develop effective means of nomination and support for election therefore directly influences the chances of victory for the candidates and thus for their parties. The standard example of the problem of social choice theory, the "paradox of voting," is paradoxical precisely because all are voting to win desired outcomes, and yet there is no majority-preferred outcome. Even if there happens to be a majority-preferred policy, the conditions under which it is truly a stable equilibrium are extremely fragile and thus all too amenable to defeat. In other words, majorities in Congress are hard to attain and at least as hard to maintain. And the only reason to employ scarce campaign resources to mobilize supporters is that such mobilization increases the odds of victory. Its opposite, the failure to act when there are broadly shared interests—the problem of collective action—reduces the prospects of victory, whether at the ballot box or in government. Scholars may recognize these as manifestations of theoretical problems and call them "impossibility results" to emphasize their generic importance. Politicians recognize the consequences of these impossibility results by their adverse effects on their chances of winning—of securing what it is in their interests to secure.

So why have politicians so often turned to political parties for solutions to these problems? Their existence creates incentives for their use. It is, for example, incredibly difficult to win election to major office without the backing of a major party. It is only a little less certain that legislators who seek to lead a policy proposal through the congressional labyrinth will first turn to their party for assistance. But such incentives tell us only that an ongoing political institution is used when it is useful. Why form political parties in the first place? . . .

First, parties are institutions. This means, among other things, that they have some durability. They may be endogenous institutions, yet party reforms are meant not as short-term fixes but as alterations to last for years, even decades. Thus, for example, legislators might create a party rather than a temporary majority coalition to increase their chances of winning not just today but into the future. Similarly, a long and successful political career means winning office today, but it also requires winning elections throughout that career. A standing, enduring organization makes that goal more likely.

Second, American democracy chooses by plurality or majority rule. Election to office therefore requires broad-based support wherever and from whomever it can be found. So strong are the resulting incentives for a two-party system to emerge that the effect is called Duverger's law (Duverger 1954). It is in part the need to win vast and diverse support that has led politicians to create political parties.

Third, parties may help officeholders win more, and more often, than alternatives. Consider the usual stylized model of pork barrel politics. All winners get a piece of the pork for their districts. All funded projects are paid for by tax revenues, so each district pays an equal share of the costs of each project adopted, whether or not that district receives a project. Several writers have argued that this kind of legislation leads to "universalism," that is, adoption of a "norm" that every such bill yields a project to every district and thus passes with a "universal" or unanimous coalition. Thus everyone "wins." . . . As a result, expecting to win only a bit more than half the time and lose the rest of the time, all legislators prefer consistent use of the norm of universalism. But consider an alternative. Suppose some majority agree to form a more permanent coalition, to control outcomes now and into the future, and develop institutional means to encourage fealty to this agreement. If they successfully accomplish this, they will win regularly. Members of this institutionalized coalition would prefer it to universalism, since they always win a project in either case, but they get their projects at lower cost under the institutionalized majority coalition, which passes fewer projects. Thus, even in this case with no shared substantive interests at all, there are nonetheless incentives to form an enduring voting coalition—to form a political party. And those in the excluded minority have incentives to counterorganize. United, they may be more able to woo defectors to their side. If not, they can campaign to throw those rascals in the majority party out of office.

In sum, these theoretical problems affect elective office seekers and officeholders by reducing their chances of winning. Politicians therefore may turn to political parties as institutions designed to ameliorate them. In solving these theoretical problems, however, from the politicians' perspective parties are affecting who wins and loses and what is won or lost. And it is to parties that politicians often turn, because of their durability as institutionalized solutions, because of the need to orchestrate large and diverse groups of people to form winning majorities, and because often more can be won through parties. Note that this argument rests on the implicit assumption that winning and losing hang in the balance. Politicians may be expected to give up some of their personal autonomy only when they face an imminent threat of defeat without doing so or only when doing so can block opponents' ability to build the strength necessary to win.

This is, of course, the positive case for parties, for it specifies conditions under which politicians find them useful. Not all problems are best solved, perhaps even solved at all, by political parties. Other arrangements, perhaps interest groups, issue networks, or personal electoral coalitions, may be superior at different times and under different conditions. The party may even be part of the problem. In such cases politicians turn elsewhere to seek the means to win. Thus this theory is at base a theory of ambitious politicians seeking to achieve their goals. Often they have done so through the agency of the party, but sometimes, this theory implies, they will seek to realize their goals in other ways.

The political party has regularly proved useful. Their permanence suggests that the appropriate question is not When parties? but How much parties and how much other means? That parties are endogenous implies that there is no single, consistent account of the political party—nor should we expect one. Instead, parties are but a (major) part of the institutional context in which current historical conditions—the problems—are set, and solutions are sought with permanence only by changing that web of institutional arrangements. Of these the political party is by design the most malleable, and thus it is intended to change in important ways and with relatively great frequency. But it changes in ways that have, for most of American history, retained major political parties and, indeed, retained two major parties.

REFERENCES

Arrow, Kenneth J. 1951. *Social Choice and Individual Values.* New York: Wiley.

Broder, David S. 1972. *The Party's Over: The Failure of Politics in America.* New York: Harper and Row.

Crotty, William. 1984. *American Political Parties in Decline.* 2d ed. Boston: Little, Brown.

Duverger, Maurice. 1954. *Political Parties: Their Organization and Activities in the Modern State.* New York: Wiley.

Eldersveld, Samuel J. 1982. *Political Parties in American Society.* New York: Basic Books.

Ferguson, Thomas. 1983. "Party Realignment and American Industrial Structures: The Investment Theory of Political Parties in Historical Perspective". In *Research in Political Economy,* vol. 6, ed. Paul Zarembka, pp. 1–82. Greenwich, Conn.: JAI Press.

Fiorina, Morris P. 1980. "The Decline of Collective Responsibility in American Politics". *Daedalus* 109 (summer): 25–45.

Jacobson, Gary C. 1992. *The Politics of Congressional Elections.* 3d ed. New York: Harper-Collins.

Kernell, Samuel. 1986. *Going Public: New Strategies of Presidential Leadership.* Washington, D.C.: CQ Press.

Kirkpatrick, Jeane J. 1978. *Dismantling the Parties: Reflections on Party Reform and Party Decomposition.* Washington, D.C.: American Enterprise Institute of Public Policy Research.

Lowi, Theodore. 1985. *The Personal President: Power Invested, Promise Unfulfilled.* Ithaca, N.Y.: Cornell University Press.

Neustadt, Richard E. 1960. *Presidential Power: The Politics of Leadership.* New York: Wiley.

_____ . 1990. *Presidential Power and the Modern Presidents: The Politics of Leadership from Roosevelt to Reagan.* New York: Free Press.

Polsby, Nelson W. 1983. *Consequences of Party Reform.* Oxford: Oxford University Press.

Popkin, Samuel, John W. Gorman, Charles Phillips, and Jeffrey A. Smith. 1976. Comment: What Have You Done for Me Lately? Toward an Investment Theory of Voting. *American Political Science Review* 70 (September): 779–805.

Ranney, Austin. 1975. *Curing the Mischiefs of Faction: Party Reform in America.* Berkeley and Los Angeles: University of California Press.

Rohde, David W. 1989. "Something's Happening Here: What It is Ain't Exactly Clear": Southern Democrats in the House of Representatives. In *Home Style and Washington Work: Studies of Congressional Politics,* ed. Morris P. Fiorina and David W. Rohde, pp. 137–163. Ann Arbor: University of Michigan Press.

_____ . 1991. *Parties and Leaders in the Postreform House.* Chicago: University of Chicago Press.

Schlesinger, Joseph A. 1966. *Ambition and Politics: Political Careers in the United States.* Chicago: Rand McNally.

_____ . 1975. The Primary Goals of Political Parties: A Clarification of Positive Theory. *American Political Science Review* 69 (September): 840–49.

_____ . 1985. The New American Political Party. *American Political Science Review* 79 (December): 1152–69.

Wattenberg, Martin P. 1990. *The Decline of American Political Parties: 1952–1988.* Cambridge: Harvard University Press.

12-2

Partisanship and Voting Behavior, 1952–1996

Larry M. Bartels

Many Americans consider themselves to be Democrats or Republicans, and a few identify with some other party. In the late 1960s and 1970s the number of Americans willing to call themselves Democrats or Republicans declined, leading political scientists to speak of a dealignment and worry about the declining importance of parties. Then partisanship appeared to rebound in the 1990s. In this essay political scientist Larry M. Bartels describes these trends and explains the importance of partisanship for the voting behavior of Americans. He argues that party identification increased in the 1980s and 1990s and that the correlation between party identification and presidential voting increased even more. He concludes by observing that changes in the behavior of elected partisans—greater partisanship among presidents and members of Congress—may have contributed to resurgent partisanship in voting in the electorate.

THE "DECLINE OF PARTIES" is one of the most familiar themes in popular and scholarly discourse about contemporary American politics. One influential journalist has asserted that "the most important phenomenon of American politics in the past quarter century has been the rise of independent voters." . . . The most persistent academic analyst of partisan decline has argued that "For over four decades the American public has been drifting away from the two major political parties," while another prominent scholar has referred to a "massive decay of partisan electoral linkages" and to "the ruins of the traditional partisan regime."

I shall argue here that this conventional wisdom regarding the "decline of parties" is both exaggerated and outdated. Partisan loyalties in the American public have rebounded significantly since the mid-1970s, especially among those who actually turn out to vote. Meanwhile, the impact of partisanship on voting behavior has increased markedly in recent years, both at the presidential level (where the overall impact of partisanship in 1996 was almost 80 percent greater

Source: Larry Bartels, "Partisanship and Voting Behavior, 1952–1996," *American Journal of Political Science* 44, no. 1 (January 2000): 35–50. Notes and bibliographic references appearing in the original have been deleted.

than in 1972) and at the congressional level (where the overall impact of partisanship in 1996 was almost 60 percent greater than in 1978). . . . My analysis suggests that "partisan loyalties had at least as much impact on voting behavior at the presidential level in the 1980s as in the 1950s"—and even more in the 1990s than in the 1980s.

The Thesis of Partisan Decline

Almost forty years ago, the authors of *The American Voter* asserted that

> Few factors are of greater importance for our national elections than the lasting attachment of tens of millions of Americans to one of the parties. These loyalties establish a basic division of electoral strength within which the competition of particular campaigns takes place. . . . Most Americans have this sense of attachment with one party or the other. And for the individual who does, the strength and direction of party identification are facts of central importance in accounting for attitude and behavior.

The so-called "Michigan model," with its emphasis on the fundamental importance of long-standing partisan loyalties, dominated the subsequent decade of academic research on voting behavior. However, over the same decade, changes in the political environment seemed to be rendering the "Michigan model" increasingly obsolete. By the early 1970s, political observers were pointing to the increasing proportion of "independents" in opinion surveys and the increasing prevalence of split-ticket voting as indications of significant partisan decline. By the mid-1970s, some political scientists were extrapolating from a decade-long trend to project a permanent demise of partisan politics. . . .

The "increase in the number of independents" in the 1960s and early '70s . . . — and the corresponding decrease in the proportion of the public who identified themselves as Democrats or Republicans—constitute the single most important piece of evidence in support of the thesis of partisan decline. These and subsequent trends are displayed in the two panels of Figure 1, which show the proportions of party identifiers (including "strong" and "weak" identifiers) and independents (including "pure" independents and "leaners"), respectively, in each of the biennial American National Election Studies from 1952 through 1996.

. . . The proportion of "strong" identifiers in the population increased from 24 percent in 1976 to 31 percent in 1996, while the proportion of "pure" independents—those who neither identified themselves as Democrats or Republicans nor "leaned" to either party in response to the traditional Michigan follow-up question—declined from 16 percent in 1976 to only 9 percent in 1996.

Figure 1. The Distribution of Party Identification, 1952–1996

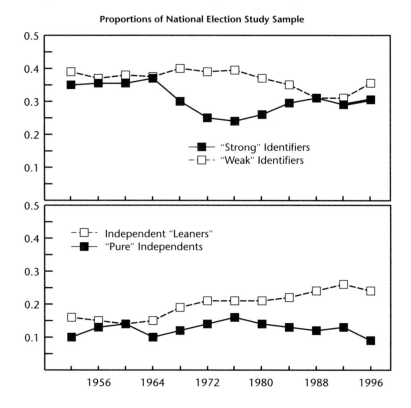

Proportions of National Election Study Sample

A Summary Measure of Partisan Voting

What significance should we attach to the shifts in the distribution of party identification documented in Figure 1? . . . To the extent that our interest in partisan loyalties is motivated by an interest in voting behavior, we would seem to need (at least) two kinds of additional information to interpret the electoral implications of changing levels of partisanship. First, are the shifts documented in Figure 1 concentrated among voters or among nonvoters? Declining partisanship among nonvoters may leave the distribution of party identification in the voting booth unchanged. And second, has the electoral *impact* of a given level of partisanship declined or increased over time? Declining *levels* of partisanship might be either reinforced or counteracted by changes in the *impact* of partisanship on electoral choices.

The first of these two questions is addressed by Figure 2, which shows separate trend lines for the proportion of ("strong" or "weak") party identifiers

Figure 2. Party Identification among Presidential Voters and Nonvoters

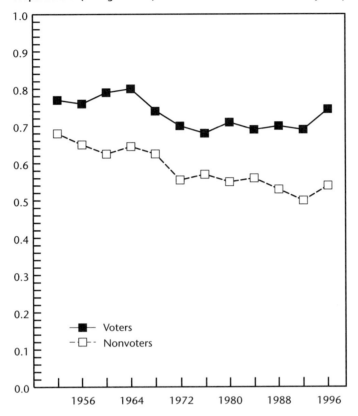

Proportions of (Strong or Weak) Identifiers in National Election Study Sample

among voters and nonvoters in presidential elections since 1952. Not surprisingly, nonvoters are less partisan than voters in every year. But what is more important to note here is that the gap in partisanship between voters and nonvoters has widened noticeably over time, from about ten percentage points in the 1950s to about twenty percentage points by the 1990s. Indeed, it appears from these results that the decline in partisanship evident in Figure 1 has been almost entirely reversed among voters: the proportion of party identifiers in the presidential electorate was 77 percent in 1952, 76 percent in 1956, and 75 percent in 1996, while the proportion among nonvoters was almost fifteen points lower in 1996 than in the 1950s. Thus, while the trend lines shown in Figure 1 suggest that the erosion of party loyalties underlying the "partisan decline" thesis has ended and probably even reversed in the last two decades, the results presented in Figure 2 suggest that these developments have been especially pronounced among actual voters.

The erosion of party loyalties among nonvoters evident in Figure 2 is of importance for any general account of the role of partisanship in contemporary American politics. It is especially important in view of evidence suggesting that declining partisanship is, at least in modest part, *responsible* for the substantial decline in turnout over the period covered by Figure 2, and that individual turnout decisions are increasingly sensitive to the strength of prospective voters' preferences for one candidate or the other, which derive in significant part from long-term partisan attachments. However, given my narrower aim here of documenting changes in the impact of partisanship *on voting behavior,* the most important implication of Figure 2 is that the distribution of partisan attachments *among those citizens who actually got to the polls* was not much different in the 1990s from what it had been in the 1950s.

Of course, the significance of partisanship in the electoral process depends not only upon the level of partisanship in the electorate, but also upon the extent to which partisanship influences voting behavior. How, if at all, has that influence changed over the four and a half decades covered by the NES data? . . . [Editors: Bartels estimates the impact of party identification on voting by taking advantage of the survey from which respondents are coded as strong Republican, weak Republican, leaning Republican, independent, leaning Democrat, weak Democrat, and strong Democrat. For each category, a statistical estimate is calculated for the effect of being in that category on voting for the alternative presidential or congressional candidates. The statistical estimate, called a probit coefficient, is averaged for the partisan categories to yield an overall measure "partisan voting." Figure 3 presents the result for elections in the 1952–1996 period.]

The Revival of Partisan Voting in Presidential Elections

. . . Figure 3 shows noticeable declines in the level of partisan voting in the presidential elections of 1964 and, especially, 1972. These declines primarily reflect the fact that Republican identifiers in 1964 and Democratic identifiers in 1972 abandoned their parties' unpopular presidential candidates by the millions, depressing the estimated effects of partisan loyalties on the presidential vote in those years. However, an even more striking pattern in Figure 3 is the monotonic increase in partisan voting in every presidential election since 1972. By 1996, this trend had produced a level of partisan voting 77 percent higher than in 1972—an average increase of 10 percent in each election, compounded over six election cycles—and 15 to 20 percent higher than in the supposed glory days of the 1950s that spawned *The American Voter.*

Figure 3. Partisan Voting in Presidential Elections

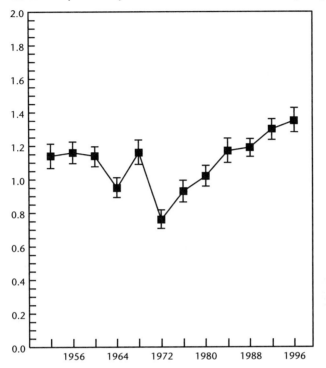

Estimated Impact of Party Identification on Presidential Vote Propensity

Note: Average probit coefficients, major-party voters only, with jackknife standard error bars.

... One possible explanation for the revival of partisan voting evident in Figure 3 is the sorting out of partisan attachments of southerners following the civil rights upheavals of the early and middle 1960s. As national party elites took increasingly distinct stands on racial issues, black voters moved overwhelmingly into the Democratic column, while white southerners defected to conservative Republican presidential candidates. What is important here is that many of these conservative white southerners only gradually shed their traditional Democratic identifications—and Democratic voting behavior at the subpresidential level— through the 1980s and '90s. Thus, it may be tempting to interpret the revival of partisan voting at the presidential level largely as a reflection of the gradual reequilibration of presidential votes and more general partisan attachments among white southerners in the wake of a regional partisan realignment.

As it happens, however, the steady and substantial increases in partisan voting over the past quarter-century evident in Figure 3 are by no means confined to the

Figure 4. Partisan Voting in Presidential Elections, White Southerners and White Nonsoutherners

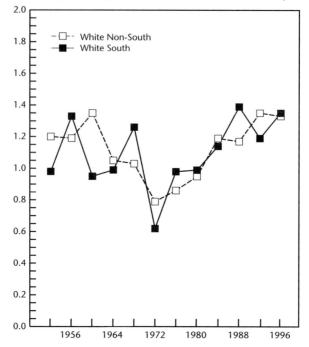

Note: Average probit coefficients, major-party voters only.

South. This fact is evident from Figure 4, which displays separate patterns of partisan voting for white southerners and white nonsoutherners. The trend lines are somewhat more ragged for these subgroups than for the electorate as a whole, especially in the South (where the year-by-year estimates are based on an average of fewer than 300 southern white voters in each election); nevertheless, the general pattern in Figure 3 is replicated almost identically in both subgroups in Figure 4. The absolute level of partisan voting in the 1964 and 1972 elections is only slightly lower among southern whites than among nonsouthern whites, and the substantial increase in partisan voting since 1972 appears clearly (indeed, nearly monotonically) in both subgroups.

It should be evident from Figure 4 that the revival of partisan voting in presidential elections documented in Figure 3 is a national rather than a regional phenomenon. Indeed, additional analysis along these lines suggests that the same pattern is evident in a wide variety of subgroups of the electorate, including voters under 40 and those over 50 years of age, those with college educations and those without high school diplomas, and so on. Thus, any convincing explanation of this partisan revival will presumably have to be based upon broad changes in the national political environment, rather than upon narrower demographic or generational developments.

Partisan Voting in Congressional Elections

My analysis so far has focused solely on the impact of partisan loyalties on voting behavior in presidential elections. However, there are a variety of reasons to suppose that the trends evident in presidential voting might not appear at other electoral levels. For one thing, I have already argued that the significant dips in partisanship at the presidential level evident in Figure 3 are attributable primarily to the parties' specific presidential candidates in 1964 and 1972. If that is so, there is little reason to expect those dips—or the subsequent rebounds—in levels of partisan voting to appear at other electoral levels.

In any case, analysts of congressional voting behavior since the 1970s have been more impressed by the advantages of incumbency than by any strong connections between presidential and congressional votes—except insofar as voters may go out of their way to split their tickets in order to produce divided government. Thus, it would not be surprising to find a longer, more substantial decline in the level of partisan voting in congressional elections than in the analysis of presidential voting summarized in Figure 3.

... Figure 5 clearly shows a substantial decline in partisan voting in congressional elections from the early 1960s through the late 1970s. Indeed, the level of partisan voting declined in seven of the eight congressional elections between 1964 and 1978; by 1978, the average impact of partisanship on congressional voting was only a bit more than half what it had been before 1964. Although the overall impact of partisanship at the presidential and congressional levels was generally similar for much of this period, the declines at the congressional level were less episodic and longer lasting than those at the presidential level.

What is more surprising is that the revival of partisanship evident in presidential voting patterns since 1972 is also evident in congressional voting patterns since 1978. While the trend is later and less regular at the congressional level than at the presidential level, the absolute increases in partisan voting since 1980 have been of quite similar magnitude in presidential and congressional elections. While partisan voting remains noticeably less powerful in recent congressional elections than it was before 1964—or than it has been in recent presidential

Figure 5. Partisan Voting in Presidential and Congressional Elections

Estimated Impact of Party Identification on Presidential and Congressional Vote Propensities

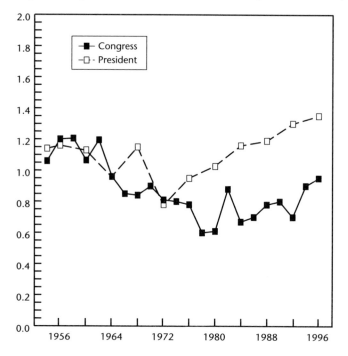

Note: Average probit coefficients, major-party voters only.

elections—the impact of partisanship on congressional votes in 1996 was almost 60 percent greater than in 1978.

An interesting feature of the resurgence of partisan voting in congressional elections documented in Figure 5 is that it appears to be concentrated disproportionately among younger and better-educated voters. For example, voters under the age of 40 were noticeably less partisan in their voting behavior than those over the age of 50 in almost every election from 1952 through 1984, but virtually indistinguishable from the older voters in the late 1980s and 1990s. Similarly, levels of partisan voting were distinctly lower among voters with some college education than among those without high school diplomas before 1982, but not thereafter. These patterns suggest that the resurgence of partisan voting reflects some positive reaction by younger and better-educated voters to the political developments of the past two decades, rather than simply a "wearing off" of the political stimuli of the 1960s and 1970s.

Discussion

If the analysis presented here is correct, the American political system has slipped, with remarkably little fanfare, into an era of increasingly vibrant partisanship in the electorate, especially at the presidential level but also at the congressional level. How might we account for this apparent revival of partisan voting?

One plausible hypothesis is that increasing partisanship in the electorate represents a response at the mass level to increasing partisanship at the elite level. "If parties in government are weakened," [political scientist Martin] Wattenberg argued, "the public will naturally have less of a stimulus to think of themselves politically in partisan terms." But then the converse may also be true: in an era in which parties in government seem increasingly consequential, the public may increasingly come to develop and apply partisan predispositions of exactly the sort described by the authors of *The American Voter.*

Why might parties in government seem more relevant in the late 1990s than they had a quarter-century earlier? The ascensions of two highly partisan political leaders—Ronald Reagan in 1981 and Newt Gingrich in 1995—may provide part of the explanation. So too may the increasing prominence of the Religious Right in Republican party nominating politics over this period. At a more structural level, the realignment of partisan loyalties in the South in the wake of the civil rights movement of the 1960s may be important, despite the evidence presented in Figure 4 suggesting that the revival of partisan voting has been a national rather than a regional phenomenon.

Regional realignment in the South and the influence of ideological extremists in both parties' nominating politics have combined to produce a marked polarization of the national parties at the elite level. By a variety of measures . . . votes on the floor of Congress have become increasingly partisan since the 1970s. . . . These changes in the composition of the parties' congressional delegations have been "reinforced by the operation of those reform provisions that were intended to enhance collective control" by party leaders in Congress, including a strengthened Democratic caucus and whip system. The new Republican congressional majority in 1995 produced further procedural reforms "delegating more power to party leaders than any House majority since the revolt against Joe Cannon in 1910."

We know less than we should about the nature and extent of mass-level reactions to these elite-level developments. However, the plausibility of a causal link between recent increases in partisanship at the elite and mass levels is reinforced by the fact that the decline in partisan voting in the electorate in the 1960s and 1970s was itself preceded by a noticeable decline in party voting in Congress from the 1950s through the early 1970s. Moreover, some more direct evidence suggests that citizens have taken note of the increasing strength of partisan cues from Washington. For example, the proportion of NES survey respondents perceiving "important differences" between the Democratic and Republican parties increased noticeably in 1980 and again in 1984 and reached a new all-time high (for the period since 1952) in 1996.

Even more intriguingly, [political scientist John] Coleman has documented a systematic temporal relationship between the strength of partisanship in government and the strength of partisanship in the electorate. Analyzing data from 1952 through 1990, Coleman found a strong positive correlation across election years (.60) between the strength of partisanship in NES surveys and the proportion of House budget votes with opposing party majorities—and an even stronger correlation (.66) between mass partisanship and opposing party majorities on budget authorization votes. While the detailed processes underlying this aggregate relationship are by no means clear, the strength of the correlation at least suggests that students of party politics would do well to examine more closely the interrelationship of mass-level and elite-level trends. . . .

12-3

Parties as Problem Solvers

Morris P. Fiorina

Political parties receive conflicting reviews. Some people view parties as self-serving entities that generate unnecessary conflict, make essential compromise more difficult, and serve as obstacles to solving important national problems. Others view party competition as the means for aggregating a variety of interests, generating policy alternatives, coordinating action across branches of government, and holding elected officials accountable. In this essay, political scientist Morris Fiorina evaluates the role of parties in addressing the nation's problems in the first decade of the new millennium.

SOME TWENTY-FIVE YEARS AGO I wrote an article entitled "The Decline of Collective Responsibility in American Politics." In that article (henceforth referenced as DOCR), I updated the classic arguments for party responsibility in light of which the politics of the 1970s looked seriously deficient. . . . [I] noted that in the 1970s party cohesion had dropped to a level not seen since before the Civil War. As a result, national politics had degenerated into a free-for-all of unprincipled bargaining in which participants blithely sacrificed general interests in their pursuit of particularistic constituency interests. The unified Democratic government of President Jimmy Carter that failed to deal with national problems such as runaway inflation and successive energy crises exemplified the sorry state of national politics. Moreover, not only had policy failure become more likely, but because voting for members of Congress increasingly reflected the particularistic activities and personal records of incumbents, members had little fear of being held accountable for their contribution to the failures of national politics. In that light, I sympathetically resurrected the arguments of early to midcentury political scientists who advocated more responsible parties. Although not all problems were amenable to government solution, unified political parties led by strong presidents were more likely to act decisively to meet the challenges facing the country, and when they took their collective performance records to the electorate for ratification or rejection, the voters at least had a good idea of whom to reward or blame.

Source: Morris P. Fiorina, "Parties as Problem Solvers," in *Promoting the General Welfare: New Perspectives on Government Performance,* eds. Alan S. Gerber and Eric M. Patashnik (Washington, D.C.: Brookings Institution Press, 2006), 237–253. Notes appearing in the original have been deleted.

Looking back at these essays, the 1980s clearly was the decade of party responsibility for me. But . . . the prevalence of divided government in the late twentieth century had raised doubts in my mind about the arguments articulated a decade earlier. These doubts cumulated into a change of position explicated at length in *Divided Government* and later writings. In brief, as the parties became more distinct and cohesive during the 1980s, voters seemed to show little appreciation for the changes. Rather than entrust control of government to one unified party, Americans were increasingly voting to split control of government—at the state as well as the national level. And whether that was their actual goal or not—a matter of continuing debate—polls showed that majorities were happy enough with the situation, whatever political scientists thought of the supposed programmatic inefficiency and electoral irresponsibility of divided government. By the early 1990s, I had come to appreciate the electorate's point of view.

Moving from one side of an argument to the other in a decade suggests that the protagonist either was wrong earlier or (worse!) wrong later. But there is another less uncomplimentary possibility—namely, that the shift in stance did not reflect blatant error in the earlier argument so much as changes in one or more unrecognized but important empirical premises, which vitiate the larger argument. . . . By 1990 I had come to believe that in important respects the parties we were observing in the contemporary era were different in composition and behavior from the ones described in the political science literature we had studied in graduate school. Parties organized to solve the governance problems of one era do not necessarily operate in the same way as parties organized to solve the problems of later eras.

This chapter considers the capacity of the contemporary party system to solve societal problems and meet contemporary challenges. I do so by revisiting DOCR and reconsidering it against the realities of contemporary politics. I begin by briefly contrasting American politics in the 1970s and the 2000s.

Politics Then and Now

DOCR reflected the politics of the 1970s, a decade that began with divided government (then still regarded as something of an anomaly), proceeded through the resignations of a vice president and president followed by the brief administration of an unelected president, then saw the restoration of the "normal order"—unified Democratic government—in 1976, only to see it collapse at the end of the decade in the landslide rejection of a presidency mortally wounded by international humiliation, stagflation, and energy crises. Contemporary critics placed much of the responsibility for the "failed" Carter presidency at the feet of Carter himself—his obsession with detail, his inability to delegate, his political

tin ear, and so forth—but I felt then that the critics were giving insufficient attention to larger developments and more general circumstances that would have
posed serious obstacles for presidents who possessed much stronger executive
and political skills than Carter.

Political Conditions in the 1970s

Not only did Jimmy Carter's 1976 victory restore the presidency to the Democrats, but large Democratic majorities also controlled both the House and Senate.
It seemed that the great era of government activism that had been derailed by
the war in Vietnam would resume. Such was not to be. After four years of political frustration Carter was soundly defeated, the Republicans captured the Senate with a remarkable gain of twelve seats, and the Democrats lost thirty-three
seats in the House. What happened?

Basically, the country faced a series of new problems, and the Democratic
Party failed to deal with them in a manner satisfactory to electoral majorities in
the nation as a whole and in many states and districts. Gas lines in particular, and
the energy crisis in general, were something new in modern American experience, as were double-digit inflation and interest rates near 20 percent. Middle-
class tax revolts were a startling development that frightened Democrats and
energized Republicans, and a succession of foreign policy setbacks led many to
fear that the United States was ill prepared to deal with new challenges around
the world. In the face of such developments Democratic majorities in Congress
failed to deliver. Indeed, they seemed fixated on old, ineffective solutions like
public works spending and trade restrictions. The honeymoon between Carter
and congressional Democrats ended fairly quickly, and the partnership was
under strain for most of Carter's administration. Members worked to protect
their constituencies from the negative effects of the new developments and worried much less about the fate of Carter or the party as a whole. As Figure 1 shows,
this was a period of low party cohesion, and although cross-party majorities were
not as common as in the late 1960s, Figure 2 shows that they still were common.

The generation of congressional scholars who contributed to the literature of
the 1950s and 1960s had defended the decentralized Congresses of the period
against the centralizing impulses of presidential scholars and policy wonks. True,
Congress did not move fast or efficiently, nor did it defer to presidential leadership, but most scholars would have characterized this as pragmatic incremental-
ism rather than the "deadlock of democracy." Congress reflected and was
responsive to the heterogeneity of interests in the country. . . .

To a younger generation of scholars, however, the failings of the decentralized Congresses and disorganized parties were cause for concern. Serious

Figure 1. The Decline and Resurgence of Party in Government
Party Unity, 1954–98

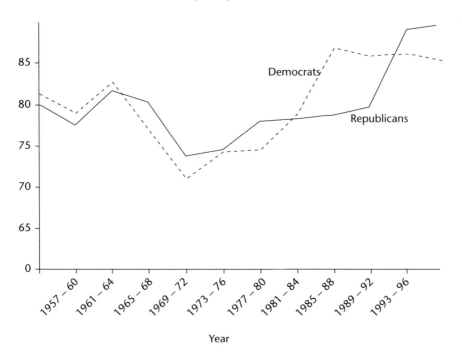

Year

Source: Harold W. Stanley and Richard G. Niemi, eds., *Vital Statistics on American Politics, 2005–2006* (Washington, DC: CQ Press, 2005), Table 5.8.

problems faced the country, presidents were held responsible for solving these problems, but incumbent members of Congress seemingly could win reelection by abandoning their presidents and parties in favor of protecting parochial constituency interests. By emphasizing their individual records, members of Congress had adapted to an era of candidate-centered politics. Historically speaking, they had far less to gain or lose from the effects of presidential coattails, nor need they be very concerned about midterm swings against their president's party. Collective responsibility traditionally provided by the political parties was at a low ebb. *Pluribus* was running rampant, leaving *unum* in the electoral dust.

Political Conditions Now

In retrospect, the trends decried in DOCR had already bottomed out by the Carter presidency. The cross-party majorities that passed President Reagan's budget and tax cuts may have obscured the fact, but party unity and party differences

Figure 2. The Decline and Resurgence of Party in Government
Party Votes, 1953–98

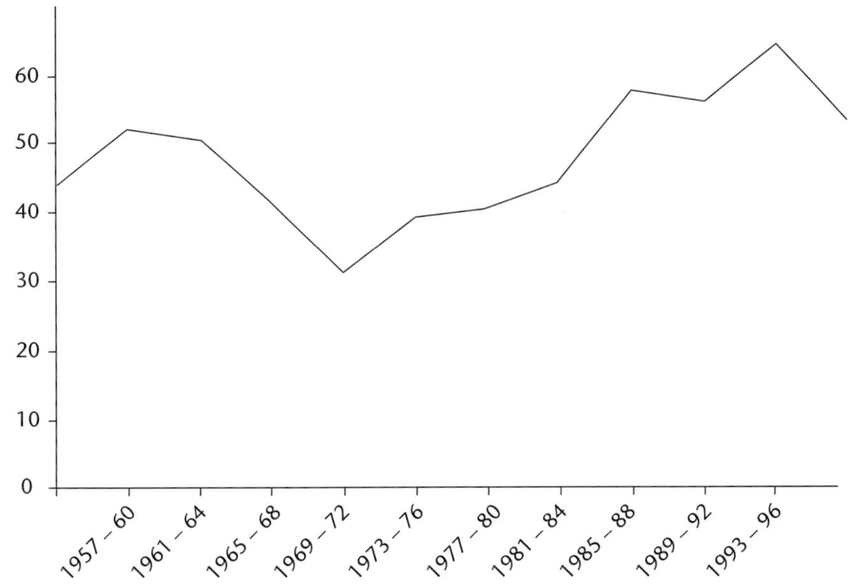

Source: Harold W. Stanley and Richard G. Niemi, eds., *Vital Statistics on American Politics, 2005–2006* (Washington, DC: CQ Press, 2005), Table 5.7.

already were on the rise and continued rising in succeeding years (Figures 1 and 2). In a related development, the electoral advantages accruing to incumbency already were beginning to recede as national influences in voting reasserted themselves. And a new breed of congressional leaders emerged to focus the efforts of their parties in support of or opposition to presidential proposals. In 1993 President Clinton's initial budget passed without a single Republican vote in the House or Senate, and unified Republican opposition contributed greatly to the demise of the administration's signature health care plan.

And then came 1994, when the Republicans finally had success in an undertaking they had sporadically attempted for a generation—nationalizing the congressional elections. In the 1994 elections, personal opposition to gun control or various other liberal policies no longer sufficed to save Democrats in conservative districts whose party label overwhelmed their personal positions. The new Republican majorities in Congress seized the initiative from President Clinton to the extent that he was asked at a press conference whether he was "still relevant." When congressional Republicans overreached, Clinton reasserted his relevance, beating back Republican attempts to cut entitlement programs and saddling them with the blame for the government shutdowns of 1995–96.

Table 1. APSA Report after Forty Years

Fate of proposal	Democrats	Republicans	System
Full implementation	13	6	5
Partial implementation	7	5	5
De facto movement	8	9	5
No change	3	10	3
Negative movement	2	3	2

Source: Grossly adapted from Denise Baer and David Bositis, *Politics and Linkage in a Democratic Society* (Upper Saddle River, N.J.: Prentice-Hall, 1993), appendix.

At the time, the Republican attempt to govern as a responsible party struck many political scientists as unprecedented in the modern era, but, as Baer and Bositis pointed out, politics had been moving in that direction for several decades. Indeed, a great deal of what the 1950 APSA [American Political Science Association] report called for already had come to pass (Table 1). Now, a decade later, it is apparent that the Congress elected in 1994 was only the leading edge of a new period in national politics. Party unity and presidential support among Republicans hit fifty-year highs during the first term of President George W. Bush, and in 2002 the president pulled off the rare feat of leading his party to seat gains in a midterm election. After his reelection in 2004, President Bush spoke in terms clearly reminiscent of those used by responsible party theorists. On the basis of a 51 percent popular majority, he claimed a mandate to make his tax cuts permanent and transform Social Security. Moreover, early in 2005 when the president was asked why no one in his administration had been held accountable for mistakes and miscalculations about Iraq, he replied in words that should have warmed the hearts of responsible party theorists: "We had an accountability moment, and that's called the 2004 election. And the American people listened to different assessments made about what was taking place in Iraq, and they looked at the two candidates, and chose me, for which I'm grateful." No president in living memory had articulated such clear statements of collective party responsibility legitimized by electoral victory.

In sum, the collective responsibility DOCR found wanting in the 1970s seems clearly present in the 2000s. Why, then, am I troubled by the operation of something I fervently wished for in the 1970s?

The Problems with Today's Responsible Parties

In 2002 a Republican administration ostensibly committed to free enterprise endorsed tariffs to protect the U.S. steel industry, a policy condemned by economists across the ideological spectrum. Also in 2002 Congress passed and President Bush signed an agricultural subsidy bill that the left-leaning *New York Times* decried as an "orgy of pandering to special interest groups," the centrist *USA Today* called "a congressional atrocity," and the right-leaning *Economist* characterized as "monstrous." In 2003 Congress passed and the president signed a special interest–riddled prescription drug plan that was the largest entitlement program adopted since Medicare itself in 1965, a fiscal commitment that immediately put the larger Medicare program on a steep slide toward bankruptcy. In 2004 congressional Republicans proposed and President Bush supported a constitutional amendment to ban gay marriage, a divisive proposal that had no chance of passing. After his reelection, President Bush declared his highest priority was to avert a crisis in a Social Security system he insisted was bankrupt, by establishing a system of personal accounts, while disinterested observers generally pronounced the situation far from crisis and in need of relatively moderate reform—especially compared to Medicare. In 2005 the Republican Congress passed and President Bush signed a pork-filled transportation bill that contained 6,371 congressional earmarks, forty times as many as contained in a bill vetoed by an earlier Republican president in 1987. Meanwhile, at the time of this writing Americans continue to die in a war of choice launched on the basis of ambiguous intelligence that appears to have been systematically interpreted to support a previously adopted position.

The preceding are only some of the more noteworthy lowlights of public policies adopted or proposed under the responsible party government of 2000–05. All things considered, if someone wished to argue that politics in the 1970s was better than today, I would find it hard to rebut them. Why? Are today's problems and challenges so much more difficult than those of the 1970s that the decentralized, irresponsible parties of that time would have done an even poorer job of meeting them than the more responsible parties of today? Or are today's responsible parties operating in a manner that was not anticipated by those of us who wished for more responsible parties? In the remainder of this chapter, I will focus on the latter possibility.

What Didn't DOCR Anticipate?

With the benefit of hindsight, one potentially negative effect of political competition by cohesive, differentiated parties is to raise the stakes of politics. Certainly, majority control of institutions always is valuable; committee chairs, agenda control, staff budgets, and numerous other benefits go to the majority.

But if majority control of the House or Senate means relatively little for policy-making because moderate Republicans and Democrats hold the balance of power, which party formally holds control means less than when policy is decided within each party caucus. Similarly, the knowledge that the president's program either will be rubber-stamped by a supportive congressional majority or killed by an opposition majority makes unified control of all three institutions that much more valuable. The fact that the parties have been so closely matched in the past decade makes the competition that much more intense.

With the political stakes ratcheted upward, politics naturally becomes more conflictual. The benefits of winning and the costs of losing both increase. Informal norms and even formal rules come under pressure as the legislative majority strives to eliminate obstacles to its agenda. Meanwhile, the minority is first ignored, then abused. House Democrats under Jim Wright marginalized House Republicans in the 1980s, and the Republicans have enthusiastically returned the favor since taking control in 1994. Meanwhile Senate Majority Leader Bill Frist threatens the minority Democrats with the "nuclear option"—a rules change that effectively eliminates the filibuster on presidential appointments. In sum, the increasing disparity between majority and minority status further raises the electoral stakes and makes politics more conflictual.

In retrospect, it is probable that the development of more responsible parties was a factor—certainly not the only one—that contributed to the rise of the permanent campaign. With majority status that much more valuable, and minority status that much more intolerable, the parties are less able to afford a hiatus between elections in which governing takes precedence over electioneering. All else now is subordinated to party positioning for the next election. Free trade principles? Forget about them if Pennsylvania and Ohio steel workers are needed to win the next election. Budget deficits? Ignore them if a budget-busting prescription drug plan is needed to keep the opposition from scoring points with senior citizens. Politics always has affected policies, of course, but today the linkage is closer and stronger than ever before.

A second problem with cohesive parties that offer voters a clear choice is that voters may not like clear choices. The APSA report asserted that responsible parties would offer voters "a proper range of choice." But what is "proper"? Voters may not want a clear choice between repeal of *Roe v. Wade* and unregulated abortion, between private Social Security accounts and ignoring inevitable problems, between launching wars of choice and ignoring developing threats. Despite much popular commentary to the contrary, the issue positions of the electorate as a whole are not polarized; voters today remain, as always, generally moderate, or, at least, ambivalent. But candidates and their parties are polarized, and the consequence is candidate evaluations and votes that are highly polarized, which is what we have seen in recent elections.

Even if voters *were* polarized on issues and wished the parties to offer clear choices, they would still be dissatisfied if there were more than one issue and the opinion divisions across issues were not the same. For example, contemporary Republicans are basically an alliance between economic and social conservatives, and Democrats an alliance between economic and social liberals. So, in which party does someone who is an economic conservative and a social liberal belong? An economic liberal and a social conservative? Such people might well prefer moderate positions on both dimensions to issue packages consisting of one position they like a great deal and another they dislike a great deal.

The bottom line is that the majoritarianism that accompanies responsible parties may be ill suited for a heterogeneous society. With only one dimension of conflict a victory by one party can reasonably be interpreted to mean that a majority prefers its program to that of the other party. But with more than one dimension a victory by one party by no means guarantees majority support for its program(s). Indeed, . . . given variations in voter intensity on different issues, a party can win by constructing a coalition of minorities—taking the minority position on each issue.

American politics probably appeared to have a simpler and clearer structure at the time the APSA report was written. Race was not on the agenda. Social and cultural issues were largely dormant in the midcentury decades, their importance diminished by the end of immigration in the 1920s, the Great Depression, and World War II. A bipartisan consensus surrounded foreign and defense policy. Under such conditions it is understandable that a midcentury political scientist could have felt that all the country needed was two parties that advocated alternative economic programs. For example, in 1962 political historian James McGregor Burns wrote, "It is curious that majoritarian politics has won such a reputation for radicalism in this country. Actually it is moderate politics; it looks radical only in relation to the snail-like progress of Madisonian politics. The Jeffersonian strategy is essentially moderate because it is essentially competitive; in a homogeneous society it must appeal to the moderate, middle-class independent voters who hold the balance of power."

To most contemporary observers the United States looks rather less homogeneous than it apparently did to observers of Burns's era. Compared to 1950, our present situation is more complex with a more elaborate political issue space and less of a tendency to appeal to the moderate voter, as we discuss below.

Burns's contention that majoritarian politics is moderate politics is quite interesting in light of the contemporary discussion of the polarization of American politics. Although the electorate is not polarized, there is no question that the political class—the variegated collection of candidates, activists, interest group spokespersons, and infotainment media—is polarized. And, where we can measure it well,

Figure 3. Polarization of Congress since the 1960s

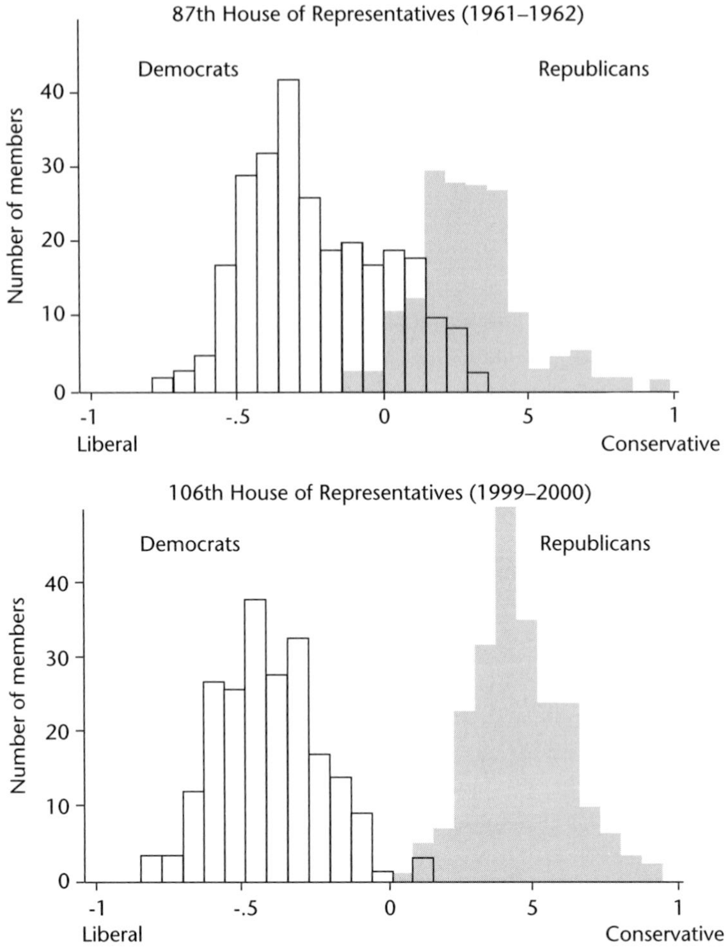

87th House of Representatives (1961–1962)

106th House of Representatives (1999–2000)

Source: Keith Poole, http://voteview.com/dwnomin.htm.

there is little doubt that the political class has become increasingly polarized over the past several decades. Figure 3 illustrates the oft-noted fact that moderates have disappeared from Congress: the area of overlap where conservative Democrats and liberal Republicans meet has shrunk to almost nothing, and it has done so at the same time as the parties were becoming more responsible—indeed, figures like these often are cited as indicators of party responsibility.

Why would polarization accompany party responsibility? Logically it need not. Indeed, the APSA report asserted that "[n]eeded clarification of party policy in itself will not cause the parties to differ more fundamentally or more sharply than they have in the past." But as I have argued elsewhere, today's parties are not the same as the parties described in midcentury textbooks. The old distinctions between "amateurs" and "professionals" or "purists" and "professionals" no longer have the same conceptual value because the amateurs have won, or perhaps more accurately, the professionals now are purists. At the time the responsible party theorists wrote, parties nominated candidates on the basis of their service to the party and their connections to party leaders, or, in more competitive areas, their electability. Aside from times when a party was bitterly divided, issue positions were seldom a litmus test of a candidate's suitability. Material motivations—control of offices, patronage—were dominant, but civil service, public sector unionization, conflict of interest laws, social welfare programs, and other developments have lessened the personal material rewards that once motivated many of those active in politics. Today, ideological motivations are relatively more important than previously. Candidates must have the right set of issue stances to attract support, and many of the potential supporters would prefer to lose with a pure ideological candidate than to win with a mushy moderate. Some candidates themselves no doubt feel the same.

These developments have contributed to a basic shift in party electoral strategy in the contemporary United States. At midcentury, the conventional wisdom expressed by Burns was in accord with political science theory—that two-party competition induces parties to move toward the center to capture the median voter. But in the last decade of the century we saw a shift to what now seems to be the prevailing strategy of concentrating on the party base—doing whatever is necessary to maximize loyalty and turnout by core party constituencies. Thus, the aforementioned forcing of a Senate vote on gay marriage was an entirely symbolic gesture toward the evangelical Christian base of the Republican Party. It had nothing to do with governing; it was a costly signal that the Bush administration was on their side.

Seemingly, today's parties no longer strive to maximize their vote, only to suffice—to get more votes than the other party. At one time a maximal victory was desirable because it would add credibility to the victors' claim that the voters had given them a mandate. But as the previously quoted remarks of President Bush indicate, at least some of today's politicians consider any victory, narrow or not, a mandate.

Parties composed of issue activists and ideologues behave differently from the parties that occupied the political science literature of the mid-twentieth century. At midcentury, each party appealed to a different swath of the American public, Democrats primarily to blue-collar workers and Republicans to middle-class-professionals and managers. Because such large social groupings were far from homogeneous internally, the party platform had to tolerate internal heterogeneity to maintain itself and compete across a reasonably broad portion of the country. As Turner put it, "[Y]ou cannot give Hubert Humphrey [liberal Democratic Senator from Minnesota] a banjo and expect him to carry Kansas. Only a Democrat who rejects part of the Fair Deal can carry Kansas, and only a Republican who moderates the Republican platform can carry Massachusetts."

Although both parties continue to have support in broad social groupings like blue-collar workers and white-collar professionals, their bases now consist of much more specifically defined groups. Democrats rely on public-sector unions, environmentalists, prochoice and other liberal cause groups. Republicans rely on evangelicals, small business organizations, prolife and other conservative cause groups. Rather than compromise on a single major issue such as economics, a process that midcentury political scientists correctly saw as inherently moderating, parties can now compromise across issues by adding up constituency groups' most preferred positions on a series of independent issues. Why should conservative mean prolife, low taxes, procapital punishment, and preemptive war, and liberal mean just the opposite? What is the underlying principle that ties such disparate issues together? The underlying principle is political, not logical or moral. Collections of positions like these happen to be the preferred positions of groups that now constitute important parts of the party bases.

At one time political scientists saw strong political parties as a means of controlling interest groups. Parties and groups were viewed as competing ways of organizing political life. If parties were weak, groups would fill the vacuum; if parties were strong, they would harness group efforts in support of more general party goals. Two decades ago, I was persuaded by this argument, but time has proved it suspect. Modern parties and their associated groups now overlap so closely that it is often hard to make the distinction between a party activist and an issue activist. As noted above, the difference between party professionals and purists does not look nearly so wide as it once did.

Although more speculative, I believe that unbiased information and policy effectiveness are additional casualties of the preceding developments. The APSA report asserts, "As a means of achieving responsibility, the clarification of party policy also tends to keep public debate on a more realistic level, restraining the inclination of party spokesmen to make unsubstantiated statements and charges. Recent experience shows just the opposite. Policies are proposed and opposed relatively more on the basis of ideology and the demands of the base, and relatively less on the basis of their likelihood of solving problems. Disinformation and outright lies become common as dissenting voices in each party leave or are silenced. The most disturbing example comes out of congressional passage of the 2003 Medicare prescription drug add-on bill. Political superiors threatened to fire Medicare's chief actuary if he informed Congress that the add-on would be 25–50 percent more costly than the administration publicly claimed. The administration apparently was willing to lie to members of its own party to assure passage of a bill whose basis was mostly political. More recently, President Bush introduced his campaign to add personal accounts to Social Security by claiming that Social Security was bankrupt and that personal accounts were a means of restoring the system to fiscal solvency. Although many experts see merit in the idea of personal savings accounts, most agreed that implementing them would increase Social Security's fiscal deficits in the coming decades. Even greater agreement surrounded rejection of the claim that Social Security was bankrupt. Although politically difficult, straightforward programmatic changes in the retirement age, the tax base, or the method of indexing future benefits would make Social Security solvent for as long as actuaries can reasonably predict.

Moreover, because parties today focus on their ability to mobilize the already committed, the importance of performance for voting declines in importance relative to ideology and political identity. It was telling that in 2004 John Kerry frequently was criticized for not having a plan to end the war in Iraq that was appreciably different from President Bush's. This seems like a new requirement. In 1952 did Dwight Eisenhower have a specific plan to end the war in Korea that differed from President Truman's? "I will go to Korea" is not exactly a plan. In 1968 did Richard Nixon have a specific plan to end the war in Vietnam that differed from President Johnson's? A "secret plan" to end the war is not exactly a precise blueprint that voters could compare to the Johnson policy. Some decades ago voters apparently felt that an unpopular war was sufficient reason to punish an incumbent, regardless of whether the challenger offered a persuasive "exit strategy."

A final consideration relates to the preceding ones. Because today's parties are composed relatively more of issue activists than of broad demographic groupings, they are not as deeply rooted in the mass of the population as was the case for much of our history. The United States pioneered the mass party, but, as Steven Schier has argued, in recent decades the parties have practiced a kind of exclusive politics. The mass-mobilization campaigns that historically characterized American elections gave way to the high-tech media campaigns of the late twentieth century. Voter mobilization by the political parties correspondingly fell. Late-century campaigns increasingly relied on television commercials, and there is some evidence that such ads demobilize the electorate. In a kind of "back to the future" development, the two most recent presidential elections have seen renewed party effort to get out the vote, with a significant impact, at least in 2004. But modern computing capabilities and rich databases enable the parties to practice a kind of targeted mobilization based on specific issues that was more difficult to do in earlier periods. It is not clear that such activities make the parties more like those of yesteryear, or whether they only reinforce the trends I have previously discussed. One-third of the voting age population continues to eschew a party identification, a figure that has not appreciably changed in three decades.

Discussion

In sum, the parties today are far closer to the responsible party model than those of the 1970s, a development that some of us wished for some decades ago, but it would be difficult to argue that today's party system is more effective at solving problems than the disorganized decentralized party system that it replaced. Rather than seek power on the basis of coherent programs, the parties at times throw fundamental principles to the wind when electoral considerations dictate, just as the decentralized parties of the mid-twentieth century did. At other times they hold fast to divisive positions that have only symbolic importance—President Bush reiterated his support for a constitutional amendment to ban gay marriage in his 2005 State of the Union address—for fear of alienating ideologically committed base elements. On issues like Social Security and the war in Iraq, facts are distorted and subordinated to ideology. Mandates for major policy changes are claimed on the basis of narrow electoral victories.

To be sure, I have painted with a broad brush, and my interpretations of recent political history may prove as partial and inaccurate as some of those advanced in DOCR. In particular, I am sensitive to the possibility that unified Democratic government under present conditions might be significantly different from the unified Republican government we have experienced—Nils Gilman argues that the features of responsible parties discussed above are really Republican features. But even if true, this implies that an earlier generation of political scientists failed to appreciate that Republican and Democratic responsible party government would be significantly different, let alone identify the empirical bases for such differences. What this reconsideration has demonstrated to me is the difficulty of making broad recommendations to improve American politics, even when seemingly solid research and argument underlie many of the component parts, which is the reason I will venture no such recommendations here. It is possible that this paper is as much a product of its temporal context as DOCR was. As Aldrich argues, the political parties periodically reinvent themselves better to deal with the problems they face. That, in fact, is my hope—that the next reinvention of the parties results in organizations that are better than the current models at dealing with the problems our society faces.

Chapter 13

Interest Groups

13-1

The Scope and Bias of the Pressure System

E. E. Schattschneider

In the mid twentieth century, many observers believed that James Madison's vision of America—as a multitude of groups or factions, none of which dominated the government—had been realized. E. E. Schattschneider provided an alternative view. In the following essay, which was originally published in 1960, Schattschneider argued that moneyed interests dominated mid-twentieth-century politics. In his view the dominance of moneyed interests limited the scope of government action and created a bias in the pressures placed on policymakers. Early in the twenty-first century, the issues raised by Schattschneider remain relevant to debates over the influence of organized and moneyed interests in American government and politics.

THE SCOPE OF CONFLICT is an aspect of the scale of political organization and the extent of political competition. The size of the constituencies being mobilized, the inclusiveness or exclusiveness of the conflicts people expect to develop leave a bearing on all theories about how politics is or should be organized. In other words, nearly all theories about politics have something to do with the question of who can get into the fight and who is to be excluded. . . .

Source: E. E. Schattschneider, "The Scope and Bias of the Pressure System," in *The Semi-Sovereign People* (New York: Holt, Rinehart, Winston, 1960), 20–45. Some notes appearing in the original have been deleted.

If we are able . . . to distinguish between public and private interests and between organized and unorganized groups we have marked out the major boundaries of the subject; *we have given the subject shape and scope.* . . . [W]e can now appropriate the piece we want and leave the rest to someone else. For a multitude of reasons *the most likely field of study is that of the organized, special-interest groups.* The advantage of concentrating on organized groups is that they are known, identifiable, and recognizable. The advantage of concentrating on special-interest groups is that they have one important characteristic in common; they are all exclusive. This piece of the pie (the organized special-interest groups) we shall call the *pressure system.* The pressure system has boundaries we can define; we can fix its scope and make an attempt to estimate its bias.

It may be assumed at the outset that all organized special-interest groups have some kind of impact on politics. A sample survey of organizations made by the Trade Associations Division of the United States Department of Commerce in 1942 concluded that "From 70 to 100 percent (of these associations) are planning activities in the field of government relations, trade promotion, trade practices, public relations, annual conventions, cooperation with other organizations, and information services."

The subject of our analysis can be reduced to manageable proportions and brought under control if we restrict ourselves to the groups whose interests in politics are sufficient to have led them to unite in formal organizations having memberships, bylaws, and officers. A further advantage of this kind of definition is, we may assume, that the organized special-interest groups are the most self-conscious, best developed, most intense and active groups. Whatever claims can be made for a group theory of politics ought to be sustained by the evidence concerning these groups, if the claims have any validity at all.

The organized groups listed in the various directories (such as *National Associations of the United States,* published at intervals by the United States Department of Commerce) and specialty yearbooks, registers, etc., and the *Lobby Index,* published by the United States House of Representatives, probably include the bulk of the organizations in the pressure system. All compilations are incomplete, but these are extensive enough to provide us with some basis for estimating the scope of the system.

By the time a group has developed the kind of interest that leads it to organize, it may be assumed that it has also developed some kind of political bias because *organization is itself a mobilization of bias in preparation for action.* Since these groups can be identified and since they have memberships (i.e., they include and exclude people), it is possible to think of the *scope* of the system.

When lists of these organizations are examined, the fact that strikes the student most forcibly is that *the system is very small.* The range of organized, identifiable, known groups is amazingly narrow; there is nothing remotely universal about it. There is a tendency on the part of the publishers of directories of associations to place an undue emphasis on business organizations, an emphasis that is almost inevitable because the business community is by a wide margin the most highly organized segment of society. Publishers doubtless tend also to reflect public demand for information. Nevertheless, the dominance of business groups in the pressure system is so marked that it probably cannot be explained away as an accident of the publishing industry.

The business character of the pressure system is shown by almost every list available. *National Associations of the United States* lists 1,860 business associations out of a total of 4,000 in the volume, though it refers without listing to 16,000 organizations of businessmen. One cannot be certain what the total content of the unknown associational universe may be, but, taken with the evidence found in other compilations, it is obvious that business is remarkably well represented. Some evidence of the overall scope of the system is to be seen in the estimate that 15,000 national trade associations have a gross membership of about one million business firms. The data are incomplete, but even if we do not have a detailed map this is the shore dimly seen.

Much more directly related to pressure politics is the *Lobby Index, 1946–1949* (an index of organizations and individuals registering or filing quarterly reports under the Federal Lobbying Act), published as a report of the House Select Committee on Lobbying Activities. In this compilation, 825 out of a total of 1,247 entries (exclusive of individuals and Indian tribes) represented business. A selected list of the most important of the groups listed in the *Index* (the groups spending the largest sums of money on lobbying) published in the *Congressional Quarterly Log* shows 149 business organizations in a total of 265 listed.

The business or upper-class bias of the pressure system shows up everywhere. Businessmen are four or five times as likely to write to their congressmen as manual laborers are. College graduates are far more apt to write to their congressmen than people in the lowest educational category are.

The limited scope of the business pressure system is indicated by all available statistics. Among business organizations, the National Association of Manufacturers (with about 20,000 corporate members) and the Chamber of Commerce of the United States (about as large as the N.A.M.) are giants. Usually business associations are much smaller. Of 421 trade associations in the metal-products industry listed in *National Associations of the United States,* 153 have a membership of less than 20. The median membership was somewhere between 24 and 50. Approximately the same scale of memberships is to be found in the lumber, furniture, and paper industries, where 37.3 percent of the associations listed had a membership of less than 20 and the median membership was in the 25 to 50 range.

The statistics in these cases are representative of nearly all other classifications of industry.

Data drawn from other sources support this thesis. Broadly, the pressure system has an upper-class bias. There is overwhelming evidence that participation in voluntary organizations is related to upper social and economic status; the rate of participation is much higher in the upper strata than it is elsewhere. The general proposition is well stated by [political scientist Paul] Lazarsfeld:

> People on the lower SES levels are less likely to belong to any organizations than the people on high SES (Social and Economic Status) levels. (On an A and B level, we find 72 percent of these respondents who belong to one or more organizations. The proportion of respondents who are members of formal organizations decreases steadily as SES level descends until, on the D level only 35 percent of the respondents belong to any associations).[1]

The bias of the system is shown by the fact that *even non-business organizations reflect an upper-class tendency.*

Lazarsfeld's generalization seems to apply equally well to urban and rural populations. The obverse side of the coin is that large areas of the population appear to be wholly outside the system of private organization. A study made by Ira Reid of a Philadelphia area showed that in a sample of 963 persons, 85 percent belonged to no civic or charitable organization and 74 percent belonged to no occupational, business, or professional associations, while another Philadelphia study of 1,154 women showed that 55 percent belonged to no associations of any kind.[2]

A *Fortune* farm poll taken some years ago found that 70.5 percent of farmers belonged to no agricultural organizations. A similar conclusion was reached by two Gallup polls showing that perhaps no more than one third of the farmers of the country belonged to farm organizations, while another *Fortune* poll showed that 86.8 percent of the low-income farmers belonged to no farm organizations. All available data support the generalization that the farmers who do not participate in rural organizations are largely the poorer ones. . . .

The class bias of associational activity gives meaning to the limited scope of the pressure system, because *scope and bias are aspects of the same tendency.* The data raise a serious question about the validity of the proposition that special-interest groups are a universal form of political organization reflecting *all* interests. As a matter of fact, to suppose that everyone participates in pressure-group activity and that all interests get themselves organized in the pressure system is to destroy the meaning of this form of politics. The pressure system makes sense only as the political instrument of a segment of the community. It gets results by being selective and biased; *if everybody got into the act, the unique advantages of this form of organization would be destroyed, for it is possible that if all interests could be mobilized the result would be a stalemate.*

Special-interest organizations are most easily formed when they deal with small numbers of individuals who are acutely aware of their exclusive interests. To describe the conditions of pressure-group organization in this way is, however, to say that it is primarily a business phenomenon. Aside from a few very large organizations (the churches, organized labor, farm organizations, and veterans' organizations) the residue is a small segment of the population. *Pressure politics is essentially the politics of small groups.*

The vice of the groupist theory is that it conceals the most significant aspects of the system. The flaw in the pluralist heaven is that the heavenly chorus sings with a strong upper-class accent. Probably about 90 percent of the people cannot get into the pressure system.

The notion that the pressure system is automatically representative of the whole community is a myth fostered by the universalizing tendency of modern group theories. *Pressure politics is a selective process* ill designed to serve diffuse interests. The system is skewed, loaded, and unbalanced in favor of a fraction of a minority.

On the other hand, pressure tactics are not remarkably successful in mobilizing general interests. When pressure-group organizations attempt to represent the interests of large numbers of people, they are usually able to reach only a small segment of their constituencies. Only a chemical trace of the fifteen million Negroes in the United States belong to the National Association for the Advancement of Colored People. Only one five-hundredth of 1 percent of American women belong to the League of Women Voters, only one sixteen-hundredth of 1 percent of the consumers belong to the National Consumers' League, and only 6 percent of American automobile drivers belong to the American Automobile Association, while about 15 percent of the veterans belong to the American Legion.

The competing claims of pressure groups and political parties for the loyalty of the American public revolve about the difference between the results likely to be achieved by small-scale and large-scale political organization. Inevitably, the outcome of pressure politics and party politics will be vastly different. . . .

. . . Everything we know about politics suggests that a conflict is likely to change profoundly as it becomes political. It is a rare individual who can confront his antagonists without changing his opinions to some degree. Everything changes once a conflict gets into the political arena—*who* is involved, *what* the conflict is about, the resources available, etc. It is extremely difficult to predict the outcome of a fight by watching its beginning because we do not even know who else is going to get into the conflict. The logical consequence of the exclusive emphasis on the determinism of the private origins of conflict is to assign zero value to the political process.

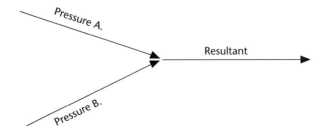

The very expression "pressure politics" invites us to misconceive the role of special-interest groups in politics. The word "pressure" implies the use of some kind of force, a form of intimidation, something other than reason and information, to induce public authorities to act against their own best judgment. [This is reflected in the famous statement by political scientist Earl Latham, in his 1952 book *The Group Basis of Politics,* that] the legislature is a "referee" who "ratifies" and "records" the "balance of power" among the contending groups.[3]

It is hard to imagine a more effective way of saying that Congress has no mind or force of its own or that Congress is unable to invoke new forces that might alter the equation.

Actually the outcome of political conflict is not like the "resultant" of opposing forces in physics. To assume that the forces in a political situation could be diagramed as a physicist might diagram the resultant of opposing physical forces is to wipe the slate clean of all remote, general, and public considerations for the protection of which civil societies have been instituted.

Moreover, the notion of "pressure" distorts the image of the power relations involved. *Private conflicts are taken into the public arena precisely because someone wants to make certain that the power ratio among the private interests most immediately involved shall not prevail.* To treat a conflict as a mere test of the strength of the private interests is to leave out the most significant factors. This is so true that it might indeed be said that the only way to preserve private power ratios is to keep conflicts out of the public arena.

The assumption that it is only the "interested" who count ought to be re-examined in view of the foregoing discussion. The tendency of the literature of pressure politics has been to neglect the low-tension force of large numbers because it *assumes that the equation of forces is fixed at the outset.*

Given the assumptions made by the group theorists, the attack on the idea of the majority is completely logical. The assumption is that conflict is monopolized narrowly by the parties immediately concerned. There is no room for a majority when conflict is defined so narrowly. It is a great deficiency of the group theory that it has found no place in the political system for the majority. The force of the majority is of an entirely different order of magnitude, something not to be measured by pressure-group standards.

Instead of attempting to exterminate all political forms, organizations, and alignments that do not qualify as pressure groups, would it not be better to attempt to make a synthesis, covering the whole political system and finding a place for all kinds of political life?

One possible synthesis of pressure politics and party politics might be produced by *describing politics as the socialization of conflict*. That is to say, the political process is a sequence: conflicts are initiated by highly motivated, high-tension groups so directly and immediately involved that it is difficult for them to see the justice of competing claims. As long as the conflicts of these groups remain *private* (carried on in terms of economic competition, reciprocal denial of goods and services, private negotiations and bargaining, struggles for corporate control or competition for membership), no political process is initiated. Conflicts become political only when an attempt is made to involve the wider public. Pressure politics might be described as a stage in the socialization of conflict. This analysis makes pressure politics an integral part of all politics, including party politics.

One of the characteristic points of origin of pressure politics is a breakdown of the discipline of the business community. The flight to government is perpetual. Something like this is likely to happen wherever there is a point of contact between competing power systems. It is the *losers in intrabusiness conflict who seek redress from public authority. The dominant business interests resist appeals to the government.* The role of the government as the patron of the defeated private interest sheds light on its function as the critic of private power relations.

Since the contestants in private conflicts are apt to be unequal in strength, it follows that *the most powerful special interests want private settlements* because they are able to dictate the outcome as long as the conflict remains private. If A is a hundred times as strong as B he does not welcome the intervention of a third party because he expects to impose his own terms on B; he wants to isolate B. He is especially opposed to the intervention of public authority, because public authority represents the most overwhelming form of outside intervention. Thus, if $A/B = 100/1$, it is obviously not to A's advantage to involve a third party a million times as strong as A and B combined. Therefore, it is the weak, not the strong, who appeal to public authority for relief. It is the weak who want to socialize conflict, i.e., to involve more and more people in the conflict until the balance of forces is changed. In the schoolyard it is not the bully but the defenseless smaller boys who "tell the teacher." When the teacher intervenes, the balance of power in the schoolyard is apt to change drastically. It is the function of public authority to *modify private power relations by enlarging the scope of conflict.* Nothing could be more mistaken than to suppose that public authority merely registers the dominance of the strong over the weak. The mere existence of public order has already ruled out a great variety of forms of private pressure. Nothing could be more confusing than to suppose that the refugees from the business community who come to Congress for relief and protection *force* Congress to do their bidding.

Evidence of the truth of this analysis may be seen in the fact that the big private interests do not necessarily win if they are involved in public conflicts with petty interests. The image of the lobbyists as primarily the agents of big business is not easy to support on the face of the record of congressional hearings, for example. The biggest corporations in the country tend to avoid the arena in which pressure groups and lobbyists fight it out before congressional committees. To describe this process exclusively in terms of an effort of business to intimidate congressmen is to misconceive what is actually going on.

It is probably a mistake to assume that pressure politics is the typical or even the most important relation between government and business. The pressure group is by no means the perfect instrument of the business community. What does big business want? The *winners* in intrabusiness strife want (1) to be let alone (they want autonomy) and (2) to preserve the solidarity of the business community. For these purposes pressure politics is not a wholly satisfactory device. The most elementary considerations of strategy call for the business community to develop some kind of common policy more broadly based than any special-interest group is likely to be.

The political influence of business depends on the kind of solidarity that, on the one hand, leads all business to rally to the support of *any* businessman in trouble with the government and, on the other hand, keeps internal business disputes out of the public arena. In this system businessmen resist the impulse to attack each other in public and discourage the efforts of individual members of the business community to take intrabusiness conflicts into politics.

The attempt to mobilize a united front of the whole business community does not resemble the classical concept of pressure politics. The logic of business politics is to keep peace within the business community by supporting as far as possible all claims that business groups make for themselves. The tendency is to support all businessmen who have conflicts with the government and support all businessmen in conflict with labor. In this way *special-interest politics can be converted into party policy.* The search is for a broad base of political mobilization grounded on the strategic need for political organization on a wider scale than is possible in the case of the historical pressure group. Once the business community begins to think in terms of a larger scale of political organization the Republican party looms large in business politics.

It is a great achievement of American democracy that business has been forced to form a political organization designed to win elections, i.e., has been forced to compete for power in the widest arena in the political system. On the other hand, *the power of the Republican party to make terms with business rests on the fact that business cannot afford to be isolated.*

The Republican party has played a major role in *the political organization of the business community,* a far greater role than many students of politics seem to have realized. The influence of business in the Republican party is great, but it is never absolute because business is remarkably dependent on the party. The business community is too small, it arouses too much antagonism, and its aims are too narrow to win the support of a popular majority. The political education of business is a function of the Republican party that can never be done so well by anyone else.

In the management of the political relations of the business community, the Republican party is much more important than any combination of pressure groups ever could be. The success of special interests in Congress is due less to the "pressure" exerted by these groups than it is due to the fact that Republican members of Congress are committed in advance to a general probusiness attitude. The notion that business groups coerce Republican congressmen into voting for their bills underestimates the whole Republican posture in American politics.

It is not easy to manage the political interests of the business community because there is a perpetual stream of losers in intrabusiness conflicts who go to the government for relief and protection. It has not been possible therefore to maintain perfect solidarity, and when solidarity is breached the government is involved almost automatically. The fact that business has not become hopelessly divided and that it has retained great influence in American politics has been due chiefly to the overall mediating role played by the Republican party. There has never been a pressure group or a combination of pressure groups capable of performing this function.

NOTES

1. Paul F. Lazarsfeld, Bernard Berelson, and Hazel Gaudet. *The People's Choice* (New York: Columbia University Press, 1948), p. 145.

2. Ira Reid and Emily Ehle, "Leadership Selection in the Urban Locality Areas," *Public Opinion Quarterly* (1950), 14:262–284. See also Norman Powell, *Anatomy of Public Opinion* (New York: Prentice Hall, 1951), pp. 180–181.

3. Earl Latham, *The Group Basis of Politics* (Ithaca: Cornell University Press, 1952), pp. 35–36.

13-2

The Evolution of Interest Groups

John R. Wright

In the following essay John R. Wright provides an overview of the development of interest groups in America. Interest groups form, Wright explains, as a net result of two factors—societal disturbances and collective action problems. Societal disturbances create common interests for groups of individuals, who then join forces to pursue those interests. All groups then face the collective action problem known as free riding—the tendency for group members to benefit from others' contributions to the provision of a public good without contributing themselves. Interest groups must find a way to encourage people to join and contribute in order to achieve their political goals.

THE RAPID ECONOMIC and social development in the United States immediately following the Civil War created a new and uncertain political environment for members of Congress. Congress emerged as the dominant force in national policy making, and members' electoral constituencies became far more heterogeneous and complex than ever before. In this new and uncertain political environment, the informational needs of members of Congress were greater than at any previous time, and it was in this environment that the American interest group system evolved.

Although the evolution of interest groups in the United States did not begin in earnest until after the Civil War, the groundwork for their development was laid much earlier in several key provisions of the U.S. Constitution. These constitutional provisions have had a profound effect on the American political party system, which in turn has had a major impact on the interest group system.

Constitutional Underpinnings

The place of special interests in American politics today is largely a consequence of two competing political values expressed in the U.S. Constitution: a concern for liberty and freedom of political expression on the one hand, and the desire to

Source: John R. Wright, "The Evolution of Interest Groups," in *Interest Groups and Congress*, John R. Wright (Boston: Allyn & Bacon, 1996), 11–22. Some notes appearing in the original have been deleted.

prevent tyranny on the other. James Madison's *Federalist* No. 10 is the classic justification for the various constitutional checks and balances, which disperse power and make it difficult for any single group of citizens to control the entire government. Madison, whose thinking was strongly influenced by the English philosopher David Hume, believed that it is natural for people to differ, and in differing, to form into factions, or parties. The problem with factions, according to Madison and his contemporaries Jefferson and Hamilton, is their potential for subverting government and the public good. Factions, in Madison's words, are mischievous.

Madison's primary concern in *Federalist* No. 10 was with *majority* factions—typically, but not exclusively, political parties as we know them today—not minority factions such as contemporary interest groups. Although he recognized that minority factions could lead to disorder and conflict, Madison believed that it is the possibility of tyranny by the majority that poses the greatest threat to individual liberties. Madison did not recommend that factions be forbidden or repressed, a practice that would conflict with the fundamental values of liberty and freedom of expression, but instead that their negative tendencies be held in check and controlled through explicit constitutional safeguards.

Formal mechanisms in the U.S. Constitution for controlling majority factions include the requirements that the president be elected separately from members of Congress and that members of Congress reside in the states from which they are elected. These provisions disperse power horizontally—across national institutions of government—and vertically—from national to local political jurisdictions. Separation of the executive and legislative branches eased fears among the smaller states in 1787 that large states, which presumably would control the Congress, would also control the presidency; and geographic representation ensured that control over elected representatives would rest with local rather than national interests, thereby lessening the influence of the national government over state decisions.

These basic constitutional provisions have had a profound effect on the abilities of modern political parties to control and manage American government. Historically, control of the government has frequently been divided between the two major political parties, neither of which has been capable of exerting much discipline over its members. A single party has controlled the presidency and a majority in the U.S. House and Senate in just 43 of the 70 Congresses—61 percent—that have convened from 1855 to 1993. Even in times of single-party control of the government, voting defections within both major parties have been common. Since World War II, a majority of Democrats has voted against a majority of Republicans only 44 percent of the time on average in the U.S. House of Representatives and only 45 percent of the time on average in the U.S. Senate.

American legislators have little incentive to toe the party line for the simple reason that a cohesive majority is not required to maintain control of the government or to preclude calling new elections, as is the case in parliamentary regimes. In the absence of party discipline, American legislators look to their geographic constituencies rather than to their parties for voting cues.

Madison and his contemporaries succeeded brilliantly in designing a constitutional system to attenuate the power of majority factions, but in doing so, they also created unanticipated opportunities for minority factions to be influential. When political parties are unable to take clear responsibility for governing, and when they cannot maintain cohesion and discipline among those elected under their labels, special interests have opportunities to gain access to the key points of decision within the government. David Truman explains that when a single party succeeds regularly in electing both an executive and a majority in the legislature, channels of access "will be predominantly those within the party leadership, and the pattern will be relatively stable and orderly."[1] He notes, however, that when "the party is merely an abstract term referring to an aggregation of relatively independent factions," as in the case of the United States, then the channels of access "will be numerous, and the patterns of influence within the legislature will be diverse, constantly shifting, and more openly in conflict."[2]

One important consequence of this "diffusion of access" is that legislators will be much more accessible to interests within their local constituencies, especially *organized* interests. Simply put, interest groups will thrive in an environment in which legislators take their behavioral cues from heterogeneous constituencies rather than from cohesive political parties. E. E. Schattschneider has summed up the situation succinctly:

> If the parties exercised the power to govern effectively, *they would shut out the pressure groups.* The fact that American parties govern only spasmodically and fitfully amid a multitude of lapses of control provides the opportunity for the cheap and easy use of pressure tactics.[3]

Although the constitution makes no specific mention of interest groups, or even political parties for that matter, it has influenced the evolution of both. The weakness of the political parties in their ability to control and manage the government is an intended consequence of the efforts by the founding fathers to inhibit majority factions; the prevalence of special interests, however, is an unintended consequence of weak parties. The U.S. Constitution indirectly laid the groundwork for a strong interest group system, but that system, unlike the political party system, did not evolve right away. It took nearly 70 years from the development of the first party system in 1800 until groups began to form and proliferate at a significant rate.

Table 1. Selected Organizations and Their Founding Dates

American Medical Association	1847
National Grange	1867
National Rifle Association	1871
American Bankers Association	1875
American Federation of Labor	1886
Sierra Club	1892
National Association of Manufacturers	1895
National Audubon Society	1905
National Association for the Advancement of Colored People	1909
U.S. Chamber of Commerce	1912
American Jewish Congress	1918
American Farm Bureau Federation	1919
National League of Cities	1924

The Formation and Maintenance of Interest Groups

Although trade unions and associations have historical roots dating to the beginning of the republic, interest groups of regional or national scope as we know them today did not develop significantly until after the Civil War, and even then, pronounced growth did not really begin to take place until the late 1800s. Table 1 lists a few of the early organizations and their founding dates.

In what is known as the "disturbance theory" of interest group formation, David Truman argued that organizations will form when the interests common to unorganized groups of individuals are disturbed by economic, social, political, or technological change.[4] As society becomes increasingly complex and interconnected, Truman argued that individuals have greater difficulty resolving their differences and grievances on their own and instead must seek intervention from the government. It is at this time that political organizations will begin to take shape. Once interest groups begin to form, they will then tend to form in "wavelike" fashion, according to Truman, because policies designed to address one group's needs typically disturb the interests of other unorganized citizens, who then form groups to seek governmental intervention to protect and advance their particular interests.

The period from 1870 to 1900 was rife with disturbances favorable to the formation of interest groups in the United States. The economic, social, and political upheaval following the Civil War destabilized relationships within and between numerous groups of individuals. The completion of the railroads and the introduction of the telegraph dramatically altered communication and transportation patterns; immigration and population growth gave rise to new economic and social relationships; and commercial and territorial expansion in the West, combined with the task of maintaining order and rebuilding the infrastructure in the South, increased demands for routine services such as post offices, law enforcement, internal improvements, customs agents, and so forth. The process of industrialization created further economic and political tensions and uncertainties. The period 1870 to 1900 witnessed three economic depressions: a major one from 1873 to 1879, a minor one in the mid-1880s, and the collapse of 1893. Overall, the period from 1870 to 1900 was one when conditions were finally right for the widespread growth of organized interests in the United States.

Margaret Susan Thompson points out that in addition to the unprecedented economic and social upheaval at the end of the Civil War, political conditions in the 1870s were also favorable to the formation of groups and, in particular, the lobbying of Congress.[5] Two factors—the ascendancy of congressional power associated with the impeachment proceedings against Andrew Johnson and the growing heterogeneity of congressional constituencies—were instrumental in the growth of congressional lobbying and interest group activity. Congress, by enacting a comprehensive program on reconstruction in 1865 over the determined opposition of the president, established political preeminence over federal policy making and, as a consequence, became the focal institution for receiving and processing the conflicting demands of many newly recognized interests. Then, as congressional constituencies diversified economically and socially, the presence of multiple and competing interests began to force legislators to develop "representational priorities."[6] Thompson notes that legislators at this time had to determine which were their "meaningful" constituencies, and organization was the critical means by which interests achieved such designation. Thompson refers to the nascent organization of interests during the 1870s as "clienteles" rather than interest groups, for even though numerous subgroups of the population began making significant demands on the government during the 1870s, there was not a great deal of formal organization then as we know it today. Still, even these nascent groups began to provide important information to members of Congress about the interests and priorities of their constituents.

One example of how interest groups formed in response to economic and political disturbances during the post–Civil War period is provided by the organization of postal workers. Even before the Civil War, the volume of mail had grown tremendously in response to the development of railroads and the resulting decrease in the costs of postage. But in 1863, another significant increase in the volume of mail occurred when Congress lowered the long-distance postage rates. This created additional strains for letter carriers and postal clerks who already were greatly overworked. Then, in 1868, the Post Office Department refused to apply the "eight-hour" law—a law enacted that same year by Congress stipulating that eight hours constituted a day's work for laborers, workmen, and mechanics—to letter carriers on the grounds that they were government employees, not laborers, workmen, or mechanics. Finally, implementation of civil service following passage of the Pendleton Act in 1883 eliminated what little political clout the letter carriers had enjoyed. Once the patronage system was eliminated, politicians lost interest in the letter carriers and no longer intervened on their behalf.

In response to these deteriorating circumstances, the letter carriers organized into the National Association of Letter Carriers in 1889. Once organized, the letter carriers had a significant advantage over the unorganized postal clerks in the competition for wages. At the time, wages for all postal workers, letter carriers and clerks alike, were provided through a single congressional appropriation to the Post Office Department, and the letter carriers used their organizational clout to claim a disproportionate share of the annual appropriation. Thus, the postal workers came under pressure to organize as well, and so in predictable "wavelike" fashion, the National Association of Post Office Clerks was established in 1894.

Changing economic, social, and political conditions are necessary but not sufficient circumstances for the formation and development of organized interests. Even when environmental conditions are favorable to the formation of groups, there is still a natural proclivity for individuals *not* to join political interest groups. The reason is that individuals do not always have to belong to political groups in order to enjoy the benefits they provide. Wheat farmers, for example, benefit from the price supports that Congress establishes for wheat even though they do not belong to the National Association of Wheat Growers (NAWG), which lobbies for price supports. Similarly, individuals do not have to belong to environmental groups in order to reap the benefits of a cleaner environment brought about by the lobbying efforts of groups such as the Sierra Club and the National Wildlife Federation. More generally, the lobbying benefits provided by groups such as the wheat growers and the environmentalists are consumed *jointly* by all citizens affected; that is, Congress does not guarantee a higher price for wheat only to farmers who have paid dues to the National Association of Wheat Growers, and it does not and cannot restrict the benefit of a clean environment only to individuals who have paid their dues to environmental groups.

Unlike lobbying benefits, which are available even to those who do not contribute to lobbying efforts, the costs of lobbying are borne only by those who actually pay their dues to political groups or otherwise participate in lobbying activities. This creates a major organizational problem, for when it is possible to get something for nothing, many individuals will rationally choose to free ride on the efforts of others. When there are thousands of wheat farmers, for example, and the annual dues to the National Association of Wheat Growers are $100 or less, individual wheat farmers might very well conclude that their single contributions are not very important, that the NAWG will manage quite nicely without their money because there are so many other wheat farmers paying dues, and that there are much better uses for the $100 in light of the fact that the government will still provide price supports for their crop. The problem for the NAWG is that if every wheat farmer reasoned this way there would be no national association, and thus probably no price supports for wheat.

Given the natural proclivity for individuals to be free riders, all organizations must provide incentives of one sort or another to induce individuals to pay dues and otherwise contribute to the collective efforts of the organization. Generally speaking, individuals do not join interest groups because of benefits that can be consumed jointly; they join because of benefits that can by enjoyed *selectively* only by those individuals who pay dues to political groups. There are three main types of selective benefits. A selective *material* benefit includes such things as insurance and travel discounts and subscriptions to professional journals and other specialized information. A second type of selective benefit is what Peter Clark and James Q. Wilson have labelled *solidary* incentives. These, too, derive only from group membership and involve benefits such as "socializing, congeniality, the sense of group membership and identification, the status resulting from membership, fun and conviviality, the maintenance of social distinctions, and so on."[7] The third basic type of selective benefit is an *expressive* incentive. Expressive incentives are those that individuals attach to the act of expressing ideological or moral values such as free speech, civil rights, economic justice, or political equality. Individuals obtain these benefits when they pay dues or contribute money or time to an organization that espouses these values. What is important in receiving these benefits is the feeling of satisfaction that results from expressing political values, not necessarily the actual achievement of the values themselves.

Most organizations provide a mix of these various benefits, although different kinds of organizations typically rely more heavily on one type of benefit than another. Professional and trade associations, for example, are more likely to offer selective material benefits than purposive benefits, whereas environmental groups and other organizations claiming to lobby for the public interest rely more heavily on expressive benefits. Expressive benefits are also common in organizations relying heavily on mass mailings to attract and maintain members. Many direct mail approaches use negatively worded messages to instill feelings of guilt and fear in individuals, with the hope that people will contribute money to a cause as a means of expressing their support for certain values or else assuaging their guilt and fear.

That individuals are not drawn naturally to interest groups and must instead be enticed to join makes it very difficult for groups to get started. Organizations often need outside support in the form of a patron—perhaps a wealthy individual, a nonprofit foundation, or a government agency—to get over the initial hurdle of organizing collective action. In one of the leading studies on the origins and maintenance of interest groups, Jack Walker discovered that 89 percent of all citizen groups and 60 percent of all nonprofit occupational groups (e.g., the National Association of State Alcohol and Drug Abuse Directors) received financial assistance from an outside source at the time of their founding.[8] Many of these organizations continued to draw heavily from outside sources of support to maintain themselves once they were launched. Walker concluded that "the number of interest groups in operation, the mixture of group types, and the level and direction of political mobilization in the United States at any point in the country's history will be determined by the composition and accessibility of the system's major patrons of political action."[9]

In summary, the proficiency that contemporary interest groups have achieved in attracting and maintaining members has evolved from a combination of factors. Most fundamental to their evolution has been a constitutional arrangement that has not only encouraged their participation but also created unanticipated opportunities for them to exert influence. Changing economic, social, and political circumstances have also played critical roles at various times throughout American history. However, even under conditions favorable to their development, the formation and maintenance of interest groups requires leadership and creative approaches for dealing with the natural inertia that individuals exhibit toward collective activities. The number of groups continues to grow each year, however, as does the diversity of the issues and viewpoints they represent.

NOTES

1. David B. Truman, *The Governmental Process: Political Interests and Public Opinion* (New York: Knopf, 1951), p. 325.

2. Ibid., p. 325.

3. E. E. Schattschneider, *Party Government* (New York: Holt, Rinehart and Winston, 1941), p. 192.

4. David B. Truman, *The Governmental Process,* Chapters 3 and 4.

5. Margaret Susan Thompson, *The Spider Web: Congress and Lobbying in the Age of Grant* (Ithaca, N.Y.: Cornell University Press, 1985).

6. Thompson, *The Spider Web,* pp. 130–131.

7. Peter B. Clark and James Q. Wilson, "Incentive Systems: A Theory of Organizations," *Administrative Science Quarterly* 6 (1961): 134–135.

8. Jack L. Walker, "The Origins and Maintenance of Interest Groups in America," *American Political Science Review* 77 (1983): 390–406.

9. Ibid., p. 406.

13-3

Buying Time: Moneyed Interests and the Mobilization of Bias in Congressional Committees

Richard L. Hall and Frank W. Wayman

Lobbyists often are thought to be in the business of influencing legislators' votes by offering campaign contributions. Richard Hall and Frank Wayman argue that lobbying is more likely to influence legislators' participation, particularly in the committee setting, than their voting behavior.

AT LEAST SINCE Madison railed about the mischiefs of faction, critics of U.S. political institutions have worried about the influence of organized interests in national policy making. In this century, one of the most eloquent critics of the interest group system was E. E. Schattschneider, who warned of the inequalities between private, organized, and upper-class groups on the one hand and public, unorganized, and lower-class groups on the other. The pressure system, he argued in *The Semisovereign People,* "mobilized bias" in national policy making in favor of the former, against the interests of the latter, and hence against the interests of U.S. democracy. Such concerns have hardly abated thirty years since the publication of Schattschneider's essay. In particular, the precipitous growth in the number and financial strength of political action committees has refueled the charge that moneyed interests dominate the policy making process. The current Congress is *The Best Congress Money Can Buy* according to one critic, one where *Honest Graft* is an institutional imperative. "The rising tide of special-interest money," one close observer concludes, "is changing the balance of power between voters and donors, between lawmakers' constitutional constituents and their cash constituents."

Despite the claims of the institutional critics and the growing public concern over PACs during the last decade, the scientific evidence that political money matters in legislative decision making is surprisingly weak. Considerable research on members' voting decisions offers little support for the popular view that PAC money permits interests to buy or rent votes on matters that affect them. Based on an examination of 120 PACs in 10 issue areas over four

Source: Richard L. Hall and Frank W. Wayman, "Buying Time: Moneyed Interests and the Mobilization of Bias in Congressional Committees," *American Political Science Review* 84, no. 3 (September 1990): 797–805, 809–815. Notes appearing in the original have been deleted.

congresses, one recent study concludes flatly that PAC contributions do not affect members' voting patterns. Another study, designed to explore the "upper bounds" of PAC influence on House roll calls, emphasizes "the relative inability of PACs to determine congressional voting." . . . Does money matter?

. . . We revisit the question by developing a theoretical account of the constrained exchange between legislator and donor quite different from the one evident in the substantial literature cited above. In particular, we adopt the premise that PACs are rational actors, seeking to maximize their influence on the legislative outcomes that affect their affiliates; but we take issue with the standard account of PAC rationality. Our approach does not lead us to predict a strong causal relationship between PAC money and floor votes. House members and interest group representatives are viewed as parties to an implicit cooperative agreement, but the constraints on member behavior and the rational calculations of group representatives limit the extent to which votes become the currency of exchange. Instead, we advance two hypotheses about the effect of money on congressional decision making.

First, we suggest that in looking for the effects of money in Congress, one must look more to the politics of committee decision making than those of the floor. . . .

Second, and more importantly, our account of the member-donor exchange leads us to focus on the *participation* of particular members, not on their votes. This variable, we believe, is a crucial but largely neglected element of congressional decision making. It is especially important in any analysis of interest group influence in a decentralized Congress. In their famous study of lobbying on foreign trade policy, for instance, Bauer, Pool, and Dexter concluded that a member's principal problem is "not how to vote but what to do with his time, how to allocate his resources, and where to put his energy." . . . If money does not necessarily buy votes or change minds, in other words, it can buy members' time. The intended effect is to mobilize bias in congressional committee decision making.

[We seek to determine whether moneyed interests mobilize bias in committee decision making.] Analyzing data from three House committees on three distinct issues, we find that they do. In the final section we briefly discuss the implications of the findings for our understanding of money, interest groups, and representation in Congress. . . .

The Rational PAC Revised

The literature on PAC contribution strategies and members' roll call voting behavior . . . suggests two puzzles. First, if group strategists are reasonably rational, why would they continue to allocate scarce resources to efforts where the expected political benefits are so low? Second, if PAC allocation strategies are designed to influence members' votes, why do they contribute so heavily to their strongest supporters and occasionally to their strongest opponents? Is it the case that PACs are systematically irrational and, by extension, that claims about the influence of money on legislative process almost certainly exaggerated? We believe that the premise of rationality need not be rejected but that theoretical work in this area requires a more complete account of rational PAC behavior. . . . Simply put, interest group resources are intended to accomplish something different from, and more than, influencing elections or buying votes. Specifically, we argue that PAC money should be allocated in order to *mobilize* legislative support and *demobilize* opposition, particularly at the most important points in the legislative process.

This argument turns directly on what we already know about the nature of legislators' voting decisions from a very rich literature. The simple but important point is that a number of powerful factors exist that predispose a member to vote a certain way, among them party leaders, ideology, constituency, and the position of the administration. Kingdon notes, moreover, that members' votes on particular issues are also constrained by their past voting histories. Members attach some value to consistency, independent of the other factors that influence their voting behavior. A third and related point is that the public, recorded nature of the vote may itself limit the member's discretion: a risk-averse member may fear the appearance of impropriety in supporting major campaign contributors in the absence of some other, legitimate force pushing her in the same direction. Finally, the dichotomous nature of the vote acts as a constraint. Money must not only affect members' attitudes at the margin but do so enough to push them over the threshold between *nay* and *yea*. In short, the limits on member responsiveness to messages wrapped in money are substantial, perhaps overwhelming, at least insofar as floor voting is concerned.

. . . The rational PAC should expect little in the way of marginal benefits in votes bought for dollars spent, especially when individual PAC contributions are limited by the Federal Election Campaign Act to ten thousand dollars—a slight fraction of the cost of the average House race. Individual votes, that is, simply aren't easy to change; and even if some are changed, the utility of the votes purchased depends on their net cumulative effect in turning a potentially losing coalition into a winning one. For the rational PAC manager, the expected marginal utility approximates zero in most every case. All other things being equal, scarce resources should be allocated heavily elsewhere and to other purposes.

How, then, should the strategic PAC distribute its resources? The first principle derives from the larger literature on interest group influence in Congress. Well aware of the decentralized nature of congressional decision making, interest groups recognize that resources allocated at the committee stage are more efficiently spent. Interest group preferences incorporated there have a strong chance of surviving as the bill moves through subsequent stages in the sequence, while provisions not in the committee vehicle are difficult to attach later. Second, the nature of the committee assignment process increases the probability that organized interests will find a sympathetic audience at the committee or subcommittee stage. Members seek and often receive positions that will permit them to promote the interests that, in turn, help them to get reelected. Finally, the less public, often informal nature of committee decision making suggests that members' responsiveness to campaign donors will receive less scrutiny. Indeed, a long tradition of research on subgovernments emphasizes that such clientelism flourishes at the committee stage. In short, groups will strategically allocate their resources with the knowledge that investments in the politics of the appropriate committee or subcommittee are likely to pay higher dividends than investments made elsewhere. Indeed, this principle is especially important in the House, where the sheer size of the chamber's membership, the greater importance of the committee stage, and the frequent restrictions on floor participation recommend a more targeted strategy.

If PACs concentrate at the committee level, what, specifically, do they hope to gain there? Purchasing votes is one possibility; and, in fact, the rationale for allocating campaign money to buy votes in committee is somewhat stronger than for vote-buying on the floor. But even within committee, PACs still tend to give to their strongest supporters. In addition, committee votes, like floor votes, are dichotomous decisions. And despite the lower visibility of committee decision making, the factors of constituency, ideology, party, and administration are almost certainly at work. In fact, . . . there is little evidence that contributions influence voting in committee any more than they do voting on the floor.

The alternative hypothesis that we test here is that political money alters members' patterns of legislative involvement, a point that emerges from an older literature on interest group influence in Congress. Stated somewhat differently, the object of a rational PAC allocation strategy is not simply the *direction* of legislators' preferences but the *vigor* with which those preferences are promoted in the decision making process. Such strategies should take the form of inducing sympathetic members to get actively involved in a variety of activities that directly affect the shape of committee legislation: authoring or blocking a legislative vehicle; negotiating compromises behind the scenes, especially at the staff level; offering friendly amendments or actively opposing unfriendly ones; lobbying colleagues; planning strategy; and last and sometimes least, showing up to vote in favor of the interest group's position. . . .

Several arguments support this view. First, participation is crucial to determining legislative outcomes; and voting is perhaps the least important of the various ways in which committee members participate. Second, while members' voting choices are highly constrained, how they allocate their time, staff, and political capital is much more discretionary. . . . The member's level of involvement is something that a strategic PAC can reasonably expect to affect. The contribution need not weigh so heavily in a member's mind that it changes his or her position in any material way; it need only weigh heavily enough to command some increment of legislative resources. The minimum threshold that must be passed is thus a fairly modest one, and the potential effect of contributions on behavior is one of degree. Specifically, the member will allocate scarce legislative resources on the group's behalf so long as the marginal utility of the contribution to the member exceeds the expected marginal utility of the most valuable remaining use of the member's resources.

A third advantage of this view is that it explains the ostensibly anomalous tendency of PACs to contribute so heavily to members who are almost certain to win reelection and almost certain to support the group's point of view. Such behavior now appears quite rational. It is precisely one's supporters that one wants to mobilize: the more likely certain members are to support the group, the more active it should want them to be. Furthermore, this view of purposive PACs makes sense of the evidence that PACs sometimes contribute to members who will almost certainly oppose them and whose involvement in an issue stands to do the group harm. The PAC may have no hope of changing the opponent's mind, but it may, at the margin at least, diminish the intensity with which the member pursues policies that the organization does not like. The intent of the money, then, is not persuasion but demobilization: "We know you can't support us, but please don't actively oppose us." However, we should not expect the demobilizing effect of money to be nearly so strong as the mobilizing effect. The message provided through contributions to one's supporters is widely perceived as a legitimate one: in asking for help, the group is encouraging members to do precisely what they would do were resources plentiful. In contrast, contributions to opponents are meant to encourage them to go against their predispositions: the implicit message is to "take a walk" on an issue that they may care about. In short, the expected effects are not symmetric; the mobilization hypothesis is on stronger theoretical ground. . . .

The Data: Money and Mobilization on Three Committees

The data for this investigation are drawn from staff interviews and markup records of three House committees on three issues: (1) the Dairy Stabilization

Act, considered by the Agriculture Committee in 1982; (2) the Job Training Partnership Act (JTPA), considered by Education and Labor in 1982; and (3) the Natural Gas Market Policy Act, considered by Energy and Commerce during 1983–84.

Several features of these cases make them particularly appropriate for exploring the effects of money on the participation of committee members. First, all were highly significant pieces of legislation, the stakes of each measuring in the billions of dollars. At issue in the Natural Gas Market Policy Act was the deregulation of natural gas prices, a proposal that would transfer billions of dollars from one region to another, from consumer to industry, and within the industry from interstate pipelines and distributors to the major natural gas producers. Annual spending on the Job Training Partnership Act was expected at the time of its passage to be in the four-to-five-billion-dollar range, and it replaced one of the most important domestic programs of the 1970s. While more narrow than these in scope, the Dairy Stabilization Act also entailed significant economic effects. The principal purpose of the act was to adjust the scheduled support price for milk downward by as much as a dollar per hundredweight over two years, creating budget savings of 4.2 billion dollars for fiscal years 1983–85 and decreasing the profitability of milk production by as much as 30% for the typical dairy farmer. In each case, then, evidence of the influence of PAC money on congressional decision making can hardly be counted narrow or trivial. The deliberations in each case bore in significant ways on major interests, both public and private.

A second feature relevant to this investigation follows from the economic importance attached to these issues. All three were salient among actors other than the private groups immediately affected, a feature that the considerable research on roll call voting suggests should depress the effect of PAC contributions on congressional decision making. . . .

At two levels, then, past research indicates that our selection of cases is biased against our argument. It suggests that high salience issues should exhibit little PAC influence on legislative behavior, yet each of the cases here commanded the attention of a wide range of political actors. Second, past research suggests that we will find little PAC influence in precisely these three policy areas. Should we find support for the hypothesis that money mobilizes support (or demobilizes opposition) at the committee level, we should be on reasonably solid ground to conclude that (1) the results of this exploration are apt to generalize to other committees and other issues and (2) the null results of past research are more likely to be artifacts of the legislative behavior and the legislative stage studied than evidence that moneyed interests do not matter in congressional decision making. . . .

Table 1. PAC Money and Committee Participation: 1982 Dairy Stabilization Act

Independent Variables	Unstandardized 2SLS Coefficient	t-statistic
Intercept	.01	.05
Number of dairy cows in district	.27**	2.21
Dairy PAC contributions to supporters	.26**	2.42
Dairy PAC contributions to opponents	−.11	-.61
Membership on reporting subcommittee	.17**	3.54
Committee or subcommittee leadership position	.35**	4.50
Freshman status	−.02	-.31

Note: Adjusted R-squared = .60; number of observations = 41. All variables are measured on a 0–1 scale. The contributions term is the predicted value from the first-stage equation.
**Statistically significant at .05 level, one-tailed test.

Results and Interpretations

In estimating [a] model of participation, we explicitly account for the possibility that contributions are effectively endogenous, that is, that in allocating contributions to committee members during the previous election cycle, a group may attempt to anticipate who the principal players will be on issues it cares about .... In each of the three cases, the model performs quite well, explaining over 55% of the variance in participation. More importantly, the analysis provides solid support for the principal hypothesis of this study, that moneyed interests mobilize bias in committee decision making.

This finding is clear for all three cases. The campaign contributions that dairy industry PACs gave to their likely supporters significantly increased their participation, even when we controlled for the importance of the issue to individual members' districts, whether they sat on the subcommittee of jurisdiction, and whether they held a leadership position (Table 1). ...

The results of the job training case are also clear, and the specific estimates are striking in their similarity to the dairy stabilization case. As Table 2 shows, the contributions that labor groups made to their supporters had a substantial, statistically significant effect on participation during Education and Labor deliberations. Remarkably, the unstandardized coefficient for the money support variable is almost identical in size to the analogous coefficient in the dairy stabilization model despite the fact that the two cases are drawn from different committees with qualitatively different jurisdictions and policy environments. In each case, a change in the money support variable from its minimum to its maximum value moves a member approximately one-fourth of

Table 2. PAC Money and Committee Participation: 1982 Job Training
Partnership Act

Independent Variables	Unstandardized 2SLS Coefficient	t-statistic
Intercept	.13	.77
CETA expenditures in district	.03	.23
Labor union net contributions to supporters	.25*	1.62
Labor union net contributions to opponents	−.18	−.80
Membership on reporting subcommittee	.19**	2.61
Committee or subcommittee leadership position	.47**	4.55
Freshman status	−.05	−.51

Note: Adjusted R-squared = .56; number of observations = 32. All variables are measured on a 0–1 scale. The net contributions term is the predicted value from the first-stage equation.
*Statistically significant at .10 level, one-tailed test.
**Statistically significant at .05 level, one-tailed test.

the way along the participation scale, almost exactly one standard deviation. In both cases, likewise, this coefficient is greater than that for subcommittee membership, a variable generally considered central to understanding participation in the postreform House. As in the dairy stabilization case, finally, the Education and Labor bill provides some support for the demobilization hypothesis. While it fails to meet conventional levels of statistical significance, the size of the money-opposition term proves negative and substantively significant, nearly matching the size of subcommittee membership.

The results regarding moneyed interests and mobilization are only slightly less compelling in the natural gas case, a case complicated both by divisions within the industry and the apparent importance of both organized and unorganized interests. As we note[d] above, such conditions are likely to mitigate the efficacy of interest group efforts, and they complicate the measurement of anticipated support and opposition. Still, the mobilization hypothesis finds strong support in the behavior of Energy and Commerce members. . . . A change in the money support variable from its minimum to its maximum moves a Commerce Committee member approximately one-sixth of the way along the participation scale. . . .

As Table 3 shows, finally, the demobilization hypothesis is not supported in the natural gas case. While the coefficient on the money opponents interaction is slight, its positive sign is inconsistent with our prediction. The foundation for the demobilization hypothesis being theoretically weaker, however, the null result here, as well as the weak results in the dairy and job training cases,

Table 3. PAC Money and Committee Participation: 1984 Natural Gas
Market Policy Act

Independent Variables	Unstandardized 2SLS Coefficient	t-statistic
Intercept	.08	.40
Natural gas production in district	.32*	1.65
Natural gas price increase effect on district	.17*	1.35
High production/high inflation interaction	−.18	−1.28
Producer-intrastate net contributions to supporters	.17**	1.69
Producer-intrastate net contributions to opponents	.01	.06
Membership reporting subcommittee	.23**	3.17
Committee or subcommittee leadership position	.54**	4.77
Freshman status	.13*	1.31

Note: Adjusted R-squared = .57; number of observations = 42. All variables are measured on a 0–1 scale. The net contributions term is the predicted value from the first stage equation.
*Statistically significant at .10 level, one-tailed test.
**Statistically significant at .05 level, one-tailed test.

are not altogether surprising. The theoretically stronger hypothesis, that money mobilizes a pro-PAC bias at the committee level, is confirmed in all three. . . .

Finally, most of the variables that tap members' institutional positions prove to be strong determinants of committee participation. While the coefficients on freshman status differ in sign, both subcommittee membership and leadership position are positive, statistically significant, and substantiv[e]ly large in all three cases. Even on issues that are widely perceived among the committee membership to be important, issues where the organized interests in the policy environment are themselves active, the opportunities and resources provided by formal institutional position are major factors in determining who makes the laws at the committee stage. Such findings are generally consistent with findings from other committees and larger samples of issues and reinforce the assumption that the model of participation employed here is specified correctly.

Conclusion

We have elaborated a theory of the member-group exchange relationship that comprehends the general patterns of PAC contributions reported in the literature. House members and interest group representatives are parties to an implicit cooperative agreement, but the constraints on member behavior and the rational calculations of group strategists limit the extent to which votes become the basis for exchange. This view suggests expectations about the effects of money on congressional decision making quite different from the ones that motivate the substantial research on the subject. We should find little causal connection between contributions and votes, especially on the floor—an expectation generally supported, although not adequately explained, in the literature. We should expect to find an important connection between contributions and the legislative involvement of sympathetic members, especially in committee— a relationship that empirical research to date has altogether ignored.

In order to test this view of moneyed interests and congressional decision making, we investigated the participation of House members on three issues in three committees. In each case, we found solid support for our principal hypothesis: moneyed interests are able to mobilize legislators already predisposed to support the group's position. Conversely, money that a group contributes to its likely opponents has either a negligible or negative effect on their participation. While previous research on these same issues provided little evidence that PAC money purchased members' votes, it apparently did buy the marginal time, energy, and legislative resources that committee participation requires. Moreover, we found evidence that (organized) producer interests figured more prominently than (unorganized) consumer interests in the participation decisions of House committee members—both for a case in which the issue at stake evoked high district salience and one where it did not. And we found little evidence that committee members respond to the interests of unemployed workers except insofar as those interests might be represented in the activities of well-financed and well-organized labor unions. Such findings suggest several implications for our understanding of political money, interest groups, and the legislative process.

The first and most important implication is that moneyed interests *do* affect the decision-making processes of Congress, an implication that one does not easily derive from the existing political science literature on contributions. In fact, it matters most at that stage of the legislative process that matters most and for a form of legislative behavior likely to have a direct bearing on outcomes. . . . Parliamentary suffrage gives a member relatively little leverage over the shape of legislation, especially at the committee stage. Only a small fraction of the decisions that shape a bill ever go to a vote, either in committee or on the floor. The vast majority are made in authoring a legislative vehicle, formulating amendments, negotiating specific provisions or report language behind the scenes, developing legislative strategy, and in other activities that require substantial time, information, and energy on the part of member and staff. While such efforts by no means guarantee that a particular member will influence the final outcome, they are usually a precondition for such influence.

A second and related implication of this investigation, then, is that empirical research should expand its view of the legislative purposes of political money and the other group resources that may accompany it. We focus here on committee participation; but the more general implication is that group expenditures may do much more than buy votes, or they may buy votes under certain conditions and affect other forms of legislative behavior under others. Such a suggestion, of course, usually appears in the various studies that examine the relationship between contributions and floor roll calls, but it needs to be elevated from the status of footnote or parenthetic remark to a central element of future research designs. Even for a small set of issues and a single group, the legislative strategies available are several, sometimes mixed. To speculate beyond the research reported here, for instance, we believe groups allocate their various resources (1) to mobilize strong supporters not only in House committees but also on the Senate floor, in dealings with executive agencies, and in various other decision-making forum[s] relevant to the group's interests; (2) to demobilize strong opponents; and (3) to effect the support of swing legislators. We require greater knowledge of the frequency and efficacy of such strategies, in any case, before we denigrate the role of moneyed interests in Congress, especially when the overwhelming weight of the evidence provided by Washington journalists and political insiders suggests that they matter a great deal.

Finally, the argument presented here provides a very different slant on the role of interest groups as purveyors of information in the deliberations of representative assemblies. A common defense of group lobbying activity, in fact, is that it provides ideas and information although its effect on member preferences is slight. Members (and their staffs) tend to consume information selectively, relying on sources with whom they already agree and discounting sources with whom they usually disagree. The view that we have advanced here suggests that while this may in fact describe how such information is used, it does not render it inconsequential. In light of the extraordinary demands on each congressional office, information—gathering it; analyzing it; turning it into speeches, amendments, and bills; using it to develop legislative strategy—can be very costly. Such costs, more than anything, limit the extent to which a nominal member will be a meaningful player in the decision-making process on a particular bill. At the very least, then, money-induced activity will distort the "representativeness of deliberations," a standard that democratic theorists since John Stuart Mill have used to evaluate the legitimacy of legislative assemblies. But it may also affect the "representativeness of decisions." By selectively subsidizing the information costs associated with participation, groups affect the *intensity* with which their positions are promoted by their legislative agents. In short, not all preferences weigh equally in legislative deliberations; and the resources of moneyed interests at least partly determine the weights.

The extent to which such efforts are damaging to representative government, as Schattschneider claimed, depends in part on the balance of interests and resources apparent in the relevant set of groups that are organized for political action. On any given issue, the efforts of one interest to mobilize supporters in Congress may be at least partially offset by the efforts of some competing group to mobilize its own supporters; indeed, there is some evidence that such countervailing efforts occurred in the natural gas case. But for those who believe that money is an illegitimate resource in such efforts—that pluralism requires something more than a competition among moneyed interests—the results of this study can only be disturbing.

Chapter 14

News Media

14-1

The Market and the Media

James T. Hamilton

With good reason, the news media have long been called the "fourth branch" of government. In a democracy citizens need news to monitor the performance of their representatives. Conversely, officeholders and those who wish to replace them need to be able to communicate with their constituencies. Moreover, with officeholders needing to coordinate with one another across the institutions that divide them, "news," as Woodrow Wilson aptly observed, "is the atmosphere of politics." The First Amendment to the Constitution recognizes the news media's special role by placing freedom of the press alongside freedoms of speech and religion as deserving categorical protection from government infringement. More than in any other Western democracy, the news media developed in America as private business enterprises virtually free of government regulation or investment. Modern news, James Hamilton reminds us, is as much a product of business as it ever was. As technology creates new audiences and products, the business of news has undergone significant market adjustment.

Source: James T. Hamilton, "The Market and the Media," in *The Press*, by Geneva Overholser and Kathleen Hall Jamieson, eds. (Oxford University Press: 2005), 351–371. Some notes appearing in the original have been deleted.

SINCE MARKET FORCES have played the most decisive role in transforming the delivery of news, the history of the American press from the 1970s to the present is economic history. Although journalists may not explicitly consider economics as they cover the day's events, the stories, reporters, firms, and media that ultimately survive in the marketplace depend on economic factors. The decisions of producers and editors are driven by supply and demand: Who cares about a particular piece of information? What is an audience willing to pay for the news, or what are advertisers willing to pay for the attention of readers, listeners, or viewers? How many consumers share particular interests in a topic? How many competitors are vying for readers' or viewers' attention, and what are these competitors offering as news? What are the costs of generating and transmitting a story? Who owns the outlet? What are the owners' goals? What are the property rights that govern how news is produced, distributed, and sold? News is a commercial product.

News outlets that cover public affairs have always struggled with the tension between giving people what they want to know and giving them what they need to know. The low probability that any reader has of influencing the outcome of a policy debate leaves many readers "rationally ignorant" about the details of governing.[1] From an investment perspective, why learn about global warming if your actions have little chance of affecting policy? News outlets do face strong demand for entertaining news, or information that helps people in their role as consumers or workers. Some people may also express a demand for news about politics, though the set of viewers that prefers politics covered as a sport or drama may exceed that which prefers detailed analysis.

In this essay I argue that since the 1970s news coverage has shifted to an increasing emphasis on what people want to know and away from information that they may need as voters. I identify three economic factors that help account for this shift: changes in technology, product definition and differentiation, and media ownership. I will examine in detail how each has affected news content over time. I then focus on network evening news programs in a case study that demonstrates how these economic factors have shaped news coverage. After providing a snapshot of current media coverage, I conclude with a section analyzing the implications of these alterations in the ways in which news is defined, distributed, and consumed.

What's Different: Technology, Products, and Owners

Three technological changes have affected the way in which images and information have entered households since 1970: the growth of cable television; the advent of the Internet; and the increased use of satellite technology to transmit news across continents and into homes. The spread of cable television in the 1980s and 1990s and introduction of direct-broadcast satellite delivery meant that by

2003 at least 85 percent of television households subscribed to multichannel delivery systems. The average number of channels per home went from 7.1 in 1970 to 71.2 in 2001. The average number of channels viewed weekly for at least ten minutes went from 4.5 to 13.5 channels per television household.[2] This proliferation of channels meant that news on cable could focus on specific niches. Rather than attempting to garner 10 million viewers (the audience attracted by the *NBC Nightly News* in 2003), a cable news program could be successful by attracting less than 1 million viewers. The result is that cable channels can focus their products on particular types of news: sports stories on ESPN; business news on CNBC; storm data on the Weather Channel; and news that appeals to a conservative audience on FOX News Channel. Both the network evening news programs and daily newspapers have broader audiences than cable channels. If survey respondents are asked to rate themselves on an ideological scale of liberalism and conservatism, the average rating for consumers of the network evening news programs and daily newspapers is the same as the national sample average. The regular consumers of the FOX News Channel, however, have the most conservative ideological rating in the survey. Cable political shows such as *Crossfire* and *Hardball*, in contrast, attract audiences more likely to rate themselves as liberal.

The relatively small audiences of some cable news programs yield profits because of low production budgets. Since talk can be cheap, cable news programs often feature journalists acting as political pundits. Political pundits, who offer a mixture of fact and opinion, face many market constraints. Since readers have the freedom to sample and ignore stories across the portfolio of topics covered in a paper, those writing for newspapers can aim for a relatively educated audience and afford to write about topics that may not be of interest to many. Television pundits, in contrast, operate in a medium where viewers of a particular program all consume the same story. If these pundits pick topics of little interest, they risk losing viewers, who may be less educated (than newspaper readers) and more likely to search for entertainment than enlightenment from television. The result is that pundits choose different languages to talk about politics, depending on the avenue of expression.

To see these differences, consider the case of George Will, who writes a syndicated column and appears as a commentator on ABC News programming.[3] As I demonstrate in my book *All the News That's Fit to Sell*, the print George Will uses a greater variety of terms and longer words than the television George Will. When composing for a print audience, Will uses more abstract terms such as those relating to inspiration, as well as more numeric terms. He writes about groups rather than individuals, as reflected in a greater focus on core values and institutions. In television appearances, Will changes expression to comply with the greater demands for entertainment. He uses more human-interest language. He makes more self-references. He simplifies and summarizes, and at the same time hedges his bets through qualifications (higher use of ambivalent language). His statements on television focus more on the present and emphasize motion. On television, Will offers opinions that are marked by greater activity and realism. Although George Will has developed a brand name for expression, he changes the delivery of his product to suit the audience demands and cost constraints of the medium. . . .

A second technological change affecting news markets is the spread of the Internet. Competition for attention across sites has driven the price of news on nearly all Internet sites to zero (the marginal delivery cost of the information). This explosion of free information has many ramifications. Consumption of high-quality newspapers, for example, is now possible around the world. If one looks at the top one hundred newspapers in the United States, the circulation of the top five (the *Wall Street Journal*, *USA Today*, the *New York Times*, *Los Angeles Times*, and *Washington Post*) accounted for 21.5 percent of the total newspaper circulation in 1999.[4] If you look at the links generated on the Internet by these top one hundred newspapers, however, the top five papers in terms of links (which included *USA Today*, the *New York Times*, and the *Washington Post*) accounted for 41.4 percent of the total links. In part this reflects the advantages of established brands on the Internet, since familiarity with a product's existence and reputation can lead to its consumption. . . .

The low cost of entry to placing information on the Internet has had many effects on news. The ability of news outlets, and columnists such as Matt Drudge, to post instantly during any time of the day has extended news cycles and created additional pressure on traditional news outlets to run with breaking news.[5] The lack of large investment in sites means that news provided may not be heavily edited or screened, which can give rise to a spread of rumor and gossip. The archiving of data on the Internet and easy accessibility make it easier for errors in reporting to propagate, as journalists access information collected by others and incorporate it into stories. The widespread existence of government and nonprofit Web sites lowers the cost of information generation and analysis for reporters. Journalists writing about campaign finance, for example, can readily locate data at the individual contributor level at the Federal Election Commission Web site or at Opensecrets.org. Similarly, reporters writing about the environment can use government data aggregated by the nonprofit Environmental Defense, which posts detailed pollution data by the zip code level at Scorecard.org.

Widespread use of satellite technology to beam images across the country and the world marks a third change in news reporting. During the 1970s the three evening network news programs had an "oligopoly of image," where viewers tuned in the programs in part to see the first pictures of the day's breaking stories. The deployment of satellite technology across the country, however, soon meant that local television stations had the ability to import stories quickly from other parts of the country and to go live to events in their own city. The ability of local stations to share in network feeds or tap into other sources of pictures meant that local news programs began to offer viewers images of national or international stories, which in turn put pressure on the evening news to offer a differentiated product (including more interpretative or contextual material). The existence of satellite technology also meant that international coverage could take place in real time, including the coverage of the Iraq War by embedded reporters.

These technological changes have put increased pressures on traditional news outlets to compete for readers and viewers. The growth in cable channels and cable/direct broadcast satellite subscription has eroded the market share of the network evening news programs and focused attention on retaining viewers. The network evening news programs have a core audience of faithful viewers and a set of marginal viewers, those who may tune in to the news or choose another program depending on what has happened in the world or what types of news the networks choose to focus on. News directors will select a mix of stories aimed at capturing the marginal viewers while not alienating the average or regular viewers. The result of competition from cable is a mix of stories that leaves average viewers somewhat frustrated and marginal viewers somewhat placated.

Survey data from the Pew Center for the People and the Press in 2000 show the tension between the interests of the average (i.e., regularly view) and marginal (i.e., sometimes view) consumers of the network nightly news programs.[6] A majority of the regular viewers are over fifty (54.8 percent) and female (53.9 percent). The marginal viewers are much younger. Females aged eighteen to thirty-four account for 20.6 percent of those who sometimes view the national news, and males aged eighteen to thirty-four account for 17.5 percent of these sometime viewers. In contrast, eighteen-to-thirty-four-year-old females are only 9.1 percent of the regular audience, and males of that age group only 9.2 percent of the regular viewers. These demographic differences translate into predictable and sharp differences between the interests of marginal and average viewers. Marginal viewers are not as attached to the news. When asked whether they enjoyed keeping up with the news, 68.1 percent of average viewers responded that they did "a lot" versus only 37.0 percent for the marginal viewers. A majority of marginal viewers said that they followed national or international news closely "only when something important or interesting is happening." Marginal viewers also were more likely to report that they watched the news with "my remote in hand" and switched channels when they were not interested in a topic.

What captures the interests of occasional viewers differs from the type of news favored by loyal viewers. The marginal and average viewers have the same top two news interests, crime and health, which may explain the prevalence of these news categories on the network evening news. The two sets of viewers differ markedly, however, in their interest in politics. For the average viewer of network news, news about political figures and events in Washington ranked fifth out of thirteen news types. This same category of news ranked tenth among marginal viewers. Political news about Washington was followed very closely by 28.4 percent of the average viewers, versus 12.3 percent of the marginals. Sports ranked sixth and entertainment news ranked twelfth among the regular viewers. These topics ranked much more highly among marginal viewers, who ranked them third and eighth among the thirteen news topics.

Viewers who are younger than fifty may also merit attention for another reason—they are more highly valued by advertisers. Reasons offered for why advertisers pay more for viewers under fifty include a belief that their brand preferences are not as fixed and the fact that they watch less television and hence are harder to reach. The rewards for capturing relatively younger viewers offer another reason for news directors to pay less attention to the (older) loyal watchers. One way to forge a compromise between the interests of average and marginal viewers is to cover the political issues of interest to younger viewers. The January 2000 Pew survey asked respondents to indicate the priority they attached to twenty political issues. When I examined the number of minutes or number of stories devoted on each network to these issues in 2000, I found that the higher the priority attached to an issue at the start of the year by the eighteen-to-thirty-four set, the more attention devoted over the year by the network news. The priorities of older viewers had no impact or a negative effect on coverage devoted by the networks. The survey data indicate that females in the age range care relatively more about issues such as dealing with the problems of families with children and strengthening gun control laws. Searching for marginal viewers and those valued by advertisers may thus lead the networks to talk about issues often associated with the Democratic Party. The competition generated by technology, and the influence of advertiser values, thus generate pressure to provide network stories that may give rise to perceptions of media bias. Among those identifying themselves as very conservative, 37.4 percent reported in 2000 that they viewed the national nightly network news as very biased. Among survey respondents who labeled themselves as very liberal, only 16.6 percent saw network news programs the same way.

Product Changes

In print and broadcast, there has been a substantial change in the content and style of news coverage since 1970. These product changes are numerous: a decrease in hard news (e.g., public-affairs coverage) and an increase in soft news (e.g., entertainment, human-interest stories); an increase in negative tone to cover elections; less focus on watchdog stories (e.g., those dealing with the operation of government); and an increase in the mix of opinion and interpretation in news coverage. These product changes also have many origins. Emphasis on cost cutting and profits has led to declines in international coverage. Competition across media and the pressure for product differentiation within a market have led some outlets to specialize in soft news. The drive to entertain can transform political coverage into horse-race coverage, with a focus on who is ahead in the polls and a tone that is often critical of candidates and events. In publicly traded companies, pressures to meet market earnings expectations can mean more focus on pleasing readers and viewers and less room for journalists to exercise their own news judgment. Changes in rules by the Federal Communications Commission (FCC) have reduced station worries about whether views expressed on air are "fair" and removed specific requirements that broadcasters provide a minimum amount of public-affairs coverage. In this section I describe the dimensions of news product changes since 1970. These changes in product attributes result from an interplay of demand and supply factors, though I do not attempt here to specify which factors generate particular product alterations.

Content analysis by the Committee of Concerned Journalists (CCJ) in 1998 captured broad changes in the media by examining for 1977, 1987, and 1997 one month of coverage on the three network evening news programs, each cover story during the year for *Time* and *Newsweek*, and each front-page story for the *New York Times* and *Los Angeles Times*. For this sample of 3,760 stories, the CCJ found that straight news accounts (e.g., what happened yesterday) went from 52 percent of stories in 1977 to only 32 percent in 1997. Story topics in traditional hard-news areas (i.e., government, military, and domestic and foreign affairs) went from 66.3 percent of all reports to 48.9 percent. Feature stories such as those about entertainment, celebrities, lifestyle, and celebrity crime grew from 5.1 percent in 1977 to 11.1 percent in 1997. Crime stories went from 8.4 percent to 11.4 percent and personal health from 0.7 percent to 3.5 percent. Attention also grew for stories about science (2.7 percent to 5.9 percent) and religion (0.5 percent to 3.7 percent).[7] . . .

As hard-news coverage declined, the tone of many stories about elections grew more critical. Assessing coverage of major-party presidential nominees in *Time* and *Newsweek* from 1960 to 1992, [Thomas] Patterson found that unfavorable references to the candidates grew from approximately 25 percent in 1960 to 60 percent in 1992. Studying front-page election stories in the *New York Times*, he found that in the 1960s the candidates and other partisan sources set the tone of nearly 70 percent of the articles. By 1992, journalists set the tone for the reports about 80 percent of the time. Kiku Adatto documented similar patterns of a shrinking role for the candidate and increasing role for the reporter on network television coverage of presidential campaigns. She found that in 1968 the average sound bite for a presidential candidate on the network evening news was 42.3 seconds. By the 1988 campaign this figure dropped to 9.8 seconds (and decreased further to 8.4 seconds in the 1992 general election). What replaced the words of the candidates was strategy coverage provided by reporters, who gave viewers their assessment of why the candidate was engaged in a particular strategy and how the candidate was faring in the horse race. Critical coverage also greeted the eventual winners. A study for the Council for Excellence in Government found that in the first year of the presidencies of Ronald Reagan (1981), Bill Clinton (1993), and George W. Bush (2001), coverage of the administration on network television news was negative in tone by a ratio of nearly two to one. The critical eye reporters used in covering government emerged in part from journalists' experience with government deception during both the Vietnam War and Watergate.[8] . . .

Product changes are evident too in the percentage of journalists saying that a particular media role was extremely important. In 1971 76 percent of journalists said investigating government claims was an extremely important mass media role, 61 percent said the same for providing analysis of complex problems, and 55 percent for discussing national policy. These figures dropped in 1992 to 67 percent for investigating government, 48 percent for analysis of complex problems, and 39 percent for national problems. Journalists in 1992 were much more likely (69 percent) to say that getting information to the public quickly was an extremely important role, versus 56 percent in 1971.[9]

In extended interviews with journalists, Howard Gardner, Mihaly Csikszent-mihalyi, and William Damon also found that journalists were frustrated: 51 percent said changes in the media were negative, versus 24 percent indicating that the changes were positive. Sixty-four percent of the journalists they interviewed said the demands to comply with business goals in journalism were increasing, and 63 percent said there was a perceived drop in ethics and values in the media. Many of those interviewed pointed to the drive for market share as a prime force undercutting the performance of journalists.[10]

Changes in government regulation also affected the extent and kind of information provided. Prior to 1987, the FCC's fairness doctrine required broadcasters to provide free and equal time to parties that dissented from controversial views that stations chose to air. While the policy may have promoted perceptions of fairness, empirical evidence indicates that the policy may have chilled speech by discouraging stations from presenting viewpoints that might trigger demands for free response time on air.[11] Once the fairness doctrine was abolished by the FCC, the genre of informational programming immediately expanded on radio. This radio genre, which includes news programming and the talk-radio format made famous by Rush Limbaugh, became both a popular and controversial force in public-affairs debates in the 1990s.

Ownership

Change in ownership of news media outlets is a third factor affecting content. There are many theories about why ownership matters: publicly traded firms could be more likely to focus on profits than journalism properties (e.g., newspapers) owned by individuals or families; outlets owned by groups, whether a newspaper in a chain or a broadcast station owned by a network may be less likely to identify with the problems of a specific city; and the concentration of ownership in a small number of firms may crowd out a diverse set of views.

Calculating how ownership has changed over time requires defining a medium and a market. Between 1970 and 1998, the number of daily newspapers declined from 1,748 to 1,489 and average circulation dropped from 62,202 to 56,183. The number of weekly newspapers, however, grew from 7,612 to 8,193 and average circulation jumped from 3,660 to 9,067. The number of cities with two or more fully competing dailies with different ownership declined from 37 in 1973 to 19 in 1996. The number of newspaper groups dropped from 157 in 1970 to 129 in 1996. In the same period, the percentage of dailies owned by chains grew from 50.3 percent to 76.2 percent and the percentage of daily circulation accounted for by these group-owned papers increased from 63.0 percent to 81.5 percent. The fifteen largest newspaper chains generated slightly more than half of the daily circulation of newspapers in the United States in 1998.[12]

At a broad level, the media have not become significantly more concentrated (in terms of the concentration of sales in a specific number of firms) over this time period. It is estimated that in terms of revenues, the top fifty media firms (which include newspaper, broadcast, cable, publishing, music, and film companies) accounted for 79.7 percent of all media industry revenues in 1986 and 81.8 percent in 1997; the share of the top four firms grew from 18.8 percent to 24.1 percent.[13] . . . One study looked at how ownership had changed between 1960 and 2000 for ten local media markets in the United States. After counting for each local market the number of broadcast outlets, cable systems, direct-broadcast satellite systems, and daily newspapers available, the study found that the percentage growth in the total number of media outlets available averaged more than 200 percent between 1960 and 2000. The percentage increase in the number of owners in the market averaged 140 percent.[14]

The actual impact of group or chain ownership in media outlets is a topic of spirited empirical debate. Reviewing the social science evidence on the impact of chain ownership on newspaper operation in 1994, Edwin Baker concluded, "Chain ownership's primary documented effects are negative. However, the findings seem tepid, hardly motivating any strong critique of chain ownership or prompting any significant policy interventions." Lisa George found that as the number of owners in a local newspaper market goes down, product differentiation between newspapers increases and the number of topical reporting beats covered in the market overall goes up. The Project for Excellence in Journalism found that in local television markets, stations affiliated with networks produced higher-quality news programs than those actually owned and operated by the networks, that stations owned by a company also operating a newspaper in the market generated higher-quality local television news programs, and that locally owned stations were not obviously superior to other stations in news production.[15]

The Changing Nature of Network News

The transformation of the network evening news programs since 1970 offers a case study of the impact of changes in technology, news definitions, and ownership.[16] In 1969 the daily debates among network news executives and reporters about what stories to include in the evening news broadcasts centered around which domestic politics and foreign policy stories to cover. Each television network was part of a media company. For each of the three networks, the founder or an early leader was still involved and identified with the operation of the organization. Network news operations were expected to generate prestige, part of which reflected back on the owners and broadcasters. The FCC routinely examined the number of hours of public-affairs programming provided when stations had their licenses renewed. A reputation for covering public affairs well in the news provided added security when licenses were up for renewal. If viewers did not enjoy the hard-news stories provided in the evening news programs, they had few other options on the dial. The average television household received seven channels. At the dinner hour more than one-third of all television households watched the network evening news. The stories they saw were news to most viewers. National news programs were not on earlier in the afternoon, and local news programs lacked the technology and time to cover national events on their own. Decision makers on network news programs felt a responsibility to provide viewers with information they needed as citizens. The large audience share and focus on politics attracted significant scrutiny of the programs, which were a frequent target of criticism from the White House.[17]

In 2000 the daily debates in network story conferences centered on whether to include domestic political stories or softer news items about health and entertainment topics. Foreign coverage was not often on the agenda, except in cases of military action. Each network was part of a publicly traded conglomerate. Network news operations were expected by corporate managers and Wall Street analysts to generate profits. The FCC no longer scrutinized public affairs coverage and license renewals were virtually assured. Television households received an average of sixty-three channels. Viewers at the dinner hour could watch sitcoms, entertainment news, sports news, and news on PBS. The three major network news programs combined captured only 23 percent of all television households. Viewers often came to the network news programs with a sense of the day's headline stories, after watching news on cable channels or local television programs containing stories and footage from around the nation. Network decision-makers felt pressure to gain ratings, which translated into a competition to discover and serve viewers' interests. Anchors and reporters were promoted as celebrities. Political criticisms of news coverage focused more on the content of cable news programs, though press critics faulted the network evening news shows for an increasing shift to soft-news stories.

To see the shift in news content, consider how the network evening news treated a consistent set of stories over time. Each year, *People* magazine selects its "25 Most Intriguing People" of the year, which consist of a set of soft-news personalities (i.e., television stars, movie actors, sports figures, persons involved in famous crimes, and royalty) and a set of famous figures from business and politics. In 1974–78, 40 percent of the soft-news personalities on the *People* list were covered in stories on at least one of the three major network evening news programs. In 1994–98, this figure rose to 52 percent. For those soft-news personalities that generated coverage over the course of the year they were listed by *People*, on ABC the "Intriguing" person averaged 9.9 stories and 1,275 seconds in coverage per year in 1974–78. This grew to 17.2 stories and 2,141 seconds of annual average coverage by 1994–98. NBC's reputation of providing more soft news than the other two networks is confirmed by its average of 25.6 stories and 3,238 seconds of coverage in 1994–98.

By many measures hard-news coverage dropped over this period. Each year, *Congressional Quarterly* identifies the key votes that take place in the U.S. Senate and House. In 1969–73, 82 percent of these major votes were covered on at least one of the network evening news programs on the day of or day after the congressional action. Yet for the period 1994–98, only 62 percent of the *CQ* votes generated network stories. A similar pattern holds for the key legislative votes identified each year by two ideological interest groups, the Americans for Democratic Action (ADA) and the American Conservative Union (ACU). The percentage of key interest-group votes in Congress that generated stories on the nightly news dropped from 64 percent in 1969–73 to 44 percent in 1994–98. The shift on the network news away from a headline service toward more background reporting is evident in the fact that those bills that were covered got more time on the evening news programs. On ABC, for example, the mean overage length for *CQ* bills went from 117 seconds in 1969–73 to 211 seconds in 1994–98.

Statistical analysis shows that many factors contributed to these changes in coverage. *People*'s intriguing personalities were more likely to be covered over the course of a year on the network evening news in the era (i.e., 1984 or later) when the FCC had deregulated much of broadcast television. Coverage of *CQ* votes declined in election years (when they were probably crowded out by campaign stories) and dropped as cost cutting became more prominent in network news operations. Interest-group vote coverage declined on each network as the percentage of households with cable increased, indicating how broadcast television shifted away from some forms of hard news as competition increased from cable. In the period 1969 to 1999, the number of network evening news stories mentioning soft-news terms such as *actor, sex,* or *movie* increased along with the percentage of households with cable. In the post-deregulation era, stories about hard-news topics such as education or Medicaid or NATO declined.

Network evening news anchors not only covered celebrities, they became them. News products have always been what economists call experience goods, which means that companies have always sought ways to signal to potential customers what today's version of events will look like in their papers or programs. The pressure for journalists to become part of the news product, however, is increasing as the number of news outlets expands. In a world of four broadcast television channels, a consumer can easily switch among viewing options to sample content. In a world where channels can number in the hundreds, sampling becomes more time-consuming.[18] If viewers recognize and enjoy watching a particular journalist on television, they may be more likely to watch a given channel because of this familiarity. The personalities of those who present the information become shortcuts for viewers to find their news niche. The changing salary rewards in network evening news programs provide evidence of how journalists have become part of the product in news.

Although network anchors deliver the news, they are rewarded in the marketplace for delivering viewers to advertisers. The salary patterns for network evening news anchors suggest that the value attached to the personal ability of these stars to deliver viewers increased markedly during the 1990s. . . . When consumers have many more choices, the value of a known commodity can increase. Network anchors become a way for channels to create a brand image in viewers' minds. If anchors become more important in drawing viewers to programs, this may translate into higher returns for anchors in salary negotiations. . . . The amount in salary that an anchor received for attracting a thousand viewing households increased from a range of $0.13 to $0.31 (in 1999 dollars) in 1976 to a range of $0.86 to $1.07 in 1999. Another way to view this is to look at the ratio of the anchor's salary to the ad price on the evening news programs. In 1976 anchors such as Walter Cronkite and John Chancellor were paid the equivalent of 28 ads per year, while in 1999 this had grown to 149 ads for Dan Rather and Tom Brokaw. The marked increase in the amount paid per viewing household, salary expressed in ad revenues, and the absolute magnitude of the salary took place in the 1990s. This was a time of declining absolute audiences, but rising importance of anchors in attracting viewers. The increased value placed on anchors is consistent with these personalities playing a growing role in attracting viewers in a multichannel universe.

Current News Markets

The expanding opportunities for individuals to consume media products has meant declining market shares for most traditional news media outlets. The percentage of survey respondents saying that they were regular consumers of a specific news outlet dropped substantially between May 1993 and April 2002 in Pew surveys: from 77 percent to 57 percent for local television news; 60 percent to 32 percent for nightly network news; and 52 percent to 24 percent for network television news magazines. Between 1994 and 2002, Pew surveys indicated drops in regular consumption from 47 percent to 41 percent for radio and 58 percent to 41 percent for newspapers. Respondents reporting regular consumption of online news grew from 2 percent in April 1996 to 25 percent in April 2002; NPR's figures also increased during that period, from 13 percent to 16 percent. In April 2002, 33 percent of survey respondents reported that they were regular consumers of cable television news. . . .

The multiplication of news outlets on cable and the Internet means [also] that an individual is more likely today than in the 1970s or 1980s to find a news outlet closer to his or her ideal news source. The creation of niche programming and content means that individuals may be more likely to find what they want. But the division of the audience into smaller groups also means that any one channel may be less likely to attract viewers, less likely to amass advertiser revenue, and hence less able to devote resources to programming. There may be a trade-off between cable channels' catering to individual topical interests and the quality of programming that can be supported by the audience size. On the Internet, the drive of competition means that price eventually equals marginal costs (zero), so sites are searching for ways to generate revenue. This means that breaking news becomes a commodity essentially offered for free. The lack of revenue may mean that sites simply repeat readily available information rather than generate their own coverage. In a study of Internet content during the 2000 presidential primaries, the Committee of Concerned Journalists found that one-quarter of the political front pages on Internet sites they studied had no original reporting.[19] The time pressure to provide news generated by the Internet and the lack of resources to do original reporting may increase the likelihood that information cascades occur. When initial news reports get facts wrong, the tendency of reporters to rely on the work of others and the quick multiplication effects can mean that bad information propagates. . . .

An additional dilemma for hard-news consumers is the economic pressures that may push some outlets away from offering the type of news they prefer. If advertisers value younger viewers and younger viewers demonstrate a higher willingness to switch channels, then broadcast programs may end up at the margins, putting more soft-news topics into previously hard-news programs. This explains in part the increased emphasis on entertainment and human-interest stories on the network news broadcasts. Media bias can also emerge as a commercial product, in at least two forms. If networks are targeting relatively younger female viewers, and these viewers express more interest in issues such as gun control and the problems of families with children, the network news programs may focus on traditionally Democratic (liberal) issues out of economic necessity. The development of niche programs on cable can also generate programs targeted at viewers with a particular ideology. The FOX News Channel. for example, attracts a relatively conservative audience and offers the cable news program with the largest audience—*The O'Reilly Factor*. The added variety arising from the expansion of cable programming means that viewers uninterested in politics can more readily avoid it. In 1996 viewers with cable who had low levels of political interest (i.e., had low levels of political information) were much less likely to watch presidential debates than viewers who had broadcast channels.[20] Those who were not interested in politics but had only broadcast television did end up watching these debates, since their options were limited. The greater entertainment options provided by cable television also appear to affect who votes. Among viewers with high interest in entertainment programming, those with cable are much less likely to vote (perhaps because they are able to avoid political programming by watching the many entertainment channels offered on cable). . . .

Changes in news markets from 1970 to today have brought new media, generated more diverse offerings, and added opportunities to find both hard and soft news. In pushing for the deregulation of broadcast television in the 1980s, FCC chairman Mark Fowler declared famously, "The public's interest . . . defines the public interest."[21] The competition for interested audiences has clearly driven many of the recent changes in journalism. Whether the aggregation of individuals pursuing the stories they want to know about yields the type of information they need to know about as citizens and voters is a question pursued further in other chapters in this volume.

NOTES

1. Anthony Downs, *An Economic Theory of Democracy* (New York: Harper Books, 1957). Downs coined the term *rational ignorance* to refer to the fact that the small probability that an individual has of influencing public policy decisions means that it may be rational to remain ignorant of current affairs, if one views information only as an instrument in making decisions and calculates the personal payoffs from keeping up with public affairs. There may still be a demand expressed for political coverage, from those who feel a duty to be informed, people who find the details of politics and policies inherently interesting, or people who derive entertainment from politics as drama, horse race, or scandal. The logic of rational ignorance may help explain why Delli Carpini and Keeter find that "despite the numerous political, economic, and social changes that have occurred since World War II, overall political knowledge levels in the United States are about the same today as they were forty to fifty years ago" (*What Americans Know about Politics and Why It Matters*. New Haven, Conn.: Yale University Press, 1996, 270).

2. For data on channel availability and consumption, see Ed Papazian, ed., *TV Dimensions 2002* (New York: Media Dynamics, 2002).

3. To study the market for pundits, I analyzed a sample of the print offerings and broadcast transcripts of fifty-six pundits in 1999 using the text analysis software DICTION. See chapter 8 in Hamilton, *All the News That's Fit to Sell,* (Princeton, N.J.: Princeton University Press, 2004).

4. For analysis of news markets on the Internet, see chapter 7 in Hamilton, *All the News That's Fit to Sell.*

5. See Kovach and Rosensteil, *Warp Speed* (New York: Century Foundation Press, 1999), and Kalb, *One Scandalous Story* (New York: Free Press, 2001), for discussions of the time pressures on journalists created by the speed of information transmission and the Internet.

6. See chapter 3 in Hamilton, *All the News That's Fit to Sell*, for an analysis of the network news audience.

7. Committee of Concerned Journalists, *Changing Definitions of News* (Washington, D.C.: Committee of Concerned Journalists, 1998), available from www.journalism.org.

8. Patterson, *Out of Order* (New York: Knopf, 1993); Adatto, *Picture Perfect* (New York: Basic Books, 1993); Council for Excellence in Government, *Government: In and Out of the News*, study by the Center for Media and Public Affairs, 2003, available at http://www.excelgov.org/displaycontent.asp?keyword=prnHomePage. Patterson's *Out of Order* also includes a discussion of distrust between reporters and politicians.

9. Weaver and Wilhoit, *The American Journalist in the 1990s* (Mahwah, N.J.: Lawrence Erlbaum, 1996).

10. Gardner, Csikszentmihalyi, and Damon, *Good Work* (New York: Basic Books, 2001).

11. Thomas W. Hazlett and David W. Sosa, "Was the Fairness Doctrine a 'Chilling Effect'?: Evidence from the Post-Deregulation Radio Market," *Journal of Legal Studies* 26, no. 1 (1997): 279–301.

12. For data on newspaper markets, see Compaine and Gomery, *Who Owns the Media?* 3rd ed. (Mahwah, N.J.: Lawrence Erlbaum, 2000).

13. Ibid.

14. Scott Roberts, Jane Frenette, and Dione Stearns, "A Comparison of Media Outlets and Owners for Ten Selected Markets: 1960, 1980, 2000" (working paper, Media Ownership Working Group, Federal Communications Commission, Washington, D.C., 2002).

15. For discussion of the impact of media ownership and concentration on content, see Peter O. Steiner, "Program Patterns and Preferences, and the Workability of Competition in Radio Broadcasting," *Quarterly Journal of Economics* 66 (1952): 194-223; Demers, *The Menace of the Corporate Newspaper* (Ames: Iowa State University Press, 1996); Bagdikian, *The Media Monopoly* (Boston: Beacon Press, 1997); McChesney, *Rich Man, Poor Democracy* (Urbana: University of Illinois Press, 2000); Jeff Chester, "Strict Scrutiny: Why Journalists Should Be Concerned about New Federal and Industry Media Deregulation Proposals," *Harvard International Journal of Press/Politics* 7, no. 2 (2002): 105–15; and Roberts and Kunkel, eds., *Breach of Faith* (Fayetteville: University of Arkansas Press, 2002). The quotation on ownership studies comes from C. Edwin Baker, "Ownership of Newspapers: The View from Positivist Social Science" (research paper, Joan Shorenstein Center on the Press, Politics and Public Policy, Kennedy School of Government, Harvard University, Cambridge, Mass., 1994), 19. See also Lisa George, "What's Fit to Print: The Effect of Ownership Concentration on Product Variety in Daily Newspaper Markets" (working paper, Michigan State University, East Lansing, Mich., 2001), and Project for Excellence in Journalism, *Does Ownership Matter in Local Television News? A Five-Year Study of Ownership and Quality*, updated April 29, 2003, http://www.journalism. org/resources/research/reports/ownership/default.asp.

16. This section excerpts and summarizes analysis from chapters 6 and 8 of Hamilton, *All the News That's Fit to Sell*.

17. In 1969 the founders or early leaders of each network still served as the chairman of the board: William S. Paley (CBS); David Sarnoff (RCA, which owned NBC); and Leonard Goldenson (ABC). For an overview of the networks that focuses on the 1980s, see Auletta, *Three Blind Mice* (New York: Random House, 1992). Data on channels per television household come from Ed Papazian, ed., *TV Dimensions 2001* (New York: Media Dynamics, 2001), which indicates (on p. 22) that averages were 7.1 for 1970 and 63.4 for 2000. Larry M. Bartels and Wendy M. Rahn, in "Political Attitudes in the Post-Network Era" (paper prepared for the Annual Meeting of the American Political Science Association, Washington, D.C., September, 2000), report that the sum of the Nielsen ratings for the three network evening news programs was close to 36 in 1970–71 and 23 in 1999–2000. For the text of Vice President Spiro Agnew's speech attacking network television news on November 13, 1969, see James Keogh, *President Nixon and the Press* (New York: Funk & Wagnalls, 1972).

18. In summer 2001 DirecTV, a digital satellite service, offered subscribers more than 225 channels (see www.directv.com). The average number of channels received in U.S. television households grew from 28 in 1988 to 49 in 1997. Households clearly have favorites among these channels. The average number of channels viewed per household, where viewing is defined as "10 or more continuous minutes per channel," was 12 in 1997. See Nielsen Media Research, *1998 Report on Television* (New York: Nielsen Media Research, 1998), 19.

19. Committee of Concerned Journalists, *ePolitics: A Study of the 2000 Presidential Campaign on the Internet* (Washington, D.C.: Committee of Concerned Journalists, 2000), available from www.journalism.org.

20. See Matthew A. Baum and Samuel Kernell, "Has Cable Ended the Golden Age of Presidential Television?" *American Political Science Review* 93, no. 1 (1999): 99–114.

21. See Hamilton, *All the News That's Fit to Sell*, 1.

14-2

The New Washington Press Corps: As Mainstream Media Decline, Niche and Foreign Outlets Grow

Project for Excellence in Journalism

Doomsday predictions of the demise of the newspaper have been around for as long as anyone can remember. In the past, what were perceived as fatal events or dire trends really just marked a healthy consolidation (the demise of the afternoon edition in the 1960s and 1970s), the transformation of the newspaper to some new format, or the arrival of a new medium (say, radio news in the 1930s) that competed for consumers' attention. Similarly, the declining quality of news reporting has been a perennial topic for hand wringing.

The fateful day may finally have arrived. Newspapers across the country are for sale at depressed prices. Unable to find buyers, some are declaring bankruptcy and shutting down their presses. Newspaper subscriptions have become more discretionary since nearly nine in ten homes have access to cable news and use of broadband internet is exploding. During the recession beginning in 2008, growing numbers of readers decided the newspaper was an expense they could forego. Advertisers were not far behind.

As newspapers scoured their organizations to find savings and stave off bankruptcy, most took a hard look at their Washington bureaus. This essay reports the results from the Pew Project for Excellence in Journalism's census of Washington news bureaus. The findings are truly bleak. Far fewer professional journalists are covering the federal government than a decade ago, and their numbers continue to shrink precipitously. In the vacuum a different kind of journalism is growing, one based on the needs of businesses and other organizations in the private sector for specialized information.

READ THE HEADLINES and it would be easy to conclude that as the new Obama Administration takes power, facing an array of domestic and international crises, it will be monitored by a substantially depleted Washington press corps.

Source: Project for Excellence in Journalism, *The New Washington Press Corps: As Mainstream Media Decline, Niche and Foreign Outlets Grow,* February 11, 2009, www.journalism.org.

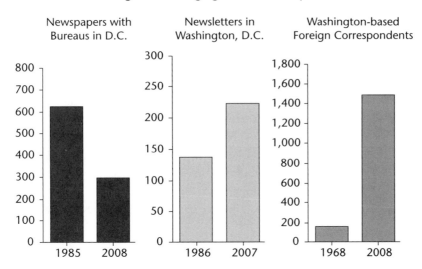

Figure 1. Changing D.C. Press Corps

It isn't exactly so. The corps of journalists covering Washington, D.C., at the dawn of the Obama Administration is not so much smaller as it is dramatically transformed. And that transformation will markedly alter what Americans know and not know about the new government, as well as who will know it and who will not.

A careful accounting of the numbers, plus detailed interviews with journalists, lawmakers, press association executives and government officials, reveals that what we once thought of as the mainstream news media serving a general public has indeed shrunk—perhaps far more than many would imagine. A roll call of the numbers may shock.

But as the mainstream media have shrunk, a new sector of niche media has grown in its place, offering more specialized and detailed information than the general media to smaller, elite audiences, often built around narrowly targeted financial, lobbying and political interests. Some of these niche outlets are financed by an economic model of high-priced subscriptions, others by image advertising from big companies like defense contractors, oil companies, and mobile phone alliances trying to influence policy makers.

In addition, the contingent of foreign reporters in Washington has grown to nearly ten times the size it was a generation ago. And the picture they are sending abroad of the country is a far different one than the world received when the information came mainly via American based wire services and cable news.

Consider a few examples:

Climate Wire, an on-line newsletter launched less than a year ago to cover the climate policy debate for a small, high-end audience, deploys more than twice the reporting power around Capitol Hill than the Hearst News Service, which provides Washington news for the chain's 16 daily newspapers.

The Washington bureau of *Mother Jones*, a San Francisco-based, left-leaning non-profit magazine, which had no reporters permanently assigned to the nation's capital a decade ago, today has seven, about the same size as the now-reduced *Time* magazine bureau.[1] The Washington bureau of the Arab satellite channel *Al Jazeera*, which opened a modest bureau when George W. Bush took office eight years ago, now has 105 staff members in its various services accredited to cover Congress,[2] similar in size to that of CBS News—both radio and television—at 129. . . .

Collectively, the implications of these changes are considerable. For those who participate in the American democracy, the "balance of information" has been tilted away from voters along Main Streets thousands of miles away to issue-based groups that jostle for influence daily in the corridors of power. . . .

The Numbers

There is no comprehensive registry of journalists in the nation's capital providing a definitive database on the changing make-up of Washington's Fourth Estate. But media directories and accreditation officials at different agencies and government press galleries offer some sense of the numbers, and the different trend lines at each sketch a consistent, reinforcing story.

First, the changes in the Washington press corps did not begin in the last three or four years with the growth of the Internet and the subsequent decline in advertising revenue—let alone with the current economic slowdown. The number of journalists in Washington appeared to peak in the mid-1990s and has been sliding for 15 years. The peak for newspapers was probably closer to 20 years ago.

Second, heading into 2008, the number of journalists in Washington was not appreciably different than it was four years earlier, and it remained more than twice the size of the Washington press corps at the time of Watergate, perhaps a high water mark for the prestige of Washington reporting.

While, there is considerable evidence of more substantial cutbacks in the last six months of 2008, the real story is in where those journalists work and the kind of coverage they are providing.

That story begins with the startling degree to which the mainstream press serving the general public and oriented to covering government according to the geographic lines around which representative democracy was designed has shrunk.

Since the mid-1980s, the number of U.S. wire services and newspapers accredited to cover Congress—either specific newspapers or bureaus representing newspaper chains—has fallen 72%, according to an audit of congressional directories.

In 1985, reporters representing 564 of these outlets carried Hill credentials. By the early months of 2007, well before the latest round of cutbacks, that number had fallen to 160.The number of magazines and general interest periodicals fell 75% to 22, down from 89.

Among the hardest hit are the regional newspapers from around the nation, those who cover the interests of Washington as they pertain to particular states, communities and regions—and who, more than any other media, do the work of covering specific elected representatives and state congressional delegations and interests. Since the mid-1990s, the rolls of the Regional Reporters Association—a group of Washington-based reporters working for smaller, regional newspapers around the country—have shrunk by more than 60%, from around 200 to 73 at the end of 2008.

Of the nation's 1,400 newspapers, 32—representing just 23 states—had their own bureaus in Washington at the beginning of 2008, according to Hudson's Washington News Media Contacts Directory. That is half the number of the mid-1980s, when 71 newspapers were representing 35 states. Add, in some additional cutbacks announced late in 2008, the number covering the Obama Administration is almost certainly lower—probably closer to 25.

Some might think that this is because more outlets are now represented by corporate bureaus—those representing a chain of multiple newspapers. Not so. In the same time period, the number of papers represented by corporate bureaus in Washington dropped by more than half to 262, down from 551.

Something similar, though far less drastic, has occurred in local television and radio. Though the amount of Washington coverage used is more limited, the number of local TV and radio stations with access to feeds and news stories from corporate news bureaus in Washington has fallen 37% from the mid-1980s to 92 stations, down from 146, according to Hudson's Directory. The number of states represented by that number is unchanged at 42. (Nearly all of these are corporate bureaus or syndicated operations serving client stations. Only two local TV or radio stations operate independent bureaus, about the same as 20 years earlier when there were three.) . . .

The numbers are similarly down for the television networks. The number of news executives, correspondents and anchors in Washington for the three traditional broadcast networks has dropped by more than half since the 1980s, according to Hudson's, from 110 in 1985 to 51 in early 2008—and that was before a round of cutbacks in 2008. Moreover, the sense is that the cutbacks in off-air staff, camera, sound and producers are even greater. Indeed, Hudson's lists include 84 executives and correspondents in Washington in its 2008 edition for the six cable and broadcast news divisions, less than the 127 included in 1985 when there were just four divisions (ABC, NBC, CBS and CNN).

Figure 2. Newspapers with Bureaus in D.C.

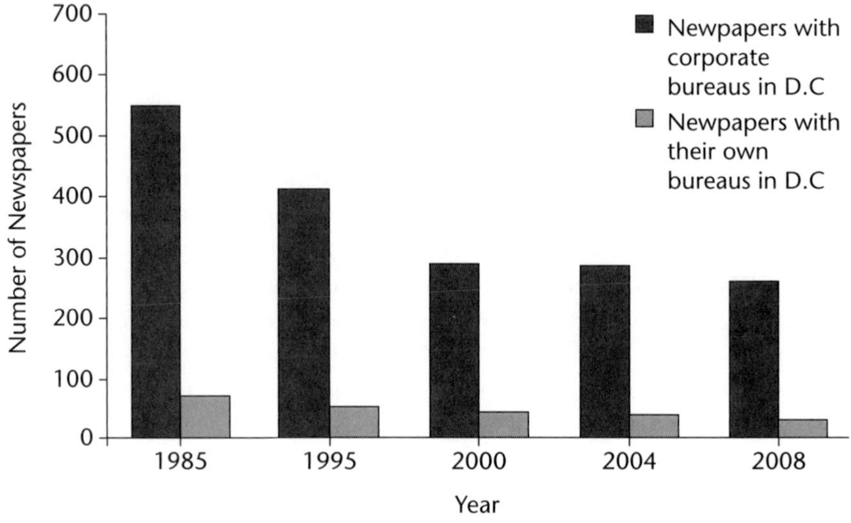

Source: Hudson's Washington News Media Contacts Directory

ABC News, for example, listed a staff of 38 in 1985, with two correspondents assigned to the State Department, three to the White House and three to Congress. In 2008, the directory listed the staff size at 12.

Robin Sproul, Vice-President and Washington Bureau Chief for ABC, says part of this shrinkage reflects a transfer of news shows from Washington to New York—Nightline is one recent example—but that economic belt-tightening also has played a role. . . . As with executives at other networks, Sproul's main concern as the Obama presidency begins is how to keep and build on the existing audience for Washington news in an environment of stiff competition from cable, satellite and a growing variety of online competitors—some of which she called "completely unreliable." "How do we continue to tell the story to people in their 20s, early 30s, and mid-30s? How do we reach them? How do we know where to reach them and how do they know they can trust us? These are the challenges," she said.

The weekly news magazines, another former important element of the Washington press corps has been buffeted by many of the same forces that affect daily newspapers. The two most prominent news weeklies, *Time* and *Newsweek*, now operate with less than half the Washington staff they had in the mid-1980s. *Time*, which at the beginning of 2008 operated with an editorial staff of 14, according to Hudson['s] listings, will end the year with just over half

Figure 3. Newspapers and Wires Covering Federal Agencies

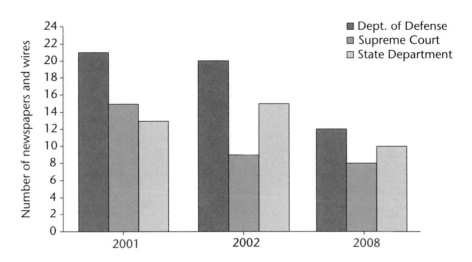

Source: 2001 and 2002 data from "Who's Got the Beat," *American Journalism Review,* Oct. 2002; 2008 data PEJ research

that many. *Newsweek,* which deployed a Washington staff of 23 to cover the first year of the George W. Bush Presidency, dipped to 14 at one point before rebuilding to 20 as it prepares to cover the early months of the Obama [A]dministration. . . .

All of this means that fewer federal agencies and less of the U.S. government are being regularly monitored. The number of mainstream wire services and newspapers staffing the Pentagon as a full-time beat appears to have dropped from 21 to 12 since 2001. At the State Department, the number has fallen from 15 to 10, and at the Supreme Court, it has gone from 15 in 2001 to eight today. In some instances, such as the Pentagon, the staffing drop could be attributed in part to a less intense volume of news. However, many of the outlets dropping away are those who have suffered significant cuts.

There were no comparable independent figures for network television beat reporting, but list[s] of beat assignments provided by the networks themselves frequently suggest a wider net of coverage than government officials say is real. Viewers who think the correspondent they see on air is working a story, developing sources and always on the scene may be laboring under a misimpression. Although network correspondents are listed as covering beats such as the State Department, agencies or even Congress, often they are no longer on scene anymore.

During the final five months of Condoleezza Rice's tenure as Secretary of State, only one network television correspondent joined her on overseas trips. That correspondent, Laura Logan of CBS, traveled just once. And not a single network television correspondent showed up for Rice's farewell news conference held shortly before she left office.[3] . . .

The number of journalists accredited to the White House shrunk dramatically . . . tighter budgets at large dailies have forced cut backs on coverage [of] out-of-town presidential trips to such an extent that some complain a long-standing White House print travel pool is effectively broken. For years, the pool has covered virtually every presidential trip. Interest in President Obama's initial months could revive the pool in the short-term, but there is concern that costs could eventually kill it.

A Grim 2008

If the numbers show that the decline in mainstream media presence in Washington is really a continuation of a trend that dates back to the mid-1980s, then 2008 will almost certainly be considered a turning point. For these figures do not reflect by and large the cutbacks that befell Washington in the last six to 12 months.

For that, it becomes useful to look at what has happened bureau by bureau.

Consider that during the course of 2008, a host of bureaus—corporate and individual—simply vanished altogether, while others were reduced exponentially. Newhouse Newspapers, Copley and the Copley News Service, Cox (in March of 2009), the (Salt Lake City) *Deseret News*, the *Fairbanks News-Miner*, the *Portland Press-Herald/Maine Sunday Telegram*, the (MA) *Lowell Sun* and the (Harrisburg, PA) *Patriot-News* all closed their Washington bureaus in 2008. Among individual newspapers, the *Los Angeles Times*, *Chicago Tribune*, *Baltimore Sun*, *Orlando Sentinel* and the *Ft. Lauderdale Sun-Sentinel* all became part of a single Tribune Co., bureau in November 2008.

Others hang on by a thread. The Stephens Media Group's Washington bureau, which counted six correspondents as recently as 2006, today has one. *Newsday*, which had a staff of 15 in Washington when George W. Bush took office in 2001, has just one correspondent today. *Business Week*, which had 20 staffers three years ago, now has three. . . .

Among the major U.S. dailies, only the *New York Times* and the *Wall Street Journal* have managed to maintain their Washington bureau staffing levels at or near historic highs.

Figure 4.

Staffing in Washington Bureaus number of FTE staff			
News Service	**Staff at peak**	**Staff at end of 2008**	**2009**
Newhouse Newspapers	26	Closed	—
Copley and Copley News Service	9	Closed	—
Hearst News Service	16	4	—
Gannett	28*	25	Cuts expected
Cox	20	14	Expected to close
Los Angeles Times	54	(Bureau Closed)+	+The combined Tribune Co. bureau now employs 35 journalists in total, down from the 95 who worked for the seven surviving Tribune papers at their peak.
Chicago Tribune	20	(Bureau Closed)+	
Baltimore Sun	12	(Bureau Closed)+	
Hartford Courant	5	(Bureau Closed)+	
Stephen's Media Group	6	1	1
Newsday	15	1	1
Business Week	20	3	3

Represents staffing levels in early 2007, which may not have been the peak.
+*The seven surviving Tribune papers include the Los Angeles Times, Chicago Tribune, Baltimore Sun, Hartford Couran , Sun Sentinel (South Florida), Orlando Sentinel and Allentown Pennsylvania Morning Call.*

Source: PEJ Research

Salt Lake Tribune Correspondent Thomas Burr, the current president of the Regional Reporters Association, which represents smaller papers around the country, says 15 of his members vanished in the months since he took over the organization in July of 2008. That represents roughly 20% of his membership and includes the *Deseret News*, ending more than six decades of Washington coverage from that paper. "It seems like just about every time I send out an email [to members], somebody's address bounces back," Burr said. "We sometimes joke that we're becoming an endangered species." . . .

The Rise of Niche

If the mainstream media have shrunk so dramatically, even before the last year, how is it that the overall numbers of journalists in Washington have not?

The answer is that a new Washington media have evolved, but they are far from the more egalitarian or citizen-based media that advocates of the digital age might imagine. Instead, this new Washington media cohort is one substantially aimed at elites, often organized by industry, by corporate client, or by niche political interest.

It represents the dramatic expansion of a once small niche sector of the Washington press corps—a group that as recently as a decade ago amounted to a couple of Capitol Hill newspapers that covered the nuts and bolts of Congress for staffers and lobbyists and a disparate collection of trade magazines and print newsletters that tracked narrow issues for those working industries ranging from aviation and health care, to energy and construction. For the most part, mainstream media journalists—and much of Washington itself—looked down upon the work of these publications as both boring and peripheral to the "real" challenge of covering Washington politics. The dream of many niche sector journalists was to land work with a major mainstream outlet.

Not any more. Today, many of Washington's most experienced and talented journalists no longer explain the workings of the federal government to those in the general public, but to specialty audiences whose interests tend to be both narrow and deep.

These are publications with names like *Climate Wire*, *Energy Trader*, *Traffic World*, *Government Executive* and *Food Chemical News*. Their audiences vary, but most readers find the content increasingly important—even crucial—for their job, their business and their industry. Because of this, readers—usually with employer support—are willing to pay significant subscription fees—high enough that some are profitable with small readerships and little advertising. . . .

The number of niche publications in Washington has been rising since the 1980s. Hudson's listings of specialty magazines, newsletters and periodicals, for example, jumped up by roughly one-third between 1985 and 2008 and by nearly 20% between 2004 and 2008. . . .

Today, it is the niche, not the mainstream, media that blanket coverage of Congress and other important arms of the federal government. And the reports today are not only daily but often more instantaneous than that.

Among the biggest and best known is Bloomberg News. The news agency offers some coverage that the general public can see on its website or via aggregators such as Yahoo!, but its bread and butter is a top-line base of about 275,000 clients worldwide, which include financial institutions, business groups, government agencies, well-to-do individuals, or anyone else with economic interests and a willingness to pay $18,000-plus a year per lease for the terminal needed to receive the service.

The company, which had no regular presence on Capitol Hill in the mid-1980s, had 112 staff members accredited in 2008, close behind the 134 of the Associated Press. It also has experienced, respected beat reporters covering key federal agencies, including the Pentagon, the State Department, Treasury and the White House. Its White House correspondent, Edwin Chen, who once covered both Congress and the president for the *Los Angeles Times*, will become president of the White House Correspondents Assn. in the spring of 2009. . . .

The growth of this niche media has been fueled by a perfect storm of events—a dramatic rise in federal spending and an accompanying jump in potential readership concentrated in and around Capitol Hill and the offices of K Street lobbyists that value the information produced by these publications enough to pay the full cost of gathering it. Meanwhile, rapid IT advances allowed publishers to create niche online publications that could deliver information faster, at lower costs, to ever more targeted audiences and make a profit. . . .

If there is a ground zero to this growth of niche media in Washington, it is Capitol Hill, where publications such as *Roll Call, The Hill, Politico,* the *National Journal* and *CQ* jostle for an edge in reporting even the smallest details affecting a legislative proposal, tidbits of insider gossip, or whiffs of political deals, whether formal or informal. Many of these publications have been reporting events on Capitol Hill for decades, but unspoken gentlemen's agreements that long defined a series of spheres of dominance tended to discourage direct competition—until IT advances and the prospect of major profits transformed the environment into a competitive free-for-all somewhat akin to a 1930s New York City newspaper war. . . .

The Implications of The New Washington Media

If the press corps in Washington aimed at the American public in general is shrinking, and the one aimed at self-defined specialized groups is growing, what does that mean about the kind of monitoring of government the press engages in? And how might that change how public opinion is formed and shaped, and does that have implications for policy and the political process?

The answers are necessarily somewhat subjective, but the evidence, and even the feelings of the journalists involved in the process, suggest a growing knowledge gap between those who place high value on information and—organized usually inside professional settings, are willing to pay a premium for that information—and a general citizenry organized more loosely by geography that will find it harder to keep tabs on what is going on.

In short, those influencing policy have access to more information than ever, while those affected by those policies—but not organized to shape them—are likely to be less informed.

The decline of regional newspaper bureaus, for instance, means that sometimes entire state congressional delegations are either under-covered or uncovered completely. Few, for example, believe a national daily or news magazine would have invested the reporting time to follow up the suspicious travel patterns of Southern California Congressman Randy "Duke" Cunningham. Those initial tips led the Washington-based Copley News Service and the *San Diego Union-Tribune* to unearth corrupt practices serious enough to send Cunningham to jail and win them the 2006 Pulitzer for national reporting.

Less dramatic, yet still important, stories also disappear with the closure of smaller bureaus. Voters in Maine, for example, will likely not see, any time soon, the story *Portland Press-Herald/Maine Sunday Telegram* Washington correspondent Jonathan Kaplan was researching when he was laid off last July. The story, about the curious relationship between his state's two senators, Olympia Snow and Susan Collins, is of little interest to any newspaper outside the state, and with no other Washington-based reporter writing solely from the perspective of Maine residents; he was probably the only one with the time and the interest to report it. The *Press-Herald* was the last newspaper with its own Washington bureau in a state that in the mid-1980s had four. An Associated Press regional reporter in Washington is assigned to track developments of interest to Maine residents, but he also has other responsibilities, including covering for three other states and national labor issues.

"In a small state like Maine, most people have met Snow[e] or Collins, but people don't know who they really are, what they do, how they interact and how they make decisions," said Kaplan. . . .

As local outlets abandon coverage of national affairs, one worry is that different public perspectives are lost. Media more closely tied to far away communities tend to see national politics differently than the elite media in New York and Washington. Former Knight Ridder and now McClatchy Bureau Chief John Walcott believes that writing for regional newspapers played an important role in his bureau's more skeptical coverage of the run up to the Iraq war than was provided by the national press. At a panel honoring the bureau for winning the first I. F. Stone Award from Harvard last year for that coverage, Wolcott was asked why his bureau was different.

"One distinction between the way we looked at this march to war and the way the *Washington Post* and *New York Times* did was driven by the fact that we don't own newspapers in Washington or New York," he said. "We're not writing for those people. We were writing, and it was very much on my mind the whole time, for the mothers and the fathers and the sisters and brothers and the sons and the daughters of the people who were going to be sent to fight this war because we own the paper in Columbus, Georgia where Fort Benning is; [in] Lexington, Kentucky, near Fort Campbell; in Fort Worth, Texas, near Fort Hood; [in] Wichita and Kansas City near Fort Riley. That's who we were writing for, and that's who we were thinking about. Is the administration making a case that justifies sending those young men and women into what the administration was arguing were going to be clouds of sarin gas and heaven knows what else? Whereas in Washington, it was all about what was going on inside the Beltway. I think it's a different perspective.". . .

There are some examples that suggest the niche media and the opinion media can, on occasion, function as a watchdog on government, even if their audience is specialized and small.

Joshua Marshall, editor-publisher of the political blog, Talking Points Memo, is widely credited with uncovering the political dimension behind the firings of several highly regarded federal prosecutors, which eventually led to the resignation of Attorney General Alberto Gonzales and won Marshall a George Polk Award for his work. "Noting a similarity between firings in Arkansas and California, Marshall and his staff . . . connected the dots and found a pattern of federal prosecutors being forced from office for failing to do the Bush Administration's bidding," noted the Polk Awards announcement.

Roll Call was the first to report the arrest of former Idaho Sen. Larry Craig for allegedly attempting to solicit sex in a Minneapolis Airport public toilet, beating the *Idaho Statesman*, which had been working on a related story about Craig. And it was *Government Executive*, a small circulation business magazine for federal government managers, who exposed Census Bureau mismanagement of a $650 million program to eliminate paperwork by equipping 2010 census-takers with hand-held computers.

But these are largely exceptions for a part of the Washington media known more for its ability to report exhaustively on narrow, complex issues, than for aggressive investigative or what some call public service journalism. In the end, virtually all of those interviewed for this study expressed concern about the potential impact a shrinking flow of information to the general public would have on the democratic process.

The migration of respected bylines from daily newspapers to a thriving group of niche publications also carries implications of its own about the current state of America's democracy. To the applause of the public at large, incoming president Barack Obama campaigned to "end the failed policies . . . that put special interests ahead of working families." But as he adjusts to Washington, he will deal with a media that has seen talent and experience flow away from mainstream outlets that serve "main street" and moved instead to niche publications that serve Washington's special interests. . . .

Almost certainly, the federal government is going to play an enlarged role in American lives in the Obama era. And one adage almost certainly applies—as government grows and tries to [e]ffect change, so will the efforts of special interests to shape that change. The news media in place to cover that transformation is very different from the one even Obama's predecessor arrived to find eight years earlier. Elites who are plugged into the new fragmented niche media of

Washington will know how that government is growing and what it means, and they will be learning it through new media channels. Their fellow citizens who rely on local or network television or their daily newspapers, however, will be harder pressed to learn what their elected representatives are doing. . . .

NOTES

1. As of January 2009, *Time* had eight in its Washington bureau, down from more than 30 in the mid-1980s.

2. This means accredited to cover the 110th Congress, whose term concluded at the end of 2008.

3. State Department Correspondents Assn. records. Interest in the State Department may well jump during the early months of a new secretary of state's time in office. Typically, network correspondents jostle for position at briefings and fight hard to grab a sought-after seat on the first foreign trip. NBC, ABC, CNN and Fox all were present at Hillary Clinton's first public appearance as Secretary of State in the department's 8th floor ceremonial reception room. How long this interest remains depends on the public interest in the secretary and story itself.

14-3

Free Falls, High Dives, and the Future of Democratic Accountability

Scott L. Althaus

The previous essay discusses how newspapers have fallen on hard times as citizens have gravitated to cable television and the internet for political news. The traditional newspapers have been fairly successful in attracting consumers to their Web sites; they have been almost uniformly unsuccessful in persuading consumers that they should pay for access. Whether the newspaper industry succeeds depends on developing a viable business model that fits the public's evolving news consumption preferences.

Much of what we know about the public's news consumption habits comes from public opinion surveys asking respondents how frequently they use some medium. Respondents' answers, however, are subject to forgetfulness and guess work. In this essay Scott Althaus employs measurements developed by the news and advertising industries to confirm that consumption of news— especially via the print media—has been steadily declining over the past two decades. But Althaus discovers interesting deviations in the trend. Whenever important events occur, the public ratchets up its news consumption, benefitting some news media more than others.

THE HEALTH of a democracy rests on the vigilance of its citizens, and democracy works best when citizens pay attention to the governing process. Different models of democracy envision different roles for citizens to fulfill, but every theory of democracy agrees that the most basic role of the citizen is to hold leaders accountable for what they have done or intend to do.[1]

Yet we know little about the conditions under which citizens are most likely to exercise such vigilance by going out and seeking political information. Recent scholarship has demonstrated that threats of various sorts can motivate people to gather information.[2] It would seem that citizen interest in politics should be most acute when the political stakes are perceived as high, or when the risk of

Source: Scott L. Althaus, "Free Falls, High Dives, and the Future of Democratic Accountability," in *The Politics of News: The News of Politics,* ed. Doris A. Graber, Denis McQuail, and Pippa Norris (Washington, D.C.: CQ Press, 2007), 161–169, 171–181, 184–189. Some notes appearing in the original have been deleted.

future harm is great. For example, citizen knowledge of politics over the latter half of the twentieth century hit an all-time high in the 1960s, presumably because of the social turmoil occurring during that decade.[3] Likewise, the American public receives higher scores on political knowledge tests given during presidential election campaigns than it does during midterm congressional elections, apparently because the highly visible presidential campaigns remind people how important it is to follow government affairs.[4] If citizen engagement in politics goes up when the political environment generates reasons to be attentive, then democratic accountability might occur most efficiently during periods of social unrest or economic hardship, as the history of "critical realignments" in American elections suggests.[5]

If vigilance follows times of trouble, then complacence should emerge in the wake of peace and prosperity. Although this prediction implies that political accountability might be harder to achieve when things are generally going well, it also suggests a reassuring explanation for one of the most vexing trends confronting American political communication scholars: the long-term decline in the size of audiences for traditional news coverage in the United States.

At the height of the Vietnam War in 1969, fully half of U.S. households tuned in to one of the three nightly news broadcasts. By 2000 the combined audience for network nightly news had dropped to less than a quarter of U.S. households. The same historical decline has affected newspaper readership. Daily newspaper circulation in the United States was approximately one newspaper per household in 1970. By 2000 weekday newspaper penetration had fallen to slightly more than one newspaper for every two households, a drop of nearly 50 percent in just thirty years.[6]

What happened between the 1960s and the turn of the twenty-first century that could explain these declines in the size of news audiences? One factor might be the end of the Vietnam War. The post-Vietnam period was a time not only of peace for Americans but also of rapidly growing prosperity. Between 1970 and 2000 per capita disposable income in the United States grew by 188 percent after controlling for inflation and changes in the price of personal commodities.[7] If times of peace and prosperity are partly responsible for the apparent demobilization of news audiences, then the public's limited amount of attention to the news in 2000 compared to 1969 could be less ominous that it might seem. As long as Americans return to the news when times again become troubled, their waning interest during good times may be of no lasting consequence. Firefighters make for pleasant company, but showing up when the house is in flames is what really counts.

If popular vigilance is an essential ingredient to successful democratic governance, then we want to know whether diminishing levels of citizen attentiveness to politics is more like a free fall or a high dive. Leaving the safety of the airplane signals a point of no return for the parachutist. Pulling the rip cord can slow down but not reverse the jumper's fall. Once on the ground, the time and expense involved in reloading the chute and flying back to altitude makes the jumper unlikely to turn around and do it again. The same may be true of interest in the news. If people reach their "tipping point" and stop paying close attention to the daily doings of political leaders, then the declining size of newspaper and broadcast news audiences may signal a long-term demobilization that results in permanently smaller and more specialized sets of niche audiences for various types of political information.[8]

But news audiences may be more resilient than they appear. Plunging headfirst from an aerial platform without a parachute sounds catastrophic, but not when the platform is a diving board suspended above a deep pool of water. The diver speeds downward but eventually bobs back up. Climbing out and scaling the ladder for another leap is easily done, and the cycle continues until the interest fades. The size of the news audience might fall when times are good, but rise again when bad times return. In such a situation, an apparent long-term decline in the health of the body politic may rapidly change for the better once a pressing need arises for renewed citizen vigilance.[9]

The difficulty in sorting out free falls from high dives comes from the challenge of identifying the unique impact of numerous factors that simultaneously influence the changing composition of news audiences over time. Comparing news habits during the Vietnam War to those at the start of the twenty-first century tells us little about the reasons for decline, as more than peace and prosperity transpired in the intervening years. The growth of cable news channels and the advent of the Internet contributed to the fragmentation of audiences for traditional news formats, just as the rise of radio and broadcast television ate away at newspaper audiences in the decades before the 1960s. Today's audiences are also lured away from news coverage by a wider range of non-news media choices than were available in 1970, from video games and personal computers to home theaters and MTV.[10] No simple comparison between the Vietnam era and today can control for the multiple influences of these other developments. To figure out not only whether the long-term contraction in the size of print and broadcast news audiences is temporary or permanent, but also how large the drop actually is, would require a census of audiences for all available news outlets. Given the complexity and scope of the contemporary media environment, such a survey may be impossible.

We have, however, a different way to approach the question that can help sort out the impact of these many competing influences. Sudden changes in the political environment following the onset of national crises provide opportunities to study the response of news audiences during times when technological advances and the state of the economy are more or less constant. This chapter considers patterns of surge and decline in news attention for [two] such cases: the Persian Gulf crisis of 1990–1991, [and] the terrorist attacks of September 11, 2001. The cases have clear and sudden starting points: the 9/11 attacks were completely unanticipated, as was Iraq's invasion of neighboring Kuwait on August 2, 1990. Moreover, the Persian Gulf crisis occurred more than two years before the advent of the World Wide Web and during a time when CNN's tiny audience and lack of cable competitors made it a novel but relatively minor player on the media scene. The timing of these two crises allows for a comparison between the dynamics of audience response in the more concentrated television news system that existed in 1991, when the three network evening news broadcasts were the main source of news for American audiences, and the highly segmented multi-outlet system that was in place by 2001. . . . Comparing the percentage of adults attending to the news before and after each precipitating event should reveal how the crisis atmosphere stimulated changes in levels of popular attention to the news.

Free Fall or High Dive?

To understand whether the American public's appetite for political news is stimulated by the loss of peace or threats to prosperity, we must start by assessing the degree to which the public sees different sources of news as useful for keeping up with national and international events. National surveys conducted since 1991 by the Pew Research Center for the People and the Press provide detailed information about the media consumption habits of the U.S. public. Figure 1 shows that when people are asked where they were most likely to turn for news about national and international issues, television news has long been the most popular source of political information in the United States.[11] In 2006, three out of four respondents named television as one of their main sources of news about national and international issues. In contrast, only about four in ten respondents mentioned newspapers as a major source of such information in 2006; one in four named the Internet; and two in ten relied on radio.

Because Pew allows respondents to mention up to two main sources of news about national and international issues, the numbers for each year can add up to far more than 100 percent. The best way to interpret these survey results is to note the trends over time and whether use of different media for surveillance changes in response to the onset of wars, major political events, or national crises. The relative importance of television, newspapers, and radio for keeping up with national and international issues has been relatively stable since 1990. Television's overwhelming popularity waned somewhat during

Figure 1. Where Amercians get most of their news about national and international issues, 1990–2006

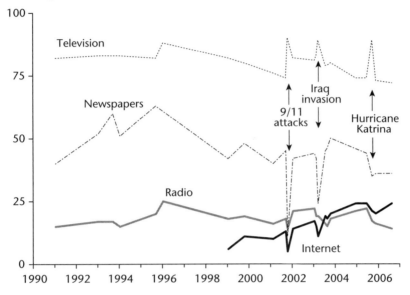

Percentage of adults

Source: Pew Research Center for People and the Press.

the late 1990s, but revived after 9/11. Newspapers are the second-most popular source for following news of global and domestic importance, but reliance on newspapers for this purpose peaked in the mid-1990s and has been waning ever since. Radio used to be the third-most mentioned source of political news, and its use for this purpose has remained relatively steady since 1990. Of the four media considered here, the Internet was the least-turned-to news medium for national and international issues until after the invasion of Iraq. But popular interest in using the Internet to follow news of the world has been building steadily since the late 1990s. Starting in July 2003 the Internet has been consistently mentioned by more people than radio as an important source of news about major events.

Yet when national crises erupt, these conventional patterns of self-reported media reliance can change quite dramatically. Figure 1 shows how reliance on television news spiked after the September 2001 attacks, the March 2003 invasion of Iraq, and Hurricane Katrina in September 2005. Short-term increases in reliance on television for news of national and international issues were accompanied by short-term declines in the use of radio and the Internet, as well as the dramatic abandonment of newspapers as a main source for political surveillance in the case of the two threats to national peace. Americans, however, did not stop reading newspapers or listening to radio news during these national crises. Instead, these data tell us merely that the perceived usefulness of the four media changed abruptly when circumstances became dire, and that television is seen as the most important news source for national and international information during times of national crisis.

Claiming to rely on a medium for keeping up with a particular kind of news does not imply doing it often. It is important to place the trends in Figure 1 into perspective. Interest in national and international news topics is not widespread in the American public. For example, Pew data show that during most of 2005 and 2006 only four in ten Americans said they paid very close attention to news about the war in Iraq.[12] For this reason, we need to examine what Americans do, not just what they say. Do sudden changes in national fortunes precipitate rapid growth in the size of news audiences for television, radio, newspapers, and the Internet? Addressing this question requires examining trends in ratings and circulation data for each medium in turn, beginning with national television news programming.

Audience Demand for Broadcast Television News

Nightly network news broadcasts hold the attention of a larger portion of Americans than any other single news product in the United States, including cable news. For example, *CBS Evening News with Katie Couric* was the lowest-rated network evening news program at the end of 2006. During the week of December 18, the average nightly audience for Couric's broadcast was 7.4 million viewers, compared to 8.5 million for ABC's *World News Tonight* and 9.5 million for NBC's *Nightly News*. Yet Couric's average nightly audience was more than two and a half times as large as the total audience for the top-rated programs on Fox, CNN, and MSNBC combined. For the week of December 18, the combined audience for Fox's *O'Reilly Factor,* CNN's *Paula Zahn Now,* and MSNBC's *Countdown with Keith Olbermann* averaged just 2.8 million viewers per night.[13] In contrast, the combined nightly audience for the three network news programs during the week of December 18 was nine times as large. Although network news audiences have been in decline for many decades, they still dwarf the nearest competitor on cable television.

To track short-term changes in the size of network news audiences over time, I combined weekly television ratings data collected by Nielsen Media Research for ABC's *World News Tonight,* CBS's *Evening News,* and NBC's *Nightly News.*[14] Translating these ratings data into the percentage of American adults tuning in to the nightly news corrects for population growth in the United States that occurred between 1990 and 2001.[15]

Figure 2. Average combined audience for evening network news broadcasts
around the time of the Persian Gulf Crisis and the 9/11 attacks

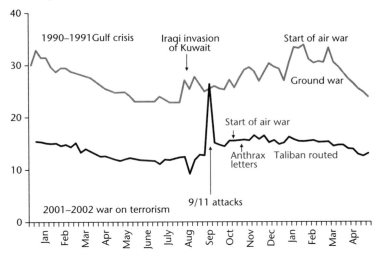

Percentage of adults

Source: Nielsen Media Research, complied from various sources.

One striking feature of these trends (see Figure 2) is that the evening news
audience was only about half as large in 2001 as it was a decade before. During
the 1990–1991 period, between 23 percent and 33 percent of American adults
watched nightly network news broadcasts, depending on the time of year.
Since January 2001 Nielsen data put the total size of nightly news audiences at
between 11 percent and 16 percent of American adults (not counting the week
of 9/11). Today's total audience for all forms of public affairs content is probably smaller than it was a decade before, but the main reason for today's
smaller network television news audience is that the once-larger broadcast
news audience of 1990–1991 is spread across a wider range of news products,
with cable, the Internet, and local television news now attracting sizable portions of a national news audience that in 1990 was shared mainly by the three
evening news programs.

Because news audiences have become fragmented, absolute differences in the
percentage of adults watching network news during each crisis period are less
telling than the relative changes in audience size within each trend. If we begin
our analysis immediately before the onset of each crisis and follow the trends
over the next several months, the two cases appear to reveal different patterns of
audience response. The Iraqi invasion of Kuwait produced an immediate four
percentage point spike in the U.S. news audience. The nightly news audience

then grew steadily during the fall as the U.S. military buildup in Saudi Arabia signaled a looming confrontation with Iraq. Nearly a third of U.S. adults were directly exposed to one of the three nightly news broadcasts during the weeks leading up to and immediately following the start of the air war on January 16, 1991. The news audience shrank somewhat in early February but jumped three percentage points during the week of ground combat, which began on February 23. A rapid victory over Iraqi ground forces was followed by an abrupt turn away from the news, and the nightly audience dropped nearly ten percentage points over the eight weeks following the close of the ground campaign.

A decade later, the tragedies of 9/11 had the immediate effect of doubling the size of the evening news audience, from 13 percent of U.S. adults in the week of September 3–9 to more than 26 percent in the week of September 10–16. Just as swiftly, however, the evening news audience contracted to 15 percent of adults in the week of September 17–23 and never rose more than 1.5 percentage points above that level in the following seven months. In contrast to frequent event-driven surges in news attention throughout the Persian Gulf crisis, network news attention in the post-9/11 United States held quite stable at about four percentage points above pre-9/11 levels for several months before declining steadily after the start of the new year in 2002. By the middle of April 2002, the size of the evening news audience had returned to the previous July's level of just 13 percent of adults.

When interpreting these postcrisis trends using the immediate precrisis period as a benchmark, it appears that the Persian Gulf crisis produced a gradual mobilization of Americans into the television news audience, but that the onset of the war on terrorism generated a smaller shock to the size of news audiences that started decaying soon after it began. During the Persian Gulf crisis, the average size of the evening news audience grew by 13.8 million persons between the last week of July 1990 and the first week of January 1991. During the onset of the war on terrorism, the growth in the evening news audience between these same two weeks was only half as large, amounting to 7.4 million more audience members in January 2002 compared to the previous July.

This interpretation of postcrisis growth in the news audience, however, requires us to ignore the left-hand side of Figure 2. The longer-term trends leading up to each precipitating event call into question whether either of these national crises fundamentally increased the size of the broadcast news audience. Network television news audiences swell during the winter months, when people spend more time indoors, and shrink in the summer months. . . . Because of the seasonal variation, a more appropriate way of measuring the impact of national crises is to calculate the size of the news audience after the precipitating event compared to its size from the same period in the previous year. This comparison paints a very different picture. During the Persian Gulf crisis an average of approximately 2.4 million more adults per day were watching evening news broadcasts in the first four months of 1991 compared to the first four months of 1990. The same comparison for the onset of the war on terrorism produces a mean difference of just less than 900,000 more audience members per day in 2002 than in 2001. Seasonal-adjusted growth in the news audience was nearly three times as large during the Persian Gulf crisis as during the current war on terrorism, but in both cases the magnitude of growth was rather small, amounting to 0.4 percent of adults in 2001–2002 and 1.3 percent in 1990–1991.[16] Seen from this perspective, the clearest impact of the Iraqi invasion of Kuwait was the increase in the amount of weekly variance around the seasonal mean rather than a shift in the mean itself. Similarly, 9 / 11 appears to have accelerated the seasonal growth curve for the evening news audience during the fall of 2001 without producing a substantive shift in its average size. . . .

In short, the daily news audience for network news broadcasts is much larger than any other daily broadcast or cable news audience in the United States. But short-term changes in the size of the network news audience are typically influenced less by the current state of national security than by the current state of the weather.

Audience Demand for Cable Television News

The size of audiences for cable news channels is hard to pin down because of the format differences between traditional network broadcasts and cable channels. Audiences for nightly news broadcasts are concentrated into a single thirty-minute time period per day, but audiences for cable news channels come and go around the clock. Cable viewership can therefore be very small for any given program but fairly large when the number of unique viewers is considered over longer periods of time. Researchers use two methods to measure audience size for cable news channels: the average number of viewers in a typical minute of a day, and the cumulative number of unique viewers that have watched the channel at some point during an entire month.

The average number of people watching cable news channels at any given minute of the day is usually quite modest by network news standards. Figure 3 shows the combined average audience per minute for the top three cable news channels: CNN, Fox, and MSNBC. The impact of the 9 / 11 attacks on long-term trends in cable news viewership is unmistakable. From January 1998 to August 2001, the combined daytime audience for the three cable channels

Figure 3. Average combined audience for CNN, Fox, and MSNBC cable
news channel during daytime and primetime hours, 1998–2005

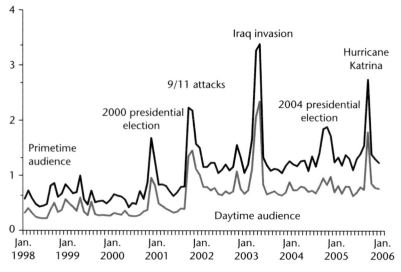

Source: Nielson Media Research, Project for Excellence in Journalism.

averaged just less than 0.4 percent of adults, or about 770,000 persons, while
the combined primetime audience per minute averaged nearly 0.7 percent of
adults, or about 1.4 million persons. From September 2001 to December 2005,
the average daytime cable audience grew to nearly 0.9 percent of adults, or
approximately 1.8 million people, while the average primetime audience
expanded to 1.4 percent of adults per minute, or 2.9 million viewers. The
increased national security threat following 9/11 effectively doubled the audience for cable news channels.

In addition to expanding the regular audience for cable news, national
crises and high-visibility political events can have even stronger short-term
effects on public attention to cable news programming. Figure 3 shows that
as recounts were ordered in several states after the 2000 presidential election,
the average cable news audience in November 2000 was three times the size
of the average cable news audience when the campaign began in September.
Likewise, comparing cable news attention in August and September 2004
shows that the start of the presidential campaign increased the size of the
primetime viewing audience by nearly a third for all three cable channels
combined. Dramatic crises had a similar effect on the size of cable news audiences. The 9/11 attacks produced a fourfold increase in the size of the average cable news audience, from 1.6 million primetime viewers in August 2001
to 4.6 million primetime viewers in September. But the average cable news

audience contracted swiftly in the months following the attacks. By January 2002 the combined per-minute audience for the three cable channels averaged 2.4 million primetime viewers, just half the size of the peak audience in September 2001. More dramatic changes in the size of the average cable news audience followed the invasion of Iraq in March 2003 and the aftermath of Hurricane Katrina in September 2005. The average minute of primetime cable news programming during the intense ground combat in April 2003 drew 3.5 million more viewers than in February 2003, a month before the invasion. The flooding of the Gulf Coast after the hurricane temporarily expanded the average audience for primetime cable news from 1.5 percent of adults in August 2005 to 2.7 percent in September, before just as swiftly snapping back to 1.4 percent in October. . . .

The cumulative number of unique cable news viewers per month may be more than twice as large as the average nightly audience for the three network newscasts, but . . . it is difficult to tell whether cable news attracts more or fewer unique viewers per month than broadcast news. It is also important to consider that this measure of the cable audience includes persons who tune in for just six minutes per month, whereas network news viewers tend to be habitually attentive. . . . Moreover, it is unclear whether even regular cable viewers are getting a mix of news comparable to that received by network audiences. A content analysis of primetime news programming on CNN, Fox, and MSNBC during late January 2002 found that cable news shows focused on a small number of "headline" stories and that much of the primetime programming took the form of personal interviews or panel discussions rather than traditional news reporting.[17] The cumulative cable news audience can include a large cross-section of the public, but this cross-section constitutes an irregular audience for news programming, tuning in to catch up with developing stories or breaking events but probably relying on noncable sources for whatever regular news diet they might choose to consume.

Audience Demand for Newspapers

Reading newspapers is relatively more habit-driven than watching television news. Eight out of ten regular newspapers readers are subscribers who have made a long-term financial commitment to a paper.[18] For this reason, levels of newspaper reading tend to remain stable even during times of national crisis.

The 1930s marked the beginning of a steady, long-term decline in American newspaper readership that has continued undisturbed by wars and other catalyzing events. Figure 4 shows a steady pattern starting with 1964, the year that the Gulf of Tonkin incident propelled the United States into a large-scale military

Figure 4. Combined national weekday readership for daily
newspapers, 1964–2006

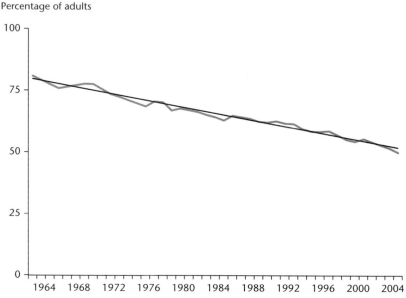

Source: Newspaper Association of America, complied from various sources.

involvement in Vietnam, and continuing through 2006.[19] The straight line in Figure 4 illustrates the predicted erosion of the newspaper audience over time, and, compared to the actual decline, shows how little impact wars and other dramatic events have had on newspaper readership over time. Daily newspaper readership during the Vietnam War started at 81 percent in 1964 but fell to 78 percent by 1970. The declining interest in newspapers continued through the 9/11 attacks[20] and the war in Iraq.

By 2006 only 50 percent of U.S. adults were estimated to read a daily newspaper. Although this sounds like a sizable news audience, research shows that only half of those readers pay regular attention to national or international news items, about the same proportion that reads the sports pages. Instead, newspaper readers disproportionately specialize in local news.[21] But because nearly nine in ten newspaper readers report paying attention to stories on the front page, it is likely that a fairly large proportion of Americans read prominent newspaper coverage of national or international news.

Audience Demand for Radio News

Like newspaper readers, the radio news audience consists mainly of habitual rather than occasional listeners. The highest levels of weekday radio news exposure occur during the morning and evening rush hours, mainly among motorists commuting between work and home.[22] Because commutes occur without regard to the weather or major events of the day, radio listeners constitute one of the most loyal and stable of news audiences.

It is important to distinguish between commercial and public radio news audiences, because commercial news-talk formats combine shorter headline-style reports with call-in discussion and interview programs, while public radio news formats tend to combine longer stories on events of the day with in-depth analysis. . . . Quarter-hour ratings the average quarter-hour radio audience for all commercial news and talk radio formats combined, excluding sports-only stations provide the average number of different persons who are listening to a format for at least five minutes in any given fifteen-minute block of time. They are therefore directly comparable in magnitude to the average audience estimates for network television and cable news. The largest audience for news formats on commercial radio listens during the morning and afternoon weekday drive times, averaging around 2 percent of American adults. . . .

Like cable, the size of the radio news audience at any given time of day is proportionally quite small, but unlike cable, it is largely unaffected by the onset of national crises. Short-lived surges in the size of the commercial radio news audience are visible for the quarterly periods including the 9/11 attacks and the 2003 invasion of Iraq, as well as the presidential elections of 2000 and 2004, but these changes are so small as to be hardly distinguishable from normal quarterly movement in the audience trends. As unresponsive as commercial news radio audiences can be, the radio audience as a whole can sometimes surge in impressive ways. An Arbitron study of radio audiences before, during, and after the 9/11 attacks found that the combined national audience for all forms of radio programming on the day of the attacks was 5 million persons above normal listening levels, a surge of roughly 2 percent of American adults within a single day.[23] . . .

The news audience for public radio is less than half the size of the audience for commercial news radio. But as with cable news, the cumulative audience for radio news can be much larger than the average audience. In 2006 the weekly cumulative audience for news-based program formats on public radio stations averaged 22.2 million unique listeners for the four public radio networks combined, which translates to 10.8 percent of the adult population.[24]

. . . According to the Pew data, the percentage of adults saying they regularly listen to NPR nearly doubled between 1994 and 1995, from 9 percent to 15 percent, but grew more slowly from that point until 2006, when 17 percent called themselves regular NPR listeners.[25] On this measure, most of the audience

Figure 5. Self-reported intentional, accidental, and back-channel
exposure to news on the Internet, 1995–2006

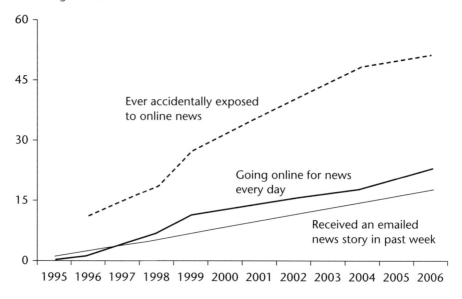

Source: Pew Research Center for People and the Press.

growth for public radio programming occurred well before the 9/11 attacks
and the Iraq war, suggesting again that the size of the radio news audience is
relatively unaffected by current events.

Audience Demand for Online News

. . . Popular access to the World Wide Web began with the advent of the
Mosaic browser in 1993. National media use surveys conducted by the Pew
Center show that online news audiences grew rapidly thereafter. Figure 5
shows that less than a quarter of a percent of adults reported visiting Internet
news sites every day in 1994. That number grew to 11 percent by 1999 and 23
percent by 2006. Not only have online news sites become more popular during a period of declining interest in traditional news outlets, but decisions to
seek out online news seem to be driven less by habit than by the occurrence
of newsworthy developments. Figure 1 showed that Americans report
slightly less dependence on the Internet for news during periods of national
crisis than during normal times, but other research suggests that breaking

news events are associated with temporary surges in the size of audiences for Internet news sites. This research suggests that event-driven interest in Internet news sites surges and declines in a way similar to that of cable news audiences, in contrast to the more stable viewership for broadcast television news, radio news, and newspapers during periods of national crisis.[26]

Although online news sites are growing in popularity, less is known about which news sites are attracting audiences and what kinds of news stories those audiences are seeking online. Research on the Internet use habits of a random sample of the population found that the most popular online news sites corresponded closely to the most popular off-line news outlets: the top six national news sites, in descending order of page-hit popularity, belonged to CNN, CBS News, *USA Today,* the *New York Times,* the *Washington Post,* and ABC News. This pattern suggests that the news stories people read online are likely to be quite similar to the stories they follow in traditional mainstream news outlets. This conclusion is underscored by the finding that visitors to online news sites, like the readers of printed newspapers, tended to pay slightly more attention to sports news than to news of national and world events.[27]

The proliferation of news outlets on the Internet has, however, produced new modes of exposure that have the potential to disseminate public affairs information far beyond the ranks of those who seek it out intentionally. The widespread use of Web portals combined with imprecise methods for locating Web-based information has caused ever more people to accidentally expose themselves to news stories online. Figure 5 shows that the percentage of Americans who have come across news stories when going online for a purpose other than to search for news rose from 11 percent in 1996 to 51 percent in 2006.[28] This number is especially impressive when we consider that only 67 percent of Americans reported ever going online at all as of 2006, which means that 76 percent of Internet users report being accidentally exposed to news stories. However, an early study on the types of people who report being accidentally exposed concluded that "those who tend to look for news online are the ones who tend to come across it by accident as well," suggesting that incidental exposure may not substantially broaden the flow of public affairs information reaching the politically disinterested.[29] . . .

The Future of Democratic Accountability

The short-term dynamics of news attention following sudden threats to national peace and prosperity offer a mix of sobering and encouraging trends. The proportion of Americans following network newscasts, newspapers, and radio news stations tended to be relatively stable before, during, and after times of national crisis. The main exception proves the rule when it comes to popular use of traditional news media: the network news audience doubled in size following the 9/11 attacks, but this surge lasted no longer than a week . . . the cable news audience surges when threats are imminent and recedes when the immediate outlook improves. Internet news audiences seem to follow a similar pattern.

Demand for news therefore seems sensitive to current events when it comes to cable and Internet audiences, but relatively inelastic when it comes to newspapers, radio, and broadcast television. Countering the long-term demobilization that might be occurring in the U.S. news audience is a short-term responsiveness when peace and prosperity are threatened that is heartening but difficult to evaluate. The proportion of Americans tuning in to Fox and CNN for anything more than a brief glimpse at the latest headlines remains unclear, but the growing popularity of Internet news outlets is another positive sign for the health of American democracy.

As encouraging as these findings may be, the long-term trends in news attentiveness give pause. Newspaper and network television news audiences keep draining steadily away, as they have for decades, while radio audiences remain stable but small. That the normally small cable news audience doubled in size after 9/11 and that the online news audience is growing over time suggests that the long-term loss of audience shares for traditional news products may partly represent changing preferences for newer news products. If so, then the shrinking audience for network broadcasts and newspapers might be driven more by changes in the technology of news delivery than by any long-term popular demobilization from the world of public affairs. If a direct transfer of audience shares from old media to new media is under way, then it is possible that today's news audience could be numerically as large in the aggregate as it was in the 1970s. . . .

The pessimistic view is that overall news consumption levels may be substantially lower today than they were in the 1970s. The steady loss of newspaper readers and network news viewers predates the advent of CNN and the World Wide Web. And given the flourishing array of entertainment media alternatives that have sprung up since the late 1960s to occupy the attention of ordinary citizens, it is unlikely that a direct transfer of audiences from old news to new news has been taking place. Instead, the new era of multimedia entertainment has almost certainly eroded the audience base for news products in the United States.[30] The question is by how much. We know that news audiences today are spread out among a broader range of information sources, but our ability to accurately measure the size of audiences for cable and Internet news remains tentative and imprecise. We do not yet have a gauge that can tell us how much less attention the American public pays to political news today compared to the

1970s. A long-term free fall in news interest could therefore be under way, albeit more gradually than some might have expected given the rapid drop-off in attention to network news since the 1980s. . . .

Conclusion

In May 2006 a previously unknown singer named Taylor Hicks was propelled to national prominence when he won the hit television show *American Idol*. Two months later, a Zogby poll found that nearly a quarter of Americans could spontaneously name Hicks as the show's most recent winner, but the same poll found that only half as many could identify Samuel Alito as the newest justice on the Supreme Court.[31] On the night of the 9/11 attacks, Nielsen Media Research found that 79.5 million viewers—nearly four in ten American adults—were tuning into any of the eleven broadcast or cable networks that were showing news coverage of the attacks. As impressive as this level of attention seems, about the same number of viewers watched the January 2001 Super Bowl.[32] Indeed, an audience of this size assembles just about every year to watch the Super Bowl.

The lesson to draw from these examples is not that the American public is stupid or intellectually lazy. Instead, these comparisons underscore how politically alert and responsive the American public could be if its interest in national and international news was as great as its interest in popular culture. It is unlikely that most Americans had even heard of the disease anthrax before late September 2001, when several letters containing anthrax spores were mailed to U.S. news organizations and government offices. Yet by early 2002 a national survey found that nine of ten adults not only knew something about the disease, but also could state correctly that the inhaled form was more deadly than the kind found on the skin.[33] It is remarkable that this level of insight occurred at a time when only half of the U.S. public understood that antibiotics do not kill viruses.[34] When the slumbering Leviathan awakes, its capacity for watchfulness can be astonishing.

Different theories of democracy envision different roles for citizens to play, with some limiting citizen involvement to participating in occasional elections and others expecting citizens to deliberate actively and frequently about important matters of public policy.[35] Contrary to popular myth, few theories of democracy require anything like a highly informed citizenry as a precondition for popular rule.[36] But the efficiency and quality of representation is likely to be enhanced under all theories of democracy as citizens become better informed about the actions of their elected representatives and the important public issues confronting the nation.[37]

The more we learn about politics, the closer our political preferences should come to resemble our political interests, and the greater the chance that our votes and voices will properly reward our political leaders for what they have done well and punish them for what they did poorly or left undone. It is the quality of popular judgment underlying the system of rewards and punishments that is threatened by waning levels of interest in public affairs and the resulting undersupply of politically informative news coverage to the attentive audience that remains. The less attention the public routinely pays to the news, the greater the chance that voters will get it wrong on election day by rewarding irresponsible leadership and bestowing punishments on those whose sober and judicious views should have rightly carried the day.

NOTES

Editors' Note: Portions of the analysis of audience demand for network news broadcasts first appeared in Scott L. Althaus, "American News Consumption During Times of National Crisis," *PS: Political Science & Politics* 35, no. 3 (2002), and are used with permission from Cambridge University Press. Unless otherwise noted, all circulation and ratings data reported in this chapter were obtained from the 2004, 2005, and 2006 editions of the Project for Excellence in Journalism's "State of the News Media" reports, available at www.journalism .org.

1. David Held, *Models of Democracy,* 2nd ed. (Stanford: Stanford University Press, 1996); Bernard Manin, *The Principles of Representative Government* (New York: Cambridge University Press, 1997).

2. Ted Brader, *Campaigning for Hearts and Minds: How Emotional Appeals in Political Ads Work* (Chicago: University of Chicago Press, 2006); George E. Marcus, W. Russell Neuman, and Michael MacKuen, *Affective Intelligence and Political Judgment* (Chicago: University of Chicago Press, 2000).

3. Michael X. Delli Carpini and Scott Keeter, *What Americans Know about Politics and Why It Matters* (New Haven: Yale University Press, 1996), 120–122.

4. Scott L. Althaus, *Collective Preferences in Democratic Politics: Opinion Surveys and the Will of the People* (New York: Cambridge University Press, 2003), 207–217.

5. Walter Dean Burnham, *Critical Elections and the Mainsprings of American Politics* (New York: Norton, 1970); Peter F. Nardulli, *Popular Efficacy in the Democratic Era: A Reexamination of Electoral Accountability in the United States, 1828–2000* (Princeton: Princeton University Press, 2005).

6. Project for Excellence in Journalism, "The State of the News Media 2006," available at www.journalism.org.

7. Personal income statistics are from the U.S. Department of Commerce's Bureau of Economic Analysis, available at www.bea.gov/bea/dn/nipaweb/index.asp. The 188 percent figure is in "chained" 2000 dollars. The growth of per capita disposable income in constant 2000 dollars, which adjusts for inflation but not for the changing price of consumer goods, is 710 percent over the 1970–2000 period.

8. Markus Prior, *Post-Broadcast Democracy: How Media Choice Increases Inequality in Political Involvement and Polarizes Elections* (New York: Cambridge University Press, 2007).

9. Michael Schudson, *The Good Citizen: A History of American Civic Life* (New York: Free Press, 1998); John Zaller, "A New Standard of News Quality: Burglar Alarms for the Monitorial Citizen," *Political Communication* 20, no. 2 (2003).

10. Prior, *Post-Broadcast Democracy.*

11. Pew's question is "How have you been getting most of your news about national and international issues? From television, from newspapers, from radio, from magazines, or from the Internet?" Up to two answers are accepted, and respondents who provide only one are prompted for (but not required to give) a second answer. Pew asks about magazines as a source of national and international news, but because the proportion relying mainly on magazines has never been higher than 10 percent since the question was first asked in 1991, this chapter focuses instead on the more popular sources of public affairs news.

12. These data are from the 2006 Pew Biennial Media Consumption Survey questionnaire reported in Pew Research Center for the People and the Press, "Online Papers Modestly Boost Newspaper Readership: Maturing Internet News Audience Broader than Deep," issued July 30, 2006. Available at http://people-press.org/reports/display.php3? ReportID=282.

13. Ratings data for the week of December 18, 2006, are from http://mediabistro.com.

14. The author compiled these data from various media sources available from the LEXIS-NEXIS database. Nielsen uses representative national samples of five thousand television households to estimate television viewing trends for all households in the United States. Electronic "people meters" continuously monitor all broadcast television, satellite, cable, and VCR viewing activity for each individual in a household.

15. Nielsen currently publishes ratings in terms of millions of audience members viewing a particular program. According to the 2000 Census, there are 205.05 million persons aged nineteen or older in the United States. Because household television penetration has been nearly universal since before 1980, simply dividing the former by the latter produces a reasonable estimate of the percentage of American adults watching nightly news programs. During the 1990–1991 period, Nielsen reported ratings information using its measure of rating points, in which each point represents 1 percent of American television households viewing a particular program. To create comparable trends for the Persian Gulf crisis, the combined rating points for all three network news broadcasts were multiplied by the mean number of persons aged nineteen or older per U.S. household (1.87, according to the 1990 Census) and then by the number of U.S. households (91.99 million in 1990). This joint product was then divided by the total number of persons aged nineteen or older (181.50 million) to estimate the percentage of adults watching nightly network news programs.

16. These percentages come from comparing the January through April averages for each case.

17. "Cable News Wars: Behind the Battle for Cable News Viewers—March 2002," *Online NewsHour,* available at www.pbs.org/newshour/media/cablenews/index.html.

18. Newspaper Association of America, "Leveraging Newspaper Assets: A Study of Changing American Media Usage Habits, 2000 Research Report," 36. Available at www.naa.org/marketscope/MediaUsage_2000.pdf.

19. Daily newspaper readership data for the total U.S. population that are used in this section were compiled from various sources by the Newspaper Association of America and are

available at www.naa.org/ReadershipPages/Research-and-Readership/readershipstatistics.aspx.

20. Audit bureau data released by the Newspaper Association of America showed that U.S. daily newspaper circulation in the period from September 31, 2001, through March 31, 2002, was 0.6 percent lower than in the prior six-month period that ended in September 2001. Felicity Barringer, "Some Big Papers Buck Trend of Circulation Drops," *New York Times,* May 7, 2002, C9.

21. Business Analysis and Research Department of the Newspaper Association of America, "Daily Newspaper Section Readership 2006." Available at www.naa.org/marketscope/readership2006/2006_newspaper_section_readership_daily.pdf.

22. Arbitron National Radio Services, "Radio Today: How America Listens to Radio," 2006 ed. Available at www.arbitron.com/downloads/NRT_2006.pdf. Unless otherwise noted, all radio audience data in this section are from Arbitron National Radio Services and available at www.arbitron.com/national_radio/home.htm.

23. Arbitron, "Radio's Role During a National Crisis," 2002. Available at www.arbitron.com/downloads/radio_911.pdf.

24. Arbitron, "Public Radio Today." Available at www.arbitron.com/downloads/Public RadioToday06.pdf. These estimates come from multiplying the drive time average quarterly hour ratings for all public radio programming reported on page 8 of the report (approximately 1.0 percent of persons twelve and older during the morning drive time, and approximately 0.6 percent of persons twelve and older during the afternoon drive time) by the combined 6 a.m. to 10 a.m. shares reported for news/talk, news-classical, news-music, and news-jazz formats (summing to 81.7 percent, found on pages 20, 22, 31, and 37).

25. National Public Radio audience data were reported in Project for Excellence in Journalism, "The State of the News Media 2006." The Pew survey estimates of NPR's audience were reported in the 2006 Pew Biennial Media Consumption survey, ibid.

26. David Tewksbury, "Exposure to the Newer Media in a Presidential Primary Campaign," *Political Communication* 23, no. 3 (2006): 313–332.

27. David Tewksbury, "The Seeds of Audience Fragmentation: Specialization in the Use of Online News Sites," *Journal of Broadcasting & Electronic Media* 49, no. 3 (2005): 332–348; David Tewksbury, "What Do Americans Really Want to Know? Tracking the Behavior of News Readers on the Internet," *Journal of Communication* 53, no. 4 (2003): 694–710.

28. These percentages were obtained by multiplying the proportion of respondents saying yes to the question, "When you go online do you ever come across news when you may have been going online for a purpose other than to get the news?" with the proportion saying yes to the question: "Do you ever go online to access the Internet or to send and receive email?"

29. David Tewksbury, Andrew J. Weaver, and Brett D. Maddex, "Accidentally Informed: Incidental News Exposure on the World Wide Web," *Journalism & Mass Communication Quarterly* 78, no. 3 (2001): 542.

30. Prior, *Post-Broadcast Democracy.*

31. Complete results from the July 2006 Zogby Poll for AOL.com are available at www.zogby.com/wfAOL%20National.pdf.

32. Lisa de Moraes, "For an Extraordinary Week, Nielsen Puts the Ratings Aside," *Washington Post,* September 20, 2001, sec. C.

33. Markus Prior, "Political Knowledge after September 11," *PS: Political Science & Politics* 35, no. 3 (2002): 523–529.

34. National Science Foundation, *Science and Engineering Indicators 2002,* Vol. 1 (Washington, D.C.: National Science Board, 2002), chap. 7.

35. C. Edwin Baker, *Media, Markets, and Democracy* (New York: Cambridge University Press, 2002); Jürgen Habermas, "Three Normative Models of Democracy," in *Democracy and Difference: Contesting the Boundaries of the Political,* ed. Seyla Benhabib (Princeton: Princeton University Press, 1996); and Held, *Models of Democracy.*

36. Scott L. Althaus, "False Starts, Dead Ends, and New Opportunities in Public Opinion Research," *Critical Review* 18, no. 1–3 (2006): 75–104.

37. ———. "Collective Preferences in Democratic Politics," in *What Americans Know,* Delli Carpini and Keeter, eds.

Constitution of the United States

We the People of the United States, in Order to form a more perfect Union, establish Justice, insure domestic Tranquility, provide for the common defence, promote the general Welfare, and secure the Blessings of Liberty to ourselves and our Posterity, do ordain and establish this Constitution for the United States of America.

ARTICLE I

Section 1. All legislative Powers herein granted shall be vested in a Congress of the United States, which shall consist of a Senate and House of Representatives.

Section 2. The House of Representatives shall be composed of Members chosen every second Year by the People of the several States, and the Electors in each State shall have the Qualifications requisite for Electors of the most numerous Branch of the State Legislature.

No Person shall be a Representative who shall not have attained to the age of twenty five Years, and been seven Years a Citizen of the United States, and who shall not, when elected, be an Inhabitant of that State in which he shall be chosen.

[Representatives and direct Taxes shall be apportioned among the several States which may be included within this Union, according to their respective Numbers, which shall be determined by adding to the whole Number of free Persons, including those bound to Service for a Term of Years, and excluding Indians not taxed, three fifths of all other Persons.][1] The actual Enumeration shall be made within three Years after the first Meeting of the Congress of the United States, and within every subsequent Term of ten Years, in such Manner as they shall by Law direct. The Number of Representatives shall not exceed one for every thirty Thousand, but each State shall have at Least one Representative; and until such enumeration shall be made, the State of New Hampshire shall be entitled to chuse three, Massachusetts eight, Rhode-Island and Providence Plantations one, Connecticut five, New-York six, New Jersey four, Pennsylvania eight, Delaware

Source: U.S. Congress, House, Committee on the Judiciary, *The Constitution of the United States of America, as Amended,* 100th Cong., 1st sess., 1987, H Doc 100-94.

one, Maryland six, Virginia ten, North Carolina five, South Carolina five, and Georgia three.

When vacancies happen in the Representation from any State, the Executive Authority thereof shall issue Writs of Election to fill such Vacancies.

The House of Representatives shall chuse their Speaker and other Officers; and shall have the sole Power of Impeachment.

Section 3. The Senate of the United States shall be composed of two Senators from each State, [chosen by the Legislature thereof,]² for six Years; and each Senator shall have one Vote.

Immediately after they shall be assembled in Consequence of the first Election, they shall be divided as equally as may be into three Classes. The Seats of the Senators of the first Class shall be vacated at the Expiration of the second Year, of the second Class at the Expiration of the fourth Year, and of the third Class at the Expiration of the sixth Year, so that one third may be chosen every second Year; [and if Vacancies happen by Resignation, or otherwise, during the Recess of the Legislature of any State, the Executive thereof may make temporary Appointments until the next Meeting of the Legislature, which shall then fill such Vacancies.]³

No Person shall be a Senator who shall not have attained to the Age of thirty Years, and been nine Years a Citizen of the United States, and who shall not, when elected, be an Inhabitant of that State for which he shall be chosen.

The Vice President of the United States shall be President of the Senate, but shall have no Vote, unless they be equally divided.

The Senate shall chuse their other Officers, and also a President pro tempore, in the Absence of the Vice President, or when he shall exercise the Office of President of the United States.

The Senate shall have the sole Power to try all Impeachments. When sitting for that Purpose, they shall be on Oath or Affirmation. When the President of the United States is tried, the Chief Justice shall preside: And no Person shall be convicted without the Concurrence of two thirds of the Members present.

Judgment in Cases of Impeachment shall not extend further than to removal from Office, and disqualification to hold and enjoy any Office of honor, Trust or Profit under the United States: but the Party convicted shall nevertheless be liable and subject to Indictment, Trial, Judgment and Punishment, according to Law.

Section 4. The Times, Places and Manner of holding Elections for Senators and Representatives, shall be prescribed in each State by the Legislature thereof; but the Congress may at any time by Law make or alter such Regulations, except as to the Places of chusing Senators.

The Congress shall assemble at least once in every Year, and such Meeting shall [be on the first Monday in December],⁴ unless they shall by Law appoint a different Day.

Section 5. Each House shall be the Judge of the Elections, Returns and Qualifications of its own Members, and a Majority of each shall constitute a Quorum to do Business; but a smaller Number may adjourn from day to day, and may be authorized to compel the

Attendance of absent Members, in such Manner, and under such Penalties as each House may provide.

Each House may determine the Rules of its Proceedings, punish its Members for disorderly Behaviour, and, with the Concurrence of two thirds, expel a Member.

Each House shall keep a Journal of its Proceedings, and from time to time publish the same, excepting such Parts as may in their Judgment require Secrecy; and the Yeas and Nays of the Members of either House on any question shall, at the Desire of one fifth of those Present, be entered on the Journal.

Neither House, during the Session of Congress, shall, without the Consent of the other, adjourn for more than three days, nor to any other Place than that in which the two Houses shall be sitting.

Section 6. The Senators and Representatives shall receive a Compensation for their Services, to be ascertained by Law, and paid out of the Treasury of the United States. They shall in all Cases, except Treason, Felony and Breach of the Peace, be privileged from Arrest during their Attendance at the Session of their respective Houses, and in going to and returning from the same; and for any Speech or Debate in either House, they shall not be questioned in any other Place.

No Senator or Representative shall, during the Time for which he was elected, be appointed to any civil Office under the Authority of the United States, which shall have been created, or the Emoluments whereof shall have been encreased during such time; and no Person holding any Office under the United States, shall be a Member of either House during his Continuance in Office.

Section 7. All Bills for raising Revenue shall originate in the House of Representatives; but the Senate may propose or concur with Amendments as on other Bills.

Every Bill which shall have passed the House of Representatives and the Senate, shall, before it become a Law, be presented to the President of the United States; If he approve he shall sign it, but if not he shall return it, with his Objections to that House in which it shall have originated, who shall enter the Objections at large on their Journal, and proceed to reconsider it. If after such Reconsideration two thirds of that House shall agree to pass the Bill, it shall be sent, together with the Objections, to the other House, by which it shall likewise be reconsidered, and if approved by two thirds of that House, it shall become a Law. But in all such Cases the Votes of both Houses shall be determined by yeas and Nays, and the Names of the Persons voting for and against the Bill shall be entered on the Journal of each House respectively. If any Bill shall not be returned by the President within ten Days (Sundays excepted) after it shall have been presented to him, the Same shall be a Law, in like Manner as if he had signed it, unless the Congress by their Adjournment prevent its Return, in which Case it shall not be a Law.

Every Order, Resolution, or Vote to which the Concurrence of the Senate and House of Representatives may be necessary (except on a question of Adjournment) shall be presented to the President of the United States; and before the Same shall take Effect, shall be approved by him, or being disapproved by him, shall be repassed by two thirds of the Senate and House of Representatives, according to the Rules and Limitations prescribed in the Case of a Bill.

Section 8. The Congress shall have Power To lay and collect Taxes, Duties, Imposts and Excises, to pay the Debts and provide for the common Defence and general Welfare of the United States; but all Duties, Imposts and Excises shall be uniform throughout the United States;

To borrow Money on the credit of the United States;

To regulate Commerce with foreign Nations, and among the several States, and with the Indian Tribes;

To establish an uniform Rule of Naturalization, and uniform Laws on the subject of Bankruptcies throughout the United States;

To coin Money, regulate the Value thereof, and of foreign Coin, and fix the Standard of Weights and Measures;

To provide for the Punishment of counterfeiting the Securities and current Coin of the United States;

To establish Post Offices and post Roads;

To promote the Progress of Science and useful Arts, by securing for limited Times to Authors and Inventors the exclusive Right to their respective Writings and Discoveries;

To constitute Tribunals inferior to the supreme Court;

To define and punish Piracies and Felonies committed on the high Seas, and Offences against the Law of Nations;

To declare War, grant Letters of Marque and Reprisal, and make Rules concerning Captures on Land and Water;

To raise and support Armies, but no Appropriation of Money to that Use shall be for a longer Term than two Years;

To provide and maintain a Navy;

To make Rules for the Government and Regulation of the land and naval Forces;

To provide for calling forth the Militia to execute the Laws of the Union, suppress Insurrections and repel Invasions;

To provide for organizing, arming, and disciplining, the Militia, and for governing such Part of them as may be employed in the Service of the United States, reserving to the States respectively, the Appointment of the Officers, and the Authority of training the Militia according to the discipline prescribed by Congress;

To exercise exclusive Legislation in all Cases whatsoever, over such District (not exceeding ten Miles square) as may, by Cession of particular States, and the Acceptance of Congress, become the Seat of the Government of the United States, and to exercise like Authority over all Places purchased by the Consent of the Legislature of the State in which the Same shall be, for the Erection of Forts, Magazines, Arsenals, dock-Yards, and other needful Buildings;—And

To make all Laws which shall be necessary and proper for carrying into Execution the foregoing Powers, and all other Powers vested by this Constitution in the Government of the United States, or in any Department or Officer thereof.

Section 9. The Migration or Importation of such Persons as any of the States now existing shall think proper to admit, shall not be prohibited by the Congress prior to the

Year one thousand eight hundred and eight, but a Tax or duty may be imposed on such Importation, not exceeding ten dollars for each Person.

The Privilege of the Writ of Habeas Corpus shall not be suspended, unless when in Cases of Rebellion or Invasion the public Safety may require it.

No Bill of Attainder or ex post facto Law shall be passed.

No Capitation, or other direct, Tax shall be laid, unless in Proportion to the Census or Enumeration herein before directed to be taken.[5]

No Tax or Duty shall be laid on Articles exported from any State.

No Preference shall be given by any Regulation of Commerce or Revenue to the Ports of one State over those of another; nor shall Vessels bound to, or from, one State, be obliged to enter, clear, or pay Duties in another.

No Money shall be drawn from the Treasury, but in Consequence of Appropriations made by Law; and a regular Statement and Account of the Receipts and Expenditures of all public Money shall be published from time to time.

No Title of Nobility shall be granted by the United States: And no Person holding any Office of Profit or Trust under them, shall, without the Consent of the Congress, accept of any present, Emolument, Office, or Title, of any kind whatever, from any King, Prince, or foreign State.

Section 10. No State shall enter into any Treaty, Alliance, or Confederation; grant Letters of Marque and Reprisal; coin Money; emit Bills of Credit; make any Thing but gold and silver Coin a Tender in Payment of Debts; pass any Bill of Attainder, ex post facto Law, or Law impairing the Obligation of Contracts, or grant any Title of Nobility.

No State shall, without the Consent of the Congress, lay any Imposts or Duties on Imports or Exports, except what may be absolutely necessary for executing it's inspection Laws: and the net Produce of all Duties and Imposts, laid by any State on Imports or Exports, shall be for the Use of the Treasury of the United States; and all such Laws shall be subject to the Revision and Controul of the Congress.

No State shall, without the Consent of Congress, lay any Duty of Tonnage, keep Troops, or Ships of War in time of Peace, enter into any Agreement or Compact with another State, or with a foreign Power, or engage in War, unless actually invaded, or in such imminent Danger as will not admit of delay.

ARTICLE II

Section 1. The executive Power shall be vested in a President of the United States of America. He shall hold his Office during the Term of four Years, and, together with the Vice President, chosen for the same Term, be elected, as follows

Each State shall appoint, in such Manner as the Legislature thereof may direct, a Number of Electors, equal to the whole Number of Senators and Representatives to which the State may be entitled in the Congress: but no Senator or Representative, or Person holding an Office of Trust or Profit under the United States, shall be appointed an Elector.

[The Electors shall meet in their respective States, and vote by Ballot for two Persons, of whom one at least shall not be an Inhabitant of the same State with themselves. And they shall make a List of all the Persons voted for, and of the Number of Votes for each; which List they shall sign and certify, and transmit sealed to the Seat of the Government of the United States, directed to the President of the Senate. The President of the Senate shall, in the Presence of the Senate and House of Representatives, open all the Certificates, and the Votes shall then be counted. The Person having the greatest Number of Votes shall be the President, if such Number be a Majority of the whole Number of Electors appointed; and if there be more than one who have such Majority, and have an equal Number of Votes, then the House of Representatives shall immediately chuse by Ballot one of them for President; and if no Person have a Majority, then from the five highest on the list the said House shall in like Manner chuse the President. But in chusing the President, the Votes shall be taken by States, the Representation from each State having one Vote; A quorum for this Purpose shall consist of a Member or Members from two thirds of the States, and a Majority of all the States shall be necessary to a Choice. In every Case, after the Choice of the President, the Person having the greatest Number of Votes of the Electors shall be the Vice President. But if there should remain two or more who have equal Votes, the Senate shall chuse from them by Ballot the Vice President.][6]

The Congress may determine the Time of chusing the Electors, and the Day on which they shall give their Votes; which Day shall be the same throughout the United States.

No Person except a natural born Citizen, or a Citizen of the United States, at the time of the Adoption of this Constitution, shall be eligible to the Office of President; neither shall any Person be eligible to that Office who shall not have attained to the Age of thirty five Years, and been fourteen Years a Resident within the United States.

In Case of the Removal of the President from Office, or of his Death, Resignation, or Inability to discharge the Powers and Duties of the said Office,[7] the Same shall devolve on the Vice President, and the Congress may by Law provide for the Case of Removal, Death, Resignation or Inability, both of the President and Vice President, declaring what Officer shall then act as President, and such Officer shall act accordingly, until the Disability be removed, or a President shall be elected.

The President shall, at stated Times, receive for his Services, a Compensation, which shall neither be encreased nor diminished during the Period for which he shall have been elected, and he shall not receive within that Period any other Emolument from the United States, or any of them.

Before he enter on the Execution of his Office, he shall take the following Oath or Affirmation:—"I do solemnly swear (or affirm) that I will faithfully execute the Office of President of the United States, and will to the best of my Ability, preserve, protect and defend the Constitution of the United States."

Section 2. The President shall be Commander in Chief of the Army and Navy of the United States, and of the Militia of the several States, when called into the actual Service of the United States; he may require the Opinion, in writing, of the principal Officer in each of the executive Departments, upon any Subject relating to the Duties of their respective Offices, and he shall have Power to grant Reprieves and Pardons for Offences against the United States, except in Cases of Impeachment.

He shall have Power, by and with the Advice and Consent of the Senate, to make Treaties, provided two thirds of the Senators present concur; and he shall nominate, and by and with the Advice and Consent of the Senate, shall appoint Ambassadors, other public Ministers and Consuls, Judges of the supreme Court, and all other Officers of the United States, whose Appointments are not herein otherwise provided for, and which shall be established by Law: but the Congress may by Law vest the Appointment of such inferior Officers, as they think proper, in the President alone, in the Courts of Law, or in the Heads of Departments.

The President shall have Power to fill up all Vacancies that may happen during the Recess of the Senate, by granting Commissions which shall expire at the End of their next Session.

Section 3. He shall from time to time give to the Congress Information of the State of the Union, and recommend to their Consideration such Measures as he shall judge necessary and expedient; he may, on extraordinary Occasions, convene both Houses, or either of them, and in Case of Disagreement between them, with Respect to the Time of Adjournment, he may adjourn them to such Time as he shall think proper; he shall receive Ambassadors and other public Ministers; he shall take Care that the Laws be faithfully executed, and shall Commission all the Officers of the United States.

Section 4. The President, Vice President and all civil Officers of the United States, shall be removed from Office on Impeachment for, and Conviction of, Treason, Bribery, or other high Crimes and Misdemeanors.

ARTICLE III

Section 1. The judicial Power of the United States, shall be vested in one supreme Court, and in such inferior Courts as the Congress may from time to time ordain and establish. The Judges, both of the supreme and inferior Courts, shall hold their Offices during good Behaviour, and shall, at stated Times, receive for their Services, a Compensation, which shall not be diminished during their Continuance in Office.

Section 2. The judicial Power shall extend to all Cases, in Law and Equity, arising under this Constitution, the Laws of the United States, and Treaties made, or which shall be made, under their Authority;—to all Cases affecting Ambassadors, other public Ministers and Consuls;—to all Cases of admiralty and maritime Jurisdiction;—to Controversies to which the United States shall be a Party;—to Controversies between two or more States;—between a State and Citizens of another State;[8]—between Citizens of different States;—between Citizens of the same State claiming Lands under Grants of different States, and between a State, or the Citizens thereof, and foreign States, Citizens or Subjects.

In all Cases affecting Ambassadors, other public Ministers and Consuls, and those in which a State shall be Party, the supreme Court shall have original Jurisdiction. In all the other Cases before mentioned, the supreme Court shall have appellate Jurisdiction, both as to Law and Fact, with such Exceptions, and under such Regulations as the Congress shall make.

The Trial of all Crimes, except in Cases of Impeachment, shall be by Jury; and such Trial shall be held in the State where the said Crimes shall have been committed; but when not committed within any State, the Trial shall be at such Place or Places as the Congress may by Law have directed.

Section 3. Treason against the United States, shall consist only in levying War against them, or in adhering to their Enemies, giving them Aid and Comfort. No Person shall be convicted of Treason unless on the Testimony of two Witnesses to the same overt Act, or on Confession in open Court.

The Congress shall have Power to declare the Punishment of Treason, but no Attainder of Treason shall work Corruption of Blood, or Forfeiture except during the Life of the Person attainted.

ARTICLE IV

Section 1. Full Faith and Credit shall be given in each State to the public Acts, Records, and judicial Proceedings of every other State. And the Congress may by general Laws prescribe the Manner in which such Acts, Records and Proceedings shall be proved, and the Effect thereof.

Section 2. The Citizens of each State shall be entitled to all Privileges and Immunities of Citizens in the several States.

A Person charged in any State with Treason, Felony, or other Crime, who shall flee from Justice, and be found in another State, shall on Demand of the executive Authority of the State from which he fled, be delivered up, to be removed to the State having Jurisdiction of the Crime.

[No Person held to Service or Labour in one State, under the Laws thereof, escaping into another, shall, in Consequence of any Law or Regulation therein, be discharged from such Service or Labour, but shall be delivered up on Claim of the Party to whom such Service or Labour may be due.][9]

Section 3. New States may be admitted by the Congress into this Union; but no new State shall be formed or erected within the Jurisdiction of any other State; nor any State be formed by the Junction of two or more States, or Parts of States, without the Consent of the Legislatures of the States concerned as well as of the Congress.

The Congress shall have Power to dispose of and make all needful Rules and Regulations respecting the Territory or other Property belonging to the United States; and nothing in this Constitution shall be so construed as to Prejudice any Claims of the United States, or of any particular State.

Section 4. The United States shall guarantee to every State in this Union a Republican Form of Government, and shall protect each of them against Invasion; and on Application of the Legislature, or of the Executive (when the Legislature cannot be convened) against domestic Violence.

ARTICLE V

The Congress, whenever two thirds of both Houses shall deem it necessary, shall propose Amendments to this Constitution, or, on the Application of the Legislatures of two thirds of the several States, shall call a Convention for proposing Amendments, which, in either Case, shall be valid to all Intents and Purposes, as Part of this Constitution, when ratified by the Legislatures of three fourths of the several States, or by Conventions in three fourths thereof, as the one or the other Mode of Ratification may be proposed by the Congress; Provided [that no Amendment which may be made prior to the Year One thousand eight hundred and eight shall in any Manner affect the first and fourth Clauses in the Ninth Section of the first Article; and][10] that no State, without its Consent, shall be deprived of its equal Suffrage in the Senate.

ARTICLE VI

All Debts contracted and Engagements entered into, before the Adoption of this Constitution, shall be as valid against the United States under this Constitution, as under the Confederation.

This Constitution, and the Laws of the United States which shall be made in Pursuance thereof; and all Treaties made, or which shall be made, under the Authority of the United States, shall be the supreme Law of the Land; and the Judges in every State shall be bound thereby, any Thing in the Constitution or Laws of any State to the Contrary notwithstanding.

The Senators and Representatives before mentioned, and the Members of the several State Legislatures, and all executive and judicial Officers, both of the United States and of the several States, shall be bound by Oath or Affirmation, to support this Constitution; but no religious Test shall ever be required as a Qualification to any Office or public Trust under the United States.

ARTICLE VII

The Ratification of the Conventions of nine States, shall be sufficient for the Establishment of this Constitution between the States so ratifying the Same.

Done in Convention by the Unanimous Consent of the States present the Seventeenth Day of September in the Year of our Lord one thousand seven hundred and Eighty seven and of the Independence of the United States of America the Twelfth. IN WITNESS whereof We have hereunto subscribed our Names,

George Washington,
President and
deputy from Virginia.

New Hampshire:	John Langdon,
	Nicholas Gilman.
Massachusetts:	Nathaniel Gorham,
	Rufus King.
Connecticut:	William Samuel Johnson,
	Roger Sherman.
New York:	Alexander Hamilton.
New Jersey:	William Livingston,
	David Brearley,
	William Paterson,
	Jonathan Dayton.
Pennsylvania:	Benjamin Franklin,
	Thomas Mifflin,
	Robert Morris,
	George Clymer,
	Thomas FitzSimons,
	Jared Ingersoll,
	James Wilson,
	Gouverneur Morris.
Delaware:	George Read,
	Gunning Bedford Jr.,
	John Dickinson,
	Richard Bassett,
	Jacob Broom.
Maryland:	James McHenry,
	Daniel of St. Thomas Jenifer,
	Daniel Carroll.
Virginia:	John Blair,
	James Madison Jr.
North Carolina:	William Blount,
	Richard Dobbs Spaight,
	Hugh Williamson.
South Carolina:	John Rutledge,
	Charles Cotesworth Pinckney,
	Charles Pinckney,
	Pierce Butler.
Georgia:	William Few,
	Abraham Baldwin.

[The language of the original Constitution, not including the Amendments, was adopted by a convention of the states on September 17, 1787, and was subsequently ratified by the states on the following dates: Delaware, December 7, 1787; Pennsylvania, December 12, 1787; New Jersey, December 18, 1787; Georgia, January 2, 1788;

Connecticut, January 9, 1788; Massachusetts, February 6, 1788; Maryland, April 28, 1788; South Carolina, May 23, 1788; New Hampshire, June 21, 1788.

Ratification was completed on June 21, 1788.

The Constitution subsequently was ratified by Virginia, June 25, 1788; New York, July 26, 1788; North Carolina, November 21, 1789; Rhode Island, May 29, 1790; and Vermont, January 10, 1791.]

Amendments

Amendment I

(First ten amendments ratified December 15, 1791.)

Congress shall make no law respecting an establishment of religion, or prohibiting the free exercise thereof; or abridging the freedom of speech, or of the press; or the right of the people peaceably to assemble, and to petition the Government for a redress of grievances.

Amendment II

A well regulated Militia, being necessary to the security of a free State, the right of the people to keep and bear Arms, shall not be infringed.

Amendment III

No Soldier shall, in time of peace be quartered in any house, without the consent of the Owner, nor in time of war, but in a manner to be prescribed by law.

Amendment IV

The right of the people to be secure in their persons, houses, papers, and effects, against unreasonable searches and seizures, shall not be violated, and no Warrants shall issue, but upon probable cause, supported by Oath or affirmation, and particularly describing the place to be searched, and the persons or things to be seized.

Amendment V

No person shall be held to answer for a capital, or otherwise infamous crime, unless on a presentment or indictment of a Grand Jury, except in cases arising in the land or naval forces, or in the Militia, when in actual service in time of War or public danger; nor shall any person be subject for the same offence to be twice put in jeopardy of life or limb; nor shall be compelled in any criminal case to be a witness against himself, nor be deprived of life, liberty, or property, without due process of law; nor shall private property be taken for public use, without just compensation.

Amendment VI

In all criminal prosecutions, the accused shall enjoy the right to a speedy and public trial, by an impartial jury of the State and district wherein the crime shall have been committed, which district shall have been previously ascertained by law, and to be informed of the nature and cause of the accusation; to be confronted with the witnesses against him; to have compulsory process for obtaining witnesses in his favor, and to have the Assistance of Counsel for his defence.

Amendment VII

In Suits at common law, where the value in controversy shall exceed twenty dollars, the right of trial by jury shall be preserved, and no fact tried by a jury, shall be otherwise re-examined in any Court of the United States, than according to the rules of the common law.

Amendment VIII

Excessive bail shall not be required, nor excessive fines imposed, nor cruel and unusual punishments inflicted.

Amendment IX

The enumeration in the Constitution, of certain rights, shall not be construed to deny or disparage others retained by the people.

Amendment X

The powers not delegated to the United States by the Constitution, nor prohibited by it to the States, are reserved to the States respectively, or to the people.

Amendment XI (Ratified February 7, 1795)

The Judicial power of the United States shall not be construed to extend to any suit in law or equity, commenced or prosecuted against one of the United States by Citizens of another State, or by Citizens or Subjects of any Foreign State.

Amendment XII (Ratified June 15, 1804)

The Electors shall meet in their respective states and vote by ballot for President and Vice-President, one of whom, at least, shall not be an inhabitant of the same state with themselves; they shall name in their ballots the person voted for as President, and in distinct ballots the person voted for as Vice-President, and they shall make distinct lists of all persons voted for as President, and of all persons voted for as Vice-President, and of the number of votes for each, which lists they shall sign and certify, and transmit sealed to the seat of the government of the United States, directed to the President of the Senate;—The President of the Senate shall, in the presence of the Senate and House of Representatives, open all the certificates and the votes shall then be counted;—The person having the greatest number of votes for President, shall be the President, if such number be a majority of the whole number of Electors appointed; and if no person have such majority, then from the persons having the highest numbers not exceeding three on the list of those voted for as President, the House of Representatives shall choose immediately, by ballot, the President. But in choosing the President, the votes shall be taken by states, the representation from each state having one vote; a quorum for this purpose shall consist of a member or members from two-thirds of the states, and a majority of all the states shall be necessary to a choice. [And if the House of Representatives shall not choose a President whenever the right of choice shall devolve upon them, before the fourth day of March next following, then the Vice-President shall act as President, as in the case of the death or other constitutional disability of the President.—][11] The person having the greatest number of votes as Vice-President, shall be the Vice-President, if such number be a majority of the whole number of Electors appointed, and if no person have a majority, then from the two highest numbers on the list, the Senate shall choose the Vice-President; a quorum for the purpose shall consist of two-thirds of the whole number of Senators, and a majority of the whole number shall be necessary to a choice. But no person constitutionally ineligible to the office of President shall be eligible to that of Vice-President of the United States.

Amendment XIII (Ratified December 6, 1865)

Section 1. Neither slavery nor involuntary servitude, except as a punishment for crime whereof the party shall have been duly convicted, shall exist within the United States, or any place subject to their jurisdiction.

Section 2. Congress shall have power to enforce this article by appropriate legislation.

Amendment XIV (Ratified July 9, 1868)

Section 1. All persons born or naturalized in the United States, and subject to the jurisdiction thereof, are citizens of the United States and of the State wherein they reside. No State shall make or enforce any law which shall abridge the privileges or immunities of citizens of the United States; nor shall any State deprive any person of life, liberty, or property, without due process of law; nor deny to any person within its jurisdiction the equal protection of the laws.

Section 2. Representatives shall be apportioned among the several States according to their respective numbers, counting the whole number of persons in each State, excluding Indians not taxed. But when the right to vote at any election for the choice of electors for President and Vice President of the United States, Representatives in Congress, the Executive and Judicial officers of a State, or the members of the Legislature thereof, is denied to any of the male inhabitants of such State, being twenty-one years of age,[12] and citizens of the United States, or in any way abridged, except for participation in rebellion, or other crime, the basis of representation therein shall be reduced in the proportion which the number of such male citizens shall bear to the whole number of male citizens twenty-one years of age in such State.

Section 3. No person shall be a Senator or Representative in Congress, or elector of President and Vice President, or hold any office, civil or military, under the United States, or under any State, who, having previously taken an oath, as a member of Congress, or as an officer of the United States, or as a member of any State legislature, or as an executive or judicial officer of any State, to support the Constitution of the United States, shall have engaged in insurrection or rebellion against the same, or given aid or comfort to the enemies thereof. But Congress may by a vote of two-thirds of each House, remove such disability.

Section 4. The validity of the public debt of the United States, authorized by law, including debts incurred for payment of pensions and bounties for services in suppressing insurrection or rebellion, shall not be questioned. But neither the United States nor any State shall assume or pay any debt or obligation incurred in aid of insurrection or rebellion against the United States, or any claim for the loss or emancipation of any slave; but all such debts, obligations and claims shall be held illegal and void.

Section 5. The Congress shall have power to enforce, by appropriate legislation, the provisions of this article.

Amendment XV (Ratified February 3, 1870)

Section 1. The right of citizens of the United States to vote shall not be denied or abridged by the United States or by any State on account of race, color, or previous condition of servitude.

Section 2. The Congress shall have power to enforce this article by appropriate legislation.

Amendment XVI (Ratified February 3, 1913)

The Congress shall have power to lay and collect taxes on incomes, from whatever source derived, without apportionment among the several States, and without regard to any census or enumeration.

Amendment XVII (Ratified April 8, 1913)

The Senate of the United States shall be composed of two Senators from each State, elected by the people thereof, for six years; and each Senator shall have one vote. The electors in each State shall have the qualifications requisite for electors of the most numerous branch of the State legislatures.

When vacancies happen in the representation of any State in the Senate, the executive authority of such State shall issue writs of election to fill such vacancies: *Provided,* That the legislature of any State may empower the executive thereof to make temporary appointments until the people fill the vacancies by election as the legislature may direct.

This amendment shall not be so construed as to affect the election or term of any Senator chosen before it becomes valid as part of the Constitution.

Amendment XVIII (Ratified January 16, 1919)[13]

Section 1. After one year from the ratification of this article the manufacture, sale, or transportation of intoxicating liquors within, the importation thereof into, or the exportation thereof from the United States and all territory subject to the jurisdiction thereof for beverage purposes is hereby prohibited.

Section 2. The Congress and the several States shall have concurrent power to enforce this article by appropriate legislation.

Section 3. This article shall be inoperative unless it shall have been ratified as an amendment to the Constitution by the legislatures of the several States, as provided in the Constitution, within seven years from the date of the submission hereof to the States by the Congress.

Amendment XIX (Ratified August 18, 1920)

The right of citizens of the United States to vote shall not be denied or abridged by the United States or by any State on account of sex.

Congress shall have power to enforce this article by appropriate legislation.

Amendment XX (Ratified January 23, 1933)

Section 1. The terms of the President and Vice President shall end at noon on the 20th day of January, and the terms of Senators and Representatives at noon on the 3d day of January, of the years in which such terms would have ended if this article had not been ratified; and the terms of their successors shall then begin.

Section 2. The Congress shall assemble at least once in every year, and such meeting shall begin at noon on the 3d day of January, unless they shall by law appoint a different day.

Section 3.[14] If, at the time fixed for the beginning of the term of the President, the President elect shall have died, the Vice President elect shall become President. If a President shall not have been chosen before the time fixed for the beginning of his term, or if the President elect shall have failed to qualify, then the Vice President elect shall act as President until a President shall have qualified; and the Congress may by law provide for the case wherein neither a President elect nor a Vice President elect shall have qualified, declaring who shall then act as President, or the manner in which one who is to act shall be selected, and such person shall act accordingly until a President or Vice President shall have qualified.

Section 4. The Congress may by law provide for the case of the death of any of the persons from whom the House of Representatives may choose a President whenever the right of choice shall have devolved upon them, and for the case of the death of any of the persons from whom the Senate may choose a Vice President whenever the right of choice shall have devolved upon them.

Section 5. Sections 1 and 2 shall take effect on the 15th day of October following the ratification of this article.

Section 6. This article shall be inoperative unless it shall have been ratified as an amendment to the Constitution by the legislatures of three-fourths of the several States within seven years from the date of its submission.

Amendment XXI (Ratified December 5, 1933)

Section 1. The eighteenth article of amendment to the Constitution of the United States is hereby repealed.

Section 2. The transportation or importation into any State, Territory, or possession of the United States for delivery or use therein of intoxicating liquors, in violation of the laws thereof, is hereby prohibited.

Section 3. This article shall be inoperative unless it shall have been ratified as an amendment to the Constitution by conventions in the several States, as provided in the Constitution, within seven years from the date of the submission hereof to the States by the Congress.

Amendment XXII (Ratified February 27, 1951)

Section 1. No person shall be elected to the office of the President more than twice, and no person who has held the office of President, or acted as President, for more than two years of a term to which some other person was elected President shall be elected to the office of the President more than once. But this Article shall not apply to any person holding the office of President when this Article was proposed by the Congress, and shall not prevent any person who may be holding the office of President, or acting as President, during the term within which this Article become operative from holding the office of President or acting as President during the remainder of such term.

Section 2. This article shall be inoperative unless it shall have been ratified as an amendment to the Constitution by the legislatures of three-fourths of the several States within seven years from the date of its submission to the States by the Congress.

Amendment XXIII (Ratified March 29, 1961)

Section 1. The District constituting the seat of Government of the United States shall appoint in such manner as the Congress may direct:

A number of electors of President and Vice President equal to the whole number of Senators and Representatives in Congress to which the District would be entitled if it were a State, but in no event more than the least populous State; they shall be in addition to those appointed by the States, but they shall be considered, for the purposes of the election of President and Vice President, to be electors appointed by a State; and they shall meet in the District and perform such duties as provided by the twelfth article of amendment.

Section 2. The Congress shall have power to enforce this article by appropriate legislation.

Amendment XXIV (Ratified January 23, 1964)

Section 1. The right of citizens of the United States to vote in any primary or other election for President or Vice President, for electors for President or Vice President, or for Senator or Representative in Congress, shall not be denied or abridged by the United States or any State by reason of failure to pay any poll tax or other tax.

Section 2. The Congress shall have power to enforce this article by appropriate legislation.

Amendment XXV (Ratified February 10, 1967)

Section 1. In case of the removal of the President from office or of his death or resignation, the Vice President shall become President.

Section 2. Whenever there is a vacancy in the office of the Vice President, the President shall nominate a Vice President who shall take office upon confirmation by a majority vote of both Houses of Congress.

Section 3. Whenever the President transmits to the President pro tempore of the Senate and the Speaker of the House of Representatives his written declaration that he is unable to discharge the powers and duties of his office, and until he transmits to them a written declaration to the contrary, such powers and duties shall be discharged by the Vice President as Acting President.

Section 4. Whenever the Vice President and a majority of either the principal officers of the executive departments or of such other body as Congress may by law provide, transmit to the President pro tempore of the Senate and the Speaker of the House of Representatives their written declaration that the President is unable to discharge the powers and duties of his office, the Vice President shall immediately assume the powers and duties of the office as Acting President.

Thereafter, when the President transmits to the President pro tempore of the Senate and the Speaker of the House of Representatives his written declaration that no inability exists, he shall resume the powers and duties of his office unless the Vice President and a majority of either the principal officers of the executive department or of such other body as Congress may by law provide, transmit within four days to the President pro tempore of the Senate and the Speaker of the House of Representatives their written declaration that the President is unable to discharge the powers and duties of his office. Thereupon Congress shall decide the issue, assembling within forty-eight hours for that purpose if not in session. If the Congress, within twenty-one days after receipt of the latter written declaration, or, if Congress is not in session, within twenty-one days after Congress is required to assemble, determines by two-thirds vote of both Houses that the President is unable to discharge the powers and duties of his office, the Vice President shall continue to discharge the same as Acting President; otherwise, the President shall resume the powers and duties of his office.

Amendment XXVI (Ratified July 1, 1971)

Section 1. The right of citizens of the United States, who are eighteen years of age or older, to vote shall not be denied or abridged by the United States or by any State on account of age.

Section 2. The Congress shall have power to enforce this article by appropriate legislation.

Amendment XXVII (Ratified May 7, 1992)

No law varying the compensation for the services of the Senators and Representatives shall take effect, until an election of Representatives shall have intervened.

NOTES

1. The part in brackets was changed by section 2 of the Fourteenth Amendment.
2. The part in brackets was changed by the first paragraph of the Seventeenth Amendment.
3. The part in brackets was changed by the second paragraph of the Seventeenth Amendment.
4. The part in brackets was changed by section 2 of the Twentieth Amendment.
5. The Sixteenth Amendment gave Congress the power to tax incomes.
6. The material in brackets has been superseded by the Twelfth Amendment.
7. This provision has been affected by the Twenty-fifth Amendment.
8. These clauses were affected by the Eleventh Amendment.
9. This paragraph has been superseded by the Thirteenth Amendment.
10. Obsolete.
11. The part in brackets has been superseded by section 3 of the Twentieth Amendment.
12. See the Nineteenth and Twenty-sixth Amendments.
13. This Amendment was repealed by section 1 of the Twenty-first Amendment.
14. See the Twenty-fifth Amendment.

CREDITS

1. Designing Institutions

1–1: Reprinted by permission of the publisher from *The Logic of Collective Action: Public Goods and the Theory of Groups* by Mancur Olson Jr., pp. 1–19, Cambridge, Mass.: Harvard University Press, Copyright © 1965, 1971 by the President and Fellows of Harvard College.

1–2: Reprinted (excerpted) with permission from *Science*, December 3, 1968, pp. 1243–1248. Copyright 1968 AAAS. Reprinted with permission from AAAS.

1–3: Excerpted from Robert D. Putnam, "The Prosperous Community: Social Capital and the Public Life," *The American Prospect* no. 13 (spring 1993). Copyright 1993 by New Prospect, Inc.; reprinted in *Bowling Alone: The Collapse and Revival of American Community* (Simon and Schuster, 2000). Reprinted by permission. The author is the Peter and Isabel Malkin Professor of Public Policy at Harvard University.

2. The Constitutional Framework

2–1: Excerpted from the article originally appearing in the *American Political Science Review* 55, no. 4 (December 1961): 799–816. Reprinted with the permission of Cambridge University Press. Some notes appearing in the original have been deleted.

3. Federalism

3–1: Excerpted from James Buchanan, "Federalism as an Ideal Political Order and an Objective for Constitutional Reform." *Publius: The Journal of Federalism* 25 (Spring 1995): 19–27. By permission of Oxford University Press, Inc.

3–3: From *A Separate Peace* by Jonathan Rauch. Copyright 2007 by *The Atlantic Monthly*. Reproduced with permission of *The Atlantic Monthly* in the format Textbook via Copyright Clearance Center.

4. Civil Rights

4–1: Excerpted from the article originally appearing in *Perspectives on Politics,* Volume 3, Issue 3 (2005): 557–561. Reprinted with the permission of Cambridge University Press. Some notes appearing in the original have been deleted.

4–2: Reprinted with permission. Copyright © *The Public Interest*, no. 144, summer 2001, Washington, D.C.

5. Civil Liberties

5–1: Sunstein, Cass R.; *Republic.com 2.0* © 2007 Princeton University Press. Reprinted by permission of Princeton University Press.

5-4: Excerpted from Lee Epstein, ed., *Contemplating Courts* (Washington, D.C.: CQ Press, 1995), pp. 390–419. Some notes and bibliographic references appearing in the original have been deleted.

7. The Presidency

7–1: Reprinted by permission of the estate of Richard E. Neustadt.

7–2: This article originally appeared in the March 2, 2009 issue of *The New Yorker.*

7-4: Excerpted from Samuel Kernell, *Going Public: New Strategies of* Presidential Leadership, 3d edition (Washington, D.C.: CQ Press, 1997), pp. 1–12, 17–26, 34–38, 57–64; and Samuel Kernell, *Going Public: New Strategies of Presidential Leadership,* 4th edition (Washington, D.C.: CQ Press, 2006), pp. 40–57. Some notes appearing in the original have been deleted.

8. The Bureaucracy

8–1: Excerpted from John E. Chubb and Paul E. Peterson, eds. *Can the Government Govern?* (Washington, D.C.: Brookings Institution Press, 1989), 267–285. Reprinted by permission. Some notes appearing in the original have been deleted.

8–2: Reprinted with permission from Government Executive.com, March 25, 2005. Copyright 2009 by National Journal Group, Inc. All rights reserved.

8–3: Lewis, David E.; *The Politics of Presidential Appointments.* Princeton University Press. Reprinted by permission of Princeton University Press.

9. The Judiciary

9–1: From Scalia, Antonin; *A Matter of Interpretation.* © 1997 Princeton University Press. Reprinted by permission of Princeton University Press.

9–2: From *Active Liberty: Interpreting Our Democratic Constitution* by Stephen Breyer, copyright © 2005 by Stephen Breyer. Used by permission of Alfred A. Knopf, a division of Random House, Inc.

9–4: Excerpted from Sarah A. Binder and Forrest Maltzman, "Congress and the Politics of Judicial Appointments," in *Congress Reconsidered* 8th ed., by Lawrence C. Dodd and Bruce I. Oppenheimer (CQ Press: 2005), 297–318. Some notes appearing in the original have been deleted.

10. Public Opinion

10–1: Originally published in Herbert Asher, *Polling and the Public: What Every Citizen Should Know,* 4th edition (Washington, D.C.: CQ Press, 1998), pp. 141–169.

10–2: Excerpted from the article originally published in *American Political Science Review* 89, no. 3 (September 1995): 543–564. Reprinted with the permission of Cambridge University Press. Notes appearing in the original have been deleted.

10–3: Michael Schudson is Professor of Communication at the University of California, San Diego and author of *The Good Citizen: A History of American Civic Life* (1998) and *The Sociology of News* (2003). Reprinted with permission.

10–4: Excerpt pp. 11–26 from *Culture War? The Myth of a Polarized America* by Morris P. Fiorina. Copyright © 2005 by Pearson Education, Inc. Reprinted by permission.

11. Voting, Campaigns, and Elections

11–1: Excerpted from Samuel L. Popkin, *The Reasoning Voter: Communication and Persuasion in Presidential Campaigns,* 2nd ed. (Chicago: University of Chicago Press, 1994), pp. 212–219. Copyright © 1991, 1994 by the University of Chicago. All rights reserved. Reprinted by permission. Notes appearing in the original have been deleted.

11–3: Excerpted from Darrell M. West, from "Overview of Ads" in *Air Wars: Television Advertising in Election Campaigns, 1952–2008,* 5th ed. (Washington, D.C.: CQ Press: 2010), 1–24. Notes appearing in the original have been deleted.

12. Political Parties

12–1: Originally published in John H. Aldrich, *Why Parties? The Origin and Transformation of Political Parties in America* (Chicago: University of Chicago Press, 1995), pp. 14–27. Copyright © 1995 by the University of Chicago. All rights reserved. Reprinted by permission. Notes appearing in the original have been deleted.

12–2: Excerpted from Larry Bartels, "Partisanship and Voting Behavior, 1952–1996," *American Journal of Political Science,* Vol. 4 (1), 2000, pp. 35–50. Reproduced with permission from Blackwell Publishing, Ltd. Notes appearing in the original have been deleted.

12–3: Morris P. Fiorina, "Parties as Problem Solvers," in *Promoting the General Welfare: New Perspectives on Government Performance,* eds. Alan S. Gerber and Eric M. Patashnik (Washington, D.C.: Brookings Institution Press, 2006), 237–253. Reprinted by permission. Some notes appearing in the original have been deleted.

13. Interest Groups

13–1: From *Semi-Sovereign People* Re-Issue, A Realist View of Democracy in America 1st edition by E. E. Schattschneider. © 1975. Reprinted with permission of Wadsworth, a division of Cengage Learning, Inc. Reproduced by permission. www.cengage.com/permissions.

13–2: Excerpts pp.11–22 from *Interest Groups and Congress* by John R. Wright. Copyright © 2003 by Pearson Education, Inc. Reprinted by permission.

13–3: Richard L. Hall and Frank W. Wayman, "Buying Time: Moneyed Interests and the Mobilization of Bias in Congressional Committees," *American Political Science Review* 84, no. 3 (September 1990): 797–820. Reprinted with the permission of Cambridge University Press.

14. New Media

14–1: James T. Hamilton, "The Market and the Media," in *The Press,* by Geneva Overholser and Kathleen Hall Jamieson, eds. (Oxford University Press: 2005), 351–371. By permission of Oxford University Press, Inc. Some notes appearing in the original have been deleted.

14–2: Reprinted with permission by Pew Research Center's Project for Excellence in Journalism.

Short Third Edition

Practical Argument

Laurie G. Kirszner

University of the Sciences, Emeritus

Stephen R. Mandell

Drexel University

bedford/st.martin's

Macmillan Learning

Boston | New York

For Bedford/St. Martin's

Vice President, Editorial, Macmillan Learning Humanities: Edwin Hill
Editorial Director, English: Karen S. Henry
*Senior Publisher for Composition, Business and Technical Writing, Developmental
   Writing:* Leasa Burton
Executive Editor: John E. Sullivan III
Developmental Editor: Sherry Mooney
Production Editor: Matt Glazer
Media Producer: Sarah O'Connor
Production Supervisor: Lisa McDowell
Marketing Manager: Joy Fisher Williams
Assistant Editor: Jennifer Prince
Copy Editor: Diana Puglisi George
Indexer: Mary White
Photo Editor: Angela Boehler
Photo Researcher: Sheri Blaney
Permissions Editor: Christine Volboril
Senior Art Director: Anna Palchik
Text Design: Jerilyn Bockorick
Cover Design: John Callahan
Cover Photos: (bike) Science Photo Library/Getty Images;
   (backpack) SarapulSar38/Getty Images
Composition: Cenveo Publisher Services
Printing and Binding: RR Donnelley and Sons

1 0 9 8 7 6

f e d c b a

For information, write: Bedford/St. Martin's, 75 Arlington Street,
Boston, MA 02116   (617-399-4000)

ISBN 978-1-319-03019-3

Acknowledgments
*Text credits and copyrights appear at the back of the book on pages C-1–C-3, which
constitute an extension of the copyright page. Art acknowledgments and copyrights appear
on the same page as the art selections they cover.*

In recent years, many college composition programs have integrated argumentation into their first-year writing sequence, and there are good reasons for this. Argumentation is central to academic and public discourse, so students who are skilled at argumentation are able to participate in the dynamic, ongoing discussions that take place both in their classrooms and in their communities. Clearly, argumentation teaches valuable critical-thinking skills that are necessary for academic success and for survival in today's media-driven society.

What has surprised and troubled us as teachers, however, is that many college argument texts are simply too difficult. Frequently, a divide exists between the pedagogy of these texts and students' ability to understand it. In many cases, technical terminology and excessively abstract discussions lead to confusion instead of clarity. The result is that students' worst fears are realized: instead of feeling that they are part of a discourse community, they see themselves as marginalized outsiders who will never be able to understand, let alone master, the principles of argumentation.

Recognizing that students struggle to master important principles of argumentative thinking and writing, we drew on our years of classroom experience to create an innovative book: *Practical Argument*, Short Third Edition. In this third edition, *Practical Argument* remains a straightforward, accessible, and visually appealing introduction to argumentative writing that explains concepts in understandable, everyday language and illustrates them with examples that actually mean something to students. *Practical Argument*, Short Third Edition, is an alternative for instructors who see currently available argument texts as too big, too complicated, and too intimidating for their students.

In short, our goal in this text is to demystify the study of argument. To this end, we focus on the things that students need to know, omitting the overly technical concepts they often struggle with. For example, *Practical Argument* emphasizes the basic principles of classical argument and downplays the more complex Toulmin logic, treating it as an alternative way of envisioning argument. *Practical Argument* works because its approach is "practical"; it helps students to make connections between what they learn in the classroom and what they experience outside of it. As they do so, they become comfortable with the rhetorical skills that are central to effective argumentation. We believe there's no other book like it.

Organization

Practical Argument, Short Third Edition, includes in one book everything students and instructors need for an argument course.

- **Part 1, Understanding Argument,** discusses the role of argument in everyday life and the value of studying argument, offers definitions of what argument is and is not, explains the means of persuasion (appeals to *logos*, *pathos*, and *ethos*), and defines and illustrates the basic elements of argument (thesis, evidence, refutation, and concluding statement).

- **Part 2, Reading and Responding to Arguments,** explains and illustrates critical thinking and reading; visual argument; writing a rhetorical analysis; logic and logical fallacies; and Rogerian argument, Toulmin logic, and oral arguments.

- **Part 3, Writing an Argumentative Essay,** traces and illustrates the process of planning, drafting, and revising an argumentative essay.

- **Part 4, Using Sources to Support Your Argument,** covers locating and evaluating print and online sources; summarizing, paraphrasing, quoting, and synthesizing sources; documenting sources in MLA style; and using sources reponsibly.

- **Appendixes.** Appendix A provides instruction on writing literary arguments, and Appendix B covers APA documentation style.

Key Features

Concise in a Thoughtful Way

Practical Argument, Short Third Edition, covers everything students need to know about argument but doesn't overwhelm them. It limits technical vocabulary to what students and instructors actually need to understand and discuss key concepts in argument and argumentative writing. In short, *Practical Argument* is argument made accessible.

Argument Step by Step, Supported by Helpful Apparatus

Practical Argument, Short Third Edition, takes students through a step-by-step process of reading and responding to others' arguments and writing, revising, and editing their own arguments. The book uses a classroom-tested, exercise-driven approach that encourages students to participate actively in their own learning process. Chapters progress in a clear, easy-to-understand sequence: students are asked to read arguments, identify their key elements, and develop a response to an issue in the form of a complete, documented argumentative essay based on in-book focused research.

Exercises and writing assignments for each selection provide guidance for students as they work toward creating a finished piece of writing. Throughout the text, checklists, grammar-in-context and summary boxes, and source and gloss notes provide support. In addition, more than a dozen unique templates for paragraph-length arguments—located with the end-of-chapter exercises—provide structures that students can use for guidance as they write definition arguments, cause-and-effect arguments, evaluation arguments, proposal arguments, and ethical arguments. Sentence templates also frequently appear in the questions that follow the readings, providing an opportunity for students to work up to arguments at the paragraph level.

A Thematically Focused Approach with Compelling Chapter Topics

Students learn best when they care about and are engaged in an issue. For this reason, *Practical Argument*, Short Third Edition, uses readings and assignments to help students learn argumentation in the context of one high-interest contemporary issue per chapter. Chapter topics include media violence, free speech, online education, technology and privacy, and how modern technology does, or does not, change the meaning of plagiarism—issues that have real meaning in students' lives.

Readings on Relevant and Interesting Issues

Forty-three accessible professional readings—on issues that students will want to read about and debate—are presented in the text, including selections from journals and blogs. This mix of scholarly and cultural works blends student concerns, such as the cost of higher education, with thought-provoking reflections on more universal questions, such as ethical consumption and the intricacies of free speech. Many visual selections enhance the readings throughout the book, while seventeen sample student essays, more than in any other argument book, provide both realistic models for student writers and additional student voices. Each of these student essays, including complete MLA and APA research papers, is annotated to further assist students in their own writing process.

To help students better understand the context of the sources included in *Practical Argument*, each is marked with an icon that shows how it was originally presented.

An Open and Inviting Full-Color Design

The fresh, contemporary look of *Practical Argument*, Short Third Edition, will engage students. This open, colorful design eliminates the sea of dense type that is typical of many other argument books. Over a hundred photographs and other visuals—such as graphic novel excerpts, cartoons, advertisements, templates, charts and graphs, Web pages, and fine art—provide appealing and instructive real-world examples. The use of open space and numerous images reinforces the currency of the book's themes and also creates an inviting and visually stimulating format.

Two Versions

Practical Argument, Short Third Edition, is also available in a full-size edition that includes expanded coverage of argumentative strategies and a reader comprising debates and casebooks on current and engaging topics. To order the full-size version of *Practical Argument*, use ISBN **978-1-319-02856-5**.

New to This Edition

Essays, Topics, and Images

The third edition includes twenty-four engaging new professional essays on such timely topics as self-driving cars and free speech on college campuses. These essays have been carefully selected for their high-interest subject matter as well as for their effectiveness as sources and as teaching models for student writing.

More Help with the Writing Process and Academic Writing

In response to instructor requests, we have expanded the templates, making them more useful to students and adding interactivity in the Launch-Pad; included additional annotations in the MLA paper to guide students in the integration of source material; simplified the coverage of Rogerian argument; and provided more background on the rhetorical situation. We have also provided more help with academic writing, including additional material on finding sources as well as expanded examples of MLA and APA documentation. We have substantially expanded our coverage of how to refute opposing arguments, providing students with a firm grasp of how to usefully incorporate conflicting viewpoints into their writing.

Get the Most Out of Your Course with *Practical Argument*

Bedford/St. Martin's offers resources and format choices that help you and your students get even more out of your book and course. To learn more about or to order any of the following products, contact your Macmillan sales representative, email sales support (**sales_support@bfwpub.com**), or look for *Practical Argument*, Short Third Edition, at **macmillanlearning.com**.

LaunchPad for Practical Argument: *Where Students Learn*

LaunchPad provides engaging content and new ways to get the most out of your book. Get an **interactive e-book** combined with **useful, highly relevant materials** in a fully customizable course space; then assign and mix our resources with yours.

- Auto-graded **reading quizzes, comprehension quizzes on argument topics**, and **interactive writing templates** help students to engage actively with the material you assign.

- **Pre-built units**—including readings, videos, quizzes, discussion groups, and more—are **easy to adapt and assign** by adding your own materials and mixing them with our high-quality multimedia content and ready-made assessment options, such as **LearningCurve** adaptive quizzing. The LearningCurve now includes argument modules focusing on topic, purpose, and audience; arguable claims; reasoning and logical fallacies; and persuasive appeals (*logos, pathos,* and *ethos*).

- LaunchPad also provides access to a **Gradebook** that provides a clear window on the performance of your whole class, individual students, and even results of individual assignments.

- A **streamlined interface** helps students focus on what's due, and social commenting tools let them **engage**, make connections, and learn from each other. Use LaunchPad on its own or integrate it with your school's learning management system so that your class is always on the same page.

To get the most out of your book, order LaunchPad for *Practical Argument* packaged with the print book. (LaunchPad for *Practical Argument* can also be purchased on its own.) An activation code is required. To order LaunchPad for *Practical Argument* with the print book, use ISBN **978-1-319-07348-0**.

Choose from Alternative Formats of *Practical Argument*

Bedford/St. Martin's offers a range of affordable formats, allowing students to choose the one that works best for them. For further details, look for *Practical Argument*, Short Third Edition, at **macmillanlearning.com.**

- *Paperback edition with readings* To order the paperback *Practical Argument: A Text and Anthology*, Third Edition, use **ISBN 978-1-319-02856-5.**

- *Other popular e-book formats* For details, visit **macmillanlearning .com/ebooks.**

Select Value Packages

Add value to your text by packaging one of the following resources with *Practical Argument*, Short Third Edition. To learn more about package options for any of the following products, contact your Bedford/St. Martin's sales representative or visit **macmillanlearning.com.**

    Writer's Help 2.0 is a powerful online writing resource that helps students find answers whether they are searching for writing advice on their own or as part of an assignment.

- **Smart search**
  Built on research with more than 1,600 student writers, the smart search in Writer's Help 2.0 provides reliable results even when students use novice terms such as *flow* and *unstuck.*

- **Trusted content from our best-selling handbooks**
  Choose *Writer's Help 2.0, Hacker Version* or *Writer's Help 2.0, Lunsford Version* and ensure that students have clear advice and examples for all of their writing questions.

- **Adaptive exercises that engage students**
  Writer's Help 2.0 includes LearningCurve, game-like online quizzing that adapts to what students already know and helps them focus on what they need to learn.

Student access is packaged with *Practical Argument*, Short Third Edition, at a significant discount. Order ISBN 978-1-319-07350-3 for *Writer's Help 2.0, Hacker Version* or ISBN 978-1-319-07351-0 for *Writer's Help 2.0, Lunsford Version* to ensure your students have easy access to online writing support. Students who rent a book or buy a used book can purchase access to Writer's Help 2.0 at **macmillanhighered.com/writershelp2.**

    Instructors may request free access by registering as an instructor at **macmillanhighered.com/writershelp2.**

    For technical support, visit **macmillanlearning.com/getsupport.**

Portfolio Keeping, **Third Edition, by Nedra Reynolds and Elizabeth Davis,** provides all the information students need to use the portfolio method successfully in a writing course. *Portfolio Teaching*, a companion guide for instructors, provides the practical information instructors and writing program administrators need to use the portfolio method successfully in a writing course. To order *Portfolio Keeping* packaged with this text, contact your sale representative for a package ISBN.

Instructor Resources

You have a lot to do in your course. Bedford/St. Martin's wants to make it easy for you to find the support you need—and to get it quickly.

Resources for Teaching Practical Argument, Short Third Edition, is available as a PDF that can be downloaded from the Bedford/St. Martin's online catalog. In addition to chapter overviews and teaching tips, the instructor's manual includes sample syllabi, answers to questions that appear within the book, and suggested classroom activities.

Join Our Community! The Macmillan English Community is now Bedford/St. Martin's home for professional resources, featuring Bedford *Bits*, our popular blog site that offers new ideas for the composition classroom and composition teachers. Connect and converse with a growing team of Bedford authors and top scholars who blog on *Bits*: Andrea Lunsford, Nancy Sommers, Steve Bernhardt, Traci Gardner, Barclay Barrios, Jack Solomon, Susan Bernstein, Elizabeth Wardle, Doug Downs, Liz Losh, Jonathan Alexander, and Donna Winchell.

In addition, you'll find an expanding collection of additional resources that support your teaching.

- Sign up for webinars

- Download resources from our professional resources series that support your teaching

- Start a discussion

- Ask a question

- Follow your favorite members

- Review projects in the pipeline

Visit **community.macmillan.com** to join the conversation with your fellow teachers.

Acknowledgments

The following reviewers gave us valuable feedback: Joshua Beach, University of Texas at San Antonio; Jenny Billings Beaver, Rowan Cabarrus Community College; Jade Bittle, Rowan Cabarrus Community College; Shannon Blair, Central Piedmont Community College; Chris Blankenship, Emporia State University; Patricia Colella, Bunker Hill Community College; Jason DePolo, North Carolina A&T State University; Julie Dorris, Arkansas Northeastern College; Sarah Duerden, University of Sheffield; Alan Goldman, Massachusetts Bay Community College; Iris Harvey, Tarrant County Community College; Rebecca Hewett, California State University; Bruce Holmes, Stratford University; Anneliese Homan, State Fair Community College; Ann Hostestler, Goshen College; Elizabeth Hurston, Eastfield College; Ann Johnson, University of Nebraska at Omaha; Virginia Kearney, Baylor University; Audrey Lapointe, Cuyamaca College; Laurie Leach, Hawaii Pacific University; Vicki Martineau-Gilliam, National University; Gwendolyn Miller, University of Wisconsin–Parkside; Deborah Miller-Zournas, Stark State College; James Minor, South Piedmont Community College; Lani Montreal, Malcolm X College; Kathleen Moore, Community College of Vermont–Montpelier; Meltam Oztan, Kent State; Matt Pifer, Husson University; Cory Potter, Bethune-Cookman University; Mandy Reid, Indiana State University; Stuart Rosenberg, Cyprus College; Zahir Small, Santa Fe College; Kymberly Snelling, Metropolitan Community College Ft. Omaha; Rosie Soy, Hudson County Community College; Andrea Spofford, Austin Peay State University; Wes Spratlin, Motlow State Community College; Cheli Turner, Greenville Technical College; Barbara Urban, Central Piedmont Community College–Levine Campus; Sandra Zapp, Paradise Valley Community College.

We thank Jeff Ousborne, Deja Ruddick, Elizabeth Rice, and Michelle McSweeney for their valuable contributions to this text.

At Bedford/St. Martin's, Joan Feinberg, Denise Wydra, Karen Henry, Steve Scipione, Leasa Burton, and John Sullivan were involved and supportive from the start of the project. John, in particular, helped us shape this book and was with us every step of the way. In this third edition, we have had the pleasure of working with Sherry Mooney, our smart, talented, and creative editor. Her addition to our team has made *Practical Argument* a much better book. Matt Glazer patiently and efficiently shepherded the book through the production process. Others on our team included Jennifer Prince, who helped with many details; Joy Fisher Williams and Gillian Daniels, who were instrumental in marketing the book; Sheri Blaney, who found art and obtained permission for it; Christine Volboril, who handled text permissions; and our outstanding copy editor, Diana P. George. We are grateful for their help.

Finally, we would like to thank each other for lunches past—and for many, many lunches to come.

Laurie G. Kirszner
Stephen R. Mandell

CONTENTS

1   The Four Pillars of Argument   23

PART

2 Reading and Responding to Arguments 57

PART
3 Writing an Argumentative Essay   251

7

Planning, Drafting, and Revising an Argumentative Essay   253

PART

4 Using Sources to Support Your Argument   285

8 Finding and Evaluating Sources   287

11 Using Sources Responsibly 369

1

Understanding Argument

Ron Chapple/Getty Images

An Introduction to Argument

Recognizing Arguments

Arguments are everywhere. Whenever you turn on the television, read a newspaper or magazine, talk to friends and family, enter an online discussion, or engage in a debate in one of your classes, you encounter arguments. In fact, it is fair to say that much of the interaction that takes place in society involves argument. Consider, for example, a lawyer who tries to persuade a jury that a defendant is innocent, a doctor who wants to convince a patient to undergo a specific form of treatment, a lawmaker who wants to propose a piece of legislation, an executive who wants to institute a particular policy, an activist who wants to pursue a particular social agenda, a parent who wants to convince a child to study harder, a worker who wants to propose a more efficient way of performing a task, an employee who thinks that he or she deserves a raise, or a spokesperson in an infomercial whose goal is to sell something: all these people are engaging in argument.

In college, you encounter arguments on a daily basis; in fact, both class discussions and academic writing often take the form of argument. Consider, for example, the following questions that might be debated (and written about) in a first-year writing class:

- Do the benefits of fracking outweigh its risks?
- How free should free speech be?
- Are helicopter parents ruining their children's lives?
- How far should schools go to keep students safe?
- Do bystanders have an ethical responsibility to help in a crisis?

What these questions have in common is that they all call for argumentation. To answer these questions, students would be expected to state their opinions and support them.

> ### WHY INSTRUCTORS ASSIGN ARGUMENT
>
> Instructors assign argumentative essays for a number of reasons. Here are just a few:
>
> - To encourage students to develop and defend a position
> - To help students think critically about their own and other people's ideas
> - To give students the tools they need to convince others of the validity of their ideas
> - To help students learn to resolve conflicting points of view

World War I propaganda poster (1917)

Defining Argument

Now for the obvious question: exactly what is an argument? Perhaps the best way to begin is by explaining what argument is *not*. An argument (at least an academic argument) is not a **quarrel** or an angry exchange. The object of argument is not to attack someone who disagrees with you or to beat an opponent into submission. For this reason, the shouting matches that you routinely see on television or hear on talk radio are not really arguments. Argument is also not **spin**—the positive or biased slant that politicians routinely put on facts—or **propaganda**—information (or misinformation) that is spread to support a particular viewpoint. Finally, argument is not just a contradiction or denial of someone else's position. Even if you establish that an opponent's position is wrong or misguided, you still have to establish that your own position has merit by presenting evidence to support it.

There is a basic difference between **formal arguments**—those that you develop in academic discussion and writing—and **informal arguments**—those that occur in daily life, where people often get into arguments about politics, sports, social issues, and personal relationships. These everyday disputes are often just verbal fights in which one person tries to outshout another. Although they sometimes include facts, they tend to rely primarily on emotion and unsupported opinions. Moreover, such everyday arguments do not have the formal structure of academic arguments: they do not establish a logical link between a particular viewpoint and reliable supporting evidence. There is also no real effort to address opposing arguments. In general, these arguments tend to be disorganized, emotional disputes that have more to do with criticizing an opponent than with advancing and supporting a position on an issue. Although such informal arguments can serve as starting points for helping you think about issues, they do not have the structure or the intellectual rigor of formal arguments.

So exactly what is an argument—or, more precisely, what is an academic argument? An **academic argument** is a type of formal argument that takes a stand, presents evidence, includes documentation, and uses logic to convince an audience to accept (or at least consider) the writer's position. Of course, academic arguments can get heated, but at their core they are civil exchanges. Writers of academic arguments strive to be fair and to show respect for others—especially for those who present opposing arguments.

Keep in mind that arguments take positions with which reasonable people may disagree. For this reason, an argument never actually proves anything. (If it did, there would be no argument.) The best that an argument can do is to convince other people to accept (or at least acknowledge) the validity of its position.

An angry exchange is not an academic argument.

Flying Colours Ltd./Getty Images

WHAT KINDS OF STATEMENTS ARE NOT DEBATABLE?

To be suitable for argument, a statement must be **debatable**: in other words, there must be conflicting opinions or conflicting facts that call the validity of the statement into question. For this reason, the following types of statements are generally *not* suitable for argument:

- **Statements of fact:** A statement of fact can be verified, so it is not debatable. For example, there is no point in arguing that your school makes instructors' lectures available as podcasts. This is a question of fact that can easily be checked. You can, however, argue that making instructors' lectures available as podcasts would (or would not) enhance education at your school. This is a debatable statement that can be supported by facts and examples.

- **Statements of personal preference or taste:** Expressions of personal preference or taste are not suitable for argument. For example, if you say that you don't like the taste of a particular soft drink, no one can legitimately argue that you are wrong. This statement is beyond dispute because it is a matter of personal taste. You could, however, argue that soft drinks should not be sold in school cafeterias because they contribute to obesity. To support this position, you would supply evidence—facts, statistics, and expert opinion.

> **NOTE**
>
> Although personal expressions of religious belief are difficult to debate, the interpretation of religious doctrine is a suitable subject for argument—and so are the political, social, philosophical, and theological effects of religion on society.

It is a mistake to think that all arguments have just two sides—one right side and one wrong side. In fact, many arguments that you encounter in college focus on issues that are quite complex. For example, if you were considering the question of whether the United States should ban torture, you could certainly answer this question with a yes or a no, but this would be an oversimplification. To examine the issue thoroughly, you would have to consider it from a number of angles:

- Should torture be banned in all situations?

- Should torture be used as a last resort to elicit information that could prevent an imminent attack?

- What actually constitutes torture? For example, is sleep deprivation torture? What about a slap on the face? Loud music? A cold cell? Are "enhanced interrogation techniques"—such as waterboarding—torture?

- Who should have the legal right to approve interrogation techniques?

If you were going to write an argument about this issue, you would have to take a position that adequately conveyed its complex nature—for example, "Although torture may be cruel and even inhuman, it is sometimes necessary." To do otherwise might be to commit the **either/or fallacy** (see p. 151)—to offer only two choices when there are actually many others.

Arguments in Real Life

In blogs, social media posts, work-related proposals, letters to the editor, emails to businesses, letters of complaint, and other types of communication, you formulate arguments that are calculated to influence readers. Many everyday situations call for argument:

- A proposal to the manager of the UPS store where you work to suggest a more efficient way of sorting packages

- A letter to your local newspaper in which you argue that creating a walking trail would be good use of your community's tax dollars

- An email to your child's principal asking her to extend after-school hours

- A letter to a credit card company in which you request an adjustment to your bill

- A blog post in which you argue that the federal government could do more to relieve the student loan burden

Because argument is so prevalent, the better your arguing skills, the better able you will be to function—not just in school but also in the wider world. When you have a clear thesis, convincing support, and effective refutation of opposing arguments, you establish your credibility and go a long way toward convincing readers that you are someone worth listening to.

Presenting a good argument does not guarantee that readers will accept your ideas. It does, however, help you to define an issue and to express your position clearly and logically. If you present yourself as a well-informed, reasonable person who is attuned to the needs of your readers—even those who disagree with you—you increase your chances of convincing your audience that your position is worth considering.

Arguments are also central to our democratic form of government. Whether the issue is taxation, health care, border control, the environment, abortion, gun ownership, energy prices, gay marriage, terrorism, or cyber-bullying, political candidates, media pundits, teachers, friends, and family members all try to influence the way we think. So in a real sense, argument is the way that all of us participate in the national (or even global) conversation about ideas that matter. The better you understand the methods of argumentation, the better able you will be to recognize, analyze, and respond to the arguments that you hear. By mastering the techniques of argument, you will become a clearer thinker, a more informed citizen, and a person who is better able to influence those around you.

Black Lives Matter protest

Andrew Burton/Getty Images

Winning and Losing Arguments

People often talk of "winning" and "losing" arguments, and of course, the aim of many arguments is to defeat an opponent. In televised political debates, candidates try to convince viewers that they should be elected. In a courtroom, a defense attorney tries to establish a client's innocence. In a job interview, a potential employee tries to convince an employer that he or she is the best-qualified applicant. However, the goal of an argument is not always to determine a winner and a loser. Sometimes the goal of an argument is to identify a problem and suggest solutions that could satisfy those who hold a number of different positions on an issue.

If, for example, you would like your college bookstore to lower the price of items (such as sweatshirts, coffee mugs, and backpacks) with a school logo, you could simply state your position and then support it with evidence. A more effective way of approaching this problem, however, might be to consider all points of view and find some middle ground. For example, how would lowering these prices affect the bookstore? A short conversation with the manager of the bookstore might reveal that the revenue generated by these products enables the bookstore to discount other items—such as art supplies and computers—as well as to hire student help. Therefore, decreasing the price of products with college logos would negatively affect some students. Even so, the high prices also make it difficult for some students to buy these items.

To address this problem, you could offer a compromise solution: the price of items with college logos could be lowered, but the price of other items—such as magazines and snacks—could be raised to make up the difference.

The Rhetorical Situation

In everyday use, the term *rhetoric* has distinctly negative connotations. When a speech is described as being nothing but *rhetoric*, the meaning is clear: the speech consists of empty words and phrases calculated to confuse and manipulate listeners. When writing instructors use the term *rhetoric*, however, it means something quite different: it refers to the choices someone makes to structure a message—written, oral, or visual.

The **rhetorical situation** refers to the factors that influence the creation of any type of communication—especially its words, images, and structure. Applied to argument, the rhetorical situation refers to five factors you should consider when planning an effective argument. Although every rhetorical situation is different, all rhetorical situations involve the following five elements:

- The writer
- The purpose
- The audience
- The question
- The context

Considering the Writer

Every argument begins with a writer, the person who creates the text. For this reason, it is important to understand how your biases or preconceptions could affect what you produce. For example, if you were home schooled, you might have very definite ideas about education. Likewise, a former Navy Seal might have preconceptions concerning the war in Afghanistan. Strongly held beliefs like these can, and often do, color your arguments. The following factors can affect the tone and content of an argument:

age

education

gender

ethnicity

cultural experiences

political affiliation

religion

sexuality

social standing

Before you plan an argument, ask yourself what preconceived ideas you may have about a particular topic. Do your beliefs prevent you from considering all sides of an issue, reaching a logical and fair conclusion, or acknowledging the validity of opposing arguments? It is important that you present yourself as a fair and open-minded person, one whom readers trust. For this reason, you should maintain a reasonable tone and avoid the use of words or phrases that indicate bias.

Considering the Purpose

A writer's **purpose** is his or her reason for writing. The purpose of an argument is to present a position and to change (or at least influence) people's ideas about an issue. In addition to this general purpose, a writer may have more specific goals. For example, you might want to criticize the actions of others or call into question a particular public policy. You may also want to take a stand on a controversial topic or convince readers that certain arguments are weak. Finally, you may want to propose a solution to a problem or convince readers to adopt a certain course of action.

When you write an argument, you may want to state your purpose directly—usually in your introduction. (Key words in your thesis statement can indicate the direction the argument will take as well as the points that you will discuss.) At other times, especially if you think readers will not readily accept your ideas, you may want to indicate your purpose later in your essay or simply imply it.

Considering the Audience

When you write argumentative essays, you don't write in a vacuum; you write for real people who may or may not agree with you. As you are writing, it is easy to forget this fact and address a general group of readers. However, doing this would be a mistake. Defining your audience and keeping this audience in mind as you write is important because it helps you decide what material to include and how to present it.

One way to define an audience is by its **traits**—the age, gender, interests, values, preconceptions, and level of education of audience members. Each of these traits influences how audience members will react to your ideas, and understanding them helps you determine how to construct your argument. For instance, suppose you were going to write an essay with the following thesis:

> Although college is expensive, its high cost is justified.

How you approach this subject would depend on the audience you were addressing. For example, college students, parents, and college administrators would have different ideas about the subject, different perspectives, different preconceptions, and different levels of knowledge. Therefore, the argument you write for each of these audiences would be different from the others in terms of content, organization, and type of appeal.

- **College students** have a local and personal perspective. They know the school and have definite ideas about the value of the education they are getting. Most likely, they come from different backgrounds and have varying financial needs. Depending on their majors, they have different expectations about employment (and salary) when they graduate. Even with these differences, however, these students share certain concerns. Many probably have jobs to help cover their expenses. Many also have student loans that they will need to start paying after graduation.

  An argumentative essay addressing this audience could focus on statistics and expert opinions that establish the worth of a college degree in terms of future employment, job satisfaction, and lifetime earnings.

- **Parents** probably have limited knowledge of the school and the specific classes their children are taking. They have expectations—both realistic and unrealistic—about the value of a college degree. Some parents may be able to help their children financially, and others may be unable to do so. Their own life experiences and backgrounds probably color their ideas about the value of a college education. For example, parents who have gone to college may have different ideas about the value of a degree from those who haven't.

  An argumentative essay addressing this audience could focus on the experience of other parents of college students. It could also include statistics that address students' future economic independence and economic security.

- **College administrators** have detailed knowledge about college and the economic value of a degree. They are responsible for attracting students, scheduling classes, maintaining educational standards, and providing support services. They are familiar with budget requirements, and they understand the financial pressures involved in running a school. They also know how tuition dollars are spent and how much state and federal aid the school needs to stay afloat. Although they are sympathetic to the plight of both students and parents, they have to work with limited resources.

An argumentative essay addressing this audience could focus on the need to make tuition more affordable by cutting costs and providing more student aid.

Another way to define an audience is to determine whether it is *friendly*, *hostile*, or *neutral*.

- A **friendly audience** is sympathetic to your argument. This audience might already agree with you or have an emotional or intellectual attachment to you or to your position. In this situation, you should emphasize points of agreement and reinforce the emotional bond that exists between you and the audience. Don't assume, however, that because this audience is receptive to your ideas, you do not have to address its concerns or provide support for your points. If readers suspect that you are avoiding important issues or that your evidence is weak, they will be less likely to take your argument seriously—even though they agree with you.

- A **hostile audience** disagrees with your position and does not accept the underlying assumptions of your argument. For this reason, you have to work hard to overcome their preconceived opinions, presenting your points clearly and logically and including a wide range of evidence. To show that you are a reasonable person, you should treat these readers with respect even though they happen to disagree with you. In addition, you should show that you have taken the time to consider their arguments and that you value their concerns. Even with all these efforts, however, the best you may be able to do is get them to admit that you have made some good points in support of your position.

- A **neutral audience** has no preconceived opinions about the issue you are going to discuss. (When you are writing an argument for a college class, you should assume that you are writing for a neutral audience.) For this reason, you need to provide background information about the issue and about the controversy surrounding it. You should also summarize opposing points of view, present them logically, and refute them effectively. This type of audience may not know much about an issue, but it is not necessarily composed of unsophisticated or unintelligent people. Moreover, even though such readers are neutral, you should assume that they are **skeptical**—that is, that they will question your assumptions and require supporting evidence before they accept your conclusions.

> **NOTE**
>
> Some audiences are so diverse that they are difficult to categorize. In this case, it is best to define the audience yourself—for example, *concerned parents*, *prudent consumers*, or *serious students*—and then address them accordingly.

Keep in mind that identifying a specific audience is not something that you do at the last minute. Because your audience determines the kind of argument you present, you should take the time to make this determination before you begin to write.

Considering the Question

All arguments begin with a question that you are going to answer. To be suitable for argument, this question must have more than one possible answer. If it does not, there is no basis for the argument. For example, there is no point trying to write an argumentative essay on the question of whether head injuries represent a danger for football players. The answer to this question is so obvious that no thoughtful person would argue that they are not. The question of whether the National Football League is doing enough to protect players from head injuries, however, is one on which reasonable people could disagree. Consider the following information:

- In recent years, the NFL has done much to reduce the number of serious head injuries.

- New protocols for the treatment of players who show signs of head trauma, stricter rules against helmet-to-helmet tackles, and the use of safer helmets have reduced the number of concussions.

- Even with these precautions, professional football players experience a high number of head injuries, with one in three players reporting negative effects—some quite serious—from repeated concussions.

Because there are solid arguments on both sides of this issue, you could write an effective argument in which you address this question.

Considering the Context

An argument takes place in a specific **context**—the set of circumstances that surrounds the issue. As you plan your argument, consider the social, historical, and cultural events that define the debate.

Assume that you were going to argue that the public school students in your hometown should be required to purchase iPads. Before you begin your argument, you should give readers the background—the context—they will need to understand the issue. For example, they should know that school officials have been debating the issue for over a year. School administrators say that given the advances in distance learning as well as the high quality of online resources, iPads will enhance the educational experience of students. They also say that it is time to bring the schools' instructional methods into the twenty-first century. Even so, some parents say that requiring the purchase of iPads will put an undue financial burden on them. In addition, teachers point out that a good deal of new material will have to be developed to take advantage of this method of instruction. Finally, not all students will have access at home to the high-speed Internet capacity necessary for this type of instruction.

If it is not too complicated, you can discuss the context of your argument in your introduction; if it requires more explanation, you can discuss it in your first body paragraph. If you do not establish this context early in your essay, however, readers will have a difficult time understanding the issue you are going to discuss and the points you are going to make.

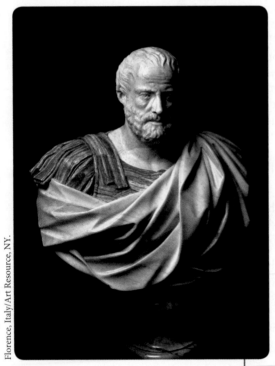

Aristotle

Logos, Pathos, and Ethos

To be effective, your argument has to be persuasive. **Persuasion** is a general term that refers to how a speaker or writer influences an audience to adopt a particular belief or to follow a specific course of action.

In the fifth century BCE, the philosopher Aristotle considered the issue of persuasion. Ancient Greece was primarily an oral culture (as opposed to a written or print culture), so persuasive techniques were most often used in speeches. Public officials had to speak before a citizens' assembly, and people had to make their cases in front of various judicial bodies. The more persuasive the presentation, the better the speaker's chance of success. In *The Art of Rhetoric*, Aristotle examines the three different means of persuasion that a speaker can use to persuade listeners (or writers):

- The appeal to reason (*logos*)
- The appeal to the emotions (*pathos*)
- The appeal to authority (*ethos*)

The Appeal to Reason (Logos)

According to Aristotle, argument is the appeal to reason or logic (*logos*). He assumed that, at their core, human beings are logical and therefore would respond to a well-constructed argument. For Aristotle, appeals to reason focus primarily on the way that an argument is organized, and this organization is determined by formal logic, which uses deductive and inductive reasoning to reach valid conclusions. Aristotle believed that appeals to reason convince an audience that a conclusion is both valid and true (see Chapter 5 for a discussion of deductive and inductive reasoning and logic). Although Aristotle believed that ideally, all arguments should appeal to reason, he knew that given the realities of human nature, reason alone was not always enough. Therefore, when he discusses persuasion, he also discusses the appeals to *ethos* and *pathos*.

Logos *in Action*

Notice how the ad below for the Toyota Prius, a popular hybrid automobile, appeals primarily to reason. It uses facts as well as a logical explanation

Car shot for Toyota Prius Harmony ad © Trevor Pearson. Background for Toyota Prius Harmony ad © Mark Holthusen Photography. Reproduced with permission of the photographers and Toyota Sales USA.

of how the car works to appeal to reason (as well as to the consumer's desire to help the environment).

You can assess the effectiveness of *logos* (the appeal to reason) in an argument by asking the following questions:

- Does the argument have a clear thesis? In other words, can you identify the main point the writer is trying to make?

- Does the argument include the facts, examples, and expert opinion needed to support the thesis?

- Is the argument well organized? Are the points the argument makes presented in logical order?

- Can you detect any errors in logic (**fallacies**) that undermine the argument's reasoning?

The Appeal to the Emotions (Pathos)

Aristotle knew that an appeal to the emotions (***pathos***) could be very persuasive because it adds a human dimension to an argument. By appealing to an audience's sympathies and by helping them to identify with the subject being discussed, emotional appeals can turn abstract concepts into concrete examples that can compel people to take action. After December 7, 1941, for example, explicit photographs of the Japanese attack on Pearl Harbor helped convince Americans that retaliation was both justified and desirable. Many Americans responded the same way when they saw pictures of planes crashing into the twin towers of the World Trade Center on September 11, 2001.

Although an appeal to the emotions can add to an already strong argument, it does not in itself constitute proof. Moreover, certain kinds of emotional appeals—appeals to fear, hatred, and prejudice, for example—are considered unfair and are not acceptable in college writing. In this sense, the pictures of the attacks on Pearl Harbor and the World Trade Center would be unfair arguments if they were not accompanied by evidence that established that retaliation was indeed necessary.

Pathos *in Action*

The following ad makes good use of the appeal to the emotions. Using a picture of polar bears defaced by graffiti, the ad includes a caption encouraging people to respect the environment. Although the ad contains no supporting evidence, it is effective nonetheless.

What will it take before we respect the planet?

Courtesy of WWF.org, reproduced with permission

You can assess the effectiveness of *pathos* (the appeal to the emotions) in an argument by asking the following questions:

- Does the argument include words or images designed to move readers?

- Does the argument use emotionally loaded language?

- Does the argument include vivid descriptions or striking examples calculated to appeal to readers' emotions?

- Are the values and beliefs of the writer apparent in the argument?

- Does the tone seem emotional?

The Appeal to Authority (Ethos)

Finally, Aristotle knew that the character and authority of a speaker or writer (*ethos*) could contribute to the persuasiveness of an argument. If the person making the argument is known to be honorable, truthful, knowledgeable, and trustworthy, audiences will likely accept what he or she is saying. If, on the other hand, the person is known to be deceitful, ignorant, dishonest, uninformed, or dishonorable, audiences will probably dismiss his or her argument—no matter how persuasive it might seem. Whenever you analyze an argument, you should try to determine whether the writer is worth listening to—in other words, whether the writer has **credibility**.

(For a discussion of how to establish credibility and demonstrate fairness in your own writing, see Chapter 7.)

Ethos *in Action*

The following ad uses an appeal to authority. It uses an endorsement by the popular tennis star Venus Williams to convince consumers to buy Reebok sneakers. (Recent studies suggest that consumers react positively to ads that feature products endorsed by famous athletes.)

You can assess the effectiveness of *ethos* (the appeal to authority) in an argument by asking the following questions:

- Does the person making the argument demonstrate knowledge of the subject?

- What steps does the person making the argument take to present its position as reasonable?

- Does the argument seem fair?

- If the argument includes sources, do they seem both reliable and credible? Does the argument include proper documentation?

- Does the person making the argument demonstrate respect for opposing viewpoints?

Venus Williams in an ad endorsing Reebok

AP Photo/Kathy Willens

The Rhetorical Triangle

The relationship among the three kinds of appeals in an argument is traditionally represented by a triangle.

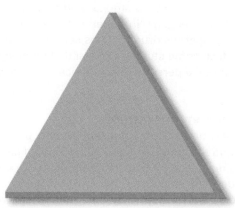

LOGOS (reason)
Focuses on the text

ETHOS (authority)
Focuses on the writer

PATHOS (emotions)
Focuses on the audience

In the diagram above—called the **rhetorical triangle**—all sides of the triangle are equal, implying that the three appeals occur in an argument in equal measure. In reality, however, this is seldom true. Depending on the audience, purpose, and situation, an argument may include all three appeals or just one or two. Moreover, one argument might emphasize reason, another might stress the writer's authority (or credibility), and still another might appeal mainly to the emotions. (In each of these cases, one side of the rhetorical triangle would be longer than the others.) In academic writing, for example, the appeal to reason is used most often, and the appeal to the emotions is less common. As Aristotle recognized, however, the three appeals often work together (to varying degrees) to create an effective argument.

Each of the following paragraphs makes an argument against smoking, illustrating how the appeals are used in an argument. Although each paragraph includes all three of the appeals, one appeal outweighs the others. (Keep in mind that each paragraph is aimed at a different audience.)

APPEAL TO REASON (*LOGOS*)

Among young people, the dangers of smoking are clear. According to the World Health Organization, smoking can cause a variety of problems in young people—for example, lung problems and shortness of breath. Smoking also contributes to heart attacks, strokes, and coronary artery disease (72). In addition, teenage smokers have an increased risk of developing lung cancer as they get older (CDC). According to one study, teenage smokers see doctors or other health professionals at higher rates than those who do not smoke (Ardly 112). Finally, teenagers who smoke tend to abuse alcohol and marijuana as well as engage in other risky behaviors (CDC). Clearly, tobacco is a dangerous drug that has serious health risks for teenage smokers. In fact, some studies suggest that smoking takes thirteen to fourteen years off a person's life (American Cancer Society).

APPEAL TO THE EMOTIONS (*PATHOS*)

Every day, almost four thousand young people begin smoking cigarettes, and this number is growing (Family First Aid). Sadly, most of you have no idea what you are getting into. For one thing, smoking yellows your teeth, stains your fingers, and gives you bad breath. The smoke also gets into your hair and clothes and makes you smell. Also, smoking is addictive; once you start, it's hard to stop. After you've been smoking for a few years, you are hooked, and as television commercials for the nicotine patch show, you can have a hard time breaking the habit. Finally, smoking is dangerous. In the United States, one out of every five deaths can be attributed to smoking (Teen Health). If you have ever seen anyone dying of lung cancer, you understand how bad long-term smoking can be. Just look at the pictures on the Internet of diseased, blackened lungs, and it becomes clear that smoking does not make you look cool or sophisticated, no matter what cigarette advertising suggests.

APPEAL TO AUTHORITY (*ETHOS*)

My advice to those who are starting to smoke is to reconsider—before it's too late. I began using tobacco over ten years ago when I was in high school. At first, I started using snuff because I was on the baseball team and wanted to imitate the players in the major leagues. It wasn't long before I had graduated to cigarettes—first a few and then at least a pack a day. I heard the warnings from teachers and the counselors from the D.A.R.E. program, but they didn't do any good. I spent almost all my extra money on cigarettes. Occasionally, I would stop—sometimes for a few days, sometimes for a few weeks—but I always started again. Later, after I graduated, the health plan at my job covered smoking cessation treatment, so I tried everything—the patch, Chantix, therapy, and even hypnosis. Again, nothing worked. At last, after I had been married for four years, my wife sat me down and begged me to quit. Later that night, I threw away my cigarettes and haven't smoked since. Although I've gained some weight, I now breathe easier, and I am able to concentrate better than I could before. Had I known how difficult quitting was going to be, I never would have started in the first place.

When you write an argumentative essay, keep in mind that each type of appeal has its own particular strengths. Your purpose and audience as well as other elements of the rhetorical situation help you determine what strategy to use. Remember, however, that even though most effective arguments use a combination of appeals, one appeal predominates. For example, even though academic arguments may employ appeals to the emotions, they do so sparingly. Most often, they appeal primarily to reason by using facts and statistics—not emotions—to support their points.

 For more practice, see the LearningCurve on Persuasive Appeals (*pathos, ethos,* and *logos*) in the LaunchPad for *Practical Argument*.

Butch Dill/AP Photos

The Four Pillars of Argument

Is a College Education Worth the Money?

In recent years, more and more high school graduates have been heading to college, convinced that higher education will enhance their future earning power. At the same time, the cost of a college education has been rising, and so has the amount of student-loan debt carried by college graduates. (During 2014, average tuition and fees at nonprofit private colleges rose 3.7 percent, to $31,231, while tuition for in-state students at four-year public schools went up 2.9 percent to $9,139. On average, 2015 graduates with student-loan debt owed over $35,000.) This situation has led some observers to wonder if the high cost of college actually pays off—not only in dollars but also in future job satisfaction. Will a college degree protect workers who are threatened by high unemployment, the rise of technology, the declining power of labor unions, and the trend toward outsourcing? Given the high financial cost of college, do the rewards of a college education—emotional and intellectual as well as financial—balance the sacrifices that students make in time and money? These and other questions have no easy answers.

Later in this chapter, you will be introduced to readings that highlight the pros and cons of investing in a college education, and you will be asked to write an argumentative essay in which you take a position on this controversial topic.

In a sense, you already know a lot more than you think you do about how to construct an argumentative essay. After all, an argumentative essay is a variation of the thesis-and-support essays that you have been writing in your college classes: you state a position on a topic, and then you support this position. However, argumentative essays also involve some special concerns in terms of structure, style, and purpose. Throughout this book, we introduce you to the unique features of argument. In this chapter, we focus on structure.

The Elements of Argument

An argumentative essay includes the same three sections—*introduction*, *body*, and *conclusion*—as any other essay. In an argumentative essay, however, the introduction includes an argumentative **thesis statement**, the body includes both the supporting **evidence** and the **refutation** of opposing arguments, and the conclusion includes a strong, convincing **concluding statement** that reinforces the position stated in the thesis.

The following diagram illustrates one way to organize an argumentative essay.

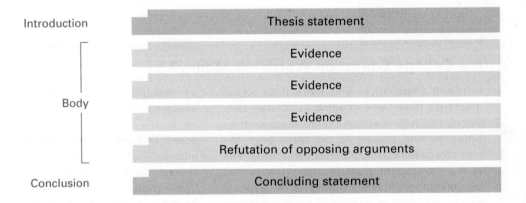

Introduction	Thesis statement
Body	Evidence
	Evidence
	Evidence
	Refutation of opposing arguments
Conclusion	Concluding statement

The elements of an argumentative essay are like the pillars of an ancient Greek temple. Together, the four elements—thesis statement, evidence, refutation of opposing arguments, and concluding statement—help you build a strong argument.

Ancient Greek temple

AP Photo/Alessandro Fucarini

Thesis Statement

A **thesis statement** is a single sentence that states your position on an issue. An argumentative essay must have an **argumentative thesis**—one that takes a firm stand. For example, on the issue of whether colleges should require all students to study a language other than English, your thesis statement could be any of the following (and other positions are also possible):

- Colleges should require all students to study a foreign language.

- Colleges should require all liberal arts majors to study a foreign language.

- Colleges should require all students to take Spanish, Chinese, or Farsi.

- Colleges should not require any students to study a foreign language.

An argumentative thesis must be **debatable**—that is, it must have at least two sides, stating a position with which some reasonable people might disagree. To confirm that your thesis is debatable, you should see if you can formulate an **antithesis**, or opposing argument. For example, the statement, "Our school has a foreign-language requirement" has no antithesis because it is simply a statement of fact; you could not take the opposite position because the facts would not support it. However, the following thesis statement takes a position that *is* debatable (and therefore suitable for an argumentative thesis):

THESIS   Our school should institute a foreign-language requirement.

ANTITHESIS Our school should not institute a foreign-language requirement.

(For more on thesis statements, see Chapter 7.)

Evidence

Evidence is the material—facts, observations, expert opinion, examples, statistics, and so on—that supports your thesis statement. For example, you could support your position that foreign-language study should be required for all college students by arguing that this requirement will make them more employable, and you could cite employment statistics to support this point. Alternatively, you could use the opinion of an expert on the topic—for example, an experienced college language instructor—to support the opposite position, arguing that students without an interest in language study are wasting their time in such courses.

You will use both *facts* and *opinions* to support the points you make in your arguments. A **fact** is a statement that can be verified (proven to be true). An **opinion** is always open to debate because it is simply a personal judgment. Of course, the more knowledgeable the writer is, the more credible his or her opinion is. Thus, the opinion of a respected expert on language study will carry more weight than the opinion of a student with no particular expertise on the issue. However, if the student's opinion is supported by facts, it will be much more convincing than an unsupported opinion.

FACTS

- Some community colleges have no foreign-language requirements.
- Some selective liberal arts colleges require all students to take two years or more of foreign-language study.
- At some universities, undergraduates must take as many as fourteen foreign-language credits.
- Some schools grant credit for high school language classes, allowing these courses to fulfill the college foreign-language requirement.

UNSUPPORTED OPINIONS

- Foreign-language courses are not as important as math and science courses.
- Foreign-language study should be a top priority on university campuses.
- Engineering majors should not have to take a foreign-language course.
- It is not fair to force all students to study a foreign language.

SUPPORTED OPINIONS

- The university requires all students to take a full year of foreign-language study, but it is not doing enough to support those who need help. For example, it does not provide enough student tutors, and the language labs have no evening hours.
- According to Ruth Fuentes, chair of the Spanish department, nursing and criminal justice majors who take at least two years of Spanish have an easier time finding employment after graduation than students in those majors who do not study Spanish.

Refutation

Because every argument has more than one side, you should not assume that your readers will agree with you. On the contrary, readers usually need to be convinced that your position on an issue has merit.

This means that you need to do more than just provide sufficient evidence in support of your position; you also need to **refute** (disprove or call into question) arguments that challenge your position, possibly acknowledging the strengths of those opposing arguments and then pointing out their shortcomings. For example, if you take a position in favor of requiring foreign-language study for all college students, some readers might argue that college students already have to take too many required courses. After acknowledging the validity of this argument, you could refute it by pointing out that a required foreign-language course would not necessarily be a burden for students because it could replace another, less important required course. (For more on refutation, see Chapter 7.)

Concluding Statement

After you have provided convincing support for your position and refuted opposing arguments, you should end your essay with a strong **concluding statement** that reinforces your position. (The position that you want readers to remember is the one stated in your thesis, not the opposing arguments that you have refuted.) For example, you might conclude an essay in support of a foreign-language requirement by making a specific recommendation or by predicting the possible negative outcome of *not* implementing this requirement.

CHECKLIST

Does Your Argument Stand Up?

When you write an argumentative essay, check to make sure it includes all four of the elements you need to build a strong argument.

- ☐ Do you have an argumentative **thesis**?
- ☐ Do you include solid, convincing **evidence** to support your thesis?
- ☐ Do you include a **refutation** of the most compelling arguments against your position?
- ☐ Do you include a strong **concluding statement**?

⬇ The following student essay includes all four of the elements that are needed to build a convincing argument.

WHY FOREIGN-LANGUAGE STUDY SHOULD BE REQUIRED

NIA TUCKSON

Introduction

"What do you call someone who speaks three languages? Trilingual.   1
What do you call someone who speaks two languages? Bilingual. What do
you call someone who speaks only one language? American." As this old
joke illustrates, many Americans are unable to communicate in a language
other than English. Given our global economy and American companies'
need to conduct business with other countries, this problem needs to be

Thesis statement

addressed. A good first step is to require all college students to study a
foreign language.

First body paragraph:
Evidence

After graduation, many students will work in fields in which speaking   2
(or reading) another language will be useful or even necessary. For example,
health-care professionals will often be called on to communicate with
patients who do not speak English; in fact, a patient's life may depend on
their ability to do so. Those who work in business and finance may need
to speak Mandarin or Japanese; those who have positions in the military
or in the foreign service may need to speak Persian or Arabic. A working
knowledge of one of these languages can help students succeed in their
future careers, and it can also make them more employable.

Second body paragraph:
Evidence

In addition to strengthening a résumé, foreign-language study can also   3
give students an understanding of another culture's history, art, and literature.
Although such knowledge may never be "useful" in a student's career, it
can certainly enrich the student's life. Too narrow a focus on career can
turn college into a place that trains students rather than educates them.
In contrast, expanding students' horizons to include subjects beyond those
needed for their careers can better equip them to be lifelong learners.

Third body paragraph:
Evidence

When they travel abroad, Americans who can speak a language   4
other than English will find that they are better able to understand
people from other countries. As informal ambassadors for the United
States, tourists have a responsibility to try to understand other
languages and cultures. Too many Americans assume that their own
country's language and culture are superior to all others. This shortsighted

attitude is not likely to strengthen relationships between the United States and other nations. Understanding a country's language can help students to build bridges between themselves and others.

Some students say that learning a language is not easy and that it takes a great deal of time. College students are already overloaded with coursework, jobs, and family responsibilities, and a new academic requirement is certain to create problems. In fact, students may find that adding just six credits of language study will limit their opportunities to take advanced courses in their majors or to enroll in electives that interest them. However, this burden can be eased if other, less important course requirements—such as physical education—are eliminated to make room for the new requirement.

5 Fourth body paragraph: Refutation of opposing argument

Some students may also argue that they, not their school, should be able to decide what courses are most important to them. After all, a student who struggled in high school French and plans to major in computer science might understandably resist a foreign-language requirement. However, challenging college language courses might actually be more rewarding than high school courses were, and the student who struggled in high school French might actually enjoy a college-level French course (or study a different language). Finally, a student who initially plans to major in computer science may actually wind up majoring in something completely different—or taking a job in a country in which English is not spoken.

6 Fifth body paragraph: Refutation of opposing argument

Entering college students sometimes find it hard to envision their personal or professional futures or to imagine where their lives may take them. Still, a well-rounded education, including foreign-language study, can prepare them for many of the challenges that they will face. Colleges can help students keep their options open by requiring at least a year (and preferably two years) of foreign-language study. Instead of focusing narrowly on what interests them today, American college students should take the extra step to become bilingual—or even trilingual—in the future.

7 Conclusion

Concluding statement

◑ EXERCISE 1.1

The following essay, "Raise the Drinking Age to Twenty-Five," by Andrew Herman, includes all four of the basic elements of argument discussed so far. Read the essay, and then answer the questions that follow it, consulting the diagram on page 24 if necessary.

This commentary appeared on August 22, 2007, on BG Views, a website for Bowling Green State University and the citizens of its community.

RAISE THE DRINKING AGE TO TWENTY-FIVE

ANDREW HERMAN

As a new school year begins, as dorms fill with new and returning students alike, a single thought frequents the minds of every member of our population: newfound freedom from a summer of jobs and familial responsibilities. 1

But our return to school coexists with a possibly lethal counterpart: college drinking. 2

Nearly everyone is exposed to parties during college, and one would be hard pressed to find a college party without alcohol. Most University students indicate in countless surveys they have used alcohol in a social setting before age 21. 3

It is startling just how ineffective current laws have been at curbing underage drinking. 4

> "It is startling just how ineffective current laws have been."

A dramatic change is needed in the way society addresses drinking and the way we enforce existing laws, and it can start with a simple change: making the drinking age 25. 5

Access and availability are the principal reasons underage drinking has become easy to do. Not through direct availability, but through access to legal-aged "friends." 6

In a college setting, it is all but impossible not to know a person who is older than 21 and willing to provide alcohol to younger students. Even if unintentional, there is no verification that each person who drinks is of the appropriate age. 7

However, it should be quite easy to ensure underage individuals don't have access to alcohol. In reality, those who abstain from alcohol are in the minority. Countless people our age consider speeding tickets worse than an arrest for underage consumption. 8

Is it truly possible alcohol abuse has become so commonplace, so acceptable, that people forget the facts? 9

Each year, 1,400 [college students] die from drinking too much. 600,000 are victims of alcohol-related physical assault and 17,000 are a result of drunken driving deaths, many being innocent bystanders. 10

Perhaps the most disturbing number: 70,000 people, overwhelmingly female, are annually sexually assaulted in alcohol-related situations. 11

These numbers are difficult to grasp for the sheer prevalence of alcoholic destruction. Yet, we, as college students, are responsible for an overwhelming portion of their incidence. It is difficult to imagine anyone would wish to assume the role of rapist, murderer, or victim. We all assume these things could never happen to us, but I am certain victims in these situations thought the same. The simple 12 truth is that driving under the influence is the leading cause of death for teens. For 10- to 24-year-olds, alcohol is the fourth-leading cause of death, made so by factors ranging from alcohol poisoning to alcohol-related assault and murder.

For the sake of our friends, those we love, our futures, and ourselves, we 13 must take a stand and we must do it now.

Advocates of lowering the drinking age assert only four countries world- 14 wide maintain a "21 standard," and a gradual transition to alcohol is useful in reducing the systemic social problems of substance abuse.

If those under the age of 21 are misusing alcohol, it makes little sense to 15 grant free rein to those individuals to use it legally. A parent who observes their children abusing the neighbor's dog would be irresponsible to get one of their own without altering such dangerous behavior.

Increasing the drinking age will help in the search for solutions to griev- 16 ous alcoholic problems, making it far more difficult in college environments to find legal-aged providers.

By the time we are 25, with careers and possibly families of our own, there 17 is no safety net to allow us to have a "Thirsty Thursday." But increasing the legal age is not all that needs to be done. Drinking to get drunk needs to exist as a social taboo rather than a doorway to popularity.

Peer pressure can become a tool to change this. What once was a factor 18 greatly contributing to underage drinking can now become an instrument of good, seeking to end such a dangerous practice as excessive drinking. Laws on drinking ages, as any other law, need to be enforced with the energy and vigor each of us should expect.

Alcohol is not an inherently evil poison. It does have its place, as do all 19 things in the great scheme of life.

But with alcohol comes the terrible risk of abuse with consequences many 20 do not consider. All too often, these consequences include robbing someone of his life or loved one. All communities in the country, our own included, have been touched by such a tragedy.

Because of this, and the hundreds of thousands of victims each year in 21 alcohol-related situations, I ask that you consider the very real possibility of taking the life of another due to irresponsible drinking.

If this is not enough, then take time to think, because that life could very 22 well be your own.

Identifying the Elements of Argument

1. What is this essay's thesis? Restate it in your own words.

2. List the arguments Herman presents as evidence to support his thesis.

3. Summarize the opposing argument the essay identifies. Then, summarize Herman's refutation of this argument.

4. Restate the essay's concluding statement in your own words.

Is a College Education Worth the Money?

Butch Dill/AP Photos

Reread the At Issue box on page 23, which summarizes questions raised on both sides of this issue. As the following sources illustrate, reasonable people may disagree about this controversial topic.

As you review the sources, you will be asked to answer some questions and to complete some simple activities. This work will help you understand both the content and the structure of the sources. When you have finished, you will be ready to write an essay in which you take a position on the topic "Is a College Education Worth the Money?"

SOURCES

This essay appeared in the *New York Times* on May 27, 2014.

IS COLLEGE WORTH IT? CLEARLY, NEW DATA SAY

DAVID LEONHARDT

Rising Value of a College Degree

The pay of people with a four-year college degree has risen compared to that 1
of those with a high school degree but no college credit. The relative pay of
people who attended college without earning a four-year degree has stayed flat.

Ratio of average hourly pay, compared with pay of people with a high school degree

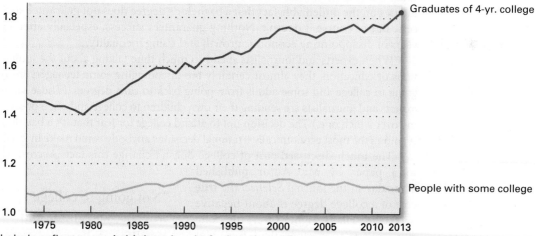

Labels reflect group's highest level of education. "Graduates of 4-year
college," for instance, excludes people with graduate degrees.

Data from: *New York Times* analysis of Economic Policy Institute data

Some newly minted college graduates struggle to find work. Others accept jobs 2
for which they feel overqualified. Student debt, meanwhile, has topped $1 trillion.

It's enough to create a wave of questions about whether a college educa- 3
tion is still worth it.

A new set of income statistics answers those questions quite clearly: Yes, col- 4
lege is worth it, and it's not even close. For all the struggles that many young college graduates face, a four-year degree has probably never been more valuable.

The pay gap between college graduates and everyone else reached a record 5
high last year, according to the new data, which is based on an analysis of Labor
Department statistics by the Economic Policy Institute in Washington. Americans with four-year college degrees made 98 percent more an hour on average in
2013 than people without a degree. That's up from 89 percent five years earlier,
85 percent a decade earlier, and 64 percent in the early 1980s.

The pay of people with a four-year college degree has risen compared to that of those with a high school degree but no college credit. The relative pay of people who attended college without earning a four-year degree has stayed flat. 6

There is nothing inevitable about this trend. If there were more college graduates than the economy needed, the pay gap would shrink. The gap's recent growth is especially notable because it has come after a rise in the number of college graduates, partly because many people went back to school during the Great Recession. That the pay gap has nonetheless continued growing means that we're still not producing enough of them. 7

"We have too few college graduates," says David Autor, an M.I.T. economist, who was not involved in the Economic Policy Institute's analysis. "We also have too few people who are prepared for college." 8

It's important to emphasize these shortfalls because public discussion today—for which we in the news media deserve some responsibility—often focuses on the undeniable fact that a bachelor's degree does not guarantee success. But of course it doesn't. Nothing guarantees success, especially after 15 years of disappointing economic growth and rising inequality. 9

When experts and journalists spend so much time talking about the limitations of education, they almost certainly are discouraging some teenagers from going to college and some adults from going back to earn degrees. (Those same experts and journalists are sending their own children to college and often obsessing over which one.) The decision not to attend college for fear that it's a bad deal is among the most economically irrational decisions anybody could make in 2014. 10

The much-discussed cost of college doesn't change this fact. According to a paper by Mr. Autor published Thursday in the journal *Science*, the true cost of a college degree is about negative $500,000. That's right: Over the long run, college is cheaper than free. Not going to college will cost you about half a million dollars. 11

> "Not going to college will cost you about half a million dollars."

Mr. Autor's paper—building on work by the economists Christopher Avery and Sarah Turner—arrives at that figure first by calculating the very real cost of tuition and fees. This amount is then subtracted from the lifetime gap between the earnings of college graduates and high school graduates. After adjusting for inflation and the time value of money, the net cost of college is negative $500,000, roughly double what it was three decades ago. 12

This calculation is necessarily imprecise, because it can't control for any pre-existing differences between college graduates and nongraduates— differences that would exist regardless of schooling. Yet other research, comparing otherwise similar people who did and did not graduate from college, has also found that education brings a huge return. 13

In a similar vein, the new Economic Policy Institute numbers show that the benefits of college don't go just to graduates of elite colleges, who typically 14 go on to earn graduate degrees. The wage gap between people with only a bachelor's degree and people without such a degree has also kept rising.

Tellingly, though, the wage premium for people who have attended college without earning a bachelor's degree—a group that includes community-college graduates—has not been rising. The big economic returns go to people with four-year degrees. Those returns underscore the importance of efforts to reduce the college dropout rate, such as those at the University of Texas, which Paul Tough described in a recent *Times Magazine* article. 15

But what about all those alarming stories you hear about indebted, jobless college graduates? 16

The anecdotes may be real, yet the conventional wisdom often exaggerates the problem. Among four-year college graduates who took out loans, average debt is about $25,000, a sum that is a tiny fraction of the economic benefits of college. (My own student debt, as it happens, was almost identical to this figure, in inflation-adjusted terms.) And the unemployment rate in April for people between 25 and 34 years old with a bachelor's degree was a mere 3 percent. 17

I find the data from the Economic Policy Institute especially telling because the institute—a left-leaning research group—makes a point of arguing that education is not the solution to all of the economy's problems. That is important, too. College graduates, like almost everyone else, are suffering from the economy's weak growth and from the disproportionate share of this growth flowing to the very richest households. 18

The average hourly wage for college graduates has risen only 1 percent over the last decade, to about $32.60. The pay gap has grown mostly because the average wage for everyone else has fallen—5 percent, to about $16.50. "To me, the picture is people in almost every kind of job not being able to see their wages grow," Lawrence Mishel, the institute's president, told me. "Wage growth essentially stopped in 2002." 19

From the country's perspective, education can be only part of the solution to our economic problems. We also need to find other means for lifting living standards—not to mention ways to provide good jobs for people without college degrees. 20

But from almost any individual's perspective, college is a no-brainer. It's the most reliable ticket to the middle class and beyond. Those who question the value of college tend to be those with the luxury of knowing their own children will be able to attend it. 21

Not so many decades ago, high school was considered the frontier of education. Some people even argued that it was a waste to encourage Americans from humble backgrounds to spend four years of life attending high school. Today, obviously, the notion that everyone should attend 13 years of school is indisputable. 22

But there is nothing magical about 13 years of education. As the economy becomes more technologically complex, the amount of education that people need will rise. At some point, 15 years or 17 years of education will make more sense as a universal goal. 23

That point, in fact, has already arrived. 24

⊙AT ISSUE: SOURCES FOR STRUCTURING AN ARGUMENT

1. Paraphrase this essay's thesis statement by filling in the following template.
   Because _____ ,
   a four-year college degree is now more important than ever.

2. To support his position, Leonhardt relies largely on statistics. Where does he include other kinds of supporting evidence?

3. Look at the graph that follows paragraph 1, and read its caption. What does this image add to the essay? Would Leonhardt's argument have been as convincing without the graph? Why or why not?

4. In paragraph 8, Leonhardt quotes economist David Autor. How do you suppose Marty Nemko (p. 37) would respond to Autor's statements?

5. In paragraph 16, Leonhardt asks a question to introduce an argument opposed to his position. What is this argument? Does he refute it effectively in the discussion that follows?

6. In paragraph 22, Leonhardt begins his conclusion with an **analogy**. What two things is he comparing? What point is he making? Do you think this concluding strategy is effective? Why or why not? How else could he have ended his essay?

This undated essay is from MartyNemko.com.

WE SEND TOO MANY STUDENTS TO COLLEGE

MARTY NEMKO

Among my saddest moments as a career counselor is when I hear a story like 1 this: "I wasn't a good student in high school, but I wanted to prove to myself that I can get a college diploma—I'd be the first one in my family to do it. But it's been six years and I still have 45 units to go."

I have a hard time telling such people the killer statistic: According to the 2 U.S. Department of Education, if you graduated in the bottom 40 percent of your high school class and went to college, 76 of 100 won't earn a diploma, even if given 8½ years. Yet colleges admit and take the money from hundreds of thousands of such students each year!

Even worse, most of those college dropouts leave college having learned 3 little of practical value (see below) and with devastated self-esteem and a mountain of debt. Perhaps worst of all, those people rarely leave with a career path likely to lead to more than McWages. So it's not surprising that when you hop into a cab or walk into a restaurant, you're likely to meet workers who spent years and their family's life savings on college, only to end up with a job they could have done as a high school dropout.

Perhaps yet more surprising, even the high school students who are fully 4 qualified to attend college are increasingly unlikely to derive enough benefit to justify the often six-figure cost and four to eight years it takes to graduate—and only 40 percent of freshmen graduate in four years; 45 percent never graduate at all. Colleges love to trumpet the statistic that, over their lifetimes, college graduates earn more than nongraduates. But that's terribly misleading because you could lock the college-bound in a closet for four years and they'd earn more than the pool of non-college-bound—they're brighter, more motivated, and have better family connections. Too, the past advantage of college graduates in the job market is eroding: ever more students are going to college at the same time as ever more employers are offshoring ever more professional jobs. So college graduates are forced to take some very nonprofessional jobs. For example, Jill Plesnarski holds a bachelor's degree in biology from the private ($160,000 published total cost for four years) Moravian College. She had hoped to land a job as a medical research lab tech, but those positions paid so little that she opted for a job at a New Jersey sewage treatment plant. Today, although she's since been promoted, she must still occasionally wash down the tower that holds raw sewage.

Or take Brian Morris. After completing his bachelor's degree in liberal 5 arts from the University of California, Berkeley, he was unable to find a decent-paying job, so he went yet deeper into debt to get a master's degree from the private Mills College. Despite those degrees, the best job he could land was teaching a three-month-long course for $3,000. At that point, Brian was married and had a baby, so to support them, he reluctantly took a job as a truck driver. Now Brian says, "I just *have* to get out of trucking."

Colleges are quick to argue that a college education is more about enlight- 6 enment than employment. That may be the biggest deception of all. There is a Grand Canyon of difference between what the colleges tout in their brochures and websites and the reality.

Colleges are businesses, and students are a cost item while research is a profit center. So colleges tend to educate students in the cheapest way

> "Colleges are businesses, and students are a cost item." 7

possible: large lecture classes, with small classes staffed by rock-bottom-cost graduate students and, in some cases, even by undergraduate students. Professors who bring in big research dollars are almost always rewarded, while even a fine teacher who doesn't bring in the research bucks is often fired or relegated to the lowest rung: lecturer.

So, no surprise, in the definitive *Your First College Year* nationwide sur- 8 vey conducted by UCLA researchers (data collected in 2005, reported in 2007), only 16.4 percent of students were very satisfied with the overall quality of instruction they received and 28.2 percent were neutral, dissatisfied, or very dissatisfied. A follow-up survey of seniors found that 37 percent reported being "frequently bored in class," up from 27.5 percent as freshmen.

College students may be dissatisfied with instruction, but despite that, do 9 they learn? A 2006 study funded by the Pew Charitable Trusts found that 50 percent of college *seniors* failed a test that required them to do such basic tasks as interpret a table about exercise and blood pressure, understand the arguments of newspaper editorials, or compare credit card offers. Almost 20 percent of seniors had only basic quantitative skills. For example, the students could not estimate if their car had enough gas to get to the gas station.

What to do? Colleges, which receive billions of tax dollars with minimum 10 oversight, should be held at least as accountable as companies are. For example, when some Firestone tires were defective, the government nearly forced it out of business. Yet year after year, colleges turn out millions of defective products: students who drop out or graduate with far too little benefit for the time and money spent. Yet not only do the colleges escape punishment; they're rewarded with ever greater taxpayer-funded student grants and loans, which allow colleges to raise their tuitions yet higher.

What should parents and guardians do? 11

1. If your student's high school grades and SAT or ACT are in the bottom 12 half of his high school class, resist colleges' attempts to woo him. Their marketing to your child does *not* indicate that the colleges believe he will succeed there. Colleges make money whether or not a student learns, whether or not she graduates, and whether or not he finds good employment. If a physician recommended a treatment that cost a fortune and

required years of effort without disclosing the poor chances of it working, she'd be sued and lose in any court in the land. But colleges—one of America's most sacred cows—somehow seem immune.

So let the buyer beware. Consider nondegree options: 13

- Apprenticeship programs (a great portal to apprenticeship websites: www.khake.com/page58.html)

- Short career-preparation programs at community colleges

- The military

- On-the-job training, especially at the elbow of a successful small business owner

2. Let's say your student *is* in the top half of his high school class and is moti- 14
   vated to attend college by more than the parties, being able to say she went to college, and the piece of paper. Then have her apply to perhaps a dozen colleges. Colleges vary less than you might think, yet financial aid awards can vary wildly. It's often wise to choose the college that requires you to pay the least cash and take on the smallest loan. College is among the few products where you don't get what you pay for—price does not indicate quality.

3. If your child is one of the rare breed who, on graduating high school, knows 15
   what he wants to do and isn't unduly attracted to college academics or the *Animal House* environment that college dorms often are, then take solace in the fact that in deciding to forgo college, he is preceded by scores of others who have successfully taken that noncollege road less traveled. Examples: the three most successful entrepreneurs in the computer industry, Bill Gates, Michael Dell, and Apple cofounder Steve Wozniak, all do not have a college degree. Here are some others: Malcolm X, Rush Limbaugh, Barbra Streisand, PBS *NewsHour's* Nina Totenberg, Tom Hanks, Maya Angelou, Ted Turner, Ellen DeGeneres, former governor Jesse Ventura, IBM founder Thomas Watson, architect Frank Lloyd Wright, former Israeli president David Ben-Gurion, Woody Allen, Warren Beatty, Domino's pizza chain founder Tom Monaghan, folksinger Joan Baez, director Quentin Tarantino, ABC-TV's Peter Jennings, Wendy's founder Dave Thomas, Thomas Edison, Blockbuster Video founder and owner of the Miami Dolphins Wayne Huizenga, William Faulkner, Jane Austen, McDonald's founder Ray Kroc, Oracle founder Larry Ellison, Henry Ford, cosmetics magnate Helena Rubinstein, Benjamin Franklin, Alexander Graham Bell, Coco Chanel, Walter Cronkite, Walt Disney, Bob Dylan, Leonardo DiCaprio, cookie maker Debbi Fields, Sally Field, Jane Fonda, Buckminster Fuller, DreamWorks cofounder David Geffen, *Roots* author Alex Haley, Ernest Hemingway, Dustin Hoffman, famed anthropologist Richard Leakey, airplane inventors Wilbur and Orville Wright, Madonna, satirist H. L. Mencken, Martina Navratilova, Rosie O'Donnell, Nathan Pritikin (Pritikin diet), chef Wolfgang Puck, Robert

Redford, oil billionaire John D. Rockefeller, Eleanor Roosevelt, NBC mogul David Sarnoff, and seven U.S. presidents from Washington to Truman.

4. College is like a chain saw. Only in certain situations is it the right tool. 16 Encourage your child to choose the right tool for her post–high school experience.

➲ AT ISSUE: SOURCES FOR STRUCTURING AN ARGUMENT

1. Which of the following statements best summarizes Nemko's position? Why?

   ■ "We Send Too Many Students to College" (title)

   ■ "There is a Grand Canyon of difference between what the colleges tout in their brochures and websites and the reality" (para. 6).

   ■ "Colleges, which receive billions of tax dollars with minimum oversight, should be held at least as accountable as companies are" (10).

   ■ "College is like a chain saw. Only in certain situations is it the right tool" (16).

2. Where does Nemko support his thesis with appeals to logic? Where does he appeal to the emotions? Where does he use an appeal to authority? Which of these three kinds of appeals do you find the most convincing? Why?

3. List the arguments Nemko uses to support his thesis in paragraphs 2–4.

4. In paragraph 4, Nemko says, "Colleges love to trumpet the statistic that, over their lifetimes, college graduates earn more than nongraduates." In paragraph 6, he says, "Colleges are quick to argue that a college education is more about enlightenment than employment." How does he refute these two opposing arguments? Are his refutations effective?

5. Nemko draws an analogy between colleges and businesses, identifying students as a "cost item" (7). Does this analogy—including his characterization of weak students as "defective products" (10)—work for you? Why or why not?

6. What specific solutions does Nemko propose for the problem he identifies? To whom does he address these suggestions—and, in fact, his entire argument?

7. Reread paragraph 15. Do you think the list of successful people who do not hold college degrees is effective support for Nemko's position? What kind of appeal does this paragraph make? How might you refute its argument?

This personal essay is from talk.onevietnam.org, where it appeared on May 9, 2011.

WHAT DOES IT MEAN TO BE A COLLEGE GRAD?

JENNIE LE

After May 14th, I will be a college graduate. By fall, there will be no more a cappella rehearsals, no more papers or exams, no more sleepless nights, no more weekday drinking, no more 1 AM milk tea runs, no more San Francisco Bay Area exploring. I won't be with the people I now see daily. I won't have the same job with the same awesome boss. I won't be singing under Sproul every Monday. I won't be booked with weekly gigs that take me all over California. I won't be lighting another VSA Culture Show. 1

I will also have new commitments: weekly dinner dates with my mom, brother/sister time with my other two brothers, job hunting and career building, car purchasing and maintenance. In essence, my life will be—or at least feel—completely different. From what college alumni have told me, I will soon miss my college days after they are gone. 2

But in the bigger picture, outside of the daily tasks, what does it mean to hold a college degree? My fellow graduating coworker and I discussed the importance (or lack thereof) of our college degrees: while I considered hanging up my two diplomas, she believed that having a bachelor's was so standard and insubstantial, only a professional degree is worth hanging up and showing off. Nowadays, holding a college degree (or two) seems like the norm; it's not a very outstanding feat. 3

> "Nowadays, holding a college degree (or two) seems like the norm."

However, I'd like to defend the power of earning a college degree. Although holding a degree isn't as powerful as it was in previous decades, stats still show that those who earn bachelor's degrees are likely to earn twice as much as those who don't. Also, only 27 percent of Americans can say they have a bachelor's degree or higher. Realistically, having a college degree will likely mean a comfortable living and the opportunity to move up at work and in life. 4

Personally, my degrees validate my mother's choice to leave Vietnam. She moved here for opportunity. She wasn't able to attend college here or in Vietnam or choose her occupation. But her hard work has allowed her children to become the first generation of Americans in the family to earn college degrees: she gave us the ability to make choices she wasn't privileged to make. Being the fourth and final kid to earn my degree in my family, my mom can now boast about having educated children who are making a name for themselves (a son who is a computer-superstar, a second son and future dentist studying at UCSF, another son who is earning his MBA and manages at Mattel, and a daughter who is thankful to have three brothers to mooch off of). 5

For me, this degree symbolizes my family being able to make and take the 6 opportunities that we've been given in America, despite growing up with gang members down my street and a drug dealer across from my house. This degree will also mean that my children will have more opportunities because of my education, insight, knowledge, and support.

Even though a college degree isn't worth as much as it was in the past, 7 it still shows that I—along with my fellow graduates and the 27 percent of Americans with a bachelor's or higher—will have opportunities unheard of a generation before us, showing everyone how important education is for our lives and our futures.

⊃ AT ISSUE: SOURCES FOR STRUCTURING AN ARGUMENT

1. What purpose do the first two paragraphs of this essay serve? Do you think they are necessary? Do you think they are interesting? How else could Le have opened her essay?

2. Where does Le state her thesis? Do you think she should have stated it more forcefully? Can you suggest a more effectively worded thesis statement for this essay?

3. In paragraph 3, Le summarizes an opposing argument. Paraphrase this argument. How does she refute it? Can you think of other arguments against her position that she should have addressed?

4. In paragraphs 5–6, Le includes an appeal to the emotions. Does she offer any other kind of supporting evidence? If so, where? What other kinds of evidence do you think she should include? Why?

5. Echoing a point she made in paragraph 4, Le begins her conclusion with "Even though a college degree isn't worth as much as it was in the past, . . ." Does this concluding statement undercut her argument, or is the information presented in paragraph 4 enough to address this potential problem?

This essay appeared on CNN.com on June 3, 2011.

COLLEGE IS A WASTE OF TIME

DALE STEPHENS

I have been awarded a golden ticket to the heart of Silicon Valley: the Thiel 1 Fellowship. The catch? For two years, I cannot be enrolled as a full-time student at an academic institution. For me, that's not an issue; I believe higher education is broken.

I left college two months ago because it rewards conformity rather than 2 independence, competition rather than collaboration, regurgitation rather than learning, and theory rather than application. Our creativity, innovation, and curiosity are schooled out of us.

Failure is punished instead of seen as a learning opportunity. We think of 3 college as a stepping-stone to success rather than a means to gain knowledge. College fails to empower us with the skills necessary to become productive members of today's global entrepreneurial economy.

College is expensive. The College Board Policy Center found that the cost of 4 public university tuition is about 3.6 times higher today than it was 30 years ago, adjusted for inflation. In the book *Academically Adrift*, sociology professors Richard Arum and Josipa Roksa say that 36 percent of college graduates showed no improvement in critical thinking, complex reasoning, or writing after four years of college. Student loan debt in the United States, unforgivable in the case of bankruptcy, outpaced credit card debt in 2010 and will top $1 trillion in 2011.

Fortunately, there are 5 productive alternatives to college. Becoming the next Mark Zuckerberg or mastering the phrase "Would you like fries with that?" are not the only options.

> "Fortunately, there are productive alternatives to college."

The success of people who never completed or attended college makes us 6 question whether what we need to learn is taught in school. Learning by doing—in life, not classrooms—is the best way to turn constant iteration into true innovation. We can be productive members of society without submitting to academic or corporate institutions. We are the disruptive generation creating the "free agent economy" built by entrepreneurs, creatives, consultants, and small businesses envisioned by Daniel Pink in his book, *A Whole New Mind: Why Right Brainers Will Rule the Future.*

We must encourage young people to consider paths outside college. 7 That's why I'm leading UnCollege: a social movement empowering individuals to take their education beyond the classroom. Imagine if millions of my peers copying their professors' words verbatim started problem-solving in the real world. Imagine if we started our own companies, our own projects, and our own organizations. Imagine if we went back to learning as practiced in French salons, gathering to discuss, challenge, and support each other in improving the human condition.

A major function of college is to signal to potential employers that one is 8 qualified to work. The Internet is replacing this signaling function. Employers are recruiting on LinkedIn, Facebook, StackOverflow, and Behance. People are hiring on Twitter, selling their skills on Google, and creating personal portfolios to showcase their talent. Because we can document our accomplishments and have them socially validated with tools such as LinkedIn Recommendations, we can turn experiences into opportunity. As more and more people graduate from college, employers are unable to discriminate among job seekers based on a college degree and can instead hire employees based on their talents.

Of course, some people want a formal education. I do not think everyone 9 should leave college, but I challenge my peers to consider the opportunity cost of going to class. If you want to be a doctor, going to medical school is a wise choice. I do not recommend keeping cadavers in your garage. On the other hand, what else could you do during your next 50-minute class? How many e-mails could you answer? How many lines of code could you write?

Some might argue that college dropouts will sit in their parents' base- 10 ments playing *Halo 2*, doing Jell-O shots, and smoking pot. These are valid but irrelevant concerns, for the people who indulge in drugs and alcohol do so before, during, and after college. It's not a question of authorities; it's a question of priorities. We who take our education outside and beyond the classroom understand how actions build a better world. We will change the world regardless of the letters after our names.

⊖ AT ISSUE: SOURCES FOR STRUCTURING AN ARGUMENT

1. In paragraph 1, Stephens says, "I believe higher education is broken." Is this statement his essay's thesis? Explain.

2. List Stephens's criticisms of college education.

3. Why does Stephens begin by introducing himself as a winner of a Thiel Fellowship? Is this introductory strategy an appeal to *logos, ethos,* or *pathos*? Explain.

4. List the evidence that Stephens uses to support his position. Do you think this essay needs more supporting evidence? If so, what kind of support would you suggest Stephens add?

5. In paragraphs 9 and 10, Stephens considers possible arguments against his thesis. What are these opposing arguments? Does he refute them effectively?

6. Throughout this essay, Stephens uses the pronoun *we* (as well as the pronoun *I*). Do these first-person pronouns refer to college students in general? To certain kinds of students? To Thiel fellows? Explain.

This article first appeared in the online publication "Examining the Value of a College Degree," produced by PayScale.

COLLEGE IS WORTH IT—SOME OF THE TIME

BRIDGET TERRY LONG

Is it still worthwhile to attend college? This has been a constant question, and as an economist and higher education researcher, I can wholeheartedly say yes. The data are clear: individuals with at least some college education make more money than those with only a high school degree. And let us not forget about the non-monetary returns, such as better working conditions, lower rates of disability, and increased civic engagement.

However, the conversation has become more complicated as research has pointed to another important fact: yes, college is worth it, but not always.

> "We no longer think that all educations are financially good investments—the specifics matter."

We no longer think that all educations are financially good investments—the specifics matter. The answer for any student depends upon three important factors: the college attended, the field of study, and the cost or debt taken.

First, the college a student attends makes a difference, as we can see from the Payscale data. But these recent data underscore a longer-term trend. In a 1999 study, a co-author and I documented increasing inequality among college-educated workers.[1] While those near the top of the income distribution (i.e., the 90th percentile) experienced larger returns to their educations over time, after accounting for inflation, those near the bottom of the distribution (i.e., the 10th percentile) earned less in 1995 than 1972. Our examination of the reasons behind these changes highlights the important role of increasing segregation in higher education, where the top students have become more and more concentrated at institutions with much greater resources. The colleges rated "most competitive" often spend more than three times per student than "less competitive" colleges.

However, selectivity rating alone does not necessarily predict which schools have the highest rates of student success. A 2009 study documents the fact that graduation rates differ not only by college selectivity but also within a selectivity group. For example, among colleges rated as "very competitive," six-year graduation rates averaged from 30 percent for the bottom 10 schools to 82 percent for the top 10 schools.[2] Selectivity does not necessarily guarantee high levels of degree completion.

[1]Hoxby, Caroline and Bridget Terry Long. (1999) "Explaining Rising Inequality among the College-Educated." National Bureau of Economic Research (NBER) Working Paper No. 6873.
[2]Hess, Frederick M., Mark Schneider, Kevin Carey, and Andrew P. Kelly. (2009) *Diplomas and Dropouts: Which Colleges Actually Graduate Their Students (and Which Don't)*. American Enterprise Institute.

A large part of the problem to understanding which colleges are good 5 investments is the lack of good measures of college quality. Most existing measures rely heavily on the academic achievements of students before they even step foot on the college campus. Meanwhile, there are few measures of the quality of the postsecondary learning experience or the value-added to the student. Hence, we rely on indicators such as earnings and loan default rates. While it is helpful to have this information to establish minimum thresholds of what might be a financially worthwhile education, they are not sufficient to help students compare possible colleges and make the decision about where they, as individuals, might maximize their benefits.

The second thing that increasingly matters in college investments is the 6 field of study. While many students do not work in the field of their college major, typically, students majoring in engineering and the sciences reap the largest benefits. However, income is not the only thing that varies by major: as emphasized by the Great Recession, unemployment rates also differ by field of study. Interestingly, although education majors may not make the most money, they have among the lowest unemployment rates.

The first two factors, the chosen college and major, focus on potential benefits, 7 but those benefits must be compared to costs to determine whether a college education is worthwhile. We focus most of our attention on price and debt load as a measure of the burden of college costs. Debt is a reality of higher education today, and some debt is fine if it makes possible a beneficial educational investment. However, the level of debt that is reasonable depends greatly on the school attended and major. One might judge $10,000 of total debt for an engineering degree to be fine, while the opposite would be true for a six-week certificate program.

Unfortunately, students typically have such poor counseling on how much 8 debt is appropriate given their plans, and with large levels of unmet financial need, many turn to multiple sources of debt, such as credit cards and private loans, without fully understanding how this will affect them over the longer term. Moreover, recent graduates (or dropouts) fresh out of school have little appreciation for how their investments may pay off 10 years from now when their current reality is living at home with their parents. In other words, it's difficult to internalize long-term benefits when the costs are so heavily weighed up front.

Ultimately, knowing whether college is a good investment depends on 9 which college, which major, at what price (or debt). Looking at the averages is no longer as meaningful, given the importance of match for an individual student with specific interests, talents, and resources. And while I would underscore the fact that for the vast majority of students, most combinations of college/major/debt they would choose are worthwhile investments, we have reached a time when the benefits of college may not far exceed the costs for increasing numbers of students.

Even if only a small percentage of investments are "bad"—ones in which 10 the college attended has low levels of success and gives credentials with little value while making students take out large amounts of debt—we have reached an enrollment level in which a small percentage translates into thousands and thousands of students each year. And that is a problem that cannot be ignored.

➲ AT ISSUE: SOURCES FOR STRUCTURING AN ARGUMENT

1. In paragraph 1, Long introduces herself as "an economist and higher education researcher." Why do you think she does this? Is she appealing here to *logos*, *ethos*, or *pathos*?

2. Long begins her essay with a question. What attitude toward college tuition does she assume her readers have? How can you tell? How else might she have opened her discussion?

3. According to Long, in what sense has "the conversation [about whether college is a worthwhile investment] become more complicated" (para. 2)? What "three important factors" does she consider?

4. Outline the structure of this essay, filling in the template below with Long's thesis statement and key points.

   Thesis statement:

   Support

   - *First important factor:* _____

   - *Second important factor:* _____

   - *Third important factor:* _____

5. In paragraphs 9 and 10, what does Long conclude about the value of a college education? What reservations does she have? How does the discussion in these paragraphs answer the question she asks in paragraph 1?

6. Could Long's entire essay be seen as a refutation of the position she takes in the essay's first paragraph? Explain.

7. If Long were making recommendations about how to solve the "problem that cannot be ignored" (10), what do you think she might recommend?

This economic letter was originally posted by the Federal Reserve Bank of San Francisco at www.frbsf.org, where it appeared on May 5, 2014.

IS IT STILL WORTH GOING TO COLLEGE?

MARY C. DALY AND LEILA BENGALI

Media accounts documenting the rising cost of a college education and rela- 1 tively bleak job prospects for new college graduates have raised questions about whether a four-year college degree is still the right path for the average American. In this *Economic Letter*, we examine whether going to college remains a worthwhile investment. Using U.S. survey data, we compare annual labor earnings of college graduates with those of individuals with only a high school diploma. The data show college graduates outearn their high school counterparts as much as in past decades. Comparing the earnings benefits of college with the costs of attending a four-year program, we find that college is still worth it. This means that, for the average student, tuition costs for the majority of college education opportunities in the United States can be recouped by age 40, after which college graduates continue to earn a return on their investment in the form of higher lifetime wages.

Earnings Outcomes by Educational Attainment

A common way to track the value of going to college is to estimate a college 2 earnings premium, which is the amount college graduates earn relative to high school graduates. We measure earnings for each year as the annual labor income for the prior year, adjusted for inflation using the consumer price index (CPI-U), reported in 2011 dollars. The earnings premium refers to the difference between average annual labor income for high school and college graduates. We use data on household heads and partners from the Panel Study of Income Dynamics (PSID). The PSID is a longitudinal study that follows individuals living in the United States over a long time span. The survey began in 1968 and now has more than 40 years of data including educational attainment and labor market income. To focus on the value of a college degree relative to less education, we exclude people with more than a four-year degree.

Figure 1 shows the earnings premium relative to high school graduates 3 for individuals with a four-year college degree and for those with some college but no four-year degree. The payoff from a degree is apparent. Although the premium has fluctuated over time, at its lowest in 1980 it was about $15,750, meaning that individuals with a four-year college degree earned about 43 percent more on average than those with only a high school degree. In 2011, the latest data available in our sample, college graduates earned on average about $20,050 (61 percent) more per year than high school graduates.

Over the entire sample period the college earnings premium has averaged about $20,300 (57 percent) per year. The premium is much smaller, although not zero, for workers with some college but no four-year degree.

Figure 1: Earnings Premium over High School Education

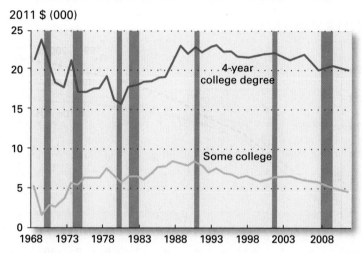

Data from: PSID and authors' calculations. Premium defined as difference in mean annual labor income. Blue bars denote NBER recession dates.

A potential shortcoming of the results in Figure 1 is that they combine the earnings outcomes for all college graduates, regardless of when they earned a degree. This can be misleading if the value from a college education has varied across groups from different graduation decades, called "cohorts." To examine whether the college earnings premium has changed from one generation to the next, we take advantage of the fact that the PSID follows people over a long period of time, which allows us to track college graduation dates and subsequent earnings.

Using these data we compute the college earnings premium for three college graduate cohorts, namely those graduating in the 1950s–60s, the 1970s–80s, and the 1990s–2000s. The premium measures the difference between the average annual earnings of college graduates and high school graduates over their work lives. To account for the fact that high school graduates gain work experience during the four years they are not in college, we compare earnings of college graduates in each year since graduation to earnings of high school graduates in years since graduation plus four. We also adjust the estimates for any large annual fluctuations by using a three-year centered moving average, which plots a specific year as the average of earnings from that year, the year before, and the year after.

Figure 2 shows that the college earnings premium has risen consistently   6
across cohorts. Focusing on the most recent college graduates (1990s–2000s)
there is little evidence that the value of a college degree has declined over time,
and it has even risen somewhat for graduates five to ten years out of school.

Figure 2: College Earnings Premium by Graduation Decades

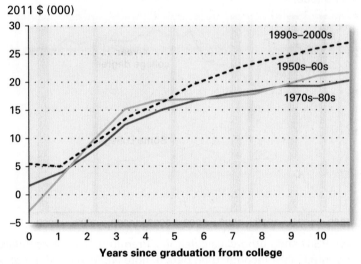

Data from: PSID and authors' calculations. Premium defined as
difference in mean annual labor income of college graduates in each
year since graduation and earnings of high school graduates in years
since graduation plus four. Values are three-year centered moving
averages of annual premiums.

The figure also shows that the gap in earnings between college and high   7
school graduates rises over the course of a worker's life. Comparing the earnings gap upon graduation with the earnings gap 10 years out of school illustrates this. For the 1990s–2000s cohort the initial gap was about $5,400, and in
10 years this gap had risen to about $26,800. Other analysis confirms that col-
lege graduates start with higher annual earnings, indicated by an initial earnings gap, and experience more rapid growth in earnings than members of
their age cohort with only a high school degree. This evidence tells us that the
value of a college education rises over a worker's life.

Of course, some of the variation in earnings between those with and with-   8
out a college degree could reflect other differences. Still, these simple estimates
are consistent with a large and rigorous literature documenting the substantial
premium earned by college graduates (Barrow and Rouse 2005, Card 2001,
Goldin and Katz 2008, and Cunha, Karahan, and Soares 2011). The main message from these and similar calculations is that on average the value of college
is high and not declining over time.

Finally, it is worth noting that the benefits of college over high school also depend on employment, where college graduates also have an advantage. High school graduates consistently face unemployment rates about twice as high as those for college graduates, according to Bureau of Labor Statistics data. When the labor market takes a turn for the worse, as during recessions, workers with lower levels of education are especially hard-hit (Hoynes, Miller, and Schaller 2012). Thus, in good times and in bad, those with only a high school education face a lower probability of employment, on top of lower average earnings once employed. 9

The Cost of College

Although the value of college is apparent, deciding whether it is worthwhile means weighing the value against the costs of attending. Indeed, much of the debate about the value of college stems not from the lack of demonstrated benefit but from the overwhelming cost. A simple way to measure the costs against the benefits is to find the breakeven amount of annual tuition that would make the average student indifferent between going to college versus going directly to the workforce after high school. 10

> "Although the value of college is apparent, deciding whether it is worthwhile means weighing the value against the costs of attending."

To simplify the analysis, we assume that college lasts four years, students enter college directly from high school, annual tuition is the same all four years, and attendees have no earnings while in school. To focus on more recent experiences yet still have enough data to measure earnings since graduation, we use the last two decades of graduates (1990s and 2000s) and again smooth our estimates by using three-year centered moving averages. 11

We calculate the cost of college as four years of tuition plus the earnings missed from choosing not to enter the workforce. To estimate what students would have received had they worked, we use the average annual earnings of a high school graduate zero, one, two, and three years since graduation. 12

To determine the benefit of going to college, we use the difference between the average annual earnings of a college graduate with zero, one, two, three, and so on, years of experience and the average annual earnings of a high school graduate with four, five, six, seven, and so on years of experience. Because the costs of college are paid today but the benefits accrue over many future years when a dollar earned will be worth less, we discount future earnings by 6.67 percent, which is the average rate on an AAA bond from 1990 to 2011. 13

With these pieces in place, we can calculate the breakeven amount of tuition for the average college graduate for any number of years; allowing more time to regain the costs will increase our calculated tuition ceiling. 14

If we assume that accumulated earnings between college graduates and non-graduates will equalize 20 years after graduating from high school (at age 38), the 15 resulting estimate for breakeven annual tuition would be about $21,200. This amount may seem low compared to the astronomical costs for a year at some prestigious institutions; however, about 90 percent of students at public four-year colleges and about 20 percent of students at private nonprofit four-year colleges faced lower annual inflation-adjusted published tuition and fees in 2013–14 (College Board 2013). Although some colleges cost more, there is no definitive evidence that they produce far superior results for all students (Dale and Krueger 2011).

Table 1 shows more examples of maximum tuitions and the corresponding 16 percent of students who pay less for different combinations of breakeven years and discount rates. Note that the tuition estimates are those that make the costs and benefits of college equal. So, tuition amounts lower than our estimates make going to college strictly better in terms of earnings than not going to college.

Table 1: Maximum Tuitions by Breakeven Age and Discount Rates

	Breakeven age	
	33 (15 yrs after HS)	38 (20 yrs after HS)
Accumulated earnings with constant annual premium	$880,134	$830,816
Discount rate	Maximum tuition (% students paying less)	
5%	$14,385 (53–62%)	$29,111 (82–85%)
6.67%*	$9,869 (37–53%)	$21,217 (69–73%)
9%	$4,712 (0–6%)	$12,653 (53–62%)

*Average AAA bond rate 1990–2011 (rounded; Moody's).

Data from: PSID, College Board, and authors' calculations. Premia held constant 15 or 20 years after high school (HS) graduation. Percent range gives lower and upper bounds of the percent of full-time undergraduates at four-year institutions who faced lower annual inflation-adjusted published tuition and fees in 2013–14.

Although other individual factors might affect the net value of a college 17 education, earning a degree clearly remains a good investment for most young people. Moreover, once that investment is paid off, the extra income from the college earnings premium continues as a net gain to workers with a college degree. If we conservatively assume that the annual premium stays around $28,650, which is the premium 20 years after high school graduation for graduates in the 1990s–2000s, and accrues until the Social Security normal retirement age of 67, the college graduate would have made about $830,800 more than the high school graduate. These extra earnings can be spent, saved, or reinvested to pay for the college tuition of the graduate's children.

Conclusion

Although there are stories of people who skipped college and achieved finan- 18
cial success, for most Americans the path to higher future earnings involves a four-year college degree. We show that the value of a college degree remains high, and the average college graduate can recover the costs of attending in less than 20 years. Once the investment is paid for, it continues to pay dividends through the rest of the worker's life, leaving college graduates with substantially higher lifetime earnings than their peers with a high school degree. These findings suggest that redoubling the efforts to make college more accessible would be time and money well spent.

References

Barrow, L., and Rouse, C.E. (2005). "Does college still pay?" *The Economist's Voice* 2(4), pp. 1–8.

Card, D. (2001). "Estimating the return to schooling: progress on some persistent econometric problems." *Econometrica* 69(5), pp. 1127–1160.

College Board. (2013). "Trends in College Pricing 2013."

Cunha, F., Karahan, F., and Soares, I. (2011). "Returns to Skills and the College Premium." *Journal of Money, Credit, and Banking* 43(5), pp. 39–86.

Dale, S., and Krueger, A. (2011). "Estimating the Return to College Selectivity over the Career Using Administrative Earnings Data." *NBER Working Paper* 17159.

Goldin, C., and Katz, L. (2008). *The Race between Education and Technology.* Cambridge and London: The Belknap Press of Harvard University Press.

Hoynes, H., Miller, D., and Schaller, J. (2012). "Who Suffers During Recessions?" *Journal of Economic Perspectives* 26(3), pp. 27–48.

⊘ AT ISSUE: SOURCES FOR STRUCTURING AN ARGUMENT

1. Why does the title of this essay include the word "still"? What does *still* imply in this context?

2. This essay is an "economic letter" from the Federal Reserve Bank of San Francisco, and its language is more technical, and more math- and business-oriented, than that of the other readings in this chapter. In addition, this reading selection *looks* somewhat different from the others. What specific format features set this reading apart from others in the chapter?

3. What kind of supporting evidence do the writers use? Do you think they should have included any other kinds of support—for example, expert opinion? Why or why not?

4. In paragraph 10, the writers make a distinction between the "value of college" and the question of whether a college education is "worthwhile." Explain the distinction they make here.

5. For the most part, this report appeals to *logos* by presenting factual information. Does it also include appeals to *pathos* or *ethos*? If so, where? If not, should it have included these appeals?

TEMPLATE FOR STRUCTURING AN ARGUMENT

Write a one-paragraph argument in which you take a position on the topic of whether a college education is a good investment. Follow the template below, filling in the lines to create your argument.

> Whether or not a college education is worth the money is a controversial topic. Some people believe that _____
> _____
> _____. Others challenge this position, claiming that _____
> _____.
> However, _____
> _____. Although both sides of this issue have merit, it seems clear that a college education (is/is not) a worthwhile investment because _____
> _____.

⊗ EXERCISE 1.2

Interview two classmates on the topic of whether a college education is a worthwhile investment. Revise the one-paragraph argument that you drafted above so that it includes your classmates' views on the issue.

⊗ EXERCISE 1.3

Write an essay on the topic "Is a College Education Worth the Money?" Cite the readings on pages 33–54, and be sure to document your sources and to include a works-cited page. (See Chapter 10 for information on documenting sources.)

⊗ EXERCISE 1.4

Review the four-point checklist on page 27, and apply each question to your essay. Does your essay include all four elements of an argumentative essay? Add any missing elements. Then, label your essay's thesis statement, evidence, refutation of opposing arguments, and concluding statement.

⊗ EXERCISE 1.5

Read the short essay that follows. What, if anything, do you think should be added to the writer's discussion to make it more convincing? Should anything be deleted or changed? Incorporating what you have learned about the structure and content of an effective argument, write a one-paragraph response to the essay.

This essay appeared on Businessweek.com in March 2011.

PRACTICAL EXPERIENCE TRUMPS FANCY DEGREES

TONY BRUMMEL

So you got great grades and earned your bachelor's degree? Congratulations. 1
You may have been better off failing college and then starting a venture and
figuring out why you didn't pass your classroom tests.

Being successful in business is absolutely not contingent on having a bach- 2
elor's degree—or any other type of degree, for that matter. A do-or-die work
ethic, passion, unwavering persistence, and vision mean more than anything
that can be taught in a classroom. How many college professors who teach
business have actually started a business?

I am the sole owner of the top independent rock 3
record label (according to Nielsen-published market
share). Historically, the music industry is thought of
as residing in New York City, Los Angeles, and

> "I have blazed
> my own trail."

Nashville. But I have blazed my own trail, segregating my business in its own
petri dish here in Chicago. I started the business as a part-time venture in 1989
with $800 in seed capital. In 2009, Victory Records grossed $20 million. We've
released more than 500 albums, including platinum-selling records for the
groups Taking Back Sunday and Hawthorne Heights.

Because I never went to college and didn't automatically have industry 4
contacts, I had to learn all of the business fundamentals through trial and error
when I started my own company. The skills I learned on my own have carried
me through 20 years of business. Making mistakes forces one to learn.

If you have a brand that people care about and loyal, hard-working 5
employees coupled with a robust network of smart financial advisers, fellow
entrepreneurs, and good legal backup, you will excel. There are plenty of people with degrees and MBAs who could read the books and earn their diplomas
but cannot apply what they learned to building a successful enterprise.

❯ EXERCISE 1.6

Study the image that opens this chapter. What argument could it suggest
about the issue of whether a college education is worth the money?

PART

2

Reading and Responding to Arguments

Thinking and Reading Critically

AT ISSUE

Do Violent Media Images Trigger Violent Behavior?

In recent years, the popular media seem to have become increasingly violent. This is particularly true of visuals in video games and on some Internet sites, but graphically violent images also appear regularly in films, on TV, in comic books, and even in newspapers. Some research has suggested that these violent images can have a negative effect on those who view them, particularly on adolescents and young children. In fact, some media critics believe that these violent images have helped to create an increasingly violent culture, which in turn has inspired young people to commit violent crimes (including school shootings) such as the massacres at Virginia Tech in 2007 and Newtown, Connecticut, in 2012. The shooter who killed 12 people and injured 58 others at the premiere of *The Dark Knight Rises* in Aurora, Colorado, on July 20, 2012, was a devotee of violent role-playing video games, and some news reports emphasized that fact. Other observers, however, argue that violent media images are not to blame for such events—and that, in fact, these images may provide a safe outlet for aggression.

In this chapter and in the chapter that follows, you will be asked to read essays and study images that shed light on the relationship between media violence and violent behavior. In the process, you will learn critical-thinking and active reading strategies that will help you learn to examine and interpret texts and images.

Now that you understand the structure of an argumentative essay, you can turn your attention to reading arguments more closely. These arguments may be the subject of class discussion, or they may be source material for the essays you write. In any case, you will need to know how to get the most out of reading them.

Thinking Critically

When you **think critically**, you do not simply accept ideas at face value. Instead, you question these ideas, analyzing them in order to understand them better. You also challenge their underlying assumptions and form your own judgments about them. Throughout this book, discussions and readings encourage you to think critically. The box below shows you where in this text to find material that will help you develop your critical-thinking skills.

USING CRITICAL-THINKING SKILLS

Reading (see Chapter 2): When you read a text, you use critical-thinking skills to help you understand what the text says and what it suggests. You ask questions and look for answers, challenging the ideas you read and probing for information. *Previewing, highlighting,* and *annotating* are active reading strategies that require you to use critical-thinking skills.

Analyzing Visual Texts (see Chapter 3): When you examine an image, you use critical-thinking skills to help you understand what you are seeing, using previewing, highlighting, and annotating to help you analyze the image and interpret its persuasive message.

Writing a Rhetorical Analysis (see Chapter 4): When you write a rhetorical analysis of a text, you use critical-thinking skills to analyze its elements and to help you understand how the writer uses various appeals and rhetorical strategies to influence readers. Critical-thinking skills can also help you to understand the argument's context. Finally, you use critical-thinking skills to evaluate the overall effectiveness of the argument.

Analyzing an Argument's Logic (see Chapter 5): When you analyze an argument's logic, you use critical-thinking skills to help you understand the relationships among ideas and the form the argument takes as well as to determine whether its conclusions are both valid and true. You also use critical-thinking skills to identify any **logical fallacies** that may undermine the argument.

Writing an Essay (see Chapter 7): When you plan an essay, you use critical-thinking skills to probe a topic, to consider what you already know and what you need to find out, to identify your essay's main idea, and to decide how to support it—that is, which ideas to include and how to arrange them. As you draft and revise, you use critical-thinking skills to evaluate your supporting evidence, to make sure your arguments are reasonable and fair, and to decide whether ideas are arranged effectively within paragraphs and in the essay as a whole. *Freewriting, brainstorming, clustering,* and *outlining* are activities that require you to use critical-thinking skills.

Refuting Opposing Arguments (see Chapter 7): When you refute opposing arguments, you use critical-thinking skills to identify and evaluate arguments against your position—and to challenge or possibly argue against them.

Evaluating Sources (see Chapter 8): When you evaluate sources, you use critical-thinking skills to assess your sources in terms of their *accuracy, credibility, objectivity,* and *comprehensiveness* and to determine whether a source is trustworthy and appropriate for your purpose and audience.

Summarizing (see Chapter 9): When you summarize a passage, you use critical-thinking skills to identify the writer's main idea.

Paraphrasing (see Chapter 9): When you paraphrase a passage, you use critical-thinking skills to identify the writer's main idea, the most important supporting details and examples, and the ways in which key ideas are related.

Synthesizing (see Chapter 9): When you synthesize, you use critical-thinking skills to analyze sources and integrate them with your own ideas.

Reading Critically

When you read an argument, you should approach it with a critical eye. Contrary to what you may think, **reading critically** does not mean arguing with every idea you encounter. What it does mean is commenting on, questioning, and evaluating these ideas.

As a critical reader, you do not simply accept that what you are reading is true. Instead, you assess the accuracy of the facts in your sources, and you consider whether opinions are convincingly supported by evidence. You try to judge the appropriateness and reliability of a writer's sources, and you evaluate the scope and depth of the evidence and the relevance of that evidence to the topic. You also consider opposing arguments carefully, weighing them against the arguments developed in your sources. Finally, you watch out for possible **bias** in your sources—and you work hard to keep your own biases in check.

GUIDELINES FOR READING CRITICALLY

As a critical reader, you need to read carefully, keeping the following guidelines in mind:

- Assess the accuracy of a source's information.
- Be sure opinions are supported convincingly.
- Evaluate the supporting evidence.
- Consider opposing arguments.
- Be on the lookout for bias—in your sources and in yourself.

 **LaunchPad**
macmillan learning

For more practice, see the LearningCurve on Reading Critically in the LaunchPad for *Practical Argument.*

Becoming an Active Reader

Reading critically means being an active rather than a passive reader. Being an **active reader** means participating in the reading process by taking the time to preview a source and then to read it carefully, highlighting and annotating it. This process will prepare you to discuss the source with others and to respond in writing to what you have read.

Previewing

When you approach an argument for the first time, you **preview** it, skimming the argument to help you form a general impression of the writer's position on the issue, the argument's key supporting points, and the context for the writer's remarks.

Begin by looking at the title, the first paragraph (which often contains a thesis statement or overview), and the last paragraph (which often includes a concluding statement or a summary of the writer's key points). Also look at the topic sentences of the essay's body paragraphs. In addition, note any headings, words set in boldface or italic type, and bulleted or numbered lists in the body of the argument. If the argument includes visuals—charts, tables, graphs, photos, and so on—look at them as well. Finally, if an argument includes a headnote or background on the author or on the text, be sure to read this material. It can help you to understand the context in which the author is writing.

When you have finished previewing the argument, you should have a good general sense of what the writer wants to communicate.

Close Reading

Now, you are ready to read through the argument more carefully. As you read, look for words and phrases that help to shape the structure of the argument and signal the arrangement of the writer's ideas. These words and phrases will help you understand the flow of ideas as well as the content and emphasis of the argument.

COMPREHENSION CLUES

- Phrases that signal emphasis (the *primary* reason, the *most important* problem)

- Repeated words and phrases

- Words and phrases that signal addition (*also, in addition, furthermore*)

- Words and phrases that signal time sequence (*first, after that, next, then, finally*)

- Words and phrases that identify causes and effects (*because, as a result, for this reason*)

- Words and phrases that introduce examples (*for example, for instance*)

- Words and phrases that signal comparison (*likewise, similarly, in the same way*)

- Words and phrases that signal contrast (*although, in contrast, on the other hand*)

- Words and phrases that signal contradiction (*however, on the contrary*)

- Words and phrases that signal a move from general to specific (*in fact, specifically, in other words*)

- Words and phrases that introduce summaries or conclusions (*to sum up, in conclusion*)

⬤ EXERCISE 2.1

"Violent Media Is Good for Kids" is an essay by Gerard Jones, a comic book writer and author of several books about popular media. In this essay, which begins on the following page, Jones argues that violent comic books and video games serve a useful function for young people.

In preparation for class discussion and other activities that will be assigned later in this chapter, preview the essay. Then, read it carefully, and answer the questions that follow it.

This article appeared in *Mother Jones* on June 28, 2000.

VIOLENT MEDIA IS GOOD FOR KIDS

GERARD JONES

At 13 I was alone and afraid. Taught by my well-meaning, progressive, English-teacher parents that violence was wrong, that rage was something to be overcome and cooperation was always better than conflict, I suffocated my deepest fears and desires under a nice-boy persona. Placed in a small, experimental school that was wrong for me, afraid to join my peers in their bumptious rush into adolescent boy-hood, I withdrew into passivity and loneli-ness. My parents, not trusting the violent world of the late 1960s, built a wall between me and the crudest elements of American pop culture.

A scene from Gerard Jones and Will Jacobs's comic book *Monsters from Outer Space*. 2
© Gerard Jones, Gene Ha, Will Jacobs.

Then the Incredible Hulk smashed through it.

One of my mother's students con-vinced her that Marvel Comics, despite their apparent juvenility and violence, were in fact devoted to lofty messages of pacifism and tolerance. My mother borrowed some, thinking they'd be good for me. And so they were. But not because they preached lofty messages of benevolence. They were good for me because they were juvenile. And violent.

The character who caught me, and freed me, was the Hulk: overgendered 4 and undersocialized, half-naked and half-witted, raging against a frightened world that misunderstood and persecuted him. Suddenly I had a fantasy self to carry my stifled rage and buried desire for power. I had a fantasy self who was a self: unafraid of his desires and the world's disapproval, unhesitating and effec-tive in action. "Puny boy follow Hulk!" roared my fantasy self, and I followed.

I followed him to new friends—other sensitive geeks chasing their own 5 inner brutes—and I followed him to the arrogant, self-exposing, self-assertive, superheroic decision to become a writer. Eventually, I left him behind, followed more sophisticated heroes, and finally my own lead along a twisting path to a career and an identity. In my 30s, I found myself writing action movies and comic books. I wrote some Hulk stories, and met the geek-geniuses who created him. I saw my own creations turned into action figures, cartoons, and computer games. I talked to the kids who read my stories. Across generations, genders, and ethnicities I kept seeing the same story: people pulling themselves out of emotional traps by immersing themselves in violent stories. People integrating the scariest, most fervently denied fragments of their psyches into fuller senses of selfhood through fantasies of superhuman combat and destruction.

I have watched my son living the same story—transforming himself into a 6 bloodthirsty dinosaur to embolden himself for the plunge into preschool, a Power Ranger to muscle through a social competition in kindergarten. In the first grade, his friends started climbing a tree at school. But he was afraid: of falling, of the centipedes crawling on the trunk, of sharp branches, of his friends' derision. I took my cue from his own fantasies and read him old Tarzan comics, rich in combat and bright with flashing knives. For two weeks he lived in them. Then he put them aside. And he climbed the tree.

A scene from Gerard Jones and Gene Ha's comic book *Oktane.* © Gerard Jones, Gene Ha, Will Jacobs.

But all the while, especially in the wake of 7 the recent burst of school shootings, I heard pop psychologists insisting that violent stories are harmful to kids, heard teachers begging parents to keep their kids away from "junk culture," heard a guilt-stricken friend with a son who loved Pokémon lament, "I've turned into the bad mom who lets her kid eat sugary cereal and watch cartoons!"

That's when I started the research. 8

"Fear, greed, power-hunger, rage: these 9 are aspects of our selves that we try not to experience in our lives but often want, even need, to experience vicariously through stories of others," writes Melanie Moore, Ph.D., a psychologist who works with urban teens. "Children need violent entertainment in order to explore the inescapable feelings that they've been taught to deny, and to reintegrate those feelings into a more whole, more complex, more resilient selfhood."

Moore consults to public schools and local 10 governments, and is also raising a daughter. For the past three years she and I have been studying the ways in which children use violent stories to meet their emotional and developmental needs—and the ways in which adults can help them use those stories healthily. With her help I developed *Power Play*, a program for helping young people improve their self-knowledge and sense of potency through heroic, combative storytelling.

We've found that every aspect of even the trashiest pop-culture story can 11 have its own developmental function. Pretending to have superhuman powers helps children conquer the feelings of powerlessness that inevitably come with being so young and small. The dual-identity concept at the heart of many superhero stories helps kids negotiate the conflicts between the inner self and the public self as they work through the early stages of socialization. Identification with a rebellious, even destructive, hero helps children learn to push back against a modern culture that cultivates fear and teaches dependency.

At its most fundamental level, what we call "creative violence"—head- 12 bonking cartoons, bloody video games, playground karate, toy guns—gives children a tool to master their rage. Children will feel rage. Even the sweetest and most civilized of them, even those whose parents read the better class of literary magazines, will feel rage. The world is uncontrollable and incomprehensible; mastering it is a terrifying, enraging task. Rage can be an energizing emotion, a shot of courage to push us to resist greater threats, take more control, than we ever thought we could. But rage is also the emotion our culture distrusts the most. Most of us are taught early on to fear our own. Through immersion in imaginary combat and identification with a violent protagonist, children engage the rage they've stifled, come to fear it less, and become more capable of utilizing it against life's challenges.

> "Rage can be an energizing emotion."

I knew one little girl who went around exploding with fantasies so violent 13 that other moms would draw her mother aside to whisper, "I think you should know something about Emily. . . ." Her parents were separating, and she was small, an only child, a tomboy at an age when her classmates were dividing sharply along gender lines. On the playground she acted out *Sailor Moon*° fights, and in the classroom she wrote stories about people being stabbed with knives. The more adults tried to control her stories, the more she acted out the roles of her angry heroes: breaking rules, testing limits, roaring threats.

A Japanese cartoon series about magical girls

Then her mother and I started helping her tell her stories. She wrote them, 14 performed them, drew them like comics: sometimes bloody, sometimes tender, always blending the images of pop culture with her own most private fantasies. She came out of it just as fiery and strong, but more self-controlled and socially competent: a leader among her peers, the one student in her class who could truly pull boys and girls together.

The title character of *Oktane* gets nasty.
© Gerard Jones, Gene Ha, Will Jacobs.

I worked with an older girl, a 15 middle-class "nice girl," who held herself together through a chaotic family situation and a tumultuous adolescence with gangsta rap. In the mythologized street violence of Ice T, the rage and strutting of his music and lyrics, she found a theater of the mind in which she could be powerful, ruthless, invulnerable. She avoided the heavy drug use that sank many of her peers, and flowered in college as a writer and political activist.

I'm not going to argue that violent entertainment is harmless. I think it 16 has helped inspire some people to real-life violence. I am going to argue that it's helped hundreds of people for every one it's hurt, and that it can help far more if we learn to use it well. I am going to argue that our fear of "youth violence" isn't well-founded on reality, and that the fear can do more harm than the reality. We act as though our highest priority is to prevent our children from growing up into murderous thugs—but modern kids are far more likely to grow up too passive, too distrustful of themselves, too easily manipulated.

We send the message to our children in a hundred ways that their craving 17 for imaginary gun battles and symbolic killings is wrong, or at least dangerous. Even when we don't call for censorship or forbid *Mortal Kombat*, we moan to other parents within our kids' earshot about the "awful violence" in the entertainment they love. We tell our kids that it isn't nice to play-fight, or we steer them from some monstrous action figure to a pro-social doll. Even in the most progressive households, where we make such a point of letting children feel what they feel, we rush to substitute an enlightened discussion for the raw material of rageful fantasy. In the process, we risk confusing them about their natural aggression in the same way the Victorians° confused their children about their sexuality. When we try to protect our children from their own feelings and fantasies, we shelter them not against violence but against power and selfhood.

The people who lived during the reign of Victoria (1819–1901), queen of Great Britain and Ireland, who are often associated with prudish behavior.

Identifying the Elements of Argument

1. What is Jones's thesis? Restate it in your own words.

2. What arguments does Jones present as evidence in support of his thesis?

3. What arguments against his position does Jones identify? How does he refute them?

4. Paraphrase Jones's concluding statement.

Highlighting

After you read an argument, read through it again, this time highlighting as you read. When you **highlight**, you use underlining and symbols to identify the essay's most important points. (Note that the word *highlighting* does not necessarily refer to the underlining done with a yellow highlighter pen.) This active reading strategy will help you to understand the writer's ideas and to see connections among those ideas when you reread.

How do you know what to highlight? As a general rule, you look for the same signals that you looked for when you read the essay the first time—for example, the essay's thesis and topic sentences and the words and phrases that identify the writer's intent and emphasis. This time, however, you physically mark these elements and use various symbols to indicate your reactions to them.

SUGGESTIONS FOR HIGHLIGHTING

- Underline key ideas—for example, ideas stated in topic sentences.

- Box or circle words or phrases you want to remember.

- Place a check mark or a star next to an important idea.

- Place a double check mark or double star next to an especially significant idea.

- Draw lines or arrows to connect related ideas.

- Write a question mark near an unfamiliar reference or a word you need to look up.

- Number the writer's key supporting points or examples.

Here is how a student, Katherine Choi, highlighted the essay "When Life Imitates Video" by John Leo, which appears below. Choi was preparing to write an essay about the effects of media violence on children and adolescents. She began her highlighting by underlining and starring the thesis statement (para. 2). She then circled references to Leo's two key examples, "Colorado massacre" (1) and "Paducah, Ky." (7) and placed question marks beside them to remind herself to find out more about them. In addition, she underlined and starred some particularly important points (2, 8, 9) as well as what she identified as the essay's concluding statement (11).

This essay first appeared in *U.S. News & World Report* on May 3, 1999.

WHEN LIFE IMITATES VIDEO
JOHN LEO

? Marching through a large building using various bombs and guns to pick off 1
victims is a conventional video-game scenario. In the Colorado massacre, Dylan Klebold and Eric Harris used pistol-grip shotguns, as in some video-arcade games. The pools of blood, screams of agony, and pleas for mercy must have been familiar—they are featured in some of the newer and more realistic kill-for-kicks games. "With each kill," the *Los Angeles Times* reported, "the

teens cackled and shouted as though playing one of the morbid video games they loved." And they ended their spree by shooting themselves in the head, the final act in the game *Postal*, and, in fact, the only way to end it.

Did the sensibilities created by the modern, video kill games play a role 2 in the Littleton massacre? Apparently so. Note the cool and casual cruelty, the outlandish arsenal of weapons, the cheering and laughing while hunting down victims one by one. All of this seems to reflect the style and feel of the video killing games they played so often.

No, there isn't any direct connection between most murderous games and 3 most murders. And yes, the primary responsibility for protecting children from dangerous games lies with their parents, many of whom like to blame the entertainment industry for their own failings.

But there is a cultural problem here: We are now a society in which the 4 chief form of play for millions of youngsters is making large numbers of people die. Hurting and maiming others is the central fun activity in video games played so addictively by the young. A widely cited survey of 900 fourth-through eighth-grade students found that almost half of the children said their favorite electronic games involve violence. Can it be that all this constant training in make-believe killing has no social effects?

Dress rehearsal. The conventional argument is that this is a harmless 5 activity among children who know the difference between fantasy and reality. But the games are often played by unstable youngsters unsure about the difference. Many of these have been maltreated or rejected and left alone most of the time (a precondition for playing the games obsessively). Adolescent feelings of resentment, powerlessness, and revenge pour into the killing games. In these children, the games can become a dress rehearsal for the real thing.

Psychologist David Grossman of Arkansas State University, a retired 6 Army officer, thinks "point and shoot" video games have the same effect as military strategies used to break down a soldier's aversion to killing. During World War II, only 15 to 20 percent of all American soldiers fired their weapon in battle. Shooting games in which the target is a man-shaped outline, the Army found, made recruits more willing to "make killing a reflex action."

Video games are much more powerful versions of the military's primitive 7 discovery about overcoming the reluctance to shoot. Grossman says Michael Carneal, the schoolboy shooter in Paducah, Ky, showed the effects of video- game lessons in killing. Carneal coolly shot nine times, hitting eight people, five of them in the head or neck. Head shots pay a bonus in many video games. Now the Marine Corps is adapting a version of *Doom*, the hyperviolent game played by one of the Littleton killers, for its own training purposes.

More realistic touches in video games help blur the boundary between 8 fantasy and reality—guns carefully modeled on real ones, accurate-looking wounds, screams, and other sound effects, even the recoil of a heavy rifle. Some newer games seem intent on erasing children's empathy and concern for others. Once the intended victims of video slaughter were mostly gangsters or aliens. Now some games invite players to blow away ordinary people who have done nothing wrong—pedestrians, marching bands, an elderly woman with a walker. In these games, the shooter is not a hero, just a violent sociopath. One ad for a Sony game says: "Get in touch with your gun-toting, testosterone-pumping, cold-blooded murdering side."

These killings are supposed to be taken as harmless over-the-top jokes. 9 But the bottom line is that <u>the young are being invited to enjoy the killing of vulnerable people picked at random.</u> This looks like the final lesson in a course to eliminate any lingering resistance to killing.

SWAT teams and cops now turn up as the intended victims of some 10 video-game killings. This has the effect of exploiting resentments toward law enforcement and making real-life shooting of cops more likely. This sensibility turns up in the hit movie *Matrix*: world-saving hero Keanu Reeves, in a mandatory Goth-style, long black coat packed with countless heavy-duty guns, is forced to blow away huge numbers of uniformed law-enforcement people.

"We have to start worrying about what we are putting into the minds of 11 our young," says Grossman. "Pilots train on flight simulators, drivers on driv- ing simulators, and now we have our children on murder simulators." If we want to avoid more Littleton-style massacres, we will begin taking the social effects of the killing games more seriously.

⤳ EXERCISE 2.2

Look carefully at Katherine Choi's highlighting of John Leo's essay on pages 68–70. How would your own highlighting of this essay be similar to or different from hers?

⤳ EXERCISE 2.3

Reread "Violent Media Is Good for Kids" (pp. 64–67). As you read, highlight the essay by underlining and starring important points, boxing or circling key words, writing question marks beside references that need further explanation, or drawing lines and arrows to connect related ideas.

Annotating

As you highlight, you should also annotate what you are reading. **Annotating** means making notes—of your questions, reactions, and ideas for discussion or writing—in the margins or between the lines. Keeping this kind of informal record of ideas as they occur to you will prepare you for class discussion and provide a useful source of material when you write.

As you read an argument and think critically about what you are reading, use the questions in the following checklist to help you make useful annotations.

Questions for Annotating

- ☐ What issue is the writer focusing on?
- ☐ Does the writer take a clear stand on this issue?
- ☐ What is the writer's thesis?
- ☐ What is the writer's purpose (his or her reason for writing)?
- ☐ What kind of audience is the writer addressing?
- ☐ Does the argument appear in a popular periodical or in a scholarly journal?
- ☐ Does the writer seem to assume readers will agree with the essay's position?

- ☐ What evidence does the writer use to support the essay's thesis? Does the writer include enough evidence?
- ☐ Does the writer consider (and refute) opposing arguments?
- ☐ Do you understand the writer's vocabulary?
- ☐ Do you understand the writer's references?
- ☐ Do you agree with the points the writer makes?
- ☐ Do the views the writer expresses agree or disagree with the views presented in other essays you have read?

🔊 The following pages, which reproduce Katherine Choi's highlighting of John Leo's essay on pages 68–70, also include her marginal annotations. In these annotations, Choi put Leo's thesis and some of his key points into her own words and recorded a few questions that she intended to explore further. She also added notes to clarify his references to two iconic school shootings. Finally, she identified arguments against Leo's position and his refutation of these arguments.

This essay first appeared in *U.S. News & World Report* on May 3, 1999.

WHEN LIFE IMITATES VIDEO
JOHN LEO

Marching through a large building using various bombs and guns to pick off   1
victims is a conventional video-game scenario. In the Colorado massacre,
Dylan Klebold and Eric Harris used pistol-grip shotguns, as in some video-
arcade games. The pools of blood, screams of agony, and pleas for mercy must
have been familiar—they are featured in some of the newer and more realistic
kill-for-kicks games. "With each kill," the *Los Angeles Times* reported, "the
teens cackled and shouted as though playing one of the morbid video games
they loved." And they ended their spree by shooting themselves in the head,
the final act in the game *Postal*, and, in fact, the only way to end it.

*Columbine H.S.,
1999*

Thesis
His position: "video kill games" can lead to violent behavior

✳

Opposing arguments

Refutation

True? _____

Date of survey?

(He means "training" does have negative effects, right?)

Opposing argument

Refutation

Quotes psychologist (= authority)

1997 _____

✳

Did the sensibilities created by the modern, video kill games play a role 2
in the Littleton massacre? Apparently so. Note the cool and casual cruelty, the
outlandish arsenal of weapons, the cheering and laughing while hunting down
victims one by one. All of this seems to reflect the style and feel of the video
killing games they played so often.

No, there isn't any direct connection between most murderous games and 3
most murders. And yes, the primary responsibility for protecting children
from dangerous games lies with their parents, many of whom like to blame the
entertainment industry for their own failings.

But there is a cultural problem here: We are now a society in which the 4
chief form of play for millions of youngsters is making large numbers of
people die. Hurting and maiming others is the central fun activity in video
games played so addictively by the young. A widely cited survey of 900 fourth-
through eighth-grade students found that almost half of the children said their
favorite electronic games involve violence. Can it be that all this constant
training in make-believe killing has no social effects?

Dress rehearsal. The conventional argument is that this is a harmless 5
activity among children who know the difference between fantasy and reality. But the games are often played by unstable youngsters unsure about the
difference. Many of these have been maltreated or rejected and left alone
most of the time (a precondition for playing the games obsessively). Adolescent feelings of resentment, powerlessness, and revenge pour into the
killing games. In these children, the games can become a dress rehearsal for
the real thing.

Psychologist David Grossman of Arkansas State University, a retired 6
Army officer, thinks "point and shoot" video games have the same effect as
military strategies used to break down a soldier's aversion to killing. During
World War II, only 15 to 20 percent of all American soldiers fired their
weapon in battle. Shooting games in which the target is a man-shaped outline,
the Army found, made recruits more willing to "make killing a reflex action."

Video games are much more powerful versions of the military's primitive 7
discovery about overcoming the reluctance to shoot. Grossman says Michael
Carneal, the schoolboy shooter in Paducah, Ky, showed the effects of video-
game lessons in killing. Carneal coolly shot nine times, hitting eight people,
five of them in the head or neck. Head shots pay a bonus in many video games.
Now the Marine Corps is adapting a version of *Doom*, the hyperviolent game
played by one of the Littleton killers, for its own training purposes.

More realistic touches in video games help blur the boundary between 8
fantasy and reality—guns carefully modeled on real ones, accurate-looking
wounds, screams, and other sound effects, even the recoil of a heavy rifle.
Some newer games seem intent on erasing children's empathy and concern
for others. Once the intended victims of video slaughter were mostly gangsters
or aliens. Now some games invite players to blow away ordinary people who
have done nothing wrong—pedestrians, marching bands, an elderly woman
with a walker. In these games, the shooter is not a hero, just a violent sociopath.

One ad for a Sony game says: "Get in touch with your gun-toting, testosterone-pumping, cold-blooded murdering side."

These killings are supposed to be taken as harmless over-the-top jokes. 9 But the bottom line is that the young are being invited to enjoy the killing of vulnerable people picked at random. This looks like the final lesson in a course to eliminate any lingering resistance to killing.

SWAT teams and cops now turn up as the intended victims of some 10 video-game killings. This has the effect of exploiting resentments toward law enforcement and making real-life shooting of cops more likely. This sensibility turns up in the hit movie *Matrix*: world-saving hero Keanu Reeves, in a mandatory Goth-style, long black coat packed with countless heavy-duty guns, is forced to blow away huge numbers of uniformed law-enforcement people.

"We have to start worrying about what we are putting into the minds of 11 our young," says Grossman. "Pilots train on flight simulators, drivers on driving simulators, and now we have our children on murder simulators." If we want to avoid more Littleton-style massacres, we will begin taking the social effects of the killing games more seriously.

Recommendation for action

⊙ EXERCISE 2.4

Reread Gerard Jones's "Violent Media Is Good for Kids" (pp. 64–67). As you read, refer to the "Questions for Annotating" checklist (p. 71), and use them as a guide as you write your own reactions and questions in the margins of Jones's essay. In your annotations, note where you agree or disagree with Jones, and briefly explain why. Quickly summarize any points that you think are particularly important. Look up any unfamiliar words or references you have identified, and write down brief definitions or explanations. Think about these annotations as you prepare to discuss the Jones essay in class (and, eventually, to write about it).

⊙ EXERCISE 2.5

Exchange books with another student, and read his or her highlighting and annotating. How are your written responses similar to the other student's? How are they different? Do your classmate's responses help you to see anything new about Jones's essay?

⊙ EXERCISE 2.6

The following letter to the editor of a college newspaper takes a position on the issue of how violent media—in this case, video games—influence young people. Read the letter, highlighting and annotating it.

Now, consider how this letter is similar to and different from Gerard Jones's essay (pp. 64–67). First, identify the writer's thesis, and restate it in your own words. Then, consider the benefits of the violent video games the writer identifies. Are these benefits the same as those Jones identifies?

In paragraph 4, the writer summarizes arguments against her position. Does Jones address any of these same arguments? If so, does he refute them in the same way this writer does? Finally, read the letter's last paragraph. How is this writer's purpose for writing different from Jones's?

This letter to the editor was published on October 22, 2003, in *Ka Leo o Hawai'i*, the student newspaper of the University of Hawaii at Manoa.

DON'T WITHHOLD VIOLENT GAMES

JESSICA ROBBINS

Entertainment and technology have changed. Video games today are more graphic and violent than they were a few years ago. There is a concern about children being influenced by the content of some of these video games. Some states have already passed laws which ban minors from the viewing or purchasing of these video games without an accompanying adult. I believe this law should not exist.

Today's technology has truly enriched our entertainment experience. Today's computer and game consoles are able to simulate shooting, killing, mutilation, and blood through video games. It was such a problem that in 1993 Congress passed a law prohibiting the sale or rental of adult video games to minors. A rating system on games, similar to that placed on movies, was put into place, which I support. This helps to identify the level of violence that a game might have. However, I do not believe that this rating should restrict people of any age from purchasing a game.

Currently there is no significant evidence that supports the argument that violent video games are a major contributing factor in criminal and violent behavior. Recognized universities such as MIT and UCLA described the law as misguided, citing that "most studies and experiments on video games containing violent content have not found adverse effects." In addition, there actually are benefits from playing video games. They provide a safe outlet for aggression and frustration, increased attention performance, along with spatial and coordination skills.

> "[T]here actually are benefits from playing video games."

Some argue that there is research that shows real-life video game play is 4 related to antisocial behavior and delinquency, and that there is need for a law to prevent children from acting out these violent behaviors. This may be true, but researchers have failed to indicate that this antisocial and aggressive behavior is not mostly short-term. We should give children the benefit of the doubt. Today's average child is competent and intelligent enough to recognize the difference between the digital representation of a gun and a real 28-inch military bazooka rocket launcher. They are also aware of the consequences of using such weapons on real civilians.

Major software companies who create video games should write 5 Congress and protest this law on the basis of a nonexistent correlation between violence and video games. If the law is modified to not restrict these games to a particular age group, then these products will not be unfairly singled out.

➲ EXERCISE 2.7

The following document, a statement on media violence released by the American Psychological Association (APA) in 2015, includes a list of specific recommendations. What position does this document take? Draft a thesis statement that summarizes this position. Then, consider how Gerard Jones (pp. 64–67) would respond to this thesis—and to the APA's specific recommendations.

This document was posted to APA.org to replace the outdated 1985 resolution on violence on television.

VIOLENCE IN MASS MEDIA
AMERICAN PSYCHOLOGICAL ASSOCIATION

On the recommendation of the Board of Directors and the Board for the 1 Advancement of Psychology in the Public Interest, Council voted to adopt the following resolution, as amended, as APA policy, replacing the 1985 resolution on television violence:

Whereas the consequences of aggressive and violent behavior have 2 brought human suffering, lost lives, and economic hardship to our society as well as an atmosphere of anxiety, fear, and mistrust;

Whereas in recent years the level of violence in American society and 3 the level of violence portrayed in television, film, and video have escalated markedly;

Whereas the great majority of research studies have found a relation   4
between viewing mass media violence and behaving aggressively;

Whereas the conclusion drawn on the basis of over 30 years of research   5
and a sizeable number of experimental and field investigations (Huston, et al.,
1992; NIMH, 1982; Surgeon General, 1972) is that viewing mass media violence leads to increases in aggressive attitudes, values, and behavior, particularly in children, and has a long-lasting effect on behavior and personality,
including criminal behavior;

Whereas viewing violence desensitizes the viewer to violence, resulting in   6
calloused attitudes regarding violence toward others and a decreased likelihood to take action on behalf of a victim when violence occurs;

Whereas viewing violence increases viewers' tendencies for becoming   7
involved with or exposing themselves to violence;

Whereas viewing violence increases fear of becoming a victim of violence,   8
with a resultant increase in self-protective behaviors and mistrust of others;

Whereas many children's television programs and films contain some   9
form of violence, and children's access to adult-oriented media violence is
increasing as a result of new technological advances;

Therefore be it resolved that the American Psychological Association: 10

1. urges psychologists to inform the television and film industry personnel who
   are responsible for violent programming, their commercial advertisers, legislators, and the general public that viewing violence in the media produces
   aggressive and violent behavior in children who are susceptible to such effects;

2. encourages parents and other child care providers to monitor and supervise television, video, and film viewing by children;

3. supports the inclusion of clear and easy-to-use warning labels for violent
   material in television, video, and film programs to enable viewers to make
   informed choices;

4. supports the development of technologies that empower viewers to prevent the broadcast of violent material in their homes;

5. supports the development, implementation, and evaluation of school-
   based programs to educate children and youth regarding means for critically viewing, processing, and evaluating video and film portrayals of
   both aggressive and prosocial behaviors;

6. requests the television and film industry to reduce direct violence in "real
   life" fictional children's programming or violent incidents in cartoons
   and other television or film productions, and to provide more programming designed to mitigate possible effects of television and film violence,
   consistent with the guarantees of the First Amendment;

7. urges the television and film industry to foster programming that models
   prosocial behaviors and seeks to resolve the problem of violence in society;

8. offers to the television and film industry assistance in developing programs that illustrate psychological methods to control aggressive and violent behavior, and alternative strategies for dealing with conflict and anger;

9. supports revision of the Film Rating System to take into account violence content that is harmful to children and youth;

10. urges industry, government, and private foundations to develop and implement programs to enhance the critical viewing skills of teachers, parents, and children regarding media violence and how to prevent its negative effects;

11. recommends that the Federal Communications Commission (FCC) review, as a condition for license renewal, the programming and outreach efforts and accomplishments of television stations in helping to solve the problem of youth violence;

12. urges industry, government, and private foundations to support research activities aimed at the amelioration of the effects of high levels of mass media violence on children's attitudes and behavior (DeLeon, 1995).

Writing a Critical Response

Sometimes you will be asked to write a **critical response**—a paragraph or more in which you analyze ideas presented in an argument and express your reactions to them.

Before you can respond in writing to an argument, you need to be sure that you understand the writer's position and that you have a sense of how supporting ideas are arranged—and why. You also need to consider how convincingly the writer conveys his or her position.

If you have read the argument carefully, highlighting and annotating it according to the guidelines outlined in this chapter, you should have a good idea what the writer wants to communicate to readers as well as how successfully the argument makes its point.

Before you begin to write a critical response to an argument, you should consider the questions in the checklist on page 78.

Begin your critical response by identifying your source and its author; then, write a clear, concise summary of the writer's position. Next, analyze the argument's supporting points one by one, considering the strength of the evidence that is presented. Also consider whether the writer addresses all significant opposing arguments and whether those arguments are refuted convincingly. Quote, summarize, and paraphrase the writer's key points as you go along, being careful to quote accurately and not to misrepresent the writer's ideas or distort them by quoting out of context. (For information

CHECKLIST

Questions for Critical Reading

☐ What is the writer's general subject?

☐ What purpose does the writer have for presenting this argument?

☐ What is the writer's position?

☐ Does the writer support ideas mainly with facts or with opinion?

☐ What evidence does the writer present to support this position?

☐ Is the evidence convincing? Is there enough evidence?

☐ Does the writer present opposing ideas and refute them effectively?

☐ What kind of audience does the writer seem to be addressing?

☐ Does the writer see the audience as hostile, friendly, or neutral?

☐ Does the writer establish himself or herself as well informed? As a fair and reasonable person?

☐ Does the writer seem to exhibit bias? If so, how does this bias affect the argument?

on summarizing, paraphrasing, quoting, and synthesizing sources, see Chapter 9.) As you write, identify arguments you find unconvincing, poorly supported, or irrelevant. At the end of your critical response, sum up your assessment of the argument in a strong concluding statement.

⬇ Katherine Choi, the student who highlighted and annotated "When Life Imitates Video" by John Leo (pp. 71–73), used those notes to help her develop the following critical response to Leo's article.

RESPONSE TO "WHEN LIFE IMITATES VIDEO"

KATHERINE CHOI

Article's source and author identified

Summary of writer's position

Analysis of supporting evidence

In "When Life Imitates Video," John Leo takes the position that   1
"video kill games" (para. 2) can actually lead to violent behavior. In fact, he suggests a cause-and-effect connection between such games and the notorious 1999 murder spree at Colorado's Columbine High School, which occurred shortly before Leo wrote his essay.

Although Leo acknowledges in paragraph 3 that there is no "direct   2
connection" between video games and this crime and agrees that parents

bear the "primary responsibility" for keeping violent games out of the hands of their children, he insists that our culture is also responsible. He is very critical of our society's dependence on violent video games, which he considers "training in make-believe killing" (para 4). This argument is convincing, up to a point. The problem is that Leo's primary support for this argument is a reference to an unnamed "widely cited survey" (para. 4), for which he provides no date. In addition, his use of a weak rhetorical question at the end of paragraph 4 instead of a strong statement of his position does little to help to support his argument.

Leo cites an opposing argument at the beginning of paragraph 5— the "conventional argument" that video games are harmless because children can tell the difference between fantasy and reality. He refutes this argument with unsupported generalizations rather than with specifics, pointing out the possibility that the games will often be played by "unstable youngsters" who channel their "adolescent feelings of resentment, powerlessness, and revenge" into the games.

3 Analysis of Leo's discussion of an opposing argument

The key piece of supporting evidence for Leo's claim that video games are dangerous comes in paragraph 6 with the expert opinion of a psychology professor who is also a retired army officer. The professor, David Grossman, draws an analogy between adolescents' video games and military training games designed to encourage soldiers to shoot their enemies. Although this analogy is interesting, it is not necessarily valid. For one thing, the army training Grossman refers to took place during World War II; for another, the soldiers were aware that the games were preparing them for actual combat.

4 Analysis of supporting evidence

In paragraph 7, Leo goes on to cite Grossman's comments about the young shooter in a 1997 attack in Paducah, Kentucky, and the Marines' use of *Doom* to train soldiers. Again, both discussions are interesting, and both are relevant to the connection between video games and violence. The problem is that neither discussion establishes a cause-and-effect relationship between violent video games and violent acts.

5 Analysis of supporting evidence

It may be true, as Leo observes, that video games are becoming more and more violent and that the victims in these games are increasingly likely to be police officers. Still, Leo fails to make his point because he never establishes that real-life violence is also increasing; therefore, he is not able to demonstrate a causal connection. His concluding

6

Concluding statement

statement—"If we want to avoid more Littleton-style massacres, we will begin taking the social effects of the killing games more seriously"—combines a frightening prediction and a strong recommendation for action. Unfortunately, although Leo's essay will frighten many readers, it does not convincingly establish the need for the action he recommends.

Work Cited

Leo, John. "When Life Imitates Video." *Practical Argument*, 3rd ed., edited by Laurie G. Kirszner and Stephen R. Mandell. Bedford/St. Martin's, 2017, pp. 68–70.

TEMPLATE FOR WRITING A CRITICAL RESPONSE

Write a one-paragraph critical response to Gerard Jones's essay on pages 64–67. Use the following template to shape your paragraph.

According to Gerard Jones, violent media can actually have positive effects on young people because _____
_____
_____
_____. Jones also believes that violent media are a positive influence on children because _____
_____.
Jones makes some good points. For example, he says that _____
_____
_____
_____. However, _____
_____
_____. All in
all, _____
_____.

⊖ EXERCISE 2.8

Expand the one-paragraph critical response that you wrote above into a more fully developed critical response to Gerard Jones's essay on pages 64–67. Refer to the highlighting and annotations that you did for Exercises 2.3 and 2.4. (If you like, you can expand your response with references to recent news events involving violent acts.)

Decoding Visual Arguments

Do Violent Media Images Trigger Violent Behavior? (continued)

In Chapter 2, you read essays focusing on whether violence on TV and in other popular media can be blamed (at least in part) for the violence in our society. Now, you will be introduced to a variety of visual texts that offer additional insights into this issue. At the same time, you will learn how to use the critical-reading strategies that you practiced in Chapter 2 to help you to **decode**, or interpret, visual texts and to use visuals as springboards for discussion and writing or as sources in your essays.

A **visual argument** can be an advertisement, a chart or graph or table, an infographic, a diagram, a Web page, a photograph, a drawing, or a painting. Like an argumentative essay, a visual argument can take a position. Unlike an argumentative essay, however, a visual argument communicates its position (and offers evidence to support that position) largely through images rather than words.

Thinking Critically about Visual Arguments

When you approach a visual argument—particularly one that will be the subject of class discussion or writing—you should do so with a critical eye. Your primary goal is to understand the point that the creator of the visual is trying to make, but you also need to understand how the message is conveyed. In addition, you need to evaluate whether the methods used to persuade the audience are both logical and convincing.

VISUALS VERSUS VISUAL ARGUMENTS

Not every visual is an argument; many simply present information. For example, a diagram of a hunting rifle, with its principal parts labeled, tells viewers what the weapon looks like and how it works. However, a photo of two toddlers playing with a hunting rifle could make a powerful argument about the need for gun safety. Conversely, a photo of a family hunting trip featuring a teenager proudly holding up a rifle while his parents look on approvingly might make a positive argument for access to guns.

Using Active Reading Strategies with Visual Arguments

As you learned in Chapter 2, being a critical reader involves responding actively to the text of an argument. The active reading strategies that you practiced in Chapter 2—*previewing, close reading, highlighting,* and *annotating*—can also be applied to visual arguments.

When you approach a visual argument, you should look for clues to its main idea, or message. Some visuals, particularly advertising images, include words (sometimes called *body copy*) as well, and this written text often conveys the main ideas of the argument. Apart from words, however, the images themselves can help you understand the visual's purpose, its intended audience, and the argument that it is making.

COMPREHENSION CLUES

- The individual images

- The relative distance between images (close together or far apart)

- The relative size of the images

- The relationship between images and background

- The use of empty space

- The use of color and shading (for example, contrast between light and dark)

- If people are pictured, their activities, gestures, facial expressions, positions, body language, dress, and so on

APPEALS: *LOGOS, PATHOS,* AND *ETHOS*

As you study a visual argument, you should consider the appeal (or appeals) that the visual uses to convince its audience.

- An ad produced by Mothers Against Drunk Drivers (MADD) that includes statistics about alcohol-related auto fatalities might appeal to logic (*logos*).

- Another MADD ad could appeal to the emotions (*pathos*) by showing photographs of an accident scene.

- Still another ad could appeal to authority (*ethos*) by featuring a well-known sports figure warning of the dangers of drunk driving.

(For more on these appeals, see pp. 14–21.)

The following illustration makes a strong visual argument, using the image of a young child holding a mutilated teddy bear to make an emotional appeal to those concerned about children's exposure to television violence.

This illustration by Todd Davidson first appeared in the *Age* newspaper, Melbourne, Australia, on March 22, 1998.

© Todd Davidson/Illustration Source

The visual on the previous page includes three dominant images: the child, the teddy bear, and a giant TV screen projecting an image of a hand holding a knife. The placement of the child in the center of the visual, with the teddy bear on one side and the knife on the other, suggests that the child (and, by extension, all children) is caught between the innocence of childhood and the violence depicted in the media. The hand holding the knife on the television screen is an extension of the child's actual arm, suggesting that the innocent world of the child is being taken over by the violent world of the media.

To emphasize this conflict between innocence and violence, the teddy bear is set against a dark background, while the TV, with its disturbing image, is paradoxically set against a light background. (The image of the child is split, with half against each background, suggesting the split between the two worlds the child is exposed to.) The child's gaze is directed at his mutilated teddy bear, apparently the victim of his own violent act. The expression on the child's face makes it clear that he does not understand the violence he is caught up in.

Because it treats subject matter that is familiar to most people—TV violence and children's vulnerability to it—this visual is easy to understand. Its powerful images are not difficult to interpret, and its message is straightforward: TV violence is, at least in part, responsible for real-world violence. The visual's accessibility suggests that it is aimed at a wide general audience (rather than, for example, child psychologists or media analysts).

The visual's purpose is somewhat more complex. It could be to criticize the media, to warn parents and others about the threat posed by media violence, or to encourage the audience to take action.

Now, turn your attention to the two graphs on the facing page. These graphs, which appeared in the 2012 *Washington Post* article "Ten-Country Comparison Suggests There's Little or No Link between Video Games and Gun Murders," by Max Fisher, appeal to logic by providing statistics as evidence to support the article's position. Thus, the graphs present a strong visual argument about the relationship between violent video games and crime—an argument that is more powerful than the argument the article alone would present.

The graphs use a simple, open design and a minimum of words to make their information accessible to most people who will look at them. The main idea, or message, they convey is summarized by the article's thesis statement, supporting the idea that contrary to expectations, the data suggest "a slight downward shift in violence as video game consumption increases."

This idea is likely to come as a surprise to most people, who might assume a causal relationship between violent video games and violent crime. However, as the graphs show, this is not the case. Thus, the graphs serve as a clear **refutation** of a commonly held assumption. Because the two graphs (and the article in which they appeared) present information that is intended to contradict the audience's probable assumptions, their purpose seems to be to convince people to change the way they look at video games.

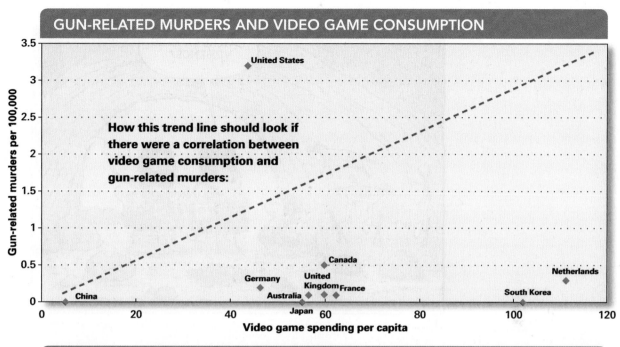

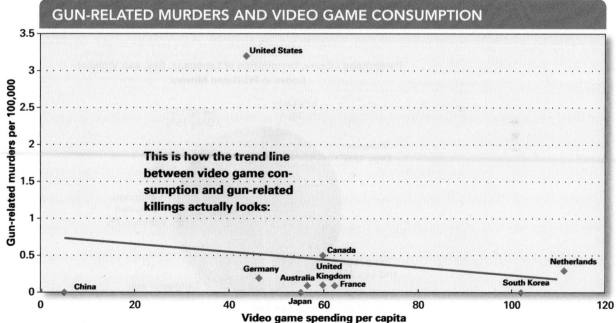

⊜ EXERCISE 3.1

Look at the visuals on the pages that follow, and then answer the questions on page 91.

Bob Engelhart, Violent Video Games

Bob Englehart. Courtesy of Cagle Cartoons.

Parenthood Library, Distribution of Language, Sex, and Violence Codes in PG-Rated Movies

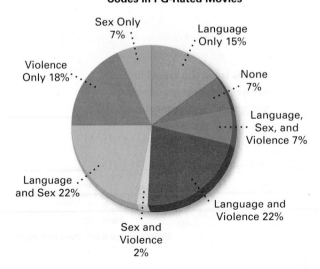

From Amy I. Nathanson & Joanne Cantor (1998), *Protecting Children from Harmful Television: TV Ratings and the V-Chip.* From *Parenthood in America,* University of Wisconsin–Madison General Library System.

Boy Playing Violent Video Game

Jochen Tack/imageBROKER/Agefotostock

Ways to Die in Children's Cartoons

A study in the *British Medical Journal* indicated that two thirds of cartoon movies included the deaths of characters, compared with half in adult films. Parents are five times as likely to die in cartoon films compared with adult dramas.

Type of Death, by Percentage of Films

Type of death	Children's animated films	Comparison films
No on-screen deaths	33.3	50.0
Animal attacks	11.1	0
Falling	11.1	33.3
Other murder	8.9	4.4
Drowning	6.7	1.1
Gunshot	6.7	14.4
Magic	6.7	0
Illness/medical complications	4.4	8.9
Other injury	4.4	2.2
Stabbing/impaling	4.4	2.2
Motor vehicle crash	2.2	8.9
Killed in combat	0	3.3
Suicide	0	1.1

Lauren Dazzara, Why Gaming Is a Positive Element in Life

© Loz Dizarra

Identifying the Elements of a Visual Argument

1. Do you see all of the visuals on pages 87–90 as arguments, or do you think some were created solely to present information?

2. What main idea, or message, does each visual communicate? State the main idea of each visual in a single sentence.

3. What elements in each visual support this main idea?

4. If the visual includes words as well as images, are the words necessary?

5. What purpose does each visual seem designed to achieve?

6. What kind of audience do you think each visual is aimed at?

7. Does the visual appeal primarily to *logos, pathos,* or *ethos*?

8. Do you think the visual is effective? That is, is it likely to have the desired effect on its intended audience?

Highlighting and Annotating Visuals

Now, it is time to look more closely at visuals and to learn how to *highlight* and *annotate* them. Unlike highlighting and annotating a written text, marking a visual text involves focusing your primary attention not on any words that appear but on the images.

After previewing the visual by looking at its overall appearance, begin highlighting to identify key images—perhaps by starring, boxing, or circling them—and then consider drawing lines or arrows to connect related images. Next, go on to make annotations on the visual, commenting on the effectiveness of its individual images in communicating the message of the whole. As in the case of a written text, your annotations can be in the form of comments or questions.

⏺ The visual on the following page shows how a student, Jason Savona, highlighted and annotated an advertisement for *Grand Theft Auto IV,* a popular violent video game.

Rockstar North, Advertisement for *Grand Theft Auto IV*

Top of gun = taller than
tallest building

Huge lone figure
looking down on city

"Liberty City" skyline
(looks like NY)

Hazy yellow sky

The Advertising Archives

Dark image stands out
against lighter background

Name of game centered; large type in
contrasting black and white for emphasis

⊜ EXERCISE 3.2

Look at the visual on the following page, and then highlight and annotate
it to identify its most important images and their relationship to one
another. When you have finished, think about how the images work
together to communicate a central message to the audience. What
argument does this visual make?

© Nate Londa

➡ EXERCISE 3.3

Interview a classmate about his or her experiences with video games—or with actual violence. Does your classmate see any links between the kinds of videos that are watched by friends and family members and the violence (or lack of violence) that occurs in his or her community? Write a paragraph summarizing your interview.

➡ EXERCISE 3.4

Study the following three visuals (and their captions), all of which appear in Gerard Jones's essay, "Violent Media Is Good for Kids" (pp. 64–67). Look at each visual with a critical eye, and then consider how effectively each one supports the central argument that Jones makes in his essay.

A scene from Gerard Jones and Will Jacobs's comic book *Monsters from Outer Space*.

© Gerard Jones, Gene Ha, Will Jacobs.

A scene from Gerard Jones and Gene Ha's comic book *Oktane*.

© Gerard Jones, Gene Ha, Will Jacobs.

The title character of *Oktane* gets nasty.

© Gerard Jones, Gene Ha, Will Jacobs.

Responding Critically to Visual Arguments

As you learned in Chapter 2, a **critical response** analyzes the ideas in a text and expresses your reactions to them. When you respond in writing to a visual argument, you rely on your highlighting and annotations to help you understand the writer's ideas and see how the words and images work together to make a particular point.

As you prepare to write a critical response to a visual argument, keep in mind the questions in the following checklist.

CHECKLIST

Questions for Responding to Visual Arguments

☐ In what source did the visual appear? What is the target audience for this source?

☐ For what kind of audience was the visual created? Hostile? Friendly? Neutral?

☐ For what purpose was the visual created?

☐ Who (or what organization) created the visual? What do you know about the background and goals of this person or group?

(*continued*)

☐ What issue is the visual addressing?

☐ What position does the visual take on this issue? How can you tell? Do you agree with this position?

☐ Does the visual include words? If so, are they necessary? What points do they make? Does the visual need more—or different— written text?

☐ Does the visual seem to be a *refutation*—that is, an argument against a particular position?

☐ Is the visual effective? Attractive? Interesting? Clear? Convincing?

When you write a critical response, begin by identifying the source and purpose of the visual. Then, state your reaction to the visual, and examine its elements one at a time, considering how effective each is and how well the various elements work together to create a convincing visual argument. End with a strong concluding statement that summarizes your reaction.

⬇ The critical response that follows was written by the student who highlighted and annotated the advertisement for *Grand Theft Auto IV* on page 92.

RESPONSE TO *GRAND THEFT AUTO IV*
JASON SAVONA

The advertisement for *Grand Theft Auto IV* presents a disturbing preview of the game. Rather than highlighting the game's features and challenges, this ad promotes the game's violence. As a result, it appeals more to those who are looking for video games that depict murder and other crimes than to those who choose a video game on the basis of the skill it requires.

The "hero" of this game is Niko Bellic, a war veteran from Eastern Europe who has left his country to build a new life in the fictional Liberty City. Instead of finding peace, he has found a new kind of war. Now,

1   Identification of visual's source

Reaction to visual

2   Analysis of visual's elements

trapped in the corrupt world of organized crime, Bellic is willing to do whatever it takes to fight his way out. His idea of justice is vigilante justice: he makes his own rules. The ad conveys this sense of Bellic as a loner and an outsider by showing him as a larger-than-life figure standing tall and alone against a background of the Liberty City skyline.

In the ad, Niko Bellic holds a powerful weapon in his huge hands,   3 and the weapon extends higher than the tallest building behind it, dominating the picture. Clearly, Bellic means business. As viewers look at the picture, the dark image of the gun and the man who holds it comes to the foreground, and everything else—the light brown buildings, the city lights, the yellow sky—fades into the background. In the center, the name of the game is set in large black-and-white type that contrasts with the ad's hazy background, showing the importance of the product's name.

This image, clearly aimed at young players of violent video games,   4 would certainly be appealing to those who want to have a feeling of

Concluding statement   power. What it says is, "A weapon makes a person powerful." This is a very dangerous message.

TEMPLATE FOR RESPONDING TO VISUAL ARGUMENTS

Write a one-paragraph critical response to the visual you highlighted and annotated in Exercise 3.2 on pages 92–93. Use the following template to shape your paragraph.

The visual created by Nate Londa shows _____
_____.

This visual makes a powerful statement about _____.
_____ The central image shows _____
_____
_____ The background enhances the central image because
_____
_____.
_____ The visual includes words as well as images.
These words suggest _____
_____.

The goal of the organization that posted the visual seems to be to _____
_____.
_____ The visual (is/is not) effective because _____
_____.

● EXERCISE 3.5

Consulting the one-paragraph critical response that you wrote above, write a more fully developed critical response to the visual on page 93. Refer to the highlighting and annotating that you did for Exercise 3.2.

AP Photo/Sakchai Lalit

Writing a Rhetorical Analysis

Is It Ethical to Buy Counterfeit Designer Merchandise?

The demand for counterfeit designer merchandise—handbags, shoes, and jewelry—has always been great. Wishing to avoid the high prices of genuine designer goods, American consumers spend hundreds of millions of dollars per year buying cheap imitations that are made primarily in factories in China (and in other countries as well). According to United States Customs and Border Protection statistics, the counterfeit goods seized in 2013 had a retail value of over $1.7 billion. In 2014, that figure went down to $1.2 billion, but much more counterfeit merchandise gets into the United States than is seized. However hard they try, law enforcement officials cannot seem to stem the tide of counterfeit merchandise that is sold in stores, in flea markets, and by street vendors as well as through the Internet. As long as people want these illegal goods, there will be a market for them.

Purchasing counterfeit designer goods is not a victimless crime, however. Buyers are stealing the intellectual property of legitimate businesses that, unlike the manufacturers of fakes, pay their employees fair wages and provide good working conditions. In addition, because counterfeit goods are of low quality, they do not last as long as the genuine articles. This is not a serious problem when people are buying fake watches and handbags, but it can be life threatening when the counterfeit products include pharmaceuticals, tools, baby food, or automobile parts.

Later in this chapter, you will read a rhetorical analysis of an essay that takes a position on this issue, and you will be asked to write a rhetorical analysis of your own about another essay on this topic.

What Is a Rhetorical Analysis?

When you write a **rhetorical analysis,** you systematically examine the strategies a writer employs to achieve his or her purpose. In the process, you explain how these strategies work together to create an effective (or ineffective) argument. To carry out this task, you consider the argument's **rhetorical situation**, the writer's **means of persuasion**, and the **rhetorical strategies** that the writer uses.

OVERVIEW: "LETTER FROM BIRMINGHAM JAIL" BY MARTIN LUTHER KING JR.

Here and throughout the rest of this chapter, we will be analyzing "Letter from Birmingham Jail" by Martin Luther King Jr., which can be found online.

In 1963, civil rights leader Martin Luther King Jr. organized a series of nonviolent demonstrations to protest the climate of segregation that existed in Birmingham, Alabama. He and his followers met opposition not only from white moderates but also from some African-American clergymen who thought that King was a troublemaker. During the demonstrations, King was arrested and jailed for eight days. He wrote his "Letter from Birmingham Jail" on April 16, 1963, from the city jail in response to a public statement by eight white Alabama clergymen titled "A Call for Unity." This statement asked for an end to the demonstrations, which the clergymen called "untimely," "unwise," and "extreme." (Their letter was addressed to the "white and Negro" population of Birmingham, not to King, whom they considered an "outsider.")

King knew that the world was watching and that his response to the white clergymen would have both national and international significance. As a result, he used a variety of rhetorical strategies to convince readers that his demands were both valid and understandable and that contrary to the opinions of some, his actions were well within the mainstream of American social and political thought. Today, King's "Letter from Birmingham Jail" stands as a model of clear and highly effective argumentation.

Martin Luther King Jr.
in Birmingham Jail
(April 1963)

Considering the Rhetorical Situation

Arguments do not take place in isolation. They are written by real people
in response to a particular set of circumstances called the **rhetorical situation**
(see pp. 9–14). The rhetorical situation consists of the following five
elements:

- The writer
- The writer's purpose
- The writer's audience
- The question
- The context

By analyzing the rhetorical situation, you are able to determine why the writer made the choices he or she did and how these choices affect the argument.

ANALYZING THE RHETORICAL SITUATION

To help you analyze the rhetorical situation of an argument, look for information about the essay and its author.

1. **Look at the essay's headnote.** If the essay you are reading has a headnote, it can contain useful information about the writer, the issue being discussed, and the structure of the essay. For this reason, it is a good idea to read headnotes carefully.

2. **Look for clues within the essay.** The writer's use of particular words and phrases can sometimes provide information about his or her preconceptions as well as about the cultural context of the argument. Historical or cultural references can indicate what ideas or information the writer expects readers to have.

3. **Search the Web.** Often, just a few minutes online can give you a lot of useful information—such as the background of a particular debate or the biography of the writer. By looking at titles of the other books or essays the writer has written, you may also be able to get an idea of his or her biases or point of view.

The Writer

Begin by trying to determine whether anything in the writer's background (for example, the writer's education, experience, race, gender, political beliefs, religion, age, and experiences) has influenced the content of the argument. Also consider whether the writer seems to have any preconceptions about the subject.

ANALYZING THE WRITER

- What is the writer's background?

- How does the writer's background affect the content of the argument?

- What preconceptions about the subject does the writer seem to have?

If you were analyzing "Letter from Birmingham Jail," it would help to know that Martin Luther King Jr. was pastor of the Dexter Avenue Baptist Church in Montgomery, Alabama. In 1956, he organized a bus boycott that led to a United States Supreme Court decision that outlawed segregation on Alabama's buses. In addition, King was a leader of the Southern Christian Leadership Conference and strongly believed in nonviolent protest. His books include *Stride towards Freedom* (1958) and *Why We Can't Wait* (1964). His "I Have a Dream" speech, which he delivered on the steps of the Lincoln Memorial on August 28, 1963, is considered by scholars to be one of the most influential speeches of the twentieth century. In 1964, King won the Nobel Prize for peace.

In "Letter from Birmingham Jail," King addresses the injustices that he sees in America—especially in the South—and makes a strong case

"I Have a Dream" speech, Washington, D.C. (August 1963)

Hulton-Deutsch Collection/Corbis

for civil rights for all races. Throughout his argument, King includes numerous references to the Bible, to philosophers, and to political and religious thinkers. By doing so, he makes it clear to readers that he is aware of the social, cultural, religious, and political implications of his actions. Because he is a clergyman, King suggests that by battling injustice, he, like the apostle Paul, is doing God's work. This point is made clear in the following passage (para. 3):

> But more basically, I am in Birmingham because injustice is here. Just as the prophets of the eighth century B.C. left their villages and carried their "thus saith the Lord" far beyond the boundaries of their home towns, and just as the Apostle Paul left his village of Tarsus and carried the gospel of Jesus Christ to the far corners of the Greco-Roman world, so am I compelled to carry the gospel of freedom beyond my own home town. Like Paul, I must constantly respond to the Macedonian call for aid.

The Writer's Purpose

Next, consider what the writer hopes to achieve with his or her argument. In other words, ask yourself if the writer is trying to challenge people's ideas, persuade them to accept new points of view, or influence their behavior.

ANALYZING THE WRITER'S PURPOSE

- Does the writer state his or her purpose directly, or is the purpose implied?
- Is the writer's purpose simply to convince or to encourage action?
- Does the writer rely primarily on logic or on emotion?
- Does the writer have a hidden agenda?

It is clear that Martin Luther King Jr. wrote "Letter from Birmingham Jail" to convince readers that even though he had been arrested, his actions were both honorable and just. To get readers to understand that, like Henry David Thoreau, he is protesting laws that he considers wrong, he draws a distinction between just and unjust laws. For him, a law is just if it "squares with the moral law or the law of God" (16). A law is unjust if it "is out of harmony with the moral law" (16). As a clergyman and a civil rights leader, King believed that he had an obligation both to point out the immorality of unjust laws and to protest them—even if it meant going to jail.

The Writer's Audience

To analyze the writer's audience, begin by considering whether the writer seems to see readers as friendly, hostile, or neutral. (For a discussion of types of audiences, see pp. 10–13). Also, determine how much knowledge the writer assumes that readers have. Then, consider how the writer takes into account factors like the audience's race, religion, gender, education, age, and ethnicity. Next, decide what preconceptions the writer thinks readers have about the subject. Finally, see if the writer shares any common ground with readers.

ANALYZING THE WRITER'S AUDIENCE

- Who is the writer's intended audience?

- Does the writer see the audience as informed or uninformed?

- Does the writer see the audience as hostile, friendly, or neutral?

- What values does the writer think the audience holds?

- What does the writer seem to assume about the audience's background?

- On what points do the writer and the audience agree? On what points do they disagree?

In "Letter from Birmingham Jail," King aims his argument at more than one audience. First, he speaks directly to eight clergymen from Birmingham, who are at worst a hostile audience and at best a skeptical one. They consider King to be an outsider whose actions are "unwise and untimely" (1). Before addressing their concerns, King tries to establish common ground, referring to his readers as "fellow clergymen" and "my Christian and Jewish brothers." He then goes on to say that he wishes that the clergymen had supported his actions instead of criticizing them. King ends his letter on a conciliatory note by asking his readers to forgive him if he has overstated his case or been unduly harsh.

In addition to addressing clergymen, King also speaks to white moderates, who he assumes are sympathetic to his cause but concerned about his methods. He knows that he has to influence this segment of his audience if he is to gain wide support for his cause. For this reason, King uses a restrained tone and emphasizes the universality of his message, ending his letter with a plea that is calculated to console and inspire those people who need reassurance (50):

Let us all hope that the dark clouds of racial prejudice will soon pass away and the deep fog of misunderstanding will be lifted from our fear-drenched communities, and in some not too distant tomorrow the radiant stars of love and brotherhood will shine over our great nation with all their scintillating beauty.

The Question

Try to determine what question the writer is trying to answer. Is the question suitable for argument? Decide if there are good arguments on both sides of the issue. For example, what issue (or issues) is the writer confronting? Does he or she address them adequately?

ANALYZING THE QUESTION

- What is the central question of the argument?
- Are there solid arguments on both sides of the issue?
- Has the writer answered the question fully enough?

The question King attempts to answer in "Letter from Birmingham Jail" is why he has decided to come to Birmingham to lead protests. Because the answer to this question is complicated, King addresses a number of issues. Although his main concern is with racial segregation in Alabama, he also is troubled by the indifference of white moderates who have urged him to call off his protests. In addition, he feels that he needs to explain his actions (for example, engaging in nonviolent protests) and address those who doubt his motives. King answers his critics (as well as his central question) by saying that because the people of the United States are interconnected, the injustices in one state will eventually affect the entire country.

The Context

The **context** is the situation that creates the need for the argument. As you analyze an argument, try to determine the social, historical, economic, political, and cultural events that set the stage for the argument and the part that these events play in the argument itself.

ANALYZING THE CONTEXT

- What situation (or situations) set the stage for the argument?
- What social, economic, political, and cultural events triggered the argument?
- What historical references situate this argument in a particular place or time?

The immediate context of "Letter to Birmingham Jail" is well known: Martin Luther King Jr. wrote an open letter to eight white clergymen in which he defended his protests against racial segregation. However, the wider social and political context of the letter is less well known.

In 1896, the U.S. Supreme Court ruled in *Plessy v. Ferguson* that "separate but equal" accommodations on railroad cars gave African Americans the equal protection guaranteed by the Fourteenth Amendment of the U.S. Constitution. Well into the twentieth century, this decision was used to justify separate public facilities—including restrooms, water fountains, and even schools and hospitals—for blacks and whites.

In the mid-1950s, state support for segregation of the races and discrimination against African Americans had begun to be challenged. For example, Supreme Court decisions in 1954 and 1955 found that segregation in the public schools and other publicly financed locations was unconstitutional. At the same time, whites and blacks alike were calling for an end to racial discrimination. Their actions took the form of marches, boycotts, and sit-ins (organized nonviolent protests whose participants refused to move from a public area). Many whites, however, particularly in the South, strongly resisted any sudden changes in race relations.

King's demonstrations in Birmingham, Alabama, took place within this larger social and political context. His campaign was a continuation of the push for equal rights that had been gaining momentum in the United States for decades. King, along with the Southern Christian Leadership

Segregated water fountains in North Carolina (1950)

© Elliott Erwitt/Magnum

Conference, had dispatched hundreds of people to Birmingham to engage in nonviolent demonstrations against those who were determined to keep African Americans from gaining their full rights as citizens.

Considering the Means of Persuasion: *Logos, Pathos, Ethos*

In the introduction to this book, you learned how writers of argument use three means of persuasion—*logos*, *pathos*, and *ethos*—to appeal to readers. You also saw how the **rhetorical triangle** represents the way these three appeals come into play within an argument. (See p. 19 for more information about the rhetorical triangle.) Of course, the degree to which a writer uses each of these appeals depends on the rhetorical situation. Moreover, a single argument can use more than one appeal—for example, an important research source would involve both the logic of the argument (*logos*) and the credibility of the writer (*ethos*). In "Letter from Birmingham Jail," King uses all three appeals.

The Appeal to Reason (Logos)

In "Letter from Birmingham Jail," King attempts to demonstrate the logic of his position. In paragraph 15, for example, he says that there are two types of laws—just and unjust. He then points out that he has both a legal and a moral responsibility to "disobey unjust laws." In paragraph 16, King supports his position with references to various philosophers and theologians—for example, St. Thomas Aquinas, Martin Buber, and Paul Tillich. He also develops the logical argument that even though all Americans should obey the law, they are responsible to a higher moral authority—God.

The Appeal to the Emotions (Pathos)

Throughout "Letter from Birmingham Jail," King attempts to create sympathy for his cause. In paragraph 14, for example, he catalogues the injustices of life in the United States for African Americans. He makes a particularly emotional appeal by quoting a hypothetical five-year-old boy who might ask, "Daddy, why do white people treat colored people so mean?" In addition, he includes vivid images of racial injustice to provoke anger against those who deny African Americans equal rights. In this way, King creates sympathy (and possibly empathy) in readers.

The Appeal to Authority (Ethos)

To be persuasive, King has to establish his credibility. In paragraph 2, for example, he reminds readers that he is the president of the Southern Christian Leadership Conference, "an organization operating in every southern state." In paragraph 3, he compares himself to the apostle Paul, who carried the gospel "to the far corners of the Greco-Roman world." In addition, King attempts to show readers that what he is doing is well within the mainstream of American political and social thought. By alluding to Thomas Jefferson, Henry David Thoreau, and the 1954 U.S. Supreme Court decision that outlawed segregation in public schools, he tries to demonstrate that he is not the wild-eyed radical that some believe him to be. Thus, King establishes himself in both secular and religious terms as a leader who has the stature and the authority to present his case.

Considering the Writer's Rhetorical Strategies

Writers use various **rhetorical strategies** to present their ideas and opinions. Here are a few of the elements that you should examine when analyzing and evaluating an argument.

Thesis

The **thesis**—the main idea or claim that the argument supports—is of primary importance in every argument. When you analyze an argument, you should always ask, "What is the essay's thesis, and why does the writer state it as he or she does?" You should also consider at what point in the argument the thesis is stated and what the effect of this placement is.

In "Letter from Birmingham Jail," Martin Luther King Jr. begins by telling readers that he is "confined here in the Birmingham city jail" and that he is writing his letter to answer clergymen who have called his demonstrations "unwise and untimely." King clearly (and unapologetically) states his thesis ("But more basically, I am in Birmingham because injustice is here") at the beginning of the third paragraph, right after he explains his purpose, so that readers will have no doubt what his position is as they read the rest of his argument.

Organization

The **organization** of an argument—how a writer arranges ideas—is also important. For example, after stating his thesis, King tells readers why he is in Birmingham and what he hopes to accomplish: he wants unjust laws to be abolished and the 1954 Supreme Court ruling to be enforced. King then **refutes**—disproves or calls into question—the specific charges that were leveled at him by the white clergymen who want him to stop his protests.

The structure of "Letter from Birmingham Jail" enables King to make his points clearly, logically, and convincingly:

- King begins his argument by addressing the charge that his actions are untimely. If anything, says King, his actions are not timely enough: after all, African Americans have waited more than 340 years for their "constitutional and God-given rights" (14).

- He then addresses the issue of his willingness to break laws and makes the distinction between just and unjust laws.

- After chiding white moderates for not supporting his cause, he addresses their claim that he is extreme. According to King, this charge is false: if he had not embraced a philosophy of nonviolent protest, the streets of the South would "be flowing with blood" (29).

- King then makes the point that the contemporary church must recapture the "sacrificial spirit of the early church" (42). He does this by linking his struggle for freedom with the "sacred heritage of our nation and the eternal will of God" (44).

- King ends his argument by asserting both his humility and his unity with the white clergy.

Evidence

To convince an audience, a writer must support the thesis with **evidence**—facts, observations, expert opinion, and so on. King presents a great deal of evidence to support his arguments. For instance, he uses numerous examples (both historical and personal) as well as many references to philosophers, political thinkers, and theologians (such as Jesus, St. Paul, St. Augustine, Amos, Martin Luther, and Abraham Lincoln). According to King, these figures, who were once considered "extremists," were not afraid of "making waves" when the need arose. Now, however, they are well within the mainstream of social, political, and religious thought. King also presents reasons, facts, and quotations to support his points.

Stylistic Techniques

Writers also use stylistic techniques to make their arguments more memorable and more convincing. For example, in "Letter from Birmingham Jail," King uses figurative devices such as *similes*, *metaphors*, and *allusions* to enhance his argument.

Simile　A **simile** is a figure of speech that compares two unlike things using the word *like* or *as*.

Like a boil that can never be cured so long as it is covered up but must be opened with all its ugliness to the natural medicines of air and light, injustice must be exposed, . . . before it can be cured. (24)

Isn't this like condemning a robbed man because his possession of money precipitated the evil act of robbery? (25)

Metaphor A **metaphor** is a comparison in which two dissimilar things are compared without the word *like* or *as*. A metaphor suggests that two things that are very different share a quality.

Frankly, I have yet to engage in a direct-action campaign that was "well timed" in the view of those who have not suffered unduly from the disease of segregation. (13)

[W]hen you see the vast majority of your twenty million Negro brothers smothering in an airtight cage of poverty . . . (14)

Allusion An **allusion** is a reference within a work to a person, literary or biblical text, or historical event in order to enlarge the context of the situation being written about. The writer expects readers to recognize the allusion and to make the connection to the text they are reading.

I would agree with St. Augustine that "an unjust law is no law at all." (15)

Of course, there is nothing new about this kind of civil disobedience. It was evidenced sublimely in the refusal of Shadrach, Meshach, and Abednego to obey the laws of Nebuchadnezzar, on the ground that a higher moral law was at stake. (21) [King expects his audience of clergymen to recognize this reference to the Book of Daniel in the Old Testament.]

In addition to those figurative devices, King uses stylistic techniques such as *parallelism*, *repetition*, and *rhetorical questions* to further his argument.

Parallelism **Parallelism**, the use of similar grammatical structures to emphasize related ideas, makes a passage easier to follow.

In any nonviolent campaign there are four basic steps: collection of the facts to determine whether injustices exist; negotiation; self-purification; and direct action. (6)

Shallow understanding from people of good will is more frustrating than absolute misunderstanding from people of ill will. Lukewarm acceptance is much more bewildering than outright rejection. (23)

I wish you had commended the Negro sit-inners and demonstrators of Birmingham for their sublime courage, their willingness to suffer, and their amazing discipline in the midst of great provocation. (47)

Repetition   Intentional **repetition** involves repeating a word or phrase for emphasis, clarity, or emotional impact.

> "Are you able to accept blows without retaliating?" "Are you able to endure the ordeal of jail?" (8)

> If I have said anything in this letter that overstates the truth and indicates an unreasonable impatience, I beg you to forgive me. If I have said anything that understates the truth and indicates my having patience that allows me to settle for anything less than brotherhood, I beg God to forgive me. (49)

Rhetorical questions   A **rhetorical question** is a question that is asked to encourage readers to reflect on an issue, not to elicit a reply.

> One may well ask: "How can you advocate breaking some laws and obeying others?" (15)

> Will we be extremists for hate or for love? (31)

Assessing the Argument

No rhetorical analysis of an argument would be complete without an assessment of its effectiveness—whether the rhetorical strategies the writer uses create a clear and persuasive argument or whether they fall short. When you write a rhetorical analysis, you can begin with an assessment of the argument as a whole and go on to support it, or you can begin with a discussion of the various rhetorical strategies that the writer uses and then end with your assessment of the argument.

After analyzing "Letter from Birmingham Jail," you could reasonably conclude that King has written a highly effective argument that is likely to convince his readers that his presence in Birmingham is both justified and necessary. Using *logos*, *pathos*, and *ethos*, he constructs a multifaceted argument that is calculated to appeal to the various segments of his audience—Southern clergymen, white moderates, and African Americans. In addition, King uses similes, metaphors, and allusions to enrich his argument and to make it more memorable, and he uses parallelism, repetition, and rhetorical questions to emphasize ideas and to reinforce his points. Because it is so clear and powerful, King's argument—in particular, the distinction between just and unjust laws—addresses not only the injustices that were present in 1963 when it was written but also the injustices and inequalities that exist today. In this sense, King has written an argument that has broad significance beyond the audiences for which it was originally intended.

Preparing to Write a Rhetorical Analysis

As you read, ask the following questions:

☐ Who is the writer? Is there anything in the writer's background that might influence what is (or is not) included in the argument?

☐ What is the writer's purpose? What does the writer hope to achieve?

☐ What question has the writer decided to address? How broad is the question?

☐ What situation created the need for the argument?

☐ At what points in the argument does the writer appeal to logic? To the emotions? How does the writer try to establish his or her credibility?

☐ What is the argument's thesis? Where is it stated? Why?

☐ How does the writer organize the argument? How effective is this arrangement of ideas?

☐ What evidence does the writer use to support the argument? Does the writer use enough evidence?

☐ Does the writer use similes, metaphors, and allusions?

☐ Does the writer use parallelism, repetition, and rhetorical questions?

☐ Given your analysis, what is your overall assessment of the argument?

Sample Rhetorical Analysis

In preparation for a research paper, Deniz Bilgutay, a student in a writing class, read the following essay, "Terror's Purse Strings" by Dana Thomas, which makes an argument against buying counterfeit designer goods. Deniz then wrote the rhetorical analysis that appears on pages 115–117. (Deniz Bilgutay's research paper, "The High Cost of Cheap Counterfeit Goods," uses "Terror's Purse Strings" as a source. See Appendix B.)

This essay appeared in the *New York Times* on August 30, 2007.

TERROR'S PURSE STRINGS

DANA THOMAS

Luxury fashion designers are busily putting final touches on the handbags   1
they will present during the spring-summer 2008 women's wear shows, which
begin next week in New York City's Bryant Park. To understand the importance of the handbag in fashion today consider this: According to consumer
surveys conducted by Coach, the average American woman was buying two
new handbags a year in 2000; by 2004, it was more than four. And the average
luxury bag retails for 10 to 12 times its production cost.

"There is a kind of an obsession with bags," the designer Miuccia Prada ₂ told me. "It's so easy to make money."

Counterfeiters agree. As soon as a handbag hits big, counterfeiters around the ₃ globe churn out fake versions by the thousands. And they have no trouble selling them. Shoppers descend on Canal Street in New York, Santee Alley in Los Angeles, and flea markets and purse parties around the country to pick up knockoffs for one-tenth the legitimate bag's retail cost, then pass them off as real.

"Judges, prosecutors, defense attorneys shop here," a private investigator ₄ told me as we toured the counterfeit section of Santee Alley. "Affluent people from Newport Beach." According to a study by the British law firm Davenport Lyons, two-thirds of British consumers are "proud to tell their family and friends" that they bought fake luxury fashion items.

At least 11 percent of the world's clothing is fake, according to 2000 figures ₅ from the Global Anti-Counterfeiting Group in Paris. Fashion is easy to copy: counterfeiters buy the real items, take them apart, scan the pieces to make patterns, and produce almost-perfect fakes.

Most people think that buying an imitation handbag or wallet is harmless, a victimless crime. But the counterfeiting rackets are run by crime syndicates that also deal in narcotics, weapons, child prostitution, human trafficking,

> "At least 11 percent of the world's clothing is fake . . ."   ₆

and terrorism. Ronald K. Noble, the secretary general of Interpol,° told the House of Representatives Committee on International Relations that profits from the sale of counterfeit goods have gone to groups associated with Hezbollah, the Shiite terrorist group, paramilitary organizations in Northern Ireland, and FARC, the Revolutionary Armed Forces of Colombia.

An international criminal police organization

Sales of counterfeit T-shirts may have helped finance the 1993 World ₇ Trade Center bombing, according to the International AntiCounterfeiting Coalition. "Profits from counterfeiting are one of the three main sources of income supporting international terrorism," said Magnus Ranstorp, a terrorism expert at the University of St. Andrews, in Scotland.

Most fakes today are produced in China, a good many of them by children. ₈ Children are sometimes sold or sent off by their families to work in clandestine factories that produce counterfeit luxury goods. Many in the West consider this an urban myth. But I have seen it myself.

On a warm winter afternoon in Guangzhou, I accompanied Chinese police ₉ officers on a factory raid in a decrepit tenement. Inside, we found two dozen children, ages 8 to 13, gluing and sewing together fake luxury-brand handbags. The police confiscated everything, arrested the owner, and sent the children out. Some punched their timecards, hoping to still get paid. (The average Chinese factory worker earns about $120 a month; the counterfeit factory worker earns half that or less.) As we made our way back to the police vans, the children threw bottles and cans at us. They were now jobless and, because the factory owner housed them, homeless. It was *Oliver Twist* in the 21st century.

What can we do to stop this? Much like the war on drugs, the effort to ₁₀ protect luxury brands must go after the source: the counterfeit manufacturers.

The company that took me on the Chinese raid is one of the only luxury-goods makers that works directly with Chinese authorities to shut down factories, and it has one of the lowest rates of counterfeiting.

Luxury brands also need to teach consumers that the traffic in fake 11 goods has many victims. But most companies refuse to speak publicly about counterfeiting—some won't even authenticate questionable items for concerned customers—believing, like Victorians,° that acknowledging despicable actions tarnishes their sterling reputations.

So it comes down to us. If we stop knowingly buying fakes, the supply 12 chain will dry up and counterfeiters will go out of business. The crime syndicates will have far less money to finance their illicit activities and their terrorist plots. And the children? They can go home.

The people who lived during the reign of Victoria (1819–1901), queen of Great Britain and Ireland, who are often associated with prudish behavior

A POWERFUL CALL TO ACTION

DENIZ BILGUTAY

In her *New York Times* essay, "Terror's Purse Strings," writer Dana Thomas uses the opening of New York's fashion shows as an opportunity to expose a darker side of fashion—the impact of imitation designer goods. Thomas explains to her readers why buying counterfeit luxury items, like fake handbags, is a serious problem. Her first goal is to raise awareness of the dangerous ties between counterfeiters who sell fake luxury merchandise and international criminal organizations that support terrorism and child labor. Her second goal is to explain how people can be a part of the solution by refusing to buy the counterfeit goods that finance these criminal activities. By establishing her credibility, building her case slowly, and appealing to both logic and emotions, Thomas succeeds in writing an interesting and informative argument.

1 Context

Topic

Analysis of writer's purpose

Thesis statement: Assessment of essay

For Thomas's argument to work, she has to earn her readers' trust. She does so first by anticipating a sympathetic, well-intentioned, educated audience and then by establishing her own credibility. To avoid sounding accusatory, Thomas assumes that her readers are unaware of the problem posed by counterfeit goods. She demonstrates this by presenting basic factual information and by acknowledging what "most people think" or what "many in the West consider": that buying counterfeit goods is harmless. She also acknowledges her readers' high level of education by

2 Analysis of writer's audience

Writer's use of similes, metaphors, allusions

drawing comparisons with history and literature—specifically, the Victorians and *Oliver Twist*. To further earn the audience's trust, she uses her knowledge and position to gain credibility. As the Paris correspondent for *Newsweek* and as the author of a book on luxury goods, Thomas has credibility. Showing her familiarity with the world of fashion by referring to a conversation with renowned designer Miuccia Prada, she further establishes this credibility. Later in the article, she shares her experience of witnessing the abuse that accompanies the production of fake designer handbags. This anecdote allows her to say, "I've seen it myself," confirming her knowledge not just of the fashion world but also of the world of counterfeiting. Despite her authority, she does not distance herself from readers. In fact, she goes out of her way to identify with them, using informal style and first person, noting "it comes down to us" and asking what "we" can do.

In Thomas's argument, both the organization and the use of evidence are effective. Thomas begins her article with statements that are easy to accept, and as she proceeds, she addresses more serious issues. In the first paragraph, she simply asks readers to "understand the importance of the handbag in fashion today." She demonstrates the wide-ranging influence and appeal of counterfeit designer goods, pointing out that "at least 11 percent of the world's clothing is fake." Thomas then makes the point that the act of purchasing these seemingly frivolous goods can actually have serious consequences. For example, crime syndicates and possibly even terrorist organizations actually run "the counterfeiting rackets" that produce these popular items. To support this point, she relies on two kinds of evidence—quotations from terrorism experts (specifically, the leader of a respected international police organization as well as a scholar in the field) and her own personal experience at a Chinese factory. Both kinds of evidence appeal to our emotions. Discussions of terrorism, especially those that recall the terrorist attacks on the United States, create fear. Descriptions of child labor in China encourage readers to feel sympathy.

Thomas waits until the end of her argument to present her thesis because she assumes that her readers know little about the problem she is discussing. The one flaw in her argument is her failure to provide the evidence needed to establish connections between some causes and their effects. For example in paragraph 7, Thomas says that the sale of counterfeit T-shirts "may have helped finance the 1993 Word Trade Center bomb-

Writer's use of ethos

Analysis of the writer

Analysis of essay's organization

Writer's use of logos

Writer's use of evidence

Writer's use of pathos

Analysis of the essay's weakness

3

4

ing." By using the word *may*, she qualifies her claim and weakens her argument. The same is true when Thomas says that profits from the sale of counterfeit goods "have gone to groups associated with Hezbollah, the Shiite terrorist group." Readers are left to wonder what specific groups are "associated with Hezbollah" and whether these groups are in fact terrorist organizations. Without this information, her assertion remains unsupported. In spite of these shortcomings, Thomas's argument is clear and well organized. More definite links between causes and effects, however, would have made it more convincing than it is.

⊙ EXERCISE 4.1

Read the following essay, "Sweatshop Oppression," by Rajeev Ravisankar. Then, write a one-paragraph rhetorical analysis of the essay. Follow the template on page 119, filling in the blanks to create your analysis.

This opinion essay was published in the *Lantern*, the student newspaper of the Ohio State University, on April 19, 2006.

SWEATSHOP OPPRESSION
RAJEEV RAVISANKAR

Being the "poor" college students that we all are, many of us undoubtedly place an emphasis on finding the lowest prices. Some take this to the extreme and camp out in front of a massive retail store in the wee hours of the morning on Black Friday,° waiting for the opportunity to buy as much as we can for as little as possible. 1

The Friday after Thanksgiving, traditionally the biggest shopping day of the year

What often gets lost in this rampant, low-cost driven consumerism is the high human cost it takes to achieve lower and lower prices. Specifically, this means the extensive use of sweatshop labor. 2

Many of us are familiar with the term sweatshop,° but have difficulty really understanding how abhorrent the hours, wages, and conditions are. Many of these workers are forced to work 70–80 hours per week making pennies per hour. Workers are discouraged or intimidated from forming unions. 3

A work environment with long hours, low wages, and difficult or dangerous conditions

They must fulfill certain quotas for the day and stay extra hours (with no pay) if these are not fulfilled. Some are forced to sit in front of a machine for 4 hours as they are not permitted to take breaks unless the manager allows them to do so. Unsanitary bathrooms, poor ventilation, and extreme heat, upward of 90 degrees, are also prevalent. Child labor is utilized in some factories as well.

Facing mounting pressure from labor rights activists, trade unions, student protests, and human-rights groups, companies claimed that they would make improvements. Many of the aforementioned conditions, however, persist. In many cases, even a few pennies more could make a substantial difference in the lives of these workers. Of course, multinational corporations are not interested in giving charity; they are interested in doing anything to increase profits. Also, many consumers in the West refuse to pay a little bit more even if it would improve the lives of sweatshop workers.

> "[Corporations] are interested in doing anything to increase profits."

Free-market economic fundamentalists have argued that claims made by those who oppose sweatshops actually have a negative impact on the plight of the poor in the developing world. They suggest that by criticizing labor and human-rights conditions, anti-sweatshop activists have forced companies to pull out of some locations, resulting in workers losing their jobs. To shift the blame in this manner is to neglect a simple fact: Companies, not the anti-sweatshop protestors, make the decision to shift to locations where they can find cheaper labor and weaker labor restrictions.

Simply put, the onus should always be on companies such as Nike, Reebok, Adidas, Champion, Gap, Wal-Mart, etc. They are to blame for perpetuating a system of exploitation which seeks to get as much out of each worker for the least possible price.

By continuing to strive for lower wages and lower input costs, they are taking part in a phenomenon which has been described as "the race to the bottom." The continual decline of wages and working conditions will be accompanied by a lower standard of living. This hardly seems like the best way to bring the developing world out of the pits of poverty.

So what can we do about it? Currently, the total disregard for human well-being through sweatshop oppression is being addressed by a number of organizations, including University Students against Sweatshops. USAS seeks to make universities source their apparel in factories that respect workers' rights, especially the right to freely form unions.

According to an article in *The Nation*, universities purchase nearly "$3 billion in T-shirts, sweatshirts, caps, sneakers and sports uniforms adorned with their institutions' names and logos." Because brands do not want to risk losing this money, it puts pressure on them to provide living wages and reasonable conditions for workers. Campaigns such as this are necessary if we are to stop the long race to the bottom.

TEMPLATE FOR WRITING A RHETORICAL ANALYSIS

Ravisankar begins his essay by _____

_____

_____. The problem he identifies is _____

_____

_____. Ravisankar assumes his readers are _____

_____

_____. His purpose in this essay is to _____

_____

In order to accomplish this purpose, he appeals mainly to _____

_____

_____. He also appeals to _____

_____

In his essay, Ravisankar addresses the main argument against his thesis, the idea that _____

_____

_____

He refutes this argument by saying _____

_____

_____

Finally, he concludes by making the point that _____

_____

Overall, the argument Ravisankar makes is effective [or ineffective] because _____

_____

_____

_____

⊘ EXERCISE 4.2

Read the following essay, "Where Sweatshops Are a Dream," by Nicholas
D. Kristof. Then, write a rhetorical analysis of Kristof's essay. Be sure to
consider the rhetorical situation, the means of persuasion, and the writer's
rhetorical strategies. End your rhetorical analysis with an assessment of
the strengths and weaknesses of Kristof's argument.

This opinion column was published in the *New York Times* on January 15, 2009.

WHERE SWEATSHOPS ARE A DREAM

NICHOLAS D. KRISTOF

Before Barack Obama and his team act on their talk about "labor standards," I'd like to offer them a tour of the vast garbage dump here in Phnom Penh. 1

This is a Dante-like vision of hell. It's a mountain of festering refuse, a half-hour hike across, emitting clouds of smoke from subterranean fires. 2

The miasma of toxic stink leaves you gasping, breezes batter you with filth, and even the rats look forlorn. Then the smoke parts and you come across a child ambling barefoot, searching for old plastic cups that recyclers will buy for five cents a pound. Many families actually live in shacks on this smoking garbage. 3

Mr. Obama and the Democrats who favor labor standards in trade agreements mean well, for they intend to fight back at oppressive sweatshops abroad. But while it shocks Americans to hear it, the central challenge in the poorest countries is not that sweatshops exploit too many people, but that they don't exploit enough. 4

Talk to these families in the dump, and a job in a sweatshop is a cherished dream, an escalator out of poverty, the kind of gauzy if probably unrealistic ambition that parents everywhere often have for their children. 5

"I'd love to get a job in a factory," said Pim Srey Rath, a 19-year-old woman scavenging for plastic. "At least that work is in the shade. Here is where it's hot." 6

Another woman, Vath Sam Oeun, hopes her 10-year-old boy, scavenging beside her, grows up to get a factory job, partly because she has seen other children run over by garbage trucks. Her boy has never been to a doctor or a dentist and last bathed when he was 2, so a sweatshop job by comparison would be far more pleasant and less dangerous. 7

I'm glad that many Americans are repulsed by the idea of importing products made by barely paid, barely legal workers in dangerous factories. Yet sweatshops are only a symptom of poverty, not a cause, and banning them closes off one route out of poverty. At a time of tremendous economic distress and protectionist pressures, there's a special danger that tighter labor standards will be used as an excuse to curb trade. 8

> "[S]weatshops are only a symptom of poverty, not a cause."

When I defend sweatshops, people always ask me: But would you want to work in a sweatshop? No, of course not. But I would want even less to pull a 9 rickshaw. In the hierarchy of jobs in poor countries, sweltering at a sewing machine isn't the bottom.

My views on sweatshops are shaped by years living in East Asia, watching 10 as living standards soared—including those in my wife's ancestral village in southern China—because of sweatshop jobs.

Manufacturing is one sector that can provide millions of jobs. Yet sweat- 11 shops usually go not to the poorest nations but to better-off countries with more reliable electricity and ports.

I often hear the argument: Labor standards can improve wages and work- 12 ing conditions, without greatly affecting the eventual retail cost of goods. That's true. But labor standards and "living wages" have a larger impact on production costs that companies are always trying to pare. The result is to push companies to operate more capital-intensive factories in better-off nations like Malaysia, rather than labor-intensive factories in poorer countries like Ghana or Cambodia.

Cambodia has, in fact, pursued an interesting experiment by working 13 with factories to establish decent labor standards and wages. It's a worthwhile idea, but one result of paying above-market wages is that those in charge of hiring often demand bribes—sometimes a month's salary—in exchange for a job. In addition, these standards add to production costs, so some factories have closed because of the global economic crisis and the difficulty of compet- ing internationally.

The best way to help people in the poorest countries isn't to campaign 14 against sweatshops but to promote manufacturing there. One of the best things America could do for Africa would be to strengthen our program to encourage African imports, called AGOA, and nudge Europe to match it.

Among people who work in development, many strongly believe (but few 15 dare say very loudly) that one of the best hopes for the poorest countries would be to build their manufacturing industries. But global campaigns against sweatshops make that less likely.

Look, I know that Americans have a hard time accepting that sweatshops 16 can help people. But take it from 13-year-old Neuo Chanthou, who earns a bit less than $1 a day scavenging in the dump. She's wearing a "Playboy" shirt and hat that she found amid the filth, and she worries about her sister, who lost part of her hand when a garbage truck ran over her.

"It's dirty, hot, and smelly here," she said wistfully. "A factory is better."   17

SAVE FREEDOM OF SPEECH

BUY WAR BONDS

Understanding Logic and Recognizing Logical Fallacies

How Free Should Free Speech Be?

Ask almost anyone what makes a society free and one of the answers will be free speech. The free expression of ideas is integral to freedom itself, and protecting that freedom is part of a democratic government's job: in a sense, this means that most people see free speech as one of the cornerstones of equality. Everyone's opinion can, and indeed must, be heard.

But what happens when those opinions are offensive, or even dangerous? If free speech has limits, is it still free? When we consider the question abstractly, it's very easy to say no. How can it be free if there are limits to how free it is, and who gets to decide those limits? It's dangerous to give anyone that kind of authority. After all, there is no shortage of historical evidence linking censorship with tyranny. When we think of limiting free speech, we think of totalitarian regimes, like Nazi Germany.

But what happens when the people arguing for the right to be heard are Nazis themselves? In places like Israel and France, where the legacy of Nazi Germany is still all too real, there are some

things you simply cannot say. Anti-Semitic language is considered "hate speech," and those who perpetuate it face stiff fines, if not imprisonment. It might seem outrageous to those of us who live in the United States. If you live in Israel, however, chances are that the legacy of the Holocaust is not that far away. And there are people in France who can still remember the day Nazi troops marched into Paris. Should they have to listen to what neo-Nazis have to say?

On American college campuses, free speech is often considered fundamental to a liberal education, and in many ways, encountering ideas that make you feel uncomfortable is a necessary part of a college education. But the question of free speech is easy to answer when it's theoretical: when the issue is made tangible by racist language or by a discussion of a traumatic experience, it becomes much more difficult to navigate. For example, should African-American students have to listen to "the n-word" in a discussion of *Huckleberry Finn*? Should a nineteen-year-old rape survivor have to sit through a

(*continued*)

(continued)

discussion of rape in American literature? Advocates of unlimited free speech respond to these objections by pointing out that censorship is a slippery slope: once you can penalize a person for saying something hateful, there will be no end to the subjects that will be off-limits.

Later in this chapter, you will be asked to think more about this issue. You will be given several sources to consider and asked to write a logical argument that takes a position on how free free speech should be.

The word *logic* comes from the Greek word *logos*, roughly translated as "word," "thought," "principle," or "reason." **Logic** is concerned with the principles of correct reasoning. By studying logic, you learn the rules that determine the validity of arguments. In other words, logic enables you to tell whether a conclusion correctly follows from a set of statements or assumptions.

Why should you study logic? One answer is that logic enables you to make valid points and draw sound conclusions. An understanding of logic also enables you to evaluate the arguments of others. When you understand the basic principles of logic, you know how to tell the difference between a strong argument and a weak argument—between one that is well reasoned and one that is not. This ability can help you cut through the tangle of jumbled thought that characterizes many of the arguments you encounter daily—on television, radio, and the Internet; in the press; and from friends. Finally, logic enables you to communicate clearly and forcefully. Understanding the characteristics of good arguments helps you to present your own ideas in a coherent and even compelling way.

Kobe Bryant, who played for the Los Angeles Lakers, arguing with a referee

Mark Ralston/Getty

Specific rules determine the criteria you use to develop (and to evaluate) arguments logically. For this reason, you should become familiar with the basic principles of *deductive* and *inductive reasoning*—two important ways information is organized in argumentative essays. (Keep in mind that a single argumentative essay might contain both deductive reasoning and inductive reasoning. For the sake of clarity, however, we will discuss them separately.)

What Is Deductive Reasoning?

Most of us use deductive reasoning every day—at home, in school, on the job, and in our communities—usually without even realizing it.

Deductive reasoning begins with **premises**—statements or assumptions on which an argument is based or from which conclusions are drawn. Deductive reasoning moves from general statements, or premises, to specific conclusions. The process of deduction has traditionally been illustrated with a **syllogism**, which consists of a *major premise*, a *minor premise*, and a *conclusion*:

Thomas Jefferson

MAJOR PREMISE	All Americans are guaranteed freedom of speech by the Constitution.
MINOR PREMISE	Sarah is an American.
CONCLUSION	Therefore, Sarah is guaranteed freedom of speech.

A syllogism begins with a **major premise**—a general statement that relates two terms. It then moves to a **minor premise**—an example of the statement that was made in the major premise. If these two premises are linked correctly, a **conclusion** that is supported by the two premises logically follows. (Notice that the conclusion in the syllogism above contains no terms that do not appear in the major and minor premises.) The strength of deductive reasoning is that if readers accept the major and minor premises, the conclusion must necessarily follow.

Thomas Jefferson used deductive reasoning in the Declaration of Independence. When, in 1776, the Continental Congress asked him to draft this document, Jefferson knew that he had to write a powerful argument that would convince the world that the American colonies were justified in breaking away from England. He knew how compelling a deductive argument could be, and so he organized the Declaration of Independence to reflect the traditional structure of deductive logic. It contains a major premise, a minor premise (supported by evidence), and a conclusion. Expressed as a syllogism, here is the argument that Jefferson used:

MAJOR PREMISE	When a government oppresses people, the people have a right to rebel against that government.
MINOR PREMISE	The government of England oppresses the American people.
CONCLUSION	Therefore, the American people have the right to rebel against the government of England.

In practice, deductive arguments are more complicated than the simple three-part syllogism suggests. Still, it is important to understand the basic structure of a syllogism because a syllogism enables you to map out your argument, to test it, and to see if it makes sense.

Constructing Sound Syllogisms

A syllogism is **valid** when its conclusion follows logically from its premises. A syllogism is **true** when the premises are consistent with the facts. To be **sound**, a syllogism must be *both* valid and true.

Consider the following valid syllogism:

MAJOR PREMISE	All state universities must accommodate disabled students.
MINOR PREMISE	UCLA is a state university.
CONCLUSION	Therefore, UCLA must accommodate disabled students.

In the valid syllogism above, both the major premise and the minor premise are factual statements. If both these premises are true, then the conclusion must also be true. Because the syllogism is both valid and true, it is also sound.

However, a syllogism can be valid without being true. For example, look at the following syllogism:

MAJOR PREMISE	All recipients of support services are wealthy.
MINOR PREMISE	Dillon is a recipient of support services.
CONCLUSION	Therefore, Dillon is wealthy.

As illogical as it may seem, this syllogism is valid: its conclusion follows logically from its premises. The major premise states that *recipients of support services*—all such *recipients*—are wealthy. However, this premise is clearly false: some recipients of support services may be wealthy, but more are probably not. For this reason, even though the syllogism is valid, it is not true.

Keep in mind that validity is a test of an argument's structure, not of its soundness. Even if a syllogism's major and minor premises are true, its conclusion may not necessarily be valid.

Consider the following examples of invalid syllogisms.

Syllogism with an Illogical Middle Term

A syllogism with an illogical middle term cannot be valid. The **middle term** of a syllogism is the term that occurs in both the major and minor premises but not in the conclusion. (It links the major term and the minor term together in the syllogism.) A middle term of a valid syllogism must refer to *all* members of the designated class or group—for example, *all* dogs, *all* people, *all* men, or *all* women.

Consider the following invalid syllogism:

MAJOR PREMISE   All dogs are mammals.

MINOR PREMISE   Some mammals are porpoises.

CONCLUSION   Therefore, some porpoises are dogs.

Even though the statements in the major and minor premises are true, the syllogism is not valid. *Mammals* is the middle term because it appears in both the major and minor premises. However, because the middle term *mammal* does not refer to *all mammals*, it cannot logically lead to a valid conclusion.

In the syllogism that follows, the middle term *does* refer to all members of the designated group, so the syllogism is valid:

MAJOR PREMISE	All dogs are mammals.
MINOR PREMISE	Ralph is a dog.
CONCLUSION	Therefore, Ralph is a mammal.

Syllogism with a Key Term Whose Meaning Shifts

A syllogism that contains a key term whose meaning shifts cannot be valid. For this reason, the meaning of a key term must remain consistent throughout the syllogism.

Consider the following invalid syllogism:

MAJOR PREMISE	Only man is capable of analytical reasoning.
MINOR PREMISE	Anna is not a man.
CONCLUSION	Therefore, Anna is not capable of analytical reasoning.

In the major premise, *man* refers to mankind—that is, to all human beings. In the minor premise, however, *man* refers to males. In the following valid syllogism, the key terms remain consistent:

MAJOR PREMISE	All educated human beings are capable of analytical reasoning.
MINOR PREMISE	Anna is an educated human being.
CONCLUSION	Therefore, Anna is capable of analytical reasoning.

Syllogism with Negative Premise

If *either* premise in a syllogism is negative, then the conclusion must also be negative.

The following syllogism is not valid:

MAJOR PREMISE	Only senators can vote on legislation.
MINOR PREMISE	No students are senators.
CONCLUSION	Therefore, students can vote on legislation.

Because one of the premises of the syllogism above is negative ("No students are senators"), the only possible valid conclusion must also be negative ("Therefore, no students can vote on legislation").

If *both* premises are negative, however, the syllogism cannot have a valid conclusion:

MAJOR PREMISE	Disabled students may not be denied special help.
MINOR PREMISE	Jen is not a disabled student.
CONCLUSION	Therefore, Jen may not be denied special help.

In the syllogism above, both premises are negative. For this reason, the syllogism cannot have a valid conclusion. (How can Jen deserve special help if she is not a disabled student?) To have a valid conclusion, this syllogism must have only one negative premise:

MAJOR PREMISE	Disabled students may not be denied special help.
MINOR PREMISE	Jen is a disabled student.
CONCLUSION	Therefore, Jen may not be denied special help.

Recognizing Enthymemes

An **enthymeme** is a syllogism with one or two parts of its argument—usually, the major premise—missing. In everyday life, we often leave out parts of arguments—most of the time because we think they are so obvious (or clearly implied) that they don't need to be stated. We assume that the people hearing or reading the arguments will easily be able to fill in the missing parts.

Many enthymemes are presented as a conclusion plus a reason. Consider the following enthymeme:

Robert has lied, so he cannot be trusted.

In the statement above, the minor premise and the conclusion are stated, but the major premise is only implied. Once the missing term has been supplied, the logical structure of the enthymeme becomes clear:

MAJOR PREMISE	People who lie cannot be trusted.
MINOR PREMISE	Robert has lied.
CONCLUSION	Therefore, Robert cannot be trusted.

It is important to identify enthymemes in arguments you read because some writers, knowing that readers often accept enthymemes uncritically, use them intentionally to unfairly influence readers.

Consider this enthymeme:

Because Liz receives a tuition grant, she should work.

Although some readers might challenge this statement, others will accept it uncritically. When you supply the missing premise, however, the underlying assumptions of the enthymeme become clear—and open to question:

MAJOR PREMISE   All students who receive tuition grants should work.

MINOR PREMISE   Liz receives a tuition grant.

CONCLUSION   Therefore, Liz should work.

Perhaps some people who receive tuition grants should work, but should everyone? What about those who are ill or who have disabilities? What about those who participate in varsity sports or have unpaid internships? The enthymeme oversimplifies the issue and should not be accepted at face value.

At first glance, the following enthymeme might seem to make sense:

North Korea is ruled by a dictator, so it should be invaded.

However, consider the same enthymeme with the missing term supplied:

MAJOR PREMISE   All countries governed by dictators should be invaded.

MINOR PREMISE   North Korea is a country governed by a dictator.

CONCLUSION   Therefore, North Korea should be invaded.

Once the missing major premise has been supplied, the flaws in the argument become clear. Should *all* nations governed by dictators be invaded? Who should do the invading? Who would make this decision? What would be the consequences of such a policy? As this enthymeme illustrates, if the major premise of a deductive argument is questionable, then the rest of the argument will also be flawed.

BUMPER-STICKER THINKING

Bumper stickers often take the form of enthymemes:

- Self-control beats birth control.

- Peace is patriotic.

- A woman's place is in the House . . . and in the Senate.

- Ban cruel traps.

- Evolution is a theory—kind of like gravity.

- I work and pay taxes so wealthy people don't have to.
- The Bible says it, I believe it, that settles it.
- No one needs a mink coat except a mink.
- Celebrate diversity.

Most often, bumper stickers state just the conclusion of an argument and omit both the major and minor premises. Careful readers, however, will supply the missing premises and thus determine whether the argument is sound.

Bumper stickers on a car. © Dave G. Houser/Corbis.

⊜ EXERCISE 5.1

Read the following paragraph. Then, restate its main argument as a syllogism.

Drunk Driving Should Be Legalized

In ordering states to enforce tougher drunk driving standards by making it a crime to drive with a blood-alcohol concentration of .08 percent or higher, government has been permitted to criminalize the content of drivers' blood instead of their actions. The assumption that a driver who has been drinking automatically presents a danger to society even when no harm has been caused is a blatant violation of civil liberties. Government should not be concerned with the probability and propensity of a drinking driver to cause an accident; rather, laws should deal only with actions that damage person or property. Until they actually commit a crime, drunk drivers should be liberated from the force of the law. (From "Legalize Drunk Driving," by Llewellyn H. Rockwell Jr., WorldNetDaily.com)

⊘ EXERCISE 5.2

Read the following paragraphs. Then, answer the questions that follow.

Animals Are Equal to Humans

According to the United Nations, a person may not be killed, exploited, cruelly treated, intimidated, or imprisoned for no good reason. Put another way, people should be able to live in peace, according to their own needs and preferences.

Who should have these rights? Do they apply to people of all races? Children? People who are brain damaged or senile? The declaration makes it clear that basic rights apply to everyone. To make a slave of someone who is intellectually handicapped or of a different race is no more justifiable than to make a slave of anyone else.

The reason why these rights apply to everyone is simple: regardless of our differences, we all experience a life with its mosaic of thoughts and feelings. This applies equally to the princess and the hobo, the brain surgeon and the dunce. Our value as individuals arises from this capacity to experience life, not because of any intelligence or usefulness to others. Every person has an inherent value, and deserves to be treated with respect in order to make the most of their unique life experience. (Excerpted from "Human and Animal Rights," by Animal Liberation.org)

1. What unstated assumptions about the subject does the writer make? Does the writer expect readers to accept these assumptions? How can you tell?

2. What kind of supporting evidence does the writer provide?

3. What is the major premise of this argument?

4. Express the argument that is presented in these paragraphs as a syllogism.

5. Evaluate the syllogism you constructed. Is it true? Is it valid? Is it sound?

⊘ EXERCISE 5.3

Read the following five arguments, and determine whether each is sound. (To help you evaluate the arguments, you may want to try arranging them as syllogisms.)

1. All humans are mortal. Max is human. Therefore, Max is mortal.

2. Alison should order eggs or oatmeal for breakfast. She won't order eggs, so she should order oatmeal.

3. The cafeteria does not serve meat loaf on Friday. Today is not Friday. Therefore, the cafeteria will not serve meat loaf.

4. All reptiles are cold-blooded. Geckos are reptiles. Therefore, geckos are cold-blooded.

5. All triangles have three equal sides. The figure on the board is a triangle. Therefore, it must have three equal sides.

● EXERCISE 5.4

Read the following ten enthymemes, which come from bumper stickers. Supply the missing premises, and then evaluate the logic of each argument.

1. If you love your pet, don't eat meat.

2. War is terrorism.

3. Real men don't ask for directions.

4. Immigration is the sincerest form of flattery.

5. I eat local because I can.

6. Don't blame me; I voted for the other guy.

7. I read banned books.

8. Love is the only solution.

9. It's a child, not a choice.

10. Think. It's patriotic.

Writing Deductive Arguments

Deductive arguments begin with a general principle and reach a specific conclusion. They develop that principle with logical arguments that are supported by evidence—facts, observations, the opinions of experts, and so on. Keep in mind that no single structure is suitable for all deductive (or inductive) arguments. Different issues and different audiences will determine how you arrange your ideas.

In general, deductive essays can be structured in the following way:

INTRODUCTION	Presents an overview of the issue
	States the thesis
BODY	Presents evidence: point 1 in support of the thesis
	Presents evidence: point 2 in support of the thesis
	Presents evidence: point 3 in support of the thesis
	Refutes the arguments against the thesis
CONCLUSION	Brings argument to a close
	Concluding statement reinforces the thesis

> **EXERCISE 5.5**
>
> The following student essay, "College Should Be for Everyone," includes all the elements of a deductive argument. The student who wrote this essay was responding to the question, "Should everyone be encouraged to go to college?" After you read the essay, answer the questions on pages 136–137, consulting the outline on page 133 if necessary.

COLLEGE SHOULD BE FOR EVERYONE

CRYSTAL SANCHEZ

Overview of issue	Until the middle of the twentieth century, college was largely for the rich. The G.I. Bill, which paid for the education of veterans returning from World War II, helped to change this situation. By 1956, nearly half of those who had served in World War II, almost 7.8 million people, had taken advantage of this benefit (U.S. Department of Veterans Affairs). Even today, however, college graduates are still a minority of the population. According to the U.S. Census Bureau, only 27.5 percent of Americans age twenty-five or older have a bachelor's degree. In many ways, this situation is not good for the country. Why should college be just for the privi-
Thesis statement	leged few? Because a college education provides important benefits, such as increased wages for our citizens and a stronger democracy for our nation, every U.S. citizen should have the opportunity to attend college.
Evidence: Point 1	One reason everyone should have the opportunity to go to college is that a college education gives people a chance to discover what they are good at. It is hard for people to know if they are interested in statistics or public policy or marketing unless they have the chance to explore these sub- jects. College—and only college—can give them this opportunity. Where else can a person be exposed to a large number of courses taught by experts in a variety of disciplines? Such exposure can open new areas of interest and lead to a much wider set of career options—and thus to a better life (Stout). Without college, most people have limited options and never realize their true potential. Although life and work experiences can teach a person a lot of things, the best education is the broad kind that college offers.
Evidence: Point 2	Another reason everyone should have the opportunity to go to college is that more and more jobs are being phased out or moved over- seas. Americans should go to college to develop the skills that they will

1

2

3

need to get the best jobs that will remain in the United States. Over the last few decades, midlevel jobs have been steadily disappearing. If this trend continues, the American workforce will be divided in two. One part will consist of low-wage, low-skill service jobs, such as those in food preparation and retail sales, and the other part will be high-skill, high-wage jobs, such as those in management and professional fields like business and engineering. According to a recent report, to compete in the future job market, Americans will need the skills that colleges teach. Future workers will need to be problem solvers who can think both critically and creatively and who can adapt to unpredictable situations. They will also need a global awareness, knowledge of many cultures and disciplines, and the ability to communicate in different forms of media. To master these skills, Americans have to be college educated ("Ten Skills for the Future Workforce").

Perhaps the best reason everyone should have the opportunity to go to college is that education is an essential component of a democratic society. Those without the ability to understand and analyze news reports are not capable of contributing to the social, political, and economic growth of the country. Democracy requires informed citizens who will be able to analyze complicated issues in areas such as finance, education, and public health; weigh competing claims of those running for public office; and assess the job performance of elected officials. By providing students with the opportunity to study subjects such as history, philosophy, English, and political science, colleges and universities help them to acquire the critical-thinking skills that they will need to participate fully in American democracy.

4   Evidence: Point 3

Some people oppose the idea that everyone should have the opportunity to attend college. One objection is that educational resources are limited. Some say that if students enter colleges in great numbers they will overwhelm the higher-education system (Stout). This argument exaggerates the problem. As with any other product, if demand rises, supply will rise to meet that demand. In addition, with today's extensive distance-learning options and the availability of open educational resources—free, high-quality, digital materials—it will be possible to educate large numbers of students at a reasonable cost ("Open Educational Resources"). Another objection to encouraging everyone to attend college is that underprepared students will require so much help that they will take time and attention away from better students. This argument is actually a red herring.° Most schools already provide resources, such as tutoring and

5   Refutation of opposing arguments

An irrelevant side issue used as a diversion

136   **Part 2**   Reading and Responding to Arguments

writing centers, for students who need them. With some additional funding, these schools could expand the services they already provide. This
course of action will be expensive, but it is a lot less expensive than leaving millions of young people unprepared for jobs of the future.

A college education gave the returning veterans of World War II   6
many opportunities and increased their value to the nation. Today, a college education could do the same for many citizens. This country has an
obligation to offer all students access to an affordable and useful education. Not only will the students benefit personally, but the nation will also.

Concluding statement

If we do not adequately prepare students for the future, then we will all
suffer the consequences.

Works Cited

"Open Educational Resources." *Center for American Progress*, 7 Feb.
2012, www.americanprogress.org/issues/labor/news/2012
/02/07/11114/open-educational-resources/.

Stout, Chris. "Top Five Reasons Why You Should Choose to Go to College." *Ezine Articles*, 2008, ezinearticles.com/?Top-Five-Reasons-
Why-You-Should-Choose-To-Go-To-College&id=384395.

"Ten Skills for the Future Workforce." *The Atlantic,* 22 June 2011,
www.theatlantic.com/education/archive/2011/06/ten-skills-for-future
-work/473484/.

United States, Census Bureau. "Bachelor's Degree Attainment Tops 30
Percent for the First Time, Census Bureau Reports." *US Census
Bureau Newsroom*, 23 Feb. 2012, www.census.gov/newsroom
/releases/archives/education/cb12-33.html.

---, Department of Veterans Affairs. "Born of Controversy: The GI Bill of
Rights." *GI Bill History*, 20 Oct. 2008, www.va.gov/opa/publications
/celebrate/gi-bill.pdf.

Identifying the Elements of a Deductive Argument

1. Paraphrase this essay's thesis.

2. What arguments does the writer present as evidence to support her
thesis? Which do you think is the strongest argument? Which is the
weakest?

3. What opposing arguments does the writer address? What other
opposing arguments could she have addressed?

4. What points does the conclusion emphasize? Do you think that any other points should be emphasized?

5. Construct a syllogism that expresses the essay's argument. Then, check your syllogism to make sure it is sound.

What Is Inductive Reasoning?

Inductive reasoning begins with specific observations (or evidence) and goes on to draw a general conclusion. You can see how induction works by looking at the following list of observations:

- Nearly 80 percent of ocean pollution comes from runoff.

- Runoff pollution can make ocean water unsafe for fish and people.

- In some areas, runoff pollution has forced beaches to be closed.

- Drinking water can be contaminated by runoff.

- More than one third of shellfish growing in waters in the United States are contaminated by runoff.

- Each year, millions of dollars are spent to restore polluted areas.

- There is a causal relationship between agricultural runoff and water-borne organisms that damage fish.

After studying these observations, you can use inductive reasoning to reach the conclusion that runoff pollution (rainwater that becomes polluted after

Sign warning of contaminated water

© Krista Kennella/ZUMA PRESS

it comes in contact with earth-bound pollutants such as fertilizer, pet waste, sewage, and pesticides) is a problem that must be addressed.

Children learn about the world by using inductive reasoning. For example, very young children see that if they push a light switch up, the lights in a room go on. If they repeat this action over and over, they reach the conclusion that every time they push a switch, the lights will go on. Of course, this conclusion does not always follow. For example, the light bulb may be burned out or the switch may be damaged. Even so, their conclusion usually holds true. Children also use induction to generalize about what is safe and what is dangerous. If every time they meet a dog, the encounter is pleasant, they begin to think that all dogs are friendly. If at some point, however, a dog snaps at them, they question the strength of their conclusion and modify their behavior accordingly.

Scientists also use induction. In 1620, Sir Francis Bacon first proposed the **scientific method**—a way of using induction to find answers to questions. When using the scientific method, a researcher proposes a hypothe-

REACHING INDUCTIVE CONCLUSIONS

Here are some of the ways you can use inductive reasoning to reach conclusions:

- **Particular to general:** This form of induction occurs when you reach a general conclusion based on particular pieces of evidence. For example, suppose you walk into a bathroom and see that the mirrors are fogged. You also notice that the bathtub has drops of water on its sides and that the bathroom floor is wet. In addition, you see a damp towel draped over the sink. Putting all these observations together, you conclude that someone has recently taken a bath. (Detectives use induction when gathering clues to solve a crime.)

- **General to general:** This form of induction occurs when you draw a conclusion based on the consistency of your observations. For example, if you determine that Apple Inc. has made good products for a long time, you conclude it will continue to make good products.

- **General to particular:** This form of induction occurs when you draw a conclusion based on what you generally know to be true. For example, if you believe that cars made by the Ford Motor Company are reliable, then you conclude that a Ford Focus will be a reliable car.

- **Particular to particular:** This form of induction occurs when you assume that because something works in one situation, it will also work in another similar situation. For example, if Krazy Glue fixed the broken handle of one cup, then you conclude it will probably fix the broken handle of another cup.

sis and then makes a series of observations to test this hypothesis. Based on these observations, the researcher arrives at a conclusion that confirms, modifies, or disproves the hypothesis.

Making Inferences

Unlike deduction, which reaches a conclusion based on information provided by the major and minor premises, induction uses what you know to make a statement about something that you don't know. While deductive arguments can be judged in absolute terms (they are either **valid** or **invalid**), inductive arguments are judged in relative terms (they are either **strong** or **weak**).

You reach an inductive conclusion by making an **inference**—a statement about what is unknown based on what is known. (In other words, you look at the evidence and try to figure out what is going on.) For this reason, there is always a gap between your observations and your conclusion. To bridge this gap, you have to make an **inductive leap**—a stretch of the imagination that enables you to draw an acceptable conclusion. Therefore, inductive conclusions are never certain (as deductive conclusions are) but only probable. The more evidence you provide, the stronger and more probable your conclusions (and your argument) are.

Public-opinion polls illustrate how inferences are used to reach inductive conclusions. Politicians and news organizations routinely use public-opinion polls to assess support (or lack of support) for a particular policy, proposal, or political candidate. After surveying a sample population—registered voters, for example—pollsters reach conclusions based on their responses. In other words, by asking questions and studying the responses of a sample group of people, pollsters make inferences about the larger group—for example, which political candidate is ahead and by how much. How solid these inferences are depends to a great extent on the sample populations the pollsters survey. In an election, for example, a poll of randomly chosen individuals will be less accurate than a poll of registered voters or likely voters. In addition, other factors (such as the size of the sample and the way questions are worded) can determine the relative strength of the inductive conclusion.

As with all inferences, a gap exists between a poll's data—the responses to the questions—and the conclusion. The larger and more representative the sample, the smaller the inductive leap necessary to reach a conclusion and the more accurate the poll. If the gap between the data and the conclusion is too big, however, the pollsters will be accused of making a **hasty generalization** (see p. 150). Remember, no matter how much support you present, an inductive conclusion is only probable, never certain. The best you can do is present a convincing case and hope that your audience will accept it.

Constructing Strong Inductive Arguments

When you use inductive reasoning, your conclusion is only as strong as the **evidence**—the facts, details, or examples—that you use to support it. For this reason, you should be on the lookout for the following problems that can occur when you try to reach an inductive conclusion.

Generalization Too Broad

The conclusion you state cannot go beyond the scope of your evidence. Your evidence must support your generalization. For instance, you cannot survey just three international students in your school and conclude that the school does not go far enough to accommodate international students. To reach such a conclusion, you would have to consider a large number of international students.

Insufficient Evidence

The evidence on which you base an inductive conclusion must be **representative**, not atypical or biased. For example, you cannot conclude that students are satisfied with the course offerings at your school by sampling just first-year students. To be valid, your conclusion should be based on responses from a cross section of students from all years.

Irrelevant Evidence

Your evidence has to support your conclusion. If it does not, it is **irrelevant**. For example, if you assert that many adjunct faculty members make substantial contributions to your school, your supporting examples must be adjunct faculty, not tenured or junior faculty.

Exceptions to the Rule

There is always a chance that you will overlook an exception that may affect the strength of your conclusion. For example, not everyone who has a disability needs special accommodations, and not everyone who requires special accommodations needs the same services. For this reason, you should avoid using words like *every*, *all*, and *always* and instead use words like *most*, *many*, and *usually*.

⊙ EXERCISE 5.6

Read the following arguments, and decide whether each is a deductive argument or an inductive argument and write "D" or "I" on the lines below.

1. Freedom of speech is a central principle of our form of government. For this reason, students should be allowed to wear T-shirts that call for the legalization of marijuana. _____

2. The Chevy Cruze Eco gets twenty-seven miles a gallon in the city and forty-six miles a gallon on the highway. The Honda Accord gets twenty-seven miles a gallon in the city and thirty-six miles a gallon on the highway. Therefore, it makes more sense for me to buy the Chevy Cruze Eco. _____

3. In Edgar Allan Poe's short story "The Cask of Amontillado," Montresor flatters Fortunato. He lures him to his vaults where he stores wine. Montresor then gets Fortunato drunk and chains him to the wall of a crypt. Finally, Montresor uncovers a pile of building material and walls up the entrance to the crypt. Clearly, Montresor has carefully planned to murder Fortunato for a very long time. _____

4. All people should have the right to die with dignity. Garrett is a terminally ill patient, so he should have access to doctor-assisted suicide. _____

5. Last week, we found unacceptably high levels of pollution in the ocean. On Monday, we also found high levels of pollution. Today, we found even higher levels of pollution. We should close the ocean beaches to swimmers until we can find the source of this problem. _____

⊘ EXERCISE 5.7

Read the following arguments. Then, decide whether they are deductive or inductive. If they are inductive arguments, evaluate their strength. If they are deductive arguments, evaluate their soundness.

1. *The Farmer's Almanac* says that this winter will be very cold. The National Weather Service also predicts that this winter will be very cold. So, this should be a cold winter.

2. Many walled towns in Europe do not let people drive cars into their centers. San Gimignano is a walled town in Europe. It is likely that we will not be able to drive our car into its center.

3. The window at the back of the house is broken. There is a baseball on the floor. A few minutes ago, I saw two boys playing catch in a neighbor's yard. They must have thrown the ball through the window.

4. Every time I go to the beach I get sunburned. I guess I should stop going to the beach.

5. All my instructors have advanced degrees. George Martin is one of my instructors. Therefore, George Martin has an advanced degree.

6. My last two boyfriends cheated on me. All men are terrible.

7. I read a study published by a pharmaceutical company that said that Accutane was safe. Maybe the government was too quick to pull this drug off the market.

8. Chase is not very good-looking, and he dresses badly. I don't know how he can be a good architect.

9. No fictional character has ever had a fan club. Harry Potter does, but he is the exception.

10. Two weeks ago, my instructor refused to accept a late paper. She did the same thing last week. Yesterday, she also told someone that because his paper was late, she wouldn't accept it. I'd better get my paper in on time.

⊙ EXERCISE 5.8

Read the inductive paragraph below, written by student Pooja Vaidya, and answer the questions that follow it.

Years ago, when my friend took me to a game between the Philadelphia Eagles and the Dallas Cowboys in Philadelphia, I learned a little bit about American football and a lot about the behavior of football fans. Many of the Philadelphia fans were dressed in green and white football jerseys, each with a player's name and number on the back. One fan had his face painted green and wore a green cape with a large white *E* on it. He ran up and down the aisles in his section and led cheers. When the team was ahead, everyone joined in. When the team fell behind, this fan literally fell on his knees, cried, and begged the people in the stands to support the Eagles. (After the game, several people asked him for his autograph.) A group of six fans sat without shirts. They wore green wigs, and each had one letter of the team's name painted on his bare chest. Even though the temperature was below freezing, none of these fans ever put on his shirt. Before the game, many fans had been drinking at tailgate parties in the parking lot, and as the game progressed, they continued to drink beer in the stadium. By the beginning of the second half, fights were breaking out all over the stadium. Guards grabbed the people who were fighting and escorted them to a holding area under the stadium where a judge held "Eagles Court." At one point, a fan wearing a Dallas jersey tried to sit down in the row behind me. Some of the Eagles fans were so threatening that the police had to escort the Dallas fan out of the stands for his own protection. When the game ended in an Eagles victory, the fans sang the team's fight song as they left the stadium. I concluded that for many

Eagles fans, a day at the stadium is an opportunity to engage in behavior that in any other context would be unacceptable and even abnormal.

1. Which of the following statements could you *not* conclude from this paragraph?

    a. All Eagles fans act in outrageous ways at games.

    b. At football games, the fans in the stands can be as violent as the players on the field.

    c. The atmosphere at the stadium causes otherwise normal people to act abnormally.

    d. Spectator sports encourage fans to act in abnormal ways.

    e. Some people get so caught up in the excitement of a game that they act in uncharacteristic ways.

2. Paraphrase the writer's conclusion. What evidence is provided to support this conclusion?

3. What additional evidence could the writer have provided? Is this additional evidence necessary, or does the conclusion stand without it?

4. The writer makes an inductive leap to reach the paragraph's conclusion. Do you think this leap is too great?

5. Does this paragraph make a strong inductive argument? Why or why not?

Philadelphia Eagles fans

© Chris Graythen/Getty Images Sports

Writing Inductive Arguments

Inductive arguments begin with evidence (specific facts, observations, expert opinion, and so on), draw inferences from the evidence, and reach a conclusion by making an inductive leap. Keep in mind that inductive arguments are only as strong as the link between the evidence and the conclusion, so the stronger this link is, the stronger the argument will be.

Inductive essays frequently have the following structure:

INTRODUCTION	Presents the issue
	States the thesis
BODY	Presents evidence: facts, observations, expert opinion, and so on
	Draws inferences from the evidence
	Refutes the arguments against the thesis
CONCLUSION	Brings argument to a close
	Concluding statement reinforces the thesis

⊖ EXERCISE 5.9

The following essay includes all the elements of an inductive argument. After you read the essay, answer the questions on page 146, consulting the outline above if necessary.

This essay appeared in *Slate* on September 2, 2006.

PLEASE DO NOT FEED THE HUMANS

WILLIAM SALETAN

Dug

In 1894, Congress established Labor Day to honor those who "from rude 1 nature have delved° and carved all the grandeur we behold." In the century since, the grandeur of human achievement has multiplied. Over the past four decades, global population has doubled, but food output, driven by increases in productivity, has outpaced it. Poverty, infant mortality, and hunger are receding. For the first time in our planet's history, a species no longer lives at the mercy of scarcity. We have learned to feed ourselves.

We've learned so well, in fact, that we're getting fat. Not just the United 2 States or Europe, but the whole world. Egyptian, Mexican, and South African women are now as fat as Americans. Far more Filipino adults are now overweight than underweight. In China, one in five adults is too heavy, and the rate of overweight children is 28 times higher than it was two decades ago. In Thailand, Kuwait, and Tunisia, obesity, diabetes, and heart disease are soaring.

Hunger is far from conquered. But since 1990, the global rate of malnutri- 3 tion has declined an average of 1.7 percent a year. Based on data from the World Health Organization and the U.N. Food and Agriculture Organization, for every two people who are malnourished, three are now overweight or obese. Among women, even in most African countries, overweight has surpassed underweight. The balance of peril is shifting.

Fat is no longer a rich man's disease. For middle- and high-income Amer- 4 icans, the obesity rate is 29 percent. For low-income Americans, it's 35 percent. Among middle- and high-income kids aged 15 to 17, the rate of overweight is 14 percent. Among low-income kids in the same age bracket, it's 23 percent. Globally, weight has tended to rise with income. But a study in Vancouver, Canada, published three months ago, found that preschoolers in "food-insecure" households were twice as likely as other kids to be overweight or obese. In Brazilian cities, the poor have become fatter than the rich.

Technologically, this is a triumph. In the early days of our species, even the 5 rich starved. Barry Popkin, a nutritional epidemiologist at the University of North Carolina, divides history into several epochs. In the hunter-gatherer era, if we didn't find food, we died. In the agricultural era, if our crops perished, we died. In the industrial era, famine receded, but infectious diseases killed us. Now we've achieved such control over nature that we're dying not of starvation or infection, but of abundance. Nature isn't killing us. We're killing ourselves.

You don't have to go hungry anymore; we can fill you with fats and carbs 6 more cheaply than ever. You don't have to chase your food; we can bring it to you. You don't have to cook it; we can deliver it ready-to-eat. You don't have to eat it before it spoils; we can pump it full of preservatives so it lasts forever. You don't even have to stop when you're full. We've got so much food to sell, we want you to keep eating.

What happened in America is happening everywhere, only faster. Fewer 7 farmers' markets, more processed food. Fewer whole grains, more refined ones. More sweeteners, salt, and trans fats. Cheaper meat, more animal fat. Less cooking, more eating out. Bigger portions, more snacks.

Kentucky Fried Chicken and Pizza Hut are spreading across the planet. 8 Coca-Cola is in more than 200 countries. Half of McDonald's business is overseas. In China, animal-fat intake has tripled in 20 years. By 2020, meat consumption in developing countries will grow by 106 million metric tons, outstripping growth in developed countries by a factor of more than five. Forty years ago, to afford a high-fat diet, your country needed a gross national product per capita of nearly $1,500. Now the price is half that. You no longer have to be rich to die a rich man's death.

Soon, it'll be a poor man's death. The rich have Whole Foods, gyms, and per- 9 sonal trainers. The poor have 7-Eleven, Popeye's, and streets unsafe for walking. When money's tight, you feed your kids at Wendy's and stock up on macaroni and cheese. At a lunch buffet, you do what your ancestors did: store all the fat you can.

That's the punch line: Technology has changed everything but us. We 10 evolved to survive scarcity. We crave fat. We're quick to gain weight and slow to lose it. Double what you serve us, and we'll double what we eat. Thanks to technology, the deprivation that made these traits useful is gone. So is the link between flavors and nutrients. The modern food industry can sell you sweetness without fruit, salt without protein, creaminess without milk. We can fatten you and starve you at the same time.

> "We evolved to survive scarcity."

And that's just the diet side of the equation. Before technology, adult men had 11 to expend about 3,000 calories a day. Now they expend about 2,000. Look at the new Segway scooter. The original model relieved you of the need to walk, pedal, or balance. With the new one, you don't even have to turn the handlebars or start it manually. In theory, Segway is replacing the car. In practice, it's replacing the body.

In country after country, service jobs are replacing hard labor. The folks 12 who field your customer service calls in Bangalore are sitting at desks. Nearly everyone in China has a television set. Remember when Chinese rode bikes? In the past six years, the number of cars there has grown from six million to 20 million. More than one in seven Chinese has a motorized vehicle, and households with such vehicles have an obesity rate 80 percent higher than their peers.

The answer to these trends is simple. We have to exercise more and 13 change the food we eat, donate, and subsidize. Next year, for example, the U.S. Women, Infants, and Children program, which subsidizes groceries for impoverished youngsters, will begin to pay for fruits and vegetables. For 32 years, the program has fed toddlers eggs and cheese but not one vegetable. And we wonder why poor kids are fat.

The hard part is changing our mentality. We have a distorted body image. 14 We're so used to not having enough, as a species, that we can't believe the problem is too much. From China to Africa to Latin America, people are trying to fatten their kids. I just got back from a vacation with my Jewish mother and Jewish mother-in-law. They told me I need to eat more.

The other thing blinding us is liberal guilt. We're so caught up in the idea 15 of giving that we can't see the importance of changing behavior rather than filling bellies. We know better than to feed buttered popcorn to zoo animals, yet we send it to a food bank and call ourselves humanitarians. Maybe we should ask what our fellow humans actually need.

Identifying the Elements of an Inductive Argument

1. What is this essay's thesis? Restate it in your own words.

2. Why do you think Saletan places the thesis where he does?

3. What evidence does Saletan use to support his conclusion?

4. What inductive leap does Saletan make to reach his conclusion? Do you think he should have included more evidence?

5. Overall, do you think Saletan's inductive argument is relatively strong or weak? Explain.

Recognizing Logical Fallacies

When you write arguments in college, you follow certain rules that ensure fairness. Not everyone who writes arguments is fair or thorough, however. Sometimes you will encounter arguments in which writers attack the opposition's intelligence or patriotism and base their arguments on questionable (or even false) assumptions. As convincing as these arguments can sometimes seem, they are not valid because they contain **fallacies**—errors in reasoning that undermine the logic of an argument. Familiarizing yourself with the most common logical fallacies can help you to evaluate the arguments of others and to construct better, more effective arguments of your own.

The following pages define and illustrate some logical fallacies that you should learn to recognize and avoid.

Begging the Question

The fallacy of **begging the question** assumes that a statement is self-evident (or true) when it actually requires proof. A conclusion based on such assumptions cannot be valid. For example, someone who is very religious could structure an argument the following way:

MAJOR PREMISE	Everything in the Bible is true.
MINOR PREMISE	The Bible says that Noah built an ark.
CONCLUSION	Therefore, Noah's Ark really existed.

A person can accept the conclusion of this syllogism only if he or she also accepts the major premise, which has not been proven true. Some people might find this line of reasoning convincing, but others would not—even if they were religious.

Begging the question occurs any time someone presents a debatable statement as if it were true. For example, look at the following statement:

> You have unfairly limited my right of free speech by refusing to print my editorial in the college newspaper.

This statement begs the question because it assumes what it should be proving—that refusing to print an editorial violates a person's right to free speech.

Circular Reasoning

Closely related to begging the question, **circular reasoning** occurs when someone supports a statement by restating it in different terms. Consider the following statement:

> Stealing is wrong because it is illegal.

Waterfall, by M. C. Escher. The artwork creates the illusion of water flowing uphill and in a circle. Circular reasoning occurs when the conclusion of an argument is the same as one of the premises.

The conclusion of the statement on the previous page is essentially the same as its beginning: stealing (which is illegal) is against the law. In other words, the argument goes in a circle.

Here are some other examples of circular reasoning:

- Lincoln was a great president because he is the best president we ever had.

- I am for equal rights for women because I am a feminist.

- Illegal immigrants should be deported because they are breaking the law.

All of the statements above have one thing in common: they attempt to support a statement by simply repeating the statement in different words.

Weak Analogy

An **analogy** is a comparison between two items (or concepts)—one familiar and one unfamiliar. When you make an analogy, you explain the unfamiliar item by comparing it to the familiar item.

Although analogies can be effective in arguments, they have limitations. For example, a senator who opposed a government bailout of the financial industry in 2008 made the following argument:

> This bailout is doomed from the start. It's like pouring milk into a leaking bucket. As long as you keep pouring milk, the bucket stays full. But when you stop, the milk runs out the hole in the bottom of the bucket. What we're doing is throwing money into a big bucket and not fixing the hole. We have to find the underlying problems that have caused this part of our economy to get in trouble and pass legislation to solve them.

The problem with using analogies such as this one is that analogies are never perfect. There is always a difference between the two things being compared. The larger this difference, the weaker the analogy—and the weaker the argument that it supports. For example, someone could point out to the senator that the financial industry—and by extension, the whole economy—is much more complex and multifaceted than a leaking bucket. To analyze the economy, the senator would have to expand his discussion beyond this single analogy (which cannot carry the weight of the entire argument) as well as supply the evidence to support his contention that the bailout was a mistake from the start.

Ad Hominem Fallacy (Personal Attack)

The **ad hominem fallacy** occurs when someone attacks the character or the motives of a person instead of focusing on the issues. This line of reasoning is illogical because it focuses attention on the person making the argument, sidestepping the argument itself.

Consider the following statement:

> Dr. Thomson, I'm not sure why we should believe anything you have to say about this community health center. Last year, you left your husband for another man.

The above attack on Dr. Thomson's character is irrelevant; it has nothing to do with her ideas about the community health center. Sometimes, however, a person's character may have a direct relation to the issue. For example, if Dr. Thomson had invested in a company that supplied medical equipment to the health center, this fact would have been relevant to the issue at hand.

The ad hominem fallacy also occurs when you attempt to undermine an argument by associating it with individuals who are easily attacked. For example, consider this statement:

> I think your plan to provide universal heath care is interesting. I'm sure Marx and Lenin would agree with you.

Instead of focusing on the specific provisions of the health-care plan, the opposition unfairly associates it with the ideas of Karl Marx and Vladimir Lenin, two well-known Communists.

Creating a Straw Man

This fallacy most likely got its name from the use of straw dummies in military and boxing training. When writers create a **straw man**, they present a weak argument that can easily be refuted. Instead of attacking the real issue, they focus on a weaker issue and give the impression that they have effectively refuted an opponent's argument. Frequently, the straw man is an extreme or oversimplified version of the opponent's actual position. For example, during a debate about raising the minimum wage, a senator made the following comment:

> Those who oppose raising the minimum wage are heartless. They obviously don't care if children starve.

The Granger Collection

Ad hominem attack against Charles Darwin, originator of the theory of evolution by natural selection

© SOTK2011/Alamy

Instead of focusing on the minimum wage, the senator misrepresents the opposing position so that it appears cruel. As this example shows, the straw man fallacy is dishonest because it intentionally distorts an opponent's position to mislead readers.

Hasty or Sweeping Generalization (Jumping to a Conclusion)

A **hasty or sweeping generalization** (also called **jumping to a conclusion**) occurs when someone reaches a conclusion that is based on too little evidence. Many people commit this fallacy without realizing it. For example, when Richard Nixon was elected president in 1972, film critic Pauline Kael is supposed to have remarked, "How can that be? No one I know voted for Nixon!" The general idea behind this statement is that if Kael's acquaintances didn't vote for Nixon, then neither did most other people. This assumption is flawed because it is based on a small sample.

Sometimes people make hasty generalizations because they strongly favor one point of view over another. At other times, a hasty generalization is simply the result of sloppy thinking. For example, it is easier for a student to simply say that an instructor is an unusually hard grader than to survey the instructor's classes to see if this conclusion is warranted (or to consider other reasons for his or her poor performance in a course).

Either/Or Fallacy (False Dilemma)

The **either/or fallacy** (also called a **false dilemma**) occurs when a person says that there are just two choices when there are actually more. In many cases, the person committing this fallacy tries to force a conclusion by presenting just two choices, one of which is clearly more desirable than the other. (Parents do this with young children all the time: "Eat your carrots, or go to bed.")

Politicians frequently engage in this fallacy. For example, according to some politicians, you are either pro-life or pro-choice, pro–gun control or anti–gun control, pro-stem-cell research or anti-stem-cell research. Many people, however, are actually somewhere in the middle, taking a much more nuanced approach to complicated issues.

Consider the following statement:

> I can't believe you voted against the bill to build a wall along the southern border of the United States. Either you're for protecting our border, or you're against it.

This statement is an example of the either/or fallacy. The person who voted against the bill might be against the wall but not against all immigration restrictions. The person might favor loose restrictions for some people (for example, migrant workers) and strong restrictions for others (for example, drug smugglers). By limiting the options to just two, the speaker oversimplifies the situation and attempts to force the listener to accept a fallacious argument.

© Ferhat/Shutterstock.com

The either/or fallacy occurs when a writer presents just two choices when there are actually more.

Equivocation

The fallacy of **equivocation** occurs when a key term has one meaning in one part of an argument and another meaning in another part. (When a term is used **unequivocally**, it has the same meaning throughout the argument.) Consider the following old joke:

> The sign said, "Fine for parking here," so because it was fine, I parked there.

Obviously, the word *fine* has two different meanings in this sentence. The first time it is used, it means "money paid as a penalty." The second time, it means "good" or "satisfactory."

Most words have more than one meaning, so it is important not to confuse the various meanings. For an argument to work, a key term has to have the same meaning every time it appears in the argument. If the meaning shifts during the course of the argument, then the argument cannot be sound.

Consider the following statement:

> This is supposed to be a free country, but nothing worth having is ever free.

In this statement, the meaning of a key term shifts. The first time the word *free* is used, it means "not under the control of another." The second time, it means "without charge."

Red Herring

This fallacy gets its name from the practice of dragging a smoked fish across the trail of a fox to mask its scent during a fox hunt. As a result, the hounds lose the scent and are thrown off the track. The **red herring** fallacy occurs when a person raises an irrelevant side issue to divert attention from the real issue. Used skillfully, this fallacy can distract an audience and change the focus of an argument.

Political campaigns are good sources of examples of the red herring fallacy. Consider this example from the 2016 presidential race:

> I know that Donald Trump says that he is for the "little guy," but he lives in a three-story penthouse in the middle of Manhattan. How can we believe that his policies will help the average American?

The focus of his argument should have been on Trump's policies, not on the fact that he lives in a penthouse.

Here is another red herring fallacy from the 2016 political campaign:

Person trying to follow the argument.

The actual issue being argued.

Red herring, a distraction not related to the argument.

> Hillary Clinton wants us to vote for her, but she will be sixty-nine when she becomes president. I think that this is a problem.

Again, the focus of these remarks should have been on Clinton's qualifications, not on her age.

Slippery Slope

The **slippery-slope** fallacy occurs when a person argues that one thing will inevitably result from another. (Other names for the slippery-slope fallacy are the **foot-in-the-door fallacy** and the **floodgates fallacy**.) Both these names suggest that once you permit certain acts, you inevitably permit additional acts that eventually lead to disastrous consequences. Typically, the slippery-slope fallacy presents a series of increasingly unacceptable events that lead to an inevitable, unpleasant conclusion. (Usually, there is no evidence that such a sequence will actually occur.)

We encounter examples of the slippery-slope fallacy almost daily. During a debate on same-sex marriage, for example, an opponent advanced this line of reasoning:

> If we allow gay marriage, then there is nothing to stop polygamy. And once we allow this, where will it stop? Will we have to legalize incest—or even bestiality?

Whether or not you support same-sex marriage, you should recognize the fallacy of this slippery-slope reasoning. By the last sentence of the passage above, the assertions have become so outrageous that they approach parody. People can certainly debate this issue, but not in such a dishonest and highly emotional way.

© Lon C. Diehl/Photoedit, Inc.

Beware the slippery-slope fallacy

You Also (Tu Quoque)

The **you also** fallacy asserts that a statement is false because it is inconsistent with what the speaker has said or done. In other words, a person is attacked for doing what he or she is arguing against. Parents often encounter this fallacy when they argue with their teenage children. By introducing an irrelevant point— "You did it too"—the children attempt to distract parents and put them on the defensive:

- How can you tell me not to smoke when you used to smoke?

- Don't yell at me for drinking. I bet you had a few beers before you were twenty-one.

- Why do I have to be home by midnight? Didn't you stay out late when you were my age?

Arguments such as these are irrelevant. People fail to follow their own advice, but that does not mean that their points have no merit. (Of course, not following their own advice does undermine their credibility.)

Appeal to Doubtful Authority

Writers of research papers frequently use the ideas of recognized authorities to strengthen their arguments. However, the sources offered as evidence need to be both respected and credible. The **appeal to doubtful authority** occurs when people use the ideas of nonexperts to support their arguments.

Not everyone who speaks as an expert is actually an authority on a particular issue. For example, when movie stars or recording artists give their opinions about politics, climate change, or foreign affairs— things they may know little about—they are not speaking as experts; therefore, they have no authority. (They *are* experts, however, when they discuss the film or music industries.) A similar situation occurs with the pundits who appear on television news shows. Some of these individuals have solid credentials in the fields they discuss, but others offer opinions even though they know little about the subjects. Unfortunately, many viewers accept the pronouncements of these "experts" uncritically and think it is acceptable to cite them to support their own arguments.

How do you determine whether a person you read about or hear is really an authority? First, make sure that the person actually has expertise in the field he or she is discussing. You can do this by checking his

Comedian/actor Amy Schumer boosts her credibility on the issue of gun control by appearing with her cousin, Senator Charles Schumer.

© Andrew Burton/Getty Images

or her credentials on the Internet. Second, make sure that the person is not biased. No one is entirely free from bias, but the bias should not be so extreme that it undermines the person's authority. Finally, make sure that you can confirm what the so-called expert says or writes. Check one or two pieces of information in other sources, such as a basic reference text or encyclopedia. Determine if others—especially recognized experts in the field—confirm this information. If there are major points of discrepancy, dig further to make sure you are dealing with a legitimate authority.

Misuse of Statistics

The **misuse of statistics** occurs when data are misrepresented. Statistics can be used persuasively in an argument, but sometimes they are distorted—intentionally or unintentionally—to make a point. For example, a classic ad for toothpaste claims that four out of five dentists recommend Crest toothpaste. What the ad neglects to mention is the number of dentists who were questioned. If the company surveyed several thousand dentists, then this statistic would be meaningful. If the company surveyed only ten, however, it would not be.

Misleading statistics can be much subtler (and much more complicated) than the example above. For example, one year, there were 16,653 alcohol-related deaths in the United States. According to the National Highway Traffic Safety Administration (NHTSA), 12,892 of these 16,653 alcohol-related deaths involved at least one driver or passenger

"That's what I want to say. See if you can find some statistics to prove it."

Cartoonstock.com

who was legally drunk. Of the 12,892 deaths, 7,326 were the drivers themselves, and 1,594 were legally drunk pedestrians. The remaining 3,972 fatalities were nonintoxicated drivers, passengers, or nonoccupants. These 3,972 fatalities call the total number into question because the NHTSA does not indicate which drivers were at fault. In other words, if a sober driver ran a red light and killed a legally drunk driver, the NHTSA classified this death as alcohol-related. For this reason, the original number of alcohol-related deaths—16,653—is somewhat misleading. (The statistic becomes even more questionable when you consider that a person is automatically classified as intoxicated if he or she refuses to take a sobriety test.)

Post Hoc, Ergo Propter Hoc (After This, Therefore Because of This)

The **post hoc** fallacy asserts that because two events occur closely in time, one event must cause the other. Professional athletes commit the post hoc fallacy all the time. For example, one major league pitcher wears the same shirt every time he has an important game. Because he has won several big games while wearing this shirt, he believes it brings him luck.

Many events seem to follow a sequential pattern even though they actually do not. For example, some people refuse to get a flu shot because they say that the last time they got one, they came down with the flu. Even though there is no scientific basis for this link, many people insist that it is true. (The more probable explanation for this situation is that the flu vaccination takes at least two weeks to take effect, so it is possible for someone to be infected by the flu virus before the vaccine starts working.)

Another health-related issue also illustrates the post hoc fallacy. Recently, the U.S. Food and Drug Administration (FDA) studied several natural supplements that claim to cure the common cold. Because the study showed that these products were not effective, the FDA ordered the manufacturers to stop making false claims. Despite this fact, however, many people still buy these products. When questioned, they say the medications actually work. Again, the explanation for this phenomenon is simple. Most colds last just a few days. As the FDA pointed out in its report, people who took the medications would have begun feeling better with or without them.

Non Sequitur (It Does Not Follow)

The **non sequitur** fallacy occurs when a conclusion does not follow from the premises. Frequently, the conclusion is supported by weak or irrelevant evidence—or by no evidence at all. Consider the following statement:

> Megan drives an expensive car, so she must be earning a lot of money.

Megan might drive an expensive car, but this is not evidence that she has a high salary. She could, for example, be leasing the car or paying it off over a five-year period, or it could have been a gift.

Non sequiturs are common in political arguments. Consider this statement:

> Gangs, drugs, and extreme violence plague today's prisons. The only way to address this issue is to release all nonviolent offenders as soon as possible.

This assessment of the prison system may be accurate, but it doesn't follow that because of this situation, all nonviolent offenders should be released immediately.

Scientific arguments also contain non sequiturs. Consider the following statement that was made during a debate on climate change:

> Recently, the polar ice caps have thickened, and the temperature of the oceans has stabilized. Obviously, we don't need to do more to address climate change.

A non sequitur
fallacy

NON SEQUITUR © 2006 Wiley Ink, Inc. Dist. By UNIVERSAL UCLICK. Reprinted with permission.
All rights reserved.

Even if you accept the facts of this argument, you need to see more evidence before you can conclude that no action against climate change is necessary. For example, the cooling trend could be temporary, or other areas of the earth could still be growing warmer.

Bandwagon Fallacy

The **bandwagon fallacy** occurs when you try to convince people that something is true because it is widely held to be true. It is easy to see the problem with this line of reasoning. Hundreds of years ago, most people believed that the sun revolved around the earth and that the earth was flat. As we know, the fact that many people held these beliefs did not make them true.

The underlying assumption of the bandwagon fallacy is that the more people who believe something, the more likely it is to be true. Without supporting evidence, however, this form of argument cannot be valid. For example, consider the following statement made by a driver who was stopped by the police for speeding:

> Officer, I didn't do anything wrong. Everyone around me was going the same speed.

As the police officer was quick to point out, the driver's argument missed the point: he was doing fifty-five miles an hour in a thirty-five-mile-an-hour zone, and the fact that other drivers were also speeding was irrelevant. If the driver had been able to demonstrate that the police officer was mistaken—that he was driving more slowly or that the speed limit was actually sixty miles an hour—then his argument would have had merit. In this case, the fact that other drivers were going the same speed would be relevant because it would support his contention.

The bandwagon fallacy

Cartoonstock.com

Since most people want to go along with the crowd, the bandwagon fallacy can be very effective. For this reason, advertisers use it all the time. For example, a book publisher will say that a book has been on the *New York Times* bestseller list for ten weeks, and a pharmaceutical company will say that its brand of aspirin outsells other brands four to one. These appeals are irrelevant, however, because they don't address the central questions: Is the book actually worth reading? Is one brand of aspirin really better than other brands?

⊙ EXERCISE 5.10

Determine which of the following statements are logical arguments and which are fallacies. If the statement is not logical, identify the fallacy that best applies.

1. Almost all the students I talked to said that they didn't like the senator. I'm sure he'll lose the election on Tuesday.

2. This car has a noisy engine; therefore, it must create a lot of pollution.

3. I don't know how Professor Resnick can be such a hard grader. He's always late for class.

4. A vote for the bill to limit gun sales in the city is a vote against the Second Amendment.

5. It's only fair to pay your fair share of taxes.

6. I had an internship at a government agency last summer, and no one there worked very hard. Government workers are lazy.

7. It's a clear principle of law that people are not allowed to yell "Fire!" in a crowded theater. By permitting protestors to hold a rally downtown, Judge Cohen is allowing them to do just that.

8. Of course this person is guilty. He wouldn't be in jail if he weren't a criminal.

9. Schools are like families; therefore, teachers (like parents) should be allowed to discipline their kids.

10. Everybody knows that staying out in the rain can make you sick.

11. When we had a draft in the 1960s, the crime rate was low. We should bring back the draft.

12. I'm not a doctor, but I play one on TV. I recommend Vicks Formula 44 cough syrup.

13. Some people are complaining about public schools, so there must be a problem.

14. If you aren't part of the solution, you're part of the problem.

15. All people are mortal. James is a person. Therefore, James is mortal.

16. I don't know why you gave me an F for handing in someone else's essay. Didn't you ever copy something from someone else?

17. First, the government stops us from buying assault rifles. Then, it limits the number of handguns we can buy. What will come next? Soon, they'll try to take away all our guns.

18. Shakespeare was the world's greatest playwright; therefore, *Macbeth* must be a great play.

19. Last month, I bought a new computer. Yesterday, I installed some new software. This morning, my computer wouldn't start up. The new software must be causing the problem.

20. Ellen DeGeneres is against testing pharmaceutical and cosmetics products on animals, and that's good enough for me.

⊙ EXERCISE 5.11

Read the following essay, and identify as many logical fallacies in it as you can. Make sure you identify each fallacy by name and are able to explain the flaws in the writer's arguments.

This essay is from Buchanan.org, where it appeared on October 31, 1994.

IMMIGRATION TIME-OUT

PATRICK J. BUCHANAN

Proposition 187 "is an outrage. It is unconstitutional. It is nativist. It is racist."

—AL HUNT, *Capital Gang*, CNN

That outburst by my columnist colleague, about California's Prop. 187— 1 which would cut off social welfare benefits to illegal aliens—suggests that this savage quarrel is about more than just money. Indeed, the roots of this dispute over Prop. 187 are grounded in the warring ideas that we Americans hold about the deepest, most divisive issues of our time: ethnicity, nation, culture.

What do we want the America of the years 2000, 2020, and 2050 to 2 be like? Do we have the right to shape the character of the country our grandchildren will live in? Or is that to be decided by whoever, outside America, decides to come here?

By 2050, we are instructed by the chancellor of the University of California at Berkeley, Chang Lin-Tin, "the majority of Americans will trace their roots to Latin America, Africa, Asia, the Middle East, and Pacific Islands." 3

Now, any man or woman, of any nation or ancestry can come here—and become a good American. 4

We know that from our history. But by my arithmetic, the chancellor is saying Hispanics, Asians, and Africans will increase their present number of 65 million by at least 100 million in 60 years, a population growth larger than all of Mexico today. 5

What will that mean for America? Well, South Texas and Southern California will be almost exclusively Hispanic. Each will have tens of millions of people whose linguistic, historic, and cultural roots are in Mexico. Like Eastern Ukraine, where 10 million Russian-speaking "Ukrainians" now look impatiently to Moscow, not Kiev, as their cultural capital, America could see, in a decade, demands for Quebec-like status for Southern California. Already there is a rumbling among militants for outright secession. A sea of Mexican flags was prominent in that L.A. rally against Prop. 187, and Mexican officials are openly urging their kinsmen in California to vote it down. 6

If no cutoff is imposed on social benefits for those who breach our borders, and break our laws, the message will go out to a desperate world: America is wide open. All you need do is get there, and get in. 7

Consequences will ensue. Crowding together immigrant and minority populations in our major cities must bring greater conflict. We saw that in the 1992 L.A. riot. Blacks and Hispanics have lately collided in D.C.'s Adams-Morgan neighborhood, supposedly the most tolerant and progressive section of Washington. The issue: bilingual education. Unlike 20 years ago, ethnic conflict is today on almost every front page. 8

Before Mr. Chang's vision is realized, the United States will have at least two official languages. Today's steady outmigration of "Anglos" or "Euro-Americans," as whites are now called, from Southern Florida and Southern California, will continue. The 50 states will need constant redrawing of political lines to ensure proportional representation. Already we have created the first "apartheid districts" in America's South. 9

Ethnic militancy and solidarity are on the rise in the United States; the old institutions of assimilation are not doing their work as they once did; the Melting Pot is in need of repair. On campuses we hear demands for separate dorms, eating rooms, clubs, etc., by black, white, Hispanic, and Asian students. If this is where the campus is headed, where are our cities going? 10

> "Ethnic militancy and solidarity are on the rise."

If America is to survive as "one nation, one people," we need to call a 11 "time-out" on immigration, to assimilate the tens of millions who have lately arrived. We need to get to know one another, to live together, to learn together America's language, history, culture, and traditions of tolerance, to become a new national family, before we add a hundred million more. And we need soon to bring down the curtain on this idea of hyphenated-Americanism.

If we lack the courage to make the decisions—as to what our country will 12 look like in 2050—others will make those decisions for us, not all of whom share our love of the America that seems to be fading away.

⊖ EXERCISE 5.12

Choose three of the fallacies that you identified in "Immigration Time-Out" for Exercise 5.11. Rewrite each statement in the form of a logical argument.

 **LaunchPad**
macmillan learning

For more practice, see the LearningCurve on Reasoning and Logical Fallacies in the Launchpad for *Practical Argument*.

How Free Should Free Speech Be?

Printed by permission of the
Norman Rockwell Family Agency.
Copyright 1943 the Norman
Rockwell Family Entities.

Go back to page 123, and reread the At Issue box that gives background on how free free speech should be. As the following sources illustrate, this question has a number of possible answers.

As you read this source material, you will be asked to answer questions and to complete some simple activities. This work will help you understand both the content and the structure of the sources. When you are finished, you will be ready to write an argument—either inductive or deductive—that takes a new position on how free free speech should actually be.

SOURCES

This article originally appeared on TheDailyBeast.com on January 1, 2014.

SHOULD NEO-NAZIS BE ALLOWED FREE SPEECH?

THANE ROSENBAUM

Over the past several weeks, free speech has gotten costlier—at least in France 1 and Israel.

In France, Dieudonne M'Bala M'Bala, an anti-Semitic stand-up comic 2 infamous for popularizing the quenelle, an inverted Nazi salute, was banned from performing in two cities. M'Bala M'Bala has been repeatedly fined for hate speech, and this was not the first time his act was perceived as a threat to public order.

Meanwhile, Israel's parliament is soon to pass a bill outlawing the word 3 Nazi for non-educational purposes. Indeed, any slur against another that invokes the Third Reich could land the speaker in jail for six months with a fine of $29,000. The Israelis are concerned about both the rise of anti-Semitism globally, and the trivialization of the Holocaust—even locally.

To Americans, these actions in France and Israel seem positively un- 4 democratic. The First Amendment would never prohibit the quenelle, regardless of its symbolic meaning. And any lover of *Seinfeld* would regard banning the "Soup Nazi" episode as scandalously un-American. After all, in 1977 a federal court upheld the right of neo-Nazis to goose-step right through the town of Skokie, Illinois, which had a disproportionately large number of Holocaust survivors as residents. And more recently, the Supreme Court upheld the right of a church group opposed to gays serving in the military to picket the funeral of a dead marine with signs that read, "God Hates Fags."

While what is happening in France and Israel is wholly foreign to Ameri- 5 cans, perhaps it's time to consider whether these and other countries may be right. Perhaps America's fixation on free speech has gone too far.

Actually, the United States is an outlier among democracies in granting 6 such generous free speech guarantees. Six European countries, along with Brazil, prohibit the use of Nazi symbols and flags. Many more countries have outlawed Holocaust denial. Indeed, even encouraging racial discrimination in France is a crime. In pluralistic nations like these with clashing cultures and historical tragedies not shared by all, mutual respect and civility helps keep the peace and avoids unnecessary mental trauma.

Yet, even in the United States, free speech is not unlimited. Certain pro- 7 scribed categories have always existed—libel, slander and defamation, obscenity, "fighting words," and the "incitement of imminent lawlessness"—where the First Amendment does not protect the speaker, where the right to speak is curtailed for reasons of general welfare and public safety. There is no freedom to shout "fire" in a crowded theater. Hate crime statutes exist in many jurisdictions where bias-motivated crimes are given more severe penalties. In 2003, the Supreme Court held that speech intended to intimidate, such as cross burning, might not receive First Amendment protection.

Yet, the confusion is that in placing limits on speech we privilege physical [8] over emotional harm. Indeed, we have an entire legal system, and an attitude toward speech, that takes its cue from a nursery rhyme: "Sticks and stones can break my bones but names can never hurt me."

All of us know, however, and despite what we tell our children, names do, [9] indeed, hurt. And recent studies in universities such as Purdue, UCLA, Michigan, Toronto, Arizona, Maryland, and Macquarie University in New South Wales show, among other things, through brain scans and controlled studies with participants who were subjected to both physical and emotional pain, that emotional harm is equal in intensity to that experienced by the body, and is even more long-lasting and traumatic. Physical pain subsides; emotional pain, when recalled, is relived.

Pain has a shared circuitry in the human brain, and it makes no distinc- [10] tion between being hit in the face and losing face (or having a broken heart) as a result of bereavement, betrayal, social exclusion, and grave insult. Emotional distress can, in fact, make the body sick. Indeed, research has shown that pain relief medication can work equally well for both physical and emotional injury.

We impose speed limits on driving and regulate food and drugs because we know that the costs of not doing so can lead to accidents and harm. Why should speech be exempt from public welfare concerns when its social costs can be even more injurious? [11]

> "We impose speed limits on driving and regulate food and drugs because we know that the costs of not doing so can lead to accidents and harm."

In the marketplace of ideas, there is a difference between trying to persuade and trying to injure. One can object to gays in the military without ruining the one moment a father has to bury his son; [12] neo-Nazis can long for the Third Reich without re-traumatizing Hitler's victims; one can oppose Affirmative Action without burning a cross on an African-American's lawn.

Of course, everything is a matter of degree. Juries are faced with similar [13] ambiguities when it comes to physical injury. No one knows for certain whether the plaintiff wearing a neck brace can't actually run the New York Marathon. We tolerate the fake slip and fall, but we feel absolutely helpless in evaluating whether words and gestures intended to harm actually do cause harm. Jurors are as capable of working through these uncertainties in the area of emotional harms as they are in the realm of physical injury.

Free speech should not stand in the way of common decency. No right [14] should be so freely and recklessly exercised that it becomes an impediment to civil society, making it so that others are made to feel less free, their private space and peace invaded, their sensitivities cruelly trampled upon.

⊃ AT ISSUE: HOW FREE SHOULD FREE SPEECH BE?

1. Rosenbaum waits until the end of paragraph 6 to state his thesis. Why? What information does he include in paragraphs 1–5? How does this material set the stage for the rest of the essay?

2. Rosenbaum develops his argument with both inductive and deductive reasoning. Where does he use each strategy?

3. What evidence does Rosenbaum use to support his thesis? Should he have included more evidence? If so, what kind?

4. In paragraph 11, Rosenbaum makes a comparison between regulating free speech and regulating driving and food and drugs. How strong is this **analogy**? At what points (if any) does this comparison break down?

5. Where does Rosenbaum address arguments against his position? Does he refute these arguments? What other opposing arguments could he have addressed?

6. What point does Rosenbaum reinforce in his conclusion? What other points could he have emphasized?

This op-ed originally ran in the *Wall Street Journal* on September 24, 2014.

THE UNFREE SPEECH MOVEMENT

SOL STERN

This fall the University of California at Berkeley is celebrating the 50th anni- 1
versary of the Free Speech Movement, a student-led protest against campus
restrictions on political activities that made headlines and inspired imitators
around the country. I played a small part in the Free Speech Movement, and
some of those returning for the reunion were once my friends, but I won't be
joining them.

Though the movement promised greater intellectual and political free- 2
dom on campus, the result has been the opposite. The great irony is that while
Berkeley now honors the memory of the Free Speech Movement, it exercises
more thought control over students than the hated institution that we rose up
against half a century ago.

We early-1960s radicals believed ourselves anointed as a new "tell it like it 3
is" generation. We promised to transcend the "smelly old orthodoxies" (in
George Orwell's phrase) of Cold War liberalism and class-based, authoritarian
leftism. Leading students into the university administration building for the
first mass protest, Mario Savio, the Free Speech Movement's brilliant leader
from Queens, New York, famously said: "There's a time when the operation of
the machine becomes so odious—makes you so sick at heart—that you can't
take part. . . . And you've got to indicate to the people who run it, to the people who own it that unless you're free, the machine will be prevented from
working at all."

The Berkeley "machine" now promotes Free Speech Movement kitsch. 4
The steps in front of Sproul Hall, the central administration building where
more than 700 students were arrested on Dec. 2, 1964, have been renamed the
Mario Savio Steps. One of the campus dining halls is called the Free Speech
Movement Cafe, its walls covered with photographs and mementos of the glorious semester of struggle. The university requires freshmen to read an admir-
ing biography of Savio, who died in 1996, written by New York University
professor and Berkeley graduate Robert Cohen.

Yet intellectual diversity is hardly embraced. Every undergraduate under- 5
goes a form of indoctrination with a required course on the "theoretical or
analytical issues relevant to understanding race, culture, and ethnicity in
American society," administered by the university's Division of Equity and
Inclusion.

How did this Orwellian inversion occur? It happened in part because the 6
Free Speech Movement's fight for free speech was always a charade. The struggle was really about using the campus as a base for radical politics. I was a

27-year-old New Left graduate student at the time. Savio was a 22-year-old sophomore. He liked to compare the Free Speech Movement to the civil-rights struggle—conflating the essentially liberal Berkeley administration with the Bull Connors of the racist South.

During one demonstration Savio suggested that the campus cops who 7 had arrested a protesting student were "poor policemen" who only "have a job to do." Another student then shouted out: "Just like Eichmann." "Yeah. Very good. It's very, you know, like Adolf Eichmann," Savio replied. "He had a job to do. He fit into the machinery."

I realized years later that this moment may have been the beginning of the 8 1960s radicals' perversion of ordinary political language, like the spelling "Amerika" or seeing hope and progress in Third World dictatorships.

Before that 1964–65 academic year, most of us radical students could not 9 have imagined a campus rebellion. Why revolt against an institution that until then offered such a pleasant sanctuary? But then Berkeley administrators made an incredibly stupid decision to establish new rules regarding political activities on campus. Student clubs were no longer allowed to set up tables in front of the Bancroft Avenue campus entrance to solicit funds and recruit new members.

The clubs had used this 40-foot strip of sidewalk for years on the 10 assumption that it was the property of the City of Berkeley and thus constitutionally protected against speech restrictions. But the university claimed ownership to justify the new rules. When some students refused to comply, the administration compounded its blunder by resorting to the campus police. Not surprisingly, the students pushed back, using civil-disobedience tactics learned fighting for civil rights in the South.

The Free Speech Movement was born on Oct. 1, 1964, when police tried 11 to arrest a recent Berkeley graduate, Jack Weinberg, who was back on campus after a summer as a civil-rights worker in Mississippi. He had set up a table on the Bancroft strip for the Berkeley chapter of the Congress of Racial Equality (CORE). Dozens of students spontaneously sat down around the police car, preventing it from leaving the campus. A 32-hour standoff ensued, with hundreds of students camped around the car.

Mario Savio, also back from Mississippi, took off his shoes, climbed onto 12 the roof of the police car, and launched into an impromptu speech explaining why the students had to resist the immoral new rules. Thus began months of sporadic protests, the occupation of Sproul Hall on Dec. 2 (ended by mass arrests), national media attention, and Berkeley's eventual capitulation.

That should have ended the matter. Savio soon left the political arena, saying that he had no interest in becoming a permanent student leader. But others had mastered the new world of political theater, understood the weakness of American liberalism, and soon turned their ire on the Vietnam War.

"But others had mastered the new world of political theater, understood the weakness of American liberalism, and soon turned their ire on the Vietnam War." 13

Mario Savio at a victory rally on the University of California campus in Berkeley (December 9, 1964)

AP Photo.

The radical movement that the Free Speech Movement spawned eventu- 14 ally descended into violence and mindless anti-Americanism. The movement waned in the 1970s as the war wound down—but by then protesters had begun their infiltration of university faculties and administrations they had once decried. "Tenured radicals," in *New Criterion* editor Roger Kimball's phrase, now dominate most professional organizations in the humanities and social studies. Unlike our old liberal professors, who dealt respectfully with the ideas advanced by my generation of New Left students, today's radical professors insist on ideological conformity and don't take kindly to dissent by conservative students. Visits by speakers who might not toe the liberal line—recently including former Secretary of State Condoleezza Rice and Islamism critic Ayaan Hirsi Ali—spark protests and letter-writing campaigns by students in tandem with their professors until the speaker withdraws or the invitation is canceled.

On Oct. 1 at Berkeley, by contrast, one of the honored speakers at the Free 15 Speech Movement anniversary rally on Sproul Plaza will be Bettina Aptheker, who is now a feminist-studies professor at the University of California at Santa Cruz.

Writing in the Berkeley alumni magazine about the anniversary, Ms. 16 Aptheker noted that the First Amendment was "written by white, propertied men in the 18th century, who never likely imagined that it might apply to women, and/or people of color, and/or all those who were not propertied, and even, perhaps, not citizens, and/or undocumented immigrants. . . . In other words, freedom of speech is a Constitutional guarantee, but who gets to exercise it without the chilling restraints of censure depends very much on one's location in the political and social cartography. We [Free Speech Movement] veterans were too young and inexperienced in 1964 to know this, but we do now, and we speak with a new awareness, a new consciousness, and a new urgency that the wisdom of a true freedom is inexorably tied to who exercises power and for what ends." Read it and weep—for the Free Speech Movement anniversary, for the ideal of an intellectually open university, and for America.

⊙ AT ISSUE: HOW FREE SHOULD FREE SPEECH BE?

1. In your own words, summarize Stern's thesis. Where does he state it?

2. At what point (or points) in the essay does Stern appeal to *ethos*? How effective is this appeal?

3. In paragraph 4, Stern says, "The Berkeley 'machine' now promotes Free Speech Movement kitsch." First, look up the meaning of *kitsch*. Then, explain what Stern means by this statement.

4. Stern supports his points with examples drawn from his own experience. Is this enough? What other kinds of evidence could he have used?

5. In paragraph 5, Stern says that every undergraduate at Berkeley "undergoes a form of indoctrination." What does he mean? Does Stern make a valid point, or is he **begging the question**?

6. Why does Stern discuss Bettina Aptheker in paragraphs 15–16? Could he be accused of making an **ad hominem** attack? Why or why not?

This code came out of a June 1992 meeting of the American Association of University Professors.

ON FREEDOM OF EXPRESSION AND CAMPUS SPEECH CODES

AMERICAN ASSOCIATION OF UNIVERSITY PROFESSORS

Freedom of thought and expression is essential to any institution of higher 1 learning. Universities and colleges exist not only to transmit existing knowledge. Equally, they interpret, explore, and expand that knowledge by testing the old and proposing the new.

This mission guides learning outside the classroom quite as much as in 2 class, and often inspires vigorous debate on those social, economic, and political issues that arouse the strongest passions. In the process, views will be expressed that may seem to many wrong, distasteful, or offensive. Such is the nature of freedom to sift and winnow ideas.

On a campus that is free and open, no idea can be banned or forbidden. 3 No viewpoint or message may be deemed so hateful or disturbing that it may not be expressed.

> "On a campus that is free and open, no idea can be banned or forbidden."

Universities and colleges are also 4 communities, often of a residential character. Most campuses have recently sought to become more diverse, and more reflective of the larger community, by attracting students, faculty, and staff from groups that were historically excluded or underrepresented. Such gains as they have made are recent, modest, and tenuous. The campus climate can profoundly affect an institution's continued diversity. Hostility or intolerance to persons who differ from the majority (especially if seemingly condoned by the institution) may undermine the confidence of new members of the community. Civility is always fragile and can easily be destroyed.

In response to verbal assaults and use of hateful language some campuses 5 have felt it necessary to forbid the expression of racist, sexist, homophobic, or ethnically demeaning speech, along with conduct or behavior that harasses. Several reasons are offered in support of banning such expression. Individuals and groups that have been victims of such expression feel an understandable outrage. They claim that the academic progress of minority and majority alike may suffer if fears, tensions, and conflicts spawned by slurs and insults create an environment inimical to learning. These arguments, grounded in the need to foster an atmosphere respectful of and welcome to all persons, strike a deeply responsive chord in the academy. But, while we can acknowledge both the weight of these concerns and the thoughtfulness of those persuaded of the need for regulation, rules that ban or punish speech based upon its content cannot be justified. An institution of higher learning fails to fulfill its mission if it asserts the power to proscribe ideas—and racial or ethnic slurs, sexist epithets, or homophobic insults almost always express ideas, however repugnant. Indeed, by proscribing any ideas, a university sets an example that profoundly disserves its academic mission. Some may seek to defend a distinction between the regulation of the content of speech and the regulation of the manner (or style) of speech. We find this distinction untenable in practice because offensive style or opprobrious phrases may in fact have been chosen precisely for their expressive power. As the United States Supreme Court has said in the course of rejecting criminal sanctions for offensive words: Words are often chosen as much for their emotive as their cognitive force. We cannot sanction the view that the Constitution, while solicitous of the cognitive content of individual speech, has little or no regard for that emotive function which, practically speaking, may often be the more important element of the overall message sought to be communicated. The line between substance and style is thus too uncertain to sustain the pressure that will inevitably be brought to bear upon disciplinary rules that attempt to regulate speech. Proponents of speech codes sometimes reply that the value of emotive language of this type is of such a low order that, on balance, suppression is justified by the harm suffered by those who are directly affected, and by the general damage done to the learning environment. Yet a college or university sets a perilous course if it seeks to differentiate between high-value and low-value speech, or to choose which groups are to be protected by curbing the speech of others. A speech code unavoidably implies an institutional competence to distinguish permissible expression of hateful thought from what is proscribed as thoughtless hate. Institutions would also have to justify shielding some, but not other, targets of offensive language—not to political preference, to religious but not to philosophical creed, or perhaps even to some but not to other religious affiliations. Starting down this path creates an even greater risk that groups not originally protected may later demand similar solicitude—demands the institution that began the process of banning some speech is ill equipped to resist.

Distinctions of this type are neither practicable nor principled; their very 6 fragility underscores why institutions devoted to freedom of thought and expression ought not adopt an institutionalized coercion of silence.

Moreover, banning speech often avoids consideration of means more 7 compatible with the mission of an academic institution by which to deal with incivility, intolerance, offensive speech, and harassing behavior:

1. Institutions should adopt and invoke a range of measures that penalize conduct and behavior, rather than speech, such as rules against defacing property, physical intimidation or harassment, or disruption of campus activities. All members of the campus community should be made aware of such rules, and administrators should be ready to use them in preference to speech-directed sanctions.

2. Colleges and universities should stress the means they use best—to educate—including the development of courses and other curricular and co-curricular experiences designed to increase student understanding

and to deter offensive or intolerant speech or conduct. Such institutions should, of course, be free (indeed encouraged) to condemn manifestations of intolerance and discrimination, whether physical or verbal.

3. The governing board and the administration have a special duty not only to set an outstanding example of tolerance, but also to challenge boldly and condemn immediately serious breaches of civility.

4. Members of the faculty, too, have a major role; their voices may be critical in condemning intolerance, and their actions may set examples for understanding, making clear to their students that civility and tolerance are hallmarks of educated men and women.

5. Student personnel administrators have in some ways the most demanding role of all, for hate speech occurs most often in dormitories, locker-rooms, cafeterias, and student centers. Persons who guide this part of campus life should set high standards of their own for tolerance and should make unmistakably clear the harm that uncivil or intolerant speech inflicts.

To some persons who support speech codes, measures like these—relying as 8 they do on suasion rather than sanctions—may seem inadequate. But freedom of expression requires toleration of "ideas we hate," as Justice Holmes put it. The underlying principle does not change because the demand is to silence a hateful speaker, or because it comes from within the academy. Free speech is not simply an aspect of the educational enterprise to be weighed against other desirable ends. It is the very precondition of the academic enterprise itself.

⊙ AT ISSUE: HOW FREE SHOULD FREE SPEECH BE?

1. The writers of this statement rely primarily on deductive reasoning. Construct a syllogism that includes the selection's major premise, minor premise, and conclusion.

2. At what audience is this statement aimed—students, instructors, administrators, or the general public? How do you know?

3. What problem do the writers address? Where do they present their solution?

4. In paragraph 5, the writers discuss the major arguments against their position. Why do they address opposing arguments so early in the selection? How effectively do the writers refute these arguments?

5. Paragraph 7 is followed by a numbered list. What information is in this list? Why did the writers decide to set it off in this way?

6. What do the writers mean when they say that free speech "is the very precondition of the academic exercise itself" (para. 8)?

This essay first appeared in the *Washington Post* on February 20, 2015.

PROGRESSIVE IDEAS HAVE KILLED FREE SPEECH ON CAMPUS

WENDY KAMINER

Is an academic discussion of free speech potentially traumatic? A recent panel 1
for Smith College alumnae aimed at "challenging the ideological echo chamber" elicited this ominous "trigger/content warning" when a transcript appeared in the campus newspaper: "Racism/racial slurs, ableist slurs, antisemitic language, anti-Muslim/Islamophobic language, anti-immigrant language, sexist/misogynistic slurs, references to race-based violence, references to antisemitic violence."

No one on this panel, in which I participated, trafficked in slurs. So what 2
prompted the warning?

Smith President Kathleen McCartney had joked, "We're just wild and 3
crazy, aren't we?" In the transcript, "crazy" was replaced by the notation: "[ableist slur]."

One of my fellow panelists mentioned that the State Department had for a 4
time banned the words "jihad," "Islamist," and "caliphate"—which the transcript flagged as "anti-Muslim/Islamophobic language."

I described the case of a Brandeis professor disciplined for saying "wet- 5
back" while explaining its use as a pejorative. The word was replaced in the transcript by "[anti-Latin@/anti-immigrant slur]." Discussing the teaching of *Huckleberry Finn*, I questioned the use of euphemisms such as "the n-word" and, in doing so, uttered that forbidden word. I described what I thought was the obvious difference between quoting a word in the context of discussing language, literature, or prejudice and hurling it as an epithet.

Two of the panelists challenged me. The audience of 300 to 400 people 6
listened to our spirited, friendly debate—and didn't appear angry or shocked. But back on campus, I was quickly branded a racist, and I was charged in the Huffington Post with committing "an explicit act of racial violence." McCartney subsequently apologized that "some students and faculty were hurt" and made to "feel unsafe" by my remarks.

Unsafe? These days, when students talk about threats to their safety and 7
demand access to "safe spaces," they're often talking about the threat of unwelcome speech and demanding protection from the emotional disturbances sparked by unsettling ideas. It's not just rape that some women on campus fear: It's discussions of rape. At Brown University, a scheduled debate between two feminists about rape culture was criticized for, as the *Brown Daily Herald* put it, undermining "the University's mission to create a safe and supportive environment for survivors." In a school-wide e-mail, Brown President Christina Paxon emphasized her belief in the existence of rape culture and invited

students to an alternative lecture, to be given at the same time as the debate. And the *Daily Herald* reported that students who feared being "attacked by the viewpoints" offered at the debate could instead "find a safe space" among "sexual assault peer educators, women peer counselors and staff" during the same time slot. Presumably they all shared the same viewpoints and could be trusted not to "attack" anyone with their ideas.

How did we get here? How did a verbal defense of free speech become 8 tantamount to a hate crime and offensive words become the equivalent of physical assaults?

> "How did a verbal defense of free speech become tantamount to a hate crime and offensive words become the equivalent of physical assaults?"

You can credit—or blame—progres- 9 sives for this enthusiastic embrace of censorship. It reflects, in part, the influence of three popular movements dating back decades: the feminist anti-porn crusades, the pop-psychology recovery movement, and the emergence of multiculturalism on college campuses.

In the 1980s, law professor Catharine 10 MacKinnon and writer Andrea Dworkin showed the way, popularizing a view of free speech as a barrier to equality. These two impassioned feminists framed pornography—its production, distribution, and consumption—as an assault on women. They devised a novel definition of pornography as a violation of women's civil rights, and championed a model anti-porn ordinance that would authorize civil actions by any woman "aggrieved" by pornography. In 1984, the city of Indianapolis adopted the measure, defining pornography as a "discriminatory practice," but it was quickly struck down in federal court as unconstitutional. "Indianapolis justifies the ordinance on the ground that pornography affects thoughts," the court noted. "This is thought control."

So MacKinnnon and Dworkin lost that battle, but their successors are 11 winning the war. Their view of allegedly offensive or demeaning speech as a civil rights violation, and their conflation of words and actions, have helped shape campus speech and harassment codes and nurtured progressive hostility toward free speech.

The recovery movement, which flourished in the late '80s and early '90s, 12 adopted a similarly dire view of unwelcome speech. Words wound, anti-porn feminists and recovering co-dependents agreed. Self-appointed recovery experts, such as the best-selling author John Bradshaw, promoted the belief that most of us are victims of abuse, in one form or another. They broadened the definition of abuse to include a range of common, normal childhood experiences, including being chastised or ignored by your parents on occasion. From this perspective, we are all fragile and easily damaged by presumptively hurtful speech, and censorship looks like a moral necessity.

These ideas were readily absorbed on college campuses embarking on a 13 commendable drive for diversity. Multiculturalists sought to protect historically disadvantaged students from speech considered racist, sexist, homophobic or otherwise discriminatory. Like abuse, oppression was defined broadly. I remember the first time, in the early '90s, that I heard a Harvard student describe herself as oppressed, as a woman of color. She hadn't been systematically deprived of fundamental rights and liberties. After all, she'd been admitted to Harvard. But she had been offended and unsettled by certain attitudes and remarks. Did she have good reason to take offense? That was an irrelevant question. Popular therapeutic culture defined verbal "assaults" and other forms of discrimination by the subjective, emotional responses of self-proclaimed victims.

This reliance on subjectivity, in the interest of equality, is a recipe for 14 arbitrary, discriminatory enforcement practices, with far-reaching effects on individual liberty. The tendency to take subjective allegations of victimization at face value—instrumental in contemporary censorship campaigns—also leads to the presumption of guilt and disregard for due process in the progressive approach to alleged sexual assaults on campus.

This is a dangerously misguided approach to justice. "Feeling realities" 15 belong in a therapist's office. Incorporated into laws and regulations, they lead to the soft authoritarianism that now governs many American campuses. Instead of advancing equality, it's teaching future generations of leaders the "virtues" of autocracy.

⊙ AT ISSUE: HOW FREE SHOULD FREE SPEECH BE?

1. Should Kaminer have given more background information about the problem she discusses? What additional information could she have provided?

2. Kaminer devotes the first six paragraphs of her essay to describing a panel discussion. Why do you think she begins her essay in this way? How does this discussion prepare readers for the rest of the essay?

3. In paragraph 8, Kaminer asks two questions. What is the function of these questions?

4. According to Kaminer, what are "feeling realities" (para. 15)? In what sense are "feeling realities" harmful?

5. Does Kaminer ever establish that the situation she discusses is widespread enough to be a problem? Could she be accused of setting up a **straw man**?

6. What does Kaminer want to accomplish? Is her purpose to convince readers of something? To move them to action? What is your reaction to her essay?

This opinion piece was originally published on March 21, 2015, in the *New York Times*.

IN COLLEGE AND HIDING FROM SCARY IDEAS

JUDITH SHULEVITZ

Katherine Byron, a senior at Brown University and a member of its Sexual 1 Assault Task Force, considers it her duty to make Brown a safe place for rape victims, free from anything that might prompt memories of trauma.

So when she heard last fall that a student group had organized a debate about 2 campus sexual assault between Jessica Valenti, the founder of feministing.com, and Wendy McElroy, a libertarian, and that Ms. McElroy was likely to criticize the term "rape culture," Ms. Byron was alarmed. "Bringing in a speaker like that could serve to invalidate people's experiences," she told me. It could be "damaging."

Ms. Byron and some fellow task force members secured a meeting with 3 administrators. Not long after, Brown's president, Christina H. Paxson, announced that the university would hold a simultaneous, competing talk to provide "research and facts" about "the role of culture in sexual assault." Meanwhile, student volunteers put up posters advertising that a "safe space" would be available for anyone who found the debate too upsetting.

The safe space, Ms. Byron explained, was intended to give people who 4 might find comments "troubling" or "triggering," a place to recuperate. The room was equipped with cookies, coloring books, bubbles, Play-Doh, calming music, pillows, blankets, and a video of frolicking puppies, as well as students and staff members trained to deal with trauma. Emma Hall, a junior, rape survivor, and "sexual assault peer educator" who helped set up the room and worked in it during the debate, estimates that a couple of dozen people used it. At one point she went to the lecture hall—it was packed—but after a while, she had to return to the safe space. "I was feeling bombarded by a lot of viewpoints that really go against my dearly and closely held beliefs," Ms. Hall said.

Safe spaces are an expression of the conviction, increasingly prevalent 5 among college students, that their schools should keep them from being "bombarded" by discomfiting or distressing viewpoints. Think of the safe space as the live-action version of the better-known trigger warning, a notice put on top of a syllabus or an assigned reading to alert students to the presence of potentially disturbing material.

Some people trace safe spaces back to the feminist consciousness-raising 6 groups of the 1960s and 1970s, others to the gay and lesbian movement of the early 1990s. In most cases, safe spaces are innocuous gatherings of like-minded people who agree to refrain from ridicule, criticism, or what they term microaggressions—subtle displays of racial or sexual bias—so that everyone can relax enough to explore the nuances of, say, a fluid gender identity. As long as all parties consent to such restrictions, these little islands of self-restraint seem like a perfectly fine idea.

> "As long as all parties consent to such restrictions, these little islands of self-restraint seem like a perfectly fine idea."   7

But the notion that ticklish conversations must be scrubbed clean of controversy has a way of leaking out and spreading. Once you designate some spaces as safe, you imply that the rest are unsafe. It follows that they should be made safer.

This logic clearly informed a campaign undertaken this fall by a Colum- 8 bia University student group called Everyone Allied Against Homophobia that consisted of slipping a flier under the door of every dorm room on campus. The headline of the flier stated, "I want this space to be a safer space." The text below instructed students to tape the fliers to their windows. The group's vice president then had the flier published in the *Columbia Daily Spectator*, the student newspaper, along with an editorial asserting that "making spaces safer is about learning how to be kind to each other."

A junior named Adam Shapiro decided he didn't want his room to be a 9 safer space. He printed up his own flier calling it a dangerous space and had that, too, published in the *Columbia Daily Spectator*. "Kindness alone won't allow us to gain more insight into truth," he wrote. In an interview, Mr. Shapiro said, "If the point of a safe space is therapy for people who feel victimized by traumatization, that sounds like a great mission." But a safe-space mentality has begun infiltrating classrooms, he said, making both professors and students loath to say anything that might hurt someone's feelings. "I don't see how you can have a therapeutic space that's also an intellectual space," he said.

I'm old enough to remember a time when college students objected to 10 providing a platform to certain speakers because they were deemed politically unacceptable. Now students worry whether acts of speech or pieces of writing may put them in emotional peril. Two weeks ago, students at Northwestern University marched to protest an article by Laura Kipnis, a professor in the university's School of Communication. Professor Kipnis had criticized— O.K., ridiculed—what she called the sexual paranoia pervading campus life.

The protesters carried mattresses and demanded that the administration 11 condemn the essay. One student complained that Professor Kipnis was "erasing the very traumatic experience" of victims who spoke out. An organizer of the demonstration said, "we need to be setting aside spaces to talk" about "victim-blaming." Last Wednesday, Northwestern's president, Morton O. Schapiro, wrote an op-ed article in the *Wall Street Journal* affirming his commitment to academic freedom. But plenty of others at universities are willing to dignify students' fears, citing threats to their stability as reasons to cancel debates, disinvite commencement speakers, and apologize for so-called mistakes.

At Oxford University's Christ Church college in November, the college cen- 12 sors (a "censor" being more or less the Oxford equivalent of an undergraduate dean) canceled a debate on abortion after campus feminists threatened to disrupt it because both would-be debaters were men. "I'm relieved the censors have made this decision," said the treasurer of Christ Church's student union, who had pressed for the cancellation. "It clearly makes the most sense for the safety—both physical and mental—of the students who live and work in Christ Church."

A year and a half ago, a Hampshire College student group disinvited an 13 Afrofunk band that had been attacked on social media for having too many white musicians; the vitriolic discussion had made students feel "unsafe."

Last fall, the president of Smith College, Kathleen McCartney, apologized 14 for causing students and faculty to be "hurt" when she failed to object to a racial epithet uttered by a fellow panel member at an alumnae event in New York. The offender was the free-speech advocate Wendy Kaminer, who had been arguing against the use of the euphemism "the n-word" when teaching American history or *The Adventures of Huckleberry Finn*. In the uproar that followed, the Student Government Association wrote a letter declaring that "if Smith is unsafe for one student, it is unsafe for all students."

"It's amazing to me that they can't distinguish between racist speech and 15 speech about racist speech, between racism and discussions of racism," Ms. Kaminer said in an email.

The confusion is telling, though. It shows that while keeping college-level 16 discussions "safe" may feel good to the hypersensitive, it's bad for them and for everyone else. People ought to go to college to sharpen their wits and broaden their field of vision. Shield them from unfamiliar ideas, and they'll never learn the discipline of seeing the world as other people see it. They'll be unprepared for the social and intellectual headwinds that will hit them as soon as they step off the campuses whose climates they have so carefully controlled. What will they do when they hear opinions they've learned to shrink from? If they want to change the world, how will they learn to persuade people to join them?

Only a few of the students want stronger anti-hate-speech codes. Mostly 17 they ask for things like mandatory training sessions and stricter enforcement of existing rules. Still, it's disconcerting to see students clamor for a kind of intrusive supervision that would have outraged students a few generations ago. But those were hardier souls. Now students' needs are anticipated by a small army of service professionals—mental health counselors, student-life deans, and the like. This new bureaucracy may be exacerbating students' "self-infantilization," as Judith Shapiro, the former president of Barnard College, suggested in an essay for *Inside Higher Ed*.

But why are students so eager to self-infantilize? Their parents should 18 probably share the blame. Eric Posner, a professor at the University of Chicago Law School, wrote on *Slate* last month that although universities cosset students more than they used to, that's what they have to do, because today's under-graduates are more puerile than their predecessors. "Perhaps overprogrammed children engineered to the specifications of college admissions offices no longer experience the risks and challenges that

"Their parents should probably share the blame."

breed maturity," he wrote. But "if college students are children, then they should be protected like children."

Another reason students resort to the quasi-medicalized terminology of 19 trauma is that it forces administrators to respond. Universities are in a double bind. They're required by two civil-rights statutes, Title VII and Title IX, to ensure that their campuses don't create a "hostile environment" for women and other groups subject to harassment. However, universities are not supposed to go too far in suppressing free speech, either. If a university cancels a talk or punishes a professor and a lawsuit ensues, history suggests that the university will lose. But if officials don't censure or don't prevent speech that may inflict psychological damage on a member of a protected class, they risk fostering a hostile environment and prompting an investigation. As a result, students who say they feel unsafe are more likely to be heard than students who demand censorship on other grounds.

The theory that vulnerable students should be guaranteed psychological 20 security has roots in a body of legal thought elaborated in the 1980s and 1990s and still read today. Feminist and anti-racist legal scholars argued that the First Amendment should not safeguard language that inflicted emotional injury through racist or sexist stigmatization. One scholar, Mari J. Matsuda, was particularly insistent that college students not be subjected to "the violence of the word" because many of them "are away from home for the first time and at a vulnerable stage of psychological development." If they're targeted and the university does nothing to help them, they will be "left to their own resources in coping with the damage wrought." That might have, she wrote, "lifelong repercussions."

Perhaps. But Ms. Matsuda doesn't seem to have considered the possibility 21 that insulating students could also make them, well, insular. A few weeks ago, Zineb El Rhazoui, a journalist at *Charlie Hebdo*, spoke at the University of Chicago, protected by the security guards she has traveled with since supporters of the Islamic State issued death threats against her. During the question-and-answer period, a Muslim student stood up to object to the newspaper's apparent disrespect for Muslims and to express her dislike of the phrase "I am Charlie."

Ms. El Rhazoui replied, somewhat irritably, "Being Charlie Hebdo means 22 to die because of a drawing," and not everyone has the guts to do that (although she didn't use the word guts). She lives under constant threat, Ms. El Rhazoui said. The student answered that she felt threatened, too.

A few days later, a guest editorialist in the student newspaper took Ms. El 23 Rhazoui to task. She had failed to ensure "that others felt safe enough to express dissenting opinions." Ms. El Rhazoui's "relative position of power," the writer continued, had granted her a "free pass to make condescending attacks on a member of the university." In a letter to the editor, the president and the vice president of the University of Chicago French Club, which had sponsored the talk, shot back, saying, "El Rhazoui is an immigrant, a woman, Arab, a human-rights activist who has known exile, and a journalist living in very real fear of death. She was invited to speak precisely because her right to do so is, quite literally, under threat."

You'd be hard-pressed to avoid the conclusion that the student and her 24 defender had burrowed so deep inside their cocoons, were so overcome by their own fragility, that they couldn't see that it was Ms. El Rhazoui who was in need of a safer space.

⊘ AT ISSUE: HOW FREE SHOULD FREE SPEECH BE?

1. What are "safe spaces"? According to Shulevitz, what is the problem of designating "some spaces as safe" (para. 7)?

2. In paragraph 9, Shulevitz quotes Adam Shapiro, a student, who says, "I don't see how you can have a therapeutic space that's also an intellectual space." What does Shapiro mean? Do you agree with him?

3. Does Shulevitz use inductive or deductive reasoning to make her case? Why do you think that she chose this strategy?

4. Where does Shulevitz discuss arguments against her position? Does she present these arguments fairly? Explain.

5. Does Shulevitz appeal mainly to *ethos, pathos*, or *logos*?

6. In paragraph 17, Shulevitz says, "Only a few of the students want stronger anti-hate-speech codes." Does this admission undercut her argument? Why or why not?

This essay was posted on Slate.com on February 12, 2015.

UNIVERSITIES ARE RIGHT TO CRACK DOWN ON SPEECH AND BEHAVIOR

ERIC POSNER

Lately, a moral panic about speech and sexual activity in universities has 1 reached a crescendo. Universities have strengthened rules prohibiting offensive speech typically targeted at racial, ethnic, and sexual minorities; taken it upon themselves to issue "trigger warnings" to students when courses offer content that might upset them; banned sexual acts that fall short of rape under criminal law but are on the borderline of coercion; and limited due process protections of students accused of violating these rules.

Most liberals celebrate these developments, yet with a certain uneasiness. 2 Few of them want to apply these protections to society at large. Conservatives and libertarians are up in arms. They see these rules as an assault on free speech and individual liberty. They think universities are treating students like children. And they are right. But they have also not considered that the justification for these policies may lie hidden in plain sight: that students *are* children. Not in terms of age, but in terms of maturity. Even in college, they must be protected like children while being prepared to be adults.

There is a popular, romantic notion that students receive their university 3 education through free and open debate about the issues of the day. Nothing could be farther from the truth. Students who enter college know hardly anything at all—that's why they need an education. Classroom teachers know students won't learn anything if they blab on about their opinions. Teachers are dictators who carefully control what students say to one another. It's not just that sincere expressions of opinion about same-sex marriage or campaign finance reform are out of place in chemistry and math class. They are out of place even in philosophy and politics classes, where the goal is to educate students (usually about academic texts and theories), not to listen to them spout off. And while professors sometimes believe there is pedagogical value in allowing students to express their political opinions in the context of some text, professors (or at least, good professors) carefully manipulate their students so that the discussion serves pedagogical ends.

That's why the contretemps about a recent incident at Marquette Univer- 4 sity is far less alarming than libertarians think. An inexperienced instructor was teaching a class on the philosophy of John Rawls, and a student in the class argued that same-sex marriage was consistent with Rawls' philosophy. When another student told the teacher outside of class that he disagreed, the teacher responded that she would not permit a student to oppose same-sex marriage in class because that might offend gay students.

While I believe that the teacher mishandled the student's complaint, 5 she was justified in dismissing it. The purpose of the class was to teach Rawls' theory of justice, not to debate the merits of same-sex marriage. The fact that a student injected same-sex marriage into the discussion does not mean that the class was required to discuss it. The professor might reasonably have believed that the students would gain a better understanding of Rawls' theory if they thought about how it applied to issues less divisive and hence less likely to distract students from the academic merits of the theory.

Teaching is tricky. Everyone understands that a class is a failure if students refuse to learn because they feel bullied or intimidated, or if ideological arguments break out that have nothing to do with understanding an idea. It is the responsibility of the professor to conduct the class in such a way that maximal learning occurs, not maximal speech. That's why no teacher would permit students to launch into anti-Semitic diatribes in a class about the Holocaust, however sincerely the speaker might think that Jews were responsible for the Holocaust or the Holocaust did not take place. And even a teacher less scrupulous about avoiding offense to gay people would draw a line if a student in the Rawls class wanted to argue that Jim Crow or legalization of pedophilia is entailed by the principles of justice. While advocates of freedom of speech like to claim that falsehoods get squeezed out in the "marketplace of ideas," in classrooms they just receive an F.

> "It is the responsibility of the professor to conduct the class in such a way that maximal learning occurs, not maximal speech."

Most of the debate about speech codes, which frequently prohibit students from making offensive comments to one another, concerns speech outside of class. Two points should be made. First, students who are unhappy with the codes and values on campus can take their views to forums outside of campus—to the town square, for example. The campus is an extension of the classroom, and so while the restrictions in the classroom are enforced less vigorously, the underlying pedagogical objective of avoiding intimidation remains intact.

Second, and more important—at least for libertarian partisans of the free 8 market—the universities are simply catering to demand in the marketplace for education. While critics sometimes give the impression that lefty professors and clueless administrators originated the speech and sex codes, the truth is that universities adopted them because that's what most students want. If students want to learn biology and art history in an environment where they needn't worry about being offended or raped, why shouldn't they? As long as universities are free to choose whatever rules they want, students with different views can sort themselves into universities with different rules. Indeed, students who want the greatest speech protections can attend public universities, which (unlike private universities) are governed by the First Amendment.

Libertarians might reflect on the irony that the private market, in which they normally put faith, reflects a preference among students for speech restrictions.

And this brings me to the most important overlooked fact about speech 9 and sex code debates. Society seems to be moving the age of majority from 18 to 21 or 22. We are increasingly treating college-age students as quasi-children who need protection from some of life's harsh realities while they complete the larval stage of their lives. Many critics of these codes discern this transformation but misinterpret it. They complain that universities are treating adults like children. The problem is that universities have been treating children like adults.

A lot of the controversies about campus life become clearer from this 10 perspective. Youngsters do dumb things. They suffer from lack of impulse control. They fail to say no to a sexual encounter they do not want, or they misinterpret a *no* as *yes*, or in public debate they undermine their own arguments by being needlessly offensive. Scientific research confirms that brain development continues well into a person's 20s. High schools are accustomed to dealing with the cognitive limitations of their charges. They see their mission as advancing the autonomy of students rather than assuming that it is already in place. They socialize as well as educate children to act civilly by punishing them if they don't. Universities have gradually realized that they must take the same approach to college students.

One naturally wonders why this has become necessary. Perhaps over- 11 programmed children engineered to the specifications of college admissions offices no longer experience the risks and challenges that breed maturity. Or maybe in our ever-more technologically advanced society, the responsibilities of adulthood must be delayed until the completion of a more extended period of education.

Yet college students have not always enjoyed so much autonomy. The 12 modern freedoms of college students date back only to the 1960s, when a wave of anti-authoritarianism, inspired by the Vietnam War and the civil rights movement, swept away strict campus codes in an era of single-sex dorms. The modern speech and sex codes have surfaced as those waters recede back to sea. What is most interesting is that this reaction comes not from parents and administrators, but from students themselves, who, apparently recognizing that their parents and schools have not fully prepared them for independence, want universities to resume their traditional role *in loco parentis*.

If all this is true, then maybe we can declare a truce in the culture wars 13 over education. If college students are children, then they should be protected like children. Libertarians should take heart that the market in private education offers students a diverse assortment of ideological cultures in which they can be indoctrinated. Conservatives should rejoice that moral instruction and social control have been reintroduced to the universities after a 40-year drought. Both groups should be pleased that students are kept from harm's way, and kept from doing harm, until they are ready to accept the responsibilities of adults.

185

⊘ AT ISSUE: HOW FREE SHOULD FREE SPEECH BE?

1. This article begins with a series of examples. Are these examples self-evident, or does Posner need to supply more material—for example, source information or evidence that the policies he mentions are widespread?

2. In paragraph 2, Posner says, "Most liberals celebrate these developments." He then goes on to talk about conservatives and libertarians. What logical fallacy does he seem to be committing?

3. In paragraph 3, Posner says, "Teachers are dictators who carefully control what students say to one another." Do you agree? How could you refute this statement?

4. What is Posner's purpose in writing this essay? Does he want to present information, change people's ideas, or move readers to action? Do you think that he achieves his purpose? Explain.

5. Posner makes a number of unsupported general statements in this essay. For example, in paragraph 8, he says that universities adopted speech and sex codes "because that's what most students want." Identify two or three of these general statements, and determine what kinds of evidence Posner would need to support them.

6. In his conclusion, Posner speculates on why universities should assume the responsibility of socializing students. Do you agree? Why or why not?

TEMPLATE FOR WRITING A DEDUCTIVE ARGUMENT

Write a one-paragraph **deductive** argument in which you argue *against* your school imposing speech codes. Follow the template below, filling in the blanks to create your argument.

One of the basic principles of the United States government is the constitutional guarantee of freedom of speech. With few exceptions, all Americans _____ _____ _____. In college _____ _____.

For example, _____ _____. By having the right to express themselves freely, _____ _____ _____. Therefore, _____ _____.

Not everyone agrees with this view, however. Some people argue that _____ _____ _____ _____. This argument misses the point. When a university limits the speech of some students because others may be upset by their comments, _____ _____ _____.

For this reason, colleges should _____ _____ _____.

TEMPLATE FOR WRITING AN INDUCTIVE ARGUMENT

Write a one-paragraph **inductive** argument in which you argue *in favor of* your school imposing speech codes. Follow the template below, filling in the blanks to create your argument.

> The number of students demanding protection from distasteful ideas is growing yearly. Some students complain that _____
> _____
> _____.These students want _____
> _____.
> A number of studies have shown that so-called safe spaces and trigger warnings go a long way toward calming students' fears and creating a hospitable learning environment. For example, some students _____
> _____. As a result, _____
> _____
> _____.The best way for colleges to deal with this problem is to _____
> _____.
> Free speech advocates, however, argue that _____
> _____
> _____
> _____. Although this may be true, _____
> _____
> _____.
> For this reason, it would make sense to _____
> _____
> _____.

⊜ EXERCISE 5.13

Interview several of your classmates as well as one or two of your instructors about how free free speech should be. Then, edit the deductive and inductive arguments you wrote using the templates above so that they include some of these comments.

⊘ EXERCISE 5.14

Write an essay in which you take a position on the question, "Should Universities Be Able to Place Limits on Free Speech?" Make sure that your essay is organized primarily as either a deductive argument or an inductive argument. Use the readings on pages 165–186 as source material, and be sure to document all information that you get from these sources. (See Chapter 10 for information on documenting sources.)

⊘ EXERCISE 5.15

Review the logical fallacies discussed on pages 147–160. Then, reread the essay you wrote for Exercise 5.14, and check to see if it contains any fallacies. Underline any fallacies you find, and identify them by name. Then, rewrite each statement so it expresses a logical argument. Finally, revise your draft to eliminate any fallacies you found.

⊘ EXERCISE 5.16

Review the four pillars of argument discussed in Chapter 1. Does your essay include all four elements of an effective argument? Add anything that is missing. Then, label the key elements of your essay.

6

Rogerian Argument, Toulmin Logic, and Oral Arguments

AT ISSUE

Is Online Education Better Than Classroom Education?

Chances are good that you have either taken an online course, or that you know someone who has. The National Center for Education Statistics found that as of 2014, one in four undergraduate students took at least one online course, and that number is expected to more than double in the coming years. In fact, from 2012 to 2013, online courses accounted for nearly three-quarters of the increase in enrollment for colleges in the United States. Given these facts, some educators wonder if students in online courses are getting what they pay for. Is online instruction as effective as meeting regularly on campus?

The appeal of online education is clear. For students, online education offers flexible scheduling, more time for work or family, and extra money, because online courses eliminate the need to commute to and from school. For colleges and universities, online education programs are cost-effective and profitable because they enable schools to reach new student populations, both nationally and internationally, without the expense of classrooms, offices, libraries, and bookstores.

But despite the advantages of online education, questions remain about its efficacy. For example, some educators ask if virtual classrooms are able to duplicate the dynamic educational atmosphere of face-to-face instruction. Others question whether students learn as well from education delivered by technology as they do from classroom instruction. Still others point out that because online instruction requires more self-discipline than on-campus classes, students find it easy to procrastinate and fall behind on their work.

Later in this chapter, you will be asked to think more about this issue. You will be given several sources to consider and asked to write an argument—using one of the three approaches discussed in this chapter—that takes a position on whether online education is better than classroom instruction.

A confrontational argument

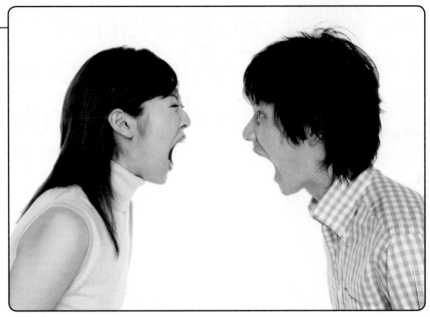

BloomImage/Getty Images

Understanding Rogerian Argument

The traditional model of argument is **confrontational**—characterized by conflict and opposition. This has been the tradition since Aristotle wrote about argument in ancient Greece. The end result of this model of argument is that someone is a winner and someone is a loser or someone is right and someone is wrong.

Arguments do not always have to be confrontational, however. In fact, the twentieth-century psychologist Carl Rogers contended that in many situations, this method of arguing can actually be counterproductive, making it impossible for two people to reach agreement. According to Rogers, attacking opponents and telling them that they are wrong or misguided puts them on the defensive. The result of this tactic is frequently ill will, anger, hostility—and conflict. If you are trying to negotiate an agreement or convince someone to do something, these are exactly the responses that you do not want. To solve this problem, Rogers developed a new approach to argument—one that emphasizes cooperation over confrontation.

Rogerian argument begins with the assumption that people of good will can find solutions to problems that they have in common. Rogers recommends that you consider those with whom you disagree as colleagues, not opponents. Instead of entering into the adversarial relationship that is assumed in classical argument, Rogerian argument encourages you to enter into a cooperative relationship in which both you and your readers search for **common ground**—points of agreement about a problem. By taking this approach, you are more likely to find a solution that will satisfy everyone.

Structuring Rogerian Arguments

Consider the following situation. Assume that you bought a video game console that stopped working one week after the warranty expired. Also assume that the manager of the store where you purchased the game console has refused to exchange it for another console. His point is that because the warranty has expired, the store has no obligation to take the product back. As a last resort, you write a letter to the game console's manufacturer. If you were writing a traditional argument, you would state your thesis—"It is clear that I should receive a new game console"—and then present arguments to support your position. You would also refute opposing arguments, and you would end your letter with a strong concluding statement.

Because Rogerian arguments begin with different assumptions, however, they are structured differently from classical arguments. In a Rogerian argument, you would begin by establishing common ground—by pointing out the concerns you and the video game console's manufacturer share. For example, you could say that as a consumer, you want to buy merchandise that will work as advertised. If the company satisfies your needs, you will continue to buy its products. This goal is shared by the manufacturer. Therefore, instead of beginning with a thesis statement that demands a yes or no response, you would point out that you and the manufacturer share an interest in solving your problem.

Establishing common ground

© Jose Luis Pelaez/Getty Images

Rogerian argument could resolve your problem.

© shvili/iStock/Getty Images

Next, you would describe *in neutral terms*—using impartial, unbiased language—the manufacturer's view of the problem, defining the manufacturer's concerns and attempting to move toward a compromise position. For example, you would explain that you understand that the company wants to make a high-quality product that will satisfy customers. You would also say that you understand that despite the company's best efforts, mistakes sometimes happen.

In the next section of your letter, you would present your own view of the problem fairly and objectively. This section plays a major role in convincing the manufacturer that your position has merit. Here, you should also try to concede the strengths of the manufacturer's viewpoint. For example, you can say that although you understand that warranties have time limits, your case has some unique circumstances that justify your claim.

Then you would explain how the manufacturer would benefit from granting your request. Perhaps you could point out that you have been satisfied with other products made by this manufacturer and expect to purchase more in the future. You could also say that instead of requesting a new game console, you would be glad to send the console back to the factory to be repaired. This suggestion shows that you are fair and willing to compromise.

Finally, your Rogerian argument would reinforce your position and end with a concluding statement that emphasizes the idea that you are certain that the manufacturer wants to settle this matter fairly.

◉ EXERCISE 6.1

Read through the At Issue topics listed in this book's table of contents. Choose one topic, and then do the following:

1. Summarize your own position on the issue.

2. In a few sentences, summarize the main concerns of someone who holds the opposite position.

3. Identify some common ground that you and someone who holds the opposite position might have.

4. Write a sentence that explains how your position on the issue might benefit individuals (including those who hold opposing views) or society in general.

Writing Rogerian Arguments

Rogerian arguments are typically used to address issues that are open to compromise. By making it clear that you understand and respect the opinions of others, you avoid an "I win / you lose" situation and demonstrate empathy and respect for all points of view. In this sense, Rogerian arguments are more like negotiations than classical arguments. Thus, in a Rogerian argument, you spend a good deal of time defining the common ground that exists between you and those with whom you disagree. Ideally, you demonstrate that it is possible to reach a consensus, one that represents the common ground that exists between opposing sides. The more successful you are in accomplishing this goal, the more persuasive your argument will be. Of course with some issues—usually the most polarizing—a consensus is difficult or even impossible to achieve. In these cases, the best you can hope for is to convince people to agree on just one or two points. With other issues, however, you will be able to demonstrate to readers how they would benefit by moving toward your position.

> **NOTE**
>
> Although the Rogerian approach to argument can be used to develop a whole essay, it can also be part of a more traditional argument. In this case, it frequently appears in the refutation section, where opposing arguments are addressed.

In general, a Rogerian argument can be structured in the following way:

INTRODUCTION	Introduces the problem, pointing out how both the writer and reader are affected (establishes common ground)
BODY	Presents the reader's view of the problem
	Presents the writer's view of the problem (includes evidence to support the writer's viewpoint)
	Shows how the reader would benefit from moving toward the writer's position (includes evidence to support the writer's viewpoint)
	Lays out possible compromises that would benefit both reader and writer (includes evidence to support the writer's viewpoint)
CONCLUSION	Strong concluding statement reinforces the thesis and emphasizes compromise

⊘ EXERCISE 6.2

The following student essay includes all the elements of a Rogerian argument. This essay was written in response to the question, "Is it fair for instructors to require students to turn off their cell phones in class?" After you read the essay, answer the questions on page 199, consulting the outline above if necessary.

WHY CELL PHONES DO NOT BELONG IN THE CLASSROOM

ZOYA KAHN

Some college students think it is unfair for instructors to require   1
them to turn off their cell phones during class. Because they are accustomed to constant cell phone access, they don't understand how such a
rule is justified. Granted, a strict, no-exceptions policy requiring that cell
phones be turned off all over campus is not fair, but neither is a policy
that prevents instructors from imposing restrictions ("Official Notices").

Common ground   Both students and instructors know that cell phone use—including texting—during class can be disruptive. In addition, most would agree that the primary goal of a university is to create a respectful learning environment and that cell phone use during class undercuts this goal. For this reason, it is in everyone's interest for instructors to institute policies that require students to turn off cell phones during class.

Thesis statement

Many students believe that requiring them to turn off their cell phones is unfair because it makes them feel less safe. Students are understandably concerned that, with their phones turned off, they will be unreachable during an emergency. For example, text message alerts are part of the emergency response system for most universities. Similarly, cell phones are a way for friends and family to contact students if there is an emergency. For these reasons, many students think that they should be free to make their own decisions concerning cell use. They believe that by turning their phones to vibrate or silent mode, they are showing respect for their classmates. As one student points out, "Only a small percentage of students will misuse their phones. Then, why should every student have to sacrifice for someone's mistakes?" (SchoolBook). After all, most students are honest and courteous. However, those few students who are determined to misuse their phones will do so, regardless of the school's phone policy.

2

Reader's view of the problem

To protect the integrity of the school's learning environment, instructors are justified in requiring students to turn off their phones. Recent studies have shown how distracting cell phones can be during a class. For example, a ringing cell phone significantly impairs students' performance, and a vibrating phone can be just as distracting (End et al. 56–57). In addition, texting in class decreases students' ability to focus, lowers test performance, and lessens students' retention of class material (Tindell and Bohlander 2). According to a recent study, most students believe that texting causes problems, "including a negative impact on classroom learning for the person who is texting, and distraction for those sitting nearby" (Tindell and Bohlander 4). Even more disturbing, cell phones enable some students to cheat. Students can use cell phones to text test questions and answers, to search the Web, and to photograph exams. Although asking students to turn off their phones will not prevent all these problems, it will reduce the abuses, and this will benefit the majority of students.

3 *Writer's view of the situation*

Benefits for reader of writer's position

Students have good reasons for wanting to keep their phones on, but there are even better reasons for accepting some reasonable restrictions. First, when students use cell phones during class, they distract themselves (as well as their classmates) and undermine everyone's ability to learn. Second, having their cell phones on gives students a false sense of security. A leading cell phone company has found that cell phones can actually "detract from school safety and crisis preparedness" in numerous ways. For example, the use of cell phones during a crisis can overload the cell phone system and make it useless. In addition, cell phones make it easy for students to spread rumors and, in some cases, cell phone use has created more panic than the incidents that actually caused the rumors ("Cell Phones").

4

Possible compromise

One possible compromise is for instructors to join with students to create cell phone policies that take into consideration various situations and settings. For example, instructors could require students to turn off their phones only during exams. Instructors could also try to find ways to engage students by using cell phone technology in the classroom. For example, in some schools teachers take advantage of the various functions available on most cell phones—calculators, cameras, dictionaries, and Internet browsers ("Cell Phones"). In addition, schools should consider implementing alternative emergency alert systems. Such compromises would ensure safety, limit possible disruptions, reduce the potential for academic dishonesty, and enhance learning.

5

It is understandable that students want instructors to permit the use of cell phones during class, but it is also fair for instructors to ask students to turn them off. Although instructors should be able to restrict cell phone use, they should also make sure that students understand the need for this policy. It is in everyone's best interest to protect the integrity of the classroom and to make sure that learning is not compromised by cell phone use. To ensure the success of their education, students should be willing to turn off their phones.

6

Concluding statement

Works Cited

"Cell Phones and Text Messaging in Schools." *National School Safety and Security Services*, 2012, www.schoolsecurity.org/trends/cell -phones-and-text-messaging-in-schools/.

End, Christian M., Shaye Worthman, Mary Bridget Mathews, and Katharina
      Wetterau. "Costly Cell Phones: The Impact of Cell Phone Rings on Aca-
      demic Performance." *Teaching of Psychology*, vol. 37, no. 1, 2010, pp.
      55–57. *Academic Search Complete*, doi: 10.1080/00986280903425912.

"Official Notices." UCLA Registrar's Office, Department of Student
      Affairs, 24 Oct. 2011, www.registrar.ucla.edu/soc/notices.htm.

SchoolBook. "Time to Repeal the Cell Phone Ban, Students Say." New
      York Public Radio, 2 Nov. 2011, www.wnyc.org/story/303205-time
      -to-repeal-the-cellphone-ban-students-say/.

Tindell, Deborah R., and Robert W. Bohlander. "The Use and Abuse of
      Cell Phones and Text Messaging in the Classroom: A Survey of Col-
      lege Students." *College Teaching*, vol. 60, no. 1, 2012, pp. 1–9. *ERIC
      Institute of Education Services*, eric.ed.gov/?id=EJ951966.

Identifying the Elements of a Rogerian Argument

1. How does the writer attempt to establish common ground? Do you think she is successful?

2. What evidence does the writer supply to support her position?

3. Other than reinforcing the writer's position, what else is the conclusion trying to accomplish?

4. How does the concluding statement reinforce agreement and compromise?

5. How would this essay be different if it were written as a traditional (as opposed to a Rogerian) argument?

Understanding Toulmin Logic

Another way of describing the structure of argument was introduced by the philosopher Stephen Toulmin in his book *The Uses of Argument* (1958). Toulmin observed that although formal logic is effective for analyzing classical arguments, it is inadequate for describing the arguments you encounter in everyday life. Although Toulmin was primarily concerned with the structures of arguments at the level of sentences or paragraphs, his model is also useful when dealing with longer arguments.

In its simplest terms, a **Toulmin argument** has three parts—the *claim*, the *grounds*, and the *warrant*. The **claim** is the main point of the essay— usually stated as the thesis. The **grounds** are the evidence that a writer uses to support the claim. The **warrant** is the **inference**—either stated or implied—that connects the claim to the grounds.

A basic argument using Toulmin logic would have the following structure.

CLAIM	Online education should be a part of all students' education.
GROUNDS	Students who take advantage of online education get better grades and report less stress than students who do not.
WARRANT	Online education is a valuable educational option.

Notice that the three-part structure above resembles the **syllogism** that is the backbone of classical argument. (See pp. 125–129 for a discussion of syllogisms.)

> **NOTE**
>
> When you use Toulmin logic to construct an argument, you still use deductive and inductive reasoning. You arrive at your claim inductively from facts, observations, and examples, and you connect the grounds and the warrant to your claim deductively.

Constructing Toulmin Arguments

Real arguments—those you encounter in print or online every day—are not as simple as the three-part model above implies. To be convincing, arguments often contain additional parts. To account for the demands of everyday debates, Toulmin expanded his model to include the following six interconnected elements.

CLAIM	The **claim** is the main point of your essay. It is a debatable statement that the rest of the essay will support. *Online education should be a part of all students' education.*
GROUNDS	The **grounds** are the concrete evidence that a writer uses to support the claim. These are the facts and observations that support the thesis. They can also be the opinions of experts that you locate when you do research. *Studies show that students who take advantage of online education often get better grades than students who do not.*

Research indicates that students who take advantage of online education are under less stress than those who are not.

WARRANT

The **warrant** is the inference that links the claim with the grounds. The warrant is often an unstated assumption. Ideally, the warrant should be an idea with which your readers will agree. (If they do not agree with it, you will need to supply **backing**.)

Online education is a valuable educational option.

BACKING

The **backing** consists of statements that support the warrant.

My own experience with online education was positive. Not only did it enable me to schedule classes around my job, but it also enabled me to work at my own pace in my courses.

QUALIFIERS

The **qualifiers** are statements that limit the claim. For example, they can be the real-world conditions under which the claim is true. These qualifiers can include words such as *most, few, some, sometimes, occasionally, often,* and *usually.*

Online education should be a required part of most students' education.

REBUTTALS

The **rebuttals** are exceptions to the claim. They are counterarguments that identify the situations where the claim does not hold true.

Some people argue that online education deprives students of an interactive classroom experience, but a course chat room can give students a similar opportunity to interact with their classmates.

➲ EXERCISE 6.3

Look through this book's table of contents, and select an At Issue topic that interests you (ideally, one that you know something about). Write a sentence that states your position on this issue. (In terms of Toulmin argument, this statement is the *claim.*)

Then, supply as many of the expanded Toulmin model elements as you can, consulting the description of these elements above.

Claim: _____

_____

Grounds: _____

_____

_____

Warrant: _____

_____

_____

Backing: _____

_____

Qualifiers: _____

_____

_____

Rebuttals: _____

_____

Writing Toulmin Arguments

One of the strengths of the Toulmin model is that it emphasizes that presenting effective arguments involves more than stating ideas in absolute
terms. Unlike the classical model of argument, the Toulmin model encourages writers to make realistic and convincing points by including claims
and qualifiers and by addressing opposing arguments in down-to-earth
and constructive ways. In a sense, this method of constructing an argument reminds writers that arguments do not exist in a vacuum. They are
often quite subtle and are aimed at real readers who may or may not agree
with them.

In general, a Toulmin argument can be organized in the following way:

INTRODUCTION	Introduces the problem
	States the claim (and possibly the qualifier)
BODY	Possibly states the warrant
	Presents the backing that supports the warrant
	Presents the grounds that support the claim
	Presents the conditions of rebuttal
	States the qualifiers
CONCLUSION	Brings the argument to a close
	Strong concluding statement reinforces the claim

➲ EXERCISE 6.4

The following student essay, which includes all the elements of a Toulmin argument, was written in response to the question, "Are cheerleaders athletes?" After you read the essay, answer the questions on page 205, consulting the outline on the previous page if necessary.

COMPETITIVE CHEERLEADERS ARE ATHLETES

JEN DAVIS

Recently, the call to make competitive cheerleading an official   1
college sport and to recognize cheerleaders as athletes has gotten
stronger. Critics of this proposal maintain that cheerleading is simply
entertainment that occurs on the sidelines of real sporting events.
According to them, although cheerleading may show strength and skill,
it is not a competitive activity. This view of cheerleading, however,
misses the point. Because competitive cheerleading pits teams against
each other in physically and technically demanding athletic contests,
it should be recognized as a sport. For this reason, those who participate   Claim and qualifier
in the sport of competitive cheerleading should be considered athletes.

Acknowledging cheerleaders as athletes gives them the respect   2 Warrant
and support they deserve. Many people associate cheerleading with   Backing
pom-poms and short skirts and ignore the strength and skill competitive
cheerleading requires. Like athletes in other female-dominated sports,
cheerleaders unfortunately have had to fight to be taken seriously. For   Grounds
example, Title IX, the law that mandates gender equity in college
sports, does not recognize competitive cheerleading as a sport. This
situation demonstrates a very narrow definition of sports, one that
needs to be updated. As one women's sports advocate explains,
"What we consider sports are things that men have traditionally
played" (qtd. in Thomas). For this reason, women's versions of long-
accepted men's sports—such as basketball, soccer, and track—are easy
for people to respect and to support. Competitive cheerleading, however, departs from this model and is not seen as a sport even though

those who compete in it are skilled, accomplished athletes. As one coach points out, the athleticism of cheerleading is undeniable: "We don't throw balls, we throw people. And we catch them" (qtd. in Thomas).

Backing

Grounds

Recent proposals to rename competitive cheerleading "stunt" or "team acrobatics and tumbling" are an effort to reshape people's ideas about what cheerleaders actually do. Although some cheerleading squads have kept to their original purpose—to lead fans in cheering on their teams—competitive teams practice rigorously, maintain impressive levels of physical fitness, and risk serious injuries. Like other sports, competitive cheerleading involves extraordinary feats of strength and skill. Cheerleaders perform elaborate floor routines and ambitious stunts, including flips from multilevel human pyramids. Competitive cheerleaders also do what all athletes must do: they compete. Even a critic concedes that cheerleading could be "considered a sport when cheerleading groups compete against one another" (Sandler). Competitive cheerleading teams do just that; they enter competitive contests, are judged, and emerge as winners or losers.

3

Rebuttal

Qualifiers

Those in authority, however, are slow to realize that cheerleading is a sport. In 2010, a federal judge declared that competitive cheerleading was "too underdeveloped and disorganized" to qualify as a legitimate varsity sport under Title IX (Tigay). This ruling was shortsighted. Before competitive cheerleading can develop as a sport, it needs to be *acknowledged* as a sport. Without their schools' financial support, cheerleading teams cannot recruit, offer scholarships, or host competitions. To address this situation, several national groups are asking the National Collegiate Athletic Association (NCAA) to designate competitive cheerleading as an "emerging sport." By doing this, the NCAA would show its support and help competitive cheerleading to develop and eventually to flourish. This does not mean, however, that all cheerleaders are athletes or that all cheerleading is a sport. In addition, the NCAA does have reason to be cautious when it comes to redefining competitive cheerleading. Some schools have taken sideline cheerleading teams and recategorized them just so they could comply with Title IX. These efforts to sidestep the purpose of the law are, as one expert puts it, "obviously transparent and unethical" (Tigay). Even so, fear of possible abuse

4

should not keep the NCAA from doing what is right and giving legitimate athletes the respect and support they deserve.

Competitive cheerleaders are athletes in every sense of the word.   5
They are aggressive, highly skilled, physically fit competitors. For this
reason, they deserve to be acknowledged as athletes under Title IX and
supported by their schools and by the NCAA. Biased and outdated ideas
about what is (and what is not) a sport should not keep competitive
cheerleading from being recognized as the sport it is. As one proponent   Concluding statement
puts it, "Adding flexibility to the definition of college athletes is a com-
mon sense move that everyone can cheer for" ("Bona Fide"). It is time to
give competitive cheerleaders the support and recognition they deserve.

Works Cited

"Bona Fide Athletes." *USA Today*, 16 Oct. 2009, www.usatoday.com
/story/opinion/2019/10/16/bona-fide-athletes/81582044/. Editorial.

Sandler, Bernice R. "Certain Types of Competition Define Sports." *USA
Today*, 22 Oct. 2009, usatoday30.usatoday.com/printedition
/news/20091022/letters22_st2.art.htm.

Thomas, Katie. "Born on the Sideline, Cheering Clamors to Be a Sport."
New York Times, 22 May 2011, www.nytimes.com/2011/05/23/sports
/gender-games-born-on-sideline-cheering-clamors-to-be-sport.html.

Tigay, Chanan. "Is Cheerleading a Sport Protected by Title IX?" *CQ
Researcher*, 25 Mar. 2011, p. 276. library.cqpress.com/cqresearcher
/document.php?id=cqresrre2011032500.

Identifying the Elements of a Toulmin Argument

1. Summarize the position this essay takes as a three-part argument that includes the claim, the grounds, and the warrant.

2. Do you think the writer includes enough backing for her claim? What other supporting evidence could she have included?

3. Find the qualifier in the essay. How does it limit the argument? How else could the writer have qualified the argument?

4. Do you think the writer addresses enough objections to her claim? What other arguments could she have addressed?

5. Based on your reading of this essay, what advantages do you think Toulmin logic offers to writers? What disadvantages does it present?

Understanding Oral Arguments

Many everyday arguments—in school, on the job, or in your community—are presented orally. In many ways, an oral argument is similar to a written one: it has an introduction, a body, and a conclusion, and it addresses and refutes opposing points of view. In other, more subtle ways, however, an oral argument is different from a written one. Before you plan and deliver an oral argument, you should be aware of these differences.

The major difference between an oral argument and a written one is that an audience cannot reread an oral argument to clarify information. Listeners have to understand an oral argument the first time they hear it. To help your listeners, you need to design your presentation with this limitation in mind, considering the following guidelines:

- **An oral argument should contain verbal signals that help guide listeners.** Transitional phrases such as "My first point," "My second point," and "Let me sum up" are useful in oral arguments, where listeners do not have a written text in front of them. They alert listeners to information to come and signal shifts from one point to another.

- **An oral argument should use simple, direct language and avoid long sentences.** Complicated sentences that contain elevated language and numerous technical terms are difficult for listeners to follow. For this reason, your sentences should be straightforward and easy to understand.

- **An oral argument should repeat key information.** A traditional rule of thumb for oral arguments is, "Tell listeners what you're going to tell them; then tell it to them; finally, tell them what you've told them." In other words, in the introduction of an oral argument, tell your listeners what they are going to hear; in the body, discuss your points, one at a time; and finally, in your conclusion, restate your points. This intentional repetition ensures that your listeners follow (and remember) your points.

- **An oral argument should include visuals.** Visual aids can make your argument easier to follow. You can use visuals to identify your points as you discuss them. You can also use visuals—for example, charts, graphs, or tables—to clarify or reinforce key points as well as to add interest. Carefully selected visuals help increase the chances that what you are saying will be remembered.

Planning an Oral Argument

The work you do to plan your presentation is as important as the presentation itself. Here is some advice to consider as you plan your oral argument:

1. **Choose your topic wisely.** Select a topic that is somewhat controversial so listeners will want to hear your views. You can create interest in a topic, but it is easier to appeal to listeners if they are already interested in what you have to say. In addition, try to choose a topic that you know something about. Even though you will probably do some research, the process will be much easier if you are already familiar with the basic issues.

2. **Know your audience.** Consider your audience and its needs before you begin to plan your presentation. For example, how much do listeners already know about your topic? Are they well informed, or do they know little about it? If listeners are unfamiliar with your topic, you will have to supply background information and definitions of key terms. If they already know a lot, you can dispense with this material and discuss your subject in more depth. Also, assess your audience members' likely response to your presentation. Will they be receptive? Hostile? Neutral? The answers to these questions will help you decide which arguments will most likely be effective (and which will not).

3. **Know your time limit.** Most oral presentations have a time limit. If you run over your allotted time, you risk boring or annoying your listeners. If you finish too soon, it will seem as if you don't know much about your subject. As you prepare your argument, include all the information that you can cover within your time limit. Keep in mind

Ann Heisenfelt/AP Photo

Visual aids can help listeners follow an oral presentation.

that you will not be able to go into as much detail in a short speech as you will in a long speech, so plan accordingly.

4. **Identify your thesis statement.** Like a written argument, an oral argument should have a debatable thesis statement. Keep this statement simple, and make sure that it clearly conveys your position. Remember that in an oral argument, your listeners have to understand your thesis the first time they hear it. (See Chapter 7 for more on developing a thesis statement.)

5. **Gather support for your thesis.** Assume that your listeners are **skeptical**, that is, that they are not easily convinced. Even if you think that your audience is friendly, you still need to make a persuasive case. Don't make the mistake of thinking that listeners will automatically accept all your ideas just because they agree with your main point. For this reason, you need to support your thesis with compelling evidence if you expect listeners to conclude that your position is valid. Supporting evidence can be in the form of facts, observations, expert opinion, or statistics. Some of your support can come from your own experiences, but most will come from your research.

6. **Acknowledge your sources.** Remember that all of the information you get from your research needs to be acknowledged. As you deliver your presentation, let listeners know where the information you are using comes from—for example, "According to a 2015 editorial in the *New York Times . . .*" or "As Kenneth Davis says in his book *America's Hidden History. . . .*" This strategy enhances your credibility by showing that you are well informed about your topic. (Including source information also helps you protect yourself from unintentional **plagiarism**. See Chapter 11.)

7. **Prepare your speaking notes.** Effective speakers do not read their speeches. Instead, they prepare **speaking notes**—often on index cards—that list the points they want to make. (Microsoft's PowerPoint, as well as some other presentation software packages, has a section on each slide for speaking notes. Although the notes are displayed on the computer screen, they are not visible to the audience.) These notes guide you as you speak, so you should make sure that there are not too many of them and that they contain just key information. (If you use note cards, it is a good idea to number them so that you can be sure that they are in the correct order.)

8. **Prepare visual aids.** Visual aids help you to communicate your thesis and your supporting points more effectively. Visuals increase interest in your presentation, and they also strengthen your argument by reinforcing your points and making them easier for listeners to follow and to understand. In addition, visuals can help establish your credibility and thus improve the persuasiveness of your argument.

You can use the following types of visual aids in your presentations:

- Diagrams
- Photographs
- Slides
- Smartboards, flip charts
- Overhead transparencies
- Document cameras
- Handouts, objects

In order moving clockwise from top left:
© deomis/Shutterstock.com; © Peter Vaclavek/
Shutterstock.com; © Tarapong Siri/
Shutterstock.com; © deomis/Shutterstock.com

In addition to these kinds of visual aids, you can also use **presentation software**, such as Microsoft's PowerPoint or the Web-based application *Prezi* (Prezi.com). With presentation software, you can easily create visually appealing and persuasive slides. You can insert scanned photographs or drawings into slides, or you can cut and paste charts, graphs, and tables into them. You can even include YouTube videos and MP3 files. Keep in mind, however, that the images, videos, or sound files that you use must support your thesis; if they are irrelevant, they will distract or confuse your listeners. (See pp. 218–221 for examples of PowerPoint slides.)

9. **Practice your presentation.** As a general rule, you should spend as much time rehearsing your speech as you do preparing it. In other words, practice, practice, practice. Be sure you know the order in which you will present your points and when you will move from one visual to another. Rehearse your speech aloud with just your speaking notes and your visuals until you are confident that you can get through your presentation effectively. Try to anticipate any problems that may arise with your visuals, and solve them at this stage of the process. If possible, practice your speech in the room in which you will actually deliver it. Bring along a friend, and ask for feedback. Finally, cut or add material as needed until you are certain that you can stay within your time limit.

CHECKLIST

Designing and Displaying Visuals

☐ Use images that are large enough for your audience to see and that will reproduce clearly.

(continued)

☐ Make lettering large enough for your audience to see. Use 40- to 50-point type for titles, 25- to 30-point type for major points, and 20- to 25-point type for less important points.

☐ Use bulleted lists, not full sentences or paragraphs.

☐ Put no more than three or four points on a single visual.

☐ Make sure there is a clear contrast between your lettering and the background.

☐ Don't show your listeners the visual before you begin to speak about it. Display the visual only when you discuss it.

☐ Face your listeners when you discuss a visual. Even if you point to the screen, always look at your listeners. Never turn your back on your audience.

☐ Introduce and discuss each visual. Don't simply show or read the visual to your audience. Always tell listeners more than they can read or see for themselves.

☐ Don't use elaborate visuals or special effects that will distract your audience.

⊖ EXERCISE 6.5

Look through the table of contents of this book, and select three At Issue topics that interest you. Imagine that you are planning to deliver an oral argument to a group of college students on each of these topics. For each topic, list three visual aids you could use to enhance your presentation.

Delivering Oral Arguments

Delivery is the most important part of a speech. The way you speak, your interaction with the audience, your posture, and your eye contact all affect your overall presentation. In short, a confident, controlled speaker will have a positive impact on an audience, while a speaker who fumbles with note cards, speaks in a shaky voice, or seems disorganized will lose credibility. To make sure that your listeners see you as a credible, reliable source of information, follow these guidelines:

1. **Accept nervousness.** For most people, nervousness is part of the speech process. The trick is to convert this nervousness into energy that you can channel into your speech. The first step in dealing with nervousness is to make sure that you have rehearsed enough. If you have prepared adequately, you will probably be able to handle any problem you may encounter. If you make a mistake, you can correct it. If you forget something, you can fit it in later.

DEALING WITH NERVOUSNESS

If nervousness is a problem, the following strategies can help you to relax:

- **Breathe deeply.** Take a few deep breaths before you begin speaking. Research has shown that increased oxygen has a calming effect on the brain.

- **Use visualization.** Imagine yourself delivering a successful speech, and fix this image in your mind. It can help dispel anxiety.

- **Empty your mind.** Consciously try to eliminate all negative thoughts. Think of your mind as a room full of furniture. Imagine yourself removing each piece of furniture until the room is empty.

- **Drink water.** Before you begin to speak, take a few sips of water. Doing so will eliminate the dry mouth that is a result of nervousness. Don't, however, drink water during your speech.

- **Keep things in perspective.** Remember, your speech is a minor event in your life. Nothing that you do or say will affect you significantly.

2. **Look at your audience.** When you speak, look directly at the members of your audience. At the beginning of the speech, make eye contact with a few audience members who seem to be responding positively. As your speech progresses, look directly at as many audience members as you can. Try to sweep the entire room. Don't focus excessively on a single person or on a single section of your audience.

3. **Speak naturally.** Your presentation should sound like a conversation, not a performance. This is not to suggest that your presentation should include slang, ungrammatical constructions, or colloquialisms; it should conform to the rules of standard English. The trick is to maintain the appearance of a conversation while following the conventions of public speaking. Achieving this balance takes practice, but it is a goal worth pursuing.

4. **Speak slowly.** When you give a presentation, you should speak more slowly than you do in normal conversation. This strategy gives listeners time to process what they hear—and gives you time to think about what you are saying.

5. **Speak clearly and correctly.** As you deliver your presentation, speak clearly. Do not drop endings, and be careful to pronounce words correctly. Look up the pronunciation of unfamiliar words in a dictionary, or

ask your instructor for help. If you go though an entire speech pronouncing a key term or a name incorrectly, your listeners will question your competence.

6. **Move purposefully.** As you deliver your speech, don't pace, move your hands erratically, or play with your note cards. Try to stand in one spot, with both feet flat on the floor. Move only when necessary—for example, to point to a visual or to display an object. If you intend to distribute printed material to your listeners, do so only when you are going to discuss it. (Try to arrange in advance for someone else to give out your handouts.) If you are not going to refer to the material in your presentation, wait until you have finished your speech before you distribute it. Depending on the level of formality of your presentation and the size of your audience, you may want to stand directly in front of your audience or behind a podium.

7. **Be prepared for the unexpected.** Don't get flustered if things don't go exactly as you planned. If you forget material, work it in later. If you make a mistake, correct it without apologizing. Most of the time, listeners will not realize that something has gone wrong unless you call attention to it. If someone in the audience looks bored, don't worry. You might consider changing your pace or your volume, but keep in mind that the person's reaction might have nothing to do with your presentation. He or she might be tired, preoccupied, or just a poor listener.

Remember to project confidence and control as you speak.

© Wavebreak Media/Agefotostock

8. **Leave time for questions.** End your presentation by asking if your listeners have any questions. As you answer questions, keep in mind the following advice:

   ■ *Be prepared.* Make sure you have anticipated the obvious counterarguments to your position, and be prepared to address them. In addition, prepare a list of websites or other resources that you can refer your audience to for more information.

   ■ *Repeat a question before you answer it.* This technique enables everyone in the audience to hear the question, and it also gives you time to think of an answer.

   ■ *Keep control of interchanges.* If a questioner repeatedly challenges your answer or monopolizes the conversation, say that you will be glad to discuss the matter with him or her after your presentation is finished.

   ■ *Be honest.* Answer questions honestly and forthrightly. If you don't know the answer to a question, say so. Tell the questioner you will locate the information that he or she wants and send it by email. Above all, do not volunteer information that you are not sure is correct.

   ■ *Use the last question to summarize.* When you get to the last question, end your answer by restating the main point of your argument.

Composing an Oral Argument

The written text of an oral argument is organized just as any other argument is: it has an introduction that gives the background of the issue and states the thesis, it has a body that presents evidence that supports the thesis, it identifies and refutes arguments against the thesis, and it ends with a concluding statement.

In general, an oral argument can be structured in the following way:

INTRODUCTION	Presents the background of the issue
	States the thesis
BODY	Presents evidence: Point 1 in support of the thesis
	Presents evidence: Point 2 in support of the thesis
	Presents evidence: Point 3 in support of the thesis
	Refutes opposing arguments
CONCLUSION	Brings the argument to a close
	Concluding statement restates thesis
	Speaker asks for questions

● **EXERCISE 6.6**

The following oral argument was presented by a student in a speech course in response to the assignment, "Argue for or against the advantages of a 'gap year' between high school and college." (Her PowerPoint slides appear at the end of the speech.) After you read this argument, answer the questions on page 221, consulting the outline on the previous page if necessary.

AN ARGUMENT IN SUPPORT OF THE "GAP YEAR"

CHANTEE STEELE

College: even the word sounded wonderful when I was in high   1
school. Everyone told me it would be the best time of my life. They told me that I would take courses in exciting new subjects and that I'd make lifelong friends. [Show slide 1.] What they didn't tell me was that I would be anxious, confused, and uncertain about my major and about my future. Although this is only my second year in college, I've already changed my major once, and to be honest, I'm still not sure I've made the right decision. But during the process of changing majors, my adviser gave me some reading material that included information about a "gap year." A gap year is a year off between high school and college when students focus on work or community service and learn about themselves—something that would have benefited me. Although gaining popularity in the United States, the gap year still suggests images of spoiled rich kids who want to play for a year before going to college. According to educator Christina Wood, however, in the United Kingdom a gap year is common; it is seen as a time for personal growth that helps students mature (36). [Show slide 2.] In fact, 230,000 British students take a gap year before going to college. As the rest of my speech

Thesis statement   will show, a well-planned gap year gives students time to mature, to explore potential careers, and to volunteer or travel.

Evidence: Point 1 in   [Show slide 3.] Apparently I'm not alone in my uncertainty about my   2
support of thesis   major or about my future. As Holly Bull, a professional gap-year counselor, explains, "The National Research Center for College and University Admissions estimates that over 50 percent of students switch majors at

least once" (8). As they go from high school to college, most students have little time to think about what to do with their lives. A gap year before college would give them time to learn more about themselves. According to Wood, "Gap years provide valuable life experiences and maturity so students are more ready to focus on their studies when they return" (37). A year off would give some students the perspective they need to mature and to feel more confident about their decisions. Bull agrees, noting that the gap year helps students choose or confirm the area of study they want to pursue, that it makes them "instantly more mature," and that it "boosts their excitement about learning" (7–8).

The gap year gives students many options to explore before going to college. [Show slide 4.] This slide shows just some of the resources students can use as they prepare for their gap year. As you can see, they can explore opportunities for employment, education, and volunteer work. There are even resources for students who are undecided. As David Lesesne, the dean of admissions at Sewanee, says, "Some students do very interesting and enriching things: hike the Appalachian Trail, herd sheep in Crete, play in a rock band, [or even] attend school in Guatemala" (qtd. in Wood 37). Many other students, especially in these economic hard times, use the gap year to earn money to offset the high cost of their education (Wood 35).

3 Evidence: Point 2 in support of thesis

Taking a gap year can also help students to get into better colleges. According to an article by the dean of admissions at Harvard, "Occasionally students are admitted to Harvard or other colleges in part because they accomplished something unusual during a year off" (Fitzsimmons, McGrath, and Ducey). Depending on the scope of their service or work, a gap year could enable students to earn scholarships that they were not eligible for before. In fact, some colleges actually recommend that students take time off after high school. Harvard is one of several U.S. colleges that "encourages admitted students to defer enrollment for one year to travel, pursue a special project or activity, work, or spend time in another meaningful way" (Fitzsimmons, McGrath, and Ducey). Furthermore, evidence shows that a gap year can help students to be more successful after they begin in college. One Middlebury College admissions officer has calculated that "a single gap semester was the strongest predictor of academic success at his school"

4 Evidence: Point 3 in support of thesis

(Bull 7). Given this support for the gap year and given the resources that are now available to help students plan it, the negative attitudes about it in the United States are beginning to change.

Refutation of opposing arguments

In spite of these benefits, parental concerns about "slackerdom" and money are common. Supporters of the gap year acknowledge that students have to be motivated to make the most of their experiences. Clearly, the gap year is not for everyone. For example, students who are not self-motivated may not benefit from a gap year. In addition, parents worry about how much money the gap year will cost them. This is a real concern when you add the year off to the expense of four years of college (Wood 37). However, if finances are a serious concern, students can spend their gap year working in their own communities or taking advantage of a paid experience like AmeriCorps—which, as the AmeriCorps website shows, covers students' room and board *and* offers an educational stipend after students complete the program. [Show slide 5.] Additionally, parents and students should consider the time and money that is wasted when a student who is not ready for college starts school and then drops out.

5

After considering the benefits of a gap year, I have concluded that more students should postpone college for a year. Many students (like me) are uncertain about their goals. We welcome new opportunities and are eager to learn from new experiences and may find a year of service both emotionally and intellectually rewarding. Given another year to mature, many of us would return to school with a greater sense of purpose, focus, and clarity. In some cases, the gap year could actually help us get

6

Concluding statement

into better schools and possibly get more financial aid. If we intend to take the college experience seriously, spending a gap year learning about our interests and abilities would help us to become better, more confident, and ultimately more focused students. [Show slide 6.]

Are there any questions?

7

Works Cited

Bull, Holly. "Navigating a Gap Year." *TeenLife*, Feb. 2011, pp. 6–9.

Fitzsimmons, William, et al. "Time Out or Burn Out for the Next Generation." *Harvard College Office of Admissions*, 2011, college.harvard .edu/admissions/preparing-college/should-i-take-time.

Wood, Christina. "Should You Take a 'Gap Year'?" *Careers and Colleges*, Fall 2007, pp. 36–37.

Slide 1

© Ana Blazic/istockphoto.com

Slide 2

230,000 students between 18 and 25 take a Gap
Year in the U.K.

—Tom Griffiths, founder and director
of GapYear.com

(qtd. in Christina Wood, "Should You Take a 'Gap Year'?,"
Careers and Colleges, Fall 2007)

Slide 3

50% of students change their major at least once.
—National Research Center for College
and University Admissions

Slide 4

A Few Links for the Potential "Gapster"

(links from Holly Bull, "The Possibilities of the Gap
Year," *Chronicle of Higher Education* 52.44 [2006])

Employment

Cool Works: CoolWorks.com (domestic jobs)

Working Abroad: WorkingAbroad.org (jobs overseas)

Education

Global Routes: GlobalRoutes.org (semester-long courses)

Sea-mester: Seamester.com (sea voyage programs)

Volunteer Work

AmeriCorps: AmeriCorps.gov

City Year: CityYear.org

Thoughtful Texts for Fence Sitters

Karl Haigler and Rae Nelson, *The Gap-Year
Advantage* (Macmillan, 2005)

Colin Hall, *Taking Time Off* (Princeton Review, 2003)

Charlotte Hindle and Joe Bindloss, *The Gap Year
Book* (Lonely Planet, 2005)

Slide 5

Courtesy of Corporation for National and Community Service. Reproduced by permission.

Slide 6

In order moving clockwise from top left: © Roger Cracknell 01/classic/Alamy; © Ben Blankenburg/iStock/Getty Images; © Steve Stock/Alamy; David Cordner/Getty Images

Identifying the Elements of an Oral Argument

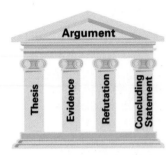

1. Where does this oral argument include verbal signals to help guide readers?

2. Does this oral argument use simple, direct language? What sections of the speech, if any, could be made simpler?

3. Where does this oral argument repeat key information for emphasis? Is there any other information that you think should have been repeated?

4. What opposing arguments does the speaker identify? Does she refute them convincingly?

5. How effective are the visuals that accompany the text of this oral argument? Are there enough visuals? Are they placed correctly? What other information do you think could have been displayed in a visual?

6. What questions would you ask this speaker at the end of her speech?

Is Online Education Better Than Classroom Education?

© Karl Dolenc/iStock/Getty Images

Go back to page 191, and reread the At Issue box, which gives background about whether online education is better than classroom instruction. As the following sources illustrate, this question has a number of possible answers.

After you review the sources listed below, you will be asked to answer some questions and to complete some simple activities. This work will help you to understand both the content and the structure of the sources. When you are finished, you will be ready to develop an argument—using one of the three alternative approaches to argument discussed in this chapter—that takes a position on whether online education is better than classroom learning.

SOURCES

The Evolution of Online Schooling

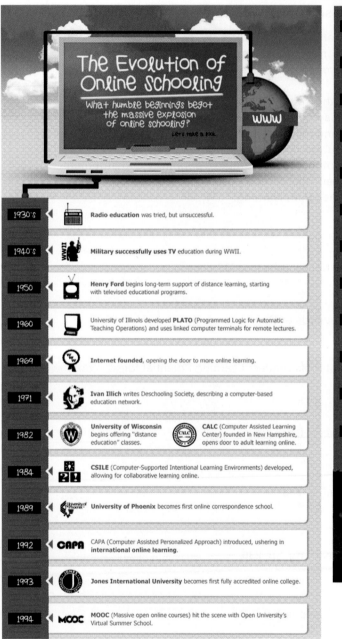

1930's — Radio education was tried, but unsuccessful.

1940's — Military successfully uses TV education during WWII.

1950 — Henry Ford begins long-term support of distance learning, starting with televised educational programs.

1960 — University of Illinois developed PLATO (Programmed Logic for Automatic Teaching Operations) and uses linked computer terminals for remote lectures.

1969 — Internet founded, opening the door to more online learning.

1971 — Ivan Illich writes Deschooling Society, describing a computer-based education network.

1982 — University of Wisconsin begins offering "distance education" classes. CALC (Computer Assisted Learning Center) founded in New Hampshire, opens door to adult learning online.

1984 — CSILE (Computer-Supported Intentional Learning Environments) developed, allowing for collaborative learning online.

1989 — University of Phoenix becomes first online correspondence school.

1992 — CAPA (Computer Assisted Personalized Approach) introduced, ushering in international online learning.

1993 — Jones International University becomes first fully accredited online college.

1994 — MOOC (Massive open online courses) hit the scene with Open University's Virtual Summer School.

1995 — University of Illinois develops Mallard, a web-based course management system allowing flexibility for graduate students to serve as online professors.

1996 — Duke starts Global Executive MBA program, combining online learning with on-campus classes in Europe, Asia, and Latin America.

1997 — California Virtual University opens offering 1,500 online courses. Blackboard founded, allowing for a more personalized online learning experience

1999 — U.S. Department of Education establishes the Distance Learning Education Demonstration Program, allows financial aid distributions for distance learners.

2000 — First online law school opens: Concord University School of Law.

2001 — Moodle introduced: this open-source software enabled educators to create better online learning websites.

2003 — Coalition for Christian Colleges and Universities' GlobalNet accommodates 1 million online learners.

2004 — Sakai initiated a Collaboration and Learning Environment (CLE), initiating a collaborative online learning environment.

2010 — Online education revolution begins. FREE online courses Top colleges offer some free online courses collaborative online learning environment.

2011 — Nearly 1/3 of all college students enrolled in at least one online class.

2012 — Harvard Open Courses are opened to the public, offering online classes to mimic real Harvard classrooms.

Today — Over 6 million students enrolled in online classes. Twice as many students earn online degrees as traditional degrees.

References:
- techcrunch.com/2012/08/09/online-education-degrees-now-dwarf-traditional-universities/
- docs.moodle.org/24/en/Online_Learning_History
- seacsstudentweb.org/a-history-of-online-learning.php
- innovativelearning.com/online_learning/timeline.html
- bakersguide.com/articles/127-distance-education-timeline

Brought to you by: collegedegreesearch.net

www.collegedegreesearch.net

⊃ AT ISSUE: SOURCES FOR USING ALTERNATIVE APPROACHES TO ARGUMENT

1. What is the purpose of this infographic? How successful is it in achieving this purpose?

2. What kind of audience does this infographic seem to be addressing? How can you tell?

3. What is this infographic's main idea or message? Write a one-sentence summary of this main idea.

4. Where does the infographic appeal to *ethos*? Is this appeal necessary? Why or why not?

5. How clear is this infographic? What other arrangement (or arrangements) of words, numbers, color, and spacing could have been used?

6. If you were going to write an argumentative essay in favor of online education, which information in this infographic would you find most useful? Which information would you find least useful? Explain.

This essay is from the online newspaper *Community College Times*. It appeared on November 16, 2011.

THE RISKS AND REWARDS OF ONLINE LEARNING

CHRIS BUSTAMANTE

In 2008, investors wanted to buy Rio Salado College, the nation's largest online public community college headquartered in Tempe, Ariz. The offer was more than $400 million with plans to convert it into a national, for-profit, online school.

Rio Salado wasn't for sale, but the offer proved how much demand exists for serving students who find traditional education systems inconvenient and need the flexibility of online formats.

Online learning may not be the first thing that comes to mind when community colleges consider providing support for student success. But that mindset is changing. It has to. The 2011 Sloan Survey of Online Learning reported that more than six million college students in the fall of 2010 took at least one online course, comprising nearly one-third of all college and university students. The growth rate in online course enrollment far exceeds the growth rate of the overall higher education student population.

Still, there is healthy skepticism about the proliferation of online learning and views still differ about its value. According to surveys by the Pew Research Center and the *Chronicle of Higher Education*, less than 30 percent of the public believes that online and classroom courses provide the same educational value. Half of college presidents share that belief.

Any way you look at it, online learning is an increasingly vital part of producing the number of qualified graduates needed to meet future workforce demands—when it is done correctly.

A Calculated Risk

In 1996, Rio Salado, one of 10 Maricopa Community Colleges, took a calculated risk and began offering courses online—16 to start—just when the Internet was taking off. Critics at the time challenged the quality of online education and claimed that students wouldn't adjust well to such a radical change in their learning environment. But Maricopa and Rio Salado pushed ahead, determined to create an innovative, nontraditional, and nimble approach that is responsive to and supportive of changing student needs.

The risks have proven to be worth it. While no one could have predicted the economic environment that students and higher education face today, making the decision to move online proved to be provident for the college and students. Rio Salado extended educational access to students who found traditional college to be out of reach in Arizona, nationwide, and around the world.

The college currently serves nearly 70,000 students each year, with more than 41,000 enrolled in 600-plus online courses.

Keeping Costs Down

To keep costs down, Rio Salado supports more than 60 certificate and degree 8 programs with just 22 residential faculty and more than 1,400 adjunct faculty. Our "one-course, many sections" model uses a master course approved by the resident faculty and taught by adjunct faculty in more than 6,000 course sections. The college's cost to educate students is as much as 48 percent less than peer institutions nationwide.

Without the expense of a traditional campus, Rio Salado has been able to 9 focus on building and improving its RioLearn platform, a customized learning management system that provides access to course-related resources, instructors, fellow students, and other support services.

Focused on Student Support

Meeting students' needs means providing access to robust, comprehensive 10 support services that are customized for their complex lifestyles, whether they are a working adult, an active military student accessing their coursework online, or someone taking in-person classes in adult basic education, incarcerated reentry, early college, or workforce training programs. Today's students need the resources of round-the-clock instructional and technology helpdesks, tutoring, and virtual library services. Additionally, we never cancel an online class and offer the flexibility of 48 start dates a year.

Students also need real-time support to keep them on track. Predictive 11 analytic technology allows the college to monitor online student engagement and predict by the eighth day of class the level of success students will have in a course. When needed, instructors facilitate interventions to minimize risks and support successful course completion.

Building a culture of unified support focused on completion won't happen overnight. It took 30 years for Rio Salado to get to this point. Our upside-down faculty model has made it possible for the college to adapt a corporate "systems approach," and all Rio Salado staff and faculty participate in a training program to instill a unified commitment to helping students complete their degree programs. 12

Technical Challenges

Staying ahead of the online curve comes with its share of challenges. Rio Salado 13 had to build its own learning management system because there wasn't one available that would support all of the features that our faculty and students wanted. In partnership with Microsoft and Dell, RioLearn was designed to be scalable to more than 100,000 students.

However, a few years ago, it didn't fully support Mac users. Although stu- 14 dents could access their coursework, they had to switch Internet browsers to do so. A new version of RioLearn was launched in 2010 to help students access their courses, regardless of the platform they are using.

We've also learned that many of our students are co-enrolled in traditional 15
colleges and universities. They come to Rio Salado for flexibility, affordability,
and convenience to accelerate their degree on their terms. They bank credits and
ultimately transfer those credits to complete their degrees at another institution.

A recent report examines Rio Salado's efforts and the experience and per- 16
spectives of more than 30 institutions throughout the U.S. addressing similar
challenges to ensure student success—especially for low-income, minority,
and adult students—and pursuing promising approaches to increase college
completion rates.

Reimagining the System

Our country can't continue to allow millions of people who are college mate- 17
rial to fall through the cracks. We must find new, convenient, and high-quality
educational options for students who might
otherwise have missed out on a college education. That means serving more students in
more places—especially where college enroll-
ments have been capped—through efforts
such as online early college initiatives, by cre-
ating cohorts at the high-school level and developing open-source courses.

> "We must find new, convenient, and high-quality educational options for students."

With tuition rising faster than the rate of inflation, and the best-paying jobs 18
requiring some form of postsecondary degree, specialized certification, or licen-
sure, we have to find solutions that lower costs for students. We need to innovate. We need new models of education to leverage public resources through
private and public partnerships and increase the capacity to serve nontraditional
students through productive and cost-efficient means.

It's encouraging to see the rapid growth in affordable online learning. It 19
has broken down the barriers of time, distance, and affordability without sacrificing high-quality academics. But shoring up its credibility and value for
students means heeding some of the lessons learned over the past 15 years.
The stakes for getting it right are certainly high and getting higher.

⊘ AT ISSUE: SOURCES FOR USING ALTERNATIVE APPROACHES TO ARGUMENT

1. According to Bustamante, "[T]here is healthy skepticism about the proliferation of online learning" (para. 4). What does he mean? What reservations, if any, do you have about the rise of online education?

2. In this essay, where does the claim appear? How is this claim quali- fied? How does the qualifier set up the rest of the essay?

3. Bustamante's article focuses on the development of one school's online education program. Do you think the risks and rewards he dis- cusses also apply to other schools' online offerings? What factors might account for any differences in other schools' experiences with online learning?

4. What is Bustamante's purpose? What does he want readers to take away from his essay?

5. Does Bustamante ever address opposing arguments? If he does, where? If he does not, should he have addressed them? Explain.

6. What does Bustamante mean when he says that we must reimagine the system of higher education? What problems does he see with the current educational system? How will online education help solve these problems?

This essay was published in the *Daily Nebraskan*, the student newspaper of the University of Nebraska, on November 29, 2011.

RELIANCE ON ONLINE MATERIALS HINDERS LEARNING POTENTIAL FOR STUDENTS

DAVID SMITH

Students of today should be thankful for the . . . plethora of ways available for them to learn. Compared to our grandparents, parents, and even older siblings, we have access to modes of communication and education that would not have been possible even 10 years ago. 1

Students today, not just in college but in high school, middle school, and elementary school, take in and process astounding amounts of information on a daily basis. We have access to TV and the Internet, social media outlets such as Twitter and Facebook, and a nearly inexhaustible supply of ways to keep in contact with and learn about one another. 2

This variety has begun to work its way into academia, as well; more and more, it seems, organized instruction is moving beyond the classroom and into cyberspace. Pencils and paper, once the sole staples of the educational experience, are slowly being ousted by keyboards, webcams, and online dropboxes. 3

Here at the University of Nebraska–Lincoln, this growing prevalence is easy to see. Just look at Blackboard and how some courses are completely dependent upon it. Blackboard has everything from grade tracking and homework assignments to the administration of quizzes and exams. 4

Look at MyRED, which now handles everything from class enrollment and scheduling to residence hall contracts and meal plans. 5

Look at things such as the Love Library's EBSCO search engine, which gives students access to a greater wealth of information than even the most practiced scholar would know what to do with, and online courses such as the Keller Plan, which allow students to complete coursework and earn credit without having to leave their dorm rooms. 6

> "While the Internet has certainly made learning easier, has it made it better?"

It's clear to even the most casual observer that taking in and processing information is far easier for the students of today than it was for the students of 100, 50, or even 10 years ago. 7

But it begs the question: While the Internet has certainly made learning easier, has it made it better? Not necessarily. 8

Think for a moment about the fundamental differences between a traditional course, taught in a classroom, and one conducted entirely via Blackboard's online services. 9

In the former, students are bound by structure and organization. They 10 must attend class on a regular basis or suffer the consequences, typically (though not always) complete regular homework assignments for points, and are constantly reminded of the work that needs to be done by the ever-present figure (or specter) of the professor.

Such is not the case with classes taken outside the classroom. The 11 instructions for such courses are, at least in my experience, pared down to the following: "Read this by this date, this by this date, and this by this date. There are quizzes on Day X, Day Y, and Day Z, and the final exam can be taken at any time during finals week in the testing center. Have a nice semester."

Now, I know that college is supposed to be a place of greater expectations, 12 of increased responsibilities and better time management skills. I get that, I really do. But the sad truth is that all too often, giving a student that kind of freedom doesn't end well.

By removing the sense of structure from a course, you remove the stu- 13 dent's notion that he or she is under any sort of pressure, any sort of time constraint. By removing a constantly present instructor, you remove what is, in many cases, the sole source of motivation students have to do well in a class. You take away the sense of urgency, the sense of immediate requirement, and by extension the student's drive.

Readings are put off or forgotten, material review sessions (if there are 14 any) are blown off or missed, and quizzes and exams are ultimately bombed. More often than not, the student will get caught up with work from the other, more traditional courses on their schedule—the ones they remember they have homework in because it was assigned in class this afternoon or the ones they have to study for because the professor reminded them about the upcoming exam the other day. Unfortunately, another marked difference between traditional and online courses is that the latters are typically far less forgiving when it comes to things such as deadlines and extensions, making it next to impossible for students to get out of the holes they dig themselves into.

The Internet is a powerful tool. It allows us to share, distribute, and 15 absorb more information in a single year than our ancestors absorbed in a lifetime, and its capacity to do those things is constantly growing. What people, educators in particular, need to realize is that no matter how powerful a tool it becomes, the Internet should never become anything more than that: a tool.

There will never be an adequate online substitute for the watchful eye 16 and the stern voice of a professor, or the pressure of an exam time limit that is about to expire, or the dismay and subsequent motivation to improve that can come from a handed-back assignment with a failing grade scrawled on it.

Now . . . off to class. 17

⊙ AT ISSUE: SOURCES FOR USING ALTERNATIVE APPROACHES TO ARGUMENT

1. Paragraph 8 expresses Smith's thesis in the form of a question and answer. Paraphrase this thesis statement in one sentence.

2. Why does Smith spend his first seven paragraphs discussing the amount of information currently available to students?

3. In paragraph 8, Smith says that his previous statement "begs the question." What does he mean? Is this statement actually an example of **begging the question**? Explain.

4. How, according to Smith, is online education different from class-room learning? What problems does Smith identify with online learning?

5. In paragraph 13, Smith says that online courses remove "the sense of structure from a course." What evidence does he present to support this statement?

6. What does Smith mean in paragraph 15 when he says that what we "need to realize is that no matter how powerful a tool it becomes, the Internet should never become anything more than that: a tool"? What is he warning against here?

7. Where does Smith use the techniques of Rogerian argument? Does he use these techniques often enough? Does he use them effectively? Explain.

8. In paragraph 16, Smith says, "There will never be an adequate online substitute for the watchful eye and the stern voice of a professor." Do you agree? Do you think this highlights a disadvantage of online edu-cation (as Smith intends) or an advantage?

This essay is from the October 9, 2011, edition of the *Daily Trojan*, the student newspaper of the University of Southern California.

ONLINE EDUCATION NEEDS CONNECTION

ELENA KADVANY

From the most trivial of issues (who went to what party this weekend?) to the most traditional of society's establishments (newspapers, music and book industries, Postal Service), the Internet has transformed our lives. But one area remains to be revolutionized digitally: education. 1

Online education is on the rise, pitting those who support the idea of a virtual university for its ability to increase access and revenue against those who believe there is no substitute for real-time, traditional educational experiences. 2

There's one thing wrong with the entire conversation, however: Viewing online education as a new higher-education business model that must supplant the current system is a close-minded view. Why not look at it as a means by which we can strengthen and innovate education by blending digital and traditional elements? 3

Online education began mostly as distance-learning programs for graduate degrees that lend themselves to the medium like engineering or business. 4

USC's Viterbi School of Engineering has a well-established Distance Education Network that offers more than 30 master's degree programs. 5

Now, in times of financial crisis, schools across the country, especially in California, are searching for ways to reinvent themselves. This has led to an expansion of digital courses into the undergraduate sphere. 6

But there is a distinct danger in allowing finance-driven ideas to dominate the dialogue about schools' futures and education in general, especially for undergraduates whose educational experiences and life tracks are so defined by their first four years on a campus. 7

> "[T]here is a distinct danger in allowing finance-driven ideas to dominate."

This is not to say that universities should completely reject online learning. It's great to be able to listen to lectures at home or gain access to classes you can't physically attend or afford. 8

Higher learning, however, is about a level of personal interaction and commitment that can't be re-created online. 9

Before transferring to USC, I spent a semester at the University of San Francisco, where I took a hybrid service-learning Spanish class. It combined conventional in-class instruction twice a week with a once-a-week class online with Blackboard, in addition to a requirement of outside community service hours. 10

This kind of blending shows the innovative potential universities should 11
recognize and seize. The idea of a virtual university should not replace the
traditional, but instead should merge with it.

For undergraduates, hybrid classes could be incredibly valuable and much 12
more engaging for a generation that spends so much time online.

Some of the University of California schools have submitted courses in 13
response to an online education pilot project proposed by the University's
Office of the President.

Sebastian Thrun, a professor at Stanford University renowned for leading 14
the team that built Google's self-driving car, now offers a free online course,
"Introduction to Artificial Intelligence." Enrollment in this class has jumped
from 58,000 to 130,000 across the world in the past month, according to the
New York Times. USC is lucky enough to have generous alumni that keep it
more than afloat financially. But as many universities choose to go digital,
USC might want to follow suit.

The potential of all things online is vast. And there's no match for the 15
value of real-time, person-to-person educational experiences.

There's no reason universities can't take advantage of both. 16

◯ AT ISSUE: SOURCES FOR USING ALTERNATIVE APPROACHES TO ARGUMENT

1. In paragraph 2, Kadvany says that online education pits those who
   support virtual education against those who support traditional classroom education. Do the essays in this At Issue section confirm or
   challenge Kadvany's point? Explain.

2. In paragraph 3, Kadvany says that it is wrong to view online education as a "higher-education business model" that will displace classroom education. Why does she use the term "business model"? Does
   she expect this term to have positive or negative connotations for her
   readers? How can you tell?

3. How has the financial crisis helped to promote the idea of online education? According to Kadvany, what is the danger of letting "finance-
   driven ideas" (para. 7) dominate the conversation about education?

4. In paragraph 9, Kadvany says that the personal interaction and
   commitment that characterize higher learning "can't be re-created
   online." What evidence does she present to support this statement?
   How convincing is this evidence? What additional evidence could she
   have used?

5. Does Kadvany ever use the techniques of Rogerian argument? If so,
   where? If not, should she have used them?

This essay is from the December 14, 2011, edition of the *MetroWest Daily News*.

SHORT DISTANCE LEARNING

JOHN CRISP

The end of the semester at my college always inclines me toward reflection, relief, and mild melancholy. I suspect my students feel the same way, with more inclination, perhaps, toward relief. Five classes have met with me about 30 times each over the course of 15 weeks, five communities of individuals that materialize, coalesce, and disperse in a few months.

Whatever its merits, I've never developed much enthusiasm for online learning. Its proponents contend that a community of learners can develop among students scattered by geography but connected by the Internet, and I'm not in a position to say they're wrong.

> "I've never developed much enthusiasm for online learning."

In fact, my purpose isn't to disparage online education. Along with the trend toward a part-time professoriate, the proliferation of online education is probably the most prominent tendency in higher education during the last decade.

Still, I prefer the face-to-face classroom, which seems to me to preserve a fine touch of humanity that warrants reflection during this week of final exams.

Who was in my classes this semester? Many are traditional students, fresh from high school and on their way to a four-year college or university, after a sojourn at my community college. Many are bright, capable, and articulate. Others are shy and reserved. A few are sullen or downright surly. But they're not always my most interesting students.

Consider the young woman who, a decade after high school, finds herself slogging through a developmental writing course before she can even attempt freshman composition. Pardon the cliché, but sometimes you do see a light go on in a student. She begins to listen to her instructor's and classmates' every word, to take notes and to think, to become absorbed in her writing, which over the course of the semester really does get better.

It doesn't always work like that, by any means. Other students are taking my developmental writing class for the second or third time. I like them, but they miss too much class. Some of them have tattoos that betray their gangbanger history; some have been thieves and some have been in prison. And how well can you learn to write amid the violence and futility in the barrio?

Many of them say that's all in the past now, and I believe them. Will they pass this semester? I'm not sure. If they don't, what will become of them?

Momentous life passages occurred as the classes proceeded: At least two 9 women in my five classes this semester were pregnant and one gave birth. Two students died. One young man, a veteran who had survived tours in Iraq and Afghanistan, was killed in the second week of the semester, hit by a car while out for his morning jog.

In mid-semester, a young woman in the same class lost control of her car 10 on the way home from school and died in a one-vehicle rollover. When I told the class the next week that she wouldn't be coming back, there were some tears. So we learned about more than just writing this semester.

A middle-aged woman expressed conservative religious beliefs then 11 admitted that she spent two years in prison for marijuana possession. Several veterans can't sleep at night and some of them drink too much. A young man came to class so depressed that I took him to one of the college's counselors, and he never came back.

Another young man and a young woman sat on opposite sides of the class 12 and never spoke up or spoke to anyone else. Then they began to sit together and talk to each other. A lot. Now I occasionally see them around the campus together. Does that happen in online classes?

In short, it's all there, a rich mixture of human experiences in one ephem- 13 eral microcosm: birth, mating, sickness, death, frustration, laughter, story-telling, aspiration, failure, and learning.

Good luck, students; the pleasure was mine. 14

⦿ AT ISSUE: SOURCES FOR USING ALTERNATIVE APPROACHES TO ARGUMENT

1. Where does Crisp attempt to establish his credibility? How effective is this appeal to *ethos*?

2. To whom is Crisp addressing his argument? Teachers? Students? Parents? Administrators? Others? How do you know?

3. In paragraph 3, Crisp says that his purpose "isn't to disparage online education." What is his purpose?

4. In paragraph 4, Crisp says that he prefers traditional classroom instruction because it preserves "a fine touch of humanity." What does he mean? What evidence does he present in paragraphs 5–12 to support this point? How convincing is this evidence?

5. Draw a **rhetorical triangle** (p. 19) that represents the relative importance of the various appeals in this essay. Which appeal does the longest side of the triangle represent? Which does the shortest side represent? Do you think this is a good balance?

6. In paragraph 2, Crisp briefly addresses an opposing argument. Does he accurately characterize the case for online learning? Should he have spent more time addressing opposing arguments?

7. Crisp ends his essay with a single sentence. Is this sentence an effective concluding statement? Why or why not?

8. Suppose Crisp wanted to present his ideas in a speech. What parts of his essay would you suggest he expand? What parts would you advise him to condense or delete? What visuals would you suggest he include?

This article was originally published in *Liberal Education* in the Fall 2013 issue.

A PLEA FOR CLOSE LEARNING

SCOTT L. NEWSTOK

"At the School" (1910), French postcard envisioning learning in the year 2000. Private Collection © Look and Learn/Bridgeman Images.

What an exciting year for distance learning! Cutting-edge communication 1 systems allowed universities to escape the tired confines of face-to-face education. Bold new technologies made it possible for thousands of geographically dispersed students to enroll in world-class courses.

Innovative assessment mechanisms let professors supervise their pupils 2 remotely. All this progress was good for business, too. Private entrepreneurs leapt at the chance to compete in the new distance-learning marketplace, while Ivy League universities bustled to keep pace.

True, a few naysayers fretted about declining student attention spans and 3 low course-completion rates. But who could object to the expansively democratic goal of bringing first-rate education to more people than ever before? The new pedagogical tools promised to be not only more affordable than traditional classes, but also more effective at measuring student progress. In the words of one prominent expert, the average distance learner "knows more of the subject, and knows it better, than the student who has covered the same ground in the classroom." Indeed, "the day is coming when the work done [via distance learning] will be greater in amount than that done in the class-rooms of our colleges." The future of education was finally here.

2013, right? Think again: 1885. The commentator quoted above was Yale 4 classicist (and future University of Chicago President) William Rainey Harper, evaluating *correspondence courses.* That's right: you've got (snail) mail. Journalist Nicholas Carr has chronicled the recurrent boosterism about mass mediated education over the last century: the phonograph, instructional radio, televised lectures. All were heralded as transformative educational tools in their day. This should give us pause as we recognize that massive open online courses, or MOOCs, are but the latest iteration of distance learning.

> "This should give us pause as we recognize that massive open online courses, or MOOCs, are but the latest iteration of distance learning."

In response to the current enthusiasm for MOOCs, skeptical faculty 5 (Aaron Bady, Ian Bogost, and Jonathan Rees, among many others) have begun questioning venture capitalists eager for new markets and legislators eager to dismantle public funding for American higher education. Some people pushing for MOOCs, to their credit, speak from laudably egalitarian impulses to provide access for disadvantaged students. *But to what are they being given access?* Are broadcast lectures and online discussions the sum of a liberal education? Or is it something more than "content" delivery?

"Close Learning"

To state the obvious: there's a personal, human element to liberal education, what 6 John Henry Newman once called "the living voice, the breathing form, the expressive countenance" (2001, 14). We who cherish personalized instruction would benefit from a pithy phrase to defend and promote this millennia-tested practice. I propose that we begin calling it *close learning,* a term that evokes the laborious, time-consuming, and costly but irreplaceable proximity between teacher and student. Close learning exposes the stark deficiencies of mass distance learning, such as MOOCs, and its haste to reduce dynamism, responsiveness, presence.

Techno-utopians seem surprised that "blended" or "flipped" classrooms— 7 combining out-of-class media with in-person discussions—are more effective than their online-only counterparts, or that one-on-one tutoring strengthens the utility of MOOCs. In spite of all the hype about interactivity, "lecturing" à la MOOCs merely extends the cliché of the static, one-sided lecture hall, where distance learning begins after the first row. As the philosopher Scott Samuelson (2013) suggests, "The forces driving online education, particularly MOOCs, aren't moving us toward close learning. We should begin by recognizing that close learning is the goal and then measure all versions of our courses by that standard. Many giant lecture-hall courses are going to be found wanting, as will many online courses, and all (or almost all) MOOCs. In the end, we're still going to need a lot of face-to-face learning if we want to promote close learning."

The old-fashioned Socratic seminar is where we actually find interactive 8 learning and open-ended inquiry. In the close learning of the live seminar, spontaneity rules. Both students and teachers are always at a crossroads, collaboratively deciding where to go and where to stop; how to navigate and how to detour; and how to close the distance between a topic and the people discussing it. For the seminar to work, certain limits are required (most centrally, a limit in size). But these finite limits enable the infinity of questioning that is close learning. MOOCs claim to abolish those limits, while they paradoxically reinstate them. Their naïve model assumes that there is always total transparency, that passively seeing (watching a lecture or a virtual simulation) is learning.

A Columbia University neuroscientist, Stuart Firestein, recently published a 9 polemical book titled *Ignorance: How It Drives Science*. Discouraged by students regurgitating his lectures without internalizing the complexity of scientific inquiry, Firestein created a seminar to which he invited his colleagues to discuss what they don't know. As Firestein repeatedly emphasizes, it is informed ignorance, not information, that is the genuine "engine" of knowledge. His seminar reminds us that mere data transmission from teacher to student doesn't produce liberal learning. It's the ability to interact, to think hard thoughts alongside other people.

In a seminar, a student can ask for clarification, and challenge a teacher; a 10 teacher can shift course when spirits are flagging; a stray thought can spark a new insight. Isn't this the kind of nonconformist "thinking outside the box" that business leaders adore? So why is there such a rush to freeze knowledge and distribute it in a frozen form? Even Coursera cofounder Andrew Ng concedes that the real value of a college education "isn't just the content. . . . The real value is the interactions with professors and other, equally bright students" (quoted in Oremus 2012).

The business world recognizes the virtues of proximity in its own human 11 resource management. (The phrase "corporate campus" acknowledges as much.) Witness, for example, Yahoo's controversial decision to eliminate telecommuting and require employees to be present in the office. CEO Marissa Mayer's memo reads as a mini-manifesto for close learning: "To become the absolute best place to work, communication and collaboration will be important, so we need to be working side-by-side. That is why it is critical that we are all present in our offices. Some of the best decisions and insights come from hallway and cafeteria discussions, meeting new people, and impromptu team meetings. Speed and quality are often sacrificed when we work from home. We need to be one Yahoo!, and that starts with physically being together" (quoted in Swisher 2013).

Why do boards of directors still go through the effort of convening in 12 person? Why, in spite of all the fantasies about "working from anywhere" are "creative classes" still concentrating in proximity to one another: the entertainment industry in Los Angeles, information technology in the Bay Area, financial capital in New York City? The powerful and the wealthy are well aware that computers can accelerate the exchange of information and facilitate "training," but not the development of knowledge, much less wisdom.

Close learning transcends disciplines. In every field, students must incline 13 toward their subjects: leaning into a sentence, to craft it most persuasively; leaning into an archival document, to determine an uncertain provenance; leaning into a musical score, to poise the body for performance; leaning into a data set, to discern emerging patterns; leaning into a laboratory instrument, to interpret what is viewed. MOOCs, in contrast, encourage students and faculty to lean back, not to cultivate the disciplined attention necessary to engage fully in a complex task. Low completion rates for MOOCs (still hovering around 10 percent) speak for themselves.

Technology as Supplement

Devotion to close learning should not be mistaken for an anti-technology 14 stance. (Contrary to a common misperception, the original Luddites simply wanted machines that made high-quality goods, run by trained workers who were adequately compensated.) I teach Shakespeare, supposedly one of the mustiest of topics. Yet my students navigate the vast resources of the Internet, evaluate recorded performances, wrestle with facsimiles of original publications, listen to pertinent podcasts, survey decades of scholarship in digitized form, circulate their drafts electronically, explore the cultural topography of early modern London, and contemplate the historical richness of the English language. Close learning is entirely compatible with engaging in meaningful conversations outside the classroom: faculty can correspond regularly with students via e-mail and keep in close contact via all kinds of new media. But this is all in service of close learning, and the payoff comes in the classroom.

Teachers have always employed "technology"—including the book, one 15 of the most flexible and dynamic learning technologies ever created. But let's not fixate upon technology for technology's sake, or delude ourselves into thinking that better technology overcomes bad teaching. At no stage of education does technology, no matter how novel, ever replace human attention. Close learning can't be automated or scaled up.

As retrograde as it might sound, gathering humans in a room with real 16 time for dialogue still matters. As educators, we must remind ourselves—not to mention our legislators, our boards, our administrators, our alumni, our students, and our students' parents—of the inescapable fact that our "product" is close learning. This is why savvy parents have always invested in intensive human interaction for their children. (Tellingly, parents from Silicon Valley deliberately restrict their children's access to electronic distractions, so that they might experience the free play of mind essential to human development.)

What remains to be seen is whether we value this kind of close learning at 17 all levels of education enough to defend it, and fund it, for a wider circle of Americans—or whether we will continue to permit the circle to contract, excluding a genuinely transformative intellectual experience from those without means. Proponents of distance education have always boasted that they provide access, but are they providing access to *close learning?*

References

Firestein, S. 2012. *Ignorance: How It Drives Science.* New York: Oxford University Press.

Newman, J. H. 2001. "What Is a University?" In *Rise and Progress of Universities and Benedictine Essays,* edited by M. K. Tilman, 6–17. Notre Dame, IN: University of Notre Dame Press.

Oremus, W. 2014. "The New Public Ivies: Will Online Education Startups like Coursera End the Era of Expensive Higher Education?" *Slate,* July 17, http://www.slate.com/articles/technology/future_tense/2012/07 /coursera_udacity_edx_will_free_online_ ivy_league_courses_end _the_era_of_expensive_ higher_ed_.html.

Swisher, K. 2013. " 'Physically Together': Here's the Internal Yahoo No-Work-from-Home Memo for Remote Workers and Maybe More." *AllThingsD,* February 22. http://allthingsd.com/20130222/physically -together-heres-the-internal-yahoo-no-work-from-home-memo-which -extends-beyond-remote-workers.

⊘ AT ISSUE: SOURCES FOR USING ALTERNATIVE APPROACHES TO ARGUMENT

1. What effect does Newstok want his introduction to have on readers? How can you tell? In your opinion, is his strategy successful?

2. In paragraph 5, Newstok asks whether an education "is something more than 'content' delivery." What does he mean?

3. According to Newstok, what is "close learning" (para. 6)? What are its advantages over online education?

4. Where does Newstok address the major arguments against his position? How effectively does he refute them?

5. Use Toulmin logic to analyze Newstok's essay, identifying the argument's claim, its grounds, and its warrant. Does Newstok appeal only to *logos*, or does he also appeal to *pathos* and *ethos*? Explain.

6. Is Newstok's argument primarily deductive or inductive? Why do you think that he chose this structure?

This essay originally appeared in the January 2013 issue of *Techniques*.

OLD FLAMES AND NEW BEACONS
RAY MCNULTY

A few years ago, I saw a video of a pop concert. It looked just like concerts of 1
my youth: a well-lit stage amid a darkened crowd flecked with small wavering
lights. I laughed when I realized, however, that the swaying glow was coming
not from cigarette lighters but from LCD screens.

This juxtaposition of old flames and new beacons reminds me of distance 2
learning. Once the realm of correspondence schools, whose matchbook cover
advertisements promised the chance to learn from home, distance learning
has evolved into myriad interactive opportunities that cater to the spectrum of
learners' needs. Striking a match on the correspondence school model, technology has ignited a virtual wildfire of prospects for education.

Educators have long pondered the technology question. Most of their stu- 3
dents know nothing firsthand about, or can scarcely remember, a time before
laptops and cellphones. Yet, though they
recognize the value of technology, many
educators still do not take full advantage of it
in their teaching. They are flummoxed by
what they perceive as an all-or-nothing choice.
If they integrate virtual learning strategies,

> "They are flummoxed by what they perceive as an all-or-nothing choice."

will they work themselves into obsolescence? If they maintain the status quo,
will they be able to fully engage students? These are understandable questions,
but I do not believe the answer is mutually exclusive.

Light Sources

Emerging teaching models combine the best of classroom methods with the 4
litheness of online learning to offer more pathways to learning for more students. Three particularly strong new models of this ilk are gaining popularity
in American education: flipped classroom, blended classroom, and supported
distance learning. Technology-infused, these learning models suit all types of
curricula, including career and technical education (CTE), which leads the
way in applied learning by keeping current with technological advances across
disciplines. They also echo CTE's core goal of providing learners with relevant
skills and knowledge to prepare them for successful careers.

The flipped classroom model reverses the traditional lecture/application 5
cycle. Educators post recorded lectures online and assign digital materials to
further students' understanding. Pre-class work by students frees teachers to
focus class meetings on discussions to reinforce understanding and hands-on
activities for practice in application. Continuous access to lectures supports

rigor in learning by enabling students to review lessons, in whole or in part, as many times as needed to grasp content. Relevancy is heightened through increased opportunities for hands-on activities. Further, when students have greater responsibility for content, they practice essential skills, such as self-motivation and time management, which become additional assets for employability and career success.

The blended classroom model involves mixing in-class lectures with online assignments, giving students opportunities for both group and independent learning. Classroom and online activities are balanced depending on content and learning goals. This model works particularly well for large or especially diverse groups of learners because it supports differentiated instruction to ensure that all students not only meet expectations but are also stretched in their learning. 6

Supported distance learning—technology-delivered coursework with low or no classroom residency requirements—is education's fastest growing sector. The National Center for Education Statistics reports that between 2005 and 2010, distance learning course enrollment among American public high school students increased by 77 percent to 1.3 million students, representing 53 percent of public high school districts. An estimated 18 percent of undergraduates will enroll in distance learning for 80 percent or more of their coursework by 2013, according to coursehero.com. 7

Snuffing Out the Myths

The rising popularity of online learning models invites a hard look at the myths and realities of what these approaches offer. 8

First, there is the erroneous perception that distance learning is only for adults. Distance and hybrid learning options are relevant across levels, from high school to graduate to career advancement programs, and capture more nontraditional students. The flexibility appeals to learners for many reasons. Some are encouraged—sometimes subsidized—by employers, others are self-motivated for career entry, advancement, or change. Others are pursuing new dreams. Learners who struggle in traditional programs find that asynchronous delivery and other elements of distance learning allow them to eliminate obstacles and forge pathways to learning success. 9

A recent Penn Foster blog asked students for feedback about why they had chosen distance learning. Some responses were expected: people with jam-packed lives sought portability and flexibility, employers were paying the fees, and lower costs. Others revealed simple but important personal reasons. One student shared that fluorescent classroom lighting gave her headaches; working at home eliminated the issue. Many respondents mentioned that music—from classical to classic rock—helped them concentrate. Several posters were happy to leave behind noisy classrooms, social pressures, and bullying. For many students, learning had become joyful and purposeful instead of forced. 10

Another myth: when it comes to employability, online learning cre- 11
dentials are not valid or valuable. Every consumer service sector has highs
and lows in quality. Some remote courses are designed well and led by great
teachers; some are not. Some programs are accredited; others are not. Wise
students research options to ensure that courses or programs support their
academic needs and professional goals. Industries often work on content
development with reputable programs—traditional and online—to ensure
courses align with industry standards in many fields. Some top-rated companies now look to online learning to enhance employees' credentials
while keeping them engaged in the workforce. Employers also recognize
the value in skills required to successfully complete online programs, such
as self-motivation, task focus, ability to work independently, and time
management.

Then there is the idea that hybrid and distance learning work only for 12
purely "academic" subjects, not for courses or programs that require hands-on
time in labs, practicums, or internships for credentialing. A good example of
success in distance learning for a hands-on profession is Penn Foster's veteri-
nary technician program. Our vet tech students complete accredited coursework online with support from peers and advisors. When they are ready for
internships, an advisor helps connect them with an onsite learning position
with one of the school's many partners. The approach works: 100 percent of
Penn Foster's vet tech students have passed the independent credentialing
exams required for employment in the field.

The vet tech program debunks the notion that distance learners must go 13
it alone, without the valuable and vibrant dialog with teachers and peers or
well-appointed libraries and other learning resources available on traditional
campuses. Flipped and blended classrooms feature classroom or campus time,
so these concerns are irrelevant to those models.

Students enrolled in well-supported distance learning need not worry 14
about isolation either. Quality distance learning programs provide many
options for students to engage with peers and teachers through online forums,
via email, by phone, and, sometimes, in person with local classmates. In the
vet tech program, students regularly connect with peers in online forums, and
they work closely, if remotely, with advisors throughout the program, especially when it comes time to arrange for internships.

Tending to the Future

The go-it-alone myth strikes a chord with many educators. If students have 15
the main responsibility for their learning, what is the teacher's role? Changes
in teaching theory and practice do not change the qualities of a good teacher.
The most effective teachers are still those who are most inspired by the possibility and responsibility of helping to shape the future and who aspire to
inspire their students. Certainly, distance and hybrid learning models change
the educator's role, but they do not negate it. High-quality programs and

courses rely on good teachers who continually seek ways to engage all types of learners so they can succeed not only in the world they live in now, but also in the one they are only beginning to dream up.

Teaching distance or hybrid model classes is different, but it offers some 16 unique advantages.

In distance learning, the biggest practical differences for teachers tend 17 to be asynchronistic teaching cycles and limited (or no) face-to-face time. Because distance learners set their own pace, teachers may find they are working with more students concurrently than is possible in a classroom. Staggered learning timelines make this possible, and many educators enjoy simultaneously teaching various stages of their lessons rather than following a sequential path for a set term. Although in-person contact is reduced, there are many opportunities for one-to-one contact by phone and online.

Flipped and blended classrooms shift the educator's role from a "sage on 18 the stage" to one of an applied learning coach. With students taking on more pre-class prep, educators have more time to facilitate discussions and hands-on activities.

One of the most exciting advantages these dynamic models have for 19 teachers is the flexibility to explore "next practices," innovative and sometimes as-yet untested ideas that may (or may not) evolve into best practices. Next practices speak to the ideals of what education can accomplish, and these teaching models support the creativity educators need to think ahead to those ideals.

In fact, it's a bit like switching from cigarette lighters to LCD screens at a 20 concert. The old flame was good in its time, but technology offers a new beacon. As an educator, how will you choose to light up learning?

⊖ AT ISSUE: SOURCES FOR USING ALTERNATIVE APPROACHES TO ARGUMENT

1. Explain the essay's title.

2. Regarding technology, how does McNulty characterize students? How does he characterize instructors? Based on your experiences, are these characterizations fair? Accurate? Explain.

3. Define the following terms that McNulty introduces in paragraph 4.

   ■ Flipped classroom

   ■ Blended classroom

   ■ Supported distance learning

   Why does he discuss these new models of instruction? How does his discussion prepare readers for the rest of his essay?

4. Much of this essay involves "snuffing out the myths" (para. 8) associated with online learning. What are these myths? How successfully does McNulty refute them?

5. Throughout his essay, McNulty uses headings. What is the purpose of these headings? Do they help readers, or do they just get in the way? Explain.

6. Who is McNulty's intended audience? How can you tell?

This piece first appeared online at HybridPedagogy.com on January 5, 2012.

TRADING CLASSROOM AUTHORITY FOR ONLINE COMMUNITY

PETE RORABAUGH

Early web commenters referred to the Internet as a primitive, lawless place like the "Wild West." Plenty still needs to change to make certain parts of the web more civil and useful, but some aspect of the "Wild West" spirit is applicable to a discussion of student-directed learning. Too much civilization and society makes us compartmentalized and complacent. The West was a challenging place for European immigrants because it required an expansive sense of responsibility. You could no longer be just an apothecary or a cobbler. You had to provide for your own food and shelter from the resources around you; you had to decide just "what to do" with all this freedom. 1

Digital culture is having a similar effect on the practice of education, and that's a good thing. Students have to own their learning more. They can't just follow the dotted line on the ground that leads to their assignment, their grade, their degree. 2

Consider four core values for the classroom in general and the online classroom: **show up**, **be curious**, **collaborate**, and **contribute**. The online classroom is more student-directed in the sense that students are more "on their own" than they are in a traditional classroom. With more authors, contexts, and platforms to consider, digital media literacy insists that students filter, evaluate, and prioritize information with more critical proficiency than traditional students. Traditional students could trust the stability of the worksheet and the textbook. Digital education by its mere existence insists on more progressive practices for teachers and students. Digital culture has already started affecting dominant cultural epistemology° by shifting some focus away from experts and giving it to participants. 3

A type of philosophy focused on the study of knowledge

Students in the digital environment, whether in a hybrid or fully online classroom, carry more responsibility for their own progress. To succeed, they have to monitor their own progress more directly, engage with the insights of their peers, and ponder the external relevance of their work. A revolution is growing online that takes this trend to an extreme—digital citizens are building educational communities without institutions. "Learning" no longer means, or needs to mean, "going to school." It can just mean developing good observation and critical thinking skills. 4

> "A revolution is growing online that takes this trend to an extreme—digital citizens are building educational communities without institutions."

What this means for the online classroom is twofold: **1.** We recognize and communicate the shift from a follow-the-leader framework to a framework in 5 which the authority is more equally distributed between teacher and students. **2.** We have to model this new approach to learning in our classrooms (whether analog or digital). Students might be happy to see the culture of experts and talking heads dissolve, but if they want to be part of the revolution then they have to be ready to share the work that the experts used to do. For example, we might have students blogging publicly instead of submitting their work to the instructor as a one-to-one transaction. In this move, students become content creators, instead of content consumers—creators of their own educations instead of consumers—textbook creators instead of consumers.

Traditional classrooms, the ones inspired by factories, create ideal students 6 who follow instructions well. ("Changing Education Paradigms," a video from RSA animate, offers a cogent argument for this shift in thinking about education.) The web and digital culture create ideal citizens who investigate things "just because." These students reach for *Wikipedia* or Google Maps on their iPhones to get immediate clarification when they need help. Our online classrooms should harness this educational holster mentality. Don't understand something? Ask the class, email a group of professionals, call the company, interview your grandmother. And this is the beauty of digital and critical pedagogy; when it's done right, it connects us to each other and to the world.

⊙ AT ISSUE: SOURCES FOR USING ALTERNATIVE APPROACHES TO ARGUMENT

1. Rorabaugh begins his essay by comparing the Internet to the Wild West. In what respects is this **analogy** valid? In what respects is it not?

2. Where in this essay does the claim appear? How is the claim qualified? How does the qualifier set up the rest of the essay?

3. Rorabaugh makes a number of statements that he assumes are self-evident. For example, in paragraph 2 he says that in the online classroom "[s]tudents have to own their learning more," and in paragraph 3 he says, "The online classroom is more student-directed." Identify other statements like these. Are they really self-evident, or do they require support?

4. Rorabaugh is clearly a supporter of online learning. Does this prevent him from seeing problems associated with online learning? Explain.

5. What preconceptions about online learning does Rorabaugh assume his readers have? How do you know?

6. Suppose Rorabaugh wanted to rewrite his essay as a Rogerian argument. What changes in his essay's tone and emphasis would he have to make?

TEMPLATE FOR WRITING A ROGERIAN ARGUMENT

Write a one-paragraph **Rogerian** argument in which you argue that the drawbacks of online education have to be addressed before it can be successful. Follow the template below, filling in the blanks to create your argument.

With more and more students taking online courses, both the students and the colleges benefit. For example, _____

_____

_____. In addition, _____

_____.

However, online education does have some drawbacks. For instance, _____

_____

_____.

These problems could be easily solved. First, _____

_____. Second, _____

_____.

If these problems are addressed, both students and colleges would benefit because _____

_____.

TEMPLATE FOR WRITING A TOULMIN ARGUMENT

Write a one-paragraph **Toulmin** argument in which you argue in favor of online education. Follow the template below, filling in the blanks to create your argument.

Many colleges and universities have instituted online education programs. These programs are the best way _____
_____.

If colleges are going to meet the rising demand for education, they _____
_____
_____.

The online course I took _____
_____
_____.

Recent studies show that _____
_____. In addition, _____
_____. However, some people argue that _____
_____
_____. They also say that _____
_____.

These arguments _____
_____.

For this reason, online education is _____
_____
_____.

⊙ EXERCISE 6.7

Discuss your ideas about online learning with one or two of your classmates. Consider both the strengths and the limitations of this method of teaching. What types of classes do you think it is best suited for? Which classes do you think it would not work for? Then, edit the Rogerian and Toulmin arguments that you wrote on the previous templates so that they include some of these comments.

❯ EXERCISE 6.8

Write an argumentative essay on the topic, "Is Online Education Better Than Classroom Education?" Use the principles of either Rogerian argument or Toulmin logic to structure your essay. Cite sources in the Reading and Writing about the Issue section on pages 222–247, and be sure to document the sources you use and to include a works-cited page. (See Chapter 10 for information on documenting sources.)

❯ EXERCISE 6.9

Review the four pillars of argument that are discussed in Chapter 1. Does your essay include all four elements of an effective argument? Add anything that is missing. Then, label the elements of your argument.

❯ EXERCISE 6.10

Assume that you have been asked to present the information in the essay you wrote for Exercise 6.8 as an oral argument. What information would you include? What information would you eliminate? Find two or three visuals that you would use when you deliver your speech. Then, make an outline of your speech and indicate at what points you would display these visuals.

Writing an Argumentative Essay

free!

2014/2015
UC SANTA CRUZ

Campus Food & Garden Guide

Where to find sustainable food at UC Santa Cruz and discover ways to engage in your campus and community food system!

FOOD SYSTEMS WORKING GROUP

DINING HALLS • CAMPUS EATERIES • CAMPUS GARDENS • FOOD SYSTEMS RELATED ACADEMIC COURSES • STUDENT AND COMMUNITY ORGANIZATIONS • VOLUNTEER OPPORTUNITIES • STUDENT INTERNSHIPS & PROJECTS • FARMERS' MARKETS

9TH EDITION

Planning, Drafting, and Revising an Argumentative Essay

Should College Campuses Go Green?

In recent years, more and more American colleges and universities have become "green campuses," emphasizing **sustainability**—the use of systems and materials that will not deplete the earth's natural resources. Various schools have taken steps such as the following:

- Placing an emphasis on recycling and reducing nonbiodegradable waste
- Creating green buildings and using eco-friendly materials in construction projects
- Instituting new curricula in environmental science
- Monitoring their greenhouse gas emissions and evaluating their carbon footprint
- Growing crops on campus to feed students
- Hiring full-time "sustainability directors"
- Encouraging students to use bikes instead of cars
- Purchasing wind-generated electricity to supply the campus's energy
- Eliminating trays in college cafeterias

Although many schools have launched ambitious programs and projects to reduce their energy dependence, some have been more cautious, citing the high cost of such programs and the need to allocate resources elsewhere. Moreover, some critics of the green movement object to the notion that colleges should help to make students "sustainability literate." Such critics consider the green movement to be an expression of political correctness that at best does no more than pay lip service to the problem and at worst threatens academic freedom by furthering a political agenda.

The question remains whether the green movement that is spreading rapidly across college campuses is here to stay or just a fad—or something between these two extremes. This chapter takes you through the process of writing an argumentative essay on the topic of whether college campuses should go green. (Exercises guide you through the process of writing your own argumentative essay on a topic of your choice.)

Before you can write a convincing argumentative essay, you need to understand the **writing process**. You are probably already familiar with the basic outline of this process, which includes *planning, drafting,* and *revising.* This chapter reviews this familiar process and explains how it applies to the specific demands of writing an argument.

Choosing a Topic

The first step in planning an argumentative essay is to choose a topic you can write about. Your goal is to select a topic that you have some emotional stake in—not simply one that interests you. If you are going to spend hours planning, writing, and revising an essay, then you should care about your topic. At the same time, you should be able to keep an open mind about your topic and be willing to consider various viewpoints. Your topic also should be narrow enough to fit the boundaries of your assignment—the time you have to work on the essay and its length and scope.

Typically, your instructor will give you a general assignment, such as the following.

> **Assignment**
> Write a three- to five-page argumentative essay on a topic related to college services, programs, facilities, or curricula.

The first thing you need to do is narrow this general assignment to a topic, focusing on one particular campus service, program, facility, or curriculum. You could choose to write about any number of topics—financial aid, the writing center, athletics, the general education curriculum—taking a position, for example, on who should receive financial aid, whether to expand the mission of the writing center, whether college athletes should receive a salary, or why general education requirements are important for business majors.

If you are interested in the environment, however, you might decide to write about the green movement that is spreading across college campuses, perhaps using your observations of your own campus's programs and policies to support your position.

> **Topic**
> The green movement on college campuses

TOPICS TO AVOID

Certain kinds of topics are not appropriate for argumentative essays. For one thing, some topics are just not arguable. For example, you could not write an argumentative essay on a statement of fact, such as the fact that many colleges saw their endowments decline after the financial crisis of 2008. (A fact is not debatable, so there can be no argument.)

Some familiar topics also present problems. These issues—the death penalty, abortion rights, and so on—are important (after all, that's why they are written about so often), but finding an original argument on either side of the debate can be a challenge. For example, you might have a hard time finding something new to say that would convince some readers that the death penalty is immoral or that abortion is a woman's right. In many people's minds, these issues are "settled." When you write on topics such as these, some readers' strong religious or cultural beliefs are likely to prevent them from considering your arguments, however well supported they might be.

Finally, topics that are very narrow or depend on subjective value judgments—or that take a stand on issues readers simply will not care much about, such as whether one particular video game or TV reality show is more entertaining than another—are unlikely to engage your audience (even if these topics are compelling to you and your friends).

⊘ EXERCISE 7.1

In response to the boxed assignment on the previous page, list ten topics that you could write about. Then, cross out any that do not meet the following criteria:

- The topic interests you.

- You know something about the topic.

- You care about the topic.

- You are able to keep an open mind about the topic.

- The topic fits the boundaries of your assignment.

Now, choose one topic to write an essay about.

For more practice, see the LearningCurve on Recognizing Topics and Main Ideas in the LaunchPad for *Practical Argument*.

Thinking about Your Topic

Before you can start to do research, develop a thesis statement, or plan the structure of your argument, you need to think a bit about the topic you have chosen. You can use *invention strategies,* such as **freewriting** (writing without stopping for a predetermined time), **brainstorming** (making quick notes on your topic), or **clustering** (creating a diagram to map out your thoughts) to help you discover ideas you might write about. You can also explore ideas in a writing journal or in conversations with friends, classmates, family members, or instructors.

Freewriting

People say green is good, but I'm not sure why. Do we really need a separate, smelly container for composting? Won't the food decompose just as fast in a landfill? In middle school, we learned about the "three Rs" to save the environment—one was Recycle, but I forget the other two. Renew? Reuse? Remember? Whatever. OK, I know not to throw trash on the ground, and I know we're supposed to separate trash and recycling, etc. I get that. But does all this time and effort really do any good?

Brainstorming

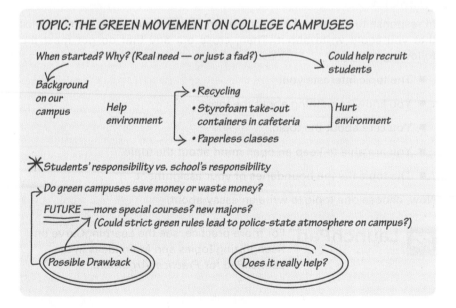

TOPIC: THE GREEN MOVEMENT ON COLLEGE CAMPUSES

When started? Why? (Real need — or just a fad?) — Could help recruit students

Background on our campus

Help environment
- Recycling
- Styrofoam take-out containers in cafeteria — Hurt environment
- Paperless classes

＊Students' responsibility vs. school's responsibility

Do green campuses save money or waste money?

FUTURE —more special courses? new majors?
(Could strict green rules lead to police-state atmosphere on campus?)

Possible Drawback   Does it really help?

Clustering

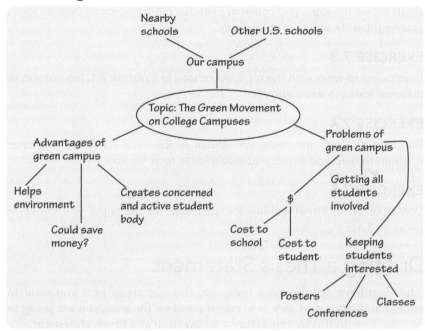

When you finish exploring ideas, you should be able to construct a quick **informal outline** that lists the ideas you plan to discuss.

Informal Outline

Topic: The Green Movement on College Campuses
    History/background
        National
        Our campus
    Positive aspects
        Helps environment
        Attracts new students
    Negative aspects
        Cost
        Enforcement
    Future

By grouping your ideas and arranging them in a logical order, an informal outline like the one above can help lead you to a thesis statement that expresses the position you will take on the issue.

⊙ EXERCISE 7.2

Focusing on the topic you chose in Exercise 7.1, freewrite to explore ideas you might write about in your essay.

⊙ EXERCISE 7.3

Continuing to work with the topic you chose in Exercise 7.1, brainstorm to discover ideas to write about.

⊙ EXERCISE 7.4

Still working with the topic you chose in Exercise 7.1, draw a cluster diagram to help you explore possible ideas to write about.

⊙ EXERCISE 7.5

Construct an informal outline for an essay on the topic you chose in Exercise 7.1.

Drafting a Thesis Statement

After you have decided on a topic and thought about how you want to approach it, your next step is to take a stand on the issue you are going to discuss. You do this by expressing your position as a **thesis statement**.

A thesis statement is the central element of any argumentative essay. It tells readers what your position is and perhaps also indicates why you are taking this position and how you plan to support it. As you draft your thesis statement, keep the following guidelines in mind:

- An argumentative thesis statement is not simply a statement of your topic; rather, it expresses the point you will make about your topic.

  TOPIC   The green movement on college campuses

  THESIS STATEMENT   College campuses should go green.

- An argumentative thesis statement should be specific, clearly indicating to readers exactly what position you will take in your essay.

  TOO GENERAL   Colleges need to do more to get students involved in environmental issues.

  REVISED   Colleges should institute programs and classes to show students the importance of using sustainable resources.

- An argumentative thesis statement should get right to the point, avoiding wordy, repetitive language.

WORDY	Because issues that revolve around the environment are so crucial and important, colleges should do more to increase student involvement in campus projects that are concerned with sustainability.
REVISED	Because environmental issues are so important, colleges should take steps to involve students in campus sustainability projects.

- Many argumentative thesis statements include words such as *should* and *should not*.

  - College campuses should _____.
  - Because _____, colleges should _____.
  - Even though _____, colleges should not _____.

> **NOTE**
>
> At this point, any thesis that you come up with is tentative. As you think about your topic and as you read about it, you will very likely modify your thesis statement, perhaps expanding or narrowing its scope, rewording it to make it more precise, or even changing your position. Still, the thesis statement that you decide on at this point can help you focus your exploration of your topic.

TENTATIVE THESIS STATEMENT

College campuses should go green.

⊘ EXERCISE 7.6

List five possible thesis statements for the topic you chose in Exercise 7.1. (To help you see your topic in several different ways, you might experiment by drafting at least one thesis statement that evaluates, one that considers causes and/or effects, and one that proposes a solution to a problem.) Which thesis statement seems most promising for your essay? Why?

Understanding Your Purpose and Audience

When you write an argument, your primary purpose is to convince your audience to accept your position. Sometimes you will have other goals as well. For example, you might want to change readers' ideas about an issue, perhaps by challenging a commonly held assumption, or even to move readers to take some action in support of your position.

To make the best possible case to your audience, you need to understand who your audience is—what knowledge, values, beliefs, and opinions your readers might have. You will also need to have some idea whether your audience is likely to be receptive, hostile, or neutral to the ideas you propose.

In most cases, it makes sense to assume that your readers are receptive but **skeptical**—that they have open minds but still need to be convinced. However, if you are writing about a topic that is very controversial, you will need to assume that at least some of your readers will not support your position and may, in fact, be hostile to it. If this is the case, they will be scrutinizing your arguments very carefully, looking for opportunities to argue against them. Your goal in this case is not necessarily to win readers over but to make them more receptive to your position—or at least to get them to admit that you have made a good case even though they may disagree with you. At the same time, you also have to work to convince those who probably agree with you or those who are neutral (perhaps because the issue you are discussing is something they haven't thought much about).

An audience of first-year college students who are used to the idea that sound environmental practices make sense might find the idea of a green campus appealing—and, in fact, natural and obvious. An audience of faculty or older students might be more skeptical, realizing that the benefits of green practices might be offset by the time and expense they could involve. College administrators might find the long-term goal of a green campus attractive (and see it as a strong recruitment tool), but they might also be somewhat hostile to your position, anticipating the considerable expense that would be involved. If you wrote an argument on the topic of green campuses, you would need to consider these positions—and, if possible, address them.

⊖ EXERCISE 7.7

Consider how different audiences might respond to the thesis statement you found the most promising in Exercise 7.6. Identify five possible groups of readers on your college campus—for example, athletes, history majors, or part-time faculty. Would you expect each group to be receptive, hostile, or neutral to your position? Why?

 **LaunchPad** macmillan learning   For more practice, see the LearningCurve on Topic, Purpose, and Audience in the Launch-Pad for *Practical Argument*.

Gathering Evidence

After you have a sense of who your audience will be and how these readers might react to your thesis, you can begin to collect **evidence** to support your thesis. As you look for evidence, you need to evaluate the usefulness and relevance of each of your sources, and you need to be alert for possible bias.

Evaluating the Evidence in Your Sources

As you read each potential source, consider the quality of the supporting evidence that the writer marshals to support his or her position. The more compelling the evidence, the more willing you should be to accept the writer's ideas—and, perhaps, to integrate these ideas into your own essay.

> **NOTE**
>
> Don't forget that if you use any of your sources' ideas, you must document them. See Chapter 10 for information on MLA documentation format and Appendix B for information on APA documentation format.

To be convincing, the evidence that is presented in the sources you review should be *accurate*, *relevant*, *representative*, and *sufficient*:

- **Accurate** evidence comes from reliable sources that are quoted carefully—and not misrepresented by being quoted out of context.

- **Relevant** evidence applies specifically (not just tangentially) to the topic under discussion.

- **Representative** evidence is drawn from a fair range of sources, not just those that support the writer's position.

- **Sufficient** evidence is enough facts, statistics, expert opinion, and so on to support the essay's thesis.

(For more detailed information on evaluating sources, see Chapter 8.)

> **NOTE**
>
> Remember, the evidence you use to support your own arguments should also satisfy the four criteria listed above.

Detecting Bias in Your Sources

As you select sources, you should be alert for **bias**—a writer's use of preconceived ideas (rather than factual evidence) as support for his or her arguments. A writer who demonstrates bias may not be trustworthy, and you should approach such a writer's arguments with skepticism. To determine whether a writer is biased, follow these guidelines:

- *Consider what a writer explicitly tells you* about his or her beliefs or opinions. For example, if a writer mentions that he or she is a lifelong member of the Sierra Club, a vegan, and the owner of a house heated by solar energy, then you should consider the possibility that he or she might downplay (or even disregard) valid arguments against a green campus rather than presenting a balanced view.

- *Look for slanted language.* For example, a writer who mocks supporters of environmental issues as *politically correct* or uses pejorative terms such as *hippies* for environmentalists should not earn your trust.

- *Consider the supporting evidence* the writer chooses. Does the writer present only examples that support his or her position and ignore valid opposing arguments? Does the writer quote only those experts who agree with his or her position—for example, only pro- (or only anti-) environmental writers? A writer who does this is presenting an unbalanced (and therefore biased) case.

- *Consider the writer's tone.* A writer whose tone is angry, bitter, or sarcastic should be suspect.

- *Consider any overtly offensive statements or characterizations* that a writer makes. A writer who makes negative assumptions about college students (for example, characterizing them as selfish and self-involved and therefore dismissing their commitment to campus environmental projects) should be viewed with skepticism.

> **NOTE**
>
> Be aware of any biases you hold that might affect the strength or logic of your own arguments. See "Being Fair," page 268.

◆ EXERCISE 7.8

What evidence might you use to support the thesis statement you decided on in Exercise 7.6?

◆ EXERCISE 7.9

In writing an essay that supports the thesis statement you have been working with in this chapter, you might find it difficult to remain objective. What biases do you have that you might have to watch for as you research and write about your topic?

◆ EXERCISE 7.10

Gather evidence to support your thesis statement, evaluating each source carefully (consulting Chapter 8 as necessary). Be on the lookout for bias in your sources.

USING ANALOGIES AS EVIDENCE

An **analogy** is an extended comparison between two items, situations, or concepts on the basis of a number of shared characteristics. This kind of comparison explains a difficult or unfamiliar concept in terms of something more familiar. **Argument by analogy** is a strategy that makes the case that a position about an issue is valid because it is analogous to a comparable position on another issue—a position you expect your readers to accept. For example, you could develop a comparison between the relatively recent green campus movement and the earlier movement to make campuses fully accessible for students with disabilities.

However, this kind of argument has limitations. For more information, see the discussion of weak analogy in Chapter 5.

Refuting Opposing Arguments

As you plan your essay and read sources that will supply your supporting evidence, you will encounter evidence that contradicts your position. You may be tempted to ignore this evidence, but if you do, your argument will not be very convincing. Instead, as you review your sources, identify the most convincing arguments against your position and prepare yourself to **refute** them (that is, disprove them or call them into question), showing them to be illogical, unfair, or untrue. Indicating to readers that you are willing to address these arguments—and that you can respond effectively to them—will help convince them to accept your position.

Of course, simply saying that your opponent's position is "wrong" or "stupid" is not convincing. You need to summarize opposing arguments accurately and clearly identify their weaknesses. In the case of a strong opposing argument, be sure to acknowledge its strengths before you refute it; if you do not, readers may see you as uninformed or unfair. For example, you could refute the argument that a green campus is too expensive by acknowledging that although expenditures are high at first, in the long run, a green campus is not all that costly considering its benefits. Also be careful not to create a **straw man**—that is, do not distort an opposing argument by oversimplifying it so it can be easily refuted (for example, claiming that environmentalists believe that sustainability should always be a college's first priority in its decisions about allocating resources). This unfair tactic will discourage readers from trusting you and thus will undermine your credibility.

Strategies for Refuting Opposing Arguments

In order to do a convincing job of refuting an argument that challenges your position, you need to consider where such an argument might be weak and on what basis you could refute it.

WEAKNESS IN OPPOSING ARGUMENT	REFUTATION STRATEGY
Factual errors or contrary-to-fact statements	Identify and correct the errors, perhaps explaining how they call the writer's credibility into question
Insufficient support	Point out that more facts and examples are needed; note the kind of support (for example, statistics) that is missing.
Illogical reasoning	Identify fallacies in the writer's argument, and explain why the logic is flawed. For example, is the writer setting up a straw man or employing the either/or fallacy? (See Chapter 5 for more on logic.)
Exaggerated or overstated claims	Identify exaggerated statements, and explain why they overstate the case.
Biased statements	Identify biased statements, and show how they exhibit the writer's bias. (See page 261, "Detecting Bias in Your Sources.")
Irrelevant arguments	Identify irrelevant points and explain why they are not pertinent to the writer's argument.

⊙ EXERCISE 7.11

Read paragraphs 7 and 8 of the student essay on page 283. Summarize the opposing argument presented in each of these paragraphs. Then, consulting the list above, identify the specific weakness of each opposing argument. Finally, explain the strategy the student writer uses to refute the argument.

Revising Your Thesis Statement

Before you can begin to draft your argumentative essay and even before you can start to arrange your ideas, you need to revise your tentative thesis statement so it says exactly what you want it to say. After you have gathered and evaluated evidence to support your position and considered the merits of opposing ideas, you are ready to refocus your thesis and state it in more definite terms. Although a tentative thesis statement such as

"College campuses should go green" is a good start, the thesis that guides your essay's structure should be more specific. In fact, it will be most useful as a guide if its phrasing actually acknowledges opposing arguments.

> ### REVISED THESIS STATEMENT
>
> Despite the expense, colleges should make every effort to create green campuses because doing so improves their own educational environment, ensures their own institution's survival, and helps solve the global climate crisis.

❯ EXERCISE 7.12

Consulting the sources you gathered in Exercise 7.10, list all the arguments against the position in your thesis statement. Then, list possible refutations of each of these arguments. When you have finished, revise your thesis statement so that it is more specific, acknowledging the most important argument against your position.

After you have revised your thesis statement, you will have a concise blueprint for the essay you are going to write. At this point, you will be ready to plan your essay's structure and write a first draft.

Structuring Your Essay

As you learned in Chapter 1, an argumentative essay, like other essays, includes an introduction, a body, and a conclusion. In the introduction of an argumentative essay, you state your thesis; in the body paragraphs, you present evidence to support your thesis and you address opposing arguments; and in your conclusion, you bring your argument to a close and reinforce your thesis with a strong concluding statement. As you have seen, these four elements—thesis, evidence, refutation, and concluding statement—are like the four pillars of the ancient Greek temple, supporting your argument so that it will stand up to scrutiny.

> ## SUPPLYING BACKGROUND INFORMATION
>
> Depending on what you think your readers know—and what you think they need to know—you might decide to include a background paragraph that supplies information about the issue you are discussing. For example, in an essay about green campuses, you might briefly sum up the history of the U.S. environmental movement and trace its rise on college campuses. If you decide to include a background paragraph, it should be placed right after your introduction, where it can prepare readers for the discussion to follow.

Understanding basic essay structure can help you as you shape your essay. You should also know how to use induction and deduction, how to identify a strategy for your argument, and how to construct a formal outline.

Using Induction and Deduction

Many argumentative essays are structured either **inductively** or **deductively**. (See Chapter 5 for explanations of induction and deduction.) For example, the body of an essay with the thesis statement that is shown on page 265 could have either of the following two general structures:

INDUCTIVE STRUCTURE

- Colleges are taking a number of steps to follow green practices.
- Through these efforts, campuses have become more environmentally responsible, and their programs and practices have made a positive difference.
- Because these efforts are helping to save the planet, they should be expanded.

DEDUCTIVE STRUCTURE

- Saving the planet is vital.
- Green campuses can help to save the planet.
- Therefore, colleges should create green campuses.

These structures offer two options for arranging material in your essay. Many argumentative essays, however, combine induction and deduction or use other strategies to shape their ideas.

Identifying a Strategy for Your Argument

There are a variety of different ways to structure an argument, and the strategy you use depends on what you want your argument to accomplish. In this text, we discuss five options for presenting material: *definition arguments, cause-and-effect arguments, evaluation arguments, proposal arguments,* and *ethical arguments.*

Any of the five options listed above could guide you as you develop an essay on green campuses:

- You could structure your essay as a **definition argument**, explaining the concept of a green campus and giving examples to show how it operates.
- You could structure your essay as a **cause-and-effect argument**, showing how establishing a green campus could have positive results for students and for the campus.

- You could structure your essay as an **evaluation argument**, assessing the strengths and weaknesses of various programs and policies designed to create and sustain a green campus.

- You could structure your essay as a **proposal argument**, recommending a particular program, service, or course of action and showing how it can support a green campus.

- You could structure your essay as an **ethical argument**, explaining why creating a green campus is the right thing to do from a moral or ethical standpoint.

Constructing a Formal Outline

If you like, you can construct a **formal outline** before you begin your draft. (Later on, you can also construct an outline of your finished paper to check the logic of its structure.) A formal outline, which is more detailed and more logically organized than the informal outline shown on page 257, presents your main points and supporting details in the order in which you will discuss them.

A formal outline of the first body paragraph of the student essay on page 280 would look like this:

I. Background of the term *green*
   A. 1960s environmental movement
      1. Political agenda
      2. Environmental agenda
   B. Today's movements
      1. Eco-friendly practices
      2. Green values

Following a formal outline makes the drafting process flow smoothly, but many writers find it hard to predict exactly what details they will use for support or how they will develop their arguments. In fact, your first draft is likely to move away from your outline as you develop your ideas. Still, if you are the kind of writer who prefers to know where you are going before you start on your way, you will probably consider the time you devote to outlining to be time well spent.

⊘ EXERCISE 7.13

Look back at the thesis you decided on earlier in this chapter, and review the evidence you collected to support it. Then, construct a formal outline for your argumentative essay.

Establishing Credibility

Before you begin drafting your essay, you need to think about how to approach your topic and your audience. The essay you write will use a combination of logical, emotional, and ethical appeals, and you will have to be careful to use these appeals reasonably. (See pp. 14–21 for information on these appeals.) As you write, you will concentrate on establishing yourself as well-informed, reasonable, and fair.

Being Well-Informed

If you expect your readers to accept your ideas, you will need to establish yourself as someone they should believe and trust. This involves showing your audience that you have a good command of your material—that is, that you know what you are talking about.

If you want readers to listen to what you are saying, you need to earn their respect by showing them that you have done your research, that you have collected evidence that supports your argument, and that you understand the most compelling arguments against your position. For example, discussing your own experiences as a member of a campus or community environmental group, your observations at a Greenpeace convention, and essays and editorials that you have read on both sides of the issue will encourage your audience to accept your ideas on the subject of green campuses.

Being Reasonable

Even if your evidence is strong, your argument will not be convincing if it does not seem reasonable. One way to present yourself as a reasonable person is to **establish common ground** with your readers, stressing possible points of agreement instead of attacking those who might disagree with your position. For example, saying, "We all want our planet to survive" is a more effective strategy than saying, "Those who do not support the concept of a green campus are out to destroy our planet." (For more on establishing common ground, see the discussion of Rogerian argument in Chapter 6.)

Another way to present yourself as a reasonable person is to **maintain a reasonable tone**. Try to avoid absolutes (words like *always* and *never*); instead, use more conciliatory language (*in many cases, much of the time,* and so on). Try not to use words and phrases like *obviously* or *as anyone can see* to introduce points whose strength may be obvious only to you. Do not brand opponents of your position as misguided, uninformed, or deluded; remember, some of your readers may hold opposing positions and will not appreciate your unfavorable portrayal of them.

Finally, be very careful to treat your readers with respect, addressing them as your intellectual equals. Avoid statements that might insult them or their beliefs ("Although some ignorant or misguided people may still think . . ."). And never assume that your readers know less about your topic than you do; they may actually know a good deal more.

Being Fair

If you want readers to respect your point of view, you need to demonstrate respect for them by being fair. It is not enough to support your ideas convincingly and maintain a reasonable tone. You also need to avoid unfair tactics in your argument and take care to avoid **bias**.

In particular, you should be careful not to *distort evidence, quote out of context, slant evidence, make unfair appeals,* or *use logical fallacies.* These unfair tactics may influence some readers in the short term, but in the long run such tactics will alienate your audience.

- **Do not distort evidence. Distorting** (or misrepresenting) **evidence** is an unfair tactic. It is not ethical or fair, for example, to present your opponent's views inaccurately or to exaggerate his or her position and then argue against it. If you want to argue that green programs on college campuses are a good idea, it is not fair to attack someone who expresses reservations about their cost by writing, "Mr. McNamara's concerns about cost reveal that he has basic doubts about saving the planet." (His concerns reveal no such thing.) It is, however, fair to acknowledge your opponent's reasonable concerns about cost and then go on to argue that the long-term benefits of such programs justify their expense.

- **Do not quote out of context.** It is perfectly fair to challenge someone's stated position. It is not fair, however, to misrepresent that position by **quoting out of context**—that is, by taking the words out of the original setting in which they appeared. For example, if a college dean says, "For schools with limited resources, it may be more important to allocate resources to academic programs than to environmental projects," you are quoting the dean's remarks out of context if you say, "According to Dean Levering, it is 'more important to allocate resources to academic programs than to environmental projects.'"

- **Do not slant evidence.** An argument based on slanted evidence is not fair. **Slanting** involves choosing only evidence that supports your position and ignoring evidence that challenges it. This tactic makes your position seem stronger than it actually is. Another kind of slanting involves using biased language to unfairly characterize your opponents or their positions—for example, using a dismissive term such as *tree hugger* to describe a concerned environmentalist.

- **Do not make unfair appeals.** If you want your readers to accept your ideas, you need to avoid **unfair appeals** to the emotions, such as appeals to your audience's fears or prejudices. For example, if you try to convince readers of the importance of using green building materials by saying, "Construction projects that do not use green materials doom future generations to a planet that cannot sustain itself," you are likely to push neutral (or even receptive) readers to skepticism or to outright hostility.

- **Do not use logical fallacies.** Using **logical fallacies** (flawed arguments) in your writing will alienate your readers. (See Chapter 5 for information about logical fallacies.)

MAINTAINING YOUR CREDIBILITY

Be careful to avoid phrases that undercut your credibility ("Although this is not a subject I know much about") and to avoid apologies ("This is just my opinion"). Be as clear, direct, and forceful as you can, showing readers you are confident as well as knowledgeable. And, of course, be sure to proofread carefully: grammatical and mechanical errors and typos will weaken your credibility.

Drafting Your Essay

Once you understand how to approach your topic and your audience, you will be ready to draft your essay. At this point, you will have selected the sources you will use to support your position as well as identified the strongest arguments against your position (and decided how to refute them). You may also have prepared a formal outline (or perhaps just a list of points to follow).

As you draft your argumentative essay, keep the following guidelines in mind:

- **Follow the general structure of an argumentative essay.** State your thesis in your first paragraph, and discuss each major point in a separate paragraph, moving from least to most important point to emphasize your strongest argument. Introduce each body paragraph with a clearly worded topic sentence. Discuss each opposing argument in a separate paragraph, and be sure your refutation appears directly after your mention of each opposing argument. Finally, don't forget to include a strong concluding statement in your essay's last paragraph.

- **Decide how to arrange your material.** As you draft your essay, you may notice that it is turning out to be an ethical argument, an evaluation argument, or another kind of argument that you recognize. If this is the case, you might want to ask your instructor how you can arrange your material so it is consistent with this type of argument.

- **Use evidence effectively.** As you make your points, select the evidence that supports your argument most convincingly. As you write, summarize or paraphrase relevant information from your sources, and respond to this information in your own voice, supplementing material that you find in your sources with your own original ideas and conclusions. (For information on finding and evaluating sources, see Chapter 8; for information on integrating source material, see Chapter 9.)

- **Use coordination and subordination to make your meaning clear.** Readers shouldn't have to guess how two points are connected; you should use coordination and subordination to show them the relationship between ideas.

Choose **coordinating conjunctions**—*and, but, or, nor, for, so,* and *yet*—carefully, making sure you are using the right word for your purpose. (Use *and* to show addition; *but, for,* or *yet* to show contradiction; *or* to present alternatives; and *so* to indicate a causal relationship.)

Choose **subordinating conjunctions**—*although, because,* and so on—carefully, and place them so that your emphasis will be clear. Consider the following two sentences.

> Achieving a green campus is vitally important. Creating a green campus is expensive.

If you want to stress the idea that green measures are called for, you would connect the two sentences like this:

> Although creating a green campus is expensive, achieving a green campus is vitally important.

If, however, you want to place emphasis on the high cost, you would connect the two sentences as follows:

> Although achieving a green campus is vitally important, creating a green campus is expensive.

- **Include transitional words and phrases.** Be sure you have enough transitions to guide your readers through your discussion. Supply signals that move readers smoothly from sentence to sentence and paragraph to paragraph, and choose signals that make sense in the context of your discussion.

SUGGESTED TRANSITIONS FOR ARGUMENT

- To show causal relationships: *because, as a result, for this reason*

- To indicate sequence: *first, second, third; then; next; finally*

- To introduce additional points: *also, another, in addition, furthermore, moreover*

- To move from general to specific: *for example, for instance, in short, in other words*

- To identify an opposing argument: *however, although, even though, despite*

- To grant the validity of an opposing argument: *certainly, admittedly, granted, of course*

- To introduce a refutation: *however, nevertheless, nonetheless, still*

GRAMMAR IN CONTEXT

Using Parallelism

As you draft your argumentative essay, you should express corresponding words, phrases, and clauses in **parallel** terms. The use of matching parts of speech to express corresponding ideas strengthens your argument's impact because it enables readers to follow your line of thought.

In particular, use parallelism in sentences that highlight *paired items* or *items in a series*.

- **Paired Items**

  UNCLEAR   Creating a green campus is important because <u>it sets</u> an example for students and the <u>environment will be protected</u>.

  PARALLEL   Creating a green campus is important because it <u>sets</u> an example for students and <u>protects</u> the environment.

- **Items in a Series**

  UNCLEAR   Students can do their part to support a green campus in four ways—by <u>avoiding</u> bottled water, use of electricity <u>should be limited</u>, and they <u>can recycle</u> packaging and also <u>educating</u> themselves about environmental issues is a good strategy.

  PARALLEL   Students can do their part to support a green campus in four ways—by <u>avoiding</u> bottled water, by <u>limiting</u> use of electricity, by <u>recycling</u> packaging, and by <u>educating</u> themselves about environmental issues.

- **Define your terms.** If the key terms of your argument have multiple meanings—as *green* does—be sure to indicate what the term means in the context of your argument. Terms like *environmentally friendly*, *climate change*, *environmentally responsible*, *sustainable*, and *sustainability literacy* may mean very different things to different readers.

- **Use clear language.** An argument is no place for vague language or wordy phrasing. If you want readers to understand your points, your writing should be clear and direct. Avoid vague words like *good*, *bad*, *right*, and *wrong*, which are really just unsupported judgments that do nothing to help you make your case. Also avoid wordy phrases such as *revolves around* and *is concerned with*, particularly in your thesis statement and topic sentences.

- **Finally, show your confidence and your mastery of your material.** Avoid qualifying your statements with phrases such as *I think, I* *believe, it seems to me,* and *in my opinion.* These qualifiers weaken your argument by suggesting that you are unsure of your material or that the statements that follow may not be true.

 **LaunchPad**
macmillan learning

For more practice, see the LearningCurve on Parallelism in the LaunchPad for *Practical Argument.*

➲ EXERCISE 7.14

Keeping the above guidelines in mind, write a draft of an argumentative essay that develops the thesis statement you have been working with.

Revising Your Essay

After you have written a draft of your essay, you will need to revise it. **Revision** is "re-seeing"—looking carefully and critically at the draft you have written. Revision is different from editing and proofreading (discussed on p. 278), which focus on grammar, punctuation, mechanics, and the like. In fact, revision can involve substantial reworking of your essay's structure and content. The strategies discussed on the pages that follow can help you revise your arguments.

Asking Questions

Asking some basic questions, such as those in the three checklists that follow, can help you as you revise.

CHECKLIST

Questions about Your Essay's Purpose and Audience

☐ What was your primary purpose in writing this essay? What other purposes did you have?

☐ What appeals, strategies, and evidence did you use to accomplish your goals?

☐ Who is the audience for your essay? Do you see your readers as receptive, hostile, or neutral to your position?

☐ What basic knowledge do you think your readers have about your topic? Did you provide enough background for them?

☐ What biases do you think your readers have? Have you addressed these biases in your essay?

☐ What do you think your readers believed about your topic before reading your essay?

☐ What do you want readers to believe now that they have read your essay?

CHECKLIST

Questions about Your Essay's Structure and Style

☐ Do you have a clearly stated thesis?

☐ Are your topic sentences clear and concise?

☐ Do you provide all necessary background and definitions?

☐ Do you refute opposing arguments effectively?

☐ Do you include enough transitional words and phrases to guide readers smoothly through your discussion?

☐ Have you avoided vague language and wordy phrasing?

☐ Do you have a strong concluding statement?

CHECKLIST

Questions about Your Essay's Supporting Evidence

☐ Do you support your opinions with *evidence*—facts, observations, examples, statistics, expert opinion, and so on?

☐ Do you have enough evidence to support your thesis?

☐ Do the sources you rely on present information accurately and without bias?

☐ Are your sources' discussions directly relevant to your topic?

☐ Have you consulted sources that represent a wide range of viewpoints, including sources that challenge your position?

The answers to the questions in the checklists may lead you to revise your essay's content, structure, and style. For example, you may want to look for additional sources that can provide the kind of supporting evidence you need. Or, you may notice you need to revise the structure of your essay, perhaps rearranging your points so that the most important point is placed last, for emphasis. You may also want to revise your essay's introduction and conclusion, sharpening your thesis statement or adding a stronger concluding statement. Finally, you may decide to add more background material to help your readers understand the issue you are writing about or to help them take a more favorable view of your position.

Using Outlines and Templates

To check the logic of your essay's structure, you can prepare a revision outline or consult a template.

- To make sure your essay's key points are arranged logically and supported convincingly, you can construct a **formal outline** of your draft. (See p. 267 for information on formal outlines.) This outline will indicate whether you need to discuss any additional points, add supporting evidence, or refute an opposing argument more fully. It will also show you if paragraphs are arranged in a logical order.

- To make sure your argument flows smoothly from thesis statement to evidence to refutation of opposing arguments to concluding statement, you can refer to one of the paragraph **templates** that appear throughout this book. These templates can help you to construct a one-paragraph summary of your essay.

Getting Feedback

After you have done as much as you can on your own, it is time to get feedback from your instructor and (with your instructor's permission) from your school's writing center or from other students in your class.

Instructor Feedback You can get feedback from your instructor in a variety of different ways. For example, your instructor may ask you to email a draft of your paper to him or her with some specific questions ("Do I need paragraph 3, or do I have enough evidence without it?" "Does my thesis statement need to be more specific?"). The instructor will then reply with corrections and recommendations. If your instructor prefers a traditional face-to-face conference, you may still want to email your draft ahead of time to give him or her a chance to read it before your meeting.

Writing Center Feedback You can also get feedback from a writing center tutor, who can be either a student or a professional. The tutor can give you another point of view about your paper's content and organization and also help you focus on specific questions of style, grammar, punctuation, and mechanics. (Keep in mind, however, that a tutor will not edit or proofread your paper for you; that is your job.)

Peer Review Finally, you can get feedback from your classmates. **Peer review** can be an informal process in which you ask a classmate for advice, or it can be a more structured process, involving small groups working with copies of students' work. Peer review can also be conducted electronically. For example, students can exchange drafts by email or respond to one another's drafts that are posted on the course website. They can also use Word's comment tool, as illustrated in the following example.

DRAFT

Colleges and universities have no excuse for ignoring the threat of global climate change. Campus leaders need to push beyond efforts to recycle or compost and instead become models of sustainability. Already, many universities are hard at work demonstrating that reducing their institution's environmental impact is not only possible but worthwhile. They are overhauling their entire infrastructure, their buildings, systems, and even curriculum. While many students, faculty, staff, and administrators are excited by these new challenges, some still question this need to go green. Is it worth the money? Is it promoting "a moral and behavioral agenda rather than an educational one"? (Butcher). In fact, greening will ultimately save institutions money while providing their students with a good education. Colleges should make every effort to create green campuses because by doing so they will help solve the global climate crisis.

Comment [LB]: Your first two sentences are a little abrupt. Maybe you could ease into your argument more slowly?

Comment [KS]: I like these two questions. They really got me thinking.

Comment [PL]: Could you be more specific? I'm not sure what you mean.

Comment [PL]: You definitely talk about this in your paper, but you also talk about other reasons to go green. You might consider revising this thesis statement so it matches your argument.

FINAL VERSION

Over the last few years, the pressure to go green has led colleges and universities to make big changes. The threats posed by global climate change are inspiring campus leaders to push beyond efforts to recycle to become models of sustainability. Today, in the interest of reducing their environmental impact, many campuses are seeking to overhaul their entire infrastructure—their buildings, their systems, and even their curriculum. While many students, faculty, staff, and administrators are excited by these new challenges, some question this need to go green. Is it worth the money? Is it promoting "a moral and behavioral agenda rather than an educational one"? (Butcher). In fact, greening will ultimately save institutions money while providing their students with the educational opportunities necessary to help them solve the crisis of their generation. Despite the expense, colleges should make every effort to create green campuses because by doing so they will improve their own educational environment, ensure their own institution's survival, and help solve the global climate crisis.

GUIDELINES FOR PEER REVIEW

Remember that the peer-review process involves *giving* feedback as well as receiving it. When you respond to a classmate's work, follow these guidelines:

- Be very specific when making suggestions, clearly identifying errors, inconsistencies, redundancy, or areas that need further development.

- Be tactful and supportive when pointing out problems.

- Give praise and encouragement whenever possible.

- Be generous with your suggestions for improvement.

⊘ EXERCISE 7.15

Following the guidelines for revision discussed earlier, get some feedback from others, and then revise your argumentative essay.

Adding Visuals

After you have gotten feedback about the ideas in your paper, you might want to consider adding a **visual**—such as a chart, graph, table, photo, or diagram—to help you make a point more forcefully. For example, in a paper on the green campus movement, you could include anything from photos of students recycling to a chart comparing energy use at different schools. Sometimes a visual can be so specific, so attractive, or so dramatic that its impact will be greater than words would be. At other times, a visual can expand and support a verbal argument.

You can create a visual yourself, or you can download one from the Internet, beginning your search with Google Images. If you download a visual and paste it into your paper, be sure to include a reference to the visual in your discussion to show readers how it supports your argument.

> **NOTE**
>
> Don't forget to label your visual with a figure number, to use proper documentation, and to include a caption explaining what the visual shows, as the student paper that begins on page 280 does. (For information on how to document visuals, see Chapter 10.)

Polishing Your Essay

The final step in the writing process is putting the finishing touches on your essay. At this point, your goal is to make sure that your essay is well organized, convincing, and clearly written, with no distracting grammatical or mechanical errors.

Editing

When you **edit** your revised draft, you review your essay's overall structure, style, and sentence construction, but you focus on grammar, punctuation, and mechanics. Editing is an important step in the writing process because an interesting, logically organized argument will not be convincing if readers are distracted by run-ons and fragments, confusingly placed modifiers, or incorrect verb forms. (Remember, your grammar checker will spot some grammatical errors, but it will miss many others.)

GRAMMAR IN CONTEXT

Pronoun-Antecedent Agreement

A pronoun must always agree in number with its **antecedent**, the word to which it refers. Every pronoun must clearly refer to a particular antecedent.

CONFUSING	College administrators, faculty members, and staff members must work hard to show every student that a green campus will benefit <u>them</u>.
REVISED	College administrators, faculty members, and staff members must work hard to show every student that a green campus will benefit <u>him or her</u>.

 **LaunchPad**
macmillan learning

For more practice, see the LearningCurve on Nouns and Pronouns in the LaunchPad for *Practical Argument*.

Proofreading

When you **proofread** your revised and edited draft, you carefully read every word, trying to spot any remaining punctuation or mechanical errors, as well as any typographical errors (typos) or misspellings that your spell checker may have missed. (Remember, a spell checker will not flag a correctly spelled word that is used incorrectly.)

GRAMMAR IN CONTEXT

Contractions versus Possessive Pronouns

Be especially careful not to confuse the contractions *it's, who's, they're,* and *you're* with the possessive forms *its, whose, their,* and *your.*

INCORRECT	<u>Its</u> not always clear <u>who's</u> responsibility it is to promote green initiatives on campus.
CORRECT	<u>It's</u> not always clear <u>whose</u> responsibility it is to promote green initiatives on campus.

Choosing a Title

After you have edited and proofread your essay, you need to give it a title. Ideally, your title should create interest and give readers clear information about the subject of your essay. It should also be appropriate for your topic. A serious topic calls for a serious title, and a thoughtfully presented argument deserves a thoughtfully selected title.

A title does not need to surprise or shock readers. It also should not be long and wordy or something many readers will not understand. A simple statement of your topic ("Going Green") or of your position on the issue ("College Campuses Should Go Green") is usually all that is needed. If you like, you can use a quotation from one of your sources as a title ("Green Is Good").

➲ EXERCISE 7.16

Evaluate the suitability and effectiveness of the following titles for an argumentative essay on green campuses. Be prepared to explain the strengths and weaknesses of each title.

- Green Campuses

- It's Not Easy Being Green

- The Lean, Clean, Green Machine

- What Students Can Do to Make Their Campuses More Environmentally Responsible

- Why All Campuses Should Be Green Campuses

- Planting the Seeds of the Green Campus Movement

- The Green Campus: An Idea Whose Time Has Come

Checking Format

Finally, make sure that your essay follows your instructor's guidelines for documentation style and manuscript format. (The student paper on p. 280 follows MLA style and manuscript format. For additional sample essays illustrating MLA and APA documentation style and manuscript format, see Chapter 10 and Appendix B, respectively.)

🔽 The following student essay, "Going Green," argues that colleges should make every effort to create green campuses.

GOING GREEN
SHAWN HOLTON

Introduction

Over the last few years, the pressure to go green has led colleges   1
and universities to make big changes. The threats posed by climate
change are encouraging campus leaders to push beyond early efforts,
such as recycling, to become models of sustainability. Today, in the
interest of reducing their environmental impact, many campuses are
seeking to overhaul their entire infrastructure. Although many students,
faculty, staff, and administrators are excited by these new challenges,
some question this need to go green. Is it worth the money? Is it
promoting "a moral and behavioral agenda rather than an educational
one"? (Butcher). In fact, greening will ultimately save institutions money
while providing their students with the educational opportunities
necessary to help them solve the crisis of their generation. Colleges

Thesis statement

should make every effort to create green campuses because by doing so
they will improve their own educational environment, ensure their own
institution's survival, and help solve the global climate crisis.

Body paragraph:
Background of green
movement

Although the green movement has been around for many years,   2
green has become a buzzword only relatively recently. Green political
parties and groups began forming in the 1960s to promote environmentalist goals ("Environmentalism"). These groups fought for "grassroots
democracy, social justice, and nonviolence" in addition to environmental protections and were "self-consciously activist and unconventional"
in their strategies ("Environmentalism"). Today, however, *green* denotes
much more than a political movement; it has become a catchall word
for anything eco-friendly. People use *green* to describe everything from
fuel-efficient cars to fume-free house paint. Green values have become
more mainstream in response to evidence that human activities, particularly those that result in greenhouse-gas emissions, may be causing
global warming at a dramatic rate ("Call for Climate Leadership" 4). To
fight this climate change, many individuals, businesses, and organizations are choosing to go green, making sustainability and preservation
of the environment a priority.

Greening a college campus means moving toward a sustainable campus that works to conserve the earth's natural resources. It means reducing the university's carbon footprint by focusing on energy efficiency in every aspect of campus life. This is no small task. Although replacing incandescent light bulbs with compact fluorescent ones and offering more locally grown food in dining halls are valuable steps, meaningful sustainability requires more comprehensive changes. For example, universities also need to invest in alternative energy sources, construct new buildings and remodel old ones, and work to reduce campus demand for nonrenewable products. Although these changes will eventually save universities money, in most cases, the institutions will need to spend money now to reduce costs in the long term. To achieve this transformation, many colleges are—individually or in cooperation with other schools—establishing formal "climate commitments," setting specific goals, and developing tools to track their investments and evaluate their progress.

> 3 Body paragraph: Definition of *green* as it applies to colleges

Despite these challenges, there are many compelling reasons to act now. Saving money on operating costs, thus making the school more competitive in the long term, is an appealing incentive. In fact, many schools have made solid and sometimes immediate gains by greening some aspect of their campus. For example, by changing its parking and transit systems to encourage more carpooling, biking, and walking, Cornell University has saved 417,000 gallons of fuel and cut costs by $36 million over the last twelve years ("Call for Climate Leadership" 10). By installing geothermal wells and replacing its old power plant with a geothermal pump system, the University of Central Missouri is saving 31 percent in energy costs, according to a case study in *Climate Neutral Campus Report* (Trane). These changes were not merely a social, or even a political, response, but a necessary part of updating the campus. Betty Roberts, the UCM vice president for administration, was faced with the problem of how to "make a change for the benefit of the institution . . . with no money." After saving several million dollars by choosing to go green, Roberts naturally reported that the school was "very happy!" with its decision (qtd. in Trane). There is more to be gained than just savings, however. Oberlin College not only saves money by generating its own solar energy (as shown in Fig. 1) but also makes money by selling its excess electricity back to the local power company (Petersen). Many other schools have taken similar steps, with similarly positive results.

> 4 Body paragraph: First argument in support of thesis

Body paragraph: Second argument in support of thesis

AP Photo/The Morning Journal/Paul M. Walsh.

Fig. 1. Solar panels on the roof of the Adam Joseph Lewis Center for Environmental Studies, Oberlin College. 2008. Oberlin.edu.

Attracting the attention of the media, donors, and—most significantly—prospective students is another practical reason for schools to go green. As one researcher explains, "There is enough evidence nationwide to detect an arms-race of sorts among universities competing for green status" (Krizek et al. 27). The *Princeton Review* now includes a "green rating," and according to recent studies, more than two thirds of college applicants say that they consider green ratings when choosing a school (Krizek et al. 27). A school's commitment to the environment can also bring in large private donations. For example, Carnegie Mellon University attracted $1.7 million from the National Science Foundation for its new Center for Sustainable Engineering (Egan). The University of California, Davis, will be receiving up to $25 million from the Chevron Corporation to research biofuel technology ("Call for Climate Leadership" 10). While greening certainly costs money, a green commitment can also help a school remain financially viable.

Body paragraph: Third argument in support of thesis

In addition to these practical reasons for going green, universities also have another, perhaps more important, reason to promote and model sustainability: doing so may help solve the climate crisis. Although an individual school's reduction of emissions may not noticeably affect global warming, its graduates will be in a position to make a huge impact. College is a critical time in most students' personal and professional development. Students are making choices about what kind of adults they will be, and they are also receiving the training, education, and experience that they will need to succeed in the working world. If universities can offer time, space, and incentives—both in and out of the classroom—to help students develop creative ways to live sustainably, these schools have the potential to change the thinking and habits of a whole generation.

Many critics of greening claim that becoming environmentally friendly is too expensive and will result in higher tuition and fees. However, often a very small increase in fees, as little as a few dollars a semester, can be enough to help a school institute significant change. For example, at the University of Colorado–Boulder, a student-initiated $1 increase in fees allowed the school to purchase enough wind power to reduce its carbon emissions by 12 million pounds ("Call for Climate Leadership" 9). Significantly, the students were the ones who voted to increase their own fees to achieve a greener campus. Although university faculty and administrators' commitment to sustainability is critical for any program's success, few green initiatives will succeed without the enthusiastic support of the student body. Ultimately, students have the power. If they think their school is spending too much on green projects, then they can make a change or choose to go elsewhere.

7 Refutation of first opposing argument

Other critics of the trend toward greener campuses believe that schools with commitments to sustainability are dictating how students should live rather than encouraging free thought. As one critic says, "Once [sustainability literacy] is enshrined in a university's public pronouncements or private articles, then the institution has diminished its commitment to academic inquiry" (Butcher). This kind of criticism overlooks the fact that figuring out how to achieve sustainability requires and will continue to require rigorous critical thinking and creativity. Why not apply the academic skills of inquiry, analysis, and problem solving to the biggest problem of our day? Not doing so would be irresponsible and would confirm the perception that universities are ivory towers of irrelevant knowledge. In fact, the presence of sustainability as both a goal and a subject of study has the potential to reaffirm academia's place at the center of civil society.

8 Refutation of second opposing argument

Creating a green campus is a difficult task, but universities must rise to the challenge or face the consequences. If they do not commit to changing their ways, they will become less and less able to compete for students and for funding. If they refuse to make a comprehensive commitment to sustainability, they also risk irrelevance at best and institutional collapse at worst. Finally, by not rising to the challenge, they will be giving up the opportunity to establish themselves as leaders in addressing the climate crisis. As the coalition of American College and

9 Conclusion

University Presidents states in its Climate Commitment, "No other institution has the influence, the critical mass and the diversity of skills needed to successfully reverse global warming" ("Call for Climate Leadership" 13). Now is the time for schools to make the choice and pledge to go green.

Concluding statement

Works Cited

Butcher, Jim. "Keep the Green Moral Agenda off Campus." *Times Higher Education*, 19 Oct. 2007, www.timeshighereducation.com/news /keep-the-green-moral-agenda-off-campus/310853.article.

"A Call for Climate Leadership." *American College and University Presidents Climate Commitment*, Aug. 2009, www2 .presidentsclimatecommitment.org/html/documents/ACUPCC _InfoPacketv2.pdf

Egan, Timothy. "The Greening of America's Campuses." *New York Times*, 8 Jan. 2006, www.nytimes.com/2006/01/08/education /edlife/egan_environment.html?scp=1&amp%3Bsq=The&_r=0.

"Environmentalism." *Encyclopaedia Britannica Online*, 2015, www.britannica.com/topic/environmentalism.

Krizek, Kevin J., Dave Newport, James White, and Alan R. Townsend. "Higher Education's Sustainability Imperative: How to Practically Respond?" *International Journal of Sustainability in Higher Education*, vol. 13, no. 1, 2012, pp. 1 -33. DOI: 10.1108/14676371211190281.

Petersen, John. "A Green Curriculum Involves Everyone on Campus." *Chronicle of Higher Education*, vol. 54, no. 41, 2008, p. A25. *ERIC Institute of Education Services*, eric.ed.gov/?id=EJ801316.

Trane. "University of Central Missouri." *Climate Neutral Campus Report*, Kyoto Publishing, 14 Aug. 2009, secondnature.org/wp-content /uploads/09-8-14_ClimateNeutralCampusReportReleased.pdf.

➲ EXERCISE 7.17

Find a visual that will strengthen your argument, and add it to your essay. Be sure to document it appropriately and to include a descriptive caption. Then, edit and proofread your paper, paying special attention to parenthetical documentation and your works-cited page. When you have finished, add a title, and print out a final copy of your essay.

4

Using Sources to Support Your Argument

Finding and Evaluating Sources

Is Technology a Serious Threat to Our Privacy?

It is increasingly common to share personal details on social media and online dating sites. The number of people who have profiles on online sites is staggering: Facebook currently has over 1.44 billion users worldwide, Twitter has over 236 million users, and Instagram has 300 million. Even newer apps like Yik Yak have millions of users, and one in five adults between the ages of twenty-five and thirty-four have used an online dating site. Studies have shown that the longer people use these sites, the more information they reveal without thinking about the possible consequences.

According to a 2015 Huffington Post report, 25 percent of Facebook users don't bother using their privacy settings. In addition, 63 percent of Facebook profiles are set on "visible to the public," meaning that anyone can access information. Even more disturbing is that every time a user visits a site with a "like" button, Facebook gets a notice, even if the user doesn't push the button. Not

surprisingly, the Internet has become the primary tool for those who want to access personal information: employers routinely use social-networking sites to find out about job candidates, advertisers buy their data to target consumers, and cybercriminals use information from these sites to steal users' identities.

In response to complaints, the federal government has begun to focus on the issue of cyberprivacy. As a result of pressure from the Federal Trade Commission, Facebook, Twitter, and Google have agreed to submit to privacy audits, and in response to complaints by users, Mark Zuckerberg, creator of Facebook, has repeatedly revised the site's privacy policies. Although privacy audits expose important weaknesses, critics claim that the only way to absolutely ensure privacy is for people to disengage from social media entirely and to avoid sharing personal information online. Others disagree, saying that social networks are a fact of

(*continued*)

(*continued*)

life and that people have to learn to use them responsibly. In other words, people should have no expectation of privacy when they post information about themselves online.

Later in this chapter, you will be asked to evaluate a number of research sources to determine if they are acceptable for an argumentative essay on the topic of technology and privacy. In Chapter 9, you will learn how to integrate sources into an essay on this general topic. In Chapter 10, you will see an MLA paper on one aspect of the topic: whether it is ethical for employers to access information posted on job applicants' social-networking sites. Finally, in Chapter 11, you will learn how to use sources responsibly while considering the question "Where should we draw the line with plagiarism?"

Finding Sources

In some argumentative essays, you can use your own ideas as evidence in support of your position. In many others, however, you have to do **research**—collect information (in both print and electronic form) from magazines, newspapers, books, journals, and other sources—to supplement your own ideas.

The obvious question is, "How does research help you to construct better arguments?" The answer is that research enables you to explore the ideas of others, consider multiple points of view, and expand your view of your subject. As you do so, you get a sense of the issues surrounding your topic, and as a result, you are able to develop a strong thesis and collect the facts, examples, statistics, quotations, and expert opinion that you will need to support your points. In addition, by taking the time to find reliable, up-to-date sources, you demonstrate to readers that your discussion is credible and that you are someone worth listening to. In short, doing research enables you to construct intelligent, authoritative, and convincing arguments.

Finding Information in the Library

When most students do research, they immediately go to the Internet—or, more specifically, to the Web. Unfortunately, by doing this, they ignore the most reliable source of high-quality information available to them: their college library.

Your college library contains both print and electronic resources that you cannot find anywhere else. Although the Internet gives you access to an almost unlimited amount of material, it does not offer the consistently high level of reliable information found in your college library. For this reason, you should always begin your research by surveying the resources of the library.

The best way to access your college library is to visit its website, which is the gateway to a great deal of information—for example, its online catalog, electronic databases, and reference works.

> **The Online Catalog:** The **online catalog** lists all the books, journals, newspapers, magazines, and other material housed in the library. Once you gain access to this catalog, you can type in keywords that will lead you to sources related to your topic.

NOTE

Many libraries have a **discovery service** that enables you to use a single search box to access a wide variety of content—for example, the physical items held by a library, content from e-books, journal articles, government documents, and electronic databases. Most discovery services return high-quality results quickly and (like Google) rank them according to relevancy.

> **Online Databases:** All college libraries subscribe to **databases**—collections of digital information that you access through a keyword search. The library's online databases enable you to retrieve bibliographic citations as well as the full text of articles from hundreds of publications. Some of these databases—for example, *Expanded Academic ASAP* and *Proquest Research Library*—provide information on a wide variety of topics. Others—for example, *Business Source Premier* and *Sociological Abstracts*—provide information on a particular subject area. Before selecting a database, check with the reference librarian to determine which will be most useful for your topic.
>
> **Reference Works:** All libraries contain **reference works**—sources of accurate and reliable information such as dictionaries, encyclopedias, and almanacs. These reference works are available both in print and in electronic form. **General encyclopedias**—such as the *New Encyclopaedia Britannica* and the *Columbia Encyclopedia*—provide general information on a wide variety of topics. **Specialized reference works**—such as *Facts on File* and the *World Almanac*—and **special encyclopedias**—such as the *Encyclopedia of Law and Economics*—offer detailed information on specific topics.

NOTE

Although a general encyclopedia can provide an overview of your topic, encyclopedia articles do not usually treat topics in enough depth for college-level research. Be sure to check your instructor's guidelines before you use a general encyclopedia in your research.

Finding Information on the Internet

Although the Internet gives you access to a vast amount of information, it has its limitations. For one thing, because anyone can publish on the Web, you cannot be sure if the information found there is trustworthy, timely, or authoritative. Of course, there are reliable sources of information on the Web. For example, the information on your college library's website is reliable. In addition, Google Scholar provides links to some scholarly sources that are as good as those found in a college library's databases. Even so, you have to approach this material with caution; some articles accessed through Google Scholar are pay-per-view, and others are not current or comprehensive.

A **search engine**—such as Google or Bing—helps you to locate and to view documents that you search for with keywords. Different types of search engines are suitable for different purposes:

- **General-Purpose Search Engines: General-purpose search engines** retrieve information on a great number of topics. They cast the widest possible net and bring in the widest variety of information. The disadvantage of general-purpose search engines is that you get a great deal of irrelevant material. Because each search engine has its own unique characteristics, you should try a few of them to see which you prefer. The most popular general-purpose search engines are Google, Bing, Yahoo!, Ask, and AOL Search.

- **Specialized Search Engines: Specialized search engines** focus on specific subject areas or on a specific type of content. The advantage of specialized search engines is that they eliminate the need for you to wade through pages of irrelevant material. By focusing your search on a specific subject area, you are more likely to locate information on your particular topic. (You are able to narrow your search to a specific subject area when you use a general-purpose search engine, but a specialized search engine narrows your search for you.) You can find a list of specialized search engines on the Search Engine List (thesearchenginelist.com).

- **Metasearch Engines:** Because each search engine works differently, results can (and do) vary. For this reason, if you limit yourself to a single search engine, you can miss a great deal of useful information. **Metasearch engines** solve this problem by taking the results of several search engines and presenting them in a simple, no-nonsense format. The most popular metasearch engines are Dogpile, Kartoo, Mamma, Surfwax, Yippy, and Zoo.

Evaluating Sources

Whenever you locate a source—print or electronic—you should always take the time to evaluate it. When you **evaluate** a source, you assess the

Sources must be
evaluated carefully.

Viorika Prikhodko/iStock/Getty Images

objectivity of the author, the credibility of the source, and its relevance to
your argument. (Although a librarian or an instructor has screened the
print and electronic sources in your college library for general accuracy
and trustworthiness, you cannot simply assume that these sources are suitable for your particular writing project.)

Material that you access online presents particular problems. Because
anyone can publish on the Internet, the information you find there has to
be evaluated carefully for accuracy. Although some material on the Internet (for example, journal articles that are published in both print and digital format) is reliable, other material (for example, personal websites and
blogs) may be unreliable and unsuitable for your research. To be reasonably certain that the information you are accessing is appropriate, you
have to approach it critically.

As you locate sources, make sure that they are suitable for your
research. (Remember, if you use an untrustworthy source, you undercut
your credibility.)

To evaluate sources, you use the same process that you use when you
evaluate anything else. For example, if you are thinking about buying a laptop computer, you use several criteria to help you make your decision—for
example, price, speed, memory, reliability, and availability of technical support. The same is true for evaluating research sources. You can use the following criteria to decide whether a source is appropriate for your research:

- Accuracy

- Credibility

- Objectivity
- Currency
- Comprehensiveness
- Authority

The illustrations on page 293 show where to find information that can help you evaluate a source.

Accuracy   A source is **accurate** when it is factual and free of errors. One way to judge the accuracy of a source is to compare the information it contains to that same information in several other sources. If a source has factual errors, then it probably includes other types of errors as well. Needless to say, errors in spelling and grammar should also cause you to question a source's general accuracy.

You can also judge the accuracy of a source by checking to see if the author cites sources for the information that is discussed. Documentation can help readers determine both the quality of information in a source and the range of sources used. It can also show readers what sources a writer has failed to consult. (Failure to cite an important book or article should cause you to question the writer's familiarity with a subject.) If possible, verify the legitimacy of some of the books and articles that a writer cites by seeing what you can find out about them online. If a source has caused a great deal of debate or if it is disreputable, you will probably be able to find information about the source by researching it on Google.

Credibility   A source is **credible** when it is believable. You can begin checking a source's credibility by determining where a book or article was published. If a university press published the book, you can be reasonably certain that it was **peer reviewed**—read by experts in the field to confirm the accuracy of the information. If a commercial press published the book, you will have to consider other criteria—the author's reputation and the date of publication, for example—to determine quality. If your source is an article, see if it appears in a **scholarly journal**—a periodical aimed at experts in a particular field—or in a **popular magazine**—a periodical aimed at general readers. Journal articles are almost always acceptable research sources because they are usually documented, peer reviewed, and written by experts. (They can, however, be difficult for general readers to understand.) Articles in high-level popular magazines, such as the *Atlantic* and the *Economist*, may also be suitable—provided experts wrote them. However, articles in lower-level popular magazines—such as *Sports Illustrated* and *Time*—may be easy to understand, but they are seldom acceptable sources for research.

You can determine how well respected a source is by reading reviews written by critics. You can find reviews of books by consulting *Book*

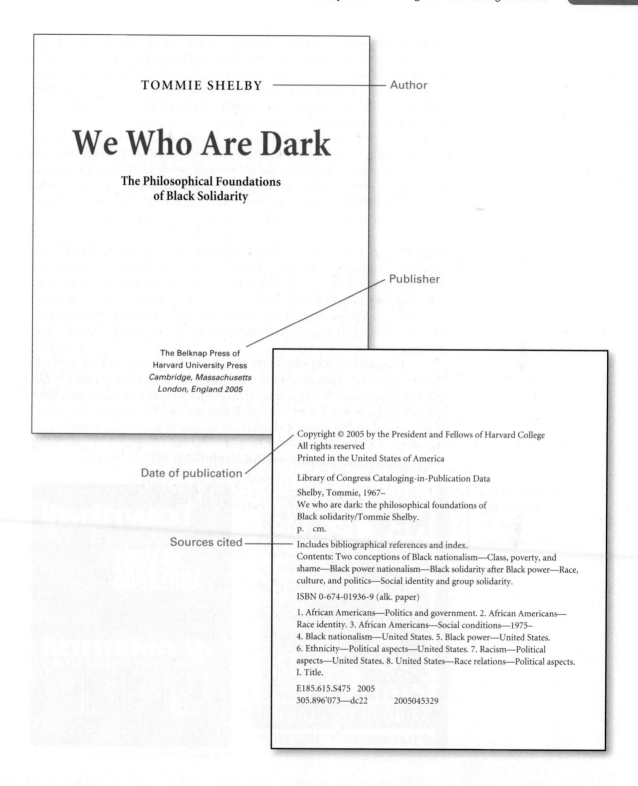

TOMMIE SHELBY ——————— Author

We Who Are Dark

**The Philosophical Foundations
of Black Solidarity**

Publisher

The Belknap Press of
Harvard University Press
*Cambridge, Massachusetts
London, England 2005*

Copyright © 2005 by the President and Fellows of Harvard College
All rights reserved
Printed in the United States of America

Library of Congress Cataloging-in-Publication Data

Shelby, Tommie, 1967–
We who are dark: the philosophical foundations of
Black solidarity/Tommie Shelby.
p. cm.

Date of publication

Sources cited ——— Includes bibliographical references and index.
Contents: Two conceptions of Black nationalism—Class, poverty, and
shame—Black power nationalism—Black solidarity after Black power—Race,
culture, and politics—Social identity and group solidarity.

ISBN 0-674-01936-9 (alk. paper)

1. African Americans—Politics and government. 2. African Americans—
Race identity. 3. African Americans—Social conditions—1975–
4. Black nationalism—United States. 5. Black power—United States.
6. Ethnicity—Political aspects—United States. 7. Racism—Political
aspects—United States. 8. United States—Race relations—Political aspects.
I. Title.

E185.615.S475 2005
305.896'073—dc22   2005045329

Review Digest—either in print or online—which lists books that have been reviewed in at least three magazines or newspapers and includes excerpts of reviews. In addition, you can consult the *New York Times Book Review* website—www.nytimes.com/pages/books/index.html—to access reviews printed by the newspaper since 1981. (Both professional and reader reviews are also available at Amazon.com.)

Finally, you can determine how well respected a source is by seeing how often other scholars in the field refer to it. **Citation indexes** indicate how often books and articles are mentioned by other sources in a given year. This information can give you an idea of how important a work is in a particular field. Citation indexes for the humanities, the social sciences, and the sciences are available online and in your college library.

Objectivity   A source is **objective** when it is not unduly influenced by personal opinions or feelings. Ideally, you want to find sources that are objective, but to one degree or another, all sources are **biased**. In short, all sources—especially those that take a stand on an issue—reflect the opinions of their authors, regardless of how hard they may try to be impartial. (Of course, an opinion is perfectly acceptable—as long as it is supported by evidence.)

As a researcher, you should recognize that bias exists and ask yourself whether a writer's assumptions are justified by the facts or are simply the result of emotion or preconceived ideas. You can make this determination by looking at a writer's choice of words and seeing if the language is slanted or by reviewing the writer's points and seeing if his or her argument is one-sided. Get in the habit of asking yourself whether you are being offered a legitimate point of view or simply being fed propaganda.

The covers of the liberal and conservative magazines shown here suggest different biases.

© Roz Chast/The New Yorker

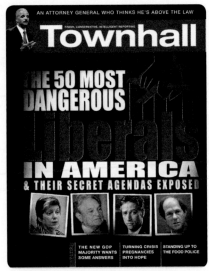

© Yasamin Khalili/Townhall Magazine

Currency A source is **current** when it is up-to-date. (For a book, you can find the date of publication on the copyright page, as above. For an article, you can find the date on the front cover of the magazine or journal.) If you are dealing with a scientific subject, the date of publication can be very important. Older sources might contain outdated information, so you want to use the most up-to-date source that you can find. For other subjects—literary criticism, for example—the currency of the information may not be as important as it is in the sciences.

Comprehensiveness A source is **comprehensive** when it covers a subject in sufficient depth. The first thing to consider is whether the source deals specifically with your subject. (If it treats your subject only briefly, it will probably not be useful.) Does it treat your subject in enough detail? Does the source include the background information that you need to understand the discussion? Does the source mention other important sources that discuss your subject? Are facts and interpretations supported by the other sources you have read, or are there major points of disagreement? Finally, does the author include documentation?

How comprehensive a source needs to be depends on your purpose and audience as well as on your writing assignment. For a short essay for an introductory course, editorials from the *New York Times* or the *Wall Street Journal* might give you enough information to support your argument. If you are writing a longer essay, however, you might need to consult journal articles (and possibly books) about your subject.

Authority A source has **authority** when a writer has the expertise to write about a subject. Always try to determine if the author is a recognized authority or simply a person who has decided to write about a particular topic. For example, what other books or articles has the author written? Has your instructor ever mentioned the author's name? Is the author mentioned in your textbook? Has the author published other works on the same subject or on related subjects? (You can find this information on Amazon.com.)

You should also determine if the author has an academic affiliation. Is he or she a faculty member at a respected college or university? Do other established scholars have a high opinion of the author? You can often find this information by using a search engine such as Google or by consulting one of the following directories:

Contemporary Authors
Directory of American Scholars
International Who's Who
National Faculty Directory
Who's Who in America
Wilson Biographies Plus Illustrated

⊘ EXERCISE 8.1

Assume that you are preparing to write an argumentative essay on the topic of whether information posted on social-networking sites threatens privacy. Read the sources that follow, and evaluate each source for accuracy, credibility, objectivity, currency, comprehensiveness, and authority.

- Nicholas Thompson, "Bigger Brother: The Exponential Law of Privacy Loss"

- *USA Today* editorial board, "Time to Enact 'Do Not Track'"

- Rebecca MacKinnon, "Privacy and Facebook"

This essay appeared in the December 5, 2011, edition of the *New Yorker*.

BIGGER BROTHER: THE EXPONENTIAL LAW OF PRIVACY LOSS

NICHOLAS THOMPSON

This past Tuesday, Facebook made a deal with the F.T.C.: from now on, the social-networking company can no longer humbug us about privacy. If we're told that something we post on the site will be private, it will stay that way, unless we give Facebook permission to make it public. Or at least sort of. For a while. Facebook has been relentless in its effort to make more of what it knows about us—the music we listen to, the photos we take, the friends we have—available to more people, and it will surely figure out creative ways, F.T.C. or no F.T.C., to further that campaign. The company's leadership sincerely believes that the more we share the better the world will be. Mark Zuckerberg, the C.E.O., has said that in ten years we'll share a thousand times as much as we do now. That seems to be both an observation and a goal.

Meanwhile, Zynga has announced that it's going to raise about a billion dollars in an impending I.P.O. Zynga makes social games like *FarmVille*, in which people harvest and sell virtual tomatoes. The games sound inane to non-players, and Zynga employees claim that their workplace is run like a labor camp; yet the company is worth perhaps ten billion dollars. Why? Partly because they collect and analyze fifteen terabytes of data a day from their users. They watch carefully in order to learn how to hook people and what enticements to offer someone frustrated about his slow-growing tomato crop. (There's a segment from *Bloomberg West* in which an analyst compares Zynga to a drug dealer.) According to Zynga's recent S.E.C. filings, its total number of players is stagnant, but the amount of money it can extract from each one is growing. Data is the currency of the Web right now. Whoever has the most detailed data about you will get rich. Zynga has great data, and Zynga is about to get very rich.

> "Whoever has the most detailed data about you will get rich."

Last week also brought the news that a company called Carrier IQ has 3 installed software on about a hundred and fifty million phones that lets it and its customers—such as Sprint, A.T. & T., and Apple—know an awful lot about you. It tracks location, stores the numbers you dial, and even records the Websites you browse when you're not connected to a cell network. The point of the software is to help the phone companies improve their networks and serve you better. But this is done in a mysterious (and perhaps nefarious) way. Most people don't know they have it, and it's not easy to remove. It's also not clear exactly what it's recording, though a bevy of new lawsuits and government investigations will now try to figure that out. At the very least, there's one more company that you've never heard of that knows a heck of a lot about you. "The excuse proffered thus far—improved service— is at best feeble when compared to the extent of the potential invasion of privacy," Stephen Wicker, a professor in electrical and computer engineering at Cornell, told me.

These are just three stories from the past seven days. There'll surely be 4 more soon. Together, they've made me think of something I'll call The Exponential Law of Privacy Loss (or TELPL, pronounced "tell people"). The more we do online, the better companies get at tracking us, and the more accurate and detailed the data they glean from us becomes. The amount of data that they have grows exponentially over time.

It's impossible to exactly measure what percent of our time is spent con- 5 nected to the Internet: texting, shopping, surfing, browsing, sleeping. But, my best estimation is that, a few years ago, we lived roughly ten percent of our lives online, and companies captured about ten percent of what we did. Now it's about thirty percent, and the companies capture thirty percent of that—which means roughly nine times as much as a few years ago. Eventually, when we live seventy percent of our lives online, digital companies will capture and store about seventy percent of that. I'm not sure what will happen to the formula when we spend our entire lives online. Ideally, we won't get there.

This tracking isn't all bad; it may not even be mostly bad. People keep 6 letting Facebook broadcast more of their preferences and habits, and they love it. The more that advertisers know about you, the more willing they are to do things like buy advertisements on Websites, supporting journalism such as this. Carrier IQ makes our phones more efficient, and I have yet to hear of any specific harm done to any specific person by their system. Still, the Law is real. The F.T.C. can slow things down, but only a little. All of us are still becoming corporate data at an ever faster rate, for better and for worse.

This editorial was published in *USA Today* on December 11, 2011.

TIME TO ENACT "DO NOT TRACK"

USA TODAY EDITORIAL BOARD

Facebook's 800 million users are probably feeling a little more secure since the social media giant agreed to privacy measures forced by the Federal Trade Commission (FTC) late last month. But they'd be wise to stay cautious. Plenty of incentive for mischief remains, and not only on Facebook.

The agreement requires Facebook to stop letting users mark their profile information as private and then making it public without their permission. Facebook also promised that it will warn users of privacy policy changes before enacting them.

But the agreement won't stop Facebook from monitoring and sharing users' Web-browsing habits, which is a way for the company and others like it to make money. It's an unsatisfying ending to a two-year investigation, but more important, it's a marker of how difficult it will be to maintain privacy in an increasingly wired world.

The weakness in the FTC's agreement is that it didn't establish any guidelines about Internet tracking, the method by which Facebook collects data about its users even when they're not on the network itself. As company representatives recently acknowledged to *USA Today,* Facebook automatically compiles a log of every Web page its users visit that has a Facebook plug-in, such as the ubiquitous "like" button.

Other online giants, such as Google and Yahoo, use similar methods to monitor users' Web-browsing. This lets them tailor their pages and advertisements to appeal to different visitors.

Online tracking companies, which help sites compile these browsing records, claim that your personal details are not connected to your name, meaning your privacy is not compromised when they share information with advertisers or others. But as the *Wall Street Journal* discovered last year, at least one tracking company collected Web surfers' names and other personally identifiable information and passed it on to clients.

The implication is that tracking companies and advertisers could know your name, e-mail address, hometown, medical history, political affiliation, and more. Such information could be used in troubling ways. A health insurance company, for example, could guess your medical conditions. Or a potential employer could find out whether you spend your time gambling online.

> "Such information could be used in troubling ways."

If you don't like that prospect, your only option is to use a Web browser that 8 offers a "Do Not Track" mechanism, such as Mozilla Firefox or Internet Explorer 9. Once you activate the feature, it signals websites you visit indicating that you do not want your data tracked by third parties. But existing Do Not Track mechanisms can't control what websites do; they can only communicate your preference.

That's why the FTC has called for a tougher and more universal version of 9 Do Not Track, a move that the online advertising industry argues would hamper Internet innovation. These fears are overblown. Behavioral advertising, which targets viewers based on their Web-browsing history, is large and growing, but it still accounts for less than 5% of all online advertising. So ads that rely on tracking are hardly the Internet's only revenue stream.

Measures that would create a legally enforceable Do Not Track mechanism 10 or otherwise address privacy concerns are languishing in Congress. Lawmakers should give Web users more tools to control their personal information. Until that happens, your online habits will reveal much more about you than just what you put on your Facebook profile.

This essay is from MacKinnon's book *Consent of the Networked* (2012).

PRIVACY AND FACEBOOK
REBECCA MACKINNON

As protests mounted in reaction to Iran's presidential elections on June 12, 1 2009, Facebook actively encouraged members of the pro-opposition Green Movement to use the social networking platform. By mid-June, more than four hundred members of Facebook's fast-growing Farsi-speaking community volunteered their time to create a Farsi version of Facebook. Thanks to efforts by Facebook enthusiasts all around the world, the platform has been made accessible in seventy languages—including many languages spoken in countries where regimes are known not to tolerate dissent.

Then in December 2009, Facebook made a sudden and unexpected alteration 2 of its privacy settings. On December 9, to be precise, people who logged in got an automatic pop-up message announcing major changes. Until that day, it was possible to keep one's list of Facebook "friends" hidden not only from the general Internet-surfing public but also from one another. That changed overnight without warning. An array of information that Facebook previously had treated as private, suddenly and without warning became publicly available information by default. This included a user's profile picture, name, gender, current city, what professional and regional "networks" one belonged to within Facebook, the "causes" one had signed on to support, and one's entire list of Facebook friends.

The changes were driven by Facebook's need to monetize the service 3 but were also consistent with founder Mark Zuckerberg's strong personal conviction that people everywhere should be open about their lives and actions. In Iran, where authorities were known to be using information and contacts obtained from people's Facebook accounts while interrogating Green Movement activists detained from the summer of 2009 onward, the implications of the new privacy settings were truly frightening. Soon after the changes were made, an anonymous commenter on the technology news site ZDNet confirmed that Iranian users were deleting their accounts in horror:

> A number of my friends in Iran are active student protesters of the government. They use Facebook extensively to organize protests and meetings, but they had no choice but to delete their Facebook accounts today. They are terrified that their once private lists of friends are now available to "everyone" that wants to know. When that "everyone" happens to include the Iranian Revolutionary Guard and members of the Basij militia, willing to kidnap, arrest, or murder to stifle dissent, the consequences seem just a bit more serious than those faced from silly pictures and status updates. I realize this may not be an issue for the vast majority of American Facebook users, but it's just plain irresponsible to do this without first asking consent. It's even more egregious because Facebook threw out the original preference (the one that requested Facebook keep the list of friends private) and replaced it with a mandate, publicizing what was once private information—with no explicit consent. If given the choice to remain a Facebook user with those settings, or quit, my friends would have quit rather than risk that information being seen by the wrong people. Instead, Facebook published it anyways. It's a betrayal of trust for the sake of better targeted advertising.

The global outcry over the exposure of people's friend lists in December 4 2009 was so strong that within roughly a day after the dramatic change, Facebook made an adjustment so that users could once again hide their friend lists from public view. People's friends could still see one another, however, and there was no way to hide them. Everybody's "causes" and "pages" were still publicly exposed by default, another serious vulnerability for activists. People kept complaining—many by creating protest groups within Facebook itself, where hundreds of thousands of people from all around the world posted angry messages. The groups had names like "Facebook! Fix the Privacy Settings!" and "Hide Friend List and Fan Pages! We Need Better Privacy Controls!" and "We

> "People's friends could still see one another, however, and there was no way to hide them."

Want Our Old Privacy Settings Back!" Scrolling through these pages, you see people posting from all over the world, with large numbers of Arab, Persian, Turkish, Eastern European, and Chinese names.

Eventually Facebook fixed this problem as well, adjusting the privacy 5 options so that information about what pages users follow, or groups they have joined, can be made private. Meanwhile, however, lives of people around the world had been endangered unnecessarily—not because any government pressured Facebook to make changes, but because Facebook had its own reasons and did not fully consider the implications for the service's most vulnerable users, in democratic and authoritarian countries alike.

❯ EXERCISE 8.2

Write a one- or two-paragraph evaluation of each of the three sources you read for Exercise 8.1. Be sure to support your evaluation with specific references to the sources.

Evaluating Websites

The Internet is like a freewheeling frontier town in the old West. Occasionally, a federal marshal may pass through, but for the most part, there is no law and order, so you are on your own. On the Internet, literally anything goes— exaggerations, misinformation, errors, and even complete fabrications. Some websites contain reliable content, but many do not. The main reason for this situation is that there is no authority—as there is in a college library—who evaluates sites for accuracy and trustworthiness. That job falls to you, the user.

Another problem is that websites often lack important information. For example, a site may lack a date, a sponsoring organization, or even the name of the author of the page. For this reason, it is not always easy to evaluate the material you find there.

© Steve Hix/Somos Images/Corbis

Most sources found in a college library have been evaluated by a reference librarian for their suitability as research sources.

When you evaluate a website (especially when it is in the form of a blog or a series of posts), you need to begin by viewing it skeptically—unless you know for certain that it is reliable. In other words, assume that its information is questionable until you establish that it is not. Then apply the same criteria you use to evaluate any sources—*accuracy, credibility, objectivity, currency, comprehensiveness,* and *authority.*

The Web page pictured on page 303 shows where to find information that can help you evaluate a website.

Accuracy

Information on a website is **accurate** when it is factual and free of errors. Information in the form of facts, opinions, statistics, and interpretations is everywhere on the Internet, and in the case of Wiki sites, this information is continually being rewritten and revised. Given the volume and variety of this material, it is a major challenge to determine its accuracy. You can assess the accuracy of information on a website by asking the following questions:

- **Does the site contain errors of fact?** Factual errors—inaccuracies that relate directly to the central point of the source—should immediately disqualify a site as a reliable source.

- **Does the site contain a list of references or any other type of documentation?** Reliable sources indicate where their information comes from. The authors know that people want to be sure that the information they are using is accurate and reliable. If a site provides no documentation, you should not trust the information it contains.

- **Does the site provide links to other sites?** Does the site have links to reliable websites that are created by respected authorities or sponsored by trustworthy institutions? If it does, then you can conclude that your source is at least trying to maintain a certain standard of quality.

- **Can you verify information?** A good test for accuracy is to try to verify key information on a site. You can do this by checking it in a reliable print source or on a good reference website such as *Encyclopedia.com.*

Credibility

Information on a website is **credible** when it is believable. Just as you would not naively believe a stranger who approached you on the street, you should not automatically believe a site that you randomly encounter on the Web. You can assess the credibility of a website by asking the following questions:

- **Does the site list authors, directors, or editors?** Anonymity—whether on a website or on a blog—should be a red flag for a researcher who is considering using a source.

Sponsoring organization

Advisory board

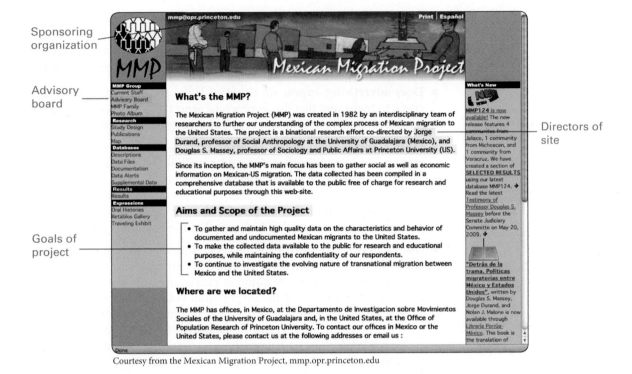

Directors of site

Goals of project

Courtesy from the Mexican Migration Project, mmp.opr.princeton.edu

- **Is the site refereed?** Does a panel of experts or an advisory board decide what material appears on the website? If not, what standards are used to determine the suitability of content?

- **Does the site contain errors in grammar, spelling, or punctuation?** If it does, you should be on the alert for other types of errors. If the people maintaining the site do not care enough to make sure that the site is free of small errors, you have to wonder if they will take the time to verify the accuracy of the information presented.

- **Does an organization sponsor the site?** If so, do you know (or can you find out) anything about the sponsoring organization? Use a search engine such as Google to determine the purpose and point of view of the organization.

Objectivity Information on a website is **objective** when it limits the amount of **bias** that it displays. Some sites—such as those that support a particular political position or social cause—make no secret of their biases. They present them clearly in their policy statements on their home pages. Others, however, try to hide their biases—for example, by referring only to sources that support a particular point of view and not mentioning those that do not.

Keep in mind that bias does not automatically disqualify a source. It should, however, alert you to the fact that you are seeing only one side of an issue and that you will have to look further to get a complete picture. You can assess the objectivity of a website by asking the following questions:

- **Does advertising appear on the site?** If the site contains advertising, check to make sure that the commercial aspect of the site does not affect its objectivity. The site should keep advertising separate from content.

- **Does a commercial entity sponsor the site?** A for-profit company may sponsor a website, but it should not allow commercial interests to determine content. If it does, there is a conflict of interest. For example, if a site is sponsored by a company that sells organic products, it may include testimonials that emphasize the virtues of organic products and ignore information that is skeptical of their benefits.

- **Does a political organization or special-interest group sponsor the site?** Just as you would for a commercial site, you should make sure that the sponsoring organization is presenting accurate information. It is a good idea to check the information you get from a political site against information you get from an educational or a reference site— *Ask.com* or *Encyclopedia.com*, for example. Organizations have specific agendas, and you should make sure that they are not bending the truth to satisfy their own needs.

- **Does the site link to strongly biased sites?** Even if a site seems trustworthy, it is a good idea to check some of its links. Just as you can judge people by the company they keep, you can also judge websites by the sites they link to. Links to overly biased sites should cause you to reevaluate the information on the original site.

USING A SITE'S URL TO ASSESS ITS OBJECTIVITY

A website's **URL** (uniform resource locator) can give you information that can help you assess the site's objectivity.

Look at the domain name to identify sponsorship. Knowing a site's purpose can help you determine whether a site is trying to sell you something or just trying to provide information. The last part of a site's URL can tell you whether a site is a commercial site (.com and .net), an educational site (.edu), a nonprofit site (.org), or a governmental site (.gov, .mil, and so on).

See if the URL has a tilde (~) in it. A tilde in a site's URL indicates that information was published by an individual and is unaffiliated with the sponsoring organization. Individuals can have their own agendas, which may be different from the agenda of the site on which their information appears or to which it is linked.

AVOIDING CONFIRMATION BIAS

Confirmation bias is a tendency that people have to accept information that supports their beliefs and to ignore information that does not. For example, people see false or inaccurate information on websites, and because it reinforces their political or social beliefs, they forward it to others. Eventually, this information becomes so widely distributed that people assume that it is true. Numerous studies have demonstrated how prevalent confirmation bias is. Consider the following examples:

- A student doing research for a paper chooses sources that support her thesis and ignores those that take the opposite position.

- A prosecutor interviews witnesses who establish the guilt of a suspect and overlooks those who do not.

- A researcher includes statistics that confirm his hypothesis and excludes statistics that do not.

    When you write an argumentative essay, do not accept information just because it supports your thesis. Realize that you have an obligation to consider all sides of an issue, not just the side that reinforces your beliefs.

Currency Information on a website is **current** when it is up-to-date. Some sources—such as fiction and poetry—are timeless and therefore are useful whatever their age. Other sources, however—such as those in the hard sciences—must be current because advances in some disciplines can quickly make information outdated. For this reason, you should be aware of the shelf life of information in the discipline you are researching and choose information accordingly. You can assess the currency of a website by asking the following questions:

- **Does the website include the date when it was last updated?** As you look at Web pages, check the date on which they were created or updated. (Some websites automatically display the current date, so be careful not to confuse this date with the date the page was last updated.)

- **Are all links on the site live?** If a website is properly maintained, all the links it contains will be **live**—that is, a click on the link will take you to other websites. If a site contains a number of links that are not live, you should question its currency.

- **Is the information on the site up-to-date?** A site might have been updated, but this does not necessarily mean that it contains the most up-to-date information. In addition to checking when a website was last updated, look at the dates of the individual articles that appear on the site to make sure they are not outdated.

Comprehensiveness Information on a website is **comprehensive** when it covers a subject in depth. A site that presents itself as a comprehensive source should include (or link to) the most important sources of information that you need to understand a subject. (A site that leaves out a key source of information or that ignores opposing points of view cannot be called comprehensive.) You can assess the comprehensiveness of a website by asking the following questions:

- **Does the site provide in-depth coverage?** Articles in professional journals—which are available both in print and online—treat subjects in enough depth for college-level research. Other types of articles—especially those in popular magazines and in general encyclopedias, such as *Wikipedia*—are often too superficial (or untrustworthy) for college-level research.

- **Does the site provide information that is not available elsewhere?** The website should provide information that is not available from other sources. In other words, it should make a contribution to your knowledge and do more than simply repackage information from other sources.

- **Who is the intended audience for the site?** Knowing the target audience for a website can help you to assess a source's comprehensiveness. Is it aimed at general readers or at experts? Is it aimed at high school students or at college students? It stands to reason that a site that is aimed at experts or college students will include more detailed information than one that is aimed at general readers or high school students.

Authority Information on a website has **authority** when you can establish the legitimacy of both the author and the site. You can determine the authority of a source by asking the following questions:

- **Is the author an expert in the field that he or she is writing about?** What credentials does the author have? Does he or she have the expertise to write about the subject? Sometimes you can find this information on the website itself. For example, the site may contain an "About the Author" section or links to other publications by the author. If this information is not available, do a Web search with the author's name as a keyword. If you cannot confirm the author's expertise (or if the site has no listed author), you should not use material from the site.

- **What do the links show?** What information is revealed by the links on the site? Do they lead to reputable sites, or do they take you to sites that suggest that the author has a clear bias or a hidden agenda? Do other reliable sites link back to the site you are evaluating?

- **Is the site a serious publication?** Does it include information that enables you to judge its legitimacy? For example, does it include a statement of purpose? Does it provide information that enables you to determine the criteria for publication? Does the site have a board of advisers? Are these advisers experts? Does the site include a mailing address and a phone number? Can you determine if the site is the domain of a single individual or the effort of a group of individuals?

- **Does the site have a sponsor?** If so, is the site affiliated with a reputable institutional sponsor, such as a governmental, educational, or scholarly organization?

⊙ EXERCISE 8.3

Consider the following two home pages—one from the website for the *Chronicle of Higher Education*, a publication aimed at college instructors and administrators, and the other from the website for *Glamour*, a publication aimed at general readers. Assume that on both websites, you have found articles about privacy and social-networking sites. Locate and label the information on each home page that would enable you to determine the suitability of using information from the site in your paper.

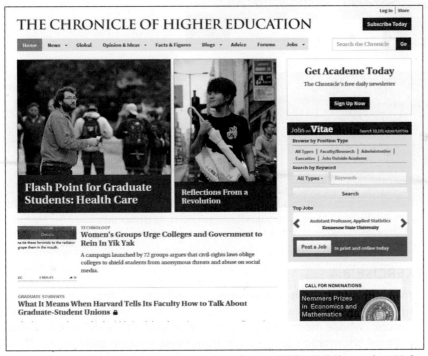

Courtesy of The Chronicle of Higher Education, www.chronicle.com; © Nabil K. Mark Photography; © Mark Leong/Redux

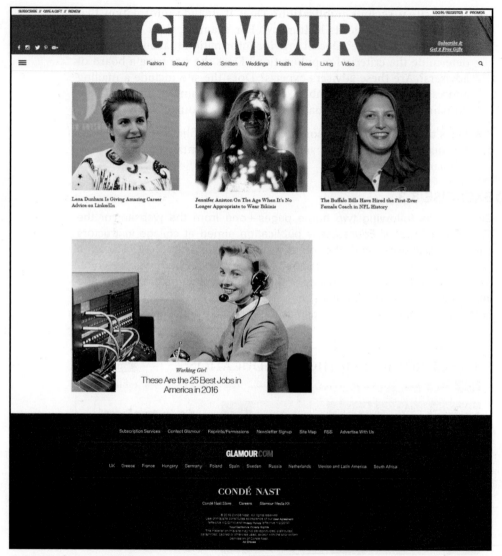

Courtesy of Glamour, © Conde Nast; Jason Merritt/Getty Images (Lena Dunham); TC: Wireimage/Getty Images (Jen Aniston); TR: AP/Wire Photo (Kathryn Smith); Bottom: Superstock/Getty Images (phone operator)

◯ EXERCISE 8.4

Here are the **mission statements**—statements of the organizations' purposes—from the websites for the *Chronicle of Higher Education* and *Glamour*, whose home pages you considered in Exercise 8.3. What additional information can you get from these mission statements? How do they help you to evaluate the sites as well as the information that might appear on the sites?

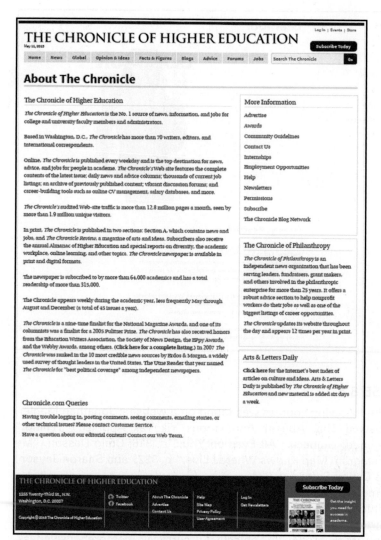

Courtesy of The Chronicle of Higher Education, www.chronicle.com

Cover Photo by: Steven Pan/Glamour; © Conde Nast

◉ EXERCISE 8.5

Each of the following sources was found on a website: Jonathan Mahler, "Who Spewed That Abuse? Anonymous Yik Yak App Isn't Telling," p. 310; Jennifer Golbeck, "All Eyes on You," p. 316; Craig Desson, "My Creepy Instagram Map Knows Where I Live," p. 322; and Sharon Jayson, "Is Online Dating Safe?," p. 324.

Assume that you are preparing to write an essay on the topic of whether information posted on social-networking sites threatens privacy. First, visit the websites on which the articles appear, and evaluate each site for accuracy, credibility, objectivity, currency, comprehensiveness, and authority. Then, using the same criteria, evaluate each source.

This article originally ran in the *New York Times* on March 8, 2015.

WHO SPEWED THAT ABUSE? ANONYMOUS YIK YAK APP ISN'T TELLING

JONATHAN MAHLER

During a brief recess in an honors course at Eastern Michigan University last   1
fall, a teaching assistant approached the class's three female professors. "I think you need to see this," she said, tapping the icon of a furry yak on her iPhone.

The app opened, and the assistant began scrolling through the feed. 2 While the professors had been lecturing about post-apocalyptic culture, some of the 230 or so freshmen in the auditorium had been having a separate conversation about them on a social media site called Yik Yak. There were dozens of posts, most demeaning, many using crude, sexually explicit language and imagery.

After class, one of the professors, Margaret Crouch, sent off a flurry of 3 emails—with screenshots of some of the worst messages attached—to various university officials, urging them to take some sort of action. "I have been defamed, my reputation besmirched. I have been sexually harassed and verbally abused," she wrote to her union representative. "I am about ready to hire a lawyer."

In the end, nothing much came of Ms. Crouch's efforts, for a simple rea- 4 son: Yik Yak is anonymous. There was no way for the school to know who was responsible for the posts.

Eastern Michigan is one of a number of universities whose campuses have 5 been roiled by offensive "yaks." Since the app was introduced a little more than a year ago, it has been used to issue threats of mass violence on more than a dozen college campuses, including the University of North Carolina, Michigan State University, and Penn State. Racist, homophobic, and misogynist "yaks" have generated controversy at many more, among them Clemson, Emory, Colgate, and the University of Texas. At Kenyon College, a "yakker" proposed a gang rape at the school's women's center.

In much the same way that Facebook swept through the dorm rooms of 6 America's college students a decade ago, Yik Yak is now taking their smartphones by storm. Its enormous popularity on campuses has made it the most frequently downloaded anonymous social app in Apple's App Store, easily surpassing competitors like Whisper and Secret. At times, it has been one of the store's 10 most downloaded apps.

Like Facebook or Twitter, Yik Yak is a social media network, only without 7 user profiles. It does not sort messages according to friends or followers but by geographic location or, in many cases, by university. Only posts within a 1.5-mile radius appear, making Yik Yak well suited to college campuses. Think of it as a virtual community bulletin board—or maybe a virtual bathroom wall at the student union. It has become the go-to social feed for college students across the country to commiserate about finals, to find a party, or to crack a joke about a rival school.

Much of the chatter is harmless. Some of it is not. 8

"Yik Yak is the Wild West of anonymous 9 social apps," said Danielle Keats Citron, a law professor at University of Maryland and the author of *Hate Crimes in Cyberspace*. "It is being increasingly used by young people in a really intimidating and destructive way."

> "Much of the chatter is harmless. Some of it is not."

Colleges are largely powerless to deal with the havoc Yik Yak is wreak- 10 ing. The app's privacy policy prevents schools from identifying users without a subpoena, court order, or search warrant, or an emergency request from a law-enforcement official with a compelling claim of imminent harm. Schools can block access to Yik Yak on their Wi-Fi networks, but banning a popular social media network is controversial in its own right, arguably tantamount to curtailing freedom of speech. And as a practical matter, it doesn't work anyway. Students can still use the app on their phones with their cell service.

Yik Yak was created in late 2013 by Tyler Droll and Brooks Buffington, fra-   11
ternity brothers who had recently graduated from Furman University in South Carolina. Mr. Droll majored in information technology and Mr. Buffington in accounting. Both 24, they came up with the idea after realizing that there were only a handful of popular Twitter accounts at Furman, almost all belonging to prominent students, like athletes. With Yik Yak, they say, they hoped to create a more democratic social media network, one where users didn't need a large number of followers or friends to have their posts read widely.

"We thought, 'Why can't we level the playing field and connect every-   12
one?'" said Mr. Droll, who withdrew from medical school a week before classes started to focus on the app.

"When we made this app, we really made it for the disenfranchised,"   13
Mr. Buffington added.

Just as Mark Zuckerberg and his roommates introduced Facebook at   14
Harvard, Mr. Buffington and Mr. Droll rolled out their app at their alma mater, relying on fraternity brothers and other friends to get the word out.

Within a matter of months, Yik Yak was in use at 40 or so colleges in the   15
South. Then came spring break. Some early adopters shared the app with college students from all over the country at gathering places like Daytona Beach and Panama City. "And we just exploded," Mr. Buffington said.

Mr. Droll and Mr. Buffington started Yik Yak with a loan from Mr. Droll's   16
parents. (His parents also came up with the company's name, which was inspired by the 1958 song, "Yakety Yak.") In November, Yik Yak closed a $62 million round of financing led by one of Silicon Valley's biggest venture capital firms, Sequoia Capital, valuing the company at hundreds of millions of dollars.

The Yik Yak app is free. Like many tech start-ups, the company, based   17
in Atlanta, doesn't generate any revenue. Attracting advertisers could pose a challenge, given the nature of some of the app's content. For now, though, Mr. Droll and Mr. Buffington are focused on extending Yik Yak's reach by expanding overseas and moving beyond the college market, much as Facebook did.

Yik Yak's popularity among college students is part of a broader reaction   18
against more traditional social media sites like Facebook, which can encourage public posturing at the expense of honesty and authenticity.

"Share your thoughts with people around you while keeping your pri-   19
vacy," Yik Yak's home page says. It is an attractive concept to a generation of smartphone users who grew up in an era of social media—and are thus

inclined to share—but who have also been warned repeatedly about the permanence of their digital footprint.

In a sense, Yik Yak is a descendant of JuicyCampus, an anonymous online 20 college message board that enjoyed a brief period of popularity several years ago. Matt Ivester, who founded JuicyCampus in 2007 and shut it in 2009 after it became a hotbed of gossip and cruelty, is skeptical of the claim that Yik Yak does much more than allow college students to say whatever they want, publicly and with impunity. "You can pretend that it is serving an important role on college campuses, but you can't pretend that it's not upsetting a lot of people and doing a lot of damage," he said. "When I started JuicyCampus, cyberbullying wasn't even a word in our vernacular. But these guys should know better."

Yik Yak's founders say the app's overnight success left them unprepared 21 for some of the problems that have arisen since its introduction. In response to complaints, they have made some changes to their product, for instance, adding filters to prevent full names from being posted. Certain keywords, like "Jewish," or "bomb," prompt this message: "Pump the brakes, this yak may contain threatening language. Now it's probably nothing and you're probably an awesome person but just know that Yik Yak and law enforcement take threats seriously. So you tell us, is this yak cool to post?"

In cases involving threats of mass violence, Yik Yak has cooperated with 22 authorities. Most recently, in November, local police traced the source of a yak—"I'm gonna [gun emoji] the school at 12:15 p.m. today"—to a dorm room at Michigan State University. The author, Matthew Mullen, a freshman, was arrested within two hours and pleaded guilty to making a false report or terrorist threat. He was spared jail time but sentenced to two years' probation and ordered to pay $800 to cover costs connected to the investigation.

In the absence of a specific, actionable threat, though, Yik Yak zealously 23 protects the identities of its users. The responsibility lies with the app's various communities to police themselves by "upvoting" or "downvoting" posts. If a yak receives a score of negative 5, it is removed. "Really, what it comes down to is that we try to empower the communities as much as we can," Mr. Droll said.

When Yik Yak appeared, it quickly spread across high schools and middle 24 schools, too, where the problems were even more rampant. After a rash of complaints last winter at a number of schools in Chicago, Mr. Droll and Mr. Buffington disabled the app throughout the city. They say they have since built virtual fences—or "geo-fences"—around about 90 percent of the nation's high schools and middle schools. Unlike barring Yik Yak from a Wi-Fi network, which has proved ineffective in limiting its use, these fences actually make it impossible to open the app on school grounds. Mr. Droll and Mr. Buffington also changed Yik Yak's age rating in the App Store from 12 and over to 17 and over.

Toward the end of last school year, almost every student at Phillips Exeter 25 Academy in New Hampshire had the app on his or her phone and checked it constantly to read the anonymous attacks on fellow students, faculty members, and deans.

"Please stop using Yik Yak immediately," Arthur Cosgrove, the dean of 26 residential life, wrote in an email to the student body. "Remove it from your phones. It is doing us no good."

At Exeter's request, the company built a geo-fence around the school, but 27 it covered only a few buildings. Students continued using the app on different parts of the sprawling campus.

"We made the app for college kids, but we quickly realized it was getting 28 into the hands of high schoolers, and high schoolers were not mature enough to use it," Mr. Droll said.

The widespread abuse of Yik Yak on college campuses, though, suggests 29 that the distinction may be artificial. Last spring, Jordan Seman, then a sopho- more at Middlebury College, was scrolling through Yik Yak in the dining hall when she happened across a post comparing her to a "hippo" and making a sexual reference about her. "It's so easy for anyone in any emotional state to post something, whether that person is drunk or depressed or wants to get revenge on someone," she said. "And then there are no consequences."

In this sense, the problem with Yik Yak is a familiar one. Anyone who has 30 browsed the comments of an Internet post is familiar with the sorts of intoler- ant, impulsive language that the cover of anonymity tends to invite. But Yik Yak's particular design can produce especially harmful consequences.

"It's a problem with the Internet culture in general, but when you add this 31 hyper-local dimension to it, it takes on a more disturbing dimension," says Elias Aboujaoude, a Stanford psychiatrist and the author of *Virtually You*. "You don't know where the aggression is coming from, but you know it's very close to you."

Jim Goetz, a partner at Sequoia Capital who recently joined Yik Yak's 32 board, said the app's history of misuse was a concern when his firm consid- ered investing in the company. But he said he was confident that Mr. Droll and Mr. Buffington were committed to ensuring more positive interactions on Yik Yak, and that over time, the constructive voices would overwhelm the destructive ones.

"It's certainly a challenge to the company," Mr. Goetz said. "It's not going 33 to go away in a couple of months."

Ms. Seman wrote about her experience being harassed on Yik Yak in the 34 school newspaper, the *Middlebury Campus*, prompting a schoolwide debate over what to do about the app. Unable to reach a consensus, the paper's edito- rial board wrote two editorials, one urging a ban, the other arguing that the problem wasn't Yik Yak but the larger issue of cyberbullying. (Middlebury has not taken any action.)

Similar debates have played out at other schools. At Clemson, a group of 35 African-American students unsuccessfully lobbied the university to ban Yik Yak when some racially offensive posts appeared after a campus march to pro- test the grand jury's decision not to indict a white police officer in the fatal shooting of an unarmed black teenager in Ferguson, Mo. "We think that in the educational community, First Amendment rights are very important," said

Leon Wiles, the school's chief diversity officer. "It's just problematic because you have young people who use it with no sense of responsibility."

During the fall, Maxwell Zoberman, the sophomore representative to the student government at Emory, started noticing a growing number of yaks singling out various ethnic groups for abuse. "Fave game to play while driving around Emory: not hit an Asian with a truck," read one. 36

"Guys stop with all this hate. Let's just be thankful we arn't black," read another. 37

After consulting the university's code, Mr. Zoberman discovered that statements deemed derogatory to any particular group of people were not protected by the school's open expression policy, and were in fact in violation of its discriminatory harassment rules. Just because the statements were made on an anonymous social-media site should not, in his mind, prevent Emory from acting to enforce its own policies. "It didn't seem right that the school took one approach to hate speech in a physical medium and another one in a digital medium," he said. 38

Mr. Zoberman drafted a resolution to have Yik Yak disabled on the school's Wi-Fi network. He recognized that this would not stop students from using the app, but he nevertheless felt it was important for the school to take a stand. 39

After Mr. Zoberman formally proposed his resolution to the student government, someone promptly posted about it on Yik Yak. "The reaction was swift and harsh," he said. "I seem to have redirected all of the fury of the anonymous forum. Yik Yak was just dominated with hateful and other aggressive posts specifically about me." One compared him to Hitler. 40

A few colleges have taken the almost purely symbolic step of barring Yik Yak from their servers. John Brown University, a Christian college in Arkansas, did so after its Yik Yak feed was overrun with racist commentary during a march connected to the school's World Awareness Week. Administrators at Utica College in upstate New York blocked the app in December in response to a growing number of sexually graphic posts aimed at the school's transgender community. 41

In December, a group of 50 professors at Colgate University—which had experienced a rash of racist comments on the app earlier in the fall—tried a different approach, flooding the app with positive posts. 42

Generally speaking, though, the options are limited. A student who felt that he or she had been the target of an attack on Yik Yak could theoretically pursue defamation charges and subpoena the company to find out who had written the post. But it is a difficult situation to imagine, given the cost and murky legal issues involved. Schools will probably just stand back and hope that respect and civility prevail, that their communities really will learn to police themselves. 43

Yik Yak's founders say their start-up is just experiencing some growing pains. "It's definitely still a learning process for us," Mr. Buffington said, "and we're definitely still learning how to make the community more constructive." 44

"Yik Yak's founders say their start-up is just experiencing some growing pains."

Golbeck's essay appeared in the September/October 2014 issue of *Psychology Today*.

ALL EYES ON YOU
JENNIFER GOLBECK

Every day, nearly everywhere I go, I'm being followed. That's not paranoia. It's 1
a fact. Consider:

On my local Washington, D.C., streets, I am constantly watched. The city 2
government alone has hundreds of traffic and surveillance cameras. And then
there are the cameras in parks, office buildings, ATM lobbies, and, of course,
around every federal building and landmark. On an average day, my image is
captured by well over 100 cameras.

When I'm online and using social media, a wealth of information about 3
my interests and routines is collected behind the scenes. I employ an add-on
on my browser that blocks companies from tracking my searches and visits. In
just one recent month, it reported blocking nearly 16,000 separate attempts to
access my data online.

I'm monitored offline, too. Anytime I use a reward card at a supermarket, 4
department store, or other retail outlet, my purchase is recorded, and the data
either sold to other marketers or used to predict my future purchases and guide
me to make them in that store. Department store tracking based on purchase
records can even conclude that a woman is pregnant and roughly when she is due.

My own devices report on me. I carry an iPhone, which tracks and records 5
my every movement. This will help me find my phone if I ever lose it (I haven't
yet), but it also provides Apple with a treasure trove of data about my daily habits.

Data on any call I place or email I send may be collected by the National 6
Security Agency. Recent news reports have revealed that the federal intelligence arm may be collecting metadata on phone and Internet traffic—when
Americans communicate and with whom, if not the actual content of those
communications. As Barton Gellman, Pulitzer Prize–winning intelligence
reporter for the *Washington Post*, said during a recent panel discussion, it's
not that the NSA knows everything about everyone, but that "it *wants* to be
able to know anything about anybody."

Thirty years after 1984, Big Brother is here. He's everywhere. In many 7
cases, we've invited him in. So the question we have to ask now is, How does
this constant surveillance affect us and what, if anything, can we do about it?

"Get Over It."

There's no question our privacy has been eroded with the help of technology. 8
There's also little question that those most responsible aren't much inclined to
retreat. As Scott McNealy, cofounder of Sun Microsystems, famously said:
"You have zero privacy anyway. Get over it."

Privacy is an intangible asset. If we never think about it, we may not realize it's gone. Does it still matter? Elias Aboujaoude, a professor of psychiatry at Stanford University and the author of *Virtually You: The Dangerous Powers of the E-Personality*, insists that it does. "We cannot afford to just 'get over it,' for nothing short of our self-custody seems to be at stake," he says. "At its heart, this is about our psychological autonomy and the maintenance of some semblance of control over the various little details that make us us."

> "Does it still matter?" ⁹

In the modern surveillance environment, with so much personal information accessible by others—especially those with whom we have not chosen to share that information—our sense of self is threatened, as is our ability to manage the impression others have of us, says Ian Brown, senior research fellow at the Oxford Internet Institute.   10

If people treat us differently based on what they have discovered online, if the volume of data available about us eradicates our ability to make a first impression on a date or a job interview, the result, Brown believes, is reduced trust, increased conformity, and even diminished civic participation. The impact can be especially powerful when we know that our information was collected and shared without our consent.   11

To be sure, we are responsible for much of this. We're active participants in creating our surveillance record. Along with all of the personal information we voluntarily, often eagerly, share on social networks and shopping sites—and few of us take advantage of software or strategies to limit our digital footprint—we collectively upload 144,000 hours of video footage a day to YouTube. And with tech enthusiasts trumpeting personal drones as the next hot item, we may soon be equipped to photograph ourselves and, just as easily, our neighbors, from above.   12

Most of us try to curate the public identities we broadcast—not only through the way we dress and speak in public, but also in how we portray ourselves on social-media platforms. The problem arises when we become conscious that uninvited observers are also tuning in. "The most fundamental impact surveillance has on identity," Brown says, "is that it reduces individuals' control over the information they disclose about their attributes in different social contexts, often to such powerful actors as the state or multinational corporations." When we discover that such entities—and third parties to which our information may be sold or shared—make decisions about us based on that data, our sense of self can be altered.   13

The Right to Be Forgotten

There are existential threats to our psyches in a world where nothing we do can be forgotten, believes Viktor Mayer-Schönberger, professor of Internet governance and regulation at the Oxford Internet Institute. His book, *Delete: The Virtue of Forgetting in the Digital Age*, relates the experiences of people whose lives were negatively affected because of information available about them online.   14

In 2006, for example, psychotherapist Andrew Feldmar drove from his   15
Vancouver home to pick up a friend flying in to Seattle. At the United States
border, which Feldmar had crossed scores of times, a guard decided to do an
Internet search on him. The query returned an article Feldmar had written for
an academic journal five years earlier, in which he revealed that he'd taken
LSD in the 1960s. The guard held Feldmar for four hours, fingerprinted him,
and asked him to sign a statement that he had taken drugs almost 40 years
earlier. He was barred from entry into the U.S.

Aboujaoude relates the story of "Rob," a nurse in a public hospital emer-   16
gency room chronically short on staff. His willingness to fill in when the ER
needed extra hands led to significant overtime pay. When a website published
an "exposé" of seemingly overpaid public employees, Rob's name and salary
were posted as an example. He was then hounded by hate mail—both paper
and electronic. People called his house, and his daughter was harassed at
school. Eventually the stress and constant criticism made him feel as if he were
becoming paranoid and led him to Aboujaoude as a therapy patient.

The ability to forget past events, Mayer-Schönberger says, or at least to let   17
them recede in our minds, is critical for decision making. Psychologists often
note that our ability to forget is a valuable safety valve. As we naturally forget
things over time, we can move on and make future choices without difficult or
embarrassing episodes clouding our outlook. But when our decisions are tan-
gled up in the perfect memory of the Internet—when we must factor in the
effect of our online footprint before every new step—"we may lose a fundamental human capacity: to live and act firmly in the present," he says.

The result can be demoralizing and even paranoia-inducing. Lacking the   18
power to control what, when, and with whom we share, Mayer-Schönberger
explains, our sense of self may be diminished, leading to self-doubt internally
and self-censorship externally, as we begin to fixate on what others will think
about every potentially public action and thought, now and in the future.

Under normal circumstances, the passage of time allows us to shape our nar-   19
rative, cutting out or minimizing less important (or more embarrassing) details to
form a more positive impression. When we can't put the past behind us, it can
affect our behavior and intrude on our judgment. Instead of making decisions
fully in the present, we make them while weighed down by every detail of our past.

The effects are not trivial. A range of people, from a long-reformed crimi-   20
nal seeking a fresh slate to a sober former college party girl in the job market,
can find that the omnipresence of public
records and posted photos permanently
holds them back. At its worst, these
weights can inhibit one's desire to
change. If we can never erase the record
of one mistake we made long ago, if we're
convinced it will only continue to hinder

> "With easily accessible digital reminders, bygones cannot be bygones."

our progress, what motivation do we have to become anyone different from
the person who made that mistake? For that matter, why bother moving

beyond conflicts with others if the sources of those disputes remain current online? With easily accessible digital reminders, bygones cannot be bygones. It's no accident that the most successful legal campaign yet against permanent digital records hinges on "the right to be forgotten."

A Spanish lawyer, Mario Costeja González, sued Google over search 21 results that prominently returned a long-ago news article detailing a government order that he sell his home to cover unpaid debts. The European Court of Justice ruled in his favor, asserting, based on an older legal concept allowing ex-convicts to object to the publication of information related to their crimes, that each of us has the right to be forgotten. Even if the information about the man's foreclosure is true, the court ruled, it is "irrelevant, or no longer relevant," and should be blocked from Google's (and other browsers') searches.

Google is now working to implement a means for European users to 22 request that certain information be removed from their searches, a process it is finding to be more complicated than many observers had imagined. No similar verdict has been handed down in the U.S., and privacy experts believe that Congress is unlikely to take up the issue anytime soon.

Do Cameras Make Us More Honorable, or Just Paranoid?

Trust is perennially strained in our workplaces, where more employees than ever 23 are being overseen via cameras, recorded phone calls, location tracking, and email monitoring. Studies dating back two decades have consistently found that employees who were aware that they were being surveilled found their working conditions more stressful and reported higher levels of anxiety, anger, and depression. More recent research indicates that, whatever productivity benefits management hopes to realize, increased surveillance on the office floor leads to poorer performance, tied to a feeling of loss of control as well as to lower job satisfaction.

Outside the workplace, we expect more freedom and wider opportunity 24 to defend our privacy. But even as we become more savvy about online tracking, we're beginning to realize just how little we can do about so-called "passive" surveillance—the cameras recording our movements as we go about our business—especially because so much of this observation is covert. The visual range of surveillance cameras has expanded even as their physical size has shrunk, and as satellites and drones become more accurate from increasing distances, social scientists have begun to explore how near-constant surveillance, at least in the public sphere, affects our behavior. The research so far identifies both concerns and potential benefits. We tend, for example, to be more cooperative and generous when we suspect someone is watching—a recent Dutch study found that people were more likely to intervene when witnessing a (staged) crime if they knew they were being watched, either by others or by a camera. But we don't become more generous of spirit. Pierrick Bourrat, a graduate student at the University of Sydney, and cognitive scientist Nicolas Baumard of the École Normale Supérieure in Paris, recently published a study on how we judge other people's bad behavior. They found that when subjects believed they were being watched, they rated others' actions more severely. A possible explanation: When we think we're being observed, we adjust our behavior to project an image of moral uprightness through harsher-than-usual judgment of others.

But adjusting our behavior in the presence of cameras to project an image aligned with presumed social norms can have a downside. The Oxford Internet Institute's Brown sees a cooling effect on public discourse, because when people think they're being watched, they may behave, consciously or not, in ways that comply with what they presume governmental or other observers want. That doesn't mean we trust the watchers. A recent Gallup poll found that only 12 percent of Americans have "a lot of trust" that the government will keep their personal information secure; we trust banks three times as much. 25

When Users Strike Back

What would happen if we really tried to root out all of the surveillance in our life and took action to erase ourselves from it? We think such knowledge would equal power, but it may just bring on paranoia. Pulitzer Prize–winning investigative journalist Julia Angwin tried for a year to prevent her life from being monitored. She used a disposable cell phone. She installed encryption software on her email accounts. She even developed a fake identity ("Ida Tarbell") to prevent her online and commercial activities from being tied to her true self. 26

Angwin detailed these efforts in her book, *Dragnet Nation*, which, while ultimately hopeful, relates a draining journey during which she lost trust in nearly every institution that holds her data. Even with her resources and single-mindedness, Angwin could achieve only partial success: Her past personal data, after all, were stored in bits and pieces by hundreds of brokers that traffic in information, and she had no means of turning back the clock. 27

The efforts also affected her worldview: "I wasn't happy with the toll that my countersurveillance techniques had taken on my psyche. The more I learned about who was watching me, the more paranoid I became. By the end of my experiment, I was refusing to have digital conversations with my close friends without encryption. I began using my fake name for increasingly trivial transactions; a friend was shocked when we took a yoga class together and I casually registered as Ida Tarbell." 28

The Next Level

Modern surveillance does have some clear benefits. Cameras in public spaces help the authorities detect crime and catch perpetrators, though they catch us in the dragnet as well. Cell phone tracking and networked late-model cars allow us to be found if we become lost or injured, and mapping apps are incredibly useful for directing us where we want to go. These features save lives—but all of them constantly transmit our location and generate a precisely detailed record of our movements. Our social media history helps providers put the people and content we prefer front and center when we log on, and our online searches and purchase records allow marketers to offer us discounts at the places we shop most, all the while collecting data on our personal 29 preferences and quirks. Given the difficulty of completely avoiding the monitoring, it may be somewhat reassuring to acknowledge this tradeoff.

Laura Brandimarte of Carnegie Mellon University and her colleagues have 30 studied people's willingness to disclose personal information. They found that when entities give people more control over the publication of their information, people disclose more about themselves—even if it is also clear that the information will be accessed and seen by others more often than it currently is.

Their work demonstrates the concept of illusion of control. In many situations, 31 we tend to overestimate the control we have over events, especially when we get cues that our actions matter. The risk to our private information comes not just from what we've shared but from how much of it is sold or made available to others. And yet when we feel that we have been given more control over our information's dissemination, our privacy concerns decrease and our disclosure increases, even though that apparent control does not actually diminish the possibility that our data will be shared. "The control people perceive over the publication of personal information makes them pay less attention to the lack of control they have over access by others," Brandimarte says.

In other words, we are simply not very sophisticated when it comes to 32 making choices about what to share.

When it comes to privacy-protection, the first issue for social-media users 33 to grapple with is inertia: According to a range of surveys of U.S. Facebook users, for example, as many as 25 percent have never checked or adjusted their privacy settings to impose even the most basic restriction on their postings: not making them public.

There is a growing availability of privacy fixes for homes, cell phones, and 34 computers. Whether they will be able to keep up with tracking mechanisms is unclear. But evidence suggests that even if they work as advertised, we may not be savvy enough to use them.

So we have limited options to protect our privacy, and few of us take 35 advantage even of those. What's the ultimate cost? Aboujaoude argues that our need for privacy and true autonomy is rooted in the concept of individuation, the process by which we develop and maintain an independent identity. It's a crucial journey that begins in childhood, as we learn to separate our own identity from that of our parents, and continues through adulthood.

Many psychologists emphasize that maintaining self-identity requires a 36 separation from others, and Aboujaoude believes that, in today's environment, control over personal information is a critical piece of the process. "You are a psychologically autonomous individual," he says, "if you have the option to keep your person to yourself and dole out the pieces as you see fit."

And who do we become if we don't have that option? We may soon find out. 37

I Married a P.I.

When we worry about who might be watching us, we tend to focus our concern 38 on Facebook, the NSA, or marketers. But we may want to consider our own partners as well.

Sue Simring, an associate professor at Columbia University's School of   39
Social Work and a psychotherapist with four decades of experience working
primarily with couples, says the ease with which people can now monitor each
other has radically changed her work. "It used to be that, unless you literally
discovered them [in flagrante], there was no way to know for sure that people
were having an affair," she says.

No more.   40

When spouses stray today, their digital trail inevitably provides clues for   41
the amateur sleuth with whom they share a bed. Simring describes one case in
which a man had carried on an affair for years while traveling for work. He
managed to keep it secret until a technical glitch started sending copies of his
text messages to his wife's iPad.

But the easy availability of tools to track a partner can cut both ways.   42
In the case of another couple that Simring worked with, the husband was
convinced that his wife was having an affair. Determined to catch her, he
undertook increasingly complex and invasive surveillance efforts, eventually monitoring all of her communications and installing spy cameras in
their home to catch her in the act. The more he surveilled, the more his
paranoia grew. It turned out that the wife was not having an affair, but
because of the trauma the husband's surveillance caused her, she ended the
marriage.

This essay was posted to the online newspaper *The Start* on February 27, 2015.

MY CREEPY INSTAGRAM
MAP KNOWS WHERE I LIVE

CRAIG DESSON

U.S. Congressman Aaron Schock's reputation took a hit this week when the   1
Associated Press used geo-location data from his Instagram account to show
how he was flying on private jets provided by campaign donors, expensed
massages, and bought Katy Perry tickets for his interns.

The reporters involved explained that "the AP extracted location data   2
associated with each image, then correlated it with flight records showing airport stopovers and expenses later billed for air travel against Schock's office
and campaign records."

To track somebody on Instagram the way AP did for the Schock story   3
isn't difficult. There is a program called Creepy that will create a Google map
showing where you've been, based on what you've shared on Instagram, Twitter,
and Flickr.

I ran Creepy on my own Instagram account and found it wouldn't be   4
hard for a stranger to figure out where I live in the Annex.

This is the map the program made about my account, and with a bit of   5
deductive logic it's clear I live just north of Bloor and Spadina.

The photos taken around Front St. are all interiors of offices, because that's   6
where I've worked for the past two and a half years. The photos taken along
major streets such as King and Bloor portray me hanging out with friends.

Then there is the funny collection of dots north of Bloor in the Annex   7
that link to Instagram photos of an apartment's interior.

You don't need to be Sherlock Holmes to guess that's my home.   8

It's true that 20 years ago, a phonebook might have led a stranger to my   9
home address. But I would at least know that I had a listed number. The trouble with Instagram tracking is that most users have no idea their photo-sharing
app is also building a detailed history of where they work and live.

If Aaron Schock, a congressman with paid communications people,   10
couldn't figure this out, then it's likely most members of the public have no
idea this is going on.

USA Today posted this article to its website on March 27, 2014.

IS ONLINE DATING SAFE?

SHARON JAYSON

Change may be coming to the rapidly growing dating industry as concern   1
mounts about the privacy and safety of all online and mobile users.

Sen. Al Franken, D-Minn., introduced legislation Thursday requiring   2
companies to get customers' permission before collecting location data off
their mobile devices and sharing it with others.

It's a move that would greatly affect dating websites and apps. As mobile dating proliferates, the focus no longer is just on daters leery of scams or sexual predators, but on keeping their locations confidential.

"This stuff is advancing at a faster and faster rate, and we've got to try and catch up," Franken says. "This is about Americans' right to privacy and one of the most private things is your location."

> "As mobile dating proliferates, the focus no longer is just on daters leery of scams or sexual predators, but on keeping their locations confidential."

Illinois, New York, New Jersey, and Texas have laws that require Internet 5 dating sites to disclose whether they conduct criminal background checks on users and to offer advice on keeping safe.

"I see more regulation about companies stating what kind of information 6 they actually use and more about their specific operation(s)," says analyst Jeremy Edwards, who authored a report on the industry last fall for IBIS-World, a Santa Monica, Calif.–based market research company. "I expect them to have to be more explicit in what they do with their data and what they require of users."

According to a Pew Research Center report in October, 11% of American 7 adults—and 38% of those currently "single and looking" for a partner—say they've used online dating sites or mobile dating apps.

"We entrust some incredibly sensitive information to online dating sites," 8 says Rainey Reitman of the San Francisco, Calif.–based Electronic Frontier Foundation, a nonprofit that advocates for user privacy amid technology development. "People don't realize how much information they're exposing even by doing something as slight as uploading a photograph."

He adds, "Many online apps are very cavalier about collecting that 9 information and perhaps exposing it in a way that would make you uncomfortable."

Dating services eHarmony, Match.com, and Spark Networks and 10 ChristianMingle signed an agreement in 2012 with the California attorney general's office to protect customers with online safety tools. These include companies checking subscribers against national sex offender registries and providing a rapid abuse reporting system for members.

However, cyberdating expert Julie Spira of Los Angeles says such reports 11 are sometimes little more than revenge.

"When people get reported, sometimes it's because they got jilted," she 12 says. "How do you quantify when someone feels rejected and pushes the report button, and when somebody really feels scared?"

Match.com, which has 1.9 million paid subscribers, has been screening all 13 subscribers against sexual offender registries since the summer of 2011, according to spokesman Matthew Traub. Earlier that year, a woman sued the dating site saying she was assaulted by someone she met through it.

Edwards believes dating sites are doing what they can to help users be safe. 14

"It's difficult for these companies to do much else than provide information and tips," he says. "Meeting someone through one of these websites does not present any greater risk than meeting someone in a bar or any other setting. There's no real added risk because you don't know who anyone is when you meet them for the first time." 15

⤵ EXERCISE 8.6

Read the blog post below and then answer the questions on page 327.

This article first appeared on Mashable.com on February 6, 2012.

SHOULD ATHLETES HAVE SOCIAL MEDIA PRIVACY? ONE BILL SAYS YES

SAM LAIRD

Should universities be allowed to force student athletes to have their Facebook and Twitter accounts monitored by coaches and administrators?   1

No, says a bill recently introduced into the Maryland state legislature.   2

The bill would prohibit institutions "from requiring a student or an applicant for admission to provide access to a personal account or service through an electronic communications device"—by sharing usernames, passwords, or unblocking private accounts, for example.   3

Introduced on Thursday, Maryland's Senate Bill 434 would apply to all students but particularly impact college sports. Student-athletes' social media accounts are frequently monitored by authority figures for instances of indecency or impropriety, especially in high-profile sports like football and men's basketball.   4

> "Student-athletes' social media accounts are frequently monitored. . . ."

In one example, a top football recruit reportedly put his scholarship hopes in jeopardy last month after a series of inappropriate tweets.   5

The bill's authors say that it is one of the first in the country to take on the issue of student privacy in the social media age, according to the *New York Times*.   6

Bradley Shear is a Maryland lawyer whose work frequently involves sports and social media. In a recent post to his blog, Shear explained his support for Senate Bill 434 and a similar piece of legislation that would further extend students' right to privacy on social media.   7

"Schools that require their students to turn over their social media user names and/or content are acting as though they are based in China and not in the United States," Shear wrote.   8

But legally increasing student-athletes' option to social media privacy could also help shield the schools themselves from potential lawsuits.   9

On his blog, Shear uses the example of Yardley Love, a former University of Virginia women's lacrosse player who was allegedly murdered by her ex-boyfriend, who played for the men's lacrosse team.   10

If the university was monitoring the lacrosse teams' social media accounts   11
and missed anything that could have indicated potential violence, it "may have
had significant legal liability for negligent social media monitoring because it
failed to protect Love," Shear wrote.

On the other hand, if the school was only monitoring the accounts of its   12
higher-profile football and basketball players, Shear wrote, then that could
have been considered discrimination and the university "may have been sued
for not monitoring the electronic content of all of its students."

Do you think universities should be allowed to force their athletes into   13
allowing coaches and administrators to monitor their Facebook and Twitter
accounts?

Questions

1. What steps would you take to determine whether Laird's information
   is accurate?

2. How could you determine whether Laird is respected in his field?

3. Is Laird's blog written for an audience that is knowledgeable about
   his subject? How can you tell?

4. Do you think this blog post is a suitable research source? Why or why
   not?

5. This blog post was written in 2012. Do you think it is still relevant
   today? Why or why not?

Summarizing, Paraphrasing, Quoting, and Synthesizing Sources

AT ISSUE

Is Technology a Serious Threat to Our Privacy? (continued)

In Chapter 8, you learned how to evaluate sources for an essay about the dangers of posting personal information online. In this chapter, you will learn how to take notes from various sources that address this issue.

As you saw in Chapter 8, before you can decide which material to use to support your arguments, you need to evaluate a variety of potential sources. After you decide which sources you will use, you can begin thinking about where you might use each source and about how to integrate information from the sources you have chosen into your essay in the form of *summary*, *paraphrase*, and *quotation*. When you actually write your argument, you will *synthesize* the sources into your paper, blending them with your own ideas and interpretations (as the student writer did when she wrote the MLA research paper in Chapter 10).

Summarizing Sources

A **summary** restates the main idea of a passage (or even of an entire book or article) in concise terms. Because a summary does not cover the examples or explanations in the source, and because it omits the original source's rhetorical strategies and stylistic characteristics, it is always much shorter than the original. Usually, in fact, it consists of just a sentence or two.

WHEN TO SUMMARIZE

Summarize when you want to give readers a general sense of a passage's main idea or a source's position on an issue.

When you summarize information, you do not include your own opinions, but you do use your own words and phrasing, not those of your source. If you want to use a particularly distinctive word or phrase from your source, you may do so—but you must always place such words in quotation marks and **document** them. If you do not, you will be committing **plagiarism**. (See Chapter 10 for information on documenting sources; see Chapter 11 for information on using sources responsibly.)

The following paragraph appeared in a newspaper opinion essay.

ORIGINAL SOURCE

When everyone has a blog, a MySpace page, or Facebook entry, everyone is a publisher. When everyone has a cellphone with a camera in it, everyone is a paparazzo. When everyone can upload video on YouTube, everyone is a filmmaker. When everyone is a publisher, paparazzo, or filmmaker, everyone else is a public figure. We're all public figures now. The blogosphere has made the global discussion so much richer—and each of us so much more transparent. ("The Whole World Is Watching," Thomas L. Friedman, *New York Times*, June 27, 2007, p. 23)

The following effective summary conveys a general but accurate sense of the original paragraph without using the source's phrasing or including the writer's own opinions. (One distinctive and hard-to-reword phrase is placed in quotation marks.) Parenthetical documentation indicates the source of the material.

EFFECTIVE SUMMARY

The popularity of blogs, social-networking sites, cell phone cameras, and YouTube has enhanced the "global discussion" but made it very hard for people to remain anonymous (Friedman 23).

Notice that this one-sentence summary is much shorter than the original passage and that it does not include all the original's examples. Still, it accurately communicates a general sense of the source's main idea.

The following summary is not acceptable. Not only does it express the student writer's opinion, but it also uses the source's exact words without putting them in quotation marks or providing documentation. (This constitutes plagiarism.)

UNACCEPTABLE SUMMARY

It seems to me that blogs, social-networking sites, cell phone cameras, and YouTube are everywhere, and what this means is that we're all public figures now.

SUMMARIZING SOURCES

Do

- Convey the main idea of the original passage.

- Be concise.

- Use your own original words and phrasing.

- Place any words borrowed from your source in quotation marks.

- Include documentation.

Do not

- Include your own analysis or opinions.

- Include digressions.

- Argue with your source.

- Use your source's syntax or phrasing (unless you are quoting).

⊛ EXERCISE 9.1

Write a two-sentence summary of the following passage. Then, edit your summary so that it is only one sentence long. Be sure your summary conveys the main idea of the original passage and includes proper documentation.

We're living at a time when attention is the new currency: with hundreds of TV channels, billions of Web sites, podcasts, radio shows, music downloads, and social networking, our attention is more fragmented than ever before.

Those who insert themselves into as many channels as possible look set to capture the most value. They'll be the richest, the most successful, the most connected, capable, and influential among us. We're all publishers now, and the more we publish, the more valuable connections we'll make.

Twitter, Facebook, Flickr, Foursquare, Fitbit, and the SenseCam give us a simple choice: participate or fade into a lonely obscurity. (Pete Cashmore, "Privacy Is Dead, and Social Media Hold Smoking Gun," *CNN.com*, October 28, 2009)

Paraphrasing Sources

A **paraphrase** is different from a summary. While a summary gives a general overview of the original, a paraphrase presents the source's ideas in detail, including its main idea, its key supporting points, and perhaps even its examples. For this reason, a paraphrase is longer than a summary. In fact, it may be as long as the original.

WHEN TO PARAPHRASE

Paraphrase when you want to communicate the key points discussed in a source—particularly a complex or complicated passage—in clear, accessible language.

Like a summary, a paraphrase uses your own words and phrasing, not the language and syntax of the original. Any words or phrases from your source must be placed in quotation marks. When you paraphrase, you may not always follow the order of the original source's ideas, but you should try to convey the writer's emphasis and most important points.

The following paragraph is from an editorial that appeared in a student newspaper.

ORIGINAL SOURCE

Additionally, as graduates retain their Facebook accounts, employers are increasingly able to use Facebook as an evaluation tool when making hiring decisions. Just as companies sometimes incorporate social functions into their interview process to see if potential hires can handle themselves responsibly, they may also check out a student's Facebook account to see how the student chooses to present him or herself. This may seem shady and underhanded, but one must understand that social networks are not anonymous; whatever one chooses to post will be available to all. Even if someone goes to great pains to keep an employer-friendly profile, his or her friends may still tag pictures of him or her which will be available to whoever wants to see them. Not only can unexpected Facebook members get information by viewing one's profile, but a user's personal information can also leak out by merely registering for the service. Both the user agreement and the privacy policy indicate that Facebook can give information to third parties and can supplement its data with information from newspapers, blogs, and instant messages. ("Beware What You Post on Facebook," *The Tiger*, Clemson University, August 4, 2006)

The following paraphrase reflects the original paragraph's emphasis and clearly communicates its key points.

EFFECTIVE PARAPHRASE

Because students keep their accounts at social-networking sites after they graduate, potential employers can use the information they find there to help them evaluate candidates' qualifications. This process is comparable to the way a company might evaluate an applicant in person in a social situation. Some people may see the practice of employers checking applicants' Facebook pages as "shady and underhanded," but these sites are not intended to be anonymous or private. For example, a person may try to maintain a profile that will be appropriate for employers, but friends may post inappropriate pictures. Also, people can reveal personal information not only in profiles but also simply by registering with Facebook. Finally, as Facebook states in its membership information, it can supply information to others as well as provide data from other sources. ("Beware")

Notice that this paraphrase includes many of the details presented in the original passage and quotes a distinctive phrase, but its style and sentence structure are different from those of the original.

The following paraphrase is not acceptable because its phrasing and sentence structure are too close to the original. It also borrows words and phrases from the source without attribution or documentation.

UNACCEPTABLE PARAPHRASE

As more and more college graduates keep their Facebook accounts, employers are increasingly able to use them as evaluation tools when they decide whom to hire. Companies sometimes set up social functions during the interview process to see how potential hires handle themselves; in the same way, they can consult a Facebook page to see how an applicant presents himself or herself. This may seem underhanded, but after all, Facebook is not anonymous; its information is available to all. Many people try to keep their profiles employer friendly, but their friends sometimes tag pictures of them that employers will be able to see. Besides, students' personal information is available not just on their profiles but also in the form they fill out when they register. Finally, according to their user agreement and their privacy policy, Facebook can give information to third parties and also add data from other sources.

PARAPHRASING SOURCES

Do

- Convey the source's ideas fully and accurately.
- Use your own words and phrasing.
- Convey the emphasis of the original.
- Simplify and clarify complex language and syntax.
- Put any words borrowed from the source in quotation marks.
- Include documentation.

Do not

- Use the exact words or phrasing of your source (unless you are quoting).
- Include your own analysis or opinions.
- Argue with or contradict your source.
- Wander from the topic of the source.

⊙ EXERCISE 9.2

Write a paraphrase of the passage you summarized in Exercise 9.1. How is your paraphrase different from your summary?

⊙ EXERCISE 9.3

The following paragraph is from the same Clemson University student newspaper article that was excerpted on pages 332–333. Read the paragraph, and then write a paraphrase that communicates its key ideas. Before you begin, circle any distinctive words and phrases that might be difficult to paraphrase, and consider whether you should quote them. Be sure to include documentation.

> All these factors make clear the importance of two principles: Responsibility and caveat emptor. First, people should be responsible about how they portray themselves and their friends, and employers, authorities, and the owners must approach this information responsibly and fairly. Second, "let the buyer beware" applies to all parties involved. Facebook users need to understand the potential consequences of the information they share, and outside viewers need to understand that the material on Facebook is often only a humorous, lighthearted presentation of one aspect of a person. Facebook is an incredibly valuable communications tool that will link the college generation more tightly than any before it, but users have to understand that, like anything good in life, they have to be aware of the downsides.

Quoting Sources

When you **quote** words from a source, you need to quote accurately—that is, every word and every punctuation mark in your quotation must match the source *exactly*. You also need to be sure that your quotation conveys the meaning its author intended and that you are not distorting the meaning by **quoting out of context** or by omitting an essential part of the passage you are quoting.

WHEN TO QUOTE

Quote a source's words only in the following situations:

- Quote when your source's words are distinctive or memorable.

- Quote when your source's words are so direct and concise that a paraphrase would be awkward or wordy.

- Quote when your source's words add authority or credibility to your argument (for example, when your source is a well-known expert on your topic).

- Quote an opposing point when you will go on to refute it.

Remember, quoting from a source adds interest to your paper—but only when the writer's words are compelling. Too many quotations—especially long quotations—distract readers and make it difficult for them to follow your discussion. Quote only when you must. If you include too many quotations, your paper will be a patchwork of other people's words, not an original, unified whole.

QUOTING SOURCES

Do

- Enclose borrowed words in quotation marks.
- Quote accurately.
- Include documentation.

Do not

- Quote out of context.
- Distort the source's meaning.
- Include too many quotations.

◑ EXERCISE 9.4

Read the following paragraphs from a newspaper column that appeared in the *Calgary Herald*. (The full text of this column appears in Exercise 9.5.) If you were going to use these paragraphs as source material for an argumentative essay, which particular words or phrases do you think you might want to quote? Why?

> How do users not know that a server somewhere is recording where you are, what you ate for lunch, how often you post photos of your puppy, what you bought at the supermarket for dinner, the route you drove home, and what movie you watched before you went to bed?
>
> So why do we act so surprised and shocked about the invasion of the privacy we so willingly relinquish, and the personal information we forfeit that allows its captors to sell us products, convict us in court, get us fired, or produce more of the same banality that keeps us logging on?
>
> We, all of us, are digital captives. (Shelley Fralic, "Don't Fall for the Myths about Online Privacy," *Calgary Herald*, October 17, 2015.)

◑ EXERCISE 9.5

Read the newspaper column that follows, and highlight it to identify its most important ideas. (For information on highlighting, see Chapter 2.) Then, write a summary of one paragraph and a paraphrase of another paragraph. Assume that this column is a source for an essay you are writing on the topic, "Is Technology a Serious Threat to Our Privacy?" Be sure to include documentation.

This column is from the *Calgary Herald*, where it appeared on October 17, 2015.

DON'T FALL FOR THE MYTHS ABOUT ONLINE PRIVACY

SHELLEY FRALIC

If you are a Facebooker—and there are 1.5 billion of us on the planet, so 1 chances are about one in five that you are—you will have noticed yet another round of posts that suggest in quasi-legalese that you can somehow block the social network's invasion of your privacy.

This latest hoax cautions that Facebook will now charge $5.99 to keep 2 privacy settings private, and the copyright protection disclaimers making the rounds this week typically begin like this: "As of date-and-time here, I do not give Facebook or any entities associated with Facebook permission to use my pictures, information, or posts, both past and future. By this statement, I give notice to Facebook it is strictly forbidden to disclose, copy, distribute, or take any other action against me based on this profile and/or its contents. The content of this profile is private and confidential information."

Well, no, it's not. 3

This is a new-age version of an old story, oft-told. No one reads the 4 fine print. Not on contracts, not on insurance policies, and not on social media sites that are willingly and globally embraced by perpetually plugged-in gossipmongers, lonely hearts, news junkies, inveterate sharers, and selfie addicts.

Facebook's fine print, like that of many Internet portals, is specific and 5 offers users a variety of self-selected "privacy" options.

But to think that any interaction with it, and its ilk, is truly private is 6 beyond absurd.

How can there still be people out there who still don't get that Netflix and 7 Facebook, Instagram and Twitter, Google and Tinder and pretty much every keystroke or communication we register on a smartphone or laptop, not to mention a loyalty card and the GPS in your car, are constantly tracking and sifting and collating everything we do?

How do users not know that a server somewhere is recording where you 8 are, what you ate for lunch, how often you post photos of your puppy, what you bought at the supermarket for dinner, the route you drove home, and what movie you watched before you went to bed?

So why do we act so surprised and shocked about the invasion of the pri- 9 vacy we so willingly relinquish, and the personal information we forfeit that allows its captors to sell us products, convict us in court, get us fired, or produce more of the same banality that keeps us logging on?

We, all of us, are digital captives. 10

But do we have to be so stupid about it? 11

And the bigger question is this: If we, the adults who should know better, 12 don't get it, what are we teaching our kids about the impact and repercussions of their online lives? What are they learning about the voluntary and wholesale abandonment of their privacy? What are we teaching them about "sharing" with strangers?

Worried about future generations not reading books or learning how to 13 spell properly or write in cursive? Worry more, folks, that Internet ignorance is the new illiteracy.

Meantime, when another Facebook disclaimer pops up with a plea to 14 share, consider this clever post from a user who actually read the fine print:

"I hereby give my permission to the police, the NSA, the FBI and CIA, 15 the Swiss Guard, the Priory of Scion, the inhabitants of Middle Earth,

Agents Mulder and Scully, the Goonies, ALL the Storm Troopers and Darth Vader, the Mad Hatter, Chuck Norris, S.H.I.E.L.D., The Avengers, The Illuminati . . . to view all the amazing and interesting things I publish on Facebook. I'm aware that my privacy ended the very day that I created a profile on Facebook."

Yes, it did.   16

Working Source Material into Your Argument

When you use source material in an argumentative essay, your goal is to integrate the material smoothly into your discussion, blending summary, paraphrase, and quotation with your own ideas.

To help readers follow your discussion, you need to indicate the source of each piece of information clearly and distinguish your own ideas from those of your sources. Never simply drop source material into your discussion. Whenever possible, introduce quotations, paraphrases, and summaries with an **identifying tag** (sometimes called a *signal phrase*), a phrase that identifies the source, and always follow them with documentation. This practice helps readers identify the boundaries between your own ideas and those of your sources.

It is also important that you include clues to help readers understand why you are using a particular source and what the exact relationship is between your source material and your own ideas. For example, you may be using a source to support a point you are making or to disagree with another source.

Using Identifying Tags

Using identifying tags to introduce your summaries, paraphrases, or quotations will help you to accomplish the goals discussed above (and help you to avoid accidental plagiarism).

> **SUMMARY WITH IDENTIFYING TAG**
> <u>According to Thomas L. Friedman</u>, the popularity of blogs, social-networking sites, cell phone cameras, and YouTube has enhanced the "global discussion" but made it hard for people to remain anonymous (23).

Note that you do not always have to place the identifying tag at the beginning of the summarized, paraphrased, or quoted material. You can also place it in the middle or at the end:

IDENTIFYING TAG AT THE BEGINNING

<u>Thomas L. Friedman notes</u> that the popularity of blogs, social-networking sites, cell phone cameras, and YouTube has enhanced the "global discussion" but made it hard for people to remain anonymous (23).

IDENTIFYING TAG IN THE MIDDLE

The popularity of blogs, social-networking sites, cell phone cameras, and YouTube, <u>Thomas L. Friedman observes</u>, has enhanced the "global discussion" but made it hard for people to remain anonymous (23).

IDENTIFYING TAG AT THE END

The popularity of blogs, social-networking sites, cell phone cameras, and YouTube has enhanced the "global discussion" but made it hard for people to remain anonymous, <u>Thomas L. Friedman points out</u> (23).

TEMPLATES FOR USING IDENTIFYING TAGS

To avoid repeating phrases like *he says* in identifying tags, try using some of the following verbs to introduce your source material. (You can also use "According to . . . ," to introduce a source.)

For Summaries or Paraphrases

[Name of writer]	notes	acknowledges	proposes	that [summary or paraphrase].
The writer	suggests	believes	observes	
The article	explains	comments	warns	
The essay	reports	points out	predicts	
	implies	concludes	states	

For Quotations

As [name of writer]	notes,	acknowledges,	proposes,	" _____[quotation]_____ ."
As the writer	suggests,	believes,	observes,	
As the article	warns,	reports,	points out,	
As the essay	predicts,	implies,	concludes,	
	states,	explains,		

Working Quotations into Your Sentences

When you use quotations in your essays, you may need to edit them to provide context or to make them fit smoothly into your sentences. If you do edit a quotation, be careful not to distort the source's meaning.

Adding or Changing Words When you add or change words in a quotation, use **brackets** to indicate your edits.

> **ORIGINAL QUOTATION**
> "Twitter, Facebook, Flickr, FourSquare, Fitbit, and the SenseCam give us a simple choice: participate or fade into a lonely obscurity." (Cashmore)

> **WORDS ADDED FOR CLARIFICATION**
> As Cashmore observes, "Twitter, Flickr, FourSquare, Fitbit, and the SenseCam [as well as similar social-networking sites] give us a simple choice: participate or fade into a lonely obscurity."

> **ORIGINAL QUOTATION**
> "The blogosphere has made the global discussion so much richer—and each of us so much more transparent" (Friedman 23).

> **WORDS CHANGED TO MAKE VERB TENSE LOGICAL**
> As Thomas L. Friedman explains, increased access to cell phone cameras, YouTube, and the like continues to "[make] the global discussion so much richer—and each of us so much more transparent" (23).

Deleting Words When you delete words from a quotation, use **ellipses**—three spaced periods—to indicate your edits. However, never use ellipses to indicate a deletion at the beginning of a quotation.

> **ORIGINAL QUOTATION**
> "Just as companies sometimes incorporate social functions into their interview process to see if potential hires can handle themselves responsibly, they may also check out a student's Facebook account to see how the student chooses to present him or herself" ("Beware").

> **UNNECESSARY WORDS DELETED**
> "Just as companies sometimes incorporate social functions into their interview process, . . . they may also check out a student's Facebook account . . ." ("Beware").

DISTORTING QUOTATIONS

Be careful not to distort a source's meaning when you add, change, or delete words from a quotation. In the following example, the writer intentionally deletes material from the original quotation that would weaken his argument.

Original Quotation

"This incident is by no means an isolated one. Connecticut authorities are investigating reports that seven girls were sexually assaulted by older men they met on MySpace" ("Beware").

Distorted

"This incident is by no means an isolated one. [In fact,] seven girls were sexually assaulted by older men they met on MySpace" ("Beware").

⬣ EXERCISE 9.6

Look carefully at the quotations that accompany this chapter's opening images (p. 328). Select three quotations, and summarize each quotation in one sentence. Then, compose an original sentence that quotes each statement. Be sure to acknowledge each source in an identifying tag and to integrate the borrowed material smoothly into each sentence.

⬣ EXERCISE 9.7

Reread the summary you wrote for Exercise 9.1 and the paraphrase you wrote for Exercise 9.3. Add three different identifying tags to each, varying the verbs you use and the position of the tags. Then, check to make sure you have used correct parenthetical documentation. (If the author's name is included in the identifying tag, it should not also appear in the parenthetical citation.)

Synthesizing Sources

In a **synthesis**, you combine summary, paraphrase, and quotation from several sources with your own ideas to support an original conclusion. A synthesis sometimes identifies similarities and differences among ideas, indicating where sources agree and disagree and how they support or challenge one another's ideas. Transitional words and phrases identify points of similarity (*also*, *like*, *similarly*, and so on) or difference (*however*, *in contrast*, and so on). When you write a synthesis, you include identifying tags and parenthetical documentation to identify each piece of information you get from a source and to distinguish your sources' ideas from one another and from your own ideas.

The following effective synthesis is excerpted from the student paper in Chapter 10. Note how the synthesis blends information from three sources with the student's own ideas to support her point about how the Internet has affected people's concepts of "public" and "private."

EFFECTIVE SYNTHESIS

Student's original point

Paraphrase

Student's own ideas

Quotation

Student's evaluation of source

Quotation

Part of the problem is that the Internet has fundamentally altered our notions of "private" and "public" in ways that we are only just beginning to understand. As Shelley Fralic observes in "Don't Fall for the Myths about Online Privacy," Facebook's privacy options do not really protect its users' privacy. On sites like Facebook, people often reveal intimate details of their lives to hundreds—perhaps even thousands—of strangers. This situation is unprecedented and, at least for the foreseeable future, irreversible. As *New York Times* columnist Thomas L. Friedman observes, "When everyone has a blog, a MySpace page, or Facebook entry, everyone is a publisher. . . . When everyone is a publisher, paparazzo, or filmmaker, everyone else is a public figure." Given the public nature of the Internet, the suggestion that we should live our lives by the same rules we lived by twenty years ago simply does not make sense. As Friedman notes, in the Internet age, more and more of "what you say or do or write will end up as a digital fingerprint that never gets erased" (23).

Compare the effective synthesis above with the following unacceptable synthesis.

UNACCEPTABLE SYNTHESIS

"The sheer volume of personal information that people are publishing online—and the fact that some of it could remain visible permanently—is changing the nature of personal privacy." On sites like Facebook, people can reveal the most intimate details of their lives to millions of total strangers. This development is unprecedented and, at least for the foreseeable future, irreversible. "When everyone has a blog, a MySpace page, or Facebook entry, everyone is a publisher. . . . When everyone is a publisher, paparazzo, or filmmaker, everyone else is a public figure" (Friedman 23). Given the changes in our understanding of privacy and the essentially public nature of the Internet, the analogy that Hall makes between a MySpace post and a private conversation seems of limited use. In the Internet age, more and more of "what you say or do or write will end up as a digital fingerprint that never gets erased."

Unlike the effective synthesis, the unacceptable synthesis above does not begin with a topic sentence that states the point the source material in the paragraph will support. Instead, it opens with an out-of-context quotation whose source is not identified. This quotation could have been paraphrased—

its wording is not particularly memorable—and, more important, it should have been accompanied by documentation. (If source information is not provided, the writer is committing plagiarism even if the borrowed material is set in quotation marks.) The second quotation, although it includes parenthetical documentation (Friedman 23), is dropped into the paragraph without an identifying tag; the third quotation, also from the Friedman article, is not documented at all, making it appear to be from Hall. All in all, the paragraph is not a smoothly connected synthesis but a string of unconnected ideas. It does not use sources effectively and responsibly, and it does not cite them appropriately.

⊘ EXERCISE 9.8

Write a synthesis that builds on the paraphrase you wrote for Exercise 9.2. Add your own original ideas—examples and opinions—to the paraphrase, and also blend in information from one or two of the other sources that appear in this chapter. Use identifying tags and parenthetical documentation to introduce your sources and to distinguish your own ideas from ideas expressed in your sources.

Documenting Sources: MLA

When you are building an argument, you use sources for support. To acknowledge the material you borrow and to help readers evaluate your sources, you need to supply documentation. In other words, you need to tell readers where you found your information. If you use documentation responsibly, you will also avoid **plagiarism**, an ethical offense with serious consequences. (See Chapter 11 for more on plagiarism.)

WHY DOCUMENT SOURCES?

- To acknowledge the debt that you owe to your sources

- To demonstrate that you are familiar with the conventions of academic discourse

- To enable readers to judge the quality of your research

- To avoid plagiarism

- To make your argument more convincing

MLA documentation consists of two parts: **parenthetical references** in the text of your paper and a **works-cited list** at the end of the paper. (The references are keyed to the works-cited list.)

Using Parenthetical References

The basic parenthetical citation consists of the author's last name and a page number:

(Fielding 213)

If the author is referred to in the sentence, include only the page number in the parenthetical reference.

> According to environmental activist Brian Fielding, the number of species affected is much higher (213).

Here are some other situations you may encounter:

- When referring to a work by two authors, include both authors' names.

> (Stange and Hogarth 53)

- When citing a work with no listed author, include a short version of the title.

> ("Small Things" 21)

- When citing a source that is quoted in another source, indicate this by including the abbreviation *qtd. in.*

> According to Kevin Kelly, this narrow approach is typical of the "hive mind" (qtd. in Doctorow 168).

- When citing two or more works by the same author, include a short title after the author's name.

> (Anderson, *Long Tail* 47)

- If a source does not include page numbers, or if you are referring to the entire source rather than to a specific page, cite the author's name in the text of your paper rather than in a parenthetical reference.

You must document *all* information that is not **common knowledge**, whether you are summarizing, paraphrasing, or quoting. (See p. 374 for an explanation of common knowledge.) With direct quotations, include the parenthetical reference and a period *after* the closing quotation marks.

> According to Doctorow, this is "authorship without editorship. Or authorship fused with editorship" (166).

When quoting a passage of more than four lines, indent the entire passage half an inch from the left margin, and do not use quotation marks. Place the parenthetical reference *after* the final punctuation mark.

Doctorow points out that *Wikipedia*'s history pages can be extremely informative:

> This is a neat solution to the problem of authority—if you want to know what the fully rounded view of opinions on any controversial subject looks like, you need only consult its entry's history page for a blistering eyeful of thorough debate on the subject. (170)

Preparing the Works-Cited List

Start your works-cited list on a new page following the last page of your paper. Center the heading Works Cited at the top of the page. List entries alphabetically by the author's last name—or by the first word (other than an article such as *a* or *the*) of the title if an author is not given. Double-space within and between entries. Each entry should begin at the left-hand margin, with subsequent lines indented one-half inch. (This format can be automatically generated if you use the "hanging indent" option in your word processing program.)

Here are some additional guidelines:

- Italicize all book and periodical titles.

- Use a short version of a publisher's name (Penguin rather than Penguin Books), and abbreviate *University Press* (as in Princeton UP or U of Chicago P).

- If you are listing more than one work by the same author, include the author's name in the first entry, and substitute three unspaced hyphens followed by a period for the second and subsequent entries.

- Put quotation marks around the title of a periodical article or a section of an edited book or anthology, and provide the inclusive page numbers: 44–99. For page numbers larger than 99, give the last two digits of the second number if the first is the same: 147–69 (but 286–301).

When you have completed your list, double-check your parenthetical references to make sure they match the items in your works-cited list.

The following models illustrate the most common kinds of references.

Periodicals

For periodical articles found online or through a full-text database, see page 355.

Guidelines for Citing a Periodical Article

To cite a print article in MLA style, include the following:

1. Author, last name first

2. Title of the article, in quotation marks

3. Title of the periodical, in italics

4. Volume and issue numbers

5. Date or year of publication

6. Page number(s) of the article

   (See images on page 349.)

> ┌——1——┐ ┌————————— 2 ————————————
> Carton, Evan. "American Scholars: Ralph Waldo Emerson, Joseph
> ————————————— 2 —————————————
> Smith, John Brown, and the Springs of Intellectual Schism."
> ┌————— 3 —————┐┌——4——┐ ┌—5—┐ ┌—6—┐
> *New England Quarterly,* vol. 85, no. 1, 2012, pp. 5–37.

Journals

Journals are periodicals published for experts in a field. Cite both volume number and issue number when available. In cases where only an issue number is available, cite just the issue.

> Minkler, Lanse. "Economic Rights and Political Decision-Making."
> *Human Rights Quarterly*, vol. 31, no. 2, 2009, pp. 369–93.
> Picciotto, Joanna. "The Public Person and the Play of Fact."
> *Representations*, no. 105, 2009, pp. 85–132.

Magazines

Magazines are periodicals published for a general audience. Do not include a magazine's volume and issue number, but do include the date (day, month, and year for weekly publications; month and year for those published less frequently). If pages are not consecutive, give the first page followed by a plus sign.

> Aviv, Rachel. "The Death Treatment." *The New Yorker,* 22 June
> 2015, pp. 56–65.
> Rice, Andrew. "Mission from Africa." *The New York Times Magazine,*
> 12 Apr. 2009, pp. 30+.

Copyright Page

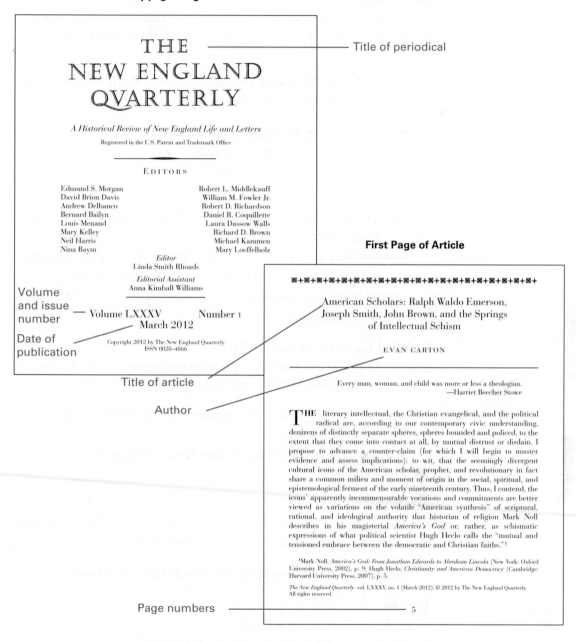

Title of periodical

THE
NEW ENGLAND
QVARTERLY

A Historical Review of New England Life and Letters

Registered in the U.S. Patent and Trademark Office

EDITORS

Edmund S. Morgan
David Brion Davis
Andrew Delbanco
Bernard Bailyn
Louis Menand
Mary Kelley
Neil Harris
Nina Baym

Robert L. Middlekauff
William M. Fowler Jr.
Robert D. Richardson
Daniel R. Coquillette
Laura Dassow Walls
Richard D. Brown
Michael Kammen
Mary Loeffelholz

Editor
Linda Smith Rhoads

Editorial Assistant
Anna Kimball Williams

Volume and issue number

Volume LXXXV   Number 1

Date of publication

March 2012

Copyright 2012 by The New England Quarterly
ISSN 0028–4866

Title of article

Author

First Page of Article

American Scholars: Ralph Waldo Emerson, Joseph Smith, John Brown, and the Springs of Intellectual Schism

EVAN CARTON

Every man, woman, and child was more or less a theologian.
—Harriet Beecher Stowe

THE literary intellectual, the Christian evangelical, and the political radical are, according to our contemporary civic understanding, denizens of distinctly separate spheres, spheres bounded and policed, to the extent that they come into contact at all, by mutual distrust or disdain. I propose to advance a counter-claim (for which I will begin to muster evidence and assess implications): to wit, that the seemingly divergent cultural icons of the American scholar, prophet, and revolutionary in fact share a common milieu and moment of origin in the social, spiritual, and epistemological ferment of the early nineteenth century. Thus, I contend, the icons' apparently incommensurable vocations and commitments are better viewed as variations on the volatile "American synthesis" of scriptural, rational, and ideological authority that historian of religion Mark Noll describes in his magisterial *America's God* or, rather, as schismatic expressions of what political scientist Hugh Heclo calls the "mutual and tensioned embrace between the democratic and Christian faiths."[1]

[1]Mark Noll, *America's God: From Jonathan Edwards to Abraham Lincoln* (New York: Oxford University Press, 2002), p. 9; Hugh Heclo, *Christianity and American Democracy* (Cambridge: Harvard University Press, 2007), p. 5.

The New England Quarterly, vol. LXXXV, no. 1 (March 2012). © 2012 by The New England Quarterly. All rights reserved.

Page numbers

5

Newspapers

Include both the letter of the section and the page number. If an article continues on to a nonconsecutive page, give just the first page followed by a plus sign.

> Darlin, Damon. "Software That Monitors Your Work, Wherever You Are." *The New York Times*, 12 Apr. 2009, pp. B2+.

Editorial, Letter to the Editor, or Review

Include authors and titles where available as well as a descriptive label—for example Editorial, Letter, or Review. In the case of reviews, include the title and author of the work that is reviewed.

> Bernath, Dan. "Letter to the Editor." *The Washington Post*, 12 Apr. 2009, p. A16. Letter.
>
> Franklin, Nancy. "Whedon's World." Review of *Dollhouse*, directed by Joss Whedon. *The New Yorker*, 2 Mar. 2009, p. 45.
>
> "World Bank Responsibility." *The Wall Street Journal*, 28 Mar. 2009, p. A10. Editorial.

Political Cartoon or Comic Strip

Include the author and title (if available) of the cartoon or comic strip, followed by a descriptive label and publication information.

> Adams, Scott. "Dilbert." *The Chicago Tribune,* 10 Mar. 2012, p. C9. Comic strip.
>
> Pett, Joel. *Lexington Herald-Leader,* 30 Apr. 2012, p. A12. Cartoon.

Advertisement

Cite the name of the product or company that is advertised, followed by the descriptive label and the publication information.

> Maxwell House. *Rolling Stone,* 18 June 2015, p. 35. Advertisement.

Books
Guidelines for Citing a Book

To cite a book in MLA style, include the following:

1. Author, last name first

2. Title, in italics

3. Full publisher's name

4. Date of publication

```
┌─────1─────┐  ┌──────2──────┐  ┌──────3──────┐ ┌─4─┐
```
Kahneman, Daniel. *Thinking, Fast and Slow*. Farrar, Straus and Grioux, 2011.

Copyright Page

Date of publication

Farrar, Straus and Giroux
18 West 18th Street, New York 10011

Copyright © 2011 by Daniel Kahneman
All rights reserved
Printed in the United States of America
First edition, 2011

Grateful acknowledgment is made for permission to reprint the following previously published material: "Judgment Under Uncertainty: Heuristics and Biases" from Science, New Series. Vol. 185, No. 4157, copyright © 1974 by Amos Tversky and Daniel Kahneman. Reprinted by permission of Science. "Choices, Values, and Frames" from The American Psychologist, copyright © 1983 by Daniel Kahneman and Amos Tversky. Reprinted by permission of the American Psychological Association.

Grateful acknowledgment is made for permission to reprint the following images: Image on page 19 courtesy of Paul Ekman Group, LLC. Image on page 57 from "Cues of Being Watched Enhance Cooperation in a Real-World Setting" by Melissa Bateson, Daniel Nettle, and Gilbert Roberts, Biology Letters (2006); reprinted by permission of Biology Letters. Image on page 100 from Mind Sights by Roger N. Shepard (New York: W.H. Freeman and Company, 1990); reprinted by permission of Henry Holt and Company. Image on page 300 from "Human Amygdala Responsivity to Masked Fearful Eye Whites" by Paul J. Whalen et al., Science 306 (2004). Reprinted by permission of Science.

Library of Congress Cataloging-in-Publication Data
Kahneman, Daniel, 1934–
    Thinking, fast and slow / Daniel Kahneman. — 1st ed.
        p. cm.
    Includes bibliographical references and index.
    ISBN 978-0-374-27563-1 (alk. paper)
    1. Thought and thinking. 2. Decision making. 3. Intuition. 4. Reasoning. 1. Title.

BF441 .K238 2011
153.4'2—dc23

Designed by Abby Kagan

www.fsgbooks.com

1   3   5   7   9   10   8   6   4   2

Title Page

Title of book

THINKING,

FAST AND SLOW

Author

DANIEL

KAHNEMAN

Publisher

FARRAR, STRAUS AND GIROUX   NEW YORK

Book by One Author

List the author, last name first, followed by the title (italicized). Include the full publisher's name, abbreviated when called for, and end with the date of publication.

> Skinner, Quentin. *Forensic Shakespeare*. Oxford UP, 2014.

Book by Two Authors

List authors in the order in which they are listed on the book's title page. List the first author with last name first, but list the second author with first name first.

> Singer, Peter, and Jim Mason. *The Way We Eat: Why Our Food Choices Matter*. Rodale, 2006.

Book by Three or More Authors

List only the first author, last name first, followed by the abbreviation et al. ("and others").

> Gould, Harvey, et al. *Advanced Computer Simulation Methods*. Pearson Education, 2009.

Two or More Books by the Same Author

List the entries alphabetically by title. In each entry after the first, substitute three unspaced hyphens, followed by a period, for the author's last name.

> Friedman, Thomas L. *Hot, Flat, and Crowded: Why We Need a Green Revolution—and How It Can Renew America*. Farrar, Strauss and Giroux, 2008.
>
> ---. *The World Is Flat: A Brief History of the Twenty-First Century*. Farrar, Strauss and Giroux, 2005.

Edited Book

If your focus is on the *author*, include the name of the editor (or editors) after the title, preceded by the abbreviation Ed. (for "edited by"). If the book is an edited collection of essays by different authors, treat it as an anthology.

> Whitman, Walt. *The Portable Walt Whitman*. Edited by Michael Warner, Penguin Classics, 2004.

If your focus is on the *editor*, begin with the editor's name followed by editor or editors.

> Michael Warner, editor. *The Portable Walt Whitman*. Penguin
> Classics, 2004.

Translation

> Bolaño, Roberto. *The Savage Detectives*. Translated by Natasha
> Wimmer, Picador, 2008.

Revised Edition

> Smith, Steven S., et al., *The American Congress*. 4th ed., Cambridge
> UP, 2006.

Anthology

Include the name of the editor (or editors) of the anthology, followed by editor or editors.

> Browning, John Edgar, and Caroline Joan S. Picart, editors.
> *Speaking of Monsters*, Palgrave, 2012.

Work in an Anthology

> Malone, Dan. "Immigration, Terrorism, and Secret Prisons."
> *Keeping Out the Other: Immigration Enforcement Today*,
> edited by David C. Brotherton and Philip Kretsedemas,
> Columbia UP, 2008, pp. 44–62.

More Than One Work in the Same Anthology

To avoid repeating the entire anthology entry, you may provide a cross-reference from individual essays to the entire anthology.

> Adelson, Glenn et al., editors. *Environment: An Interdisciplinary*
> *Anthology*, Yale UP, 2008.
> Lesher, Molly. "Seeds of Change." Adelson, pp. 131–37.
> Marshall, Robert. "The Problem of the Wilderness." Adelson,
> pp. 288–92.

Section or Chapter of a Book

> Leavitt, Steven D., and Stephen J. Dubner. "Why Do Drug Dealers Still Live with Their Moms?" *Freakonomics: A Rogue Economist Explores the Hidden Side of Everything,* Morrow, 2006, pp. 49-78.

Introduction, Preface, Foreword, or Afterword

> Christiano, Thomas, and John Christman. Introduction. *Contemporary Debates in Political Philosophy.* Edited by Thomas Christiano and John Christman, Wiley, 2009, pp. 1–20.

Multivolume Work

> McNeil, Peter, editor. *Fashion: Critical and Primary Sources.* Berg Publishers, 2009. 4 vols.

Article in a Reference Work

A **reference work** is a book (print or electronic)—such as an encyclopedia, a dictionary, a bibliography, an almanac, or a handbook—that contains factual information. If the entries in a reference work are arranged alphabetically, do not include page numbers or volumes. When citing a familiar encyclopedia that publishes new editions regularly, include only the edition (if given) and year. If the article's author is given, include that as well. For less well-known reference encyclopedias, include publication information.

> "Human Rights." *Encyclopedia Americana.* 2003 ed.
>
> "Seagrass Beds." *Ocean: A Visual Encyclopedia.* DK Publishing, 2015.

> **NOTE**
>
> Keep in mind that many instructors do not consider encyclopedia articles acceptable research sources. Before including a citation for an encyclopedia article in your works-cited list, check with your instructor.

Audiovisual Sources

TV Show

> "A Desperate Man." *NCIS,* written by Nicole Mirante-Matthews, directed by Leslie Libman, CBS, 10 Jan. 2012.

Film

The Tree of Life. Directed by Terrence Malick, performances by Brad
Pitt, Sean Penn, and Jessica Chastain, Fox Searchlight, 2011.

Internet Sources

Citing Internet sources can be problematic because they sometimes lack
basic information—for example, dates of publication or authors' names.
When citing Internet sources, include all the information you can find.

- For sites that are online editions of printed works, include as much of
  the original print information as is available, as well as the URL.

- For sites that exist only online, include (when available) the author,
  title, overall website title (if part of a larger project), the date it was last
  updated, and the URL.

- For works that are accessed through a library database, include the
  name of the database (in italics) and the URL or Digital Object Identifier (DOI). A DOI is a unique series of numbers assigned to electronic
  documents. The DOI remains the same regardless of where on the
  Internet a document is located.

For particularly long URLs (three lines or greater), you may use the
URL for the main website on which you found the content instead of the
URL for the specific page which you are referencing. However, your
instructor may not require a URL, so be sure to confirm their preference.
It is always a good idea, however, to keep a record of the URLs for yourself
in case you need to revisit your source.

If you type a URL into a works-cited entry that carries over to the next
line, make sure that you break it at an appropriate place—for example,
after a slash or a hyphen. If you paste a URL into a works-cited entry,
Word will do this for you.

Guidelines for Citing a Website

To cite a website in MLA style, follow these guidelines:

1. Author (if any)

2. Title (if any)

3. Name of website or sponsor

4. Date the site was last updated

5. DOI or URL

Author

Title

City of publication

Date of last update

Sponsor

Foodsafety.gov

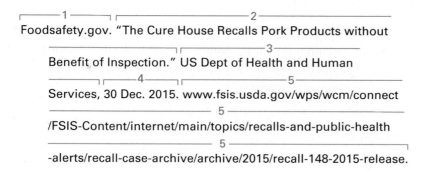

Foodsafety.gov. "The Cure House Recalls Pork Products without Benefit of Inspection." US Dept of Health and Human Services, 30 Dec. 2015. www.fsis.usda.gov/wps/wcm/connect /FSIS-Content/internet/main/topics/recalls-and-public-health -alerts/recall-case-archive/archive/2015/recall-148-2015-release.

Entire Website

Include (if available) the author, title of the website, date of last update, and the URL.

Document within a Website

"Uniform Impunity: Mexico's Misuse of Military Justice to Prosecute
   Abuses in Counternarcotics and Public Security Operations."
   Human Rights Watch, Apr. 2009, www.hrw.org/report/2009/04/29
   /uniform-impunity/mexicos-misuse-military-justice-prosecute
   -abuses-counternarcotics.

Online Video

Baggs, Amanda. "In My Language." *YouTube*, 14 Jan. 2007,
   www.youtube.com/watch?v=JnyIM1hI2jc.

Blog Posts and Blog Comments

Caryl, Christian. "Burma: How Much Change?" *NYR Daily*, NYREV,
   17 Nov. 2015, www.nybooks.com/daily/2015/11/17/burma
   -election-how-much-change/.
Cimons, Marlene. "Why Cities Could Be the Key to Solving the
   Climate Crisis." *Thinkprogress.org*, Center for American
   Progress Action Fund, 10 Dec. 2015, thinkprogress.org
   /climate/2015/12/10/3730938/cities-key-to-climate-crisis/.

Tweet

Begin with the author's real name, followed by the user name in parentheses. Include only the user name if the real name is unknown. Next, include the entire text of the tweet in quotation marks, followed by the date, the time, and the medium (Tweet).

Curiosity Rover. "Can you see me waving? How to spot #Mars
in the night sky: https://youtu.be/hv8hVvJlcJQ." *Twitter*,
5 Nov. 2015, 11:00 a.m., twitter.com/marscuriosity/status
/672859022911889408.

Podcast

Koenig, Sarah. "The Alibi." *Serial,* Chicago Public Radio,
3 Oct. 2014, serialpodcast.org/season-one/1/the-alibi.

Ogg, Erica. "Google Tries to Rehab Its Antitrust Image." *CNET News
Daily Podcast*, CBS Interactive, 8 May 2009, www.cnet.com
/news/cnet-news-daily-podcast-google-tries-to-rehab-its
-antitrust-image/.

Online Book

Doctorow, Cory. *Content: Selected Essays on Technology,
Creativity, Copyright, and the Future of the Future,* Tachyon,
2008. *Craphound.com.*

Part of an Online Book

Zittrain, Jonathan L. "The Lessons of *Wikipedia*." *The Future of the
Internet and How to Stop It,* Yale UP, 2008. *futureoftheinternet.org.*

Article in an Online Scholarly Journal

Johnston, Rebecca. "Salvation or Destruction: Metaphors
of the Internet." *First Monday*, vol. 14, no. 4, 2009,
firstmonday.org/article/view/2370/2158.

Magazine Article Accessed Online

Marantz, Andrew. "What to Do When Your App Is Racist." *The New
Yorker*, 29 Jul. 2015, www.newyorker.com/business/currency
/what-to-do-when-your-app-is-racist.

Newspaper Article Accessed Online

Possley, Maurice, and Ken Armstrong. "The Verdict: Dishonor."
Chicago Tribune, 11 Jan. 1999, www.chicagotribune.com/news
/watchdog/chi-020103trial1-story.html.

Article from a Library Database

Hartley, Richard D. "Sentencing Reform and the War on Drugs: An
Analysis of Sentence Outcomes for Narcotics Offenders
Adjudicated in the US District Courts on the Southwest
Border." *Criminal Justice Policy Review,* vol. 19, no. 4, 2008,
pp. 414-37. *Sage Premier,* doi: 10.1177/1043986208323264.

Legal Case

When citing a court opinion, provide the plaintiffs' names, the legal
citation (volume, abbreviation of the source, page numbers), the name
of the court, the year of the decision, and any relevant information
about where you found it. In many cases, online versions of the opinions will include only the first page; in those cases, supply that page
number followed by a plus sign.

Miranda v. Arizona, 384 US 436+. Supreme Court of the US. 1966.
FindLaw, Thompson Reuters, caselaw.findlaw.com
/us-supreme-court/384/436.html.

Government Document

Include the government agency or body issuing the document, followed by
publication information.

United States, Department of Homeland Security, *Estimates of the
Unauthorized Immigrant Population Residing in the United
States, Office of Immigration Policy,* Feb. 2009, www.dhs.gov
/sites/default/files/publications/ois_ill_pe_2011_0.pdf.

 **LaunchPad** macmillan learning   For more practice, see the LearningCurve on
Working with Sources (MLA) in the LaunchPad
for *Practical Argument.*

⬇The following student research paper, "Should Data Posted on
Social-Networking Sites Be 'Fair Game' for Employers?" by Erin Blaine,
follows MLA documentation style as outlined in the preceding pages.

MLA PAPER GUIDELINES

- An MLA paper should have a one-inch margin all around and be double-spaced.

- Indent the first line of every paragraph. Number all pages, including the first, consecutively. Type your name, followed by the page number, in the upper right-hand corner.

- An MLA paper does not typically have a title page. Type the following information at the top of the paper, one inch from the left-hand margin:

  Name

  Instructor

  Course

  Date submitted

- Center the title of the paper. Capitalize all important words of the title, except prepositions, articles, coordinating conjunctions, and the *to* in infinitives—unless the word is the first or last word of the title. Titles should never be italicized, underlined, or followed by a period.

- Begin the **works-cited list** on a new numbered page, after the body of the paper. (See page 347 for a discussion of the works-cited list.)

- Citations should follow MLA documentation style.

NOTE

In the student essay that follows, note that the green annotations explain the student's choice of sources and the orange annotations highlight features of the student's use of documentation.

Blaine 1

Erin Blaine

Professor Adams

Humanities 101

4 March 2015

Should Data Posted on Social-Networking Sites

Be "Fair Game" for Employers?

The popularity of social-networking sites such as   1
Facebook and Twitter has increased dramatically over the last
several years, especially among college students and young
professionals. These sites provide valuable opportunities for
networking and for connecting socially. At the same time, however, potential employers, human resources professionals, and
even college admissions officers routinely use these sites to
evaluate applicants. Because it is so easy to access social-
networking sites and because they provide valuable information,
this trend is certain to continue. Some people are concerned
about this development, arguing that social-networking sites
should be off-limits to potential employers because they do not
have the context they need to evaluate information. As long as
applicants have freely posted information in a public forum,
however, there is no reason for an employer not to consult this
information during the hiring process.

The number of employers and universities using social-   2
networking sites to evaluate candidates is growing every year.
A recent survey found that 24 percent of college admissions
officers acknowledged visiting sites like Facebook to learn more
about applicants, and 12 percent said that the information they
found "negatively impacted the applicant's admissions chances"
("Online Behavior"). This practice also occurs in the business
world, where the numbers are even more striking. A study conducted by CareerBuilder found that 43 percent of employers use

This source and
the following
one supply
statistics that
support the
main point of
the paragraph.

Parenthetical
reference
identifies the
source, which is
included in the
works-cited list.

Blaine 2

social-networking sites such as Facebook, Twitter, and LinkedIn to help them evaluate potential employees ("Number of Employers"). According to the *New York Times*, 75 percent of recruiters are required by their companies to research applicants online, and 70 percent of recruiters have rejected applicants because of information they found. The practice of checking social media is so common that some employers use outside companies, such as Social Intelligence Corp., to do Internet background checks on job candidates (Preston).

Not everyone is happy with this practice, though, and   3
some have strong objections. Becca Bush, a college student in Chicago, argues that employers should not have the right to use social media to evaluate potential employees. "It's a violation of privacy," she says. "Twenty years ago, people still did the same things as now," but the information "wasn't as widespread" (qtd. in Cammenga). Marc S. Rotenberg, president of the Electronic Privacy Information Center, agrees, saying, "Employers should not be judging what people in their private lives do away from the workplace" (qtd. in Preston). Rotenberg goes on to say that privacy settings on sites like Facebook are often misunderstood. According to him, "People are led to believe that there is more limited disclosure than there actually is" (qtd. in Preston). Some people mistakenly think that looking at an applicant's Facebook page is illegal (Cammenga). Even though it is not, this practice can lead to discrimination, which *is* illegal. An online search can reveal characteristics that an applicant is not required to disclose to employers—for example, race, age, religion, sex, national origin, marital status, or disability (Preston).

Given the realities of the digital age, however, admissions   4
committees and job recruiters are acting reasonably when they access social-networking sites. As a practical matter, it would be

Blaine 3

almost impossible to prevent employers from reviewing online sites as part of informal background and reference checks. Moreover, those who believe that it is unethical for recruiters to look at the online profiles of prospective job candidates seem willing to accept the benefits of social-networking sites but unwilling to acknowledge that these new technologies bring new responsibilities and liabilities. Finally, the problems associated with employers' use of social-networking sites would not be an issue in the first place if users of social-networking sites took full advantage of the available measures to protect themselves.

Part of the problem is that the Internet has fundamentally altered our notions of "private" and "public" in ways that we are only just beginning to understand. As Shelley Fralic observes in "Don't Fall for the Myths about Online Privacy," Facebook's privacy options do not really protect its users' privacy, and thinking they do "is beyond absurd" (1). On sites like Facebook, people can reveal intimate details of their lives to millions of strangers. This situation is unprecedented and, at least for the foreseeable future, irreversible. As *New York Times* columnist Thomas L. Friedman observes, "When everyone has a blog, a MySpace page, or Facebook entry, everyone is a publisher. . . . When everyone is a publisher, paparazzo, or film-maker, everyone else is a public figure." Given the changes in our understanding of privacy and the public nature of the Internet, the suggestion that we should live our lives by the same rules we lived by twenty years ago simply does not make sense. As Friedman notes, in the Internet age, more and more of "what you say or do or write will end up as a digital fingerprint that never gets erased" (23).

5

Because the source and the author are named in an identifying tag, only the page numbers are needed parenthetically.

Ellipses indicate that words have been left out of a quotation.

Including a recognized authority, such as Friedman, adds credibility.

Blaine 4

Rather than relying on outdated notions of privacy,   6
students and job seekers should accept these new conditions
and take steps to protect themselves. Most college and career
counseling services have easy-to-follow recommendations for
how to maintain a positive online reputation. First on almost
everyone's list is the advice, "Adjust your privacy settings."
Northwestern University's Career Services says it simply:
"Use your settings wisely and employers will not have access
to the contents of your sites" ("Using Social Networking").
Understanding and employing these settings is a user's
responsibility; misunderstanding such protections is no excuse.
As Mariel Loveland suggests, those who want extra help can
hire an online reputation-management company such as
Reputation.com or Integrity Defenders or use services such as
those offered by Reppler. The "Reppler Image Score" enables
social-networking users to identify questionable material
"across different social networks" and to rate its "professionalism and consistency."

The most important way for people to protect themselves   7
against the possible misuse of personal information is for them
to take responsibility for the information they post online.
According to a recent article in *Education Week*, even middle
school students should keep their future college and career
plans in mind when they post information online ("Online
Behavior"). In preparing students to apply for college, many
high school counselors stress the "golden rule": "students
should never post anything online they wouldn't want their

Internet source includes no page number in the parenthetical documentation.

Distinctive key phrases are quoted directly.

Not every summary or paraphrase needs to include a quotation.

Blaine 5

parents to see" ("Online Behavior"). Students and job seekers must realize that a commonsense approach to the Internet requires that they develop good "digital grooming" habits (Bond). For example, one self-described "cautious Internet user" says that she "goes through the information on her [Facebook] account every few weeks and deletes statuses, messages, and other things" (Bond). She understands that a potential employer coming across an applicant's membership in a Facebook group such as "I Sold My Grandma for Crack-Cocaine!" or a picture of a student posing with an empty liquor bottle may not understand the tone, the context, or the joke. Students should also be careful about "friends" who have access to their online social networks, asking themselves whether these people really know them and would have good things to say about them if a prospective employer contacted them for a reference. According to one high school principal, 75 percent of the students at his school admitted to accepting a friend request from someone they did not know ("Online Behavior"). Getting students to consider the repercussions of this kind of choice is central to many social-media education programs.

Although social-networking sites have disadvantages, they also have advantages. These sites provide an excellent opportunity for job seekers to connect with potential employers and to get their names and résumés in circulation. For example, a job seeker can search the LinkedIn networks of a company's executives or human resources staff for mutual connections. In addition, a job seeker can post information calculated to appeal to potential employers. Recruiters are just as likely to hire

8

Brackets indicate that a quotation has been edited for clarity.

Paraphrasing provides readers with the key points of a source.

Blaine 6

candidates based on social-media screening as they are to reject them. A recent article reports the following:

A quotation of more than four lines of text is double-spaced, indented one inch from the left margin, and typed as a block, without quotation marks. Parenthetical documentation comes after the final punctuation.

> However, one third (33 percent) of employers who research candidates on social networking sites say they've found content that made them more likely to hire a candidate. What's more, nearly a quarter (23 percent) found content that directly led to them hiring the candidate, up from 19 percent last year. ("Number of Employers")

In today's job market, people should think of their networks as extensions of themselves. They need to take an active role in shaping the image they want to project to future employers.

As Thomas L. Friedman argues in his column, "The Whole World Is Watching," access to information creates opportunities as well as problems. Quoting Dov Seidman, Friedman maintains that the most important opportunity may be the one to "out-behave your competition." In other words, just as the Internet allows negative information to travel quickly, it also allows positive information to spread. So even though students and job seekers should be careful when posting information online, they should not miss the opportunity to take advantage of the many opportunities that social-networking sites offer.

Blaine 7

Works Cited

Bond, Michaelle. "Facebook Timeline a New Privacy Test." *USA Today*, 2 Nov. 2011, www.usatoday.com/tech/news /internetprivacy/story/2011-11-02/facebook-timeline -privacy/51047658/1.

Cammenga, Michelle. "Facebook Might Be the Reason You Don't Get That Job." *Hub Bub*, Loyola University Chicago's School of Communication, 23 Feb. 2012, blogs.luc.edu /hubbub/reporting-and-writing/employers-screen-facebook/.

Fralic, Shelley. "Don't Fall for the Myths about Online Privacy." *Calgary Herald*, 17 Oct. 2015, p. 1.

Friedman, Thomas L. "The Whole World Is Watching." *The New York Times,* 27 June 2007, p. A23.

Loveland, Mariel. "Reppler Launches 'Reppler Image Score,' Rates Social Network Profile Content for Potential Employers." *Scribbal*, 27 Sept. 2011, www.scribbal.com/reppler-launches -rates-social-network-profile-content-09-27-11/.

"Number of Employers Passing on Applicants Due to Social Media Posts Continues to Rise." *CareerBuilder*, 26 June 2014, www.careerbuilder.com/share/aboutus/pressreleasesdetail .aspx?sd=6%2F26%2F2014&id=pr829&ed=12%2F31%2F2014.

"Online Behavior Jeopardizing College Plans; Admissions Officers Checking Social-Networking Sites for Red Flags." *Education Week,* 14 Dec. 2011, p. 11. *Academic One File*, www.edweek .org/ew/articles/2011/12/08/14collegeadmit.h31.html.

Preston, Jennifer. "Social Media History Becomes a New Job Hurdle." *The New York Times*, 20 July 2011, www.nytimes .com/2011/07/21/technology/social-media-history-becomes -a-new-job-hurdle.html?_r=0.

"Using Social Networking in Your Employment Search." *University Career Services*, Northwestern University, 2011, www.northwestern.edu/careers/job-intern-prep/social -media-advice/index.html.

The works-cited list includes full information for all sources cited in the paper.

Be sure that your data comes from recent sources.

Tim Roberts/Getty Images

Using Sources Responsibly

Where Should We Draw the Line with Plagiarism?

In recent years, a number of high-profile plagiarism cases have put a spotlight on how much "borrowing" from other sources is acceptable. Some critics—and many colleges and universities—draw little distinction between intentional and unintentional plagiarism, arguing that any unattributed borrowing is theft. Others are more forgiving, accepting the fact that busy historians or scientists (or students) might not realize that a particular sentence in their notes was not their original idea or might accidentally incorporate a source's exact words (or its unique syntax or phrasing) into their own work without attribution.

In the age of the Internet, with its "cut-and-paste" culture, plagiarism has become easier to commit; however, with the development of plagiarism-detection software, it is also now much easier to detect. Still, some colleges and universities are uncomfortable with the idea of using such software, arguing that it establishes an atmosphere of distrust.

On college campuses, as in the professional world, questions like the following have arisen: What exactly constitutes plagiarism? How serious a matter is it? Is there a difference between intentional and unintentional plagiarism? Is plagiarizing a few sentences as bad as plagiarizing an entire paper? Why do people commit plagiarism? What should be done to prevent it? How should it be punished? What are its short- and long-term consequences?

These are some (although by no means all) of the questions that you might think about as you consider the sources at the end of this chapter. After reading these sources, you will be asked to write an argumentative essay that takes a position on the issue of what exactly constitutes plagiarism and how it should be dealt with.

Understanding Plagiarism

Plagiarism is the act of using the words or ideas of another person without attributing them to their rightful author—that is, presenting those borrowed words and ideas as if they are your own. When you plagiarize, you fail to use sources ethically or responsibly.

TWO DEFINITIONS OF PLAGIARISM

From *MLA Handbook* Eighth Edition (2016)

Merriam-Webster's Collegiate Dictionary defines plagiarizing as committing "literary theft." Plagiarism is presenting another person's ideas, information, expressions, or entire work as one's own. It is thus a kind of fraud: deceiving others to gain something of value. While plagiarism only sometimes has legal repercussions (e.g., when it involves copyright infringement—violating an authors' exclusive legal right to publication), it is always a serious moral and ethical offense.

From *Publication Manual of the American Psychological Association*, Sixth Edition (2009)

Researchers do not claim the words and ideas of another as their own; they give credit where credit is due (APA Ethics Code Standard 8.11, Plagiarism). Quotation marks should be used to indicate the exact words of another. *Each time* you paraphrase another author (i.e., summarize a passage or rearrange the order of a sentence and change some of the words), you need to credit the source in the text.

The key element of this principle is that authors do not present the work of another as if it were their own work. This can extend to ideas as well as written words. If authors model a study after one done by someone else, the originating author should be given credit. If the rationale for a study was suggested in the Discussion section of someone else's article, that person should be given credit. Given the free exchange of ideas, which is very important to the health of intellectual discourse, authors may not know where an idea for a study originated. If authors do know, however, they should acknowledge the source; this includes personal communications.

For many people, defining plagiarism is simple: it is not "borrowing" but stealing, and it should be dealt with severely. For others, it is a more slippery term, seen as considerably more serious if it is intentional than if it is accidental (for example, the result of careless research methods). Most colleges and universities have guidelines that define plagiarism strictly and have penalties in place for those who commit it. To avoid committing unintentional plagiarism, you need to understand exactly what it is and why it occurs. You also need to learn how to use sources responsibly and to understand what kind of information requires documentation and what kind does not.

Avoiding Unintentional Plagiarism

Even if you do not intentionally misuse the words or ideas of a source, you are still committing plagiarism if you present the work of others as your own. The most common errors that lead to unintentional plagiarism—and how to avoid them—are listed below.

COMMON ERROR	HOW TO AVOID IT
No source information is provided for borrowed material (including statistics).	Always include full parenthetical documentation and a works-cited list that make the source of your information clear to readers. (See Chapter 10.)
A source's ideas are presented as if they are your own original ideas.	Keep track of the sources you consult, and always keep full source information with your sources. Never cut and paste material from an electronic source directly into your paper.
The boundaries of borrowed material are unclear.	Be sure to use an identifying tag *before* and parenthetical documentation *after* borrowed material. (See Chapter 9.)
The language of paraphrases or summaries is still too close to that of the original source.	Be careful to use original phrasing and syntax when you write summaries and paraphrases. (See Chapter 9.)

(Continued)

COMMON ERROR	HOW TO AVOID IT
A friend's or tutor's words or ideas appear in your paper.	Any help you receive should be in the form of suggestions, not additions.
Material you wrote for another course is used in your paper.	Always get permission from *both* instructors if you want to reuse work you did for another course, and be sure the material you use is substantially revised.

To avoid unintentional plagiarism, you need to maintain control over your sources, keeping track of all the material you use so that you remember where you found each piece of information.

As you take notes, be careful to distinguish your sources' ideas from your own. If you are copying a source's words into your notes, put them in quotation marks. (If you are taking notes by hand, circle the quotation marks; if you are typing your notes, put the quotation marks in boldface.) If you photocopy material, write the full source information on the first page, and staple the pages together. When you download material from the Internet, be sure the URL appears on every page. Finally, never cut and paste material from a source directly into your paper.

INTERNET SOURCES AND PLAGIARISM

The Internet presents a particular challenge for students as they try to avoid plagiarism. Committing plagiarism (intentional or unintentional) with electronic sources is easy because it is simple to cut and paste material from online sources into a paper. However, inserting even a sentence or two from an Internet source (including a blog, an email, or a website) into a paper without quotation marks and documentation constitutes plagiarism.

It is also not acceptable to use a visual (such as a graph, chart, table, or photograph) found on the Internet without acknowledging its source. Finally, even if an Internet source does not identify its author, the words or ideas you find there are not your own original material, so you must identify their source.

As you draft your paper, be sure to quote your sources' words accurately (even punctuation must be reproduced exactly as it appears in the source). Be careful not to quote out of context, and be sure that you are presenting your sources' ideas accurately when you summarize or paraphrase. (For information on quoting, paraphrasing, and summarizing source material, see Chapter 9.)

INTENTIONAL PLAGIARISM

Deliberately plagiarizing from a source, handing in another student's paper as your own, or buying a paper from an Internet site is never acceptable. Such acts constitute serious violations of academic integrity. Creating your own original work is an important part of the educational experience, and misrepresenting someone else's work as your own undermines the goals of education.

Cartoon by Loos Diallo from Whitman Pioneer.

Knowing What to Document

Documentation is the practice of identifying borrowed material and providing the proper bibliographic information for each source. Different academic disciplines require different formats for documentation—for example, English uses MLA, and psychology uses APA. For this reason, you should be sure to check with your instructor to find out what documentation style he or she requires. (For information on MLA and APA documentation formats, see Chapter 10 and Appendix B, respectively.)

Regardless of the discipline, the following kinds of information should always be documented:

- Quotations from a source
- Summaries or paraphrases of a source's original ideas
- Opinions, judgments, and conclusions that are not your own
- Statistics from a source
- Visuals from a source
- Data from charts or graphs in a source

The following kinds of information, however, do not require documentation:

- **Common knowledge**—that is, factual information that can be found in several different sources (for example, a writer's date of birth, a scientific fact, or the location of a famous battle)
- Familiar quotations—anything from proverbs to frequently quoted lines from Shakespeare's plays—that you expect readers will recognize
- Your own original opinions, judgments, and conclusions

◯ EXERCISE 11.1

Which of the following statements requires documentation, and why?

1. Doris Kearns Goodwin is a prize-winning historian.

2. Doris Kearns Goodwin's *The Fitzgeralds and the Kennedys* is a 900-page book with about 3,500 footnotes.

3. In 1994, Lynne McTaggart accused Goodwin of borrowing material from a book that McTaggart wrote.

4. My own review of the background suggests that Goodwin's plagiarism was unintentional.

5. Still, these accusations left Goodwin to face the "slings and arrows" of media criticism.

6. As Goodwin explains, "The more intensive and far-reaching a historian's research, the greater the difficulty of citation."

7. In her defense, Goodwin argued that the more research a historian does, the harder it is to keep track of sources.

8. Some people still remain convinced that Goodwin committed plagiarism.

9. Goodwin believes that her careful research methods, which she has described in exhaustive detail, should have prevented accidental plagiarism.

10. Some of Goodwin's critics have concluded that her reputation as a historian was hurt by the plagiarism charges.

❯ EXERCISE 11.2

Assume you are using the following editorial as a source. Identify two pieces of information you would need to document (for example, statistics). Then, identify two pieces of information you would *not* need to document (for example, common knowledge).

This unsigned newspaper editorial appeared on August 11, 2006.

CHEATERS NEVER WIN

AUSTIN AMERICAN-STATESMAN

We live in the era of cut and paste, thanks to the Internet, which provides students with countless materials to plagiarize. 1

If you think that's an exaggeration, do an Internet search of "free term papers." You'll find cheathouse.com, Cheater.com, Schoolsucks.com, echeat.com, and Free Essay Network (freeessay.com) among the 603 million results that turn up. 2

One site, 24hourtermpapers.com, even boasts of providing "custom term papers" within 24 hours (at $23.95 per page), targeting college students who put off writing papers until the 11th hour. A disclaimer warns that "these term papers are to be used for research purposes only. Use of these papers for any other purpose is not the responsibility of 24 Hour Term Papers." Funny that they say that, because the site provides the student with a nice package to hand directly to the professor: All term papers are "sent within the due date," with a bibliography page thrown in for no extra charge. 3

A student who pays such a steep price for a term paper is not likely to use it only as a resource. One of the perks of being a student today is unlimited access to a slew of research tools, from the library to an online research database the institution pays for the student to use. 4

Student Judicial Services at the University of Texas defines plagiarism as "representing as your own work any material that was obtained from another 5 source, regardless of how or where you acquired it." This includes borrowing ideas or even structure. And "by merely changing a few words or rearranging several words or sentences, you are not paraphrasing. Making minor revisions to borrowed text amounts to plagiarism," the Web site warns.

But those warnings go unheeded by many. The Center for Academic 6 Integrity found last year that more than 70 percent of college students admitted to having cheated at least once, more than 60 percent admitted to plagiarizing, and nearly 40 percent said they have plagiarized from the Internet.

Strict disciplinary action should follow students who are caught trying to 7 claim someone else's work as their own. The more it goes unnoticed, the easier it is for students to keep stealing. Educators should devote time and attention to properly educating students on what plagiarism is and why it's stupid to do it.

In the end, the plagiarizer has the most to lose, whether he or she gets 8 caught or not. Many of the online papers are not worthy of copying, especially if a student wants to excel in college. By stealing someone else's work and labeling it as their own, students forgo the opportunity to learn how to research, develop ideas, and translate them into quality writing. Not to mention tarnishing a reputation, if the student gets caught.

> "In the end, the plagiarizer has the most to lose, whether he or she gets caught or not."

Cheathouse.com and other sites like it might get students a passing grade 9 in a course, but it only puts them a step behind everyone else who is developing the skills needed to thrive in the workplace. Employers won't be as forgiving as teachers or disciplinary committees. The day will come when the "I'm a student. I'm still learning" excuse will fall on deaf ears.

Revising to Eliminate Plagiarism

As you revise your papers, scrutinize your work carefully to be sure you have not inadvertently committed plagiarism.

The following paragraph (from page 28 of *Hot, Flat, and Crowded* by Thomas L. Friedman) and the four guidelines that follow it will help you to understand the situations in which accidental plagiarism is most likely to occur.

> So if you think the world feels crowded now, just wait a few decades. In 1800, London was the world's largest city with one million people. By 1960, there were 111 cities with more than one million people. By 1995 there were 280, and today there are over 300, according to

UN Population Fund statistics. The number of megacities (with ten million or more inhabitants) in the world has climbed from 5 in 1975 to 14
in 1995 and is expected to reach 26 cities by 2015, according to the UN.
Needless to say, these exploding populations are rapidly overwhelming
infrastructure in these megacities—nineteen million people in Mumbai
alone—as well as driving loss of arable land, deforestation, overfishing,
water shortages, and air and water pollution.

1. **Be sure you have identified your source and provided appropriate
   documentation.**

PLAGIARISM
The world is becoming more and more crowded, and some twenty-
six cities are expected to have populations of over 10 million by 2015.

This student writer does not quote directly from Friedman's discussion,
but her summary of his comments does not represent her original ideas
and therefore needs to be documented.

The following correct use of source material includes both an **identifying tag** (a phrase that identifies Friedman as the source of the ideas) and
a page number that directs readers to the exact location of the material the
student is summarizing. (Full source information is provided in the works-
cited list.)

CORRECT
According to Thomas L. Friedman, the world is becoming more and
more crowded, and twenty-six cities are expected to have populations of over 10 million by 2015 (28).

2. **Be sure you have placed quotation marks around borrowed words.**

PLAGIARISM
According to Thomas L. Friedman, the exploding populations of megacities around the world are overwhelming their infrastructure (28).

Although the passage above provides parenthetical documentation and
includes an identifying tag indicating the source of its ideas, it uses
Friedman's exact words without placing them in quotation marks.

To avoid committing plagiarism, the writer needs to either place
quotation marks around Friedman's words or paraphrase his comments.

CORRECT (BORROWED WORDS IN QUOTATION MARKS)
According to Thomas L. Friedman, the "exploding populations" of
large cities around the world are "rapidly overwhelming infrastructure in these megacities" (28).

CORRECT (BORROWED WORDS PARAPHRASED)
According to Thomas L. Friedman, the rapid rise in population of large cities around the world poses a serious threat to their ability to function (28).

3. **Be sure you have indicated the boundaries of the borrowed material.**

PLAGIARISM
The world is becoming more and more crowded, and this will lead to serious problems in the future. Soon, as many as twenty-six of the world's cities will have populations over 10 million. It is clear that "these exploding populations are rapidly overwhelming infrastructure in these megacities" (Friedman 28).

In the passage above, the student correctly places Friedman's words in quotation marks and includes appropriate parenthetical documentation. However, she does not indicate that other ideas in the passage, although not quoted directly, are also Friedman's.

To avoid committing plagiarism, the student needs to use identifying tags to indicate the boundaries of the borrowed material, which goes beyond the quoted words.

CORRECT
According to Thomas L. Friedman, the world is becoming more and more crowded, and this will lead to serious problems in the future. Soon, Friedman predicts, as many as twenty-six of the world's cities will have populations of over 10 million, and this rise in population will put a serious strain on the cities' resources, "rapidly overwhelming infrastructure in these megacities" (28).

4. **Be sure you have used your own phrasing and syntax.**

PLAGIARISM
If you feel crowded now, Thomas L. Friedman says, just wait twenty or thirty years. In 1800, London, with a million inhabitants, was the largest city in the world; over 111 cities had more than a million people by 1960. Thirty-five years later, there were 280; today, according to statistics provided by the UN Population Fund, there are more than 300. There were only five megacities (10 million people or more) in 1975 and fourteen in 1995. However, by 2015, the United Nations predicts, there might be twenty-six. These rapidly growing populations threaten to overwhelm the infrastructure of the megacities (Mumbai alone has 19 million people), destroying arable land, the forests, and fishing and causing water shortages and water and air pollution (28).

The student who wrote the paragraph on the preceding page does provide an identifying tag and parenthetical documentation to identify the source of her ideas. However, her paragraph's phrasing and syntax are almost identical to Friedman's.

In the following paragraph, the writer correctly paraphrases and summarizes Friedman's ideas, quoting a few distinctive passages. (See Chapter 9 for information on paraphrase and summary.)

CORRECT

As Thomas L. Friedman warns, the world has been growing more and more crowded and is likely to grow still more crowded in the years to come. Relying on UN population data, Friedman estimates that there will be some twenty more "megacities" (those with more than 10 million people) in 2015 than there were in 1975. (In 1800, in contrast, only one city in the world—London—had a million inhabitants.) Obviously, this is an alarming trend. Friedman believes that these rapidly growing populations are "overwhelming infrastructure in these megacities" and are bound to strain resources, leading to "loss of arable land, deforestation, [and] overfishing" and creating not only air and water pollution but water shortages as well (28).

NOTE

Do not forget to document statistics that you get from a source. For example, Thomas L. Friedman's statistics about the threat of rising population are the result of his original research, so you need to document them.

⊙ EXERCISE 11.3

The following student paragraph synthesizes information from two different sources (which appear on pp. 380–381, following the student paragraph), but the student writer has not used sources responsibly. (For information on synthesis, see Chapter 9.) Read the sources and the paragraph, and then make the following changes:

- Insert quotation marks where the student has quoted a source's words.

- Edit paraphrased and summarized material if necessary so that its syntax and phrasing are not too close to those of a source.

- Add parenthetical documentation where necessary to acknowledge the use of a source's words or original ideas.

- Add identifying tags where necessary to clarify the scope of the borrowed material or to differentiate material from the two sources.

- Check every quoted passage once more to see if the quotation adds something vital to the paragraph. If it does not, summarize or paraphrase the source's words instead.

STUDENT PARAGRAPH

In recent years, psychologists have focused on the idea that girls (unlike boys) face a crisis of self-esteem as they approach adolescence. Both Carol Gilligan and Mary Pipher did research to support this idea, showing how girls lose their self-confidence in adolescence because of sexist cultural expectations. Women's groups have expressed concern that the school system favors boys and is biased against girls. In fact, boys are often regarded not just as classroom favorites but also as bullies who represent obstacles on the path to gender justice for girls. Recently, however, this impression that boys are somehow privileged while girls are shortchanged is being challenged.

Source 1

That boys are in disrepute is not accidental. For many years women's groups have complained that boys benefit from a school system that favors them and is biased against girls. "Schools shortchange girls," declares the American Association of University Women. . . . A stream of books and pamphlets cite research showing not only that boys are classroom favorites but also that they are given to schoolyard violence and sexual harassment.

In the view that has prevailed in American education over the past decade, boys are resented, both as the unfairly privileged sex and as obstacles on the path to gender justice for girls. This perspective is promoted in schools of education, and many a teacher now feels that girls need and deserve special indemnifying consideration. "It is really clear that boys are Number One in this society and in most of the world," says Patricia O'Reilly, a professor of education and the director of the Gender Equity Center, at the University of Cincinnati.

The idea that schools and society grind girls down has given rise to an array of laws and policies intended to curtail the advantage boys have and to redress the harm done to girls. That girls are treated as the second sex in school and consequently suffer, that boys are accorded privileges and consequently benefit—these are things everyone is presumed to know. But they are not true.

—CHRISTINA HOFF SOMMERS, "THE WAR AGAINST BOYS"

Source 2

Girls face an inevitable crisis of self-esteem as they approach adolescence. They are in danger of losing their voices, drowning, and facing a devastating dip in self-regard that boys don't experience. This is the picture that Carol Gilligan presented on the basis of her research at the Emma Willard School, a private girls' school in Troy, N.Y. While Gilligan did not refer to genes in her analysis of girls' vulnerability, she did cite both the "wall of Western culture" and deep early childhood socialization as reasons.

Her theme was echoed in 1994 by the clinical psychologist Mary Pipher's surprise best seller, *Reviving Ophelia* (Putnam, 1994), which spent three years on the *New York Times* best-seller list. Drawing on case studies rather than systematic research, Pipher observed how naturally outgoing, confident girls get worn down by sexist cultural expectations. Gilligan's and Pipher's ideas have also been supported by a widely cited study in 1990 by the American Association of University Women. That report, published in 1991, claimed that teenage girls experience a "free-fall in self-esteem from which some will never recover."

The idea that girls have low self-esteem has by now become part of the academic canon as well as fodder for the popular media. But is it true? No.

—ROSALIND C. BARNETT AND CARYL RIVERS, "MEN ARE FROM EARTH, AND SO ARE WOMEN. IT'S FAULTY RESEARCH THAT SETS THEM APART"

Where Should We Draw the Line with Plagiarism?

Reread the At Issue box on page 369. Then, read the sources on the following pages. As you read these sources, you will be asked to answer questions and to complete some activities. This work will help you to understand the content and structure of the material you read. When you have read the sources, you will be ready to write an argumentative essay in which you take a position on the topic, "Where Should We Draw the Line with Plagiarism?"

Tim Roberts/Getty Images

SOURCES

In this *Slate* article, Shafer accuses a *New York Times* reporter of plagiarism. As evidence, he presents the opening paragraphs from the source (a *Bloomberg News* story), the accused reporter's *New York Times* article, and—for contrast—two other newspaper articles that report the same story without relying heavily on the original source.

This article appeared in *Slate* on March 5, 2008.

SIDEBAR:° COMPARING THE COPY

JACK SHAFER

A short news story printed alongside a longer related article

How different can four news stories generated by the same assignment be? Compare the opening paragraphs of these pieces about the 2005 mad cow disease conference call: the *Bloomberg News* version; the *New York Times* version,

> "How different can four news stories generated by the same assignment be?"

which lifts passages from *Bloomberg* without attribution; and the starkly different pieces run by the globeandmail.com and the *Omaha World-Herald*.

Opening paragraphs from the July 15, 2005, *Bloomberg News* story by Daniel Goldstein:

The U.S. plans to resume imports of Canadian cattle, after an appellate court cleared the way to end a ban imposed two years ago because of mad-cow disease.° Cattle prices fell and shares of beef producer Tyson Foods Inc. surged.

A brain disease that can be transmitted to humans through consumption of contaminated beef

The first shipments from Canada may arrive at U.S. slaughterhouses in days, U.S. Agriculture Secretary Mike Johanns said today in a conference call. "If things go well, it could very well be next week." USDA and Canadian officials are coordinating how to certify animals for shipment, he said.

A U.S. appellate court° yesterday ruled in favor of the government, which argued Canadian cattle under 30 months of age don't pose a risk of mad-cow disease. Tyson's beef business had a loss of $19 million in the quarter ended April 2, as the lack of available cattle boosted costs and led to plant closings. Canada before the ban supplied about 5 percent of U.S. beef.

A higher court that hears appeals of rulings that were made by a lower court

Opening paragraphs from the July 16, 2005, *New York Times* story by Alexei Barrionuevo:

The United States Agriculture Department said on Friday that it planned to resume imports of Canadian cattle within days, after an appellate court lifted a two-year-old injunction imposed because of mad cow disease.

The first shipments from Canada could arrive at American slaughter- 6 houses as early as next week, Agriculture Secretary Mike Johanns said in a conference call with reporters. Officials in Canada and the United States are coordinating how to certify the animals for shipment, he said.

"We want to make sure everything is in place," he said. "If things go well, 7 it could very well be next week."

The news sent shares of the beef producer Tyson Foods and McDonald's 8 restaurants surging. Cattle prices fell. Shares of Tyson rose 7.5 percent in early trading, and closed at $19.47 a share, a 5 percent increase, while McDonald's closed at $30.99 a share, up 4.7 percent.

Tyson's beef business recorded a loss of $19 million in the quarter ended 9 April 2. The company was hurt by the ban on cattle from Canada, which increased costs and led to temporary plant closings. Before the ban, Canada supplied about 5 percent of the nation's beef.

A United States appeals court ruled on Thursday in favor of the govern- 10 ment, which had argued that Canadian cows under 30 months of age did not pose a risk of bovine spongiform encephalopathy, or mad cow disease.

Opening paragraphs from the July 15 globeandmail.com story by Terry Weber, time stamped 12:28 p.m.:

The United States is taking immediate steps to reopen the border to Canadian 11 cattle imports, Agriculture Secretary Mike Johanns said Friday.

During a webcast, Mr. Johanns said that Washington has been in touch 12 with Ottawa and that the two sides are now going through the logistical steps necessary to resume trade of live cattle for the first time since May, 2003.

"Our hope is we're talking about days and not weeks," he said. "If things 13 go well, it could very well be next week, but we have not set a specific date."

Late Thursday, a three-member U.S. appeal court panel in Seattle 14 overturned a temporary injunction issued by Montana Judge Richard Cebull halting the U.S. Department of Agriculture's March plan to reopen the border.

Judge Cebull had sided with U.S. ranchers group R-Calf in its argument 15 that reopening the border exposed U.S. ranchers and consumers to unnecessary risks from mad-cow disease. The USDA had been planning to ease restrictions by allowing cattle younger than 30 months to be imported.

Mr. Johanns noted that Canadian officials had already anticipated the 16 ruling and taken steps to meet U.S. requirements, should Thursday's favor reopening the border.

"It [the reopening] could be as early as next week, but we want to make 17 sure everything is in place," he said.

Those requirements, he said, including ensuring that animals being 18 imported into the U.S. meet minimal-risk rule criteria, getting documents to U.S. customs to confirm the shipments are appropriate for entry.

Opening paragraphs from the July 15 *Omaha World-Herald* story by Chris Clayton:

Canadian cattle could start arriving at U.S. feedlots and meatpacking plants as early as next week, U.S. Agriculture Secretary Mike Johanns said Friday. 19

Thursday's unanimous decision by the 9th U.S. Circuit Court of Appeals lifting a lower court's injunction gives U.S. and Canadian officials a nearly two-week window to begin shipping live cattle from Canada before another court hearing, scheduled late this month in Montana. 20

No date has been set, but Johanns said he will move as "expeditiously as possible" to begin importing Canadian cattle once officials work out the ground rules. Canadian and USDA officials anticipated the requirements would be in place at whatever time the legal issues were resolved. 21

"Our hope is we are talking about days, not weeks," Johanns said. "It could be as early as next week, but we want to make sure everything is in place. . . . If things go well, it could very well be next week, but we haven't set a specific date" [*ellipsis in the original*]. 22

Johanns has lamented the closed border since becoming agriculture secretary in late January, saying that it hurts U.S. cattle feeders and meatpackers because the United States continued to import boxed beef from Canada. 23

Higher cattle prices because of tight supplies caused meatpackers to scale back production at U.S. facilities. Industry officials claim to have lost as many as 8,000 meatpacking jobs because of the closed border. 24

"I'm just worried that many of those jobs were impacted in a very permanent way," Johanns said. "My hope is that restructuring now will be abated and this industry can start getting back to a normal flow of commerce here." 25

About 1 million cattle were imported from Canada in the year before the border closed in May 2003 when Canada reported its first case of mad-cow disease, or bovine spongiform encephalopathy. 26

⊘ AT ISSUE: SOURCES FOR UNDERSTANDING PLAGIARISM

1. Identify the passages in the *New York Times* story that you think are too close to the original *Bloomberg News* story.

2. Identify passages in the other two excerpts that convey the same information as the *Times* story (paraphrased or summarized).

3. In his introduction, Shafer says that the passages from the Toronto *Globe and Mail* and the *Omaha World-Herald* are "starkly different" from the *Bloomberg News* story. Do you agree?

4. Can you identify any passages in the *Globe and Mail* or *Omaha World-Herald* excerpts that you believe are too close to the original source?

5. On the basis of what you see here, do you agree with Shafer that the *New York Times* reporter is guilty of plagiarism? Explain your conclusion.

This essay appeared in the *Washington Post* on September 3, 2004.

HOW TO FIGHT COLLEGE CHEATING

LAWRENCE M. HINMAN

Recent studies have shown that a steadily growing number of students cheat or 1 plagiarize in college—and the data from high schools suggest that this number will continue to rise. A study by Don McCabe of Rutgers University showed that 74 percent of high school students admitted to one or more instances of serious cheating on tests. Even more disturbing is the way that many students define cheating and plagiarism. For example, they believe that cutting and pasting a few sentences from various Web sources without attribution is not plagiarism.

Before the Web, students certainly plagiarized—but they had to plan 2 ahead to do so. Fraternities and sororities often had files of term papers, and some high-tech term-paper firms could fax papers to students. Overall, however, plagiarism required forethought.

Online term-paper sites changed all that. Overnight, students could order 3 a term paper, print it out, and have it ready for class in the morning—and still get a good night's sleep. All they needed was a charge card and an Internet connection.

One response to the increase in cheating has been to fight technology with 4 more technology. Plagiarism-checking sites provide a service to screen student papers. They offer a color-coded report on papers and the original sources from which the students might have copied. Colleges qualify for volume discounts, which encourages professors to submit whole classes' worth of papers—the academic equivalent of mandatory urine testing for athletes.

The technological battle between term-paper mills and anti-plagiarism services will undoubtedly continue to escalate, with each side constructing more elaborate countermeasures to outwit the other. The cost of both plagiarism and its detection will also undoubtedly continue to spiral. 5

> "The cost of both plagiarism and its detection will also undoubtedly continue to spiral."

But there is another way. Our first and 6 most important line of defense against academic dishonesty is simply good teaching. Cheating and plagiarism often arise in a vacuum created by routine, lack of interest, and overwork. Professors who give the same assignment every semester, fail to guide students in the development of their projects, and have little interest in what the students have to say contribute to the academic environment in which much cheating and plagiarism occurs.

Consider, by way of contrast, professors who know their students and 7 who give assignments that require regular, continuing interaction with them about their projects—and who require students to produce work that is a meaningful development of their own interests. These professors create an environment in which cheating and plagiarism are far less likely to occur. In this context, any plagiarism would usually be immediately evident to the professor, who would see it as inconsistent with the rest of the student's work. A strong, meaningful curriculum taught by committed professors is the first and most important defense against academic dishonesty.

The second remedy is to encourage the development of integrity in our stu- 8
dents. A sense of responsibility about one's intellectual development would pre-clude cheating and plagiarizing as inconsistent with one's identity. It is precisely this sense of individual integrity that schools with honor codes seek to promote.

Third, we must encourage our students to perceive the dishonesty of their 9
classmates as something that causes harm to the many students who play by the rules. The argument that cheaters hurt only themselves is false. Cheaters do hurt other people, and they do so to help themselves. Students cheat because it works. They get better grades and more advantages with less effort. Honest students lose grades, scholarships, recommendations, and admission to advanced pro-grams. Honest students must create enough peer pressure to dissuade potential cheaters. Ultimately, students must be willing to step forward and confront those who engage in academic dishonesty.

Addressing these issues is not a luxury that can be postponed until a more 10
convenient time. It is a short step from dishonesty in schools and colleges to dishonesty in business. It is doubtful that students who fail to develop habits of integrity and honesty while still in an academic setting are likely to do so once they are out in the "real" world. Nor is it likely that adults will stand up against the dishonesty of others, particularly fellow workers and superiors, if they do not develop the habit of doing so while still in school.

⊘AT ISSUE: SOURCES FOR UNDERSTANDING PLAGIARISM

1. In the first five paragraphs of this essay, Hinman provides background on how plagiarism by students has been changed by the Internet. Sum-marize the plagiarism situation before and after the development of the Internet.

2. The essay's thesis is stated in paragraph 6. Restate this thesis in your own words.

3. Does Hinman view plagiarism-detection sites as a solution to the problem of college cheating? What are the limitations of such sites?

4. According to Hinman, what steps can "committed professors" (para. 7) take to eliminate academic dishonesty?

5. In paragraphs 8 and 9, Hinman suggests two additional solutions to the problem of plagiarism. What solutions does he propose? Given what you know about college students, do you think Hinman's sug-gestions are realistic? Explain.

387

6. Hinman does not address arguments that challenge his recommen-dations. What opposing arguments might he have presented? How would you refute these opposing arguments?

7. This essay was published more than ten years ago. Do you think Hinman's observations and recommendations are still valid? Why or why not?

This article is from the August 1, 2010, edition of the *New York Times*.

PLAGIARISM LINES BLUR FOR STUDENTS IN DIGITAL AGE

TRIP GABRIEL

At Rhode Island College, a freshman copied and pasted from a Web site's frequently asked questions page about homelessness—and did not think he needed to credit a source in his assignment because the page did not include author information.

At DePaul University, the tip-off to one student's copying was the purple shade of several paragraphs he had lifted from the Web; when confronted by a writing tutor his professor had sent him to, he was not defensive—he just wanted to know how to change purple text to black.

And at the University of Maryland, a student reprimanded for copying from *Wikipedia* in a paper on the Great Depression said he thought its entries—unsigned and collectively written—did not need to be credited since they counted, essentially, as common knowledge.

Professors used to deal with plagiarism by admonishing students to give credit to others and to follow the style guide for citations, and pretty much left it at that.

But these cases—typical ones, according to writing tutors and officials responsible for discipline at the three schools who described the plagiarism—suggest that many students simply do not grasp that using words they did not write is a serious misdeed.

It is a disconnect that is growing in the Internet age as concepts of intellectual property, copyright, and originality are under assault in the unbridled exchange of online information, say educators who study plagiarism.

Digital technology makes copying and pasting easy, of course. But that is the least of it. The Internet may also be redefining how students—who came of age with music file-sharing, *Wikipedia*, and Web-linking—understand the concept of authorship and the singularity of any text or image.

"Now we have a whole generation of students who've grown up with information that just seems to be hanging out there in cyberspace and doesn't seem to have an author," said Teresa Fishman, director of the Center for Academic Integrity at Clemson University. "It's possible to believe this information is just out there for anyone to take."

Professors who have studied plagiarism do not try to excuse it—many are champions of academic honesty on their campuses—but rather try to understand why it is so widespread.

In surveys from 2006 to 2010 by Donald L. McCabe, a co-founder of the Center for Academic Integrity and a business professor at Rutgers University, about 40 percent of 14,000 undergraduates admitted to copying a few sentences in written assignments.

Perhaps more significant, the number who believed that copying from the 11 Web constitutes "serious cheating" is declining—to 29 percent on average in recent surveys from 34 percent earlier in the decade.

Sarah Brookover, a senior at the Rutgers campus in Camden, N.J., said 12 many of her classmates blithely cut and paste without attribution.

"This generation has always existed in a world where media and intellec- 13 tual property don't have the same gravity," said Ms. Brookover, who at 31 is older than most undergraduates. "When you're sitting at your computer, it's the same machine you've downloaded music with, possibly illegally, the same machine you streamed videos for free that showed on HBO last night."

Ms. Brookover, who works at the campus library, has pondered the differ- 14 ences between researching in the stacks and online. "Because you're not walking into a library, you're not physically holding the article, which takes you closer to 'this doesn't belong to me,'" she said. Online, "everything can belong to you really easily."

> "Online, 'everything can belong to you really easily.'"

A University of Notre Dame anthropologist, Susan D. Blum, disturbed by 15 the high rates of reported plagiarism, set out to understand how students view authorship and the written word, or "texts" in Ms. Blum's academic language.

She conducted her ethnographic research among 234 Notre Dame under- 16 graduates. "Today's students stand at the crossroads of a new way of conceiving texts and the people who create them and who quote them," she wrote last year in the book *My Word! Plagiarism and College Culture*, published by Cornell University Press.

Ms. Blum argued that student writing exhibits some of the same qualities 17 of pastiche that drive other creative endeavors today—TV shows that constantly reference other shows or rap music that samples from earlier songs.

In an interview, she said the idea of an author whose singular effort cre- 18 ates an original work is rooted in Enlightenment ideas of the individual. It is buttressed by the Western concept of intellectual property rights as secured by copyright law. But both traditions are being challenged. "Our notion of authorship and originality was born, it flourished, and it may be waning," Ms. Blum said.

She contends that undergraduates are less interested in cultivating a 19 unique and authentic identity—as their 1960s counterparts were—than in trying on many different personas, which the Web enables with social networking.

"If you are not so worried about presenting yourself as absolutely unique, 20 then it's O.K. if you say other people's words, it's O.K. if you say things you don't believe, it's O.K. if you write papers you couldn't care less about because they accomplish the task, which is turning something in and getting a grade," Ms. Blum said, voicing student attitudes. "And it's O.K. if you put words out there without getting any credit."

The notion that there might be a new model young person, who freely 21
borrows from the vortex of information to mash up a new creative work,
fueled a brief brouhaha earlier this year with Helene Hegemann, a German
teenager whose best-selling novel about Berlin club life turned out to include
passages lifted from others.

Instead of offering an abject apology, Ms. Hegemann insisted, "There's no 22
such thing as originality anyway, just authenticity." A few critics rose to her
defense, and the book remained a finalist for a fiction prize (but did not win).

That theory does not wash with Sarah Wilensky, a senior at Indiana Uni- 23
versity, who said that relaxing plagiarism standards "does not foster creativity,
it fosters laziness."

"You're not coming up with new ideas if you're grabbing and mixing and 24
matching," said Ms. Wilensky, who took aim at Ms. Hegemann in a column in
her student newspaper headlined "Generation Plagiarism."

"It may be increasingly accepted, but there are still plenty of creative 25
people—authors and artists and scholars—who are doing original work,"
Ms. Wilensky said in an interview. "It's kind of an insult that that ideal is gone,
and now we're left only to make collages of the work of previous generations."

In the view of Ms. Wilensky, whose writing skills earned her the role of 26
informal editor of other students' papers in her freshman dorm, plagiarism
has nothing to do with trendy academic theories.

The main reason it occurs, she said, is because students leave high school 27
unprepared for the intellectual rigors of college writing.

"If you're taught how to closely read sources and synthesize them into your 28
own original argument in middle and high school, you're not going to be tempted
to plagiarize in college, and you certainly won't do so unknowingly," she said.

At the University of California, Davis, of the 196 plagiarism cases referred 29
to the disciplinary office last year, a majority did not involve students ignorant
of the need to credit the writing of others.

Many times, said Donald J. Dudley, who oversees the discipline office on 30
the campus of 32,000, it was students who intentionally copied—knowing it
was wrong—who were "unwilling to engage the writing process."

"Writing is difficult, and doing it well takes time and practice," he said. 31

And then there was a case that had nothing to do with a younger genera- 32
tion's evolving view of authorship. A student accused of plagiarism came to
Mr. Dudley's office with her parents, and the father admitted that he was the
one responsible for the plagiarism. The wife assured Mr. Dudley that it would
not happen again.

⊘ AT ISSUE: SOURCES FOR UNDERSTANDING PLAGIARISM

1. Gabriel begins inductively, presenting three paragraphs of evidence
   before he states his thesis. Is this the best strategy, or should these
   examples appear later in his discussion? Explain.

2. In paragraph 5, Gabriel notes that "many students simply do not grasp that using words they did not write is a serious misdeed." Is this his thesis statement? Does he take a position, or is he just presenting information?

3. Why, according to Gabriel, is plagiarism so widespread? Do you think the reasons he cites in any way excuse plagiarism—at least accidental plagiarism? Does Gabriel seem to think they do?

4. What is *pastiche* (para. 17)? What is a collage (25)? How does the concept of pastiche or collage apply to plagiarism? Do you see the use of pastiche in TV shows or popular music (17) as different from its use in academic writing? Why or why not?

5. Summarize Sarah Wilensky's views (23–28) on the issue Gabriel discusses. Do you agree with her? Do you agree with Helene Hegemann's statement, "There's no such thing as originality anyway, just authenticity" (22)?

6. Do you think the anecdote in paragraph 32 is a strong ending for this article? Does the paragraph need a more forceful concluding statement? Explain.

This essay appeared on the *New Yorker*'s "Book Bench" blog on August 4, 2010.

TOO HARD *NOT* TO CHEAT IN THE INTERNET AGE?

ELIZABETH MINKEL

A deeply troubling article sat atop the *New York Times'* most-emailed list yesterday (no, not the one about catching horrible diseases at the gym). "Plagiarism Lines Blur for Students in Digital Age," the headline proclaimed, pinpointing a problem, weaving a theory, and excusing youthful copycats in one fell swoop. The story here is that a large number of college students today are acting as college students always have—baldly lifting whole passages for their term papers from other sources. But it's the Digital Age now, and between unverifiable, unattributed information sitting around online and the general ease with which young people obtain, alter, and share creative content on the Internet, students can't seem to figure out that cheating on a paper is wrong. In fact, a lot of them can't even tell that they're cheating, and the Internet is to blame. 1

Really? When I was in college (I graduated three years ago), I was well aware of the necessity of avoiding minefields of unattributed—and often incorrect—information on the Web. *Wikipedia* was never an acceptable source, perhaps because my professors knew they'd get students like the one from the University of Maryland who, when "reprimanded for copying from *Wikipedia* . . . said he thought its entries—unsigned and collectively written—did not need to be credited since they counted, essentially, as common knowledge." There are probably only two types of people pulling these excuses: the crafty, using the Digital Age argument to their advantage, and the completely clueless, who, like plenty in preceding generations, just don't understand the concept of plagiarism. The *Times* asked current students to weigh in (helpfully labelling them "Generation Plagiarism"), and one wrote: 2

"I never 'copy and paste' but I will take information from the Internet and change out a few words then put it in my paper. So far, I have not encountered any problems with this. Thought [*sic*] the information/words are technically mine because of a few undetectable word swaps, I still consider the information to be that of someone else." 3

The student goes on to say that, "In the digital age, plagiarism isn't and shouldn't be as big of a deal as it used to be when people used books for research." The response leaves me just as confused as I believe he is,

"I'm pretty convinced that he'd still be fuzzy on plagiarism if he'd lived back when people actually used books." 4

but I'm pretty convinced that he'd still be fuzzy on plagiarism if he'd lived back when people actually used books. But what I've found most frustrating in the ensuing debate is the assertion that these students are a part of some new *Reality Hunger*–type wave of open-source everything—if every song is sampled, why shouldn't writers do the same? The question is interesting, complicated, and divisive, but it has little bearing on a Psych 101 paper.

Excusing plagiarism as some sort of modern-day academic mash-up   5 won't teach students anything more than how to lie and get away with it. We should be teaching students how to produce original work—and that there's plenty of original thinking across the Internet—and leave the plagiarizing to the politicians.

⊘ AT ISSUE: SOURCES FOR UNDERSTANDING PLAGIARISM

1. Minkel's essay is a refutation of Trip Gabriel's article (p. 389), whose headline she accuses of "pinpointing a problem, weaving a theory, and excusing youthful copycats in one fell swoop" (para.1). Do you agree that Gabriel's article excuses plagiarism, or do you think it simply identifies a problem? Explain.

2. In paragraph 1, Minkel summarizes Gabriel's article. Is this a fair and accurate summary?

3. When Minkel quotes the student in paragraphs 3 and 4, is she setting up a **straw man**? Why or why not?

4. How would you characterize Minkel's tone? For example, is she angry? Frustrated? Condescending? Annoyed? Is this tone appropriate for her audience? (Note that this essay first appeared in the *New Yorker*, a magazine likely to be read by educated readers.)

5. In paragraph 2, Minkel identifies herself as a recent college graduate. Why? Is she appealing here to *ethos*, *pathos*, or *logos*?

6. Evaluate Minkel's last paragraph, particularly her concluding statement. Does this paragraph accurately express her reasons for criticizing Gabriel's article? What, if anything, do you think she should add to her conclusion? Why?

This essay appeared in *Newsday* on May 18, 2003.

THE TRUTH ABOUT PLAGIARISM

RICHARD A. POSNER

Plagiarism is considered by most writers, teachers, journalists, scholars, and even members of the general public to be the capital intellectual crime. Being caught out in plagiarism can blast a politician's career, earn a college student expulsion, and destroy a writer's, scholar's, or journalist's reputation. In recent days, for example, the *New York Times* has referred to "widespread fabrication and plagiarism" by reporter Jayson Blair as "a low point in the 152-year history of the newspaper."

In James Hynes' splendid satiric novella of plagiarism, *Casting the Runes*, the plagiarist, having by black magic murdered one of the historians whom he plagiarized and tried to murder a second, is himself killed by the very same black magic, deployed by the widow of his murder victim.

There is a danger of overkill. Plagiarism can be a form of fraud, but it is no accident that, unlike real theft, it is not a crime. If a thief steals your car, you are out the market value of the car, but if a writer copies material from a book you wrote, you don't have to replace the book. At worst, the undetected plagiarist obtains a reputation that he does not deserve (that is the element of fraud in plagiarism). The real victim of his fraud is not the person whose work he copies, but those of his competitors who scruple to enhance their own reputations by such means.

> "There is a danger of overkill."

The most serious plagiarisms are by students and professors, whose undetected plagiarisms disrupt the system of student and scholarly evaluation. The least serious are those that earned the late Stephen Ambrose and Doris Kearns Goodwin such obloquy° last year. Popular historians, they jazzed up their books with vivid passages copied from previous historians without quotation marks, though with footnote attributions that made their "crime" easy to detect.

Abusive language

(One reason that plagiarism, like littering, is punished heavily, even though an individual act of plagiarism usually does little or no harm, is that it is normally very difficult to detect—but not in the case of Ambrose and Goodwin.) Competing popular historians might have been injured, but I'm not aware of anyone actually claiming this.

Confusion of plagiarism with theft is one reason plagiarism engenders indignation; another is a confusion of it with copyright infringement. Wholesale copying of copyrighted material is an infringement of a property right, and legal remedies are available to the copyright holder. But the copying of brief passages, even from copyrighted materials, is permissible under the doctrine of "fair use," while wholesale copying from material that is in the public domain—material that never was copyrighted, or on which the copyright has expired—presents no copyright issue at all.

Plagiarism of work in the public domain is more common than otherwise. 7 Consider a few examples: *West Side Story* is a thinly veiled copy (with music added) of *Romeo and Juliet*, which in turn plagiarized Arthur Brooke's *The Tragicall Historye of Romeo and Juliet*, published in 1562, which in turn copied from several earlier Romeo and Juliets, all of which were copies of Ovid's story of Pyramus and Thisbe.

Paradise Lost plagiarizes the book of Genesis in the Old Testament. Classical 8 musicians plagiarize folk melodies (think only of Dvorak, Bartok, and Copland) and often "quote" (as musicians say) from earlier classical works. Edouard Manet's most famous painting, *Déjeuner sur l'herbe*, copies earlier paintings by Raphael, Titian, and Courbet, and *My Fair Lady* plagiarized Shaw's play *Pygmalion*, while Woody Allen's movie *Play It Again, Sam* "quotes" a famous scene from *Casablanca*. Countless movies are based on books, such as *The Thirty-Nine Steps* on John Buchan's novel of that name or *For Whom the Bell Tolls* on Hemingway's novel.

Many of these "plagiarisms" were authorized, and perhaps none was 9 deceptive; they are what Christopher Ricks in his excellent book *Allusions to the Poets* helpfully terms *allusion* rather than *plagiarism*. But what they show is that copying with variations is an important form of creativity, and this should make us prudent and measured in our condemnations of plagiarism.

Especially when the term is extended from literal copying to the copying 10 of ideas. Another phrase for copying an idea, as distinct from the form in which it is expressed, is dissemination of ideas. If one needs a license to repeat another person's idea, or if one risks ostracism by one's professional community for failing to credit an idea to its originator, who may be forgotten or unknown, the dissemination of ideas is impeded.

I have heard authors of history textbooks criticized for failing to document 11 their borrowing of ideas from previous historians. This is an absurd criticism. The author of a textbook makes no claim to originality; rather the contrary— the most reliable, if not necessarily the most exciting, textbook is one that confines itself to ideas already well accepted, not at all novel.

It would be better if the term *plagiarism* were confined to literal copying, 12 and moreover literal copying that is not merely unacknowledged but deceptive. Failing to give credit where credit is due should be regarded as a lesser, indeed usually merely venial, offense.

The concept of plagiarism has expanded, and the sanctions for it, though 13 they remain informal rather than legal, have become more severe, in tandem with the rise of individualism. Journal articles are no longer published anonymously, and ghostwriters demand that their contributions be acknowledged.

Replaceable

Individualism and a cult of originality go hand in hand. Each of us sup- 14 poses that our contribution to society is unique rather than fungible° and so deserves public recognition, which plagiarism clouds.

This is a modern view. We should be aware that the high value placed on 15 originality is a specific cultural, and even field-specific, phenomenon, rather than an aspect of the universal moral law.

Judges, who try to conceal rather than to flaunt their originality, far 16 from crediting their predecessors with original thinking like to pretend that there is no original thinking in law, that judges are just a transmission belt for rules and principles laid down by the framers of statutes or the Constitution.

Resorting to plagiarism to obtain a good grade or a promotion is fraud   17 and should be punished, though it should not be confused with "theft." But I think the zeal to punish plagiarism reflects less a concern with the real injuries that it occasionally inflicts than with a desire on the part of leaders of professional communities, such as journalists and historians, to enhance their profession's reputation.

Journalists (like politicians) have a bad reputation for truthfulness, and   18 historians, in this "postmodernist"° era, are suspected of having embraced an extreme form of relativism and of having lost their regard for facts. Both groups hope by taking a very hard line against plagiarism and fabrication to reassure the public that they are serious diggers after truth whose efforts, a form of "sweat equity," deserve protection against copycats.

Postmodernism is a school of criticism that denies concepts such as scientific certainty and absolute truth.

Their anxieties are understandable; but the rest of us will do well to keep   19 the matter in perspective, realizing that the term *plagiarism* is used loosely and often too broadly; that much plagiarism is harmless and (when the term is defined broadly) that some has social value.

⊘ AT ISSUE: SOURCES FOR UNDERSTANDING PLAGIARISM

1. According to Posner, how do most people define *plagiarism*? How is the definition he proposes different from theirs? Do you think this definition is too broad? Too narrow?

2. Why does Posner believe that the plagiarisms committed by students and professors are the most serious? Can you think of an argument against this position?

3. How do the examples Posner cites in paragraphs 7 and 8 strengthen his argument? Do you agree that the examples he gives here constitute plagiarism? Why or why not?

4. Explain the connection the author makes in paragraph 16 between judges and plagiarism. (Note that Posner himself is a federal judge.)

5. Why, according to Posner, do journalists and historians think plagiarism should be punished severely?

6. According to Posner, "the truth about plagiarism" is that "much plagiarism is harmless and (when the term is defined broadly) that some has social value" (para. 19). Does the evidence he presents in this essay support this conclusion? What connection do you see between this position and his comments about the rise of individualism and the "cult of originality" in paragraphs 13–15?

This article first appeared on July 25, 2014, on Politico.com.

PLAGIARISM AND BUZZFEED'S ACHILLES' HEEL

DYLAN BYERS

1. In 2013, the satirical website *The Onion* wrote an article titled "BuzzFeed Writer Resigns in Disgrace after Plagiarizing '10 Llamas Who Wish They Were Models.'" It appealed to reporters because it was a clever knock on the state of digital journalism—and because it resonated with a widely held perception about BuzzFeed.

2. High-profile plagiarism cases are always met with a certain amount of schadenfreude from the media's chattering classes, as well as calls for the defendant's head, but the response to BuzzFeed editor Benny Johnson's serial plagiarism has been especially intense.

3. There's a reason for that: In the eyes of many journalists, BuzzFeed is constantly walking a fine line between aggregation, or "curation," and theft. Go to BuzzFeed.com and click on any one of its lists. In very fine print, buried below each photo, there will be a link to another site—usually Reddit—which is where the photograph came from.

4. Is this plagiarism? Of course not. Does it feel a little seedy? Yeah, a bit.

5. In 2012, as BuzzFeed was growing into the Internet sensation it is today, *Slate*'s Farhad Manjoo (now with the *New York Times*) wrote a lengthy post explaining "the secret to BuzzFeed's monster online success."

6. "How does this one site come up with so many simple ideas that people want to spread far and wide? What's their secret?" he wrote. "The answer, in short, is that BuzzFeed's staff finds stuff elsewhere on the Web, most often at Reddit. They polish and repackage what they find. And often—and, from what I can tell, deliberately—their posts are hard to trace back to the original source material."

7. Because BuzzFeed is so popular, Manjoo wrote, its "pilfered" lists all but eclipse the original sources of content: "Once you understand how central Reddit is to BuzzFeed, it's like spotting the wizard behind the curtain. Whenever you see a popular BuzzFeed post, search Reddit, and all will be revealed."

8. Jonah Peretti, BuzzFeed's founder, told Manjoo that there was "nothing wrong" with picking up other people's content "because few things on the Web are really original."

9. Gawker's Adrian Chen (now with the *New Inquiry*) also wrote an extensive analysis of BuzzFeed's "plagiarism problem" in 2012.

10. "BuzzFeed has built a lucrative business on organizing the internet's confusing spectacle into listicles easily comprehended by even the most numbed office workers," Chen wrote. "But the site's approach to all content as building blocks for viral lists puts it in an awkward position in relation to internet etiquette and journalistic ethics."

"For example," Chen wrote, "the BuzzFeed listicle '21 Pictures That Will 11 Restore Your Faith in Humanity,' appears to be an almost exact replica of a couple of posts on an obscure site called Nedhardy . . . BuzzFeed slapped together many of the same pictures, presented it as an original idea, and it went Avian-Flu-level-viral, ending up with more than seven million page views."

Is *this* plagiarism? It's certainly closer to it. Somehow, the Internet came 12 to accept it: The *New York Times* reported, Huffington Post aggregated, BuzzFeed curated. Maybe "repackaging funny things found on Reddit is just how the Internet works these days," Chen wrote.

Text, of course, was a different story. You couldn't publish someone else's 13 articles or *Wikipedia* entries and just throw a link to the original source at the bottom. When BuzzFeed reporters wrote, they were subject to the same rules as everyone else. Sure you could draw facts from elsewhere—everyone does —but you had to write it in your own language.

At some point, Johnson probably got lazy and started inserting text into 14 his posts the same way he had been inserting photographs—by pressing Ctrl+C and Ctrl+V. His mistake was that he forgot to put quote marks around it and add "according to."

It didn't help reporters' perception of BuzzFeed that, when the first 15 instances of plagiarism were brought to editor-in-chief Ben Smith's attention, he called them "serious failures" of attribution, rather than "plagiarism," and simply "corrected" the posts.

"Ben, you can't 'correct' articles that were clearly plagiarized. I know you 16 know this!" Gawker's J. K. Trotter wrote on Twitter.

BuzzFeed is currently conducting an internal review of Johnson's work 17 before deciding on how to proceed. Whatever Johnson's fate, his plagiarism is one more instance in which the public spotted the wizard behind BuzzFeed's curtain. And the wizard seems a little seedy.

> "Meanwhile, *The Onion*'s satire has become reality."

Meanwhile, *The Onion*'s satire has become 18 reality.

"Journalism today," one *Bloomberg News* 19 journalist tweeted: "accused of plagiarism 'for an article it did about former President George H. W. Bush's socks.'"

Update (July 26) 20

Late Friday evening Smith announced Johnson had been fired after an 21 internal review found 40 instances of plagiarism.

⊘ AT ISSUE: SOURCES FOR UNDERSTANDING PLAGIARISM

1. Do you consider the material typically posted on BuzzFeed to be plagiarized? Explain. (If you are not familiar with BuzzFeed, visit the site and read a few posts.)

2. What does "Achilles' heel" mean? In what sense does plagiarism constitute BuzzFeed's Achilles' heel?

3. Why does Byers begin and end his discussion with paragraphs about *The Onion* (para. 1, 18–19)? Is this an effective strategy? Why or why not?

4. In paragraph 3, Byers says that many journalists believe that "BuzzFeed is constantly walking a fine line between aggregation, or 'curation,' and theft." What distinction is he making here? Do you see a difference between BuzzFeed's "aggregation" or "curation" and outright theft? Does Byers?

5. Byers quotes Farhad Manjoo, Adrian Chen, and others. What positions do his sources take on the issue of BuzzFeed and plagiarism?

6. Do you think it matters that Benny Johnson's "repackaging" of material from other sources was done deliberately rather than accidentally? Why or why not?

7. An update to this article notes that Johnson was fired from BuzzFeed "after an internal review found 40 instances of plagiarism." Do you think this punishment was justified? Why or why not?

8. Does Byers take a position on the issue of BuzzFeed and plagiarism? If so, what is that position? Do you see this essay as an argument? Which of the four elements of an argumentative essay are present here? Which are absent?

This summary was posted on July 24, 2014, on the WriteCheck.com blog.

OK OR NOT?

K. BALIBALOS AND J. GOPALAKRISHNAN

OK or not? This is an age-old question on plagiarism that arises during the 1
writing process, whether from researching a topic, incorporating and paraphrasing sources, or supporting arguments within a paper. Students commonly
find themselves in situations in which ethical questions are raised, and, all too
often, students wonder whether the decisions they made were the right ones.

This new poll series brings to light common scenarios—specifically 2
focused on plagiarism and perhaps a few examples on other forms of academic misconduct—and helps students better think critically about situations
in order to make ethical choices. All polls can be found on the WriteCheck
page on Facebook.

POLL QUESTION #1
**"OK or not? You and a partner collaborate on a paper by sharing notes and
paraphrasing the same ideas."**

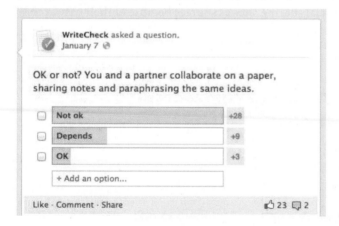

We started off the series by asking about collaboration because collaborating with 3
peers is a common thing to do among students. Students "collaborate" to
complete schoolwork and to help their friends in need. But collaborating with
peers can sometimes cross ethical boundaries. For example, in this question,
has the student copied-and-pasted the other student's work? The question
doesn't really get into that concern, but we do know that the students shared
the same ideas by "paraphrasing." This is where the question gets tricky. If

done properly, meaning the student wrote the idea in his/her own words and included citations, then paraphrasing is acceptable. Plagiarism is, by definition, the taking of another person's work or ideas.

The Results

The majority of respondents (28) chose "not OK" in response to student collaboration on a paper. However, two viewers who weighed in had a different perspective. 4

English Instructor, Beth Calvano, made the following comment: "If the paper is supposed to be individual, this scenario is not okay. If, according to plagiarism rules, it is not acceptable to use another person's ideas without citing that individual, collaborating in this way is not ethical. Your paper should consist of your own notes and original ideas." 5

Facebook fan Quenna Corchado agreed with Calvano, adding: "I think it's okay if they are citing. It doesn't matter if they are using the same sources as long as they cite it. They are helping each other out, so it makes sense that they are using the same notes and paraphrasing the same thing. What is important is to cite everything accordingly, which doesn't make it plagiarism." 6

Overall, it can be concluded from these responses that it is "OK" to share notes and paraphrase the same idea with proper attribution, unless the assignment is supposed to be done individually. 7

POLL QUESTION #2
"OK or not? You do a Google search of your subject and use *Wikipedia*, blogs, and other social sharing sites as sources because of their easy access."

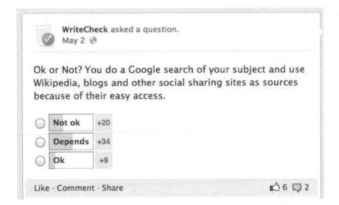

This situation resonates with students because of the amount of free, available information due in part to the mass connectivity of the digital age. Nowadays, *Wikipedia* is synonymous with accessibility and reader-friendly information since it provides accurate information on nearly every topic one might be researching. The number of blogs on the internet grows exponentially by the day since anyone has the ability to create a blog and share their thoughts. And, of course, social sites are a normal part of millions of people's lives. However, 8 just because information is available on the web doesn't mean that it's reputable to use as a source in your academic paper.

The Results

Based on 34 respondents, "depends" was the top answer, followed by "not OK" (20 respondents). 9

To provide some insight, Jason Chu from Plagiarism.org weighed in with the following comment: "It's OK to use Google search, *Wikipedia*, and social sharing sites as the starting point for doing research for a paper. But you should NOT rely on these sources alone. In fact, *Wikipedia* entries typically list references that are great to use in your research in support of your paper. But, by and large, sources that rely heavily on crowd-sourced or shared content — like *Wikipedia* or Yahoo! Answers — do not carry the same authority as a peer-reviewed journal article, for example." 10

Jessica from WriteCheck argued that it was "not OK," citing educator insight that social sites should never be cited in research papers. Academic writing requires looking at primary or secondary sources, which are typically presented in academic journals, whereas *Wikipedia* is written for the general public. 11

Overall, it can be concluded that the answer is "depends." Social sites like *Wikipedia* can be used as a starting point for research papers, but adding academic credibility to your sources will result in a more thorough and scholarly research paper. 12

POLL QUESTION #3
"OK or not? You get 2 assignments with enough overlap to submit the same paper to both."

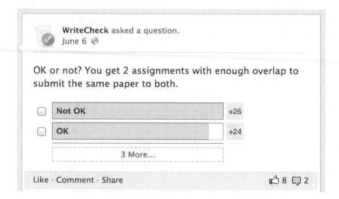

The most recent poll was inspired by a recent article on the *Ethicist*, a blog on the *New York Times*, entitled, "Can I Use the Same Paper for Multiple College Courses?" Some readers see it as a stroke of genius, while others view it as the mark of laziness. Some suggest that it is cheating, while others opine that you are only cheating yourself. *International Business Times* writer James DiGioia 13 disagreed with *The Ethicist* in his article, "*The Ethicist* Is Wrong: Self-Plagiarism Is Cheating." Given those different opinions, we wanted to see what our WriteCheck community thought. "Is it OK to submit one paper for two assignments?"

The Results

The results were evenly split among the poll respondents between "not OK" 14 and "OK." *The Ethicist* describes why this situation is tricky, explaining that emotionally, our hearts cry that "this *must* be unethical, somehow," but aside from these emotions, he argued that there were no grounds that inherently make submitting papers to multiple assignments unethical.

Unlike James DiGioia, Jason Chu of Plagiarism.org agreed somewhere in 15 the middle, saying: "OK — if instructor approval is received. Not OK otherwise."

In summary, although debatable, it could be concluded that submitting a 16 paper to multiple assignments is "OK" with approval from both instructors. Otherwise, it may be a violation of university-wide academic integrity codes and generally accepted principles that assignments are unique to a class.

Conclusion

These three scenarios are real-life situations that students may face at one 17 point in their academic journeys. Some scenarios may appear more straight-forward than others, however, no plagiarism allegation is simple. Self-plagiarism, for example, may make more sense in a professional or scholarly environment because of copyright issues. Self-plagiarism is a gray area, and a relatively new term within academia, and is still to be explored. *Wikipedia* also is a newly introduced site, becoming popular only within the last decade.

While definitions and rules of plagiarism are debated, learning the defini- 18 tions and how to cite properly, as well as working with instructors when a question arises are all ways to avoid plagiarism and academic misconduct.

Have you encountered situations where you asked yourself "OK or not?" 19

⊘ AT ISSUE: SOURCES FOR UNDERSTANDING PLAGIARISM

1. This blog post reports the results of a survey, and it also makes a point. In one sentence, summarize the main point of the post.

2. Which of the writers' three scenarios, if any, do you see as "not OK"? Why? With which majority opinions, if any, do you disagree? Explain.

3. For what purpose did the writers design this poll? Where do they state this purpose?

4. Who is the intended audience for the three poll questions? Is this the same audience as the one the writers expected to read the results of the poll? How can you tell?

5. In poll question #2, what conclusions do the writers draw about the use of *Wikipedia*? What problems does this site, as well as "blogs and other social sharing sites," present for college students?

6. Do you think the writers' conclusion takes a strong enough stand on the issue discussed? Is this post actually an argument? Why or why not?

This essay originally appeared in the *Los Angeles Times* on June 17, 2012.

ESSAY MILLS: A COARSE LESSON IN CHEATING

DAN ARIELY

Sometimes as I decide what kind of papers to assign to my students, I worry about essay mills, companies whose sole purpose is to generate essays for high school and college students (in exchange for a fee, of course). 1

The mills claim that the papers are meant to be used as reference material to help students write their own, original papers. But with names such as echeat.com, it's pretty clear what their real purpose is. 2

Professors in general are concerned about essay mills and their effect on learning, but not knowing exactly what they provide, I wasn't sure how concerned to be. So together with my lab manager Aline Grüneisen, I decided to check the services out. We ordered a typical college term paper from four different essay mills. The topic of the paper? Cheating. 3

Here is the prompt we gave the four essay mills: 4

"When and why do people cheat? Consider the social circumstances involved in dishonesty, and provide a thoughtful response to the topic of cheating. Address various forms of cheating (personal, at work, etc.) and how each of these can be rationalized by a social culture of cheating." 5

We requested a term paper for a university-level social psychology class, 12 pages long, using 15 sources (cited and referenced in a bibliography). The paper was to conform to American Psychological Assn. style guidelines and needed to be completed in the next two weeks. All four of the essay mills agreed to provide such a paper, charging us in advance, between $150 and $216 for the paper. 6

Right on schedule, the essays came, and I have to say that, to some degree, they allayed my fears that students can rely on the services to get good grades. What we got back from the mills can best be described as gibberish. A few of the papers attempted to mimic APA style, but none achieved it without glaring errors. Citations were sloppy. Reference lists contained outdated and unknown sources, including blog posts. Some of the links to reference material were broken. 7

> "What we got back from the mills can best be described as gibberish."

And the writing quality? Awful. The authors of all four papers seemed to have a very tenuous grasp of the English language, not to mention how to format an essay. Paragraphs jumped bluntly from one topic to another, often simply listing various forms of cheating or providing a long stream of examples that were never explained or connected to the "thesis" of the paper. 8

One paper contained this paragraph: "Cheating by healers. Healing is 9
different. There is harmless healing, when healers-cheaters and wizards offer
omens, lapels, damage to withdraw, the husband-wife back and stuff. We read
in the newspaper and just smile. But these days fewer people believe in
wizards."

This comes from another: "If the large allowance of study undertook on 10
scholar betraying is any suggestion of academia and professors' powerful
yearn to decrease scholar betraying, it appeared expected these mind-set
would component into the creation of their school room guidelines."

And finally, these gems: 11

"By trusting blindfold only in stable love, loyalty, responsibility and hon- 12
esty the partners assimilate with the credulous and naive persons of the past."

"Women have a much greater necessity to feel special." 13

"The future generation must learn for historical mistakes and develop the 14
sense of pride and responsibility for its actions."

It's hard to believe that students purchasing such papers would ever do 15
so again.

And the story does not end there. We submitted the four essays to 16
WriteCheck.com, a website that inspects papers for plagiarism, and found that
two of the papers were 35% to 39% copied from existing works. We decided to
take action on the two papers with substantial plagiarizing and contacted the
essay mills requesting our money back. Despite the solid proof we provided to
them, the companies insisted they did not plagiarize. One company even threatened to expose us by calling the dean and saying we had purchased the paper.

It's comforting in a way that the technological revolution has not yet 17
solved students' problems. They still have no other option but to actually work
on their papers (or maybe cheat in the old-fashioned way and copy from
friends). But I do worry about the existence of essay mills and the signal that
they send to our students.

As for our refund, we are still waiting. 18

⊘ AT ISSUE: SOURCES FOR UNDERSTANDING PLAGIARISM

1. Consider the title of this essay. What does the word *coarse* mean?
   What does it suggest in this context?

2. What is an essay mill? Look up the word *mill*. Which of the definitions
   provided applies to the word as it is used in the phrase *essay mill*?

3. Why does Ariely decide to investigate the services provided by essay
   mills? What does he want to find out? Is he successful?

4. What does Ariely conclude about the four companies he surveys?
   Does he provide enough evidence to support his conclusion? If not,
   what kind of evidence should he add?

5. In paragraph 15, Ariely says, "It's hard to believe that students purchasing such papers would ever do so again." Given the evidence Ariely presents, how do you explain the continued popularity of essay mills?

6. What information does Ariely provide in his conclusion? Do you think he is departing from his essay's central focus here, or do you think the concluding paragraph is an appropriate and effective summary of his ideas? Explain.

TERM PAPERS FOR SALE ADVERTISEMENT (WEB PAGE)

⊘ AT ISSUE: SOURCES FOR UNDERSTANDING PLAGIARISM

1. The Web page above is from a site that offers papers for sale to students. What argument does this Web page make? What counter-argument could you present?

2. Identify appeals to *logos*, *pathos*, and *ethos* on the TermPaperWriter .org page. Which appeal dominates?

3. Study the images of students on the page. What message do these images convey?

4. Unlike the TermPaperWriter.org page, many other sites that offer papers for sale include errors in grammar, spelling, and punctuation. Search the Web for some other sites that offer papers for sale. What errors can you find? Do such errors weaken the message of these ads, or are they irrelevant?

5. One site promises its papers are "100% plagiarism free." Does this promise make sense? Explain.

TEMPLATE FOR WRITING AN ARGUMENT ABOUT PLAGIARISM

Write a one-paragraph argument in which you take a position on where to draw the line with plagiarism. Follow the template below, filling in the blanks to create your argument.

> To many people, plagiarism is theft; to others, however, it is not that simple. For example, some define *plagiarism* as _____ _____ ; others see it as _____ _____. Another thing to consider is _____ _____. In addition, _____ _____. Despite these differences of opinion, plagiarism is often dealt with harshly and can ruin careers and reputations. All things considered, _____ _____.

⊙ EXERCISE 11.4

Discuss your feelings about plagiarism with two or three of your class-mates. Consider how you define *plagiarism*, what you believe causes it, whether there are degrees of dishonesty, and so on, but focus on the *effects* of plagiarism—on those who commit it and on those who are its victims. Then, write a paragraph that summarizes the key points of your discussion.

⊙ EXERCISE 11.5

Write an argumentative essay on the topic, "Where Should We Draw the Line with Plagiarism?" Begin by defining what you mean by *plagiarism*, and then narrow your discussion down to a particular group—for example, high school or college students, historians, scientists, or journalists. Cite the sources on pages 383–409, and be sure to document the sources you use and to include a works-cited page. (See Chapter 10 for information on documenting sources.)

⊙ EXERCISE 11.6

Review the four pillars of argument discussed in Chapter 1. Does your essay include all four elements of an effective argument? Add anything that is missing. Then, label the elements of your argument.

⊙ WRITING ASSIGNMENTS: USING SOURCES RESPONSIBLY

1. Write an argument in which you take a position on who (or what) is to blame for plagiarism among college students. Is plagiarism always the student's fault, or are other people (or other factors) at least partly to blame?

2. Write an essay in which you argue that an honor code will (or will not) eliminate (or at least reduce) plagiarism and other kinds of academic dishonesty at your school.

3. Reread the essays by Posner and Balibalos and Gopalakrishnan in this chapter. Then, write an argument in which you argue that only intentional plagiarism should be punished.

4. Do you consider student plagiarism a victimless crime that is best left unpunished? If so, why? If not, how does it affect its victims—for example, the student who plagiarizes, the instructor, the other students in the class, and the school?

Writing Literary Arguments

When you write an essay about literature, you have a number of options. For example, you can write a **response** (expressing your reactions to a poem, play, or story), or you can write an **explication** (focusing on a work's individual elements, such as a poem's imagery, meter, figurative language, and diction). You can also write an **analysis** of a work's theme, a character in a play or a story, or a work's historical or cultural context. Another option, which is discussed in the pages that follow, is to write a literary argument.

What Is a Literary Argument?

When you write a literary argument, you do more than just respond to, explicate, or analyze a work of literature. When you develop a **literary argument**, you take a position about a literary work (or works), support that position with evidence, and refute possible opposing arguments. You might, for example, take the position that a familiar interpretation of a well-known work is limited in some way, that a work's impact today is different from its impact when it was written, or that two apparently very different works have some significant similarities.

It is important to understand that not every essay about literature is a literary argument. For example, you might use a discussion of Tillie Olsen's short story "I Stand Here Ironing," with its sympathetic portrait of a young mother during the Great Depression, to support an argument in favor of President Franklin D. Roosevelt's expansion of social welfare programs. Alternatively, you might use Martín Espada's poem "Why I Went to College" to support your own decision to continue your education. However, writing a literary argument involves much more than discussing a literary work in order to support a particular position or referring to a character to shed light on your own intellectual development or to explain a choice you made. A literary argument *takes a stand* about a work (or works) of literature.

Stating an Argumentative Thesis

When you develop an argumentative thesis about literature, your goal is to state a thesis that has an edge—one that takes a stand on your topic. Like any effective thesis, the thesis of a literary argument should be clearly worded and specific; it should also be more than a statement of fact.

INEFFECTIVE THESIS (TOO GENERAL)	In "A&P," Sammy faces a difficult decision.
EFFECTIVE THESIS (MORE SPECIFIC)	Sammy's decision to quit his job reveals more about the conformist society in which "A&P" is set than about Sammy himself.
INEFFECTIVE THESIS (STATES A FACT)	The theme of *Hamlet* is often seen as an Oedipal conflict.
EFFECTIVE THESIS (TAKES A STAND)	Although many critics have identified an Oedipal conflict in *Hamlet*, Shakespeare's play is also a story of a young man who is struggling with familiar problems—love, family, and his future.

Here are three possible thesis statements that you could support in a literary argument:

- Charlotte Perkins Gilman's short story "The Yellow Wallpaper," usually seen as a feminist story, is actually a ghost story.

- The two characters in August Strindberg's play *The Stronger* seem to be rivals for the affection of a man, but they are really engaged in a professional rivalry to see who gives the better performance.

- Although many readers might see Wilfred Owen's "Dulce et Decorum Est" as the more powerful poem because of its graphic imagery of war, Carl Sandburg's understated "Grass" is likely to have a greater impact on modern readers, who have been overexposed to violent images.

(For more on developing a thesis statement, see Chapter 7.)

Choosing Evidence

Like any argument, a literary argument relies on evidence. Some of this evidence can be found in the literary work itself. For example, to make a point about a character's antisocial behavior, you would cite specific examples of such behavior from the work. To make a point about a poet's use of biblical allusions, you would present examples of such allusions from the poem.

> **NOTE**
>
> Be careful not to substitute plot summary for evidence. For example, summarizing everything that happens to a character will not convince your readers that the character is motivated by envy. Choose only *relevant* examples—in this case, specific instances of a character's jealous behavior, including relevant quotations from the literary work.

Evidence can also come from **literary criticism**—scholarly articles by experts in the field that analyze and evaluate works of literature. For example, to argue that a particular critical theory is inaccurate, outdated, or oversimplified, you would quote critics who support that theory before you explain why you disagree with their interpretation. (For more on evaluating potential sources for your essay, see Chapter 8.)

Writing a Literary Argument

The structure of a literary argument is similar to the structure of any other argument: it includes a **thesis statement** in the introduction, supporting **evidence**, **refutation** of opposing arguments, and a strong **concluding statement**. However, unlike other arguments, literary arguments follow specific conventions for writing about literature:

- In your essay's first paragraph, include the author's full name and the title of each work you are discussing.

- Use present tense when discussing events in works of literature. For example, if you are discussing "I Stand Here Ironing," you would say, "The mother *worries* [not *worried*] about her ability to provide for her child." There are two exceptions to this rule. Use past tense when referring to historical events: "The Great Depression *made* things difficult for mothers like the narrator." Also use past tense to refer to events that came before the action described in the work: "The mother is particularly vulnerable because her husband *left* her alone to support her children."

- Italicize titles of plays and novels. Put titles of poems and short stories in quotation marks.

- If you quote more than four lines of prose (or more than three lines of poetry), indent the entire quotation one inch from the left-hand margin. Do not include quotation marks, and add the parenthetical documentation after the end punctuation. Introduce the quotation with a colon, and do not add extra line spaces above or below it.

- When mentioning writers and literary critics in the body of your essay, use their full names ("Emily Dickinson") the first time you mention them and their last names only ("Dickinson," not "Miss Dickinson" or "Emily") after that.

- Use **MLA documentation style** in your paper, and include a works-cited list. (See Chapter 10 for information on MLA documentation.)

- In your in-text citations (set in parentheses), cite page numbers for stories, act and scene numbers for plays, and line numbers for poems. Use the word *line* or *lines* for the first in-text citation of lines from each poem. After the first citation, you may omit the word *line* or *lines*.

The following literary argument, "Confessions of a Misunderstood Poem: An Analysis of 'The Road Not Taken,'" takes a stand in favor of a particular way of interpreting poetry.

CONFESSIONS OF A MISUNDERSTOOD POEM: AN ANALYSIS OF "THE ROAD NOT TAKEN"

MEGAN MCGOVERN

Introduction (identifies titles and authors of works to be discussed)

In his poem "Introduction to Poetry," Billy Collins suggests that rather than dissecting a poem to find its meaning, students should use their imaginations to experience poetry. According to Collins, they should "drop a mouse into a poem / and watch him probe his way out" (lines 5–6). However, Collins overstates his case when he implies that analyzing a poem to find out what it might mean is a brutal or deadly process, comparable to tying the poem to a chair and "beating

1

it with a hose" (15). Rather than killing a poem's spirit, a careful and methodical dissection can often help the reader better appreciate its subtler meanings. In fact, with patient coaxing, a poem often has much to "confess." One such poem is Robert Frost's familiar but frequently misunderstood "The Road Not Taken." An examination of Frost's "The Road Not Taken" reveals a complex and somewhat troubling message about the arbitrariness of our life choices and our need to idealize those choices.

On the surface, Frost's poem seems to have a fairly simple meaning. The poem's speaker talks about coming to a fork in the road and choosing the "less-traveled" path. Most readers see the fork in the road as a metaphor: the road represents life, and the fork repre-sents an individual's choices in life. By following the less-traveled road, the speaker is choosing the less conventional—and supposedly more emotionally rewarding—route. At the end of the poem, the speaker indicates his satisfaction when he says his choice "made all the difference" (line 20). However, Frost himself, referring to "The Road Not Taken," advised readers "'to be careful of that one; it's a tricky poem—very tricky,'" encouraging readers not to accept the most appealing or obvious interpretation (qtd. in Savoie 7–8). Literary critic Bojana Vujin urges readers to look for "poetic booby traps such as irony or deceit" in this poem and to enjoy the pleasures and rewards of discovering instances of "deliberate deceit on the poet's part" (195). In fact, after the speaker's tone and word choice are care-fully examined, the poem's message seems darker and more compli-cated than it did initially.

The speaker's tone in the first three stanzas suggests indecision, regret, and, ultimately, lack of power. Rather than bravely facing the choice between one common path and one uncommon path, the speaker spends most of the poem considering two seemingly equal roads, "sorry" not to be able to "travel both" (2). Even after choosing "the other" road in line 6, the speaker continues for two more stanzas to weigh his options. The problem is that the two roads are, in fact, indistinguishable. As several critics have observed, "the difference between the two roads, at least when

The word *lines* is omitted from the in-text citation after the first reference to lines of a poem.

Thesis statement

2 Refutation of opposing argument

3 Evidence: Analysis and explication of Frost poem

Evidence: Literary
criticism

it comes to the amount of treading they have been exposed to, is but
an illusion: "'they both that morning equally lay' and neither is
particularly travelled by" (Vujin 197). The roads are worn "really
about the same" (10). If there is virtually no difference between the
two, then why does Frost draw our attention to this fork in the
road—this seemingly critical moment of choice? If Frost had wanted
to dramatize a meaningful decision, the roads would be different in
some significant way.

Evidence: Literary
criticism

One critic, Frank Lentricchia, argues that Frost is demonstrating   4
"'that our life-shaping choices are irrational, that we are fundamentally out of control'" (qtd. in Savoie 13). Similarly, another critic
contends that Frost wants his readers "to feel his characters'
inner conflicts and to feel as conflicted as his characters, who are

Evidence: Analysis and
explication of Frost poem

all too often lost in themselves" (Plunkett). These two critical views
help to explain the speaker's indecision in the first three stanzas.
The speaker impulsively chooses "the other" road but cannot accept
the arbitrariness of his choice; therefore, he cannot stop considering
the first road. He exclaims in the third stanza, "Oh, I kept the first
for another day!" (13). In the next two lines, when he finally gives up
the possibility of following that first road, he predicts, "Yet knowing
how way leads on to way, / I doubted if I should ever come back"
(14–15). Here, the speaker further demonstrates a lack of control
over his own decisions. He describes a future guided not by his own
active, meaningful choices but rather by some arbitrary force. In a
world where "way leads on to way," he is a passive traveler, not a
decisive individualist.

Evidence: Analysis and
explication of Frost poem

Given the indecision that characterizes the previous stanzas, the   5
poem's last two lines are surprisingly decisive: "I took the one less
traveled by / And that has made all the difference" (19–20). Is the
speaker contradicting himself? How has he suddenly become clear
about the rightness of his decision? In fact, the last stanza does not
make sense unless the reader perceives the irony in the speaker's tone.
The speaker is imagining himself in the future, "ages and ages hence,"
telling the story of his moment at the crossroads (17). He imagines
how he will, in hindsight, give his choice meaning and clarity that it
did not have at the time. As Vujin argues, the poem's speaker is

already "mythologizing his self and his life" (198). The narrator, rather than anticipating the satisfaction that will come from having made the right and braver choice, is anticipating rewriting his own life story to make sense of an ultimately arbitrary chain of events. Vujin explains, "This is not a poem about individuality; this is a poem about self-deceit and the rewriting of one's own history" (198). Reading the last stanza ironically allows readers to make sense of the poem as a whole.

Evidence: Literary criticism

There are many possible interpretations of "The Road Not Taken," most of which can be supported with evidence from the poem itself. However, to understand these interpretations, readers need to take the poem apart, look at how its parts fit together, and reach a thoughtful and logical conclusion. To do so, readers must go against some of Billy Collins's well-meaning advice and be willing to tie the poem—and themselves—to a chair: to read it carefully, ask questions, and stay with it until it confesses.

6 Conclusion

Works Cited

Collins, Billy. "Introduction to Poetry." *Sailing Alone around the Room*. Random House, 1998, p. 16.

Frost, Robert. "The Road Not Taken." *Mountain Interval*. Henry Holt, 1920, *Bartleby.com*, www.bartleby.com/119/1.html.

Plunkett, Adam. "Robert Frost Was Neither Light Nor Dark." *New Republic*, 13 Jun. 2014, newrepublic.com/article/118046/art-robert-frost-tim-kendall-reviewed-adam-plunkett.

Savoie, John. "A Poet's Quarrel: Jamesian Pragmatism and Frost's 'The Road Not Taken.'" *New England Quarterly*, vol. 77, no. 1, 2004, pp. 5–24. *Academic Search Premier*, www.ebscohost.com/academic/academic-search-premier.

Vujin, Bojana. "'I Took the Road Less Traveled By': Self-Deception in Frost's and Eliot's Early Poetry." *Annual Review of the Faculty of Philosophy*, vol. 36, no. 1, 2011, pp. 195–203.

⊘ The following literary argument, "Not Just a 'Girl,'" argues against the commonly held position that a key character in the 1925 Ernest Hemingway short story "Hills Like White Elephants" is a stereotype.

NOT JUST A "GIRL"
LOREN MARTINEZ

Introduction

    In Ernest Hemingway's famous story "Hills Like White Elephants," [1] a couple, "the American and the girl with him," talk and drink while waiting for a train to Madrid (Hemingway 69). Most readers agree that the subject of their discussion is whether "the girl," called Jig, should have an abortion. Most of the story is told through dialogue, and although the word *abortion* is never mentioned, most readers agree that the pregnancy is the source of the tension between them. However, there are other aspects of the story about which readers do not agree. For example, some critics believe that Hemingway's portrayal of "the girl" is unfair or sexist. More specifically, some see in her the qualities of "the typically submissive Hemingway woman" (Nolan 19). How-

Thesis statement

ever, a close reading of the story reveals the opposite to be true: "the girl" is not a one-dimensional stereotype but a complex, sympathetically drawn character.

Refutation of opposing arguments

    Most critics who see Hemingway's portrayal of Jig as sexist base [2] their interpretation on Hemingway's reputation and not on the story itself. For example, feminist critic Katherine M. Rogers points out that because Hemingway himself "openly expressed fear of and hostility to women" (263), it "seems fair" to see his male characters "as representative of Hemingway himself" (248). However, although "the American" in this story may see Jig as just "a pleasant pastime," it would be an oversimplification to confuse the character's opinion of her with the writer's as Rogers would encourage us to do (251). For example, one could argue (as many critics have done) that because the name "Jig" has sexual connotations, it reveals the author's sexism (Renner 38). However, as critic Howard Hannum points out, she is referred to by this name only twice in the story, both times by the male character himself, not by the narrator (qtd. in Renner 38). Critic Stanley Renner agrees with Hannum, rejecting the idea that Hemingway's choice to refer to the character as "the girl" is equally "belittling" (38).

Renner argues that this use of the word *girl* is necessary to show how the character changes and matures in this story. In fact, he sees "her achievement of mature self-knowledge and assertion [as] the main line of development in the story" (39). All in all, the evidence suggests that "the girl," not "the American," is actually the story's protagonist. Given this central focus on "the girl" and the complexity of her character, the accusations that Hemingway's sexism has led him to create a stereotype do not seem justified.

When students who are not familiar with Hemingway's reputation as a misogynist read "Hills Like White Elephants," they tend to sympathize more often with "the girl" than with "the American" (Bauer 126) and to see the female character's thoughtfulness and depth. Although "the American" refers to the abortion as "'really an awfully simple operation'" (Hemingway 72), downplaying its seriousness, "the girl" has a "more mature understanding" of what her decision might mean (Bauer 130). She recognizes that it is not so "simple," and she is not naive enough to think that having the baby will save the relationship. In fact, she responds to his own naive comments with sarcasm. He claims that they will be "'all right and happy'" if she goes through with the operation; he says he's "'known lots of people who have done it.' 'So have I,' said the girl. 'And afterward they were all so happy'" (Hemingway 73). Despite her sarcasm and her resistance to his suggestions, the man continues to insist that this problem will be easy to fix. Finally, the girl becomes irritated with him and, as readers can see by the dashes that end his lines midsentence, cuts him off, finishing his lines for him as he tries to tell her again how "perfectly simple" the operation is (Hemingway 76). Readers understand her pain and frustration when she finally says, "'Would you please please please please please please please stop talking?'" (Hemingway 76).

3 Evidence: First point in support of thesis

The argument that "the girl" is a flat, stereotypical character portrayed in sexist terms is hard to support. In fact, a stronger argument could be made that it is the man, "the American," who is the stereotype. As critic Charles J. Nolan Jr. points out, "Hemingway highlights Jig's maturity and superiority as he excoriates the selfishness and insensitivity of her companion" (19). Moreover, "the girl" is certainly the central character in this story—the one in conflict, the one who must

4 Evidence: Second point in support of thesis

make the final decision, and the one who grows over the course of the story. At times, she seems willing to listen to the man, even going so far as to say, "'Then I'll do it. Because I don't care about me'" (Hemingway 74). However, soon after, she responds defiantly to his comment, "'You mustn't feel that way'" with "'I don't feel any way'" (Hemingway 75). Thus, as Renner notes, Hemingway's dialogue reveals "the self-centered motives of his male character" while at the same time dramatizing the female character's complex inner struggle (38). By the end of the story, the shallow "American" still expects things to be all right between them. But when the man asks, "'Do you feel better?'" Hemingway shows the girl's quiet power—and her transformation—by giving her the final understated words of the story: "'I feel fine. . . . There's nothing wrong with me. I feel fine'" (Hemingway 77). Although we do not learn what her decision is, we can see that she is now in control: she has decided to shut down the conversation, and what the man has to say no longer matters.

Conclusion

In "Hills Like White Elephants," "the girl" proves herself to be neither "'weak *in* character'" nor "'weak *as* character'" as some have described Hemingway's female characters (Bauer 126). Far from being weak *in* character, she constantly questions and pushes against the male character's suggestions. And far from being weak *as* a character, she acts as the protagonist in this story, winning the reader's sympathies. A stereotypically drawn female character would not be able to carry off either of these feats. Although Hemingway may demonstrate sexism in his other stories—and demonstrate it in his own life—readers who evaluate *this* story will discover a complex, conflicted, sympathetic female character.

Concluding statement

5

Works Cited

Bauer, Margaret D. "Forget the Legend and Read the Work: Teaching Two Stories by Ernest Hemingway." *College Literature*, vol. 30, no. 3, 2003, pp. 124–37. *Academic Search Premier*, www.ebscohost .com/academic/academic-search-premier.

Hemingway, Ernest. "Hills Like White Elephants." *Men without Women*. Charles Scribner's, 1927, pp. 69–77.

Nolan, Charles J., Jr. "Hemingway's Women's Movement." *Hemingway Review*, vol. 4, no. 1, 1984, pp. 14–22. *Academic Search Premier*, www.ebscohost.com/academic/academic-search-premier.

Renner, Stanley. "Moving to the Girl's Side of 'Hills Like White Elephants.'" *Hemingway Review*, vol. 15, no. 1, 1995, pp. 27–41. *Academic Search Premier*, www.ebscohost.com/academic/academic-search-premier.

Rogers, Katherine M. *The Troublesome Helpmate: A History of Misogyny in Literature*. U of Washington P, 1996.

AP Photo/The Journal and Courier, Tom Leniniger

B

Documenting Sources: APA

American Psychological Association (APA) documentation style is commonly used in the social sciences. In APA style, parenthetical references refer readers to sources in the list of references at the end of the paper.* Parenthetical citations must be provided for all sources that are not common knowledge, whether you are summarizing, paraphrasing, or quoting.

Using Parenthetical References

In APA style, parenthetical references refer readers to sources in the list of references at the end of the paper. A typical parenthetical reference includes the author's last name (followed by a comma) and the year of publication: (Vang, 2015). Here are some guidelines for specific situations.

- If the author's last name appears in the text, follow it with the year of publication, in parentheses: According to Vang (2015), recent studies suggest . . .

- When quoting from a source, include a page number, if available: (Vang, 2015, p. 33). Once you have cited a source, you can refer to the author a second time without the publication date so long as it is clear you are referring to the same source: Vang also found . . .

- If no author is identified, use a shortened version of the title: ("Mind," 2015).

- If you are citing multiple works by the same author or authors published in the same year, include a lowercase letter with the year: (Peters, 2014a), (Peters, 2014b), and so on.

---

*American Psychological Association, *Publication Manual of the American Psychological Association*, Sixth Edition (2010).

- When a work has two authors, cite both names, separated by an ampersand, and the year: (Tabor & Garza, 2006). For three to five authors, in the first reference, cite all authors, along with the year; for subsequent references, cite just the first author, followed by et al. When a work has six or more authors, cite just the first author, followed by et al. and the year: (McCarthy et al., 2010).

- Omit page numbers or dates if the source does not include them. (Try to find a .pdf version of an online source; it will usually include page numbers.)

- If you quote a source found in another source, cite the original author and the source in which you found it: Psychologist Gary Wells asserted . . . (as cited in Doyle, 2005, p. 122).

- Include in-text references to personal communications and interviews by providing the person's name, the phrase "personal communication," and the date: (J. Smith, personal communication, February 12, 2015). Do not include these sources in your reference list.

If a direct quotation is forty words or less, include it within quotation marks without separating it from the rest of the text. When quoting a passage of more than forty words, indent the entire block of quoted text one-half inch from the left margin, and do not enclose it in quotation marks. It should be double-spaced, like the rest of the paper. Place parenthetical documentation one space after the final punctuation.

Preparing a Reference List

Start your list of references on a separate page at the end of your paper. Center the title References at the top of the page, and follow these guidelines:

- Begin each reference flush with the left margin, and indent subsequent lines one-half inch. Double-space the reference list within and between entries.

- List your references alphabetically by the author's last name (or by the first major word of the title if no author is identified).

- If the list includes references for two sources by the same author, alphabetize them by title.

- Italicize titles of books and periodicals. Do not italicize article titles or enclose them in quotation marks.

- For titles of books and articles, capitalize the first word of the title and subtitle as well as any proper nouns. Capitalize words in a periodical title as they appear in the original.

When you have completed your reference list, go through your paper and make sure that every reference cited is included in the list in the correct order.

Examples of APA Citations

The following are examples of APA citations.

Periodicals

Article in a journal paginated by volume

Shah, N. A. (2006). Women's human rights in the Koran: An interpretive approach. *Human Rights Quarterly*, *28*, 868–902.

Article in a journal paginated by issue

Lamb, B., & Keller, H. (2007). Understanding cultural models of parenting: The role of intracultural variation and response style. *Journal of Cross-Cultural Psychology*, *38*(1), 50–57.

Magazine article

Von Drehle, D. (2015, April 20). Line of fire. *Time*, *185*(14), 24–28.

Newspaper article

DeParle, J. (2009, April 19). Struggling to rise in suburbs where failing means fitting in. *The New York Times,* pp. A1, A20–A21.

Books

Books by one author

Jordan, Jennifer A. (2015). *Edible memory: The lure of heirloom tomatoes and other forgotten foods*. Chicago, IL: University of Chicago Press.

Books by two to seven authors

McFadden, J., & Al-Khalili, J. (2014). *Life on the edge: The coming of age of quantum biology.* New York, NY: Crown.

Books by eight or more authors

Barrett, J. M., Smith, V., Wilson, R. T., Haley, V. A., Clarke, P., Palmer, N. B., . . . Fraser, D. (2012). *How to cite references in APA style.* New York: Cambridge University Press.

Edited book

Brummett, B. (Ed.). (2008). *Uncovering hidden rhetorics: Social issues in disguise*. Los Angeles, CA: Sage.

Essay in an edited book

Alberts, H. C. (2006). The multiple transformations of Miami. In H. Smith & O. J. Furuseth (Eds.), *Latinos in the new south: Transformations of place* (pp. 135–151). Burlington, VT: Ashgate.

Translation

Piketty, T. (2015). *The Economics of inequality* (A. Goldhammer, Trans.). Cambridge, MA: Harvard University Press.

Revised edition

Johnson, B., & Christensen, L. B. (2008). *Educational research: Quantitative, qualitative, and mixed approaches* (3rd ed.). Los Angeles, CA: Sage.

Internet Sources
Entire website

Secretariat of the Convention on Biological Diversity. (2015). *Convention on biological diversity*. Retrieved from https://www.cbd.int/

Web page within a website

The great divide: How Westerners and Muslims view each other. (2006, July 6). In *Pew global attitudes project*. Retrieved from http://pewglobal.org/reports/display.php?ReportID=253

University program website

National security archive. (2009). Retrieved from George Washington University website: http://www.gwu.edu/~nsarchiv/

Journal article found on the Web with a DOI

Because websites change and disappear without warning, many publishers have started adding a **Digital Object Identifier (DOI)** to their articles. A DOI is a unique number that can be retrieved no matter where the article ends up on the Web.

To locate an article with a known DOI, go to the DOI system website at http://dx.doi.org/ and type in the DOI number. When citing an article that has a DOI (usually found on the first page of the article), you do not need to include a URL in your reference or the name of the database in which you may have found the article.

Geers, A. L., Wellman, J. A., & Lassiter, G. D. (2009). Dispositional
optimism and engagement: The moderating influence of goal
prioritization. *Journal of Personality and Social Psychology, 94,*
913–932. doi:10.1037/a0014746

Journal article found on the Web without a DOI

Bendetto, M. M. (2008). Crisis on the immigration bench: An ethical
perspective. *Brooklyn Law Review, 73,* 467–523. Retrieved from
http://brooklaw.edu/students/journals/blr.php/

Journal article from an electronic database

The name and URL of the database are not required for citations if a DOI is available. If no DOI is available, provide the home page URL of the journal or of the book or report publisher.

Staub, E., & Pearlman, L. A. (2009). Reducing intergroup prejudice
and conflict: A commentary. *Journal of Personality and Social
Psychology, 11,* 3–23. Retrieved from http://www.apa.org/journals
/psp/

Electronic book

Katz, R. N. (Ed.). (2008). *The tower and the cloud: Higher education
in an era of cloud computing.* Retrieved from http://net
.educause.edu/ir/library/pdf/PUB7202.pdf

Video blog post

Green, J. (2015, July 7). Understanding the financial crisis in Greece
[Video file]. Retrieved from https://www.youtube.com
/watch?v=tigaryz-1y4

Presentation slides

Hall, M. E. (2009) *Who moved my job!? A psychology of job-loss
"trauma"* [Presentation slides]. Retrieved from http://www.cew
.wisc.edu/docs/WMMJ%20PwrPt-Summry2.ppt

Student Essay

The following research paper, "The High Cost of Cheap Counterfeit Goods," follows APA format as outlined in the preceding pages.

APA PAPER GUIDELINES

- An APA paper should have a one-inch margin all around and be double-spaced throughout.

- The first line of every paragraph should be indented, and all pages of the paper, including the first, should be numbered consecutively.

- Every page should have a page header (an abbreviated title in all upper-case letters) typed one-half inch from the top of the page.

- An APA paper has four sections: the *title page*, the *abstract*, the *body of the paper*, and the *reference list*:

  1. The **title page** (page 1) should include a running head (in all upper-case letters) at the top:

     Running Head: COUNTERFEIT GOODS

  2. The title page should also include the title of the paper (upper- and lower-case letters), your name (first name, middle initial, last name), and your school.

  3. The **abstract** (page 2) should be a 150- to 250-word summary of the paper. Type the word **Abstract** (centered); skip one line; and do not indent. After the abstract, skip one line and type *Keywords* (italicized and indented), followed by keywords that will help researchers find your essay in a database.

  4. The **body of the paper** should begin on page 3. After the title page, each page of the paper should include the running head (in all upper-case letters), typed flush left, one-half inch from the top of the page:

     COUNTERFEIT GOODS

  5. The **reference list** should begin on a new page, after the body of the paper. (See pages A-14–A-15 for a discussion of how to format the reference list.)

- Citations should follow APA documentation style.

Running Head: COUNTERFEIT GOODS   1

The High Cost of Cheap Counterfeit Goods

Deniz A. Bilgutay

Humanities 101, Section 1

Professor Fitzgerald

March 4, 2015

Abstract

The global trade in counterfeit products costs manufacturers of luxury goods millions of dollars each year. Although this illegal trade threatens the free market, employs underage labor, and may even fund terrorism, many people consider it a victimless crime. Studies show that some consumers even take pride in buying knock-off products. But a closer look at this illicit trade in counterfeit goods shows that consumers in the United States—and around the world—do not understand the ethical implications of the choices they make. Consumers should stop supporting this illegal business, and law enforcement officials should prosecute it more vigorously than they currently do. In the final analysis, this illegal practice hurts legitimate businesses and in some cases endangers the health and safety of consumers.

Keywords: counterfeiting, terrorism, ethics, crime

COUNTERFEIT GOODS   3

The High Cost of Cheap Counterfeit Goods

For those who do not want to pay for genuine designer

products, a fake Louis Vuitton bag or knock-off Rolex watch

might seem too good to pass up. Such purchases may even be

a source of pride. According to one study, two-thirds of British

consumers said they would be "proud to tell family and

friends" that they bought inexpensive knock-offs (Thomas,

2007). The trade in counterfeit goods, however, is a crime—and

not a victimless crime. A growing body of evidence suggests

that the makers and distributers of counterfeit goods have

ties to child labor, organized crime, and even terrorism. In

addition, the global economic cost of counterfeiting is esti-

mated at $600 billion a year, according to recent data from the

International Chamber of Commerce (Melik, 2011). For these

reasons, consumers should stop buying these products and

funding the illegal activities that this activity supports.

Much of the responsibility for the trade in counterfeit

goods can be placed on the manufacturers and the countries

that permit the production and export of such goods. For exam-

ple, China, which dominates the world counterfeit trade, is

doing very little to stop this activity. According to a recent arti-

cle in *USA Today* by Calum MacLeod (2011), "a major obstacle

is China's *shanzhai* culture, whereby some Chinese delight in

making cheap imitations, sometimes in parody, of expensive,

famous brands." Chinese counterfeiters have gone so far as to

create entire fake stores: fake Starbucks stores, fake Abercrom-

bie & Fitch stores, and even fake Apple stores. Although some

of these copycats have been prosecuted, there is a high level

of tolerance, even admiration, for counterfeiting in China.

This attitude towards *shanzhai* is reflected in the country's

lax intellectual property protection laws. As one Chinese

intellectual property lawyer observed, "The penalties don't

Introduction

Thesis
statement

outweigh the benefits" (as cited in MacLeod, 2011). Given this situation, the production of counterfeit goods in China is not likely to slow down any time soon.

Despite such cultural justifications for counterfeiting, there is still an ethical problem associated with the purchase of knock-offs. As Dana Thomas (2007) has written in *The New York Times*, many of these counterfeit products are made by children who are "sold or sent off by their families to work in clandestine factories." To American consumers, the problem of children laboring in Chinese factories may be remote, but it is serious. If it is reasonable to place blame for this flourishing market on the countries that allow it, it is also reasonable to blame the people who buy most of the counterfeit goods—namely, consumers in the United States and Europe. According to a report by U.S. Customs and Border Patrol, 62% of fake goods seized in the United States in 2011 were produced in China (as cited in Coleman, 2012). In Europe, the numbers are even higher. According to *The Wall Street Journal*, 85% of goods seized in the European Union come from China (Nairn, 2011). Consequently, the simple act of buying a counterfeit Coach handbag implicates the consumer in the practice of forced child labor.

Immoral labor practices are not the only reason why the counterfeit market needs to be stopped. Organized crime is behind much of the counterfeit trade, so "every dollar spent on a knockoff Gap polo shirt or a fake Kate Spade handbag may be supporting drug trafficking, . . . and worse" ("Editorial: The True Cost," 2007). Consumer dollars may also be supporting narcotics, weapons, and child prostitution (Thomas, 2007).

This illicit international system also helps to finance groups even more sinister than crime syndicates. American consumers of counterfeit goods should understand that profits from

COUNTERFEIT GOODS 5

counterfeit goods support terrorist and extremist groups, including Hezbollah, paramilitary organizations in Northern Ireland, and
FARC, a revolutionary armed faction in Colombia (Thomas, 2007).
According to the International Anti-Counterfeiting Coalition, the
sale of knock-off T-shirts may even have funded the 1993 attack
on the World Trade Center. Some observers speculate that terrorists annually receive about 2% of the roughly $500 billion trade in
counterfeit goods ("Editorial: The True Cost," 2007). According to
Ronald K. Noble, secretary-general of the international law
enforcement agency Interpol, crime involving counterfeit merchandise "is becoming the preferred method of funding for a
number of terrorist groups" (as cited in Langan, 2003).

    Beyond the moral and ethical implications of its links to
child labor, crime, and terrorism, counterfeit merchandise also
undermines the mainstay of Western business—respect for intellectual property. In the context of a vast international market of
counterfeit luxury goods, the issue of intellectual property can
seem insignificant. But the creation of new products requires
time, energy, and money, and "unrestrained copying robs creators of the means to profit from their works" (Sprigman, 2006).
Copyright law exists to make sure that inventors and producers
will be motivated to create original work and be fairly compensated for it. This principle applies to the designers of luxury
goods and fashion items as well. Christopher Sprigman (2006)
disagrees, however, noting that although intellectual property
law does little to protect fashion designs, this is as it should be.
"Trend-driven consumption," says Sprigman, is good for the
fashion industry because the industry's ability to create trends
"is based on designers' relative freedom to copy." But even
this argument—which addresses the influences of legitimate
fashion designers and manufacturers—cannot be used to
justify allowing counterfeiters to copy Prada handbags or Hugo

Marginal annotations:

Evidence: Point 3

Evidence: Point 4

Opposing argument

Refutation

COUNTERFEIT GOODS   6

Boss suits and pass them off as genuine branded articles. Such
illicit activity creates no trends—other than perhaps increasing
the market for counterfeit products, which siphons off more
profits from original designers.

Evidence:
Point 5

The knock-off market is not limited to fashion and luxury
goods. For example, fake products such as shoddy brake pads
have directly injured many consumers. In addition, each year
millions of people in the United States and abroad buy counterfeit drugs that do not work and in many cases are dangerous.
Some sources estimate that the majority of drugs used to treat
life-threatening diseases in Africa are counterfeit. Not coincidentally, many of the same people who are making and distributing counterfeit luxury goods are also manufacturing these
drugs ("Editorial: The True Cost," 2007).

Conclusion

It is time for people to realize the harm that is done by
counterfeit merchandise and stop buying it. One way to combat this problem is to educate consumers about the effects of
their purchases. As James Melik (2011) of the BBC explains,
"People try to save money without realising that the purchase
of counterfeit goods can actually harm themselves, the economy and ultimately, their own pockets." Melik urges consumers to "think twice" before buying "products which promote
and fund crime." Another way to confront the problem is for
law enforcement to address this issue aggressively. Not only
should local authorities do more to stop this illegal trade, but
national governments should also impose sanctions on countries that refuse to honor international treaties concerning intellectual property. Only by taking this issue seriously can we
ensure that this "victimless" crime does not continue to spread
and claim more victims.

COUNTERFEIT GOODS   7

                        References

Coleman, S. (2012, January 20). China still accounts for majority
        of US counterfeit goods. *Canadian Manufacturers and
        Exporters*. Retrieved from http://www.cme-mec.ca/?lid
        =JCKNC-E742G-1W6JA&comaction=show&cid=DVU6K
        -CVBRZ-C6TZQ

Editorial: The true cost: Illegal knockoffs of name-brand products
        do widespread harm [Editorial]. (2007, December 2). *The
        Columbus* [OH] *Dispatch*, p. 4G.

Langan, M. (2003, July 24). Counterfeit goods make real
        terrorism. *Pittsburgh Post-Gazette*, p. A17.

MacLeod, C. (2011, August 2). China takes knock-offs to a
        new level, copying entire stores. *USA Today*. Retrieved
        from http://www.usatoday.com/money/industries
        /technology/2011-07-31-China-counterfeiting-fake-Western
        -goods-stores_n.htm

Melik, J. (2011, December 18). Fake goods save money but at
        what cost? *BBC News*. Retrieved from http://www.bbc
        .co.uk/news/business-16087793

Nairn, G. (2011, October 18). Countering the counterfeiters. *The
        Wall Street Journal*. Retrieved from http://online.wsj.com
        /article/SB10001424052970204226204576600462442044764
        .html

Sprigman, C. (2006, August 22). The fashion industry's piracy
        paradox [Online forum comment]. Retrieved from http://
        www.publicknowledge.org/node/597

Thomas, D. (2007, August 30). Terror's purse strings. *The New
        York Times*, p. A23.

Accurate evidence: Evidence from reliable sources that is quoted carefully and in context.

Ad hominem fallacy: The logical fallacy of undermining an argument by attacking the person who is making the argument instead of addressing the argument itself.

Allusion: A reference within a work to a person, literary or biblical text, or historical event. This shorthand device reminds the reader of something that enlarges the context of the situation being written about.

Analogy: An extended comparison that explains an unfamiliar item, concept, or situation by comparing it to a more familiar one.

Annotating: Making notes of your questions, reactions, and ideas on the document itself.

Antithesis: An opposing statement that tests whether an argumentative **thesis** is debatable.

Appeal to doubtful authority: The use of nonexperts to support an argument.

Applied ethics: The field of philosophy that applies **ethical principles** to real-life issues (such as abortion, the death penalty, animal rights, or doctor-assisted suicide).

Argument: A logical and persuasive presentation of **evidence** that attempts to convince people to accept (or at least to consider) the writer's position.

Argument by analogy: An argument that claims that its position is valid because it is similar in some ways to a position on another issue that readers are likely to accept.

Backing: In a **Toulmin argument**, the evidence that supports the warrant.

Bandwagon appeal: An attempt to convince people that something is true because it is widely held to be true.

Begging-the-question fallacy: An illogical assumption that a statement is self-evident (or true) when it actually requires proof.

Bias: Preconceived ideas or prejudices, which are often used in an argument instead of factual **evidence**.

Brainstorming: Making quick notes on a topic to generate ideas.

Causal chain: A sequence of events in which one event causes the next, which in turn causes the next, and so on.

Cause-and-effect argument: An argument that explains an event or a situation by considering its likely causes or outcomes.

Circular reasoning: An attempt to support a statement by simply repeating the statement in different terms.

Claim: In a **Toulmin argument**, the main point, usually stated as a **thesis**.

Clustering: Creating a diagram to map out your thoughts.

Common ground: Points of agreement that are shared by those on opposing sides of an argument.

Common knowledge: Factual information (such as a writer's date of birth, a scientific fact, or the location of a famous battle) that can be found in several credible sources. Common knowledge does not require documentation.

Conclusion: The last part of a **syllogism**.

Confirmation bias: The tendency that people have to accept information that supports their own beliefs and to ignore information that does not.

Confrontational argument: A kind of argument that is characterized by conflict and opposition.

Contributory causes: The less important causes in a **causal argument**.

Credibility: Trustworthiness. A credible source is believable.

Criteria for evaluation: Standards by which a subject (or source) is evaluated.

Critical response: A passage in which a writer examines the ideas that are presented in an argument and evaluates them.

Current source: A source containing up-to-date information. Current sources are especially important in discussions of scientific subjects and may be less important in other subjects.

Debatable thesis: A thesis statement that presents a position with which people might disagree.

Deductive reasoning: A form of reasoning that moves from general statements (or **premises**) to specific conclusions. See **inductive reasoning**.

Definition argument: An argument that is based on the idea that something fits or does not fit a particular definition of a key term.

Dictionary definition: A structure for definition that consists of the term to be defined, the general class to which the term belongs, and the qualities that differentiate the term from other items in the same class.

Dilemma: A choice between two or more unfavorable alternatives.

Distortion: An unfair tactic of argument in which the writer misrepresents evidence—for example, by presenting an opponent's view inaccurately or by exaggerating his or her position.

Documentation: Information that identifies the sources used in an argument.

Editing and proofreading: The final steps in the writing process, which check that an essay is well organized, convincing, and clearly written and has no distracting grammatical, spelling, and mechanical errors.

Either/or fallacy: Faulty reasoning that presents only two choices when there are actually three or more choices.

Enthymeme: A **syllogism** with one or two parts of its argument (usually the major premise) missing.

Equivocation: The use of two different meanings for the same key term in an argument.

Ethical argument: An argument that focuses on whether something should be done because it is good or right.

Ethical dilemma: A conflict between two or more possible actions, each of which will potentially have negative outcomes.

Ethical principles: A set of ideas or standards that guides someone to an ethically correct conclusion.

Ethics: The field of philosophy that studies the standards by which an act can be judged right or wrong or good or bad.

Ethos: An appeal to the trustworthiness or credibility of a speaker or writer.

Evaluate: To express an opinion about the quality of something.

Evaluation argument: An argument that presents a positive or negative judgment, asserts that someone else's positive or negative judgment is not accurate or justified, or demonstrates that one thing is or is not superior to another.

Evidence: The facts, observations, expert opinion, examples, and statistics that support a thesis statement. In a **Toulmin argument**, the evidence is called the **grounds**.

Fact: A statement that can be verified (proven to be true).

Fallacy: An error in reasoning that undermines the logic of an argument.

False dilemma: See **either/or fallacy**.

Formal argument: An argument developed according to set rhetorical principles in academic discussion and writing. See **informal argument**.

Formal outline: A presentation of an essay's main and subordinate points that uses a number/letter system to designate the order in which the points will be discussed.

Freewriting: Writing continuously for a set time to generate ideas without worrying about spelling or grammar.

Grounds: In a **Toulmin argument**, the evidence that is used to support the claim.

Hasty generalization: An error in reasoning that occurs when a conclusion is based on too little evidence or when the gap between the evidence and conclusion is too wide.

Highlighting: Using underlining and symbols to identify an essay's most important points.

Identifying tag: A phrase that identifies the source of a **quotation**, **paraphrase**, or **summary**.

Immediate cause: In a **causal argument**, the cause that occurs right before an event.

Inductive leap: In **inductive reasoning**, a stretch of the imagination that enables a writer to draw a reasonable conclusion from the existing information.

Inductive reasoning: A form of reasoning that begins with specific observations (or evidence) and moves to a general conclusion. See **deductive reasoning**.

Inference: A statement that uses what is known to draw a conclusion about what is unknown.

Informal argument: An **argument** that occurs in daily life about politics, sports, social issues, and personal relationships. See **formal argument**.

Informal outline: A list of the ideas that will be discussed in an essay. See **formal outline**.

Jumping to a conclusion: See **hasty generalization**.

Logic: The principles of correct reasoning that enable someone to tell whether a conclusion correctly follows from a set of statements or assumptions.

Logical fallacy: A flawed argument.

Logos: An appeal to logic.

Main cause: In a **causal argument**, the most important cause.

Major premise: See **syllogism**.

Means of persuasion: The appeals—*logos*, *pathos*, and *ethos*—that writers use to persuade their audience.

Metaphor: A comparison in which two dissimilar things are compared without the word *like* or *as*.

Middle term: The term in a **syllogism** that appears in both the major and minor premises but not in the conclusion.

Minor premise: See **syllogism**.

Misuse of statistics fallacy: When data are misrepresented.

Non sequitur fallacy: Illogical reasoning that occurs when a conclusion does not follow from the premises or is supported by weak or irrelevant evidence or by no evidence at all.

Objective source: A source that is not unduly influenced by personal opinions or feelings.

Operational definition: A definition of how something acts or works that transforms an abstract concept into something concrete, observable, and possibly measurable.

Opinion: A personal judgment; therefore, an idea that is open to debate.

Parallelism: The use of the same or a similar structure in the repetition of words, phrases, or clauses.

Paraphrase: A passage that presents a source's ideas in detail, including its main idea and key supporting points and perhaps key examples.

Parenthetical references: In MLA and APA **documentation**, citations that identify the source of a paraphrase, quotation, or summary.

Pathos: An appeal to the emotions.

Peer review: The process of having colleagues examine and critique written work. Informally, school work is read by friends or classmates; formally, scholarly work is read by experts in the field to confirm its accuracy.

Persuasion: The act of influencing an audience to adopt a particular belief or to follow a specific course of action.

Plagiarism: The use of the words or ideas of another person without attributing them to their rightful author.

Popular magazine: A periodical that is aimed at general readers. It generally is not an acceptable source for research.

Post hoc fallacy: Faulty reasoning that asserts that because two events occur closely in time, one event must have caused the other.

Premises: Statements or assumptions on which an **argument** is based or from which a conclusion is drawn.

Previewing: During active reading, forming a general impression of a writer's position on an issue, the argument's key supporting points, and the context for the writer's remarks.

Propaganda: Biased or misleading information that is spread about a particular viewpoint, person, or cause.

Proposal argument: An argument that attempts to convince people that a problem exists and that a particular solution is both practical and desirable.

Qualifiers: In a **Toulmin argument**, statements that limit the **claim**.

Quotation: Words or sentences taken directly from a source.

Quoting out of context: Removing a quotation from its original setting for the purpose of distorting its meaning.

Reading critically: Questioning or challenging material instead of simply accepting it as true. This often involves assessing the accuracy of facts in sources and considering the evidence that supports them.

Reason: In a **Toulmin argument**, a statement that supports the **claim**.

Rebuttals: In a **Toulmin argument**, refutations of opposing arguments.

Red herring fallacy: An irrelevant side issue that diverts attention from the real issue.

Refutation: The section of an argumentative essay that identifies opposing arguments and presents arguments against them.

Refute: To disprove or call into question.

Relevant evidence: **Evidence** that applies specifically (not just tangentially) to the topic under discussion.

Remote causes: In a **causal argument**, incidents that occurred in the past but may have had a greater impact than more recent events.

Representative evidence: **Evidence** that is drawn from a fair range of sources, not just from sources that support a particular position.

Revision: The careful and critical review of a draft.

Rhetoric: The effect of various elements working together to form a convincing and persuasive **argument**.

Rhetorical analysis: A systematic examination of the strategies that a writer employs to achieve his or her purpose.

Rhetorical question: A question that encourages readers to reflect on an issue but does not call for a reply.

Rhetorical situation: The combination of the writer, the writer's purpose, the writer's audience, the topic, and the context.

Rhetorical strategies: The ways in which argument writers present ideas and opinions, including but not limited to thesis, organization, evidence, and stylistic techniques (**simile, metaphor, allusion, parallelism**, repetition, and **rhetorical questions**).

Rhetorical triangle: A graphic representation of the three kinds of appeals in an argument—*logos* (reason), *ethos* (credibility), and *pathos* (values and beliefs).

Rogerian argument: A model of argument that assumes that people of good will can avoid conflict by identifying **common ground** and points of agreement. It is based on the work of Carl Rogers, a twentieth-century psychologist who felt that traditional confrontational arguments could be counterproductive.

Scholarly journal: A periodical that is usually written by experts, documented, and peer reviewed.

Scientific method: A way of using induction to find answers to questions. It involves proposing a hypothesis, making a series of observations to test the hypothesis, and arriving at a conclusion that confirms, modifies, or disproves the hypothesis.

Self-evident: A proposition that requires no proof or explanation.

Simile: A figure of speech that compares two unlike things by using *like* or *as*.

Skeptical: Having an open mind but still needing to be convinced.

Slanting: An unfair tactic that makes an argument appear stronger by presenting only evidence that supports a particular position and ignoring evidence that challenges it.

Slippery-slope fallacy: An illogical argument that holds that one thing will cause a series of events that ends in an inevitable, unpleasant conclusion, usually with no evidence that such a sequence will actually occur.

Straw man fallacy: An intentional oversimplification of an opposing argument to make it easier to refute.

Sufficient evidence: Evidence that includes enough facts, statistics, and expert opinion to support the essay's thesis.

Summary: A concise restatement of the main idea of a passage (or article or book) without the examples, explanations, and stylistic devices of the source.

Sweeping generalization: See **hasty generalization**.

Syllogism: A model for **deductive reasoning** that includes a **major premise**, a **minor premise**, and a **conclusion**. Some types of syllogisms are:

   Sound syllogism: A syllogism that is both true and valid.

   True syllogism: A syllogism in which the **premises** are consistent with the **facts**.

   Valid syllogism: A system in which a conclusion follows logically from its premises.

Synthesis: A combination of **summary**, **paraphrase**, **quotation**, and a writer's own ideas that supports an original conclusion.

Taking a stand: Expressing a position in the form of a **thesis statement**.

Thesis: The position that an argument supports.

Thesis statement: A single sentence in an argumentative essay that states a position on an issue.

Thinking critically: Questioning rather than accepting ideas at face value.

Toulmin argument: An argument that includes the **claim** (the main point), the grounds (the **evidence** a writer uses to support the claim), and the **warrant** (the inference—either stated or implied—that connects the claims to their grounds).

Unfair appeal: An appeal to an audience's fears or prejudices.

Visual: An image—such as a chart, graph, table, photo, drawing, or diagram.

Visual argument: An advertisement, chart, graph, table, diagram, Web page, photograph, painting, or other representation that communicates a position through images.

Warrant: In a **Toulmin argument**, the inference or assumption, either stated or implied, that connects a claim to its grounds.

Works-cited list: An alphabetical list of sources that appears at the end of an essay that follows MLA style.

Writing process: The process of planning, drafting, revising, and editing an argument.

You-also fallacy (*tu quoque*): An illogical assertion that a statement is false because the speaker has said or done the opposite. It attacks a person for doing the thing that he or she is arguing against.

Text Credits

American Psychological Association. "Violence in Mass Media." Copyright © 2016 by the American Psychological Association. From the *Council Policy Manual*. Reproduced with permission. The official citation that should be used in referencing this material is http://www.apa.org/about/policy/media.aspx. No further reproduction or distribution is permitted without written permission from the American Psychological Association.

Dan Ariely. "Essay Mills: A Coarse Lesson in Cheating." From *Los Angeles Times*, June 17, 2012. Reproduced with the permission of the author.

Austin American-Statesman. "Cheaters Never Win." From *The Austin American-Statesman*, August 11, 2006. Copyright © 2006 Austin American-Statesman. Reproduced with permission. All rights reserved.

K. Balibalos and J. Gopalakrishnan. " 'Okay or Not?' A New Poll Series about Plagiarism." From *WriteCheck*, July 24, 2013. Copyright © 2013 Turnitin, LLC. Reproduced with permission.

Tony Brummel. "Practical Experience Trumps Fancy Degrees." From *Bloomberg Business Week*, March 2011. Reproduced with permission of Bloomberg L.P. Copyright © 2015. All rights reserved.

Patrick Buchanan. "Immigration Time-Out." From http://buchanan.org/blog/immigration-time-out-163, October 31, 1994. Copyright © 1994 Patrick Buchanan. Reproduced with permission of Friedman, Inc. All rights reserved.

Chris Bustamante. "The Risks And Rewards Of Online Learning." From *The Community College Times*, November 16, 2011. Copyright © 2011 American Association of Community and Junior Colleges. Reproduced with permission. All rights reserved.

Dylan Byers. "Plagiarism and BuzzFeed's Achilles' Heel." From Politico, July 25, 2014. Copyright © 2014 Politico. Reproduced with permission of Politico via Copyright Clearance Center.

John Crisp. "Short Distance Learning." From *The Metro West Daily News*, December 14, 2011. Copyright © 2011 John Crisp. Reproduced with permission of the author. All rights reserved.

Mary C. Daly and Leila Bengali. "Is It Still Worth Going to College?" From *FRBSF Economic Letter*, May 5, 2014. © 2014 Federal Reserve Bank of San Francisco. Reproduced with permission.

Craig Desson. "My Creepy Instagram map knows where I live." From *The Toronto Star*, February 27, 2015. © 2015 Copyright Toronto Star Newspapers Ltd. Reproduced with permission.

Shelley Fralic. "Fralic: Don't fall for the myths about online privacy." From *Calgary Herald*, October 17, 2015. © 2015 Postmedia Network Inc. Material republished with the express permission of Calgary Herald, a division of Postmedia Network Inc.

Trip Gabriel. "Plagiarism Lines Blur For Students In Digital Age." From *The New York Times*, August 1, 2010. Copyright © 2010 The New York Times. All rights reserved. Used by permission and protected by the Copyright Laws of the United States. The printing, copying, redistribution, or retransmission of this Content without express written permission is prohibited.

Jennifer Golbeck. "All Eyes on You." From *Psychology Today*, September/October 2014. Reproduced with permission of the author.

Andrew Herman. "Raise The Drinking Age to 25." From *The BG News*, August 22, 2007. Copyright © 2007 BG News. Reproduced with permission. All rights reserved.

Lawrence M. Hinman. "How To Fight College Cheating." From *The Washington Post*, September 3, 2004. Copyright © 2004 Lawrence Hinman. Reproduced with permission of the author. All rights reserved.

Sharon Jayson. "Online and Mobile Dating Face Privacy, Safety Concerns." From *USA Today*, March 27, 2014. Copyright © 2014 Gannett. All rights reserved. Used by permission and protected by the Copyright Laws of the United States. The printing, copying, redistribution, or retransmission of this Content without express written permission is prohibited.

Gerard Jones. "Violent Media Is Good For Kids." From *Mother Jones*, June 28, 2000. Copyright © 2000 The Foundation for National Progress. Reproduced with permission of The Foundation for National Progress. All rights reserved.

Elena Kadvany. "Online Education Needs Connection." From *The Daily Trojan*, October 9, 2011. Copyright © 2011 The Daily Trojan. Reproduced with permission. All rights reserved.

Wendy Kaminer. "The Progressive Ideas Behind the Lack of Free Speech on Campus." From *The Washington Post*, February 20, 2015. Reproduced with permission of the author.